Standards for Middle and High School Literacy Coaches

© 2006 by Carnegie Corporation of New York
Published by the International Reading Association

The four coaching standards are organized in two parts—leadership standards and content area literacy standards. Correlation of book chapters and standards are shown in *italics*. Standard 4 refers to different subject areas; these are indicated in **bold**.

LEADERSHIP STANDARDS

Standard 1: Skillful Collaborators *(Chapter 13)*

Content area literacy coaches are skilled collaborators who function effectively in middle school and/or high school settings.

Standard 2: Skillful Job-Embedded Coaches *(Chapter 13)*

Content area literacy coaches are skilled instructional coaches for secondary teachers in the core content areas of English language arts, mathematics, science, and social studies.

Standard 3: Skillful Evaluators of Literacy Needs *(Chapter 13)*

Content area literacy coaches are skilled evaluators of literacy needs within various subject areas and are able to collaborate with secondary school leadership teams and teachers to interpret and use assessment data to inform instruction.

CONTENT AREA LITERACY STANDARDS

Standard 4: Skillful Instructional Strategists *(Chapters 6, 7, 8, 9, 10, 11)*

Content area literacy coaches are accomplished middle and high school teachers who are skilled in developing and implementing instructional strategies to improve academic literacy in **English language arts**.

Standard 4: Skillful Instructional Strategists *(Chapters 6, 7, 8, 9, 10, 11)*

Content area literacy coaches are accomplished middle and high school teachers who are skilled in developing and implementing instructional strategies to improve academic literacy in **mathematics**.

Standard 4: Skillful Instructional Strategists *(Chapters 6, 7, 8, 9, 10, 11)*

Content area literacy coaches are accomplished middle and high school teachers who are skilled in developing and implementing instructional strategies to improve academic literacy in **science**.

Standard 4: Skillful Instructional Strategists *(Chapters 6, 7, 8, 9, 10, 11)*

Content area literacy coaches are accomplished middle and high school teachers who are skilled in developing and implementing instructional strategies to improve academic literacy in **social studies**.

Content Area Reading and Literacy

Succeeding in Today's Diverse Classrooms

Fifth Edition

Donna E. Alvermann
University of Georgia

Stephen F. Phelps
Buffalo State College

Victoria G. Ridgeway
Clemson University

PEARSON

Boston   New York   San Francisco
Mexico   City   Montreal   Toronto   London   Madrid   Munich   Paris
Hong Kong   Singapore   Tokyo   Cape Town   Sydney

Executive Editor: Aurora Martinez
Series Editorial Assistant: Lynda Giles
Executive Marketing Manager: Krista Clark
Composition and Prepress Buyer: Linda Cox
Manufacturing Manager: Megan Cochran
Cover Coordinator: Linda Knowles
Editorial-Production Coordinator: Mary Beth Finch
Editorial-Production Service: Stratford Publishing Services
Electronic Composition: Stratford Publishing Services

For related titles and support materials, visit our on-line catalog at www.ablongman.com

Between the time Web site information is gathered and then published, it is not unusual for some sites to have closed. Also, the transcription of URLs can result in unintended typographical errors. The publisher would appreciate notification where these errors occur so that they may be corrected in subsequent editions.

Photo Credits: Chapter 1: Tom Lindfors Photography; Chapter 2: Frank Siteman; Chapter 3: Tom Lindfors Photography; Chapter 4: Frank Siteman; Chapter 5: Frank Siteman; Chapter 6: © Joanthan Nourok/PhotoEdit; Chapter 7: Tom Lindfors Photography; Chapter 8: Tom Lindfors Photography; Chapter 9: Tom Lindfors Photography; Chapter 10: Tom Lindfors Photography; Chapter 11, Frank Siteman; Chapter 12: © Cindy Charles/PhotoEdit

Library of Congress Cataloging-in-Publication Data

Alvermann, Donna E.
    Content reading and literacy : succeeding in today's diverse classrooms / Donna E.
    Alvermann, Stephen F. Phelps, Victoria G. Ridgeway—5th ed.
        p.   cm.
    Includes bibliographical references and index.
    ISBN 0-205-48938-9
        1. Content area reading—United States   2. Reading (Secondary)—United States
    3. Multicultural education—United States   4. Reading (Secondary)—Social aspects—
    United States   5. Teenagers—Books and reading—United States.   I. Phelps, Stephen F.
    II. Ridgeway, Victoria G.   III. Title.

LBI050.455.A47 2007
428.4071'2—dc22

                                                                                2006041570

Printed in the United States of America.

10   9   8   7   6   5   4   3   2   1   RRD-VA   11   10   09   08   07   06

Donna: For Jack
Steve: For Sarah
Victoria: In memory of my brother, Jack

Contents

■ ■ ■ ■ ■ ■ ■ ■ ■ ■ ■ ■

11 Studying and Study Strategies   337

Preface and Acknowledgments

The Greek philosopher Heraclitus said, "Nothing endures but change." And so it is. This edition represents several changes, including the addition of a third author, Victoria Ridgeway. As a 20-year veteran science teacher, she is ever mindful of the pressures on content area teachers to "cover the material." When asked about the most important message for content area teachers to understand, she replies: "Sometimes content area teachers view content reading and learning strategies as something to do in *addition* to teaching content; when in reality the strategies enable teachers to teach content more effectively and efficiently." But adding a new member to the author team is not the only change. In the two years since our last edition, much has transpired on the national scene that has practical implications for literacy education, generally, and content area teaching and learning, specifically.

For example, nationally, the No Child Left Behind legislation has been extended to middle and high schools through the Striving Readers Initiative. The result has been more attention to adolescent literacy, particularly as it applies to content area teaching and learning. A survey conducted by the Alliance for Excellent Education indicated that for the first time, the public sees that investing in elementary school improvement does not inevitably lead to success in the high school years. Readers of this text are well positioned to address issues related to adolescent literacy because the fifth edition reflects the latest in research on literacy instruction and its implications for student learning. In addition to updating each of the chapters so as to incorporate the most current research, we have created a new feature for identifying myths about content literacy instruction that need to be dispelled. Accompanying each description of a dispelled myth is a policy-related issue that is expected to have an impact on content area teachers' instruction. At a time when national policies direct much of what happens at the local level, teachers need to be aware of various misconceptions surrounding those policies.

The diversity of cultures and languages reflected in classrooms in the United States and elsewhere in the English-speaking world continues to increase. Thus, in our latest edition of *Content Reading and Literacy: Succeeding in Today's Diverse Classrooms*, we continue our emphasis on how to teach English learners the academic literacy strategies and skills they need to comprehend their subject-matter texts. We also continue to provide a balance in the content areas that are represented in the examples, lessons, vignettes, and scenarios. To ensure that instructors who have students enrolled from different discipline areas can locate relevant content-specific examples easily, we again reference this information by content areas in the index of the book.

Finally, one of the most noticeable changes in this edition is a new chapter on literacy coaches, which will prove useful for those preparing to become literacy coaches and those who may benefit from working with literacy coaches as they begin their teaching careers or seek to improve their practices as veteran teachers. This new chapter highlights why literacy coaching at the middle and high school levels is a sign of the times and how you, the reader, can benefit from the literacy coach's expertise.

As in previous editions, the new strategies and examples used in *Content Reading and Literacy: Succeeding in Today's Diverse Classrooms* have been field-tested with preservice and inservice subject-matter specialists who view themselves as active facilitators of students' content area learning. Once again, we are indebted to the many prospective and practicing teachers in our classes who have contributed in substantive ways to this book. Their stories about literacy-related events that have made a difference in their instruction, as well as their suggestions for strategies that appeal to a wide range of student abilities and interests, continue to keep this book practical (and, we hope, interesting to read).

IMPORTANT FEATURES OF THIS TEXT

New in This Edition

The 5th edition of *Content Reading and Literacy: Succeeding in Today's Diverse Classrooms* introduces a new co-author and three new features.

Victoria Gentry Ridgeway, a former secondary school science teacher, who now teaches preservice and inservice teacher education courses at Clemson University, brings a host of practical experiences to bear on improving adolescents' literacy achievement. Her current work also takes her into the classrooms of both urban and rural schools where she is able to see firsthand how the ideas introduced in this book play out in the real world.

A new chapter entitled **Literacy Coaches: A sign of the Times** is in response to the growing need in school districts for qualified professionals who can assist teachers in closing the literacy achievement gap that presently exists. This chapter focuses on the qualifications, roles, and responsibilities of literacy coaches at the middle and high school levels, and their relationships with the classroom teachers with whom they work. It also makes important connections between a coach's current knowledge base and the body of research commonly referred to as scientifically-based reading instruction.

Dispelling Policy Myths is a new feature that helps readers identify myths about content literacy instruction and teaches them to be critical consumers of information. This feature is especially good for launching discussions of vital information about the conditions of teaching and learning that are typically omitted from a content area methods text. For example, consider the following myth and its policy implications:

Dispelling Policy Myths

Dispelling a Myth

The literacy community, knowing the importance of the new literacies for students' success in the Information Age, is taking a leadership role in this area. As a result, literacy educators are making gains in influencing national and state policy makers to support assessments that would allow students to demonstrate their competencies in using the new literacies.

Policy Implications

In fact, just the opposite is happening. As literacy educators, we seem to be taking a

backseat to policy makers. For example, the new framework for the National Assessment of Educational Progress in Reading that will be in place by 2009 does not allow students to use any form of technology other than the traditional paper and pencil. Nor, according to Leu et al. (2005), does any state in the United States assess students' ability to "locate, read, critically evaluate, and comprehend information in an online environment" (p. 5).

New Vignettes for Chapter Openers   Several new vignettes introduce readers to the central ideas of a chapter and provide an easy and motivating way to engage with the chapter's content. For example, here is the vignette that Victoria Ridgeway wrote for Chapter 1:

In 1974 I had six years of teaching experience in junior high and high schools under my belt. I considered myself a good science teacher. In the fall of that year, I was asked to attend a district-level meeting on content area reading. After all my efforts to evade the meeting failed, I grudgingly went, taking papers to grade so that I could at least accomplish something while I endured what I believed would be a useless meeting. I was, after all, a science teacher—not a reading teacher. What did I need to know about reading? My students seemed to be illiterate (they did not read their assignments and rarely did their homework). I believed I could teach science without reading—I taught a hands-on activities-based course.

During that meeting, Joy Monahan presented instructional ideas that she claimed would help students learn content. I was singularly uninterested until she challenged us to try "just a few of these strategies" for two or three weeks and report the results to her. At the time, I was teaching in a school that tracked students according to academic achievement. I taught both ends of the spectrum—students designated "basic" and those designated "gifted." I decided to show this Ms. Monahan that she could teach me nothing about teaching science.

That particular year I had a student, Amy.*, who had been a thorn in my side since the first day of school. She had learned to remove all the bolts securing the legs to the tops of the science tables in my room and did so with regularity. When the bolts were removed, the next student to enter the room and throw his/her books on the table had to move quickly to avoid the collapsing table. I never could her at this game. Amy was one of those students

*pseudonym

who, by her very presence in the classroom, was disruptive. I had a lot to teach Amy, and as it turned out she had much more to teach me.

In the ensuing few weeks, I selected two of the instructional ideas presented by Ms. Monahan (they were the ideas that required the least amount of effort on my part) and tried them with my "basic" classes, teaching the "gifted" classes in my normal (and brilliant) way. I gave both groups the same test, designed for the "gifted" class. I reasoned that I could allow the "basic" students to drop one test grade and thus my little experiment would do them little harm.

When I graded the tests for both classes, I was astounded. The "basic" group' is average was higher than that of the "gifted" class. I was transformed from a cynic to a convert in the time it took to grade those papers. My "basic" students had learned material that I previously thought too difficult for them. In fact, I had also noticed that these students were doing their assigned reading and homework and actively participating in class. Most important to me, their behavior had changed from apathetic to cooperative. This little experiment was a turning point in my life.

Marginal Icons

"Technology Tip" boxes provide practical and innovative ways to incorporate information communication technologies in teaching across the curriculum.

"Tips for Struggling Readers and Writers" boxes feature practical advice grounded in the research and in- classroom practice on how to teach children who have difficulty comprehending assigned reading materials.

"A Response from Our Readers" boxes are included throughout several chapters to illustrate how users of previous editions are adapting strategies and materials for use in their own classes.

Evidence-based research icons in every chapter highlight current research on content area teaching and learning and provide a solid ground on which to build one's instruction effectively.

Standards icons denoting various subject areas are included in each chapter to help preservice teachers make the connection to the ways content area literacy instruction helps them meet the standards in their disciplines.

Writing icons throughout the chapters point to writing examples.

ACKNOWLEDGMENTS

We would like to thank the many students and colleagues who have shared their experiences and given us invaluable feedback on this book. We particularly thank Michael Kibby and Cynthia Greenleaf for taking the time to give us their advice. We would also like to express our appreciation to those who played roles in the editing and production of the book. Specifically, we want to acknowledge the expert guidance and support we received from our editor, Aurora Martinez, often under quite challenging circumstances. We also thank Kevin Shannon and Mekea Harvey, Aurora's assistants at Allyn and Bacon, and Dennis Troutman at Stratford Publishing Services, each of whom made sure that we received answers to our questions on a timely basis and clarified procedures when we were uncertain.

Content Literacy and the Reading Process

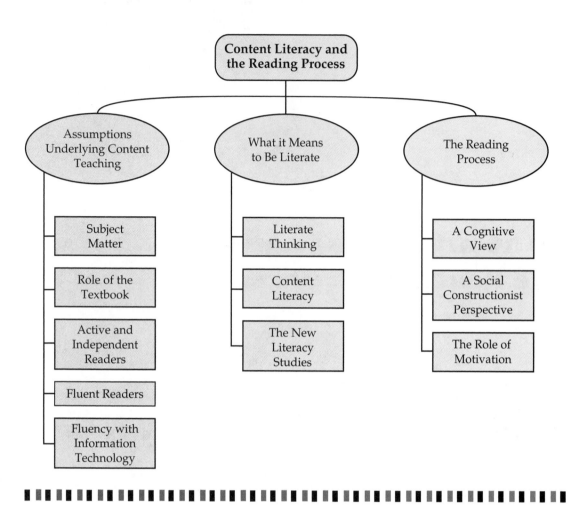

V ictoria, one of the authors of this edition, remembers her first encounter with reading and science in the following vignette.

■ ■ ■ ■ ■ ■ ■

In 1974 I had six years of teaching experience in junior high and high schools under my belt. I considered myself a good science teacher. In the fall of that year, I was asked to attend a district-level meeting on content area reading. After all my efforts to evade the meeting failed, I grudgingly went, taking papers to grade so that I could at least accomplish something while I endured what I believed would be a useless meeting. I was, after all, a science teacher—not a reading teacher. What did I need to know about reading? My students seemed to be illiterate (they did not read their assignments and rarely did their homework). I believed I could teach science without reading—I taught a hands-on activities-based course.

During that meeting, Joy Monahan presented instructional ideas that she claimed would help students learn content. I was singularly uninterested until she challenged us to try "just a few of these strategies" for two or three weeks and report the results to her. At the time, I was teaching in a school that tracked students according to academic achievement. I taught both ends of the spectrum—students designated "basic" and those designated "gifted." I decided to show this Ms. Monahan that she could teach me nothing about teaching science.

That particular year I had a student, Amy*, who had been a thorn in my side since the first day of school. She had learned to remove all the bolts securing the legs to the tops of the science tables in my room and did so with regularity. When the bolts were removed, the next student to enter the room and throw his/her books on the table had to move quickly to avoid the collapsing table. I never could catch her at this game. Amy was one of those students who, by her very presence in the classroom, was disruptive. I had a lot to teach Amy, and as it turned out she had much more to teach me.

In the ensuing few weeks, I selected two of the instructional ideas presented by Ms. Monahan (they were the ideas that required the least amount of effort on my part) and tried them with my "basic" classes, teaching the "gifted" classes in my normal (and brilliant) way. I gave both groups the same test, designed for the "gifted" class. I reasoned that I could allow the "basic" students to drop one test grade and thus my little experiment would do them little harm.

When I graded the tests for both classes, I was astounded. The "basic" group's average was higher than that of the "gifted" class. I was transformed from a cynic to a convert in the time it took to grade those papers. My "basic" students had learned material that I previously thought too difficult for them. In fact, I had also noticed that these students were doing their assigned reading and homework and actively participating in class. Most important to me, their behavior had changed from apathetic to cooperative. This little experiment was a turning point in my life.

∎∎∎∎∎∎

Imagine teaching an athlete like Venus Williams to play tennis until third or fourth grade and because she is the best young player in the world, concluding that she needs no more instruction. Now imagine that after three or four years with little to no instruction, Venus Williams is expected to play tennis, and play well, at Wimbledon—a different context from the one in which she originally learned to play the game. There is a large crowd, the court is clay, the stakes are very high. Although this scenario seems unimaginable, think of children in elementary schools, learning to read using narrative text. After several years with little to no instruction in reading expository text, they are expected

---

*pseudonym

to read high school textbooks with comprehension. There are parallels in these two scenarios that are difficult to ignore. Think about these parallels as you consider the assumptions underlying content area teaching.

ASSUMPTIONS UNDERLYING CONTENT TEACHING

Most content area teachers assume it is their responsibility to cover their subject matter in a timely, accurate, and effective manner (Alvermann & Moore, 1991; Moore, 1996). They also assume, for the most part, that textbooks are necessary for teaching and learning content (Wade & Moje, 2000). Finally, content area teachers tend to assume that by the time students enter middle school and high school, they are strategic in their approach to reading and learning (Alvermann & Nealy, 2004). These assumptions influence teachers' instructional decision making, their use of textbooks, and their perceptions of active and independent readers.

Subject Matter

The historical roots of content area reading instruction go back several decades. Prior to the twentieth century, the predominant mode of instruction in American secondary schools was one of imitation and memorization. In the early part of the twentieth century, the work of humanist educators such as John Dewey and developmentalists interested in individual growth factors began to emphasize child-centered curricula over rote memorization. With the cognitive revolution in psychology in the early 1970s came the notion that reading and writing should be taught as thinking processes rather than in the mechanical manner advocated by the behaviorists, who had preceded the cognitivists. Although other writers at that time were beginning to publish books on reading at the secondary school level, Herber's (1970) text, *Teaching Reading in the Content Areas,* is generally regarded as the first to demonstrate how teachers can simultaneously teach content and process (reading). It is also one of the first content area methods texts to emphasize the importance of teachers' decision making.

As a content area teacher you take pride, and rightfully so, in knowing a lot about the subject matter you teach and how best to engage students in learning. You also recognize that you are responsible for monitoring students' learning and pacing their instruction accordingly. If these were the only two factors you had to take into consideration when making instructional decisions, it would be a relatively simple task to decide what to teach, when, and at what pace. Unfortunately, instructional decision making is complicated by what Newmann (1988) refers to as the addiction to coverage:

> We are addicted to coverage. This addiction seems endemic in high schools . . .
> but it affects all levels of the curriculum, from kindergarten through college.

> We expose students to broad surveys of the disciplines and to endless sets of skills and competencies. . . . The press for broad coverage causes many teachers to feel inadequate about leaving out so much content and apologetically mindful of the fact that much of what they teach is not fully understood by their students. (p. 346)

Addiction to coverage is dangerous because it tends to produce a false dichotomy between content knowledge and process knowledge. When *knowing what* takes precedence over *knowing how,* as it typically does when preparing students for standardized tests pressures teachers to cover a wide variety of topics in an inadequate space of time, students are deprived of the opportunity to learn how bits of knowledge fit together and generalize to other areas of the curriculum or to real life. In short, students are denied the kind of instruction that leads to active and independent learning.

Role of the Textbook

Textbooks and other learning materials provide a focus for several chapter sections in this book. For example, in Chapter 3, we explore how hypertext and other forms of electronic media have led to a new relationship between text and reader. In Chapter 4, we consider the decision making involved in choosing appropriate materials to use in planning content literacy lessons or longer units of instruction. Here, however, we focus on three assumptions underlying the use of textbooks. One is that textbooks will help to structure loosely coupled curricular goals and objectives. By most estimates, textbooks do indeed structure from 67 to 90 percent of all classroom instruction (Woodward & Elliott, 1990), but this varies according to the type of instructional approach—transmission or participatory—that teachers espouse (Wade & Moje, 2000).

A second assumption is that students will use their textbooks to learn course content. This assumption may or may not be borne out. It depends on whether students view their textbooks or their teachers as the ultimate source of knowledge. Some researchers (Hinchman & Zalewski, 1996; Smith & Feathers, 1983a, 1983b) have found that students perceive their teacher, not the textbook, as the primary source of knowledge. Students generally find their teacher easier to understand than the textbook, especially if they believe they will be tested on what the teacher says in class. Other researchers (e.g., Fournier & Graves, 2002) found evidence that teachers put the responsibility for acquiring the information contained in the text squarely on their students' shoulders. Still other researchers (Ratekin, Simpson, Alvermann, & Dishner, 1985) have reported that in some content area classrooms it is the custom for teachers to use the textbook as a "safety net"—something to fall back on—rather than as a vital link and a basis for class discussions. When teachers use texts as safety nets, more often than not they substitute lecturing for discussions of assigned readings.

A third assumption is that textbooks will present the content in a coherent and unbiased fashion. We know from experience that this is not always so. If you have ever attempted to read a poorly organized text, one in which the author seems to jump from one topic to another, then you know what we mean when we say coherency cannot be taken for granted. Similarly, if you have ever discovered biases in a textbook's content, then you know that text-book authors, like everyone else, have particular ways of viewing the world and reporting on it. However, given appropriate planning strategies, even the most biased of texts can lead to excellent classroom discussions in which students learn to look at both sides of an issue for sources of possible misunder-standing. We firmly believe that in today's diverse classrooms, opportunities for students to respond to biased texts should be welcomed. Taking advantage of such opportunities can contribute toward building appreciation for individual differences.

Using textbooks wisely requires teachers who know both the content and the processes needed to understand that content. In the opening vignette, Victoria recounted how she discovered that her students *could* read their text-books. As the year progressed, students in her class became actively involved in their own learning.

Active and Independent Readers

Content area teachers love their subject matter. Why else would someone choose to spend five days a week immersed in science, history, mathematics, or literature? We want our students to love science or history or mathematics or literature as much as we do and choose to read and learn about our subjects independently. What do active and independent readers look like?

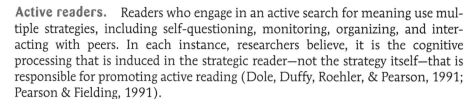

Active readers.   Readers who engage in an active search for meaning use multiple strategies, including self-questioning, monitoring, organizing, and interacting with peers. In each instance, researchers believe, it is the cognitive processing that is induced in the strategic reader—not the strategy itself—that is responsible for promoting active reading (Dole, Duffy, Roehler, & Pearson, 1991; Pearson & Fielding, 1991).

Active readers *generate questions* before they read, as they read, and when they have finished reading. Before reading a chapter in a social studies book, for example, active readers ask themselves what the selection is likely to cover, whether they know anything about the topic or are interested in it, and what they intend to do with the information presented. As they read, they question the meanings of unfamiliar words or ask how a certain event is likely to trigger a reaction. After reading the chapter, active readers ask whether their prediction of what the chapter would cover was accurate, whether they learned anything new, and how they might apply what they learned to something they already know. In fact, a fairly robust finding by researchers is that teaching students to generate their own questions leads to active learning and improved comprehension of text (National Reading Panel, 2000; Wade & Moje, 2000).

Active readers *monitor,* or periodically check, their understanding of what they have read. Although monitoring can include self-questioning, it is used here to describe the two-part process that readers go through when they (1) become aware of a breakdown in comprehension and (2) apply fix-up strategies to regain understanding.

ACTIVITY   To experience monitoring for yourself, read the following question, then the short paragraph.

> *Question:* Why would a love of french fries ruin a marriage?
>
> *Three-sentence paragraph:* The hamburger chain owner was afraid his love for french fries would ruin his marriage. He was worried. He decided to go on a daily exercise program.*

When you read the paragraph for the purpose of monitoring your comprehension, you might have called to mind what happens to people when they overindulge in fried foods. Thus, you might have inferred that the hamburger chain owner's love of french fries had caused him to put on weight, which in turn threatened his marriage—if, of course, it can be assumed that the owner's wife disliked overweight men. Suppose, however, that the owner did not eat any french fries; maybe he simply worked long hours and went home with the smell of fries on his clothes. Might this have contributed to the man's fear that his marriage was in trouble? In fact, any number of inferences could be drawn, depending on the knowledge and past experiences a reader brings to the task.

The point is, you are now aware from monitoring your reading that there is more than one plausible interpretation. Consequently, if you are like most active readers, you will try to resolve the ambiguity and potential loss of understanding by selecting from an array of fix-up strategies. What are some strategies that you could apply in the exercise involving the hamburger chain owner? You could ask to see the remainder of the text, in the anticipation that forthcoming information would provide some clue as to which inference is correct. Or, you might reread the three-sentence paragraph to see if there is any evidence to suggest one inference over the other. As you can see, the third sentence ("He decided to go on a daily exercise program.") lends support to the "overweight" inference, although students have argued that a daily exercise program would keep the hamburger chain owner away from home even more, and that it could conceivably add to the objectionable-odor problem.

---

*Adapted from C. J. Gordon, "Modeling inference awareness across the curriculum," *Journal of Reading, 29* (444–447, 1985).

Active readers attempt to make sense of the large body of facts, interpretations, and principles presented in their various textbooks by *organizing* such information into meaningful units. They may do this in one of several ways: by graphically organizing the information so as to form a semantic map or structured overview, by writing summaries, by constructing outlines and taking notes, or by elaborating on the text by drawing from their background knowledge and past experiences whatever associations seem most helpful in bridging from the *known* ("in the head") to the *unknown* ("on the page").

Regardless of which organizing strategy they choose, active readers are skilled in separating important information from unimportant information. When students experience difficulty in organizing what they have read, it is quite often because they are insensitive to what is important. Sometimes this insensitivity is due to a reader's inability to identify information that an author deems important; at other times it is due to a reader's strong sense of personal relevancy. For instance, Winograd (1984) found that eighth graders who were having difficulty reading tended to identify importance on the basis of what held high personal interest for them (such as sentences containing rich visual detail), whereas good readers tended to identify important information on the basis of its superordinate or subordinate placement within the text structure. Young adolescents have difficulty organizing large bodies of information partially because they rely on personal relevance as a criterion for attributing importance.

EVIDENCE-BASED RESEARCH

Although we recognize that readers often reflect on what they have read and actively construct meaning from texts without the benefit of *peer interaction,* there is growing support for placing a greater emphasis on socially constructed meaning (Gee, 1996; Davis, Sumara, & Luce-Kapler, 2000; Lankshear & Knobel, 2003). Engaged readers, whether in gifted, regular, or basic level classes, enjoy opportunities for open-forum discussions, in which a free-flowing exchange of ideas enriches and refines their understandings of what was read and heightens their motivation to read further (Alvermann, 2000). Discussions of this type, unlike lecturing and recitations, provide learners for whom English is a second language with excellent opportunities to practice English and learn content simultaneously (Met, 1994). Interactions with peers also enable students from diverse cultural groups to learn from one another.

Independent readers.   Independent readers typically are independent learners, and vice versa. We agree with Herber and Nelson-Herber's (1987) claims that the similarities between the two are numerous and that independence can be developed by capitalizing on the following five principles:

1. *Independence comes from practice.* Readers develop independence when they have sufficient opportunities across the curriculum to establish their own purposes for reading, to make connections between their own experiences and those they read about, to use valid criteria in making judgments about the quality and value of what they read, and to apply what they have learned in one content area to another.

2. *Independence develops by design, not chance.* As students grow in independence, they require less and less in the way of structured learning activities. In the beginning, however, they are dependent on teacher modeling and guidance to show them how to apply the reading and reasoning processes necessary for understanding important concepts. As time goes on, responsibility is gradually released, as students assume more and more of the responsibility for applying what they have learned to new areas of study and new materials (Pearson & Gallagher, 1983).

3. *Independence is a relative state.* This is true for all of us. As a science teacher, Victoria feels confident in reading text related to biology and chemistry. However, even a simple mathematics text baffles her! How many of us can read an insurance document or a credit card agreement with ease? Teachers must keep in mind that in order to develop and nurture independence, the maturity level of the student must be matched with appropriate resources.

4. *Independence can be achieved in groups.* Herber and Nelson-Herber (1987) advocate small-group learning experiences to develop students' independence in reading. We agree with their view "that students can be as much in charge of their reading and reasoning processes and their use of ideas when interacting in cooperative groups as when working individually" (p. 586). There is ample research to support this view on cooperative learning, which we discuss in Chapter 3.

5. *Independence means forever "becoming."* No one is ever totally independent as a learner. Occasionally, we all rely on others to help us interpret, clarify, or elaborate on what we read. Helping students become independent readers and learners will require time, skill, and patience.

Fluent Readers

EVIDENCE-
BASED
RESEARCH

What does it mean to read fluently, and what assumptions do we often make about older readers' fluency (or lack thereof)? First, a common definition of fluency in relation to reading in the content areas focuses on students' ability to comprehend texts of various types with speed, accuracy, and appropriate expression (National Reading Panel, 2000). Another less common definition is one that focuses on students' fluency with information technology (American Association of University Women Educational Foundation, 2000). We believe both are important in terms of their implications for content literacy teaching and learning.

An assumption that is often made about older students is that they have attained a satisfactory level of fluency in reading assigned content area materials. Unfortunately, this is not always the case. In fact, among readers who struggle to comprehend, difficulties with fluency are often the culprit. Why is this so? Theoretically, readers have only a limited amount of attention, and when that attention is diverted to decoding words and pausing in appropriate places, overall comprehension suffers (LaBerge & Samuels, 1974). Slow and laborious decoding at the word level also hampers students' ability to monitor their reading. When text processing at the word level is not automatic, Klenk and Kibby (2000) venture that readers will not "know how it sounds and feels to read text fluently" (p. 673).

EVIDENCE-BASED RESEARCH

Speed, accuracy, and appropriate expression.   The underlying assumption of fluency instruction defined in terms of a reader's speed, accuracy, and appropriate expression is that teachers will view it as a means to comprehension and not as an end in itself. Because adequate comprehension is essential for effective studying to occur, it is clear that fluency plays a pivotal role overall. The National Reading Panel (2000), while acknowledging that fluency instruction is often neglected in day-to-day classroom instruction, found sufficient research evidence to suggest that guided oral-reading procedures have a positive impact on students' fluency and comprehension across a range of grade levels and in a variety of regular and special education classrooms. Examples of these procedures are included in Chapter 7.

Fluency with Information Technology

One of several new terms to make its way into the field of reading education as a result of the information explosion associated with today's computer age is *information literacy.* It refers to what is generally defined as the ability to access, evaluate, organize, and use information culled from a variety of sources. Not to be confused with *computer literacy,* which reflects a technological know-how in manipulating software packages, information literacy requires, among other things, knowing how to formulate a search strategy for zeroing in on needed information. The topic of Internet search strategies will be discussed later. For now, it is sufficient to link information literacy to fluency with information technology.

In a report focused on how to educate students in the computer age so that they become tech savvy and capable of participating fully in e-culture (American

Technology Tip on Media Standards

A useful set of nonprint media standards for helping students achieve fluency with information technology is available through the National Research Center on English Learning and Achievement (CELA). Developed at CELA by Karen Swan, the nonprint media standards are divided into basic skills, critical literacies, and construction skills for each of three grade levels: elementary, middle, and high school. A complete listing of these standards for achieving information literacy is available at http://cela.albany.edu/reports/standards/index.html

Association of University Women Educational Foundation, 2000), the argument is made that fluency with information technology is much more than static listings of how to become more proficient at word processing or e-mailing. Instead, the authors of the report note that "fluency goals must allow for change, enable adaptability, connect to personal goals, and promote lifelong learning" (p. xi).

These goals will require that all students become fluent in skills such as designing a home page, organizing a database, communicating with others whom they may never meet in person, and evaluating personal privacy concerns. Examples of strategies for promoting fluency with information technology are found in Chapter 3.

In summary, content area reading instruction involves much more than covering the subject matter in a particular specialty area. It includes dealing with assumptions about the role of the textbook, promoting active and independent reading, and developing readers' fluency. Students who self-question, monitor their reading, organize information, and interact with their peers possess some of the strategies necessary for becoming fluent readers and independent learners. However, their overall sense of themselves as learners will depend to a large extent on how they see themselves as readers and what it means to be literate in a fast-changing world.

WHAT IT MEANS TO BE LITERATE

As individuals, we tend to approach literacy with our own agendas: we are in pursuit of *something.* Depending on our ideological frameworks, our educational backgrounds, and our social, economic, and political status in life, we may hold quite different perceptions of why we are in pursuit and what it means to be literate. For many, literacy is something to value for its intrinsic worth; for others, it may be a symbol of achievement or a means for social change; and for still others, it is something to profit from. In each of these perceptions, there is the underlying assumption that being literate means having a special capacity of one kind or another.

However, as Knoblauch (1990) pointed out, this is not necessarily the case. In observing that "literacy is one of those mischievous concepts, like virtuousness and craftsmanship, that appear to denote capacities but that actually convey value judgments," Knoblauch (p. 74) reminds us that individuals who have the motivation and status to enforce literacy as a social requirement are often the same ones whose value judgments count. Failure to take note of the power relations surrounding such judgments is tantamount to buying into the idea that literacy is a "neutral" or innocent concept. Recognizing the political nature of what it means to be literate is important to our work as educators. It may keep us from falling into the trap of equating a student's innate worthiness with her or his competence in reading and writing. It may also prevent us from being blinded by ideological leanings that sometimes propel us to act as if our own literacy agendas were innocent or pure.

Literate Thinking

From Langer's (1989) perspective, reading and writing are "tools that enable, but do not insure, literate thinking" (p. 2). She argues vigorously against the tendency to equate literate thinking with the ability to analyze or synthesize large chunks of print, a common but uninformed notion of what it means to be literate.

ACTIVITY   Langer (1989) provides an example to highlight the distinction she draws between print literacy and literate thinking:

> When a group of American students read a social studies textbook and then discuss the contents and the implications, most people would say that the students are engaging in literate thinking (within the norms of this culture). But, what if the discussion had occurred after the students had seen a television news report about the same topic? I would still want to claim that the students had engaged in literate thinking even though they had neither read nor written. Now, imagine a group of students who do not know how to read or write in English or another language engaged in the very same conversation about the television news report. I would claim that they too would have engaged in literate thinking. In contrast, imagine that the students had read the same social studies text and then completed end-of-chapter questions by locating information in the text and copying the information the questions asked them to itemize. I would claim that the kinds of literacy in this activity do not reflect the kinds of school literacy that, based on the many reports and articles in both the professional and public press, are needed and valued by American society today. That activity does not involve culturally useful literate behavior, even if the students get the answers right. (p. 2)

Do you agree or disagree with Langer's argument? Why?

The 1980s and 1990s spawned a rash of reform movements, most of which had as their goal the erasing of illiteracy as a threat to the economic well-being and worldwide competitiveness of the United States. A characteristic of most of the reforms has been their emphasis on a print- or book-focused literacy. Schools in general are concerned with students' abilities to read and write—to demonstrate what is understood—regardless of grade level. The attention educators give to functional literacy, according to Greene (1991), leaves little time for asking some difficult, but important, questions:

> [Teachers] scarcely ever ask [themselves] about the difference literacy makes in various lives. Does it overcome alienation or confirm it? Does it reduce feelings of powerlessness or intensify them? How much, after all, depends on

literacy and how much on social arrangements? How much on trust? On love? On glimpses of the half-moon? On wonderful ideas? On feeling, as Dickinson did, "a clearing" in the mind? (p. 130)

Similar concerns have been raised by Heath (1986b), whose research has shown that in many families and communities, being a competent reader and writer is not viewed as being a ticket to equality, a good job, or social mobility. In short, being literate has different meanings for different cultural groups, or as Langer (1989) so aptly puts it, "there is no right or wrong literacy, just the one that is, more or less, responsive to the demands of a particular culture" (p. 1).

(Source: CALVIN AND HOBBES © 1989 & 1995 Watterson. Dist. by UNIVERSAL PRESS SYNDICATE. Reprinted with permission. All Rights Reserved.)

Content Literacy

Generally, content literacy is defined as "the ability to use reading and writing for the acquisition of new content in a given discipline" (McKenna & Robinson, 1990, p. 184). To that we add the importance of oral language (e.g., small- and large-group discussions) and computer-mediated communication technologies in affecting students' ability to learn from reading and writing activities in their subject matter classes. Students' prior knowledge of a particular subject and their interest in learning more about it also mediate their ability to use their content literacy skills.

Content knowledge.   Content literacy is not to be confused with content knowledge, although the two concepts do share some common ground. For example, as McKenna and Robinson (1990) pointed out, the more knowledge students have about the content they are assigned to read in their textbooks,

Special Hints for Struggling Readers and Writers

Hints for helping readers who struggle to learn the content of their subject matter classes abound. For example, Ivey (2000) has developed what she calls her "working generalizations" on teaching adolescents who struggle with reading and writing. Based on her research and experience as a classroom teacher, these so-called generalizations include the following advice:

- Provide students with access to materials that hold personal interest for them and that span a wide range of difficulty levels.
- Make room in the school day for students to have time to share their literacy experiences with others through small-group discussions, buddy reading, and choral reading activities.

- Plan activities that require students to use reading and writing to complete a task that is content related and highly motivating, such as performing hands-on science experiments or communicating through e-mail with classmates who found novel ways to complete a math assignment.
- Take into account students' desires to improve their literacy skills and help them do so through initiating the reading and writing workshop concept as a part of the regular classroom routine. (See Chapter 3 for an example of the reading and writing workshop adapted from Allen [1995] for high school use.)

the more that knowledge facilitates their reading and writing—a situation which in turn sets up a cyclical pattern such that still more knowledge is acquired and applied to other tasks requiring content literacy skills.

This cyclical pattern should come as good news to content area teachers. In effect, what it says is that teachers who instruct students in a subject matter specialty are helping to improve students' abilities to read and write in that subject area by simply providing some of the necessary background information. Providing background information, however, is only half of the task. The other half involves helping students acquire content literacy, or the ability to use reading and writing strategies to learn new content. Students who have the literacy skills necessary for supplementing their knowledge of the content by reading beyond what the teacher introduces through lectures, demonstrations, and so on are well on their way to becoming independent learners.

The New Literacy Studies

In the 1980s and 1990s, an interdisciplinary group of scholars (Bloome & Green, 1992; Cazden, 1988; Cook-Gumperz, 1986; Gee, 1996; Heath, 1983; Luke, 1988; Street, 1995) began to ask questions such as "What is literacy?" "Who benefits from being literate?" and "What specific cultural meanings and practices are involved in becoming literate?" The impetus for asking these questions, all of which deal in one way or another with the differing contexts in which people read and write, was a growing mistrust in the more conventional or dominant view of literacy as a "neutral" or technical skill. No longer willing to think of reading as primarily a psychological phenomenon—one in which individuals who can decode and have the requisite background knowledge for drawing inferences are able to arrive at the right interpretation of a text—this interdisciplinary group of scholars began to document how the "right" interpretation of a text rarely holds for different individuals reading in different contexts. Their work and that of others who are similarly focused on students' multiple literacies has become known as the New Literacy Studies (NLS) (Willinsky, 1990). The NLS are distinguished from the dominant view on literacy because they focus on "what literacy events and practices mean to users in different cultural and social contexts" (Street, 2003, p. 10).

In addition, related work in the area of social cognition (Lave & Wenger, 1991; Tharp & Gallimore, 1988) and cultural studies (Lewis, 1998) has contributed to the growing sense that reading and writing are shaped by (and in turn help to shape) multiple sociocultural practices associated with becoming literate. Describing these practices as "deeply political," Gee (1999) has gone on to show how they also "fully integrate language, both oral and written, with nonlanguage 'stuff,' that is, with ways of acting, interacting, feeling, valuing, thinking, and believing, as well as with various sorts of nonverbal symbols, sites, tools, objects, and technologies" (p. 356). In summary, the NLS encompass ways of behaving, knowing, thinking, and valuing which give meaning to the uses of reading and writing that go far beyond simply mining a textbook for its literal or inferential meaning.

Rethinking content literacy practices.   The New Literacy Studies, which provide a different way of looking at literacy, are beginning to affect the ways in which teacher educators and classroom teachers think about content reading and writing instruction and how students learn from such instruction. This is especially the case among educators who subscribe to the so-called natural approaches to literacy instruction. Labeled typically as process writing and reader response, these approaches are being examined closely by individuals interested in critical literacy and critical language awareness—an awareness, that is, of why writers or speakers choose to write about certain topics, what

Technology and Multiliteracies

For information on New Literacy Studies check out Brian Street's on-line article in the May 2003 issue of Current Issues in Comparative Education at www.tc.columbia.edu/ CICE/archives/contents.html

content they include and leave out, whose interests they serve, and who is empowered (or disempowered) by the language they choose.

Some teacher educators (Kamler, 1999; Kamler & Comber, 1996), for instance, are beginning to reflect on how personal written response and other expressivist pedagogies such as reader response are teaching students to think about themselves and others in particularly naive ways—ways that rarely move them to social action and a critique of what they read or hear. Others (Lewis, 2000; Lewis, Ketter, & Fabos, 2001) are learning how to work around certain reader response approaches that emphasize personal identification at the expense of critiquing texts to look for an author's assumptions about people's identities, their goals, ways of being in the world, and so on. Although there is much to admire in these natural approaches to literacy instruction, they have come under criticism of late for what they leave out.

For instance, critics (Moje, Willes, & Fassio, 2001; Patterson, Mellor, & O'Neill, 1994) say that these approaches have major flaws, but they are flaws that can be corrected so as to enable important gains realized through student-centered instruction to move forward. One of the identified flaws is that educators who teach from a reader response perspective put too much emphasis on personal experience and individual interpretation. This leads, they say, to a naive view of the reading process, one in which it would appear that texts could somehow be neutrally produced and read. What they propose is a drawing in of the view from "without" (Green, 1991; Lemke, 1995). For example, Annette Patterson and colleagues (1994) believe it is their responsibility as literacy educators to teach students to take up a range of reading positions—some that may lead to resistant readings of what have become dominant or "mainstream" texts.

Helping students develop a facility and an interest in reading resistantly is an idea that has taken on increasing significance since its introduction in the late 1970s (Fetterly, 1978; Scott, 1990). Although some literacy educators might argue that resistant reading is just another name for critical reading, we disagree. A characteristic of resistant reading that we find absent in conventional descriptions of critical reading is the notion of "reading subtexts" as "a way of distancing ourselves and gaining some control over the reading experience" (Commeyras & Alvermann, 1996, p. 45).

The importance of reading the subtext is highlighted in Sam Wineburg's (1991) study in which he compared how historians read historical texts and how high school students read the same texts. Wineburg found that the students were quite good at identifying the main ideas and answering the comprehension questions that went with the readings, but they failed to see how the authors of the texts had constructed them as social instruments "masterfully crafted to achieve a social end" (p. 502). The historians, on the other hand, read two types of subtexts. They read the texts as rhetorical artifacts, which involved reconstructing the "authors' purposes, intentions, and goals" (p. 498). They also read the texts as human artifacts, which involved identifying "elements that work at cross-purposes with the authors' intentions, bringing to the

**EVIDENCE-
BASED
RESEARCH**

surface convictions the authors may have been unaware of or may have wished to conceal" (p. 499).

Some thought questions

1. Think back to a time when you taught students to read using a so-called natural language learning approach. Or, perhaps you were taught to read by someone who favored one or more of those approaches. Do you agree with the criticism leveled against such approaches? Why? Why not?
2. Are you a resistant reader? When and under what conditions?
3. If you do not read resistantly yourself, do you see any reason for teaching others to read in that fashion? Why? Why not?

THE READING PROCESS

In recent years, developments in cognitive psychology, sociolinguistics, and cultural anthropology have drawn attention to the need for explanations of the reading process that take into account a broad view of the everyday world of students and their families, teachers, schools, and communities. This section focuses on three aspects of the reading process: a cognitive view, a social constructionist perspective, and the role of motivation in the reading process.

A Cognitive View

A cognitive or psycholinguistic view of the reading process assumes "an active reader who constructs meaning through the integration of existing and new knowledge and the flexible use of strategies to foster, monitor, regulate, and maintain comprehension" (Dole et al., 1991, p. 242). Students who take a personal, adaptive view of reading understand that knowledge is constructed by them and that the experiences they bring to texts shape in large part what they will comprehend (Brown, Collins, & Duguid, 1989).

Technology Tip—ELLs and the New Literacies

Becoming knowledgeable about the social functions of written language within various linguistic and cultural communities can foster English language learners' (ELLs) expressive abilities. Such knowledge is vitally important for teachers whose linguistic and sociocultural backgrounds differ from those of their students. It is all part of rethinking one's teaching practices in light of the New Literacy Studies. To learn how the new literacies are affecting what counts as writing in content area classrooms, visit www.readingonline.org/electronic/JAAL/4-01_column/

One of our favorite articles of all time dates back to our days in graduate school at Syracuse University. Dr. Margaret Early, one of our professors at the time, introduced us to Cooper and Petrosky's (1976) "A Psycholinguistic View of the Fluent Reading Process." The authors of the article make the point that "in reading, the brain supplies more information than it receives from the eye about the text" (p. 191). The following activity is designed to demonstrate Cooper and Petrosky's point. See if you agree with their view of the fluent reading process.

ACTIVITY   Try your hand at using a little common sense and some prior knowledge of language and content to comprehend two paragraphs from a selection titled "The Kingdom of Kay Oss" (Roskos & Walker, 1994, p. 5).

The Kingdom of Kay Oss

Once in the land of Serenity there ruled a king called Kay Oss. The king wanted to be liked by all his people. So one day thx bxnxvolxnt dxspot dxcidxd that no onx in thx country would bx rxsponsiblx for anything. Zll of thx workxrs rxstxd from thxir dzily lzbors. "Blxss Kzy Oss," thxy xxclzimxd.

Now thx lzw mzkxrs wxrx vxry wvsx. But zs wvsx zs thxy wxrx, thxy dxcvdxd thzt thx bxst form of govxrnmxnt wzs nonx zt zll.

If you made sense of all or most of these two paragraphs with relative ease and little frustration, it might be said that you are the type of person who reads to obtain meaning rather than to identify letters or words per se. According to Frank Smith (1971), a prominent psycholinguist whose work builds on that of E. B. Huey (1908/1968):

The ability to put letters together to form words has very little to do with the actual process of [fluent] reading (as opposed to learning to read) and . . . even the ability to identify words loses its importance when one "reads for meaning." (Smith cited in Cooper & Petrosky, 1976, p. 186)

Simply put, reading is more than the linear sum of words. Think about this claim in relation to your reading of "The Kingdom of Kay Oss," and then answer the following questions:

1. Did you find that you needed only a minimum of visual cues from the printed text to understand it?
2. What prior knowledge did you call on to make sense of the selection?
3. To what extent did your knowledge of stories, in general, influence your understanding and reduce the uncertainty of the task?
4. How often did you rely on your knowledge of:
   Letter-sound associations (graphophonics)?
   Spelling patterns (orthography)?
   Relationships of words to each other (syntax)?
   Contextual meaning (semantics)?

5. Did you risk being "wrong" in your attempt to derive meaning? That is, did you use context to guess unfamiliar words or just skip them?
6. Did you maintain sufficient speed when reading the selection to overcome the limitations of visual processing and short-term memory?

If you find yourself agreeing with Cooper and Petrosky's (1976) claim that "in reading, the brain supplies more information than it receives from the eye about the text" (p. 191), then you will probably feel right at home when you read about the top-down model of text processing discussed later in this chapter. If you have doubts about this claim, you may feel more comfortable with the interactive model of reading, also discussed later in the chapter.

Prior knowledge and schema theory.   Prior knowledge can cover a wide range of ideas, skills, and attitudes. When we use the term, we are focusing particularly on a reader's previous or existing knowledge of the subject matter of the text. What a person already knows about a topic is probably the single most influential factor with respect to what he or she will learn.

EVIDENCE-BASED RESEARCH

Cognitive psychologists use the word *schema* to describe how people organize the raw data of everyday experiences into meaningful patterns. A schema is a collection of organized and interrelated ideas or concepts. Schemata (the plural form) are fluid; they overlap and intertwine, and they are constantly modified to assimilate or accommodate new information. Schemata enable people to draw generalizations, form opinions, and understand new experiences (Anderson, 1984).

Schemata are frequently explained using the example of restaurants, probably because everyone has had some experience in going out to eat. Your schema for going to a restaurant might include the following: Someone will ask you what you would like to eat; that person or another will bring food, usually the food you asked for; you will pay for this food; you will not have to wash the dishes. Depending on actual experiences with dining out, individual restaurant schemata will vary. If your culinary adventures are mostly at fast-food outlets in your hometown on the East Coast, you would know just what to do at a Burger King in Cody, Wyoming, but you might not be sure which fork to use or which wine to order in a fancy restaurant. If your experiences were more varied, however, you would probably know about such things as making reservations, tipping, à la carte menus, and the specialties at different kinds of ethnic restaurants. You would not expect to order chicken wings at the Russian Tea Room in New York City, even if you had never been there before.

Schemata operate similarly in reading. They act as a kind of mental filing system from which the individual can retrieve relevant existing knowledge and into which new information can be filed. As you read, your schema for a topic helps you to anticipate, to infer, to decide what is or is not important, to build relationships between ideas, and to decide what information merits close attention. After reading, you use your schema as a topic to help you recall what you have read and put it into your own words.

Schemata, which are sometimes referred to as prior knowledge structures, play a large role in the reading process. They determine which of several interpretations of a text is the most probable. For example, this famous sentence taken from the work of Bransford and McCarrell (1974) illustrates how one's culture can influence the meaning that is made of print:

> The notes were sour because the seam split.

Although they may be familiar with all of the words and the syntax or ordering of those words, readers in the United States typically have difficulty constructing meaning for this sentence until they are provided with clues such as *bagpipe* or *Scottish musical instrument*.

Making connections between theory and practice.   Victoria likes to remind students in her content literacy classes of the importance of applying in their own classrooms what they know about prior knowledge and schema theory. She uses a series of three short passages to make her point. We include those passages here, along with several self-reflection questions aimed at helping you make connections between theory and practice.

The first passage illustrates the fact that prior knowledge must be *activated* to be of use. Note that no title is provided in order to demonstrate the difficulty in comprehending material for which prior knowledge, although available, has not been activated.

Passage:

The procedure is actually quite simple. First you arrange items into different groups. Of course one group may be sufficient depending on how much there is to do. If you have to go somewhere else due to lack of facilities, that is the next step; otherwise, you are pretty well set. It is important not to overdo things. That is, it is better to do too few things at once than too many. In the short run this may not seem important but complications can easily arise. A mistake can be expensive as well. The manipulation of the appropriate mechanisms should be self-explanatory, and we need not dwell on it here. At first, the whole procedure will seem complicated. Soon, however, it will become just another facet of life. It is difficult to foresee any end to the necessity for this task in the immediate future, but then, one never can tell. After the procedure is completed, one arranges the materials into different groups again. Then they can be put into their appropriate places. Eventually they will be used once more and the whole cycle will then have to be repeated. However, that is part of life. (Bransford, 1979, pp. 134–135)

Self-reflection questions
1. If we had provided a title, such as "Washing Clothes," would the passage have made more sense immediately?

2. Would simply providing a title be adequate for activating your students' background knowledge about topics you regularly assign them to read? What else might you want to do to activate their knowledge more fully?

The second passage illustrates the importance of activating *appropriate* prior knowledge. Failure to do so can lead to confusion and misinterpretation of the text. For example, read the following passage twice: first, from the perspective of a *prisoner*, and then from a *wrestler's* perspective. After each of the readings, choose the best answer from the four possible ones that follow the question "How had Rocky been punished for his aggressiveness?"

Passage:

Rocky slowly got up from the mat, planning his escape. He hesitated a moment and thought. Things were not going well. What bothered him most was being held, especially since the charge against him had been weak. He considered his present situation. The lock that held him was strong but he thought he could break it. He knew, however, that his timing would have to be perfect. Rocky was aware that it was because of his early roughness that he had been penalized so severely—much too severely from his point of view. The situation was becoming frustrating; the pressure had been grinding on him for too long. He was being ridden unmercifully. Rocky was getting angry now. He felt he was ready to make his move. He knew that his success or failure would depend on what he did in the next few seconds. (Anderson, Reynolds, Schallert, & Goetz, 1977, p. 372)

Comprehension question: How had Rocky been punished for his aggressiveness?
A. He had been demoted to the "B" team.
B. His opponent had been given points.
C. He lost his privileges for the weekend.
D. He had been arrested and imprisoned.

Self-reflection questions
1. Have you ever read something only to find out later that you had activated inappropriate background knowledge? How did it affect your comprehension? How did it make you feel?
2. As a teacher, or prospective teacher, what might you do instructionally to ensure that students activate appropriate background knowledge for reading the materials required in your content area?

The third passage demonstrates why prior knowledge must be *sufficient* to be of use in comprehending text. For example, you may have had experience playing baseball—even bowling—but the batsmen and bowlers in "Today's Cricket" do not play by the rules you might expect. In short, if you grew up in the United States, it is likely you are as "lost" as we are when it comes to comprehending a sport played mainly in England and other parts of the Commonwealth.

Passage:

"Today's Cricket"

The batsmen were merciless against the bowlers. The bowlers placed their men in slips and covers. But to no avail. The batsmen hit one four after another along with an occasional six. Not once did a ball look like it would hit their stumps or be caught. ("Wood's 100 Helps," 1978)

Self-reflection questions

1. Would knowing that "bowl" (as used in cricket) means "to put a batsman out by bowling the balls off the wicket" (*Webster's New World Dictionary*, 1991, p. 166) improve your understanding of the game? Why? Why not? What prior knowledge do you still lack?
2. If you were teaching a class in which your students were expected to read a story about cricket, how would you provide them with sufficient background knowledge?

In summary, as illustrated previously, it is one thing to develop a theoretical understanding of prior knowledge; it is quite another to apply that understanding in an actual classroom situation. However, we contend (and believe you would agree) that looking for ways to bridge theory and practice is well worth the effort.

EVIDENCE-BASED RESEARCH

Three models of the reading process.   The bottom-up, top-down, and interactive models of the reading process are all concerned with a reader's schemata, but to varying degrees. The bottom-up model, sometimes referred to as the automaticity model (LaBerge & Samuels, 1976), is based on the idea that one can focus attention selectively on only one thing at a time. By this line of reasoning, until readers can decode the words of a text automatically, they will be unable to devote a sufficient amount of attention to comprehending the text and fluency will suffer, as noted earlier. As its name implies, the bottom-up model of the reading process assumes that meaning resides primarily in the text and that pieces of information are chunked incrementally to produce comprehension. Letters and their associated sounds are chunked to make words, words are chunked to make sentences, and so on.

According to the top-down model of the reading process, what the reader already knows is thought to determine in large part what he or she will be able to comprehend. For example, even if *triskaidekaphobia* is pronounced accurately, the reader may not be able to comprehend its meaning in text:

Claudia's bout with triskaidekaphobia prevented her from ever staying on the thirteenth floor of a hotel.

In order for comprehension to occur, the reader would have to associate the meaning of the word *triskaidekaphobia* (fear of the number 13) with some previous experience or knowledge that linked the number 13 with unlucky. Proponents of the top-down model of reading argue that meaning resides largely in one's head, and it is the reader's schemata more than the print on the page that account for what is comprehended and what is not. As its name implies, the top-down model assumes that comprehending begins when a reader accesses appropriate background experiences and knowledge to make sense of print. In other words, unlike the bottom-up model, in which the reader incrementally chunks bigger and bigger pieces of information, the top-down model proposes that the reader makes educated guesses to predict the meaning of the print.

The interactive model of the reading process incorporates features of both the bottom-up and top-down models. Proponents of this model argue that the degree to which a reader uses print or prior knowledge will depend largely on the familiarity of the topic being read, how interested the reader is in the topic, and the purpose for which he or she is reading. For example, if you have read about different models of reading in the past and have an interest in learning more about them or reviewing what you know, you may be reading this section of the chapter using a top-down process approach.

Alternatively, you may be reading along at a pretty good clip, making predictions about what you will find on the printed page, and slowing to examine more closely words such as *automaticity* and *triskaidekaphobia*. Perhaps you decoded a large word or looked for a familiar word part (such as *automatic*) in it. If you processed the information in this fashion, you were reading interactively. That is, you were using, alternately, what you knew from prior knowledge and what you were able to infer from your knowledge of the English language and the conventions of print.

Along with a majority of other literacy educators, we believe the interactive model of the reading process is a good descriptor of how students typically read their content area texts. They connect what they know about language, decoding, and vocabulary to their background experiences and prior knowledge. They also take into account the demands of the reading task or the reasons for which they are reading.

Metacognition.   Metacognition, simply put, means knowing about knowing. It is a term used to describe students' awareness of *what* they know, their understanding of *how* to be strategic readers, and their knowledge of *when* (i.e., under what conditions) to evaluate the adequacy of their comprehension (Paris, Lipson, & Wixson, 1983). Metacognition is an awareness of what resources (materials, skills, and knowledge) one can call up to meet the demands of a particular task (Baker & Brown, 1980). For example, before reading a textbook chapter on the Holocaust, students might take a mental inventory of the information about the topic they have gleaned previously from books, films, and magazine accounts. They might also assess their interest in pursuing the topic further, their ability to read strategically, and/or their understanding of the purpose for the assignment. Developing such an awareness, however, does not ensure that they will succeed in comprehending the portion of text on the Holocaust. They will also need to monitor their reading.

EVIDENCE-BASED RESEARCH

Monitoring involves evaluating the trustworthiness of certain assumptions or inferences one makes while reading. It also involves applying any of a number of fix-up strategies when comprehension falters or breaks down completely. Moving backward and forward in text searches, concentrating on only the important information, making mental images, and contrasting new ideas with previous experiences are some of the most common fix-up strategies (Brown & Campione, 1994). As you might imagine, there is an important difference between knowing something is not making sense and doing something about it. Knowledge that is treated as separate and distinct from the situations in which it is learned and put to use is less helpful than knowledge that is contextually situated.

A lifespan developmental perspective on reading.   Reading development has traditionally been considered synonymous with early reading development. Recently, Alexander (n.d.) proposed a lifespan developmental perspective that attempts to explain how reading develops across the lifespan, "from womb to tomb" (p. 5). This view of reading holds promise for those of us engaged in educating adolescents because it helps us consider the development of literacy as students move beyond the early grades. Three stages are described in the lifespan developmental model: (a) acclimation, (b) competence, and (c) proficiency/expertise.

Alexander identifies three main factors that influence lifespan development of reading expertise across these three stages. The first factor, knowledge of

Hints for Struggling Readers and Writers

It is helpful to keep in mind Stanovich's (1980) interactive-compensatory model when working with readers who struggle to decode texts. According to this model, they will tend to rely more than good readers on context for word recognition and hence have less freed-up capacity for comprehension than good readers. The instructional implications of the interactive-compensatory model for content area teachers include the following:

■ Provide readers who struggle to decode their assigned texts with opportunities to hear those texts read aloud, perhaps through tape-assisted instruction, and to write down what they want to remember.
■ Give readers for whom word recognition is a problem supplemental materials that

include visual clues to word meaning. Also consider the use of manipulatives in science and math areas.

■ Allot extra time for readers who struggle to complete their assignments. Consider assigning fewer pages, perhaps concentrating on the key ideas in a passage or chapter.
■ Encourage struggling readers to use the Internet. Sometimes the symbols and icons that are bothersome to good readers are the very means through which struggling readers make meaning. Writing e-mails to classmates about where to find information for a report can also be an important literacy tool for readers who struggle with content area assignments.

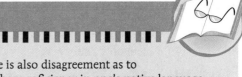

English Language Learners

Among educators in the United States there is considerable disagreement over whether second-language learners use the same cognitive monitoring processes as native English speakers when reading (Garcia, 2000).

There is also disagreement as to whether proficiency in one's native language and oral proficiency in the second language are prerequisites for ESL reading instruction.

language and of content topics, includes domain knowledge related to language and reading as well as knowledge about specific topics referenced in the text. The more you read, the more you learn about language and reading, and since you must read about *something*, you also acquire increased topic knowledge as you read. Across the lifespan, knowledge about language and topic knowledge increase. The second factor described by Alexander is interest. Interest can be situational (temporary interest induced by the context) or individual (representing a long-term involvement in a particular topic or field). Over time, the relative importance of these two kinds of interest shifts. In the acclimation stage, situational interest is important whereas individual interest becomes more and more important as a reader passes through competence to proficiency. The third factor is a reader's strategic processing, which changes as reading competence develops. In the acclimation stage, surface-processing strategies such as re-reading, altering reading rate, or skipping unfamiliar words are important. Over time, deep-processing strategies that involve personalization and transformation of text develop and are more important.

As those of us who have taught in middle and high schools know, readers in the acclimation stage can be found at all grade levels. If we want to help adolescents to grow to be competent readers on their way to proficiency, we must help them increase their knowledge of language in general and specific topics about which they read, offer them interesting books, magazines, and media so they will have the desire to read, and model deep-processing strategies so that they can develop their own strategic reading skills.

A Social Constructionist Perspective

Have you ever been in a situation in which you realized that the presence of others whom you judged to be more competent than yourself made you a better thinker, reader, or writer? If you have experienced this, you are likely to have little or no difficulty understanding a social constructionist view of learning. The term *social constructionism* is frequently used synonymously with *social constructivism*, although there are many good reasons for not conflating the two concepts (Hruby, 2001). For purposes of this chapter, we concentrate on social constructionism. Both concepts are theories of learning; they are not theories of teaching per se. To understand the differences between social constructionism and social constructivism, it is useful to first define constructivist learning theory.

Constructivist learning theory.   Constructivism has become a catch-all term for a collection of theoretical approaches to learning that rely for their explanation on the cognitive processes individuals use in making sense of their lived experiences. Literacy educators generally limit their attention to four versions of constructivism: Piagetian constructivism, radical constructivism, sociohistorical constructivism, and social constructivism (Eisenhart, Finkel, & Marion, 1996; Phillips, 2000). Piagetian constructivism holds that conceptual development results from an individual's ability to assimilate and accommodate new information into existing knowledge structures. To count as learning, however, this newly assimilated (or accommodated) information must correspond with an authoritative body of knowledge external to the individual. Motivation for such learning rests in the individual and in the materials (content) to be learned.

Radical constructivism also situates motivation for learning in the person and the content to be learned. However, unlike Piagetian constructivism, radical constructivism assumes that evidence of new learning rests on an individual's ability to make personal sense of her or his own experiences; that is, radical constructivists have no need to apply some sort of external litmus test to determine the "correctness" of a student's personally constructed knowledge. Teachers who adhere to either Piagetian or radical constructivism view students as "autonomous actors who learn by building up their own understandings of their worlds in their heads" (Eisenhart, Finkel, & Marion, 1996, p. 278).

In contrast to these two perspectives are sociohistorical constructivism and social constructivism. Sociohistorical constructivism embraces Vygotsky's (1978) activity theory, whereas social constructivism is more closely associated with Bruner (1986), at least among literacy educators. Both sociohistorical and social constructivism are concerned with how factors outside the head, such as the culture of a classroom, influence what students do in the name of learning.

Social constructionist learning theory.   The view that "truth" is made, not found, and the centrality of language in mediating what people come to understand about their lived experiences are features that most readily distinguish a social constructionist perspective from a constructivist perspective. Gavelek and Raphael (1996) describe how a teacher who subscribes to social constructionist learning theory would elicit students' responses:

> The teacher's role would shift from asking questions to ensure that students arrive at the "right" meaning to creating prompts that encourage students' exploratory talk. . . . Teachers would encourage talk that elicits a range of

possible interpretations among individuals reading and responding at any given time. Teachers would also encourage talking about previously read texts because individuals construct different readings at different periods in life or within different contexts. . . . Textual meaning is not "out there" to be acquired: It is something that is constructed by individuals through their interactions with each other and the world. In classrooms, these interactions take the form of discussions, and the teacher helps guide and participates in them. Underlying the processes of interpretations and justifications in discussions is language. (p. 183)

In an attempt to give you a sense of how meaning is socially constructed, we have included a two-sentence short story by Richard Brautigan (1971) and an accompanying small-group activity.

Story: "It's very hard to live in a studio apartment in San Jose with a man who's learning to play the violin." That's what she told the police when she handed them the empty revolver. (p. 197)

ACTIVITY   Gather a group of three or four individuals, and respond to the following prompts after someone in the group has read aloud Brautigan's story:

- Explain what happened.
- Elaborate on why it happened.
- Defend why you know you're right.

After completing the activity, reflect on the process. As you discussed your responses to the story, did you notice the role that language played in mediating your own and other people's interpretations? How would you explain your choice of language in constructing your interpretation? Why is your interpretation as viable as other people's interpretations? What previous experiences have you had that might possibly account for your interpretation of the story? Reflecting on questions such as these will help you understand how individuals go about socially constructing the meanings of all sorts of texts, not just short stories.

Technology Tip

To experience what is involved in reading a passage that illustrates a constructivist perspective on learning, see "What Is Really True? A Lesson in Understanding Constructivism." This lesson was developed by Lloyd Rieber, one of Donna's colleagues at the University of Georgia, and can be accessed at http://it.coe.uga.edu/~lrieber/constructlesson.html.

Such reflections will also illustrate Brock and Gavelek's (1998) point that although our cultural histories do not determine how we experience or respond to texts, these histories do in fact channel or help to frame our responses. In fact, the very idea that reading is a socially constructed practice draws on some of the most basic assumptions from cultural anthropology and sociolinguistics (Cook-Gumperz, 1986; Gee, 1988; Heath, 1983). One such assumption is that "students of different races, different social classes, and different genders may produce readings which challenge dominant or authoritative meanings because they have available to them different sets of values and beliefs" (Patterson, Mellor, & O'Neill, 1994, p. 66). However, it should come as no surprise that students who share common cultural backgrounds and who are contemporaries of one another may still respond to and interpret the same text very differently. This is to be expected given that each student will have had unique life experiences and different ways of using language to interpret those experiences.

Of course, nothing is as simple as it might first seem. Social constructionist learning theory will only buy us so much. Learning and teaching in a complex world involves much more than language, and it is this fact that drives home the following point:

> The suggestion that all knowledge is language-based—and, hence, formulated and explicit—would imply that agents must be aware (or capable of being aware) of their knowledge. As such, statements like "My dog knows how to dig holes" or "My heart knows how to beat" are nonsensical. In other words, underpinning the claim that all knowledge is socially constructed is a presumption that "the human" is separable from the non- and sub-human. The same sort of separation is implicit in debates of nature versus nurture. (Davis, Sumara, & Luce-Kapler, 2000, p. 17)

Suffice it to say that for the purposes of this book, we will leave the discussion on socially constructed learning where we started. That is, it is a helpful construct for thinking about how the cognitive processes of reading are always "embedded in, enabled by, and constrained by the social phenomenon of language" (Davis et al., 2000, p. 67).

The Role of Motivation

EVIDENCE-BASED RESEARCH

Listening to the voices of students is key to understanding what motivates them to learn. Based on her review of research on student motivation, Barbara McCombs (1995) of the Mid-Continent Regional Educational Laboratory writes:

> The support is overwhelmingly on the side of learner-centered practices that honor individual learner perspectives and needs for competence, control, and belonging. The voices of the students themselves provide even more

support for this perspective. . . . When students are asked what makes school a place where they want to learn, they report that they want (a) rigor and joy in their schoolwork, (b) a balance of complexity and clarity, (c) opportunities to discuss personal meanings and values, (d) learning activities that are relevant and fun, and (e) learning experiences that offer choice and require action. (p. 10)

EVIDENCE-BASED RESEARCH

Middle-grade students' motivations for reading as measured by the *Motivations for Reading Questionnaire* extend and complement this view of the importance of intrinsically appealing learner-centered instruction. Approximately 600 students in a large mid-Atlantic city school system (55 percent African American, 43 percent Caucasian, and 2 percent Asian and Hispanic) said they do not avoid difficult reading activities. Motivational dimensions related to enjoyment, curiosity, and a sense of efficacy were the best predictors of the frequency with which they read (Wigfield, Wilde, Baker, Fernandez-Fein, & Scher, 1996).

When students are positively motivated, they view themselves as competent readers who are in control of their comprehension processes; they are said to be strategic in their approach to reading. Sometimes, however, students adopt tactics that result in an avoidance of reading or of spending time on assignments. When this occurs, they are said to be using strategies in a self-serving, or negative, fashion. Both positive and negative types of motivation for reading are present among students, regardless of ability level, socioeconomic status, or racial and ethnic background. Knowledge of how both types of motivation manifest themselves in subject matter classrooms is vital to understanding the reading process and to planning for instruction.

Positive strategies.   Strategic readers take pride in what they are able to learn independently from text. They view reading as a means of gaining control of their academic environment. They also develop feelings of self-worth and confidence in their ability to achieve desired goals (Weiner, 1986). This sense of control can lead to increased achievement in their subject matter classes; it can also lead to better peer relations. For example, Charley comes to mind here. Charley was 13 years old and in the eighth grade when Donna first met him. She was observing his math teacher, Ms. Wilthey, model for the class how to sort through and discard extraneous information in a word problem. The object was to choose only relevant numbers on which to perform certain mathematical operations. Charley initially showed little interest in the teacher's lesson. However, when Ms. Wilthey challenged the class to come up with different ways of solving a set of math problems for homework that night, Charley consulted "The Library of Math Forum Problems" (http://mathforum.org/library/problems/sets/funpow_all.html) and brought in numerous examples to share with the class.

As young adolescents move from the middle grades into secondary school, their perceptions of their control become stronger. According to Paris, Wasik, and Turner (1991), greater "perceived control leads to greater effort in the use of particular learning strategies. Successful students persist in the face of failure and choose appropriate tactics for challenging tasks more often than students who do not understand what controls learning outcomes" (p. 626).

For students to experience a sense of control in becoming competent readers, they must believe four things. First, they must believe that they are capable of assuming responsibility for their own learning and have the ability to complete their assignments. Second, they must believe that they have a voice in setting their own objectives for reading and in determining suitable standards of excellence. Third, they must be convinced of the usefulness of certain strategies for accomplishing specific objectives. Finally, they must believe that their successes as readers are contingent on the effort and skill they invest in becoming strategic readers (Paris, Wasik, et al., 1991).

**EVIDENCE-
BASED
RESEARCH**

Avoidance strategies.   Giving up on, or withdrawing from, situations that involve learning from text is a tactic students may use when the material they are assigned to read seems too difficult or uninteresting. This tactic may even be used by students for whom the material is neither too difficult nor uninteresting. Why? To the best of our knowledge, disengaged readers for one reason or another devalue reading; they tend to invest their time in other endeavors. Their attention is focused elsewhere, perhaps on a subject requiring less reading, a part-time job, or extracurricular activities. David O'Brien (1998) captured this kind of student in his description of Denise, an underachieving junior at Jefferson High. When David taught her in the Jeff Literacy Lab, Denise was working 20 hours a week at a local pizza shop. He described her thusly: "Denise has been in the Literacy Lab for 3 years. She views her reading ability as a weak link in a relatively strong chain of other accomplishments. . . . She noted: 'I don't read unless I have to.' She likes the computer activities, but she does not seem to connect computers with reading and writing" (p. 38). Another avoidance strategy students use involves shifting the blame for reading difficulties from themselves to someone or something else. For example, students may complain that their teachers dislike them, that they are distracted easily, or that other teachers load them up with homework. The least desirable avoidance strategy is the one used by students who free themselves of the responsibility for reading text to learn by copying assignments, cheating on tests, or repeatedly seeking the assistance of a friend or family member (Paris, et al., 1991).

Each of these avoidance strategies shares certain attributes with the others. First, they all help to preserve students' positive self-perceptions because "passing the buck" leads to short-term success at preserving self-esteem. Second, they eventually lead to the *passive failure syndrome* (Johnston & Winograd, 1985), in which students, over time, fail to learn the necessary content and skills that make regular advancement in school an attainable goal. Third, students' sense of "beating the system" may lead to a false idea of what it takes to succeed in any endeavor, whether reading or something else.

Self-motivation.   The idea that teachers can cultivate within students the will, or self-motivation, to use their reading and writing skills in all areas of the curriculum is a central theme of this book. In fact, the underlying goal of most literacy instruction in middle and secondary schools is to enable students to use reading and writing as tools for learning the content of their coursework. However, teachers know that all too often adolescents do not make the effort that is necessary for this learning to take place (Bishop, 1989). Why this apathy?

Here are some answers to that question from the students' perspectives:

- Henri (a newly arrived student from outside the U.S.) talks about his apathy in physics class: "I know that I should work hard, do my homework, listen in class, but well, see, it's just that I don't want to stand out as being a hard worker. I know I can do the work, but I just don't want to stand out."
- Patricia (a third-year Latin student) explains how she plays down her abilities in order to strike a "just-right" balance: "See, I don't want to be called the class brain or something. . . . I do just enough to get by. That way no one knows."
- Dan (a tenth grader) never tries in history class and thus never risks the stigma of having tried and failed: "I don't know . . . studying for a quiz in history isn't worth the effort, I guess. Look at it this way: if I tried and didn't make it then I'd say to myself, 'Dumb . . . you should have just slacked off.'"

Other answers to the apathy question come from teachers. For example, Janis Gabay, the 1990 National Teacher of the Year, argued that adolescents (especially minorities) are often labeled as "unmotivated" when actually it is a

A Response from Our Readers

Marlene Willis,* a middle-grades teacher and graduate student enrolled in Donna's content literacy methods course at the University of Georgia, wrote the following response after reading the section on students' use of both positive and avoidance strategies in Chapter 1 of this book:

I, as well as many students of my generation, persisted and felt that hard work would pay off; however, too many students today lack the drive to succeed. I felt that I was in control of my destiny. Students I encounter daily seem to leave their fates to chance. Clearly, an understanding of what controls learning outcomes is important. That successful students persist when faced with failure and have a repertoire of tactics for challenging tasks is not surprising to me. How to instill in adolescents the four things that Paris, Wasik, and Turner (1991) say students need to believe remains the million-dollar question for me. . . . The real challenge as I see it is to first halt the fears adolescents (all of us) have of being labeled over- or underachievers (as well as a myriad of other revolting things) and then to find ways to propel students to become independent learners.

*Adapted with permission of Marlene S. Willis.

matter of their having no sense of ownership and no incentive to participate in classroom activities. To Gabay's (1991) way of thinking,

> Teachers can help their students become self-motivated in a number of ways: by tapping students' prior knowledge; setting forth clear expectations and goals so students know what they are aspiring to in a specific lesson, unit, or semester; conveying to students the difficulty of the challenge but emphasizing the supports the teacher will provide to ensure their success; giving lots of genuine praise for the incremental, tentative steps students take; holding students accountable in a way that includes self-evaluation of their progress; acknowledging each student through a significant nod, a smile, or an encouraging comment (not always in front of the whole class)—especially for that student at risk of "disconnecting"; and by modeling the enthusiasm that teaching and learning engender so students can see a tangible example of self-motivation, commitment, and effort. (p. 7)

Perhaps one of the most useful things to bear in mind as we work to increase our students' self-motivation is a statement attributed to John F. Kennedy. Speaking on the importance of developing each child's potential to its fullest, Kennedy (cited in Inos & Quigley, 1995) said, "Not every child has an equal talent or an equal ability or equal motivation, but children have the equal right to develop their talent, their ability, and their motivation" (p. 1). We think this statement and its implications for classroom practice capture our sentiments exactly.

Dispelling Policy Myths

Dispelling a Myth

"Every teacher is a teacher of reading." When Victoria heard that statement as a former science teacher, she remembers thinking "If I had wanted to teach reading, I'd have majored in it." Somehow, content area teachers tend to think of content area literacy strategies as something they have to make time for *in addition to* teaching their content. In reality, content area literacy strategies make teaching content more effective and efficient. It isn't *in addition to*—it's *a way to* teach content.

Policy Implications

In August 2005, the Alliance for Excellent Education released findings from a public opinion survey on high schools. For the first time, the public identified improvement of high schools as the most important priority for educational reform. Other findings indicate that the public believes:

- Investing in elementary school does not automatically result in success in high school.
- Improving the nation's abysmal literacy rate is the key to improving student achievement.
- Too many students drop out of high school, and as a result they and the nation suffer.
- A high school diploma does not insure that graduates are prepared for college or workplace training.
- It is not too late to help poorly performing students in high school.

Will YOU be part of the solution?

SUMMARY

A pervasive and legitimate concern of middle and high school content area teachers is how to help students learn from texts. In the English language arts curriculum that concern is broadened to include an emphasis on how to help readers evaluate the connotations and associations evoked by the experience of transacting with texts. In all areas of the curriculum, the goal is to support adolescents' literacy growth by providing them with access to materials they can and want to read (Moore, Bean, Birdyshaw, & Rycik, 1999). Ensuring that all students, including those who struggle with fluency in reading and who are learning English as a second language, become active and independent learners is a primary goal of content area educators. Teachers' pedagogical subject matter knowledge and their understanding of the role that textbooks and the Internet (through its various Web sites) play in classroom instruction are vital links to reaching that goal.

Traditional definitions of what it means to be literate have given way to a broadened view of literacy—one that includes informational, computer, media, scientific, and technological literacies. These multiple literacies require skills that extend far beyond the conventional reading and writing competencies associated with print literacy. They also require that teachers attend to more than a cognitive view of the reading process. Constructivist and social constructionist perspectives on that process, as well as students' motivations for becoming literate, must be taken into account as important mediators of students' ability to learn in various content areas.

SUGGESTED READINGS

Barton, D., Hamilton, M., & Ivanic, R. (2000). *Situated literacies: Reading and writing in context.* New York: Routledge.

Bruce, B. C. (Ed.). (2003). *Literacy in the information age.* Newark, DE: International Reading Association.

Cope, B., & Kalantzis, M. (Eds.). (2000). *Multiliteracies: Literacy learning and the design of social futures.* New York: Routledge.

Freebody, P., Luke, A., & Gilbert, P. (1991). Reading positions and practices in the classroom. *Curriculum Inquiry, 21,* 435–457.

Lankshear, C., & Knobel, M. (2003). *New literacies: Changing knowledge and classroom learning.* Philadelphia, PA: Open University Press.

Spivey, N. N. (1997). *The constructivist metaphor: Reading, writing, and the making of meaning.* San Diego, CA: Academic Press.

CHAPTER 2

Language, Diversity, and Culture

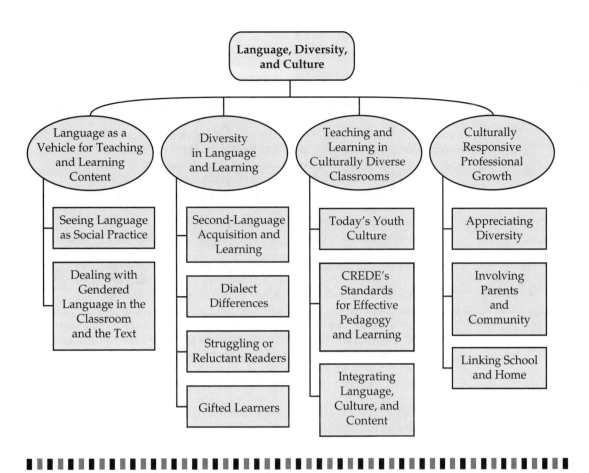

We open this chapter with a thumbnail sketch of Katya, one of several students who participated in a year-long study of adolescents' perceptions of classroom talk about their assigned reading materials. The sketch, compiled by Steve Phelps, a researcher in the study (Alvermann et al., 1996b), evokes images of why we believe teaching and learning in today's culturally diverse classrooms must entail more than simply attending to the assigned literacy tasks. Important as those tasks are, they cannot be isolated from the influences affecting students' everyday lives. As you read Steve's description of Katya, which he assembled from observing her in class and interviewing her in private, think of questions that you would like to ask her or her social studies teacher, Mr. Williams (pseudonyms are used throughout).

▮▮▮▮▮▮▮

Katya had come to the United States with her mother and three siblings from the Ukraine two years before the time of the study. They were members of the local Ukrainian Pentecostal Christian community. Katya said she attended church daily. Because her English was limited, both in vocabulary and in syntax, Katya had enrolled in two classes of English as a second language (ESL) as well as an after-school English program. She said she spoke Ukrainian at home. In her high school, Katya was referred to as "one of the Russian students," seemingly because the faculty and staff did not differentiate between the Ukraine and Russia.

Katya was very reserved and shy in class. To help overcome her difficulties with the language, Mr. Williams paired her with Ahmed, an Arabian student she had known the previous year in a biology class. Although Katya rarely uttered a word in class discussions, she (along with Ahmed) was one of the more diligent and attentive students in class when it came to reading, note-taking, and following the teacher's lectures. The only instances in which Katya attempted to enter into public discourse were occasional and nearly inaudible one-word responses when the class was going over the answers to a worksheet.

Although it would be easy to attribute Katya's lack of participation to her shyness or difficulty with the English language, there were brief flashes of evidence that suggested she was willing to share interesting information. For example, when she spoke with Steve about her life in the Ukraine and when she and Ahmed paged through a magazine prior to the start of class, Katya was animated and insightful. Katya's grades were in the low 90s, and on the final state Regent's Exam, which was part multiple choice and part essay, Katya got a 76. Although she did relatively well in her other subjects as well, she was unable to graduate at the end of the year because she did not have enough physical education credits. (Phelps & Weaver, 1999)

▮▮▮▮▮▮▮

What questions came to mind as you read this sketch? For us, one nagging question was, "What might Mr. Williams have done to create spaces for Katya's private voice in the public discourse of the classroom?" However, as we ask it, we think back to other studies of student voice in which researchers have found that attempts to empower others is not something one can do *to* or *for* another person (Alvermann, 1995–1996; Orner, 1992; Perry & Delpit, 1998). In fact, some educators have begun to ask themselves, "Whose interests are served when students speak?" The answers, as you might expect, are layered and complex. It is this complexity, along with others, that we invite you to explore in the following pages.

The chapter is divided into four major sections, which reflect its four purposes. The purpose of the first section is to explore issues concerning language as a vehicle for teaching and learning in culturally diverse classrooms. The purpose of the second section is to describe issues regarding the various needs of English language learners (ELLs), or English learners (ELs) as they are referred to in California. The purpose of the third section is to examine the need for integrating language, culture, and content given today's youth culture. The purpose of the fourth section is to suggest ways of synchronizing professional growth opportunities so that they focus on culturally responsive teaching.

LANGUAGE AS A VEHICLE FOR TEACHING AND LEARNING CONTENT

A major influence on how we currently view the teaching and learning of content literacy is the work of Lev Vygotsky, a Russian psychologist. Although Vygotsky's (1978) theory of learning took shape in the early years of the twentieth century, educators in North America did not learn of it until edited translations of his work appeared in English in the 1960s and 1970s. In a nutshell, Vygotsky believed that "mental functioning in the individual originates in social, communicative processes" (Wertsch, 1991, p. 13), which are embedded in an array of cultural, historical, and institutional contexts. In other words, a Vygotskian perspective on learning does not assume that students will learn independently but rather that they will benefit from engaging socially in groups where others more knowledgeable than themselves can guide their learning (Vygotsky, 1978).

This emphasis on the social, communicative processes of language as a mediator of even the most private forms of thinking has had a profound influence on how we view the reading process, as described in Chapter 1. Its influence is highlighted again here: first, in our look at language as social practice, and next in our discussion of ways to deal with the gendered nature of classroom language and text.

Seeing Language as Social Practice

What a person says (or does) and what other people hear (or see) will vary greatly depending on the social and cultural contexts in which such communication takes place. Even though the people involved may be speaking the same language, there is room for misinterpretation. Consider, for example, the following story told by James Gee (1996), a sociolinguist whose work informs much of what we believe about language as a mediating force in what gets said and understood in content area classrooms. In this story, Gee illustrates how language in the social context of a biker bar (or pub) reveals much more about the narrator (himself) than his proficiency in using English:

> Imagine I park my motorcycle, enter my neighborhood "biker bar," and say to my leather-jacketed and tattooed drinking buddy, as I sit down: "May I have a match for my cigarette, please?" What I have said is perfectly grammatical English, but it is "wrong" nonetheless, unless I have used a heavily ironic tone of voice. It is not just *what* you say, but *how* you say it. And in this bar, I haven't said it in the "right way." I should have said something like "Gotta match?" or "Give me a light, wouldya?"
>
> But now imagine I say the "right" thing ("Gotta match?" or "Give me a light, wouldya?"), but while saying it, I carefully wipe off the bar stool with a napkin to avoid getting my newly pressed designer jeans dirty. In this case, I've still got it all

wrong. In *this* bar they just don't do that sort of thing: I have *said* the right thing, but my "saying–doing" combination is nonetheless wrong. It's not just what you say or even just how you say it, it's also who you are and what you're doing while you say it. It is not enough just to say the right "lines." (p. viii)

What you have just read is an example of a Discourse, with a capital *D*. Briefly defined, Discourses are ways of speaking, thinking, and behaving in the world. Whether in biker bars or in classrooms, Discourses operate as ways of sorting individuals and groups. When this sorting leads to different expectations for students, we need to be concerned. As Gee (1996) reminds us:

Each Discourse incorporates a usually taken for granted and tacit "theory" of what counts as a "normal" person and the "right" ways to think, feel, and behave. These theories crucially involve viewpoints on the distribution of social goods like status, worth, and material goods in society (who should and who should not have them). The biker bar "says" that "tough guys" are "real men"; the school "says" that certain children—often minority children and those from lower socioeconomic groups—are not suited for higher education and professional careers. (p. ix)

Some questions to get you thinking

1. What are some Discourses in which you claim membership (e.g., student, teacher, administrator, citizen, sister, mother)?
2. How would others recognize you as a member of these Discourses?
3. Do you change your ways of speaking, thinking, and behaving when you move from one Discourse to another? Why?
4. What connections can you make between the example of the Discourse of the biker bar and the Discourses you are apt to find in various school settings?

Developing an awareness of how different Discourses construct the social realities of the classrooms in which we teach is an important first step in dealing with some of these realities. Just as learning subject matter can be described as learning a kind of Discourse (Soetaert & Bonamie, 1999), so also can learning how to do school literacy. In the following section, you will learn how reading—and "doing"—gendered literacy is part of school literacy.

Dealing with Gendered Language in the Classroom and the Text

Currently, there is a great deal of emphasis placed on student-centered literacy practices, such as personal response to texts in book clubs, literature circles, and cooperative-learning groups. However, little attention has been paid to classroom language that leads to stereotyping. In the two sections that follow on the language of classroom and text, we provide anecdotal evidence of how such stereotyping inevitably narrows students' thinking and creates potentially unproductive learning environments.

Language of the classroom.

> I think the girls, we're like, we dominate, we rule the class.
> —*Jamaica*

> Since we've been talking about sexism [in books], the girls got their own point of view and the boys got their own . . . [and] we're always against each other.
> —*David*

Spoken passionately and with conviction, these statements reflected attitudes that existed in David Hinson's seventh-grade language arts class following a class reading of a play about a girls' soccer team that defeats a boys' soccer team (Alvermann et al., 1996b). The discussion of this play eventually led a student to ask, "Should boys be allowed to join an all-girls' softball team?" Although a few students said yes, most of them flatly rejected the idea.

The proverbial battle lines between the sexes were drawn when Cherie announced: "An all-girls' team talks about 'girl talk' so boys would ruin everything." The boys, sensing they were being cast as the outsiders, retorted with statements like, "It just shows the stupidity of women." As the name-calling escalated, the students seemed bent on excluding each other's ideas along sexist lines rather than questioning the source of those ideas and why they might hold currency among their peers.

We believe that incidents such as this one can lead eventually to patterns of discourse that students internalize and act on in a variety of ways. When language of the classroom centers on the meanings boys and girls attach to being male or female, as in the example just given, gender becomes something students *do*—a way of being in the world. Over time, as stereotypes form and become more firmly inscribed each time gender is socially constructed through classroom talk, students shape their identities to fit the language they hear.

ACTIVITY   Record on a sheet of paper for three consecutive class sessions any language you hear that treats males and females in stereotypical ways. Keep notes on who uses that language and how the persons to whom it is directed tend to react. Share your findings on how gendered classroom language affects the way individuals think and feel about themselves.

Language of the text.   Reading texts in which an author's language socially constructs gender can also inscribe stereotypes. However, gender is but one of several filters through which readers experience texts. Social class, race, ethnicity, and culture are others. Consider, for instance, the overlapping filters

that are operating in the following examples from Sally Randall's eighth-grade language arts classroom:

Example 1:

Rather than assign the questions at the end of an excerpt from *The Pearl* (Steinbeck, 1989) in the class anthology, Ms. Randall asked the students to consider a series of quotations from the selection. One quotation helped students consider how an author's gendered way of writing can influence the language they use in discussing the text.

> Kino had wondered often at the iron in his patient, fragile wife. She, who was obedient and respectful and cheerful and patient, she could arch her back in child pain with hardly a cry. She could stand fatigue and hunger almost better than Kino himself. In the canoe she was like a strong man. (p. 677)

After students had read this quotation aloud, Ms. Randall asked them to consider why Steinbeck wrote the description of Kino's wife in this way. The first student to respond said Juana (Kino's wife) had the physical characteristics of a man but still gave Kino the honor and respect he deserved because he was a man. Ms. Randall then underlined the word *almost* and the phrase *like a strong man*. She asked the class to think about what those words implied. A student spoke up to say that Juana may have had qualities like a man but they were also women's qualities. Exchanges such as these allow students to explore multiple perspectives.

Example 2:

The Pearl became the focus of another discussion in Ms. Randall's class. This time the students were asked to consider who was the more dominant character—Kino or Juana. Most of them concluded it had to be Kino because he was the man, and he made all the decisions for his family. Ms. Randall asked, "Do you think this is pretty common in literature for the man to be the dominant one?" Heads nodded in agreement, with Paula explaining it this way:

> Well, it kind of just started in the beginning. Adam was made first, and that was kind of like the man was the head of the family. And so it was just kind of in all the stories. That's just like in real life. That's just the way.

With this example, it is easy to see how the language of the classroom and the language of the text conspire to socially construct what it means to be male and, by implication, what it means to be female. Here, the weight of religion, literary history, and culture combine to leave little doubt in Paula's mind that this is just the way life is, has always been, and will always be.

Interrupting the status quo.   Strategies that support students as they begin to question the source of the ideas or the values expressed in the texts they read and hear discussed in class are most effective when they call into question inequities associated with gender bias. For example, Wayne Williams, a physics teacher who collaborated in a two-year action research project with Barbara Guzzetti, a literacy

**EVIDENCE-
BASED
RESEARCH**

A Response from Our Readers

Elizabeth Armstrong-Yazzie,* a student enrolled in Josephine Young's content literacy course at Arizona State University, wrote the following response after reading Paula's interpretation of male dominance in Steinbeck's story.

> I could see how many European American students might think in that way but what about students from other cultures? For example, what would Navajo students think of the quotations? The Navajo tribe is a matrilineal society. Traditional Navajos do not believe in the Adam and Eve creation story. They have their own creation story. Some Navajos may not have even heard of the Adam and Eve creation story.
>
> This is a reminder that you should not assume that your students will understand everything you discuss in class. Be prepared to explain a lot and ask if your students are familiar with what you're talking about and if they understand it. I can't help but wonder how different the Navajo students' interpretations would be of the excerpt.

*Adapted with permission of Elizabeth Armstrong-Yazzie.

teacher educator (Guzzetti & Williams, 1996), employed a simple but effective strategy for intervening in a gendered interactional style that favored boys' voices over girls' voices in his classroom. Briefly, Mr. Williams had been unaware during the first year of the study that the boys in his class generally believed that the girls' questioning style indicated an inability on their part to learn difficult concepts. In the second year of the study, Mr. Williams presented his subject matter in a way that demonstrated science involves an active questioning and exploring of ideas. In doing this, he was able to communicate that females' ways of talking should be viewed positively, rather than negatively, and that questioning is the first step in scientific inquiry.

DIVERSITY IN LANGUAGE AND LEARNING

We begin this section on second-language learning, dialect differences, struggling readers, and gifted learners with a cautionary note. It is easy to fall into the trap of generalizing about an individual based on one aspect of that person's group membership. How many times, for example, have you heard or taken part in conversations that narrowly define someone on the basis of their race, gender, age, ability, religion, and so on? Generalizing group characteristics to an individual is misleading in other ways as well. A case in point is Katya. If you were her teacher, why would it be important to identify her in more than one way?

Although Katya's nationality is Ukrainian, this is only one of her multiple group memberships. Katya, the individual, is simultaneously a woman and a member of the Pentecostal Christian community. Although she did not disclose information related to her social class or racial makeup, we do know she has at least one exceptionality—Katya is multilingual. She speaks Ukrainian, Russian, and English. Thus, if you were Katya's teacher, you would want to consider her multiple group memberships when planning for instruction, facilitating group discussions, devising assessments, or making any number of other instructional decisions. Without knowledge of the different norms, values, myths, traditions, and symbols that have meaning for different cultural groups, you will find it difficult to access or build on your students' rich and diverse backgrounds when introducing new concepts and strategies for learning from texts.

Although developing an awareness of your students' cultural backgrounds is important, it is not enough. Too often we think of "other" people as having a diverse set of beliefs and values and yet remain blind to our own. It is as if we simply do not see what looks and feels so "normal" to us. Try the following activity to gain insight into your own cultural norms.

ACTIVITY   Fold a sheet of notebook paper in half the long way. On the left side, state the values and beliefs you hold most dear. On the right side, briefly state how you practice or "live out" each of them. For instance, give examples of how you practice them. Then review both sides, noting as you go any statements that seem particularly narrow or finite. Inspect your more "absolute" ways of believing and valuing to see if you have a blind spot that may interfere in teaching a culturally diverse group of students. Think of how you might compensate for that blind spot.

Second-Language Acquisition and Learning

The distinction between second-language acquisition and second-language learning is not simply a dichotomous one; it is more like a continuum, with the two terms serving as the imaginary poles. However, the distinction is useful in drawing attention to Krashen's (1989) claim that second-language development is more a matter of acquisition than of learning through formal methods.

According to Gee (1996), "acquisition is a process of acquiring something (usually subconsciously) by exposure to models, a process of trial and error, and practice within social groups, without formal teaching" (p. 138). For example, first-language development for native English speakers is primarily a matter of acquisition, though as most of us remember from classes in English grammar, some formal schooling was also involved. Like Gee (1996), we believe that we are better at performing what we *acquire* than what we *learn*:

> For most of us, playing a musical instrument, or dancing, or using a second language, are skills we attained by some mixture of acquisition and learning. But it is a safe bet that, over the same amount of time, people are better at (performing) these activities if acquisition predominated during that time. (p. 139)

We also believe language differences should be more than tolerated; they need to be celebrated and affirmed. As teachers, we need to help students appreciate that having two or more languages or dialects at their command gives them the prerogative to choose from among them as circumstances dictate. To literacy educator David Bloome's (1992) way of thinking,

> We need to replace the LEP (limited English proficiency) mentality with the LTEP (limited to English proficiency) mentality. Bilingualism and multilingualism need to be viewed as normal, healthy, and prevalent states of life (both for individuals and for communities). Monolingualism needs to be viewed as the aberration. (p. 7)

To appreciate the implications of Bloome's thinking for content teaching and learning, it helps to familiarize yourself with the major approaches to educating second-language learners. Advocates of sheltered English, content-based ESL, transitional bilingual, and two-way bilingual programs express strong rationales for preferring one type of instruction to another. With California's passage of Proposition 227 decreeing English-only instruction in the waning years of the past century, educators have had to rethink what it means to teach students whose primary or native language (L1) is something other than English. Because sheltered English instruction is increasingly the approach of choice in school districts throughout the United States (Echevarria, Vogt, & Short, 2000), we devote a proportionately greater amount of attention to it here. We include briefer descriptions of other approaches, however, because of their viability and presence in the research literature on bilingual education (Garcia, 2000; Ovado, 2003).

Sheltered English instruction.   We are living in a time when adolescents' language backgrounds are becoming increasingly diverse but those of their teachers are not. What happens to students who come to school without the proficiency in English to keep up with their peers in the various subject matter areas? How are such students expected to meet the high standards set by state and national reform movements? More and more frequently, schools are turning to sheltered English instruction as an approach that prepares ELLs to comprehend the content of their subject matter classes at the same time that they receive instruction in reading, writing, speaking, and listening in English.

Through various adaptations in their instruction, English-speaking teachers are able to make adjustments in the language demands put on students who are not yet fluent in English but who, with supportive teaching techniques, can understand grade-level content standards and concepts (Echevarria, Vogt, & Short, 2000). These adjustments may include scaffolding their instruction (e.g., modeling teacher thinking, providing analogies, and elaborating on student responses), providing necessary background information and experiences, and organizing their lessons in ways that simplify syntactic structures (e.g., using more active than passive verbs). Teachers in sheltered classrooms may also employ strategies that emphasize visual cues and other concrete means for helping students apply what they know in their primary language to learning content in English. Students are expected to gain proficiency enough to enter mainstream classes in one year (Mora, Wink, & Wink, 2001).

The downside of sheltered English instruction is that "many ELLs receive much of their instruction from content area teachers or aides who have not had appropriate professional development to address their second-language development needs" (Echevarria, Vogt, & Short, 2000, p. 4). The demand for teachers knowledgeable in the implementation of sheltered English instruction simply exceeds the supply. Although the sheltered approach to teaching involves many of the same instructional methods and strategies that regular classroom teachers use, most teachers who have not had coursework and experience in second-language acquisition lack the skills necessary for linguistically and culturally responsive instruction. Without knowledge of the ELL's second-language development needs, a teacher is at a distinct disadvantage, as is the learner who is the recipient of such instruction.

EVIDENCE-BASED RESEARCH

However, in schools that have initiated systemwide sheltered instruction taught by appropriately educated staff, the story is quite different. In these schools, it is highly likely that students whose first language is other than English will acquire academic literacy through instruction that shows them how to pool their emerging knowledge of English with what they know about the content and the tasks necessary for comprehending that content. The Sheltered Instruction Observational Protocol (SIOP) model (Echevarria, Vogt, & Short, 2000) is one example of a well-researched tool for planning and implementing sheltered English instruction in subject matter classrooms. Originally designed as an observation instrument, the SIOP is also used as a source of concrete examples of the features of sheltered instruction that make it possible for ELLs to acquire a second language and academic content simultaneously. Specific suggestions and strategies that take into account sheltered English instruction can be found in Chapters 4 and 6–10.

Content-based ESL.   This instructional approach uses academic content (sometimes packaged thematically) as a vehicle for second-language learning. Unlike sheltered English instruction in which ELLs work alongside their native-English-speaking peers, students enrolled in content-based ESL classes are all ELLs. Also, unlike sheltered instruction in which content learning and language development are merged, the primary goal of content-based ESL instruction is to prepare ELLs for regular English-medium classrooms (Echevarria, Vogt, & Short, 2000). The two approaches, however, do share a common problem: the demand for ESL and sheltered English teachers far exceeds the supply.

ESL teachers, who typically are monolingual English speakers, often serve as "cultural brokers" by introducing learners to the mainstream culture as well as to the English language (Adamson, 1993). Critics of ESL programs charge that students are unable to keep up with their mainstream peers because they are pulled out of their content area classes and taught by teachers who emphasize English as a second language over subject matter learning.

Bilingual programs. The Bilingual Education Act, the law that had supported the education of English language learners (ELLs) for 34 years, was repealed in 2002 and replaced with the No Child Left Behind Act (NCLB). In what is viewed as an attempt to emphasize a clean break with the past, the Bush Administration insisted that the law's provisions be renumbered. The section dealing with English learners, which in the past was referred to as Title VII, the Bilingual Education Act, has become Title III, which is officially called the English Language Acquisition, Language Enhancement, and Academic Achievement Act (www.nabe.org/advocacy/nclb.html, no page given).

EVIDENCE-
BASED
RESEARCH

What research says about bilingual education program effectiveness. Bernhardt (2003) argues that literacy researchers historically have overgeneralized the "sameness" in first- and second-language (L1 and L2) reading processes. To Bernhardt's thinking, "the mere existence of a *first*-language (regardless of whether it is only oral, or oral and literate) renders the *second*-language reading

Dispelling Policy Myths

Dispelling a Myth

The No Child Left Behind Act (NCLB) makes it illegal to have transitional bilingual and two-way bilingual education programs.

According to the National Association for Bilingual Education, "NCLB neither prohibits nor encourages bilingual instruction. It does, however, strike all references to bilingual education, bilingualism, and biliteracy from federal education law. Developing students' native-language proficiency, an important priority of Title VII, is not among the goals of Title III" (www.nabe.org/advocacy/nclb.html, no page given).

Policy Implications

Supporters of NCLB, including some well-intentioned advocates for language-minority students, have argued that by including ELLs in NCLB's new accountability system—based on high-stakes testing and demands that schools show adequate yearly progress—in effect has forced schools to pay attention to these students. Although the National Association for Bilingual Education (NABE) agrees that this is likely the case, for NABE the question that remains is whether or not this attention will be beneficial. For example, a growing number of educators believe that there is a problem with the NCLB's reliance on a single test score to label schools as failing or succeeding. For ELLs, the problem is particularly acute, with the result that NABE has joined together with a group of more than 35 education and civil rights organizations to advocate for a thorough overhaul of NCLB's accountability system (www.nabe.org/advocacy/nclb.html, no page given).

process considerably different from the first-language reading process because of the nature of information stored in memory" (p. 112).

This disagreement about whether L1 and L2 reading processes are the same or different has implications for content literacy instruction. Scholars on both sides of the divide generally acknowledge that we lack direct experimental evidence of the need for a unique form of instruction for second-language readers. What is important, it seems, is that content area teachers adhere to the "Five Standards for Effective Pedagogy and Student Outcomes" (Center for Research on Education, Diversity and Excellence, 2003b) discussed later in this chapter (see Teaching and Learning in Culturally Diverse Classrooms).

EVIDENCE-BASED RESEARCH

A National Study of School Effectiveness for Language Minority Students' Long-Term Academic Achievement published by the Center for Research on Education, Diversity and Excellence (2003a) found that bilingual programs that were sustained for five to six years assisted ELLs in maintaining the greatest gains in both their native language and English in all content areas. Moreover, the fewest high school dropouts came from these programs. ELLs who attended only English mainstream programs were the most likely students to drop out of school. When ELLs who had been schooled in all-English-medium programs (e.g., ESL and sheltered English) first exited a language support program, they outperformed their peers in bilingual programs when tested in English. However, by the middle school years, ELLs schooled in bilingual programs reached the same achievement levels as ELLs schooled all in English and by high school they outperformed them. Thomas and Collier (2002), the researchers who conducted the study, note:

> In order to close the average achievement gap between ELLs and native English speakers, language support programs must be well implemented . . . sustained for 5–6 years, and demonstrate achievement gains of more than the average yearly progress of the non-ELL group each year until the gap is closed. Even the most effective language support programs can only close half of the achievement gap in 2–3 years. (pp. 3–4)

ACTIVITY   Read the following announcement that was posted on the Web site of the National Association for Bilingual Education. In groups of two or three, discuss the assumptions that one could draw from this announcement. Then answer the following question: Why is bilingual education such a controversial topic in the United States?

> In late August, 2005, the U.S. Department of Education decided not to release a controversial research study that it commissioned. Findings from the two-year study, which was conducted by a panel of experts in bilingual education, pointed to the superiority of bilingual education programs when compared to all-English immersion programs in teaching students whose first language is other than English. "It's a shame that the Department

refuses to stand behind its own report," said James Crawford, executive director of the National Association for Bilingual Education (NABE). The study, which cost U.S. taxpayers $1.8 million, was conducted by the National Literacy Panel on Language Minority Children and Youth, convened by SRI International and the Center for Applied Linguistics. Researchers were hand-picked by the Administration to ensure that only those who met with its approval were included (http://www.nabe.org/press/press9.html, no page given).

Dialect Differences

In the classroom communities in which we work, dialect is frequently the most salient feature of cultural diversity, and it is often a contentious issue. The dilemma is twofold. How does one teach the codes of power while at the same time respecting students' culture and language? How does one disentangle form and meaning in language? Dialect can be a very powerful way of expressing meaning; at the same time, it can be a powerful barrier to communication. Bidialectical speakers—that is, individuals who are facile in using both dialect and "standard" forms of English—recognize this dilemma, but they also know how advantageous it is to "own" more than one language.

EVIDENCE-BASED RESEARCH

We think Gloria Ladson-Billings (1994) presents a useful way of thinking about dialect differences in her book, *The Dreamkeepers*. Ladson-Billings describes the classroom practices of eight teachers who differ in personal style and methods but who share an ability to teach in a manner that affirms and reinforces African American students' belief in themselves and their cultural identities. Patricia Hilliard, one of the eight teachers in Ladson-Billings's study, is an African American teacher who has taught in both public and private schools in a large urban area. Like Lisa Delpit (1995), Hilliard is wary of instructional approaches that fail "to make students cognizant of the power of language and the language of power" (Ladson-Billings, 1994, p. 82). In Hilliard's words (cited in Ladson-Billings, 1994),

> I get so sick and tired of people trying to tell me that my children don't need to use any language other than the one they come to school with. Then those same people turn right around and judge the children negatively because of the way they express themselves. My job is to make sure that they can use *both* languages, that they understand that their language is valid but that the demands placed upon them by others mean that they will constantly have to prove their worth. We spend a lot of time talking about language, what it means, how you can use it, and how it can be used against you. (p. 82)

One way that Patricia Hilliard affirms and reinforces her students' cultural identities while she simultaneously teaches them the value of knowing both dialect and "standard" forms of English is through an activity that involves what she calls the "translation" process. Placing a transparency of the lyrics of their favorite rap on the overhead projector (double-spaced so she can write between the lines), Hilliard proceeds to engage her students in a translation activity. In talking with students about the process, she compares it to what interpreters do when they translate from one language to another. Hilliard (cited in Ladson-Billings, 1994) explains her objective for doing the activity as follows:

> I want the children to see that they have some valuable knowledge to contribute. I don't want them to be ashamed of what they know but I also want them to know and be comfortable with what school and the rest of the society requires. When I put it in the context of "translation" they get excited. They see it is possible to go from one to the other. It's not that they are not familiar with Standard English . . . they hear Standard English all the time on TV. It's certainly what I use in the classroom. But there is rarely any connection made between the way they speak and Standard English. I think that when they can see the connections and know that they can make the shifts, they become better at both. They're bilingual! (p. 84)

The point that Patricia Hilliard is making is one that linguists also make; that is, we are all speakers of one dialect or another. Whose dialect counts is often a matter of politics, however. Addressing this issue, Wayne O'Neil (1998), head of the Department of Linguistics and Philosophy at the Massachusetts Institute of Technology, wrote the following in response to the public's outrage over a school board's resolution to teach Ebonics in Oakland, California, in 1996:

> We assume . . . that there are standard versions of [all] languages, the pinnacles that each dialect speaker is supposed to aspire to, but that which normally—for reasons of class, or race, or geography—she or he is not able to reach. On this view, dialects are diminished varieties of a standard ("legitimate") language, a value judgment that has no standing in linguistics. For, on the scientific point of view, all . . . languages are rule-governed systems of equal complexity and interest—instantiations of the capacity for language that each infant enters the world with. (p. 41)

Ebonics, commonly known among linguists as Black English or African American Vernacular English (AAVE), was the term used in the Oakland school board resolution. Although members of the board never intended for Ebonics to replace Standard English, the media's distortion of the resolution led to this interpretation (Perry & Delpit, 1998). Amid much furor and heated debates through the press and TV talk shows, African Americans appeared divided on the issue. In addressing this divisiveness and the implications of Ebonics for teachers, the well-known African American educator Lisa Delpit (1998) stated,

> I have been asked often enough recently, "What do you think about Ebonics? Are you for it or against it?" My answer must be neither. . . . It exists. It is the language spoken by many of our African American children. It is the language they heard as their mothers nursed them and changed their diapers and played peek-a-boo with them. It is the language through which they first encountered love, nurturance, and joy. (p. 17)

Technology Tip

To view a five-minute demonstration of a CD-ROM portraying a two-day high school multigrade lesson in ecological science, go to www.crede.ucsc.edu/products/multimedia/cdr oms.html# and then click on "The Mara Mills Case: A Video Ethnography of Biological Science in a Sheltered English Classroom," by Annela Teemant, Stefinee Pinnegar, Roland Tharp, and Carl Harris (2001). Each study in the case highlights one of the five standards for effective pedagogy promoted by the Center for Research on Education, Diversity and Excellence (CREDE, 2003b). The teacher, students, a science educator, a second-language educator, and teacher educators all give their perspectives on teaching.

Note: You will need to have QuickTime installed on your computer for you to be able to see the live demonstration. A free copy of QuickTime can be installed by going to www.apple.com/quicktime/download.

Delpit went on to add, however, that she, like most teachers and parents, believes that children who are not taught the power code of Standard English will not have equal access to good jobs and leadership positions. Therefore, Delpit recommends the following: help children who speak Ebonics learn Standard English so that through acquiring an additional form of linguistic expression they are able to code switch when necessary and still retain pride in the language with which they grew up.

Struggling or Reluctant Readers

We are all struggling or reluctant readers at times. Reflect for a moment on the type of text you struggle with or are reluctant to put much effort into understanding. Perhaps it is the owner's manual for your new computer, the technical jargon in the latest consumer price index, or the symbolism in a much touted film that all of your friends are wild about. Whatever your struggle or reluctance, it typically consists of more than an ability to decode text, broadly defined. The same is true for adolescents who struggle with reading or are reluctant to approach a task that reminds them of past struggles and perhaps even failure.

Even with the best literacy instruction in the early grades, some adolescents will enter secondary school with numerous and debilitating reading difficulties. These difficulties may be associated with poor motivation, low self-esteem, inadequate cognitive processing strategies, underdeveloped technical vocabularies, boredom with a curriculum that seemingly has little relevance to their everyday lives, and so on. For the purposes of this book, we are less interested in the causes of reading difficulties than with the instructional strategies and activities that teachers can use in working with struggling readers.

**EVIDENCE-
BASED
RESEARCH**

Staying focused on what adolescents who struggle with reading bring to their coursework is an important instructional principle—one that is backed by years of research and practice (Moore, Alvermann, & Hinchman, 2000; Readence, Moore, & Rickelman, 2000). In fact, many of the teachers we know take struggling readers' prior knowledge into consideration when planning instruction, teaching content, and assessing learning. Examples of how they do this can be found in Chapters 4–6. Here, we focus on some general principles of instruction that we believe are helpful when working with adolescents who struggle with reading.

**EVIDENCE-
BASED
RESEARCH**

For example, we believe that scaffolding instruction through appropriate comprehension monitoring, self-questioning, and small-group discussion strategies (Palincsar, 1986; Rothenberg & Watts, 2000) provides struggling readers with the support they need to comprehend the content of their subject matter classes. We also believe that direct instruction in vocabulary (Harmon, 2000), summarizing, using text structure, and certain information processing strategies such as those outlined in Flood and Lapp (2000) can make a difference in struggling readers' comprehension of their assigned readings. Finally, we believe struggling adolescent readers benefit from instruction that facilitates writing across the curriculum (Andrews, 2000), provides access to a range of reading materials (Bintz, 1993; Ivey, 1999b), and encourages them to participate in their own assessment, such as engaging in portfolio conferences (Young et al., 2000). These strategies, as well as others, are highlighted in the chapters that follow, along with examples of their application in actual classroom practice and how to teach them, taking struggling readers' needs into account.

Before concluding this section, a caveat is in order. We believe, like Ivey (1999a), that "whereas terminology or categories such as problem, average, superior, or low, middle, high may provide a general sense of how much students have developed as readers, they offer limited information about the complexities of individual experiences" (p. 188). Thus, planning instruction based on how a student has been labeled as a reader (e.g., struggling, low, and disabled) is a practice that lacks pedagogical soundness.

Technology Tip for Motivating Struggling Readers

In an article entitled "Guiding Readers to New Understandings through Electronic Text," Patterson and Pipkin (2001) discuss the merits of encouraging struggling or reluctant readers to engage with a variety of interactive features of electronic texts. They suggest that teachers, librarians, and professional development specialists check out TappedIn (version 2) at http://ti2.sri.com/tappedin/. This site offers K–12 educators opportunities for threaded discussions, file sharing, and private messaging on topics of their own choosing, such as motivating struggling readers in content area classrooms.

Gifted Learners

ACTIVITY   Read and respond in writing to excerpts from an article (below) that appeared in the *Washington Post* on August 25, 2005. A good research project would be to do a follow-up to this story to learn what has happened to the "gifted" label since this news item was published.

Group Seeks to End Gifted Designation

By Lori Aratani
Washington Post Staff Writer
Thursday, August 25, 2005; GZ21

In Montgomery County, where many high school graduates move on to top-notch colleges, a proposal to do away with the designation "gifted and talented" might be seen as blasphemous.

But members of the Equity in Education Coalition, launched a few months ago by concerned parents and community activists, are calling on Montgomery County public school educators to do just that.

They say children suffer when some are labeled gifted and others are not. Evie Frankl of Silver Spring, co-chair of the Montgomery County Education Forum, one of the coalition's member groups, said such designations can give some students an unfair advantage over others.

"It sets up a system by which certain kids head off on a track that prepares them for [high level] courses by giving them an enriched curriculum," Frankl said. "But kids who are not ID'd as gifted and talented take a much more remedial set of courses, so they're not prepared for honors and AP courses in high school."

Added Denise Young of Silver Spring, another member of the coalition, "You don't need to stamp kids [gifted and talented] in order to figure out what they need."

School system officials, pointing to new test scores that show black and Hispanic students making significant progress in reading and math, said the county offers all children the same quality of education. They say that while there are achievement gaps between white and Asian students and their black and Hispanic counterparts, those gaps are narrowing.

Frankl said it's important the community understand that the group is not calling for an end to gifted and talented programs but for an expansion of the programs' reach. "What we want to do is incorporate the gifted and talented program into what every child gets," she said.

In Montgomery County, educators begin identifying students as gifted and talented at the end of second grade, using what they call global screening, a process that includes parent and teacher input and test scores from specially designated exams. If a child is not identified as gifted and talented at that time, parents can appeal the decision. They also have the option of asking that their child be reevaluated at any time during his or her school career, said system spokesman Brian Edwards.

Edwards said the county does everything it can to ensure that all students have access to the programs. He noted that Montgomery is one of the few systems that screens all students for eligibility, rather than just a select few. He said that while there are proportionately fewer black and Hispanic students in the program than there are white and Asian students, educators have worked to devise strategies to identify children who might not fit the traditional definition of gifted and talented.

Frankl said that the system has made strides but that it can do more. "Now is a good time to get rid of the label and think about kids as kids," she said (www.washingtonpost.com/wp-dyn/content/article/2005/08/ 24/ AR2005082401173_pf.html, no page given).

The nation's response to educating the gifted has historical underpinnings that are perhaps best captured in Richard Hofstadter's (1970) *Anti-Intellectualism in American Life*. Extending Alexis de Tocqueville's (1833/1983) characterization of American democracy in antebellum times, Hofstadter wrote,

> Again and again . . . it has been noticed that intellect in America is resented as a kind of excellence, as a claim to distinction, as a challenge to egalitarianism, as a quality which almost certainly deprives a man or woman of the common touch. (p. 51)

In short, intellect is viewed as "foreign to a society built on practicality and consensual understandings" (Resnick & Goodman, 1994, p. 110). In such a culture, gifted young people tend to stand out as special. This label of exceptionality has brought with it a host of tensions tied to issues of social and economic inequality. For example, placements in gifted and talented classes reflect an underrepresentation of minority and poor children (Mehan, 1991). They also reflect the misguided practice of automatically assigning ELLs to basic or general-level classes, rather than gifted classes, because their proficiency in the dominant language (English) fuels the perception that they are incapable of handling a challenging curriculum.

Regardless of how restrictive or flexible one's definition of giftedness, adolescents who are highly creative and insightful will benefit from literacy instruction that offers opportunities for independent inquiry using the Internet, innovative problem solving, and expressive writing—activities that should be a part of all classrooms, but especially those in which gifted and talented students live and work (Ruddell, 1997). Keeping in mind that students of high ability who come from different cultures or from backgrounds of extreme poverty have the same potential to succeed as those students from the dominant culture will ensure that they have equal access to all literacy practices, not just those of a basic nature.

TEACHING AND LEARNING IN CULTURALLY DIVERSE CLASSROOMS

Although we weave suggestions for teaching culturally diverse students throughout this book, we focus here on the importance of standards and of integrating language, culture, and content in teaching culturally diverse students. However, first we invite you to consider the range of cultural diversity present among today's youth and the implications of this for you as a classroom teacher. Such consideration will no doubt heighten your awareness of the need to gear up to teach content reading and literacy in ways that are culturally relevant for all students, not just those who are most like you.

Today's Youth Culture

Each moment that teachers spend interacting with adolescents in content area classrooms is embedded in what social anthropologists Vered Amit-Talai and Helena Wulff (1995) refer to as "a range of cultural possibilities" (p. 231). They use this term to express the view that youth culture cannot be localized (and taught to) as if the classroom were a separate world of its own. Youth culture is produced at home, in school, on the streets, with friends, in malls, among siblings, through TV, music, and the Internet, and so on. To ignore this fact is to teach as if "teachers and students relate to one another undistracted by the classism, racism, and sexism that rage outside the classroom" (Brodkey, 1989, p. 139).

Although we discussed diversity issues that dealt with language, reading ability, and achievement motivation in the previous section, we barely touched the surface of the diversity present in today's youth culture. Consider, for example, the differences in working-class youth's discourse and school discourse. Patrick Finn (1999), an educator born into a working-class Irish Catholic family on the south side of Chicago, has devoted a lifetime to exploring these differences and what they mean for literacy teaching and learning. According to Finn, there are two kinds of education in the United States:

> First, there is empowering education, which leads to powerful literacy, the kind of literacy that leads to positions of power and authority. Second, there is domesticating education, which leads to functional literacy, or literacy that makes a person productive and dependable, but not troublesome (pp. ix–x).

Arguing against the second kind, which is based in conspiracy theory, Finn places the responsibility on schools for educating all youth in ways that are empowering, not simply domesticating.

Differences also abound in how adolescents view themselves in terms of ethnic identity. For example, among Hispanics (a label given to diverse groups of people by the federal government 30 years ago), popular youth culture has proclaimed a "Latino/Latina Revolution" led by Ricky Martin, Jennifer Lopez, and Christina Aguilera (Trujillo, 2000). According to Trujillo, a poll taken by the vice president of quepasa.com revealed that of 5,000 people responding, 37 percent chose Latino, 31 percent chose Hispanic, and the remaining 32 percent wanted to be identified as Mexican, Cuban, Puerto Rican, or whatever their national origin. Among Native Americans, as well as among Asian and Asian American youth, there is also the problem of being grouped together as if there were no differences among tribal groups or countries of national origin. Teachers who take the time to understand the differences between the Hopis and the Apaches or between Vietnamese and Chinese youth, for example, are on the road to achieving a more equitable and culturally responsive pedagogy (Henze & Hauser, 1999).

Finally, in matters of sexual orientation, differences also exist among heterosexual, gay, lesbian, bisexual, and transgender communities of people. Although sexual orientation is not typically a category to which authors of content area reading texts devote space, we include it here because of its place in the wider spectrum of multicultural education and because of the increasing number of publications dealing with homosexuality (Allan, 1999; Young, 2000) in professional journals focused on literacy teaching and learning. Whether coming from homes with gay or lesbian parents or embracing their own issues of sexual orientation, teenagers today need teachers who are as accepting of them and their literacy needs (e.g., appropriate reading materials and informational texts) as they are of students from various racial, ethnic, socioeconomic, linguistic, and religious backgrounds.

CREDE's Standards for Effective Pedagogy and Learning

**EVIDENCE-
BASED
RESEARCH**

The Center for Research on Education, Diversity and Excellence (CREDE) offers research-based standards for effective pedagogy and learning (CREDE, 2003b). According to CREDE, the standards reflect the pedagogical recommendations on which researchers are in agreement for all cultural and linguistic groups in the United States, for all age levels, and for all content areas. Although the standards describe effective instructional methods for all students (including mainstream youth), for students at risk for educational failure, these standards are especially important.

STANDARDS

- Standard I—Teachers and Students Producing Together
  Facilitate learning through joint productive activity among teacher and students.
- Standard II—Developing Language and Literacy across the Curriculum
  Develop competence in the language and literacy of instruction across the curriculum.
- Standard III—Making Meaning: Connecting School to Students' Lives
  Contextualize teaching and curriculum in the experiences and skills of students' homes and communities.

- Standard IV—Teaching Complex Thinking
  Challenge students toward cognitive complexity.
- Standard V—Teaching through Conversation
  Engage students through dialogue, especially the Instructional Conversation.

(http://crede.ucsc.edu/products/print/occreports/g1.html, no page given)

Integrating Language, Culture, and Content

Being able to adjust one's lesson in the midst of teaching is part of a teacher's repertoire of instructional decision-making skills. Fred Genesee (1994), who researches second-language immersion programs in the United States and Canada, cites studies showing that teachers make as many as 1,300 instructional decisions each day. These decisions are most effective when teachers integrate their subject matter expertise with what they have learned about their students' language and culture.

What's to be gained from this type of instruction?   Sheltered English classrooms are considered by some educators as being the only viable means for reaching large numbers of second-language learners. They provide academic support in the second language (English), which is akin to Russian psychologist Lev Vygotsky's (1978) notion of the zone of proximal development (ZPD). Envisioning ESL instruction as scaffolding—a temporary prop that helps move students from what they know (their native language) to what they need to know (English)—is a form of ZPD. Stated in more technical terms, the ZPD is

Technology Tip—Instructional Conversation in Science

View a demonstration of an instructional conversation, a component of *teaching through conversation*, one of the five standards for effective pedagogy and learning of the Center for Research on Education, Diversity and Excellence. The URL for this CD-ROM demonstration is http://crede.ucsc.edu/products/multimedia /ta_demo.html.

In this demo, the teacher first asks students what they have accomplished on a science bumper-sticker activity so she can assist them in clarifying the next steps they should take. The conversation concludes by focusing on the degree to which students have understood the concepts underlying the activity.

Note: You will need to have QuickTime installed on your computer to view the live demonstration. A free copy of QuickTime can be installed by going to www.apple.com/quicktime/download.

the distance between a speaker's ability to handle English without guidance and his or her level of potential development under the guidance of more English-fluent adults or peers. The ZPD takes on added significance when one considers that ESL learners often experience "a pattern of insecurity or ambivalence about the value of their own cultural identity as a result of their interactions with the dominant group" (Cummins, 1994b, p. 45). Teachers who plan instruction with the ZPD in mind increase their chances of helping students learn to use elements of their own culture to understand those of the dominant culture.

Teachers who take into account students' cultural backgrounds, while being sensitive to the fact that not all young people from the same culture group think or respond in the same way, create favorable learning conditions in which students view themselves as capable and engaged learners. For example, in a news release that appeared soon after his ground-breaking book *Teaching Reading to Black Adolescent Males: Closing the Achievement Gap* (2005) was published, Alfred Tatum, who grew up in a poverty-stricken neighborhood in Chicago, offered the following advice to teachers:

■ *Establish a broader definition of literacy instruction that guides the selection of text.* It must focus on skill and strategy knowledge, content knowledge, and identity development. "It is imperative that these young men have the requisite skills to read text independently. It is also imperative that they become 'smarter' as a result of their reading," he says.

■ *Identify a core of "must-read" texts for African American adolescent males.* These include James Baldwin's The Fire Next Time and Ralph Ellison's Invisible Man.

■ *Discuss texts in culturally responsive ways.* "Students benefit when they can extend the ideas contained in texts into their own lives," he says.

■ *Examine your disposition toward using texts with African American adolescent males.* Many teachers back down when they encounter resistance from their students to read beyond the required material, Tatum says. "However, no research currently shows that having students read less advances their academic and other literacy needs" (Northern Illinois University's Office of Public Affairs, 2005, n.p.).

CULTURALLY RESPONSIVE PROFESSIONAL GROWTH

Appreciating Diversity

Allan Neilsen (1991) made the interesting observation that "while we often talk about differentiated curriculum and instruction for younger learners, we tend to act as though teachers, as learners, are 'all grown up' and all the same" (p. 67). That such is not the case is clearly the message Irvine (1990) hoped to get across when she wrote

Teacher education appears to be suspended in a serious time warp, training future educators in the pedagogy of decades past and pretending that . . . graduates will teach . . . highly motivated, achievement-oriented . . . middle-class students from two-parent families. . . . By the Year 2010, 38 percent of all children will come from a minority group. Demographic data confirm that working mothers, poor single mothers, teenage mothers, declining fertility rates among white middle-class women, increasing fertility rates among poor minority women, the influx of immigrants, and the growing underclass will dramatically change how we will administer schools and teach students.

Teacher education professionals must hastily respond to this problem of the growing, at-risk, minority student population, decreasing minority teacher pools, and increasing numbers of majority teacher education students. The profession must respond with the expectation that, at least in the near future, the majority of minority students' teachers will be white females who are unfamiliar with minority students' language, lifestyle, culture, family, and community. (p. 18)

Synchronizing professional growth opportunities so that they take into account the ever-widening gap between the number of minority students enrolled in school and the number of minority teachers available to instruct them in content literacy is a complex task. It involves educating all teachers— minority and nonminority—in a manner that helps them to understand the central role of culture in their lives and the lives of their students. Architects of such professional growth opportunities, Ladson-Billings (1994) argues, must ensure that teachers come away with more than a "foods-and-festivals" approach to understanding culture. She also maintains that it is foolhardy for any group to believe that "culture is what other people have; what we have is just *truth*."

Creating safe environments that foster classroom appreciation of diversity does not mean engaging in "neutral" discussions in which feelings of conflict or issues of power are submerged in teachers' and students' making-nice talk. On the contrary, according to Henze and Hauser (1999), such issues can (and should) be raised. They offer the following strategies for engaging in this kind of talk:

In order to foster discussion about issues such as conflict or power, along with less emotionally charged topics relating to cultural values and practices, teachers need to establish an environment in which students feel comfortable expressing their views. Several strategies can be employed. For example, teachers can validate the knowledge of students at the outset through an activity where they create shared understandings of topics to be addressed, such as culture or ethnicity [see Give One/Get One handout in Figure 2.1]. Teachers can use self-disclosure as a way to humanize themselves and model the process of honest reflection. Another way in which many teachers establish safe conditions for dialogue is by setting up ground rules at the outset. For example, the class might agree that no individuals should dominate the conversation, that students have a right to pass if they do not want to share certain things about themselves, and that the opinions of others should be respected even if they disagree. (p. 3)

Give One/Get One: Sample Handout

A. Write (or draw) by yourself for _____ minutes putting down three answers to the following question:

What do you think of when you hear the term "culture"?

1. _____

2. _____

3. _____

B. Now get up and walk around. Give an idea from your list to another person—preferably someone you don't know very well—and get an idea from that person's list to add to your own. Write down the other person's name next to his or her idea. You have _____ minutes.

1. _____

2. _____

3. _____

FIGURE 2.1   Give one/get one: sample handout (*Source:* Adapted with permission from R. C. Henze & M. E. Hauser (1999). *Personalizing culture through anthropological and educational perspectives*, Educational Practice Report No. 4, p. 24. Santa Cruz, CA: Center for Research on Education, Diversity and Excellence.)

Involving Parents and Community

Parents are a child's first teacher. Thus, it makes sense that a focus on culturally responsive teaching strategies should include the need to develop parent and community partnerships in content literacy learning. In the past, a deficit model of home–school relations assumed inappropriately that schools needed to exert a good deal of influence on certain low-income parents' literate interactions with their children in order to "make up" for perceived inadequacies in the home. This manner of thinking has largely given way to one of mutual understanding in which each party (parents and teachers) develops an awareness of the other's specific cultural practices. As Cairney (2000) noted, "In this way schooling can be adjusted to meet the needs of families. Parents, in turn, can also be given the opportunity to observe and understand the definitions of literacy that schools support" (p. 59).

With this change in focus has come an increased appreciation of intergenerational literacy programs (Gadsden, 2000), which are rich with implications for culturally responsive teaching if we pay attention to what we can learn from them as teachers. There is also room in this new reciprocal way of thinking about home–school partnerships for students to see their cultures reflected in a positive light through both the school curriculum and culturally responsive teaching. In short, no longer is it necessary for students to endure what Rosalinda Barrera refers to as the "culturalectomies" that children of her generation experienced growing up under the deficit model of home–school relations (Jimenez et al., 1999, p. 217).

However, communicating with parents who are from a culture different from one's own can present challenges at times. For example, we are reminded of a research study that Lee Gunderson (2000) conducted in which he interviewed teenagers from various immigrant groups (refugees, landed immigrants, and entrepreneurs). What he learned about these youth, their parents, and himself in the process of doing this study is worth repeating here because it illustrates what all of us—firmly established citizens and newly landed immigrants alike—need to know if we are to be culturally responsive educators. In Gunderson's words,

> I am an immigrant, a Norwegian-American-Canadian. Like millions of native English-speaking individuals in Australia, Canada, New Zealand, and the United States, my parents' first culture and language, in my case Norwegian, has withered away. . . . First- and second-generation immigrants remember their struggles learning a new language and a new culture. Most often, however, they are convinced that their losses were a consequence of their heroic or pioneer-like efforts to forge new lives for themselves and their families. They view their losses as part of the price they have paid to become members of a new society. Their willingness to sacrifice signifies in their minds their dedication to family and to the democratic ideals of their new country. They are members of the most recognizable diasporas. . . . The individuals of the third, fourth, and fifth generations are the lost ones whose first cultures like unsettled spirits haunt their angst-filled reveries. Becoming an American, an Australian, or a Canadian means the surrender of first languages and first cultures. Children and grandchildren have little sense of what has been lost.
>
> Perhaps in recognizing this loss in our own lives, we will be one step further along the path to becoming culturally responsive educators. At the very least, we will have stopped a moment to consider what it might be like to walk in the shoes of the adolescents who come to our classes each day speaking a different language, holding on to cultural practices that still make sense to them, and wishing for a teacher or two who will understand all of this. (p. 693)

Linking School and Home

In their report of a study that focused on using math literacy to link home and school, Civil, Andrade, and Gonzalez (2002) emphasize the importance of teaching in ways that respect students' construction of meaning and the connections they make outside of school, in the home. This approach, the researchers argue, is important for all students, but in particular for those who come from economically underprivileged homes in which English is not the first language. Viewing parents as intellectual resources, Civil, Andrade, and Gonzalez developed a series of mathematics workshops for a core group of mothers who were Mexican immigrants and for their children's teachers. The workshops, which had as their premise that "we are all learners," were jointly negotiated by the mothers and the teachers, and the information gained from them became curriculum building blocks for teaching and learning math literacy in school. For example,

> One of the [middle school] teachers used his household visits . . . to develop a sophisticated curriculum plan around the idea of "build your dream home." Through this project, students learned many of the required mathematical skills and concepts in a familiar context—that of house construction. Furthermore, several of their family members were involved in the final projects, the making of a model for their dream home. Another teacher, knowing that her students' families were quite knowledgeable about gardening, developed a theme centered on this topic. This theme allowed her to explore in depth topics in measurement, geometry, and graphing, that while they are grade-appropriate, they are often barely touched on. (www.crede.ucsc.edu/research/md/4.2es.html, no page given)

English teachers, like the mathematics teachers in the preceding example, can also support second-language learners by providing prompt and helpful feedback on their written language. When editing the writing of ELLs, Carroll et al., (1996) recommend that teachers focus on the students' rich and colorful language, rather than simply correcting their grammatical errors. This attention to the positive aspects of second-language learners' written work will demonstrate "acknowledgment and respect for immigrant/ELL students, their families, their experiences and the language they use at home and in their communities" (Rubenstein-Avila, 2003, p. 133).

SUMMARY

Envisioning language as social practice opens the door to new ways of thinking about content literacy teaching and learning in culturally diverse classrooms. With this envisioning comes an awareness of students' different ways of dialoging with the world. Listening to students' views, and especially to the views of those who come from linguistic and ethnic minority backgrounds, can provide important clues about what is valued or devalued in the curriculum and why (Nieto, 1994). Just as the sorting practices of the school present their own special set of challenges, so too do the demographic changes in the U.S. student population. English language learners represent one of the fastest growing groups of students in U.S. secondary schools. According to the National Clearinghouse for English Acquisition and Language Instruction Educational Programs, English language learners as a whole speak more than 460 different languages and represent multiple countries that include Mexico, Vietnam, Laos, China, Korea, Russia, Haiti, and Japan, among others (www.ncela.gwu.edu/resabout/ells/1_characteristics.htm, n.p.).

The makeup of the U.S. student population is also expected to change. Unlike the two-thirds white (non-Hispanic) majority in our schools today, by 2010, approximately four of every ten students in grades kindergarten through 12 will represent minority groups (Hodgkinson, 1992; Hoffman, 1999). At the same time, the number of minority teachers is expected to decline. These trends point to the need for all teachers to sharpen their instructional skills in the area of integrating language, content, and culture.

SUGGESTED READINGS

Baker, J. (2002). Trilingualism. In L. Delpit & J. K. Dowdy (Eds.), *The skin that we speak: Thoughts on language and culture in the classroom* (pp. 49–61). New York: New Press.

de la Luz Reyes, M., & Molner, L. A. (1991). Instructional strategies for second-language learners in the content areas. *Journal of Reading, 35,* 96–103.

Delpit, L. (2002). No kinda sense. In L. Delpit & J. K. Dowdy (Eds.), *The skin that we speak: Thoughts on language and culture in the classroom* (pp. 31–48). New York: New Press.

Flores-Gonzalez, N. (2002). *School kids/street kids: Identity development in Latino students.* New York: Teachers College Press.

Gandara, P., Maxwell-Jolly, J., & Driscoll, A. (2005). *Listening to teachers of English language learners: A survey of California teachers' challenges, experiences, and professional development needs.* Santa Cruz, CA: The Center for the Future of Teaching and Learning.

Godina, H. (1999). High school students of Mexican background in the midwest: Cultural differences as a constraint to effective literacy instruction. In T. Shanahan & F. V. Rodriguez-Brown (Eds.), *48th Yearbook of the National Reading Conference* (pp. 266–279). Chicago: National Reading Conference.

Jimenez, R. T. (2003). Literacy and Latino students in the United States: Some considerations, questions, and new directions. *Reading Research Quarterly, 38,* 122–128.

Mason, P. A., & Schumm, J. S. (Eds.). (2003). *Promising practices for urban reading instruction.* Newark, DE: International Reading Association.

Rickford, J., & Rickford, A. (1995). Dialect readers revisited. *Linguistics and Education, 7,* 107–128.

Creating a Favorable Learning Environment

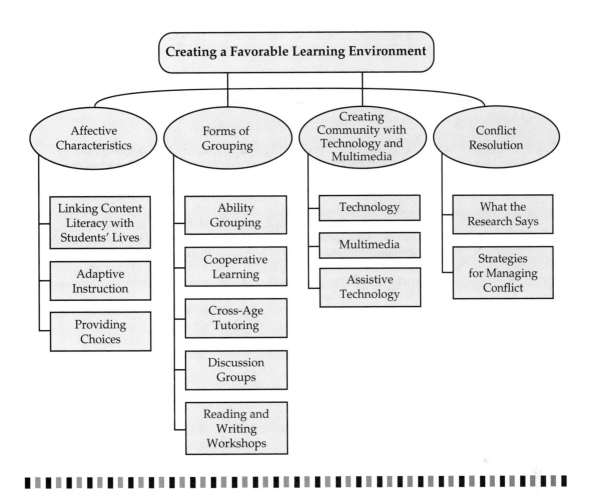

Creating a favorable learning environment involves more than just teaching to the standards. Although standards are important, as Todd Goodson, a professor at Kansas State University, reminds us in his account of "Teaching in the Time of Dogs," it is the time we spend responding to the spontaneity of students' concerns that must be our starting point. For "in the classroom there's one thing you can be sure of," writes Goodson (2004), "and that's that anything can happen" (www.writingproject.org/cs/nwpp/print/nwpr/1979).

∎∎∎∎∎∎∎

Teaching in the Time of Dogs

by Todd Goodson

A number of years ago, I was a middle school teacher. One morning I was standing outside my classroom as my first-hour group assembled when one of my students approached me in tears.

"Mr. Goodson," she sobbed, "I think my neighbor skinned his dog."

As she stood there crying, and I stood there looking at her, it occurred to me at that moment that I really had no clue how to handle this situation. I knew there were interpersonal and cultural and ethical and perhaps even legal issues unfolding in front of me, but I didn't even know what they were, much less what I, as a teacher, was obligated to do. But as a crowd of curious middle-schoolers gathered around us, I knew I had to do something. I decided to start with the obvious question.

"What makes you think your neighbor skinned his dog?" I asked.

"Because it's hanging from his clothesline," she wailed.

Her answer didn't help my state of mind all that much. For a moment I wondered whether it was the neighbor's *dog's skin* or the neighbor's *skinned dog* hanging from the clothesline, but I decided it probably didn't matter. (Except, of course, to the dog.) The real problem at the moment was my student, still standing there, crying, waiting for me to resolve this matter. I decided on a bold course of action.

"Have you told your mother about this?" I asked.

She shook her head no. "I saw it on my way to school," she said.

"Why don't you go down to the office and call your mother?" I suggested, and I was more than a little grateful when she nodded and turned away, leaving me to curse those idiot education professors who didn't prepare me for this encounter.

A few minutes after she left to call her mother, she came back to my classroom. She wasn't upset anymore. In fact she bounced to her seat and started whispering and giggling with her friends. I drifted through the room and back to her seat.

"Is everything all right?" I asked, now thoroughly puzzled by her dramatic change in mood.

She seemed confused, as if she didn't know what I was talking about.

"Your neighbor's dog," I reminded her.

"Oh, yeah," she said. "It was just a coyote."

"Great," I said. And I suppose it probably was. (Except, of course, for the coyote.)

Years passed. Today I'm an "idiot education professor," trying to figure out a way to teach young people things they can only really learn from experience and writing about the curious magic of literacy and its teaching.

(Note: To read more than this excerpt from "Teaching in the Time of Dogs," visit www.writingproject.org/cs/nwpp/print/nwpr/1979)

∎∎∎∎∎∎∎

When Donna first read this anecdotal account of the art of teaching, she couldn't wait to share it with students in her content literacy methods class at the University of Georgia. "Teaching in the Time of Dogs" (thanks to Todd Goodson's gift as a storyteller) is what this chapter on creating a favorable learning environment is all about. Thus, as you read, keep this story in mind, and remember that "the art of teaching, like the art of writing, lies as much in how we respond to the irregular as in how we plan to create regularity" (Goodson, 2004, n.p.).

AFFECTIVE CHARACTERISTICS

A favorable learning environment supports students as they grapple with issues of affect that influence how they feel about school and their willingness to engage in academic activities. Affective characteristics of instruction that concern teachers in this kind of environment include those of linking content literacy with students' lives and providing students with choices. In advocating that classrooms become places in which the integration of heart, head, voice, and hand is the norm rather than the exception, Shelby Wolf and colleagues (Wolf, Edmiston, & Enciso, 1997) remind us of the need to teach in a manner that joins the cognitive and affective domains of knowing. As Vygotsky (1986) has written,

> Thought is not begotten by thought; it is engendered by motivation, i.e., by our desires and needs, our interests and emotions. Behind every thought there is an affective-volitional tendency, which holds the answer to the last "why" in the analysis of thinking. A true and full understanding of another's thought is possible only when we understand its affective-volitional basis. (p. 252)

We know, from our own experiences as teachers, the validity of Vygotsky's thinking. Time and time again, we have learned to rely on the affective currents in our classrooms as guideposts to what is possible in the cognitive domain. Working hard not to separate the cognitive from the affective is a way of life. It is an approach to teaching that we find both challenging and rewarding.

Linking Content Literacy with Students' Lives

The learning cycle.   Creating a favorable learning environment, to our way of thinking, should involve helping students link content literacy learning to their own lives. One way of assisting them in this process is to think of learning as being "controlled as much by experiences students bring to the learning situation as it is by the way the information is presented" (Marshall, 1996, p. 81). This view of learning, which Marshall calls *the learning cycle* (Figure 3.1), rests on the notion that students' earlier learning experiences tend to dictate in large part their attitude and willingness to engage in new learning.

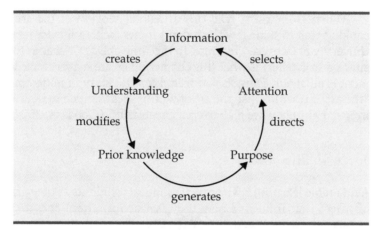

FIGURE 3.1   The learning cycle (*Source:* N. Marshall (1996).
The Students: Who are they and how do I reach them? In D. Lapp, J. Flood, &
N. Farnan (Eds.), *Content area reading and learning*, p. 82.) Copyright 1982 by
Allyn and Bacon. Reprinted by permission.

Like the schema-theoretic view of the reading process described in Chapter 1,
the learning cycle is heavily dependent on prior knowledge. In Marshall's (1996)
words,

> To understand [the learning cycle], it is easiest to begin with *prior knowledge*.
> Since all new learning is based on existing knowledge, the previous experiences
> of the students are central to the complete cycle. Furthermore, prior knowledge
> helps [generate] reasons for learning or not learning. Depending on *purpose* for
> learning, attention is directed differently. . . . *Attention* is limited; we cannot
> pay attention to everything in a new situation. For learning to be efficient,
> therefore, attention must be directed to the most important *information*. Once
> the information is encountered, it needs to be *understood*. . . . Finally, to be able
> to use new information as the basis of subsequent learning, students must use
> the new understanding to *modify* existing knowledge. (p. 82)

We see the learning cycle as a useful heuristic for thinking about ways to
link content literacy with students' lives. First, it suggests that teachers need to
take students' prior knowledge into account when planning their instruction.
Second, it implies that students will have their own purposes for engaging in (or
avoiding) certain learning activities. A closer look at the learning cycle suggests
that teaching and learning are not simply mirror processes. As Wenger (1998)
pointed out, instruction itself does not cause learning; instead, it creates the
conditions and context in which learning can take place:

> Learning and teaching are not inherently linked. Much learning takes place
> without teaching, and indeed much teaching takes place without learning. To
> the extent that teaching and learning are linked in practice, the linkage is one

not of cause and effect but of resources and negotiation. . . . Learning is an emergent, ongoing process, which may use teaching as one of its many structuring resources. In this regard, teachers and instructional materials become resources for learning in much more complex ways than through their pedagogical intentions. (pp. 266–267)

We like to think of teachers and instructional materials as offering opportunities for engagement in learning. Thought of in this way, teaching involves creating a favorable learning environment, one in which students become invested in their own learning. Moreover, in this kind of environment, it is often the case that the things students learn extend beyond what the teacher is hired to teach. Such learning is sometimes referred to as "stolen knowledge" (Brown & Duguid, 1996, p. 49). In other words, a literate environment contains the resources and opportunities students need to participate in a community of learners who are legitimately free to "steal" the knowledge they need to make sense of the content and social practices they are expected to acquire. As Brown and Duguid explain, the need to steal knowledge arises from the fact that "relatively little of the complex web of actual practice can be made the subject of explicit instruction" (p. 50). Much remains implicit, where it is always available to be stolen as needed.

A strategy for linking content literacy to students' lives.   Short warm-up activities can demonstrate to students the usefulness of determining what they know and do not know about a certain topic prior to reading about it. Such activities also can shed light on how willing (or unwilling) students may be to engage in learning about the topic. For example, a strategy called Creative Thinking–Reading Activity (CT-RA) (Ruddell, 1996), which takes no more than 10 or 15 minutes to complete, offers students a chance to brainstorm solutions to the topic at hand using their everyday knowledge. This kind of activity rewards students for using ideas from their practical store of knowledge to solve textbook-related problems. The CT-RA includes the following steps (Ruddell, 1996, p. 103):

1. Develop with students the rules for brainstorming:
   a. Think of as many ideas as you can.
   b. No criticism of any ideas—even your own.
   c. Go for any freewheeling thought—the wilder the idea the better.
   d. Build on others' ideas and combine ideas when you can.
2. Give students the creative thinking task (only one) and allow five minutes for brainstorming. For example, a task might be to estimate the amount of industrial toxins that seep into their local waterways or reservoir.
3. Share ideas in large group.
4. Announce a single criterion for students to evaluate and select an answer; for example, "Which of [the solutions to the problem] do you think is the wildest?"
5. Share these responses.

We like the CT-RA strategy because it provides spaces for ESL students and students who are less academically inclined to contribute their ideas—ideas that might otherwise be overlooked or dismissed. We also like it because we have observed students asking their peers for clarification in the small-group brainstorming portion of the strategy. According to Canales (1996), "asking questions for clarification is particularly critical for ESL students" (p. 7).

Bridging out-of-school literacies and content literacy learning.   *School's Out!* (Hull & Schultz, 2002) presents an edited collection of teachers' and researchers' insights into the connections youth make between the literacies they use outside school and those they learn as part of the regular school curriculum. The book challenges the notion that there is a great divide between the literate practices learners use in school and out. To Hull and Schultz's way of thinking,

> Sometimes this dichotomy relegates all good things to out-of-school contexts and everything repressive to school. Sometimes it dismisses the engagement of children with non-school learning as merely frivolous or remedial or incidental. What we want to argue . . . is that, rather than setting formal and informal education systems and contexts in opposition to each other, we might do well to look for overlap or complementarity or perhaps a respectful division of labor. (p. 3)

Policy debates over what counts as literacy (and by extension, content literacy instruction) are not only counterproductive, they are also irrelevant if one embraces the argument made in *School's Out!* As shown repeatedly by the contributors to this book, Dewey (1899/1998) was correct in his belief that much can be learned from observing the overlap between formal education and everyday life. Without romanticizing the connections between these two worlds, *School's Out!* chronicles the tensions inherent in them and offers insights into ways of better understanding how to bridge formal and informal learning.

For example, in a chapter by Ellen Skilton-Sylvester (2002), we learn how a Cambodian girl dealt with peer pressure and partially overcame the stereotype that being interested in school writing marked her as being "unpopular" among her peers. In this instance, Nan's prolific out-of-school writing could have been the bridge to better in-school writing performance had peer pressure not intervened. As it was, much of what Nan was able to accomplish as a writer in her home and community remained invisible to her teachers. This finding has implications for what you, as a content area teacher with students like Nan in your classroom, will need to consider as you work toward creating a favorable learning environment for all learners, including those for whom peer pressure is very much a part of their world in and out of school.

Adaptive Instruction

Teaching students how to assume responsibility for their own learning involves adapting one's instruction to fit the needs of various types of learners. Adaptive instruction is particularly germane to teaching students who are members of special populations, such as ESL students, gifted students, slower learners, and students with learning disabilities. As defined by Corno and Snow (1986), adaptive teaching is student-centered:

> [It] arranges environmental conditions to fit learners' individual differences. As learners gain in aptitude through experience with respect to the instructional goals at hand, such teaching adapts by becoming less intrusive. Less intrusion, less teacher or instructional mediation, increases the . . . need for more learner self-regulation. (p. 621)

Generally, adaptive instruction follows five principles (Strother, 1985):

1. Students should receive instruction based on their assessed capabilities, not their weaknesses.
2. Materials and methods should be chosen on the basis of flexibility and appeal to students' interests.
3. Students should play an active role in setting goals and evaluating their progress toward those goals.
4. Alternative activities and materials should be available for students who require additional assistance.
5. Cooperative, rather than competitive, approaches to learning should be stressed.

A point worth emphasizing here is that adapting instruction for struggling readers and English language learners is not synonymous with dumbing down

Struggling Readers and ELLs— Writing with SPAWN Prompts

SPAWN, the acronym derived from five categories of writing options originally developed by Martin, Martin, and O'Brien (1984) and recently reintroduced by Brozo (2003), is an especially effective strategy to use with struggling readers and English language learners, who may benefit specifically from extra attention paid to their particular life experiences. The five writing options include:

S—*Special Powers.* Students are given the power to change some aspect of the text or topic. Their writing should explain *what* was changed, *why,* and the *effects* of the change.

P—*Problem Solving.* Students are asked to write possible solutions to problems posed

or suggested by the books being read or material being studied.

A—*Alternative Viewpoints.* Students write about a topic or retell a story from a unique perspective.

W—*What If?* Students are asked to respond to a change the teacher has introduced in some aspect of the topic or story (an option similar to Special Powers).

N—*Next.* Students are asked to write in anticipation of what the author will discuss next, explaining the logic behind their conjecture.

(Brozo, 2003, p. 44)

the curriculum. Just the opposite case is true. Like Rubenstein-Avila (2003), we believe that being sensitive to the needs of youth who struggle with reading or who are learning English as a second language "is best reflected by conveying to students that we have high expectations for all learners" (p. 129).

Providing Choices

Lynn Rhodes and Nancy Shanklin (1993), two experts in assessing literacy learning in grades K–8, say that providing students with choices in materials, activities, and time lines for finishing an assignment increases a teacher's chance of communicating genuine purposes for reading and writing. Rhodes and Shanklin also recommend that teachers follow students' leads whenever possible. Sometimes these leads are more subtle than direct, but when teachers pick up on them, they demonstrate a willingness to meet the student halfway.

EVIDENCE-BASED RESEARCH

Providing choices can extend to the kinds of questions teachers are willing to entertain. This is an area of particular interest to Donna and Steve. In our multi-case study of five school sites throughout the United States, we were well aware of the questions that students and teachers considered "safe" to ask (Alvermann et al., 1996b). We are uncomfortable with this kind of self-censoring behavior. We also found evidence in our research that supports Kathe Jervis's (1996) observation that "even in schools which seek to create diverse and integrated school communities, silence about race prevails" (p. 546). A willingness to hear the hard questions that children ask, Jervis argues, is basic to exploring issues of discrimination and equity.

Self-censorship of these hard questions leads to what Dwight Boyd (1996) calls the "'munch, stomp, and dress up' view of multiculturalism" (p. 612). That is, when students and teachers limit themselves to asking safe questions, they are left with a superficial approach to understanding differences—one that leads to discussing a culture's food, dance, and clothing style preferences rather than its moral values and beliefs. In moving away from so-called safe discussions, teachers would provide students with choices regarding what is talked about in the curriculum. Given the litigious nature of our society, it is not a move that we expect to see in the near future. However, we agree with Jervis and Boyd that in failing to address the hard questions students might ask, we limit our ability to understand how they see the world. In turn, this places a limitation on the success that might be had in creating open and viable learning environments.

FORMS OF GROUPING

Tracking is but one, though still very common, way of grouping students for instruction at the middle and high school levels. A system for deciding who should learn what and at what pace, tracking remains a controversial issue in the United States. Despite legal attempts to end or limit the amount of tracking in secondary schools, it is a system that has proven "extraordinarily resilient and resistant to change" (Welner & Oakes, 1996, p. 466). Nonetheless, in many reform-oriented school districts throughout the country, alternative forms of grouping such as cooperative learning groups, cross-age tutoring, small-group discussions, and reading and writing workshops are gaining in popularity.

Ability Grouping

In general, schools group students for instruction in one of three ways: curriculum tracking, ability-group tracking, or within-class grouping. *Curriculum tracking* involves scheduling students' courses so that they follow a particular sequence and prepare students for life after high school. This gives rise to the familiar college preparatory, general, and vocational tracks of secondary schools.

Ability-group tracking, or between-class grouping, involves assigning students to a particular class section (such as history honors or general math) based on their past performance in that subject area. Such grouping is intended to reduce the heterogeneity of an instructional group and thus make the teacher's job more manageable. At the high school level, ability-group tracking is often synonymous with curriculum tracking. A special kind of tracking, called block scheduling, is found in some schools and consists of grouping students for a large block of time each day.

Within-class grouping, which is more common at the elementary level than at the middle and secondary levels, consists of separating students into smaller instructional groups once they have been assigned to a particular class; for example, an English teacher might do within-class grouping to accommodate differences in students' reading or writing abilities (Glatthorn, 1991).

Arguments for. Traditionally, those who favor ability-group tracking do so on the grounds that it affords teachers the opportunity to adapt their instruction in a way that challenges the faster learner and supports the slower learner. Proponents say that high-ability students become bored with schooling when the pace of instruction is slowed down to accommodate less able students. According to Feldhusen (1989), "grouping gifted and talented youth for at least part of the school day and offering a differentiated curriculum leads to higher achievement, engenders better attitudes and motivation, and does no harm to less able youth" (p. 4).

Arguments against. Hargreaves (1967) and Oakes (1985) concluded that higher-track students feel more positively toward school than lower-track students do, partly because they are exposed to more competent teachers and teachers with better attitudes. Reading practices also seem to vary according to tracks, with higher-track students receiving instruction that allows them to exercise critical thinking skills and lower-track students being held more to factual recall.

A Response from Our Readers

Abel Hernandez, a student in one of Professor Josephine Young's content literacy classes at Arizona State University, wrote the following reflection after reading the section on the pros and cons of ability grouping in an earlier edition of our text, *Content Reading and Literacy: Succeeding in Today's Diverse Schools.* With Mr. Hernandez's permission, we quote from his written reflection:

> As an affected member of a minority group who was impressed upon at an early age the effects of grouping, my feelings on this issue run deep. When I was in grades first through sixth I attended a segregated school that consisted of Hispanics/Mexicans. I was happy at that school and really did not mind being in such a school. It was not until I moved from Texas to Arizona that I began to appreciate the blatant discrimination that I had experienced as a child.
>
> Upon transferring, I, as well as the rest of my family, met with the principal of the [new] school. He strongly advised, encouraged, and suggested that I be placed in the special education classes at the school until the

administration determined what level of education I had. My sister vehemently disagreed and informed the teacher that if I was placed in a special education class she would have no problem with filing a lawsuit against the school on the theory of alleged bias and discrimination because of my ethnicity.

> During my first day in class I happened to meet the special education students, and what a coincidence that all of them were Hispanics. To this day, I find it amazing the effects that tracking and grouping had on those children's lives. I can imagine what effect this would have had on me had my sister not championed my right to an education based on equal opportunity and not on my ethnicity or similarity to others like me.
>
> I believe there is a place for tracking and grouping but when it is done solely based on the color of one's skin, then it becomes intolerable. Grouping for the sake of the students' education is commendable, but when it is done for the convenience of the school, that is when the line has to be drawn.*

*Courtesy of Abel Hernandez.

Cooperative Learning

In cooperative-learning groups, students work together in small groups (of four or five individuals) to set goals and to learn from one another, with the incentive being a group reward for combined individual efforts. "The principal idea behind cooperative learning methods is that by rewarding groups as well as individuals for their academic achievement, peer norms will come to favor rather than oppose high achievement" (Slavin, 1984a, p. 54).

In cooperative-learning groups, students come to rely less on the teacher and more on one another. Acting as peer tutors, they learn more because they are actively engaged with the text or other instructional materials. Slavin (1984b) demonstrated the value of cooperative learning in culturally diverse classrooms and with students who have disabilities that could potentially interfere with their learning. By engaging students in cooperative learning, teachers set the stage for acceptance of diversity and valuing of individual contributions. Linguistically

EVIDENCE-BASED RESEARCH

diverse students are known to benefit from cooperative learning because they become more actively involved and spend more time in meaningful exchanges with their peers than they otherwise would (Reyes & Molner, 1991).

Three widely used cooperative-learning techniques developed by Slavin and colleagues at the Johns Hopkins Center for Social Organization of Schools are Student Teams–Achievement Divisions (STAD), Teams–Games–Tournament (TGT), and Jigsaw II. As indicated in Figure 3.2, the three techniques share certain features: there are four or five members to a team, and each team is heterogeneously grouped according to ability, gender, ethnicity, and race. The three cooperative learning techniques are described by Lehr (1984) as follows:

> In STAD . . . team members study worksheets on material that the teacher has presented through lecture or discussion. Students may use any means of mastering the material, and they are given answer sheets so that it is clear that they are to master concepts, not merely fill in blanks on the sheet. They are told to study until all team members understand the subject. The students are quizzed individually, and the team's overall score is determined by the extent to which each student improved his or her performance over past efforts. A base score is set 5 points below each student's average, and [students] earn points up to a maximum of 10 for each point that exceeds their base score. This system allows low-performing students to contribute maximum points to the team by showing improvement or completing a perfect paper. Teams with the highest scores are recognized weekly in a class newspaper, as are students who exceed their own past records.
>
> The same procedures are used in TGT. However, rather than taking quizzes, students play academic games with other class members with similar past performance records. In preparation for the tournaments, which are held once or twice a week, teams hold regular practices when teammates help each other review skills taught by the teacher. Each student is then assigned to a tournament table to compete with representatives of two other teams with similar performance records. At the end of each game, the players at each table compare their scores to determine the top, middle, and low scorers at the various tables. Top scorers receive 6 points, middle scorers 4, and low scorers 2. Team scores are determined by adding the results for teammates, and these scores are then added to previous game scores in the tournament for a cumulative score. The games involve answering questions presented on cards or sheets and pertaining to the subject being studied. As in STAD, high-scoring teams and tournament winners receive recognition in a weekly class newspaper.
>
> As originally developed by Aronson and his colleagues at the University of California, Santa Cruz, Jigsaw involves teams of five or six members, each of whom is given one segment of the day's lesson and made responsible for teaching it to others. Students who get the same segment meet in counterpart groups to help each other work out the best ways of teaching it and to anticipate the kinds of questions they might have to answer. Since the only way students can gain information about lesson segments other than their own is to listen to their teammates, the Jigsaw technique also becomes a method for enhancing listening and questioning skills. In Jigsaw II, a modification,

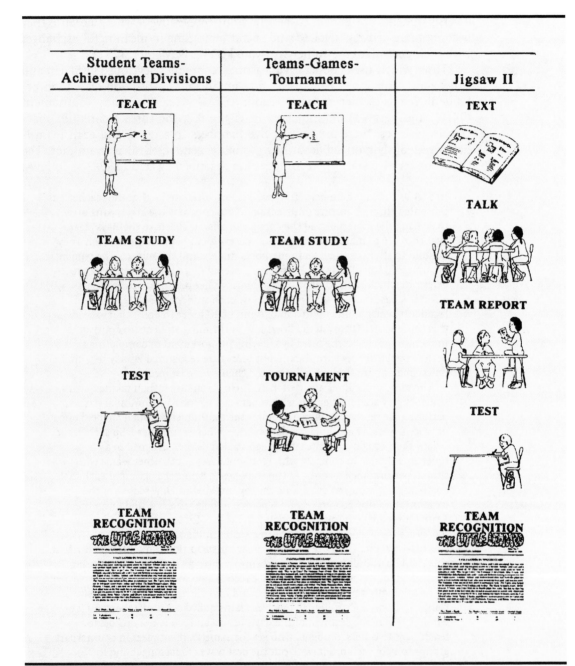

FIGURE 3.2   Basic schedule of activities for STAD, TGT, and Jigsaw II (*Source:* From R. E. Slavin, *Student Team Learning: A Practical Guide to Cooperative Learning,* © 1991, National Education Association. Reprinted with permission.)

students work in four- to five-member teams. Instead of receiving different lesson segments, all read a common text from which each is given a topic on which to become an expert. Students with the same topics meet, discuss, and return to their teams to teach what they have learned. After this, the entire class is quizzed for individual and team scores, as in STAD.*

EVIDENCE-BASED RESEARCH

Cooperative learning of a more informal nature than that prescribed in STAD, TGT, and Jigsaw II is generally defined as any collaborative act that involves two or more students working together to accomplish specific pedagogical tasks (Gumperz, Cook-Gumperz, & Szymanski, 1999). This type of grouping arrangement, when used in conjunction with content literacy instruction, has been found to be a highly effective means for improving students' understanding of academic subject matter (National Reading Panel, 2000). For example, Heather Thomas (1999) describes a tenth-grade biology class in which the teacher made extensive use of cooperative learning groups. In these groups, students helped each other complete various tasks at workstations throughout the room while "talking science" (Lemke, 1990)—that is, while using scientific vocabulary to formulate and test task-related hypotheses. Cooperative learning has expanded school-wide in some districts across the United States. For example, *The Reading Edge*, a comprehensive reading curriculum for middle school students, is based on a cooperative-learning model. According to a recent evaluation study (Daniels, Madden, & Slavin, in press), seven schools using *The Reading Edge* gained an average of 24.6 percentage points in the number of students passing their state reading assessments, compared to only 2.2 percentage point gains for matched control groups. The schools participating in the study were all impoverished and from both urban and rural areas.

Cross-Age Tutoring

The middle grades, in particular, lend themselves to the use of cross-age tutoring because of the school-within-a-school concept that most restructured middle schools espouse. The physical setting and the emphasis on the concept of community within the middle school support older students' teaching younger students to deal with their assignments. As the authors of *Turning Points* (Carnegie Council on Adolescent Development, 1989) note,

> Cross-age tutoring could take place . . . during the part of the day reserved for activities outside the core instructional program for younger and older students. Cross-age tutoring has shown consistent positive effects on achievement outcomes for both tutors and tutees. Tutors encounter

---

*Lehr, F. (1984). ERIC/RCS: Cooperative learning. *Journal of Reading, 27*(5), 458–461. Reprinted with permission of the International Reading Association.

opportunities to review basic skills without embarrassment, gain experience in applying academic abilities, and develop insight into the process of teaching and learning. Tutees receive individualized instruction and work with positive role models. (p. 52)

Cross-age tutoring differs from cooperative learning on several counts. First, cross-age tutoring usually occurs in dyads as opposed to small groups of four or five members. Second, cross-age tutoring is characterized by the transfer of very specific information and usually involves some form of basic skills practice, whereas cooperative learning tends to focus on higher-order thinking. Third, cross-age tutoring focuses on rewarding the individual, whereas cooperative learning rewards the group (although, certainly, individuals are also rewarded as members of the group) (Indrisano & Paratore, 1991).

Guidelines from the research on cross-age tutoring offer insights on how to pair the student partners. Generally, these guidelines hold for peer tutoring as well—that is, for partners who are approximately the same age but with varying achievement levels (Rekrut, 1994).

EVIDENCE-BASED RESEARCH

1. The age level of the tutor and learner may vary depending on the situation. Although older, more accomplished students typically serve as the tutors, they may not always be superior achievers. For example, we know of instances in which low-achieving high school students have served as successful tutors to struggling readers at the elementary level.
2. Same-sex pairs are preferable, but if such pairings are impossible, research has shown that older girls can successfully tutor younger boys.
3. Tutors need to be taught to work with their partners without making value judgments.
4. Post-tutoring debriefings should be ongoing and should give attention to both content and process skills.
5. Affective objectives, such as self-confidence and self-esteem building, are as important in cross-age tutoring as concept mastery and skill reinforcement.

Discussion Groups

EVIDENCE-BASED RESEARCH

As teachers we have always valued classroom discussion as a means for enriching and refining students' understandings. Recently, we had the opportunity to learn how students feel about this form of classroom communication. Findings from a multicase study involving adolescents at five culturally diverse sites throughout the United States (Alvermann et al., 1996b) indicate that students perceive discussions as helping them understand what they read. They know what they like and dislike about large- and small-group discussions; they also know how various topics and tasks influence their participation. In sum, students told us that classroom discussions provide them with opportunities for testing their own ideas while learning to respect the ideas of others.

Definitions of discussion.   Multiple definitions exist for what discussion is or should be, but we prefer one developed largely from David Bridges's work with classroom teachers in Cambridge, UK:

1. Discussants should put forth multiple points of view and stand ready to change their minds about the matter under discussion.
2. Students should interact with one another as well as with the teacher.
3. Interactions should exceed the typical two- or three-word phrases common to recitation lessons. (Alvermann, Dillon, & O'Brien, 1987, p. 7)

These three criteria are helpful in distinguishing between a true discussion and what sometimes passes as one—a recitation in disguise. Recitations are rarely more than fast-paced exchanges between teachers and students in which teachers elicit answers to a series of preplanned questions. Little room is left for the substantive exchange of ideas because the teacher's evaluation of a student's answer is the signal to move on to the next question.

ACTIVITY   Consider the following excerpt from a fictionalized account of an interaction between Lennie and his teacher in Betsy Byars's well-known book, *The TV Kid* (1976). Is it an example of a discussion or a recitation? Why do you think so?

> "Do you think he was just talking about *one* year passing?" the teacher went on. "Or do you think, Lennie, the poet was seeing his whole life as a year, that he was seeing his whole life slipping past?"
> "I'm not sure," Lennie's hand was still on his chin as if ready to stroke a long gray beard.
> "Class?"
> "His whole life slipping past," the class chorused together. They had had this teacher so long that they could tell, just from the way she asked a question, what they were supposed to answer. (p. 70)

Purposes.   Small-group discussions, like whole-class discussions, should stimulate students to think for themselves rather than rely solely on their teachers or their texts for ideas. The old notion that thinking must originate within the individual before it is ready to be shared with others has given way to the belief that some of the best thinking may result from a discussion group's collective efforts (Sternberg, 1987). In fact, there is empirical evidence to suggest that "student-led small-group discussions of nonfiction are superior to both lecture and whole-class discussion in helping students recall and understand essays . . . [and] in preparing students to write analytic, opinion essays" (Sweigart as cited in Nystrand, Gamoran, & Heck, 1992, p. 3).

**EVIDENCE-
BASED
RESEARCH**

Discussion groups can take many forms. Common interests, problem solving, subject mastery, and current issues are but a few of the possible foci for small-group discussion. Regardless of the focus, one thing remains constant—the need to keep in mind that as group size increases, proportionately fewer members participate. A rule of thumb is that a discussion group should consist of no more individuals than are essential for completing the task the group has taken on.

Reading and Writing Workshops

The reading and writing workshop is a form of grouping most often associated with Nancie Atwell's first edition of *In the Middle* (1987). This book is often credited with changing the way middle school language arts teachers structure their classrooms to make them more inviting as literate environments. A few high school teachers have also used the concept of reading/writing workshop to break through some of the barriers that struggling readers have constructed after experiencing years of frustration with classroom literacy activities. For example, Janet Allen (1995), working with a group of ninth-grade "basic" students—all struggling readers—in rural Maine immersed them in a year-long encounter with all types of reading materials. Through daily read alouds, independent reading and writing time (including computer access), group sharing, journaling, conferencing, portfolios, and minilessons involving strategies and skills, by the end of the year the 15 struggling readers in Janet's reading/writing workshop realized that it is never too late to experience the joy of reading.

Reading/Writing Workshop and the Struggling Reader

Creating a safe environment for readers who struggle with school literacy tasks involves the following:

■ Providing sufficient time for students to complete reading and writing activities.

■ Building in student choice, not only in types of literacy materials and equipment available but also in types of assessments and classroom routines.

■ Supporting students by teaching them the strategies they will need to make connections between what they know and what they are expected to learn.

■ Having a variety of resources from which to choose: for example, young adult literature collections; class sets of paperbacks for whole-group shared reading; multiple copies of single titles for guided reading and literature circles; and access to computers and recorded, unabridged books.

Taking what she had learned in her own classroom from working with adolescents who either could not or would not read, Allen helped to launch the Orange County (FL) Literacy Project for students who were previously unsuccessful in school. This project involved setting up literacy workshop classrooms (patterned after Allen's reading and writing workshop) in several pilot schools in Orange County. The concept has since spread to all middle schools in Orange County as well as to other middle schools and high schools in Florida and beyond (Allen & Gonzalez, 1998). Although quick to point out that the reading/writing workshop is no magic formula or recipe for success in working with struggling readers (meaning that teachers must adapt, not adopt, the concept), Allen and Gonzalez describe four components of a literacy environment that are crucial to a workshop's success. (See boxed inset on page 78.).

CREATING COMMUNITY WITH TECHNOLOGY AND MULTIMEDIA

EVIDENCE-BASED RESEARCH

Technology, and in particular the Internet, is revolutionizing how adolescents relate to print and nonprint media. Changes are occurring rapidly in what counts as reading and writing—so much so in fact, that entire books (Cope & Kalantzis, 2000; Reinking et al., 1998; Sefton-Green, 1999), as well as research reports from major foundations (Kaiser Family Foundation, 2003), and policy documents (National Reading Panel, 2000), are focused on exploring the challenges of the digital arts for young people's literacy needs. Some literacy scholars, such as the late Alan Purves (1998), have theorized how the advent of hypertext—print and nonprint texts interlinked by the mere click of a computer mouse—has led to a new relationship between reader/writer and text. These developments strongly suggest that technology and media use in schools must be taken into account in any discussion of how to create favorable learning environments for adolescents in the twenty-first century.

Technology

Interest in using technology and multimedia to motivate students' interest in content area learning is not new, but the resources that are fast becoming available make it easier to use them in creating a favorable learning environment. In this section, we begin by focusing on a newcomer to education—the cyber school and the need to recognize students' use of new literacies.

Cyber schools, also called on-line schools, deliver the majority of their instruction to students through a Web site posted on the Internet instead of in a school building. Although cyber schools differ in their organizational structure, typically students work at their own pace and spend anywhere from 20 to 80 percent of their time on the Internet. Other differences between cyber schools and traditional schools include avenues for interaction and assessment. For example, teachers may spend as much as one-third of their time interacting one-on-one with students using the telephone or e-mail, and parents of students enrolled in cyber schools are expected to supervise their children's work. Assessments usually take the form of portfolios and a combination of online and offline tests (Long, 2004). Although research on cyber schools is spotty to date and likely does not represent accurately the number of such schools springing up across the United States (Long, 2004), we do know from Kinzer's (2005) report on the intersection of traditional schools, communities, and technology that students' use of new literacies is reflective of the ease with which they are learning content through interactive communication software.

Given this picture, therefore, one would expect to find increasingly more state and national assessments focused on these new literacies. Such is not the case, however, as Leu and his colleagues (2005) have documented in their recent review of the research on the use of new information communication technologies in the United States. For example, Leu et al. noted that "Not a single state allows all students to use a word processor, if they wish to do so, on their state writing assessments, despite research [see Russell & Plati, 2000] suggesting that nearly 20% more students would pass their state writing assessments if they were permitted to use word processors" (p. 5). Moreover, according to Leu, Ataya, and Coiro (2002), state and national assessments do not include any of the new literacies that students need for competing successfully in the Information Age.

EVIDENCE- BASED RESEARCH

ACTIVITY   In groups of two or three, discuss the assumptions that one could draw from the information included in the Dispelling Policy Myths box.

Dispelling Policy Myths

Dispelling a Myth

The literacy community, knowing the importance of the new literacies for students' success in the Information Age, is taking a leadership role in this area. As a result, literacy educators are making gains in influencing national and state policy makers to support assessments that would allow students to demonstrate their competencies in using the new literacies.

Policy Implications

In fact, just the opposite is happening. As literacy educators, we seem to be taking a

backseat to policy makers. For example, the new framework for the National Assessment of Educational Progress in Reading that will be in place by 2009 does not allow students to use any form of technology other than the traditional paper and pencil. Nor, according to Leu et al. (2005), does any state in the United States assess students' ability to "locate, read, critically evaluate, and comprehend information in an online environment" (p. 5).

Yet, despite what is a rather gloomy situation on the assessment front, classroom teachers continue to acknowledge the role that new information communication technologies and the new literacies play in their students' lives. For example, Linda Hardin, a veteran language arts teacher at Beck Middle School in Greenville, South Carolina, used the Internet to build a sense of community within her eighth-grade classroom as part of a history project to put Greenville's history on the Web. This interdisciplinary project involved all sections of her language arts class—80 students in all. The class, becoming what Hardin (1999) described as "tourists in their own town" (p. 7), documented parts of Greenville's history, including the controversy surrounding the Reedy River, which the Cherokees had fought to keep prior to the Revolutionary War. Initially conceiving of their project in linear fashion, the students soon learned one of the advantages of the Web. With the help of an Internet tool called WebQuest, they learned how to organize the information they were obtaining from interviews with longtime residents of Greenville, from Web surfing, from hometown library searches, and from e-mailing messages to historians across the United States in a "hyperbranching" rather than linear manner. In effect, the students in Ms. Hardin's language arts classes were learning how to publish their history on the Internet in a way that allowed endless revisions and invited future links as newly discovered maps, photos, or updates to a story came in. As Hardin (1999) noted, "for us, it was like putting the index at the beginning of a book and allowing the reader to jump around from page to page rather than reading the entire text first" (p. 9).

Multimedia

Teachers may find it useful to take adolescents' out-of-school multimedia interests into account when planning ways to build a community of learners within their classrooms, being careful, of course, not to appropriate for school purposes the very things students find most pleasurable in their out-of-school pursuits (Luke, 1997, 2000). Teachers we know who have done this successfully have been ones who have built on their students' interests in computers, video, and the Web.

For example, Marcella Kehaus (2000) developed a teen writers' on-line community (www.TeenLit.com) for students interested in writing for audiences beyond their classroom peers and teacher. Frustrated by the limited number of publishing opportunities for her own students, Kehaus, along with one of her teacher friends, developed the TeenLit.com Web site. This site, which receives on average 1,500 visitors a week, provides a forum for teens to publish and discuss their work, review books they have read, and engage in discussions with other teen writers on the Web.

Another teacher, Pat Egenberger (1999) of Ustach Middle School in Modesto, California, transformed a required class research project into a community-building activity. Students in Egenberger's eighth-grade English class created a 20-minute video that not only integrated language arts, science, and social studies but also led them to new understandings and appreciation of Pam

Conrad's (1985) *Prairie Song*, a novel they had previously read. Using questions that they generated from their reading of Conrad's novel (e.g., "What was it like living in a soddy?" and "Were there really grasshopper storms?"), the students divided into teams of two or three to research the answers to their questions. They relied on multimedia resources from their school library and from the Internet. After writing short scripts about the information they had located, students formed video crews and took turns taping each other as they shared this information. Reflecting on the project, Egenberger wrote,

> In general, the students were surprised that what we had just done was a form of research. It didn't have to be frustrating, dreary, and solitary. Creating a class video gave them an audience for their work. A necessary school task was transformed into a community effort and celebration. (p. 57)

Assistive Technology

The use of assistive technological devices and equipment for youth who have disabilities is a way of enhancing the classroom learning environment and ensuring that access to high-quality content literacy instruction is an option for all students. Assistive technology, also known as enabling or supportive technology, provides a variety of multimodal tools (visual, auditory, kinesthetic, and tactile) that students with special needs typically require if they are to achieve greater independence and become more successful learners. For example,

> Word processing software assists children with learning disabilities in several ways. First, it reduces the frustration these children experience with awkward letter formation. Typing on a keyboard is much easier than forming letters by hand, especially since each letter appears precisely formed on the screen. Moreover, looking at letters on the keyboard may increase letter-recognition skills. Finally, word processors provide children with the opportunity to use spell checkers to improve accuracy in spelling, an area that is often difficult for children with learning disabilities. (Leu & Kinzer, 2003, p. 454)

High-speed connectivity to the Internet serves as a gateway to the World Wide Web and offers teachers resources that they can use to extend their students' knowledge of the content areas. However, often Web-based thematic units employ traditional methods and materials that are not directly pertinent to the specific learning outcomes a teacher may have in mind. This is especially problematic when some of the students in a class have learning disabilities. In such cases, experts in assistive technology recommend that the teacher impose an external structure on a collection of Web sites by doing the following:

1. Selecting only those sites that are directly relevant to the learning objectives;
2. Informing the student of the learning activities for each site; and
3. Sequencing how students should access the sites (e.g., establish the order in which a student ideally views sites for the first time). (Gardner & Wissick, 2002, n.p.)

Another recommendation involves imposing a structure on Internet searches. This is what a high school science teacher in Donna's content literacy class did. He used TrackStar (http://altec.org/index.php) to organize information and activities on biomes for students in his class who were part of the school's inclusion program. TrackStar is a noncommercial site that directs students "to a single Web address, where a *track* takes over and provides structure, sequence, and annotations for Web-based learning" (Gardner & Wissick, 2002, n.p.) By using this kind of assistive technology, the teacher was able to keep students focused, attentive, and engaged in reading about biomes around the world.

CONFLICT RESOLUTION

Resolving conflicts that arise among adolescents is central to the process of creating and maintaining a favorable learning environment, one in which students are free to express themselves as long as they show respect to others and take responsibility for their own actions. Often easier to write about than to do, conflict resolution is a process that requires some special skills on the part of teachers and students alike. In content literacy classrooms in which collaboration is encouraged, it is especially important that students have some understanding of this process. Best introduced by the teacher in preparation for independent group work, conflict resolution may include one or more of the following strategies: problem solving, listening to negative feedback or criticism and responding appropriately, mediating the conflicts of others, compromising, accepting the answer "no," and coping with failure (Warger & Rutherford, 1997).

What the Research Says

A review of the research on understanding peer conflict (Laursen, Hartup, & Koplas, 1996) suggests that "classmates with no history of rewarding exchange and no emotional investment in one another [will] appear unconcerned about future interaction" (p. 94). This is unfortunate but all the more reason for teachers to work toward creating a learning environment in which all students have reason to feel valued for their contributions, regardless of race, ethnicity, class, gender, ability, physical size, sexual orientation, religious background, and other identity markers that set individuals apart and open them to unfair ridicule.

Having to endure the bullying behaviors of others is the consequence most often cited by those who are the target of school bias. Interestingly, bullying, which has been defined as "repeated oppression, physical or psychological, of a less powerful person by a more powerful person or group" (Rigby cited in Koki, 2000, p. 1), is more of a problem in mainland United States than it is in Hawaii and other Pacific Island schools under U.S. jurisdiction. Thought to be a result of the Western ideal of rugged individualism, bullying is less evident in

Tech Tips for Teaching Tolerance and Conflict Resolution

Teaching Tolerance, a project of the Southern Poverty Law Center, is a Web site that offers practical ideas that teachers can use to promote respect for differences and appreciation of diversity. At www.tolerance.org/teach/index.jsp, you will find teaching resources related to conflict resolution, opportunities for examining your role in teaching tolerance, and current events that lead to discussions of the need for tolerance.

Education World, the Web site of the National Education Association, offers a special theme page on bullying (www.education-world.com/a_special/bully_2000.shtml) that is current and links to many related sites on conflict resolution.

cultures in which peer/family/community support are traditionally valued over one's personal goals (Koki, 2000).

Strategies for Managing Conflict

Some of the best suggestions for managing classroom conflict that results from bullying comes from William Kreidler's book *Creative Conflict Resolution* (1984). Although written two decades ago, this book offers practical and easy-to-initiate strategies for resolving problems before they become more serious. We include two of those strategies here, adapted to fit our notion of what would work in the classrooms with which we are most familiar—our own.

Negotiating a solution to a problem.   This strategy, which is easily adapted across content areas, consists of the following steps:

1. Write "negotiate" and "negotiating" on the board and ask students to brainstorm meanings for the two words.
2. After five minutes of brainstorming, invite individuals to share their definitions with the whole class. If the idea that negotiating is a way of solving problems between people so that everyone can win does not come out in the discussion, suggest it and seek student feedback.
3. List the following procedure for negotiating a problem:
   - State what you think the problem is.
   - Say what you want.
   - Tell what the limits are (what can or cannot be changed).
   - Work out an agreement.
   - Ask if everyone is able to live with the negotiated outcome. If not, address individual concerns privately, in a small group, or as a whole class, depending on the case.

4. Walk students through the process using the following situation:
   Jill, one of the students in your TGT cooperative learning group, is not summariz-ing correctly the assigned readings in the social studies text. This is causing you and other students to answer test questions incorrectly during the tournament. Resentment is building.
5. After the class has negotiated a solution to the problem, ask students to describe a situation in which this type of negotiation would not work. Then ask them to explain what they would do in such a situation.

Building respect and community.   This strategy for managing classroom conflict that stems from general disrespect toward others and little sense of community is best introduced early in the school year and revisited occasionally so that students can gauge for themselves whether or not any change has occurred in their learning environment. The procedure consists of the following steps:

1. Engage students in a discussion of the actions, words, and body language that signal respect or disrespect for others. Point out that you need not like someone to behave respectfully toward him or her.
2. Ask class members to think about their learning environment and the things they would like to change (as well as those aspects of the environ-ment they would like to keep the same).
3. Give each student an index card and pencil and request that individuals describe what they would change (and would not change) about the class learning environment. They may choose to sign their cards or remain anonymous. Post the cards on the bulletin board.
4. After a few days (having allowed enough time for students to read and think about the cards on the bulletin board), open a class discussion focused on the following questions:
   - How would it feel to learn in the environment that you envision?
   - Is it a vision worth working toward?
   - If so, how would we begin working toward it?

In following up on any progress the class is making, you would need to ensure that discussions focus on both the positives and the negatives associ-ated with change. For example, you might ask individuals to recall situations in which respect was shown, how it made them feel, what events tended to derail good intentions, how those derailments were addressed, and where the class currently stands in relation to its goal of creating a more favorable learning environment. Time spent in teaching conflict resolution to adolescents is time well spent, as Van Slyck and Stern (1999) noted. According to these experts on youth-oriented conflict resolution, research has shown that "learning conflict resolution principles and techniques increases social support and decreases victimization" (p. 179)—changes that ultimately lead to higher self-esteem and less depression or anxiety among adolescents.

EVIDENCE-
BASED
RESEARCH

SUMMARY

A favorable learning environment supports students as they grapple with issues of affect (e.g., how they feel about school and their willingness, or unwillingness, to engage with the academic tasks teachers assign) that influence how they feel about school and their willingness to engage in the academic activities that are part of the schooling process. Although tracking by ability level is not likely to disappear in the near future, there are numerous alternatives for grouping, including cooperative learning, cross-age tutoring, discussion groups, and reading/writing workshops.

The use of technology and various media forms to create a community of learners is a literacy practice that increasingly more teachers are choosing as they strive to motivate student interest and learning in their content area classes. This practice requires that teachers be sensitive to the pleasures young people draw from the media and not appropriate them for school use in ways that would cause students to abandon their interests in reading and writing with media outside of school. It also requires that teachers take time to help adolescents express their dislikes and disagreements in ways that resolve or manage conflicts before they become serious threats to classroom life and beyond. Treating conflict resolution as a necessary and natural part of creating a favorable learning environment is a first step toward ensuring that students will have opportunities to express themselves freely as they read, write, speak, and listen to others discuss the content of your classroom.

SUGGESTED READINGS

Ambrosini, M., & Morretta, T. M. (2003). *Poetry workshop for middle school.* Newark, DE: International Reading Association.

Coloroso, B. (2003). *The bully, the bullied, and the bystander: From preschool to high school, how parents and teachers can help break the cycle of violence.* New York: HarperResource.

Delpit, L., & Dowdy, J. K. (2002). *The skin that we speak: Thoughts on language and culture in the classroom.* New York: New Press.

Golub, J. N. (2000). *Making learning happen: Strategies for an interactive classroom.* Portsmouth, NH: Boynton/Cook.

Staudt, C. (2005). *Changing how we teach and learn with handheld computers.* Thousand Oaks, CA: Corwin Press.

Tatum, A. W. (2000). Breaking down barriers that disenfranchise African American adolescent readers in low-level tracks. *Journal of Adolescent & Adult Literacy, 44,* 52–64.

Planning for Content Literacy

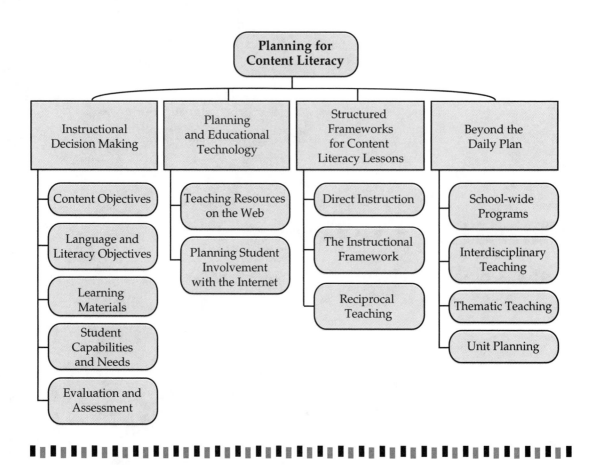

Victoria keeps a professional journal, and she shares selected journal entries on a listserve with her students, people just like the readers of this book. Her entries offer a look into the thinking of a teacher trying to plan effective lessons. Student replies are often more honest than she imagined they might be, as the following exchange illustrates (Ridgeway, 1997).

■ ■ ■ ■ ■ ■ ■

At the end of one difficult day, Victoria wrote to her students about trying to teach them about planning:

> I was not greatly pleased with class today, and I'm not sure why. I didn't "cover" everything I wanted to, but that isn't the reason for the ambivalent feelings about class. I just felt "off" for some reason. I feel as though I said a little about a lot of things and in the process didn't get my message across. When planning, you must take into consideration your students, your

content, your teaching style, as well your actual class activities. Maybe I shouldn't have tried to cover even more pre-teaching strategies. When will I learn??? You guys probably feel inundated already, and we've only just begun! Anyway, I think I've answered my own question. I tried to do too much—in too much detail—and ended up not really accomplishing what I had originally intended. Well, spilled milk, I guess. [The entry continues with ideas for revising the lesson and planning ahead for upcoming classes].

A student responded to this journal entry:

I'm not sure that your "message" of determining the what, how, when and why components [of planning] is something you can teach us in a 75 minute block of instruction. You can tell us, but I think it's something that we have to learn for ourselves for it to really sink in. It'll sink in the first time I'm in front of a group of kids trying to review for a test and I say to myself, "Hey knucklehead, this isn't working. Maybe if I do this with the entire class instead of breaking up into groups. Or, this is taking too long. Maybe I shouldn't spend so much time brainstorming." It seems to me that your job here is to plant seeds of knowledge in the barren soil of our minds. They might not germinate today, or tomorrow, but hopefully they'll spring up next year or the year after when we really need them.

Have you ever heard of the acronym MEGO? It stands for "My eyes glaze over." You achieved MEGO yesterday after about the third graphic organizer you showed us. By about the sixth or seventh organizer, we were somewhere else, dreaming of Pegasus, and flying ships and woodsmen made of tin.

Victoria replied to the listserve immediately with thanks for the honest response and several ideas for how she could have presented her lesson more effectively by involving students in hands-on planning experiences. This exchange illustrates several important points about planning for instruction. First of all, lessons do not always go as planned. Even experienced and effective teachers have those "off" days. Second, good teachers are always evaluating their work, looking for ways to improve. They listen to their students as part of that process. Finally, as Victoria's student acknowledges, some things have to be learned through experience.

■ ■ ■ ■ ■ ■ ■

Observing an effective and well-organized teacher can be deceptive. When a class is actively engaged in some kind of learning activity, whether it is instruction on how to graph a math equation, discussion of a poem, a chemistry experiment, or a conversation in Spanish, teacher and students can make learning seem logical, purposeful, almost effortless. Even when students become confused or ask for help, the teacher appears to know just what to do, how to ask the right question or rephrase instructions in a way that gets everybody back on track. Classroom veterans know, however, that good teaching is far from effortless. Rather, effective instruction is usually the result of thoughtful planning and careful preparation.

We too recognize that there is no one best way to plan for teaching. How a teacher prepares for the classroom will vary according to the particular style or preference of the teacher, the subject matter, the materials available, and, of course, the students. Experience is also an influential factor in the planning process. New teachers and those who are preparing for a new curriculum or a new topic are more likely to explicitly lay out objectives and teaching strategies, whereas veterans can draw on previous lessons and classroom experience, updating and adapting as needed to maximize effectiveness.

We also acknowledge, as Robert Burns says, "The best-laid schemes o' mice an' men gang aft a-gley." Teaching can always be something of an adventure, and what actually happens in the classroom will usually be different from what one planned, as Victoria illustrates in the opening anecdote. An idea that seemed wonderful while sitting at the dining room table on Sunday afternoon may turn out to be a turkey on Monday morning. Most teachers can also relate instances when they abandoned a planned lesson to pursue a "teachable moment," an idea that evolved in the classroom and became more immediate, more important, more instructive than whatever had originally been on the agenda. With experience, teachers learn to anticipate both the potential problems and the opportunities for serendipity, and they learn how to adjust instruction as they meet the needs of the moment.

Nevertheless, most good teaching and learning happen by design. What occurs in a classroom is usually the result of a complex decision-making process that begins well before the bell rings, evolves throughout the class period, and continues even after the class has ended as the teacher evaluates how students reacted and what they learned and also thinks about what to do next. Thus, we cannot emphasize enough the importance of intentionally planning for literacy learning in your content specialty. To experience effectiveness as a content area teacher, it is crucial that your students receive instruction in how to use reading, writing, listening, speaking, and visual and critical analysis to make meaning of the content they are expected to learn. In this chapter we discuss some of the ways in which teachers design their instruction; we examine some of the decisions involved in planning for content area instruction and describe some frameworks for structuring content area literacy lessons.

INSTRUCTIONAL DECISION MAKING

Lesson planning, whether for a single day's activities, a two- or three-week unit, or an entire marking period, involves many complex and interrelated decisions. We have said that there is no single best way to plan, and a teacher may begin the planning process from any number of points. A chemistry teacher may begin by previewing chapter objectives in a teacher's manual. The French teacher may decide that students need more practice with translation from French to English. The geometry teacher may plan a day of review for a unit test on triangles. A language arts–social studies team may center their planning on a medieval fair, complete with costumes, games, entertainment, and food. Whatever their starting points, these teachers will need to consider what they want students to learn, the learning materials that are available, the capabilities and prior knowledge of students, and the specific instructional strategies and evaluation options that would be most effective. This section describes some of those factors that must be considered in teacher decision making.

Content Objectives

What do students need to learn? On the surface, this would seem like a simple question. However, if we were to examine a topic such as the American Revolution, we would see that the answer is far from simple. What is important for students to know about the American Revolution? When it occurred? Who the principals were? Why it was fought? What the outcomes were? Any or all of these might arguably be essential.

Taken as a collection of isolated facts, the American Revolution can be pretty confusing: Townsend Acts, 1776, Washington, Boston Tea Party, Jefferson, Cornwallis, "Give me liberty or give me death"! This information will be easier to learn, and ultimately more meaningful, to the extent that the various parts can be related to each other. Therefore, it would be useful to organize a topic such as this around one or two key ideas. For instance, the history teacher may decide to organize his or her class's study of the Revolution around a theme as follows: "The American Revolution came about because people wanted the opportunity to make their own decisions." This central idea, or *organizing concept* (Phelps, 1984), could help the teacher to focus the various events, personalities, and ideas in the unit. Furthermore, it introduces a theme that may be revisited throughout the U.S. history curriculum as the class studies Jacksonian democracy, the Civil War, the rise of labor unions, or the suffrage movement. Figure 4.1 shows a planning web for the American Revolution centered on this organizing concept.

Our American Revolution example is broad and pertinent to a unit of study that may take a matter of weeks to complete. However, single class sessions may also be organized around a key idea. For instance, a high school geometry teacher may plan a lesson around the computation of the area of a circle, centered on the mathematical expression $A = \pi r^2$. That single mathematical sentence contains all the essential components of the lesson: multiplication, area, radius, π. If students learn those components and the relations between them they will have achieved the teacher's content objective; they will be able to compute the area of a circle.

An organizing concept may be broad or narrow. It may express a theme such as "the difficulty of making personal choices" when a class is reading Robert Cormier's novel *The Chocolate War* (1974), or it may be a more functional concept such as "vegetative propagation and sexual reproduction in plants" in a

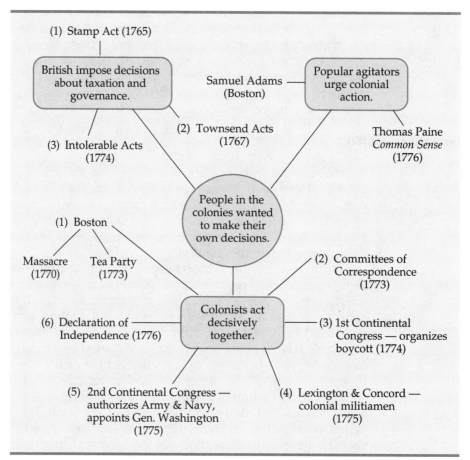

FIGURE 4.1   **Planning web for the American Revolution**

biology class. A teacher's primary objectives may also include content processes. That is, teachers want to help their students to think like a writer, a mathematician, a scientist, a historian, or a linguist. Good teaching should be grounded on clearly articulated content objectives, however they may be defined or articulated. Learning will be more meaningful when teachers (and students) see the big picture, and the overall point of classroom activity. Individual facts, ideas, or skills will be easier to learn when they can be related to each other and to a central concept or process. It will make it less likely that students will be involved in busywork such as filling out worksheets or copying down notes with no apparent pedagogical purpose other than to give the appearance of meaningful activity.

We want to stress that we are not talking about behavioral objectives. Nor do we believe it is necessary for teachers to laboriously write down objectives for every lesson using a particular formula or taxonomy, although this may be required in some schools and may have some utility in a methods course as a way to get teachers to think systematically about what they are doing. Content area teaching is based on a curriculum of ideas that students are expected to learn, and it is sufficient that teachers have some part of that curriculum clearly in mind as they plan what they are going to do and what they are going to have students do in class.

Language and Literacy Objectives

In addition to the content that teachers intend students to learn, certain skills will be required. For example, basic computational skills, using a calculator, and working with a protractor and compass are needed in the study of geometry. Working with laboratory equipment, including setup, cleanup, and safety procedures, is an important component of science study. In this text, our emphasis is on the language and literacy skills that students will need in order to be effective learners.

EVIDENCE-BASED RESEARCH

Particularly when working with students from diverse backgrounds, who may have less access to the conventions and forms of discourse commonly accepted in mainstream academic settings, teachers may need to provide frequent explicit skill instruction (Au, 1998; National Reading Panel, 2000). In the course of planning, teachers will want to think about the reading and writing activities that go along with learning and decide how their teaching will help students achieve those objectives.

The term *skills* has fallen into disfavor, especially among advocates of a natural language approach to literacy instruction, who object to attempts to fragment and isolate so-called literacy subskills and teach them individually through direct instruction and drill (Goodman, 1986; Weaver, 1988). Therefore, we use the term *literacy skills* advisedly. We do not mean to imply that there is a finite list of discrete skills, many unique to particular content areas, that should be systematically taught. However, we recognize that reading a chemistry chapter to prepare for a quiz, reading a short story and writing a personal response, or using the Internet to search for information for a history project each requires some special skills, and that these skills must be learned, usually through explicit instruction, in order for students to be successful.

As experts in their content specialties, teachers generally have a good deal of experience with reading and writing science, literature, social studies, mathematics, technology, and so on, but they may not be consciously aware of these abilities. The purpose of reading a text such as this one and taking a course on content area literacy is to increase teachers' sensitivity to the literacy requirements implied in a content area lesson. As teachers plan, they make decisions about what students will read and write; they analyze the literacy skills inherent in the subject and the reading material. They ask themselves, "How is this reading selection organized? What is there about the selection that makes it easy to understand or that is likely to be difficult? In order to complete this written assignment, what will students need to know or understand? How can I help them with this?"

Good teachers anticipate which skills may be difficult for students and plan to assist with those skills within the context of content area learning. If the biology chapter has an unusually heavy load of technical vocabulary based on Latin and Greek roots, the teacher may wish to use one or more strategies for helping students to master vocabulary. If students need some assistance with note taking and report writing, the teacher could include appropriate instruction in daily plans as students gather information and begin drafting their written products. Other language- and literacy-related abilities that will be useful in content area classes include speaking and listening skills, working effectively with peers, preparing for tests, and abilities such as critical thinking, analysis, or prediction. (In the following chapters, we describe many teaching and learning strategies that integrate literacy learning with content learning.) Deciding what kinds of talking, listening, reading, and writing students will do and determining ways to assist students with those processes are important components of the planning process.

Learning Materials

While planning, teachers also consider what materials are at hand and what will be needed. Such things as laboratory equipment, math manipulatives, audio and video recordings, and various teacher-made materials may be used to demonstrate concepts, create interest, involve students, or provide essential background information. Regarding reading materials, teachers will think about textbooks, possible complementary readings from trade books or periodicals, worksheets and directions, exams, charts and diagrams, and reference materials.

Students of all cultural backgrounds will benefit when teachers introduce readings that authentically present diverse cultures, especially when the authors come from diverse cultural groups (Au, 1998). Writing assignments imply basic materials such as pen or pencil and paper, as well as journals, notebooks, computers and printers, and the possible formats for final written products such as newspapers, student-made books, formal reports or essays, posters, letters, electronic transmission, or bulletin boards.

Student Capabilities and Needs

Another important aspect of planning is accommodation of student needs. Teachers will try to anticipate what students already know, what strengths or aptitudes they may have, and what difficulties they are likely to encounter. In Chapter 2 we considered some of the factors that contribute to classroom diversity. In our mobile, diverse, and rapidly evolving society, it is impossible to talk about a "typical" classroom. Students bring varied cultural understandings, varied language backgrounds, and a wide variety of previous experiences to school. Students will also range widely in their interests, in their aptitudes for a particular subject, and in their reading and writing abilities. In addition, many students with identified learning difficulties or disabilities are included in regular classrooms, sometimes with the support of specialists and sometimes without.

The growing diversity in classrooms presents both challenges and opportunities for teachers. Traditional instruction based on textbook readings, lectures, memorization, and formal academic expository writing will simply not serve the needs of all learners.

One way in which teachers are able to successfully meet the needs of diverse students is through *instructional scaffolding.* Just as a construction crew may erect a scaffold to support them as they work and then gradually dismantle the scaffold as the work is completed, so a teacher can plan a supportive framework for student learning and then gradually withdraw it as students take over more responsibility for their own learning. For example, Randi Reppen (1994/1995) describes how she taught different genres of writing to students in a fifth-grade social studies class who were learning English as a second language. Students learned each style of writing by reading and discussing examples, with the teacher explicitly pointing out the features of the genre and comparing it with other genres. Then the teacher modeled by writing at the overhead projector for the whole class, asking students for input and describing what she was doing and why. Control over learning was gradually turned over to students, first by having them write in the particular style with peers in a small group and finally by having each student produce an individual piece of writing.

Planning to use flexible and varied patterns of in-class grouping can also help a teacher capitalize on diverse student backgrounds and meet varied student needs (Au, 1998). Alternating among whole-class instruction, various small-group activities, paired-learning tasks, and individual assignments allows students to assist each other, provides more opportunities to participate, and generally creates a learning environment based on student activity rather than passivity. Active learning environments are especially important when teaching students of diverse ability and background. In fact, Bill Bigelow (1994) suggests several interlocking components that have allowed him and his colleagues to turn passive learners into active learners:

- Students need to experience ideas, not just hear about them. Bigelow recommends role-playing and simulations.
- Assignments need to be flexible and take into account students' interests and abilities.
- The classroom environment must be encouraging, even loving.
- Students need to understand how the ideas and skills they are learning can make a difference in their lives.
- Evaluation of students should be flexible and equitable.

Bigelow readily admits that teaching in an untracked classroom is easier said than done. Students may get off-task, miss assignments, and experience failure. However, when a teacher believes that all students can learn and plans to meet the needs of all students, the result can be a classroom that is lively, stimulating, and actively devoted to the pursuit of knowledge.

Planning content area instruction for ELLs.   Many of the general suggestions we have made are especially appropriate for students who are learning English, including flexible grouping, linking new content to prior knowledge, and instructional scaffolding. English language learners add a new dimension to teacher planning, however. In addition to knowledge of content and academic skills, they also need teachers who can help them develop their knowledge of the English language. Therefore, teachers who use a sheltered English approach scaffold their instruction by making adjustments both in the instructional tasks they plan and by adjusting their speech (Echevarria, Vogt, & Short, 2000). Teachers should also explicitly and clearly communicate both content and language objectives to students orally and in writing.

Sheltered English teachers adjust their speech by using simple subject–verb–object sentences, avoiding complex embedded constructions, and by accompanying their spoken presentations with visual representations in the form of charts, diagrams, demonstrations, real objects, or pictures. Such visual aids are also part of adjusting instruction to meet the triple goals of expanding ELLs' vocabulary and language skill, their content knowledge, and their ability to perform increasingly complex academic tasks. Additional instructional adaptations include (Echevarria, Vogt, & Short, 2000):

- Preteaching vocabulary
- Reviewing previous instruction before introducing new material
- Explicitly modeling language and literacy skills
- Planning simulations, role-playing, and hands-on experiences
- Giving ELLs support in their native language through the use of L1 reading materials, dictionaries, or bilingual peers and classroom aides
- Providing supplemental materials to support English language texts, including trade books, audiovisuals, pictures, computer-based information, audiotaped books, and specially designated textbooks with key concepts and vocabulary highlighted
- Creating graphic organizers, outlines, and study guides
- Allowing ELLs to demonstrate what they have learned through multiple channels, including hands-on activities, group projects, oral reports, and informal discussions, in addition to more formal quizzes and written assignments

A final component of sheltered English is engaging ELLs in instructional conversations that help them to improve their functional language skills. Specifically, students need opportunities to use academic language, not just social language. Peer interactions can facilitate this practice, but sheltered English teachers also directly elicit elaborated responses from ELLs. This means suppressing the instinct to compensate for students' lack of English language facility by not calling on them, speaking for them, or completing a partial response. Instead, Echevarria, Vogt, and Short (2000) recommend using prompts such as "Tell me more about that," "What do you mean by . . . ," "What else . . . ," or "How do you know?" It is also very important to provide the ELL sufficient wait time to formulate a response after a question is posed.

Although accommodating the needs of ELLs requires some specialized planning and instructional modifications, most of the specific teaching strategies recommended for ELLs are derived from those designed for mainstream classes. You will find these strategies and methods described in this and subsequent chapters.

Evaluation and Assessment

As teachers plan, they also think about how they will evaluate students' learning. Quizzes and exams, homework, worksheets, journals, essays, projects, in-class presentations, and observation of student performance are among the tools that teachers use to make both formal and informal judgments about what students have accomplished. Decisions about evaluation may come near the end of the planning process, after teachers have worked out the content objectives, materials, and learning activities for a lesson or a series of lessons in a unit. Other times, evaluation may actually be a primary influence in planning, as it is when teachers must prepare students for a departmentalized exam or other testing at the district, city, or state level. Evaluation and assessment will be treated in detail in Chapter 5.

All the decision-making factors that we have cited here are interrelated, and the interrelation is more weblike than linear. There is no single best sequence for lesson planning. Knowing something about students' reading ability will influence what kinds of reading materials they will be able to use successfully as well as the kinds of literacy objectives that might reasonably be achieved. Determining content objectives will help a teacher think of ways to draw on students' backgrounds and will also determine what will be emphasized in evaluation. Individual teachers will have their own preferred styles. Some will depend on external sources such as teachers' manuals, curriculum guides, or unit tests to help them formulate content objectives and teaching strategies, whereas others will draw on their own ideas of what should be emphasized. Some teachers may be student centered in their planning, whereas others are more content oriented.

Teachers at elementary, middle school, and high school levels will all take into account the developmental characteristics of their students as well as the relative degree to which the content areas are either distinct or integrated at each level. Specific subject matter will also make a difference; teachers in different subject areas have very different notions of what they can and cannot do in their classes, and the various subject area subcultures have a strong influence on actual instructional practices (Grossman & Stodolsky, 1995; Stodolsky, 1988).

**EVIDENCE-
BASED
RESEARCH**

PLANNING AND EDUCATIONAL TECHNOLOGY

We are neither expert nor foolhardy enough to attempt detailed predictions of where technology may take us in the future. Nevertheless, it is safe to say that computer literacy, with emphasis on the Internet, will command continued importance as an integral part of students' literacy learning. Consequently, teachers will be increasingly expected to draw on computer resources in their planning and in the delivery of instruction. As they plan, teachers will also need to consider the technological skill and sophistication of their students.

The International Society for Technology in Education (ISTE), in collaboration with the U.S. Department of Education and other sponsors, has developed recommended technology standards for students at all grade levels (ISTE, 2002; http://cnets.iste.org/currstands/cstands-netss.html). Students should be able to

STANDARDS

1. Demonstrate proficiency with basic operations and concepts
2. Understand social, ethical, and human issues (including issues of copyright, plagiarism, and citation)
3. Use technology productivity tools to enhance learning and to collaborate in constructing models, preparing publications, and producing other creative works
4. Employ technology communication tools to collaborate, publish, and interact with peers, experts, and other audiences; use a variety of media and formats to communicate information and ideas effectively
5. Apply technology research tools to locate, evaluate, and collect information; use technology tools to process data and report results; evaluate and select new information resources
6. Use technological resources to make informed decisions; employ technology to solve real-world problems

Notice the explicit and implicit literacy abilities embedded in these standards. In order to use a technology resource such as the Internet, students will need basic reading and writing skills and an understanding of how they transfer to computer environments. They will also require keyboarding abilities, an understanding of computer terminology, flexible comprehension strategies, critical and analytical

Technology Standards
Applied to Specific Content Areas

▮▮

The National Educational Technology Standards (NETS) Project has compiled a list of technology standards that apply to specific content areas. These standards were developed by professional organizations representing mathematics, science, social studies, English language arts, foreign languages, educational technology, and information literacy. To view this list for the separate content areas, check out http://cnets.iste.org/currstands.

facilities, research skills (including Internet search strategies), and the ability to effectively combine print, audio, and visual media in order to communicate their ideas. Although some of this can be learned in technology classes, teachers in all content areas need to take into account the literacy ramifications as they guide students to use technological learning and communication tools.

Planning with the Internet involves two aspects. First, teachers can find lesson plans, unit plans, and many other kinds of instructional resources on the Web. Many sites welcome postings from teachers who wish to share successful ideas with colleagues. E-mail, listserves, bulletin boards, and chat rooms make it possible to communicate with other teachers or content area specialists and get specific planning suggestions. There is also a wealth of up-to-date information relative to almost any facet of any content area that one could imagine, available in an ever-expanding and ever-changing Internet environment.

The second facet of planning with the Internet is incorporating Internet activities and other technology uses into instruction. Teachers will want to plan what students will do with computers, how the Internet can complement the curriculum, and what students will need to know and do in order to have successful experiences with the Web and other technology.

Teaching Resources on the Web

There are numerous sites that give sample lesson plans and suggestions for teaching activities—many more than we could suggest here. Some good starting points include the following:

Teachers Net

Many different resources for teachers, including lesson plans, links to other useful sites, chat rooms, and message boards.
http://teachers.net/

Teaching Resources: Content and Lesson Planning Resources

Features a host of unique links, including self-study quizzes for ESL students, art-teaching resources from the National Gallery, more than 7,000 on-line lesson plans for teachers, and paperless interactive Internet learning activities for students to use.
www.ibritt.com/resources/tr_content.htm

Kathy Schrock's Guide for Educators

Features links to other sites, organized into categories, including subject areas; also has a wealth of WebQuest information, including examples.
http://school.discovery.com/schrockguide/

MarcoPolo

Features high-quality standards-based Internet content and easy-to-access lesson plans, student activities, reviewed Web sites, and other MarcoPolo resources.
www.marcopolo-education.org/index.aspx

Youth Net

A place where youth of all ages can meet, discuss, and participate in learning projects; many student projects, school Web sites, and student home pages can be accessed through this site.
http://youth.net/

The Suggested Readings at the end of this chapter recommend other sites featuring lesson planning ideas, as does the companion Web site to this text.

In addition to lesson planning ideas, teachers will also find information on the Web to share with students. This might include useful background information, expanded coverage of a topic featured in the text, application of an important concept in some authentic context, or other information that is not included in the textbook. This is especially useful in the sciences and social studies, for which the limitations of textbook technology make it impossible for texts to include the most recent developments in science, politics, or world affairs.

For instance, a biology teacher leading his or her class in a study of genetics would not find the most recent details on mapping the human genetic code in the textbook. However, the teacher could "capture" a series of Internet pages related to this topic, including text and graphics, using Web-capturing software such as Web Whacker (www.bluesquirrel.com/products/webwhacker/index.html). This

Internet Literacy and Struggling Readers

The Internet can be a welcome change from textbooks and a motivating environment for struggling readers, but it will also present them with some special challenges (Balajthy, 1990). The very vastness of the Web can prove frustrating for readers who are not particularly adept at finding useful information quickly and easily. The disjunctive nature of hypertext environments (where the viewer can jump from screen to screen or site to site in any order) may make it difficult for some students to keep in mind the overarching structure of a site or lose track of their purpose; they may become "lost in hyperspace" (Neilsen, 1990). Also, much of the information that students may access will be conceptually challenging, with a good deal of difficult technical vocabulary.

The following suggestions can provide support for struggling readers as they use the Internet:

- Pair struggling readers with more able peers.
- Steer them to sites that have been previewed and found to be appropriate.
- Select sites that include helpful site maps and navigation tools.
- When the site does not provide navigational aids, prepare a graphic of the site's structure and explain it to students.
- Scaffold Internet searches by providing specific questions, directions, or explicit guidance.
- Preteach potentially difficult vocabulary that may be found at a site.
- Use "talking" software, such as eReader or textHelp, that gives the user a spoken version of the text on the screen.

would allow the teacher to access the sites he or she had selected even if there were no on-line links in the classroom. By using multimedia authoring software such as HyperStudio (www.hyperstudio.com/) and by linking his or her computer to a large-screen display, the teacher could develop a presentation that interspersed scientific data from the Human Genome Project or other scientific agencies with Web-based news articles on the latest developments, predictions of the future benefits of genetic mapping, and perhaps some thoughtful considerations of the social and ethical issues involved in genetic science. Such a presentation could easily be a starting point and a model for hands-on student Internet projects as well.

Planning Student Involvement with the Internet

Content area teachers plan a variety of student hands-on experiences with the Internet that involve collecting, synthesizing, organizing, creating, and presenting information. Student activities include

- Collecting hot lists, a list of sites related to a particular topic
- Evaluating Web sites using criteria provided by the teacher or developed collaboratively in class
- Other higher-level responses to selected sites, including interpretation, relation to personal experience, or synthesis with what they are learning in the classroom
- Conducting a treasure hunt in which they find answers to specific questions tailored for specific Web sites
- Downloading items for a scrapbook, a collection of photos, maps, text, and audio or video clips that can be pasted into a multimedia presentation, a Web page, or other project
- Undertaking a WebQuest—a challenging task, scenario, or problem to solve in which student groups become experts on one aspect of a topic and then recombine and synthesize what they have learned with other groups either in their classroom or in other classrooms linked through the Internet
- Collaborative Internet projects (Mike & Rabinowitz, 1998), which enable students to communicate with peers in distant schools or experts in various fields, gather and synthesize information, and make their work public through electronic or other media

The Internet and English language learners. The Internet can be an especially useful tool for ELLs (Leu & Leu, 1999). E-mailing back and forth between English-speaking peers or teachers, either in their own school or in remote schools, gives ELLs authentic communication contexts for reading and writing English. If students enter into an Internet project with a school in which a student's native language is spoken, that student can become a resource for translating back and forth between languages. This helps to illustrate the practical advantages of students' dual-language competency and helps to integrate ELLs socially and academically with their monolingual peers. A second-language learner can use the Internet to access sites in his or her home country and share information with peers as part of an Internet activity.

Internet planning guidelines.   The sheer volume of information available on the Internet, as well as the difficulty of finding just what you want, means that the Internet can consume a lot of planning time, especially for someone just beginning to explore the possibilities of the Web. Martha Rekrut, a high school English teacher in Rhode Island, describes her own initial experiences with using the Web as well as some successful Internet applications by teachers in other disciplines. She shares some guidelines for Internet beginners (Rekrut, 1999):

- Determine instructional objectives and do some preliminary research to decide if the Internet is going to be helpful.
- Integrate the Internet into the context of ongoing instruction.
- Be aware of the literacy demands of the Web.
- Develop specific objectives for each Internet session.
- Include a written component or product to be handed in at the end of each session.
- If possible, help students disseminate their findings on the Internet via e-mail, on the school's Web site, or through displays and public presentations.
- Help students evaluate their Internet experiences in discussion or in writing.

To this, we add a few other general suggestions for planning Internet activities. First, be aware of varied student expertise with computers and the Internet. It would not be surprising if you had students who were much more knowledgeable about computers and the Internet than you are, but you may need to offer basic "how-to" instruction to others. You will also want to make sure that the more tech-savvy students do not monopolize the available workstations or dominate an activity.

Second, it is usually helpful to preselect sites for students to visit, especially if class computer time is limited and students are at the beginning or intermediate stages of Internet experience. This will save time and allow you to steer students toward sites that are reliable, reasonably well organized, and accessible at busy times of the day.

Technology Tip for Teaching English Language Learners

Dave's ESL Café (www.eslcafe.com/) is a Web site designed for English language learners and their teachers. It features, among many other things, idioms, photos, pronunciation power tools, quizzes, quotes, a Today in History section, and a message exchange.

Finally, we encourage you to link book literacy with computer literacy. For instance, if students are working on a research project, you could require that they consult a certain number of book or periodical resources as well as the Internet, or you could use textbook selections as starting points for Internet exploration. Student projects should also include a student-composed written component. At the end of this chapter, we give an example of an interdisciplinary thematic unit that incorporates earth science, English, student use of the Internet and traditional print resources, student publication, and state assessments.

STRUCTURED FRAMEWORKS FOR CONTENT LITERACY LESSONS

The Learning Cycle, which we introduced in Chapter 3, is one example of a structured framework for teaching content literacy. We think it is particularly well suited for helping students make connections between the content they are expected to learn and what they already know from related experiences. As you read about other structured frameworks in this section, think about how you might use them in your own content specialty. In all probability, you will find useful ideas within each of the frameworks described. Rather than adopting any one particular framework in its entirety, you may decide to select those ideas that you feel best fit your content specialty, your students, and your own preferences.

Keep in mind as you read that the structured frameworks described here should not be confused with strategies. The latter, most of which are introduced in Chapters 6–11, can be used at various points in the learning cycle, during direct instruction, as part of Herber's (1978) Instructional Framework, or during Reciprocal Teaching (Palincsar & Brown, 1984). Strategies in and of themselves are *not* structured frameworks; rather, they may be used in any number of different frameworks (e.g., the Instructional Framework and Reciprocal Teaching both use summarizing as a strategy).

Direct Instruction

Direct instruction is useful for teaching a specific skill or process. In this approach, the teacher first states explicitly what is to be learned and models the skill or process. For example, a social studies teacher who wants students to learn how to write a summary might begin by explaining what a summary is, why it is useful, and how one is written. The teacher would then read a short passage from the history textbook and compose a summary on the overhead projector, explaining to the class the specific processes he or she was using.

After the process has been modeled for students, the teacher should involve them in guided practice. To continue our summary-writing example, the teacher could direct the class to read further from the text. The teacher then would compose another summary, but this time base it on input from the class. As an alternative form of guided practice, the teacher could have students work cooperatively in groups of two or three to compose summaries while the teacher walked around the room and offered assistance. Then the groups could compare their summaries and the teacher could help them analyze the merits of including or excluding certain information, their various choices for wording and syntax, and the accuracy with which the summaries captured the important ideas in the text.

In the direct instruction model, guided practice is followed by independent practice in which students use the skills on their own. In the case of summary writing, the teacher could ask students to read and summarize a selection from their text as a homework assignment.

The direct instruction model is most useful when there is a single, relatively straightforward content or literacy objective that can be initially modeled and taught within a one- or two-day time frame. Direct instruction can be effectively applied to such activities as computational skills in math, map reading and interpretation in geography, paragraph structure in English class, or grammatical constructions in a modern language class. Literacy skills such as using context as a vocabulary aid or understanding question–answer relationships can also be taught by direct instruction. However, as the content or literacy objectives become more complex or abstract, direct instruction may need to be followed by extended reinforcement and guided practice, especially for struggling readers (Swanson & de la Paz, 1998).

The Instructional Framework

Harold Herber (1978) developed an instructional framework for content area literacy lessons that takes into account both the content objectives and the literacy objectives of a lesson. It incorporates some of the elements of the direct instruction model. Unlike the direct instruction model, however, the Instructional Framework lends itself to conceptually complex topics that may evolve over longer periods of instruction. Herber's model consists of three major components: preparation, guidance, and independence.

During the *preparation* phase of instruction, a teacher may choose one or more means to get students ready to learn:

- Employ motivational techniques to pique students' interest and encourage them to make a personal investment in learning.
- Activate students' background knowledge.
- Where prior experience is lacking, help build up background for the new concepts that are to be studied.
- Help students anticipate what they will be learning and be purposeful in their efforts.
- Give clear and careful directions about what needs to be done, especially when the assignment involves novel processes or ideas.
- Introduce technical or difficult vocabulary that otherwise might interfere with learning.

Useful strategies for working with students' prior knowledge and building anticipation for learning are provided in Chapter 6, and Chapter 8 focuses on vocabulary development.

In the *guidance* phase of the Instructional Framework, teachers need to provide structured opportunities for students to develop both their learning processes, including their reading and writing abilities, and the concepts that constitute the subject area. The teacher helps students learn by structuring and guiding the interaction between reader and text or between writer and written product. According to Herber (1978), such guidance "must be sufficiently structured to give purpose and direction, but sufficiently open to allow personal strengths, preferences, and discoveries to emerge" (p. 220). Teachers can provide this kind of guidance through thoughtful questioning, by preparing reading or study guides, or by developing cooperative-learning activities in which students can work together on tasks with teacher assistance. A variety of guided learning strategies are described in Chapters 6–11.

Independence is the final phase of Herber's Instructional Framework, and student independence, ideally, is the ultimate goal of instruction. As teachers, we want our students to be able to use both the learning processes and the concepts of our discipline. Math teachers want their students to apply math concepts and operations to authentic, real-life situations. The earth science teacher would hope students could apply their knowledge to local issues of environmental quality. The history teacher hopes that students will use their understanding of the past in order to more intelligently understand their positions as citizens in their communities and in the nation. Such independent applications of skills and knowledge require instruction that transcends rote memorization and perfunctory "coverage." Instead, teachers need to plan instruction that allows students to guide their own learning. This happens over time in classes in which teachers provide instructional scaffolding, where guidance is highly structured and explicit at first but then gradually withdrawn as students become increasingly capable of learning on their own. Reciprocal teaching, described next, is one good example of how this works.

Reciprocal Teaching

In our discussion of accommodating diverse student capabilities, we used the term *scaffolding* to describe how teachers initially guide and support student learning and then gradually give students increasing responsibility for guiding their own learning. This is a variation of *cognitive apprenticeship* (Brown, Collins, & Duguid, 1989). Content area teachers who use cognitive apprenticeship as their approach to instruction adhere to the principle that *knowing* cannot be separated from *doing*. That is, they believe that what students are taught in school must not be different from the real-world use of such knowledge. For example, teachers who believe in this approach would argue against teaching students to memorize facts about U.S. history because it is not the way historians use such facts. In the real world, historians interpret so-called facts about certain events and people's actions surrounding those events; they do not simply read and "neutrally" record in rote fashion what they recall from their reading.

The term *apprenticeship* is used here to emphasize the central role of meaningful, authentic activity in any learning task. There is no room for activity that is not meaningful and authentic in traditional apprenticeships (in trades such as shoemaking or in professional apprenticeships such as medicine and law). However, students in middle and secondary schools are required daily to participate in activities that bear little if any resemblance to what practitioners do in the real world.

What can be done? Reciprocal teaching (Palincsar & Brown, 1984) is perhaps the best-known and most thoroughly researched application of cognitive apprenticeship to the teaching of reading comprehension. Reciprocal teaching involves direct instruction in comprehension strategies, most often the strategies of predicting, questioning, clarifying, and summarizing. Strategy instruction is provided with authentic classroom reading materials, either narrative or expository, instead of worksheets or other materials designed specifically for skill instruction. An important feature of reciprocal teaching is the use of an instructional dialogue in which the teacher initially leads in modeling the comprehension strategies, but then gradually turns the responsibility for leading the dialogue over to students. An illustration of how a teacher might initiate such a dialogue is given in Figure 4.2. We have included generic statements or questions that might prompt student participation, as well as topical statements or questions that a teacher might use to model the particular comprehension strategy. Figure 4.3 features a brief reciprocal teaching dialogue from a college class. Note how much student talk there is relative to teacher talk, and notice also that students speak to each other, asking for clarification and concrete examples. Students in this example are taking charge of their own learning.

As students become more proficient with the reading strategies, the teacher gradually fades out of the dialogue and allows students to assume leadership. In a review of research on reciprocal teaching, Rosenshine and Meister (1994) concluded that the key to its effectiveness was not so much which strategies were taught, but rather the importance of careful scaffolding of instruction. That is, teachers should present strategies in small steps, guide student practice, provide ongoing feedback and correction, and engage students in extensive independent practice.

EVIDENCE-BASED RESEARCH

Successful use of reciprocal teaching with varied student populations has been widely reported in professional literature. A review of 16 separate empirical studies indicated that reciprocal teaching generally yielded positive results with students ranging from fourth grade through adult (Rosenshine and Meister, 1994). This review also suggested that reciprocal teaching was effective with students who had developed some decoding skills but who were poor in reading comprehension. Reciprocal teaching has been successfully adapted for

The following passage is part of the discussion of the Louisiana Purchase in *A History of the United States* (Boorstin & Kelly, 2005):

> This was perhaps the greatest test of statesmanship that Jefferson ever had to face. He was on the spot. The Constitution said nothing at all about whether or how Congress could buy land from a foreign country. Again and again, Jefferson had argued that Congress had only those powers that the Constitution had assigned in so many words. Maybe the power to buy land from foreign countries had been left out of the Constitution on purpose—to prevent the United States from playing the dangerous, old-fashioned game of empire. The people of the new United States had tried to escape from the ways of the Old World, where the rulers were in the habit of buying and selling, bartering and gambling faraway lands and unknown peoples. Now would Jefferson go against everything he had been saying for years?

Questioning

Initiating: Does anybody have a good question that we should be trying to answer for this section?

Modeling (after reading the first two sentences of the passage): What does the author mean when he says Jefferson was on the spot?

Clarifying

Initiating: Is there anything that is not clear?

Modeling: I wasn't sure what the author meant when he said the power to buy land had been left out of the Constitution *on purpose*. I had to re-read the next two sentences and think about that. Maybe it means that the writers of the Constitution left some things out because they weren't good ideas.

Summarizing

Initiating: What is the main idea of this section?

Modeling: The main point here seems to be that President Jefferson had a dilemma. He had to make a choice between changing his long-held positions or taking a step into the unknown.

Predicting

Initiating: What will Jefferson decide? What will the reaction be in Congress? What makes you think that?

Modeling: Everything we've read so far seems to indicate that Jefferson will support the purchase. The author keeps suggesting that making a bold decision would be evidence of Jefferson's leadership ability. When I look at the map on this page, I see that a huge section is colored in green and labeled "Louisiana Purchase," so Congress will probably support the decision, but with a lot of debate.

FIGURE 4.2   Initiating and modeling comprehension strategies in reciprocal teaching

Excerpt from a Lesson on Reading Titles and Lead Paragraphs Using Cultural Literacy *by Hirsch (1987)*

Predicting

Teacher: Look at the chapter title, "What Every American Needs to Know." What might the author expect you to know?

Student 1: Things like the Founding Fathers, Plymouth Rock, geography, five basic food groups.

Teacher: Good predictions! Now, read paragraph one.

Questioning

Student 2: What does Hirsch mean by "cultural literacy"?

Student 3: World knowledge . . . that's what it says in paragraph one.

Clarifying

Student 2: I'm still not sure what "cultural literacy" means exactly. I need some concrete examples.

Summarizing

Student 4: "Cultural literacy" is the common background information we have stored in our minds in order to understand what we read.

Student 2: Okay, so background information means I already have ideas like the ones in the book.

Predicting

Teacher: Good. Now, look at the subheading, "The Decline of Teaching Cultural Literacy."

Student 5: I think this section will probably explain why students aren't becoming culturally literate.

FIGURE 4.3   **Strategies for reciprocal teaching**

social studies instruction of seventh- and eighth-grade students with learning disabilities who were learning English as a second language (Klingner & Vaughan, 1996) and for students in Chapter I reading classes (Alfassi, 1998).

Two fundamentals of reciprocal teaching, supported by a substantial body of educational research, would appear to account for its effectiveness: direct instruction and the gradual shift of responsibility for "teaching" from the teacher to the students (Pressley, 1998). Obviously any implementation of reciprocal teaching requires the commitment of time and effort on the part of the teacher. To suggest a general time frame, Westera and Moore (1995) found that students with low reading comprehension scores who received 12 to 16 training sessions made significant gains on standardized tests, whereas similar students who had only 6 to 8 sessions made no gains.

Reciprocal teaching involves a high degree of social interaction and collaboration, as students gradually learn to assume the role of teacher in helping their peers construct meaning from text. In essence, reciprocal teaching is authentic activity because "learning, both outside and inside school, advances through collaborative social interaction and the social construction of knowledge" (Brown, Collins, & Duguid, 1989, p. 40).

BEYOND THE DAILY PLAN

Teachers' instructional decisions clearly transcend the question of "What shall I do tomorrow?" Teachers also need a long-term view of teaching and learning. Those who understand the socially constructed nature of knowledge will plan to involve students in discussion, collaboration, and problem solving related to their content area studies. Also implied in this trend is a view of the curriculum as comprising meaningfully interrelated concepts and themes, not simply as isolated bits of information to be learned by rote. All of this implies that teachers will plan activities that enable students to make connections between content areas, between the real world and the world of the classroom, and between "knowing what" (facts and concepts) and "knowing how" (using facts and concepts in authentic ways). In the following sections, we describe the planning of a school-wide literacy program as well as two frequently recommended approaches to integrating curricula: interdisciplinary teaching and thematic teaching.

School-Wide Programs

Reading Next (Biancarosa & Snow, 2004), a report on adolescent reading commissioned by the Carnegie Corporation, asserts that a comprehensive and coordinated literacy program is a key element in effectively meeting the needs of adolescent students, especially those who find reading and writing to be challenging. Although the efforts of individual teachers are important, they cannot have the same impact as a school-wide program spearheaded by commited, enthusiastic leaders and implemented by knowledgeable teachers who coordinate instruction across disciplines. Because the needs of adolescents are quite diverse, the nature of coordinated school-wide efforts will vary to meet the needs of particular communities. In some cases, the attention to literacy by content teachers may be relatively modest, while other situations may require more intensive accommodations.

In a widely cited program, a group of teachers in the San Francisco Bay area implemented a school-wide scaffolded approach to content area instruction under the umbrella of the Strategic Literacy Initiative at WestEd Regional Educational Laboratory (Greenleaf, Schoenbach, Cziko, & Mueller, 2001; Schoenbach,

Greenleaf, Cziko, & Hurwitz, 1999). They incorporated multiple research-supported elements into a literacy program for ninth-graders in an ethnically and linguistically diverse San Francisco high school. As an alternative to traditional skills-based remedial reading instruction, WestEd facilitators and teachers developed a year-long course in Academic Literacy that featured what they call *reading apprenticeship.* Conceptualizing adolescent readers as inexperienced rather than deficient, expert adults inducted student apprentices into the strategies of content area literacy by systematically showing them how. Based on extensive assessment of students, teachers knew that ninth graders could decode and comprehend, but they needed to expand their fluency and experience with more diverse kinds of texts, all with direct, expert guidance on how to read more challenging material.

The primary goal of reading apprenticeship is to show adolescent readers that expert reading is a complex, problem-solving process by engaging them in "metacognitive conversations" about what they are reading and learning. These conversations involve teachers and students in talk about how they approach content area reading tasks, with teachers taking the lead by making their own reading processes visible as they pause to think aloud while reading to students. Reading apprenticeship involves four key dimensions that are necessary to support adolescent reading development (Schoenbach, Braunger, Greenleaf, & Litman, 2003):

- *Social dimension:* community building in the classroom, including recognizing the resources brought by each member and developing a safe environment for students to be open about their reading difficulties
- *Personal dimension:* developing students' identities and self-awareness as readers, as well as their purposes for reading and goals for reading improvement
- *Cognitive dimension:* developing readers' mental processes, including their problem-solving strategies
- *Knowledge-building dimension:* identifying and expanding the kinds of knowledge readers bring to a text and further develop through interaction with that text

The Academic Literacy course was divided into three units: Reading Self & Society, Reading Media, and Reading History. Throughout the year students read, wrote, and talked about a variety of texts in various media, including literature, history texts, and print and broadcast advertising. Reciprocal teaching, direct instruction in text structures, note taking and paraphrasing, vocabulary study, regular independent reading of self-selected works, and response log writing and sharing were used as appropriate during the year.

The program resulted in significant gains in reading comprehension on a standardized test. In one year, students' average scores moved from late seventh-grade to late ninth-grade level. Gains continued at an accelerated rate for a smaller representative sample tested in tenth grade. Students who had the most need of literacy development, such as struggling readers, English language learners, and special education students, tended to make the most gains. The Strategic Literacy Initiative has extended the Academic Literacy course to many other middle and high schools, with similarly encouraging results (Strategic Literacy Initiative, 2004a, 2004b, 2004c.) More information on the Strategic Literacy Initiative and the Academic Literacy course can be found at www.wested.org/strategicliteracy.

The results of the Academic Literacy course suggest that separate literacy classes in middle school and high school can be effective for a broad range of students if they are based on academically challenging, content-based, scaffolded instruction with a variety of texts. Reflecting on the growth of a student named Rosa as a capable and strategic reader, Greenleaf et al. (2001) contrast their Reading Apprenticeship approach with traditional skills-based remediation:

> Imagine, for a moment, that Rosa had been in a reading course focused on building basic reading skills. While such a course may have strengthened her word analysis and vocabulary skills, we doubt that Rosa would have developed the kind of intellectual and ethical engagement and personal agency she demonstrates here. When we imagine such a limited outcome, we are struck with a keen sense of loss and unfulfilled potential, not only for Rosa, but for the many young people with whom we work. (p. 110)

Interdisciplinary Teaching

In the middle grades, it is common to assign students to interdisciplinary teams in order to create a school-within-a-school climate or the feeling that each student belongs to a particular school "family." Interdisciplinary teams typically include teachers from each of the core academic areas, sometimes with the addition of specialists in reading or special education. Because each team works with the same students for the whole year, teachers and students become well acquainted. Teams often have a common planning time so they can jointly plan instruction that will enable students to see how concepts learned in one discipline can apply in another. This can create an environment that is intellectually stimulating for teachers as well as students.

In high schools, however, built-in constraints such as subject matter specialization, inflexible scheduling, and large numbers of students make interdisciplinary teaming difficult. Nevertheless, special interdisciplinary programs have been successful even in very large schools. For example, the Humanitas program is an interdisciplinary, team-based approach to humanities teaching in the Los Angeles Unified School District. The Humanitas program emphasizes building understanding of issues that have relevance to urban youth, and teachers frequently bypass textbooks in favor of primary source materials, news media, and novels. Essay questions are used to develop students' abilities to think and write in a critical vein about what they have read. The following is an essay question from a unit on culture and tradition (Aschbacher, 1991):

> The cosmology of a traditional culture permeates every aspect of that culture. This is illustrated in the following three cultural groups: the Eskimos, the Southwest Indians, and the Meso-Americans. Specifically, discuss the spirit world that each group believed in, and explain how it influenced [that group's] culture and values. Include examples from your reading in art history, literature, and social studies to illustrate and substantiate your analysis. Finally, to what extent, if any, does the spirit world affect us today? (pp. 17–18)

In many schools, there may be opportunities for teachers from two or three disciplines to work together. For example, Amy Schimberg and Heidi Grant, eighth-grade science and English teachers at John Jay Middle School in Cross River, New York, found that their disciplines had many natural connections in a mystery thematic unit designed to build on students' interest in recent high-profile crimes (Schimberg & Grant, 1998). In English class, Ms. Grant's students read and discussed several types of mysteries and learned about the literary devices used by mystery writers. At the same time, a member of the local police force visited science classes to explain and demonstrate finger-printing. Then, students were plunged into a simulated murder investigation. The crime scene was set and clues were left for the student investigators. Students analyzed chemical and physical properties in the authentic context of the "forensic lab," in which stations for analyzing fingerprints, ink, fiber evidence, a handkerchief smelling of mysterious perfume, and poisons were set up. Student teams observed the crime scene, interviewed suspects (portrayed by school staff members), conducted forensic analyses, and kept all their notes and results in investigator's notebooks and a case file. At the end of their investigations, student teams presented their conclusions to the whole class.

Individual teachers can also incorporate aspects of interdisciplinary teaching into their content areas. For instance, students who study the history of science can learn a good deal about the nature of science, the human face of science, and the links between science and society. A chemistry teacher might present students with the historical background of Mendeleev's development of the periodic table of elements, and engage them in a hands-on activity that leads them through the actual thought processes that Mendeleev employed in the 1860s (McKinney & Michalovic, 2004). Exploring biographies of scientists or learning about famous scientific episodes like the development of the Salk polio vaccine helps students learn science concepts such as the tentative nature of scientific models, the use of empirical evidence, the contributions of women and people of color to science, and the fact that scientists may draw different conclusions from the same evidence (Rudge & Howe, 2004).

Thematic Teaching

The terms *interdisciplinary teaming and thematic teaching* are often used synonymously. For us, the major distinction is that thematic teaching can be implemented successfully within a single content area classroom (e.g., a civics class), but the success of interdisciplinary teaming often depends on special organizational school structures, such as flexible block scheduling and common teacher planning periods. We think that this distinction has practical significance since so few schools throughout the United States have implemented interdisciplinary programs of study.

The single-discipline thematic unit allows teachers to incorporate a variety of materials and instructional groupings to meet the reading interests and needs of their students. To do this, teachers must identify fundamental ideas or organizing concepts within the subject and selectively abandon less important material that might have been emphasized if the goal were to cover a certain amount of content by the end of the year. For example, Rodney White (1995) suggests organizing the study of world history around a thematic unit on religion. Rather than taking a strictly chronological approach to history, with the topic of religion given brief attention in disparate chapters, students could undertake a comparative study of the historical evolution of the world's religions. This would allow them to understand both the commonalities and differences among people and to explore issues such as the separation of church and state in the United States, the contrast between Eastern and Western worlds, and relationships among Judaism, Christianity, and Islam. Such a unitary approach to world history would be especially appropriate in a culturally diverse classroom. White also suggests a culturally sensitive study of U.S. history that could be developed around the theme "What is an American?" with students thinking about and discussing questions of cultural unity versus diversity.

In science as in history, there is a movement away from teaching a collection of isolated facts. Susan Offner (1992) proposes a biology unit founded on the theme of human heredity that would tie together concepts of protein structures, enzymes, DNA, genetics, and hereditary diseases. Understandings that students consolidate in this unit would carry over to the study of the various systems of the human body, evolution, and other diverse units of the biology curriculum.

Unit Planning

Whether a thematic unit integrates learning across content areas or is developed within a single discipline, careful planning and preparation are required. The steps in planning a thematic unit follow the decision-making process described at the beginning of this chapter. The first step would be to select a unifying theme or organizing concept for the unit (Goerss, 1996). The possibilities both within and across disciplines are enormous. It may help to think of three categories of themes (Fogarty, 1994): topical themes, such as dinosaurs; conceptual themes, such as systems; and problematic themes, such as "How do humans survive?"

Timothy Shanahan (1995) warns against picking topical themes that do not allow students to inquire deeply into meaningful ideas. For instance, if a unit on dinosaurs meant reading *Jurassic Park* (Crichton, 1991), writing some dinosaur poems or science fiction, and printing out dinosaur graphics with the classroom computer, students might get some useful reading and writing practice, but they would not be learning much about dinosaurs, about science (beyond the considerably fictionalized concepts in the novel), or about math. However, a dinosaur unit that led students to explore concepts such as extinction, climatic change, evolution, chaos theory, DNA, geologic time, habitat, classification of species, and measurement would represent much more substantial learning.

Earlier in the chapter, when we discussed cognitive apprenticeship, we said that learning will be more meaningful if students are engaged in authentic activity—if they can discern meaningful purposes in what they are doing. Bette Bergeron and Elizabeth Rudenga (1996) propose an interrelated five-part framework for evaluating the authenticity of learning activities in a unit plan:

- *Purpose.* Literacy activities intended primarily for practice or evaluation will be less meaningful than those designed to communicate or share ideas.
- *Choice.* To the extent possible, students and teachers should negotiate curricular goals, activities, and materials rather than having all choices made by the teacher.
- *Audience.* Reading and writing are less purposeful if the only audience is the teacher. Learning can be shared with peers and audiences outside the classroom.
- *Resources.* Contrived learning materials are inherently less motivating and meaningful than real-life resources. Students benefit from using a variety of resources, print and nonprint.
- *Relevance.* Activities should meet relevant curriculum requirements and the development of meaningful learning.

Of course, meeting each criterion for authenticity with every learning activity would not be practical. A framework such as this, however, does give you a means to focus your planning on genuine learning rather than simply covering curriculum or keeping students occupied.

Once a thematic focus or organizing concept has been selected for a unit, teachers will begin listing overall goals, related concepts and skills, available materials, possible activities and teaching strategies, and ways to evaluate students' learning, all with the particular needs and abilities of their students in mind (Goerss, 1996). This will take some time as resources are located, materials such as study guides and handouts are developed, Internet sites are located, and new ideas for the unit come from reflection, research, and conversations with students and colleagues. To keep the ideas for a unit organized, teachers often use a web or graphic organizer to map out concepts, resources, or activities. In Figure 4.1, we illustrated a completed concept planning web for a unit on the American Revolution, and Figure 4.4 shows two generic variations of planning webs.

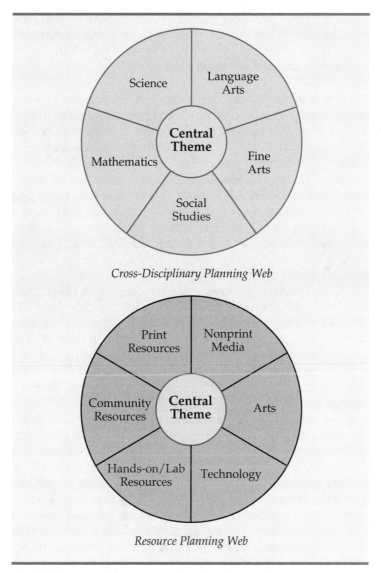

Cross-Disciplinary Planning Web

Resource Planning Web

FIGURE 4.4   Planning webs for thematic teaching

The final stages of unit planning involve planning activities, developing assessment procedures, and constructing a time line for the unit. To enhance student interest, engagement, and learning, it is best to plan a variety of activities, including whole-class, small-group, and independent activities, some that are teacher assigned, and some that are self-selected by students. J. D. Cooper (1997) suggests the use of three chronological categories of activities. *Initiating activities* should motivate students, activate prior knowledge and build background, and help students take responsibility for their own learning. *Developing activities* involve students in reading, writing, discussing, problem solving, and hands-on experience with making something, creating, or experimenting. *Culminating activities* allow students to share their learning, reflect on the ideas in the unit, and evaluate their own efforts.

Putting it all together.   Recently, Steve participated in a conference on using technology in education at which he heard a presentation by Gene Kulbago, an English teacher at Niagara Middle School in Niagara Falls, New York. Gene and his colleague, earth science teacher Mary Marcinkowski, have collaborated on an earth science research project that illustrates many of the ideas presented in this chapter. Niagara Middle is an urban middle school that serves a diverse population of students. It features a schoolwide technology program in which all students learn to use word processing, desktop publishing and presentation software, Internet browsers, digital cameras, and scanners. Although sixth graders learn basic skills in a ten-week introductory technology course, the entire three-year curriculum of the school is infused with applications of technology in virtually every content area.

Gene and Mary are experienced teachers, both professionally active in state and local teacher organizations. They teach approximately 50 eighth-grade students in an honors program, all of whom are taking Mary's earth science course for New York State Regents high school credit. In order to receive credit for this course (and as part of state high school graduation requirements), students take a statewide earth science examination at the end of the year. Ten percent of the examination is awarded for completing a research project on an appropriate earth science topic.

The seeds of the earth science research project are sown in seventh grade, in which students learn basic research skills and the format for a research paper and then apply them to a short paper on a student-selected science topic. Then in eighth grade, Mr. Kulbago and Mrs. Marcinkowski and their students embark on earth science research projects that will occupy much of their time, especially in the second half of the school year. Figure 4.5 shows a planning web for this project. After the teachers have outlined the general parameters of the project, students begin to think about topics they would like to pursue. Students have investigated a wide range of topics, such as the formation of hurricanes or tornadoes, dinosaur extinction theories, the geology of the Niagara River gorge, New York State oil and natural gas reserves, evidence for global warming, and the causes and effects of the Buffalo blizzard of 1977.

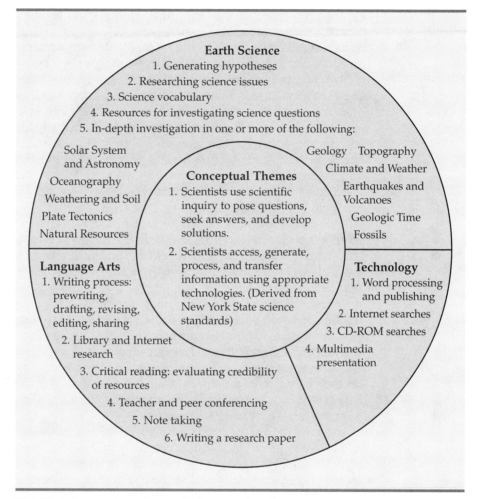

Earth Science
1. Generating hypotheses
2. Researching science issues
3. Science vocabulary
4. Resources for investigating science questions
5. In-depth investigation in one or more of the following:

Solar System
and Astronomy
Oceanography
Weathering and Soil
Plate Tectonics
Natural Resources

Geology   Topography
Climate and Weather
Earthquakes and
Volcanoes
Geologic Time
Fossils

Conceptual Themes
1. Scientists use scientific inquiry to pose questions, seek answers, and develop solutions.
2. Scientists access, generate, process, and transfer information using appropriate technologies. (Derived from New York State science standards)

Language Arts
1. Writing process: prewriting, drafting, revising, editing, sharing
2. Library and Internet research
3. Critical reading: evaluating credibility of resources
4. Teacher and peer conferencing
5. Note taking
6. Writing a research paper

Technology
1. Word processing and publishing
2. Internet searches
3. CD-ROM searches
4. Multimedia presentation

FIGURE 4.5   Planning web for Earth Science Research Unit (*Source:* Gene Kulbago and Mary Marcinkowski, Niagara Middle School, Niagara Falls, New York.)

With guidance from their teachers, students begin collecting information for their projects. They are required to gather information from both electronic and traditional print resources. To get students started, the teachers have selected 18 sample Internet sites that feature reliable and useful earth science information along with links to other sites. Gene posts these on his own Web site, which students access for reference during their projects. Gene's Web site also includes specifications for writing a research paper and a summary of MLA guidelines for style and citations. On-line, students branch out to a great variety of Web sites, due to the diversity of their topics. Gene says that most students would prefer to conduct their searches entirely on-line, but he and Mary believe that it is important that students be facile with traditional print resources as well, such as science encyclopedias, scientific journals, and science trade books. Throughout their research, students are guided to make critical judgments about the credibility of the information they are collecting, especially from the Internet, by considering the authors' knowledge, purpose, and affiliations or other credentials.

By February, students are expected to begin drafting their research papers. When students have a final draft completed, Mr. Kulbago evaluates them for adherence to MLA guidelines and other standard writing conventions. Students are then expected to revise as needed, after which Mrs. Marcinkowski evaluates the papers for their scientific content. This evaluation is followed by a conference with Mrs. Marcinkowski, and then the research papers are revised and finalized during language arts class time.

As students are completing their research papers, they begin preparing a PowerPoint multimedia presentation of their findings. These presentations are designed to highlight the major findings in a creative way that will hold audience interest, along with a concluding statement of the importance of the topic. Students share the completed multimedia presentations at a special parent night. Figure 4.6 shows sample "slides" from student Frank Accardo's multimedia presentation.

Together, the research paper and PowerPoint presentations constitute the "research" portion of the state earth science exam. Mrs. Marcinkowski calculates a final grade for the two projects by evaluating the depth of the research, the variety of resources used, the expression of students' understanding of the topic, and the appropriateness of the topic to the earth science curriculum. This then becomes 10 percent of students' earth science exam grade, added to 15 percent for a practical hands-on laboratory activity and 75 percent for a traditional pencil-and-paper examination.

It is important to note that for experienced teachers such as Gene Kulbago and Mary Marcinkowski, planning is usually ongoing and cumulative. They have developed different aspects of the earth science research unit over the three years that they have presented it, and at the end of the current school year they were already making plans for what they would add to the project next year to make it more meaningful and broad reaching. One addition will be student oral reports in order to strengthen the speaking and listening aspects of the projects. Another facet they would like to add is a social studies component so that students can also consider the historical and social contexts of scientific issues. For instance, students who chose to research the Niagara River gorge might investigate the social, political, and economic issues surrounding the development of tourist attractions at Niagara Falls, the generation of hydroelectric power, or the shared border between the United States and Canada. Considering such aspects of a topic would reflect a social constructionist view as students learned that science is not just "neutral" facts but rather has ramifications that are socially shaped and contested.

This earth science unit exemplifies good applications of integrated language processes and interdisciplinary teaching. Teachers from two disciplines, science

The Formation of the Moon

Frank Accardo
Earth Science 8
Mrs. Marcinkowski
Mr. Kulbago
June 2000

The Collision Theory

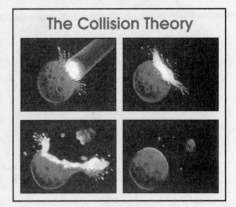

The Collision Theory

- This theory's main idea says that a large body in space collided with the earth in its early development stages causing parts to shatter.

- Later those same parts came together to form the moon.

- This can be proved believable because samples of the earth's rock were the same as the moon's.

The Capture Theory

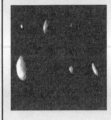

The basis of this theory states mainly that the earth and moon were formed separately and the moon revolved around the sun. But on one special occasion the earth's gravity caught the moon and pulled it into its own region, hence making it the earth's moon.

The Co-Formation Theory

The main idea of this theory says that the earth and moon were formed as a double-planet system and that they were both formed from a cloud of dust. Some experts believe that our whole universe was formed from a cloud of dust. If they were both formed from this so-called cloud of dust then it's only logical that since they were formed together they stayed together, hence their position now.

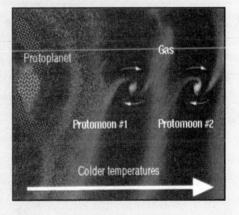

FIGURE 4.6   Multimedia slides for Earth Science Research Presentation (*Source*: Frank Anthony Accardo, Niagara Middle School, Niagara Falls, New York.)

(*continued*)

The Escape Theory

The English mathematician George H. Darwin suggested in 1879 that the earth and moon were literally formed together. Because of the earth's attraction to the sun a great bulge began to form on the side of it. At this time the earth's rotation had a much greater speed than it does now and spun a great amount faster. As the bulge grew, it began to break away from the earth. As soon as the bulge was large enough and the earth was spinning fast enough, the bulge just broke off into space. But since the newly formed moon wasn't strong enough to escape the earth's gravity, it was caught and has stayed there ever since as the earth's moon.

My Conclusion

There are so many theories on how our magnificent moon was formed and information backing each one, who knows which is actually true? Hopefully as science and mankind progress into the future we will have a better idea of the moon's actual formation and maybe we'll even know for sure how it all really happened. Until then all we can do is study the theories we have today and try and choose for ourselves which is true.

Bibliography

Bill Arnett. "The moon" Last updated: 1/5/00. 1/20/00 http://seds.lpl.arizona.edu/nineplanets/luna.html.

Gamow, George. Moon. New York. Abelard-Schuman. 1959.

Johnson. "Moon making." 2/01/00. http://www.kidsnspace.org/moon.htm.

Bibliography

"Moon." 1995 Microsoft Encarta. Version 95. CD-ROM. 1995.

University of Michigan. "The Formation of the Moon." 1/20/00 http://www.windows.umich.edu.

World Book. "How the Moon was Formed." 1/25/00. http://www.worldbook.com/fun/moon/html/formed.htm.

FIGURE 4.6   **continued**

and English, have collaborated to integrate technology, reading, writing, speaking, and listening as fundamental tools in extending student understanding of several earth science topics. In this case, the unit theme encompasses the broad topic of scientific investigation and is specifically keyed to one of the state requirements for successful completion of the earth science course. Although the disciplinary boundaries of English and science are maintained, the unit is designed to have students learn and apply skills and strategies that overlap between the two subject areas. This unit meets all the criteria for authenticity suggested by Bergeron and Rudenga (1996). Specific topics and a variety of print and nonprint resources are chosen by students. Major purposes of the project are for students to investigate meaningful topics and to communicate their findings in multiple formats to an audience of their peers. Also, the activities are all directly relevant to both local and state curriculum requirements.

SUMMARY

As you read about the various ways that teachers can plan lessons and units, we are sure you found some ideas attractive, felt others were impractical or incompatible with your situation, and thought of ways to modify other ideas to suit your style, your students, and your content area. We would not be so presumptive as to prescribe a particular planning approach for any teacher. However, we have tried to emphasize four points that will influence your planning. First, we encourage you to think about how students will use language and literacy in your content area. Second, you can look for ways to help students take charge of their own learning. Third, learning will be more meaningful and long-lasting if your students can make connections among the concepts they learn, connections between content areas, and connections to what they know and experience outside of school. Finally, there are no short-term "fixes" for the difficulties many students encounter with their content area studies, but when teachers commit to integrating literacy learning with the learning of content over a period of time, there will be visible gains in student achievement.

SUGGESTED READINGS

American Alliance for Health, Physical Education, Recreation, and Dance. (n. d.) Physical Education and Health Lesson Planning Links. Available http://www.teacherstoolkit.com/dept7.htm

Au, K. (1998). Social constructivism and the school literacy learning of students of diverse backgrounds. *Journal of Literacy Research, 30,* 297–319.

Buell, C., & Whittaker, A. (2001). Enhancing content literacy in physical education. *Journal of Physical Education, Recreation, and Dance, 72*(6), 32–37.

Bruce, B. C. (Ed.). (2003). *Literacy in the information age: Inquiries into meaning making with new technologies.* Newark, DE: International Reading Association.

Fielding, A., Schoenbach, R., & Jordan, M. (Eds.). (2003). *Building academic literacy: Lessons from Reading Apprenticeship classrooms, grades 6–12.* San Francisco, CA: Jossey-Bass.

Frank Potter's Science Gems. (n. d.). More than 14,000 science resources sorted by category (e.g., earth science, life science, physical science), subcategory (e.g., energy, waves), and grade level. Available: http://www.sciencegems.com/

Leu, D., & Leu, D. (1999). *Teaching with the Internet: Lessons from the classroom.* Norwood, MA: Gordon.

Meister, D. G., & Nolan, J. (2001). Out on a limb on our own: Uncertainty and doubt, moving from subject-centered to interdisciplinary teaching. *Teachers College Record, 103,* 608–633. (Also available at http://www.tcrecord.org).

Schoenbach, R., Greenleaf, C., Cziko, C., & Hurwitz, L. (1999). *Reading for understanding: A guide to improving reading in middle and high school classrooms.* San Francisco: Jossey-Bass.

Sleeter, C. (n. d.). *Websites for multicultural teaching resources.* Available: http://home.csumb.edu/s/sleeterchristine/world/Websites/teacher_resources.html

Weaver, C., Chaston, J., & Peterson, S. (1995). *Theme exploration: A voyage of discovery.* Portsmouth, NH: Heinemann.

Assessment of Students and Textbooks

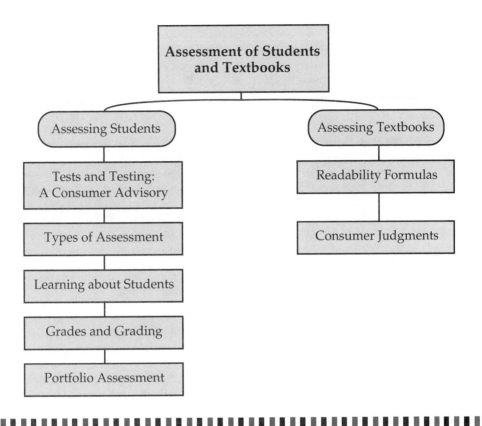

As schools and teachers are increasingly pressed to be accountable for the results of instruction, students are being assessed in schools for varied and often conflicting purposes. Various constituencies look to assessment for different reasons and engage in an ongoing and sometimes rancorous debate over how student assessment should be conducted. The issues that have been raised are far from being resolved. Given the limitations inherent in educational assessment, many of them never will be resolved. In this chapter we address some of the issues surrounding student assessment, but because of their complexity and intractability, we do not presume to settle the many theoretical and philosophical questions that exist. Instead, we concentrate on the practical day-to-day assessment decisions that teachers make.

How well can students read, write, think, and study? Can they apply what they know? How can teachers fairly and accurately reflect student knowledge through the grades they award? How difficult, interesting, and useful are available texts? This chapter explores some ways to find answers to these questions.

In the following reminiscence, Dawn Voelker, a math teacher at West Seneca (New York) Central Schools, reflects on what it was like to be on the receiving end of teacher assessment. We think it captures many of the difficulties experienced by students and teachers.

■■■■■■■

I can clearly remember my friend Kathy and I working on a project in high school. It involved research, reading, and an interview. We chose the same topic, so we decided to do the paper together. It started off great. We met every night possible and helped one another out. As time went on, she wasn't doing any of the reading and research. On the other hand, I was working my tail off. I got to the point where I didn't care because I knew we were getting separate grades anyway.

When the interviewing part came up, she made the whole thing up. I told her that she had better work harder, but she insisted she would do fine. I continued to do my project and put forth more effort than on any other paper. Kathy's laziness inspired me to work even harder. I wanted to do better than she did.

The projects were handed in, graded, and returned to us within a week. As the papers were being passed back, I glanced over at Kathy. I was expecting disappointment. Instead, she gleamed, held up her paper, and said, "I got an A minus." I thought to myself, "Great! This means I at least have an A."

When I got my paper back, there on the front was a huge C+. Below the grade was a note: "Misspellings, grammatical errors and run-ons." I felt like crawling under my desk. My face got red-hot as Kathy stared at me, waiting for me to announce my grade. Instead, I just stuck the project in my folder and stared straight ahead.

I couldn't understand why I had put forth all the effort and gotten an average grade. Just because I had misspellings and run-ons? That was completely unfair. Kathy put down anything and made it sound good and got an A. I didn't have the nerve to confront my teacher and tell him that I had worked so hard and deserved a better grade. I wanted to tell him that Kathy practically made hers up. I just didn't say anything because I trusted that he knew more about grading than I did.*

■■■■■■■

Most of us can commiserate with Dawn's dismay and confusion, yet we would be reluctant to criticize the teacher too harshly. After all, he saw only the product of Dawn's and Kathy's work, not the process of producing them.

There are many variables in a teacher's day, many things to consider as decisions are made about what will happen in the classroom. There are, of course, students. Middle-grade and high school teachers often see from 100 to 150 or more students in a day. Like Dawn and Kathy, each of these students has his or her own personality, aptitudes, interests, and effect on classroom dynamics. They represent at least 100 energetic bundles of human variability. Teachers must somehow plan instruction that meets their disparate needs and must make periodic judgments—in the form of grades—of how well individual students have learned a

*Used with permission of Dawn Voelker, West Seneca Central Schools, West Seneca, NY.

subject. Textbooks and other text and nontext materials represent another set of variables for teachers. Text materials especially will vary greatly in their levels of difficulty, interest, and utility. They may be well suited to students' needs; they may be quite inappropriate. The more you know about these variables—students and texts—the more effective you can be as a teacher.

ASSESSING STUDENTS

Experts on educational evaluation talk about two purposes for assessing students. *Formative assessment* is intended to help "form," or develop, a student. Formative assessment helps a teacher to draw conclusions about the various strengths and weaknesses of the individual, those things that might help or hinder learning. *Summative assessment* is intended to make a "summarizing" judgment of what a person has learned or done. Grades on tests, assignments, and report cards are examples of summative assessments.

Whatever the purposes of assessment, we believe that good assessment practices have certain characteristics:

1. *Good assessment draws on multiple sources of information.* No single test—whether it is a standardized, norm-referenced, commercially published test of student achievement or a teacher-made, ten-item multiple-choice pop quiz on last night's homework—can tell a teacher the "true" state of a student's knowledge.
2. *Good assessment results in information that is useful to both students and teachers.* Students need to know how they are doing, what they are doing right, and what they can do to improve. Teachers need to know about students' attitudes, interests, background knowledge, and aptitude for reading, writing, and other academic tasks.
3. *Good assessment gives students optimal conditions for showing their capabilities.* Varied assessment procedures, fairly introduced and interpreted, give students the chance to show their individual strengths.
4. *Good assessment involves students in self-assessment.* In the long run, the judgments that students make about themselves are just as important as—if not more important than—the judgments teachers make about students. Self-evaluation is an essential component of learning how to learn.
5. *Good assessment admits the potential of fallibility.* After all is said and done, teachers must acknowledge that some students will remain enigmas and that some judgments, no matter how carefully considered, may be inaccurate.

Tests and Testing: A Consumer Advisory

There are many stakeholders in the debates over student assessment, and their demands frequently conflict (Pearson, 1998). Community members have numerous concerns: Are tax dollars being well spent? Do our schools compare favorably with those in other districts or states? Are the values and culture of the community being fairly represented? Is my child learning as well as I would like? Politicians at the local, state, and national levels try to represent the many voices of their community, but they frequently view assessment as a means to further their political agendas as well. Test results may be used by politicians to promote funding for educational programs or to further attacks on public schools, teachers' unions, or particular aspects of the curriculum.

School administrators view assessment as a way to demonstrate accountability and program effectiveness, yet they must also consider how cost-effective various assessment techniques may be. Teachers are looking for ways to find out how well students are progressing, both so that they can report to other stakeholders and so that they can devise effective instruction. At the same time, teachers know that their own performance will be judged by how well their students do on statewide or district testing. Of all the voices in the assessment debate, the one least often heard is that of students, yet they have perhaps the most important stake of all.

The professed purposes of testing are as varied and contradictory as the stakeholders. Reformers of all political stripes may see tests as a means to drive school reform. Some may look to state or national assessments as a way to raise student achievement, whereas others see alternative assessment procedures as a way to complement curricular reforms and increase students' participation in their learning. Some people see assessment as a means to ensure equity for students of diverse backgrounds, whereas others point out that assessment procedures often reinforce or even create an unequal playing field for children of different economic, linguistic, or cultural backgrounds. Many teachers argue that assessment should be a professional tool that they can use to evaluate and improve instruction. However, for state boards of education, college admissions officers, and employers, assessment may provide a gatekeeping function, determining whether an individual can graduate from high school, enter college, engage in certain professions, or hold a particular job.

The conflicting demands and claims surrounding educational assessment present several very real problems to classroom teachers. Among them are

- *Validity.* How can we be sure that a particular assessment tool is really telling us what we want to know?
- *Credibility.* How well will other stakeholders—parents, administrators, taxpayers, etc.—accept the results of assessment?
- *Time.* Demands on a teacher's time are daunting. How can we get useful information without taking too much valuable instructional time?
- *Influences on curriculum and teaching.* How can we deal with the pressure to "teach to the test," to alter what and how we teach in order to increase student performance on externally imposed assessments?
- *Teacher knowledge and training.* Will we have the requisite knowledge of assessment, the curriculum, and students? Will there be opportunities for

in-service training and reflection in order to design assessments and collect, analyze, and report results?

■ *Equity*. Will assessment fairly reflect the abilities of all our students, especially those from diverse linguistic, social, or cultural backgrounds? Do we promote fairness by asking all students to take the same test in the same circumstances, or do we provide students with alternatives so that each can show what he or she is capable of doing in optimal circumstances?

While reading the following discussion of tests and testing, you should keep in mind the limitations of testing. You might think of tests as being like snapshots: some may be flattering, and some may be downright dreadful. Your friends or family might like a photo you think makes you look goofy, whereas *you* might prefer one that makes you look sleek, athletic, or intellectual, even though others say it looks nothing like you. No photo, not even a portrait by a talented photographer, is the real you. It is at best an image of you at a particular time that, by skill or accident, may communicate something of your essence.

So it is with almost any instrument or procedure designed to evaluate or assess students. A student may do well or poorly on a particular test, but the test alone cannot tell definitely why the student performed that way or whether that is typical of the student's performance. It is at best a suggestion of what was going on inside the student's head at that particular moment. However, over a period of time, after experiencing the student's oral and written output, scores on tests and assignments, and participation (or lack of it) in classroom activities, you can form a composite judgment of how well he or she is doing in your subject and of his or her general aptitude as a student. The best decisions about students will be made after carefully considering many sources of information.

Cultural bias.   Teachers who work with students of diverse cultural backgrounds must especially be aware of the cultural biases that can influence tests and testing (Gronna, Chin-Chance, & Abedi, 2000). Tests (and the curricula they are designed to assess) are generally devised by members of the dominant culture and may be inadequate for evaluating the knowledge, achievement, and ability of students from other cultures. There are several sources of cultural bias in standardized tests (Garcia, 1991; Garcia & Pearson, 1994; Helms, 1992) and in more innovative forms of testing (Au, 1998); many of these biases apply to teacher-designed tests as well:

**EVIDENCE-
BASED
RESEARCH**

1. *Content and conceptual bias.* Test content is most likely to reflect the knowledge and values of mainstream society. Test content may be more or less familiar to members of different cultures, who may therefore assign different meanings to the same concept. Even though some concepts may have been covered by the instructor, other concepts that are unfamiliar may appear in the wording of test questions or multiple-choice responses. Standardized tests also predominantly emphasize isolated skills, literal-level facts, and low-level thinking.

2. *Linguistic bias.* Lack of familiarity with academic English, with specific vocabulary, or with familiar synonyms (e.g., *canine* for *dog*) may influence test scores for students whose primary language or dialect is not standard English. Time limits will be especially problematic for bilingual students. It is difficult to decide whether bilingual students are better off being tested in English or in their native language, and a test in either language may not demonstrate what a student knows in both languages.

3. *Functional bias.* The mainstream conventions of testing, where adults request known answers to questions that have no apparent functional goal, may be perceived as foolish or nonsensical to members of other cultures. Some cultures may also prize answers that are imaginative or elaborative as opposed to literally true. Many tests are not flexible enough to fully assess the capabilities of English language learners.

4. *Consequential bias.* Results of testing are often used as graduation requirements or to place students in remedial or lower-track classes. Unfortunately, students of color and low-income students are disproportionately impacted, and this is due in part to the biases inherent in test content and procedures. To compound this problem, students in remedial programs are subjected to further testing, most of which focuses on discrete skills and isolated, literal-level facts. This results in fragmented, skills-based instruction for these students.

We take the final point in our advisory from Georgia Garcia and David Pearson (1994), who remind us of the position of power we assume as teachers:

> Assessment is a political act. Assessments tell people how they should value themselves and others. They open doors for some and close them for others. The very act of giving an assessment is a demonstration of power: One individual tells the other what to read, how to respond, how much time to take. One insinuates a sense of greater power because of greater knowledge (i.e., possession of the correct answers). The political dilemma is a problem for all students, but it is particularly acute for students from diverse cultural, linguistic, and economic backgrounds whose cultures, languages, and identities have been at best ignored and at worst betrayed in the assessment process. (p. 381)

It is our responsibility to exercise our power ethically, carefully, and compassionately.

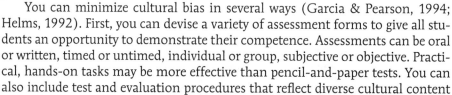

You can minimize cultural bias in several ways (Garcia & Pearson, 1994; Helms, 1992). First, you can devise a variety of assessment forms to give all students an opportunity to demonstrate their competence. Assessments can be oral or written, timed or untimed, individual or group, subjective or objective. Practical, hands-on tasks may be more effective than pencil-and-paper tests. You can also include test and evaluation procedures that reflect diverse cultural content and values. Finally, you can follow up on apparent "wrong" answers by asking students for elaborated explanations or justifications for their responses. These may reveal more about students' actual knowledge of a concept than the test results indicate.

To be useful in addressing the literacy needs of diverse students, assessment should include more than tests of academic achievement. Tatum (2005) says that comprehensive assessment must include a variety of "close-ups." Cognitive close-ups would include a student's strengths and weaknesses with words, with comprehension, and with metacognition. Pedagogical close-ups would show what kind of instruction the student was receiving, as well as whether the student found the curricula to be relevant and challenging. Psychological close-ups would consider a student's goals, self-efficacy, and emotional disposition toward school. Finally, physiological close-ups such as specific medical conditions and vision problems might require evaluation by experts other than the classroom teacher.

Types of Assessment

The professional lexicon describes several different kinds of student assessment. Some of the terms used are relatively new, and many of them seem to be used interchangeably or in such a way that their meaning is unclear or confusing. Consequently, we will give a brief definition and description of some of the more common types of assessment used in schools.

Standardized tests.   Standardized tests are commercially prepared tests used to assess the achievement of large numbers of students in reading, math, and other academic areas. They are designed so that their administration, scoring, and interpretation are uniform, or standard, across all settings. Many schools require that standardized tests be administered once or twice a year, and standardized test results are usually included in a student's cumulative school record.

Standardized tests are norm-referenced. This means that an individual's score on a test is compared with a large, demographically representative cross section of American students, called a norming population. Comparisons are made possible by converting raw test scores to derived scores such as percentiles or stanines, which indicate the position of an individual score relative to the scores of the norming population.

Standardized testing is a large and lucrative business. It is estimated that $1.8 billion was spent on commercial standardized tests in 2003 from prekindergarten through twelfth grade (Zeller, 2005). Middle school and high school students take tests of reading, math, and other content areas, as well as college placement tests such as the Scholastic Assessment Test (SAT). Recently, Educational Testing Service has announced a new test of technological literacy, The Information and Communications Technology Literacy Assessment (www.ets.org), designed to assess college students' ability to make critical evaluations of the vast amount of information available on the Internet. Such an assessment may find its way into high schools as increasing attention is paid to secondary students' digital media literacy as part of the accountability movement. Although ETS is understandably bullish on the possibilities of this new assessment, critics have questioned whether there is sufficient agreement on the nature of informational literacy skills, and whether such skills can be accurately measured (Zeller, 2005).

EVIDENCE-BASED RESEARCH

Standardized tests have been the target of considerable criticism. In a review of assessment policies, Valencia and Wixson (2000) conclude that "high-stakes standardized basic skills tests led to narrowing of the curriculum; overemphasis on basic skills and test-like instructional methods; reduction in effective instructional time and an increase in time for test preparation; inflated test scores; and pressure on teachers to improve test scores" (p. 915). Critics argue, among other things, that standardized tests actually assess a narrow and artificial set of reading abilities. The test scores, on the other hand, render those abilities into global categories of "comprehension" and "vocabulary" and a composite "total reading" score, none of which really indicates much about what a student actually can or cannot do. Critics also point out that a student's performance on standardized tests is influenced by nonreading factors such as prior knowledge, test-taking skill, physical and emotional status, and cultural background.

Standardized test results are probably not particularly useful to the content area teacher. They can give a preliminary estimate, or rough sorting, of students into "high, medium, and low ability" categories, but this estimate must be tempered by the understanding that an individual student's scores are not very precise. A difference of a few raw score points is not very significant, even though it may affect the derived percentile or stanine score. Schell (1988) points out that comprehension is very often text-specific: a reader may comprehend very differently in two texts at the same reading level. Therefore, a student who scores very high on a test of reading comprehension may still have considerable difficulty with a particular text or subject. Standardized tests are no substitute for informed teacher observation and judgment.

Standardized tests can be useful in helping teachers understand the overall status of student reading achievement, which can encourage teachers to invest in school-wide reform. In a report on the efforts of one high school to improve students' reading achievement, Brozo and Hargis (2003) explain how they began by sharing the results of standardized reading tests with the faculty. Nearly 35 percent of the students were reading one or more grade levels below their actual grade placement, and another 18 percent were reading one or more grade levels beyond expectations. Realization of this wide range of achievement spurred a commitment to initiatives designed to better meet the literacy needs of students.

Authentic assessment.   The term *authentic assessment* is used to describe a broad range of assessment tasks and data that are based on everyday situations

Dispelling Policy Myths

Dispelling a Myth

Many people believe that standardized tests are accurate indicators of an individual's ability. It is true that standardized tests are developed through rigorous application of psychometric principles, and that this does enhance their validity as measures across relatively large numbers of people. However, the statistical foundations of psychometrics are quite complex and not readily understood by laypersons. (The three of us are quick to admit that the statistics can be daunting!) The fact is that statistically speaking, there is a fairly wide error of measurement built into standardized test scores, which means that an individual reading test score actually represents the midpoint of a range of possible "true scores" of reading ability for that individual.

Policy Implications

A single standardized test should not be used to make high-stakes decisions about students. Guidelines for educational testing developed jointly by the American Educational Research Association, American Psychological Association, and National Council for Measurement in Education (1999) say that decisions about retention, tracking, or graduation should not be based on any single test, but should also take into consideration other relevant and valid information. When test results are used as a significant component in high-stakes decisions, the test should clearly address content and skills that students have had an opportunity to learn. Students who score low on such tests should be given multiple opportunities to demonstrate their mastery of the material. Special care should be taken to examine the consequences of high-stakes testing, especially for racial or ethnic minorities and students of lower socio-economic status. When students who lack proficiency with the English language are tested, results may well measure their language abilities rather than other skills or knowledge. Finally, not enough is known at present about how testing modifications may affect the scores of students with disabilities, and so scores for such students must be interpreted cautiously.

or realistic applications of content knowledge and concepts. Much of what students learn cannot be adequately assessed through multiple-choice or other objective test formats. Therefore, in order to demonstrate how well they can use what they have learned, students must engage in tasks that approximate real-world situations (Wiggins, 1998). Teacher observations, teacher–student conferences, student journals, portfolios, inquiry projects, exhibitions, hands-on activities, open-ended problem solving, essay questions, and performances are some means of authentic assessment. Although the term is used differently by many people, authentic assessments are usually teacher designed and closely related to the context of the actual teaching and learning that go on in the classroom. Teachers frequently include students as partners in the authentic assessment process.

Authentic assessment tasks are complex and challenging and frequently have several possible outcomes. Grading such tasks is also complex because several variables must often be evaluated. Both teachers and students should evaluate not just the end product but also the processes that are used to complete the task. Although authentic assessments are usually more work for students and teachers, they yield a better picture of student achievement and place a premium on application, not just rote learning.

EVIDENCE-BASED RESEARCH

In addition, authentic assessments have many potential advantages over traditional kinds of testing for students of diverse cultural backgrounds, especially for bilingual students (Garcia & Pearson, 1994). Authentic assessment is more amenable to adaptations that include cultural content and values of diverse students. When students are asked to use what they have learned in more realistic settings, they are better able to relate new learning to their own cultural-specific understandings. Bilingual students have the opportunity to show what they know in both languages and how both languages interact in the learning process. Teachers have much more flexibility in collecting and interpreting information on how students are learning and developing, and students are more likely to be judged in terms of their individual progress rather than according to externally imposed criteria.

At the same time, authentic assessment poses some potential difficulties. There is a question regarding who defines "authenticity" or what counts as "real" (Alvermann & Commeyras, 1998). When teachers define authentic tasks and the parameters for analyzing performance on those tasks, there is no guarantee that the assessment has relevance to the reality of students, or that the assessment will be free of cultural biases. Authentic assessment with culturally and linguistically diverse students requires a good deal of unbiased knowledge about student culture and language on the part of the teacher.

For example, an English teacher might work with students on descriptive writing. To decide what constitutes an "authentic" descriptive writing task for his students, the teacher would need to know not only something about their interests and experiences but also something about how writing is valued by the students, the purposes for which students use writing and language, and the linguistic and rhetorical conventions of students' vernacular. In evaluating students' written products, the teacher would also need to decide if dialect features in the writing should or could be considered separately from the persuasive power of the writing.

Both decisions—what counts as "authentic writing" and how dialect features can influence the effectiveness of the writing—might best be arrived at through discussion and negotiation with students. Therein lies what many consider to be the primary advantage of authentic assessments: student involvement. When assessment grows out of the everyday activities of the classroom, assessment becomes an integral component of instruction. Students can become active partners in determining what will be learned, how it will be learned, and how learning can best be demonstrated and evaluated.

We will expand on the potential advantages and disadvantages of authentic assessment later in this chapter when we discuss the use of student portfolios.

Performance assessment.   Performance assessment overlaps in many ways with authentic assessment, and some educators may use the terms interchangeably. The difference is that performance assessments are graded according to externally established criteria and students usually are expected to achieve some benchmark score as an index of competency in the area being tested. Performance assessments of writing, for instance, have been commonplace for more than 20 years. In a typical writing competency test, students are given one or more actual writing tasks and their written products are then given a holistic "pass/fail" by trained raters.

Performance assessments are designed to simulate real-world tasks, and they require the active participation of students in the creation of an answer or product that shows application of the student's knowledge and understanding. Performance assessment and authentic assessment may be based on the same techniques, including projects, essays, problem solving, experiments, demonstrations, or portfolios. However, performance assessments involve some sort of benchmarks or criteria for judging student performance, often called *rubrics*. Although a teacher may develop a rubric for evaluating or assigning grades to authentic assessment data such as portfolios, rubrics for evaluating performance assessments are designed to allow for comparisons across classrooms or even across schools or districts. The development and dissemination of rubrics make assessment public; all stakeholders, including parents, teachers, and students, have access to the criteria for successful performance.

In order to achieve comparability and fairness across different settings, those who rate performance assessments must undergo systematic training. For example, if a group of science teachers were selected to score the results of districtwide performance assessments, they would likely receive in-service training in which they would learn about the standards or rubrics, study benchmark responses illustrating various levels of achievement, and practice scoring sample responses.

The use of performance assessment to judge the performance of students, teachers, or programs has some advantages over traditional standardized testing and multiple-choice exams. Performance assessments are by their very nature more closely tied to what actually happens in the classroom. When the criteria for success can be clearly stated up front, both teachers and students have a better idea of what they are doing and why, and learning may take on more relevance (Hoffman, Paris, Salas, Patterson, & Assaf, 2003). Instruction is likely to focus more on practical application and less on rote learning of isolated skills and information. Performance assessments also have many of the advantages of authentic assessment for students of diverse backgrounds. Performance assessments allow for more teacher scaffolding, more freedom to work in a variety of settings and without time constraints, and more acceptance of diverse responses than do traditional tests.

On the other hand, many questions about the utility of performance assessment remain unanswered. Technical problems of validity and reliability must be resolved (Valencia & Wixson, 2000). If teachers provide assistance with performance tasks and students work in groups, there is a question of how much an assessment can tell us about the performance of individual students (Gearhart & Herman, 1995). There is always the possibility that results will be inflated if teachers "teach to the test." As with authentic assessment, there is also the question of who decides what counts as "real" and what constitutes mastery. Finally, performance assessments represent a significant increase in time and cost over traditional multiple-choice assessments.

National assessments.   National assessment of students has been a reality since 1971. The National Assessment of Educational Progress (NAEP) is a congressionally mandated program that has sampled the reading and writing abilities of 9-, 13-, and 17-year-old students since then. Adolescents' reading achievement has generally remained steady (National Center for Education Statistics, 2005). Achievement levels for 17-year-olds improved during the 1980s and early 1990s, but began to decline in the mid-1990s; the 2004 level was the same as 1971. For 13-year-olds, the picture is a little better. With slow but steady increases, the 2004 level is significantly higher than in 1971. Ninety-four percent of 13-year-olds and 80 percent of 17-year-olds were reading at a level that would allow them to locate and identify facts from simple stories or news articles and make inferences on short, uncomplicated passages. However, only 61 percent of 13-year-olds and 38 percent of 17-year-olds were reading at a level that would allow them to understand complicated information, suggesting that too many adolescents are insufficiently prepared to meet the literacy demands of the twenty-first century.

Writing was also assessed by NAEP in 2002 (Persky, Daane, & Jin, 2003). Students in the fourth, eighth, and twelfth grades completed three types of writing tasks: informative, persuasive, and narrative. Fifteen percent of eighth graders and 26 percent of twelfth graders scored below the "basic" level, and only about one-fourth of the students at these grade levels scored at the "proficient" level or above. There was also a large gender gap favoring girls in the writing assessment.

State assessments.   Many states have tried to develop more authentic types of assessments, especially of literacy. Statewide performance assessments of reading and writing "include longer and more complex reading selections from a variety of genres, higher-level comprehension questions, extended written responses, and cross-text analyses" (Valencia & Wixson, 2000, p. 917).

This movement toward establishing and assessing higher standards appears to be driven by two related assumptions. One is that raising the bar for high school graduation can accomplish systemic reform of teaching and learning at the classroom level (Valencia & Wixson, 2000). The second argument is economic: ensuring higher levels of achievement will prepare students for productive roles in the labor force (Levin, 1998). The validity of these arguments has been questioned, however. Levin suggests that although education does indeed affect economic outcomes, the specific aspects of education that make a difference are not clear. Indeed, he counters that

> [Y]ears of education provide a much better prediction of earning and occupational success than any specific attribute of education such as test scores. . . . It is generic skills with face validity that are likely to be more valuable and that can be molded through training and job experience to the specific needs of different jobs, different workplaces, and different times as technology, products, and services change over the lifetime of the worker. (p. 7)

There is also reason to question whether higher standards and more rigorous assessments have the desired effects on teaching and learning (Hamilton, 2003; Hoffman et al., 2003). Standards and tests alone cannot influence what happens in the classroom unless teachers are given sufficient professional development opportunities to implement meaningful changes and sufficient time to assess students' progress. For example, John McVay, a middle school math teacher in a suburb of New York City, estimates that if he were to do a culminating performance assessment at the end of six math units during the year and spend 15 minutes on each of his 187 students' work, he would need about 35 eight-hour student-free workdays (or 18 weekends) (Focused Reporting Project, 1999). High-stakes performance assessments are relatively intrusive, inefficient, costly, time-consuming, and difficult to administer (Madaus & O'Dwyer, 1999) and are subject to persistent questions about their reliability and validity (French, 2003; Pearson, 1998; Valencia & Wixson, 2000). There are also serious concerns that high-stakes performance assessments may further disadvantage ELLs and other students of diverse backgrounds (Au, 1998; Madaus & O'Dwyer, 1999). High-stakes tests are also likely to increase drop-out rates, and this has a disproportionate effect on African American and Latino/a students (French, 2003).

EVIDENCE-BASED RESEARCH

In their review of the research on standards and assessment policy, Valencia and Wixson (2000) summarize the issue of systemic reform:

> [I]t is clear that literacy standards and assessment do have an influence on teachers' beliefs and practice, but the influence is not always in the expected or desired direction. The effect is mediated by a large number of factors such as teachers' knowledge, beliefs, and existing practices; the economic, social, philosophical, and political conditions of the school or district; the stakes attached to the policy; and the quality of the support and lines of communication provided to teachers and administrators. It is equally clear that policy by itself is not sufficient to promote desired change; simply implementing new assessments or creating new standards does not insure improved teaching or learning. (p. 930)

Kentucky provides one example of the potential, both positive and negative, when states implement high-stakes testing. As part of a comprehensive school reform and assessment program beginning in 1991, the state required that all eighth graders and high school seniors complete a portfolio of writing across the curriculum. Senior portfolios consist of a personal experience piece, a sample of creative writing, and two pieces designed to communicate with a wider audience. At least two of the pieces must be from a content area other than English. Using well-designed criteria and benchmark examples, portfolios are scored by trained teachers. Schools face significant sanctions for low overall performance, but no minimum score is required of individual students.

Many schools found that their students initially did not do as well as expected, and this led to intensive conversations about student writing and learning (Berryman & Russell, 2001; Scott, 2005). In some schools, teachers from content areas other than English were enlisted in the scoring of portfolios. This resulted in a clearer understanding of writing instruction and assignments across the curriculum, which in turn led to changes in instruction as teachers from all disciplines attempted to align what they did more closely to the state guidelines for effective writing. Students, too, internalized the guidelines and referred to them as they wrote and revised the pieces for their portfolios. Seniors came to the portfolio tasks with several years of enculturation to the standards.

EVIDENCE-BASED RESEARCH

Scott (2005) found that while some more traditional teachers resisted buying in to the new assessment system and writing reforms, more progressive teachers felt that it was positive in that it held everyone to a single clear and reasonable standard and helped them to reflect on and improve their pedagogy. On the other hand, Scott was troubled by the way in which the portfolio work dominated class activities and limited the agency of teachers and students. While the portfolios were supposed to increase the authenticity and student "ownership" of writing, many students felt they were producing work primarily for the system and expressed frustration with the process. Scott concludes that although the performance assessments have helped teachers develop a more sophisticated and uniform understanding of writing pedagogy, it has been at the cost of the kinds of "local innovation and freedom of inquiry that many of us believe must characterize high-quality education" (p. 58).

STANDARDS

Regardless of the arguments over standards and assessment policy, the reality is that statewide assessments do pose both challenges and opportunities for teachers. One persistent issue is whether or not to "teach to the test." For example, New York State has implemented new standards and assessments for all content areas. As of 2004, all New York State students will need to pass five statewide high school Regents exams, and students are being assessed in elementary and middle school to determine whether they are on track to meet the rigorous new requirements. The new standards as well as the tasks in all these exams are challenging and imply a constructivist curriculum that emphasizes "knowing how" as well as "knowing what."

In an effort to prepare teachers and students for these new requirements, districts throughout New York have invested heavily in staff development. In many cases, school districts or individual teachers have made up parallel assessment tasks that mirror the state exams, and students have been given (sometimes extensive) practice. Practicing for the state exam is not by itself necessarily a bad thing, especially if teachers carefully deconstruct the tasks by explaining what is expected and giving guidance on how to accomplish it. However, we caution that time spent on extensive practice in test taking might be better spent by involving students in more authentic and meaningful experiences with reading and writing, mathematical problem solving, examination of primary sources, laboratory activities, and research; in fact, many districts and individual teachers have used the implementation of the new standards to do just that. Rather than focusing solely on devising, administering, and scoring practice tests, they have worked on ways to change curriculum and instruction to align more closely with the new standards.

Perhaps the most pertinent finding on "teaching to the test" comes from Langer's (2001) study of schools and teachers who "beat the odds" by having their students achieve relatively strong performance on high-stakes assessment. One key factor was that "beating the odds" teachers prepared students for high-stakes testing by carefully aligning curriculum and assessment. They were aware of what students would be asked to do and integrated those kinds of tasks, along with instruction on how to perform them, into ongoing instruction. On the other hand, teachers whose students achieved more typical results were more likely to allocate specific blocks of time to test preparation, usually involving practice and test-taking hints, separate from other kinds of instruction. In other words, the best "teaching to the test" was thoughtful teaching of needed knowledge and skills embedded in the curriculum throughout the year.

Learning about Students

In order to plan effective instruction, we need to learn as much as we can about students' norms, values, traditions, language, and beliefs as well as their reading, writing, and study skills. All these factors may affect their performance in a content area classroom. The following sections consider practical ways of assessing these variables.

Interest and attitude inventories.   Many teachers find it helpful to find out what students think about a content area or a specific topic. Knowing that several students like science fiction will help an English teacher plan the reading selections for the whole class or decide to include science fiction as a topic for small-group book talks. On the other hand, if significant numbers claim a distaste for poetry, the teacher knows that introductory poetry selections will have to be chosen carefully and that it will be necessary to do a little sales promotion on behalf of the genre. An interest, or attitude, inventory can be given at the beginning of the year or at the introduction of a new unit. A sample inventory for high school English is shown in Figure 5.1.

Struggling Readers and State Assessments

High-stakes testing can be especially problematic for struggling readers. For them, the pressure of passing a state-mandated test can result in an excess of skill-and-drill instruction. Such was the case for Kathy Bussert-Webb (1999, 2000), who describes her experiences as the teacher of ninth-grade remedial reading in a south Texas high school in which 98 percent of the student body were Mexican American, mostly native speakers of Spanish. Because the school had a poor pass rate on the Texas Achievement of Academic Skills assessment (TAAS), a high school graduation requirement, the school administration began to focus on intense, structured teaching of the skills covered on the test. For Bussert-Webb and her students, this meant a lot of reading of short passages and answering multiple-choice questions.

After becoming increasingly dissatisfied with this approach, Bussert-Webb abandoned it and did what her instincts and training led her to believe was best for her students. She focused instead on making personal connections with students, increasing their connections with reading, and having more class discussions instead of covering the curriculum. Students began reading things they cared about, such as low-rider truck magazines, young adult novels, and stories by Latino/a authors. As a result, she found her students had fewer discipline problems and off-task behaviors. Most important, they did more reading—50 percent more than her previous students—and enjoyed it. Her students had the most library points of any class in the school.

What about the TAAS? Overall, the pass rate for sophomores at the school improved dramatically, from a 59 percent pass rate in 1995 to 82 percent in 1999. All but three of Bussert-Webb's struggling readers passed, a success rate of 88 percent. The three who did not pass just missed the passing score of 70 percent, with scores of 69, 67, and 65 percent, compared to a mean score of 59 percent for the other students at the school who failed. Although it would be a mistake to read too much into these data, it is clear that Bussert-Webb's student-centered, holistic curriculum did not negatively affect her students.

A content area learning log or journal is another good source of information about students' attitudes and interests or their backgrounds. Teachers can ask students to jot down "what I liked best this week," "something I'd like to know more about," or "what I thought was hardest this week." By periodically reviewing students' log entries the teacher can get helpful feedback on what students are thinking, learning, and feeling.

Effective teaching starts with what students already know and leads them to new understandings. Therefore, it is helpful to know not only what students feel about a topic but also what they know about it. Some of this may come out in an interest inventory or in class discussions. There are also many instructional strategies that begin with what students already know or believe. You will find several such strategies discussed in later chapters, especially Chapter 6.

INVENTORY OF ATTITUDES AND INTERESTS

1. **Rate each item from 1 (least) to 5 (most). I like to read:**

   _____ Science fiction   _____ Plays

   _____ Poetry   _____ Short stories

   _____ Fantasy   _____ Biographies

   _____ Romance   _____ Adventure

   _____ Novels   _____ History

   _____ Sports   _____ Current events

   _____ War stories   _____ Mysteries

   _____ Other: _____

2. **Rate each item from 1 (least) to 5 (most). I like to write:**

   _____ Letters to friends   _____ My opinions

   _____ In a diary/journal   _____ Poems

   _____ Short stories   _____ Humorous stories

   _____ Plays, scripts   _____ Nonfiction

   _____ Other: _____

3. **Rate each item from 1 (hardest) to 5 (easiest). When I write, this is what I find hard and easy about it:**

   _____ Getting started   _____ Changing what I have written

   _____ Finding ideas to write about   _____ Letting someone else read my writing

   _____ Organizing my ideas   _____ Proofreading

   _____ Putting the words on paper

Rate the next items using this scale:

1 = Strongly disagree

2 = Disagree

3 = Not sure

4 = Agree

5 = Strongly agree

   _____ 4. I am a good writer.
            Why do you say this?

   _____ 5. I am a good reader.
            Why do you say this?

   _____ 6. I have a good vocabulary.

   _____ 7. I am good at spelling.

   _____ 8. English is difficult for me.

   _____ 9. English is a useful subject.

   _____ 10. I think English is interesting.

FIGURE 5.1   Attitude/interest inventory for high school English students

Cloze passages.   Cloze passages (Bormuth, 1968; Taylor, 1953) can be used to estimate how well students will fare with a particular text. The cloze procedure is based on the idea that humans instinctively try to bring about closure to unfinished or incomplete patterns. A cloze passage is constructed by deleting words from a text passage. Readers' success with filling in the blanks suggests their relative potential for comprehending that reading material.

The passage should be reasonably complete and coherent on its own. The length of the passage will depend on the number of words to be deleted. Although many authorities recommend that approximately 50 words be deleted, we have found this to be frustrating for many students, especially younger students and struggling readers. Because scores are ultimately converted to percentages, we have found deletion of 25, 33, or 50 words to be most convenient, as each item is then worth either four, three, or two points. Many teachers include a practice passage with five to ten items, which they use to model the cloze procedure.

Figure 5.2 presents a short cloze passage from a middle school science text. Try filling in the blanks yourself. (The deleted words are listed below the figure. Cover them while completing the passage.)

ORES

Minerals from which metals and nonmetals can be removed in usable amounts are called ores. Metals are elements that ___(1)___ certain special properties. Metals ___(2)___ shiny surfaces and are ___(3)___ to conduct electricity and ___(4)___ . Metals also have the ___(5)___ of malleability. Malleability is ___(6)___ ability of a metal ___(7)___ be hammered into thin ___(8)___ without breaking. Another property ___(9)___ metals is ductility. Ductility ___(10)___ the ability of a ___(11)___ to be pulled into ___(12)___ strands without breaking. Iron, ___(13)___ , aluminum, copper, silver, and ___(14)___ are metals. Most metals ___(15)___ found combined with other substances, or impurities, in ores. After the ores are removed from the earth by mining, the metals must be removed from the ores.

Deleted Words

1. have	6. the	11. substance
2. have	7. to	12. thin
3. able	8. sheets	13. lead
4. heat	9. of	14. gold
5. property	10. is	15. are

FIGURE 5.2   **Sample cloze passage** (*Source:* Passage taken from Charles Coble et al., *Earth Science*, p. 159. Englewood Cliffs, NJ: Prentice Hall, 1993.)

The following are instructions for constructing, administering, scoring, and interpreting a cloze passage:

1. Construction
   a. Select a passage. Copy it on a word processor with no typographical errors.
   b. Delete a word at random from the second sentence of the passage. (The first and last sentences should be left intact to give additional context to the beginning and end of the passage.) Beginning with the first deletion, every fifth word is deleted until the desired number of words have been left out. To make the task somewhat easier, delete every sixth or seventh word. It is important, however, that a specific interval be selected and maintained throughout the passage. In no circumstances should words be avoided because they seem too hard or too easy.
   c. Leave a blank space for each deleted word. All blanks should be of equal length so as not to give any clues about word length.
2. Administration
   a. Give students a copy of the cloze passage and instruct them to read through it before they do anything else.
   b. Instruct students to go back and fill in the blanks with words that they think make sense. They should be encouraged to make a guess at each blank. There should be no time limit for completing the passage.
3. Scoring
   a. Count only words that are exact replacements for (or intelligibly spelled facsimiles of) the deleted words.
   b. Figure the percentage of exact replacements. For instance, if you have left 25 blanks, each is worth four points. A student who gets 14 exact replacements scores 56 percent ($4 \times 14 = 56$).
4. Interpretation
   a. A score above 60 percent suggests that the text material is at a student's *independent level*. That is, the student should be able to read that material on his or her own with excellent understanding.
   b. A score between 40 and 60 percent suggests that the material is at the student's *instructional level*. The material would be challenging, but with appropriate help from the teacher it would be useful.
   c. A score below 40 percent suggests that the material is at the student's *frustration level*. It may be too difficult for that student.

Teachers who are used to encouraging good guesses and giving students the benefit of the doubt often feel it is unduly stringent not to count good synonyms when scoring a cloze passage. However, what constitutes a "good synonym"? Take the sentence "John got in his _____ and drove downtown," from which the word *truck* is deleted. If a student wrote *van* in the blank, a reasonable person might count that as a synonym. However, what about *car* or

Chevy or *Trans Am?* Some teachers would accept those; they are vehicles. How about *suit?* That is not a vehicle, but it fits the sentence. The point is that teachers will vary in what they will accept as a synonym, and that variance will affect the reliability of assessments using cloze passages. If only exact replacements are counted, the task is simpler and more objective.

Instead of penalizing readers for good guesses, the suggested scoring criteria for a cloze passage account for the many synonyms that good readers are likely to use. Although a score of 65 percent would be barely passing on most exams, it is an excellent score on a cloze passage.

A teacher may avoid emphasis on "right" or "wrong" answers by letting students score their own papers. When all students have completed the passage, the teacher shows them the list of deleted words. They can write the words above their "inexact" guesses. This gives students immediate feedback on their efforts and allows for a discussion of why some words did or did not fit the context. The teacher should make it clear that many of the students' guesses would make sense in the passage, even though they are not the words used by the author. That is, good synonyms are not wrong.

We need to emphasize that cloze results are only estimates and must be interpreted with caution, especially for individual students. When a class or several classes of students are sampled, however, cloze passages give practical insight into the question "How will these students do with this reading material?"

Informal content text inventories.   Teachers can also use textbook passages to devise short, informal assessments. At the beginning of the school year, students can be asked to read a two- or three-page selection from the text, followed by questions that emphasize vocabulary, comprehension at various levels, and the ability to interpret graphs and visual aids. (Chapter 7 discusses in detail the art of designing good comprehension questions.) Sharon Walpole (1998/1999) suggests asking students to write a summary of what they have read to determine which ideas they select and how they organize them. She also interviews students to assess their understanding of the structures and features of textbooks. In her interviews, she poses three general questions:

- What is that? (With reference to a particular textbook feature, such as section titles, emphasized words, glossary, or end-of-chapter activities)
- Why did the author put it there?
- How could you use it?

The results from such informal assessments can reveal a good deal about students' capabilities as readers.

Much can also be learned by privately having a student read a short passage aloud and then retell what was understood. Although multiple class sections with large numbers of students may make this impractical for many teachers, it can be especially useful with struggling readers who have learned many strategies to mask their difficulties with the printed page.

Technology Tips

▮▮

The following Web sites feature additional information on various aspects of assessment, as noted.

NAEP Reading & Writing reports:
http://nces.ed.gov/nationsreportcard/reading/
http://nces.ed.gov/nationsreportcard/writing/

Center for Research on Evaluation, Standards, and Student Testing
http://www.cse.ucla.edu/index6.htm

Funded by U.S. Department of Education; part of UCLA Center for Study of Evaluation; features many research studies on assessment- and standards-related topics.

Learning for the 21st Century
http://www.medialit.org/reading_room/article580.html
Use 21st-century assessments that measure 21st-century skills.

Grades and Grading

Giving grades to students is an almost universal reality for teachers and is almost universally ignored in reading methods textbooks. This neglect may be due in part to reluctance to confront one of the primary contradictions in the teacher's role—the conflict between maintaining standards and respecting individual students. Thomas (1986) illustrates this contradiction in his discussion of the use of the grade F. He suggests that the two extremes might be stated as follows:

> Students should get an F regardless of effort if they do not meet minimum standards for the subject.
> Students should not get an F if they have made their best effort in the subject.

This dilemma applies to all of a teacher's decisions about assigning grades to students. Should the bright student who rarely cracks a book get the same grade as the average student who diligently spends hours on assignments? Should spelling and grammar "count" toward the grade on a history project, and if so, how much? What should end-of-term grades be based on? How much should homework count? What about class participation? Should grades be used as weapons to discourage unwanted behavior?

The traditional system of giving letter grades has many significant drawbacks (Willis, 1993). First, a single letter grade gives no hint of what a student can actually do or not do, or what an individual's strengths or weaknesses might be. When letter grades are stringently applied, only a few students do well (i.e., receive an A), and less able students are demoralized by constant negative reinforcement. On the other hand, if most students receive A's and B's, the underlying meaning of grades as indices of ability becomes even less clear.

Finally, letter grades may actually undermine some teaching strategies such as cooperative learning or writer's workshop, in which the emphases are less on product and more on process, less on individual accomplishment and more on achievement of the group, shared learning, and confidence building.

EVIDENCE-BASED RESEARCH

Despite calls for more student-centered teaching and alternative means of assessment, determining grades in high schools continues to follow largely traditional and narrow formulas. A study of the grading preferences of 91 high school science teachers determined that traditional labs, quizzes, and tests were by far the most frequently used determinants of grades (Feldman, Alibrandi, & Kropf, 1998). The teachers reported that they rarely used portfolios or journals, two forms of authentic assessment frequently recommended by reformers. Another study of high school grading practices (Stiggins, Frisbie, & Griswold, 1989) also found that grading was variable, subjective, and often at odds with the recommendations of researchers and methods textbook authors.

The dilemma of grading is especially sharp for those who work with students outside the middle-class academic mainstream. Students from diverse ethnic or cultural backgrounds, students with limited proficiency in standard English, and students with identified learning problems often find themselves in an academic game with long odds; their chances for success seem to be diminished by the very system that is supposed to bring them into the mainstream (Oakes, 1986). The national drop-out rate among African American and Hispanic students is a depressing indication that too many youth give up in the face of repeated failure (Hoffman et al., 2003).

Objectivity or teacher judgment?   Even though a teacher tries to design an objective grading system, it is impossible to avoid using judgment in arriving at grades. Take, for example, multiple-choice tests, which are often referred to as "objective tests" because they supposedly have clear-cut right and wrong answers and teacher judgment does not enter into the scoring—students either know the material and answer correctly or they do not. However, anyone who has ever made up a multiple-choice test knows how difficult it is to write good, unambiguous questions that reflect important content and that have answers that are clearly "right." In selecting what will be tested and how test items will be worded, a teacher is making subjective decisions. Still other subjective decisions must be made if students challenge some questions because they were too hard or because more than one answer might be right. Teachers cannot escape professional subjectivity.

Schools or districts often adopt uniform grading systems (e.g., 90–100 = A and 80–89 = B) in an attempt to attain objectivity across classes and grade levels. However, individual teachers must still decide what will be evaluated, how much each such activity will be worth, and how a final grade on the 0–100 scale will be computed. It is a well-known fact that within every school that uses such a system, some teachers are known as "hard" markers and others "easy." This creates "a situation in which grades given by one teacher might mean something entirely different from grades given by another teacher" (Marzano & Kendall, 1996, p. 10).

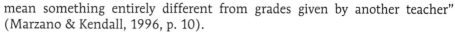

It is no wonder, then, that students are often confused about grades. Many students do not know how grades are determined or why they got a particular grade. Low achievers especially tend to attribute poor grades to external factors, to things beyond their control (Evans & Engelberg, 1985).

Every teacher comes to terms with the dilemmas of grading in his or her own way; it would be foolish and presumptuous of us to suggest that any uniform approach would be possible or desirable. However, the following subsections suggest some strategies that might help you avoid some of the pitfalls of assigning grades to students.

Tough but fair.   "Old Smitty's tough but fair. She makes you work hard, but you learn a lot in her class." We have always admired teachers with reputations like that, for whom grades are not just final marks on a report card but more indicative of a process of teaching, learning, assessing, and communicating. Barbara Walvoord and Virginia Anderson (1998) describe the power of grades to influence learning. For them, grading is only one element in the overall planning process:

> Grading . . . includes tailoring the test or assignment to the learning goals of the course, establishing criteria and standards, helping students acquire learning over time, shaping student motivation, feeding back results so students can learn from their mistakes, communicating about students' learning to the students and to other audiences, and using results to plan future teaching methods. When we talk about grading, we have student learning most in mind. (p. 1)

(*Source*: © Batom, Inc. Reprinted with special permission of North American Syndicate.)

We suggest five guidelines that will help you develop a "tough but fair" grading system:

- Select assignments, tests, or projects that reflect and measure what you value most as a teacher. For example, a math teacher who was interested in *how* his students solved problems might ask students to provide a written explanation of what they did and why as well as the answers to problems (Walvoord & Anderson, 1998).
- Provide a variety of opportunities to earn credit. Diverse students have diverse ways of learning and showing what they have learned. Figure 5.3 lists some possible credit-bearing activities that involve some combination of language and literacy ability. You might also consider extra-credit activities or revisions so that students can make up for less-than-optimal performances.
- Be clear about your grading system and standards. Begin a new year by describing clearly what must be done for credit, how different activities will be weighted, and what must be done to earn a grade of A, B, C, and so forth.
- Be clear about how you will assess specific assignments and tests. Many teachers develop *rubrics*, itemized lists of criteria that are distributed when an assignment is made and filled out and returned when the assignment is graded.
- Collaborate with students to set and achieve goals and to deconstruct the language of both official and teacher-devised standards. In Chapter 1, we suggested that students should play an active part in setting goals and evaluating their progress. This is especially important when working with culturally diverse students, who may not be familiar with the nuances of school discourse

Peer conferences	Creating a display, poster, graph, etc.
Teacher conferences	Math word problems
Participation in group work	Photographs
Writing in journal or log	Audio or video recordings
Responding to another student's journal or log	Vocabulary puzzles, analogies
Attending selected out-of-school events	Self-selected vocabulary list
Reporting to class	Writing, performing, or producing a dramatic piece
Panel presentation	Sharing a book or poem with classmates
Debate	Self-evaluation
Hosting a guest speaker	Extra reading
Demonstrating an experiment or process	Book review, oral or written

FIGURE 5.3   Opportunities to earn course credit

EVIDENCE-BASED RESEARCH

and who may feel that academic tasks are arbitrarily assigned and evaluated. In a collaborative study of how portfolios could be used as part of the grading process (Sarroub et al., 1997), university researchers and eighth-grade teachers found that students were particularly interested in decoding the "secret world of assessment," recrafting the official standards into language they could understand, and generating their own standards for assessment.

Grading systems. A social studies class of bilingual seventh-graders collaborated in setting up a grading system for a four-week unit on the theme "How does where you live influence how you live?" (Freeman & Freeman, 1989). Credit for activities and class participation was negotiated at the beginning of the unit. Among other things, students received credit for their participation in brainstorming and research, for completing the various components of the project, for their oral and written reports, and for how well they listened to others. More credit could be earned for unusual or creative work. Also, the possibility existed for making up lost credit or redoing unsatisfactory work. The teachers tried to direct students' focus toward the content of the unit and the research processes rather than to grades. The system was negotiated at the beginning of the unit and referred to infrequently while students were working on the topic.

Contracting is another grading system that involves some collaboration and negotiation with students. Teachers spell out criteria for different grades or negotiate with individual students what they hope to earn and what work they will complete. Students "contract" to complete the requirements for an A, a B, and so on. Although contracting is more time-consuming for teachers, it can have the effect of making students feel more responsible for fulfilling their contracts.

Grant Wiggins (1998), a recognized assessment authority and researcher, argues that single-letter grades at the end of a marking period provide little useful feedback for students or other stakeholders. Instead, he urges the adoption of multidimensional grading systems that would report subscores for various categories of accomplishment. Specifically, Wiggins proposes that students should be given both grades and performance indicators. Grades would be an index of expectations for an individual student—his or her ability, effort, and what Wiggins calls "habits of mind and work." Thus, struggling readers might achieve good grades for a subject, even though they do not do as well as many of their peers. However, performance indicators would measure a student's progress against grade level or exit criteria. Performance indicators would give an idea of how well a student had progressed relative to standards for a particular subject and grade level. Such a system obviously would be more complex and time-consuming than single-letter grade systems and would likely have to be adopted by an entire school or district rather than by an individual teacher.

Rubrics. Rubrics help students to know "what the teacher is looking for," make grading a large number of assignments easier for the teacher, and make

Technology Tips on Rubrics

To view an assessment rubric created by Jesse, a preservice teacher enrolled in Josephine Young's content literacy course at Arizona State University, visit www.geocities.com/jesse002/iceageintro.html. Jesse's rubric was part of a WebQuest on the Ice Age that he created for use with younger students. It includes criteria and a group evaluation and closure activity.

Alternatively, to learn how to use RubiStar, a free on-line tool for creating rubrics, visit http://rubistar.4teachers.org/index.php. Here you will see rubrics in the context of a lesson, and you will be able to view, edit, and print existing rubrics as a way of customizing them for your own content area classroom.

grading more uniform. There is no set format for developing rubrics (Wiggins, 1998). They may be holistic, giving a single descriptor for a whole performance, or they may be trait analytic, with multiple descriptors for various dimensions of a performance. Rubrics can be generic, as when an English teacher uses the same rubric for evaluating all student writing, or they may be event specific, as in the case of a rubric designed for a single project.

Usually, rubrics feature a scale of possible points to be earned, the dimensions of the task, and the criteria that must be met. An example of a rubric for Gene Kulbago and Mary Marcinkowski's earth science research project (described in Chapter 4) is given in Figure 5.4. In this case, the dimensions of the task include organization, information, and adherence to MLA and standard language conventions. The points and criteria for each dimension are also indicated.

STANDARDS

When Donna develops a rubric for her content reading and literacy course at the University of Georgia, she typically involves her students in creating criteria for the rubric. Working collaboratively with students to brainstorm ideas for a rubric does not preclude a teacher from putting forth her or his own criteria. In fact, some teachers whom Donna has observed at the middle and high school levels involve their students in brainstorming criteria that take into account their state's content standards (see Appendix E). In such cases, teachers will frequently ask their students to put the language of the standards in their own words and then devise criteria for a rubric that will take those standards into account. When this kind of student involvement and "buy-in" is achieved, the task of completing a rubric and grading student work based on it becomes much easier for the teacher. Brainstorming criteria with students that can be used in developing a rubric will result in many ideas that then need to be categorized. Categories may need to be collapsed until a manageable number of items appear in the final rubric.

Content area quizzes and tests.   Probably the most frequently used means of evaluating middle-grade and secondary school students are tests made up by

Student Name _____

Date _____

Title of Paper _____

	Concern	Possible Points	Points Earned
Organization	Paper contains an Introductory Statement which clearly defines the hypothesis.	5	
	Information is organized in such a way to make it understandable to the audience.	10	
	Paper contains a concluding statement which evaluates the hypothesis based upon information (data) discovered during research.	10	
Information	Student used a variety of informational sources, including both electronic and published (written) sources.	10	
	Student has selected appropriate sources and has evaluated them for credibility.	5	
	Student has included sufficient information in the report necessary to make a valid conclusion.	20	
MLA and Language Conventions	Paper contains a proper title page.	5	
	Paper contains a bibliography which follows the MLA style.	10	
	Paper demonstrates proper use of parenthetical documentation.	10	
	Paper demonstrates proper use of language conventions: spelling, capital letters, paragraphing, gramatical usage, etc.	10	
	Paper is reasonably neat and demontrates effort on the part of the writer.	5	
Comments			Final Score

FIGURE 5.4   Rubric for earth science research report (*Source:* Gene Kulbago, Niagara Middle School, Niagara Falls, New York.)

_____ 1. Students are likely to have the experiences and prior knowledge necessary to understand what the question calls for.

_____ 2. The vocabulary is appropriate for the intended grade level.

_____ 3. The sentence complexity is appropriate for the intended grade level.

_____ 4. Definitions and examples are clear and understandable.

_____ 5. The required reasoning skills are appropriate for the students' cognitive level.

_____ 6. Relationships are made clear through precise, logical connectives.

_____ 7. Content within items is clearly organized.

_____ 8. Graphs, illustrations, and other graphic aids facilitate comprehension.

_____ 9. The questions are clearly framed.

_____ 10. The content of the items is of interest to the intended audience.

FIGURE 5.5   Checklist for evaluating test item readability (*Source:* S. Rakow & T. Gee, "Test science, not reading," *The Science Teacher, 54,* 28–31, February 1987. Used with permission from NSTA Publications, National Science Teachers Association, 1742 Connecticut Ave., NW, Washington, DC 20009.)

teachers or provided by textbook publishers. Any test—true/false, multiple choice, short answer, or essay—must be readable in order for students to be able to respond to it. This may seem a simple requirement, but it is often overlooked. The result is that some students perform poorly not because they did not know the material but because they misunderstood the questions. Rakow and Gee (1987) devised a checklist for test items, which may be used to minimize student confusion (Figure 5.5).

It is difficult to write "foolproof" test items. In fact, the constraints of so-called objective test items frequently penalize students who are divergent thinkers or are good at inference and interpretation; they see subtleties where others see only right or wrong. Therefore, teachers sometimes use a *quiz qualifier*—simply space at the end of an objective test where students can qualify their answers. If a student feels that the answer to question number 23 could be either a or c, he or she explains why in the quiz qualifier. If the student gets the answer wrong, the teacher reads the qualification, and if it is convincing, the student gets credit for number 23.

It is also reasonable for a teacher to give students help in preparing for tests. Teachers should make it clear what will be tested and what the test will look like. Often, teachers give students practice tests or test items, especially when students are faced with departmentalized, district, or state exams. This is sometimes criticized as "teaching the test." Although such preparation should not take an inordinate amount of time away from actual content-based instruction, guided practice in test taking shows students what to expect, allows them to make a trial run and critique their results, and can result in improved performance.

Portfolio Assessment

Some time ago, Barney, an out-of-town friend and professional photographer, came to visit and brought his portfolio. In fact, Barney brought three portfolios. One was his professional portfolio, which included photos of buildings, food, manufactured products, and people. There were color prints, transparencies, and samples of actual brochures, magazines, and books that he had illustrated. It gave an impressive overview of his best work and his capability as a commercial photographer. The second portfolio was a selection of black-and-white landscapes and portraits and a series of photographs of a model, which had evolved over several years. This was a highly personal and expressive collection that showed Barney's thoughtful and artistic side. The third portfolio was a selection of Barney's newspaper photos, which he had assembled especially for a trip to New York City and meetings with newspaper photo editors.

Two aspects of Barney's portfolios are relevant to our discussion of assessment and grading: the work was self-selected, and a variety of items were included. The pictures in each portfolio were carefully selected for different purposes and indeed made very different impressions. Barney selected pieces that displayed a range of subjects, techniques, and moods, and he included finished work as well as work in progress.

Students can prepare similar portfolios of their work in content area courses. Kenneth Wolf and Yvonne Siu-Runyan (1996) define a student portfolio as "a selective collection of student work and records of progress gathered across diverse contexts over time, framed by reflection and enriched through collaboration, that has as its aim the advancement of student learning" (p. 31). They identify three portfolio models, each with a different primary purpose:

- *Ownership portfolios.* These collections of student work emphasize student choice, reflection, and self-assessment. The main purpose of an ownership portfolio is to allow students to display and reflect on their accomplishments.
- *Feedback portfolios.* These are co-constructed by the teacher and the student. They give an overall portrait of a student's development, strengths, and needs. The purposes of feedback portfolios are to guide student learning and to communicate with parents.
- *Accountability portfolios.* These are portfolios that are used as performance assessments. Accountability portfolios are assembled according to structured guidelines and are often evaluated by people other than the classroom teacher with reference to an established rubric. The purpose of these portfolios is to demonstrate student achievement for accountability or program evaluation.

There is an especially important distinction between accountability portfolios and those designed purely for classroom use, as the two uses of portfolios are in many respects at odds (Tierney et al., 1998; Valenica & Wixson, 2000;

EVIDENCE-
BASED
RESEARCH

Wiggins, 1998). Classroom-based portfolios are assembled and evaluated according to criteria established by teachers, often in collaboration with students. Their purpose is to help teachers, students, and parents understand learning, and they are often important factors in guiding teachers' instructional decisions. Interpretation of classroom-based portfolios is nuanced and sensitive to individual students and their instructional settings. Accountability portfolios, on the other hand, must meet externally imposed criteria and may form the basis for high-stakes conclusions about students, teachers, or schools. Measurement researchers have voiced serious reservations about the reliability and validity of accountability portfolios (Tierney et al., 1998; Valencia & Wixson, 2000). Although accountability portfolios certainly have the potential to influence instruction and learning, their net effect may be disruptive and counter-productive if external demands displace a teacher's professional judgment of what is best for students (Scott, 2005). In the discussion that follows, our emphasis is on classroom-based portfolios.

Sarah Drake (1998) describes a portfolio project she initiated during her second year as a history teacher at Naperville North High School in Illinois. At the beginning of the year, she told her ninth-grade ancient history and eleventh-grade U.S. history students that they would be building a portfolio that would showcase their best work and their understanding of the vital themes and narratives of history. Together, she and her students developed criteria for selecting ten items that represented their learning of history over the semester. Students included group projects, Venn diagrams, journal entries, essays, research papers, political cartoons, posters, and maps in their portfolios. They needed to write a brief explanation of why each item was chosen and a summary in which they explained the most important concept(s) they had learned.

With student input, she developed a rubric for the portfolio that evaluated students on the dimensions of historical knowledge, reasoning, and communication. Students held peer-evaluation sessions three times during the semester to help them organize their portfolios and develop their selection rationalizations. At the end of the semester, each student had a 10-minute individual conference with Ms. Drake in which they discussed the portfolio. Although students were dubious at first, Sarah found most of her students were able to recognize vital themes and narratives of history, and that their summaries expressed personal examinations and insightful reflections. She was especially pleased with the results of the portfolio interviews, during which she learned new information about students and built on relationships she had established.

Penelope Valdez (2001) describes a portfolio project that she implemented in her seventh-grade life science class. Each month, students were asked to choose a topic from class and submit a portfolio in which they do the following:

■ Explain a science concept, a science process, or knowledge of scientific equipment in detail in their own words.

- Create a product that applies to their topic in a readily understandable way. For instance, they might take photos of someone properly using and storing a microscope.
- Evaluate an item from current media that deals with the topic. Is the science in this selection accurate?

Valdez developed a brief scoring rubric for these portfolios and awarded credit to students equivalent to a test grade. Although it takes a while to evaluate the portfolios, Valdez found that the feedback she received made the effort worthwhile. Students made major improvements in their projects from month to month, and she was able to clearly see how well students knew scientific topics and could apply them.

Portfolios can be used to evaluate interdisciplinary learning. In a project that involves math, science, and technology, teams of students are given the task of designing a strong, lightweight construction beam by reinforcing concrete with one or more recyclable materials: aluminum cans, plastic milk jugs, soda bottles, or newspaper (Sanders, 1994). Students design and construct their beam, weigh it, and test its ability to support a load. They document their work with a portfolio that would be evaluated by the science, math, and technology teachers. The portfolio would include

- Sketches of all the solutions they thought of
- Notes made during the project, including hypotheses, brainstorming, or questions
- Descriptions of the science and math principles involved in their project
- Information they gathered from resources
- Graphic illustrations of how their beam performed (graphs, tables, and photos)
- A final self-assessment of the project, including a critique of their processes, the final product, and suggestions for redesign

Portfolio assessment may be adapted in many ways. In science classes, students might be asked to pick their two best lab sessions and present their procedural and observational notes along with the finished lab reports and a statement of why these labs were chosen. In social studies, students could be asked to go to their learning logs and assess their before-and-after knowledge of a subject, including examples from their work that were instrumental in changing their attitudes or understandings. In French, students might collect tape recordings of conversations from early, midway, and late in the term or the notes and drafts that led to the completed translation of a poem or piece of prose. In any course, students might include their best and worst tests, with an "improved" or corrected version of the poor test and a self-evaluation of the difference in performance. Other suggestions for portfolio contents are given in Figure 5.6.

Research indicates that portfolio assessment can be more effective than single, static measures of student achievement. Simmons (1990) reports

Math

Story problems written for others to solve
Written report of strategies used to solve a problem
Pictures or graphs illustrating problem and solution
Examples of how math concepts are applied
Computer spreadsheets

Science

Drawings
Lab notes
Photos of projects or labs
Anecdotal stories of field work
Science reports with notes and drafts

Social Studies

Charts, graphs, and maps
Oral histories
Time lines
Written reports or essays with notes and drafts

Travel brochure for region, state, or country
Creative writing
Audio- or videotapes of debates, panels, speeches,
   or presentations

All Subjects

Homework assignments
Exams or tests with self-evaluations
List of self-selected vocabulary
Content-area biographies: "My life as a scientist"
Semantic maps
Log or journal entries
Record of teacher and peer conferences
Brainstorming lists
Photographs
Record of outside reading related to content area
Audio- or videotapes
Movie or television reviews

FIGURE 5.6   Suggestions for items to include in content area portfolios

that for middle-grade students, "self-selected portfolios of their best work are significantly better than timed tests in estimating students' writing abilities" (p. 28). In another study (Garcia et al., 1990), two groups of teachers were asked to assess students with limited English proficiency. One group was given standardized test data, and the other was given portfolios of observational data with samples of student reading and writing. In all cases, the teachers who looked at the portfolios gave more complete evaluations and recommendations and more detailed requests for additional information.

Another advantage of portfolios is their potential to inform and improve instruction. In a conversation about the possibilities of portfolio assessment among researchers and teachers, Tierney et al. (1998) assert that portfolios can "serve an important role in helping teachers customize teaching and learning to the students' needs, interests, background, and circumstances" (p. 478).

Student involvement.   An oft-cited benefit of portfolio assessment is student involvement in self-evaluation and discourse about what, why, and how they are learning (Bauer & Garcia, 1997; Clark et al., 2001; Sarroub et al., 1998). To guide students' self-evaluation of their portfolio work, teachers could use questions similar to the following, adapted from Reif (1990):

What makes this your best work?
How did you go about producing it?
What problems did you encounter?
How did you solve them?

What makes your most effective work different from your least effective work?

What goals did you set for yourself?

How well did you accomplish them?

What are your goals for the next marking period?

Portfolio assessment allows students to be active participant-observers of their own growth and development. When they are asked to select, polish, arrange, and analyze their own work, they have a chance to see that learning is not haphazard or incidental to any efforts of their own. They also have more direct input into what ultimately goes on their report cards. Each student can state his or her best case to the teacher.

Pat Frey-Mason, a math teacher in an urban high school, has her students keep portfolios. When students have difficulty with certain types of problems, they are asked to work similar problems and write short reflections of what was learned in the second attempt. The problems and reflections are included in their portfolios. Excerpts from two student reflections are shown in Figure 5.7.

Implementing portfolio assessment.   Using portfolios as assessment tools represents a significant shift from traditional ways of teaching and testing. If you have not used portfolios, getting started with them will take some time, patience, and trial and error.

Because much of the effectiveness of portfolio assessment is derived from students' increased awareness of their own learning, it is not surprising that

---

Jennifer Z.: I feel that doing another problem similar to the first one helped me in a few ways. One, I got more practice at doing those types of problems. Two, the more I do those types of problems, the more used to them I become. Finally, by reading the corrections and trying the problems over, I have become more aware of my mistakes. Basically, I have become more conscious of each particular section of a problem situation. Though I still get a rush of adrenaline when working with math, I must admit after doing things over I do feel a bit more confident to get down and attack the problem.

Kelly R.: When first approaching the problem, I went through the directions and just graphed what they gave me. For example, for part (a) it said to make a graph symmetric with respect to the X axis. The easiest way I saw of doing this part of the problem was to imagine the X line being folded down the middle and just flipping the image over the line. Luckily, this method worked for parts (a) and (b) but this method didn't work for parts (c) and (d). Problems occurred when I didn't follow the methods, according to the directions. When referring to "symmetric to the origin" it requires a different method. Because I did this problem so poorly, I was given a similar problem. With this problem instead of just graphing the graphs I used a sure method to graph each one. I FOLLOWED THE DIRECTIONS!

FIGURE 5.7   Sample self-analyses from student portfolios for precalculus math
(*Source:* Supplied by Patricia Frey-Mason, Chair, Math Department, Buffalo Academy for Visual and Performing Arts, Buffalo, NY.)

students' perspectives and expectations are crucial to successful implementation of portfolios (Moje, Brozo, & Haas, 1994). Therefore, you will want to involve students from the very beginning. You will need to explain what a portfolio is, what it will include, why it is being assembled, how it is related to the curriculum, and how it will be evaluated. Although you may retain final authority over these issues, it will be helpful if you let students negotiate them with you. Students are more likely to take responsibility for their learning and to reach higher levels of achievement if they know clearly what is expected and have had a voice in determining it.

Portfolios are also likely to be more successful if you provide guidance and modeling for students as they put them together. You may wish to start with short and simple activities and group efforts before you have students undertake a complex individual portfolio project. Students will need assistance with selecting, arranging, and evaluating their portfolio contents. As students prepare their portfolios, you could use class time to demonstrate and discuss these processes. Class time can also be used to work on portfolios and get advice and assistance from peers or from you. Your feedback will be as important during portfolio preparation as it will be at the end of the process. It will also help if you negotiate incremental steps and deadlines for major portfolio projects.

Tracey Wathen describes how she implemented a two-tiered portfolio system with her middle school ESL class (Smolen et al., 1995). On Mondays, she distributed index cards to the class on which they wrote their literacy goals for the week. As the students worked on various reading and writing activities, they kept their notes, drafts, reflections, and other literacy-related materials in a working portfolio. On Fridays, students used the blank side of their goals cards to reflect on how well they had achieved their weekly goals, and they selected pieces from their working portfolios to include in a showcase ownership portfolio that displayed their growth in literacy and English language proficiency. Because students initially tended to write relatively simplistic goals ("I will read four books this week"), Tracey led the class in brainstorming reading and writing strategies and classifying them. She modeled various strategies such as predicting and visualizing story settings and emphasized them with poster charts. As a result, students began to set more complex goals, and their achievement of these goals was reflected in their portfolios.

Portfolio pros and cons.   As with other forms of assessment, portfolios have both advantages and drawbacks. On the plus side, we have repeatedly emphasized the value of portfolios in increasing students' awareness and involvement in their own learning. Portfolios can also provide detailed, authentic representations of what students have learned and what has taken place in a classroom for parents, colleagues, and administrators. Finally, portfolios can give us an opportunity to reflect on our practice as teachers. More than numeric scores on a test, portfolios allow us to take stock of what has worked, what has been learned, and what is important to learn.

By now, it is probably apparent to you that portfolios also require considerable time to introduce, create, and evaluate. That is indeed a potential drawback. Portfolio assessment takes much more teacher time and effort than simply giving a multiple-choice unit test from the teacher's manual. However, because portfolios intimately integrate assessment and instruction, many teachers believe that the time and effort are well spent (Valdez, 2001).

EVIDENCE-BASED RESEARCH

Although portfolios can help to inform teachers' instructional decisions, that potential may not always be realized. Eurydice Bauer (1999) reviewed 19 classroom studies of alternative literacy assessments, 13 of which featured portfolios. She found that some teachers had difficulty moving from assessment to instruction. She also reported few indications that alternative assessments led to more equitable instruction for struggling readers. Portfolio assessment is probably more prevalent in elementary grades and English classes, whereas teachers in other disciplines may be more resistant to any departure from traditional assessments. Indeed, teacher training, knowledge, and beliefs are all essential determinants of whether portfolios will be used, how they will be implemented, and what ultimate effects they may have on teaching and learning (Sarroub et al., 1997; Valencia & Wixson, 2000).

There is a final negative potential in portfolios that should be considered—the possible infringement of students' personal privacy (Hargreaves, 1989). If we were to substitute the term *dossier* for *portfolio,* very different images might be conveyed—images of aberrant behavior, surveillance, and control. When we ask students to engage in self-evaluation, to open up their thought processes and personal reflections for scrutiny, or to include their social relationships as part of an assessment of group projects, we are collecting very sensitive information. The information in a portfolio may be stored for future reference, subjected to interpretation according to standards imposed by a teacher or external authority, and used to make high-stakes decisions about students, all of which create a potential "threat to individual liberty, personal privacy, and human diversity" (Hargreaves, 1989, p. 138). When accountability portfolios are used in a performance assessment, teachers are subject to similar threats.

We do not mean to suggest that portfolios should not be used. We believe that the potential benefits of portfolio assessment far outweigh any potential harm. Rather, we return to a point we made when discussing the potential biases that are inherent in assessment: assessment involves responsibility. Because we are in the position of making important judgments about students, we must take special care of how judgments are made and the possible consequences.

ASSESSING TEXTBOOKS

Although less than perfect, no doubt, textbooks are still a fact of life in most content area classrooms. Teachers often have little choice of texts; a single text is available for each subject. Sometimes a department chooses more than one text for a subject, assigning different books to different tracks. Many times teachers participate with school administrators in deciding which of several competing texts should be adopted. What teachers need in any of these situations are ways to look at textbooks, to see their strengths and weaknesses and their suitability for students.

Earlier, we discussed the cloze procedure, which was originally developed to assess the difficulty of text (Taylor, 1953). It applies a kind of Goldilocks test, which suggests whether students will find the book "too hard," "too easy," or "just right."

There are two other general approaches to judging textbooks' suitability: readability formulas and consumer judgments. Readability formulas are quantitative yardsticks for estimating differences in difficulty among texts. They can be tedious to apply, but they are relatively objective and useful if a large number of texts must be formally compared. Teachers and students make consumer judgments when they look through a text, sample a few passages, and identify features they feel make the book easy or hard, interesting or dull. If teachers collaborate with one another and with students to develop a checklist of predetermined criteria, group judgments of a textbook can be quite reliable and closely correlated to the scores of readability formulas (Klare, 1984).

EVIDENCE-BASED RESEARCH

Readability Formulas

Most readability formulas rely on two assumptions. The first is that longer sentences on the average are more difficult to read than shorter ones. Theoretically, sentence length gives an estimate of syntactic complexity. The longer the sentence, the more likely it is to have imbedded clauses, passive constructions, and other features that can cause difficulty for readers. The second assumption is that unfamiliar words make text harder to read. These assumptions and the way they are applied in the use of readability formulas are not without controversy.

Fry (1977) takes the second assumption a step further and asserts that on average, long words are more likely to be unfamiliar or difficult to understand than short words. The Fry readability formula is one of the most popular methods for estimating text readability. It is useful for our purposes because it provides estimates over a wide range, from primary to college level. The procedures for using the Fry formula are given in Figure 5.8.

The use of readability formulas has caused considerable debate. First, formulas perpetuate a common but erroneous impression that educators can mechanically and precisely match student reading levels to text difficulty levels. The whole concept of "reading level" is subject to question, whether it is applied to people or to texts (Cadenhead, 1987; International Reading Association, 1982). Reading level is at best a metaphor for certain observable facts: some people read better than others; some books are harder to read than others. Two books at the "tenth-grade level" may vary considerably in the difficulties they present to

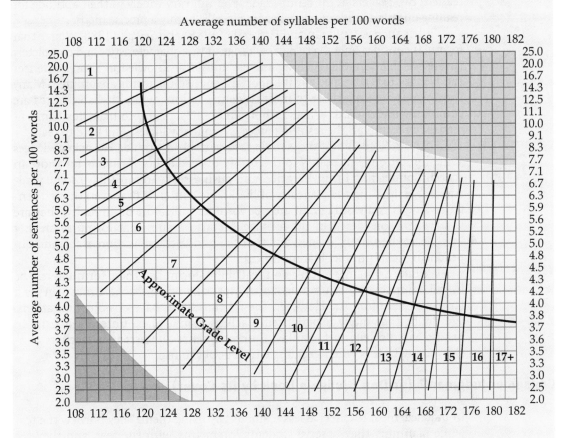

Average number of syllables per 100 words

Directions for Computing Readability

1. Randomly select three 100-word samples from the text. A word is any group of symbols with a space on each side. A number such as 1776 counts as a word; so does an initialization such as USA.

2. Count the number of sentences within each 100-word sample. If a 100-word sample ends in the middle of a sentence, figure the decimal fraction of the sentence that is included.

3. Count the number of syllables in each 100-word sample. A syllable is defined as a phonetic syllable. In numerals and initializations, each symbol counts as a

syllable. For example, 1776 counts as four syllables, and USA as three. Hint: A 100-word sample has at least 100 syllables. Make a light tic mark above each additional syllable, count the total number of tic marks, and add to 100.

4. Compute the average number of sentences and the average number of syllables per 100 words.

5. Plot these two averages on the graph. They should intersect either above or below the curved line within one of the numbered segments. The number in the segment is the approximate grade level of the text. A few books may fall in the shaded gray areas; their grade-level scores are invalid.

FIGURE 5.8   Fry readability graph (*Source*: Edward Fry, Rutgers University Reading Center, New Brunswick, NJ 08904.)

readers; two readers at the tenth-grade level will vary widely in their aptitude for reading different kinds of texts. Reading level is hardly a precise metric.

Critics such as Cullinan and Fitzgerald (1985) and Sewall (1988) charge that formulas consider only a very narrow range of text characteristics and completely ignore student variables such as interest and prior knowledge. Short sentences can be hard to read, especially if important connecting words are omitted. Many short words are unfamiliar to most students, and many multisyllabic words are commonly understood. When authors and publishers try to make textbooks fit readability formulas, the resulting prose is frequently lifeless and hard to read.

Fry (1989) defends the simple two-variable formula. He acknowledges some limitations but points to the utility of readability formulas for those in schools, publishing firms, libraries, and businesses who must have some yardstick for estimating the difficulty of books. He contends that even though sentence length and word length are not absolute indicators of difficulty, they are valid when considered in the average. He also argues that formulas are not intended to be writers' guides, and that the mindless application of formulas in producing text is in fact blatant misuse.

We take a pragmatic stance on readability formulas. These formulas can be useful adjuncts to teacher judgments, especially when teachers must survey a large number of books. However, the formulas also have obvious limitations. We doubt that many experienced teachers would place unreserved trust in results based solely on formulas. Common sense suggests that teachers consider many factors when deciding which books to use.

Consumer Judgments (or Don't Judge a Book by Its Cover)

In practice, most teachers assess textbooks by using them. They preview the text while planning, they observe students interacting with the text, and they see how students react to reading assignments. From these practical observations, they form judgments about how good the text is and how they should use it.

If a group of teachers are working on textbook adoption and need to screen several texts, they can decide among themselves what is important and possibly devise their own checklist. Science teachers are interested in what sort of laboratory activities are included in a textbook and how they are explained and illustrated. Writing style is important in a social studies text, but it would be impossible to judge style in an English anthology containing the work of many authors. Math teachers want to know what kinds of problems are featured in a text and how many problems focus on each kind of math concept. When we consider the unique content and instructional problems of foreign languages, health, industrial arts, and computer science, we must conclude that no single checklist could cover all of them.

Whatever the content area, there are some general factors to consider when judging a text. Instead of a checklist, we offer a framework that you can use to develop your own checklist for assessing text materials (Figure 5.9).

Content

Does the content complement the curriculum?

Is the content current?

Is there balance between depth and breadth of coverage?

How many new or difficult vocabulary terms are included and how are they introduced and defined?

How dense are the new concepts in the text?

Is the content generally appropriate to students' prior knowledge?

Format

Are there good graphic aids and illustrations? Are they distracting or irrelevant to the content?

How are chapters set up? Are there introductions, summaries, heads and subheads, and marginal notes?

Are layout and print attractive and easy to read?

How useful are the index, glossary, etc.?

Utility

How good are the activities at the end of the chapters?

Do text questions call for interpretation, evaluation, and application as well as literal recall?

Is there a teacher's manual? Would it be helpful?

Are quizzes or test questions provided? How good are they?

Does the text or manual suggest additional readings or related trade books?

Style

Is the writing lively and interesting to read?

Is the syntax at a suitable level of complexity?

Is the writing coherent and clear?

FIGURE 5.9   **Framework for assessing texts**

It is rare for all teachers of the same subject to agree that they are using the best available text and rarer still to find a teacher who claims to be using a perfect text. Also, considerable criticism has been aimed at texts from outside of faculty rooms. Content texts are too often written in a way that is "inconsiderate" to the reader (Anderson & Armbruster, 1984). Schallert and Roser (1996) contend that even though modern content texts have improved, they are often pointless and "contentless." They cite the lavish illustrations interspersed with incessant short, unanswered questions in many early grade texts and the frequent lack of coherent examples or explanations that tie information together in more advanced texts. Social studies texts have been attacked for their "ahistorical" bias, distracting formats, and lifeless writing (Sewall, 1988). The content of textbooks in science, social studies, and literature has been the subject of religious and political controversy. People from diverse cultures are often ignored, underrepresented, or misrepresented.

SUMMARY

There are many variables in a teacher's day—variables that require countless decisions about students, teaching methods, materials, and assessment. The more information a teacher has, the better the quality of those decisions will be. This

chapter offered many suggestions for collecting and interpreting information on students' reading and writing abilities and for utilizing that information when planning instruction and assigning grades. It also looked at ways of deciding how difficult or useful textbooks might be. All of these decisions are ultimately professional judgments. As a profession, teaching is more art than science. The teaching art has many legitimate forms of expression, and good teachers, like good artists, are constantly evolving. There is no "right" way to assign grades, no "best" test of reading ability, no "perfect" text for any subject, but good teachers keep looking and experimenting.

SUGGESTED READINGS

Hall, K. (2003). *Listening to Stephen read: Multiple perspectives on literacy.* Philadelphia: Open University Press.

Purcell-Gates, V. (2002). The irrelevancy—and danger—of the 'simple view' of reading to meaningful standards. In R. Fisher, G. Brooks, & M. Lewis (Eds.), *Raising standards in literacy* (pp. 105–116). London: Routledge.

Rhodes, L. (Ed.) (1993). *Literacy assessment: A handbook of instruments.* Portsmouth, NH: Heinemann.

Shuster, N. E. (2002, Winter). The assistive technology assessment: An Instrument for team use. *JSET ejournal, 17*(1). Available: http://jset.unlv.edu/17.1/asseds/ashton.html

Strickland, K., & Strickland, J. (1998). *Reflections on assessment: Its purposes, methods, and effects on learning.* Portsmouth, NH: Boynton/Cook.

Valencia, S., Hiebert, E., & Afflerbach, P. (Eds.) (1993). *Authentic reading assessment: Practices & possibilities.* Newark, DE: International Reading Association.

Van Kraayenoord, C. E. (2003). Toward self-assessment of literacy learning. In H. Fehring (Ed.), *Literacy assessment* (pp. 44–54). Newark, DE: International Reading Association.

Walker, B. (2000). *Diagnostic teaching of reading: Techniques for instruction and assessment* (4th ed.). Upper Saddle River, NJ: Merrill.

Preparing to Read

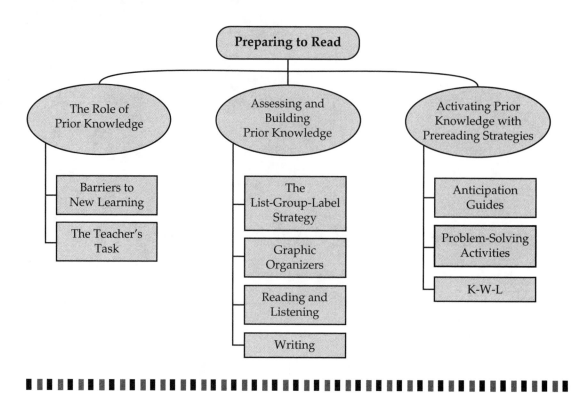

In previous chapters, we discussed the importance of helping students make connections between their own knowledge, values, and concerns and the ideas in their texts and coursework. In this chapter, we elaborate on these suggestions by describing ways to activate and build prior knowledge, create interest and motivation for reading, and focus students on their reading and learning activities.

The following scenario illustrates what can happen when students are *not* focused on a reading assignment. It is based on events that have been reported to us by teachers and students and that we have observed ourselves in many classrooms. As you read it, ask yourself how the teacher might have helped students connect with the reading assignment.

■■■■■■

The tenth-grade class had finished a short film on the geography of Japan with 20 minutes left in the period. Mr. Gregory told them to use the time to begin reading "Traditional Japan," the second chapter in the new unit. He wrote on the board: "Read Chapter 16, pages 252–257. Answer question 1, p. 255 and questions 1 and 3, p. 257 for tomorrow."

As Felicia began to read, her mind was on the track meet. In a little less than two hours, she would be running the mile relay for the first time. A series of incomprehensible dates and unpronounceable names swam before her eyes as she read. She plodded through a long passage on government written by some Japanese prince in the seventh century. Finally she came to question 1, "What principle did the Shotoku constitution stress?" Her eyes wandered back to the heading "Shotoku's Constitution." In the first paragraph, she found what she needed. She put her name and the page and question number on a clean sheet of paper and began to copy from the text: "Confucian values of orderly society and obedience to authority were especially stressed." Wasn't there something about Confucius in the unit test on China? Maybe he was an emperor or something. Oh, well. Mr. Gregory would explain it tomorrow, and she had done the first part of the assignment. If she could finish this in class, she could go get pizza with some of the girls after the track meet. She ought to do well on her leg of the relay; her quarter-mile times had been improving. Felicia thought of all their drill on the exchange of the baton. She rehearsed it in her mind . . . be sure to get a firm grip on the baton before starting to sprint . . . her eyes moved across more names and dates.

■■■■■■

Felicia's difficulty was not that she *cannot* read but that she was not *ready* to read. Before a person begins to read, whether for work, for pleasure, or for school, several interrelated factors influence how and what will be understood and remembered:

1. *Interest.* If students want to know more about a topic, curiosity will help to guide their reading. Students are more likely to recall something of interest to them.
2. *Motivation.* Reading done for pleasure is different from reading done for work or school. Reading will be less labored in a class students enjoy, more purposeful and serious when they are trying to get a good grade.
3. *Purpose.* Purpose can be either long term or short term. One purpose may be to do well on a test or in a class discussion. A student may also have a more immediate purpose, such as the need to answer a question, solve a problem, or find a particular piece of information. If students' main purpose is simply to get through the reading, their efforts will be less fruitful.
4. *Attention.* If a student's mind is on the reading, without distractions from the immediate surroundings or competing thoughts, he or she will probably comprehend more.
5. *Strategy.* Having an effective plan or strategy increases the likelihood of success, and the anticipation of success also increases motivation. Anyone may conduct reading methodically, whether it is a particular order for reading the Sunday paper or a plan for studying a difficult chemistry chapter.
6. *Prior knowledge.* In some ways, this factor is a composite of all of the above. Students' knowledge of language, of reading and study, of the world, and

particularly of the topic at hand will influence how they proceed through a text. Prior knowledge helps students set purposes, direct their attention, fill in gaps, make connections or inferences, monitor their progress, and recall what they have read.

Students vary widely in the knowledge, skill, and enthusiasm they bring to a reading assignment. Like Felicia in the previous scenario, they may frequently read without interest, motivation, or attention, without adequate purpose or strategy, and without full awareness of their pertinent prior knowledge. Good teachers recognize this and realize that preparing students well will go a long way toward making their reading successful. Most of the teaching strategies in this chapter not only help to prepare students for reading but also carry over into the reading itself. Furthermore, most of them are designed for cooperative learning or small-group interaction, or can be so adapted.

THE ROLE OF PRIOR KNOWLEDGE

EVIDENCE-BASED RESEARCH

Prior knowledge can cover a wide range of skills, ideas, and attitudes. When we use the term, we are focusing particularly on a reader's background knowledge of the subject matter of the text. What a person already knows about a topic is probably the single most influential factor in what he or she will learn. According to a recent review of effective classroom literacy instruction in the middle and high school grades, teachers who used prior knowledge activation strategies were equally effective in teaching high-, average-, and low-achieving readers. Students in these teachers' classrooms outperformed their control-group peers on a variety of comprehension measures (Alvermann, Fitzgerald, & Simpson, in press).

Barriers to New Learning

EVIDENCE-BASED RESEARCH

In Chapter 1, we discussed how people use schemata to organize and collect their thoughts and synthesize their experiences. Many research studies have demonstrated how inappropriate or missing schemata can influence learning from reading (Anderson, 1984). Distortions or misinterpretations may result when readers attempt to make sense of unfamiliar ideas by drawing on their cultural schemata. For example, Steffensen, Joag-Dev, and Anderson (1979) asked Americans and natives of India to read two letters, one about an American wedding and the other about an Indian wedding. Both the Americans and the Indians needed less time to read the letter that had culturally familiar content and recalled more information from the familiar material. Each group interpreted the same information differently, depending on its cultural perspective. For instance, some American readers thought that the dowry described in the Indian passage referred to an exchange of gifts between the families or favors given to the attendants by the bride and groom. Because the American bride was wearing her grandmother's wedding gown, one Indian reader inferred that the dress was badly out of fashion.

Problems also arise when a reader has no relevant schema or an insufficient schema, if relevant schemata are not recalled, or if an existing schema is inconsistent with information in the text. A reader will often ignore ideas in a text or discussion that conflict with conventional wisdom or supposed real-world knowledge (Alvermann, Smith, & Readence, 1985; Guzzetti & Hynd, 1998; Hynd et al., 1995). Students with reading difficulties appear to have particular trouble using their prior knowledge to modify misconceptions or to learn new information from reading. Often, a reader who is struggling to understand a difficult text will fasten on isolated details in the text, call on an inappropriate schema to fill in the gaps, and consequently make unwarranted inferences.

We should not underestimate the tenacity with which students will hold on to their beliefs, even in the face of conflicting evidence. Watson and Konicek (1990) discuss a class of students in Massachusetts who were studying heat transfer. All of them knew from experience that hats, sweaters, and blankets made them warm in winter. They conducted a series of experiments in which they wrapped thermometers in various articles of warm clothing and waited for the temperature to rise. Even when this failed to happen, they maintained their belief that the clothing made them warm. According to Watson and Konicek, several barriers make it difficult for students to change previously developed concepts. The first is stubbornness, or "the refusal to admit one's theory may be wrong" (p. 682). Second, language itself gets in the way of changing old beliefs: sweaters are "warm clothes." Third, perceptions can reinforce beliefs: when you put on a sweater, you feel warmer.

Factors such as cognitive, social, and moral development also influence the ease with which students can accommodate new ideas that conflict with everyday experience and conventional wisdom. Anyone who has ever tried teaching the difference between fact and opinion to middle-grade students will sympathize with this because the typical middle schooler will tell you, "If I agree with it, it's a fact!" Students are much too canny to accept an idea simply because a textbook or teacher says they should.

EVIDENCE-
BASED
RESEARCH

A factor that has strong potential to affect conceptual change is culture. The misinterpretations of American and Indian readers in the study by Steffensen, Joag-Dev, and Anderson (1979) resulted from cultural differences. In another study, black and white teenagers were asked to read a passage that described "sounding," a kind of verbal duel common in African American communities (Reynolds et al., 1982). The white readers tended to interpret the episode as dangerous, even violent; the black readers were more likely to see it as a nonthreatening contest of wits. Although cultural schemata determine in part how students perceive what they read, making culturally based assumptions about what students will or will not understand holds the danger of devolving to stereotypes, which may themselves create barriers to learning.

The effects of culture are much more subtle than is indicated by common stereotypes such as "Italians/Irish/Hispanics are emotional," "students from single-parent households lack discipline," and "yuppie children are achievement motivated." Shirley Brice Heath (1983) details the complex and subtle interplay of family, neighborhood, economic circumstances, and religion that influences what children learn about language and literacy. She describes how children from two small working-class communities came to school with quite different ideas about what language, reading, and writing are, how they should be used, and what should be thought about them. The culture of the school reflected yet another set of ideas—the mainstream values and attitudes of the town. What often resulted was a conflict of expectations between school and student—to the detriment of the student.

The Teacher's Task

We draw three broad implications from our understanding of how schemata affect the reading process:

1. What the reader brings to the page in the way of prior knowledge is more important to comprehension than what is actually on the page.
2. What teachers do before reading to prepare students can be more effective in promoting comprehension than what is done after reading.
3. Before reading, teachers should try to activate students' prior knowledge, assess the sufficiency and accuracy of that knowledge, and build appropriate background knowledge when necessary.

Good teachers have long understood the necessity of preparing students, and this is reflected in the teaching practices commonly used in content areas. New material is often introduced by a review of what has already been covered, by presenting essential background information via a lecture or media such as films and pictures, and by brainstorming and class discussion. Vocabulary instruction, which is another way to prepare students for reading or studying new topics, is discussed at length in Chapter 8.

ASSESSING AND BUILDING PRIOR KNOWLEDGE

This section presents some teaching strategies that help students build a schema before reading a selection. Each strategy is designed to "bridge the gap between what the reader already knows and what the reader needs to know before he or she can meaningfully learn the task at hand" (Ausubel, 1968, p. 148). Each of these techniques is relatively easy to plan and introduce in the classroom. As you read about these strategies, keep in mind how students' different sociocultural backgrounds and the varying knowledge they bring to a task will need to be taken into account.

The List-Group-Label Strategy

The strategy called List-Group-Label (Taba, 1967) is a variation on brainstorming that can be done with a whole class, in small groups, or by individual students. Students first list all the words they can think of that are associated with a new topic; then they group the words they have listed by looking for words that have something in common. Several variant groupings are usually possible, and a particular word often fits into more than one group. Once groups of words are established, students decide on a label for each group. An important part of List-Group-Label is the discussion of why words belong in a certain group.

If students' background is fairly extensive, a List-Group-Label session should be sufficient to help them activate and organize what they already know. Students will learn from one another; only where significant gaps or misconceptions exist will the teacher need to fill in additional background. List-Group-Label is also effective as a review activity after students have read about a topic.

Graphic Organizers

When a teacher and students diagram their labeled groups of ideas, they are in effect creating what Barron (1969) called a *graphic organizer,* or structured overview. Barron suggested that important vocabulary terms can be arranged in a diagram that illustrates the relationships between ideas. A typical graphic organizer, with coordinate and subordinate ideas arranged in a branching pattern, is shown in Figure 6.1. Other formats for graphic organizers are presented in Chapter 7. Like the List-Group-Label strategy, graphic organizers can also be used to review information at the end of a unit or chapter. (You probably noticed that graphic organizers present chapter content throughout this text.)

A teacher may prepare a graphic organizer ahead of time and explain it to the students while displaying it on the chalkboard or with the overhead projector. However, a graphic organizer is more effective when students participate in its development. The example in Figure 6.1 was designed to introduce a unit on the novel as a literary form. If the teacher prepared this organizer ahead of time, he or she might have included only the title and top three labels on an overhead transparency. The teacher could have introduced the new topic by asking students to discuss what they know about novels—characteristics, authors, novels they have read, and so on. The teacher could then have displayed his or her partial graphic organizer and begun to fill in some of the ideas that students generated. Where students did not volunteer essential information, the teacher could have filled in the blanks.

Reading and Listening

For mature readers, much of the background for reading a particular selection comes from previous reading experiences. They have prepared for reading by

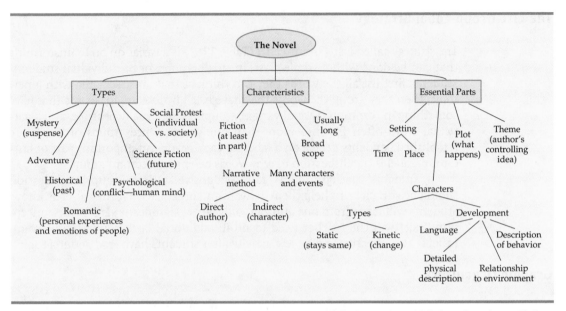

FIGURE 6.1   A graphic organizer with a branching format for a high school English class on the novel

reading (Alexander & Jetton, 2000). Similarly, a relatively simple method for building students' background for a reading selection is to have them first read another selection on the same topic. In a study with eleventh graders, Crafton (1983) found that reading two articles on the same topic improved students' comprehension of the second article. Specifically, those students generated more inferences, used more outside information and personal involvement, and focused more on higher-level information than did students who read two unrelated articles.

Reading a pertinent selection from a different textbook, a trade book, or a magazine should help to activate and build background for subsequent reading of a targeted selection in a content area text. For instance, a biology teacher introducing a unit on biomes might give the class an excerpt on rain forests from *Scientific American.* A social studies teacher who plans to introduce a unit on intergenerational family relationships might begin by reading a short essay titled "My Name" by Sandra Cisneros (1989). If time is a factor, the teacher might choose to concentrate on a particular section of the essay, such as the part in which Esperanza, a young girl growing up in a Chicano barrio and the narrator of the essay, recalls how she was named after her great-grandmother:

> A wild horse of a woman, so wild she wouldn't marry. Until my great-
> grandfather threw a sack over her head and carried her off. Just like that, as if

she were a fancy chandelier. That's the way he did it. And the story goes she never forgave him. She looked out the window her whole life, the way so many women sit their sadness on their elbow. Esperanza, I have inherited her name, but I don't want to inherit her place by the window. (p. 11)

As students listen, the teacher might ask them to pick out what Courtney Cazden (2000) calls their "strong lines"—especially memorable phrases or sentences—and be prepared to share them at the end.

Another strategy for using reading as a schema builder is called *Skinny Books* (Gilles et al., 1988). A teacher can collect several related and relevant readings from newspapers, magazines, trade books, and other sources and put them together in a folder or theme binder. For instance, for a class studying local elections, a teacher might assemble several "skinny books" with articles on various candidates, rules of voting, campaign literature, and a sample ballot (Gilles et al., 1988). Students should be given time to read and discuss these prior to reading the assigned text.

Writing

Writing is really a special kind of thinking. When students write, they must reflect on what they know, select what they wish to use, organize the selected ideas, and commit them to written language with some concern that a reader will be able to understand what is meant. Writing what they *do* know can lead them to discover what they do *not* know or what they need to find out. Writing, therefore, can also serve as a bridge between prior knowledge and new material to be learned.

A growing number of content area teachers have their students keep a journal, or learning log, for their subject. A *learning log* is a notebook dedicated to jotting, reflecting, drafting, and sometimes doodling. (We discuss learning logs in depth in Chapter 10.) Students are regularly given five to ten minutes during a period to write in their logs, and teachers periodically collect and read the logs. If the teacher responds to a particular entry by writing a short note in a student's log, it becomes a kind of private dialogue between teacher and student. Students can use their learning logs for listing, speculating, or predicting before reading.

Technology Tip

For other suggestions on how to use reading and listening activities that will prepare students from diverse cultures to read their content area texts, visit the Web site of Education World® Where Educators Go to Learn at www.education-world.com/.

After a brainstorming session or some other preliminary organizing activity, a teacher might give students five minutes for *free-writing* on a topic ("Write whatever comes to mind on the topic of insects"). For free-writing, the only requirement is that students continue writing for the time period specified (Elbow, 1973). If students protest that they do not know what to write, the teacher can spend a few minutes brainstorming and jotting ideas on the blackboard to help focus the writing activity. Free-writing products are often rough and disjointed, but the object of free-writing is not polished prose. Free-writing promotes written fluency and helps writers to begin collecting and organizing their thoughts.

A teacher might also precede a reading assignment using a strategy of previewing and predicting. A three-step process, *preview and predict* incorporates a writing component as the second step. First, students preview the assignment by reading the title and looking at the illustrations to get a sense of the content presented or, in the absence of illustrations, by reading the title and the first few paragraphs of the text. Second, students predict in writing what they think they will learn (if reading an informational text) or what they think will happen (if reading a narrative). Third, they read the selection to verify their predictions. The teacher must be sure to point out that good readers monitor their own comprehension—that it is important for the students to think about their predictions as they read and to change them if warranted.

Research dating back to the early 1980s (e.g., Graves, Cooke, & LaBerge, 1983) supports the practice of building on students' prior knowledge and

Technology Tip—Professional Standards On-Line for Active Inquiry

You can read the full text of the *National Science Education Standards* for free on-line at www.nap.edu/catalog/4962.html. As noted in an overview of these standards, they "rest on the premise that science is an active process. Learning science is something that students do, not something that is done to them. 'Hands-on' activities, while essential, are not enough. Students must have 'minds-on' experiences as well. . . . In this way, students actively develop their understanding of science by combining scientific knowledge with reasoning and thinking skills" (http://books.nap.edu/html/nses/overview. html).

To discover the degree to which other professional organizations' standards emphasize active processing of texts, visit www.ncss.org/ (social studies), www.sscnet. ucla.edu/nchs/ standards/(history), www.nctm.org/ (mathematics), www.tesol.org/assoc/standards/index.html (teaching English to speakers of other languages), www.reading.org/resources/issues/reports/learning_standards.html (English language arts), www.menc.org/publication/books/prek12st.html (music education), www.naea-reston.org/publications-list.html# standards_for_art_education (art education), and www.aahperd.org/naspe/publications-nationalstandards.html (physical education).

EVIDENCE-BASED RESEARCH

motivating interest in reading through previewing and predicting. Many educational organizations stress the importance of teaching students to become active inquirers as they read, an emphasis duly reflected in the enunciation of the organizations' professional standards. To read about these standards online, see the Technology Tip on page 172.

Throughout the rest of this chapter, you will find other activities that involve writing, some used before reading and some used after. For instance, as you read the following sections you will see many possibilities for writing activities. Some of the strategies will stimulate learning log entries or even evolve into more formal written products.

ACTIVATING PRIOR KNOWLEDGE WITH PREREADING STRATEGIES

Like Felicia at the beginning of this chapter, most middle school and high school students have a lot more on their agendas than schoolwork. After all, in addition to their academic development, they are hard at work on social, physical, and personal growth. It should not come as a surprise that many are not particularly interested in using trigonometric ratios, reading *Julius Caesar,* conjugating Spanish verbs, or learning how the valence-shell electron-pair repulsion model helps in predicting the shapes of molecules. We like to take a realistic view of this by paraphrasing Abraham Lincoln: you can interest some of your students all of the time, you can interest all of your students some of the time, but you will never get all of them excited about the valence-shell electron-pair repulsion model at the same time.

Interest is an important factor in learning, as we said at the beginning of this chapter. Many of you can probably remember teachers who, through their enthusiasm and commitment, brought to life subjects that you ordinarily dreaded. Student interest is relative, though; you might not expect great enthusiasm ("Golly, Ms. Trimble, I now realize that John Milton is the greatest writer who ever lived!"), but you would like to see some curiosity, commitment, and engagement on the part of students during the few minutes they are with you each day. Martha Ruddell (1996) suggests three principles that can serve as a basis for planning interest-generating instruction:

1. Learning occurs most rapidly and efficiently when new concepts and information build on what is already known.
2. The easiest way to gain and hold students' interest and attention is by engaging them in intellectually rich activities that require problem solving, critical thinking, and active participation.
3. Personal identification with and investment in an activity increases and sustains a learner's persistence and productivity.

A major purpose of prereading strategies is to engage students' interest by focusing a lesson on their ideas and beliefs. The strategies presented here are designed to involve students in discussions of what they know and believe, including ideas that may be contentious or contrary to the orthodoxy of the textbook and curriculum. A prereading strategy should allow students to use the discussion as a platform for understanding and organizing new information.

Anticipation Guides

An *anticipation guide* (called a prediction guide by Harold Herber, 1978) is a series of statements that are relevant both to what students already know and to the materials they are going to be studying. As part of a well-planned lesson, such a guide serves as a catalyst for activating relevant schemata and leads students into reading with some personal investment in finding out what is in the text. Anticipation guides are useful tools for effecting conceptual change. Dufflemeyer, Baum, and Merkley (1987) explain this function: "By virtue of [their] potential for provoking disagreement and bringing to the surface notions which represent a challenge to students' existing beliefs, anticipation guides serve not only as prior knowledge activators but also as springboards for modifying strongly held misconceptions about the topic" (p. 147). When students' prior knowledge is inaccurate, as is often the case, especially in math and science, confronting their

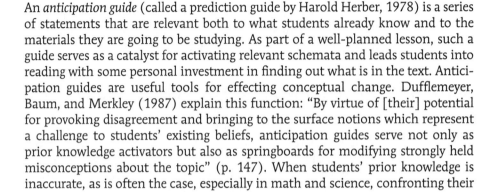

Hints for Struggling Readers

Anticipation guides are especially helpful when working with students who struggle with their textbook assignments. We recommend using these guides in conjunction with various media formats and the Internet:

- Tape-record relevant sections of a text to assist readers who struggle with decoding and need extra help in completing the guides. Signal on the tape where the information is to be used on the guide.
- Provide a list of Web sites for students to explore who do not have the requisite background knowledge to complete an anticipation guide. Ask students to add to that list as they search the Internet for related sites.
- Encourage struggling readers to use the classroom or school media center collection

of videotapes and CD-ROMs on topics that you assign for reading. Make sure that the directions and activities on the anticipation guides are stated in such a way that students can use what they learn from the media to complete the guides.

- Make use of struggling readers' everyday knowledge—knowledge that comes from out-of-school experiences—to scaffold school literacy tasks on the anticipation guide. For example, let adolescents use their interest in music CDs to scaffold text-based learning. This might involve letting them rap their answers to the guide material.
- Use sheltered English techniques that rely on visuals and manipulatives when designing anticipation guides for students who speak a language other than English as their first language.

misconceptions directly can be helpful in bringing about new understanding (Guzzetti et al., 1993).

Paul Mance, a teacher at a middle school in Angola, New York, a predominantly rural school district bordering on a Seneca Nation reservation, used an anticipation guide in his ninth-grade English class. The class was going to read *The Rising of the Moon,* a play about a rebel in the Irish Revolution. Paul began by writing on the board, "Thou shalt not kill, except . . ." and asking, "Is it ever right to take another person's life?" The students had many ideas. They discussed euthanasia (a word volunteered by a member of the class), self-defense, and war. He listed these on the board. Then he distributed the anticipation guide (Figure 6.2). After a minute or two, students began to compare responses within their small groups. The Native American students in the class had particularly telling insights on some of the issues in the guide.

When the groups had considered each of the items in the guide, the class weighed the pros and cons of each issue, bringing up many experiences and current events in support of their opinions. Then Paul asked the class, "Based on what you've discussed, and the little bit you know about this play, do you think the author would agree with you?" Again the students had a number of

---

ANTICIPATION GUIDE: *THE RISING OF THE MOON*

We are going to read a play called *The Rising of the Moon.* It is about a rebel on the run during the Irish Revolution. He tried his best to outsmart the police and avoid being captured. The play deals with many issues of basic human rights for all people.

Directions: Read the list of issues below. If you agree with a statement, make a check in column A. Be ready to explain why you agree or disagree with each item.

A	B	
(You)	(Author)	
_____	_____	1. It is always wrong to kill.
_____	_____	2. A person should be willing to die for his or her country.
_____	_____	3. People who live in the same country usually think alike.
_____	_____	4. All men are brothers.
_____	_____	5. Police are cold and unsympathetic.

Once we have discussed these items in class, read the play. If you think the author would agree with you, make a check in column B. You must be able to cite evidence from the play to support your choices in column B.

FIGURE 6.2   An anticipation guide for a ninth-grade English class
(*Source:* Paul Mance, Lake Shore Middle School, Angola, New York.)

ideas. Several students wanted to know if the playwright was Irish, and if so, which side he was on. The teacher suggested this would be a good thing to try to figure out when they read the play for homework.

The next day students sat again with their working groups. They got out their anticipation guides and literature anthologies and began to go back through each of the issues in the guide. Students frequently turned to a particular section of the play and pointed out information that supported their interpretation. Once again, Paul called the class together to review and summarize. Although there was a high degree of consensus on what the author intended, a few students remained unpersuaded on particular points. All students had a chance to explain their point of view, however. Finally, Paul asked students to pick one statement from the anticipation guide and write in their learning log why they thought the author agreed or disagreed with them on that particular issue. This log entry became the basis of an essay that students polished and submitted for a grade.

Developing anticipation guides.   The use of anticipation guides requires some planning on the part of the teacher. We suggest the following steps in preparing and using an anticipation guide:

1. Analyze the reading assignment to identify key ideas and information.
2. Think of points of congruence between text ideas and students' prior knowledge. To do this, you may need to look beyond the facts and literal information in the text. Try to find the ideas underlying the facts.
3. Anticipate ideas that may be counterintuitive or controversial, especially any misconceptions that students might have about the material.
4. Devise written statements that address students' existing schemata. Although the number of statements will vary, five to eight is recommended for most one- or two-day lessons.
5. Write a brief background or introduction to the reading assignment.
6. Write directions for students. Be sure to provide a bridge between the reader and the author. Direct students to read the text with reference to their own ideas. (Note that the guide in Figure 6.2 says, "If you think the author would agree with you . . .")
7. Have students work on the guide after a brief introduction to the topic. (Refer to the section on building prior knowledge for some good introductory techniques.)
8. Small-group discussion of the guide, both before and after reading, is an effective means for generating student involvement.

There is one mistake that teachers sometimes make in developing an anticipation guide. When a statement on a guide is too passage dependent, that is, when it is too far removed from students' personal knowledge and experience, they can only make wild guesses about whether or not it is true. This discourages student investment and curiosity and instead reinforces the impression that the textbook is much "smarter" than the reader and is therefore unapproachable. For example, to prepare eighth-grade students for a science chapter on physical properties, a teacher might draft a guide that included the following definition from the text: "A physical property is a characteristic of matter that may be observed without changing the chemical composition of the substance." If this were the only introduction the students had to the topic, they might have difficulty activating schemata for the following statements:

> You can change a physical property of an object by applying heat to the object.
> Water has a lower boiling point than alcohol.
> We use physical properties to identify and describe objects.

The definition of a physical property is too abstract, and the statements contain potentially unfamiliar technical terms from the text, such as "boiling point." The following statements should be more accessible because they appeal more directly to students' experiences:

> Heat can change objects.
> Water and alcohol are different.
> We use our senses to identify and describe objects.

Other factors that contribute to the effectiveness of anticipation guides (Dufflemeyer, 1994):

- Statements should reflect important ideas in the text.
- Statements that reflect common knowledge are less likely to stimulate thinking and discussion.
- Statements should be general rather than specific.
- Statements that challenge student beliefs will highlight discrepancies between what they believe and what is in the text.

An important element of the anticipation guide is the bridge between students' prior knowledge and ideas in the text. (Note that the guide in Figure 6.2 directs students to read the text and decide whether or not the author would agree with them. They must also be ready to support their decisions.) In what they call an *extended anticipation guide,* Frederick Dufflemeyer and colleagues (Dufflemeyer, Baum, & Merkley, 1987; Dufflemeyer & Baum, 1992) take this element a step further by asking students to paraphrase what they found in the text. In the example of an extended anticipation guide in Figure 6.3, students are asked to decide whether the text information is compatible with what they discussed before reading. Finally, students write their own paraphrase of what the text says.

ANTICIPATION GUIDE: POPULATION CHANGES

Isle Royale National Park is a large island in Lake Superior. In 1900, a few moose found their way to the island. By 1920, more than 2,000 moose lived there. Between 1920 and 1970, the number of moose on the island went up and down several times.

Directions: Below are several things that influenced the moose herd. Decide whether each one would increase (+) or decrease (−) the number of moose in the herd. Be ready to explain your choices.

+/−

_____ 1. There are approximately four moose for every square kilometer on the island.

_____ 2. A forest fire burns over a quarter of the island. This land is then grown over with moss, lichen, and new trees (moose food).

_____ 3. The birth rate of the herd goes up. The death rate goes down.

_____ 4. A pack of wolves comes to the island.

Directions: Now read pages 453–455 in your text. If what you read supports your choices, place a check in the Yes column. If the text does not support your prediction, place a check in the No column. For each item, write in your own words what actually happened.

Support?

Yes	No		In Your Own Words
____	____	1.	_____
____	____	2.	_____
____	____	3.	_____
____	____	4.	_____

FIGURE 6.3   An extended anticipation guide for a seventh-grade science lesson (*Source:* Based on W. Ramsey et al., *Holt Life Science.* New York: Holt, Rinehart & Winston, 1986.)

Applications of the anticipation guide.   Anticipation guides can be created for a variety of subjects. The guide in Figure 6.4 was developed for a first-year French class by their teacher, Beth Anne Connors. The students were going to be reading a dialogue in which a hotel clerk and a guest discussed hotel amenities, room rates, and reservations. Most of the new vocabulary in the selection was specific to travel and hotels. Several differences between hotels in France and in the United States were implied in the passage. Beth Anne began by asking the class, "Combien parmi vous est jamais resté dans un hôtel pendant un voyage?" ("How many of you have ever stayed in a hotel during a trip?") She distributed the anticipation guide and asked the students to respond to Part I in groups. In Part II of the guide, they listed in English any

ANTICIPATION GUIDE: À L'HÔTEL

Part I: We are going to read a story about a man who is trying to make hotel reservations in France. Think about the types of things that people usually expect when staying in a hotel. Read each of the following statements and then mark the appropriate column stating whether you agree or disagree with each expectation. You must be able to explain your choices.

Agree   **Disagree**

_____ _____ 1. Unless it is vacation season, you will have no trouble getting a room.

_____ _____ 2. There will be a phone and a TV in the room.

_____ _____ 3. There will be a bathroom in the room.

_____ _____ 4. The hotel will have a pool and/or other recreational facilities.

_____ _____ 5. The hotel will be reasonably priced.

Part II: In column A, list 5 words in English that will most likely appear in the text. Then read "À l'hôtel." If you find any of the words you listed, write the French word in column B. Write any other new words or phrases from the selection that you think are important at the bottom of the page.

      A. Anglais   **B. Français**

1. _____   _____

2. _____   _____

3. _____   _____

4. _____   _____

5. _____   _____

Autres mots ou phrases importantes:

FIGURE 6.4   An anticipation guide for a first-year French class (*Source:* Beth Anne Connors, Royalton-Hartland Junior-Senior High School, Middleport, New York.)

words they thought would be used in the passage. As they read the text silently, the students jotted down the French equivalents of the words they had anticipated. Additional French words were written in the bottom section. They compared their postreading lists and discussed the terms, with assistance from the teacher. The students then reread the dialogue orally in pairs. Finally, they used their vocabulary lists to write a summary of the story, in which they described one similarity and one difference between hotels in the United States and France. The teacher found that the anticipation guide made students less dependent on her for help with new vocabulary. Because they had anticipated many of the ideas and words that were found in the text, they were able to attend more to the overall meaning of the passage and were less concerned with understanding every single word.

Jennifer Ostrach was presenting a new concept to her sixth-grade math class: "When integers with unlike signs are added, the sum will be the difference between the integers and will have the sign of the greater integer." To help her students understand this concept on their own terms, she prepared the anticipation guide in Figure 6.5, which featured everyday situations she knew her students would be familiar with. She began class with a preview of the previous lesson on adding integers with like signs. Then she placed the following problem sentence on the board and asked the class to brainstorm possible solutions: +4 + −6.

After they had talked about the problem, Jennifer distributed the anticipation guide and had them work on it in groups of three or four. Students talked about their responses, read the pertinent selection in the math book, and then reexamined their responses. Then Jennifer assisted them as they wrote their

---

ANTICIPATION GUIDE: ADDING INTEGERS WITH UNLIKE SIGNS

Directions: Read each statement below and decide whether you agree with it or not. Write A (Agree) or D (Disagree) in the blank before each. Compare responses with others in your group. Be ready to explain your choices.

A or D

_____ 1. If a team wins 6 home games and loses 4 away games, they have won more games than they have lost.

_____ 2. If a football team gains 17 yards on one play and loses 9 yards on the next play, they have gained yardage.

_____ 3. If you spend $15 at the mall and find a $20 bill on the way home, you are ahead.

_____ 4. If you get a bill for $53 and a paycheck for $35, you have enough money to pay the bill.

_____ 5. If you have $8 and buy a movie ticket for $6, you will have enough to buy a supersize bucket of popcorn for $3.

_____ 6. You can add two numbers and still have less than zero.

Directions: Now read p. 408 in your math book. Note the rule for adding positive and negative integers and the examples. Go back to the statements above and see if you have changed your mind. In the space following statements 1 through 5, write an addition sentence using integers and solve the problem. After statement 6, design your own word problem like those in the guide, and give it to others in your group to solve.

FIGURE 6.5   Anticipation guide for adding integers with unlike signs
(*Source:* Jennifer Ostrach, Maryvale Middle School, Cheektowaga, New York.)

ANTICIPATION GUIDE: THE ORDER OF OPERATIONS

Directions: We have already studied the four basic number operations. Now, we are going to examine expressions that involve two or more operations. Before reading about the "Order of Operations Agreement," think about the mathematical expressions and their simplified values listed below. Based on the expression and its simplified value, predict a rule for the order in which mathematical operations are computed. Be able to explain your decisions.

Expression	Simplified Value	Predict Rule
1. $4+8\div2$	8	
2. $18\div2+7$	16	
3. $4*3+4*4$	28	
4. $10-3*5$	-5	
5. $5(3+2)$	25	
6. $36\div2*3$	54	
7. $(5-2)2$	9	
8. $2+7^2$	51	
9. $(4+8)\div2$	6	
10. $(10-3)5$	35	
11. $8+[13-5(6-4)]$	11	
12. $[2(5*5)-7][6-(12\div3)]$	86	

FIGURE 6.6   An anticipation guide for the Order of Operations

own problem sentences using the integers in the statements. As a concluding activity, each student designed a problem like those in the anticipation guide and gave it to the other students in the group to solve.

The anticipation guide in Figure 6.6 was created by Victoria's math students in her content area reading class several years ago. It is designed to be used in a middle school pre-algebra class just before students study the Order of Operations agreement. In mathematics, when several operations are necessary to simplify an expression, the order in which those operations are completed really matters. In pairs or small groups, students complete the anticipation guide in Figure 6.6 and predict the rule used to produce the simplified value of the expressions in the first column. This activity enables students to generate their own "order of operations" rules before reading about the International Agreement on Order of Operations. It also prepares students to read their mathematics text with better comprehension than if they had read it without any preparation.

Problem-Solving Activities

Another way of activating students' prior knowledge is to engage them in problem-solving activities such as those generated in a problem-based approach to learning and in designing WebQuests. Both approaches are viewed as constructivist teaching methods and thus espouse the assumption that developmentally appropriate, teacher-supported learning should be initiated and directed by the student.

Problem-Based Learning

In a problem-based learning approach, "students are presented with an ill-structured problem and instructed to work in small groups to arrive at some resolution to the problem" (Lambros, 2004, p. ix). For example, the following problem-solving activity could be aligned with the science curriculum in most high schools today:

ACTIVITY   **Lost Without a Cell Phone**

You are the member of a camera crew for an award-winning film company. You are doing a documentary on the human body and have been miniaturized and injected into a human body to film. However, you quickly find yourself trapped inside the nucleus of a pancreas cell when your micro-vehicle malfunctions. You have no way of communicating with anyone on the outside to tell them where you are or to get help. Without a propulsion system, you need to find your way out of the cell safely.

- What do you know from the problem statement?
- What additional information would you like to have?
- How will you proceed? (Lambros, 2004, p. 99)

The acquisition and structuring of knowledge in problem-based learning is thought to work as a result of engaging students in the following cognitive processes (Schmidt, 1993):

- Initial analysis of the problem and activation of prior knowledge through small-group discussion
- Elaboration on prior knowledge and active processing of new information
- Restructuring of prior knowledge
- Stimulation of curiosity related to real-world problem solving

Cognitive development is but one of the positive features associated with a problem-based learning approach. According to Lambros (2004), experienced teachers have reported that this approach can actually eliminate some of the behavioral problems that occur when students are bored or disinterested in content learning. Further, it is important to bear in mind that adolescents are at a stage in their development when career options become increasingly important. Thus, opportunities to engage with real-world problem solving take on additional relevance.

Dispelling Policy Myths

▮▮

Dispelling a Myth

A high school education should prepare students for success in postsecondary schooling. Although this is a statement that many teachers would consider central to their mission as educators, the fact is that the U.S. Census Bureau's Educational Attainment 2003 Study found only 27.2 percent of high school graduates 25 and older held a bachelor's degree. Yet, as McCain (2005) notes, "if you walk into any high school, you will find that the overwhelmingly majority of courses . . . are focused on getting students ready for postsecondary education" (p. 14). Referring to this paradox as the "myth of postsecondary education" (p. 13), and lamenting the fact that teachers often resort to "telling" rather than involving students in problem-solving activities, McCain argues for a curriculum that engages students in thinking logically and solving problems effectively   while they are still in their middle and high school years.

Policy Implications

Although there are few secondary schools that offer problem solving in the curriculum, it is the case that this approach to teaching is a standard or goal in almost every state (www.fpsp.org/Standards.pdf, no page given). For example, the Future Problem Solving Program (FPSP), a nonprofit educational corporation that serves over 250,000 students annually, has demonstrated the alignment of various states' curriculum standards with its six-step problem-solving model, which includes: (1) identifying challenges; (2) selecting an underlying problem; (3) producing solution ideas; (4) generating and selecting criteria to evaluate the merit of a proposed solution; (5) applying criteria to solution ideas; and (6) developing an action plan. (Note: For a more comprehensive view of FPSP's curricular alignment project and background information on the organization's co-founder, E.Paul Torrance, a world-renowned figure in gifted education, visit www.fpsp.org.)

Designing WebQuests

A WebQuest, as defined by Wikipedia, a free on-line encyclopedia, is "an inquiry-oriented activity in which some or all of the information that learners interact with comes from resources on the Internet" (http://en.wikipedia.org/wiki/WebQuest, no page given). Developed by Bernie Dodge in 1995, a WebQuest is usually divided into the following sections: introduction, task, process, evaluation, conclusion, and teacher page. Students typically complete WebQuests in groups, often with individuals being assigned role-playing personas (e.g., a critic, a historian, a researcher, and so on). The following Technology Tip box offers an assortment of useful Web sites designed to help students produce their own WebQuests.

When Donna introduces an activity that requires a critique of an existing WebQuest in her content literacy methods class, she typically gives her students the following rubric to use as a self-assessment guide.

Rubric for Completing a WebQuest Critique of

"A WebQuest about WebQuests" available at
http://edweb.sdsu.edu/webquest/webquestwebquest-hs.html

Information

Describe a specific topic or lesson with which you might use a WebQuest of your choice.
(1 point)
     State specifically the value (or lack of value) of a WebQuest for the topic or lesson
named. (1 point)

Personal Reaction

State the difficulties (significant or relatively insignificant ones) that you experienced
while attempting to complete this assignment "A WebQuest about WebQuests" (2 points)
     Self-assess what you learned from the assignment that could conceivably help you
make the very same assignment more meaningful to *your* students. (2 points)

Discussion

Participate in a whole group (videotaped) discussion of the points you made in your paper.
(2 points)
     Reflect on the videotaped discussion at a later time. (2 points)

K-W-L

K-W-L is a prereading strategy suggested by Donna Ogle (1986). Students first
identify what they *know* about a topic, then decide what they *want* to find out
about it, and finally discuss what they have *learned*. (Some teachers, when their
students profess that there is nothing they *want* to find out about the topic, use
the term *need* to find out instead—K-N-L). In the first phase of a K-W-L lesson,

A Response from Our Readers

Josephine Young, a professor at Arizona State
University, e-mailed us that having her students
design their own WebQuests revitalized her
content area methods class. In an e-mail to that
effect, Josephine wrote:

> This year I asked the students in content
> literacy to make WebQuests as their final
> project. I had about 90 students this semester
> . . . . If you feel like it go to www.geocities.
> com/jesse002 and click on Ice Age

WebQuest. It is a really well-designed
one. I think you could make a connection
between Hal Herber's instructional
frameworks and WebQuest design and use.
This assignment seems to be a good way for
students to integrate different dimensions of
content literacy—prior knowledge, vocabulary
study, reflection, writing, reading guides, etc.
I'm glad you mentioned WebQuests in your
book—it has revitalized my class.

Technology Tip

For examples and templates of WebQuests suitable for a wide range of content areas, visit one or more of the following Web sites:

www.qesnrecit.qc.ca/cc/inclass/webquest.htm (See the WebQuest Design Process under the major heading Learn More About WebQuests.)

webquest.sdsu.edu/literature-wq.htm (This Web site is especially suited for English teachers; see the numerous examples using literature.)

www.macomb.k12.mi.us/wq/wqdmain.htm (This Web site offers a template for students to use in designing their own WebQuests.)

www.spa3.k12.sc.us/WebQuestTemplate/webquesttemp.htm (This Web site shows how to incorporate different student roles in resolving a conflict.)

http://edweb.sdsu.edu/webquest/LessonTemplate.html (This Web site is for the more advanced/experienced WebQuest user.)

students brainstorm and discuss the ideas they have on a topic they will be reading about in their text. They can jot down their own ideas on worksheets or in their learning logs. With teacher guidance and modeling, they categorize the information they have discussed and anticipate other categories of information that they may find as they read.

Figure 6.7 shows a K-W-L worksheet developed by a high school self-contained special education class during a lesson on the U.S. Constitution. The students in this class ranged from 13 to 16 years old, and formal testing suggested their academic functioning levels ranged from second to sixth grade. The teacher, Michelle Beishline, began by reviewing the previous chapter; she asked the class to recall why the Colonists were unhappy with Great Britain. Then she asked who had heard of the Constitution and distributed a blank K-W-L worksheet. She told students to write down everything they could think under the K *(Know)* column, first individually and then in a small group. Then she called on students to share what they had written. As students volunteered, Michelle wrote their responses on a large chart on the board and interspersed some general questions: What is the Constitution? Why is it important? When do you think it was written? Who wrote it? She filled in more information under the K column as students elaborated on their answers.

Michelle then asked students what they would want to find out about the Constitution, and she asked them to list their questions under the W *(Want to Know)* column, first individually and then again in their groups. Once more, she called on students and filled in their responses on the chart on the board. Before students read the text, Michelle asked them what the most important categories of information were going to be, and the students responded with the categories in the lower left-hand corner of the chart: What was it all about? Why was it written? When? Who? The text selection on writing the Constitution was

K (Know)	W (Want to Know)	L (Learned)
—It was an important paper.	—How many people wrote it?	—55 men wrote it—farmers, merchants, and lawyers. They were called Framers.
—It had to do with freedom.	—Who wrote it?	
—A lot of people involved (John Hancock, George Washington, Ben Franklin)	—Why was it written?	—Written in Philadelphia, summer 1787.
	—How long did it take to write?	
—It happened a long time ago.	—When was it written?	—Kept secret so Framers could speak freely.
—Secret	—Were there any women in on it?	
—Had to do with Boston Tea Party.	—How long was it?	—Where was it written?
—Was written with feather pen.	—Why was it kept a secret?	—Nation needed a better government.
	—What was it all about?	—6 ideas:
Categories: What was it all about? When? Who? How?		1. protect rights of people 2. powers controlled by law 3. power is from people—voting 4. power of government divided into 3 branches 5. checks & balances 6. federalism—a central gov't that shares power with the states
		—Problems solved through compromise

FIGURE 6.7   K-W-L worksheet for "Writing the Constitution" (*Source:* Michelle Beishline, Stanley G. Falk School, Buffalo, New York.)

assigned as homework, and students were told to fill in the final column of the worksheet, L *(Learned)*. Later in the day, a teacher aide read the text aloud for a few of the students with severe reading difficulties and helped them fill out the L column. The following day, students first compared what they had written in their small groups, and then the class completed the master chart with the help of the teacher.

K-W-L lends itself to several variations. Students who have had several experiences with K-W-L could devise their own K-W-L lists in small groups, pairs, or individually. Teachers can add columns to the basic K-W-L format. For example, a "How" column could be added after the "Want to Know" column, and students could predict ways of finding answers to their initial questions.

SUMMARY

Prior knowledge is a powerful determinant of reading success. Reading about something interesting and familiar seems effortless; the reader is not really conscious of reading at all. Plowing through difficult and unfamiliar reading material, however, can be a frustrating and fruitless task. A person may read and reread with little comprehension or retention of the ideas encountered.

This chapter described many strategies for activating and building students' prior knowledge before they read. These strategies can promote motivation, purpose, and confidence in readers. Students are more likely to be successful with challenging reading material when they can discuss what they know or believe, when they get a preview of what they will be reading, or when the teacher has stimulated a need to know—an itch of curiosity that can be scratched by reading.

SUGGESTED READINGS

Anderson, R. C., & Pearson, P. D. (1984). A schema-theoretic view of basic processes in reading. In P. D. Pearson (Ed.), *Handbook of reading research* (pp. 255–292). New York: Longman.

Berkowitz, B., & DonVito, J. (2003). Powers of the president: A study in presidential decision-making (grades 7–12). *Big6 eNewsletter,* e4, 1. Available: http://www.big6.com/showarticle.php?id=333

Godina, H. (1999). High school students of Mexican background in the Midwest: Cultural differences as a constraint to effective literacy instruction. In T. Shanahan & F. V. Rodriguez-Brown (Eds.), *National Reading Conference Yearbook 48* (pp. 266–279). Chicago: National Reading Conference.

Herber, H. (1978). Prediction as motivation and an aid to comprehension. In H. Herber (Ed.), *Teaching reading in content areas* (2nd ed.). Englewood Cliffs, NJ: Prentice Hall.

Readence, J. E., Moore, D. W., & Rickelman, R. J. (2000). *Prereading activities for content area reading and learning* (3rd ed.). Newark, DE: International Reading Association.

Reading to Learn

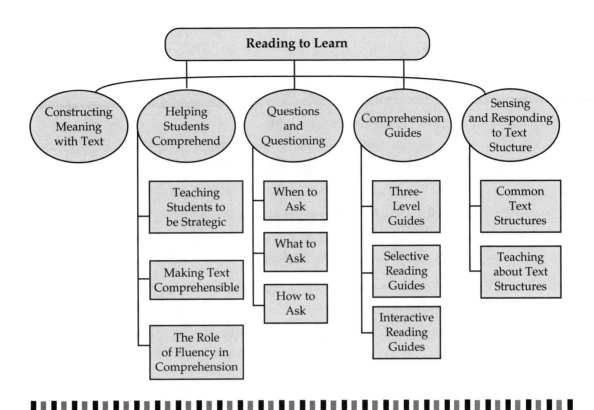

The following poem was written by Christine Woyshner, formerly a teacher in Lackawanna, New York, who was thinking back on her own days as a student. It raises some questions that are central to this chapter: What happens when a student sits down to read a content area text assignment? What strategies might the student use, and how effective are they?

■ ■ ■ ■ ■ ■ ■

'Twas the night before English and to my dismay
I had not finished the reading due the next day.
My pencils were sharpened and laid on my desk.
As far as I was concerned, I'd do my best.

We were asked to read *Hamlet.* "No problem," I thought.
I cracked open my copy the school district just bought.
"Thee, though, thou" the words they did say.
Just what the heck does that mean, anyway?

Let's see . . . that Hamlet, he seems pretty wild.
I think I'll go see what's on TV for a while.
Now *E.R.* is over, I'll return to my book,
But first I'll open the fridge for a look.

Okay, this is great. I'm up to page ten.
I still can't figure out who did what and when.
It's too bad it's so late, or I'd go to the mall.
I'd better go give my friend Pat a call.

It's getting so late, there's so much more to read.
Pat mentioned a book she thought I might need.
It's by someone named "Cliff" or something like that.
Now I can be an A student, like Pat.

Reading *Cliff's Notes* is the way to go
If you're ever stuck reading "thee, thou, and though."
Now that *Hamlet*'s behind me, I really am glad,
And reading Cliff's *Iliad* won't be so bad.*

■ ■ ■ ■ ■ ■ ■

Christine's strategies included sharpened pencils, TV and food breaks, and expert help. Some of these strategies worked, some didn't; in the end she was able to look back and reflect on the confidence she had gained from the experience.

The focus of this chapter is reading to learn, or what happens when a student opens a book and reads. Ideally, what happens is that the reader learns something about algebra, chemistry, history, or whatever the subject might be. However, as Christine's poem illustrates, text content does not transfer directly and intact into the mind of the reader; it is not like loading a text file from a disk into your computer. Although this chapter may seem to emphasize the text, we have not forgotten the importance of the reader or the fact that reading is socially situated. What is learned from reading depends, among other things, on the reader's prior knowledge, attitudes, intention, and learning strategies (Alexander, 2005) as well as the social context in which reading and learning occur (Gee, 1996). Learning implies more than just rote mastery of facts, formulas, and "who did what and when"; it also means thinking about and using that information. Rather than seeing a particular text as having a single meaning that all successful readers must apprehend, it is more accurate to think of text as representing a range of potential meanings.

Students generally view their textbooks as sources of important information, necessary for success on tests and assignments. However, they are often unsure of their own ability to understand and think about text material. Some good students develop effective strategies for learning from their texts, but many others find the increased demands of learning from their texts overwhelming. Even though they may want to learn and try to learn, the complexity and abstraction of something like Shakespearean language or the laws of physics may pose seemingly insurmountable problems.

Although the content of their studies becomes more complex, the actual strategies that middle-grade and secondary students have for learning often

---

*Reprinted with permission of Christine A. Woyshner, Temple University.

remain relatively primitive. For content area teachers, experts in their subject matter, the difficulties of their novice students can be frustrating and perplexing. How can students learn when they seem to lack the necessary background and skills? There is no easy or quick solution, but there are several things a teacher can do that will help students read to learn.

CONSTRUCTING MEANING WITH TEXT

Learning from text involves constructing meaning from the author's message. We do not mean to diminish the role of the reader; rather, we emphasize that in order for text to be a useful learning tool, a reader needs to be able to construct a mental representation of what is conveyed by it. In Chapter 1, we outlined a cognitive view of the reading process that emphasizes the mental operations of the reader in comprehension and a contrasting social constructionist view that recognizes the influences of language and social factors on a reader's understanding of text. From a cognitive standpoint (Goldman & Rakestraw, 2000), comprehension of text

> involves building coherent mental representations of information. It means processing the meaning of individual words and phrases in the text as well as how these individual words and phrases relate to one another, both within the text and within a larger, preexisting knowledge base. To accomplish this, readers rely on both text-driven and knowledge-driven processes. (p. 311)

A social constructionist would view the question of comprehension quite differently (Gergen, 1999):

> [C]onstructionists take meaning to be continuously negotiable; no arrangement of words is self-sustaining in the sense of possessing a single meaning. The meanings of "I love you," for example, border on the infinite. Such reasoning suggests that all bodies of thought are spongy or porous. Whatever is said can mean many different things; meaning can be changed as conversations develop. . . . [V]ocabulary is also porous, and every concept is subject to multiple renderings depending on the context. (p. 236)

These two viewpoints each have their merits, and they are continuously debated among researchers and theorists. (We have exchanged several faxes and e-mails regarding this passage, trying to reach a mutually satisfactory version.) There appears to be some common ground between the two. Comprehension requires transaction between the text and the reader's prior knowledge. If we include a reader's socially constructed ways of speaking, thinking, and behaving (Gee, 1996) as part of prior knowledge, then these two views of the reading process become more complementary than contradictory.

A hypothetical example may help to illustrate the complementary roles of author, reader, and social context. Steve lives in a northern city with a more than 30-year history as a hockey town; he is an ardent, season-ticket-holding hockey fan. Donna lives in the South near a major city that has only recently reacquired a major league hockey team; she is mildly interested in the sport, mostly out of courtesy to her friend Steve. Imagine that we both read a news article on the decline of fighting as a part of the sport. Donna, reading from her position as a pacifist and a relative hockey "outsider," might see that decline as a good thing. Steve, although he shares many of Donna's understandings of the world, nevertheless might find fighting to be an acceptable facet of the sport. We could talk endlessly about our interpretations of the article, and our discussion would be grounded partly on what the author of the article actually said, partly on our prior experience and beliefs about such things as sports and violence in our society, and partly on our long-standing friendship and discussions of many varied topics and ideas. In other words, our different understandings of the article would be textually, personally, and socially constructed.

Sometimes, constructing meaning with text is easy, especially when the reading material is interesting and well written and the topic is familiar. However, even the most experienced and effective reader will encounter text that must be closely read, reread, and pondered before an approximation of the author's intended message can be teased out and an interpretation of that message formed.

HELPING STUDENTS COMPREHEND

EVIDENCE-BASED RESEARCH

Comprehension is influenced by several interrelated factors, including the text itself, a reader's prior knowledge, the strategies a reader can use, and the goals and interests of the reader (Alexander & Jetton, 2000). One other important influence on comprehension is *instruction,* or what a teacher does to help students comprehend. It is important to make a distinction here between two kinds of comprehension instruction, student-centered and content-centered (Brown, 2002). Student-centered comprehension instruction involves teaching students how to use specific comprehension strategies independently. This can be done in the context of content area teaching, so that students are learning comprehension strategies and content at the same time, but in the initial stages at least, it requires a good deal of explicit emphasis on reading and thinking.

With content-centered comprehension instruction, teachers use materials such as graphic organizers or reading guides to help make text more comprehensible. This chapter, for instance, describes several kinds of reading guides that teachers may design to help students understand content area text. In this approach to comprehension, the primary objective is understanding new content-area information. Clearly, these two approaches are not mutually exclusive. Rather, it is more a matter of where emphasis is placed, on content learning or on comprehension strategy learning.

Teaching Students to Be Strategic

No scripted program, instructional package, or workbook can teach students how to be strategic comprehenders (Duffy, 2002). To teach comprehension strategies effectively, a teacher must be knowledgeable, flexible, and methodical. A knowledgeable teacher must understand which strategies fluent readers use and how to teach those strategies. Comprehension is complex, and our understanding of how comprehension works is still developing. A single comprehension term such as *inference, main idea,* or *critical thinking* may take on varied meanings in the context of different theoretical approaches. It is therefore not surprising that a review of reading methods texts and journal articles yields a confusing array of strategies and teaching suggestions.

The U.S. Congress authorized the National Reading Panel (NRP) expressly to bring clarity to the often bewildering and contradictory recommendations of educational authorities and to determine which reading strategies and instructional approaches had strong research support. The NRP's research itself was not without its critics, who charged that its definition of "scientific research" was too narrow and unscientific (Cummins, 2002); that it did not review qualitative and correlational studies; that its methodology and some of the results of its research reviews were questionable (Allington, 2002; Alvermann, 2002; Yatvin, 2002); and, of particular concern, that it excluded studies of second-language readers. Nevertheless, the NRP subgroup report on comprehension yielded a handful of recommendations for instruction that most informed readers of educational research would include on their Top Ten lists. (Every one of the NRP's recommendations for comprehension instruction has been prominently featured in each edition of this textbook.) The NRP report (National Reading Panel, 2000) lists seven categories of comprehension instruction that met the panel's criteria for strong research support:

EVIDENCE-BASED RESEARCH

- Comprehension monitoring
- Cooperative learning
- Use of graphic and semantic organizers
- Question answering
- Question generation
- Story or text structure
- Summarization

The report also notes the essential role that vocabulary development and instruction play in comprehension.

Notable omissions from the panel's findings include teaching readers to use their prior knowledge and to actively make predictions as they read, which has strong evidence-based support, and the integration of reading and writing, which can also be a powerful aid to comprehension. In addition, Alvermann (2002) notes that much of the NRP's research on comprehension instruction has been conducted on students in grades 3–8 and that teachers must therefore be cautious about applying those findings to older students. Despite the limitations of the NRP's investigations, its findings are of practical value. Of the panel's seven recommended comprehension strategies this chapter will give special attention to three: question answering, question generation, and story or text structure.

Direct instruction of comprehension strategies. Effective comprehension strategy instruction follows the direct instruction model outlined in Chapter 4. To help students learn to use a comprehension strategy independently, a teacher should introduce the strategy, model the strategy for students, guide them as they practice the strategy with easy-to-read text, and then provide continued independent practice in a variety of reading situations with frequent feedback (Baumann, 1984; Keene & Zimmerman, 1997; Pressley, 2002). Direct instruction is facilitated when both strategies and content are the subject of collaborative discourse between student and teacher and among students themselves (Langer, 2000; National Reading Panel, 2000).

EVIDENCE-BASED RESEARCH

There are clear costs and benefits to direct instruction in comprehension. Bringing students to the point where they can use a comprehension strategy independently rarely happens quickly and easily. Comprehension instruction is most effective when a few well-validated and pertinent strategies are taught, when they are discussed and practiced repeatedly over time, and when students are reading interesting content-area text that requires application of the strategies they have been taught (El Dinary, 2002; Guthrie & Ozgungor, 2002;

Comprehension Help for Students Who Struggle with Reading

Students who get to middle or high school with reading difficulties are likely to have many years of frustration, remediation, avoidance, and failure behind them. Their difficulties are often severe, complex, and seemingly intractable. Although many such students can and do make significant improvement in reading when given focused instruction by a knowledgeable specialist, it is unfair and impractical to expect content area teachers to correct all of their problems (Greenleaf, Jiménez, & Roller, 2002). Effective strategy instruction for students with reading disabilities requires intensive efforts in small-group or one-on-one settings, provided by a teacher who views that instruction as a major responsibility (Beers, 2003; Fisher, Schumaker, & Deshler, 2002). So what can classroom teachers do? Relating new information to prior knowledge, providing many examples of important concepts, comparing and contrasting concepts, and clarifying vocabulary will help students learn essential content. Involving students in classroom discussion about their reading will keep struggling readers involved. Teachers can mediate comprehension for these students by employing content-centered teaching strategies such as those discussed in this chapter in the section Making Text Comprehensible.

Ogle & Blachowicz, 2002). For teachers in the middle and secondary grades, meeting the optimal conditions of time and context for direct instruction may be impractical in the face of intense curricular pressures and high-stakes testing (Bulgren, Deshler, & Schumaker, 1997; Scanlon, Deshle, & Schumaker, 1996). However, when students are explicitly and systematically taught strategies for comprehending, teachers find noticeable improvement in achievement, critical thinking, self-confidence, and student-to-student interaction (Deshler, et al., 2005; El Dinary, 2002; Langer, 2000).

Making Text Comprehensible

If intensive student-centered comprehension instruction is impractical, teachers can still help students read, discuss, and comprehend their assignments by using teaching strategies that stress content objectives, such as K-W-L; graphic organizers, introduced in various formats before or after reading; and any of the several prereading activities detailed in the previous chapter. In this chapter, you will learn how questioning strategies, knowledge of expository text structures, and reading guides improve comprehension and how comprehension also increases when students integrate reading and discussion into their cooperative-learning activities.

The Role of Fluency in Comprehension

The ability to read fluently is an important precondition of comprehension (Rasinski et al., 2005). Fluent readers, according to the National Reading Panel (2000), are able to comprehend texts of various types with speed, accuracy, and appropriate expression. Nonfluent readers, on the other hand, expend much of their attention and effort on decoding, and are distracted by frequent and often nonsensical miscues. Nonfluent reading leaves precious few cognitive resources for comprehension. It is impossible to decode, figure out unfamiliar vocabulary, keep a reading strategy in mind, and comprehend important content all at once (Sinatra, Brown, & Reynolds, 2002).

The NRP, while acknowledging that fluency instruction is often neglected in day-to-day classroom instruction, found sufficient research evidence to suggest that guided oral-reading procedures have a positive impact on students' fluency and comprehension across a range of grade levels and in a variety of regular and special education classrooms. On the other hand, the panel did not find sufficient evidence to recommend independent silent reading as an effective way to improve reading achievement, in part because there were only ten studies that met the panel's research criteria. In criticizing this conclusion, Krashen (2002) argues that the NRP omitted a large number of relevant studies and misinterpreted the studies it did review. Admittedly, setting aside significant blocks of time for independent reading is probably impractical for most content area teachers, although it is an important component of reading-skills courses in middle school and high school. Because of its long-standing usage and the strong correlational evidence of its effectiveness, independent silent reading remains a part of this text's discussion of fluency.

Guided oral-reading procedures. Repeated reading, shared reading, paired reading, and other similar procedures make up what are generally referred to as guided oral-reading procedures. These procedures share several key characteristics. They typically involve students in rereading the same text over and over again until a specified level of proficiency is reached. They also tend to rely on one-to-one instruction through tutoring (including peer tutoring and cross-age tutoring), audiotapes, or some other means of guided oral-reading practice. Unlike whole-class, round-robin oral reading in which individuals read aloud for only a brief period of time, the guided oral-reading procedures just named maximize the amount of time any one student spends practicing fluency.

Readers need to attain a level of fluency such that difficulties with word recognition and slow, choppy reading do not interfere with comprehension and studying. However, it is an especially important goal for students who are learning English as a second language. Although the National Reading Panel (2000) did not address issues relevant to second-language learning, a growing body of research on guided oral-reading procedures used with Latina/o students tends to support the panel's findings that such procedures do indeed improve reading.

For example, Robert Jiménez and Arturo Gámez (2000) were successful in their efforts to build reading fluency and improved attitudes toward reading among a group of middle school Latina/o students who, without such instruction and opportunities for guided oral rereading, might have been viewed simply as at risk for school failure. Similar results were found for a fluency procedure called "cooperative" repeated readings used with a group of African American eighth graders who struggled with reading and who were considered at risk of school failure (Tatum, 2000). As Jiménez and Gámez noted, too often the at-risk label is applied to students who "may possess untapped potential for success in literacy" (p. 81) if given appropriate instruction.

Independent silent reading. The assumption here is that by encouraging students to read on their own, we influence the amount of time they spend practicing their literacy skills. Although procedures such as sustained silent reading, drop everything and read, and a number of incentive programs (e.g., Million Minutes and Pizza Hut's Book It) are thought to motivate students to read more, the relationship between increased voluntary reading time and reading achievement is still murky. As the National Reading Panel (2000) took pains to point out in their report, the data connecting time spent reading and

Students Who Struggle with Reading: Rereading for Comprehension

When experienced readers encounter difficult text, they will reread sentences, paragraphs, or even chapters, asking questions, seeking clarification, and reflecting in order to construct meaning. This simple but effective comprehension strategy is so automatic for many of us that we hardly realize we are doing it. Less experienced readers and those who have difficulty with reading often think that rereading difficult material is futile or somehow "cheating," because they don't see their more accomplished peers rereading, and besides, the assignment only said to *read* the chapter, not reread it or understand it. To demonstrate the value of rereading, Beers (2003) recommends choosing a short text selection and directing students to read it three times. Students should rate their comprehension after each reading on a 1–10 scale, and then discuss their ratings when they have finished. Teachers should also model their own thinking as they reread text and then give students occasional follow-up passages to reread for specific tasks. As students continue to practice this strategy, they should continue to reflect on the results and list occasions when rereading can be helpful.

reading achievement are correlational rather than causative in nature. Thus, it could be the case that reading more makes an individual a better reader, or it could be simply the fact that better readers opt to read more. The lack of conclusive evidence in support of independent silent reading does not mean that teachers should cease to encourage it. On the contrary, as Saunders and Goldenberg (1999), researchers with the Center for Research on Education, Diversity and Excellence, are quick to note, pleasure reading and teacher read-alouds are designed "to expose students to the language of expert writers and the fluency of an expert reader" (p. 5).

QUESTIONS AND QUESTIONING

Using questions to help students learn is at least as old as Socrates. Asking questions about texts is "perhaps the most common kind of academic work in comprehension instruction" (Dole et al., 1991). Good questions can guide students' search for information, lead them to consider difficult ideas, and prompt new insights.

EVIDENCE-BASED RESEARCH

Long tradition and widespread use do not mean that questioning is always effective, however. Too often, questions test what students have learned rather than helping them to learn. A high proportion of teachers' questions tend to be literal, "what's it say in the book" questions, asked after students have read (Durkin, 1978/1979). In Chapter 3, we considered the differences between discussion (which prompts thinking and learning) and recitation (which prompts memorization). In a traditional classroom recitation, the teacher dispenses questions and is at once the repository and arbiter of "correct" answers. Students are frequently given little time to formulate a reply before the teacher either calls on someone else or asks a new question. Although such recitations probably have their place in helping students to review and remember the vast curricular content they are expected to cover, they do little to help students learn as they read.

Although questioning is among the most common classroom activities, all students may not be equally prepared for question–answer situations. Responses to a teacher's questions may vary depending on a student's cultural background. Mainstream middle-class families prepare young children for school by rewarding the kinds of language behavior that are also rewarded by schools (Heath, 1991; Gee, 1996). This behavior includes answering questions that focus on labels, on information known to the questioner, and on recounts of previously learned information. Such adult–child questioning situations usually require children to give a straightforward expository response.

The same kinds of language behavior are not necessarily prized in other cultural groups, in which labels and language may be learned cooperatively in functional settings, often from siblings rather than adults. In some communities, question–answer exchanges between adults and children take on a different form from what is routinely done in schools. Shirley Brice Heath (1991) found that in their home settings, young African American children in one community were frequently asked playful or teasing questions and questions that encouraged their interpretive or analytical powers. Students from diverse cultural backgrounds may also possess extraordinary language powers that can be utilized in school settings. Lisa Delpit (1995) notes that Native American children come from communities in which storytelling, featuring a wealth of meaning with an economy of words, is highly sophisticated. Delpit also notes the "verbal adroitness, the cogent and quick wit, the brilliant use of metaphorical language, the facility in rhythm and rhyme" (p. 57) that are developed and celebrated in the African American community.

These cultural differences in language use imply a need to modify the traditional recitation session with its emphasis on single correct, literal answers. Some students may need support and guidance in formulating answers to conventional classroom questions; they may perform better when responses are formulated in small discussion groups rather than in whole-class recitations. Equally important, the kinds of questions that are asked and the answers that are rewarded should reflect the verbal strengths of students. Higher-level questions and active give-and-take in discussion facilitate learning by culturally diverse students (Hill, 1989).

Research on questioning has suggested many ways in which teachers can make their questioning more effective. To use questions well, teachers need to know when to ask, what to ask, and how to ask.

When to Ask: The Right Time and the Right Place

EVIDENCE-BASED RESEARCH

Questions appear to have different effects depending on when they are asked (Just & Carpenter, 1987). Generally, questions asked before reading tend to help readers focus on the targeted information. Prereading questions in effect tell the readers what to look for and, by implication, what to ignore. On the other hand, questions that follow reading tend to improve understanding not only of the targeted information but also of information that is not covered by the questions. Furthermore, questions seem to be more effective the closer they are to the information in the reading material. Interspersing questions within text is sometimes called "slicing the task" because it reduces the amount of text that students must read and comprehend at a given time (Wood, 1986).

These findings have some practical implications for teachers. When students are especially in need of guidance—for example, when they must digest relatively long and difficult text assignments—prereading questions help them separate the important from the unimportant by alerting them to essential ideas and information. On the other hand, when selections are more manageable or when the teacher is aiming for a broader general understanding of a selection, postreading questions might be the best approach. In practice, many teachers use a mix of prereading questions to guide students' reading and postreading questions to assess their understanding and stimulate them to reflect.

The physical proximity of questions to text is more difficult to accomplish. Obviously, a teacher cannot insert questions in students' textbooks or be there in person to ask the right questions just as a student finishes a particular passage. One solution is to give students a question guide that is keyed to particular sections of the text, with instructions to complete the answers as they go. Anytime a teacher gives students a list of questions beforehand, though, there is the probability that some students will resort to simply reading the questions and skimming the text to match words in the questions to words in the text.

What to Ask: The Relation between Questions and Answers

There are many different types of questions. At one extreme is the factual question with a single correct answer: Who is buried in Grant's tomb? When was the War of 1812? Responding to some questions, however, requires a good deal of thought: How do the presidencies of Grant and Nixon compare? What were the causes and the immediate and long-term consequences of the War of 1812? Factual questions can be useful, but they are overused in too many classrooms. According to Just and Carpenter (1987), "questions that require high-level abstraction (such as the application of a principle) produce more learning than factual questions. High-level questions probably encourage deeper processing and more thorough organization" (pp. 421–422).

Many questions asked by teachers are necessarily extemporaneous reactions to classroom situations, but questioning is most effective when it is planned in advance. Teachers who develop a core of questions can target specific information or concepts and can encourage different kinds of thinking. It is easier to plan and ask effective questions if a teacher has some way to conceptualize or categorize questions.

Different questions may prompt answers from different sources, and so it is useful to think of question–answer relationships (QARs) (Pearson & Johnson, 1978). The answer to some questions may be *textually explicit*, or literally stated in the text. A reader might paraphrase the text, point to the exact words, or read them aloud to answer the questions. Other questions may call for a response that is *textually implicit*, not directly stated but suggested or implied by the text. To formulate an answer, a reader has to think about what the author has said and perhaps integrate information from several places in the text. Sometimes the answer to a question does not come from the text at all. The reader must call on prior knowledge or beliefs to answer the question. Pearson and Johnson call this prior knowledge a reader's "script" and say that such an answer would be *scriptally implicit*.

**EVIDENCE-
BASED
RESEARCH**

In a series of studies, Taffy Raphael further developed the concept of QARs and demonstrated their potential for helping students to comprehend their reading (Raphael & Pearson, 1982; Raphael, 1982, 1984, 1986). Raphael suggested that younger students, those in second grade or below, could most easily distinguish two main sources of information—the text itself and their own background knowledge. She coined the phrase *In the Book* to describe answers that were either textually explicit or textually implicit, and she used the phrase *In My Head* for answers that were scriptally implicit.

As readers become more conceptually mature, they are able to make finer discriminations between the kinds of answers they produce, and it is possible for them to think of four different QARs. Older readers are able to see that some answers are textually explicit, which Raphael (1986) labeled *Right There*. They are also able to understand that some answers are not directly stated but rather require inferences drawn from different parts of the text. These textually implicit answers are derived by the reader *Putting It Together*.

By the middle grades, students can identify two different types of questions that call on their background knowledge. Some scriptally implicit questions require the reader to combine prior knowledge with information from the text to derive a response; hence, these are *Author and You* answers. Finally, some questions can be answered solely from the reader's knowledge base; they may even be answered without reading the text. As a reader, you are *On Your Own*.

Figure 7.1 gives a graphic representation of the various QARs, with sample questions and answers based on the story of "Goldilocks and the Three Bears." To give you a further idea of how the four QARs might work with textbook material, we invite you to try the following activity.

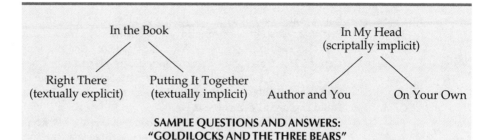

SAMPLE QUESTIONS AND ANSWERS:
"GOLDILOCKS AND THE THREE BEARS"

1. **Right There:** What were the Three Bears eating for breakfast?

   Answer: They were eating porridge.

2. **Putting It Together:** Why was Baby Bear so upset when he came home?

   Answer: Because his breakfast was gone, his chair was broken, and there was a stranger sleeping in his bed.

3. **Author and You:** What kind of a person was Goldilocks?

   Answer: She was not very nice. She was bold. She was hungry and tired, and maybe she was lost or homeless.

4. **On Your Own:** Why is it a bad idea to go into a stranger's house when no one is home?

   Answer: It is against the law; it is trespassing. The people would not like it. They might be mean people and do something bad to you.

FIGURE 7.1   Question–answer relationships

ACTIVITY

Here is a short passage titled "Why the British Lost" from a high school American history text (Boorstin & Kelley, 2005). Following it are eight questions. The first four are answered for you and labeled Right There, Putting It Together, Author and You, and On Your Own. A brief rationale is given for each relationship. See whether you can answer the last four questions and decide what the QAR is for each of them. (The answers are at the bottom of the box on page 203.)

> The British were separated from their headquarters by a vast ocean. Their lines of communication were long. The British government was badly informed. They thought the Americans were much weaker than they really were. And they expected help from uprisings of thousands of Loyalists. But these uprisings never happened.
>
> The most important explanation was that the British had set themselves an impossible task. Though they had an army that was large for that day,

how could it ever be large enough to occupy and subjugate a continent? The British knew so little of America that they thought their capture of New York City would end the war. After the Battle of Long Island in August 1776, General Howe actually asked the Americans to send him a peace commission, and cheerfully expected to receive the American surrender. But he was badly disappointed. For the colonists had no single capital that the British could capture to win the war.

American success was largely due to perseverance in keeping an army in the field throughout the long, hard years. George Washington was a man of great courage and good judgment. And Americans had the strengths of a New World—with a new kind of army fighting in new ways. Still, it is doubtful the Americans could have won without the aid of France.

Although many Americans opposed the Revolution, and some were lukewarm, it was a people's war. As many as half of all men of military age were in the army at one time or another. Each had the special power and special courage that came from fighting for himself, for his family, and for his home. (p. 100)

1. *Question:* What did the British expect from the Loyalists?
   Answer: They expected uprisings from thousands of Loyalists.
   QAR: Right There—The answer is almost a direct quote from the text.
2. *Question:* What evidence is there that the British were responsible for defeating themselves?
   Answer: The were badly informed. They were overly confident and made many poor judgments. They tried to fight a war that was too far away from their headquarters.
   QAR: Putting It Together—The reader must select information from several places in the text and make inferences about this information.
3. *Question:* What could Britain have done to win the war?
   Answers: They could have gotten better information. They could have had better generals who would have adapted to a new kind of warfare. They could have captured General Washington. They could have negotiated a treaty with France.
   QAR: Author and You—The reader must know many of the issues and events from the text, but the question also calls for the reader to use prior knowledge and reasoning to think of possible answers.
4. *Question:* What qualities are important in a leader during a time of crisis?
   Answers: During a crisis, a leader should have courage, good judgment, ability to inspire loyalty and confidence, intelligence, coolheadedness.
   QAR: On Your Own—The reader can rely entirely on prior knowledge; no knowledge of the text or the events of the American Revolution is required.

5. *Question:* In what way was the Revolution a people's war?
6. *Question:* If the United States were invaded by a foreign army, what might people in your community do?
7. *Question:* What did the British think would happen when they captured New York City?
8. *Question:* What lessons might we learn today from Britain's experience in the American Revolution?

5. *Answer:* Half of all the men served in the army. People were fighting for their own families and homes. America won because people were willing to sacrifice and keep fighting even though they met some early defeats. QAR: Putting It Together—The answer is not directly stated. The reader must infer the answer from what the authors say. 6. *Answer:* People in our community might fight back. They would join the army or go underground and fight a guerrilla war. Some people might become collaborators, though, depending on what they thought of the invaders. QAR: On Your Own—The question can be answered with background knowledge and the readers' suppositions; no knowledge of the text is necessary. 7. *Answer:* The British thought the war would end once they captured New York City. QAR: Right There—The answer is stated explicitly in the text. 8. *Answer:* We should know what we are doing before we become involved in something. We shouldn't try to take on impossible tasks. It is imprudent to enter into a war in a faraway country when the people of that country are mostly against you. Be sure you have the means and the will to follow through whatever you start. QAR: Author and You—A number of answers are possible, depending on readers' background knowledge and opinions, but a person must also have knowledge of the factors that are discussed in the text.

In her work with middle-grade students, Raphael demonstrated that students can be taught about QARs and that this knowledge of where answers come from can actually improve students' ability to answer questions (Raphael & Pearson, 1982; Raphael, 1982, 1984, 1986). There is also evidence that students maintain their use of QAR strategies over time, and that QAR training with narrative text transfers when students read expository text (Ezell et al., 1996).

A content area teacher might teach students about QARs using a procedure similar to that suggested by Raphael (1982):

1. Explain the four QARs and demonstrate them with relatively simple examples.
2. Once students appear to have grasped the relationships, give them several questions labeled Right There, Putting It Together, Author and You, or On Your Own, and have them develop answers.
3. As students become competent with this type of practice, begin posing questions without labels and instruct students to develop answers and decide which QAR applies.

QUESTION GUIDE: PACKAGING AND LABELING

Directions: Read the questions and then read the chapter. Give a complete answer for each question. Be ready to explain your answers.

Right There: Be sure you can show where in the chapter you found the following information.

1. What are the five functions of packaging mentioned in the chapter?
2. What two inexpensive materials are among the most widely used packaging materials?
3. What may be classified as "brand," "grade," or "descriptive"?

Putting It Together: You will not find answers to the following questions directly stated. Be ready to show what evidence you found for your answers.

1. What steps are involved in packaging design?
2. What are some of the disadvantages of using plastic and plastic-based containers?
3. Why are labeling laws and standards important to consumers?

Author & You: The author gives some clues, but you'll need your own ideas, too.

1. Why is the appearance of a product's packaging important?
2. Why do marketers use a combination of materials for packaging products?
3. Why should we be concerned about the materials used in packaging? Why is "green" packaging becoming more popular?

On Your Own: Draw from your own beliefs and experiences for the following answers.

1. Do products with more appealing packaging work or taste better? Give an example that supports your answer.
2. Do you recycle containers? Why or why not?

FIGURE 7.2   **QAR guide: "Packaging and Labeling"** (*Source:* Margaret A. Pyrak, Business and Marketing Education, Buffalo State College, New York.)

Throughout this instructional sequence, discussion of questions, text, and answers is essential to help illustrate and reinforce the relationships. The emphasis should be on comprehension. What is important are the answers that students supply and the sources of those answers. QAR instruction should not become a task of simply "labeling" questions as Right There, Putting It Together, and so on.

Margaret Pyrak, a preservice teacher in business education, prepared a QAR comprehension guide in one of Steve's classes (Figure 7.2). The guide was created to help students in a high school business marketing class understand key ideas in a chapter on labeling and packaging. Margaret began by introducing the definitions of each question–answer relationship to students, using examples from the movie *The Lion King*. She gave them the QAR guide to be completed as they read the chapter for homework. In class, she planned to have students compare and discuss their answers. As a follow-up, she directed students to one of the Internet sites for packaging companies listed in their textbook, as well as

Technology Tip

ReadingQuest.org, a Web site designed for social studies teachers who wish to more effectively engage their students with the content in their classes, has a discussion of how teachers can use Question–Answer Relationships and Questioning the Author, each with examples. For more suggestions on classroom questioning strategies, visit the University of Delaware's Center for Teaching Effectiveness Web site. As part of the university's handbook for teaching assistants, you will find a list of specific strategies for encouraging students to ask and answer questions at http://cte.udel.edu/ TAbook/question/html.

another site they found from a search of the keyword "packaging." Finally, she asked them to write a paragraph explaining how their Internet discoveries related to what they had learned from reading the chapter.

Instruction in QARs readily complements the kind of question–answer reading assignments and discussions often used by content teachers. All of the examples can be based on students' actual textbook reading assignments, and discussion of QARs requires minimal additional classroom time.

The QAR taxonomy is simple and intuitively easy to comprehend. In practice, however, teachers have found a few difficulties inherent in this very simplicity. Comprehension (in this case, the answers to questions) is too complex to be tidily classified by four relationships. The QAR taxonomy also implies a linear process that simply does not exist. Readers do not begin by comprehending information that is right there, then move on to putting ideas together, and end up being on their own. In fact, these kinds of comprehension occur simultaneously and interdependently.

In addition, the definitions of the four relationships are not precise. For instance, if a student answers a question with the exact words from two different paragraphs in the text, is the QAR Right There because the exact words were used or Putting It Together because the answer integrated information from different parts of the text? Often, a reader will answer a question using an Author and You or Putting It Together QAR when the information is actually Right There. The answer is not necessarily wrong just because it came from a source other than one the teacher had intended.

Despite these limitations, we believe that QARs provide a useful framework for teachers and students. First, there is a good argument for teaching students about QARs. When students are consciously aware of the different sources of information available to answer questions, they become more strategic in their reading and thinking, and their comprehension is improved (Raphael, 1984). Second, we have found that the four QARs are helpful in teacher planning. Teachers need to strike a balance between literal questions and more thought-provoking questions. Questions reflecting the Putting It Together, Author and

You, and On Your Own QARs help students to see relationships within the text, connections between text ideas and other ideas in the subject area, and associations with their own prior knowledge and experiences. Such questions frequently have more than a single good answer, which stimulates students to think rather than passively wait to be told the "right" answer.

How to Ask: Questioning Strategies

Teachers frequently devise prereading questions, assign end-of-chapter questions, or use questions to guide class recitations and discussions. This section offers some alternative questioning strategies that can help students become more actively involved in formulating and answering questions. In conjunction with instruction on QARs, these techniques can facilitate students' development of independent strategies for reading to learn.

EVIDENCE-BASED RESEARCH

Questioning the author.   Developing readers often accept uncritically the authority of the textbook without stopping to consider that texts are written by authors who have made decisions about what to include and how to present information. Questioning the Author (QtA) is an approach that helps students see that a "book's content is simply someone's ideas written down, and that this person may not have always expressed things in the clearest or easiest way for readers to understand" (Beck et al., 1997, p. 18). The researchers who developed QtA use the term "queries" to differentiate their questioning strategy from the usual teacher-dominated classroom routine of recitation in which the teacher asks questions and evaluates students' responses.

Material from content area textbooks can be classified as *expository text*, or writing that explains something. This is in contrast to *narrative text*, which tells a story, such as in novels, plays, or short stories. There are two types of QtA queries that can be used with either narrative or expository text (Beck et al., 1997). *Initiating queries* are used to begin consideration of important ideas in the text. The following are generic examples of initiating queries:

- What is the author trying to say?
- What is the author's message?

Follow-up queries are designed to guide students in evaluating and connecting ideas and constructing meaning. The following are sample follow-up queries:

- Does the author explain this clearly?
- Does the author tell us why?
- How does this connect to what the author told us before?

Whereas initiating and follow-up queries can be applied to expository or narrative text, *narrative queries* specifically help students to think about what an author is doing with character and plot:

- How do things look for this character now?
- What do you think this character is up to now, given what the author has told us?
- How has the author let you know that something has changed?
- How has the author settled this for us?

QtA strategies require thoughtful planning and implementation. The teacher must analyze the reading assignment carefully to determine key ideas (both explicit and implicit), anticipate concepts or connections that may cause comprehension difficulties for students, plan queries, and segment the text into meaningful sections to determine stopping points for discussion. QtA can be used selectively to introduce new selections that students will be completing as homework or to support students' reading of especially difficult segments.

When introducing QtA for the first time, it is a good idea to explain the purposes of QtA. Students should be told explicitly that comprehension difficulties are often as much the fault of the author as they are of the reader, and that part of the work of reading well is to question whether authors are making their ideas clear. When Doug Buehl, a high school teacher in Madison, Wisconsin, introduces QtA, he helps his students to identify the authors of their text by name and speculate on any biographical information that might be available (Buehl, 2001). After explaining the nature of QtA, students should read a selection from the text, followed by teacher queries to initiate discussion. In addition to posing queries, the teachers' role during discussion is to help students construct meaning by highlighting key points, returning students' attention to the text, and refining and interpreting student comments. Teachers also model their own thinking, fill in gaps left by the author, and guide students in summarizing and moving on through the text.

QtA obviously requires a good deal of teacher knowledge, preparation, and in-class practice. However, Beck and associates (1997) have found that QtA has resulted in more student talk, more student-initiated questions, and more emphasis on meaning and integration of ideas than in traditional question–answer sessions in which the focus is on evaluating student comprehension and recall of literal-level information from the text.

Wineburg (1991) found that high school students and actual historians read history very differently. Historians would often look first to see who the author was and then noted the author's point of view and the various subtexts that were implied. High school students who had taken four years of history courses and who had achieved high SAT scores and grade point averages seldom considered the authors of their texts. They did not question whether the author was trying to promote a particular point of view, whether information was selectively included or excluded, or whether the textbook was a trustworthy source of information. They tended to see history as a collection of facts and truths, not as something that could be interpreted either by authors or by readers; they "failed to see text as a social instrument masterfully crafted to achieve a social end" (Wineburg, 1991, p. 502). Therefore, their reading was primarily a search for information. A strategy like Questioning the Author could be used to help students develop a more critical eye, so that they might read more like historians. You will find more suggestions for this kind of critical reading in Chapter 9.

ReQuest.   Reciprocal questioning, or *ReQuest* (Manzo, Manzo, & Estes, 2001), is a relatively simple variation on classroom routine. Instead of the teacher asking questions, the students are given the opportunity to ask questions of the teacher. The ReQuest procedure works as follows:

1. Identify a text selection that has several obvious stopping points for discussion and prediction. Prepare a few higher-level questions for each section of the text.
2. Prepare students for the reading selection by previewing it, by discussing background information or selected vocabulary, or by instigating some other appropriate activity.
3. Tell students that they will be reversing roles with you. As they read the first part of the selection, they are to think of questions that they will ask you.
4. Let students read to a predetermined point. Then allow the students to ask you as many questions as they can think of. Respond without looking at the text.
5. When students have asked their questions, they close their books, and you direct questions to them. At this point, you should model higher-level questioning.
6. Repeat the reading–questioning procedure through successive segments of the text until a logical point is reached at which to make predictions about the rest of the material. Lead students to turn their predictions into one or more purpose-setting questions. Once they have completed the reading, continue the discussion by asking them for answers to their purpose-setting questions.

In our experience, students are very eager to take on the role of teacher. The questions they initially ask are often factual, but, with teacher modeling, they quickly begin asking more complex and thoughtful questions. The ReQuest procedure combines very neatly with direct instruction in questioning or other comprehension strategies (Ciardiello, 1998). If the class has previously learned about QARs, the teacher can think aloud about the sources of information used to formulate answers: "I know that information isn't right there in the book, but my previous experience would lead me to say that . . . " The amount of text covered between questioning episodes can be varied to meet the reading ability of the students and the difficulty of the material. Also, ReQuest can be a cooperative-learning activity if students are allowed to formulate their questions with a partner or in small groups.

Self-questioning.   One attribute of active readers is that they generate questions before, during, and after reading. Teaching students to ask questions about their reading improves their comprehension (National Reading Panel, 2000; Rosenshine, Meister, & Chapman, 1996). The ReQuest procedure would be one way of encouraging student self-questioning. Another approach to self-questioning was described by Singer and Donlan (1982). A group of high school students were taught that short stories generally have several general attributes in common, such as characters, goals, obstacles, outcomes, and themes. As they read short stories, these readers considered model questions about these attributes and were guided to develop their own questions. On daily quizzes, the self-questioning group significantly outperformed another group that simply answered the teacher's questions.

Instruction in self-questioning can be adapted to other genres and other content areas. Students of poetry can be guided to ask their own questions about rhyme, meter, or imagery. Social studies teachers can show their students how to ask questions about causes and effects or comparisons and contrasts. When students encounter math problems, they can be shown how to ask their own questions about what is given and what is to be found. Students familiar with the QARs can formulate their own Right There, Putting It Together, Author and You, and On Your Own questions (Helfeldt & Henk, 1990). As homework, students can be asked to make up a certain number of self-questions and answers for the next day, and their questions can become the departure point for class discussion.

You could adapt a quadrant activity similar to one that Roni Draper used in her middle school math class (McIntosh & Draper, 1995). Over several class periods, she gave her students explicit instruction in QARs and demonstrated how they applied to their mathematics text. Once students had a good working knowledge of QARs, she gave them a sheet of paper divided into four quadrants labeled Question, Answer, Relationship, and Explanation. Working alone, in pairs, or in small groups, according to their preferences, students wrote their own question in the appropriately labeled quadrant. They made a note in their math logs as to which type of QAR they thought this question was and then traded papers with someone else. In the remaining three quadrants, they answered each other's questions, wrote down what type of QAR it was, and noted the explanation for this choice. They exchanged papers again and compared their responses. Where there was disagreement between those who wrote the questions and those who answered them, discussion continued until they agreed. Draper found that this procedure facilitated mathematical communication among her students, who were thus able to clarify and consolidate their understanding of mathematical concepts.

Self-questioning has a high level of success in improving comprehension, probably because it leads to more active reading and thinking. Self-questioning is also an effective strategy for students who are learning English (Jiménez & Gámez, 1996). Formulating questions and answers helps them to express their

Questions and the Struggling Reader

In a review of research on QARs, Raphael and Gavelek (1984) note that "classroom training in QARs appeared to make average- and low-ability students look much like high-ability students in their ability to answer questions" (p. 241). It is noteworthy that self-questioning seems to be especially beneficial to poor readers (Brozo, 2000; Gillespie, 1990). Nolan (1991) used a combination of prediction and self-questioning to boost the reading comprehension of middle-grade students, and he found that those with the most severe reading difficulties made the most gains. André and Anderson (1978/1979) also found self-questioning to be particularly effective with students having low verbal ability. They hypothesized that self-questioning gave these readers a strategy much more effective than their usual "plow through the words" approach and that students with high verbal ability may already have the component skills of selecting and organizing information. When teaching questioning strategies to struggling readers, teachers should begin with simple materials and provide ample practice, support, and feedback to help students gain confidence in using the strategies correctly across a variety of reading assignments (Swanson & de la Paz, 1998).

EVIDENCE-BASED RESEARCH

thoughts in English, often by borrowing and manipulating the language of the text. Self-questioning also allows bilingual students to actively monitor their own comprehension rather than passively responding to questions posed by the teacher. When students work on activities such as self-questioning in pairs or cooperative groups, it gives them an opportunity to practice their language skills while talking about the content they are learning, all in a less formal and less threatening atmosphere than whole-class recitation (Nelson, 1996).

Questioning strategies for English language learners.   Answering questions in class can be especially daunting for students who are not academically proficient with English. In order to maintain the flow of a question-and-answer session, it is easy to overlook English language learners or to simply settle for a "yes/no" response. It is also tempting to speak for ELLs or finish their responses. Wait time, or the time between when a question is asked and when someone responds, is especially important for ELLs. Three or four seconds of silence can seem like an eternity, but it will take that long or longer for many students to formulate an answer, especially an elaborated response to a higher-level question. Be sure that students, especially ELLs, are given sufficient time to think over and complete their responses.

Teachers can draw out more extended responses by asking follow-up questions such as "Tell me more about . . . ," "What do you mean by . . . ," or "What does that remind you of?" Another technique helpful to ELLs is to restate their responses in standard English, with a prompt such as "In other words [response

A Response from Our Readers

Amanda Fredrickson, a preservice teacher enrolled in George Hruby's content literacy course at the University of Georgia, wrote the following after reflecting on the use of questions in helping students learn from and with texts: "I never realized how much thought went into the questions that my [high school] teachers asked me, but it all makes perfect sense.

Just like with life, timing is everything. *When* you ask a question all depends on *what* the teacher wants to accomplish with the question. . . . I know this sounds simple, but before reading this chapter, I never thought of questioning and questions in such a methodical manner."

restated]. Is that accurate?" (Echevarria, Vogt, & Short, 2000). Also, cooperative-learning settings will allow ELLs more opportunities to respond to questions with less anxiety about speaking in front of a large group.

COMPREHENSION GUIDES

Many variations of the reading or study guide exist, but all share a common purpose: to help students comprehend key ideas in their reading. This section describes three kinds of comprehension guide. The first is a three-level guide that features a list of statements instead of questions. The other two variations, the selective reading guide and the interactive reading guide, combine questions with specific directions for where and how to read the text. Like the QAR guide, these three guides are intended as general models to be adapted by teachers to fit their particular circumstances.

Three-Level Guides

Harold Herber (1978) suggests that students in content areas can benefit from being walked through a comprehension process similar to that used by expert readers. To accomplish this, Herber proposes that teachers devise a comprehension guide designed to support students in constructing meaning at three different levels. The *literal level* consists of specific facts and concepts that are explicitly stated. The *interpretive level* requires "reading between the lines" or drawing inferences about ideas that the author implies. The *applied level* represents comprehension that extends beyond the text to form new ideas or use ideas from the text in different contexts. Like QARs, these three levels of comprehension are neither discrete nor linear. That is, there will be a good deal of overlap among levels, and readers will move back and forth among these kinds of comprehension as they work their way through a text.

A three-level comprehension guide presents students with a list of declarative statements at each level before they read. This alerts readers to potentially important ideas and supports their search for meaning. As they read, students look for the ideas featured in the guide. After reading, the guide can be used as a departure point for discussion in small groups, as students compare their reactions to the guide and look back through the text to support their decisions.

A three-level comprehension guide designed by Amy Sanders for her class of seven 13- to 15-year-old special education students is shown in Figure 7.3. Previously, Amy had introduced the three levels of comprehension to her students and illustrated each level with a reading guide based on a short, familiar passage. Now she and her class were going to be spending three days learning about the sense of taste. The key ideas for this lesson were presented in five pages of their science text, which included two experiments to be carried out in class along with exposition on how people perceive taste.

To begin the lesson, Ms. Sanders passed out the reading guide and read through the instructions and statements with students. Note that in the guide in Figure 7.3, literal level statement 2 is intended as a distractor. It is literally *not* true

---

READING GUIDE: THE SENSE OF TASTE

I. Literal. Place a check mark next to the statements you think say the same thing the author says. (The words may be slightly different from the text.) Be prepared to show where you found this in the text.

_____ 1. Your sense organ for taste is your tongue.

_____ 2. Taste buds send messages to your tongue.

_____ 3. You don't taste food when it is dry.

_____ 4. Your tongue is sensitive to four tastes: sweet, sour, bitter, and salty.

II. Interpretive. Check the statements you think the author implies. Some thinking is required! Be ready to support your answers.

_____ 1. The front sides of your tongue taste the salt from a potato chip better than the back of your tongue.

_____ 2. Different parts of your tongue are sensitive to salt, bitter, sweet, and sour.

_____ 3. You can see your taste buds on your tongue.

_____ 4. Smell and taste work together.

III. Applied. Check the statements that you agree with, based on your experiences and what you learned from the passage. Choose *one* statement and write why you did or didn't check it.

_____ 1. If something doesn't smell good, you probably shouldn't eat it.

_____ 2. Two can do better than one.

FIGURE 7.3   Three-level comprehension guide: "The Sense of Taste"
(*Source:* Amy Sanders, Baker Victory Day Treatment Center, Lackawanna, New York.)

according to the text. Similarly, teachers may include ideas in the interpretive or applied levels that have more than one legitimate response. These distractors are intended to generate thought and discussion and to keep readers from simply checking all the items on the guide without doing the reading.

Ms. Sanders asked them to speculate what the reading passage might be about and what ideas they might be learning. Because most of her students had difficulty reading the science text on their own, she paired six of them to read the text and complete the guide together, while the seventh student worked on his own. After they had finished reading, she brought the class together to share their responses to the guide. Together, the group listed key facts and ideas from the passage and then used their list to complete a graphic organizer. They then performed the first of the two experiments, which involved finding the parts of their tongues that were more sensitive to a piece of candy and a lemon slice. They reconfirmed their reading guide responses based on their findings.

On the second day, the class went to the computer lab, in which they accessed Neuroscience Resources for Kids (http://faculty.washington.edu/chudler/tasty.html). This site was used to reinforce and extend concepts that had been encountered in the text. Although some of the material here was a good deal more challenging and technical than what had been described in the text, Amy asked her students to review their reading guides and see if the Web site supported their responses or added any new insights. She also asked each pair of students at their computer to find at least two new technical vocabulary terms related to "taste," and to be prepared to explain them to the rest of the class.

On the third day, the class reviewed the reading guide and graphic organizer and then performed the second experiment described in the text. As a culminating activity, the students were given a quiz that consisted of filling in a blank version of the graphic organizer and writing a short essay that explained the relationship between taste and smell.

STANDARDS

By combining reading, writing, the Internet, and experimentation in this lesson, Ms. Sanders was enabling her students to develop several of the concepts and abilities specified in the national content standards for science (National Research Council, 1996). These include

- Conducting a scientific investigation
- Using tools and scientific techniques to gather, analyze, and interpret data
- Developing scientific explanations that incorporate existing scientific knowledge and new evidence from observations and experiments into internally consistent, logical statements
- Communicating experimental procedures and results
- Understanding the structure and function of living systems

Selective Reading Guides

Another way to support students' learning is to create a selective reading guide that points students to important information in the text. This is similar to the

---

CARDIOVASCULAR DISEASE

Directions: Read pages 569–578 in your text, looking for answers to the following questions.

1. (p. 569) Define "hypertension." Can hypertension cause death? How?

2. (p. 570) Describe the difference between "atherosclerosis" and "arteriosclerosis." Which is more deadly? Why?

3. (pp. 571–572) Explain how you could tell if someone were having a heart attack. List three ways to prevent a heart attack.

4. (p. 573) Explain how "cardiac arrest" is different from a heart attack.

5. (pp. 573–574) Define "thrombus" and "embolus." Tell why these are dangerous.

6. (pp. 569–574 and p. 578) Compare the *causes* of cardiovascular disease with ways of *preventing* it. The first one has been done for you.

Causes	Prevention
a. Eating foods high in fat.	a. Follow a low-fat diet.
b.	b.
c.	c.
d.	d.
e.	e.

7. Based on your comparison chart, make an overall conclusion about the relationship between the causes and prevention of cardiovascular disease.

FIGURE 7.4   Selective reading guide: "Cardiovascular Disease" (*Source:* Kim Miller, Kenmore West High School, Kenmore, New York.)

kinds of end-of-chapter review questions that are found in many textbooks. However, teachers may prefer to make their own decisions regarding which facts, ideas, and terminology are most important and devise a guide that directs students to specific sections of the text. When such a guide is given to students before they read, it makes their reading more purposeful and efficient. The expectation here is that students will not necessarily need to read *all* the text but only those sections that contain essential information.

An example of a selective reading guide designed by Kim Miller, a high school health teacher, is shown in Figure 7.4. Kim introduced the guide to her class along with a brief introduction to the topic of cardiovascular disease. She explained that this is the number one killer in the United States, and asked how many students knew someone who had been affected by cardiovascular disease. Then she read through the reading guide with students, explaining the directions. She was careful to point out that some of the information asked for in the guide was explicitly stated in the text, but that there were also ideas which were implicit or which required them to use some of their prior knowledge. She suggested that students read the text through once and then go back and reread specific pages as needed to complete the guide. Students were asked to complete the reading and the guide for homework. The next day, students were put into groups of three or four to check over each other's responses, and then Mrs. Miller reassembled the whole class to compare responses, clarify any confusion, and provide additional explanations as necessary.

Interactive Reading Guides

As the name implies, an interactive reading guide (Buehl, 2001; Wood, 1988) is designed to guide the in-class reading of students as they interact in cooperative groups or pairs. Preparation of the guide begins with previewing the text selection, deciding on the main points that students need to understand, and identifying potential spots where students may have difficulty. The teacher should think about which sections of the text might be read orally or silently, which might be skimmed, or as with the selective reading guide, which passages may be skipped entirely. The guide will present specific tasks and questions that help students identify key ideas, make connections, and read critically.

The interactive reading guide in Figure 7.5 was designed for a section of a chapter in a U.S. history text on the Great Depression. Students could be given a class period to work on the reading guide, followed by another class session in which they would report on their results with guidance and feedback from the teacher. If one class period were not enough time to complete the whole reading, different segments could be assigned to each group, who would then present their findings to the whole class, as in the Jigsaw strategy described in Chapter 3.

SENSING AND RESPONDING TO TEXT STRUCTURE

A chapter in a history textbook, a poem, or a short story are not just random collections of words, facts, and ideas. Within each type of text are structures that tie ideas together. Texts "have both a content and a structure, with the knowledge of both entering into the comprehension process" (Just & Carpenter, 1987, p. 241). Teachers can aid student comprehension both by teaching students about text structure and by using the structures inherent in texts to help students organize the information that is presented (Goldman & Rakestraw, 2000).

Common Text Structures

Five kinds of structures, or organizational patterns, are commonly found in textbooks:

1. *Simple listing:* A collection of related facts or ideas, sometimes presented in order of importance. An example is the presentation of different types of bacteria in a biology text.

READING GUIDE: "THE BIG CRASH"

Directions: With your partner, follow the instructions below. You will share your results during the whole-class discussion of this section.

1. **Student A:** Read paragraph 1 on p. 601 aloud. **Group**: Listen and briefly predict some things you will be learning in the rest of this section.

2. **Student B:** Read the section on "Black Thursday" aloud. **Group:** Listen and summarize:
   - What happened to the stock market on Black Thursday?
   - What did the leading bankers decide to do?

3. **Group:** Skim the section on "The Big Crash" and read the *New York Times* page reprinted on p. 602. Together, draft a two-sentence summary:
   - Sentence 1: Explain what happened in the Big Crash.
   - Sentence 2: Give at least one statistic that illustrates what happened.

4. **Group:** Read the sections on "Unequal Distribution of Wealth" and "Other Flaws in the Economy," silently. Answer the following:
   - Give three reasons why factories were laying off workers and shutting down.
   - Consider what you have read since the beginning of this chapter. Why do the authors call the stock market a "gambling arena"?

5. **Group:** Read the next two sections, "Hoover Takes Action" and "Aid for Farmers and Business," silently. Answer the following:
   - List four things that the government did to try to help ease the effects of the Crash.
   - Why did imports and exports drop after the Hawley-Smoot Tariff Act?

6. **Student B**: Read aloud the 3rd and 4th paragraphs of the section on "The Run on Banks." **Group**: Listen and answer the following questions:
   - Give two reasons why banks were failing.
   - What did bank failures mean to the people who had money deposited?

7. **Group:** Read the next two sections, "Beginning of the Great Depression" and "Unemployed Strike Back," silently. Write a short summary of the effects that the Great Depression had on Americans.

8. **Group:** Read the rest of "The Big Crash" silently. President Hoover tried to help businesses, the unemployed, farmers, and homeowners through loans and construction projects, but he was against giving money directly to people. Answer the following and be ready to support your conclusions!
   - Why did he take this approach?
   - Do you agree or disagree with this?

FIGURE 7.5   Interactive reading guide: "The Big Crash"

2. *Sequence or time order:* A series of events that occur in a particular order. An example is a discussion of early African societies, from ancient Egypt to Timbuktu in the 1500s, in a global studies text.
3. *Compare and contrast:* A description of similarities and/or differences among two or more things. An example is the explanation of mean, median, and mode in a mathematics text.
4. *Cause and effect:* A description of events and their causes or consequences. Often, a single cause will have more than one effect, and a single event may have more than one cause. An example is a discussion of how temperature, pressure, concentration, and catalysts affect chemical reactions.
5. *Problem–solution:* Similar to cause and effect, except that outcomes are a result or solution of a perceived need or problem. An example is an explanation in a history text of how New Deal legislation was passed during the first 100 days of Roosevelt's presidency in response to the Great Depression.

Authors rarely use one of these patterns exclusively. Instead, they use multiple patterns. Within a section of text, however, the essential content is often presented via a single pattern. A chapter on color in a physics text, for example, *lists* the complementary colors and the colors of the spectrum and *compares* color by reflection with color by transmission. However, most of the chapter is concerned with how humans perceive color, and this is explained in terms of *causes and effects,* such as what happens when colored pigments are mixed, why the sky is blue, and why sunsets are red.

We will not emphasize simple listing in our discussion of text structure. It is more familiar to most students than the other structures, and it does not present as much difficulty for readers. Teaching strategies for working with lists of examples or attributes can be found in the Questions and Questioning section.

Although these five organizational patterns are commonly used throughout expository text, they are also found in narrative text and poetry. The plot of most fiction is driven by characters in search of a solution to a problem, as when Ahab seeks to destroy the white whale or Huck Finn tries to escape from his father. These problems set off chains of cause-and-effect events. Literature also makes frequent use of comparison and contrast, such as the comparisons of two lovers found in several of Shakespeare's sonnets.

Literature presents additional structural complexities, however. Although it is beyond the scope of this text to consider in detail the varied structures of poetry, drama, and novels, it is worth noting that narrative text generally follows a structure sometimes referred to as *story grammar.* Like the grammar or syntax of a sentence, a story is made up of certain components that fit together in a predictable sequence. The first common element in story structure is a *setting,* which establishes the time and place of the events. Authors also establish *characters* early in the story. An *initiating event* sets the plot in motion by establishing a problem or a conflict that one or more characters must try to resolve. What follows then are one or more episodes or *attempts* to resolve the problem, each with an *outcome*. The culmination of the plot is the *resolution* of the problem. The elements of story grammar are usually arranged in a predictable manner, although authors often manipulate story structures for literary effect. For instance, time and place may be purposely vague, the origins of a problem or conflict may only be implied, or an author might end a story without a definite resolution. Complex novels may feature numerous intertwined subplots with several characters, conflicts, attempts, and outcomes.

Teaching about Text Structures

**EVIDENCE-
BASED
RESEARCH**

There is evidence that text structure affects the reading comprehension of middle-grade and secondary students (Goldman & Rakestraw, 2000). In a study with fourth, sixth, and eleventh graders, Hare, Rabinowitz, and Schieble (1989) found "that both comparison/contrast and cause/effect texts (but not sequence texts) did pose greater difficulty for [students] than listing texts" (p. 86). Furthermore, awareness of text structures seems to have a positive effect on comprehension. Richgels et al. (1987) found that sixth graders had a high awareness of comparison/contrast structure and a low awareness of causation, and that structure-aware students were likely to use their awareness strategically as they read. Thus, the researchers believed that these students were "promising candidates for instruction in how to apply a structure strategy" while reading (p. 192). After studying fifth- and seventh-grade students' knowledge of text structure, Garner and Gillingham (1987) concluded that students benefit from direct instruction in the use of text structure. There is also evidence that students who are taught about text structures will use their knowledge to improve the structural coherence of their writing as well as to enhance their reading comprehension (Goldman & Rakestraw, 2000; Gordon, 1990; Miller & George, 1992).

Teacher modeling with Think alongs.   To introduce students to text structures, the teacher should identify and describe a specific structure, drawing simple examples from the textbook. The teacher could read aloud short passages, pointing out words that signal a particular text pattern and modeling the thinking processes that those words trigger. (A list of words commonly used to signal text patterns is given in Figure 7.6.) This modeling of thinking processes is called a Think Along (Ehlinger & Pritchard, 1994).

For example, a biology teacher might demonstrate the pattern of comparison and contrast with the following passage, which serves as a transition between two major sections of a chapter (Schraer & Stoltze, 1993):

> The problems of life in aquatic biomes are different from the problems in terrestrial biomes. For one thing, in aquatic biomes, water is always present. However, in fresh water, organisms must excrete less water, and in salt water,

Sequence/Time Order	Compare & Contrast	Cause and Effect/Problem-Solution
first, second, third, etc.	on the other hand	because
next	however	since
initially	less than, least	therefore
later	more than, most	if . . . then
following that	other	due to
finally	differently, difference	hence
before	similarly, similarity	thus
after	dissimilar	as a result
when	but	consequently
now	not only . . . but also	subsequently
in the past	either . . . or, neither . . . nor	accordingly
previously	while	eventually
presently	yet	initiated
	likewise	precipitated
	also	the outcome
	in comparison	the aftermath
	in contrast	
	conversely	

FIGURE 7.6   **Signal words for text structures**

excess salt may be excreted by organisms. Temperature changes in the course of a year are much less in aquatic environments than they are on land. Temperatures in the oceans show the least change, while those in lakes and ponds show more change. Other physical factors that affect living things in aquatic biomes are the amounts of oxygen and carbon dioxide dissolved in the water, the availability of organic and inorganic nutrients, and light intensity. (p. 854)

As the teacher reads this passage with the class, he or she could point out the use of the signal words *different from, however, less than, least,* and *while.* The teacher might also show how the comparisons and contrasts are layered, with contrasts drawn between aquatic and terrestrial biomes, fresh water and salt water, and oceans and lakes. The passage helps to bridge the information in the two sections of the chapter, and the teacher can show how this passage helps to anticipate some of the new material. Students could be involved in a discussion of why the authors use comparison and contrast and how knowledge of that structure might help them comprehend the text. Calling on students to volunteer examples from earlier lessons or their previous experience is also helpful. Once attention has been drawn to a specific structure, one of the following teaching strategies can be used to help students work with further text passages in which that structure is predominant.

EVIDENCE-BASED RESEARCH

Graphic representations.   The use of graphic and semantic organizers is one of the comprehension strategies recommended by the National Reading Panel (2000). Semantic maps are also useful for giving readers a graphic representation of the structural relationships between ideas in a passage. According to Jones, Pierce, and Hunter (1988/1989), students can be taught how to construct their own graphic representations of text ideas through a five-step teaching process:

1. Students survey the reading passage to see which organizational pattern, if any, the author appears to use.
2. Students construct a predicted outline of the passage. At first, they will need guidance to do this, perhaps with the teacher modeling on the chalkboard or overhead projector. Over time, students will become increasingly able to construct their own outlines.
3. Students read the passage.
4. The outlines are revised and completed, again with help from the teacher if needed.
5. Students use their completed outlines to formulate a written or oral summary of the passage. This can be done independently or as a cooperative-learning activity.

Jones, Pierce, and Hunter (1988/1989) suggest a general graphic form for each of several text structures (Figure 7.7). Each graphic form has associated *key frame questions* that can be used to guide students as they read the passage.

Guides to organizational patterns.   Just as a motorist uses a road map to plot a route, students can use a reading guide to help them navigate through a complicated text. The guide allows them to find the right intersections, avoid detours, recognize landmarks, and arrive at their destination with minimal delay. Teachers may design guides that can help students read assignments that feature potentially difficult organizational patterns or text structures. According to Herber (1978), an *organizational pattern guide* allows a student to "focus on the predominant pattern, using it as an aid to understanding relationships within the material and as an aid for recall after the reading has been completed" (p. 79).

For example, a sixth-grade science teacher is planning to spend a week working with a chapter on diseases. She knows from past experience that her students will have difficulty understanding the cause-and-effect relationships involved in the chapter. To help them, she devises a reading guide (Figure 7.8). On Monday, she reviews recent class discussions of cause-and-effect patterns in the text, introduces the topic of the chapter, and leads the class as they brainstorm about

(a) *Series of Events Chain*

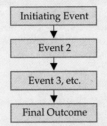

Key Frame Questions:
What is the object, procedure, or initiating event?
What are the stages or steps?
How do they lead to one another?
What is the final outcome?

(b) *Cycle*   (This form could be used for either sequence or cause/effect structures.)

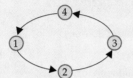

Key Frame Questions:
What are the critical events in the cycle?
How are they related?
In what ways are they self-reinforcing?

(c) *Compare/Contrast Matrix*

	Name 1	Name 2
Attribute 1		
Attribute 2		
Attribute 3		

Key Frame Questions:
What things are being compared?
How are they similar?
How are they different?

(d) *Cause/Effect Fishbone Map*   (A single cause that has multiple effects can be represented by reversing the cause and effect labels.)

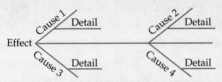

Key Frame Questions:
What are the factors that cause X?
How do they interrelate?
Are the factors that cause X the
    same as those that cause X to
    persist?

(e) *Problem-Solution Outline*

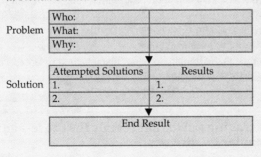

Key Frame Questions:
What was the problem?
Who had the problem?
Why was it a problem?
What attempts were made
    to solve the problem?
Did those attempts succeed?

FIGURE 7.7   **Graphic forms for representing text structures** (*Source:* From B. F. Jones, J. Pierce, & B. Hunter, "Teaching students to construct graphic representations," *Educational Leadership, 46,* 20–25, 1988/1989, December/January.)

READING GUIDE

1. **Directions:** Read the list of possible causes and effects below. As you read Chapter 6, match the causes to the effects. Note: some letters (causes) will be used more than once, and there may be more than one cause for a single effect. Be ready to back up your answers with information from the text.

CAUSES

a. skin stops microorganisms
b. white blood cells "remember" how to make antibodies
c. viruses
d. microorganisms in water or air
e. disinfectants kill germs
f. malnutrition, heredity, chemicals in air or water
g. bacteria
h. white blood cells destroy germs and damaged tissues
i. direct contact
j. mucus traps germs
k. vaccine causes the body to produce antibodies that kill bacteria
l. animal carriers
m. fungi

EFFECTS

_____ 1. infectious diseases

_____ 2. strep throat

_____ 3. disease is stopped or prevented

_____ 4. a person becomes immune

_____ 5. polio

_____ 6. infection stops and healing takes place

_____ 7. noninfectious diseases

_____ 8. infectious diseases spread from one host to another

_____ 9. diseases in plants

II. **Directions:** Below you will find some ideas about catching or preventing diseases. Check the ones you agree with, based on your own experience and what we have read and talked about. You must be able to explain why you did or didn't check each one.

_____ 1. People get sick from many different causes.

_____ 2. What you can't see won't hurt you.

_____ 3. Even though the human body has many natural defenses against disease, it still can use some help.

_____ 4. A good offense is the best defense.

FIGURE 7.8 **A reading guide that reveals the cause-and-effect structure of a chapter on diseases**

Technology Tip

There are software programs such as Timeliner and Inspiration that can be used by teachers or students to prepare and print out graphic representations of ideas. Timeliner can be used to prepare time lines of historical events. It is available in a version that can switch back and forth between English and Spanish. Inspiration can create webs, diagrams, maps, or outlines with information provided by the user.

Timeliner 5.0
Tom Snyder Productions
Watertown, MA
www.tomsnyder.com

Inspiration 7.6
Inspiration Software
Portland, OR
http://inspiration.com

diseases and their causes and cures. The teacher then distributes copies of the guide and goes over the instructions for Part I, emphasizing that there will be several possible ways to match the causes and effects. She assigns the first half of the chapter as homework. During the next three days, the teacher refers to Part I of the guide as students work their way through the chapter and carry out a lab experiment on the effect of disinfectants in preventing bacterial growth. When students have read the whole chapter, she has them complete Part II of the guide and compare responses for both parts with their lab partners. The class reviews the guide, lab work, and important vocabulary terms on Thursday. On Friday, students take a two-part chapter test. The first part consists of multiple-choice questions. For the second part of the test, students must pick one of the four statements from Part II of the reading guide and explain in writing why they agree or disagree with it.

You have probably noticed that Part I of the guide leads students to work with ideas within the predominant organizational pattern—cause and effect. Part II is what Herber (1978) calls the "so what?" part of the guide. That is, it challenges readers to draw conclusions, refer to their own experience, and in effect answer the question "So what does this all add up to?" The science teacher could have omitted this part of the guide if she felt such tasks could be addressed in other ways. She could also have given students only the items in the effects column, with directions to find the causes. This activity would be more difficult but might be effective with students who have the ability to determine causes on their own.

To develop an organizational pattern guide, first determine whether essential information and ideas are conveyed through one of the common text structures and whether this is likely to cause difficulty for students. Sequence, for instance, is inherent in most fiction and historical writing, but it may not be problematical for students unless the sequence in the text is different from the actual chronological sequence, as when an author uses flashbacks or otherwise presents events in a nonlinear fashion. The example in Figure 7.9 shows a format for comparison/contrast guides. The teacher lists comparisons, some literal and some inferred, from a passage on feudalism. Students have to decide whether or not the author actually makes those comparisons. As they explain their decisions, they will discuss the similarities and differences between serfs and free peasants, the Middle Ages and the Renaissance, and so on.

Story maps.   Research on story grammar suggests that children as young as five or six have a well-developed sense of the elements in story structure (Mandler & Johnson, 1979; Stein & Glenn, 1979). Extensive teaching of story structure beyond early elementary grades, therefore, is probably not warranted.

COMPARE AND CONTRAST: THE MIDDLE AGES

Directions: Read the list of comparisons below and then read pages 152–158 in your text. When you have finished reading, check those comparisons you believe are made either directly or indirectly by the author.

_____ 1. hopeless/hopeful

_____ 2. military service by knights/taxes

_____ 3. serfs/free peasants

_____ 4. work for the lord/pay rent

_____ 5. feudalism/national governments

_____ 6. fields of crops/raising sheep

_____ 7. Middle Ages/Renaissance

_____ 8. knights in armor/guns and cannons

_____ 9. vassal of a lord/number in a nation

Directions: Once you have finished the first part of this guide, check those statements below that you feel can be supported by what you read or your own experiences. Compare your responses with those of other members of the class. Be sure you can support your choices.

_____ 1. You get what you pay for.

_____ 2. Advances in technology often bring about the need for social and political changes.

_____ 3. Necessity is the mother of invention.

_____ 4. Guilds of the Middle Ages were much like the unions of today.

_____ 5. It takes a woman to get the job done right.

FIGURE 7.9   Comparison/contrast guide for a sixth-grade social studies lesson (_Source:_ Marilynne Crawford, Maya School, Guatemala City, Guatemala.)

"ROMEO AND JULIET"

Time & Place: **Characters:**

Middle Ages   Romeo—a Montague

Verona, Italy   Juliet—a Capulet

                                                     (Montagues & Capulets are bitter enemies)

The Event That Starts the Main Plot:

Romeo sneaks into a Capulet costume party and meets Juliet.

Characters' Response and Main Problem:

Romeo and Juliet fall in love, but they can't do anything about it because their families hate each other.

Major Events:

1. Romeo goes to Juliet's at night; they pledge their love to each other.

2. Romeo and Juliet secretly get married.

3. In a street fight, Romeo kills Juliet's cousin. He has to leave town to avoid arrest.

4. Juliet's father tells her she has to marry Paris, a young nobleman.

5. Juliet arranges to fake her death so she can escape with Romeo.

Resolution:

Romeo doesn't know the plan, sees Juliet "dead," kills himself.

Juliet wakes up, sees Romeo dead, kills herself.

Capulets and Montagues see the result of their hatred for each other.

FIGURE 7.10   Story map for _Romeo and Juliet_

**EVIDENCE-
BASED
RESEARCH**

However, as literary offerings become more sophisticated or complex, some readers may have difficulty tracking a story's development (Goldman & Rakestraw, 2000). To help readers navigate through a complex or unusual narrative, teachers may employ a variation of a story map. When working with story maps, teachers should expect varied student opinions regarding the initiating event, main problem, and what constitutes "important" events. Figure 7.10 illustrates a story map for _Romeo and Juliet_. Note that this story map does very little to involve readers in thinking about the theme of the play, Shakespeare's poetry, or the main characters and their dilemma. Outlining the structure of a story may help readers to follow the plot, but it is not sufficient engagement with a good literary work. A story map should be used as a foundation for other, more thoughtful consideration of the story.

SUMMARY

Using textbooks as tools for learning can be a challenge for many students. Through instruction and support, teachers can help students develop useful strategies for learning from reading. Thoughtful questioning can guide students' learning, especially if they are shown how to ask their own questions as they read. Readers of textbooks also need to learn how to work with different text structures and how to interpret an author's message. When teachers model these strategies and lead students through meaningful practice with content area text materials, students become more effective learners.

SUGGESTED READINGS

Allington, R. (2001). *What really matters for struggling readers: Designing research-based programs.* Portsmouth, NH: Heinemann.

Beck, I., McKeown, M., Hamilton, R., & Kucan, L. (1997). *Questioning the author: An approach for enhancing student engagement with text.* Newark, DE: International Reading Association.

Beers, K. (2003). *When kids can't read: What teachers can do. A guide for teachers 6–12.* Portsmouth, NH: Heinemann.

Block, C., & Pressley, M. (2002). *Comprehension instruction: Research-based best practice.* New York: Guilford.

Keene, E., & Zimmerman, S. (1997). *Mosaic of thought: Teaching comprehension in a reader's workshop.* Portsmouth, NH: Heinemann.

Raphael, T. (1986). Teaching question–answer relationships, revisited. *The Reading Teacher, 39,* 516–522.

Wood, K., Lapp, D., & Flood, J. (1992). *Guiding readers through text: A review of study guides.* Newark, DE: International Reading Association.

Increasing Vocabulary and Conceptual Growth

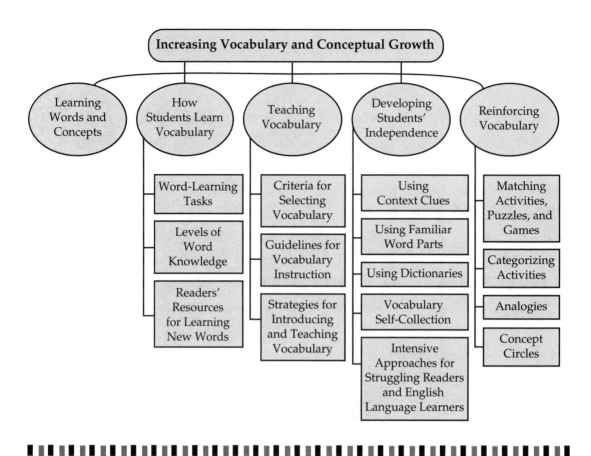

Polonius: What do you read, my lord?

Hamlet: Words, words, words.

If Hamlet is right and reading is just "words, words, words," then common sense suggests that a person who does not know the words is not going to have much success. In fact, it has long been recognized that vocabulary knowledge strongly influences reading comprehension (Nagy & Scott, 2000). Students need to learn the meanings of many new words, and to the extent that they can do this, they will be able to read and understand. Learning vocabulary is much more than memorizing words and definitions, however. In content areas, words are labels for important concepts and can only be mastered through repeated experience within meaningful context. The following anecdote from Lori Eframson, a rehabilitation counselor in Buffalo, New York, dramatically illustrates this point.

■ ■ ■ ■ ■ ■ ■

On a September day in 1973, when I was ten years old, I dove into what I thought was a pile of hay in a barn. It turned out to be only a floor-covering of hay, and I broke three vertebrae in the cervical region of my neck. This left me paralyzed from my shoulders down. My dive into the hay had changed my life forever. It also forced me to learn a whole new language—the technical language of medicine.

I spent six months in traction in a teaching hospital in Syracuse, New York. When the doctor would come to see me on his daily rounds, he would bring ten or twelve students with him and talk about me and my body as if I weren't there. I listened intently to every word he said, but understood almost none of it. None of this technical jargon was explained to me, either. Being a very curious kid, I wanted to know what they were saying about me. This was information that was very important to me, and I absorbed it all. I began to put pieces of the puzzle together. After a month or so, I found it easier to follow what the doctor was talking about. He said almost the same thing every day!

One day, he came in with his group of curious students. Before he could open his mouth, I spewed out his usual phrases. He and his students stood with their mouths hanging open as I told them about my central nervous system, the compression of the cervical, thoracic, and lumbar regions of my spine, the contraction and spasms of my muscles, the loss of sensation, and the conditions of paraplegia and quadraplegia. From this point on, the doctor would come in and say, "This is Lori. I'm going to let her tell you what's going on with her." It was kind of a joke, but I began to understand and accept my condition as I spoke about it.*

■ ■ ■ ■ ■ ■ ■

In this chapter, we first consider how readers learn vocabulary and then discuss several techniques for guiding and reinforcing students' vocabulary and conceptual growth. We emphasize ways to develop readers' strategies for learning vocabulary on their own.

LEARNING WORDS AND CONCEPTS

A close look at vocabulary development reveals several knotty questions: What exactly is a word? How many words are there that need to be learned? How are they learned? What do we mean when we say a person has "learned" a word?

On a simple typographic level, a word is a group of letters surrounded by white space. Such a definition hardly accounts for the richness of meaning that a word can represent, however. The word *fidelity*, for instance, represents a whole range of philosophical, psychological, and practical concepts in contexts ranging from ethics to matrimony to electronic sound reproduction. For our

---

*Used with the permission of Lori Eframson.

purposes, it may help to think of word *families,* or groups of words with clear relationships (Nagy & Herman, 1987). For instance, the words *specify, specifies, specific,* and *specification* are all members of the same family. Knowing the meaning of one of these words increases the chances of being able to infer the meanings of the others.

**EVIDENCE-
BASED
RESEARCH**

Nagy and Herman (1987) estimate that there are about 88,500 distinct word families in the printed English used in grades 3–9 and that the average schoolchild learns approximately 3,000 new words each year through twelfth grade. That is approximately eight new words each day! It is important to remember that these are rough averages. Students from different backgrounds vary considerably in their learning of vocabulary (White, Graves, & Slater, 1990), and students who are having reading difficulties have more trouble learning new words (Shefelbine, 1990).

It is not likely that students are absorbing eight new meanings a day from direct instruction by their teachers or by old-fashioned rote memorization. Although direct instruction is effective in teaching new word meanings, students also learn new meanings from wide reading, from conversation, and from the rich language environment of school, family, community, and mass media.

What is meant by saying a person "knows" a word is not simple. Students might understand the word *order* as something one does in a restaurant and as a general term having to do with arranging things. However, they would find new and different meanings for this word in content areas. Within social studies, they would find many meanings: a military order, a religious order, the Order of the Garter, law and order, and a new world order. Would they "know" the word if they did not understand all these? In biology, order has a specific meaning in the classification of organisms. Would it be enough to know that an *order* is a way to classify living things, or would students also need to know that *order* comes between *class* and *family,* two other words that everybody knows?

The point is that in content areas, words are more than marks on a page, more even than dictionary definitions. Content area vocabulary represents concepts, and learning the vocabulary means understanding the concepts well enough to apply them in a meaningful way. Although declarative knowledge (being able to define a term) may be sufficient for some technical vocabulary, much of the vocabulary learned in content areas requires procedural knowledge, or being able to do things with a concept, to apply it in combination with other ideas (Nagy & Scott, 2000).

HOW STUDENTS LEARN VOCABULARY

Every content area has a large collection of specialized or technical terms that denote important concepts. Sometimes these words and concepts are already familiar to students, for example, when high school seniors study *political parties.* Other words with commonly known meanings have specialized (and often different) meanings in a content area, as exemplified by the word order and by mathematical terms such as *proof, point, line,* and *root.* There are also technical terms that are specific to a particular content area, such as *abscissa, metaphor, photosynthesis,* and *archipelago.*

Word-Learning Tasks

When we talk of learning vocabulary, we are really talking of four different relationships between words and schemata or concepts (Graves & Slater, 1996; Herber, 1978). These four relationships, or word-learning tasks, are (1) known word/known concept, (2) new word/known concept, (3) known word/new concept, and (4) new word/new concept. These relationships are illustrated in Figure 8.1. In the first, a common or known word represents a concept that students understand. When seventh graders begin a unit on *weather,* they are using a familiar word to label familiar phenomena. This is more than review, however. In their study of weather, they will enlarge and refine their concept.

The second kind of word-learning task is to apply new words to familiar concepts. The teacher may introduce the terms *meteorology* and *precipitation.* Students will be familiar with rain or snow, but some may not know the generic term for "wet stuff that falls from the sky." Most have seen weather forecasts on television and heard the word *meteorologist,* but they may not know the meaning of *meteorology.*

The third word-learning task requires students to learn a new concept but use a familiar word. For example, students will have several ideas about what pressure means, but the concepts of air pressure (or barometric pressure) and how changes in pressure affect weather may be new. All students know the words *watch* and *warning,* but these terms have specific technical meanings when the National Weather Service issues a *storm watch* or *storm warning.* This word-learning task may present some special difficulties when students have to unlearn or at least suspend a known meaning for a word in order to learn a new concept. A good example is the word work. In everyday usage this refers to a variety of things that people do: go to work, *work* out an agreement, work up a sweat, and work on a problem. In physics, however, *work* has a very precise meaning: it is the amount of force applied to an object multiplied by the

Words	Concept	Examples from a Science Unit
1. Known word	Known concept	weather
2. New word	Known concept	meteorology, precipitation
3. Known word	New concept	pressure, storm watch, storm warning
4. New word	New concept	humidity, hygrometer

FIGURE 8.1   **The four word-learning tasks**

distance the object moves. By this definition, studying for a chapter test or doing 30 math problems is no work at all! This seeming paradox can be very frustrating, especially for middle-grade students. However, every content area has many examples of this kind of word.

The final word-learning task is probably the most difficult. In this case, students must learn both a new concept and a new word to describe it. Although seventh-grade students may have heard the term *humidity* used in weather reports, the concept of moisture in the air will be new for many. The term *hygrometer* and the way in which this instrument measures humidity will almost certainly be novel. These students will be developing new concepts and vocabulary within the overall schema of weather.

Levels of Word Knowledge

We have questioned what it means to know or learn a word. There is no easy answer. Words have many uses and meanings. Like people, they may be complete strangers or intimate friends, with many intervening gradations of acquaintanceship, from "Weren't we in an English class together once?" to "Hey, it's great to see you again!"

A word may be in a student's *receptive vocabulary* (recognized when seen or heard), yet may rarely or never be part of that person's *expressive vocabulary* (used in speech or in writing). Some words (and associated concepts) are learned so well in school that people never forget them. Other words are learned superficially, and all but a vague residue seems to evaporate from memory as soon as the student has taken a test or moved on to another subject.

Teachers require different levels of word and concept knowledge. To match a word and definition in a multiple-choice test, a student must recognize the word and associate it with the information given. For example, the following question could be answered even if the student had never seen a hygrometer:

A _____ is used to measure humidity.

a. thermometer   b. barometer
c. hygrometer   d. hydrometer

If the student were supposed to actually use a hygrometer to measure humidity and to explain how the hygrometer works, the task might seem much more difficult. Certainly the knowledge required would be deeper and more complex. However, if the student had practiced using a hygrometer and had been carefully taught how it works, the task might be easier than the rote memory retrieval required for the multiple-choice test.

The question of what it means to learn a word is relative. The answer depends on how the word is to be used, when it will be encountered again, how the word is taught, and how a person's knowledge is to be assessed.

Readers' Resources for Learning New Words

When a reader comes across an unfamiliar word, there are four ways he or she might approximate the meaning: context clues, morphemic analysis, expert advice, and the dictionary (Nagy & Scott, 2000).

EVIDENCE-BASED RESEARCH

Context clues.   Written and spoken contexts are the richest resources for learning new words (Nagy & Herman, 1987). What other possible explanation is there for the rapid growth in vocabulary in children and the fact that adults are constantly learning new words and new meanings for old words? When proficient readers encounter an unfamiliar word, they usually read on, content to ignore that word or derive a partial understanding as long as their overall comprehension of the passage is satisfactory. Although initial exposure to an unfamiliar word in context may have limited usefulness, seeing or hearing the word again in different contexts may build a more complete meaning, until eventually the word becomes well understood (Nagy & Scott, 2000).

Context is not always helpful, however. Unfamiliar words often appear in contexts that offer few, if any, hints to the word's meaning (Schatz & Baldwin, 1986). In fact, the context may be misleading or confusing. To demonstrate just how little help context can be, read the following passage from *A House for Mr. Biswas* by Nobel laureate V. S. Naipaul (1984) and try to figure out what the italicized word means:

> His tailless shirt flapped loose, unbuttoned all the way down, the short sleeves rolled up almost to his arm-pits. It was as though, unable to hide his *prognathous* face, he wished to display the rest of himself as well. (p. 244)

If you did not previously know the meaning of *prognathous*, you may have guessed something like "ugly" or "homely" because of the implication that the man's face should be hidden. However, nothing in the context suggests the actual meaning of the word, which is "having a protruding jaw."

Morphemic analysis.   Familiar word parts—roots and affixes—are another aid in wrestling with unfamiliar words. Using these parts to approximate meaning is sometimes called *morphemic analysis*. A *morpheme* is the technical term for the smallest unit of meaning in a language. The word *car* is a free morpheme; it can stand alone. The suffix *-s* is a bound morpheme; it has no meaning by itself, but when added to a word, as in *cars*, it carries the meaning of "more than one." *Cars* is therefore a word made up of two morphemes. Some morphemes are fairly consistent in the way they modify a root word, such as the prefixes *re-* in *reproduce* and *un-* in *unlikely*. Another large group of morphemes, many of Latin or Greek origin, combine with other morphemes to make up familiar or predictable words in science, math, and social studies (*biology, photosynthesis, centimeter, polygon, automation,* and *monopoly*).

We said at the beginning of the chapter that it is really more useful to think of words in families than as discrete entities. When a person learns one word, she or he may be able to generalize to other variations of the word. A person who knows the word *exist* may understand the words *existence* and *existent*. Morphemic generalization is not infallible, however. Knowing the variations of *exist* is not much help in understanding *existentialism*, and knowing *sign* does not help with *resignation*.

Context clues and morphemic analysis can be complementary, as in the following example from a middle-grade social studies text (Rawls & Weeks, 1985): "Energy from the earth's core can be tapped through hot water or steam near the earth's surface. This *geothermal* energy can be used to generate electricity" (p. 727). The context clearly explains the concept, and familiarity with other words containing the roots *geo* and *therm* (*geography* and *thermometer*) will reinforce the meaning of the word.

A recent review of the research on teaching contextual and morphological analyses as transferable and generalizable vocabulary learning strategies suggests the following:

1. Use of context clues is a relatively ineffective means for inferring the meanings of specific words; rather, semantic relatedness procedures and mnemonic methods are preferred approaches for teaching the meanings of specific words.
2. When definitional information is combined with contextual cues, students are more apt to learn specific new vocabulary than when contextual analysis is used in isolation.
3. Teaching contextual analysis does facilitate students' ability to infer word meanings from surrounding context, although the relative efficacy of instruction in specific context clues versus simple practice in inferring meanings from context remains in question.
4. There is some indication that students can be taught specific morphemes (e.g., prefixes) that may enable them to unlock the meanings of unknown words containing these elements; also, there is some evidence that teaching students the meanings of unfamiliar words enables them to infer the meanings of morphologically related words. However, additional research is required in this area. (Baumann, Kame'enui, & Ash, 2003, p. 774)

Expert advice.   A reader who is stumped by a word can ask for expert advice. The "expert" can be a teacher, a parent or sibling, or the student at the next desk. Often, asking someone is the simplest and most satisfying solution. By asking and receiving a good answer, the reader gets the needed information while the motivation to learn is strong and with minimal disruption of the reading process.

Dictionaries.   When context or roots and affixes fail to help with the meaning of a word, a reader can consult a dictionary or glossary. In fact, when students ask for help with a word, many well-meaning teachers tell them, "Look it up in the

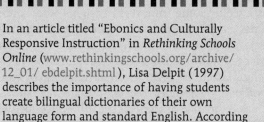

Bidialectical Dictionaries for Dialect Speakers

In an article titled "Ebonics and Culturally Responsive Instruction" in *Rethinking Schools Online* (www.rethinkingschools.org/archive/12_01/ ebdelpit.shtml), Lisa Delpit (1997) describes the importance of having students create bilingual dictionaries of their own language form and standard English. According to Delpit, "Both the students and the teacher become engaged in identifying terms and deciding upon the best translations. This can be done as generational dictionaries, too, given the proliferation of 'youth culture' terms growing out of the Ebonics-influenced tendency for the continual regeneration of vocabulary" (Delpit, 1997, n.p.). To stay current with similar issues related to culturally responsive instruction, visit the regularly updated *Rethinking Schools Online* Web site at www.rethinkingschools.org/archive/curriss.shtml.

dictionary." Although dictionaries are valuable tools, they are not always effective for learning vocabulary. Students may turn to the dictionary, read a definition, and come away no better informed than when they started. For instance, if you look up the term *radioisotope* in the dictionary, you will find the definition "radioactive isotope," which is not very useful unless you happen to know those words. Looking up *microtubule* in the glossary of a high school biology textbook yields "long, cylindrical organelles found in cilia and flagella." (Help!)

It is not that dictionaries, glossaries, and thesauruses are not useful tools or that students should never be told to look a word up. The point is that students must be shown how to use various resources for learning words. The following section on teaching strategies presents several ways to enhance students' use of context clues, morphemic analysis, and dictionaries.

TEACHING VOCABULARY

EVIDENCE-
BASED
RESEARCH

A teacher must decide how much attention to give to vocabulary, which words should be taught, and when and how they should be taught. There is an important cost–benefit ratio to consider (Graves, 1986; Graves & Prenn, 1986). Simply put, the harder the task and the deeper the knowledge expected of students, the more time that must be put into instruction, as illustrated by the earlier example about the word *hygrometer*. Given the necessity of meeting many curriculum objectives in too little time, teachers must try to keep the costs of instruction low and the benefits high. Because school reading materials present so many potentially unfamiliar words, this is quite a challenge.

To illustrate this problem, we examined two very different samples of content area text: a chapter from a sixth-grade science textbook and a short story from a ninth-grade literature anthology. We listed words from each selection that might be unfamiliar to a significant portion of students in the respective grade levels (Figures 8.2 and 8.3). Although each word is a candidate for special attention, no science or English teacher would be able to take time to teach all of the words on either list.

Examination of the two lists yields some important insights into content area vocabulary. First, it becomes easier to understand how students might encounter an average of eight unfamiliar words each day. There are some similarities between the lists. Both have common words used in uncommon ways (*eye, runner, daughter, egg, rise, game, lots*). Each list includes terms made up of two or more words (*third-person narration, preparatory school, asexual reproduction, daughter cells*). The two lists are also indicative of some of the differences between expository and narrative text. Roughly two-thirds of the terms in the science chapter (Figure 8.2) are written in boldface, explained in context, and defined in the margins of the textbook. Most of them are repeated throughout the chapter as concept builds on concept. Clearly, the science passage is dense in new words and concepts, and to understand the chapter a reader will need a pretty clear understanding of each term. To teach the vocabulary is to teach the content.

Although the short story had almost as many potentially unfamiliar words, only four of them were defined in the text (Figure 8.3), and only three appeared more than once in the story. Most ninth-grade readers could follow the plot and understand the story even if they recognized less than half of the words on the list. Except for *preparatory school* (which is defined in a footnote), none of these words are essential for adequate comprehension, although each

trait*	potato eyes
reproduction*	strawberry runners
heredity*	fertilization*
inherited*	egg*
asexual reproduction*	sperm*
sexual reproduction*	pistil*
unique	stigma*
cell*	ovary*
amoeba	stamen*
nucleus*	anther*
clone*	pollen*
oyster	budding*
cell division*	sea anemones
daughter cells*	hydra
regeneration*	
organisms	
salamander	

*Printed in boldface and defined in the margin.

FIGURE 8.2   Potentially unfamiliar terms from a chapter (about 3,800 words long) on reproduction in a sixth-grade science textbook

catkins	deterred
preparatory school*	inconceivable
genial	quadruplicate
blueprints	sward
dormitory	grandeur
Shah of Iran	perplexity
asinine	resignation
game (a game woman)	incredulity
ambitious	foil**
reserve (lack of reserve)	conflict***
rise (waited for a rise on a remark)	third-person narration**
unrepentant	omniscient**
segregated	scholarship
lots (to draw lots)	

*Defined in a footnote.

**Defined in Skill Development section at the end of the story.

***Unit theme.

FIGURE 8.3   Potentially unfamiliar terms from *The Lie* by Kurt Vonnegut (about 3,200 words long)

adds color and depth to the story. Spending an inordinate amount of time on learning this vocabulary would detract from the more important and interesting reactions to the plot, theme, and characters of the story.

Criteria for Selecting Vocabulary

Comparison of the word lists in Figures 8.2 and 8.3 suggests that the first step toward maximizing the cost–benefit ratio should be judicious choice of words with which to work. Herber (1978) suggests four criteria to keep in mind when selecting vocabulary: relation to key concepts, relative importance, students' ability and background, and potential for enhancing independent learning.

Relation to key concepts.   There is little point in spending time with a word if it is not necessary to the comprehension of the selection. Many of the words in Figure 8.3 can be eliminated under this criterion. They are not crucial to getting the gist of the narrative or understanding the conflicts in the plot.

Relative importance.   A teacher must decide the relative importance of concepts and terms. For instance, in Figure 8.2, the terms *sexual reproduction* and *asexual reproduction* are the two central ideas in the chapter. Also, some terms have relatively high value outside the specific selection at hand. Since the next chapter in the science text is about genetics, the terms *trait, heredity,* and *clone* will be used frequently in the subsequent lessons. Many terms that students learn even have resonances beyond the school year and beyond a particular content area. Consider, for instance, the cumulative nature of math curricula and the importance of math concepts in biology, chemistry, and physics.

Students' ability and background.   Which words are likely to be familiar to most students? What experience will students from diverse linguistic, social, and cultural backgrounds have with the words and concepts? Students with limited proficiency in English may know the words in their native language but not in English. Have any of the terms been studied previously, and will a quick review be enough to refresh students' understanding? What resources or skills do the students have that might allow them to figure out the words themselves? If most students know a word or can easily associate it with something familiar, that word will require less attention. For example, in Figures 8.2 and 8.3, *oyster* and *segregated* might be familiar enough that they would not need much attention.

Potential for enhancing independent learning.   Sometimes when teachers teach specific words and concepts, they also develop strategies, such as context clues, morphemic analysis, or dictionary skills, that students can use to figure out the meanings of other words they may encounter. For instance, discussion of the prefix *re-* in *regeneration* and *reproduction* will help students understand those terms, but it will also give them a strategy for understanding words such as *reaction, recycling,* and *renewable.*

Guidelines for Vocabulary Instruction

EVIDENCE-
BASED
RESEARCH

Our understanding of the research on vocabulary instruction (Baumann et al., 2003; Blachowicz & Fisher, 2000; Graves, 1986; Kibby, 1995; Stahl & Clark, 1987) leads us to six guidelines for teaching vocabulary:

1. Start with what students already know, and build new terms and concepts on that.
2. Provide students with multiple exposures to new terms and concepts. A single presentation is rarely enough to convey complex meanings.
3. Involve students in varied activities using new terms and concepts. Active engagement creates interest and strengthens learning; varied contexts help to develop fuller meanings for words.
4. Teach to promote transfer. Concentrate on words and strategies that have the widest possible application to other subjects and other reading situations.
5. Include discussion as one of the vocabulary activities. When students know they may have to explain new terms in their own words, they tend to process the meanings of the terms more thoroughly.

6. Make your classroom a word-rich environment in which students are immersed in rich language and appreciation for the power of words.

The teaching strategies presented throughout the rest of this chapter were selected to meet these guidelines.

Strategies for Introducing and Teaching Vocabulary

This section discusses several strategies for introducing and teaching content area vocabulary. Depending on the number and difficulty of the vocabulary terms in a lesson, teachers may choose to use any of these strategies before students read, while they read and discuss the text in class, or after they have read an assignment as homework.

In-class presentation.   Perhaps the least costly strategy in terms of time, yet still beneficial, is simply presenting students with a list of important vocabulary and briefly discussing each term. For instance, a teacher in an eleventh-grade history class might quickly refer to the following six terms written on the blackboard: *free enterprise, monopoly, trust, holding company, Social Darwinism,* and *laissez-faire.* The teacher asks the students if they know any of these terms, then briefly defines each, and finally tells them to pay careful attention to the terms as they read the section titled "The Age of Industry" for tomorrow's class. A simple presentation such as this may be all that is required if there are relatively few terms, if they are clearly explained in the text, and if students have sufficient ability.

Semantic mapping.   One strategy has attracted more attention than any other as a means of introducing new vocabulary, perhaps because it is so versatile and because two decades of research have shown it to be effective with learners of diverse reading abilities, ages, and ethnicities (Baumann et al., 2003). The basic idea is to place key terms into a diagram, sometimes called a *semantic map* or semantic web (Johnson & Pearson, 1984). Key words are arranged in clusters that represent the way in which semantic information is organized in one's memory. The main topic is at the center, with related concepts radiating outward from it (Figure 8.4).

A semantic map is most effective when it is developed with students' input and discussion. The example in Figure 8.4 was constructed for a tenth-grade general biology class. The teacher told students they would be studying the nervous system next and wrote those two words on the blackboard. She then asked students what they knew about the nervous system—what its function was, what the various parts were, and how they were related. As students came up with terms like *brain* and *nerves,* she added them to the growing semantic map on the board, along with terms that she added and defined herself, such as *neurons.* Through questioning, students were able to give examples of *voluntary*

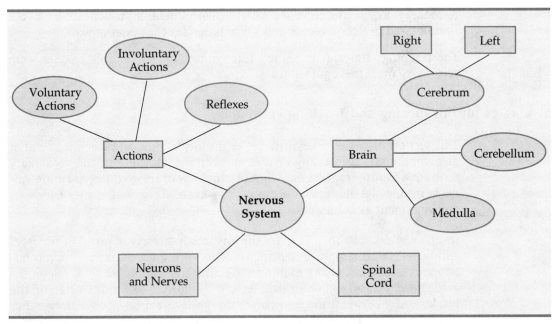

FIGURE 8.4   **Semantic map of the nervous system for a tenth-grade biology unit**

and *involuntary actions* and *reflexes.* Finally, the teacher added the terms for the various parts of the brain and explained each one briefly. Students copied the resulting map into their notebooks and referred to it frequently as they worked through the chapter. Another version of the semantic map, called the *graphic organizer* (Barron, 1969), was introduced in Chapter 6.

Concept of definition map.   Readers often have trouble giving their own definitions for words because they do not have a fully developed concept of what a definition is. Word maps have been used to teach students about three types of information that together make up the concept of a definition (Schwartz & Raphael, 1985; Schwartz, 1988). As students discuss a particular term, they are asked to consider the *category* in which it falls ("What is it?"), its properties ("What is it like?"), and *illustrations* of the term ("What are some examples?"). A completed *concept of definition map* is shown in Figure 8.5. Using such a map, students should be able to write a full definition of the term. Once students are familiar with the concept of definition map, they can develop definitions for one or two words in small groups and report their work to the whole class.

Semantic maps and graphic organizers have been successfully adopted by many teachers, who see several advantages to them. When students are involved in discussing and developing a semantic map or graphic organizer,

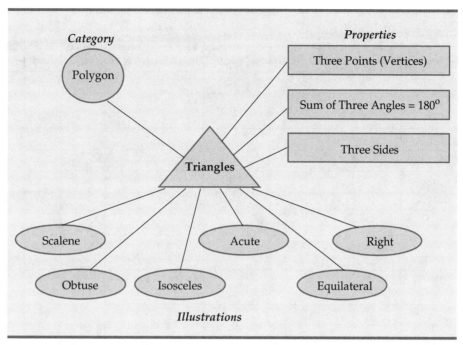

Category

Polygon

Properties

Three Points (Vertices)

Sum of Three Angles = 180°

Three Sides

Triangles

Scalene

Acute

Right

Obtuse

Isosceles

Equilateral

Illustrations

FIGURE 8.5   A concept of definition map on triangles for an eighth-grade math class

they are able to combine their prior knowledge with new information. The map or diagram also allows them to see the interrelation of the concepts they are studying—how one idea fits with another. These techniques have a solid research base. As noted earlier, semantic organizers have been shown to be particularly effective with students of diverse reading abilities, ages, and ethnic backgrounds (Baumann et al., 2003) because they allow students to use their background knowledge and experience in learning new vocabulary.

Semantic feature analysis.   Another strategy for teaching vocabulary that has been effective with diverse student groups is *semantic feature analysis* (Anders & Bos, 1986; Baumann et al., 2003; Johnson & Pearson, 1984). Semantic feature analysis helps students see relationships among key concepts and vocabulary, particularly the many dimensions of meaning that may be associated with a particular term.

The example given in Figure 8.6 was developed by Lavon Smith, a teacher of ESL in Athens, Georgia, for a reading assignment on health and diet. In the far left column of the grid, Lavon listed various foods and included spaces for students to fill in other favorites. Across the top of the grid, he listed several characteristics of foods that students were going to be reading about and discussing. He

Food	Has animal protein	Has choles-terol	Fattening	Has added sugar	Very healthful	Often eaten raw	Ethnic food	Fast food	Junk food	Gourmet food
Beef										
Mars Bar										
Egg										
Carrot										
Salmon										
Apple										
Egg roll										
Ham-burger										
Whole milk										
Whole wheat bread										

FIGURE 8.6   **Semantic feature analysis grid for a reading assignment on health and diet for an ESL class** (*Source:* Lavon Smith, Athens, Georgia.)

gave each student a copy of the grid and also displayed a copy on the overhead projector. First, the class went down the left-hand column and discussed each kind of food listed, practicing pronunciation and making sure that all students understood the terms. Then Lavon reviewed the words written across the top of the grid, briefly defining the terms *protein, cholesterol, ethnic,* and *gourmet.* The discussion of ethnic food elicited a lot of enthusiastic participation from this ethnically diverse group, and Lavon pointed out how many ethnic foods had become staples in the American diet. As they talked, the group marked each box on the grid. A plus (+) signified a positive relationship between two terms (e.g., beef has animal protein). A minus (−) meant a negative relationship (e.g., egg roll is not eaten raw). A question mark (?) indicated that the class was unsure of the relationship. Lavon left these decisions up to the class. For some columns, such as "Fast food" and "Junk food," there were diverse opinions. After the students had completed discussion of the feature analysis grid, they were assigned a four-page reading in their ESL reader. As they read, the students verified or revised their responses on the feature analysis grid. The next day they discussed the grid again as a whole class, paying special attention to the previously unknown relationships.

Possible sentences.   *Possible sentences* (Moore & Moore, 1992; Stahl & Kapinus, 1991) is a technique that requires relatively little preparation time but is quite effective for getting students actively involved in discussing, writing, and reading, all focused on key vocabulary terms. It works as follows:

1. Identify five to eight key vocabulary words and list them on the board. Pronounce each word for the students. For instance, as a math teacher you might select the words *random, outcome, event, sample space,* and *equally likely* from a unit on probability.
2. Also list a few key words that are likely to be known by students. In this case, you might use *chance* and *possible,* two words that are important in the unit.
3. Ask students to make up sentences using at least two words from the list. This can be done in small groups or individually. Record the student sentences on the board until all the words on the list have been used at least once. It does not matter if some words are used incorrectly. The following are possible sentences using the examples listed previously:
   - Each *outcome* has the same *chance* of occurring.
   - Probability is the *chance* that an *event* will happen.
4. Ask students to speculate what the unit might be about. Students then read the text, looking for the targeted vocabulary terms. They verify whether or not their sentences are "possible." That is, are the words used in the same sense in which they are used in the text?
5. Have students participate in either small-group or whole-class discussion to reach a consensus on whether their sentences are possible. If they are not, they are amended or refined as needed. A dictionary may be used if the context of the selection does not yield a satisfactory meaning.
6. As a final step, ask for new sentences using at least two of the words. This reinforces the meanings of the words and gives students yet another exposure to them.

Visual associations.   It is often easier to remember a new word and its meaning if one can connect it with a strong visual image. Verbal–visual associations are often recommended as particularly useful word-learning strategies for ELLs (Echevarria, Vogt, & Short, 2000). Gary Hopkins (Hopkins & Bean, 2000) used a strategy he called vocabulary squares to teach roots and prefixes to junior and senior high school students at Lame Deer High School on the Northern Cheyenne Reservation in Montana. He drew a square and subdivided it into four panels. (An example of a vocabulary square is shown in Figure 8.7.) In the first panel, he wrote a root or prefix that he wanted students to learn. In the second panel, he wrote the dictionary definition. The third

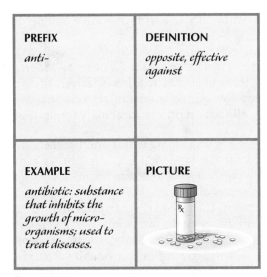

FIGURE 8.7   Vocabulary square

panel featured an example of how the root or prefix was used in a word. Then he drew a picture to illustrate the example in the fourth panel.

Instead of roots and prefixes, vocabulary squares could be modified to teach content area vocabulary terms. The first panel would contain the target word, the second square the dictionary definition, and the third square could feature a sentence using the word. An illustration would again go in the remaining space.

Selling words.   Teachers can be "wordmongers," or sellers of words. Learning vocabulary is not just a matter of strategies and instruction, costs and benefits. There is an affective dimension, too. Students need to have fun with words, to become "word-aware" and "word-curious." As good role models, teachers can nurture appreciation of words. Teachers can "sell" words by discussing connotations and ingenious usages, exploring word histories and derivations, and sharing new additions to their personal lexicon. Appendix A presents a list of books that deal with vocabulary in various content areas. Teachers might include some of these books in their classroom libraries and refer to them during class discussions. Looking up word histories, acronyms, and interesting or amusing words is a good activity for odd and idle minutes when the teacher is taking attendance or when a student has finished a test or seatwork assignment before the rest of the class. Teachers can also generate interest and appreciation for language by playing with words in riddles, puns, and language games. Several of the books in Appendix A illustrate the humor of language use and misuse. Other examples of the interest, power, and humor of words can come from newspaper clippings and cartoons.

(Source: © Tribune Media Services, Inc. All Rights Reserved. Reprinted with permission.)

ACTIVITY

- Select a concept or unit of study in your discipline. Generate a list of vocabulary terms for that concept or unit. Share your list with a colleague in your discipline. Together, categorize the list into those words that are crucial, those that would be nice to know, and those that students need to be aware of only.
- Choose one or more of the following to complete with a colleague in your discipline:
  1. Decide how you might introduce each of the crucial terms.
  2. Create a semantic feature analysis activity with your terms.
  3. Create a model concept of definition map for one or more of the vocabulary terms on your crucial list.

DEVELOPING STUDENTS' INDEPENDENCE

Teachers should try to teach more than the terms needed on the next test; they should also emphasize strategies that readers can use to deal with unfamiliar words in other contexts. This section examines some vocabulary-teaching techniques that also reinforce word-learning strategies that readers can use independently.

Using Context Clues

When we discussed how readers learn vocabulary, we said that context clues are useful but sometimes misleading. Despite the potential difficulties in relying on context, there is evidence that instruction in using context clues is especially effective when it is combined with definitional information (Baumann et al., 2003).

Target words in text. A teacher can present target words that are either taken directly from the text or from sentences composed by the teacher. Relevant portions of the text can be shown to students on the chalkboard, an overhead, or a handout. Some teachers initially cover or omit the target words and encourage students to predict the meanings of the words from the context. Students should talk about how they arrived at their predictions. That is, what in the context suggests what the target words mean? This kind of discussion helps make students more aware of how context can help with unfamiliar words.

EVIDENCE-BASED RESEARCH

When presenting target words in text, the teacher must ensure that the context is rich enough to imply the meaning of the word. Research has shown that when teachers ensure that a target word is embedded in rich context and directly teach the definition of that word, students' comprehension of text passages is improved (Baumann et al., 2003). For example, students who are taught using a definition-plus-context approach do better on measures of word knowledge and reading comprehension than students who are taught contextual clues and definitional information separately (Kolich, 1991; Stahl, 1983). Based on their meta-analysis of what type of vocabulary instruction affects comprehension, Stahl and Fairbanks (1986) reported:

> Methods that provided only definitional information about each to-be-learned word did not produce a reliable effect on comprehension. . . . Also, drill-and-practice methods, which involve multiple repetitions of the same type of information about a target word using only associative processing, did not appear to have reliable effects on comprehension. (p. 101)

Citing this evidence and other research on teaching definitions, Baumann et al. (2003) concluded that "definitional instruction alone is not likely to promote comprehension of passages that contain taught words. Additional instructional dimensions—contextual information or semantic relatedness, for example—must support or extend definition instruction" (p. 765).

Knowledge rating. To introduce a list of potentially unfamiliar words, teachers can use a strategy called *knowledge rating* (Blachowicz, 1986). Figure 8.8 presents a knowledge rating chart developed by Gretchen Bourdeau, a sixth-grade science teacher, as an introduction to a chapter on astronomy. Students who thought they could define a word checked the first column, "Know it well." Students who had heard or seen a word but were unsure what it meant checked the second column, "Heard of it." If the word was completely unfamiliar, students checked the "Clueless" column. Students were told to jot down the meanings of "Know it well" terms on the backs of their papers. They were especially motivated by this activity because it was all right not to know an answer.

RATE YOUR SPACE KNOWLEDGE

	Know it well	Heard of it	Clueless
aurora			
galaxy			
quasar			
big bang theory			
black hole			
pulsar			
neutron star			
supernova			
corona			
sunspot			
fusion			
prominence			
Milky Way			
telescope			
red giant			
nebula			
solar flare			

FIGURE 8.8 **A knowledge-rating chart for a sixth-grade science lesson** (*Source:* Gretchen Bourdeau, Oglethorpe County Middle School, Georgia.)

After they had worked on their own for about 15 minutes, Ms. Bourdeau led the class as they developed a list of the terms they knew and discussed what these words meant. Of the 17 terms, there were only 3 for which all the students were "clueless": *quasar, big bang theory,* and *prominence.* Ms. Bourdeau defined these for the class and noted that these three would need special attention as they continued their study of astronomy. At the end of the class period, students left the class with an awareness of how much they already knew about this new topic, a firm understanding of most of the vocabulary, and a significant investment of interest and attention. In the following days, as they read and discussed the chapter, the class confirmed, altered, or expanded on their understanding of these terms.

Wide reading. Regular independent reading is frequently suggested as an effective vocabulary-building strategy (Nagy, Herman, & Anderson, 1985).

Many content area teachers encourage students to read beyond their textbooks by assigning projects that require outside reading and by frequently sharing content-related books and articles with students. In fact, using literature in content areas is the subject of Chapter 12. Nonetheless, despite a large body of anecdotal evidence supporting the use of wide reading to develop young people's vocabulary knowledge, the fact remains that very few well-designed research studies have been conducted on this topic to date (Baumann et al., 2003; National Reading Panel, 2000).

Using Familiar Word Parts

Students can learn many words by morphemic generalization, especially when they use it in conjunction with context clues (Blachowicz & Zabroske, 1990; Wysocki & Jenkins, 1987). Through the intermediate grades and into high school, the number of words in content areas that are built with common roots and affixes increases dramatically. Therefore, it makes sense to help students by teaching them the strategy of morphemic analysis and by teaching them directly many of the important building blocks of the English language.

Teaching morphemic analysis.   When a new term is made up of familiar or easily analyzable parts, students should be led to infer the meaning. Good examples are *reproduce* and *regeneration* from the list in Figure 8.2. Once attention has been drawn to the prefix *re-*, students can be asked for other *re-* words they know. A general meaning for the prefix can then be derived from words such as *rebuild* and *repay*. The next step is to ask what other familiar parts they see in the two new words, leading to a discussion of *produce* and *generate*. Finally, the class can derive possible meanings for the two words.

Not all words are made up of familiar parts, however. Teachers can still help students by directly teaching the meanings of selected morphemes, as Gary Hopkins did in the vocabulary squares activity discussed previously. If students learn that the root *gen* in *regeneration* refers to "birth" or "species," they will have a clue to the relationship among the various meanings of *generation* and related words such as *gene, genetics,* and *generic*.

Etymology.   When a teacher and students talk about the meanings of roots and affixes, they are essentially discussing the origin and history of words. This is called *etymology* (from the Greek word *etumen*, which means "the real or true sense of a word"). There is much more to etymology than the study of roots and affixes, however. It is especially interesting to consider the contributions to American English that have been made by various nationalities and ethnic groups (see Figure 8.9) and to see how the language is constantly being enriched by borrowing from many vital language communities. For example, as English-speaking immigrants first encountered the Americas, they borrowed Native American words for the many places and

Borrowed words:					
Spanish:		*African:*		*Native American:*	
fiesta	alligator	banjo	yam	racoon	squash
macho	patio	jazz	phony	kayak	hickory
mesa	ranch	tote	zombie	tomato	potato
canyon	hammock	okra		moccasin	chocolate

FIGURE 8.9   **Origins of a few English words**

things they were seeing for the first time. As a result, American English has more than 300 loan words from Native American languages, primarily those of the Algonquian language family (Carver, 1991).

Regional variations in language are another source of interest. In New England, for instance, a freshwater stream is called a brook. In the north or northwest, it is called a creek (which may rhyme with "leek" or "trick," depending on regional preferences). In New York State, along the Hudson River, it may be called a kill, a Dutch derivation. In Kentucky it is called a branch. In Louisiana, it would be called a bayou, a word the French borrowed from the Choctaw natives. In Arizona, it would be an arroyo, a Spanish word.

Using Dictionaries

"Look these words up in the dictionary and write a sentence for each one." How many times do you think that assignment has been given in U.S. schools? In many content area classes, it is the only vocabulary-teaching strategy ever employed. In desperation, students often respond to the "look 'em up and write" assignment by finding something familiar in the dictionary definition, inventing a sentence that includes the familiar term, and substituting in the word they are supposed to be learning. Here are some typical results (Miller & Gildea, 1987):

I was *meticulous* about falling off the cliff. (meticulous: careful)
Our family *erodes* a lot. (erode: to eat out, to eat away)
Mrs. Morrow *stimulated* the soup. (stimulate: to stir up)

We believe that the teachers who made those assignments got pretty much what they deserved.

The best use of the dictionary is in conjunction with other strategies that encourage students to anticipate or predict word meanings. Strategies such as context clues, morphemic analysis, knowledge rating, and vocabulary self-collection are discussed in various sections of this chapter.

Vocabulary on the Internet

The Internet provides many vocabulary resources. References, word origins, and word games suitable for all grade levels and content areas can be found at the sites listed here. For more vocabulary Internet applications, see our Web site at www.ablongman.com/alvermann5e.

OneLook Dictionary
www.onelook.com/index.html
OneLook Dictionary uses more than 6 million words from more than 959 dictionaries; includes entries from dictionaries in English, French, German, Italian, and Spanish.

World Wide Words
www.worldwidewords.org
World Wide Words is devoted to the English language—its history, quirks, curiosities, and evolution; new words, weird words, questions and answers, and many articles on the English language.

Take Our Word for It, the Bi-Weekly Word-Origin Webzine
www.takeourword.com
Contains a feature called "Words to the Wise," which answers all your etymological queries.

Common Errors in English
www.wsu.edu/~brians/errors/errors.html
Includes a lengthy list of commonly misspelled words and misquoted phrases; a great quick reference guide for young writers.

ESL Idiom Page
www.eslcafe.com/idioms/id-mngs.html
Phrases such as hit the hay and easy as pie are illustrated in sentences that are fairly obvious and helpful in determining meanings for these nonliteral expressions.

Fake Out
www.eduplace.com/fakeout/
An interactive game that challenges students to correctly guess definitions. The game changes every week. For real word fanatics, there are archives of past challenges.

Vocabulary University
www.vocabulary.com
A great place for games and puzzles that promote word power. The site includes thematic word puzzles on a range of topics set up by grade level.

Given that most middle-grade and high school students have mastered the basic skill of finding a word in the dictionary, we suggest that content teachers enhance "look 'em up" assignments by modeling and giving students occasional guided practice in the following dictionary skills:

1. *One solution:* For example, *unrepentant* (Figure 8.3) is not a main entry in the *American Heritage Dictionary.* You must look up the word *repentant* and the prefix "un" and infer the meaning of the word from both definitions.
2. *Matching the dictionary definition with the context:* A character in the short story *The Lie* discusses a situation "with growing incredulity." If *incredulous* means "disbelieving or skeptical," what does this phrase mean? Why might the character be incredulous?
3. *Deciding which definition fits:* In one dictionary, the word *game* has 13 definitions. Which one fits the phrase "a game, ambitious woman"?

4. *Using the information and abbreviations in an entry:* In addition to definitions, dictionary entries may also give the part of speech of a word, variant spellings, derivation, pronunciation, and synonyms or antonyms.

When students know *how* and *when* to use a dictionary, it becomes a natural adjunct to learning new words. Keep in mind that looking up a word in the dictionary is disruptive and time-consuming. Few adult readers run to the dictionary for every unfamiliar word, and it is unrealistic to expect students to do so. When students ask for help with a word, telling them to "look it up" is probably less effective than simply providing a quick definition.

Vocabulary Self-Collection

Martha Haggard (1982, 1986) describes a simple but effective method for getting students to become more "word-aware." As they read, students identify words they think the class should learn, perhaps using sticky notes to mark them. After reading, students are organized into teams to compare and discuss the terms they identified. The procedures for *vocabulary self-collection* are as follows:

1. Each student team identifies a word that is important for learning content information. The teacher also identifies one word.
2. The teacher writes the words on the chalkboard as teams give definitions from context.
3. Class members add any information they can to each definition.
4. Teacher and students consult references for definitions that are incomplete or unclear. Final definitions are derived.
5. Students and teacher narrow the list to arrive at the final class list.
6. Students record the class list and agreed-upon definitions in their journals.
7. Students record any additional personal vocabulary in their journals.
8. Words from the class list are used in follow-up study activities.
9. Words are tested as they apply to content information.

These steps are suggested for small teams of students involved in reading content area textbooks, but they can be modified in several ways. Different teams may take responsibility for finding and teaching vocabulary on different days or in different sections of the text. Once they are familiar with the procedure, students may collect vocabulary terms individually in their content area notebook or learning log. The teacher can expand vocabulary self-collection outside the classroom and textbook by asking students to bring in and share content-related words collected from other sources.

Teachers should scaffold vocabulary self-selection by modeling their own strategies for selecting vocabulary as well as how they use context, morphemic analysis, or the dictionary to help determine word meanings (Blachowicz & Fisher, 2000). They can point out words that they have selected and explain to students how they decided the relative importance of the words. They can also demonstrate how to use textbook vocabulary aids such as bold-faced type, contextual or side-bar definitions, pronunciation keys, chapter vocabulary lists, and glossaries.

Self-collection shifts the responsibility for identifying and teaching vocabulary from the teacher to the students. This has several significant benefits. First, students are likely to identify different words from those the teacher might pick, ones they identify as unfamiliar yet important. Second, compared with teacher-compiled vocabulary lists, word study through self-collection is more directly related to students' prior knowledge and more actively involves students in their learning. Third, by selecting and discussing vocabulary on their own, students increase their sensitivity to words and develop new strategies for word learning.

Intensive Approaches for Struggling Readers and English Language Learners

The teaching strategies presented so far have been fairly economical in terms of preparation and presentation time. For some students, especially those who have reading difficulties or limited proficiency in English, a more elaborate approach may be appropriate. Students with reading difficulties tend to be dramatically less "word-wise" than capable readers, and less adept with printed language in general (Blachowicz & Fisher, 2000). They often know fewer words and have a less complete understanding of the words they do know (Shefelbine, 1990).

In an intensive year-long program developed for middle-grade struggling readers, teachers and students compiled a list of the types of context clues that helped them with word meanings. Students were shown how to use a four-step process (Blachowicz & Zabroske, 1990):

1. *Look* before, at, and after the word.
2. *Reason* about what is already known and what is in the text.
3. *Predict* a possible meaning.
4. *Resolve* by trying again or consulting a person or a dictionary.

Vocabulary Self-Collection for Struggling Readers and ELLs

Students who typically struggle to comprehend their content area texts can become avid word learners when they participate in the Vocabulary Self-Collection Strategy (VSS) (Ruddell & Shearer, 2002). The VSS is also recommended as a means of expanding English language learners' vocabulary knowledge because it provides opportunities for building on concepts that are meaningful to them in their first language and offers them choices in word learning.

Small Puppies, Big Dogs, and Struggling Readers

Alfred Tatum (2000) describes a multifaceted approach to teaching a class of eighth-grade struggling readers in a Chicago school. These African American adolescents, assigned to the class because of low reading test scores, were reluctant to read, seldom finished assignments, refused to respond, and equated "reading" with worksheets, assessment questions, and chronic inadequacy. This was Tatum's dilemma: subjecting students like these to isolated skill instruction only serves to deepen their sense of failure and alienation, but trying to engage them in meaningful reading experiences is frustrating because of their lack of skills.

Tatum identified three major barriers to student success: fear of embarrassment, lack of word attack ability, and limited vocabularies. To reduce the potential of embarrassment, he set about building a supportive classroom community in which the difficulty of reading could openly be acknowledged, miscues were considered part of learning, and students could be actively involved in teaching each other and assessing their own progress.

Within this supportive community, Tatum offered a balanced instructional program that featured skill and strategy instruction along with reading of fiction, nonfiction, and poetry relevant to the African American experience, materials that challenged students to think and talk about their social and cultural traditions. Students read and discussed each selection with a partner three times before whole-class discussions and written follow-up. Tatum guided class discussion and modeled comprehension strategies such as self-questioning and constructing graphic organizers.

Because the students had great difficulty decoding words, their attention was too often diverted from comprehension. To help with this, Tatum began an intensive study of syllables and phonogram patterns, what the students called "attacking the small puppies (syllables) to get to the big dogs (multisyllabic words)." Each day, he selected several multisyllabic words from their readings and taught students how to break them down into syllables and then blend them together into their correct pronunciations. Students were given varied activities to practice decoding and encoding these words.

Pronunciation and spelling were not the only goals, however. The meanings of the words were discussed, their use in the literature selections was highlighted, and students were encouraged to use them in writing and class discussion. The class thought up excerpts from songs to help them remember the meanings of some words. (For example, *reciprocate* was associated with "It's the big payback" from a song by James Brown.) The words on the word wall were continuously reviewed and vocabulary tests were given every other week. More than 450 multisyllabic words ended up on the word wall, and all but a handful of the students could recognize and spell words such as *ambitious, cognizant, mediocre,* and *indefatigable.*

The combination of intensive word study and culturally relevant literature brought about a dramatic shift in both students' attitude and competence. At the end of the year, 25 of 29 students, all of whom started the year several years behind grade level in reading, were promoted to high school by meeting the requirement of a grade-equivalent score of 7.0 on the Iowa Test of Basic Skills.

The students worked with context clues throughout the school year. Activities included direct teacher modeling, class discussion, frequent practice, and writing. Although using context was the major focus of instruction, these students were actually involved in an intensive program of heightened word awareness. Words, word meanings, and ways of learning words were emphasized throughout the year. In addition to context, students also considered roots and affixes, dictionary definitions, and word histories. By the third month, student teams began to lead weekly vocabulary lessons, identifying words and leading their peers to use the strategies they had developed. They also invented a contest called "Mystery Word." A photocopy from a book, magazine, or newspaper on which a word was highlighted was posted. Students wrote down what they thought the word meant and what clues they used to figure it out. At the end of the day, the student team who had posted the word reviewed all the guesses with the class and consulted a dictionary if necessary to resolve uncertainty about the meaning.

English language learners.   Vocabulary will present special challenges to students who are learning English as a second language. Students in ESL or bilingual education classes often have a difficult time making the transition to mainstream content area classes. Even when students appear to have developed English fluency in social situations, they may need more time to develop academic proficiency with the language. Some authorities estimate that it may take as long as five or more years for students to develop academic proficiency (Cummins, 1994a). Students may nevertheless be expected to pass district or state examinations in content areas, with little or no accommodation made for their language status. Vocabulary has a particularly adverse affect on ELLs' performance on such testing (Fitzgerald, 1995; Garcia & Pearson, 1994).

ELLs are likely to have more difficulty than native speakers with deriving meaning from context (Lebauer, 1985.) They will need a substantial core vocabulary to facilitate contextual learning (Blachowicz & Fisher, 2000). Although English or bilingual dictionaries can be very helpful for ELLs, they may prove frustrating for some students who cannot find inflected forms of words or who find inadequate or confusing definitions (Gonzalez, 1999). Figurative or idiomatic usages and unknown connotations will be especially problematic. Marie Vande Steeg (1991) relates the problems her high school ELLs had with life science vocabulary such as *tissue* and *organ*; some thought tissues were for blowing noses and organs were played in church. A partial or incorrect understanding of a word may interfere with understanding an entire passage.

On the other hand, students who are learning English have many strengths on which they can draw. Their basic reading processes are substantially similar to those of native speakers, although they may use certain strategies less effectively and more slowly. Among the strategies that bilingual students use in reading are the transfer of reading skills and background knowledge across languages, monitoring of comprehension, looking for cognate words, using context, and making inferences to determine word meanings (Fitzgerald, 1995; Jimenez, Garcia, & Pearson, 1996).

Teaching ELLs requires some general considerations in regard to vocabulary. Among these are patience and anticipation that there will be many unknown or confusing words, help with recognizing cognate vocabulary, and careful development of students' prior knowledge. To help students with limited proficiency in English succeed, many schools have established *sheltered English classrooms*, in which content is taught with the help of gestures, visual aids, and hands-on experiences. A sheltered English classroom operates on the following principles (Pierce, 1988):

1. The focus is on meaning rather than form. Students' language miscues are not overtly corrected.
2. Simplified sentences and controlled vocabulary are used.
3. Content area concepts are presented using a variety of clue-rich contexts, such as demonstrations, visual aids, maps, and experiments.
4. Students are involved in content-related conversational interaction.
5. New students are allowed a "silent period"; they do not have to speak until they are ready.

Vocabulary activities are particularly well suited to sheltered English classes. Teachers can model correct usage of vocabulary terms and paraphrase difficult text passages. They can also tailor the selection of vocabulary to the needs of ELLs by focusing on a few key terms rather than a long list of words and by having students keep individual word-study books.

In her life science class, in which nine different languages were represented, Marie Vande Steeg (1991) had her students use their senses to help them learn. When studying cells, they made gelatin cells using fruits and vegetables as organelles. As they ate their gelatin cells, they drew them on the board and explained them. The teacher had a lab assistant make popcorn in the back of the room to illustrate the concept of diffusion. When students smelled the popcorn, the principle of diffusion became easier to understand.

For a review of important concepts, Vande Steeg printed scientific sentences on cards with one word to each card. She gave packets of these sentence strips to students, who arranged them to make scientifically (and grammatically) correct sentences. She also printed scientific vocabulary on index cards and gave them to cooperative-learning groups to discuss. After a designated amount of time, groups took turns sharing their words with the whole class.

Mary Blake and Patricia Majors (1995) found that ELLs of intermediate proficiency can benefit most from holistic instruction that reinforces new vocabulary through reading, writing, listening, and speaking. They suggest a five-stage instructional process:

1. *Prereading activities:* The teacher presents selected vocabulary, leads students to practice pronunciation, and gives students definitions. Other activities such as knowledge rating, semantic mapping, semantic feature analysis, or contextual analysis could be used as well.
2. *Oral reading and responses:* Students and teacher take turns reading aloud with periodic stops for comprehension. Targeted vocabulary is given special attention. Students may write about the selection in their learning logs.
3. *Focused word study:* Students work with individual study cards that include the target word, a meaningful sentence, a definition, and perhaps the word written in the students' first language. Students play word games. They could also use any of the various vocabulary-reinforcing activities that are described in the next section.
4. *Evaluating word knowledge:* Students are quizzed on their understanding through crossword puzzles, cloze passages with definitions provided, and other formats.
5. *Writing workshop:* The teacher models a written summary or short composition that uses as many of the target terms as possible. The final step of the process is for students to brainstorm, draft, and revise their own written pieces featuring the new vocabulary.

In a study focused on closing the gap between ELLs and English Only (EO) native speakers, Carlo and her colleagues (2004) chose to focus on vocabulary-learning strategies such as word analysis, use of context, morphology, and cognate knowledge and introduce fewer vocabulary words. The focus on word-learning strategies resulted in a significant improvement in reading comprehension.

In content area classes with a large proportion of nonnative English speakers or students reading significantly below grade level, intensive focus on vocabulary is beneficial. Motivating such students to think about and acquire new words may be one of the best strategies for helping them overcome reading difficulties, especially if the program is combined with ample opportunities to practice reading independently.

REINFORCING VOCABULARY

Whether vocabulary terms are briefly presented, discussed after reading, or form the focus of one of the more elaborate teaching strategies we have described, it is often desirable to give students additional independent practice to reinforce the words they are learning. This may be done through discussion, games, writing, pencil-and-paper exercises, or computer activities. This section describes several different kinds of vocabulary reinforcers.

Matching Activities, Puzzles, and Games

The simplest type of reinforcing activity requires students to match words with their definitions. Teachers often use matching exercises after vocabulary has been introduced, either before or after students read a text selection. Presenting matching activities in the format of a crossword puzzle or other type of self-correcting activity adds a motivational dimension. There are many computer programs that can generate word puzzles for duplication or completion at the computer (e.g., visit www.vocabulary.com/VUhowtouse.html).

Matching activities, in whatever format, are limited in that they only require students to associate a word with a definition. Although this may be useful, it does not by itself guarantee that students will master the concepts associated with the words, the possible variations in meanings, or the association between terms. Thus, it is important to provide some practice in using words in context.

Categorizing Activities

In some vocabulary reinforcers, students are asked to consider the relationships among various terms by deciding how they might be categorized. In order to decide what words do or do not go together, students must know more than definitions. Categorizing activities develop relational knowledge and provide an opportunity for students to talk about connections among terms under study. When students know more than mere definitions, they begin to "own" (rather than "rent") words.

In a particularly difficult chapter on geometry in an eighth-grade math text, more than 60 technical terms are introduced. The chapter is typical of much

Morphology Practice for ELLs and Readers Who Struggle

Flip-a-Chip (Mountain, 2002) is a word-game strategy for building students' vocabulary and comprehension that is particularly good to use with English language learners and readers who struggle. Played with a partner, Flip-a-Chip provides students practice in working with inflectional endings (e.g., *-ing* and *-ed*), comparative and superlative suffixes (e.g., *-er* and *-est*), prefixes and roots, plurals and possessives, and more advanced morphology (e.g., a suffix like *-en* can turn adjectives into verbs, as in *dark/darken*). A cautionary note is in order here. Words should always be introduced and practiced within the context of meaningful subject matter. Simply memorizing parts and meanings of words is both ineffective and inefficient.

math material because the vocabulary is cumulative. Terms that are introduced at the beginning (*line, angle, point,* and *vertex*) must be thoroughly understood because they are used throughout the chapter. A math teacher could help students review for a chapter test by giving them the vocabulary reinforcer in Figure 8.10.

Sorting words is a very simple but effective categorizing activity that encourages active student involvement. In pairs or small groups, students are given a list of words to sort into meaningful categories. Using selected geometry terms from Figure 8.10, for instance, the teacher might tell students to sort words into the categories "angles," "polygons," "triangles," and "circles." For a more challenging activity, which would result in a greater variety of responses,

---

VOCABULARY REINFORCER

Directions: In each group of words, there is one word that does not belong with the others. Cross it out. Then pick a word from the "Labels" list to describe each group of words. You must be able to tell how the words are related.

1. _____
   acute
   right
   line
   obtuse
   vertex

2. _____
   sphere
   pyramid
   polyhedron
   cube
   parallelogram

3. _____
   prism
   arc
   chord
   radius
   diameter

4. _____
   triangle
   trapezoid
   rhombus
   circle
   pentagon

5. _____
   scalene
   diameter
   isosceles
   equilateral
   congruent sides

6. _____
   complementary
   perpendicular
   90°
   supplementary
   right triangle

Labels

RIGHT ANGLE
LINES
ANGLES
TRIANGLES

POLYGONS
CIRCLES
CONGRUENT
3-DIMENSIONAL FIGURES

FIGURE 8.10   Categorizing vocabulary reinforcer for an eighth-grade geometry lesson

students could simply be given words to sort without predetermined categories. Each group would then have to explain their arrangements.

Analogies

Analogies are another powerful tool for helping students see relationships among vocabulary terms. The traditional form of the analogy sets up a parallel relationship between four terms: A is to B as X is to Y. Several types of analogous relationships, with examples, are presented in Figure 8.11. The key to these analogies is the various relating factors. The relationship on one side of an analogy must parallel the relationship on the other side. In order to be logically correct, term A must bear the same relationship to term B that term X has to term Y. Thus, the relating factor of "Places" in Figure 8.11 is that Sacramento and Springfield are the capital cities of their respective states. The relating factor between "Action : Object" is that the stomach digests food, while the lungs breathe air. Analogies can be fairly difficult for teachers to devise and students to complete, but they are quite effective for reinforcing thinking skills and conceptual understandings.

Figure 8.12 provides an example of the use of analogies to reinforce vocabulary for a high school biology assignment. After reading and discussing the chapter, students worked in small groups to complete the analogies. Then the class went over the reinforcer, with groups taking turns explaining the reasons behind their responses and the relationships among the four terms.

Part to Whole
noun : subject :: verb : predicate

Synonym/Antonym
obscure : vague :: potent : strong
affluence : poverty :: safety : peril

People
Gandhi : India :: Martin Luther King : America

Samuel Clemens : Mark Twain :: Theodore Giesl :
   Dr. Seuss

Places
Sacramento : California :: Springfield : Illinois
Fredericksburg : Confederacy :: Gettysburg : Union

Dates
1776 : United States :: 1917 : Russia

Degree
hot : searing :: cold : frigid

Cause and Effect
virus : measles :: bacteria : food poisoning
drought : starvation :: flood : devastation

Characteristic
credit card : finance charge :: loan : interest

Action/Object
digest : stomach :: breathe : lungs

Function
legislature : make laws :: judiciary : interpret laws
keyboard : enter data :: disk drive : store data

FIGURE 8.11   Types and examples of analogies

VOCABULARY REINFORCER

Directions: Fill in the blanks with the word from the list below that best completes the analogy. Be able to explain your answer.

Example: beagle : dog :: robin : bird
Read the line as follows: Beagle is to dog as robin is to bird.

1. circulation : blood :: streaming : _____
2. capillaries : earthworm :: _____ : grasshopper
3. open circulatory system : grasshopper :: closed circulatory system :_____
4. protists : cyclosis :: hydra : _____
5. grasshopper blood : colorless :: earthworm blood :_____
6. single-celled : amoeba :: multicellular : _____
7. grasshopper : heart :: earthworm : _____
8. transport across cell membranes : _____ :: transport within a cell or organism : circulation
9. slow : fast :: open circulatory system :_____
10. earthworm : circulation :: protist : _____

Word List

earthworm	hemoglobin (red)	hydra
cyclosis	closed circulatory system	absorption
sinuses	aortic arches	cytoplasm
diffusion		

FIGURE 8.12   A vocabulary reinforcer using analogies for a high school biology unit (*Source:* Ruth Major, School 81, Buffalo, New York.)

Before students are asked to work independently with analogies, we suggest that teachers discuss analogies with them and give them several simple examples so that they become familiar with the format and the relating factors. It would also be helpful to work through the first item or two on an analogy reinforcer.

Concept Circles

Concept Circles (Wandersee, 1987), a type of graphic organizer, visually represent hierarchical and nested conceptual relationships among vocabulary words. Concept Circles use circles to represent concepts, and the position of the circles relative to each other visually represent the relationships that exist among the ideas in the conceptual scheme. The Concept Circle in Figure 8.13 is used in physics to help students understand the relationships among terms studied in mechanics. Fundamental units are at the center because all other units are derived from them. This visual representation makes it clear that units of work

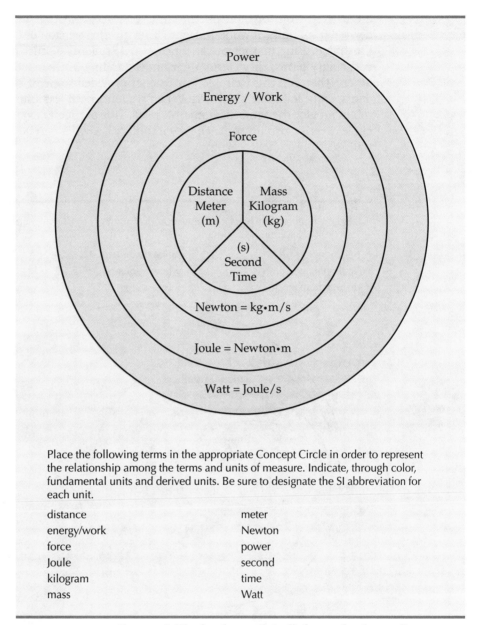

Place the following terms in the appropriate Concept Circle in order to represent the relationship among the terms and units of measure. Indicate, through color, fundamental units and derived units. Be sure to designate the SI abbreviation for each unit.

distance	meter
energy/work	Newton
force	power
Joule	second
kilogram	time
mass	Watt

FIGURE 8.13   **Concept Circles (completed) for a physics unit on mechanics**

are derived from or built on the units of force, and that units of power are derived from units of work. In Figure 8.14, another version of Concept Circles is illustrated using mathematical concepts. As students discuss placement of the vocabulary terms, they clarify their understanding of the relationships existing among them. In this example, the teacher provided some of the words for students, scaffolding their learning. When students need less scaffolding, a teacher might provide the same diagram unlabeled. This particular example of a concept circle exercise also illustrates how vocabulary activities can be used to differentially scaffold student learning.

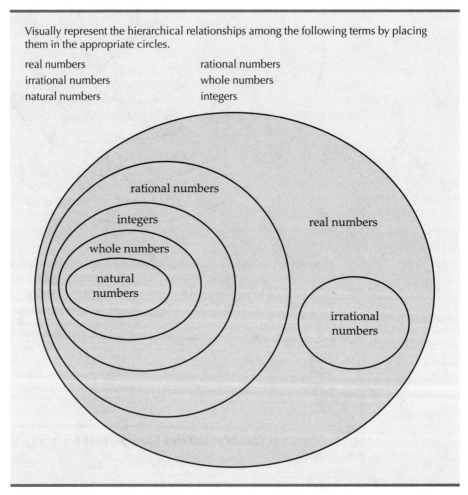

Visually represent the hierarchical relationships among the following terms by placing them in the appropriate circles.

real numbers   rational numbers
irrational numbers   whole numbers
natural numbers   integers

rational numbers

integers

whole numbers

natural numbers

real numbers

irrational numbers

FIGURE 8.14   Concept Circles (completed) for a review over real numbers

ACTIVITY   Create a reinforcement activity that emphasizes relational knowledge of vocabulary (category, analogy, concept circle) with the vocabulary list generated in the activity earlier in the chapter. If you choose to generate a categorizing activity similar to that in Figure 8.10, you will find it easier if you first generate a graphic organizer that illustrates the relationships among the terms in the vocabulary list and use that graphic organizer to select words for your categorizing activity.

Using vocabulary in writing.   Several of the vocabulary teaching strategies we have described involve writing. Using a new word in writing helps to reinforce its meaning and also gives students a greater feeling of confidence in their understanding. Students can use new terms in their learning log jottings, in written summaries, in writing paragraphs based on category exercises or graphic organizers such as Concept Circles, or in other kinds of writing assignments devised by the teacher. Cindy Borowski, a math teacher, has her students use new math vocabulary to write their own word problems. An example from one of Cindy's students is given in Figure 8.15.

DEVELOPING WORD PROBLEMS

Use at least three of the vocabulary words below to write a word problem. Please make it legible. After you have written the problem, solve the problem showing all your work.

Bob makes a salary of $400 a week, plus straight commission of 4% on

all sales. He made his sales quota of $5,000 for the week. What were his gross

earnings for the week?

$5,000 × 4% = $200

$200 + $400 = $600

Vocabulary

salary	wages	rate of commission
sales	gross earnings	quota
straight commission	graduated commission	overtime

FIGURE 8.15   Using vocabulary in writing (*Source:* Cindy Borowski, Frontier Central Schools, Hamburg, New York.)

Dispelling Policy Myths

Dispelling a Myth

When we mention the topic of vocabulary to pre- and in-service teachers, they usually assume we are talking about general vocabulary knowledge. In fact, in content literacy teaching it is the technical vocabulary that is most important. Often, the most difficult *technical* vocabulary words are the polysemantic words that students assume they know, but do not. Teachers need to emphasize multiple definitions, especially technical meanings, so that students can acquire the language of the discipline. We'll say it again: when you teach vocabulary, you teach your content!

Policy Implications

The importance of vocabulary to comprehension has long been established. In the 2009 NAEP Framework for Reading, for the first time the assessment will test word meanings in context. There will be sufficient vocabulary items to report useful information on the extent of vocabulary knowledge (www.nagb.ort/release/resolution_09.html).

SUMMARY

Content area texts introduce many new and difficult concepts, usually represented either by unfamiliar words or by familiar words used in new ways. The conceptual load of a single chapter or even a single page can be quite heavy, and the effect is cumulative. Mastering a term introduced on one page may be a prerequisite for grasping other terms presented on the next page. The demands of content area vocabulary can be especially daunting for students who are not very good readers or lack proficiency in English.

Given the pressures of extensive curricula, limited time, and a wide range of student abilities,

teachers need vocabulary strategies that can yield the greatest benefit in student learning with the least cost in planning and instructional time. Many effective strategies for introducing and reinforcing vocabulary meanings have been presented in this chapter. Students learn best when they encounter new words in various contexts, when they can relate new words to their previous experiences, and when they have varied opportunities to use new words in discussion, in writing, and in practice.

SUGGESTED READINGS

Blachowicz, C., & Fisher, P. (1996). *Teaching vocabulary in all classrooms.* Columbus, OH: Merrill.

Blachowicz, C., & Fisher, P. (2000). Vocabulary instruction. In M. Kamil, P. Mosenthal, P. D. Pearson, & R. Barr (Eds.), *Handbook of Reading Research, Volume 3* (pp. 503–523). Mahwah, NJ: Erlbaum.

Nagy, W. (1988). *Teaching vocabulary to improve reading comprehension.* Newark, DE: International Reading Association.

Nilsen, A. P., & Nilsen, D. L. F. (2002). Lessons in the teaching of vocabulary from September 11 and Harry Potter. *Journal of Adolescent & Adult Literacy, 46,* 254–260.

Pittleman, S., Heimlich, S., Berglund, R., & French, M. (1991). *Semantic feature analysis: Classroom applications.* Newark, DE: International Reading Association.

Rosenbaum, C. (2001). A word map for middle school: A tool for reflective vocabulary instruction. *Journal of Adolescent & Adult Literacy, 45,* 44–49.

Reflecting on Reading

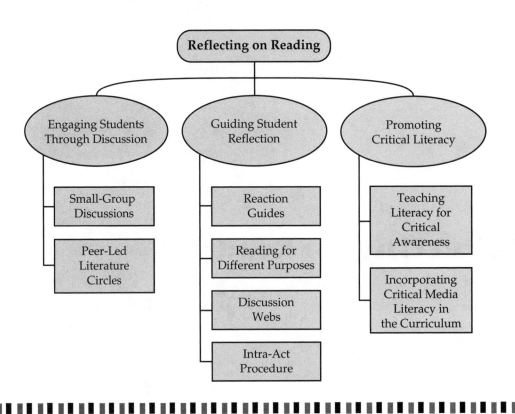

Most of you can probably remember a teacher whose class you looked forward to because you knew you were going to have a chance to think, to talk, and to come up with new and sometimes surprising ideas. Maybe it was a history teacher who helped you see the relevance behind the dry dates and names of people and places. Perhaps it was a math teacher who helped you think like a mathematician for an hour or so each week. It might have been a science teacher who gave you a little shiver when you realized how complex, how systematic, and yet how mysterious our world really is. Whatever the subject, the memorable teacher was probably one who had high expectations and for whom you worked hard. That teacher may be the very one you keep in mind as you seek a model for your own efforts in the classroom. Perhaps it was someone like José Gonzalez, a teacher in an urban high school in which nearly 40 percent of the students come from Hispanic/Latino backgrounds.

■■■■■■■

Mr. Gonzalez is leading a discussion of four stories that the class has read. The stories are quite different, written from the 1930s to the 1990s by authors from Argentina, Spain, Mexico, and Puerto Rico. Most of the 15 students are of Puerto Rican background, about half of them born in the United States. A few are recent immigrants from Central America. They have varying degrees of English proficiency, but in this class there are no language barriers to discussion, for the class is conducted entirely in Spanish. Mr. Gonzalez is particularly interested in preparing these students for success in college. As he tells a visitor, "I want them to think; I want to treat them like adults."

Mr. Gonzalez begins by asking questions about "El Cuento," the story most recently read. At first only two or three students respond as they talk about the basics of plot and character. But then they come to the most dramatic moment of the story—the death of a child—and more students become animated. Students begin talking to each other, and Mr. Gonzalez talks less, interjecting occasionally to arbitrate disputes, include other students in the discussion, or pose an alternative point of view. He asks students to reflect on similarities and differences in the social and political views of the several authors. The discussion also touches on contemporary social issues, especially those he knows are relevant to his students' lives.

During the 45 minutes of the class, the discussion ebbs and flows. At any one time, only a few students seem to be actively participating, but the individual discussants change as students engage in the conversation, argue their point of view for a while, and then drop out to reflect and listen. The atmosphere in the class is relaxed and informal, but the discussion is thoughtful, the participants animated, the listeners attentive. Nearly every student there has something to offer during the class, and it is obvious the students enjoy being treated like adults who have important thoughts to share.

▪▪▪▪▪▪▪

Mr. Gonzalez leads his students to make connections, draw conclusions, and extend their thinking in many directions. Although he shares many of his own ideas, the emphasis in this class is on what students think. According to many critics of education, too little of this sort of teaching is done in U.S. schools. Reading and writing assignments, class activities, and examinations too often require an accumulation of facts and largely ignore higher levels of thinking.

EVIDENCE-BASED RESEARCH

By placing an emphasis on what his students think as they discuss what they have read, Mr. Gonzalez is scaffolding their understandings of the four texts. Through discussion, he is helping them make connections between literature and their everyday lives. Many teachers find it difficult to let go of the traditional classroom response pattern in which they initiate a question, a student responds, and they in turn evaluate that response (the IRE pattern). Judith Langer tells teachers with whom she works that learning new response patterns, such as the one Mr. Gonzalez uses, is like "getting new bones" (Langer, cited in Allington & McGill-Franzen, 2000). Difficult as it may be, we believe that the effort spent doing so will pay dividends in the end. In fact, there is research to suggest that students at the middle and high school levels view discussions which invite a wide range of responses as helping them comprehend what they read (Alvermann et al., 1996b). This finding holds for ESL and bilingual learners as well as for students typically served through inclusion programs (Floriani, 1993; Goatley, Brock, & Raphael, 1995).

In this chapter we consider some ways that teachers can encourage students to think beyond the facts in the text, to reflect on what they have read. A reflective reader can talk or write about what he or she has read and, in the process, come up with new meanings and new ideas, often quite different or even opposed to those intended by the author.

The ability to read and think reflectively does not develop naturally; as with other learning, students must be given models, support, and continued practice. The strategies included in this chapter are designed to integrate reading, thinking, and oral language. Although a fair amount of writing is also involved, we have saved for Chapter 10 those strategies that focus primarily on writing as a means of reflecting. In this chapter, we first suggest some ideas for grouping that you might consider when engaging students in discussions of various types of texts. Then we offer several classroom-tested strategies for guiding students' reflections. Finally, we discuss ways of promoting critical literacy as a special form of reflection.

ENGAGING STUDENTS THROUGH DISCUSSION

Important as they are to student engagement in general, cognitive and motivational factors alone cannot fully account for students' willingness to participate in academic tasks that require reflecting on what they have read. The culture of the classroom also clearly plays a significant role in how readily students are willing to engage in reflection. Small-group discussions and peer-led literature circles are two vehicles for engaging students in reflecting on reading and learning with texts.

Small-Group Discussions

In a whole-class discussion, only a few students can participate at any one time. In such a situation, it is difficult to avoid domination of the discussion by the teacher and a handful of articulate students. In Chapter 3, we discussed various ways to group students. Although both small-group discussion and cooperative learning require that group members collaborate on a common task, the latter is more highly structured and typically demands greater individual accountability in relation to team effort. Small-group discussion, as its name implies, places more emphasis on members' ability to communicate orally than does cooperative learning, allowing them to voice their ideas on a topic in greater detail and to express a greater diversity of views and beliefs. Small-group discussion also reduces the competition between individual students and promotes group interdependence and a sense of community. It gives students learning English as a second language more opportunity to practice their language skills, to learn technical vocabulary, and to benefit from peer teaching.

Finally, small-group discussion activities allow students to assume and practice a variety of important roles. They may be proponents, devil's advocates, mediators, researchers, summarizers, task-minders, monitors, or spokespersons. Sometimes these roles may be assigned, but more often than not they emerge as part of the natural processes of the group.

EVIDENCE-BASED RESEARCH

Roles, although important, are not the first things that students mention when they are asked what makes a good discussion. Based on our interviews from a multicase study of classroom discussions in middle and high school classrooms throughout the United States (Alvermann et al., 1996b), we know that students are well aware of the conditions they believe are conducive to effective discussions. First is the importance of small-group discussion. The students we interviewed said that small-group, unlike whole-group, discussions provide them with greater opportunities to voice their opinions. For example, in their own words:

> **John:** I kind of like those [small groups] because you don't have to fight over, you don't have to wait and wait and wait before you have a chance to talk. You only have like five people in the group and everybody is close enough to hear you, so you just kind of say your thing when you feel like it.
>
> **Alice:** The small group is kind of nicer [*sic*] because it is more personal and people kind of listen to you more and get interested in it.
>
> **Christy:** It seems like it takes forever for [the teacher] to call on me, and by that time we have gone on to another subject, by the time I get to say anything [in whole-class discussions].
>
> **Melanie:** It [whole-group] gets me nervous to talk in front of a whole lot of people about, like, opinions and stuff. But then, small group, it's like me and my friends, so it is easier. (p. 254)

Classroom cultures that support students' perceptions of a good discussion have a second characteristic in common. According to the adolescents whom we interviewed, students should have a say in how small discussion groups are formed and the rules for participating in them. Students prefer to choose their own working groups and to make rules that will guard against off-track discussions due to members not having read their assignments in advance. Although characterizing effective small-group discussions in this way is hardly news, it is noteworthy that in the classrooms we observed, peer-group pressure was an important factor in how the groups used talk to mediate their comprehension of assigned materials. Overall, students were adamant in their belief that they had a better understanding of what they read when they listened to their peers discuss a selection.

A particular form of small-group discussion that bears special mention here is the instructional conversation (IC), which offers teachers a way to engage students in the academic language of the various content areas (Tharp &

Immersing Struggling Readers in a "Sea of Talk"

In my 20 years of teaching I had found that students in lower tracks were often relegated to classrooms that had virtually eliminated talk. I certainly understood teachers' hesitancy about involving students in discussions. I have many memories of trying to build and sustain conversation in remedial classes—experiences that haunt my dreams to this day. In seconds one comment can spark another's anger, and fists compensate for an inability to disagree with words. I also knew that if I continued a practice based on silence and worksheets, I was denying students access to a system based on one's ability to use language. Whatever it took to help students become able to carry on conversations, whether about books or life, I was willing to try. . . . Jan Duncan, a New Zealand educator, says that in our classrooms, "Reading and writing should float on a sea of talk." (Allen, 1995, p. 112)

Gallimore, 1988). Advantages of the IC include the opportunity to structure discussions so that student talk occurs more often than teacher talk and focuses on the concepts and vocabulary of particular subject matter. The IC is especially beneficial to ELLs who may have achieved considerable proficiency in everyday English usage but need more time and instruction to gain competency in academic language. Teachers who are adept at using the IC are guided by what Dalton (1998, p. 30) describes as the "three checks":

- *Clarification:* Teachers assure students' understanding (e.g., Are we clear?).
- *Validation:* Teachers provide opportunities for students to explain their reasoning (e.g., How do you know?).
- *Confirmation:* Teachers encourage students to negotiate with each other about what meaning to construct from the text (e.g., Do we agree?).

Implementing small-group discussions. Some teachers worry about implementing discussion activities designed to limit their talk while increasing the number of opportunities for student talk. Generally, they are concerned that their classrooms will become noisy and unfocused and that students will spend too much time "off task," socializing instead of working. We want to reassure you that this need not be the case and that the alternative—a virtual lack of student talk—is just as worrisome. Effective small-group discussions are in fact the product of thorough preparation and on-the-spot facilitation by the teacher. Here are several experience-based recommendations:

1. *Assign clear and manageable tasks.* Before they begin work, group members must have a clear idea of their purpose: to accomplish a specific task through reflection.

2. *Prepare and guide students for the task.*   Be sure students have enough background information. It may be necessary to model, or walk them through, a similar activity before they try the task on their own.

3. *Set limits.*   Tell students how long they have to complete their task and how much they are expected to produce. For instance, say, "You have ten minutes to come up with two different solutions to this problem." If a task has several steps, remind students occasionally how much time has elapsed and where they should be in the process.

4. *Monitor and assist group work.*   As students talk, move around the room to observe, question, encourage, and, when necessary, to keep groups focused on reflecting. Draw out reticent group members and make sure that more voluble participants give others a chance to speak. It is especially important for the teacher to avoid actively participating in group reflection.

5. *Moderate a whole-class follow-up.*   Let the various groups share and compare their conclusions and reasoning.

6. *Be a model.*   During both small- and large-group discussions, model reflective thought processes, good listening, tolerance, and ways to handle conflict.

Peer-Led Literature Circles

A literature circle occurs when a group of youngsters come together to reflect on and discuss a book they have read in common (Daniels, 1994). The discussion, which is peer led, typically is conducted by a discussion director whose job it is to prepare a list of questions for the group to answer. Others in the group assume roles such as the connector (responsible for connecting the text to everyday life experiences or to other texts), the word or phrase finder (responsible for locating language in the text that is colorful, unusual, funny, etc.), the literary luminator (responsible for identifying sections of the text the group might find interesting to read aloud), and the illustrator (responsible for visually representing his or her favorite part of the story, sharing it with other members of the group, and receiving their feedback). Students alternate in these roles so that everyone has responsibility for guiding the discussions in different ways.

An underlying assumption of peer-led literature circles is that young people can reflect on what they have read and will take responsibility for their own discussions when they are given choices and sufficient structure in which to apply them. The teacher's role is one of facilitator and guide in getting the groups to function on their own, which includes deciding how much reading will be done prior to the next group discussion and the roles each member will play in it. Although literature circles and "book clubs" (McMahon & Raphael, 1997) are similar in their goals and the procedures for realizing them, the two are distinct. The book club program, for example, is particularly useful in integrating content knowledge and the language arts, whereas literature circles are more focused on getting students to reflect on what they have read.

Recently, literature circles have been used to stimulate students' interests in reading in their second language. For example, Claudia Peralta-Nash and Julie Dutch (2000) initiated cycles of literature circles over an entire school year to engage Julie's bilingual classroom in reading and discussing books in both Spanish and English. What they discovered was that Spanish-dominant youngsters were more apt to take risks and join groups reading an English novel when they had the support of their group (self-chosen) to do so. Likewise, English-dominant students were more apt to choose books written in Spanish when they participated in discussions in which both Spanish and English were used to discuss a book selection.

Although peer-led literature circles may be slightly stilted at first, after students have had sufficient practice in making choices and assuming responsibility for organizing and carrying out discussions on their own, the creativity these circles may unleash is considerable (Burns, 1998; Peralta-Nash & Dutch, 2000). For example, students can be encouraged to analyze a book's storyline for underlying assumptions, to imaginatively create alternative solutions to a protagonist's problems, and to make text-to-life connections by exploring a literary theme in relation to their own lives. Indeed this type of activity illustrates the triarchic theory of intelligence (Sternberg & Grigorenko, 2000), which maintains that an individual's intellectual and creative abilities are not fixed but instead can be developed just like any other form of expertise. Moreover, Denig (2004), in his comparison of theories of multiple intelligences and learning styles, suggests that "teachers who use a combination of both theories may be able to improve student learning over the range of intelligences" (n.p.).

GUIDING STUDENT REFLECTION

In our experience, students usually appreciate genuine opportunities to flex their thinking muscles. The results are not always predictable; adolescents can be quirky and extravagant in developing their opinions. The concept of cognitive apprenticeship is especially pertinent here. The teacher can be a model of reflective thinking, guiding and supporting students as they think about and beyond the text. With persistence and a measure of tolerance from the teacher, students can develop their independent reflective powers.

EVIDENCE-BASED RESEARCH

Content teachers have found a number of activities that promote reflective thinking, student interaction, and the application and extension of ideas. The strategies presented here are adaptable to various content areas and age levels. Each one encourages students to think and talk about what they have read, and each one has the potential to lead to thoughtful writing as well. Reflective thinking is not just for gifted and talented students or those who are academically proficient; there is ample research evidence suggesting that students of all intellectual ability levels can benefit from instruction in higher levels of thinking (Haney & Thistlethwaite, 1991; Kennedy, Fisher, & Ennis, 1991; Sternberg et al., 2000).

Reaction Guides

When class members have completed a reading assignment, watched a videotape or movie, or attended a dramatic performance, how does the teacher get them to reflect on and talk about their reactions, with special attention to one or two issues, in small groups? To help focus the groups on such a task, the teacher could prepare a *reaction guide* similar to the reading guides discussed in previous chapters.

A reaction guide can be tailored to facilitate students' thinking along various paths. The teacher might want students to engage in an intensive analysis of the text or performance, or the goal could be to stimulate a deeper reflection. In the guide shown in Figure 9.1, the teacher wanted students to reflect on some of the specific incidents in the movie *Conrac*. He also wanted them to relate the ideas from the movie to the ongoing unit theme of prejudice, which they had been reading and talking about for the past two weeks.

To create a reaction guide, first identify a few key ideas or possible lines of thought you would like students to pursue. It is probably best to avoid crowding too much into the guide so that students can have time to fully reflect on their reading. Directions to students should make it clear that they must be able to support their responses. The actual format of the guide is flexible; it may feature questions, statements, or a checklist. Another possibility is to ask readers to reflect on polar opposites along a semantic differential scale (Bean & Bishop, 1992). For instance, to guide students' reflection on the usefulness of worms in medicine, you might ask them to respond on a five-point scale to statements such as the following:

Leeches are _____.

unwelcome bloodsuckers   anti-inflammatory agents

                1   2   3   4   5

Maggots are _____.

causes of infection   used for treating wounds

                1   2   3   4   5

James Middleton (1991) describes a strategy he uses to promote problem solving and creative thinking among his biology students. He identifies a problem in biology, asks students to think of an analogous everyday problem, and then encourages them to find solutions to both the everyday and the biological problems. The following is an example of this analogical problem solving (p. 45):

Biological Problem: How can we get rid of trapped heat from the greenhouse effect?
Everyday Problem: How can we get rid of heat in a greenhouse?

REACTION GUIDE: *CONRAC*

I. Directions: Identify the character in the movie who made each statement. We have talked about prejudice based on age, sex, social class or group, race, and religion. If you think the statement shows prejudice, write in the kind of prejudice you think is involved.

1. "Colored children need the whip."
   Character? _____
   Prejudice? _____

2. "We [teachers] are overseers, and things are tough on overseers."
   Character? _____
   Prejudice? _____

3. "You got that thin white skin. I don't have that advantage. So I just try to please the man."
   Character? _____
   Prejudice? _____

4. "Kids don't need trips; they need drill."
   Character? _____
   Prejudice? _____

5. "I'm white and I'm proud."
   Character? _____
   Prejudice? _____

II. Directions: Reflect on what you saw and heard in the movie, and your own experiences. Which of the following statements would you agree with? Be able to give examples to support your choices.

_____ 1. Anybody can learn if he or she is given the chance.

_____ 2. Prejudice is usually too strong for a single person to overcome.

_____ 3. Teachers can learn as much from students as students can learn from teachers.

_____ 4. Things like poetry and classical music are only for the upper classes.

FIGURE 9.1   Reaction guide for a movie for an eighth-grade English class

Everyday Solutions: Punch holes in the greenhouse. Turn on fans.
Biological Solutions: Punch holes in the CO_2 cloud. Create storms in the upper atmosphere.

Reading for Different Purposes

To encourage students to move beyond surface-level understanding in their reflections and to challenge them to extend and elaborate on the ideas of others, you might ask members of a class to read the same material for different purposes or from different perspectives (Dolan et al., 1979). The procedure works as follows:

1. Assign all students the same material to read. (News stories, editorials, and magazine articles on current issues are particularly well suited to this activity.)
2. After students have read the material, break the class into groups and give each group a different task, such as the following:
   a. Name an obvious and a less obvious, or hidden, purpose the author may have had.
   b. Determine one relevant and one irrelevant sentence in the text.
   c. Look for evidence of biased reporting or emotive language in the text.
   d. List three fact statements and three opinion statements, and ask students to determine which is which.
   e. Present an alternative argument to one in the text, and ask students to choose the stronger of the two.
   f. Test the author's assertions by referring to other sources.
   g. Devise a set of questions that can be answered only by consulting additional sources.
3. When groups have completed their discussions, a spokesperson for each group presents its findings to the class for discussion. For instance, the first group might ask the class to decide which of the two purposes, obvious or hidden, seems more probable and why.
4. As a follow-up, students can write a summary of their group's issue or perhaps rewrite the text leaving out the irrelevant material or substituting different words for the emotive language.

ACTIVITY   Try reading for different purposes. If you are part of a group, have each person read the following abstract from a journal article for one of the purposes listed; then compare responses. If you are working alone, read the abstract for at least two of these purposes:

1. Read from the point of view of a nutrition expert. How would you critique the abstract?
2. Read from the point of view of an athlete in training for the Olympics. How would you critique the article?
3. Name an obvious and a less obvious, or hidden, purpose the author may have had in writing the article.
4. Find one statement of fact and one opinion.
5. Devise an alternative reason for why determination of the effectiveness of supplements has been hampered.

Active persons ingest protein supplements primarily to promote muscle strength, function, and possibly size. Currently, it is not possible to form

> a consensus position regarding the benefit of protein or amino acid
> supplements in exercise training. Determination of whether supplements
> are beneficial has been hampered by the failure to select appropriate
> endpoints for evaluation of a positive effect. Furthermore, studies focused at
> a more basic level have failed to agree on the response of protein metabolism
> to exercise. An additional complication of dietary studies that is not often
> taken into account is amount of energy intake. (Wolfe, 2000, p. 551)

This procedure can be adapted or modified to fit different types of reading assignments. For example, in literature class, students can reflect on the points of view of different characters in a short story. In social studies, groups can take different slants on social issues; they might be asked, for example, to assess the Chicago Haymarket Riot of 1886 from the point of view of the workers, the strikebreakers, the police, the anarchists, the politicians, and the general public. Students can also look at events from different cultural perspectives. For instance, how might Native Americans, Hispanic Americans, and African Americans view the arrival of Columbus or the Emancipation Proclamation? A chemistry class might reflect on a chapter on air pollution from the standpoint of an environmentalist, a Los Angeles automobile commuter, and an employee and an officer of a major manufacturing firm (Frager & Thompson, 1985).

Discussion Webs

EVIDENCE-
BASED
RESEARCH

Consideration of more than one point of view gives students the opportunity to reflect on and expand their understanding of what they have read. However, when whole-class discussions are monopolized by a few highly verbal students, those who are less verbal may be unwilling or unable to think through and voice their opinions. Students who are learning English may have difficulty using their newly acquired language skills in academic settings. Female students especially may be at a disadvantage in classrooms in which male voices and male conversational styles are privileged (Alvermann, 1995/1996; Guzzetti & Williams, 1996).

A Discussion Web (Alvermann, 1992) can help to structure discussions in such a way that more students have an opportunity to contribute. Discussion Webs make it easier to keep a discussion focused and to ensure that discussants support their assertions with relevant information rather than generalizations, emotional arguments, or conversational intimidation. A Discussion Web is a graphic aid that presents a central issue or question along with spaces in which readers can fill in evidence supporting opposing points of view. The example shown in Figure 9.2 has the central question "Was Athens a true democracy?" On either side of the web, there are spaces for students to list reasons for answering no or yes to the central question.

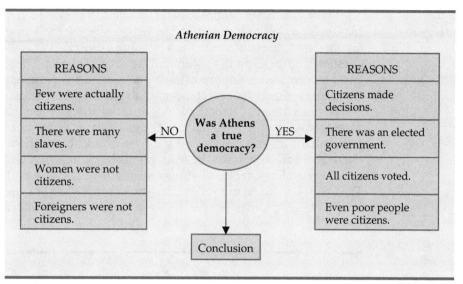

FIGURE 9.2   **Discussion Web for sixth-grade social studies unit on Athenian democracy**

The Discussion Web is used to encourage discussion and reflection as part of a five-step procedure (Alvermann, 1992):

1. Prepare students for reading using any of the strategies suggested in Chapter 6.
2. After students have read the assignment, introduce the central question and the Discussion Web. Have them discuss in pairs the points of view defined by the web and take turns jotting down reasons in the two support columns. To ensure that the students consider both sides of the issue, instruct them to give an equal number of reasons in each column.
3. After students have jotted down a few of their reasons, pair one set of partners with another. To give all members of the new groups a chance to participate, ask each member to present at least one reason to the rest of the group. Have each group compare its Discussion Webs and ask the members to reach a group conclusion. If all members cannot agree, tell them to develop a dissenting opinion, or minority report, as well. In the unlikely event of an evenly split opinion, the group is considered deadlocked.
4. When the groups of four have reached their conclusions, give each group three minutes to present its conclusion, its strongest reason (or two strongest, in the case of a deadlock), and any dissenting opinion. (If each group gives a single reason, it reduces the likelihood that the last few groups have little or nothing to say.) Finally, open the discussion up to the whole class.
5. As a follow-up activity, have students use their webs and the ideas they have heard presented to write individual answers to the central question.

Many variations on the basic Discussion Web can be created by changing the labels on the basic structure. The web may be used to stimulate a prereading discussion of students' predictions by using a central "What do you think. . . ?" question and labeling the columns "Prediction 1" and "Prediction 2." In science, students who are preparing to conduct an experiment might generate hypotheses about the outcome and list their reasons in columns labeled "Hypothesis 1" and "Hypothesis 2." In social studies or literature, readers can compare two people or characters. For example, they might compare the positions of Lincoln and Douglas on slavery or think about who was the dominant character in the trip down the Mississippi—Huck or Jim. A Discussion Web can even help students decide what information is relevant in math word problems. The web shown in Figure 9.3 was designed so that pairs of students could decide which information is needed to solve three problems. Then the pairs were

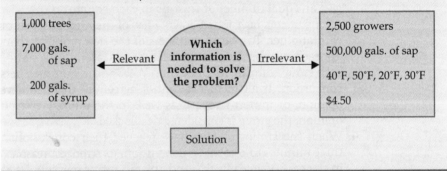

A Sappy Story

Vermont is one of the country's major producers of maple syrup. There are close to 2,500 maple growers in Vermont, each of whom taps an average of 1,000 trees. About 500,000 gallons of maple syrup are produced each year.

When the sap is running, growers collect it from their trees daily and boil it down to make the syrup. Traditionally, the season for "sugaring," as this process is called, begins on the first Tuesday in March. In reality, though, the sap runs only when temperatures rise to 40°F–50°F during the day and fall to 20°F–30°F at night.

A grower can tap 7,000 gallons of sap from 1,000 trees per season, yielding 200 gallons of syrup, which is then sold at $4.50 per half-pint.

1. On average, how many trees are there per grower?
2. How many gallons of sap are tapped per tree?
3. What is the ratio of the gallons of sap a grower taps to the gallons of syrup made from it, in simplest form?

| 1,000 trees

7,000 gals. of sap

200 gals. of syrup | ← Relevant | **Which information is needed to solve the problem?** | Irrelevant → | 2,500 growers

500,000 gals. of sap

40°F, 50°F, 20°F, 30°F

$4.50 |

Solution

FIGURE 9.3   Discussion Web for eighth-grade math (*Source:* Problem from S. Chapin, M. Illingworth, M. Landau, J. Masingila, & L. McCracken, *Middle grade mathematics: Course 3.* Needham, MA: Prentice Hall, 1995.)

combined into groups of four to compare their decisions and work together to solve the problems.

Intra-Act Procedure

Easily adapted to guide reflection in most content areas, the Intra-Act procedure (Hoffman, 1979) spurs verbal interaction around a group problem-solving task. It derives its name from the inferred *intra*personal dialogue that takes place among individuals who are engaged in an exercise of self-*act*ualization leading to concept formation. The Intra-Act procedure was developed during a time in education history when values clarification was at the forefront. Today, we see it being useful as a way to encourage students to reflect on what they read by predicting how the meaning that they construct of a particular text is likely to be the same as, different from, or some combination of how others in their peer group construct the same message.

In the following example of an Intra-Act supplied by Victoria, groups of students (no more than five students in a group) would read an article on bionic trees by Hillary Rosner, which was published by the *New York Times* on April 3, 2004, and is available for downloading at www.speechfriendly.org/cgi-bin/ nyt.cgi/http://www.nytimes.com/learning/teachers/featured_articles/200408 03tuesday.html?pagewanted=print). In her article titled "Turning Genetically Engineered Trees Into Toxic Avengers," Rosner describes a research project directed by Dr. Richard Meagher, a professor of genetics at the University of Georgia. Briefly, Dr. Meagher has genetically engineered trees to extract mercury from the soil, store it without being harmed, convert it to a less toxic form of mercury, and release it into the air.

After reading the article on bionic trees, a student leader starts the discussion by summarizing the selection as he or she understood it, and then others join in with their reactions. Because newspaper articles do not have the overt structure of textbooks with lots of headings and subheadings, Victoria recommends giving students a list of topics such as the following to guide students' discussion of the important points of the article:

- Heavy metals (like mercury) in the soil
- Logging of old-stand forests that could possibly result in the loss of wild forests
- Greenhouse gas in the atmosphere, resulting in global warming
- Loss of trees (like the American chestnut) due to disease

At the end of the discussion period, students work individually on their copy of Intra-Act (Figure 9.4), recording whether they agree (A) or disagree (D) with each statement. They also predict (by circling A or D under the names of the

	Student 1	Student 2	Student 3	Student 4	Student 5
It is okay to change a plant's genetic make-up if it is going to benefit human beings.	A D ___	A D ___	A D ___	A D ___	A D ___
Just because human beings have the capability to alter the genetic code of an organism doesn't mean we should do so.	A D ___	A D ___	A D ___	A D ___	A D ___
Dangers posed by genetically modified organisms to the environment and to human health outweigh the possible uses of such organisms.	A D ___	A D ___	A D ___	A D ___	A D ___
Global warming is a danger to the continued way of life we enjoy in the United States.	A D ___	A D ___	A D ___	A D ___	A D ___
A genetically modified tree can replace a natural tree without causing any harm to the ecosystem.	A D ___	A D ___	A D ___	A D ___	A D ___
Genetically modified organisms are dangerous to human health.	A D ___	A D ___	A D ___	A D ___	A D ___
I would feel comfortable eating a fruit or vegetable from a plant or tree that was genetically modified.	A D ___	A D ___	A D ___	A D ___	A D ___

FIGURE 9.4   **A sample Intra-Act**

other group members) how their peers will respond to the various statements, based on how they remember the discussion in which they were all involved. In the final phase of the activity, students share their responses to each of the statements and reflect on whether or not their predictions square with their peers' actual responses. It is particularly important for teachers to stress that agreement (or lack of agreement) with a statement has nothing to do with that statement's validity as such. It is also important to give students time in this final step to reflect on why they responded as they did and to encourage discussion of their reflections.

Reading for Different Purposes, the Discussion Web, and Intra-Act all require students to consider competing points of view. As you may recall from Chapter 7, this is a strategy that Wineburg (1991) found historians using frequently in his study of how experts and novices differ in the way they read history texts. The historians read to see who the author of a text was; for example, they noted the author's point of view and they took into account the various subtexts that view implied. With few exceptions (e.g., see Katz, Boran, Braun, Massie, & Kuby, 2003), students at the middle and high school levels are seldom encouraged to take a reflective, critical stance as readers. This is indeed unfortunate.

PROMOTING CRITICAL LITERACY

Developing adolescents' critical awareness through literacy practices that engage them in interpreting and evaluating all forms of text (print, nonprint, image-based, and verbal) is an important aspect of guiding students in their response to reading. When we use the word *critical* to modify literacy, as in the title of this section, we do so with the notion of critical theory in mind. If critical theory is a relatively new concept for you, or even if you know a great deal about it and its premises, we think you will find Hinchey's (1998) retelling of the following Zen parable and her analysis of it quite helpful.

> In a Zen parable, a young fish asks an elder fish to define the nature of the sea. The young one complains that although everyone talks constantly about the sea, he can't see it and he can't really get a clear understanding of what it is. The wise elder notes that the sea is all around the young one; it is where he was born and where he will die; it is a sort of envelope, and he can't see it because he is part of it.
>
> Such is the difficulty of coming to understand our own cultural beliefs and how they influence our actions. Like the fish who has trouble understanding the very sea surrounding him, we have trouble identifying the influence of our culture because we are immersed in it and are part of it; we have been since birth and we will be until death—or until an experience with a different culture shows us that things might be other than the way we've always known them to be.
>
> It is in overcoming this difficulty that critical theory is especially valuable. It offers us a new perspective to use in analyzing our experiences, as the fish would get an entirely new perspective on the sea if he were able to consider it from a beach. The lens of critical theory refocuses our vision of the place we've lived all our lives. As is true of all theory, the usefulness of critical theory is that it helps open our minds to possibilities we once found unimaginable. (Maybe standardized tests aren't reliable. Maybe tracking promotes inequality rather than equality.) Once such heresies are imagined, we can explore them. And maybe in our explorations, we can change the face of the way things *are,* forever. (p. 15)

Indeed, it must be quite obvious by now that when we refer to critical literacy, we mean a form of reading that goes well beyond responding to words on a page. Among other things, "critical literacy makes possible a more adequate and accurate 'reading' of the world" (Lankshear & McLaren, 1993, p. xviii). That is, it gives readers a way of reflecting on an author's point of view and how that view affects who we are and how we interpret the author's message. As Temple (2005) notes, critical literacy is usually traced to Paolo Freire, a Brazilian lawyer turned educator who popularized the notion that before one can learn to read the word, one must learn to read the world. Freire taught illiterate peasants in Brazil the importance of orally naming their socioeconomic problems before anchoring such insights in the written word.

Teaching Literacy for Critical Awareness

The notion that literacy is on the verge of reinventing itself (Luke & Elkins, 1998) has become more than just a handle on which to hang our observation about the unprecedented and disorienting pace at which texts and everyday literate practices are changing. Increasingly, we find our lives changing in material ways as a result of major shifts in cultural practices, economic systems, and social institutions worldwide. This is a time when literacy educators from around the globe are speculating about the ways in which new technologies will alter our current conceptions about reading and reflecting on various kinds of texts.

At the center of much of this activity is the perceived need to assist students in their critical awareness of how all texts (both print and nonprint) position them as readers and viewers within different social, cultural, and historical contexts. The implications of all this for facilitating students' thoughtful reflections on what they read were described in Chapter 1 in our discussion of rethinking content literacy practices, multiliteracies (New London Group, 1997), and the New Literacy Studies (Willinsky, 1990). Briefly, and by way of review, when we teach critical literacy awareness, it is generally for one or more of the following reasons:

- To motivate students to explore the assumptions authors seem to have been operating under when constructing their messages
- To facilitate students' thinking about the decisions authors make (and why) with regard to word choice, content (included as well as excluded), and interests served
- To encourage multiple readings of the same text from different perspectives

Here, we expand this list by considering how readers respond to hypertext and the impact of this medium on critical literacy awareness. An expert in hypertext literacy, Jay Bolter (1992) has observed that "above all, hypertext challenges our sense that each [text] is a complete, separate, and unique expression of its author" (p. 22). This observation, coupled with the potential for readers to reconstruct an author's text while at the same time leaving "tracks" for subsequent readers to follow or revise, suggests that teaching

Technology Tips for Building Critical Literacy Awareness

If you are concerned that your students lack know-how in critically evaluating Web sites, check out ways to develop this skill at www.anovember.com/articles.zack.html, or for other suggestions on how to teach students to critique the media for bias, access this book's companion site, www.ablongman.com/

alvermann5e. For information specific to educating girls to be tech-savvy in today's computing culture, visit www.aauw.org or e-mail the American Association of University Women (foundation@aauw.org) for a copy of *Tech-Savvy: Educating Girls in the New Computer Age.*

critical literacy awareness with hypertext will need to take into account the following questions:

- In manipulating the text to meet our own desire for information (or entertainment), what do we come to know about ourselves that we would not otherwise know?
- Are hypertext readings of authors' messages privileged in ways that linear readings are not? If so, what might be the consequences of this privileging?
- How does linking materials in hypertext influence readers' thinking about issues of race, class, gender, ethnicity, sexual orientation, ability, age, wellness, and other identity markers?

Incorporating Critical Media Literacy into the Curriculum

Just as the word *literacy* is used differently in various contexts, so too is the term *critical media literacy*. Depending on one's perspective or theoretical frame, the latter may be characterized as the ability to

- Reflect on the pleasures derived from popular media (e.g., TV, radio, video games, movies, music CDs, the Internet, and cyberpunk culture).
- Analyze how popular media texts shape and are shaped by youth culture.
- Map the ways in which individuals assimilate popular culture texts differently.
- Uncover the codes and practices that privilege some messages and silence others.
- Problematize the relationship between audience and mode of media production (Alvermann & Hagood, 2000).

It is important to note that in offering a range of defining characteristics for the term *critical media literacy*, we deliberately refrain from referring to it as simply visual literacy or critical viewing literacy because the emphasis on viewing

A Response from Our Readers

After Donna had taught students in her content literacy methods class at the University of Georgia how to reflect critically on what they read, Nancy Edwards (a student in that class) wrote:

> There is much to be learned by examining the assumptions in the texts we read. All too often I find myself being a passive reader, accepting what is given to me as the truth. As a graduate student, I have been asked to write critically or think critically about my readings, but not once [previous to this class] has anyone shown me how. Breaking down the process into manageable steps made it possible for me.
>
> The first step of finding and naming the assumption seems so basic, but it is a step I have not been doing on my own. Once I have narrowed down an assumption, it is much easier to think critically about it. It is far less overwhelming than trying to agree or disagree with an entire text. The second step of finding a source that opposes or modifies the original assumption was helpful in many ways. It got me thinking more "deeply" about the original assumption; it forced me to read many related articles with an authentic purpose; and it helped remind me to look at all sides of the issue at hand.
>
> Reading critically is an important tool for me as a graduate student, and as a literate person in our society. Living in a world filled with easily accessible information, we need to know how to filter through it to find our own assumptions.

implies that audiences are passive in relation to the media's messages. In guiding students' critical reflections on the media, teachers would do well to point out that audiences (such as the students themselves) are typically neither passive nor predictable. In fact, as cultural studies scholars Hall and Whannel (1998) emphasized in their analysis of the entertainment media, "the use intended by the [media] provider and the use actually made by the audience never wholly coincide, and frequently conflict" (pp. 61–62). It is this potential for conflict—the oppositional reading of a media text—that makes it possible for some audiences to perceive Madonna as nothing more than a "boy toy," whereas others observe in her the personification of resistance to patriarchy's definition of what a woman should be, do, and say.

The extent to which school curricula can incorporate literacy practices related to TV, video and computer games, music, comics, and other popular culture forms is yet to be determined (Alvermann & Hagood, 2000). Obviously, not all media texts are of equal value, and concerns about the pleasure they bring must not override all else. What we do know, however, is that when students are not required to leave their out-of-school literacies at the classroom door, they are eager responders to popular media texts, with a few offering critiques on their own that have surprised even the most seasoned of teachers (Lewis, 1998). Although some educators endorse this blurring of in-school and out-of-school literacies (Alvermann, Moon, & Hagood, 1999; Buckingham & Sefton-Green, 1994), others, although not opposed to the idea, offer a variety of caveats worth considering (Duncan, 1996).

For example, Australian educator Carmen Luke (1997), in discussing the problems of incorporating critical media literacy into the school curriculum, noted the following:

> [Asking students to critique the media texts they find pleasurable] is likely to cue a critical response which can often be an outright lie . . . [for while] students are quick to talk a good anti-sexist, anti-racist, pro-equity game . . . what they write in the essay or what they tell us in classroom discussion is no measure of what goes on in their heads. (p. 43)

In similar fashion, David Buckingham (1993) cautioned about the danger of asking young people to critique the very pleasures they derive from popular media texts. He suggests that teachers take time to engage with different media for which they have little or no background experience (such as computer games) in order to get a sense of what their students find so enjoyable. Doing so need not end up in some naive celebration of popular culture, nor does it necessarily lead to an appropriation of students' outside interests in the service of schooling. Rather, it serves as an introduction to what students value and find motivational. Sometimes the findings are totally unexpected.

For instance, when literacy teacher educators Alleen and Don Nilsen (2000) took it upon themselves to investigate the controversial Gameboy version of Pokémon and the trading cards associated with the game, they found that children were using many school-related literacy skills to improve their game playing. Banned in many schools throughout the United States for distracting kids of all ages from serious learning, the 150 Pokémon, all with their own names and descriptors for how they evolve (e.g., Bulbasaur evolves into Ivysaur, which in turn evolves into Venusaur), in fact provided much morphemic analysis and spelling practice on the side. The Nilsens also found evidence of literary allusions in the game cards (e.g., Geodude evolves into Graveller, who evolves into Golem, the creature in J. R. R. Tolkien's *The Lord of the Rings*).

EVIDENCE-
BASED
RESEARCH

Although literacy researches have begun to study the effects of teaching students to read between the lines of text in order to uncover hidden messages in magazine advertisements (e.g., Linder & Falk-Ross, 2004), it is still too early to say definitively whether or not this approach will find its way into the traditional curriculum of most U.S. classrooms. Like Linder and Falk-Ross, who found that middle school readers can gain valuable insight into the persuasive nature of advertising and the role of gender in responding to media, we are quick to remind our readers that all research (not just that done on critical media literacy) must be read with a degree of skepticism.

Approaches to teaching critical media literacy.   Before incorporating critical media literacy into an already full curriculum, teachers will want to examine various approaches to determine what best suits their classroom. Figure 9.5 provides a rough sketch of three possibilities, each with a different focus: consumerism and the media, mindless consumption versus critical analysis of

Dispelling Policy Myths

Dispelling a Myth

Programs or curriculum mandates supported by claims of "research-based" evidence should be believed and acted upon.

Policy Implications

According to Wren (2002), a misuse of the term "research-based" can lead to confusion and potential harm. For example, he notes that "often research results are skewed or biased to appear to be consistent with hypotheses proposed" (p. 6). Wren also reminds us that "Just because a well-known researcher said it, that doesn't make it so. In short, we should always remember the researcher's credo: 'Remarkable claims require remarkable evidence'" (p. 8).

Approaches to Teaching Critical Media Literacy

Approach	Perspective	Application
Viewers as Consumers	When students learn the detrimental effects of most popular media, they become wiser consumers.	"Turn off the TV" week-long initiative calls attention to and sparks discussion about the amount of TV—and commercials—young people watch.
Teacher as Liberating Guide	Students seek to become "the ideal viewer" in learning to avoid the thoughtless consumption of popular media texts.	Critiques of media texts downplay the pleasures students might derive from them. Teaching becomes a process of demystification.
Pleasures without Parameters	All media texts are equally good. Views and voices from everywhere become views and voices from nowhere; the slippery slope of relativism prevails.	Concerns for students' pleasures override all else; teachers are careful not to require students to analyze and critique that which they like (or don't like).
Media as Source of Both Pleasure and Learning	Critical media literacy is not merely a cognitive experience, nor is it solely a pleasure-seeking experience without challenges. In maximizing its educational value, it is important to acknowledge (1) the expertise students bring to the learning environment, (2) the pleasures they derive from popular media texts, and (3) the multiple readings students produce from these texts.	Teachers provide opportunities for students to explore how popular media texts position them socially, culturally, materially, and otherwise; the goal is not to spoil students' pleasure but to extend their understanding.

FIGURE 9.5   Approaches to teaching critical media literacy (*Source:* Adapted from D. E. Alvermann, J. S. Moon, & M. C. Hagood, *Popular Culture in the Classroom: Teaching and Researching Critical Media Literacy*, pp. 23–28. Newark, DE: International Reading Association and the National Reading Conference, 1999.)

popular media, or a balanced consideration of the pros and cons of media texts. The Application column should help in deciding which approach is most applicable and relevant, depending on the desired focus, the topic or topics under discussion, and classroom style. Each approach serves effectively to promote students' powers of reflection and critical awareness.

Finally, an important issue in teaching critical media literacy is students' out-of-school literacy practices. Because students are bound to develop these on their own, teachers will have to determine whether to allow them into the classroom in response to assigned readings. Of course, no teacher has the time and resources to accommodate each and every one of her students' idiosyncrasies, but the more teachers can learn about their individual responses to popular media, the more likely they will appreciate the impact of new technologies on current notions of what counts as reading and reflecting on texts of various kinds. In the following activity, a reaction paper by a graduate student in Donna's content literacy class, Allison Hanson,[*] raises the question of whether a particular student's literacy practice (list making) could or should be incorporated as a response to a reading assignment. If circumstances permit, expand the activity by engaging with a small group of your peers to address the issues raised in the reaction paper.

ACTIVITY   First, read the excerpt below in which Allison describes her teenage son's development as a reader and his passion for creating lists. Then, study carefully one of the media-related lists that her son, Paul, created. Finally, pretend that you are Paul's high school English teacher and decide whether or not you would think it appropriate to incorporate Paul's passion for creating media lists as a possible response to a reading assignment you are planning to make. If you decide it would be appropriate, explain why. If you decide it would not be appropriate, explain why not.

Excerpt from Allison's Reaction Paper

Paul began his quest for literacy in a way that would please any mother (I think). He literally taught himself how to read at four years of age. His choice of texts was a Golden Book story I had bought for him from Winn Dixie when we first moved to Conyers, Georgia. The book, *The Best Christmas Tree Ever,* was about forest animals living in a tree that was overlooked by Santa every year, and how they solved the problem. . . . I remember his second grade teacher talking about him with wonder as she explained how he enjoyed reading the encyclopedias from her class set. He felt compelled to write from encyclopedias for hours at his grandparents' house also. I loved feeding his love for books. . . . He participated eagerly in all of the summer reading programs at the library and was known to check out and devour large chapter books such as the Superman sagas. By middle school, however, his interest in reading books for pleasure fizzled out.

---

*Used with Allison Hanson's permission.

Books were clearly out in middle school, and magazines, catalogues, and video game manuals were in. Paul was also into baseball statistics from collectors' cards and newspapers. While reading a magazine or whatever, he could be seen on the floor with his writing journal or notebook paper. He would create lists for hours on end. Pages and pages of players' names and averages, special moves for video game goals, shopping lists complete with product descriptions and prices from mail order catalogues, etc., were spread around his room from corner to corner. His literacy habits have really not changed a lot since.

Although he's now a senior in high school, there is a clear difference between what Paul reads at school academically and what he reads at home for pleasure. He's reading Shakespeare and other "great" literary pieces at school. He tells me that he wishes he could go to a college where he wouldn't have to take English literature. . . . At home he still makes lists for CDs, special computer programming language codes, shoe and clothing catalogue numbers, etc.

Paul's Media-Related List*

Mass Destruction
Ace Combat
Ace Combat II
GPolice x
Street Fighter EX Plw
Soul Blade
Fighters Megamix
WCW vs. The World
WCW vs. Nitro
Dynasty Warriors
Street Fighter Collection
NFL Game Day '98
NHL '98
NCAA Football '98
NBA Action '98
PGA Tour '98
NBA Shoot Out '98
NBA In The Zone '98
NCAA Game Breaker '98
NCAA March Madness '98
Nagano Winter Olympics
Here's Adventures
Blast Corps
Croc: Legend of the Gobbos
Arkanoid
Space Invaders
Desert Demolition
Ecco: The Tides of Time
Mega Bomberman

*Source: Paul Hanson, Senior, Loganville High School

Struggling Readers and Multimedia Inquiry

In his online article "Juxtaposing Traditional and Intermedial Literacies to Redefine the Competence of Struggling Adolescents" (www.readingonline.org/newliteracies/obrien2/), David O'Brien critiques the notion of struggling readers being "at risk" in light of the New Literacy Studies framework. O'Brien focuses on a four-year collaborative project that he codesigned with his colleagues in a public high school in Indiana. The outcomes of the project demonstrated that low-achieving readers' interest in and mastery of multimedia inquiry served to redefine their literacy competencies.

SUMMARY

Teachers at the middle and high school levels are under intense pressure to cover their curricula. It seems that each year local or state authorities add new requirements regarding what should be included in a content area course. It is hardly surprising that some teachers, struggling to cover all the required topics by June, are skeptical when they are told they should also be teaching students how to apply thoughtful and critical strategies as they reflect on what they read.

Yet, thinking critically, or the ability to go beyond the text or lecture and use information in productive ways, is arguably more important than much of the information itself. State and national assessments are increasingly focusing on the sort of thinking processes discussed in this chapter. Content coverage and higher-level critical thinking are not mutually exclusive in classrooms where students are involved in talking about and reflecting on what they are reading.

SUGGESTED READINGS

Alvermann, D. E. (2000). Classroom talk about texts: Is it dear, cheap, or a bargain at any price? In B. Taylor, M. Graves, & P. van den Broek (Eds.), *Reading for meaning: Fostering comprehension in the middle grades* (pp. 136–151). New York: Teachers College Press.

Alvermann, D. E., & Hagood, M. C. (2000). Fandom and critical media literacy. *Journal of Adolescent & Adult Literacy, 43,* 436–446.

Boyd, F. (2003). Literature circles and national standards for social studies teachers: A plan for reading and discussing children's literature. *The California Reader, 36*(4), 16–21.

Connolly, B., & Smith, M. W. (2002). Teachers and students talk about talk: Class discussion and the way it should be. *Journal of Adolescent & Adult Literacy, 46,* 16–26.

Golub, J. N. (2000). *Making learning happen: Strategies for an interactive classroom.* Portsmouth, NH: Boynton/Cook.

Hobbs, R., & Frost, R. (2003). Measuring the acquisition of media-literacy skills. *Reading Research Quarterly, 38,* 330–355.

Johnson, H., & Freedman, L. (2005). *Developing critical awareness at the middle level.* Newark, DE: International Reading Association.

Pandis, M., Ward, A., & Mathews, S. R. (Eds.). (2005). *Reading, writing, thinking: Proceedings of the 13th European Conference on Reading.* Newark, DE: International Reading Association.

Thornburg, D. (1991). Strategy instruction for academically at-risk students: An exploratory study of teaching "higher-order" reading and writing in the social studies. *Reading, Writing, and Learning Disabilities, 7,* 377–406.

Writing across the Curriculum

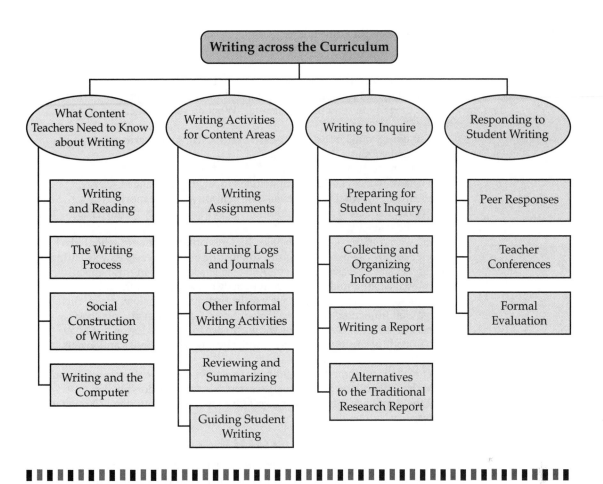

Victoria tells this story to her content reading students as an introduction to writing to learn:

■■■■■■■

Years ago, as a junior high teacher with two young daughters, going out to a movie was a special treat, one I looked forward to. One evening my husband and I went to see *The Last of the Mohicans*. As the movie began, my husband leaned over and whispered, "That guide is a traitor." Sure enough, he was. Later, he leaned over and whispered, "These troops are going to be ambushed." Sure enough, they were. This continued throughout the movie, with my husband leaning over to whisper his predictions about every 20 minutes. When the movie was over, I asked him (not very nicely, I admit) why he had taken me to a movie he had already seen.

"I've never seen that movie before," he said.

"Well, how did you know everything that was going to happen?" I asked.

"Let me ask you something," he said. "What do you do when you go to the movies?"

"I sit quietly and let the movie wash over me like some warm ocean wave, and I keep my mouth shut!" I replied.

"Well, that explains it," he said.

"Explains what?" I asked in an irritated tone, and then added, "Okay, mister smart guy, what is it that *you* do when you go to the movies?"

"I make predictions and ask questions . . . I *think* my way through the movie," he said.

And with that, he had me. I believe students often experience school like I experience movies—like some warm, comforting ocean wave—passively letting the teacher's voice wash over them. And teachers know when this happens. We can tell when a student is present in body but absent in spirit and mind. Students sort of slump down in their seats; their breathing slows down; their eyes go a bit unfocused. When we look out over a classroom and see these disengaged students, we suddenly think, "I have to jazz this lesson up! I have to do something creative!" And we frantically buy activity books and invent games to entertain students.

Let me tell you something right now: teachers are NOT entertainers. If you doubt that, take a look at the average teacher's salary. We don't make anything near what Tom Cruise makes! Our job is not to entertain. Our job is to *engage students' minds.*"

▮▮▮▮▮▮▮

One way to engage students' minds is through writing, both writing to communicate and writing to learn. Lucy Calkins (who recounts a similar situation in her book, The Art of Teaching Writing, 1994) puts it this way: "Learning isn't something we can do for (or to) our students" (p. 484). Calkins reminds us that learning is an active verb: we can create conditions conducive to learning, but the students must make the choice to learn. Teachers are charged with preparing students for a world we cannot imagine and will never experience. How can we possibly accomplish this task? Part of the answer to this question is to help students learn to think in disciplined ways. When students commit ideas and knowledge to writing, they must be more thoughtful, organized, and precise than when speaking. Writers make choices, make changes, and make meaning. Writing is thinking written down (Zinsser, 1988). Donald Murry puts it this way: "Writing, in fact, is the most disciplined form of thinking" (1984, pp. 3).

WHAT CONTENT TEACHERS NEED TO KNOW ABOUT WRITING

For English language arts teachers, much of this chapter may be "preaching to the choir." After all, teaching writing is a significant part of your job. Usually, secondary teachers leave writing and writing instruction to the English teachers. As a science teacher, Victoria readily admits, "I didn't have a clue about grammar or punctuation and what's more I didn't really care! Based on my own schooling experience, I assumed that writing was about punctuation, grammar, and spelling. Writing was for English class—*doing science* was for science class." One problem with this sort of thinking is that writing in English class is vastly different from writing in science. Victoria learned this when she returned to graduate school in literacy education, twenty years after earning a master's degree in science education. She had learned to write in third person, passive voice (Victoria says, "I hadn't a clue as to what that was—I could only do it, not name it") with lots of prepositions thrown in for good measure. Her professors in the Reading department at UGA (Donna was one!) went through dozens of red ink pens trying to break her of these habits.

Another problem with leaving writing instruction to English teachers is that writing is more than grammar and punctuation. Grammar and punctuation help us write with clarity so that our message is understood by others, but all writing is not for public consumption. Certainly, none of us want to publish our personal journals, grocery or To Do lists, or notes to ourselves jotted on sticky notes and pasted all over our computer screens. Because writing is thinking written down, writing is a powerful tool that helps students learn how mathematicians, scientists, and historians think—which, it seems to us, is a main purpose of math, science, and history in the curriculum.

Writing and Reading

EVIDENCE-
BASED
RESEARCH

Research suggests that there is an especially beneficial effect to combining writing with reading activities. Tierney et al. (1989) noted that "reading and writing in combination have the potential to contribute in powerful ways to thinking" (p. 166). When Judith Langer (1986) compared the ways in which high school juniors completed short-answer questions, took notes, and wrote essay answers, she found that writing essays not only contributed the most to their topic knowledge but also seemed to improve their thinking about the content: "When writing essays, students seem to step back from the text after reading it—they reconceptualize the content in ways that cut across ideas, focusing on larger issues or topics. In doing this, they integrate information and engage in more complex thought" (p. 406).

In another study using social studies material with high school juniors, Martin and Konopak (1987) employed a relatively simple combination of brainstorming, writing, and reading. In a three-day trial, they found this procedure helped students synthesize information from several sources and integrate new information with their prior knowledge. The researchers got similar results when they tried the same procedure with sixth-grade students (Konopak, Martin, & Martin, 1990).

Writing, then, is a potent tool for learning and reflecting across the school curriculum. Many teachers have found that writing means much more than an in-class five-paragraph essay or a one-shot term paper. As you read the following examples, consider the kinds of thinking required as students read, talk, and write:

Example 1:

At the end of the year, a sixth-grade teacher involves her class in a review of all they have studied in science, including the scientific method and famous scientists, the environment, electricity, the plant and animal kingdoms, astronomy, and meteorology. After reading *The Magic School Bus Inside the Earth* and *The Magic School Bus Inside the Human Body* by Joanna Cole, groups of students write and illustrate their own adventure stories about field trips to the labs of famous scientists, a forest ranger station, a nuclear power plant, and other places related to their studies. For three weeks, students converge on the media center with three-by-five index cards and buzz together in composing and editorial conferences. When their books are written, illustrated, laminated, and bound, they proudly show them off to visiting fifth graders who are getting a preview of their next year in school.

Example 2:

An eighth-grade history class is considering the relative effectiveness of violence and nonviolence in conflict resolution. On the first day, each cooperative learning group receives two case studies to read. Following the instructions given in Figure 10.1, they collectively write brief comparisons of the two cases. On the second day, the groups report their interpretations to the class. Through questioning, the teacher helps the class focus on the long- and short-term effects, both personal and social, of conflicts between aboriginals and colonials in New Zealand and North America, between blacks and whites during the American civil rights movement of the 1960s, and between muggers and victims on city streets. The teacher lists these cases on the blackboard and students add other historical and current events to the list. The teacher makes an assignment: pick one event, research it, and write a position paper advocating violence or nonviolence. In the following two weeks the teacher devotes part or all of several classes to media center visits, drafting, and conferencing. When students have completed their inquiries and writing, the cooperative learning groups present their individual papers in the format of an academic roundtable. As a finale, students write individually about what they have learned from their study of conflict resolution and how this relates to their personal experience.

CONTENT STANDARDS ACTIVITY

STANDARDS

Working in small groups (perhaps by disciplinary area), locate the number of times writing is referred to in the content standards of your professional organization. For a list of Web sites for those standards, see Appendix E. Prepare a short list of the different ways that writing is a tool for learning in your specific content area and share that information in whole-class discussion or with a partner from a different discipline.

REFLECTIVE WRITING: VIOLENCE VERSUS NONVIOLENCE

Directions: Read the case studies given to your group. Each one includes acts of violence and nonviolence. Complete the chart below with information you find in the case studies.

	Case Study 1	Case Study 2
A. 1. Identify act(s) of violence.		
2. What was the intended goal/objective?		
3. Was the goal/objective achieved?		
B. 1. Identify act(s) of nonviolence.		
2. What was the intended goal/objective?		
3. Was the goal/objective achieved?		

C. Decide: How are these acts similar? How do they differ? Are they more alike than different, or vice versa? Why?

D. Write: As a group, draft a brief written comparison of your two cases, including essential information from A, B, and C above. You will be presenting this in class tomorrow.

FIGURE 10.1   A reflective writing activity for a tenth-grade history class (*Source:* Reprinted by permission of Margaret Boykin, Buffalo Public Schools, #18, Buffalo, New York.)

The Writing Process

The use of writing in schools has changed as teachers have broadened their understanding of how writers work. All writers, from beginners to professional authors, go through similar processes to produce a piece of writing:

1. *Prewriting:*   This involves deciding on a topic, collecting one's thoughts, gathering data, organizing ideas mentally or on paper, and perhaps rehearsing in one's mind or in writing some of the things that will be said.
2. *Drafting:*   This is actually putting words, sentences, and paragraphs down on paper. The word *drafting* necessarily implies something unfinished or unpolished, for a piece of writing may go through many drafts before it reaches its final form. During drafting, the emphasis is on fluency and getting ideas onto paper.
3. *Revising:*   Revision literally means "to see again." As a writer reads what has been written with the eyes of a reader, he or she can look for meaning and clarity. The writer may add, delete, or rearrange information at this point. During revision, it may also be helpful to have another person read the work and share his or her impressions.

4. *Editing:*   The distinction between revising and editing is important. When revising, the focus is on content or meaning. When editing, the focus is on form, on things such as spelling, punctuation, grammatical conventions, and finding just the right word.

5. *Postwriting:*   Sometimes this is called publishing, in the sense that when a piece of writing is finished, it is often "made public." For most student writing, this means handing it in to the teacher. However, there are other audiences and venues for student writing—classmates, parents, students in other classes and grades, and school publications. Students often find opportunities to share their writing outside the school community as well. They may write letters to authors, politicians, newspapers, or students in another school. Local businesses, professionals, civic organizations, and community agencies may agree to sponsor student writing projects and respond to the final products.

Having described these phases in numerical order, we must emphasize that the writing process is *not* strictly linear; a writer does not march through the process as if it were so many steps in a recipe for apple pie. Writing is recursive. At any stage in the development of a piece of writing, the author may go back or forward in the process. While writing this text, for instance, we frequently (more often than we like to think about) revised our outline, changed our focus, gathered more information, and rewrote. As part of this process, we shared parts of the book with each other, with colleagues, and with friends. Even as we sat at our word processors, we found ourselves continuously rereading, revising, and editing.

Another important point about the writing process, especially in the context of content area teaching, is that writing activities do not always have to culminate in finished products to be useful. A lot of writing is informal and never shared with a wide audience or intended for the evaluative eye of a teacher. This informal, unfinished writing is valuable because it promotes reflective thinking. It also gives the writer (and others) an opportunity to look back and trace changes and development in learning and thinking. For this reason, many content area teachers have adopted learning logs and other informal writing activities.

When teachers are familiar with the writing process, they find it affects their expectations and their teaching in at least five important ways. First, they realize that there will be a great deal of variability in students' writing. Within a single classroom, there will be writers who are fluent and confident as well as some for whom it will be a struggle to put a few words or sentences on the page. There will also be great variability in writing styles and approaches. Although the basic writing process is similar for all writers, each individual develops his or her own preferences and strategies for writing.

Second, process-oriented teachers know that developing writers need regular and frequent practice. Competence comes with experience. When students write regularly in a variety of modes, including unfinished writing, both their ability and their confidence increase.

Third, these teachers emphasize the writing process, especially prewriting and revising, in their assignments and instruction. Rather than overwhelming students with a multipage handout titled something like "Requirements for the History 11 Term Paper," they provide students with incremental modeling, guidance, and practice in the different phases of the writing process. These teachers also confer with students regularly as they work on their writing and provide structured opportunities for students to confer with each other.

Fourth, the more teachers know about writing processes, the more they understand that *writing well is hard work*, whether you are a student or a published professional writer. Teachers who are themselves writers are in an especially good position to communicate this important message to their students, as Anne Shealy (2000), a middle school teacher, learned in a graduate writers' workshop: "I discovered that writing was almost always a difficult process, but the exertion is a natural, acceptable step in becoming a better writer. My continued development as a writer informs my teaching of writing" (p. 11).

Finally, these teachers are likely to emphasize the content of students' writing over the form. They recognize that developing writers are not perfect. Even professional authors must rely on copy editors. It does not seem sensible to hold learners to a higher standard than that applied to experts. Rather, process-oriented teachers respond primarily to the meaning in students' writing and view the mechanics as a secondary, but important, consideration.

The results of the 2002 National Assessment of Educational Progress (NAEP) writing assessment for eighth and twelfth graders support the teaching of strategies often associated with an understanding of the writing process (Persky, Daane, & Jin, 2003). For example, eighth and twelfth graders who said their teachers had them engage in various stages of the writing process scored significantly higher than their peers who reported little or no such instruction. Students who said they were sometimes or often asked to write multiple drafts performed better than those who never or rarely did more than one draft. Finally, students whose teachers talked to them about their writing outperformed those who said their teachers never talked to them about their written work.

Social Construction of Writing

Our description of writing processes has largely emphasized the individual cognitive aspects of writing, at least up to the point at which writing is shared with others. However, there are also important social dimensions to both the long-term development of writing abilities and the actual composition of a particular piece of writing. As with other facets of literacy, writing is socially constructed, and therefore involves

> the historical, cultural, and social identities the individual brings to writing, the social world in which the writing occurs, the peer and teacher interactions that surround the writing, and the classroom organization, including the

curriculum and pedagogical decisions made by the teacher and the school. (Schultz & Fecho, 2000, p. 54)

Writing is more than a set of technical skills that can be taught and learned in a normative progression; rather, it is a complex interplay of writer, audience, language, and social context.

Language, culture, and writing.   Written words, as language made tangible and subject to public scrutiny, reveal the interrelationships of language, culture, and education. In a fundamental way, to be educated in our society means to be literate. Facility with writing, especially in the direct exposition of thesis and elaboration most often associated with school writing tasks, is a significant marker of an individual's mastery of schooled literacy. Some features of written language, such as spelling, dialect, and "code-switching" miscues by ELLs, are especially apparent. However, the relation between culture and language is much deeper and more complex than what is revealed in these surface features (Gee, 1996; Heath, 1983; Delpit, 1995). *Pragmatics* is a term used by linguists to describe how people use language socially "for demonstrating intelligence, apologizing, asking for a favor, telling someone what to do, claiming allegiance with others, displaying status, getting one's point across, even telling a story" (Meier, 1998b, p. 122). People from different cultural and linguistic communities have varied strategies for negotiating these situations, and pragmatics may often be a significant source of misunderstanding both within and across cultural groups.

For example, Chinese cultural traditions place more emphasis on collectivism and "fitting in" than U.S. traditions, which are more likely to prize individualism. Native Chinese who are learning to write English tend to favor a style that emphasizes contingency, avoids strong assertions, features the collective "we" rather than the individual "I," and relies on rhetorical devices such as proverbs and analog, in contrast to native English-speaking U.S. writers, who are more direct, quicker to assert and defend polarized positions, and more likely to employ personal anecdotes (Wu & Rubin, 2000).

African American oral and written traditions also feature many unique patterns of style and pragmatics that are absent or not so richly developed in other North American language communities. These include

> characteristic intonational patterns; metaphorical language; concrete examples and analogies to make a point; rhyme, rhythm, alliteration, and other forms of repetition, including word play; use of proverbs, aphorisms, biblical quotations, and learned allusions; colorful and unusual vocabulary; arguing *to* a main point (rather than *from* a main point); making a point through indirection. (Meier, 1998a, p. 99)

These are highly prized and effective conventions in many contexts, although they may not be awarded points in the five-paragraph persuasive essay or the history term paper if standard rhetorical conventions are expected.

Social class is another factor that may denote writing styles. Hemphill (1999) found that working-class adolescents produced responses to poetry that prominently featured their own role as readers and elaborated on the characters' thoughts and actions in the narrative, whereas middle-class students were more likely to concentrate on abstracted meaning or "big ideas" and suppress explicit self-references.

Although our diverse language communities all have their individual styles and strengths, it is nevertheless important that students gain facility with standard academic English. The question is not whether students should learn Standard English spelling, grammar, and rhetoric, but how (Delpit, 1995). First, teachers of linguistically diverse students need to understand and appreciate language differences. When asked what advice she would give white teachers of Ebonics-speaking students, high school English teacher Hafeesah Dalji replied:

> Respect the language of the students. Let them know that no language is inferior or superior. Give them examples. And of course you have to feel that way, too, because if you don't there is no sense in trying to teach what you don't feel, because students will see it. You also have to be knowledgeable about Ebonics before you are able to work with students in transferring their language to Standard English. . . . A European teacher has to recognize that there is a rhythm to the language, they have to recognize the cadence of the language, they have to recognize the rich metaphors, so they can draw upon this when they are trying to tell their students, "Now let's say this in another way, in Standard English." (Dalji & Miner, 1998, pp. 114–115)

While acknowledging and appreciating language differences is an essential first step in teaching Standard English, it is not always a comfortable position for monolingual teachers who may be unfamiliar with other language forms. Teaching Standard English also has ideological and social implications that may cause discomfort for some teachers and students. To be blunt, "it is difficult to talk about black language/Ebonics in a meaningful way without simultaneously talking about racism" (Meier, 1998b, p. 120). English teacher Bob Fecho found this out when he read a poem by Nikki Giovanni with his African American students, who were initially offended that this writer whom they assumed to be white was making fun of their language (Fecho, 1998, 2000). Understanding that Giovanni was in fact an African American led Fecho and his students into a year-long study of language usage during which students investigated and debated language differences both within and across cultures.

Teaching Standard English forms to linguistically diverse students can best be accomplished by comparing and analyzing different uses of language and by explicitly modeling and teaching standard conventions. Authors such as Alice Walker, Amy Tan, or Judith Ortiz Cofer, who effectively meld or switch between linguistic and rhetorical styles, help to illustrate language differences at the same time that they validate the multicultural power of language. It is much easier to explicitly compare language forms and make students aware of standard styles and conventions in an atmosphere in which language variation is celebrated rather than suppressed. Exercises in which students translate from one style to another, write in different voices or from different points of view and for different audiences, practice specific language forms or features, and read aloud from a variety of published and student-written texts all help to increase students' metacognitive awareness of language and expand their language power.

Writing and English Language Learners.   Learning Standard English written forms is especially challenging for students who are still learning to hear and speak the language. However, ELLs are able to begin writing even as they are learning spoken English. Sarah Hudelson (1999) lists several widely accepted principles of second-language writing:

- Students need to be able to take risks and make mistakes.
- They need support through all phases of the writing process, including multiple drafts, revisions, and opportunities to share their writing with others.
- ELLs need practice writing for different purposes, including reflections on content learning, responses to literature, and inquiry writing.
- Reading different kinds of text, especially good expository writing, will have a positive influence on students' writing.
- Learning logs (described later) provide an excellent medium for ELLs to write informally about their content subjects.
- ELLs who have learned to write in their native language can transfer much of what they know about writing to English contexts. Writing development in both languages can be simultaneous and complementary.

Writing and the Computer

The personal computer gets our vote as the most useful tool for the writer since the invention of papyrus. Because computers are now commonplace in schools at all levels and in many homes, increasingly more students are discovering new writing fluency and power as they become liberated from the physical constraints of paper and pencil. Part of this new writing fluency can be attributed to the fact that youth today are quite at ease when communicating in writing on the Internet. Teachers who recognize this fact are finding new ways to teach writing genres that are particularly relevant to their content areas.

Take for example the case of Glenn Beaumont, a teacher of 12-year-olds who believed that his students' unfamiliarity with written argumentation was at the root of the difficulty they were experiencing in learning to write persuasively. Working with Wendy Morgan, a researcher from a nearby university, Beaumont arranged for a series of chat-room sessions in which students engaged in online dialogue to converse about issues that were of importance to them (e.g., the school district's plan to set up a gender-segregated middle school). The school in which the students were enrolled was in a working-class

Technology Tips—Writing Links

The following web sites are maintained by Capital Community College, Hartford, CT:

Guide to grammar and writing
http://grammar.ccc.commnet.edu/grammar/

Guide to writing research papers
www.ccc.commnet.edu/mla/

Guide to avoiding plagiarism
www.ccc.commnet.edu/mla/plagiarism.shtml

Purdue University's Online Writing Lab (OWL) for ESL students:
http://owl.english.purdue.edu/handouts/esl/eslstudent.html#purdue

neighborhood, and each classroom had six computers with Internet access. In the first few sessions, Beaumont's goal was to get the students to recognize the need to back up their assertions with facts, to listen to another person's point of view, and to evaluate the various arguments being made for their appropriateness and effectiveness. Later, he introduced other computer-mediated learning strategies to support the students' growing competency in justifying their arguments.

Although the outcomes were mixed, generally students demonstrated improvement in their persuasive writing from the first term to the second. From this on-line project, Morgan and Beaumont (2003) developed the following guidelines for other teachers interested in pursuing similar activities involving the computer and writing:

- First, become comfortable with the workings of chat-room environments yourself.
- Find "hot" topics with diverse justifiable positions.
- Model and encourage courteous acknowledgment of the views of others, requests for clarification of words and meanings, and so on.
- Trace and reward instances where students make concessions or change their point of view thoughtfully as a result of arguments made in the course of the dialogue.
- Be explicit in reminding students about the dialogic nature of argument and show them how to accommodate other points of view and incorporate the voices of others in their own subsequent writing.
- Find reasons for students to reframe and re-present their case. (p. 155)

WRITING ACTIVITIES FOR CONTENT AREAS

Writing in content areas may range from informal notes and jottings to lengthy formal research reports, complete with footnotes and bibliography. In

Dispelling Policy Myths

Dispelling a Myth

The No Child Left Behind (NCLB) reform signed into law in 2002 by President Bush focused on early literacy and beginning reading. NCLB is being extended to middle and high schools through The Striving Readers Initiative (www.reading.org/resources/issues/focus_nclb_links.html). The Striving Readers Initiative includes three components: (1) research-based interventions focused on those adolescents who read significantly below grade level, (2) professional development for content area classroom teachers that focuses on reading improvement across the curriculum, and (3) rigorous experimental evaluation. The program is funded at $24.8 million. As schools and districts begin to focus on reading, some teachers may believe that writing no longer matters. However, according to Jenkins, Johnson, and Hileman (2004), current reading assessments include both traditional multiple choice questions and performance measures in the form of Constructed Response questions which require written responses. Their research indicated that writing ability was an important source of explanation for observed individual differences in overall reading.

Policy Implications

In this age of high-stakes testing, we are mindful that we must test what we value, because we will certainly value what we test. With the extension of NCLB into middle and high schools through the Striving Readers Initiative, increased testing at middle and high school levels is sure to follow. However, this does not have to result in a superficial "teach to the test" curriculum. Judith Langer's (2000) research into successful schools examined high-performing schools and compared them to schools of average performance. Langer found that when teachers and other stakeholders study the tests, evaluate competencies required to pass high-stakes tests, and then integrate those skills into the curriculum, the focus of test preparation shifts from surface preparation to gaining knowledge and competencies that support successful learning. Writing to learn strategies are particularly helpful because they foster disciplined thinking about curricular content.

the following sections, we describe some of the useful writing activities that content teachers use.

Writing Assignments

A student's successful writing experience begins with a good writing assignment. When an assignment is precise and specific and offers the writer ample guidance, the writer is more likely to produce a satisfactory product. Five elements of an assignment can be crafted to heighten student involvement and interest and to avoid frustration and confusion.

1. *Choosing a topic.*   Writing is hard work, and enthusiasm can be especially hard to maintain when the topic is of little or no interest to the writer. The more discretion a student has in selecting what to write about, the more

care and effort he or she is likely to invest in writing. In content area classes, it is usually necessary for the teacher to specify a general topic related to the area of study. However, there are still many ways to allow student choice. In the examples presented earlier, the sixth-grade scientists chose the topics for their adventure stories, and the writers in the high school history class chose the event and point of view they presented at the round table.

2. *Specifying an audience and purpose for writing.* Writers need experience with writing for a variety of realistic purposes and for audiences other than the teacher. The sixth graders were writing to explain one area of science to a general, uninitiated audience and specifically to younger students who would be in sixth grade the next year. The high school students were writing as advocates of a particular point of view to an audience of their peers. If writers have a purpose and audience in mind, they can decide what information is needed, what voice or stance to take, and what will best meet the needs of their readers.

3. *Writing in varied modes.* There are many forms that content area writing can take. Students gain competence and avoid boredom when they have opportunities to write in different formats. (See Figure 10.2 for some possibilities.)

4. *Accommodating the writing process.* Students will need help and guidance with the various phases of the writing process. This means supporting students' prewriting decisions and data collection, allowing sufficient time for drafting and revising, and providing opportunities for teacher and peer conferences to aid revision. Supplying the necessary guidance implies that some in-class time will be used for working on the assignment.

5. *Guiding students' writing.* Students can be overwhelmed and dismayed by all the work and potential for frustration and failure built into a writing assignment that comes with a lengthy list of specifications and requirements. Instead of springing all this detail on them at once, the teacher can introduce a writing project in increments while offering guidance at each stage. Discussion, brainstorming, and semantic webbing facilitate student engagement and planning during the introduction of an assignment. Data collection, drafting, conferencing, and editing can be supported by the teacher-designed guides discussed in this chapter.

RAFT assignments. The acronym *RAFT* can help a teacher plan successful writing assignments by varying some of the elements discussed previously (Santa, Havens, & Harrison, 1996). The letters stand for Role, Audience, Format, and Topic. A writer might take many roles: reporter, scientist, famous historical figure, a character from a story, an animal, or even an inanimate object. In a given role, the writer may address a variety of real or imaginary audiences. The format may be a poem, a letter, or any of the other modes listed in Figure 10.2. We have recently adapted RAFT to RAFT[2]—Role, Audience, Format, Topic, Task. The assignment should include a Task in the form of a strong verb such as "persuade," "compare," "describe," or "explain," which will

Journals or diaries	Memos
Fiction:	Poems
Fantasy	Scripts:
Historical	Plays
Adventure	Radio
Science fiction	Television
Choose-your-own-adventure	Prophecies, predictions, visions
Children's books	Newspaper writing:
Picture books	Articles
Dictionaries	Editorials
Fact books	Features
How-to books	Advertisements
Biographies	Proposals:
Letters to real or imaginary people	Social programs
Dialogues and conversations	Grants
Thumbnail sketches of:	Research
People	Construction
Places	Position papers and responses
Important concepts	Reviews of:
Historical events	Books
Requests	Movies and TV shows
Job descriptions	Recordings
Applications and resumés	Performances
Acceptance or rejection letters	Math:
Research reports	Word problems
Science:	Problem solutions
Observations	Practical applications
Notebook	Cartoons
Lab reports	Debates
Hypotheses	Songs and raps
Interviews (real and imaginary)	Games and puzzles
Photos and captions	Posters, displays, collages
Recipes	Instructions or directions
Catalogs	Travelogues
Obituaries, epitaphs, eulogies	Quick writes

FIGURE 10.2   Possible modes for content area writing (*Source:* Adapted from S. Tschudi & J. Yates, *Teaching writing in the content areas: Senior high school.* Washington, DC: National Education Association, 1983.)

help the writer understand the tone and purpose of the writing. When studying fractions, for example, math students might write a want ad for an improper fraction or a letter from the numerator to the denominator explaining why it is the most important part of the fraction.

A word of caution is necessary concerning RAFT assignments. The purpose of using a planning device such as RAFT is to increase student motivation and interest in a writing assignment and to devise writing assignments that vary from the traditional student essay written for the teacher. As we have said,

Scaffolding Writing Instruction for Students Who Struggle

Writing instruction for struggling adolescent readers has become a focal point as a result of new accountability systems on writing and evidence of achievement gains when students refine their writing in the course of several drafts. Working from this information and a gradual-release model of instruction, Doug Fisher, a university-based instructor, accepted an invitation to co-teach a ninth-grade section on genre studies at an urban high school in San Diego (Fisher & Frey, 2003). The students in the class were all reading significantly below grade level and had to pass the genre studies class to become eligible to enroll in an English

class. Using an idea popularized in the movie *Finding Forrester* (Wolf, King, & Van Sant, 2000), Fisher asked his class of struggling readers to use a piece of writing from a well-known author's previously published work as a scaffold for creating their own original writing. This scaffold, which is consistent with a gradual-release model of instruction in that it provided support as students took on more responsibility for their own writing, resulted in increased writing and reading achievement for the class. Moreover, 19 of the 24 students made enough progress to transfer into an English I class by midyear.

EVIDENCE-BASED RESEARCH

good writing, especially good academic writing, requires hard work. Writers are likely to invest the most effort and motivation in topics that hold strong personal interest (Graves, 1983). A role or topic that may seem "creative" to one person may hold little attraction to another. Not every student will be eager to write from the point of view of a rain forest animal, Captain Ahab's second mate, the unknown variable in a two-step equation, or a red blood cell traveling through the circulatory system. One possibility is to develop assignments that allow students to choose from more than one possible role, audience, format, or topic. Another is to let students assist in determining possible roles, audiences, and so on.

An example of a RAFT[2] assignment is seen in Figure 10.3. This RAFT[2] asked students to choose a Role as one of the vocabulary terms being studied (mode, mean, median, outlier), and write a friendly letter to an Audience of another of the vocabulary terms on the Topic of measures of central tendency. The Task was to show that they understood each of the three types of measures of central tendency and how they were related to each other. This example was written by English majors in Victoria's content area reading class in response to a lesson on measures of central tendency in mathematics.

Figure 10.4 illustrates another adaptation of RAFT[2]. Alan Crawford, who invented this RAFT version, calls it Reciprocal RAFT (personal communication, January 26, 2004), one in which two groups write to each other. The example provided was written by Guatemalan teachers who were participants in the

---

Dear Outlier:

I was just wondering why you feel that you're different—you are so standoffish! You stake out a place so far away from everyone else that it messes up our fun. We do appreciate, however, the fact that you show up. Your friend, mode, never shows up unless he brings his twin brothers along, even when they aren't invited. As for mean, we've heard so much about her that we'd really love to meet her. We're beginning to think she doesn't really exist. She only shows up after we all come and go.

We're having a big party here in the middle next week. Ask your girlfriend if she'll let you off the leash to join "sum" of your colleagues for "sum" fun.

Sincerely,

Median

FIGURE 10.3   Sample RAFT² written by English majors in a content reading class in response to a math lesson

Guatemalan Reading and Writing For Critical Thinking project. In the first communication, the Role assumed by the writers was indigenous Guatemalans writing to an Audience of Spain to protest that country's treatment of them (Topic and Task). The answer from Spain (the Reciprocal part) chastises the Guatemalans for being ungrateful for all the wonderful things Spain has done for them, a tongue-in-cheek reply.

Learning Logs and Journals

EVIDENCE-BASED RESEARCH

Learning logs or content area journals have been enthusiastically and effectively adopted by many content area teachers in both middle and secondary schools. For instance, eleven- to thirteen-year-old math students who wrote in their math journals for seven to ten minutes three times a week over twelve weeks showed improvement in their conceptual understanding, procedural knowledge, and math communication compared to a similar group that did practice problems instead of journal writing (Jurdak & Abu Zein, 1998). They are among the most frequently recommended strategies for helping students learn English as a second language (Ardizzone, 1992; Arthur, 1991; Dolly, 1990). As mentioned in Chapter 6, learning logs are notebooks that are dedicated to informal writing, note taking, and musing on content area subjects. Regular log entries give students opportunities for risk-free reflection. It is a place for students to try out ideas, to put their thoughts down on paper so they can see what is there, and to develop writing fluency that can transfer to other written assignments. Learning logs are good platforms for prewriting rehearsal and drafting. Some of what students write in their logs may eventually find its way into their more formal writing. They can be excellent resources when reviewing for a quiz or test, and students might even be allowed to consult their learning logs as "lifeline" resources during an examination. Learning logs also constitute a

Initial letter of protest from indigenous Guatemalans:

Pergamino de Protesta

Guatemala hacia España:

Haz dejado mis arcas vacias.

Haz sometido a mi raza a tus viles deseos.

Haz derramado la sangre bendita de mis hijos.

Haz alterado la paz de mi suelo.

Haz cambiado sus ideales religiosos.

Y hoy, hoy España, nuestra Patria lamenta tu traicióal haber mancillado nuestra libertad.

Miriam de Serech

Edna Portales de Núñez

Letter of reply from Spain:

Derecho de Respuesta al Pergamino de Protesta de aEspaña aGuatemala.

¡Que poco reconocimiento al esfuerzo conjunto, tenza y audaz de mi gente!

¿Acaso fue fácil ingresar a un inhóspito lugar, para llevar civilización?

¡Deciis que cambiamos vuestros ideales y libertad! ¡y de qué libertad hablais? Si ni siquiera pensamiento critico teniais.

¡Deciaiis que vaciamos vuestras arcas! Pero si quereis saber, fueron ustedes quienes nos las entregaron a manos llenas, con una sonrisa de oreja a oreja, después qye nosotros les dimos los espejito!

¿De qué paz hablais?, si cuando llegamos a estas tierras matándose ustedes estaban entre si.

¡Traición! ¡De qué traición hablais? Más dijera yo, ¡Agradecidos deberiais estar por los animales, alimentos, idioma y muchos ostros beneficios más que hemos traido, de los que hoy disfrutais.

¡Que Dios les perdone por tanto odio que guardais en vuestros corazones! ¿Sabeis una cosa? El odio es un sentimiento muy malo que hace mucho daño a vuestro organismo y a nada bueno os conduce, más bien enfermedades vais a tener.

Chichicastenago 4-2-2,002

Miriam de León

Olga de Motta

Maria Luisa Salazar

FIGURE 10.4   Example of a reciprocal RAFT written by participants in the Reading and Writing for Criticial Thinking project in Guatemala

valuable record of student growth and learning over a marking period, a semester, or a year.

What students actually write in their logs varies widely. Entry topics can be specified by the teacher or left entirely to the student. Almost certainly, teachers will need to suggest topics or questions at first. Figure 10.5 lists some

Process Entries	Reaction Entries
What did I understand about the work we did in class today?	If I were the teacher, what questions would I ask about this assignment, chapter, etc.?
What didn't I understand? What was confusing?	Explain a theory, concept, vocabulary term, etc., to another person.
What problems did I have with a text assignment?	
How did I solve a problem with understanding, vocabulary, text, etc.?	Free-writing: simply write for 5–10 minutes about a specific topic, whatever comes into the writer's mind.
At what point did I get confused?	Summarize, analyze, synthesize, compare and contrast, evaluate an idea, topic, event, person, etc.
What did I like or dislike today?	
What questions do I have about what we did today?	Connection with prior knowledge or experience.
Notes, lists, or jottings relevant to my upcoming assignments.	"Unsent letters" to people, living or dead, historical or mythical, about topic of study.
My reflections on cooperative-learning group processes—what did or didn't work and why, my role, the role of other participants.	Doodles; words and pictures that reflect feelings or thoughts on a topic.
My predictions and expectations about a new topic.	Response to higher-order questions posed by the teacher.
What was the most difficult homework problem? What made it so difficult?	Reread a log entry from last week. Write a reaction to what was written.

FIGURE 10.5   Sample prompts for students' learning log entries

generic prompts that you could tailor to your subject area. *Process entries* generally ask students to reflect on *how* they have learned; *reaction entries* focus more on *what* they have learned. We think both kinds of prompts are useful, even though the distinction between the two may get blurred in students' writing.

The *double-entry journal* is another variation on content area learning logs (Bromley, 1993; Fretzin, 1992). In a double-entry journal, the writer either draws a line down the middle of the page or uses two facing pages. The left-hand side is used to jot down a stimulus for thought. This could be a personal experience, a quotation from a book, something said in class, a new vocabulary term, or an important issue or concept. On the right side, the writer can enter his or her reactions, thoughts, and feelings. At first, teachers can provide prompts for the left side of the journal. When students become familiar with the double-entry format, they can be asked to find their own prompts.

The double-entry journal format can be used across all content areas. Math students could write out a particularly difficult problem on the left side and explain their solutions on the right. Physics students could state one of the laws of thermodynamics on the left side and describe one way in which it has practical application in their lives on the right. In literature study, readers could choose characters, plot events, figurative language, or specific quotations to include on the left side, with their personal interpretations or reactions on the right. The double-entry format could also be used to have students juxtapose pros and cons on an issue, causes and effects, or comparisons and contrasts.

Pamela Carroll (2000) suggests a *triple-entry format* for journal writing. Writers make three columns or divide the page into thirds horizontally. The first space is used to note specific parts of the text that caught their fancy— words, phrases, or sentences, along with page numbers. The second space is used to note reactions to, questions about, or elaborations on the passages they have cited. The final space is reserved for a peer who reads the first two entries and then writes a response. This is most effective when students are given a few minutes following writing to converse in reader–responder pairs.

Many students may initially resist the idea of writing in a learning log, especially in science or math classes, in which writing is not traditionally required on a regular basis (Berenson & Carter, 1995). It may help to begin learning log writing with "feeling"-type prompts that have no right or wrong answers and move on to more conceptually oriented prompts after students have gotten used to the routine of learning log writing. Learning log entries will be longer and more thoughtful if you talk with the class about what they might write, specify your expectations for their learning log writing, and model entries that have been written by other students. Finally, it will help to set a timer or to have a specific time period each day or week dedicated to learning log writing.

A learning log is an excellent repository for all sorts of miscellanea. Students may use their logs to take lecture notes, to keep procedural and observational notes during labs, and to jot down new or essential vocabulary. If they are assigned reading beyond their textbooks, reactions can be noted in their logs. They may jot down quotations from their reading, their classmates, or the teacher. They can copy discussion webs or other graphic representations from the board, or they can create their own webs in the log.

Teachers have worked out different strategies for keeping track of students' learning log entries. When one or two class sections are writing in logs, it is easy to review entries on a weekly or biweekly basis. Multiple sections can turn in their logs on a staggered schedule. If teachers regularly review student logs, they get a sense of what is or is not working, both for individual students and for a whole class, and students see that the logs are important to the teacher. Reading student logs does not have to be a Herculean task. Because learning logs contain unfinished writing, the teacher should not be assigning a qualitative grade or marking mechanics. Log entries can be a messy mixture of trash and treasure, so a quick, impressionistic reading is usually sufficient to ferret out the important parts and ensure that the writer is making the expected effort. Gradebook credit can be given on a pass/fail basis for making regular entries.

Another approach to evaluating learning logs promotes students' reflections on their own learning. At the end of the grading period, have students reread their entries, select one or more that exemplify their best thinking, and put a title to only these entries. Having them flag these entries with sticky notes will help you quickly locate them. Whether they select one or several entries for you to read is your choice. Have students number pages, create a table of contents, and write an introduction in which they explain how they have used the journal/learning log and why they chose specific entries for you to read. The grade can come primarily from "bean counting"—giving points for having numbered pages, created a table of contents, etc. When Victoria taught physical science in junior high, she graded students' learning logs each quarter. She would take a week, and each day she would evaluate the learning logs from one class, making brief responses to the entries students had selected to be read.

Responding to log entries is a matter of choice. A check mark or a word or two in the margin may be enough. A teacher who prefers not to write directly in the students' logs can use sticky notes. Occasional elaborated responses to questions or observations will motivate students and make the learning log a more meaningful tool. Teachers sometimes use logs to conduct ongoing dialogues with students, and they find that this promotes a type of teacher–student communication that otherwise would not occur in daily classroom exchanges (Atwell, 1998).

Martha Dolly (1990) points out that when teacher and students carry on a dialogue in this manner, the learning log becomes a reading activity as well as a writing one for students. She says that this intertwining of reading and writing is especially beneficial for students who are learning English as a second language since it makes literacy both active and functional. Students who struggle with formal reading and writing assignments find the exchange of questions, answers, and observations stimulating.

Other Informal Writing Activities

Students can engage in informal, unfinished writing activities even if they do not keep learning logs. A teacher could use the first five minutes of class for a writing warm-up, based on one of the prompts listed in Figure 10.5. A teacher can assign brief "Entrance visas" to be written outside of class and handed in at the beginning of the next class period. "Exit visas" can be written in class and collected from students at the end of the period. Another simple writing-to-reflect activity, often called Think Writes in science, mathematics, and social studies (Mayher, Lester, & Pradl, 1983), and termed free writes in English, can be used at the beginning, middle, or end of a lesson or a unit. Students can compare their free-writing products in groups or free-write for five minutes as a follow-up to group work.

What students do after writing is an essential element in the success of an informal writing activity (Tierney, Readence, & Dishner, 2000). They need an opportunity to share their written responses so that they can see how others have interpreted the reading. This reinforces the understanding that a variety of responses are possible. When teachers write and share their responses with students, they add their experience to the discussion and serve as good reflective models.

Another informal writing activity, called *writing roulette* (Bean, 1992), can be used to reinforce content area vocabulary. The teacher provides a simple story structure consisting of three elements: a setting and a character, a problem or goal for the character, and a resolution. Students are told they must use and underline at least one word from their content unit in each section of the story. Students begin writing about the setting and character and continue for a specified time, perhaps five minutes. When the time is up, papers are exchanged within a small group, and a new time limit is set. Each student reads the paper he or she received and writes the problem section of the story. Papers are exchanged a final time so that a third student writes the resolution. The finished stories are then returned to the original authors, who share them with the small group.

Response Heuristic.   Response Heuristic (Bleich cited in Tierney & Readence, 2000) is a strategy that guides student response to learning. It is particularly well suited to poetry and to literature rich with figurative language. When using Response Heuristic, students are guided to make three levels of response using a three-column grid:

1. *Text perceptions*:   The reader records important information. Sometimes you may want students to record direct quotes, as in the example below. "As you read, jot down any words or phrases that you find interesting or that you think are particularly important." This is essentially a literal level response.
2. *Reactions*:   The reader tells what she or he thinks or feels about the text or what the author is trying to say. "What does this mean? How does it make you feel?" This is an interpretive level response.
3. *Associations*:   The reader makes connections between the text and personal knowledge, prior knowledge, and beliefs. "What else does this selection call to mind? Does this remind you of anything you have experienced?" This is an application level response.

Victoria remembers one English class studying Zora Neale Hurston's *Their Eyes Were Watching God*. The student teacher she was observing used Response Heuristic to guide her students' interpretation of the novel. She asked students to read a selection from the text and record a quote from the book that struck them as interesting, amused them, or was for some reason noticed by them. One of the concepts she was emphasizing was figurative language, and this strategy was particularly effective in teaching students how to understand figurative language. An example of Victoria's response is illustrated below:

Quote from text	Author's meaning	Your associations
"Women are the mules of the world"	I think Hurston means that women do most of the work in the world but don't get credit for it. I think she also intends to illustrate that men think women are "dumb and stubborn" as mules are usually portrayed.	It makes me think of myself, working full time both at home (cleaning, cooking, buying groceries, etc.) and teaching school when my husband was in graduate school—he went to class (on occasion) and did a lot of hunting and fishing on weekends while I took care of laundry!

What students do *after* writing is an essential element in this strategy. Students need an opportunity to share their responses so that they can see the variety of responses to the text. When teachers write and share their responses with students, they provide a valuable model for students. Response Heuristic can be adapted to suit other content areas as well. For example, in a history class you could emphasize the residual effects of events in history by using the following column headings: Event—Immediate Effect/Result—Residual Result.

Reviewing and Summarizing

Many students believe that if they have read each page, they have conscientiously fulfilled an assignment to "read Chapter 12." If there are no questions to answer, no reading guide to complete, they are content to let the teacher tell them in class what it all meant, or at least what was important. Consequently, their efforts at reading and learning are passive and less effective than if they had actively sought to consolidate what they had learned. They have omitted the final, integrative step in reading to learn—taking the time to review the text and summarize what was learned. Summarizing reinforces and consolidates the many processes involved in learning from text, such as determining important information, perceiving text structure, and drawing inferences.

EVIDENCE-
BASED
RESEARCH

Numerous studies have shown that students of varying ages benefit from learning how to produce written summaries of what they have read (Armbruster, Anderson, & Ostertag, 1987; Taylor & Beach, 1984). Hare and Borchardt (1984) found that summary writing was effective with urban African American and

Hispanic high school students. In order to write a summary, a reader must know how to perform three basic processes (Hidi & Anderson, 1986):

1. Select and delete information.
2. Condense information by combining or by substituting a general term for a group of specific terms (e.g., "farm animals" instead of "horses, goats, pigs, and sheep").
3. Transform the information into writing.

Although basic, these processes are hardly simple. As with other reading processes, students need to be shown how to summarize and need continual, long-term practice in order to effectively add summarizing to their repertoire of reading strategies.

Strategies for teaching students to summarize. Hierarchical summaries, REAP, and GIST are three formal procedures for teaching summarization. Each has several useful features. *Hierarchical summaries* are structured around the headings and subheadings found in most content area texts (Taylor & Beach, 1984). The procedure is as follows:

1. Students preview the reading selection with emphasis on headings, highlighted vocabulary, and other typographical cues.
2. Based on the preview, teacher and students together develop a skeleton outline that the teacher writes on the chalkboard, overhead projector, or projected computer screen.
3. Students read the text using the outline as a reading guide.
4. After reading, students compose main idea statements for main points in the outline and add essential supporting details, again with teacher guidance.
5. Finally, students develop a "key idea" or summarizing statement for the entire passage, which becomes the first sentence of the summary.

The hierarchical summary is a strategy that students can learn to use independently. The strategy depends, however, on the heading/subheading format of textbooks, and it would not be appropriate for narrative or other material that does not have clear graphic signals for important information and text organization.

REAP is an acronym for four stages in reading and understanding: *R*ead the text; *E*ncode into your own language; *A*nnotate by writing the message down; *P*onder, or think about, the message on your own and with others. Skilled readers make many different kinds of annotations. Sometimes they jot down a critical comment, a question, a note on the author's intentions, or, a personal reaction. The simplest kind, though, is a summary annotation. Eanet and Manzo (1976) suggest that students be introduced to summary annotations of paragraphs through a four-step sequence:

1. Show students a sample paragraph and a summary annotation. Explain what an annotation is and why readers might use annotations to help them understand and remember what they have read.

2. Show students another paragraph, this time with three annotations. One is a good summary, and the other two are flawed. Lead students to select the best summary and discover the problems with the other two.
3. Show students how to summarize by modeling the process for them with a third paragraph.
4. Have individual students develop their own summary annotations, and then in groups, analyze their summaries and combine ideas to come up with a concise and complete summary.

EVIDENCE-BASED RESEARCH

GIST stands for *Generating Interactions between Schemata and Text* (Cunningham, 1982). Using the GIST procedure, students produce progressively more condensed summaries of a text selection. To begin the GIST procedure, you need a short, coherent expository paragraph. You then proceed as follows:

1. Show students the first sentence of the paragraph, and ask them to retell it in 15 words or less. Write their summary on the chalkboard or overhead as they dictate and edit it as a group.
2. Show students the second sentence of the paragraph. Erase their first summary statement and ask students to summarize both sentences in 15 words or less.
3. Continue this procedure, one sentence at a time, until the group has summarized the entire paragraph in 15 words or less.
4. Repeat this procedure as many times as necessary until students become adept. Then, lead them to summarize an entire paragraph at one time, rather than sentence by sentence.
5. Finally, when the group has built some proficiency with the GIST procedure, have students produce summary statements individually.

All students need guided practice in summarizing before they can be expected to produce summaries independently. Initial efforts can be carried out in cooperative-learning settings to maximize student participation. Intermediate and middle-grade students and secondary students with lower reading ability will need several guided practice sessions, but they can take more responsibility for generating the outlines and summaries each time.

Teachers should not expect that students' independent efforts will be flawless, however. Summary writing is a difficult skill that requires plenty of practice. Implicit information and text passages that are long and complex will be especially problematic, even for relatively advanced students. Honors students and learning disabled students alike will struggle in learning how to summarize, as the writing examples in Figure 10.6 demonstrate.

Narrative text is generally easier to summarize than expository text, so it might be advisable to start inexperienced students with a short story in an English anthology or a chapter in a novel. If that is not practical, students will have the most initial success with relatively short passages of expository text,

Summarizing and the Struggling Reader

There are important developmental differences in the way students summarize (Anderson & Hidi, 1988/1989; Hill, 1991; Paris, Wasik, & Turner, 1991). The variability of summarizing skill within a single grade level is illustrated by the contrasting examples from two seventh graders in Figure 10.6. The students read an article, "Good-bye Communism," in a current events newspaper. The teacher placed the following list of key words on the board: *communism, independence, coup,* and *economic crisis.* Students copied these words in their notebooks to guide them in writing a short summary of important events in the article. Both summaries capture the key idea, but Adam's is short and features only two additional details, with no connections among the information in the summary. Jonathon, on the other hand, includes several key ideas with direct support and provides definitions of key terms.

Like Adam, younger or less able readers have difficulty combining ideas, rearranging information, and translating ideas into their own words. Although most students know that a summary should include important information from a passage, struggling readers are less adept than good readers at identifying what is important and are less likely to include important information in their summaries (Winograd, 1984). For Adam, including the main idea of the article in his summary is a good beginning. For his next summary, his teacher might give him a shorter selection of text to work with and model for him how to elaborate on his main point, perhaps by asking himself "who," "what," and "why" questions. She could also pair Adam with a more able student or enlist the help of a resource teacher who could give Adam more practice and support in summarizing. Even though his skill level is quite different from Jonathon's, Adam should be able to improve his reading ability through summarizing.

perhaps five or six paragraphs at most. Self-contained passages with explicitly stated main ideas and a clear structure will be the easiest to work with. For typical science, math, or social studies text material, this might mean working with a single important subsection of a chapter, perhaps a page or two in length. Able high school readers can be expected to work with longer selections of text.

EVIDENCE-BASED RESEARCH

The main ideas may seem obvious to us as expert readers and summarizers, but students learning how to summarize may pick out ideas that are personally important or interesting to them instead of trying to find the main ideas in the text. Therefore, it is helpful to point out that a summary should try to capture the ideas that would probably be important to the author (Anderson & Hidi, 1988/1989). Students who are learning how to summarize should also be allowed to work with a copy of the text to refer to. Summarizing requires careful consideration of the text, including rereading and checking for information. It is not an exercise in memorization.

ADAM'S SUMMARY

(Adam is classified as learning disabled.)

(2) The souets our go came communism The presedent chanmged The cleabrated that they were free

JONATHON'S SUMMARY

(Jonathon is in an honors class.)

GOOD-BYE COMMUNISM

COMMUNISM IS WHEN THE GOVERNMENT CONTROLS EVERYTHING. THE SOVIET UNION JUST GOT RID OF COMMUNISM. DURING THAT TIME WHEN COMMUNISM RULED MANY REPUBLICANS THREATEND TO LEAVE AND BECOME INDEPEND COUNTRIES. THE GOVERNMENT CONTROLED WHAT YOU WOULD GROW WHAT JOB YOU GOT WHAT TO BUY AND SO ON. PEOPLE WANTED TO BE FREE, THEY WANTED TO BEABLE TO DO WHAT THEY WANTED TO. NOW THAT COMMUNISM IS OVER THEY ARE FACING PROBLEMS. THEY NEED MORE FOOD FOR THE PEOPLE OTHER COUNTRIES ARE GIVING SUPPORT SUCH AS FOOD SUPPLES AND SO ON

FIGURE 10.6 **Sample summaries of a social studies reading by two seventh graders**

Guiding Student Writing

Some content area teachers say that they are reluctant to assign writing because students' written products are often not very good. When students are asked to write on a topic from a reading assignment, many simply do not have enough experience to know how to proceed. They end up churning out a vague paragraph or two that can be as hard to read as it was to write. Of course, if students do not write much, they will not get any better, and a vicious circle becomes established. If teachers can give some support and structure to students' writing, the writing will be easier and the products should improve.

Guided writing procedure. The *guided writing procedure* (Smith & Bean, 1980; Konopak, Martin, & Martin, 1987) has six steps that can be implemented over two or three days:

1. Students brainstorm on their prior knowledge of a new topic.
2. As a class or in groups, students label their ideas and organize them into a semantic web or other graphic format.
3. Each student writes on the topic.
4. Students read the assigned text selection.
5. Based on their reading, students revise their original writing.
6. A brief quiz is given on the material.

EVIDENCE-
BASED
RESEARCH

As we mentioned earlier, this writing procedure has been successfully implemented with both middle-grade and high school students. Writers in both age groups produced fewer text-explicit details and more higher-level ideas than their peers who did not write before reading (Konopak, et al., 1990; Martin & Konopak, 1987).

The guided writing procedure is also effective with students who are developing proficiency in English (Reyes & Molner, 1991). The combination of oral language, reading, and writing helps linguistically diverse students synthesize their thinking and go beyond the highly structured grammar exercises that are characteristic of many ESL writing programs. Reyes and Molner recommend modifying this procedure to include cooperative-learning formats in which second-language learners can achieve greater success. They also caution that teachers should not overemphasize form and mechanics when reading ESL students' drafts.

Writing guides. When students write after studying a textbook chapter or unit or after reading a novel, they are able to pull many ideas together, see

A Response from Our Readers

Amanda Fredrickson, an undergraduate in a course that George Hruby taught at the University of Georgia, chose to do a critique of several chapters in the third edition of *Content Reading and Literacy: Succeeding in Today's Diverse Classrooms* for her final project. Here, in her words, is what Amanda wrote regarding the need for more ideas on how to use writing as a stimulus for class discussion:

Although I think discussion is important and effective, I think students need the opportunity to reflect on their own [e.g., through journaling, quick writes, learning logs, or any other strategy for written responses]. In my opinion, having students write their own reflections first before small or whole group discussions enhances the overall effectiveness of classroom discussions. It gives students the opportunity to gather their thoughts on the topic that will be discussed and express their own individual opinion before a teacher or other students express their opinions.

meaningful relationships, and consolidate what they have learned. When discussing writing assignments earlier, we said that a teacher can help students understand what and how to write by manipulating certain elements of the task. *Writing guides* constitute a good illustration of how this can be done.

In the writing guide shown in Figure 10.7, the teacher uses the format of a grant proposal to get students to write about what they have learned in their study of genetics. This format gives writers a clear purpose (to obtain a research grant) and a voice (formal and scientific) for their writing. The hints give students guidance about what should be included in their proposals. The teacher acknowledges the importance of revising and editing by asking each student to trade papers with a fellow scientist to make sure the proposal includes the important information and is free of errors in spelling or grammar.

Same facts, different audience.   Lawrence Baines (2000) describes an activity that can be adapted to most content areas. To begin with, students are

---

WRITING GUIDE: GENETICS

Imagine you are Gregor Mendel's lab assistant. Pretend that you are writing an explanation of your findings so that you can receive a grant to further your research. Write a well-developed explanation of your findings from your experiments with pea plants. You should have a clear explanation of Mendel's research and a description of a Punnet square.

Hint: Remember that you are writing a scientific paper. Be sure to include and explain the following terms:

heredity	genetics	dominant
pure	hybrid	recessive
genotype	generation	genes
	phenotype	

Hint: Scientists are thorough people. Don't forget to explain the outcomes of each of the pairs below.

1. Two dominant genes

2. Two recessive genes

3. One dominant and one recessive gene

Give an example of the genotype and phenotype that result from each of the above combinations.

Hint: Make sure you do not lose the grant because of silly grammatical errors or spelling mistakes. Trade papers with a friend. Ask him/her to be sure that you have clearly covered the necessary information.

FIGURE 10.7   Writing guide for an eighth-grade science unit (*Source:* Reprinted by permission of Judith L. Stenroos, Buffalo Public Schools, #31, Buffalo, New York.)

SAME FACTS, DIFFERENT AUDIENCE

Directions: Select one project for each of the audiences.

1. Audience 1: Royal Maritime Commission appointed in 1912 to study the sinking.

    a. Write an investigative report that attempts to assign blame for the disaster.

    b. Write a series of recommendations for avoiding such accidents in the future.

2. Audience 2: Family members of victims.

    a. Write a letter from the steamship company expressing condolences.

    b. As an attorney, write a proposal for a lawsuit against one or more parties to the accident.

3. Audience 3: Contemporary *Titanic* fanatics.

    a. Write an advertising brochure for submersible trips to the wreck.

    b. Write a proposal to ban further exploitation of the *Titanic* wreckage.

FIGURE 10.8   Same Facts, Different Audience guide: The wreck of the *Titanic*

given a fact sheet related to a "hot topic" in current events or their content area curriculum. After a class discussion of the fact sheet, students can be divided into groups of three or four and given a worksheet that lists different audiences and possible writing topics for each. (Figure 10.8 gives an example for facts related to the sinking of the *Titanic* and subsequent discovery of the wreck.) Each group should select three projects they would like to work on and make a plan for dividing up the labor. After a day or two of in-class writing time, groups present their projects to the rest of the class, which gives them feedback on the effectiveness of the writing. This should be followed by a whole-class analysis of the different kinds of appeals that were used in the writing. The number of audiences and writing projects can be varied, and this could also be an individual writing activity instead of a cooperative group task.

Creative writing.   You may believe that so-called "creative writing" is the exclusive province of the English or language arts teacher, but there are many forms of creative writing that lend themselves to other content areas. In fact, entire genres of literature, such as science fiction and historical fiction, have been developed around concepts that come from those disciplines. You could use RAFT to develop fiction-based writing assignments around ideas in your content areas.

Jokes, riddles, cartoons, songs and raps, and advertisements are other examples of creative writing that can be adapted to various content areas. Several poetry formats lend themselves to content areas, too. An *acrostic poem* spells out a key word or phrase with the first letter of each line, as in the following example written for a geography class studying Africa:

Shifting sand dunes
Across a vast area.
Harsh landscape with
Ancient highways.
Rain is scarce
And temperatures are high.

The *cinquain* is another poetry format that lends itself to writing in content areas. It is a five-line poem with a set number of syllables in each successive line. The syllable pattern is two-four-six-eight-two. The following is an example that incorporates concepts from a middle school earth science lesson:

The moon (2)
Reflects the sun, (4)
Revolving 'round the earth, (6)
Waxing and waning and pulling (8)
The tides. (2)

The *biopoem* is frequently used as a beginning-of-the-year exercise to fire up the writing synapses and help students get acquainted with new classmates. The basic format can be adapted to include many facts and concepts focused on particular people, things, places, or events from various content areas. Figure 10.9 illustrates how an autobiographical biopoem and a biopoem based on a historical personage takes shape.

BIOPOEMS

Autobiographical Biopoem	*Historical Personage Biopoem*
Line 1: Your first name	Line 1: First name of subject
Line 2: Four adjectives that describe you	Line 2: Four adjectives that describe subject
Line 3: Resident of . . .	Line 3: Resident of . . .
Line 4: Son or daughter of . . .	Line 4: Lover of . . . (3 people, places, things)
Line 5: Brother or sister of . . .	Line 5: Who believed . . . (1 or more ideas)
Line 6: Lover of . . . (3 items)	Line 6: Who used . . . (3 methods or things)
Line 7: Who likes to . . . (3 things)	Line 7: Who wanted . . . (3 things)
Line 8: Who hates to . . . (2 things)	Line 8: Who said "_____" (Give a quote)
Line 9: Who would like to . . . (3 things)	Line 9: Who gave . . . (3 things)
Line 10: Your last name	Line 10: Last name of subject

FIGURE 10.9   Biopoem formats

Sodium

A reactive, soft solid metal, gray in color, an oxidizer

Sibling to Li and K

Lover of all halogens, especially Cl

Who feels explosive in the presence of water, producing a base as the result of the reaction

Who needs to get rid of one electron in order to have a complete outer electron shell

With an electron distribution of 2-8-1, you fear your own instability

Who gives one electron to its halogen compounds, forming ionic bonds

Provided with a willing recipient, you would love to get rid of that single outer electron

Resident of Group IA on the Periodic Chart of the Elements

Na

FIGURE 10.10   Model of a biopoem written by Victoria for physical science students

With a bit of revision to the prompts for the lines, biopoems can also be used in science, math, and other subjects. Figure 10.10 is an example of a biopoem Victoria created as a model for her physical science students when they were studying the Periodic Chart of the Elements.

The lighter side.   Not all content-related writing need be serious. Playing with language is another useful creative outlet that can lighten the classroom atmosphere and promote language development. Jokes, puns, and satire have always been used to critique leaders, highlight social issues, and score points in public discourse. Humorous writing, then, can serve a more serious purpose of engaging students in critical thinking about a topic. Students can write short pieces that feature humorous repetition, exaggeration, or unexpected associations (Weber, 2000). A class can brainstorm content-related top ten lists or variations on Ten Things to Do With a Dead Cat. (Our apologies to cat lovers for this example; we are decidedly "dog people.") Students might create wacky advertisements or want ads based on content area facts or concepts. Many other humorous variations are possible among the modes of content area writing listed in Figure 10.2.

Sydeana Martin (2000) suggests a tabloid exposé format that can be used to write about literature, history, scientific developments, or current events. This would start by sharing some humorous headlines with the class, either real or teacher created, typical of tabloids such as the *National Inquirer*. The teacher then introduces the topic, and students brainstorm tabloid headlines. Finally, students take the role of tabloid reporter and write up the topic in tabloid style.

Teaching Struggling Writers

Too often, instruction for students with writing disabilities focuses heavily on drill with spelling and mechanics. This narrow concentration, added to the difficulties that struggling writers have with handwriting, organization, and sustaining fluency, means that they often do very little actual writing. Bernice Wong and associates (Wong et al., 1997; Wong, 1997) have shown that a three-phase instructional process can lead to significant improvement in the writing of adolescents with learning disabilities. The three phases are:

1. Teacher modeling of specific expository genres combined with collaborative planning
2. Drafting at a word processor, which helps to attenuate handwriting, spelling, and fluency problems
3. Revising with peer and teacher conferences

In an instructional study, Wong et al. (1997) gave explicit instruction in writing compare-and-contrast essays to 21 struggling adolescent writers. After writing six compare-and-contrast essays, these students demonstrated significantly improved clarity and organization and utilization of facts and details to support comparisons and contrasts. Wong and associates credited this success to their explicit focus on a single genre, to the intensity of the instruction, and to the interactive dialogues among teachers and peers.

In chemistry, Ron DeLorenzo (1999) uses tongue-in-cheek mystery titles to engage student interest, build communication skills, and illustrate important science concepts. For example, he gives a detailed analysis of the temperature of hell (slightly above 246°F based on biblical reference and scientific fact, according to DeLorenzo). Other mystery topics include the following: Why do humans kiss? How can sand predict earthquakes? Why do ice cream and car batteries explode? Why is electricity free in the winter? Given some hints and guidance, students could write their own solutions to these mysteries. They could also create their own science mysteries.

WRITING TO INQUIRE

We are living in what is sometimes called the Information Age and are witnessing the rapid expansion of knowledge across many disparate fields. What is taught in science, social studies, and mathematics will almost certainly change dramatically over the next decade. In an age of rapidly changing and expanding knowledge, a well-educated person must have the ability to inquire into a topic—to investigate it, read about it, think about it, and communicate about it. All too often we find that when students in our teacher education courses reflect on their own experiences in writing a report when they were youngsters, they recall a scenario not unlike that told by Amy Haysman. As you read this excerpt from Amy's reflections, think about the problems she encountered and what specialized skills she needed to write her report.

> The one research report that really impacted my life was due on January 30, 1984. I don't think I will ever forget that date or the term paper assignment I turned into Mrs. Hudson on that cold, dreary morning. When my ninth-grade teacher had first presented this assignment in class, I was excited. I was all grown up now! I was in high school and had finally been told to do the famous, dreaded task of writing a term paper. . . . I was given a slip of paper that said, "The characterization of Lady Macbeth in *Macbeth*." "Was I supposed to know what this means?" I thought to myself. Suddenly, this coming-of-age assignment wasn't too appealing. Luckily, my teacher anticipated my panic attack and told everybody not to worry because she planned to teach us how to do the research step by step. Writing the paper was then up to us.
>
> For the next few weeks, Mrs. Hudson led the class, page by grueling page, through a 38-page folder entitled, "The Term Paper: A Guide to Research, Documentation, and Format." We were then set loose in the school library. . . . After countless hours in several libraries, I had compiled a stack of note cards too big to fit in even a jumbo-size rubber band. I decided it was time to stop researching and start writing. As I read my note cards, I realized two problems. One, I didn't really understand what was written on these cards from the 13 books I had quoted, and two, I really had no idea how to write this paper. I had not learned anything about the characterization of Lady Macbeth in my frenzy to take notes and write bibliography cards in the correct form.*

Chances are, this scenario brought back vivid memories of the term paper, one of the most dreaded of all school projects for students and teachers alike. One obvious problem for Amy was her assigned topic. Perhaps if her teacher had considered aspects of an assignment represented by the RAFT acronym she might have had a better idea of why she was writing, what she was writing about, and for whom she was writing. When students are sent forth to "do research" for little more reason than it is ninth grade and the term paper is part of the ninth-grade curriculum, the results are too often exactly as Amy describes them.

One way to make writing to inquire more authentic and engaging is to consider how professionals in various content areas use writing. In a study of the writing of five research scientists, Debby Deal (1999) found that they used a progressive combination of expressive writing (personal, tentative, and meant primarily for themselves) and transactional writing (more formal, structured, and intended to communicate ideas to others) as they moved from the early stages of designing an experiment, through data collection and analysis, to the final preparation of a report to a funding agency or an article for a professional journal. Carolyn Keys (1999) argues that science students need to be engaged in authentic scientific writing, which she says should involve the production of

**EVIDENCE-
BASED
RESEARCH**

---

*Reprinted by permission of Amy P. Haysman.

new knowledge. Traditional scientific genres that promote scientific thinking include:

1. Writing about experiments that are student designed or which may yield more than one data set
2. Writing explanations of scientific phenomena and processes
3. Writing reports based on secondhand sources
4. Biographies of one or a group of scientists
5. Persuasive expository writing on a controversial topic, such as whether dinosaurs are warm- or cold-blooded

Authentic historical inquiry should help students understand that history is not just a dry, noncontroversial recitation of facts, dates, and names of rich and powerful people but rather a frequently contentious interpretation of diverse perspectives and experiences with direct relevance to our contemporary lives. Therefore, students of history need to be guided to ask authentic questions, select and examine a variety of evidence, appreciate the context of historical events, evaluate divergent perspectives, and reach logical (albeit tentative) conclusions (Foster & Padgett, 1999).

Preparing for Student Inquiry

Asking students to embark on an extended inquiry project requires thoughtful planning and guidance. We suggest some general planning parameters here and describe more specific strategies in following sections.

Preparation should begin well before the assignment is explained and topics are selected. First, teachers need to decide on a conceptual framework within which students will select topics. By narrowing the scope of possible topic selection, teachers can do more advance preparation. They can alert media center colleagues and begin to identify resources. By placing some limits on the range of topics, teachers will be in a better position to provide resources and assistance as students pursue their research.

Establishing an overall theme for inquiry also makes it possible to build appropriate background through lecture, audiovisuals, read-aloud selections from literary works or nonfiction, primary sources, or guest speakers. For example, Cena and Mitchell (1998) describe how they began a research unit on the Middle Ages by showing a PBS video based on David Macaulay's book *Cathedral* (1973). After seeing the video and the book students were able to suggest several major themes related to life in the Middle Ages, including technology of building construction, social class distinctions, the arts, and the roles of religion, politics, and economics.

Once students understand the general issues related to their research theme, they can begin to brainstorm specific questions to investigate. Teachers should encourage reflection on the suitability of these topics—whether they are too narrow or too broad, whether the question is open or closed, and whether there are likely to be sufficient resources available for their inquiry.

As students embark on their inquiries, teachers may need to provide varied kinds of assistance. Directing students to appropriate resources, including people to interview, print sources, CD-ROMs, and Web sites, is a given. Students may also need guidance on how to evaluate their resources. Minilessons might cover any of a number of research skills that will facilitate inquiry, for example:

- Note taking
- Using indexes and tables of contents to pinpoint needed information
- Generating search terms for on-line indexes and the Internet
- Interpreting a "results" page from an Internet search
- Organizing gathered information and putting it into readable form
- Applying appropriate citation techniques
- Understanding stylistic requirements for final reports

Throughout the inquiry process, from brainstorming topics to preparation of a final draft, teachers can encourage students to share their work with each other. This kind of peer collaboration and feedback was an important part of the inquiry process of the scientists interviewed by Deal (1999).

A final consideration in planning for student inquiry is time. Not only should teachers allow sufficient time for research and writing, but it is also help-ful to establish reasonable deadlines for various stages of the inquiry process, such as topic selection, identifying resources, developing an outline, beginning a draft, and completing a draft. Teachers can monitor student progress with a checklist or by periodically looking at student research logs. Meaningful inquiry takes a good deal of time for professionals, so it would be difficult to expect much less from apprentices. Although much of the inquiry process can be done outside of class, it is reasonable to expect that concentrated periods of class time will be devoted to students' research. For instance, the early stages of inquiry might require a few days to get everybody started. Then, a specified day each week might be devoted to student projects, with two or three days reserved for the final stages of preparation and presentation.

Collecting and Organizing Information

We think that the following two techniques for collecting and organizing information, when introduced to your students over a reasonable period of time, will keep them from experiencing some of the same frustrations Amy felt when it came time to write her paper.

Research or three-search?   Term papers can be as vexing to the teacher who has to read them as they are to the students who have to write them. For example, consider Terry Phelps's (1992) recollections:

> After years of grading research papers, I began to question their value. To begin with, I hated reading the wretched things. They were usually boring strings of quotes with none of the students' own thoughts. Most students

fitted the papers to the quotes rather than vice versa. True synthesis was rare, and evidence that any learning had taken place was scant. (p. 76)

Phelps's dislike of grading term papers prompted him to look for alternatives to the traditional method of report writing. First, he wanted to develop a process that would enable students to rely more on their own ideas and interpretations and less on meaningless strings of quotations. To do this, he developed what he calls a *three-search paper* (Phelps, 1992). Named after the three search processes students must go through to produce a final written paper—reflecting, interviewing, and reading—the three-search paper discourages students from building their reports around quotations. It does this by engaging them in more personally and socially active kinds of research before sending them off to the library to find printed sources that support, expand, or explain what they have learned from personal reflection and interviews.

The three-search process for report writing begins with several reflective, or introspective, activities. Students examine sample papers that were written by former students to give them an idea of what their final papers may look like. Names are removed from the papers to preserve anonymity, and examples of both good and not-so-good papers are provided. Students also engage in a free-writing activity that encourages them to jot down whatever experiences they have had in relation to the topic on which they will write. Then, working in groups of three, students give each other feedback by focusing on what can be eliminated and what must be added to each person's list.

At the interview step, students examine the sample papers once more, this time for the purpose of noting how good writers incorporate specific examples and ask open-ended questions rather than questions that can be answered with yes or no. Then, each student interviews at least two people, including a peer and an authority on the topic he or she has chosen to research. For example, a student living outside Charlottesville, Virginia, who is planning to do a three-search paper on Thomas Jefferson, might interview a representative of the Jefferson Memorial Foundation at Monticello as well as an African American peer. The interviews might focus on these persons' views about Jefferson, author of the Declaration of Independence and owner of more than 170 slaves. (For more information, see *Confronting Thomas Jefferson, Slave Owner* by James Blackman 1992).

The final step—reading periodicals, books, pamphlets, and so forth—is usually the first step in the traditional approach to report writing. However, in the three-search process, printed sources are consulted only after students have had opportunities to reflect on previous experiences with the research topic and after they have interviewed at least two individuals. As Phelps (1992) discovered, "by this time, students are fairly well immersed in their subjects; hence, a trip to the library for the third area of research is more focused and less odious" (p. 77).

I-charts.   An inquiry chart, or *I-chart* (Hoffman, 1992), capitalizes on what students already know about a particular research topic prior to reading.

I-CHART

Name: *Dan*   Topic: *Rainforest canopy*

Subtopic:

  What are the different layers in a rainforest canopy?

What I Already Know:

  A rainforest has special kinds of plants and animals.

Resource:	Important Ideas:
1	*If there are a few high trees, others will grow higher to compete for light.*
2	*Most seedlings start on forest floors.*
3	*Rain helps leaf molds grow.*

Interesting Related Facts:

  Animals knock fruit down from the highest trees. This fruit is food for animals that can't climb trees.

Key Words:

  ecology, habitats

New Questions to Research:

  What are the names of some of the giant rainforest trees?

FIGURE 10.11   I-chart

I-charts can be the basis for whole-class, small-group, or individual inquiry. A sample I-chart is illustrated in Figure 10.11. Students list their topic and an inquiry question about the topic, along with any information they already know on the topic. Then they consult various resources, noting bibliographic information and important ideas from each. Figure 10.11 has spaces for three resources, but I-charts can be expanded to include more. It is useful, however, to limit the amount of note-taking space to discourage wholesale copying of resource text. The I-chart has a place to list key words that students will want to use in their written reports, and it also provides space for the student to jot down any new questions that arise once their inquiry is under way.

Sally Randall (2000), a teacher at Oconee County Middle School in Watkinsville, Georgia, adapted the I-chart to make it fit her eighth graders' needs. She wanted to help her students build on prior knowledge and develop critical thinking skills as they collected and organized information for writing a research report. The I-chart provided a structure that suited her instructional goals.

First, Sally prepared her students for the eighth-grade interdisciplinary unit on the wilderness by teaching specific language arts skills that they would need in researching the topic. These skills included letter writing, paraphrasing, interviewing, and reference skills for use in looking up information in source materials and in constructing a bibliography of those materials. She relied on her colleague in science to prepare the class for topics related to the wilderness unit.

After students had chosen a topic that suited their interests, they wrote proposals, listing what they already knew about the topic, what they wanted to learn, and where they would look for the information. This step in the process helped the students to narrow their topics.

Next, students brainstormed questions they had about their topics—questions that could not be answered by a simple yes or no. Following this brainstorming activity, they set up their individual I-charts. They turned their subtopics into questions. As they wrote their different subtopics/questions at the top of each of their I-charts, the students also recorded what they already knew about a particular subtopic.

Then, turning to their source materials, they began to read for information that would help them answer their questions. They also wrote letters to people in the community who they thought would be knowledgeable on their topics of interest. This appeal to outside sources opened opportunities for meeting and talking with people who represented a diversity of interests and backgrounds.

Recording the information involved students in using what they had learned about note taking and paraphrasing. It also introduced them to an efficient way of recording bibliographic information. Briefly, they drew a line on their I-charts after they had finished writing down what they had learned from a particular source. Then, on a separate sheet of paper labeled "References" they wrote the complete bibliographical information about that source, assigning a number (1, 2, 3) to each source and recording the number on the I-chart. From that point on, they only needed to refer to a source by its number when they wished to add information to their I-charts.

The I-chart is similar to, but not to be confused with, Macrorie's three-step *I-Search* (cited in Anders & Guzzetti, 1996). In the first step of this inquiry process, a student describes something he or she already knows about the topic under investigation and states a goal for learning new topic-related information. The second step entails a written description of the process used in learning the new information (i.e., the search), and the third step is an interpretation of what was found. The student then writes a conclusion and reflects on the value of what was learned and how the new information will be used.

Writing a Report

Report writing calls for some specialized skills if students are to succeed in researching and writing about what they find. One of these skills is outlining, and another is paraphrasing.

Outlining.   After Sally Randall's eighth graders had completed their I-charts, they were ready to begin the writing process. Each student had accumulated information on eight to ten subtopics (e.g., "What animals live in the rain forest?"), and they had organized their answers to the subtopic questions on their I-charts. By attaching a Roman numeral to each subtopic in their respective I-charts, the students had the beginnings of a formal outline. They added the details and interesting related facts found within their I-charts to complete the rest of their outline. As Randall (2000) noted in her discussion of the eighth graders' work, some used their outlines to create a visual display:

> The final product was a visual display for a wilderness convention much like the typical science fair. Students used the information they had learned to create a display of maps, charts, listings of facts, pictures, graphs, and timelines. They [also] created . . . a pamphlet informing the public of their expertise. These were showcased at an evening program to which we invited parents, experts who had been interviewed, and county librarians who had provided research assistance. (p. 540)

Paraphrasing.   Too often teachers assume students are able to paraphrase and find later, much to their dismay, that entire sections of a text have been copied verbatim with or without the use of quotation marks. Singer and Donlan's (1989) steps in teaching students how to paraphrase are easy to follow and demonstrate both *syntactic paraphrasing* (changing the order of the words) and *semantic paraphrasing* (substituting synonyms for the original words):

Step 1: Present a passage from a text along with a paraphrased version. Lead students to discuss how the two differ.

Step 2: Lead students to practice paraphrasing short passages from a text. Help them by identifying phrases to reword, using a dictionary to find synonyms, and modeling how long passages can be rewritten in shorter form.

Step 3: Gradually introduce longer passages and eliminate or reduce your support.

Alternatives to the Traditional Research Report

In earlier chapters, we featured several student inquiry projects that involved computer or media technology both in the research process and in the presentation of the results. It is clear from these examples that the days are long gone when research meant little more than time spent with the *Reader's Guide* and stacks of index cards. New technologies have dramatically changed the ways in which inquiry can be conducted and reported. In the following sections, we take a closer look at some alternatives to the term paper.

Multigenre reports.   Inquiry results can be reported in genres and media other than the traditional expository research paper (Moulton, 1999). Students who have learned about the Curie family of scientists, for instance, might create birth, marriage, and death certificates in order to convey important details of their lives, along with newspaper accounts of the Nobel prizes won by members of the family in 1903, 1911, and 1935. Another possibility would be to create

Evaluating Web Sources

The Internet is largely unregulated, rapidly expanding, and continuously changing. Anybody with minimal technology skills can post a Web site and say whatever they wish. Therefore, one important Internet inquiry strategy is the ability to evaluate the reliability of what is found there. The following guidelines are adapted from suggestions made by Gardner, Benham, and Newell (1999) and Foster and Padgett (1999). Most of them can be applied to other inquiry resources as well.

1. Explain extension domains. Common extensions include

   .com commercial entity
   .edu educational institution
   .gov government agency
   .mil military
   .net network resource
   .org -other type of organization, usually not-for-profit
   .web Web-related organizations

2. Is an author's name listed? Who is the author? What are his or her credentials? What is his or her affiliation and relation to the sponsors of the Web site? Is there an e-mail address, phone number, or other way to contact the author?

3. How accurate is the information? Are there references, links, or other ways to verify it? Is there any conflicting or supporting evidence?

4. How objective is the site? Why was this written? Do the language, graphics, or imagery reveal the author's perspective?

5. When was this written? Is there a date when the site was created and/or revised? Is the information current?

6. Does this site adequately cover the topic? How well does the information compare to other published resources? What is missing, hidden, or confusing? What additional information would be useful to know about this?

For more on evaluating Web sources, see our companion Web site at www.ablongman.com/alvermann5e.

Inquiry for Struggling Readers and Writers

Martha Rekrut (1997) recommends a collaborative approach to helping low achievers conduct inquiry. Inquiry topics should be of high interest to students and should be derived from questions that arise during the course of instruction. She recommends placing students in heterogeneous research groups of two, three, or four. She also says it is important to carefully teach and practice summarization or paraphrasing skills before students begin their research.

"laboratory notes" explaining one or more of the Curie discoveries. Students investigating Elizabethan theater might create posters and playbills for Shakespeare's plays. Inquiry results can also be incorporated into poems, skits or plays, and songs. Students might bring in short music clips that relate to some aspect of their research, along with a written explanation of the significance of their musical selection to their topic. Photos with captions, original artwork, and audio and video recordings are other media that can be used to present inquiry findings. These various genres and media can be motivating and provide a creative outlet for student learning, but still be based on significant data collection, synthesis, and evaluation.

Hypermedia.   Hypermedia software allows users to create computer-based files that may include text, sound, and visual images. The contents of a hypermedia file may be original creations of the person who is making the file or they may be imported to the file from another computer file, a scanner, CD-ROM, the Internet, videodisk, or audio CD. The information within a hypermedia file is connected by hyperlinks, much like the Internet, so that anyone who accesses the file may move from link to link in whatever order may be of interest. For example, if a student were to create a hypermedia file on the jazz trumpeter Miles Davis, he or she might include photos of Davis, pictures of his album covers, a discography, reviews of his recordings, a biography, sound clips from his recordings or interviews, and pictures of a trumpet with a written description of the instrument and how it is played. With many hypermedia programs, it is possible to include links to Internet sites. The student could use this file to make a presentation of his or her research or it could be accessed on the computer by other interested people. If done as an HTML file, it could be posted to the Internet for an unlimited audience.

Teachers and students have found many uses for hypermedia. Nancy Patterson (1999) describes how her eighth-grade students began their research with Native American poems. Students highlighted words and phrases they were curious about in the poems and began searching for more information on the Internet. For example, a poem about the Spanish conquistadors led some students to learn more about the Spanish Conquest, which then led to Spanish galleons and Spanish weaponry of the sixteenth century. At the same time, they were also following leads to information on the Anasazi, the Navajo, and other Native Americans of the Southwest.

Typically, Patterson's students read dozens of on-line articles as well as other information they found in library reference materials. When they accumulated sufficient information on one of their subtopics, they created a "page" file which became part of a web of links from one topic to another. Their final hypermedia products opened with their selected poem. By clicking on highlighted words in the poem, a reader could move to another page, which in turn would have links to other pages. Students created an average of 20 pages each for their final products. In contrast to the traditional research paper, Patterson found this project to be much more motivating. It also gave her students an expanded sense of what "text" is and how it can be manipulated. It allowed them to make choices about what to investigate, how to present information, and what organizational logic might link their varied findings.

Collaborative Internet projects. The Internet makes it possible for collaborative inquiry to extend beyond a single classroom to different schools, states, and countries. E-mail communications, collaboration with experts in various fields, "virtual gatherings" in which on-line presentations introduce people from different countries, electronic publishing, and shared data collection projects are a few of the collaborative Internet projects described by Mike and Rabinowitz (1998). One example is the We Are One project, which involves students from throughout the world in acting on an issue relevant in their area, and sharing their work with others (www.weareoneday.com). Teachers can find other projects or register a project of their own, along with an invitation to others to join, at the Global Schoolhouse Projects Registry (www.gsn.org/ GSH/pr/index.cfm).

There are many more applications of technology for inquiry than we could possibly catalog here, and teachers and students are continuously finding new ways to use technological tools for conducting inquiry and disseminating the results. To learn more, you might consult some of the references we have cited here as well as the Suggested Readings at the end of Chapter 4.

RESPONDING TO STUDENT WRITING

We recently met a friend, who is an English teacher, for dinner at a sidewalk café. When we had told him we might be a little late, he said that would be no problem. He was planning to spend a couple of hours there anyway, enjoying the pleasant spring weather and doing what English teachers do in the evening—reading student papers. Although English teachers may accept that as part of their turf, teachers in other disciplines usually do not. As you have been reading our recommendations for encouraging students to write, you might well have been wondering how you would read and correct all that writing. For high school teachers who have 100 or more students writing on a regular basis, that is something to consider. Fortunately, responding to student writing does not have to be an overwhelming chore for a teacher.

First, responding to writing need not be left entirely to the end of the writing process, when papers are handed in and it is too late to do anything about problems of content, clarity, or form. Second, responding does not have to be the sole responsibility of the teacher. Much of what students write can be read and responded to while it is still in process, and students can be very effective reviewers of one another's work.

Peer Responses

Throughout this chapter, we have made many suggestions for peer collaboration on writing. Group brainstorming and composing, exchanges of drafts, and conferences for revision and editing all help students get feedback on their work, see that others have similar questions or problems, and enhance the quality of their final written products. Collaboration among student writers does not occur spontaneously, however. Teachers need to take a little time to model good responses and to set some ground rules.

The key to responding to a writer's work is what Donald Graves (1983) calls "receiving." By this he means responding to what the writer is saying or letting the writer know that his or her message has come across. Teachers can show students how to receive each other's writing by modeling the process with an anonymous piece of student writing that can be duplicated or displayed on the overhead projector. (To protect the feelings of the writer, we recommend that you not use writing from any member of the class.) The teacher can begin by rephrasing the main points of the piece and commenting on its strengths and then move on to one or two questions for the writer or suggestions for possible revision. Observations and questions from the class should be invited. Once class members have discussed what would and would not be helpful comments for the writer, they might collectively establish some ground rules for peer responses. We suggest some variation of three basic rules:

1. *Be positive.* Respond to what the writer is trying to say and what the writer does well. Tearing down another person's work will only result in discouragement and hurt feelings.

PEER REVIEW

Writer: _____

Reviewer: _____

Topic/Title: _____

1. Read your partner's draft.

2. Which words or phrases struck you most? (Write them here.)

3. What do you feel the author was trying to say? Summarize it here in one sentence.

4. What are the main strengths of the draft?

5. What questions do you have for the author?

6. What one suggestion would you make to the author?

FIGURE 10.12   A peer review guide

2. *Be helpful.* Do your best to make comments that will be useful to the writer.
3. *Be specific.* Talk about specific words, phrases, or paragraphs.

To facilitate peer conferences, you might prepare a checklist or a *peer review guide* similar to the one in Figure 10.12. Such a form gives you a way to monitor peer conferences, and it could be included in a portfolio as part of the record of how a writing project developed.

Successful peer conferences depend on successful peer relations, which of course are not always conducive to helpful cooperation. Timothy Lensmire (1994) has described how social relations among students play themselves out in writing workshop activities, sometimes to the detriment of students with low social status. He concludes that teachers should recognize peer culture and social relations and take positive steps to sustain what he calls an "engaged, pluralistic classroom community" in which the voices of all students are valued and students learn to be considerate of their peers. It is unrealistic to expect that a teacher can heal all peer conflicts and maintain perfect harmony for a 45-minute period, despite whatever exchanges may be occurring in the hallways, on the street, or over the Internet or telephone. However, thoughtful modeling, guidance, and assignment of working groups can help to nourish civil and productive academic relationships.

Teacher Conferences

Teachers can respond to work in progress. In a short conference lasting two to five minutes, a teacher can read or listen to what a student is working on, ask a question or two, and respond to the writer's concerns. The goal of this kind of conference is to be helpful without being prescriptive. Teachers should confer without a pen or pencil in hand; marking a student author's draft voids the author's ownership and responsibility for the piece. Specific suggestions for adding, deleting, or altering the content of a draft may also diminish the writer's control and what Murray (1984) calls "the satisfaction of the writer's own learning, the joy and surprise of finding what [one has] to say" (p. 4). Instead, the teacher should try to adapt generic questions such as the following to each piece of writing:

> What do you think you will do next with this?
> What do you like best about this piece so far?
> What problem or difficulty are you having?
> Could you tell me more about X?
> What is the connection between X and Y?

Questions such as these generate talk that can help writers work out problems and make their own discoveries.

There are several benefits to in-process teacher conferences. First, conferences can help students develop their general writing skills. Teacher guidance and feedback can improve the actual written products. Conferencing also pays off when the time comes for teachers to make a formal evaluation of students' writing. The better the writing is, the easier it will be to read. Also, reading and responding will go faster when the teacher has been involved in the development of a piece of writing.

Formal Evaluation

All writing by students need not be subjected to formal evaluation. Learning logs, informal written reflections, and other unfinished writing can be read quickly and given a simple check mark to indicate completion of the assignment, with a brief written acknowledgment or response if appropriate. Assigning formal grades to such writing defeats the purpose of informal writing-to-learn activities, in which the process of writing (and thinking) is more important than the product.

In those pieces that are polished and handed in for grading, teachers should respond first to the content. When a teacher uses the red pencil to mark each and every mechanical or stylistic miscue, it sends two unfortunate messages to the writer. First, it signals that form is more important than content. Second, it implies that there is little hope of mastering a skill so technical and arcane. A paper covered with red marks is discouraging to a writer. Where could one possibly begin to improve such a mess?

If students are writing to show what they have learned, grades and written comments should be based primarily on content. There is no question that spelling and other mechanics are important or that numerous mechanical errors detract severely from the effectiveness of writing. However, if students are writing to show what they have learned, the information presented and the quality of the reflection and thinking should merit more weight than spelling and other mechanical aspects. If necessary, a teacher might point out one or two mechanical problems that are repeated or are especially troublesome for a reader, and it is reasonable to expect that students learn how to spell the technical vocabulary of a subject area.

Mechanics should account for a portion of a grade, and we have no quarrel with rigorous academic expectations. However, "three wrong and it's a C" requirements seem too stringent for developing writers, at least for content area assignments in which the emphasis is on mastery of ideas, not mastery of conventions.

Dialect features in writing represent a particularly sensitive, complex, and controversial aspect of evaluating student writing. As we said in our earlier discussion of dialect, there is no question that all students need to be fluent with Standard English writing conventions. However, standard conventions need to be modeled and taught in a context that recognizes the legitimacy and power of diverse language forms and the importance of an individual's voice. This implies that in some situations, nonstandard stylistic features may be appropriate. In writing for which Standard English is expected, the marking of dialect miscues should be done with consideration of the age of the writer, the instruction in standard forms that he or she may have received, and the importance of content versus form in the writing task.

For assignments such as inquiry projects whose development is complex and time-consuming, you might consider some variation on portfolio assessment, as suggested in Chapter 5. Along with the finished product, students may hand in notes, outlines, early drafts, journal entries, and conference records. Self-evaluation should also be part of the portfolio. In fact, self-evaluation can be factored into the final grade on any formal written assignment.

SUMMARY

Writing is a rigorous kind of thinking; it can be hard work even for the most adept. Teachers who understand writing processes know that students need guidance, reassurance, and plenty of practice. When teachers thoughtfully assign, guide, and respond to student writing in content areas, students benefit in many ways. They gain increased content knowledge and understanding. When students write, they learn. Whether it is a short note reflecting on a new concept or a term paper involving several weeks of effort, writing helps them to connect and clarify their thinking. Regular informal writing activities prepare students for the more formal demands of writing papers and examinations. However, perhaps more important, writing empowers. In a world of expanding information and technology, the ability to express oneself clearly in writing is likely to become more, not less, of a social, professional, and economic determinant.

SUGGESTED READINGS

Atwell, N. (1990). *Coming to know: Writing to learn in the intermediate grades*. Portsmouth, NH: Heinemann.

Atwell, N. (1991). *Side by side: Essays on teaching to learn*. Portsmouth, NH: Heinemann.

Baines, L., & Kunkel, A. (Eds.). (2000). *Going Bohemian: Activities that engage adolescents in the art of writing well*. Newark, DE: International Reading Association.

Bright, R. (1995). *Writing instruction in the intermediate grades: What is said, what is done, what is understood*. Newark, DE: International Reading Association.

Burns, M. (1995). *Writing in math class*. Sausalito, CA: Math Solutions.

Countryman, J. (1992). *Writing to learn mathematics*. Portsmouth, NH: Heinemann.

Daisey, P. (2003). The value of writing a "how-to" book to reduce the writing apprehension of secondary preservice science and mathematics teachers. *Reading Research and Instruction, 42*(3), 75–111.

Dyson, A. H., & Freedman, S. W. (2003). Writing. In J. Flood, D. Lapp, J. Squire, & J. Jensen (Eds.), *Handbook of research on teaching the English language arts* (2nd ed., pp. 967–992). Mahwah, NJ: Erlbaum.

Freedman, R. (1999). *Science and writing connections*. White Plains, NY: Seymour.

Fulwiler, T. (1987). *The journal book*. Portsmouth, NH: Boynton/Cook.

Hammann, L. A., & Stevens, R. J. (2003). Instructional approaches to improving students' writing of compare-contrast essays: An experimental study. *Journal of Literacy Research, 35*, 731–756.

Perry, T., & Delpit, L. (Eds.) (1998). *The real Ebonics debate: Power, language, and the education of African-American children*. Boston: Beacon.

Studying and Study Strategies

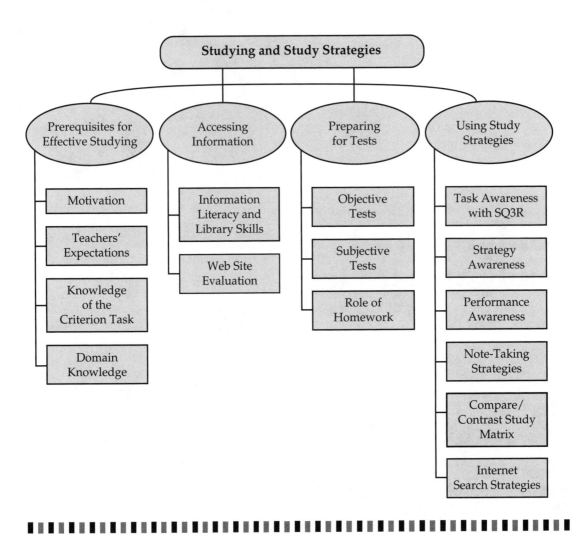

Victoria recalls the shock to her system when she first entered college. Her story may seem familiar to you:

■■■■■■

I had been a very good high school student—which is to say, I had learned to play the game of school well. Although I didn't make all As, as a senior I garnered a small scholarship from the local education association. When I went off to college, it was great—no one took up homework, there were only one or two exams for each class back then—fabulous! I played bridge and drank coffee in the canteen all quarter long . . . but when I sat my first exam, it occurred to me that perhaps I had missed something. The first test was English, but it might as well have been Greek. I didn't have a clue about gerunds or adjective clauses. I was physically ill. I knew something had to change and change fast.

During the next quarter, I studied as though my life depended on it, as indeed it did. I took notes in lecture and made notes from reading, I drew detailed diagrams, color coded and labeled. I learned some effective, if not efficient, study strategies. And my grades did improve, but it took real work—that was the first time I understood that studying *was* work. It was years before I learned about study strategies that could be effective and efficient. Most of my students, both graduates and undergraduates, say they were never really taught how to study, and based on that experience they don't really think about that in relation to their students until we discuss study strategies in content area reading. Frequently undergraduates will say that learning note-taking strategies helps them do better in the classes they are taking that semester; they complain that if just one teacher had taught them about taking notes and studying, they would have higher GPAs. They lament all the hours they've wasted because they didn't have a strategic study plan, and it makes them consider the importance of doing for their own students what wasn't done for them.

■ ■ ■ ■ ■ ■ ■

Paulo Freire and Donaldo Macedo (1987) are two literacy educators who want their students to read the world as well as the word. To Freire and Macedo's way of thinking, "to study is not easy, because to study is to create and recreate and not to repeat what others say" (p. 77). We think this definition of what makes studying difficult aptly summarizes the intent of this chapter on studying and study strategies. We view studying as an active process—one born of creative and critical thinking, not of passive acceptance and mindless regurgitation.

In this chapter, we describe several prerequisites for effective studying and accessing of information. We also provide some tips on preparing students to take tests. Finally, we present several study strategies that are designed to help students develop the metacognitive and self-regulatory processes necessary for effective studying. We hope you will think about your own history as a student as you read this chapter.

PREREQUISITES FOR EFFECTIVE STUDYING

To be effective in their studying, students need to develop a certain metacognitive awareness of the task and of themselves as readers; that is, they need to check their comprehension periodically for loss of meaning, apply appropriate fix-up strategies, monitor the effectiveness of those strategies, and evaluate their efforts to learn from studying (Baker & Brown, 1984). They also need to pay attention to what motivates them to learn. Beyond that, they can benefit from knowing their teachers' expectations of them as learners, understanding the nature of the criterion task, and possessing adequate domain knowledge.

Motivation

Students generally find studying a worthwhile activity only when they see real and meaningful purposes for doing it (Brozo, 2003) or when a reward structure is sufficient for the goals they hold as learners (e.g., studying to make good grades so they can go on to college, so they can play high school sports, be a member of the marching band, and so on).

Motivating students to study in a way that makes clear what is in it for them is of primary importance. Although it is fairly easy to teach students new study strategies, it is something else to get them to apply those strategies on their own if they find no reason to do so. The strategies we introduce in this chapter will be most effective if taught at a time when students can use them to complete an assignment in one of their content area classes.

Teachers' Expectations

**EVIDENCE-
BASED
RESEARCH**

Teachers expect students to study the content of various subject matter specialties and to pass their courses. Because studying is mostly a self-directed activity (Thomas & Rohwer, 1986), teachers are aware of the need to teach students how to be effective studiers. Just knowing that their teachers expect them to master the content is sometimes motivation enough for students to value the study strategies they are taught (Nolen & Haladyna, 1989). However, when this is not the case, it may be useful to let them experience the difference a good study strategy can make. For example, students might find that by previewing a chapter they are able to reduce the time it actually takes them to read it. Even better, as Richardson and Morgan (2000) pointed out, teacher-guided previewing can help students reduce uncertainty about a reading assignment, especially when they discover that they do know something (however little) about the material. Reassuring students in this way can create a sense of shared responsibility in that they become aware of what they know and do not know (and thus need to study) at the same time that their teacher senses the difficulties a particular assignment will entail. When a teacher's expectations for effective studying are made explicit and easy-to-use strategies are demonstrated, as in the previewing example just given, a more relaxed and productive learning environment becomes possible.

Knowledge of the Criterion Task

Test-taking skills depend on a great deal more than students' ability to comprehend textual material. For example, there is considerable evidence that instruction in study skills is effective when students' knowledge of the criterion task enables them to study in a manner that ensures a match between the study technique and the items on a test (Alvermann & Moore, 1991; Anderson & Armbruster, 1984). This being the case, why don't more teachers tell students about the criterion task so that they can study more effectively? As Otto (1990) so aptly puts it, "teachers, themselves, often don't have a clear notion of the criterion task or its importance for studying, so they can't or don't make it clear to students" (p. 369). Faced with a lack of evaluation data on which study strategies work best for which types of learners and tasks, teachers often find themselves left with but one choice: to teach a variety of such strategies in the hope that at least one of them will be applied by their students. This hit-or-miss approach to strategy instruction is complicated further by the fact that even with a clearly set criterion task, there is no guarantee that students will use an appropriate study strategy. The mismatch between task and strategy is made worse when students do not possess adequate content area, or domain, knowledge.

Domain Knowledge

Many students lack the prerequisite content knowledge to study effectively. Excessive absences or inattentiveness in class contribute to this knowledge deficit and make studying particularly difficult. Students who know little about a topic will find that their strategic knowledge cannot compensate for their lack of domain knowledge. To complicate matters further, Young, Arbreton, and Midgley (1992) observed that "all content areas may not be created equal" (p. 1). That is, students' ability to acquire knowledge in a specific domain (e.g., social studies, science, mathematics, or English) may rest partially on their motivational orientation to learning. According to Young et al., the middle-grade students they studied were more likely to enjoy learning for its own sake in mathematics and science than in English and social studies.

In classrooms of the twenty-first century, being literate in a particular domain is not limited by what students are able to access from printed texts using conventional study strategies. Instead, it is becoming increasingly common for readers who struggle with their content area textbooks to turn to electronic study aids to help them organize their thinking around a set of domain-specific tasks. Consider, for example, the case of Andrew Sheehan (Sheehan & Sheehan, 2000), a ninth grader whose writing disability and attention deficit disorder have been partially compensated for by the use of assistive technology such as a voice-to-text computer software program, an electronic pocket organizer, and a portable keyboard. In the box on the next page are Andrew's own words and some ideas that teachers may find useful in helping other students like him acquire crucial domain knowledge through special study aids.

Assistive Technology for Readers Struggling to Acquire Domain Knowledge

Electronic organizers

If memory is the library of the mind . . . I've lost my card catalog! I use an electronic pocket organizer for day-to-day survival. I type in my homework, notes, reminders, phone numbers, et cetera. . . . I can jot something down before I forget it, and all my important messages stay in one place. Handwriting is not necessary, nor is organization on a page. . . . This is far superior to having notes to myself scattered all across the globe. (Sheehan & Sheehan, 2000, p. 27)

Portable keyboards

For daily notetaking I use a product called Alpha Smart (made by Intelligent Peripheral

Devices, Inc., 20380 Town Center Lane, Suite 270, Cupertino, CA 95014; alphasmart.com). The Alpha Smart is like an overgrown organizer. This device is nearly a full-sized keyboard with an LCD screen and eight files. Each file can be used for a different school subject. Even though keyboarding is necessary, I can get down enough information in classes to serve as notes. Then I can send this information to a word processor on a Macintosh or PC and edit and print the notes. The new Alpha Smart 2000 model has a built-in spell checker, which is a big help. This device runs on three AA batteries and fits in my backpack. (Sheehan & Sheehan, 2000, p. 28)

ACCESSING INFORMATION

On-line resources abound for students interested in using the World Wide Web as a learning environment—one in which accessing information efficiently plays an important role in effective studying. How well students do in this digital environment will depend to a great extent on how well teachers prepare them to become independent learners capable of applying information literacy and library skills in critical and creative ways. Part and parcel of what it means to be information literate is the ability to evaluate Web sites and their various resources. Without critical evaluation, these resources are hardly worth accessing.

Information Literacy and Library Skills

As noted in Chapter 1, one of several new terms to make its way into the field of literacy education as a result of the information explosion on the Web is *information literacy.* It refers to what is generally defined as the ability to access, evaluate, organize, and use information culled from a variety of sources. It involves knowing how to formulate a search strategy for zeroing in on needed information. This is not easy, especially for learners who are barely acquainted

Technology Tip—Standards for Integrating Technology

A useful set of nonprint media standards for helping students access and evaluate information is available through the National Research Center on English Learning and Achievement (CELA). Developed at CELA by Karen Swan, the nonprint media standards are divided into basic skills, critical literacies, and construction skills for each of three grade levels: elementary, middle, and high school. A complete listing of these standards for achieving information literacy is available at http://cela.albany.edu/standards/index.html. A pdf file of the standards is located at http://cela.albany.edu/publication/brochure/standards.pdf.

with efficient search strategies in traditional print texts. For example, Gavin Brown's (2003) research into young adolescents' use of text characteristics to locate main ideas and details in informational texts showed that students easily located answers that required using only a single, verbatim search term cued through typographic and signaling markers. However, they experienced considerably more difficulty locating answers that required complex, multiword search terms. From Brown's research, reported in full at http://readingonline.org/articles/art_index.asp?HREF=/articles/brown/, he concluded the following:

> The real challenge in searching for main ideas and details, whether within paper-based documents or digital environments, is not the location of verbatim terms, but lies rather in the incorporation of implicit terms that need to be inferred across passages of text. The results of this research suggest that if teachers draw attention to and assist students in learning various navigation tools . . . [e.g., headings, titles, organizational structure, typographic features, page layout], then student ability to locate information should improve. Naturally, the goal in students' learning to search for main ideas and details by utilizing a variety of text and task characteristics is not simply rapid location of materials. . . . Rather, these skills are used to solve informational problems. Unless presented, developed, and exercised in such a context, they will remain rather pointless.

STANDARDS

The library skills necessary for accessing information in paper form or on the Internet when studying or completing a homework assignment are very similar to those needed in any problem-solving activity. One first defines the task and then determines which available search strategies would most likely yield the best results in terms of locating and accessing the desired information. The Information Literacy Standards (see Appendix E) form the backbone of Mike Eisenberg's and Bob Berkowitz's information problem-solving curriculum. Basically, this curriculum is a six-stage approach to teaching information literacy in the Information Age. Visit the Eisenberg and Berkowitz Web site

Information Literacy Standards and the K-W-L Strategy

As spelled out in the Information Literacy Standards of the American Association of School Libraries (see Appendix E), the nine standards are subdivided into three categories: information literacy, independent learning, and social responsibility. To better understand how these standards relate to reading and studying in content area classrooms, visit www.big6.com/ showarticle.php?id=238. There you will see how the K-W-L strategy described in Chapter 6 can be adapted and made into a chart for planning and gathering information.

(www.big6.com/showarticle.php?id=16) to learn more about their approach and to view strategies and lesson plans for helping students conduct more efficient Web searches as part of their studying routine.

Web Site Evaluation

As noted earlier, teaching students how to access resources on the Internet in a timely and effective manner is a worthwhile endeavor, but if such instruction omits or plays down the importance of Web site evaluation, then all will have been for naught. Information that is biased or inaccurate is information best left alone. As Joyce Valenza points out in her on-line article entitled "A WebQuest About Evaluating Web Sites" (http://mciunix.mciu.k12.pa.us/~spjvweb/ evalwebteach.html),

> The information source your students use most frequently is likely to be the Web. They will have little trouble actually gathering information these days. In fact they will be flooded with it. Selecting the "best stuff" is going to be their real challenge. It is up to us as teachers to help them to understand that the quality of information varies greatly. The Internet has no "filter" for quality, taste or reliability. No editorial board determines the publication of material.

As Valenza goes on to note, however, this free-for-all approach to Web publishing should not dissuade teachers from including Web-based homework assignment. Rather, she argues, it simply behooves us as teachers to offer students the guidance and practice necessary for them to become thoughtful evaluators of the Web sites they visit. What might such instruction look like? From Valenza's point of view, an effective way of teaching older students to evaluate Web sites is to assign them to small groups of four and ask each member to play a different role: that of content specialist, authority/credibility specialist, bias/purpose specialist, and usability/design specialist. Some of the questions each member could ask of a common site include the following:

Content Specialist

- Does the information seem accurate based on what you know about the topic?
- Is it important to know when the material was last revised?

Authority/Credibility Specialist

- Who is responsible for this site? (Hint: Truncate the URL section by section until you are able to find the sponsor.)
- Who else links to the site? Are they credible sources?

Bias/Purpose Specialist

- Is the site trying to persuade you or change your opinion?
- Can you distinguish facts from opinion?

Usability/Design Specialist

- Is the site easy to navigate (user-friendly)?
- Do the links on the site work?

After everyone has had an opportunity to evaluate the site, share findings within the group and across groups.

PREPARING FOR TESTS

By relieving some students' natural anxiety about taking tests, teachers may help them improve their performance. Providing students with information about the criterion task such as the number of questions about each major topic being tested and involving students in activities that help them prepare for the test are examples of how teachers reduce the demands of testing. This type of help lessens students' need to second-guess what the teacher thinks is important and unimportant. Students are also less anxious about taking tests when they know in advance that the tests will consist of objective items (multiple-choice, true/false, fill-in-the-blank) or subjective items (short answer and opinion essay). Because objective and subjective exams place different demands on students, teachers usually find it helpful to provide a separate set of test-taking tips for each type of exam.

Objective Tests

Objective tests evaluate students' recall or recognition of information. Fill-in-the-blank items require students to recall information, and multiple-choice, true/false, and matching items require them to choose from among two or more options. Although students typically find it easier to recognize a correct answer

"M.U.R.D.E.R." and the Struggling Reader

A study system that is especially helpful to struggling readers is one known by the acronym **MURDER**. Adapted from John Hayes's (1989) work in problem solving, the acronym is explained this way:

- **M**ood: set a positive mood for yourself to study in.
- **U**nderstand: Mark any information you don't understand.
- **R**ecall: After studying, stop and put what you have learned into your own words.
- **D**igest: Go back to what you did not understand and reconsider the information.
- **E**xpand: In this step, ask three kinds of questions concerning the studied material:

1. If I could speak to the author, what questions would I ask or what criticism would I offer?
2. How could I apply this material to what I am interested in?
3. How could I make this information interesting and understandable to other students?

- **R**eview: Go over the material you've covered.

(From a study guide developed by Joe Landsberger; see statement that permission is granted to freely copy, adapt, print, transmit, and distribute at www.studygs.net/murder.htm)

than to recall it, there are exceptions. For example, the student for whom English is a second language generally finds recognition tasks difficult because each option presents the possibility that vocabulary meaning will be distorted. Consequently, foils (incorrect answers) are double jeopardy for such a student.

Tips on helping students prepare for objective tests include teaching them to use mnemonic devices. For example, the first letter of each word in the sentence "George Everett's old grandfather rode a pig home yesterday" will help them recall and spell the word *geography*. Similarly, HOMES is a mnemonic for the names of the Great Lakes and ROY G BIV for the colors in the visible spectrum. In addition, imagery (such as visualizing where the Ohio River joins the Mississippi River) may help students recognize the meaning of a word (such as *confluence*) in a matching test.

List-Group-Label, a strategy introduced in Chapter 6 to assess and build on prior knowledge, is also useful in helping students review for major tests over large amounts of information. It is helpful to have students brainstorm important words and concepts and record them without looking at notes or the text. Next, students might compare their lists with each other, and consult their notes, learning logs, or textbooks to add additional terms in another color ink. Using different colors of ink helps students see those words and concepts they remembered less well and therefore need to study more carefully. Alternatively, you might provide students with a list of important terms, particularly if time is an issue. Victoria has used this technique with sticky notes, which works well for the next step, in which students sort the terms into conceptually related groups. Once students have the terms sorted, they can label each group. Or, if students need scaffolding, you can provide them with a range of the number of groups to use in the sorting, or provide the labels for them. Using sticky notes and multiple sorts, students can be guided to create their own graphic organizers, which can then be used to study independently.

Sometimes words such as *always* and *never* are included in a list of foils; when students see them, they can be almost certain that these are not the correct answers. Exceptions, of course, are instances in which the inclusive term describes a generally accepted fact, as in "All carrots are vegetables."

Objective test items may have more than one correct answer. When this occurs, it is possible that a mistake has been made, and students should check with the teacher. If the items are correctly written and students believe that more than one answer is correct, they may bring the matter up with the teacher after the test has been marked, or teachers may give students the option of justifying their answers to objective test items as part of the examination process (see Chapter 5). Doing this, of course, greatly increases the amount of time required to grade the exam.

Subjective Tests

Subjective tests, such as short-answer tests and opinion essays, evaluate students' abilities to organize, analyze, synthesize, and integrate ideas. They are easier to construct than objective tests, but they take longer to grade and are open to more dispute regarding the correctness of answers. Both holistic and analytic scoring methods have been used successfully with essays. As its name implies, *holistic scoring* is based on the overall impression a teacher has of an essay after reading it for the general meaning of its message. Unlike holistic scoring, *analytic scoring* enables a teacher to grade separate components of an essay (its content, form, argument, grammar, and so on). The analytic scoring method is time-consuming, but it gives students a clear idea of how teachers arrive at a grade.

Tips on helping students prepare for subjective tests include providing them with information on what should be included in an essay and what the point distribution will be if analytic scoring is to be used. Letting students know whether grammar, spelling, and punctuation will be taken into consideration is also helpful. (See Chapter 5 for a discussion of rubrics.)

Using the List-Group-Label procedure as the basis for paragraph-writing exercises helps students prepare for short-answer and essay tests. Students take the label for a category and turn it into a topic sentence, then write the paragraph using the remaining terms, being sure to explain what the terms mean and how they are related to each other conceptually.

Scaffolded instruction, or instruction that begins with the teacher modeling a particular process and gradually turning the responsibility for the task over to students, can be used to teach students how to write essays. Based on the ideas of Wood, Bruner, and Ross (1976), "the metaphor of a scaffold has been proposed to describe this process since a scaffold is erected at the outset of construction and gradually withdrawn as a building becomes self-supporting" (Pressley, El-Dinary, & Brown, 1992, p. 106). To provide scaffolded instruction in writing essays, teachers can show students model essays that have prompts written in the margins to indicate the types of information that should be included. A model also provides students with an idea of the form a finished product should take.

Role of Homework

Historically, opinions about the value of homework have fluctuated widely. There was a renewed interest in homework in the late 1950s after the Soviets launched Sputnik, and recently there has been a resurgent interest in the topic in response to increasing accountability measures, particularly in the early grades (Gill & Schlossman, 2004). Current research on homework has examined issues related to home school interaction, the effect of media on homework performance, and the impact of different types of homework. Van Voorhis (2003) found that middle school science students who were assigned interactive homework turned in more accurate assignments and had significantly higher science grades than those who were assigned conventional homework. Interactive homework required students to involve family members in the assignment. For example, students might interview family members about clothing styles, music, or television shows that were popular when she or he was the student's age. Interactive homework assignments that have students interviewing residents of a retirement center about life during the Great Depression, or interviewing a local pharmacist about drug interactions, or collecting data by recording the ingredients for selected products at the grocery store for a discussion in chemistry are all examples of interactive homework assignments. Interactive homework helps make connections between the curriculum and students' lives outside of school. Overall, the research literature on assigning homework supports the view that the amount of time spent doing homework is associated with students' academic achievement. Intuitively, of course, it would seem that the more conscientious a student is in completing her or his homework, the better that student will do academically. Overall, the research literature on assigning homework supports the view that the amount of time spent doing homework is associated with students' academic achievement. For example, in a booklet distributed by the U.S. Department of Education (Paulu, 1995), we learn that

EVIDENCE-BASED RESEARCH

> In the *early elementary grades,* homework can help children develop . . . [good] habits and attitudes. . . . From *fourth through sixth grades,* small amounts of homework, gradually increased each year, may support improved academic achievement. In *seventh grade and beyond,* students who complete more homework score better on standardized tests and earn better grades, on

Power Writing for Students Who Struggle with Essay Exams: A Fluency Activity

Sometimes students experience difficulty writing essay exams because they are not fluent writers. When this is the case, try power writing (Fisher & Frey, 2003), a fluency activity that requires students to write (in one minute) everything they can on a topic the teacher gives them. They can chart the number of words they write at the end of each one-minute timed activity and then note the progress they make over several days or weeks.

the average, than students who do less homework. The difference in test scores and grades between students who do more homework and those who do less increases as children move up through the grades. (p. 5)

The nature of homework varies according to the purpose for giving the assignment. Generally, there are three types of assignments: practice, preparation, and extension (LaConte, 1981). Each of these types of assignments can be interactive or conventional. When homework is given for the purpose of reinforcing new learning, it is thought of as a *practice assignment.* Research on expert and novice teachers indicates that the experts assign homework only after they have monitored and guided students' practice in class, but the novices are likely to assign material that they were unable to find time to teach in class (Leinhardt, 1983).

(Source: CALVIN AND HOBBES © 1989 & 1995 Watterson. Dist. by UNIVERSAL PRESS SYNDICATE. Reprinted with permission. All Rights Reserved.)

As their name implies, *preparation assignments* are meant to provide students with the background information they will need in order to understand new information when it is introduced in their textbook or in class discussion. The assumption is that students will acquire "hooks" on which to hang new information if they have the appropriate background knowledge. Unlike practice and preparation assignments, *extension assignments* are given to encourage students to move beyond their textbooks in acquiring, synthesizing, and using the information they find. Increasingly, with greater access to the World Wide Web, extension assignments are becoming popular with both teachers and students. Although this development has its upside, there is a downside as well. Unfortunately, too often students are left to flounder when it comes to completing an extension assignment for which they must develop their own search strategies, a topic we address later in this chapter.

USING STUDY STRATEGIES

Reading to learn specific information for the purpose of performing some criterion task is what defines studying and sets it apart from merely comprehending the information (Anderson & Armbruster, 1984). This type of reading, or studying, requires students to think about and control their own learning processes (Zimmerman, 1994). However, before students can become metacognitively aware of what these learning processes are, they must know the following (Wade & Reynolds, 1989, p. 6):

1. What to study in a particular learning situation, or *task awareness*
2. How best to learn it, or *strategy awareness*
3. Whether and to what extent they have learned it, or *performance awareness*

EVIDENCE-BASED RESEARCH

Thus, before students can actively monitor their own studying, they need to learn about and develop task, strategy, and performance awareness. Sufficient research exists on the subject of metacognitive awareness to merit basing instruction on its findings. The instructional activities for developing these three areas of awareness discussed in this section are derived from the research literature on metacognition. They have also been field-tested by Wade and Reynolds (1989).

Technology Tip

The Internet Public Library at www.ipl.org offers general homework help and a listing of numerous links to useful Web sites. For example, BJ Pinchbeck's Homework Helper at http://school.discovery.com/students/homework help/bjpinchbeck/ provides a large number of links organized by subject, with brief annotations, and offers up-to-date lesson plans by teachers for teachers in all content areas.

Task Awareness with SQ3R

Helping students locate information that is important according to external criteria (although not necessarily interesting to them) is the first step in developing their task awareness. Ways of doing this include having students brainstorm about the important ideas in a short selection they have read. After recording their responses on the chalkboard, ask them to give reasons why the ideas are important, based on external criteria. External criteria imply that information is relevant if it is one of the main ideas put forth by the author of a selection. This does not mean that internal criteria, such as students' interests, are unimportant. However, for the purpose of developing task awareness, external rather than internal criteria are employed.

To point out the importance of task awareness in answering an essay question, show students what information they would need to answer a sample question satisfactorily. As a follow-up to this activity, show students how to arrange the needed information in a hierarchical manner. Selectively focusing attention on relevant material also teaches students to self-question. For example, students might ask themselves why they placed a particular piece of information in a position subordinate to another piece of information.

EVIDENCE-BASED RESEARCH

Deciding what to study in a particular reading assignment is at the core of task awareness. An effective way to focus students' attention on important information is to introduce them to SQ3R—an acronym that stands for *S*urvey, *Q*uestion, *R*ead, *R*ecite, and *R*eview (Robinson, 1961). This study system has been in use for several decades and for good reason. It works if introduced and practiced under teacher guidance, though not perfectly for every student in every study setting (Devine & Kania, 2003). As a systematic way of previewing, questioning, and reviewing information that is read, SQ3R offers students a chance to be proactive in developing task awareness as they study expository text. In Figure 11.1, we describe the five steps in SQ3R, and then we show how these steps relate to locating and remembering information that is considered important in a selection.

Strategy Awareness

After students have analyzed the task to determine while information is relevant or irrelevant, the next step is to develop an awareness of the type of strategy needed to comprehend and remember the relevant information. For example, if an assessment or criterion task consists of taking a true/false test, a different kind of strategy is needed than would be the case if the task consists of writing an essay.

One way of teaching students how to develop an awareness of the type of strategy needed to meet a particular task is to model the process yourself. Choose a passage from your class text that is particularly dense or laced with difficult vocabulary. As you read the passage aloud, describe which strategies you use to help you remember what you are reading. List those strategies on the chalkboard under one of the two categories (observable or in-the-head study methods) shown in Figure 11.2.

Step	Description of Step	Relation to Task Awareness
Survey	Preview a selection by reading titles, headings, subheadings, captions accompanying illustrations, and a summary if one is available.	Enables a reader to locate information that the author of a selection thought important enough to highlight structurally or to illustrate through examples.
Question	Turn each title, heading, and caption into a question.	Makes clear to a reader what he or she already knows (or doesn't know) about the assigned informational text.
Read	Actively read to answer questions posed in Step 2.	Focuses attention on what the author believes is important and worth remembering.
Recite	Close the text and orally summarize what you just read; then make notes using your own words.	Improves memory and aids attention span after initial reading of the selection.
Review	Study your notes periodically, and refresh your memory of the text by using its main headings to cue your recall of the subheadings.	Keeps relevant information foremost in mind and reinforces relationships between important ideas and the evidence that supports them.

FIGURE 11.1   The SQ3R study system

Next, ask students to construct a similar list using a different passage from the class text. After they have exhausted their list of strategies, ask them to compare their list with the list in Figure 11.2. A discussion might follow in which students give their reasons for sometimes, always, or never using a particular study strategy. At this point it is important to remind student that not every strategy meets everyone's needs, nor should they feel compelled to adopt a particular strategy. Research has demonstrated that student who are effective studiers use the strategies that work for them (Swafford, 1988).

Performance Awareness

According to Wade and Reynolds (1989), "a strategy can be considered effective only when it has a strong, positive effect on learning" (p. 11). Developing students' performance awareness enables them to monitor whether or not they have understood the task and used the appropriate study strategy. If they have done both, their performance on the criterion task should reflect it. Research has shown that metacognitively aware readers know when their learning breaks down and how to adjust the strategies they are using (or adopt new ones) to remedy the problem (Ghatala, 1986).

Study Strategies	Think aloud—why you use the strategy
Observable	
• Select important information: highlight or underline	Highlighting or underlining helps to direct your attention to ideas in the text. Don't highlight or underline everything! A good rule is not to highlight or underline unless you are going to make a note summarizing the information in your own words.
• Make notes	Translating text information into your own words helps to hold your thinking. Always *make* notes—paraphrase information. Copying information verbatim provides practice in handwriting, but is not as effective as representing the information in your own words.
• Organize meaningfully	Two good ways to organize information meaningfully are outlining and drawing a diagram or graphic organizer. Either method visually organizes information so that you can immediately see how the ideas are related to each other.
In-The-Head	
• Preview	Survey or preview the reading. This helps to familiarize you with the organization of the information. You can preview the graphics, headings, subheadings, first an/or last sentences. If there is a good summary, read the summary first!
• Vary reading rate	Familier text can be read more quickly than unfamiliar text. Text about new concepts, or dense text (with many new ideas introduced in a few paragraphs) should be read slowly. Read as you might drive—quickly when the road is familiar and straight, but slowly when the road twists and turns or is—unfamiliar.
• Visualize	Make a picture in your head—see what you are reading—this helps you make sense of the reading.
• Predict	Think ahead . . . what might the author describe next? Use text structure and the author's organizational clues to think your way through the text. This helps you pay close attention.
• Make connections	Associate what you are reading with what you already know, have experienced, or have read about in other texts. This aids understanding.
• Summarize	Periodically summarize what you are reading. This helps to check your understanding and keep you focused on the task.
• Ask questions	Ask questions when you are confused, and try to answer them. Alternatively, ask questions you think a teacher might ask and try to abswer them. Self-questioning keeps you alert and on task.
• Reread	When you are confused, don't understand what you are reading, or feel lost, stop! Reread the last sentence, Sentence, paragraph, or section you understood.

FIGURE 11.2   Study Strategy awareness. Helpful Study strategies and reasons to use them.

A good way to develop performance awareness among students is to have them determine whether the strategies they use to study a selection are effective. Ask students to read a short selection, and then have them record the strategies they used on a separate sheet of paper. Next, ask them to respond to ten objective questions on the selection they have just read without looking back at the text. Finally, grade answers to the questions as a class activity, and encourage students to discuss why they think the strategies they used were or were not appropriate for the task.

Note-Taking Strategies

EVIDENCE-BASED RESEARCH

Both research (Devine & Kania, 2003) and practical experience emphasize the importance of direct instruction in teaching students how to take notes. Such instruction should explain the purpose of note taking, and it should take place over a reasonable period of time. Brozo and Simpson (1995, p. 284) provide the following criteria for helping students develop expertise in using study strategies:

1. Strategy explanations and rationales (e.g., steps, tactics, advantages)
2. Strategy modeling and talk-throughs by the teacher
3. Examples from real texts and tasks that students will encounter
4. Guided practice with real texts, followed by specific, qualitative feedback
5. Debriefing sessions that deal with questions, student doubts, and fix-up strategies
6. Frequent independent practice opportunities across appropriate texts
7. Guidelines on how to evaluate a strategy's success or failure.

Palmatier's (1973) split-page method of note taking, which is different from the double-entry journal (see Chapter 10), gives students a systematic approach to organizing and studying their class notes. Using the split-page method, teachers instruct students to

1. Use only one side of an 8½-by-11-inch sheet of paper that has been divided lengthwise by folding it into two parts. The left column should be about one-third of the paper; the right column, about two-thirds of the paper.
2. Record the lecture notes in the right column, using both subordination of ideas and spacing to indicate the importance of information.
3. Review and organize the notes by first reading over the information in the right column to obtain a sense of the major concept and then placing that concept in the left column opposite the related information in the right column.
4. If the notes are unclear or sketchy, refer to the textbook or the source that was the basis for the lecture. Additional information may be added to the back of the paper if no space remains on the front.
5. Study the notes by folding the paper so that only the left column is visible. The labels in that column serve as a focal point for recalling information found in the right column.

Read Aloud/Note-Taking Method for Readers Who Struggle

To prepare her self-contained eighth-grade reading class for the New York State English Language Arts exam, Rebecca Meyers* engaged in an action research project to determine if her students would improve their listening and note-taking skills as a result of participating in an eight-week direct-instruction approach to the split-page method of note taking. All participants were enrolled in the school's special education program and attended inclusion classes for their core academic courses.

Ms. Meyers began the project by interviewing students about note taking. Then, after obtaining a baseline measure of their note-taking skills, she read aloud a short expository passage while the students listened for important information but did not take notes. Before reading aloud the same passage for a second time, Rebecca taught her students how to set up their papers for the split-page method of note taking. On the second read-aloud, students jotted down facts in the right-hand column of their papers. The class worked as a group to classify the facts (details) they had identified into main idea topics, which were listed in the left-hand column of their papers.

In the weeks that followed, Ms. Meyers taught her students how to abbreviate words or draw stick figures that would convey their understanding of the important information they heard as she read aloud from a variety of expository and informational texts.

By scaffolding her explicit instruction of the split-page method of note taking, Rebecca was able to assist the class in moving from almost total dependence on her for structuring their notes to independence in note taking. She was also able to shorten the time that she paused between paragraphs as she read aloud from the passages. After only six sessions of explicit instruction in this method, Rebecca noted an increase in the number of facts they wrote down. She also learned from poststudy interview data that all students felt comfortable taking notes using the split-page method, although not all were comfortable using abbreviations. One girl said she could not always remember what her abbreviations stood for when she reviewed her notes.

*Used with permission of Rebecca Meyers, Wilson Middle School, Wilson, New York.

Spires and Stone (1989) suggest a way to use videotapes to provide instruction in the split-page method of note taking. Teachers' lectures can be taped and played back as students view the tapes and practice applying the split-page method. Initially, the practice sessions should be no longer than 15 minutes. As students' comfort level with the method increases, so too should the time allotted to practice sessions.

Interactive Notating System for Effective Reading and Thinking (INSERT) (Vaughn & Estes, 1986) helps readers maintain sustained engagement with text and promotes metacognitive activity in the reader. The method is quite simple, and consists of recording symbols and notes as you read, either in the margin, or on sticky notes to avoid writing in the text. The sticky notes may be transferred to split-page notes after class discussion. Procedures for the INSERT strategy are as follows:

> As you read, place one of four different marks in the margin of the text or on sticky notes to note your own knowledge or understanding. Record annotations in your own words on each sticky note as you read. You may devise any symbols you wish, but the following are commonly used:
>
> ✓ → Put a ✓ (check mark) in the margin if you read text that confirms something you already knew.
> − → Put a − (minus sign) in the margin if you read information that contradicts what you think you know.
> + → Put a + (plus sign) in the margin if you encounter new information.
> ? → Put a ? (question mark) in the margin if you encounter information that is confusing or if you want to know more about something in the text.

The number of symbols and annotations you record will vary. It is not necessary to annotate each line or idea. In very dense text, you might annotate every idea, or several per paragraph. In text about familiar information, you may not need to annotate every paragraph. After you complete your reading, construct a chart like the one below and categorize information from the reading:

✓	−	+	?
Record information and ideas that confirmed what you knew as you read the text	Record information that contradicts what you thought you knew as you read the text	Record information that was new to you	Record questions you have or ideas that were confusing to you

After all students have read, recorded symbols and annotated the text, and created their own INSERT summary charts, have them compare their charts with one or two peers. Discussion based on these charts will help to clarify information for students. INSERT is particularly powerful for struggling readers who need to develop metacognitive habits of mind. This strategy is most powerful when students create a conceptually based map from their INSERT chart.

Compare/Contrast Study Matrix

This study strategy assists students in organizing information as they read their content area assignments. It simultaneously involves them in summarizing that information in a compare/contrast pattern (Santa, 1988). Developing a sense of a text's organizational structure enables students to recall information more fully and efficiently. Thus, the compare/contrast study matrix illustrated

	anarchy	monarchy	democracy	dictatorship	oligarchy	fascism	theocracy
Who ? governs							
How do you get power?							
How is power maintained?							
How is power transferred?							
How are laws made?							
Essential elements?							
Example:							

FIGURE 11.3   Compare/contrast matrix: Social studies—forms of government
(*Source:* From V. Ridgeway's adaptation of C. M. Santa, *Content reading including study systems,* pp. 75–83, Dubuque, IA: Kendall/Hunt, 1988.)

in Figure 11.3 is a natural tool for students to use with reading assignments that present information that differs along various attributes. For example, in Figure 11.3 Victoria, uses six attributes, stated in the form of questions, to demonstrate to the students in her content literacy course how seven different types of government differ. She also asks them to include an example of each type of government (e.g., the United States is an example of a democracy).

When using the compare/contrast study matrix the first few times with your classes, we recommend that you model the procedure. This might consist of partially filling in each column and row while referring to the text. Also, you might want students to predict what they think they will find in their reading, using their predictions to fill in some of the columns and rows. Then, after reading the material, they could check the accuracy of their predictions. After students become more familiar with this study matrix, they may begin to construct similar matrices on their own.

If you are using the compare/contrast study matrix for the first time with students who find reading a struggle, it is advisable to have them listen for signal words such as *however, but, different from,* and *while* as you read aloud a passage from their textbook and model how you would fill in the matrix. As noted by at least one middle school teacher of considerable classroom experience, readers who have difficulty comprehending will find it frustrating if they have to divide their attention between learning a new study strategy and perceiving the organizational structure of their texts (Marlene Willis, personal communication, April 11, 2000). See Chapter 7 for a compare/contrast guide for teaching about text structure.

Compare/contrast matrices also help students organize information from several sources. Pertinent questions can be listed in the first column, while information from different sources is entered in each column thereafter. This helps students organize information and see patterns that exist across several sources.

■ *Use the "snatch-and-grab" reading technique.* The objective is to read Web pages superficially—that is, skim to identify a key word or phrase, surf the relevant links, bookmark sites, and compile a grab-bag of references. It is important to remind students, however, that once they have gathered a sufficient number of potentially helpful references, they will need to read the accompanying texts in a much more careful manner.

■ *Focus on refining keyword searches.* Once students have identified a keyword or phrase (e.g., printing press), teach them how to narrow the scope of their search by refining the original keyword or phrase. For example, if they were interested in the history of the printing press, they might search under *history of* or *invention of the printing press.*

■ *Provide clear search guidelines.* Providing students with clear statements of the purpose for a search, giving them an approximation of how many sites they should search, and offering tips on how to use the toolbar for efficient searches are a few of the ways you can prevent panic from setting in when you require them to do an on-line research assignment.

■ *Use the "chunking technique."* This involves teaching students who have poor organizational skills to break a complex topic into smaller, more manageable bits of information. For example, if they were searching on the topic of *September 11,* they might brainstorm keywords and phrases related to that event, such as

terrorists, rescue workers, location of buildings, and *clean-up.* By focusing on one chunk at a time, students are less likely to feel overwhelmed or waste time "getting lost" in cyberspace.

■ *Develop teaching mechanisms to overcome frustration with technology.* Students can become frustrated when the topic they are researching involves a good deal of moving back and forth between links. One mechanism for alleviating some of their frustration is to model how you would ignore certain links but click on others. Talking through your reasons for doing so and letting them predict which ones will be useful to you are ways of handling this problem.

■ *Provide short-cut lists to sites or search engines.* Give students in advance a list of bookmarks to reliable sites (e.g., those least likely to have broken links). Or, prepare a simple step-by-step handout that explains how to use search engines, and then model the process one step at a time.

■ *Evaluate nontextual features (images, graphics).* Visual elements can distract some readers, whereas others may think the visuals are merely "illustrations" of something in the written text. Teaching them to become what Leu (1997) describes as "healthy skeptics" of Web site information and modeling for them how you know certain kinds of drawings, photographs, and graphs can manipulate what you see are helpful evaluation techniques. (Sutherland-Smith, 2002, pp. 665–667)

FIGURE 11.4   Internet search strategies

Internet Search Strategies

**EVIDENCE-
BASED
RESEARCH**

Surfing the Web for information requires strategies that differ considerably from those used in locating information in paper documents. In a growing number of school districts, curriculum standards mandate that teachers help students become efficient and effective at searching on the Internet for information that can be used in completing homework assignments and studying. Among the guidelines that now exist for how teachers might accomplish this task, those developed in Australia by Sutherland-Smith (2002) in collaboration with students from two sixth-grade classes are the most helpful and explicit in their recommendations. Figure 11.4 offers a number of the strategies that worked in Sutherland-Smith's study, which spanned a ten-week term and involved students from multilingual backgrounds.

We conclude with a brief section on the importance of teaching students strategies for searching for information that will supplement their textbooks when they are studying or attempting to complete an assignment. Based on several months of firsthand observations of middle and high school students in a public library as they searched for Web sites for which they had no specific URLs (Web site addresses), we concluded that their lack of a search strategy often led to their giving up or becoming distracted by irrelevant Web site information (Alvermann et al., 2000a).

In helping these students develop independent search strategies, we began with an introduction to Ask Jeeves Kids! at www.ajkids.com. This user-friendly Web site does not teach a strategy per se, but through using it kids learn to narrow their questions, which is the first step in helping them become more efficient in their searches. For example, if one types in the question, "Where can I learn about ants?" on the Web site's home page, the reply is "Jeeves knows these answers":

Where can I learn about the insect or arachnid ant?
What if I get bit by a fire ant?
Where can I find a concise encyclopedia article on ants?
Where can I learn about ant interactions in a tropical rain forest?

If none of these answers prove satisfactory, kids are given the option to check out links from the Web site's metasearch partners or to ask a new question.

After the students we were observing in the public library became fairly comfortable with the Ask Jeeves Kids! format, we introduced them to subject matter Web sites, such as the History Channel (www.historychannel.com/home/index.html). Here, they were able to further hone their search strategies by deciding what types of information would satisfy their needs. At this Web site students have the option of searching a particular topic by century (and then decade). They can also participate in a quick poll, find out what happened in history on the day they were born, and so on. One drawback to this Web site is the overabundance of

A Response from Our Readers

Alison Pinyan,* a graduate student enrolled in Donna's content literacy course at the University of Georgia, wrote the following response after reading about the compare/contrast matrix:

> I have always had a hard time making myself read or study something that does not interest me because I'm a terrible note taker. I know that I am not alone in this. I'm sure that many children feel the same way. . . . I really liked

the compare/contrast matrix. It was a way to make a quick reference guide without having to go back and read a bunch of notes. It seems as though it would be an easy way for anyone to understand difficult concepts. I only wish my teachers knew about this method when I was in [high] school.

*Adapted with permission of Alison Pinyan.

options, most of which are unrelated to the topic the student types in to begin the search. Even so, we took advantage of this potentially distracting Web site to discuss with them the importance of staying focused (a skill we ourselves often find difficult to master).

For those students who were ready for more advanced Internet search strategies, we introduced them to some of the more popular search engines and subject directories. Yahoo! quickly became their favorite, so much so in fact that we noticed kids teaching other kids some strategies for searching Yahoo! that they had figured out on their own (mostly in relation to music Web sites). However, these self-taught strategies seemed to transfer well across topics and domains.

Dispelling Policy Myths

Dispelling a Myth

When students pass a test, teachers tend to believe that students "know" the information. However, in too many cases, students (particularly those who have learned how to play the "game of school") are merely memorizing disconnected information, and when the test is over they forget it. Knowing disconnected "facts" might have been sufficient for us and for our parents, but it won't get our students very far in the twenty-first century.

Policy Implications

As No Child Left Behind is extended to middle and high schools through the Striving Readers

Initiative, accountability is increasing. Several states have instituted End of Course (EOC) testing in up to 10 courses at the high school level. In addition to passing an exit examination, students also must pass the EOC tests. In some states, scores on EOC tests count for as much as 20 percent of the student's course grade. Teaching students effective and efficient study strategies is increasingly important in this era of high-stakes assessment.

Finally, we showed them how to avoid too many listings on a topic of their choice. For example, we took the advice of experts on teaching with the Internet (Leu & Leu, 1999) and cautioned against using words such as *the, of,* or *a* as part of the search question. We also paired less proficient navigators of the Web with more proficient ones, being careful of course to avoid pairings that might aggravate a problem rather than solve it.

SUMMARY

Being personally motivated to learn, valuing study strategies, knowing something about the criterion task, and possessing adequate domain knowledge are all factors that help students become effective studiers. Like learning to study, acquiring proficiency in Internet searches takes time, effort, and specialized knowledge. So does studying for an exam. Preparing for exams is made easier when teachers take individual differences into account and reduce the demands associated with taking tests. Test taking is also made easier for students when they become knowledgeable about the differences in objective and subjective tests. Finally, learning how to study is facilitated by developing an awareness of the task, choosing potentially useful strategies, and identifying performance criteria needed to complete the task successfully.

SUGGESTED READINGS

Caverly, D., Mandeville, T., & Nicholson, S. A. (1995). PLAN: A study-reading strategy for informational text. *Journal of Adolescent & Adult Literacy, 39,* 190–199.

Hayasaki, E. (2003). 2Rs left in high school: Out of choice or fatigue, many teachers have abandoned the term paper, leaving a hole in college-bound students' education. *Los Angeles Times,* May 19, n.p. Available: http://www.readfirst.net/2rs.html.

Manzo, A. V. (1985). Expansion modules for the ReQuest, CAT, GRP, and REAP reading/study procedures. *Journal of Reading, 28,* 498–502.

Rekrut, M. D. (2000). Peer and cross-age tutoring: The lessons of research. In D. W. Moore, D. E. Alvermann, & K. A. Hinchman (Eds.), *Struggling adolescent readers: A collection of teaching strategies* (pp. 290–295). Newark, DE: International Reading Association.

Riemberg, R. (1996). Reading to write: Self-regulated learning strategies when writing essays from sources. *Reading Research and Instruction, 35,* 365–383.

Sakta, C. G. (1999). SQRC: A strategy for guiding reading and higher level thinking. *Journal of Adolescent & Adult Literacy, 42,* 265–269.

Taylor, B. M. (1986). Teaching middle grade students to summarize content textbook material. In J. F. Baumann (Ed.), *Teaching main idea comprehension* (pp. 195–209). Newark, DE: International Reading Association.

Developing Lifetime Readers: Literature in Content Area Classes

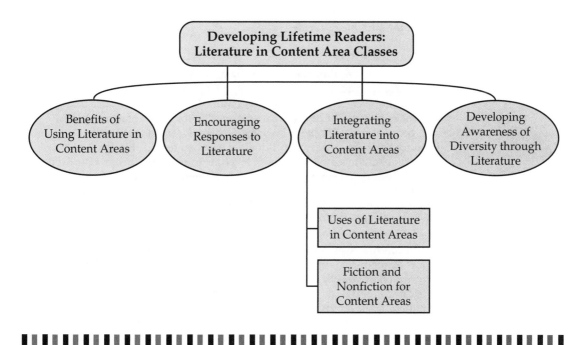

■■■

So far in this book, we have talked almost exclusively about school reading, or reading for academic purposes. In this chapter, we will take a look at the bigger picture and consider what people do with reading beyond school. At work or at leisure, each day millions of people in this country turn to a book, a magazine, a newspaper, or the Internet and read for information, for personal gain, or for pleasure. In the following anecdote, Marie Saladino, a high school history teacher, reflects on her life as a reader.[*] As you share her thoughts, consider your own uses of reading and how you have evolved as a lifetime reader.

■■■■■■■

I love to read. I can remember being four years old and demanding that my mother read to me and let me try to read parts of stories. I am certain that since reading was encouraged and worked on in my home, I had an easier time of learning in school.

I often wonder what has changed since my early days of reading. Up until eighth grade I used to read at least three books per week just for my own enjoyment. Once I entered high school, and then later in college, I never had enough time to read for personal satisfaction. In high school there was just too much going on, and in college there was so much subject matter reading.

---

[*]Used with permission of Marie Saladino.

I remember that reading was never really stressed when I was starting high school. We never read any literature except in English class, and I really did not care for the novels we had to read. I always wanted to read books related to my social studies classes. The only book we ever read in four years of social studies, besides textbooks, was *The Jungle* by Upton Sinclair. I learned that I really enjoyed reading books that were fictional yet based on real-life historical events.

Now that I am teaching I have even less time to read for pleasure than I did in college. I do try to read books that deal with the subject matter I teach. Presently the most reading I get to do is a few novels or books per year, some magazines, Sunday newspapers, and a ton of African, Asian, and American government books.

Please do not think that I never read for enjoyment. I like fictional books that deal with controversy in society. This summer I read *The Handmaid's Tale* by Margaret Atwood, *The Godfather* by Mario Puzo, *Twins* by Roxanne Pulitzer, and *Sleeping with the Enemy* by Nancy Price. All of these books were very different, but I learned a great deal from each of them. The authors got me thinking and then criticizing the direction society seems to be going. I guess the major benefit I get from reading is my thinking power. While reading I am always learning new things, analyzing what I am reading, and forming my own opinions about new topics. There is always so much to learn in the world.

■ ■ ■ ■ ■ ■ ■

This anecdote touches on several themes that will be developed in this chapter. First, it illustrates how an appreciation for reading develops over a lifetime, as the contexts, subjects, and various externally and internally imposed imperatives change. Marie mentions how the pressures of adolescence and early adulthood militated against reading for enjoyment and how she wished she had been given more opportunities to read (and enjoy reading) literature related to her content area studies. The anecdote also gives a fairly common picture of the reading activities of a professional adult, who must read extensively for work, bemoans the lack of time to read for pleasure, and yet finds great satisfaction and significance in the reading that does occur. Finally, there is social significance in what Marie reveals when she tells us her reading gets her "thinking and then criticizing the direction society seems to be going." The founders of this country guaranteed freedom of the press in order that citizens might have free access to the information they need to govern themselves. There was no more passionate believer in the necessity of an informed public than Thomas Jefferson, who said, "If a nation expects to be ignorant and free, in a state of civilization, it expects what never was and never will be." All the advances in telecommunications and mass media have not usurped the role of reading as a means for in-depth learning, reflection, and decision making.

Of course, not all adults become readers like Marie Saladino. Jim Trelease (2001), in his testament to the benefits of reading aloud, bemoans the current state of literacy and leisure reading among both adults and teenagers. Among many depressing statistics, he noted that the best-selling weekly magazines in the United States at the time were *TV Guide* and the *National Enquirer.* Still, bookstores, libraries, and publishers continue to flourish. Many newspapers and news magazines enjoy healthy circulations. The Internet has become a major source of information, entertainment, communication, and commerce. Casual observation reveals people from all walks of life reading at home, at bus stops, on lunch or coffee breaks, at the beach—wherever they have a few minutes to themselves.

With adolescents, outside-of-school reading must compete for attention with television, video games, sports, and social activities. However, research contradicts the popular conception that most adolescents would never be caught reading a book. In a canvas of 400 students in five central Illinois high schools, Moffit and Wartella (1992) found that 78 percent claimed to read books for leisure. Although reading was not a primary leisure-time activity, it was ranked third by females (after sports and being with friends) and tied for fifth place with talking on the telephone and watching television among males (who listed sports, friends, music, and "solitary activities" as their top four). More females than males claimed to read, and academically proficient students were more likely to be readers than students who received poor grades. A more recent study of 200 students in sixth and ninth grades reports similar results (Nippold, Duthie, & Larsen, 2005). Forty-three percent of the surveyed students reported reading between 20 and 60 minutes a day on average, with ninth graders reading slightly less than the younger students.

EVIDENCE-
BASED
RESEARCH

Two separate surveys of sixth graders also showed that early adolescents are engaged readers. Worthy, Moorman, and Turner (1999) queried more than 400 students about their reading preferences. Almost every one was able to cite a favorite title, type of reading, or author, evidence that their attitudes toward reading were not as negative as is often suggested. Ivey and Broaddus (2001) elicited reading preferences from 1,700 sixth graders. Highly rated materials in both studies included scary stories, humor, popular magazines, sports, and nonfiction about varied topics. The authors of both surveys were especially impressed by the wide range of materials that students enjoyed reading. However, in both studies, students' stated reading preferences did not match what they found in school. Although students reported a variety of reading interests outside of school to Ivey and Broaddus, they reported a much narrower selection of in-school titles, mostly award-winning fiction read by a whole class at the same time. Similarly, Worthy, Moorman, and Turner found that the most popular reading materials were not readily available in school, especially the preferred reading of boys and struggling readers. Teachers and librarians cited lack of money, inappropriate or objectionable content, lack of academic merit, and the fact that popular materials were either always checked out or tended to "walk away" or become lost. In both studies, students were more likely to obtain their preferred reading materials outside of school.

Given time and appropriate materials, adolescents are surprisingly complex and multidimensional readers who are willing to read when it satisfies their personal needs (Ivey, 1999a). Like many adults, they especially enjoy light reading on topics that are pleasing and important to them. Indeed, it is likely that students do not lose interest in reading as they progress through school; they just lose interest in school reading (Bintz, 1993). Adolescents' experiences with reading in school may very well influence what they read, their reasons for reading, and how often they read outside of school. If you believe that it is important for students to continue their development as readers after their school years, you will find many suggestions in this chapter that can help you expand their experiences with literature in school. In this chapter, we use the word *literature* in a broad sense to mean reading materials other than textbooks. These include fiction and nonfiction books and periodicals that students might read as part of their content area studies.

BENEFITS OF USING LITERATURE IN CONTENT AREAS

If students have positive reading experiences beyond their textbooks, their chances for becoming lifetime readers increase. There are more immediate benefits, too. Reading from fiction and nonfiction sources can enhance content area knowledge as well as readers' overall reading and thinking abilities. There are many reasons for using literature, both fiction and nonfiction, in content areas:

1. Reading increases vocabulary, including content-specific terms. (The role of wide reading in vocabulary development was cited in Chapter 8.) Through content-related literature, students increase their exposure to the language of a discipline. The examples are as diverse as the literature available. Readers of *The Hunt for Red October* (Clancy, 1984) will find many words specific to the technology of nuclear energy. David Macaulay's books, such as *Castle* (1977) and *City: A Story of Roman Planning and Construction* (1974), illustrate many terms specific to architecture and civic planning as well as vocabulary that describes the people and social institutions of the respective eras.

2. Literature is often more up-to-date than textbooks. A textbook may be several years in development; one with a 2000 copyright may only reflect information available in the early to mid 1990s. Timely written accounts of developments in science and social studies may be available only in recent periodicals and books.

3. Although textbooks tend to pile up facts, dates, and concepts in a didactic avalanche, trade books can present much of the same information in a more appealing context (Beck & McKeown, 1991). (The term *trade books* is used for books, both fiction and nonfiction, written for the general public, as distinguished from textbooks, which are designed for classroom use.) Readers incidentally learn and store away countless facts as they enjoy trade books.

4. Literature goes beyond the facts. Readers get a sharper understanding of the issues and of the various stands they might adopt by sharing the experiences of fictional characters or reading nonfiction reportage and analysis. Through

literature, students can begin to understand some of the uses and abuses of science, statistics, and political power. The social and emotional implications of topics as far-ranging as racism, immigration, war, nuclear energy, genetic engineering, ecology, and computer technology can be explored in works of fiction and nonfiction.

EVIDENCE-BASED RESEARCH

5. Literature allows readers to experience other times, other places, other people, and other cultures with empathy. For example, Spears-Bunton (1991) describes the reaction of Courtney, a white high school student in an Ohio River town in Kentucky, to the events in Harriet Jacobs's (1987) account of her life as a slave girl. When asked what she would have done in Harriet's place when the elderly slave owner made his sexual desires clear, Courtney "turned her blue eyes toward the river and replied, 'I would have run, and I would have taken my children'" (pp. 12–13).

6. Trade books can be a powerful catalyst for thoughtful analysis (Alsup, 2003; Bean, Kile, & Readence, 1996). When students read about controversial topics, they learn to exercise critical thinking. As they compare two or more views, they will find discrepancies, contradictions, and differences of interpretation; they must decide which source is most compelling, complete, or accurate. *Johnny Tremaine* (Forbes, 1945), *My Brother Sam Is Dead* (Collier & Collier, 1974), *Sarah Bishop* (O'Dell, 1980), and *Bloody Country* (Collier & Collier, 1985), for instance, present events in the Revolutionary War from the points of view of characters of different genders, ages, races, and social standings.

7. Good experiences with reading breed motivation to seek other reading experiences. This is particularly important for reluctant readers or students who have difficulty with reading. When a teacher can help a troubled reader make a connection with an interesting and readable piece of literature, that reader gains the practice and confidence necessary to read further. Many adolescents who find reading a "turnoff" surprise themselves when they find the right material.

ACTIVITY

The following is an excerpt from *Catherine, Called Birdy* (Cushman, 1994),* a young adult novel told from the point of view of a 12-year-old girl living in thirteenth-century England. As you read it, look for vocabulary, facts, and concepts about the Middle Ages, and see what you can tell about Birdy, the narrator.

> Just three days to the feast of Saint Edward, my brother Edward's saint day. When Edward was still at home, we celebrated this day each year with feasting and dancing and mock battles in the yard. Now our celebrations

include my father's face turning purple, my mother tightening her eyes and her mouth, and the cook swinging his ladle and swearing in Saxon. The cause of all the excitement is this: On this day each year, since Edward went to be a monk, my mother takes wagons full of gifts to his abbey in his honor. My father shouts that we may as well pour his precious stores in the cesspit (one day his angry liver will set him afire and I will toast bread on him). My mother calls him Pinch-Fist and Miser. The cook boils and snarls as his bacon and flour and Renish wine leave home. But each year my mother stands firm and the wagons go. This year we send:

460 salted white herring
3 wheels of cheese, a barrel of apples
4 chickens, 3 ducks, and 87 pigeons
4 barrels of flour, honey from our bees
100 gallons of ale (for no one drinks more ale than monks, my father says)
4 iron pots, wooden spoons, and a rat trap for the kitchen
goose fat for the making of everyday candles and soap (lots of candles and little soap, I wager, seeing that they are monks)
40 pounds of beeswax candles for the church
a chest of blankets, linens, and napkins
horn combs, for those who have hair
goose quills, down, and a bolt of woven cloth (black) (pp. 23–24)

A check of three randomly selected samples of this book with the Fry readability formula (see Chapter 5) estimates that it is at the seventh-grade reading level, and the cover of the book recommends it for ages 12 and up. Do you think this book might be easier to read than a typical textbook intended for sixth or seventh grade? Why might it be more motivating to learn about the Middle Ages by reading a book like this than by reading a typical middle-grade history textbook?

Throughout this chapter, we will suggest ways to complement a full curriculum with literature, from short read-alouds to the use of novels and other full-length books. Consider carefully the potential understanding and appreciation that can come from literature; it is well worth including in a busy schedule.

ENCOURAGING RESPONSES TO LITERATURE

Some people are troubled by the idea of using trade books, especially fiction, to enhance students' understanding of content area concepts. They recall all too clearly how teachers "ruined" perfectly good novels by assigning questions and papers and by wringing out, chapter by chapter, every last bit of significance and interpretation, demolishing any possibility of enjoying a book purely for the personal and emotional responses it evokes. But surely, you are thinking, there are less heavy-handed ways to use literature as a basis for understanding content area information.

How should students respond to literature? How much should students' response be influenced by a teacher? The literary theory of Louise Rosenblatt (1978) suggests some possible answers. She describes reading as a complex transaction between reader and text. How a reader responds and what meaning a reader constructs from a text are influenced by the stance or purpose that the reader chooses. Rosenblatt (1985) defines two possible stances, the *efferent* and the *aesthetic:*

> The difference between the two kinds of reading lies in the reader's "selective attention" to what is being stirred up in the experiential reservoir. The predominantly efferent reader focuses attention on public meaning, abstracting what is to be retained after reading—to be recalled, paraphrased, acted on, analyzed. In aesthetic reading, the reader's selective attention is focused primarily on what is being personally lived through, cognitively and affectively, *during* the reading event. The range of ideas, feelings, associations activated in the reservoir of symbolizations is drawn upon. . . . Any text . . . can be read either way. (pp. 101–102)

Rosenblatt (1982) makes it clear that neither teachers nor readers have to make an "all-or-nothing" choice between efferent and aesthetic purposes for reading. She maintains that any reading act falls somewhere on a continuum between efferent and aesthetic, with most reading somewhere in the middle. She also recognizes the need for both kinds of reading and the need to teach students to read for both efferent and aesthetic purposes, although she cautions that greater emphasis needs to be placed on aesthetic reading.

EVIDENCE-BASED RESEARCH

Cynthia Lewis (2000) argues that the aesthetic stance is too often limited strictly to personal identification and interpretation. She suggests that aesthetic reading also encompasses a social or critical dimension, especially when readers are reading about cultures or experiences that are quite different from their own. She cites as an example *The Watsons Go to Birmingham—1963* (Curtis, 1995), a novel about an African American family at the time of the Civil Rights movement. The interactions of this close-knit family would have a personal aesthetic appeal to all readers, who could identify with the humor, warmth, and varied personalities. However, in the details of the Watsons' experiences with and resistance to white racism, European American readers are clearly positioned as outsiders. In this instance, the aesthetic experience is not one of close personal identification but rather understanding how the characters' lives are different from one's own.

How does a teacher translate theory into practice? That is, how can you "teach" a novel and leave room for students to experience it aesthetically? First, teachers need to be receptive to students' stances. That means that teachers should listen carefully for students' reactions—whether efferent or aesthetic, positive or negative. Students need the freedom to determine their own purposes for reading and their own reactions to reading.

Obviously, the very fact that a book is assigned for reading limits student choice and suggests an efferent purpose. Therefore, teachers must be careful how assignments and questions are posed if they wish to retain the possibility of aesthetic response. Rosenblatt (1982) warns that requests for verbal responses from students are especially liable to get in the way of aesthetic reading. In their questions, adults often telegraph what the "correct" response should be or steer students toward what the adult finds pertinent or interesting.

To encourage aesthetic reading and response, teachers can begin discussion of literature by asking for the readers' responses first. Rosenblatt (1982) suggests questions such as "Did anything especially interest ... annoy ... puzzle ... frighten [or] please [you or] seem familiar [or] weird?" (p. 276). Knowledge of students, their interests and their outlooks, helps a teacher choose questions that allow them to connect with other texts, other ideas, and other experiences. It is also useful to let students connect with each other, to let them see the similarities and differences in their points of view, perhaps by using some of the ideas presented in Chapter 9 and Chapter 10 or one of the strategies discussed later in this chapter.

INTEGRATING LITERATURE INTO CONTENT AREAS

This section describes several uses of literature in content areas and suggests some resources that should facilitate your search for pertinent books.

Uses of Literature in Content Areas

EVIDENCE-BASED RESEARCH

Literature can complement any content area. For English teachers, of course, literature study represents a sizeable segment of the curriculum. Literature complements the study of history and contemporary social issues by dramatizing and personalizing issues and events. There is also support in the research literature for integrating literature into content areas. For example, Wineburg (1991), a highly respected scholar in the field of history education, draws from his research on novice and expert readers when he recommends that young people should be given more than just history textbooks to read as part of the school curriculum. Although literature is less likely to be associated with content areas such as science and math, numerous nontextbook resources provide an added dimension to these subjects as well.

Read-alouds and book talks. By talking about books and reading aloud from books in class, teachers demonstrate that experts in a content area enjoy reading and actively pursue reading related to their field. Furthermore, such teacher modeling can be contagious. Teachers who actively promote reading and share what they read create interest on the part of students and illustrate the range of reading materials available. Equally important, hearing a teacher read high-quality sources can enhance the receptive language and broaden the conceptual scope of students from diverse linguistic and cultural backgrounds.

Reading aloud to students is one of the best ways to share a love of books. Read-alouds can be anywhere from 5 to 20 minutes or more in length and might be a daily or weekly occurrence in most any content area classroom. Short read-alouds can be used to develop interest and motivation, to introduce a new topic, to illustrate practical applications of content area concepts, and to inject a measure of humor into the classroom.

Consider this example. In *Life on the Mississippi* (1961), Mark Twain writes about his experiences living and working on the great river in a book that is part travelogue, part natural history, and part tall tale. In one short passage, he describes how the river often cuts through a narrow neck of land, thereby shortening the course of the river by many miles. Using statistics creatively (but accurately), he calculates that in exactly 742 years, the Lower Mississippi will be only a mile and three-quarters long. He ends the passage with a typical Twain epigram: "One gets such wholesale returns of conjecture out of such a trifling investment of fact" (p. 120). Mark Forget describes how he uses this passage in his algebra class, first reading it aloud and then plugging Twain's numbers into an algebraic formula, calculating the slope of the line, and plotting it on a graph (Richardson, 2000). Forget also points out that this passage would be an ideal read-aloud for a geography class, with its accurate descriptions of how the river works its will and the many citations of places readily found on different kinds of maps.

The following are some dos and don'ts for reading aloud (Trelease, 2001; Richardson, 2000; Sanacore, 2000).

1. Choose a selection that you enjoy and that you think students will like as well. It should be something that will encourage discussion and further inquiry. Your listeners will appreciate humor, strong emotion, action, or the unusual.
2. Preview the material. Look for parts you might want to shorten, eliminate, or discuss.
3. Reader and audience should get comfortable. Sit or stand where your audience can see you easily, with your head above the heads of your listeners so your voice can carry; make frequent eye contact with your audience.
4. Practice. Be expressive with your reading and do not rush; vary your intonation to heighten the action or indicate different characters.
5. Encourage predictions, questions, and discussion during reading, but do not impose your own point of view or lecture as you read. Inferential and critical thinking questions can be used to follow up a read-aloud session.
6. Once you start a book or story, follow through unless it turns out to be universally unpopular. Students may not seem to be enjoying a book but will howl in protest if you decide not to finish it.

Appendix B is a list of books that contain short read-aloud selections pertinent to a variety of topics, historical events, and dates. A teacher could begin a class by reading about the physics of a curveball, what happened 100 years ago on a given day, or how dirty tricks were used in early presidential campaigns. A book-loving colleague especially recommends collections of weird and curious facts, for which he uses the delightful word *gallimaufry* (which originally referred to a kind of hash made up of leftovers). In this type of book, you can learn how crickets chirp, how Beethoven was able to compose even though he was deaf, and how the *Mariner I* space probe was lost because a minus sign was omitted from instructions fed into a computer. Such tidbits augment textbook information and add appeal to content area studies. Students also enjoy browsing through these books, even reluctant readers who would never consider the idea of reading a whole book cover to cover.

Judith Richardson (2000) illustrates suggested read-aloud selections for a wide range of content areas, including English as a second language. For ELLs, read-alouds provide exposure to intonational and syntactic patterns, vocabulary, idioms, and important cultural and conceptual information. Among the read-aloud selections that Richardson recommends is *Grab Hands and Run* (Temple, 1993), a story of a Salvadoran family waiting for Canadian citizenship. This book treats issues of politics, immigration, assimilation, language differences, and language learning, many of which are pertinent to the experiences of ELLs.

Book talks are another medium through which a teacher can promote content-related literature. When a teacher does a five- or ten-minute "show-and-tell" with a book, whether it is an old favorite or a current page-turner, students see a reader who takes pleasure from books. Book talks can also create interest for a particular author or title. A teacher may even recommend titles for specific students, just like a recommendation between friends. It is a powerful incentive to a student to have a teacher hand him or her a book and say something like "I know something about you, and I think you'll enjoy this—try it!"

Free reading time.   Some teachers have successfully instituted a regular time when everybody in the class simply reads. This activity, called *SSR* (Sustained Silent Reading) or *DEAR* (Drop Everything and Read) time, has only two simple requirements. First, everybody reads, including the teacher. Second, students must read something other than their textbooks (and the teacher is not supposed to grade papers). This second requirement might be modified in content area classes by restricting students to reading related to the subject area. That is, students in science class should be reading something relevant to science, other than the class text.

In secondary-level content area classrooms, time is probably the biggest obstacle to implementing free reading time. Even if it is impractical to schedule free reading throughout the year, teachers can institute SSR when students are working on outside reading projects, especially at the beginning, when they need to make a selection and get a good head start on reading it.

In-school free reading requires that students have access to reading materials. Some students will bring their own books to read, especially if they know independent reading will take place at a regular time. Those who do not have their own books will need to select something from the classroom library. Sanacore (1990) suggests that content area teachers stock their classroom libraries with materials that represent a variety of reading levels, lengths, and formats. Many of the titles listed in Appendix B make excellent SSR resources, along with paperbacks, periodicals, newspapers, and graphic novels.

The purpose of SSR is to give students an opportunity to practice lifetime reading skills, to read for their own purposes and pleasure. Independent reading is not a "for credit" activity. Students are not graded, nor are they expected to produce anything as a result of their reading. It might be helpful to use a part of free reading time for book talks by the teacher or by student volunteers, but otherwise it is devoted simply to reading for the sake of reading.

Independent reading is an essential component in the language development of ELLs. Reading interesting, ability-appropriate materials provides ELLs with "comprehensible input" (Krashen, 1985). Opportunities to read without academic pressure can help ELLs make a transition from easier to more difficult materials. Furthermore, reading exposes ELLs to a wider range of topics, concepts, syntactic patterns, and vocabulary than they are likely to encounter in their oral language interactions.

Janice Pilgreen (2000) describes a successful SSR program established for high school ELLs. She lists eight factors that will influence the success of such a program:

1. *Access:* Students will need a wide variety of reading materials at suitable levels.
2. *Appeal:* Magazines, comic books, and series books will be especially popular.
3. *Conducive environment:* Posters, artwork, and comfortable places to sit make it pleasant to read. Silent reading time should also be free of interruptions and distractions.
4. *Encouragement:* Teachers can model their own enjoyment of reading during free reading time and explain the benefits of reading for students' language development.
5. *Distributed time to read:* Students need regularly scheduled times for free reading throughout the week. Daily practice is optimal.
6. *Nonaccountability:* Free reading should involve no book reports, journal entries, or comprehension assessments.
7. *Follow-up activities:* Students should have opportunities to share information with each other about their reading on a voluntary basis.
8. *Staff training:* Teachers need to understand the substantial benefits of free reading time as well as how to implement a formal free reading program.

Dispelling Policy Myths

Dispelling a Myth

We have heard from some teachers that their school has discontinued Sustained Silent Reading time because the National Reading Panel (2000) found that in-school independent reading was ineffective. In fact, the NRP subgroup report on fluency acknowledged that only 14 studies were available that met their stringent criteria for experimental research. Their analysis of these studies concluded that the results were mixed and that there was insufficient evidence to recommend in-school independent reading. However, Stephen Krashen (2002) points out that the NRP misinterpreted some of the studies included in their analysis and overlooked other studies that did meet their criteria. When he added studies that involved college-age students and English language learners and reanalyzed the results, he found that SSR students did as well as or better than comparison students in 50 out of 53 comparisons. SSR students were superior in eight out of ten studies that lasted for more than a year. Krashen points out that SSR appears to have the greatest effect for students who have the greatest need, that is, struggling readers and ELLs. It is also noteworthy that in the subsection on vocabulary, the NRP recommends independent reading as an effective means for building students' word knowledge.

Policy Implications

Implementation of Sustained Silent Reading has shown consistently strong correlation with reading improvement. For example, Douglas Fisher (2004) reports on an urban high school where 75 percent of the students were English language learners and 99 percent of the student body qualified for free lunch. Although the school had an SSR program, selected observations revealed that it was not being uniformly implemented. Many students had no opportunity for independent reading in school. Teachers knew from surveying students that many did not have opportunities for free reading at home either. A review of the school's previous standardized reading test scores showed that students in classrooms where SSR was regularly practiced had higher reading scores than classes where SSR was not done. Based on this information, the faculty decided to implement a new standard at the school—the Opportunity to Read standard, which resulted in more effective school-wide implementation of SSR.

This suggests that decisions about using SSR in a school or a specific classroom should be made locally and based on the particular needs of the students in that setting. Such decisions should be made after considering multiple criteria, including data from testing, student surveys, characteristics of the student body, the availability of sufficient and suitable reading materials, administrative support, and the willingness of faculty to buy in to the program.

High school ELL students were asked to comment on the free reading program. The following samples indicate their enthusiasm (Pilgreen, 2000):

"My vocabulary is better, and I have noticed that my understanding of English has improved."

"When I began reading, I didn't want to stop, even for a minute. Now I want to read the harder books."

"Sometimes when I read I get excited, and I don't want to stop reading so I take the book home."

"I like a lot when you allowed us to read newspapers and magazines because I could get information about modern things."

"The books are getting harder and longer now than before because I used to read short easy books." (pp. 82–85)

Complementary readings. Literature can be used in a variety of ways to complement textbooks. Some teachers may have a whole class reading a single book or story during a thematic unit. For instance, a social studies class might read *Roll of Thunder, Hear My Cry* (Taylor, 1976) as part of a unit on the Great Depression. Many of the prereading, comprehension, writing, and vocabulary strategies presented in earlier chapters are appropriate when the whole class is reading the same book. To maximize students' involvement and self-direction, we especially recommend anticipation guides and K-W-L (Chapter 6), ReQuest and self-questioning (Chapter 7), vocabulary self-selection (Chapter 8), Discussion Webs (Chapter 9), and learning logs (Chapter 10).

Whole-class study of a single book requires enough copies of the book for every student to have one, which can stretch a tight school budget. There is also the problem that some students may find a particular text uninteresting or too challenging. An alternative strategy is to select several titles, all related to a single topic or theme. (You will find books related to specific themes suggested in Appendixes B, C, and D.) When several different books are available, students have a choice of what to read. Multiple titles also present the possibility of offering different cooperative-learning arrangements. If students are grouped with others reading the same book, they may work cooperatively on developing a book talk, a poster or visual display, a read-aloud, or some other presentation based on the book. Students in a group all reading different books may do book talks within their group, or the group may develop some cooperative project such as a Web site devoted to student inquiry and writing.

Complementary reading does not need to be focused on a particular topic or theme. Content teachers often assign outside reading projects, for which students are allowed to choose their own books. Social studies teacher Edwin Biloff (1996) incorporated complementary trade book reading with his eleventh-grade American history class. During their study of the Civil War, he assigned *The Killer Angels* (Shaara, 1974), a novel about the Battle of Gettysburg. Over a period of seven weeks, students read the novel, chose one of three major characters from the novel, conducted outside research in nonfiction resources on this person, and then wrote an essay that analyzed the person's character and leadership. In the essay, they were to compare the novelized treatment of their subject with the information found in the nonfiction sources.

Sprague and Cotturone (2003) describe the frustration of a high school physics teacher when she discovered that only about 10 percent of her students could readily answer questions based on short passages from their physics text. In order to motivate her students to read about physics, the teacher obtained a

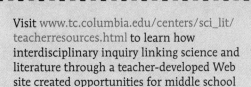

Technology Tip
for Linking Science and Literature

Visit www.tc.columbia.edu/centers/sci_lit/ teacherresources.html to learn how interdisciplinary inquiry linking science and literature through a teacher-developed Web site created opportunities for middle school students "to investigate and document their environment, and figure out ways to incorporate into the website what they saw, wondered about, and learned" (Howes, Hamilton, & Zaskoda, 2003, p. 494).

class set of *The Science of Star Wars* (Cavelos, 2000) and showed the first *Star Wars* film. Drawing on the movie and selected readings in the *Star Wars* book, she posed a series of physics problems for students to solve, resulting in a spirited exchange of ideas and information. The teacher offered extra credit for students who did additional reading in the book.

STANDARDS

Based on the success of this initial trade book reading, she divided students into small groups and gave them short selections from two other trade books, *The Einstein Paradox* (Bruce, 1997) and *Mr. Tompkins in Paperback* (Gamow, 1993). Each selection dealt with topics featured in the state physics standards. Over two 90-minute class periods, students discussed prereading questions, read the selections, and then prepared presentations for the rest of the class. Students selected presentation options in a variety of media, including PowerPoint, videos, storybooks, models, and role-playing. The presentations revealed a thorough and accurate understanding of the physics concepts involved, and students were surprised to find how much science they could learn from reading.

Fiction and Nonfiction for Content Areas

**EVIDENCE-
BASED
RESEARCH**

One major difference between lifetime readers and school readers is the matter of choice. Young people and adults who enjoy reading as a regular pastime choose their reading materials from among many genres, authors, and subjects; in school, readers are limited for the most part to what they are assigned or what is available in the school library. However, these school reading materials are not reflective of the wide range of adolescent reading preferences (Ivey & Broaddus, 2001; Worthy, Moorman, & Turner, 1999). Lack of choice in school reading is one reason frequently cited by secondary students who are willing readers outside of school but resist assigned reading (Bintz, 1993). Aliterate students, those who can read but choose not to, cited "choosing their own books" as the number one thing that would motivate them to read more (Beers, 1996). The choices teachers can offer students are constrained by time, curriculum, and resources. However, teachers recognize the importance of selecting books and readings that will appeal to readers (Palmer & Stewart, 1997).

It is difficult to assess what adolescent readers are likely to enjoy because their tastes are as varied as those of adult readers. In their study of Illinois high school students, Moffit and Wartella (1992) found a preference for romance among females and for fantasy, science fiction, and sports among males. When Bank (1986) surveyed students in grades 6–12 in the New York metropolitan area, their interests ranged across a total of 58 different topics. The top 10 topics were young people, mystery, humor, adventure, love, sex, movies, famous people, romances, and horror, but preferences varied widely by grade level, ethnicity, native language, and other student characteristics.

Boys generally lag behind girls in reading achievement and tend to spend less time reading, especially in adolescence (Brozo, 2002; Smith & Wilhelm, 2002). Teachers and librarians can make a difference, however, if they provide male readers with materials that they find motivating and accessible. For instance, boys are more inclined to read informational texts, graphic novels, and comic books. They like to read about sports, hobbies, and other active pursuits. Jon Scieszka, author and illustrator of books designed to appeal to boys, recommends a variety of titles for boys on his Web site, www.guysread.com.

The annual survey of young adult choices in literature conducted by the International Reading Association and published in the *Journal of Adolescent & Adult Literacy* confirms this interest in a wide range of topics, authors, and genres. It is important to remember, too, that nonfiction may account for as much as half of adolescents' leisure reading (Abrahamson & Carter, 1991).

With so many interests and so many available titles, it is difficult to pick a winner every time. Knowing your students and the available literature increases the possibility that you will make good choices, however. Appendixes C and D suggest some books that have been recommended to us by colleagues and teachers. These selections are far from exhaustive. To give you an idea of the range of options, we have tried to pick books that are of general interest as well as some that pertain to specific topics. In cases in which the title alone does not suggest the subject matter, we offer brief annotations. We also designate books written for young adults with a YA. This is tricky because so-called young adult books vary considerably in their format and content. Many are quite suitable for secondary school readers, but others are likely to be rejected as too immature. Ultimately, the teacher's judgment and a bit of trial and error will be necessary to match books and students.

Those who are looking for a trade book to complement a particular unit of study might find guidelines suggested by Biloff (1996) useful:

1. The reading should match students' reading levels, be interesting, represent content area concepts accurately, and complement curricular goals.
2. If choosing a novel, look for action, crisp dialogue, and empathic characters.
3. Select material for which you have special interest or expertise.

4. Consider piloting the material with a representative student sample.
5. Readings that can be coordinated with audiovisuals are especially useful.
6. Look for material that could be used in varied and interesting ways from year to year.

Picture books and graphic novels for content areas.   Picture books and so-called graphic novels tell stories and illustrate concepts from literature, science, social studies, and mathematics (Miller, 1998; Schwarz, 2002, 2004.) While picture books are familiar to most people, graphic novels are a relatively new genre. They are essentially extended comic books, and along with contemporary picture books, they treat a wide range of subjects including the environment, families, ethnic heritage, relationships, war, love, social problems, and historical events. Many picture books and graphic novels feature exceptional artistic and literary accomplishment. For instance, Art Spiegelman's graphic novel about the Holocaust, *Maus* (1986), won a Pulitzer Prize for literature.

You may think of picture books and comics as being unsuitable for serious use in middle and high school, but each can serve multiple purposes. They can be used to introduce abstract topics, develop technical vocabulary, provide information for inquiry projects, prompt writing, and provide both visual and conceptual experiences with people from diverse cultures.

The themes of many picture books and graphic novels have appeal that transcends age levels, and they are often written at fairly advanced conceptual and maturity levels. For example, Neal and Moore (1991–1992) cite *Rose Blanche* (Innocenti, 1985), a disturbing story of the Holocaust, and *The Wall* (Bunting, 1990), which tells the story of the Vietnam Veterans Memorial, as two picture books that address worldly and emotional topics in a realistic fashion. Schwarz (2004) points out that many graphic novels also give nuanced treatment to a wide range of worthy topics and lend themselves to teaching multiple literacies, including print literacy, visual literacy, and media literacy. The short format of picture books makes them especially well suited to complement the short class periods in most middle and high schools. A picture book can be read in its entirety during the period, with time left for discussion or other activities. Graphic novels are also relatively short, and their often colorful formats provide a welcome and motivating change from textbooks.

 Picture books can help make visual and verbal connections for students who are learning English. Nancy Hadaway and Jane Mundy (2000) outline a unit on weather that they developed for high school ELLs. They decided to emphasize the seasons, weather phenomena, and weather disasters. Students used informational picture books, newspaper weather reports, national weather maps, and books with weather experiments as their texts. During the course of the unit, they wrote poetry that featured weather vocabulary, created their own graphic organizers of weather concepts, wrote about their weather experiments and observations in weather journals, and made a weather collage of words and pictures. To culminate the unit, students researched weather-related disasters such as floods, tornadoes, and hurricanes. Their inquiry was scaffolded with picture books before they moved to the school library to consult standard reference materials.

Integrating popular culture.   In Chapter 9 we raised the question of how popular culture might be incorporated into school curricula. An expanded conception of adolescent literacies must take into account both the pleasure and the utility that adolescents find in such popular media as movies, television, music CDs, phones and pagers, magazines, graphic novels, electronic games, and the Internet. Whether we bid them to or not, adolescents bring these literacies into school. Lorri Neilsen (1998) tells the story of her son David, a high school junior who downloaded parts of the filmscript to the movie *Pulp Fiction* from the Internet. David and his friends memorized long passages of the movie dialogue and produced their own videotaped versions of favorite scenes. David also directed scenes from the movie for a school drama project. Neilsen explains that a movie such as *Pulp Fiction* can become a "touchstone text" for adolescents, texts that help adolescents to "make and shape meaning in their lives through literacy" (p. 4). She goes on to consider the implications of these texts for teachers and teaching. She says that adolescents like her son remind her

> that their ongoing curriculum is the lives they lead; that they teach one another and can teach their teachers; and that they will explore learning, grow in their literacy, and dream their dreams in settings often much more influential than school settings. What important paths to learning are we blocking off at the school door? How can we learn to listen to that learning and bring it into school settings and curricula? (p. 22)

In an intergenerational conversation, Tom Bean and his adolescent daughters explored the many functions of text and media for the two girls both in school and out (Bean, Bean, & Bean, 1999). Both girls had teachers who

Picture Books and Struggling Readers

The availability of picture books for both independent and content-specific reading helps to establish them as "acceptable" for *all* students (Miller, 1998). This is especially helpful for struggling readers, who can get pleasure and useful content from picture books but who might be embarrassed if they felt they were being targeted to read "kids' books." High-quality picture books with challenging ideas and interesting content can provide struggling readers with much-needed practice and confidence.

encouraged them to make connections between home, school, and peer cultures. Sixteen-year-old Shannon's social studies teacher allowed students to express their understanding of historical periods through artwork, models, and rap songs. For a science project on animals, twelve-year-old Kristen used her home computer to write about dogs, specifically the cocker spaniel that she has trained and shown. In each case, the girls were able to use their multiple literacies and interests in the service of school-based learning. If we expand our conceptions of literacy and text to incorporate popular media and culture, we will find many ways to help make such connections.

Censorship.   A discussion of using literature in content areas would not be complete without considering the problem of censorship. When community groups or parents exert pressure to remove reading materials from the school library or classroom, school boards and administrators often acquiesce, with the result that an entire class or school may be denied the right to read a particular text. The potential threat of external protests as well as personal objection to certain works of literature may also lead teachers to self-censorship. For example, the Harry Potter series has prompted numerous protests by people who object to the alleged promotion of witchcraft and magic in the books. Other books that are regularly the object of censorship attempts include *The Catcher in the Rye, Huckleberry Finn, The Diary of Anne Frank,* and *I Know Why the Caged Bird Sings.* Much contemporary young adult fiction addresses issues such as sexuality, violence, and drug use that may make teachers, parents, or administrators uncomfortable. Nevertheless, many teachers feel an ethical as well as intellectual duty to help students read critically about topics that, while potentially controversial, are relevant to important social issues and to students' lives outside of school (Alsup, 2003).

In interviews with five experienced high school English teachers, Jane Agee (1999) found that all wanted to include diverse, rich, contemporary literature in their curriculum, but all had found themselves at one time or another in risky territory because of their book choices. In very real terms, teachers who want their students to read a wide range of texts may be putting their careers in jeopardy. When schools have formal policies and procedures for handling book challenges, active book screening committees, collegial discussions of potential texts, and supportive administrators and colleagues, they are less likely to succumb to the pressures of censors. Even in the best of circumstances, however, books are banned and teachers learn to be cautious about what they bring into the classroom.

**EVIDENCE-
BASED
RESEARCH**

The teachers that Agee (1999) interviewed detailed many strategies for introducing potentially controversial texts into their curricula, and they also practiced some form of self-censorship. One defense is to carefully weigh the maturity and family backgrounds of students and decide how much of a fight a particular book is worth. Another is to communicate carefully with parents about what students will be reading and why. For instance, at the beginning of the year one teacher sent home a list of 30 films she *might* show during the year, although in practice she only used five or so a semester. Students and parents could review the list, and if there were potential problems, students could drop the class. Sometimes teachers offer to provide alternative readings if there is isolated objection to a proposed assignment.

Another proactive strategy is to include censorship issues as part of the curriculum, thus engaging students directly in the debate over their right to read. For example, to prepare for the reading of *Huckleberry Finn*, teachers often discuss the history of censorship attempts on the book. This prepares both European American and African American students to critically consider the racial issues prompted by Twain's portrayal of Huck and Jim and his use of the vernaculars of the place and time in which the story is set. Although such preparation does not settle all the controversies, it helps to diffuse them and set the stage for critical but civil discussion in which students of different backgrounds and beliefs are better prepared to understand diverse points of view.

DEVELOPING AWARENESS OF DIVERSITY THROUGH LITERATURE

In many large urban centers, linguistically or culturally diverse children often comprise half or more of the school population, a fact that challenges the very notion of a "mainstream" or "majority" culture. African American and Hispanic/Latino students represent the largest cultural minorities in schools, but they are by no means the only representatives of culturally diverse groups.

To cite one example, Grover Cleveland High School in Buffalo, New York, has approximately 1,000 students, of whom approximately 38 percent are Hispanic, 24 percent are African American, 18 percent are Asian, and 20 percent are of European origin. However, that does not tell the whole story because nearly half of these students are classified as having limited English proficiency, and their numbers encompass students from 19 different language groups, including Spanish, Vietnamese, Cambodian, Russian, Ukrainian, and Arabic. Labels such as "Hispanic" and "Asian" obscure the true diversity of these students, who include native-born Americans as well as immigrants from Puerto Rico, El Salvador, Mexico, Venezuela, Honduras, Ethiopia, Somalia, China, Japan, Korea, Vietnam, Thailand, Cambodia, and Laos. The specific demographics and ethnic mixes would differ, but most large cities would have selected schools with similar diversity.

This diversity poses both challenges and opportunities. For the students, there are the challenges and dilemmas of alienation, assimilation, and acculturation. For schools whose expectations, curricula, and methods are based on mainstream culture, there are the challenges of reaching out to an increasingly diverse student population and of fostering tolerance and understanding among all students. There is also the opportunity to celebrate this diversity, to use the varied talents of people from many cultures, and to break down the barriers between "us" and "them," while adding to the rich texture of this country's cultural tapestry.

Advantages of using multicultural literature.   Literature provides a vehicle for both meeting these challenges and realizing the potential of cultural diversity. First, several positive effects occur when students read about their own culture. Culturally relevant literature validates students' cultural identity and projects a positive image of them and their culture. In a review of African American children's literature, for instance, Bishop (1990) notes five important positive themes:

1. Warm and loving human relations, especially in the family
2. A sense of community among African Americans
3. African American history, heritage, and culture
4. A sense of continuity
5. Physical and psychological survival in the face of overwhelming odds

When such personal validation comes from books read at school, students' positive identification with the school itself is strengthened. Culturally relevant literature can also be an important tool for developing students' motivation to read. The personal appeal of reading about culturally familiar subjects can be especially effective with students who are otherwise turned off by books.

The value of reading stories by and about people of various cultures extends to all students, however, regardless of ethnic or cultural affiliation (Spears-Bunton, 1998). From a strictly curricular standpoint, reading culturally diverse literature can increase students' knowledge of history and geography and expand their understanding of literary technique (Norton, 1990). More important, readers can gain a greater understanding and appreciation of cultures other than their own when they identify with the characters in a novel. The literature of different cultures helps to break down some of the myths and stereotypes people hold.

Resistance to multicultural literature.   Unfortunately, there is evidence of resistance to the use of multicultural literature on the part of some students, teachers, administrators, community members, and politicians (McCarthy, 1998). Some object on the grounds that schools should focus on traditionally recognized and accepted "great works" that transmit values and ideas common to the mainstream culture (Bloom, 1994; Hirsch, 1987). Administrators may feel that using multicultural literature will not be accepted by parents, will interfere with a more skills-based approach to literacy, or will unfairly focus attention on particular ethnic or cultural groups (Godina, 1996).

Glazier and Seo (2005) describe discussions of *The Way to Rainy Mountain* (Momaday, 1996), a book about the Kiowa nation, in a culturally diverse ninth-grade classroom. They found that in conversations about the book, non-European American students frequently gave voice to ideas and feelings that had not been previously expressed, often in the form of personal narratives about their own cultural backgrounds and understandings. European American students, on the other hand, did not make the same text-to-self connections. When asked about his cultural background, Mark, a European American, replied, "I don't know . . . it's American. That's all I have—that's all the culture I know . . . I don't know what my culture is" (p. 696). Students like Mark did not see themselves reflected positively in the text, and the culture of the mainstream remained covert, unvoiced and unexamined.

Teachers' concerns fall into two general categories (Jordan & Purves, 1993). First, they see institutional constraints: whether literature should be used to foster cultural identity or to develop critical understanding, whether multicultural literature should bump the so-called classics from the curriculum, and whether a teacher from one cultural background can effectively teach multicultural literature to students of another culture. Second, they may feel constrained by the reactions and attitudes of their students. A teacher in an affluent suburb said, "Our students can feel superior to the literature of others as long as it deals with the suffering of others, but when it presents a point of view that they can't feel sorry for, then it is not welcome" (p. 10). In contrast, another teacher felt that her students could not relate to multicultural literature "because nothing we read at school makes them feel important. The school's lower-middle-class whites get nothing from multicultural literature" (p. 100).

The apparent resistance of some students to multicultural literature is confirmed by Richard Beach (1997), who suggests that some of the high school readers he interviewed resisted a stance that acknowledged institutional racial or gender bias and instead adopted a stance of "individual prejudice." That is, they rejected the notion that they might be prejudiced and instead attributed bias to other individuals rather than to the society as a whole. Thus, mainstream readers may deny ethnic or gender differences, profess a lack of relevant cultural knowledge, resist feelings of guilt or complicity, and contest challenges to their privileged status in society. At the same time, Beach found other readers who adopted alternative stances that allowed them to empathize with people of other cultures and to reflect on their own status in society.

These are complex issues that do not have easy answers. It is our feeling that the very resistance to multicultural literature is an argument for its inclusion in the curriculum. The United States is a pluralistic society, and the more we understand about each other the better off we will be. There is much in multicultural literature that reinforces basic beliefs and aspirations that are common across our society, while still pointing out important differences in the way people can think, act, live, and feel. It is important that we understand where our similarities and differences lie, even if our differences cannot always be easily reconciled.

Insistence that student readers must be limited to a narrow corpus of "great works" simply does not make good sense. First, it assumes the impossible, which is that we could ever agree on what should be included in such a body of work. It ignores the fact that "greatness" is a fluid concept that changes with time, location, and those who define it. Insisting that there are certain works that students must read in school is to assume that they would or could never read anything else, that their reading will be limited exclusively to what they get in school (Hughes, 1993). Finally, there is a high degree of artistic and intellectual merit in the best of multicultural fiction and nonfiction so that inclusion of such works does not displace an emphasis on reading works of quality.

There are ways that a teacher can help to reduce students' resistance to reading about other cultures. It is important, first of all, to understand why some students may be uncomfortable with what they perceive as challenges to their position or to the beliefs of their peers and family members. As models and facilitators, teachers can set a tone of tolerance and nonconfrontational dialogue. Before introducing a multicultural text in class, a teacher should prepare by learning some biographical details of the author, reviewing the historical setting of the story and the period when the author wrote, and making "cultural footnotes" on things that may be unfamiliar to students (Willis & Palmer, 1998). This will allow teachers to share factual background information, clarify potential cultural misunderstandings, and prepare students to react to the story, characters, and action, not just to the "culture" (Jordan & Purves, 1993). To that end, many of the prereading activities in Chapter 6 could be employed.

Culturally Appropriate Materials and Lesson Plans on the Internet

Young people's resistance to academic reading practices can sometimes prompt teachers to look for alternative kinds of material in an attempt to help students make connections between their everyday lives and content area learning. Sometimes these well-intentioned attempts can backfire, especially when middle-class teachers make assumptions about lower-level socioeconomic communities that are incongruent with the culture of those communities (e.g., see Hicks & Dolan, 2003). A Web site for choosing appropriate multicultural books, along with criteria for guiding your choices, is one titled "How to Choose the Best Multicultural Books," available at http://teacher.scholastic.com/products/instructor/multicultural.htm. For choices in other kinds of material, check out The CyberHunt Library at http://teacher.scholastic.com/products/instructor/cyberhunt_kids.htm. This site offers opportunities for surfing the Web in search of fascinating facts that can be used to answer puzzles and other challenges in social studies, science, sports, and the language arts. Another site you will want to explore is one maintained by the Young Adult Library Services Association (www.ala.org/yalsa), which offers information on Teen Read Week and links to electronic discussion lists. For examples of teacher and media guides to accompany young adult multicultural books, visit Cynthia Leitich Smith's Web page at www.cynthialeitichsmith.com/; it has been named one of the Top Ten writer sites on the Internet by Writer's Digest. Finally, for lesson plans that are aligned with the IRA/NCTE Standards for the English Language Arts, visit www.readwritethink.org.

Finally, it is important to bring mainstream students into the conversation, to give them a chance to tell their own stories and to consider their own culture, to recognize that culture is a multifaceted concept (Glazier & Seo, 2005). Mainstream students need to see that one can have pride and confidence in one's heritage without necessarily being oppressive to others. To that end, Beach (1997) suggests that we give students examples of people who have transcended bias in their lives. Such people can be found in most communities, and their stories are recorded in the popular media and in biographies and autobiographies. Best of all, we can strive to be such models ourselves.

EVIDENCE-BASED RESEARCH

Choosing and using multicultural literature.   Locating suitable multicultural literature, planning for its instruction, and actually teaching it requires a considerable investment of time (Willis & Palmer, 1998). Nevertheless, the results are worth the investment. Athanases (1998) reported on a year-long study of two urban tenth-grade classrooms in which teachers committed themselves to an exploration of diverse texts. During the year the classes read short stories, poems, autobiographical pieces, plays, and novels by a diverse group of authors including Amy Tan, Maya Angelou, Maxine Hong Kingston, Shakespeare, Sophocles, Langston Hughes, and Albert Camus. Both teachers encouraged students to develop their own literary responses and exploratory thinking through collaborative projects and presentations, journal writing, and open-ended questioning by both teachers and students that emphasized analysis, synthesis, and speculation over literal recall. Most important, both teachers encouraged students to explore racial issues openly and to use their personal and community knowledge to help them interpret what they were reading.

The students represented diverse academic levels, ethnic backgrounds, and language communities. African American, Chinese American, Filipino, European American, Puerto Rican, Mexican, and Central American heritages were all represented in significant numbers. Half of each class spoke a language other than English at home, and one-fourth of the students had been formally identified as at risk for school failure. During the course of the year, Athanases (1998) documented responses over a wide range of categories:

- Family and adolescent concerns
- Pride of culture and place
- Developing cultural identities
- Developing gender and sexual identities
- Learning from new experiences and ideas about cultures
- Rethinking stereotypes

Of course, there was also resistance to challenging ideas and portrayals in the literature as well as occasional tensions and conflicts during discussions. Nevertheless, the varied texts and the exploratory talk in these classes helped students make connections and discoveries that many of them recalled vividly two years afterward. In his summary of the study, Athanases (1998) notes that simply introducing diversified texts into the classroom is not enough; he says we need to "move beyond debates on *what* should be taught, to analyses of *how*—an essential step, because changing course materials alone has not historically yielded humanistic benefits" (p. 293).

For the teacher, however, deciding what should be taught is the first step. Teachers who are not familiar with or are a little overwhelmed by the growing body of multicultural literature might start by reading works that fit their particular interests or curricular needs and teaching what they are learning (Spears-Bunton, 1998). It is important to make a distinction between world literature (e.g., stories about people in Africa or Latin America) and ethnic American literature (stories about African Americans or Latino/a Americans). Selecting literature that is representative of diverse cultural backgrounds also requires sensitivity to potential cultural and gender bias.

One issue is whether the author is writing from the perspective of an "insider" or an "outsider" (Harris, 1991). Some earlier works by outsider authors tended to be paternalistic or patronizing in their portrayals of culturally diverse groups. Although many authors write with sensitivity about cultures other than their own, being an insider may give an author more license to interpret a particular ethnic group's experience. There is also a need to avoid lumping different cultures together into "cultural conglomerates" (Reimer, 1992). As we pointed out earlier, "Hispanic" does not mean just Mexican or Puerto Rican, and a term such as "Asian" or "European" encompasses many different cultures. Also, teachers should not make the mistake of assuming that all members of a particular cultural group will enjoy the same books. To do so can lead to stereotyping and damaging overgeneralization.

The following guidelines, adapted from Hansen-Krening and Mizokawa (2000) and Pang et al. (1992), can help to avoid stereotypes and choose books that accurately portray people of varying cultural identities. Good multicultural literature should have

- *An authoritative author:* If the author is not a member of the portrayed ethnic group, he or she must have some knowledge or experience that allows for credibility.
- *A culturally pluralistic theme:* Cultural diversity should be valued and issues of cultural assimilation should be treated sensitively. Also, the work should transcend the "food, festival, and folktale" approach to multicultural literature.
- *A good plot and characterization:* An interesting plot and compelling characters are what make a book enjoyable. However, plot and characters may not necessarily adhere to traditional European American literary traditions.
- *Positive and accurate portrayals:* Characters from diverse cultures should be seen as empowered people and not be stereotyped. Ethnic Americans should be accurately portrayed, but it must be clear that they are at the same time American, not foreign. Many Asian Americans and Hispanic

Americans are native born and may actually represent families whose history in the United States precedes that of many immigrants from the British Isles and Europe.

- *Accurate illustrations:* If there are pictures, they should not stereotype people's physical features, dress, and mannerisms.
- *Historical accuracy:* Books should be carefully researched by their authors.

For teachers who wish to broaden the cultural scope of their students' reading, there is both good news and bad news. The good news is that there are many diverse authors from diverse backgrounds turning out excellent works. The bad news is that many ethnic groups, most notably Hispanics/Latinos, who are the fastest-growing ethnic group in the United States, are not proportionately represented in literature (Barry, 1998). Also, in the competitive literary marketplace, many titles quickly go out of print and may be difficult to find. With this caution in mind, we offer in Appendix D a list of titles that reflect some of the diverse cultures in today's schools. We intend this list to be representative, not exhaustive. Several of the authors presented have published numerous outstanding books besides those given, and many other authors we might have included but could not because of space limitations. In addition, many of the articles and reviews cited in this chapter and in the Suggested Readings include excellent lists of culturally diverse literature. We especially recommend *Teaching and Using Multicultural Literature in Grades 9–12*, edited by Arlette Willis (1998), which has chapters on the literature of the African American, Puerto Rican, Asian/Pacific American, Native American, Mexican American, and Caribbean American communities.

SUMMARY

A local video outlet advertises with the slogan "So many movies, so little time." That is how we feel about books. For a lifetime reader, there is both joy and frustration in the great wealth of reading material available. In this chapter, we have tried to show how literature can accomplish two important purposes. First, good literature can present content area facts, concepts, and issues in a form that is often more palatable and memorable than textbooks. Second, and perhaps more important, exposure to good literature can cultivate in students a passion for lifetime reading.

SUGGESTED READINGS

Adamson, L. (1997). *Literature connections to American history, 7–12: Resources to enhance and entice.* Englewood, CO: Libraries Unlimited.

Allen, J. (1995). *It's never too late: Leading adolescents to lifelong literacy.* Portsmouth, NH: Heinemann.

American Library Association. *Best books for young adults, High-low books for young adults, and Booklist: Young adult editors' choices.* Write to ALA, Young Adult Services Division, 50 East Huron, Chicago, IL 60611.

Barry, A. (1998). Hispanic representation in literature for children and young adults. *Journal of Adolescent & Adult Literacy, 41,* 630–637.

Brozo, W., & Schmelzer, R. (1997). Wildmen, warriors, and lovers: Reaching boys through archetypal literature. *Journal of Adolescent & Adult Literacy, 41,* 4–11.

Carr, C. (2001). Not just for primary grades: A bibliography of picture books for secondary content teachers. *Journal of Adolescent & Adult Literacy, 45,* 146–153.

Commeyras, M., Bisplinghoff, B. S., & Olson, J. (Eds.). (2003). *Teachers as readers: Perspectives on the importance of reading in teachers' classrooms and lives.* Newark, DE: International Reading Association.

Copeland, M., & Goering, C. (2003). Blues you can use: Teaching the Faust theme through music, literature, and film. *Journal of Adolescent & Adult Literacy, 46,* 436–441.

International Reading Association. Young adults' choices. Annotated bibliography of newly published books appears each fall in the *Journal of Adolescent and Adult Literacy.*

National Council for the Social Studies/Children's Book Council. Notable children's trade books in the field of social studies. Appears each spring in *Social Education.*

National Science Teachers Association/Children's Book Council. Outstanding science trade books for children. Appears each spring in *Science and Children.*

Pilgreen, J. (2000). *The SSR handbook: How to organize and manage a sustained silent reading program.* Portsmouth, NH: Heinemann.

Quinn, K. B., Barone, B., Kearns, J., Stackhouse, S. A., & Zimmerman, M. E. (2003). Using a novel unit to help understand and prevent bullying in schools. *Journal of Adolescent & Adult Literacy, 46,* 582–591.

Rand, D., Parker, T., & Foster, S. (1998). *Black books galore! Guide to great African American children's books.* New York: Wiley.

Reeves, A. R. (2004). *Adolescents talk about reading: Exploring resistance to and engagement with text.* Newark, DE: International Reading Association.

Richardson, J. (2000). *Read it aloud! Using literature in the secondary content classroom.* Newark, DE: International Reading Association.

Schon, I. (2002). From *Dias de pinta* to *Las Christmas:* Noteworthy books in Spanish for adolescents. *Journal of Adolescent & Adult Literacy, 45,* 410–414.

Sprague, M., & Keeling, K. (2000). A library for Ophelia. *Journal of Adolescent & Adult Literacy, 43,* 640–647. (Novels that examine critical issues faced by girls)

Willis, A. (Ed.). (1998). *Teaching and using multicultural literature in grades 9–12: Moving beyond the canon.* Norwood, MA: Christopher Gordon.

Literacy Coaches: A Sign of the Times

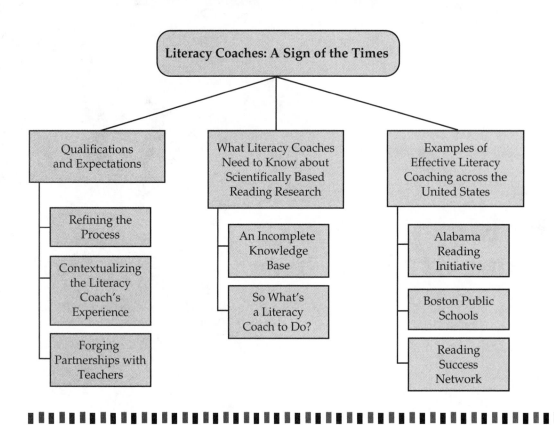

We open this chapter with a thumbnail sketch of the history of the term *literacy coach*. To help us accomplish the task in a relatively short space, we draw from *Pentimento: A Book of Portraits*, Lillian Hellman's autobiographical account of her relationships with others—images of people and ideas that influenced her once and were there for her still.

■ ■ ■ ■ ■ ■ ■

Old paint on canvas, as it ages, sometimes becomes transparent. When that happens it is possible, in some pictures, to see the original lines: a tree will show through a woman's dress, a child makes way for a dog, a large boat is no longer on an open sea. That is called pentimento because the painter "repented," changed his mind. Perhaps it would be as well to say that the old conception, replaced by a later choice, is a way of seeing and then seeing again (Hellman, 1973, p. 3).

■ ■ ■ ■ ■ ■ ■

In a number of ways, this analogy reminds Donna, Steve, and Victoria of the evolving role of literacy coaches. As early as the 1930s the concept of literacy coaches existed as support persons—reading specialists who worked with teachers to improve a school's reading program (Bean & Wilson, 1981). After World War II the old conception of literacy coach as reading specialist was gradually replaced—painted over—with the advent of the remedial reading teacher, in response to the public's concern that children were not learning to read properly through regular channels. By the 1960s, the figure of the remedial reading teacher was once again painted over—emerging this time as the reading resource person whose responsibilities were not unlike those of the earlier specialists of the 1930s. By the mid 1990s, the International Reading Association had established a Commission on the Role of the Reading Specialist (Long, 1995), and it was not long after that the concept of literacy coaches came into its own—this time with a label signifying its function and a descriptor that read "master teachers who provide essential leadership for the school's entire literacy program" (Sturtevant, 2003, p. 11).

Like the transparency of old paint in Hellman's *Pentimento*, the evolution of *literacy coach* provides a way of seeing and then seeing again. It also offers glimpses of why, despite the importance of the coach's role, there is still no one "official" written job description (Poglinco et al., 2003). It's a sign of the times, we're prone to say, when definitions of literacy coaching include responsibilities as disparate as setting up a model classroom, modeling instructional techniques in the classroom, administering a school's assessment plan, delivering professional development to teachers, and providing direct instruction to students (Bean, 2004). However, much of the disparity in what constitutes literacy coaching may ease soon, especially with the emergence of some new measures of uniformity in the qualifications and expectations for literacy coaches.

QUALIFICATIONS AND EXPECTATIONS

Recognizing the growing need for literacy coaches and the need to bring some measure of coherency to their role and responsibilities, the International Reading Association published a position statement in 2004, *The Role and Qualifications of the Reading Coach in the United States*, which recommended coaches meet the following minimum qualifications:

- Are excellent teachers of reading, preferably at the levels at which they are coaching

(A compromise position: As previous content area teachers in middle and secondary schools, Donna, Steve, and Victoria don't think literacy coaches necessarily need to be teachers of reading or have master's degrees in reading. Excellent teachers of science, math, social studies, and English can acquire knowledge of the reading processes and strategies and can, in their own right, become excellent coaches—in fact, they have the necessary content knowledge that reading teachers often lack. Since there are so few reading teachers at the high school level, this compromise makes sense to us.)

- Have in-depth knowledge of reading processes, acquisition, assessment, and instruction
- Have expertise in working with teachers to improve their practices
- Are excellent presenters and group leaders
- Have the experience or preparation that enables them to model, observe, and provide feedback about instruction for classroom teachers (n.p.)

Refining the Process

STANDARDS

The foregoing qualifications were stopgaps in the International Reading Association's move to bring some order to the field of literacy coaching. As pointed out in the 2004 position statement on *The Role and Qualifications of the Reading Coach in the United States*, IRA's stance at that time was that all coaches should meet the standards for reading specialist/literacy coach as spelled out in *Standards for Reading Professionals, Revised 2003*. In that set of standards, the expectation was that coaches regardless of their title (e.g., reading coach, literacy coach, reading specialist) should provide leadership, instruction in the form of professional development (rather than direct instruction to students), and supervision of program-wide assessments (but not the evaluation of teachers per se). As affirmed in IRA's 2004 position statement, "reading coaches who do not meet the Association's standards and who do not hold a reading specialist certificate should be working under the supervision of a reading professional who does meet those standards and holds a reading specialist certificate" (n.p.).

In 2006, the International Reading Association published *Standards for Middle and High School Literacy Coaches* in collaboration with the National Council of Teachers of English, National Council of Teachers of Mathematics, National Science Teachers Association, and the National Council for the Social Studies. The collaborators spent nearly a year and a half, with support from the Carnegie Corporation of New York, gathering empirical evidence to codify the "must have" (p. 4) competencies for coaches working at the secondary level. Described by its authors as a document that "represents an ideal" (p. 5), the report is practical in its recommendations. For instance, on the topic of securing the services of qualified literacy coaches at the middle and high school levels, the authors write: "In hiring, employers may not be able to find individuals who meet all the standards. In those cases, the goal should be for literacy coaches to meet these standards over a reasonable period of time" (p. 5).

Standards for Middle and High School Literacy Coaches (2006) is organized into two parts: leadership standards and content area literacy standards. In a section of the report titled "Challenges to Being a Secondary Literacy Coach," the authors acknowledge that coaches will need to develop expertise in working with large numbers of teachers housed in several content area departments who may not view themselves as being responsible for teaching reading and writing. From our own experiences in working at the secondary level, we know that there is a lack of awareness on the part of many teachers of the need to teach content and literacy skills simultaneously. We also recognize that it is impossible to generalize to all content area teachers. Still, based on our experiences, we believe there are useful guidelines for implementing the *Standards for Middle and High School Literacy Coaches*. To our way of thinking, developing a mutual respect is paramount. Although the coach may have information about effective literacy instruction, it is the content area teacher who knows her or his students' needs and who has the content knowledge necessary for making appropriate instructional choices from among the many available.

As a side note, when Donna and Victoria provided feedback to the International Reading Association on the latest set of standards for literacy coaches, they emphasized the importance of making certain that coaches are familiar with the standards of the various professional organizations (NCTM, NCTE, and the like) no matter what their own specialty areas might be. From experience, Donna, Steve, and Victoria know that becoming acquainted with the standards of the various disciplines is a prerequisite for helping middle and high school teachers improve their students' academic literacy. Without such knowledge, a literacy coach will be viewed as largely irrelevant in the secondary curriculum. In order to choose appropriate reading, writing, thinking, listening, and discussion strategies, one has to have knowledge not only of the pedagogical approaches available, but also knowledge of the specific content taught in a disciplinary area and the context in which such pedagogical and content knowledge meet and play out. It is toward the latter—the context in which literacy coaching takes place—that we now turn our attention.

Contextualizing the Literacy Coach's Experience

Typically there are two levels of literacy coaching: the building level and the school district level (Vogt & Shearer, 2003). At the building level, literacy coaches are resources to teachers, often providing professional materials, information about instructional strategies (including demonstration lessons in which the coaches use those strategies with students in a particular teacher's classroom), and organizing various study groups (such as teacher book clubs).

At the school district level, literacy coaches are typically in charge of designing and implementing year-long professional development for teachers as well as overseeing a district's literacy assessment plan. Literacy coaches' district-wide responsibilities also include serving as a liaison between schools and the community. This translates into working closely with special educators, community-wide service agencies, and parents to develop a supportive environment in which the combined pedagogical and content knowledge of

Dispelling Policy Myths

Dispelling a Myth

The oft-repeated motto "Every teacher a teacher of reading" sounds like a good idea, but a cursory glance at the research literature on content area reading and writing instruction for the last five decades clearly shows that it is not in synch with how most subject matter teachers think of themselves. First and foremost, these are teachers whose passion for engaging youth in a particular discipline frequently overrides whatever concern they might have for their students' literacy needs. This is not to say that they are oblivious to the difficulties some students in their classes might experience in comprehending and responding to various kinds of text (print, visual, aural, and digital). Rather, it is more often the case that subject matter teachers simply have not been adequately exposed in their undergraduate and graduate education courses to the processes involved in reading from and with a text, and to the steps that must be taken when student apathy sets in as a result of passive learning conditions.

Policy Implications

Reform-minded state boards of education, spurred on by mandates from the federal government to leave no child behind, are increasingly on the lookout for ways to improve literacy instruction in content area classrooms.

One such approach is the use of literacy coaches to provide ongoing professional development within a school—to work specifically at the middle and high school levels with subject matter teachers, modeling appropriate content literacy strategies, supervising a school's entire literacy program, ordering materials, and serving as a liaison between teachers and administrators. Recognizing the need for a large cadre of literacy coaches in schools that are not making annual yearly progress or that have no formal programs in place to close the literacy achievement gap for underserved students, the Carnegie Corporation of New York provided funding in 2005 that enabled representatives from various professional organizations to meet and draw up a set of standards for literacy coaching at the secondary level. This set of standards, published in 2006, is unique in that members of the International Reading Association, the National Council of Teachers of Mathematics, the National Council of Teachers of English, the National Science Teachers Association, and the National Council for the Social Studies collaborated on a document that reflects the need for literacy coaches who are well versed in the culture of secondary schools (middle and high) and able to provide leadership in improving academic literacy instruction in the various content areas.

the literacy coach can be used to improve teachers' instructional approaches and, ultimately, students' academic achievement in the content areas.

To accomplish both building and school district level initiatives, literacy coaches must depend to a large extent on the cooperation of teachers. As Donna, Steve, and Victoria have learned from their own experiences as teachers (and now as teacher educators), any "outsider" in a school district—and this is how a literacy coach may be perceived, at least initially—must earn the respect of the teachers with whom he or she will work. For this to happen, literacy coaches need to approach subject matter teachers with a great deal of respect for the content knowledge that the teachers possess. The goal is to build a collaborative working relationship in which teachers are viewed as the content specialists and literacy coaches as educators who have knowledge of a disciplinary field's content standards and how appropriate literacy instruction can support the achievement of those standards. Keeping in mind Hal Herber's (1978) point that content determines process—where process refers to the pedagogical knowledge associated with strategy and skill instruction—will help to ensure a favorable working relationship.

Forging Partnerships with Teachers

If there were one "magic wand" that Donna, Steve, and Victoria wish they could give to literacy coaches, it would be an instrument that conveyed instant and total knowledge about the culture of the particular secondary school in which the coaches will teach. Of course, this is exactly what makes such a wand-giving event a fantasy, or science fiction at best: regardless of the desirability of such knowledge, it will never be complete and for all practical purposes it can never be instant. No matter what type of middle or high school setting in which a literacy coach works, change is constant. What one knows today is not necessarily a guarantee that such knowledge will be viewed as a currency for negotiating a better tomorrow. Still, despite the times in which we live, fueled as they are by rapidly developing technologies and a shrinking globe, one thing we can count on for at least the foreseeable future is the maintenance of departmentalization in secondary schools. Although high schools are generally viewed as being more departmentalized than middle schools, the culture of both forms of secondary schooling suggest that "covering content"is first and foremost in most teachers' minds. With that as a given, where does the literacy coach begin?

In the following examples, we catalog effective techniques for what Victoria calls "getting a literacy coach's foot in the door." Although never a literacy coach herself (at least not by designated title), Victoria once worked full time as a science teacher in a junior high school in South Carolina where the principal made good use of both her pedagogical knowledge (i.e., how to teach content and process skills simultaneously) and her rapport with fellow teachers. Specifically, she recalls forging positive relationships with teachers using what she calls "faculty meeting commercials" and faculty development in an hour (one has to know Victoria personally to appreciate this concept, and her humor, fully).

Commercials during faculty meetings.   Describing a faculty meeting as "the principal's classroom," it was (and remains) Victoria's belief that teachers should leave such a meeting with something they can use right away in their content area classrooms. Specifically, she remembers doing a science experiment during one of the meetings to get fellow faculty to realize the importance of one's prior knowledge for understanding new concepts. She recommends that involving teachers in a prereading strategy such as K-W-L or List-Group-Label (see Chapter 6) doesn't take too long and requires little preparation (in terms of time spent duplicating materials or coming up with questions), but results in high levels of engagement when used in the classroom. The goal is that teachers, armed with this experience and a handout to remind them of ways to adapt the modeled strategy to their own content areas, will attempt to use it with their students. In reality, Victoria admits, the commercials did not always lead to such direct (and immediate) application. However, they frequently led to invitations to model the same strategies in teachers' classrooms.

Professional development in an hour.   Victoria recalls that in Orange County, Florida, where she taught back in the 1970s, literacy coaches (they were called reading resource specialists at the time) were expected to run an inservice activity each period of the day to which teachers could come if they wished. The coaches would demonstrate literacy strategies, using some of the same activities featured in this text. For example, they might develop teachers' theoretical and practical knowledge about the usefulness of strategies that tap into and/or build on students' background knowledge about a particular subject. If she were doing the same type of professional development today, Victoria emphasizes that she would enrich teachers' experiences by pointing out the various Web sites that are filled with resources for content area teaching. In particular, she would be sure to include Kathy Schrock's home page (http://kathyschrock.net/) and the *New York Times* Learning Network (www.nytimes.com/learning/).

Although excellent techniques, these examples of ways of getting one's foot in the door as a literacy coach do not guarantee any staying power, once inside. For long-term commitment to teaching content literacy, teachers will need to be supported through the use of methods such as those highlighted and described more fully in this text. However, we would be the first to point out that a thorough working knowledge of the approaches recommended in this volume will not address all of the issues a beginning (or even experienced) literacy coach can expect to meet when working with teachers in their own districts. Nor will it address the issue of teacher buy-in, or resistance as the case may be. Issues such as this one are not easily handled by the literacy coach alone. Because effective coaching calls for collaboration with teachers (Dole, 2004), the responsibilities of both content area teachers and coaches mix and mingle in complex ways.

Acknowledging that it is sometimes difficult to say "I don't know" or "I'm not sure," especially when one's reputation is on the line, is part of learning to become a literacy coach. Although an effective coach welcomes queries from teachers about a range of instructional issues, it is also the case that on occasion content area teachers may expect more guidance from literacy coaches than is reasonable. When expectations increase to the point that a coach feels overwhelmed by questions—in terms of both volume and level of specificity—it is time to say "I don't know" or "I'm not sure." Domain-specific knowledge, while useful and desirable in a coach, is also limited by the very fact that one cannot be a specialist in all content areas simultaneously (and often on short notice). Still, our experience has told us that it is better to address problems as they arise rather than pass them off with an empty promise to do something about them in the future. In the following activity, we present a scenario that calls for your consideration, either as someone who is presently coaching or preparing to become a literacy coach, or as a content area teacher.

ACTIVITY   Respond in writing to the following viewpoint. Be sure to include the pros and cons of taking this view from either a literacy coach's or a content area teacher's perspective.

Viewpoint: This is an excellent opportunity for literacy coaches to model how teachers really are researchers; for example, if a question needs answering, how might the literacy coach and teacher go about finding an answer together? Just as a teacher is not an all-knowing fount, neither is a literacy coach an inexhaustible source of solutions. If the literacy coach always answers the questions, it disenfranchises the teacher—both are, in reality, in this together.

WHAT LITERACY COACHES NEED TO KNOW ABOUT SCIENTIFICALLY BASED READING RESEARCH

In a chapter section somewhat playfully titled "SBRR and How Can You Get Some?" Walpole and McKenna (2004) provide a brief history of how scientifically based reading research (SBRR) became the watchword for the current skills-based reform movement in literacy education. As they explain, the National Reading Panel was commissioned by the U.S. Congress in 1997 to assess the extent to which generalizations could be drawn for classroom practice from the available research on reading instruction. The panel took a restrictive view of what counted as research and thereby limited its analyses to studies employing an experimental or quasi-experimental research design.

In experimental research, participants are randomly assigned to one or more intervention groups and a control group. Variables that might contribute to differences on outcome measures are carefully controlled, much like the research done in pharmaceutical labs. Needless to say, researchers often find it difficult (if not impossible) to convince schools that schedules must be interrupted in order to randomly assign students to treatment groups. Thus, they often settle for pre-existing groups, which means that their research will have a quasi-experimental design—one that is not quite as powerful a design as the true experiment, but more practical in the end.

Literacy coaches need to know the basics of research design if they are to interpret the findings in a knowledgeable way. They also need to know that certain kinds of research studies were excluded from the National Reading Panel's report (NRP, 2000) because they did not meet the Panel's criteria for being scientifically based reading research. For example, studies employing correlational methods or those adhering to a qualitative research methodology were absent from the report. The implications of such absences are discussed next.

An Incomplete Knowledge Base

**EVIDENCE-
BASED
RESEARCH**

Although better than nothing, the conclusions drawn from the National Reading Panel Report about effective comprehension instruction (see Chapter 7) must be considered in light of their limitations. Literacy coaches, for example, will need to keep in mind that while the Panel based its conclusions on 205 studies of text comprehension instruction that met their stringent criteria, these studies were designed primarily to test the effectiveness of certain cognitive processes in comprehending printed texts, often within controlled conditions that did not represent typical classroom learning environments.

Studies that took into account the sociocultural and situation-specific aspects of reading in content area classrooms (e.g., Dillon & Moje, 1998; Guzzetti & Hynd, 1998; Ivey, 1999; Moore, 1996; Obidah, 1998; Sturtevant, 1996) were excluded from consideration because they did not meet the criteria that the Panel had specified as evidence of scientifically based reading research. This resulted in a report that reflects a rather narrow and restrictive view of the reading process. In fact, six of the seven categories of comprehension instruction that the Panel found effective—self-questioning, answering a teacher's questions, comprehension monitoring, representing information using graphic organizers, making use of different text structures, and summarizing—point to strategies that content area teachers might use if their view of the reading process were one in which students work by themselves to extract information from printed texts. Also, as noted elsewhere (Wade & Moje, 2000), this rather narrow view of the reading process risks disenfranchising large groups of students for whom printed texts are not the primary means through which they learn.

A further limitation of the NRP's conclusions about effective comprehension instruction is its purposeful omission of studies that included English language learners and/or focused on the social organization of learning and instruction in large urban schools serving students who live in poverty. [Note, however, that Gutierrez et al. (2002) argue persuasively that "the issue is not poverty but rather how being a poor child becomes a debilitating condition in schools" (p. 329).] Thus, the larger issue is how schools treat poor children, many of whom speak a language other than English as their first language. Considering these limitations, then, a literacy coach might be left to wonder about the generalizability of the NRP's findings for teaching adolescents in urban schools, though granted it would be unwise to assume that urban youth would benefit any less from NRP-recommended strategies than their more economically advantaged peers.

So What's a Literacy Coach to Do?

We recommend that literacy coaches take every opportunity to inform themselves about current research and related policies in order that they may make up their own minds about the completeness or incompleteness of the knowledge base they are expected to implement. One excellent resource for keeping abreast of issues related to working with teachers and students at the middle and high school levels is the Alliance for Excellent Education (www.all4ed.org). By its own description, the Alliance for Excellent Education is a national policy, advocacy, and research organization created to help middle and high school students receive an excellent education. To inform the national debate about education policies and options, the Alliance for Excellent Education produces reports and other materials, including a biweekly newsletter, *The StraightAs,* which is also available on its Web site.

Making use of digital networked information is another way to keep abreast of what is going on in one's particular area of interest. It is also a way to experience firsthand the need to be critical consumers of the information that is offered. The fact that many teachers at the middle and high school levels fail to take advantage of this kind of information sharing is interesting, especially when they are the same teachers who expect their students to complete content area reading assignments on the Web. Literacy coaches might choose to address this issue by inviting the teachers with whom they work to read David Warlick's blog of October 10, 2005 (http://davidwarlick.com/2cents/2005/10/page/2/) in which he responded to the following question posed by Jon Pederson:

> What percentage of adults have the required skills to a) navigate this environment and b) be critical consumers of information? Can we expect our students to be proficient with these skills when adults aren't?

In response to this question, Warlick wrote:

> This is an excellent question, and I'd love to see the percents myself. The Pew Internet and American Life project has a lot of good statistics, but I'd answer the question this way. The adults who have managed to gain these skills are those who had to. People who work in professions that have access to networked, digital information and owe their success to decisions based on that information, have gained those skills, or else they don't do it any more. You learn it when you have to. It's called life-long learning. What's really

hurting our children is that most teachers *don't* have to. They can continue to teach with five-year-old textbooks, cut off from the world by four solid walls, and experience the success that their leaders expect. They won't teach contemporary literacy, because they don't need it themselves, because they're still working with an antiquated industrial age institution. (n.p.)

After reading Warlick's blog entry, a literacy coach might initiate a study group comprised of teachers interested in responding to the claims made in the blog. Do they agree? Disagree? Is Warlick's information based on reputable research? What challenges does he present? How might they address them and for what purpose?

Yet another means for helping literacy coaches keep abreast of what is happening in their field is the professional literature. A number of journals exist that are specific to literacy education. For example, the International Reading Association publishes *Reading Research Quarterly* and the *Journal of Adolescent & Adult Literacy*, both of which are available on-line as well as in hard copy. The National Reading Conference publishes the *Journal of Literacy Research* and an annual yearbook that captures what was on researchers' minds for that year. The College Reading Association's *Reading Research and Instruction* focuses on bridging research and practice. Other professional journals, though not specifically literacy oriented, often carry reports of research and essays that may tie indirectly to a literacy coach's responsibilities.

In the latter category, one of Donna's favorite journals is *Educational Horizons* because it features a column titled "From the Trenches." This column seems particularly relevant to literacy coaches inasmuch as they are continually on the firing line—caught sometimes between assisting teachers to implement an unpopular intervention and pleasing the administration in its bid to follow

Technology Tip

Blogs are increasingly popular among professionals who must depend on getting other people's views on policy-driven initiatives. For example, check out the literacy coach blog called the blahblahblog (http://npera2.tblog.com/) to see what literacy coaches and the teachers with whom they work are saying about the No Child Left Behind Act of 2001. Or read a posted entry at another blogging site that discusses the Striving Readers Initiative (www.gop.com/Blog/BlogPost.aspx?BlogPostID=224), which the U.S. Department of Education funded for the first time in 2005. Discover why Striving Readers has piqued the interest of many school districts nationwide as a result of the huge sums of money that will be available for hiring literacy coaches in districts that submit a winning proposal.

state and national policies. In the summer 2005 issue of *Educational Horizons*, Edward Rozycki, a twenty-five year veteran of the Philadelphia school district, wrote "Can We Trust 'Best Practices'?" In this piece, Rozycki proposed that one should evaluate an instructional intervention or practice by examining its positive characteristics while being on the watch for certain telltale warning signs. Among the positive signs that a purported "best practice" can be trusted, according to Rozycki, are these three characteristics: there is a firm basis for the research, an appropriate focus, and reasonable expectations.

A firm basis.   Ask yourself these questions: Is the research on a particular intervention situated within a theoretical framework that has stood the test of time and shown to be predictive of improved performance? Does it mesh with previous experience? If findings from the research go beyond previous experience, are they based on reasonable extrapolations from the theoretical framework supporting them? To what degree is the recommended practice based on wishful thinking? For example, the belief that bolstering an adolescent's self-esteem will lead to improved performance has had currency for generations; yet according to a recent article in *Scientific American* (Baumeister, Campbell, Krueger, & Vohs, 2005), self-esteem plays a minor role, at best, in improving achievement. Understanding that one study doesn't make or break a favorite hypothesis, of course, is also part of the literacy coach's arsenal of knowledge.

An appropriate focus.   The greater the degree to which research on a particular intervention addresses one's needs is another positive characteristic. As Rozycki (2005) reminds us in the following example, stretching the results of a study to fit within a particular context can lead to applications that are inappropriate:

> People tend to think of persons wearing uniforms as deporting themselves more appropriately than those wearing casual dress. And so it is that school boards are tempted to impose dress standards or uniforms on students. But student bodies are not cadres of persons in uniformed service, even if they are dressed to look like them. (p. 227)

ACTIVITY   Think of a time when you experienced the consequences of a misapplied finding from the research on literacy education. Describe the situation in writing or share the experience orally with a classmate. If possible, cite the study from which the application was inappropriately made. Then speculate as to why someone would want to stretch a finding to fit a particular context.

Reasonable expectations.   Attempting to apply the findings from an intervention study, no matter how good that study is, will backfire unless there is a reasonable set of expectations in place for implementing the intervention. In fact, one of the more common problems that literacy coaches face in working with teachers at the secondary level is getting them to buy into needs-based literacy instruction as a daily component of a schoolwide reading intervention. This problem is made even worse when students do not demonstrate improvement at the levels expected. As Walpole and McKenna (2004) wisely note, literacy coaches must come "to anticipate specific logjams in literacy growth at each grade level, and to coordinate personnel, materials, and schedules to address those logjams" (p. 162).

The negative characteristics, or warning signs, that a purported "best practice" may be of questionable value include the following: using similes or metaphors, engaging in sloganeering, and resorting to testimonials.

Similes or metaphors.   A "best practice" that is touted as effective in one domain and thus easily transported to another is suspect. As Rozycki (2005) pointed out, the following simile that compares measuring student learning to testing a river's saline level has been used to justify the No Child Left Behind Act's (2001) mandate for more frequent high-stakes testing of student progress: "Seeing whether kids are learning is like monitoring a river for salinity. You need repeated testing."

Sloganeering.   Another negative sign that should raise one's suspicions about a particular "best practice" is the use of a slogan to sell an idea, often in a misleading manner. Literacy coaches must remain on guard when they read research that suggests students must "learn to read before they read to learn." Although the slogan rolls nicely off one's tongue, it is potentially damaging from an instructional point of view. Separating the act of reading from one of its functions—reading to learn *something*—makes no sense. Though it can be argued that developmentally, beginning readers are different from skilled readers, the difference between these two groups lies more with the content or subject matter materials they are expected to read than with any overall purpose for reading.

Testimonials.   As Rozycki (2005) is quick to point out, testimonials are a dead give-away that something is amiss with a particular research study. The use of testimonials is most frequently associated with research on commercially produced literacy programs that have not been properly assessed by independent, third-party evaluators. Thus, claims such as "All school personnel in Dry Creek County found 'Intervention X' to be helpful and inspiring when used to teach adolescents how to read their content area texts critically" should be given no credence. Neither should vague references to suspect claims. For example, one thing that Steve tells his graduate students who are studying to become literacy specialists is this: When someone tells you, "The research says such-and-such," always ask for a specific citation. Say, "That's very interesting. Could you tell me where I could find that study? I'd like to read it." If the claim seems suspect and the person making the claim provides a citation, follow up on it. Does the research really say what the person claimed? Was the research done with a population of students similar to yours? If no specific citation is forthcoming, the claim has no merit.

EXAMPLES OF EFFECTIVE LITERACY COACHING ACROSS THE UNITED STATES

Increasingly, the professional literature is filled with examples of literacy coaches working in the context of Reading First, an elementary-based initiative that stems from the No Child Left Behind Act of 2001. As this edition of *Content Reading and Literacy: Succeeding in Today's Diverse Classrooms* was going to press, the Struggling Readers Initiative, which is sometimes referred to as the middle and high school version of Reading First, was barely getting off the ground. By 2006, however, we predict that there will be a large hue and cry for the increased presence of literacy coaches in secondary schools. With this in mind, we offer next three examples of effective literacy coaching in school districts across the United States. These are among several such districts that caught Elizabeth Sturtevant's attention as she prepared the Alliance for Education's first publication on literacy coaching (Sturtevant, 2003). A word of caution, however: As happens every time sampling is involved, many good programs had to be omitted. Thus, our challenge to you is to find one or more school districts in your state that employ literacy coaches at the middle and/or high school levels.

We begin our examples with the statewide Alabama Reading Initiative. Then we move to the Boston Public Schools district-wide initiative as an example of a large city's approach to literacy coaching. Finally, we travel westward for a look at what is called the Reading Success Network, which was designed by the Southern California Comprehensive Assistance Center in collaboration with WestEd (Sturtevant, 2003). In addition to having demonstrated some of the many ways that literacy coaches can effectively impact content area teachers' instruction and, in turn, students' academic literacy achievement, these three programs share some commonalities among themselves and with other successful programs involving literacy coaches. In Table 13.1, we highlight several of these commonalities.

Alabama Reading Initiative

Begun in 1998, the Alabama Reading Initiative (ARI) is a statewide K–12 initiative that includes participation of 132 middle schools and high schools (Sturtevant, 2003). This comprehensive program aims to put a literacy coach in every participating school. In order to qualify for participation in the ARI,

85 percent of a school's faculty must vote to join the initiative. As Sturtevant implies, the volunteer aspect of ARI has undoubtedly contributed to the gains in student achievement at Buckhorn High School. In addition, factors such as the following are viewed as co-contributors:

- Each ARI school must have a full-time reading specialist with in-depth, hands-on reading instruction experience.
- Teachers reinforce comprehension skills for all students, throughout the school day and across the entire curriculum.
- The principal is strongly committed to the reading initiative and knows how to provide educational leadership in the school. (Sturtevant, 2003, p. 14)

As an aside, Donna had the privilege of working briefly with two ARI professionals during the summer of 2005 when she joined them in planning a presentation for the Alliance for Excellent Education's High School Achievement Forum in Washington, DC. The two ARI participants were Tracy Wilson, the chair of the English Department and Literacy Coach at Buckhorn High School in New Market, Alabama, and Sarah Fanning, the Curriculum and Instructional Assistant at the same high school. Clearly, both of these women demonstrated in presenting their work at Buckhorn that literacy coaching is a team effort—one that leads to effective content area teaching and ultimately to student achievement on district-wide tests of academic literacy.

Boston Public Schools

With over 62,000 students enrolled, including over 18,000 in grades 9–12, and with 71 percent of all students qualifying for free and reduced lunch, Boston Public Schools may be said to represent many other large city districts across the United States that are working to close the literacy achievement gap by using many of the approaches sanctioned by the National Urban Alliance (see the associated Technology Tip for examples of these approaches). According to Sturtevant (2003), literacy coaches employed by the Boston Public Schools under the auspices of the Boston Plan for Excellence

> work with school staff on understanding and using [reading] workshop instruction. . . . They also take part in inquiry groups of teacher teams, meet with principals, and model instruction in lab sites. Upon request, they follow up in teachers' classrooms (modeling, observing, and co-teaching the strategy being studied in inquiry and the lab site). (p. 15)

Within the Boston Public Schools initiative, Fenway High School is often cited as an example of a school where students have made exceptional progress in academic literacy achievement. The school has been recognized by the U.S. Department of Education for its excellence. According to Sturtevant (2003), "the school employs a full-time literacy coordinator who co-teaches with core subject area teachers to incorporate literacy strategies and skills in the content

Technology Tip

For a comprehensive listing of projects in the National Urban Alliance that support many of the things literacy coaches are working to achieve in urban districts, check out the following site: www.nuatc.org/resources/weblinks/urban_ed/urban_education.html

areas. The coordinator also teaches a literacy foundations course for all ninth graders in the school" (pp. 15–16). By way of comment, it strikes Donna, Steve, and Victoria that indeed a literacy coach's title and responsibilities are still far from standardized across the United States.

Reading Success Network

The Reading Success Network (RSN) is equipped to provide a national cadre of trainers whose job it is to prepare teacher-coaches to work with content area teachers as they learn and practice effective strategies and approaches for teaching subject matter material. According to a description of RSN offered by Sturtevant (2003),

> Coaches and teachers participate in nine days of intensive professional development work related to analysis of data from their schools, and to build the coaching conversations that are important for success. Coaches then work in their own schools to support individual teachers and teams. They meet with teams, model, observe and discuss lessons, and help analyze student data. They also advise the principal on literacy-related issues. Importantly, the RSN maintains an ongoing network of support for the coaches. It brings them together on a regular basis to discuss common issues and coaching strategies. Principals also participate in a series of professional development sessions and attend network meetings, as they are seen as key to the success of the program. (p. 16)

	Alabama Reading Initiative	Boston Public Schools	Reading Success Network
Coaching is part of a larger professional development plan	X	X	X
Coaching is a team effort	X	X	X
Coaching requires an ongoing network of support	X	X	X

FIGURE 13.1   **Similarities among programs in approaches to coaching**

Regardless of the individual differences noted in the programs that Sturtevant (2003) surveyed, we were struck by the similarities in approaches to coaching, shown in Figure 13.1.

SUMMARY

Whether working one-on-one or with groups of teachers, experts in the area of professional support systems suggest that learning to coach is a balancing act. We couldn't agree more with two such experts, Sharon Walpole and Michael McKenna, when they write:

> To create a truly comprehensive system of professional support, we urge literacy coaches to balance time providing support inside classrooms (through observations, feedback, and modeling) with time providing support outside the classroom (through knowledge-building sessions, data-based presentations, and book clubs). We urge literacy coaches to provide support both orally (through discussion) and in writing (through confidential, written feedback about teaching). (Walpole & McKenna, 2004, p. 190)

To this balancing act, we would add (as former content area classroom teachers) the need for teachers to cooperate as fully as possible with the literacy coaches in their respective buildings and school districts. For as Hall (2004), writing in the *Carnegie Reporter*, reminds us, setting standards for literacy coaches working with middle and high school content area teachers is but the first step in improving instructional methods that can, in turn, affect students' academic literacy achievement. All the steps that follow will definitely need the input and cooperation of teachers who are well versed in their subject matter specialties and willing to give the concept of literacy coaching a try.

SUGGESTED READINGS

Blachowicz, C. L. Z., Obrochta, C., & Fogelberg, E. (2005). Literacy coaching for change. *Educational Leadership, 62*(6).

Guth, N. D., & Pettengill, S. S. (2005). *Leading a successful reading program: Administrators and reading specialists working together to make it happen.* Newark, DE: International Reading Association.

Henwood, G. F. (1999/2000). A new role for the reading specialist: Contributing toward a high school's collaborative educational culture. *Journal of Adolescent & Adult Literacy, 43,* 316–325.

Lapp, D., Fisher, D., Flood, J., & Frey, N. (2003). Dual role of the urban reading specialist. *Journal of Staff Development, 24*(2), 33–36.

Neufeld, B., & Roper, D. (2003). *Coaching: A strategy for developing instructional capacity.* Washington, DC and Providence, RI: The Aspen Institute Program on Education and the Annenberg Institute for School Reform.

Quatroche, D. J., & Bean, R. M., & Hamilton, R. L. (2001). The role of the reading specialist: A review of research. *The Reading Teacher, 55,* 282–294.

Stewart, R. A., & O'Brien, D. G. (1989). Resistance to content area reading: A focus on preservice teachers. *Journal of Reading, 32,* 396–401.

Toll, C. (2005). *The literacy coach' s survival guide: Essential questions—and answers—for literacy coaches.* Newark, DE: International Reading Association.

Word Lover's Booklist

APPENDIX

A

American Heritage Dictionaries (2002). *The American heritage dictionary for learners of English*. Boston: Houghton-Mifflin.

Ammer, Christine (1989). *Fighting words: From war, rebellion, and other combative capers*. New York: Dell.

Amner, Christine (1997). *The American heritage dictionary of idioms*. Boston: Houghton Mifflin.

Blumenfeld, Warren (1989). *Pretty ugly: More oxymorons and other illogical expressions that make absolute sense*. New York: Putnam.

Bowler, P. (1994). *The superior person's second book of weird and wondrous words*. New York: Laurel.

Bryson, B. (2002). *Bryson's dictionary of troublesome words: A writer's guide to getting it right*. New York: Broadway Books.

Burchfield, Robert, & Fowler, Henry W. (2000). *The new Fowler's modern English usage*, 3rd ed. New York: Oxford University Press.

Carver, C. (1991). *A history of English in its own words*. New York: Harper-Collins.

Clark, Audrey (2003). *The Penguin dictionary of geography*. New York: Penguin.

Cole, Chris (1999). *Wordplay: A curious dictionary of language oddities*. New York: Sterling.

Cutler, C. (1994). *O brave new words: Native American loan words in current English*. Norman: University of Oklahoma Press.

Dunkling, Leslie (1990). *A dictionary of epithets and terms of address*. New York: Routledge.

Elster, Charles (1988). *There is no zoo in zoology and other beastly mispronunciations*. New York: Collier Books.

Flexner, S. (1993). *Wise words and wives' tales: The origins, meanings, and time-honored wisdom of proverbs and folk sayings*. New York: Avon.

Freeman, M. (1993). *Hue and cry and humble pie: The stories behind the words*. New York: Plume.

Garrison, Webb (2000). *What's in a word? Fascinating stories of more than 300 everyday words and phrases*. Nashville, TN: Rutledge Hill.

Green, Jonathan (1991). *Neologisms: New words since 1960*. London: Bloomsbury.

Hendrickson, R. (1994). *Grand slams, hat tricks, and alley-oops: A sports fan's book of words*. New York: Prentice Hall.

Lederer, Richard (1989). *Anguished English*. New York: Pocket Books.

Mills, J. (1993). *Womanwords: A dictionary of words about women*. New York: Henry Holt.

Neaman, Judith, & Silver, Carole (1990). *Kind words: A thesaurus of euphemisms.* New York: Avon.

Randall, Bernice (1991). *When is a pig, a hog? A guide to confoundingly related English words.* Englewood Cliffs, NJ: Prentice Hall.

Rawson, Hugh (1989). *Wicked words: A treasury of curses, insults, put-downs, and other formerly unprintable terms from Anglo-Saxon times to the present.* New York: Crown.

Rovin, J. (1994). *What's the difference? A compendium of commonly confused and misused words.* New York: Ballantine.

Sheehan, Michael (2000). *Word parts dictionary: Standard and reverse listings of prefixes, suffixes, and combining forms.* Jefferson, NC: McFarland.

Smitherman-Donaldson, G. (2000). *Black talk: Words and phrases from the hood to the amen corner.* Boston: Mariner Books.

Spears, Richard (2001). *Contemporary American slang: An up-to-date guide to the slang of American English.* New York: McGraw-Hill.

Urdang, Laurence, LaRoche, Nancy, & Hunsinger, Walter (Eds.) (1998) *Picturesque expressions: A thematic dictionary.* New Lyme, CT: Verbatim Books.

Westbrook, Alonzo (2002) *Hip hoptionary: The dictionary of hip hop terminology.* New York: Harlem Moon.

Read-Aloud Books for Content Areas

History and Social Studies

Beyer, Rick (2003). *The greatest stories never told: 100 tales from history to astonish, bewilder, and stupefy.* New York: HarperResource.

Boardman, Barrington (1988). *Flappers, bootleggers, "Typhoid Mary" and the bomb: An anecdotal history of the United States from 1923–1945.* New York: Harper and Row.

Davis, Kenneth (2001). *Don't know much about the presidents.* New York: HarperCollins.

Farquhar, M. (2003). *A treasury of great American scandals: Tantalizing true tales of historic misbehavior by the founding fathers and others who let freedom swing.* New York: Penguin Books.

Felton, Bruce (2003). *What were they thinking? Really bad ideas throughout history.* Guilford, CT: Globe Pequot Press.

Hay, Peter (1988). *All the presidents' ladies: Anecdotes of the women behind the men in the White House.* New York: Viking.

Hoose, Phillip (1993). *It's our world, too! Stories of young people who are making a difference.* Boston: Little, Brown. (Young social activists, including those from the Revolutionary War, abolitionists, labor, and civil rights)

Kane, Joseph, Anzovin, Steven, & Podell, Janet (1997). *Famous first facts: A record of first happenings, discoveries and inventions in American history* (5th ed.). New York: Wilson.

O'Brien, C. (2004). *Secret lives of the U.S. presidents.* Philadelphia: Quirk Books.

Rossi, Melissa (2003). *What every American should know about the rest of the world: Your guide to today's hot spots, hot shots, and incendiary issues.* New York: Plume.

Spinrad, Leonard, Spinrad, Thelma, Miller, Anistatia, & Brown, Jared (1999). *On this day in history.* Paramus, NJ: Prentice Hall.

Wagman, John (1990). *On this day in America: An illustrated almanac of history, sports, science, and culture.* New York: Gallery Books.

Science and Mathematics

Adair, Robert (1990). *The physics of baseball.* New York: Harper & Row.

Aschenbach, Joel (1996). *Why things are & why things aren't.* New York: Ballantine.

Berry, A. (1993). *The book of scientific anecdotes.* Buffalo, NY: Prometheus.

Bryson, Bill (2003). *A short history of nearly everything.* New York: Broadway Books.

Flaste, Richard (Ed.). (1991). *The New York Times book of science literacy: What everyone needs to know from Newton to the knuckleball.* New York: HarperCollins.

Flatow, Ira (1992). *They all laughed: From the lightbulb to the laser.* New York: HarperCollins.

Gardner, Martin (2001). *The colossal book of mathematics: Classic puzzles, paradoxes, and problems.* New York: Norton.

Goldberg, Philip (1990). *The Babinski reflex and 70 other useful and amusing metaphors from science, psychology, business, sports and everyday life.* Los Angeles: Tarcher.

Lee, Martin (2000). *40 fabulous math mysteries kids can't resist.* New York: Scholastic.

MacEachern, Diane (1990). *Save our planet: 750 everyday ways you can help clean up the earth.* New York: Dell.

Masoff, Joy (2000). *Oh, yuck: The encyclopedia of everything nasty.* New York: Workman.

McLain, B. (2001). *What makes flamingos pink?* New York: HarperCollins. (A book of questions and answers about all sorts of science facts)

Murphree, Tom, & Miller, Mary (1998). *Watching weather (Accidental scientist series).* New York: Henry Holt.

Park, Robert (2000). *Voodoo science: The road from foolishness to fraud.* New York: Oxford University Press.

Paulos, John A. (1999). *Once upon a number: The hidden mathematical logic of stories.* New York: Basic Books.

Ray, C. (1997). *The New York Times science questions and answers.* New York: Anchor.

Roberts, R. (2001). *Serendipity: Accidental discoveries in science.* New York: Wiley.

Seff, Philip, & Seff, Nancy (1996). *Petrified lightning and more amazing stories from "Our Fascinating Earth."* Chicago: NTC/Contemporary.

Shermer, M. (2002). *Why people believe weird things: Pseudoscience, superstition, and other confusions of our time.* New York: Henry Holt.

Tahan, M. (1993). *The man who counted: A collection of mathematic adventures.* New York: Norton.

Waldbauer, Gilbert (2000). *Millions of monarchs, bunches of beetles: How bugs find strength in numbers.* Cambridge, MA: Harvard University Press.

Gallimaufry

Bathroom Readers' Institute (1998). *Uncle John's great big bathroom reader.* Ashland, OR: Bathroom Readers' Press.

Carroll, Robert (2003). *The skeptic's dictionary: A collection of strange beliefs, amusing deceptions, and dangerous delusions.* New York: Wiley.

Craughwell, Thomas (1999). *Alligators in the sewer and 444 other absolutely true stories that happened to a friend of a friend of a friend.* New York: Black Dog & Leventhal.

Drimmer, Frederick. (1988). *Born different: Amazing stories of very special people.* New York: Bantam.

Dunn, Jerry (Ed.). (1991). *Tricks of the trade: Over 79 experts reveal the secrets behind what they do.* Boston: Houghton Mifflin.

Goldberg, M. Hirsch (1984). *The blunder book: Colossal errors, minor mistakes and surprising slipups that have changed the course of history.* New York: Morrow.

Kohn, Alfie (1990). *You know what they say: The truth behind popular beliefs.* New York: HarperCollins.

Schott, Ben (2003). *Schott's original miscellany.* New York: Bloomsbury.

Seuling, Barbara (1991). *You can't count a billion dollars! And other little known facts about money.* New York: Ballantine.

Tuleja, Tad (1999). *Fabulous fallacies: More than 300 popular beliefs that are not true.* New York: BBS.

Dead Ends

Donaldson, Norman, & Donaldson, Betty (1989). *How did they die?* New York: St. Martin's.

Forbes, Malcolm (with Jeff Block) (1988). *They went that-away.* New York: Ballantine.

Panati, Charles (1988). *Extraordinary endings of practically everything and everybody.* New York: Harper & Row.

Shushan, E. R. (1990). *Grave matters.* New York: Ballantine.

Silverman, Stephen (1991). *Where there's a will.* New York: HarperCollins.

Slee, Christopher (1990). *The Chameleon book of lasts.* Huntingdon, UK: Chameleon.

Trade Books for Science, Math, and Social Studies

Discoverers and Discoveries

Adair, Gene (1989). *George Washington Carver*. Broomall, PA: Chelsea House. (YA)

Billings, Charlene (1989). *Grace Hopper: Navy admiral and computer pioneer*. Hillsdale, NJ: Enslow. (YA)

Brooks, P. (1989). *The house of life: Rachel Carson at work*. Boston: Houghton Mifflin.

Bryson, Bill (2003). *A short history of nearly everything*. New York: Broadway Books. (Everything from the Big Bang to the rise of civilizations, including many of the scientists who made important discoveries about our world and the universe)

Feynman, Richard (1999). *Meaning of it all: Thoughts of a citizen scientist*. Boulder, CO: Perseus.

Hartman, William (2003). *A traveler's guide to Mars: The mysterious landscapes of the red planet*. New York: Workman.

Kass-Simon, G., & Farnes, P. (1993). *Women in science: Righting the record*. Bloomington: Indiana University Press.

Kidd, R., Kessler, J., Kidd, J., & Morin, K. (1995). *Distinguished African American scientists of the 20th century*. Phoenix: Oryx Press.

Smith, Jane (1990). *Patenting the sun: Polio and the Salk vaccine*. New York: Morrow.

Vare, Ethlie, & Ptacek, Greg (1989). *Mothers of invention: From the bra to the bomb, forgotten women and their unforgettable ideas*. New York: Morrow.

Disasters

Ballard, Robert (with Rick Archbold) (1987). *The discovery of the Titanic*. New York: Warner/Madison.

Gale, Robert, & Hauser, Thomas (1988). *Final warning: The legacy of Chernobyl*. New York: Warner.

Lauber, Patricia (1986). *Volcano: The eruption and healing of Mt. St. Helens*. New York: Bradbury.

Petroski, Henry (1985). *To engineer is human*. New York: St. Martin's.

Preston, Richard (1994). *The hot zone*. New York: Random House. (Outbreak of the ebola virus)

Scotti, R. A. (2003). *Sudden sea: The great hurricane of 1938*. New York: Little, Brown.

Von Drehele, David (2003). *Triangle: The fire that changed America*. New York: Atlantic Monthly Press.

Ward, Kaari (Ed.). (1989). *Great disasters*. Pleasantville, NY: Reader's Digest.

Winchester, S. (2003). *Krakatoa: The day the world exploded, August 27, 1883*. (The eruption and resultant tsunami that killed nearly 40,000 people; also describes the wave of anti-Western militancy among Muslims that followed the eruption)

Ecology and the Environment

Bash, B. (1990). *Urban roosts: Where birds nest in the city*. San Francisco: Sierra Club Books.

Buckley, B., Hopkins, E., & Whitaker, R. (2004). *Weather: A visual guide*. Richmond Hill, Ontario, Canada: Firefly Books.

Kohl, J., & Kohl, H. (2000). *The view from the oak*. New York: New Press. (How animals perceive reality differently from humans)

LaBastille, Anne (1991). *Woodswoman*. New York: Dutton. (Autobiographical story of a woman who lived alone in the Adirondacks, showing both the beauties and stark realities of nature)

Lomborg, Bjorn (2001). *The skeptical environmentalist: Measuring the real state of the world*. New York: Cambridge University Press.

McDonough, William & Braungart, Michael (2002). *Cradle to cradle: Remaking the way we make things*. New York: North Point Press.

Paulsen, Gary (1994). *Father Water, Mother Woods: Essays on hunting and fishing in the North Woods*. New York: Delacorte.

Mathematics

Devlin, Keith (2000). *The math gene: How mathematical thinking evolved and why numbers are like gossip*. New York: Basic Books.

Harman, Hollis (1999). *Money sense for kids*. Hauppauge, NY: Barron's.

Livio, Mario (2003). *The golden ratio: The story of phi, the world's most astonishing number*. New York: Broadway Books.

Pappas, Theoni (1991). *Math talk: Mathematical ideas in poems for two voices*. San Carlos, CA: Wide World/Tetra.

Paulos, John (1990). *Innumeracy: Mathematical illiteracy and its consequences*. New York: Random House.

Ryan, M. (2002). *Everyday math for everyday life: A handbook for when it just doesn't add up*. New York: Warner Books.

Seife, Charles (2000). *Zero: The biography of a dangerous idea*. New York: Penguin.

Stein, Sherman (2001). *How the other half thinks: Adventures in mathematical reasoning*. New York: McGraw-Hill.

Weaver, J. (2002). *What are the odds? The chances of extraordinary events in everyday life*. New York: Prometheus.

Life Sciences

Fleischman, J. (2002). *Phineas Gage: A gruesome but true story about brain science*. New York: Houghton Mifflin.

Fridell, R. (2004). *Decoding life: Unraveling the mysteries of the genome*. New York: Lerner Publishing.

McClellan, M. (2003). *Organ and tissue transplants: Medical miracles and challenges*. Berkeley Heights, NJ: Enslow.

Skurzynski, G. (2004). *Are we alone? Scientists search for life in space*. Washington, DC: National Geographic Society.

Physics and Chemistry

Aschenbach, Joel (1999). *Captured by aliens: The search for life and truth in a very large universe.* New York: Simon & Schuster.

Blanding, Sharon, & Monteleone, John (2003). *The science of sports: How things in sports work.* New York: Barnes & Noble.

Cash, T. (2001). *101 physics tricks: Fun experiments with everyday materials.* New York: Sterling Publishers.

Dickinson, Terence (1998). *Nightwatch: A practical guide to viewing the universe,* 3rd ed. Toronto: Firefly Books.

Downie, N. (2001). *Vacuum bazookas, electric rainbow jelly, and 27 other Sunday science projects.* Princeton, NJ: Princeton University Press.

Grossblatt, Ben (2003). *Air hockey science.* New York: Tangerine Press. (The physics and technology of air hockey; includes plans and instructions for building an air hockey table)

Hawking, Stephen (2003). *The theory of everything: The origin and fate of the universe.* North Miami Beach, FL: New Millennium Press.

Le Couteur, P., & Burreson, J. (2003). *Napoleon's buttons: How 17 molecules changed history.* New York: Penguin Putnam. (A true account of how chemicals changed history. Clear explanations of organic chemistry principles and vocabulary.)

Moring, G. (2000). *The idiot's guide to understanding Einstein.* Indianapolis, IN: Alpha Books.

Morris, R. (2003). *The last sorcerers: The path from alchemy to the periodic table.* Washington, DC: Joseph Henry Press. (A history of the development of the periodic chart of the elements)

Paterniti, M. (2000). *Driving Mr. Einstein.* New York: Dell. (Fictional account of the famous physicist)

Sacks, Oliver (2002). *Uncle Tungsten: Memories of a chemical boyhood.* New York: Vintage Books.

Science Fiction and Fiction about Science

Adams, Douglas (1979). *Hitchhiker's guide to the galaxy.* New York: Harmony. (The first of a series; "Hitchhiker" fans are legion)

Anderson, M. T. (2002). *Feed.* Cambridge, MA: Candlewick Press. (YA fiction; a future world where television and computers are connected directly into people's brains and teens are driven by fashion and consumerism)

Asimov, Isaac (1987). *Fantastic voyage.* New York: Bantam. (Based on the screenplay; a journey inside the human body)

Cavelos, J. (2000). *The science of Star Wars.* New York: St. Martin's Griffin.

Clancy, Tom (1991). *The sum of all fears.* New York: Putnam. (Terrorists plant a nuclear bomb)

Cook, Robin (1997). *Chromosome 6.* New York: Berkley. (Scientists researching apes in Africa venture into cloning)

Crichton, Michael (1990). *Jurassic Park.* New York: Knopf. (Scientists use fossil DNA to clone dinosaurs for a theme park)

Defelice, Cynthia (1998). *The ghost of Fossil Glen.* New York: Avon. (YA fiction; a girl is pursued by a ghost after a near-death experience while fossil hunting)

Hesse, Karen (1996). *The music of dolphins.* New York: Scholastic. (YA fiction; child is lost at sea and adopted by dolphins; after her rescue, she is sent to a center for scientific research, where she is taught human language but yearns for her dolphin family)

Klass, David (1994). *California blue.* New York: Scholastic. (YA fiction; battle between environmentalists and community dependent on a local mill)

Lawrence, Louise (1985). *Children of the dust.* New York: Harper & Row. (Mutant and nonmutant survivors of a nuclear holocaust)

History

Colman, P. (2002). *Where the action was: Woman war correspondents in World War II.* New York: Crown Publishers.

Herbert, J. (2001). *Marco Polo for kids: His marvelous journey to China.* Chicago: Chicago Review Press.

Ross, S. (2000). *The war in Kosovo.* Austin, TX: Steck Vaughan.

Slavery Times

Armstrong, J. (1992). *Steal away . . . to freedom.* New York: Scholastic. (Story of two girls, one white, one black, and the Underground Railroad)

Clark, Margaret (1980). *Freedom crossing.* New York: Scholastic. (Underground Railroad story set in Lewiston, NY)

Cosner, Sharon (1991). *The Underground Railroad.* New York: Venture.

Franklin, John & Schweninger, Loren (2000). *Runaway slaves: Rebels on the plantation.* New York: Oxford University Press.

Hamilton, V. (1993). *Many thousand gone: African-Americans from slavery to freedom.* New York: Knopf. (African American folk tales and stories, including stories of escape from slavery)

Lester, Julius (1968). *To be a slave.* New York: Scholastic. (True narratives of the lives of slaves)

Meyers, Walter D. (1998). *Amistad: Long road to freedom.* New York: Putnam.

Rappaport, D. (1991). *Escape from slavery: Five journeys to freedom.* New York: HarperCollins.

Wisler, G. Clifton (1996). *Caleb's choice.* New York: Dutton. (YA fiction; set in Texas, the story of a white youth's entanglement in the area's sharp divisions over the Fugitive Slave Law)

Civil War

Chang, Ina (1991). *A separate battle: Women and the Civil War.* New York: Scholastic.

Clapp, Patricia (1986). *Tamarack tree.* New York: Lothrop, Lee & Shepard. (YA fiction; the siege of Vicksburg)

Freedman, R. (1987). *Lincoln: A photobiography.* Boston: Houghton Mifflin.

Hunt, Irene (1964). *Across five Aprils.* New York: Berkley. (YA fiction; life on an Illinois farm during the Civil War)

Marrin, Albert (1994). *Unconditional surrender: U.S. Grant and the Civil War.* New York: Atheneum. (Biography, illustrated with photographs)

Marrin, Albert (1994). *Virginia's general: Robert E. Lee and the Civil War.* New York: Atheneum. (Biography, illustrated with photographs)

Rinaldi, Ann (1993). *In my father's house.* New York: Scholastic. (YA fiction; story of a Southern family during the Civil War)

Shaara, Michael (1974). *The killer angels.* New York: Ballantine. (Fiction; the Battle of Gettysburg)

Immigration

Ashabranner, Brent (with Melissa Ashabranner) (1987). *Into a strange land; Unaccompanied refugee youth in America.* New York: Putnam.

Bode, Janet (1989). *New kids on the block: Oral histories of immigrant teens.* New York: Watts.

Conover, Ted (1987). *Coyotes.* New York: Vintage. (The lives of Mexicans who illegally cross the U.S. border)

Denenberg, Barry (1997). *So far from home: The diary of Mary Driscoll, an Irish mill girl.* New York: Scholastic. (YA fiction)

Hest, Amy (2003). *When Jessie came across the sea.* Cambridge, MA: Candlewick Press. (Picture book about a 13-year-old girl's journey from Eastern Europe to New York's Lower East Side)

Meltzer, M. (2002). *Bound for America: The story of the European immigrants.* Tarrytown, NY: Benchmark Books.

Paulsen, Gary (1987). *The crossing.* New York: Dell. (YA fiction; an orphaned 14-year-old attempts to cross the U.S.-Mexican border)

Rolvaag, Ole (1991). *Giants in the earth.* New York: Harper. (A story of Norwegian families who settled in the Dakotas)

Wartski, Maureen (1982). *Long way from home.* New York: Dutton. (YA fiction; a young Vietnamese refugee tries to establish himself in America)

Culturally Conscious Trade Books

African American

Busby, Margaret (Ed.). (1992). *Daughters of Africa: An international anthology of words and writings by women of African descent from the ancient Egyptian to the present.* New York: Pantheon.

Campbell, Bebe Moore (1998). *Singing in the comeback choir.* New York: Putnam.

Flake, S. G. (1998). *The skin I'm in.* New York: Jump at the Sun Hyperion Paperbacks for Children. (YA fiction; an authentic portrayal of African American teenagers; winner of the 1999 Coretta Scott King Award and chosen as the American Library Association's Best Book for Young Adults in 1999, this book humorously and cleverly pulls young reluctant readers into a world rarely represented in YA fiction)

Giovanni, Nikki (1974). *Ego-tripping and other poems for young people.* Chicago: Hill. (YA)

Giovanni, Nikki (1994). *Racism 101.* New York: Quill. (Essays on race relations)

Hamilton, Virginia (Ed.). (1985). *The people could fly: American black folktales.* New York: Knopf.

Hudson, Wade (Ed.). (1993). *Pass it on: African-American poetry for children* (Floyd Cooper, Illust.). New York: Scholastic. (Illustrated collection of poetry by such African American poets as Langston Hughes, Nikki Giovanni, Eloise Greenfield, and Lucille Clifton)

Hurston, Zora Neale (1937). *Their eyes were watching God.* New York: Harper & Row. (Story of an independent African American woman in the rural South)

Johnson, Angela (2000). *Heaven.* Thorndike, ME: Thorndike Press. (YA fiction; a fourteen-year-old girl discovers that the family she has been living with her whole life are not her real parents)

Laird, R., & Laird, T. (1997). *Still I rise: A cartoon history of African-Americans.* New York: Norton. (Graphic novel)

Lester, Julius (1987). *The tales of Uncle Remus: The adventures of Brer Rabbit.* New York: Dial.

Malcolm X (with Alex Haley) (1964). *The autobiography of Malcolm X.* New York: Ballantine.

McCall, Nathan (1994). *Makes me wanna holler: A young black man in America.* New York: Random House.

Monceaux, M., & Katcher, R. (1999). *My heroes, my people: African-Americans and Native Americans in the West.* (M. Monceaux, Illus.). New York: Farrar, Straus & Giroux. (Short biographies and illustrations; relatively easy reading; especially interesting are the many multiethnic personalities who lived, worked, and pioneered in the American West—a fascinating mingling of cultures.)

Morrison, Toni (1971). *Beloved*. New York: Knopf. (Former slave and her family; life before and after Civil War)

Myers, Walter Dean (1999). *Monster*. New York: HarperCollins. (YA fiction by prolific novelist, poet, and biographer; 16-year-old boy accused of a violent crime)

Njeri, Itabari (1990). *Every good-bye ain't gone*. New York: Random House. (A series of essays about growing up in New York City during the 1950s and 1960s by a writer of African American, East Indian, Native American, English, and French descent)

Schroeder, Alan (1989). *Ragtime Tumpie*. Boston: Little, Brown. (YA; biography of entertainer Josephine Baker)

Taylor, Mildred (1976). *Roll of thunder, hear my cry*. New York: Dial. (YA fiction; first in a series of three novels about the struggles of a black family in Mississippi in the 1930s)

Terry, Wallace (Ed.). (1985). *Bloods: An oral history of the Vietnam War by black veterans*. New York: Ballantine.

Thomas, Joyce Carol (2001). *The blacker the berry*. New York: HarperCollins. (Poems by well-known young adult author)

Wideman, John E. (1985). *Brothers and keepers*. New York: Oxford University Press. (An African American college professor explores the painful contrasts between his life and that of his brother in prison)

Asian American

Crew, Linda (1989). *Children of the river*. New York: Dell. (YA fiction; story of a Cambodian American high school student in Oregon)

Hamanaka, Sheila (1990). *The journey: Japanese Americans, racism, and renewal*. New York: Orchard. (A picture book suitable for third grade through high school)

Huynh, Quang Nhuong (1986). *Land I lost: Adventures of a boy in Vietnam*. New York: Harper & Row.

Kingston, Maxine Hong (1977). *Woman warrior: Memoirs of a girlhood among ghosts*. New York: Random House. (The struggle to keep a Chinese identity while assimilating into American society)

Kiyama, H. (1999). *The four immigrants manga*. (F. Schodt, trans.). Berkeley, CA: Stone Bridge Press. (Graphic novel)

Lee, Marie (1992). *Finding my voice*. Boston: Houghton Mifflin. (YA fiction; Ellen Sung, a Korean American, goes to Harvard as a freshman)

Mah, Adeline Yen (1999). *Chinese Cinderella: The true story of an unwanted daughter*. New York: Delacorte.

Na, An (2003). *A step from heaven*. New York: Puffin. (YA fiction; story of a Korean immigrant family)

Sone, Monica (1979). *Nisei daughter*. Seattle: University of Washington Press. (A Japanese American tells of growing up in Seattle in the 1930s and relocation during World War II)

Tan, Amy (1989). *The joy luck club*. New York: Random House. (Fiction)

Uchida, Yoshiko (1981). *A jar of dreams*. New York: Atheneum. (YA fiction; the first in a trilogy of books about an 11-year-old Japanese American girl)

Yep, Lawrence (1977). *Child of the owl*. New York: Harper & Row. (YA fiction; child struggles to balance her Chinese roots and her identity with mainstream America)

Hispanic

Alvarez, J. (2002). *Before we were free*. New York: Knopf. (YA fiction; Dominican Republic)

Anaya, Rudolfo (1976). *Bless me Ultima*. Berkeley, CA: Tonatiuh. (Fiction about a Chicano boy)

Bernardo, Anilu (1996). *Jumping off to freedom*. Houston: Piñata. (YA fiction; family leaves Cuba on a raft for the United States)

Burke, David (1999). *Street Spanish: Slang dictionary and thesaurus*. New York: Wiley.

Carlson, Lori (Ed.). (1994). *Cool salsa: Bilingual poems on growing up in the United States*. New York: Henry Holt.

Cisneros, Sandra (1986). *The house on Mango Street*. Houston: Arte Publico. (A collection of Mexican American stories)

Chavez, D. (1994). *Face of an angel*. New York: Warner. (Story of a family in rural New Mexico)

Cruz, Victor Hernandez (1989). *Rhythm, content & flavor*. Houston: Arte Publico Press. (Poetry; Puerto Rican)

Day, F. A. (1997). *Latino and Latina voices in literature for children and teenagers*. Portsmouth, NH: Heinemann.

Gonzales, B. D. (1995). *Sweet fifteen*. Houston: Piñata Books. (A girl's quinceaños celebration is changed by the death of her father just before her fifteenth birthday)

Jiménez, Francisco (2002). *Breaking through*. Boston: Houghton-Mifflin. (YA; autobiographical stories of a migrant family in California)

Mohr, Nicholasa (1979). *Felita*. New York: Dial. (YA fiction; a family faces prejudice when they move from a predominantly Hispanic neighborhood)

Ortiz Cofer, Judith (1995). *An island like you: Stories of the barrio*. New York: Orchard.

Poniatowska, Elene, & Stellweg, Carla (1992). *Frida Kahlo: The camera seduced*. San Francisco: Chronicle. (Photos and essays about the great Mexican artist)

Quinonez, Ernesto (2000). *Bodega dreams*. New York: Vintage. (Novel set in Spanish Harlem)

Rodriquez, Luis (1993). *Always running: La vida loca: Gang days in L.A.* New York: Touchstone.

Ryan, Pam Muñoz (2000). *Esperanza Rising*. New York: Scholastic. (YA fiction; daughter of wealthy Mexican loses her father, migrates to California during the Great Depression; unions, strikes, Okies, cultural conflicts, exploration of class differences)

Santiago, E. (1994). *When I was Puerto Rican*. New York: Prentice Hall. (Autobiographical stories of a young woman's acculturation to the mainland United States)

Soto, Gary (2000). *Nickel and dime*. Albuquerque: University of New Mexico Press. (Story of three Mexican American men and street life in Oakland, California)

Thomas, Piri (1967). *Down these mean streets*. New York: Vintage. (Puerto Rican)

Velasquez, Gloria (1994). *Juanita fights the school board*. Houston: Piñata Press. (YA fiction)

Islam

Ansary, T. (2002). *West of Kabul, East of New York: An Afghan American Story*. New York: Bantam.

Idilibi, Ulfat (1998). *Grandfather's tale*. (Peter Clark, Trans.). London: Quartet. (A young boy's pilgrimage to Mecca, growth into adulthood, and fulfillment of his family duties)

Morris, Neil (2003). *The atlas of Islam: People, daily life and traditions*. Hauppauge, NY: Barron's.

Sacco, J. (2001). *Palestine*. Seattle, WA: Fantagraphic Books. (Graphic novel)

Satrapi, M. (2003). *Persepolis: The story of a childhood*. Paris: L'Association. (Graphic novel)

Wormser, Richard (2002). *American Islam: Growing up Muslim in America*. New York: Walker. (Looks at the lives of two different groups, immigrants from the Middle East and African Americans)

Jewish

Brooks, Jerome (1990). *Naked in winter*. New York: Orchard. (YA fiction; a 16-year-old boy copes with moving to a new neighborhood, family troubles, and sexual awakening)

Grossman, Mendel, & Dabba, Frank (2000). *My secret camera: Life in the Lodz ghetto*. New York: Harcourt.

Klein, G. W. (1995). *All but my life*. New York: Hill & Wang. (Holocaust survivor's story; film version won documentary Oscar in 1996)

Mazer, Norma Fox (1999). *Good night Maman*. New York: Harcourt. (YA fiction)

Singer, Isaac B. (1980). *The power of light: Eight stories for Hannukah*. New York: Farrar, Straus & Giroux.

Spiegelman, A. (1986) *Maus*. New York: Pantheon Books. (Graphic novel of the Holocaust)

Native American

Bouchard, D. (1997). *The elders are watching*. Vancouver, BC: Raincoast.

Esbensen, Barbara J. (1989). *Ladder to the sky: How the gift of healing came to the Ojibway Nation*. Boston: Little, Brown.

Fleischman, Paul (1990). *Saturnalia*. New York: HarperCollins. (YA fiction; a Narrangansett boy is sold as a slave to a Boston family in the 1660s)

Hernandez, I. (1992). *Heartbeat drumbeat*. Houston: Arte Publico Press. (YA fiction; story of a girl with a Chicano father and Navajo mother)

Norman, Howard (1989). *How Glooskap outwits the ice giants and other tales of the Maritime Indians*. Boston: Little, Brown.

Rees, Celia (2003). *Sorceress*. Cambridge, MA: Candlewick Press. (YA fiction; a Native American college student begins to investigate mysteries in her past)

Thomasma, Kenneth (1984). *Soun Tetoken: Nez Perce boy*. Grand Rapids, MI: Baker. (YA fiction; the story of the Nez Perce tribe before and during the war of 1877)

Thorn, James (1989). *Panther in the sky*. New York: Ballantine. (A fictional account of Tecumseh, leader of the Shawnee tribe in the late eighteenth century)

Diverse Cultures

Carmi, D. (2001). *Samir and Yonatan*. (Yael Lotan, Trans.). New York: Scholastic. (YA fiction; Israel and Palestine)

Lynch, Chris (1996). *Blue-eyed son: A trilogy*. New York: HarperCollins. (YA fiction; three books about Mick, the younger son in an Irish American family, and his struggles to come to terms with his heritage, his family, racism, and alcoholism)

McBride, James (1996). *The color of water: A black man's tribute to his white mother*. New York: Riverhead.

Mead, Alice (1996). *Adem's cross*. New York: Farrar, Straus & Giroux. (YA fiction; the violence and brutality of war in the former Yugoslavia, as seen in the story of a minority Albanian boy in Serb-controlled territory)

Meyer, Carolyn (1996). *Gideon's people*. San Diego: Harcourt Brace/Gulliver Books. (YA fiction; family and ethnic conflicts around the relationship of Isaac, son of immigrant Jews, and his Amish friend Gideon)

Woodson, Jacqueline (1994). *I hadn't meant to tell you this*. New York: Delacorte. (YA fiction; a friendship between two girls, one an African American from a protective and relatively well-off family, the other a white girl who is the victim of abuse)

Zusak, Markus. (2000). *Fighting Ruben Wolfe*. New York: Push, Scholastic. (YA fiction; an intense tale about boxing, brotherly solidarity, and searching for self-respect in a family down on its luck as a result of economically hard times)

Standards for the Content Areas—Web Ready/At a Glance

English/Language Arts Standards

www.reading.org/resources/issues/reports/learning_standards.html/

Foreign Language Standards

www.actfl.org/i4a/pages/index.cfm?pageid=3392

Information Literacy Standards

www.ala.org/aaslTemplate.cfm?Section=Information_Power&Template=/ContentMan
agement/ContentDisplay.cfm&ContentID=19937

Literacy Coach Standards

www.reading.org/resources/issues/reports/coaching.html

Middle Web Guide to Standards-Based Reform

www.middleweb.com/SBRGuide.html

National Council for the Social Studies Standards

www.ncss.org/

National Council of Teachers of Mathematics Standards

www.nctm.org/

National Educational Technology Standards

http://cnets.iste.org/

National Science Education Standards

www.nap.edu/catalog/4962.html

National Standards for History

www.sscnet.ucla.edu/nchs/standards/

National Standards for Music Education

www.menc.org/publication/books/standards.htm

National Standards for Physical Education

www.aahperd.org/naspe/publications-nationalstandards.html

Standards for Art Education

www.naea-reston.org/publications-list.html#standards_for_art_education

Teachers of English to Speakers of Other Languages

www.tesol.org/seccss_asp?CID=113&DID=1583

References

|||||||||||||||||||

Abrahamson, R., & Carter, B. (1991, January). Non-fiction: The missing piece in the middle. *English Journal, 79,* 52–58.

Adamson, H. D. (1993). *Academic competence: Theory and classroom practice, preparing ESL students for content courses.* New York: Longman.

Agee, J. (1999, November). "There it was, that one sex scene": English teachers on censorship. *English Journal, 89,* 61–69.

Alexander, P. (2005). *The path to competence: A life-span developmental perspective on reading.* Retrieved August 29, 2005 from National Reading Conference Web site: http://www.nrconline.org.

Alexander, P. A., & Jetton, T. L. (2000). Learning from text: A multidimensional and developmental perspective. In M. L. Kamil, P. B. Mosenthal, P. D. Pearson, & R. Barr (Eds.), *Handbook of reading research: Volume 3* (pp. 285–310). Mahwah, NJ: Erlbaum.

Alfassi, M. (1998). Reading for meaning: The efficacy of reciprocal teaching in fostering reading comprehension in high school students in remedial reading classes. *American Educational Research Journal, 35,* 309–332.

Allan, C. (1999). Poets of comrades: Addressing sexual orientation in the English classroom. *English Journal, 88(6),* 97–101.

Allen, J. (1995). *It's never too late: Leading adolescents to lifelong literacy.* Portsmouth, NH: Heinemann.

Allen, J., & Gonzalez, K. (1998). *There's room for me here: Literacy workshop in the middle school.* York, ME: Stenhouse.

Allington, R. (2002). Troubling times: A short historical perspective. In R. Allington, (Ed.), *Big Brother and the national reading curriculum: How ideology trumped evidence* (pp. 3–46). Portsmouth, NH: Heinemann.

Allington, R. L., & McGill-Franzen, A. (2000, Winter). Looking back, looking forward: Excerpts from a conversation about teaching reading in the 21st century. *English Update: A Newsletter from the Center on English Learning & Achievement,* 4–5.

Alsup, J. (2003). Politicizing young adult literature. Reading Anderson's *Speak* as a critical text. *Journal of Adolescent & Adult Literacy, 47,* 158–166.

Alvermann, D. E. (1992). The discussion web: A graphic aid for learning across the curriculum. *The Reading Teacher, 45,* 92–99.

Alvermann, D. E. (1995–96). Peer-led discussions: Whose interests are served? *Journal of Adolescent & Adult Literacy, 39,* 282–289.

Alvermann, D. E. (2000). Classroom talk about texts: Is it dear, cheap, or a bargain at any price? In B. M. Taylor, M. F. Graves, & P. Van Den Broek (Eds.), *Reading for meaning* (pp. 136–151). New York: Teachers College Press.

Alvermann, D. E. (2002). Effective literacy instruction for adolescents. *Journal of Literacy Research, 34,* 189–208.

Alvermann, D. E., & Commeyras, M. (1998). Feminist poststructuralist perspectives on the language of reading assessment: Authenticity and performance. In C. Harrison, M. Bailey, & A. Dewar (Eds.), *New paradigms in reading assessment* (pp. 50–60). London: Routledge.

Alvermann, D. E., Fitzgerald, J., & Simpson, M. (in press). Teaching and learning in reading. In P. Alexander & P. Winne (Eds.), *Handbook of Educational Psychology* (2nd ed.). Mahwah, NJ: Erlbaum.

Alvermann, D. E., & Hagood, M. C. (2000). Critical media literacy: Research, theory, and practice in "new times." *Journal of Educational Research, 93*, 193–205.

Alvermann, D. E., & Moore, D. W. (1991). Secondary school reading. In R. Barr, M. L. Kamil, P. Mosenthal, & P. D. Pearson (Eds.), *Handbook of reading research: Volume 2* (pp. 951–983). New York: Longman.

Alvermann, D. E., & Nealy, A. (2004). Professional development content for reading educators at the middle and high school levels. In D. Strickland & M. Kamil (Eds.), *Improving reading achievement through professional development* (pp. 85–93). Norwood, MA: Christopher-Gordon.

Alvermann, D. E., Commeyras, M., Young, J., Hinson, D., & Randall, S. (1996). *The gendered language of texts and classrooms: Teachers and students exploring multiple perspectives and interpretations* (Instructional Resource No. 23). Athens: University of Georgia, National Reading Research Center.

Alvermann, D. E., Dillon, D. R., & O'Brien, D. G. (1987). *Using discussion to promote reading comprehension.* Newark, DE: International Reading Association.

Alvermann, D. E., Hagood, M. C., Heron, A., Hughes, P., & Williams, K. (2000a). *Critical literacy practices in after-school media clubs.* Final report submitted to the Spencer Foundation, Chicago, September 30.

Alvermann, D. E., Hagood, M. C., Heron, A., Hughes, P., & Williams, K. (2000b). *The media club study.* Paper presented at the annual meeting of the College Reading Association, St. Petersburg Beach, FL.

Alvermann, D. E., Moon, J. S., & Hagood, M. C. (1999). *Popular culture in the classroom: Teaching and researching critical media literacy.* Newark, DE: International Reading Association and the National Reading Conference.

Alvermann, D. E., O'Brien, D. G., & Dillon, D. R. (1990). What teachers do when they say they're having discussions of content reading assignments: A qualitative analysis. *Reading Research Quarterly, 25*, 296–322.

Alvermann, D. E., Olson, J., & Umpleby, R. (1993). Learning to do research together. In S. Hudelson & J. Lindfors (Eds.), *Delicate balances: Collaborative research in language education* (pp. 112–124).

Urbana, IL: National Council for Teachers of English.

Alvermann, D. E., Smith, L., & Readence, J. (1985). Prior knowledge activation and the comprehension of compatible and incompatible text. *Reading Research Quarterly, 20*, 420–436.

Alvermann, D. E., Young, J. P., Green, C., & Wisenbaker, J. M. (1999). Adolescents' perceptions and negotiations of literacy practices in after-school read and talk clubs. *American Educational Research Journal, 36*, 221–264.

Alvermann, D. E., Young, J. P., Weaver, D., Hinchman, K. A., Moore, D. W., Phelps, S. F., Thrash, E. C., & Zalewski, P. (1996b). Middle and high school students' perceptions of how they experience text-based discussions: A multicase study. *Reading Research Quarterly, 31*, 244–267.

American Association of University Women Educational Foundation (2000). *Tech-savvy: Educating girls in the new computer age.* Washington, DC: American Association of University Women Educational Foundation.

American Educational Research Association, American Psychological Association, & National Council on Measurement in Education (1999). *Standards for Educational and Psychological Testing.* Washington, DC: AERA.

Amit-Talai, V., & Wulff, H. (Eds.). (1995). *Youth cultures: A cross-cultural perspective.* New York: Routledge.

Anders, P., & Bos, C. (1986). Semantic feature analysis: An interactive strategy for vocabulary development and text comprehension. *Journal of Reading, 29*, 610–616.

Anders, P. L., & Guzzetti, B. J. (1996). *Literacy instruction in the content areas.* New York: Harcourt Brace.

Anderson-Inman, L., & Horney, M. (1994). The electrotext project: Hypertext reading patterns of middle school students. *Journal of Educational Multimedia and Hypermedia, 3*, 71–91.

Anderson, R. C. (1984). Role of the reader's schema in comprehension, learning, and memory. In R. C. Anderson, J. Osborn, & R. J. Tierney (Eds.), *Learning to read in American schools: Basal readers and content texts* (pp. 243–258). Hillsdale, NJ: Erlbaum.

Anderson, R. C., Hiebert, E., Scott, J., & Wilkinson, I. (1985). *Becoming a nation of readers: The report of the Commission on Reading.* Washington, DC: National Institute of Education.

Anderson, R. C., Reynolds, R. E., Schallert, D. L., & Goetz, E. T. (1977). Frameworks for comprehending discourse. *American Educational Research Journal, 14,* 367–382.

Anderson, T. H., & Armbruster, B. B. (1984). Studying. In P. D. Pearson, R. Barr, M. Kamil, & P. Mosenthal (Eds.), *Handbook of reading research* (pp. 657–679). New York: Longman.

Anderson, T. H., & Armbruster, B. B. (1984). Content area textbooks. In R. C. Anderson, J. Osborn, & R. Tierney (Eds.), *Learning to read in American schools: Basal readers and content texts* (pp. 193–226). Hillsdale, NJ: Erlbaum.

Anderson, V., & Hidi, S. (1988/1989). Teaching students to summarize. *Educational Leadership, 4,* 26–29.

André, M., & Anderson, T. H. (1978/1979). The development and evaluation of a self-questioning study technique. *Reading Research Quarterly, 14,* 605–623.

Andrews, S. E. (2000). Writing to learn in content area reading class. In D. W. Moore, D. E. Alvermann, & K. A. Hinchman (Eds.), *Struggling adolescent readers: A collection of teaching strategies* (pp. 217–219). Newark, DE: International Reading Association.

Applebee, A., Langer, J., Mullis, I., Latham, A., & Gentile, C. (1994). *NAEP 1992 writing report card.* Washington, DC: U.S. Department of Education, Office of Educational Research and Improvement.

Ardizzone, P. (1992, November). The journal—A tool in the ESL classroom. *Writing Teacher, 6,* 31–33.

Armbruster, B. B., Anderson, T. H., & Ostertag, J. (1987). Does text structure/summarization instruction facilitate learning from expository text? *Reading Research Quarterly, 22,* 331–346.

Arthur, B. (1991). Working with new ESL students in a junior high school reading class. *Journal of Reading, 34,* 628–631.

Aschbacher, P. R. (1991). Humanitas: A thematic curriculum. *Educational Leadership, 49(2),* 16–19.

Athanases, S. (1998). Diverse learners, diverse texts: Exploring identity and difference through literary encounters. *Journal of Literacy Research, 30,* 273–296.

Atwell, N. (1987). *In the middle: Writing, reading, and learning with adolescents.* Portsmouth, NH: Boynton/Cook.

Atwell, N. (1998). *In the middle: New understandings about writing, reading and learning* (2nd ed.). Portsmouth, NH: Heinemann.

Au, K. (1998). Social constructivism and the school literacy learning of students of diverse backgrounds. *Journal of Literacy Research, 30,* 297–319.

Au, K. H. (1980). Participation structures in reading lessons: Analysis of a culturally appropriate instructional event. *Anthropology and Education Quarterly, 11,* 91–115.

Ausubel, D. (1968). *Educational psychology: A cognitive view.* New York: Holt, Rinehart & Winston.

Baines, L. (2000). Same facts, different audience. In L. Baines & A. Kunkel (Eds.), *Going Bohemian: Activities that engage adolescents in the art of writing well,* (pp. 78–80). Newark, DE: International Reading Association.

Baker, L., & Brown, A. L. (1980). *Metacognitive skills and reading* (Tech. Rep. No. 188). Urbana: University of Illinois, Center for the Study of Reading.

Baker, L., & Brown, A. L. (1984). Metacognitive skills and reading. In P. D. Pearson, R. Barr, M. Kamil, & P. Mosenthal (Eds.), *Handbook of reading research* (pp. 353–394). New York: Longman.

Balajthy, E. (1990). Hypertext, hypermedia, and metacognition: Research and instructional implications for disabled readers. *Reading, Writing and Learning Disabilities, 6,* 183–190.

Bank, S. (1986). Assessing reading interests of adolescent students. *Educational Research Quarterly, 10(3),* 8–13.

Barron, R. (1969). The use of vocabulary as an advance organizer. In H. Herber & P. Sanders (Eds.), *Research in reading in the content areas: First year report* (pp. 29–39). Syracuse, NY: Syracuse University Reading and Language Arts Center.

Barry, A. (1998). Hispanic representation in literature for children and young adults. *Journal of Adolescent & Adult Literacy, 41,* 630–637.

Bauer, E., & Garcia, G. (1997). Blurring the lines between reading assessment and instruction: A case study of a low-income student in the lowest reading group. In C. Kinzer, K. Hinchman, & D. Leu (Eds.), *Inquiries in literacy theory and practice* (pp. 166–176). 46th Yearbook of the National Reading Conference. Chicago, IL: National Reading Conference.

Bauer, E. (1999). The promise of alternative literacy assessments in the classroom: A review of empirical studies. *Reading Research & Instruction, 38,* 153–168.

Baumann, F. J., Kame'enui, E. J., & Ash, G. W. (2003). Research on vocabulary instruction: Voltaire Redux. In J. Flood, D. Lapp, J. Squire, & J. Jensen (Eds.), *Handbook of research on teaching the English language arts* (2nd ed., pp. 752–785). Mahwah, NJ: Erlbaum.

Baumann, J. (1984). The effectiveness of a direct instruction paradigm for teaching main idea comprehension. *Reading Research Quarterly, 20,* 93–115.

Baumeister, R. F., Campbell, J. D., Krueger, J. I., & Vohs, D. D. (2005). Exploding the self-esteem myth. *Scientific American* (January), 84–91.

Beach, R. (1997). Stances of resistance and engagement in responding to multicultural literature. In T. Rogers & A. Soter (Eds.), *Reading across cultures: Teaching literature in a diverse society* (pp. 69–94). New York: Teachers College Press.

Bean, R., & Wilson, R. (1981). *Effecting change in school reading programs: The Resource role.* Newark, DE: International Reading Association.

Bean, R. M. (2004). Promoting effective literacy instruction: The challenge for literacy coaches. *The California Reader, 37*(3), 58–63.

Bean, T. (1992). Combining writing fluency and vocabulary development through writing roulette. In E. Dishner, T. Bean, J. Readence, & D. Moore (Eds.), *Reading in the content areas: Improving classroom instruction* (3rd ed., pp. 247–254). Dubuque, IA: Kendall/Hunt.

Bean, T., & Bishop, A. (1992). Polar opposites: A strategy for guiding students' critical reading and discussion. In E. Dishner, T. Bean, J. Readence, & D. Moore (Eds.), *Reading in the content areas: Improving classroom instruction* (3rd ed., pp. 247–254). Dubuque, IA: Kendall/Hunt.

Bean, T., Bean, S., & Bean, K. (1999). Intergenerational conversations and two adolescents' multiple literacies: Implications for redefining content area literacy. *Journal of Adolescent & Adult Literacy, 42,* 438–448.

Bean, T., Kile, R., & Readence, J. (1996). Using trade books to encourage critical thinking about citizenship in high school social studies. *Social Education, 60,* 227–230.

Bean, T. W. (1997). Preservice teachers' selection and use of content area literacy strategies. *Journal of Educational Research, 90,* 154–163.

Beane, J. A. (1990). *A middle school curriculum from rhetoric to reality.* Columbus, OH: National Middle School Association.

Beck, I., & McKeown, M. (1991). Social studies texts are hard to understand: Mediating some of the difficulties. *Language Arts, 68,* 482–490.

Beck, I., McKeown, M., Hamilton, R., & Kucan, L. (1997). *Questioning the author: An approach for enhancing student engagement with text.* Newark, DE: International Reading Association.

Beers, K. (1996). No time, no interest, no way! The three voices of aliteracy. *School Library Journal, 42,* 110–113.

Beers, K. (2003). *When kids can't read: What teachers can do. A guide for teachers 6–12.* Portsmouth, NH: Heinemann.

Berenson, S., & Carter, G. (1995). Changing assessment practices in science and mathematics. *School Science & Mathematics, 95,* 182–186.

Bergeron, B., & Rudenga, E. (1996). Seeking authenticity: What is "real" about thematic literacy instruction? *The Reading Teacher, 49,* 544–551.

Berliner, D., & Biddle, B. (1995). *The manufactured crisis: Myths, frauds, and the attack on America's public schools.* Reading, MA: Addison-Wesley.

Bernhardt, E. B. (2000). Second-language reading as a case study of reading scholarship in the 20th century. In M. L. Kamil, P. B. Mosenthal, P. D. Pearson, & R. Barr (Eds.), *Handbook of reading research: Volume 3* (pp. 791–811). Mahwah, NJ: Erlbaum.

Bernhardt, E. B. (2003). Challenges to reading research from a multilingual world. *Reading Research Quarterly, 38,* 112–117.

Berryman, L., & Russell, D. (2001, July). Portfolios across the curriculum: Whole school assessment in Kentucky. *English Journal, 90,* 76–83.

Biancarosa, G., & Snow, C. E. (2004). *Reading Next— A Vision for Action and Research in Middle and High School Literacy: A Report to Carnegie Corporation of New York.* Washington, DC: Alliance for Excellent

Education. Also available at: http://www.all4ed. org/publications/Reading Next/index.html.

Bigelow, B. (1994). Getting off the track: Stories from an untracked classroom. In B. Bigelow, L. Christensen, S. Karp, B. Miner, & B. Peterson (Eds.), *Rethinking our classrooms*. Milwaukee, WI: Rethinking Schools.

Biloff, E. (1996). *The Killer Angels*: A case study of historical fiction in the social studies curriculum. *Social Studies, 87*, 19–23.

Bintz, W. P. (1993). Resistant readers in secondary education: Some insights and implications. *Journal of Reading, 36*, 604–615.

Bishop, J. H. (1989). Why the apathy in American high schools? *Educational Researcher, 18*(1), 6–10, 42.

Bishop, R. (1990). Walk tall in the world: African American literature for today's children. *Journal of Negro Education, 59*, 556–565.

Blachowicz, C. (1986). Making connections: Alternatives to the vocabulary notebook. *Journal of Reading, 29*, 543–549.

Blachowicz, C. (1991). Vocabulary instruction in content classes for special needs learners: Why and how? *Reading, Writing, and Learning Disabilities, 7*, 297–308.

Blachowicz, C., & Fisher, P. (2000). Vocabulary instruction. In M. Kamil, P. Mosenthal, P. D. Pearson, & R. Barr (Eds.), *Handbook of reading research* (Vol. 3, pp. 503–523). Mahwah, NJ: Erlbaum.

Blachowicz, C., & Zabroske, B. (1990). Context instruction: A metacognitive approach for at-risk readers. *Journal of Reading, 33*, 504–508.

Blackman, J. A. (1992). Confronting Thomas Jefferson, slave owner. *Phi Delta Kappan, 74*, 220–222.

Blake, M., & Majors, P. (1995). Recycled words: Holistic instruction for LEP students. *Journal of Adolescent & Adult Literacy, 39*, 132–137.

Blanco, J. (2003). *Please stop laughing at me*. Toronto, Canada: Adams Media Corporation.

Bloom, H. (1994). *The western canon: The books and school of the ages*. New York: Harcourt Brace.

Bloome, D. (1992, April). Researching language: Languaging research. *Newsletter of the Reading & Writing Program*. Amherst: University of Massachusetts, School of Education.

Bloome, D., & Green, J. L. (1992). Educational contexts of literacy. *Annual Review of Applied Linguistics, 12*, 49–70.

Bolter, D. J. (1992). Literature in the electronic writing space. In M. Tuman (Ed.), *Literacy online: The promise (and peril) of reading and writing with computers*. Pittsburgh, PA: University of Pittsburgh Press.

Bond, L., & Roeber, E. (1995). *The status of state student assessment programs in the United States*. Washington, DC: Council of Chief State School Officers/North Central Regional Educational Laboratory.

Boorstin, D., & Kelley, B. (2005). *A history of the United States*. Needham, MA: Prentice Hall.

Bormuth, J. (1968). Cloze test readability: Criterion referenced scores. *Journal of Educational Measurement, 5*, 189–196.

Boyd, D. (1996). Dominance concealed through diversity: Implications of inadequate perspectives on cultural pluralism. *Harvard Educational Review, 66*, 609–630.

Bransford, J. D. (1979). *Human cognition: Learning, understanding, and remembering*. Belmont, CA: Wadsworth.

Bransford, J. D., & McCarrell, N. S. (1974). A sketch of a cognitive approach to comprehension. In W. B. Weimer & D. S. Palermo (Eds.), *Cognition and the symbolic processes*. Hillsdale, NJ: Erlbaum.

Brautigan, R. (1971). *Revenge of the lawn*. New York: Simon & Schuster.

Britzman, D. P. (1987). Cultural myths in the making of a teacher: Biography and social structure in teacher education. In M. Okazawa-Rey, J. Anderson, & R. Traver (Eds.), *Teachers, teaching, and teacher education* (pp. 220–233). Cambridge, MA: Harvard University Press.

Brock, C. H., & Gavelek, J. R. (1998). Fostering children's engagement with texts: A sociocultural perspective. In T. E. Raphael & K. H. Au (Eds.), *Literature-based instruction: Reshaping the curriculum* (pp. 71–94). Norwood, MA: Christopher-Gordon.

Brodkey, L., (1989). On the subjects of class and gender in "The Literacy Letters." *College English, 51*, 125–141.

Bromley, K. (1993). *Journaling: Engagements in reading, writing, and thinking*. New York: Scholastic.

Brown, A. L., & Campione, J. C. (1994). Guided discovery in a community of learners. In K. McGilly (Ed.), *Classroom lessons: Integrating cognitive theory and classroom practice* (pp. 229–270). Cambridge, MA: MIT Press.

Brown, A. L., & Palincsar, A. S. (1989). Guided, cooperative learning and individual knowledge acquisition. In L. B. Resnick (Ed.), *Knowing, learning, and instruction: Essays in honor of Robert Glaser* (pp. 393–451). Hillsdale, NJ: Erlbaum.

Brown, G. T. L. (2003, September/October). Searching informational texts: Text and task characteristics that affect performance. *Reading Online, 7*(2). Available: http://www.readingonline.org/articles/art_index.asp?HREF=brown/index.html

Brown, J. S., & Duguid, P. (1996). Stolen knowledge. In H. McLellan (Ed.), *Situated learning perspectives* (pp. 47–56). Englewood Cliffs, NJ: Educational Technology Publications.

Brown, J. S., Collins, A., & Duguid, P. (1989). Situated cognition and the culture of learning. *Educational Researcher, 18*(1), 32–42.

Brown, R. (2002). Straddling two worlds: Self-directed comprehension instruction for middle schoolers. In C. Block & M. Pressley (Eds.), *Comprehension instruction: Research-based best practice* (pp. 337–350). New York: Guilford.

Brozo, W. (2000). Hiding out in secondary classrooms: Coping strategies of unsuccessful readers. In D. Moore, D. Alvermann, & K. Hinchman (Eds.), *Struggling adolescent readers: A collection of teaching strategies* (pp. 51–56). Newark, DE: International Reading Association.

Brozo, W. (2002). *To be a boy, to be a reader: Engaging teen and preteen boys in active literacy.* Newark, DE: International Reading Association.

Brozo, W. G. (2003). Writing to learn with SPAWN prompts. *Thinking Classroom, 4*(3), 44–45.

Brozo, W., & Hargis, C. (2003). Taking seriously the idea of reform: One high school's efforts to make reading more responsive to all students. *Journal of Adolescent & Adult Literacy, 47*, 14–23.

Brozo, W., & Simpson, M. (1995). *Readers, teachers, learners: Expanding literacy in secondary schools* (2nd ed.). Columbus, OH: Merrill.

Bruce, C. (1997). *The Einstein paradox.* Reading, MA: Perseus Books.

Bruner, J. S. (1986). *Actual minds, possible worlds.* Cambridge, MA: Harvard University Press.

Buckingham, D. (1993). Just playing games. *The English & Media Magazine, 28*, 21–25.

Buckingham, D., & Sefton-Green, J. (1994). *Cultural studies goes to school: Reading and teaching popular media.* London: Taylor & Francis.

Buehl, D. (2001). *Classroom strategies for interactive learning* (2nd ed.). Newark, DE: International Reading Association.

Bulgren, J. A., Deshler, D. D., & Schumaker, J. B. (1997). Use of a recall enhancement routine and strategies in inclusive secondary classes. *Learning Disabilities Research & Practice, 12*, 198–208.

Bunting, E. (1990). *The Wall.* (R. Himler, Illust.). New York: Clarion.

Burns, B. (1998). Changing the classroom climate with literature circles. *Journal of Adolescent and Adult Literacy, 42*, 110–113.

Bussert-Webb, K. (1999). To test or teach: Reflections from a holistic teacher-researcher in south Texas. *Journal of Adolescent & Adult Literacy, 42*, 582–585.

Bussert-Webb, K. (2000). Did my holistic teaching help students' standardized test scores? *Journal of Adolescent & Adult Literacy, 43*, 572–573.

Byars, B. (1976). *The TV kid.* New York: Viking.

Cadenhead, K. (1987). Reading level: A metaphor that shapes practice. *Phi Delta Kappan, 68*, 436–441.

Cairney, T. H. (2000). Developing parent partnerships in secondary literacy learning. In D. W. Moore, D. E. Alvermann, & K. A. Hinchman (Eds.), *Struggling adolescent readers: A collection of teaching strategies* (pp. 58–65). Newark, DE: International Reading Association.

Calkins, L. (1994). *The art of teaching and writing.* Portsmouth, NH: Heinemann.

Canales, J. A. (1996, September). *Making English in the content areas comprehensible for language minority students.* Paper presented at the Denver Public Schools Secondary Literacy Conference, Denver, CO.

Carlo, M. S., August, D., McLaughlin, B., Snow, C. E., Dressler, C., Lippman, D. N., Lively, T. J., & White, C. E. (2004). Closing the gap: addressing the vocabulary needs of English-language learners in bilingual and mainstream classrooms. *Reading Research Quarterly, 39*, 188–215.

Carnegie Council on Adolescent Development (1989). *Turning points: Preparing American youth for the 21st century.* New York: Carnegie.

Carnegie Council on Adolescent Development (1996). *Great transitions: Preparing adolescents for a new century* (Abridged Version). New York: Carnegie.

Carr, E., & Ogle, D. (1987). K-W-L Plus: A strategy for comprehension and summarization. *Journal of Reading, 30,* 626–631.

Carroll, P. S. (2000). Journal to the third power. In L. Baines & A. Kunkel (Eds.), *Going Bohemian: Activities that engage adolescents in the art of writing well* (pp. 5–9). Newark, DE: International Reading Association.

Carroll, P. S., Blake, F., Camalo, R. A., & Messer, S. (1996). When acceptance isn't enough: Helping ESL students become successful writers. *English Journal, 85,* 25–33.

Carver, C. (1991). *A history of English in its own words.* New York: HarperCollins.

Cavelos, J. (2000). *The science of Star Wars.* New York: St. Martin's Griffin.

Cazden, C. (1988). *Classroom discourse: The language of teaching and learning.* Portsmouth, NH: Heinemann.

Cazden, C. B. (2000). Taking cultural differences into account. In B. C. Cope & M. Kalantzis (Eds.), *Multiliteracies: Literacy learning and the design of social futures* (pp. 249–266). New York: Routledge.

Cena, M., & Mitchell, J. (1998). Anchored instruction: A model for integrating the language arts through content area study. *Journal of Adolescent & Adult Literacy, 41,* 559–561.

Center for Research on Education, Diversity and Excellence. (2003a). *A national study of school effectiveness for language minority students' long-term academic achievement.* Available: http://www.cal.org/crede/pubs/ResBrief10.htm.

Center for Research on Education, Diversity and Excellence. (2003b). *Research evidence: Five standards for effective pedagogy and student outcomes.* (Technical Report No. G1). University of California, Santa Cruz: CREDE.

Chandler-Olcott, K., & Mahar, D. (2003). Adolescents' *anime*-inspired "fanfictions": An exploration of multiliteracies. *Journal of Adolescent & Adult Literacy, 46,* 556–566.

Christian, D. (1994). *Two-way bilingual education: Students learning through two languages* (Educational Practice Report No. 12). Santa Cruz: University of California, The National Center for Research on Cultural Diversity and Second Language Learning.

Ciardiello, A. (1998). Did you ask a good question today? Alternative cognitive and metacognitive strategies. *Journal of Adolescent & Adult Literacy, 42,* 210–219.

Cisneros, S. (1989). *The house on Mango Street.* New York: Vintage/Random House.

Civil, M., Andrade, R., & Gonzalez, N. (2002). *Linking home and school: A bridge to the many faces of mathematics* (Final Report). University of California, Santa Cruz: CREDE.

Clancy, T. (1984). *The hunt for Red October.* Annapolis, MD: Naval Institute Press.

Clark, C., Chow-Hoy, T., Herter, R., & Moss, P. (2001). Portfolios as sites of learning: Reconceptualizing the connections to motivation and engagement. *Reading Research Quarterly, 33,* 211–241.

Coble, C., Rice, D., Walla, K., & Murray, E. (1993). *Earth science.* Englewood Cliffs, NJ: Prentice Hall.

Collier, J., & Collier, C. (1974). *My brother Sam is dead.* New York: Four Winds.

Collier, J., & Collier, C. (1985). *The bloody country.* New York: Four Winds.

Commeyras, M., & Alvermann, D. E. (1996). Reading about women in world history textbooks from one feminist perspective. *Gender and Education, 8*(1), 31–48.

Conrad, P. (1985). *Prairie song.* New York: Harper & Row.

Cook-Gumperz, J. (Ed.) (1986). *The social construction of literacy.* Cambridge, UK: Cambridge University Press.

Cooper, C. R., & Petrosky, A. R. (1976). A psycholinguistic view of the fluent reading process. *Journal of Reading, 20,* 184–207.

Cooper, J. D. (1997). *Literacy: Helping children construct meaning* (3rd ed.). Boston: Houghton Mifflin.

Cope, B., & Kalantzis, M. (Eds.) (2000). *Multiliteracies: Literacy learning and the design of social futures.* London: Routledge.

Cormier, R. (1974). *The chocolate war*. New York: Dell.

Corno, L., & Snow, R. E. (1986). Adapting teaching to individual differences among learners. In M. C. Wittrock (Ed.), *Handbook of research on teaching* (3rd ed., pp. 605–629). New York: Macmillan.

Crafton, L. (1983). Learning from reading: What happens when students generate their own background information? *Journal of Reading, 26*, 586–593.

Crane, S. (1964). *The red badge of courage*. New York: Bantam. (Original work published 1895)

Crichton, M. (1991). *Jurassic Park*. New York: Ballantine.

Cullinan, B., & Fitzgerald, S. (1985, January). IRA, NCTE take stand on readability formula. *Reading Today, 2*, 1.

Cummins, J. (1994a). The acquisition of English as a second language. In K. Spangenberg-Urbschat & R. Pritchard (Eds.), *Kids come in all languages: Reading instruction for ESL students*. (pp. 36–62) Newark, DE: International Reading Association.

Cummins, J. (1994b). Knowledge, power and identity in teaching English as a second language. In E. Genesee (Ed.), *Educating second language children* (pp. 33–58). Cambridge, UK: Cambridge University Press.

Cummins, J. (1999). Alternative paradigms in bilingual education research: Does theory have a place? *Educational Researcher, 28(7)*, 26–32, 41.

Cunningham, J. (2002). The National Reading Panel report (A review). In R. Allington, (Ed.), *Big Brother and the national reading curriculum: How ideology trumped evidence* (pp. 49–74). Portsmouth, NH: Heinemann.

Cunningham, J. (1982). Generating interactions between schemata and text. In J. Niles & L. Harris (Eds.), *New inquiries in reading research and instruction, Thirty-first Yearbook of the National Reading Conference* (pp. 42–47). Washington, DC: National Reading Conference.

Curtis, C. (1995). *The Watsons go to Birmingham— 1963*. New York: Delacorte.

Cushman, K. (1994). *Catherine, called Birdy*. New York: HarperCollins.

Dalji, H., & Miner, B. (1998). "Listen to your students": An interview with Oakland high school English teacher Hafeezah AdamaDavia Dalji. In T. Perry & L. Delpit (Eds.), *The real Ebonics debate:* *Power, language, and the education of African-American children* (pp. 105–115.) Boston: Beacon.

Dalton, S. S. (1998). *Pedagogy matters: Standards for effective teaching practice*. (Research Report No. 4). Santa Cruz, CA: Center for Research on Education, Diversity, and Excellence.

Daniels, C., Madden, N., & Slavin, R. (in press). The success for all middle school: Adding content to middle grades reform. *Middle School Journal*.

Daniels, H. (1994). *Literature circles: Voice and choice in the student-centered classroom*. York, ME: Stenhouse.

Davis, B., Sumara, D., & Luce-Kapler, R. (2000). *Engaging minds: Learning and teaching in a complex world*. Mahwah, NJ: Erlbaum.

Deal, D. (1999, December). *Writing in the lab: Five research scientists talk about their use of writing in pursuit of scientific inquiry*. Paper presented at the National Reading Conference, Orlando, FL.

DeLorenzo, R. (1999). When hell freezes over: An approach to develop student interest and communication skills. *Journal of Chemical Education, 76*, 503.

Delpit, L. (1995). *Other people's children: Cultural conflict in the classroom*. New York: New Press.

Delpit, L. (1997, Fall). Ebonics and culturally responsive instruction. *Rethinking Schools Online, 12*(1), n.p. Available: http://www.rethinkingschools.org/archive/12_01/ebdelpit.shtml.

Delpit, L. (1998). What should teachers do? Ebonics and culturally responsive instruction. In T. Perry & L. Delpit (Eds.), *The real Ebonics debate: Power, language, and the education of African-American children* (pp. 17–26). Boston: Beacon.

Delpit, L., & Dowdy, J. K. (Eds.). (2002). *The skin that we speak: Thoughts on language and culture in the classroom*. New York: New Press.

Denig, S. (2004). Multiple intelligences and learning styles: Two complementary dimensions. *Teachers College Record, 106*(1), 96–111.

Deshler, D. D., Schumaker, J. B., Lenz, B. K., Bulgren, J. A., Hock, M. F., Knight, J., & Ehren, B. J. (2001). Ensuring content-area learning by secondary students with learning disabilities. *Learning Disabilities Research & Practice, 16*, 96–109.

Devine, T. G., & Kania, J. S. (2003). Studying: Skills, strategies, and systems. J. Flood, D. Lapp,

J. Squire, & J. Jensen (Eds.), *Handbook of research on teaching the English language arts* (2nd ed., pp. 942–954). Mahwah, NJ: Erlbaum.

Dewey, J. (1998). School and society. In M. Dworkin, (Ed.), *Dewey on education*. New York: Teachers College Press. (Original work published 1899)

Dillon, D. R., & Moje, E. B. (1998). Listening to the talk of adolescent girls: Lessons about literacy, school, and life. In D. E. Alvermann, K. A. Hinchman, D. W. Moore, S. F. Phelps, & D. R. Waff (Eds.), *Reconceptualizing the literacies in adolescents' lives* (pp. 193–223). Mahwah, NJ: Erlbaum.

Dolan, T., Dolan, E., Taylor, V., Shoreland, J., & Harrison, C. (1979). Improving reading through group discussion activities. In E. Lunzer & K. Gardner (Eds.), *The effective use of reading*. London: Heinemann Educational Books.

Dole, J. (2004). The changing role of the reading specialist in school reform. *The Reading Teacher, 57*, 462–471.

Dole, J. A., Duffy, G. G., Roehler, L. R., & Pearson, P. D. (1991). Moving from the old to new: Research on reading comprehension instruction. *Review of Educational Research, 61*, 239–264.

Dolly, M. (1990). Integrating ESL reading and writing through authentic discourse. *Journal of Reading, 35*, 360–365.

Drake, S. (1998). One teacher's experiences with student portfolios. *Teaching History, 23*, 60–76.

Duffelmeyer, F. (1994). Effective anticipation guide statements for learning from expository prose. *Journal of Reading, 37*, 452–457.

Duffelmeyer, F., & Baum, D. (1992). The extended anticipation guide revisited. *Journal of Reading, 35*, 654–656.

Duffelmeyer, F., Baum, D., & Merkley, D. (1987). Maximizing reader-text confrontation with an extended anticipation guide. *Journal of Reading, 31*, 146–151.

Duffy, G. (2002). The case for direct explanation of strategies. In C. Block & M. Pressley (Eds.), *Comprehension instruction: Research-based best practice* (pp. 28–41). New York: Guilford.

Duncan, B. (1996). *Mass media and popular culture* (2nd ed.). Toronto, Canada: Harcourt Brace.

Durkin, D. (1978/1979). What classroom observations reveal about reading comprehension

instruction. *Reading Research Quarterly, 14*, 481–533.

Eanet, M., & Manzo, A. (1976). R.E.A.P.—A strategy for improving reading/writing study skills. *Journal of Reading, 19*, 647–652.

Echevarria, J., Vogt, M., & Short, D. (2000). *Making content comprehensible for English language learners. The SIOP model*. Boston: Allyn & Bacon.

Egenberger, P. (1999). Integration through video: Seeing beyond the literary work into history and science. *Cyber Briefs, 1*(4), 55–58.

Ehlinger, J., & Pritchard, R. (1994). Using Think Alongs in secondary content areas. *Reading Research & Instruction, 33*, 187–206.

Eisenhart, M., Finkel, E., & Marion, S. F. (1996). Creating the conditions for scientific literacy: A re-examination. *American Educational Research Journal, 33*, 261–295.

Elbow, P. (1973). *Writing without teachers*. New York: Oxford University Press.

El Dinary, P. (2002a). Challenges of implementing transactional strategies instruction for reading comprehension. In C. Block & M. Pressley (Eds.), *Comprehension instruction: Research-based best practice* (pp. 351–364). New York: Guilford.

Evans, E., & Engelberg, R. (1985). *A developmental study of student perceptions of school grading*. Paper presented at the biennial meeting of the Society for Research in Child Development, Toronto, Ontario, April. (ERIC No. ED 256 482)

Ezell, H., Hunsicker, S., Quinque, M., & Randolph, E. (1996). Maintenance and generalization of QAR reading comprehension strategies. *Reading Research & Instruction, 36*, 64–81.

Fecho, B. (1998). Crossing boundaries of race in a critical literacy classroom. In D. Alvermann, K. Hinchman, D. Moore, S. Phelps, & D. Waff (Eds.), *Reconceptualizing the literacies in adolescents' lives* (pp. 75–101). Mahwah, NJ: Erlbaum.

Fecho, B. (2000). Critical inquiries into language in an urban classroom. *Research in the Teaching of English, 34*, 368–395.

Feldhusen, J. (1989). Issue: The sorting of students into ability groups has come under increasing fire recently. Should schools end the practice of grouping students by ability? *ASCD Update, 31*(1), 1–8.

Feldman, A., Alibrandi, M., & Kropf, A. (1998). Grading with points: The determination of report card grades by high school science teachers. *School Science & Mathematics, 98*, 140–148.

Fetterly, J. (1978). *The resisting reader.* Bloomington: Indiana University Press.

Finn, P. J. (1999). *Literacy with an attitude: Educating working-class children in their own self-interest.* Albany; State University of New York Press.

Fisher, D. (2004). Setting the "opportunity to read" standard: Resuscitating the SSR program in an urban high school. *Journal of Adolescent & Adult Literacy, 48*, 138–150.

Fisher, D., & Frey, N. (2003). Writing instruction for struggling adolescent readers: A gradual release model. *Journal of Adolescent & Adult Literacy, 46*, 396–405.

Fisher, J., Schumaker, J., & Deshler, D. (2002). Improving reading comprehension of at-risk adolescents. In C. Block & M. Pressley (Eds.), *Comprehension instruction: Research-based best practice* (pp. 351–364). New York: Guilford.

Fitzgerald, J., (1995). English-as-a-second-language learners' cognitive reading processes: A review of research in the United States. *Review of Educational Research, 65*, 145–190.

Fitzgerald, J., & Cummins, J. (1999). Bridging disciplines to critique a national research agenda for language-minority children's schooling. *Reading Research Quarterly, 34*, 378–390.

Flood, J., & Lapp, D. (2000). Reading comprehension instruction for at-risk students: Research-based practices that can make a difference. In D. W. Moore, D. E. Alvermann, & K. A. Hinchman (Eds.), *Struggling adolescent readers: A collection of strategies* (pp. 138–147). Newark, DE: International Reading Association.

Floriani, A. (1993). Negotiating what counts: Roles and relationships, texts and contexts, content and meaning. *Linguistics and Education, 5*, 241–273.

Focused Reporting Project (1999, Fall). *Changing schools in Long Beach: Independent reporting on the growth and achievement of young adolescents.* Atlanta: Edna McConnell Clark Foundation.

Fogarty, R. (1994, March.) Thinking about themes: Hundreds of themes. *Middle School Journal, 25*, 30–31.

Forbes, E. (1945). *Johnny Tremaine.* Boston: Houghton Mifflin.

Foster, S., & Padgett, C. (1999). Authentic historical inquiry in the social studies classroom. *The Clearing House, 72*, 357–363.

Fournier, D. N. E., & Graves, M. F. (2002). Scaffolding adolescents' comprehension of short stories. *Journal of Adolescent & Adult Literacy, 48*, 30–39.

Frager, A., & Thompson, L. (1985). Conflict: The key to critical reading instruction. *Journal of Reading, 28*, 676–683.

Freeman, Y., & Freeman, D. (1989). Evaluation of second-language junior and senior high school students. In K. Goodman, Y. Goodman, & W. Hood (Eds.), *The whole language evaluation book* (pp. 141–150). Portsmouth, NH: Heinemann.

Freire, P., & Macedo, D. (1987). *Literacy: Reading the word and the world.* Hedley, MA: Bergin & Garvey.

French, D. (2003, September). A new vision of authentic assessment to overcome the flaws in high stakes testing. *Middle School Journal, 35*, 14–23.

Fretzin, L. (1992, November). Double-entry journals. *Writing Teacher, 6*, 36–37.

Fry, E. (1977). Fry's readability graph: Clarifications, validity, and extension to level 17. *Journal of Reading, 21*, 242–252.

Fry, E. (1989). Reading formulas—maligned but valid. *Journal of Reading, 32*, 292–297.

Gabay, J. (1991). Issue: Motivation. ASCD *Update, 33, 7.*

Gadsden, V. (2000). Intergenerational literacy within families. In M. L. Kamil, P. Mosenthal, P. D. Pearson, & R. Barr (Eds.), *Handbook of reading research* (Vol. 3, pp. 871–887). Mahwah, NJ: Erlbaum.

Galbraith, M., Hennelly, J., & Purves, A. (1994). *Using portfolios to negotiate a rhetorical community.* Albany, NY: National Research Center on Literature Teaching & Learning.

Gamow, G. (1993). *Mr. Tompkins in paperback.* Cambridge, UK: Cambridge University Press.

Garcia, E., Rasmussen, B., Stobbe, C., & Garcia, E. (1990). Portfolios: An assessment tool in support of instruction. *International Journal of Education, 14*, 431–436.

Garcia, G. (1991). Factors influencing the English reading test performance of Spanish-speaking Hispanic children. *Reading Research Quarterly, 26,* 371–392.

Garcia, G. E. (2000). Bilingual children's reading. In M. L. Kamil, P. B. Mosenthal, P. D. Pearson, & R. Barr (Eds.), *Handbook of reading research* (Vol. 3, pp. 813–834). Mahwah, NJ: Erlbaum.

Garcia, G., & Pearson, P. D. (1994). Assessment and diversity. *Review of Research in Education, 20,* 339–391.

Gardner, H. (1999). *Intelligence reframed: Multiple intelligences for the 21st century.* New York: Basic Books.

Gardner, J. E., & Wissick, C. A. (2002). Enhancing thematic units using the World Wide Web: Tools and strategies for students with mild disabilities. *JSET e-journal, 17*(1). Retrieved October 21, 2003, from http://jset.unlv.edu/17.1/gardner/first.html.

Gardner, S., Benham, H., & Newell, B. (1999, September). Oh, what a tangled web we've woven! Helping students evaluate sources. *English Journal, 89,* 39–44.

Garner, R., & Alexander, P. (1989). Metacognition: Answered and unanswered questions. *Educational Psychologist, 24,* 143–158.

Garner, R., & Gillingham, M. (1987). Students' knowledge of text structure. *Journal of Reading Behavior, 29,* 247–259.

Gavelek, J. R., & Raphael, T. E. (1996). Changing talk about text: New roles for teachers and students. *Language Arts, 73,* 182–192.

Gearhart, M., & Herman, J. (1995, Winter). Portfolio assessment: Whose work is it? In *Evaluation Comment.* Los Angeles: UCLA Center for the Study of Evaluation & The National Center for Research on Evaluation, Standards, and Student Testing.

Gee, J. P. (1988). Legacies of literacy: From Plato to Freire through Harvey Graff. *Harvard Educational Review, 58,* 195–212.

Gee, J. P. (1996). *Social linguistics and literacies: Ideology in discourses* (2nd ed.). London: Taylor & Francis.

Gee, J. P. (1999). Reading and the new literacy studies: Reframing the National Academy of Sciences report on reading. *Journal of Literacy Research, 31,* 355–374.

Gee, J. P. (2000). Teenagers in new times: A new literacy studies perspective. *Journal of Adolescent & Adult Literacy, 43,* 412–420.

Genesee, E. (1994). *Integrating language and content: Lessons from immersion* (Educational Practice Report No. 11). Santa Cruz: University of California, National Center for Research on Cultural Diversity and Second Language Learning.

Gergen, K. (1999). *An invitation to social construction.* Thousand Oaks, CA: Sage.

Ghatala, E. S. (1986). Strategy-monitoring training enables young learners to select effective strategies. *Educational Psychologist, 21,* 43–54.

Gill, B. P., & Schlossman, S. L. (2004). Villain or savior? The American discourse on homework, 1850–2003. [Electronic version] *Theory into Practice, 43*(3), 174(8).

Gilles, C., Bixby, M., Crowley, P., Crenshaw, S., Henrichs, M., Reynolds, E., & Pyle, D. (Eds.) (1988). *Whole language strategies for secondary students.* New York: Richard C. Owen.

Gillespie, C. (1990). Questions about student-generated questions. *Journal of Reading, 34,* 250–257.

Glatthorn, A. (1991). Secondary English classroom environments. In J. Flood, J. M. Jensen, D. Lapp, & J. R. Squire (Eds.), *Handbook of research on teaching the English language arts* (pp. 438–456). New York: Macmillan.

Glazier, J., & Seo, J. (2005). Multicultural literature and discussion as mirror and window? *Journal of Adolescent & Adult Literacy, 48,* 686–700.

Goatley, V. J., Brock, C. H., & Raphael, T. E. (1995). Diverse learners participating in regular education book clubs. *Reading Research Quarterly, 30,* 352–380.

Godina, H. (1996). The canonical debate—Implementing multicultural literature and perspectives. *Journal of Adolescent & Adult Literacy, 39,* 544–549.

Goerss, B. (1996). Interdisciplinary planning within cooperative groups. *Journal of Adolescent & Adult Learning, 40,* 110–116.

Goldman, S., & Rakestraw, J. (2000). Structural aspects of constructing meaning from text. In M. Kamil, P. Mosenthal, P. D. Pearson, & R. Barr (Eds.), *Handbook of reading research* (Vol. 3, pp. 311–335). Mahwah, NJ: Erlbaum.

Gonzalez, O. (1999). Building vocabulary: Dictionary consultation and the ESL student. *Journal of Adolescent & Adult Literacy, 43,* 264–270.

Goodman, K. (1986). *What's whole in whole language?* New York: Scholastic.

Goodson, T. (2004). Teaching in the time of dogs. *The Quarterly, 26*(3). Retrieved September 3, 2005 from http://www.writingproject.org/cs/nwpp/print/nwpr/1979.

Gordon, C. (1990, Winter). Contexts for expository text structure use. *Reading Research & Instruction, 29,* 55–72.

Grady, M. (1998). *Qualitative and action research: A practioner handbook.* Bloomington, IN: Phi Delta Kappa.

Graves, D. (1983). *Writing: Teachers and children at work.* Portsmouth, NH: Heinemann.

Graves, M. (1986). Vocabulary learning and instruction. *Review of Research in Education, 13,* 49–89.

Graves, M., & Prenn, M. (1986). Costs and benefits of various methods of teaching vocabulary. *Journal of Reading 29,* 596–602.

Graves, M., & Slater, W. (1996). Vocabulary instruction in content areas. In D. Lapp, J. Flood, & N. Farnan (Eds.), *Content area reading and learning: Instructional strategies.* Boston: Allyn & Bacon.

Graves, M. F., Cooke, C. L., & LaBerge, M. J. (1983). Effects of previewing difficult short stories on low ability junior high school students' comprehension, recall, and attitudes. *Reading Research Quarterly, 18,* 262–276.

Green, B. (1991). Reading "readings": Towards a postmodernist reading pedagogy. In C. D. Baker & A. Luke (Eds.), *Towards a critical sociology of reading pedagogy.* Philadelphia: Benjamins.

Greene, M. (1991). The literacy debate and the public school: Going beyond the functional. *Educational Horizons, 69,* 129–134, 164–168.

Greenlaw, M. J. (1987). Science fiction as moral literature. *Educational Horizons, 65,* 165–166.

Greenleaf, C., Jiménez, R., & Roller, C. (2002). Conversations: Reclaiming secondary reading interventions: From limited to rich conceptions, from narrow to broad conversations. *Reading Research Quarterly, 37,* 484–496.

Greenleaf, C. L., Schoenbach, R., Cziko, C., & Mueller, F. L. (2001). Apprenticing adolescent readers to academic literacy. *Harvard Educational Review, 71,* 79–129.

Gronna, S., Chin-Chance, S., & Abedi, J. (2000, April). Differences between the performance of limited English proficient students and students who are labeled proficient in English on different content areas: Reading and mathematics. Paper presented at the meeting of the American Educational Research Association, New Orleans.

Grossman, P. L., & Stodolsky, S. S. (1995, November). Content as context: The role of school subjects in secondary school teaching. *Educational Researcher, 24,* 5–23.

Gunderson, L. (2000). Voices of the teen-aged diasporas. *Journal of Adolescent & Adult Literacy, 43,* 692–706.

Guthrie, J., & Ozgungor, S. (2002). Instructional contexts for reading engagement. In C. Block & M. Pressley (Eds.), *Comprehension instruction: Research-based best practice* (pp. 275–288). New York: Guilford.

Gutierrez, K. D., Asato, J., Pacheco, M., Moll, L. C., Olson, K., Horng, E. L., et al. (2002). "Sounding American": The consequences of new reforms on English language learners. *Reading Research Quarterly, 37,* 328–343.

Guzzetti, B. J., & Williams, W. D. (1996). Changing the pattern of gendered discussion: Lessons from science classrooms. *Journal of Adolescent & Adult Literacy, 40,* 38–47.

Guzzetti, B., & Hynd, C. (Eds.). (1998). *Perspectives on conceptual change: Multiple ways to understand knowing and learning in a complex world.* Mahwah, NJ: Erlbaum.

Guzzetti, B., & Hynd, C. (Eds.). (1998). *Theoretical perspectives on conceptual change.* Mahwah, NJ: Erlbaum.

Guzzetti, B., & Williams, W. (1996). Gender, text, and discussion: Examining intellectual safety in the science classroom. *Journal of Research in Science Teaching, 33,* 5–20.

Guzzetti, B., Snyder, T., Glass, G. V., & Gamas, W. S. (1993). Promoting conceptual change in science: A comparative meta-analysis of instructional interventions from reading education and science education. *Reading Research Quarterly, 28,* 116–159.

Hadaway, N., & Mundy, J. (2000). Children's informational picture books visit a secondary ESL classroom. In D. Moore, D. Alvermann, & K. Hinchman (Eds.), *Struggling adolescent readers: A collection of teaching strategies* (pp. 83–95). Newark, DE: International Reading Association.

Haggard, M. (1982). The vocabulary self-collection strategy: An active approach to word learning. *Journal of Reading, 26*, 203–207.

Haggard, M. (1986). The vocabulary self-collection strategy: Using student interest and world knowledge to enhance vocabulary growth. *Journal of Reading, 29*, 634–642.

Hall, B. (2004). Literacy coaches: An evolving role. *Carnegie Reporter, 3*(1). Retrieved October 15, 2005 from http://www.carnegie.org/reporter/09/literacy/.

Hall, S., & Whannel, P. (1998). The young audience. In J. Storey (Ed.), *Cultural theory and popular culture; A Reader* (2nd ed., pp. 61–67). Athens: University of Georgia Press.

Hamilton, L. (2003). Assessment as a policy tool. *Review of Research in Education, 27*, 25–68.

Haney, G., & Thistlethwaite, L. (1991). A model critical reading lesson for secondary high-risk students. *Reading, Writing and Learning Disabilities, 7*, 337–354.

Hansen-Krening, N., & Mizokawa, D. (2000). Exploring ethnic-specific literature: A unity of parents, families, and educators. In D. Moore, D. Alvermann, & K. Hinchman (Eds.), *Struggling adolescent readers: A collection of teaching strategies* (pp. 96–106). Newark, DE: International Reading Association.

Hardin, L. F. (1999, Fall/Winter). Netting the past: Putting our town's history on the web. *Bread Loaf Rural Teacher Network Magazine*, 7–9.

Hare, V., & Borchardt, K. (1984). Direct instruction of summarization skills. *Reading Research Quarterly, 20*, 62–78.

Hare, V., Rabinowitz, M., & Schieble, K. (1989). Text effects on main idea comprehension. *Reading Research Quarterly, 24*, 72–88.

Hargreaves, A. (1989). *Curriculum assessment and reform*. Philadelphia: Open University Press.

Hargreaves, D. H. (1967). *Social relations in a secondary school*. London: Routledge & Kegan Paul.

Harmon, J. M. (2000). Vocabulary teaching and learning in a seventh-grade literature-based classroom. In D. W. Moore, D. E. Alvermann, & K. A. Hinchman (Eds.), *Struggling adolescent readers: A collection of teaching strategies* (pp. 174–188). Newark, DE: International Reading Association.

Harris, V. (1991). "Have you heard about an African Cinderella story?": The hunt for multiethnic literature. *Publishing Research Quarterly, 7* (3), 23–36.

Hayes, J. R. (1989). *The complete problem solver*. Hillsdale, NJ: Erlbaum.

Heath, S. B. (1983). *Ways with words: Language, life, and work in communities and classrooms*. Cambridge, UK: Cambridge University Press.

Heath, S. B. (1986b). The functions and uses of literacy. In S. DeCastell, A. Luke, & K. Egan (Eds.), *Literacy, society, and schooling: A reader* (pp. 15–26). London: Cambridge University Press.

Heath, S. B. (1991). The sense of being literate; Historical and cross-cultural features. In R. Barr, M. L. Kamil, P. Mosenthal, & P. D. Pearson (Eds.), *Handbook of reading research* (Vol. 2, pp. 3–25). New York: Longman.

Helfeldt, J., & Henk, W. (1990). Reciprocal question-answer relationships: An instructional technique for at-risk readers. *Journal of Reading, 33*, 509–514.

Hellman, L. (1973). *Pentimento: A book of portraits*. Boston: Little, Brown.

Helms, J. (1992). Why is there no study of cultural equivalence in standardized cognitive ability testing? *American Psychologist, 47*, 1083–1101.

Hemphill, L. (1999). Narrative style, social class, and response to poetry. *Research in the Teaching of English, 33*, 275–302.

Henze, R. C., & Hauser, M. E. (1999). *Personalizing culture through anthropological and educational perspectives* (Educational Practice Report No. 4). Santa Cruz, CA: Center for Research on Education, Diversity and Excellence.

Herber H. (1978). *Teaching reading in content areas* (2nd ed.). Englewood Cliffs, NJ: Prentice Hall.

Herber, H. L. (1970). *Teaching reading in content areas*. Englewood Cliffs, NJ: Prentice Hall.

Herber, H. L., & Nelson-Herber, J. (1987). Developing independent learners. *Journal of Reading, 30*, 584–588.

Hicks, D., & Dolan, T. K. (2003). Haunted landscapes and girlhood imaginations: The power of horror fictions for marginalised readers. *Changing English, 10*(1), 45–57.

Hidi, S., & Anderson, V. (1986). Producing written summaries: Task demands, cognitive operations, and implications for instruction. *Review of Educational Research, 56*, 473–494.

Hill, H. (1989). *Effective strategies for teaching minority students.* Bloomington, IN: National Educational Service.

Hill, M. (1991). Writing summaries promotes thinking and learning across the curriculum—But why are they so difficult to write? *Journal of Reading, 34*, 536–539.

Hinchey, P. H. (1998). *Finding freedom in the classroom: A practical introduction to critical theory.* New York: Peter Lang.

Hinchman, K., & Zalewski, P. (1996). Reading for success in a tenth-grade global-studies class: A qualitative study. *Journal of Literacy Research, 28*, 91–106.

Hirsch, E. D. (1987). *Cultural literacy.* Boston: Houghton Mifflin.

Hodgkinson, H. L. (1992). *A demographic look at tomorrow.* Washington, DC: Center of Demographic Policy.

Hoffman, J. (1992). Critical reading/thinking across the curriculum: Using I-charts to support learning. *Language Arts, 68*, 121–127.

Hoffman, J. V. (1979). The intra-act procedure for critical reading. *Journal of Reading, 22*, 605–608.

Hoffman, J. V., Paris, S. G., Salas, R., Patterson, E., & Assaf, L. (2003). High-stakes assessment in the language arts: The piper plays, the players dance, but who pays the price? In J. Flood, D. Lapp, J. Squire, & J. Jensen (Eds.), *Handbook of research on teaching the English language arts* (2nd ed., pp. 619–630). Mahwah, NJ: Erlbaum.

Hoffman, L. (1999). Key statistics on public elementary and secondary schools and agencies. *Education Statistics Quarterly, 1*(4), 67–70.

Hofstadter, R. (1970). *Anti-intellectualism in American life.* New York: Knopf.

Hopkins, G., & Bean, T. (2000). Vocabulary learning with the verbal-visual word association strategy in a Native American community. In D. Moore, D. Alvermann, & K. Hinchman (Eds.), *Struggling adolescent readers: A collection of teaching strategies* (pp. 107–115). Newark, DE: International Reading Association.

Howes, E. V., Hamilton, G. W., Zaskoda, D. (2003). Linking science and literature through technology: Thinking about interdisciplinary inquiry in middle school. *Journal of Adolescent & Adult Literacy, 46*, 494–504.

Hruby, G. G. (2001). Sociological, postmodern, and new realism perspectives in social constructionism: Implications for literacy research. *Reading Research Quarterly, 36*, 48–62.

Hudelson, S. (1999, May/June). ESL writing: Principles for teaching young writers. *ESL Magazine, 2*, 8–10, 12.

Huey, E. B. (1968). *The psychology and pedagogy of reading.* Cambridge, MA: MIT Press. (Original work published 1908)

Hughes, R. (1993). *Culture of complaint.* New York: Oxford University Press.

Hull, G., & Schultz, K. (Eds.). (2002). *School's out! Bridging out-of-school literacies with classroom practice.* New York: Teachers College Press.

Hynd, C., McNish, M., Lay, K., & Fowler, P. (1995). *High school physics: The role of text in learning counterintuitive information* (Technical Report No. 46). Athens, GA: National Reading Research Center.

Indrisano, R., & Paratore, J. R. (1991). Classroom contexts for literacy learning. In J. Flood, J. M. Jensen, D. Lapp, & J. R. Squire (Eds.), *Handbook of research on teaching the English language arts* (pp. 477–488). New York: Macmillan.

Innocenti, R. (1985). *Rose Blanche.* London: Jonas Cape.

Inos, R. H., & Quigley, M. A. (1995). *Research review for inclusive practices.* November Newsletter (pp. 1–6). Honolulu, HI: Pacific Region Educational Laboratory.

International Reading Association (1982). Misuse of grade equivalents. *The Reading Teacher, 35*, 464.

International Reading Association (2004). *The role and qualifications of the reading coach in the United States: A position statement of the International Reading Association.* Newark, DE: International Reading Association.

International Society for Technology in Education (2002). *National educational technology standards for students: Connecting curriculum & technology.* Eugene, OR: International Society for Technology in Education.

Irvine, J. (1990). Transforming teaching for the 21st century. *Educational Horizons, 69*(1), 16–21.

Ivey, G. (1999a). A multicase study in the middle school: Complexities among young adolescent readers. *Reading Research Quarterly, 34,* 172–192.

Ivey, G. (1999b). Reflections on teaching struggling middle school readers. *Journal of Adolescent & Adult Literacy, 42,* 372–381.

Ivey, G. (2000). Reflections on teaching struggling middle school readers. In D. W. Moore, D. E. Alvermann, & K. A. Hinchman (Eds.), *Struggling adolescent readers: A collection of teaching strategies* (pp. 27–38). Newark, DE: International Reading Association.

Ivey, G., & Broaddus, K. (2001). "Just plain reading": A survey of what makes students want to read in middle school classrooms. *Reading Research Quarterly, 36,* 350–377.

Jacobs, H. (1987). The perils of a slave woman's life. In M. E. Washington (Ed.), *Invented lives: Narratives of black women, 1860–1960* (pp. 16–69). New York: Anchor.

Jenkins, J. R., Johnson, E., & Hileman, J. (2004). When is reading also writing: Sources of individual differences on the new reading performance assessments. *Scientific Studies of Reading, 8,* 125–151.

Jervis, K. (1996). "How come there are no brothers on that list?": Hearing the hard questions all children ask. *Harvard Educational Review, 66,* 546–576.

Jiménez, R. T., & Gámez, A. (1996). Literature-based cognitive strategy instruction for middle school Latino/a students. *Journal of Reading, 40,* 84–91.

Jiménez, R. T., & Gámez, A. (2000). Literature-based cognitive strategy instruction for middle school Latina/o students. In D. W. Moore, D. E. Alvermann, & K. A. Hinchman (Eds.), *Struggling adolescent readers: A collection of teaching strategies* (pp. 74–82). Newark, DE: International Reading Association.

Jiménez, R. T., Moll, L. C., Rodriguez-Brown, F. V., & Barrera, R. B. (1999). Latina and Latino researchers interact on issues related to literacy learning. *Reading Research Quarterly, 34,* 217–230.

Jiménez, R., Garcia, G., & Pearson, P. D. (1996). The reading strategies of bilingual Latina/o students who are successful English readers: Opportunities and obstacles. *Reading Research Quarterly, 31,* 90–112.

Johnson, D., & Pearson, P. D. (1984). *Teaching reading vocabulary* (2nd ed.). New York: Holt, Rinehart and Winston.

Johnston, P. H., & Winograd, P. N. (1985). Passive failure in reading. *Journal of Reading Behavior, 17,* 279–301.

Jones, B. F., Pierce, J., & Hunter, B. (1988/1989). Teaching students to construct graphic representations. *Educational Leadership, 46*(4), 20–25.

Jordan, S., & Purves, A. (1993). *Issues in the responses of students to culturally diverse texts: A preliminary study.* Albany, NY: National Research Center on Literature Teaching and Learning.

Jurdak, M., & Abu Zein, R. (1998). The effect of journal writing on achievement in and attitudes toward mathematics. *School Science & Mathematics, 98,* 412–419.

Just, M., & Carpenter, P. (1987). *The psychology of reading and language comprehension.* Boston: Allyn & Bacon.

Kaiser Family Foundation (2003). *Key facts: Media literacy.* (Publication Number: 3383). Retrieved October 9, 2005 from http://www.kff.org/entmedia/Media-Literacy.cfm.

Kamler, B. (1999, November). *The politics of teaching writing and the changing nature of teachers' work.* Paper presented at the annual meeting of the National Council of Teachers of English, Denver.

Kamler, B., & Comber, B. (1996). Critical literacy: Not generic—not developmental—not another orthodoxy. *Changing Education, 3*(1), 1–9.

Katz, C. A., Boran, K., Braun, T. J., Massie, M. J., & Kuby, S. A. (2003). The importance of being with Sir Ernest Shackleton at the bottom of the world. *Journal of Adolescent & Adult Literacy, 47,* 38–49.

Keene, E., & Zimmerman, S. (1997). *Mosaic of thought: Teaching comprehension in a reader's workshop.* Portsmouth, NH: Heinemann.

Kehaus, M. (2000). Working with teen writers online: Policies, procedures, and possibilities. *Journal of Adolescent & Adult Literacy, 44,* 179–183.

Kennedy, M., Fisher, M., & Ennis, R. (1991). Critical thinking: Literature review and needed research. In L. Idol & B. F. Jones (Eds.), *Educational values and cognitive instruction: Implications for reform* (pp. 11–40). Hillsdale, NJ: Erlbaum.

Keys, C. (1999). Revitalizing instruction in scientific genres: Connecting knowledge production with writing to learn in science. *Science Education, 83*, 115–130.

Kibby, M. (1995). The organization and teaching of things and the words that signify them. *Journal of Adolescent & Adult Literacy, 39*, 208–223.

Kinzer, C. K. (2005). The intersection of schools, communities, and technology: Recognizing children's use of new literacies. In R. A. Karchmer, M. H. Mallette, J. Kara-Soteriou, & D. J. Leu, Jr. (Eds.), *Innovative approaches to literacy education: Using the Internet to support new literacies* (pp. 65–82). Newark, DE: International Reading Association.

Klare, G. (1984). Readability. In P. D. Pearson (Ed.), *Handbook of reading research* (pp. 681–744). New York: Longman.

Klenk, L., & Kibby, M. (2000). Re-mediating reading difficulties: Appraising the past, reconciling the present, constructing the future. In M. L. Kamil, P. B. Mosenthal, R. Barr, & P. D. Pearson (Eds.), *Handbook of reading research* (Vol. 3, pp. 667–690). Mahwah, NJ: Erlbaum.

Klingner, J. K., & Vaughan, S. (1996). Reciprocal teaching of reading comprehension strategies for students with learning disabilities who use English as a second language. *Elementary School Journal, 96*, 275–293.

Knoblauch, C. H. (1990). Literacy and the politics of education. In A. A. Lunsford, H. Moglen, & J. Slevin (Eds.), *The right to literacy* (pp. 74–80). New York: Modern Language Association of America.

Knowles, J. (1960). *A separate peace.* New York: Macmillan.

Koki, S. (2000, February). Bullying in Pacific schools—Should we be concerned? *Pacific Education Updates*, 1–12.

Kolich, E. M. (1991). Effects of computer-assisted vocabulary training on word knowledge. *Journal of Educational Research, 84*, 177–182.

Konopak, B., Martin, S., & Martin, M. (1990). Using a writing strategy to enhance sixth-grade students' comprehension of content material. *Journal of Reading Behavior, 22*, 19–38.

Konopak, B., Sheard, C., Longman, D., Lyman, B., Slaton, E., Atkinson, R., & Thames, D. (1987). Incidental versus intentional word learning from context. *Reading Psychology, 8*, 7–21.

Krashen, S. (1985). *The input hypothesis: Issues and implications.* New York: Longman.

Krashen, S. (1989). *Language acquisition and language education.* New York: Prentice Hall.

Krashen, S. (2002). More smoke and mirrors: A critique of the National Reading Panel report on fluency. In R. Allington, (Ed.), *Big Brother and the national reading curriculum: How ideology trumped evidence* (pp. 112–124). Portsmouth, NH: Heinemann.

Krashen, S. D. (1988). Do we learn to read by reading? The relationship between free reading and reading ability. In D. Tannen (Ed.), *Linguistics in context: Connecting observation and understanding* (pp. 269–298). Norwood, NJ: Ablex.

Kreidler, W. J. (1984). *Creative conflict resolution.* Glenview, IL: Scott, Foresman.

Kuykendal, C. (1992). *From rage to hope: Strategies for reclaiming Black and Hispanic students.* Bloomington, IN: National Educational Service.

LaBerge, D., & Samuels, S. J. (1974). Toward a theory of automatic information processing in reading. In H. Singer & R. Ruddell (Eds.), *Theoretical models and processes of reading* (3rd ed., pp. 689–718). Newark, DE: International Reading Association.

LaConte, R. T. (1981). *Homework as a learning experience: What research says to the teacher.* Arlington, VA: ERIC Document Reproduction Service. (ED 217 022)

Ladson-Billings, G. (1994). *The dreamkeepers.* San Francisco: Jossey-Bass.

Lambros, A. (2004). *Problem-based learning in middle and high school classrooms: A teacher's guide to implementation.* Thousand Oaks, CA: Corwin Press.

Langer, J. (1986). Learning through writing: Study skills in the content areas. *Journal of Reading, 29*, 400–406.

Langer, J. (1989). Literate thinking and schooling. *Literacy Research Newsletter, 5*(1), 1–2.

Langer, J. (2000). *Beating the odds: Teaching middle and high school students to read and write well.*

Albany, NY: National Center on English Learning and Achievement.

Langer, J. A. (2001). Beating the odds: Teaching middle and high school students to read and write well. *American Educational Research Journal, 38,* 837–880.

Lankshear, C., & McLaren, P. (Eds.). (1993). *Critical literacy: Politics, praxis, and the postmodern.* Albany, NY: State University of New York Press.

Lankshear, C., & Knobel, M. (2003). *New literacies: Changing knowledge and classroom learning.* Philadelphia: Open University Press.

Laursen, B., Hartup, W. W., & Koplas, A. L. (1996). Towards understanding peer conflict. *Merrill-Palmer Quarterly, 42*(1), 76–102.

Lave, J., & Wenger, E. (1991). *Situated learning.* Cambridge, UK: Cambridge University Press.

Lebauer, R. (1985). Nonnative English speaker problems in content and English classes: Are they thinking or reading problems? *Journal of Reading, 29,* 136–142.

Lehr, F. (1984). ERIC/RCS: Cooperative learning. *Journal of Reading, 27,* 458–461.

Leinhardt, G. (1983, April). *Routines in expert math teachers' thoughts and actions.* Paper presented at the annual meeting of the American Educational Research Association, Montreal.

Lemke, J. (1990). *Talking science: Language, learning and values.* Norwood, NJ: Ablex.

Lemke, J. L. (1995). *Textual politics: Discourse and social dynamics.* London: Taylor & Francis.

Lensmire, T. (1994). *When children write: Critical revisions of the writing workshop.* New York: Teachers College Press.

Leu, D. J. (1997). Caity's question: Literacy as deixis on the Internet. *The Reading Teacher, 51,* 62–67.

Leu, D. J., & Kinzer, C. K. (2003). *Effective literacy instruction K-8: Implementing best practice* (5th ed.). Upper Saddle River, NJ: Merrill Prentice Hall.

Leu, D. J., & Leu, D. D. (1999). *Teaching with the Internet: Lessons from the classroom.* Norwood, MA: Gordon.

Leu, D. J., Jr., Ataya, R., & Coiro, J. L. (2002, December). *Assessing assessment strategies among the 50 states: Evaluating the literacies of our past or the literacies of our future?* Paper presented at the National Reading Conference, Miami, FL.

Leu, D. J., Jr., Mallette, M. H., Karchmer, R. A., & Kara-Soteriou, J. (2005). Contextualizing the new literacies of information and communication technologies in theory, research, and practice. In R. A. Karchmer, M. H. Mallette, J. Kara-Soteriou, & D. J. Leu, Jr. (Eds.), *Innovative approaches to literacy education: Using the Internet to support new literacies* (pp. 1–12). Newark, DE: International Reading Association.

Levin, H. (1998). Educational performance standards and the economy. *Educational Researcher, 27,* 4–11.

Lewis, C. (1998). Rock 'n' roll and horror stories: Students, teachers, and popular culture. *Journal of Adolescent & Adult Literacy, 42,* 116–120.

Lewis, C. (2000). Limits of identification: The personal, pleasurable, and critical in reader response. *Journal of Literacy Research, 32,* 253–266.

Lewis, C., Ketter, J., & Fabos, B. (2001). Reading race in a rural context. *International Journal of Qualitative Studies in Education, 14,* 317–350.

Linder, R., & Falk-Ross, F. (2004). Reading between the lines: Middle school readers uncover messages in magazine advertisements. In J. R. Dugan, P. E. Linder, M. B. Sampson, B. A. Brancato, & L. Elish-Piper (Eds.), *Celebrating the power of literacy: The twenty-sixth yearbook of the College Reading Association* (pp. 376–393). Commerce, TX: Texas A&M University.

Long, A. (2004). *Cyber schools.* Denver, CO: Education Commission of the States.

Long, R. (1995, August/September). Preserving the role of the reading specialist. *Reading Today,* p. 6.

Luke, A. (1988). *Literacy, textbooks, and ideology.* London: Falmer.

Luke, A., & Elkins, J. (1998). Reinventing literacy in new times. *Journal of Adolescent & Adult Literacy, 42,* 4–7.

Luke, C. (1997). Media literacy and cultural studies. In S. Muspratt, A. Luke, & P. Freebody (Eds.), *Constructing critical literacies: Teaching and learning textual practice* (pp. 19–49). Cresskill, NJ: Hampton Press.

Luke, C. (2000). Cyber-schooling and technological change: Multiliteracies for new times. In B. Cope & M. Kalantzis (Eds.), *Multiliteracies: Literacy learning and the design of social futures* (pp. 69–91). London: Routledge.

Macaulay, D. (1973). *Cathedral*. New York: Houghton Mifflin.

Macaulay, D. (1974). *City: A story of Roman planning and construction*. Boston: Houghton Mifflin.

Macaulay, D. (1977). *Castle*. Boston: Houghton Mifflin.

Madaus, G., & O'Dwyer, L. (1999). A short history of performance assessment: Lessons learned. *Phi Delta Kappan, 80*, 688–695.

Malcolm X (with A. Haley) (1965). *The autobiography of Malcolm X*. New York: Ballantine.

Mandler, J., & Johnson, N. (1979). Rememberance of things parsed: Story structure and recall. *Cognitive Psychology, 9*, 111–151.

Manzo, A. (1969). The ReQuest procedure. *Journal of Reading, 13*, 23–26.

Manzo, A., Manzo, U., & Albee, J. J. (2002). iREAP: Improving reading, writing, and thinking in the wired classroom. *Journal of Adolescent & Adult Literacy, 46*, 42–47.

Manzo, A., Manzo, U., & Estes, T. (2001). *Content area literacy: Interactive teaching for interacive learning*, 2nd ed. New York: Wiley.

Marshall, N. (1996). The students: Who are they and how do I reach them? In D. Lapp, J. Flood, & N. Farnan (Eds.), *Content area reading and learning* (2nd ed., pp. 79–93). Boston: Allyn and Bacon.

Martin, C., Martin, M., & O'Brien, D. (1984). Spawning ideas for writing in the content areas. *Reading World, 11*, 11–15.

Martin, M., & Konopak, B. (1987). An instructional investigation of students' ideas generated during content area writing. In J. Readence & R. S. Baldwin (Eds.), *Research in literacy: Merging perspectives* (pp. 265–271). Rochester, NY: National Reading Conference.

Martin, S. (2000). Tabloid exposé. In L. Baines & A. Kunkel (Eds.), *Going Bohemian: Activities that engage adolescents in the art of writing well* (pp. 123–124). Newark, DE: International Reading Association.

Marzano, R., & Kendall, J. (1996). *The fall and rise of standards-based education* (National Association of State Boards of Education *Issues in Brief*). Aurora, CO: Mid-Continent Regional Educational Laboratory.

Mayher, J. S., Lester, N., & Pradl, G. M. (1983). *Learning to write: Writing to learn*. Portsmouth, NH: Heinemann.

McCain, T. (2005). *Teaching for tomorrow: Teaching content and problem solving skills*. Thousand Oaks, CA: Corwin Press.

McCarthy, C. (1998). Multicultural education, minority identities, and the challenge of curriculum reform. In A. Willis (Ed.), *Teaching and using multicultural literature in grades 9–12: Moving beyond the canon* (pp. 1–16). Norwood, MA: Christopher Gordon.

McCombs, B. L. (1995). Understanding the keys to motivation to learn. In *What's noteworthy on learners, learning, schooling* (pp. 5–12). Aurora, CO: Mid-Continent Regional Educational Laboratory.

McIntosh, M., & Draper, R. (1995). Applying the question–answer relationship strategy in mathematics. *Journal of Reading, 39*, 120–131.

McKenna, M. C., & Robinson, R. D. (1990). Content literacy: A definition and implications. *Journal of Reading, 34*, 184–186.

McKinney, D., & Michalovic, M. (2004, November). Teaching the stories of scientists and their discoveries. *The Science Teacher, 71*, 46–51.

McMahon, S. I., & Raphael, T. E. (Eds.). (1997). *The book club connection*. New York: Teachers College Press.

Mchan, H. (1991). *Sociological foundations supporting the study of cultural diversity* (Research Report No. 1). Santa Cruz: University of California, National Center for Research on Cultural Diversity and Second Language Learning.

Meier, T. (1998a). Kitchen poets and classroom books: Literature from children's roots. In T. Perry & L. Delpit (Eds.), *The real Ebonics debate: Power, language, and the education of African-American children* (pp. 94–104). Boston: Beacon.

Meier, T. (1998b). Teaching teachers about black communications. In T. Perry & L. Delpit (Eds.), *The real Ebonics debate: Power, language, and the education of African-American children* (pp. 117–125.) Boston: Beacon.

Met, M. (1994). Teaching content through a second language. In F. Genesee (Ed.), *Educating second language children* (pp. 159–182). Cambridge, UK: Cambridge University Press.

Middleton, J. (1991). Student-generated analogies in biology. *The American Biology Teacher, 53,* 42–46.

Mike, D., & Rabinowitz, J. (1998). Collaborative projects on the Internet. *Language & Literacy Spectrum, 8,* 48–60.

Miller, G., & Gildea, P. (1987). How children learn words. *Scientific American, 257,* 94–99.

Miller, K., & George, J. (1992). Expository Passage Organizers: Models for reading and writing. *Journal of Reading, 35,* 372–377.

Miller, T. (1998). The place of picture books in middle-level classrooms. *Journal of Adolescent & Adult Literacy, 41,* 376–381.

Minami, M., & Ovando, C. J. (1995). Language issues in multicultural contexts. In J. A. Banks & C. A. McGee Banks (Eds.), *Handbook of research on multicultural education* (pp. 427–444). New York: Macmillan.

Moffit, M., & Wartella, E. (1992). Youth and reading: A survey of leisure reading pursuits of female and male adolescents. *Reading Research and Instruction, 31,* 1–17.

Moje, E. B., Willes, D. J., & Fassio, K. (2001). Constructing and negotiating literacy in a seventh-grade writer's workshop. In E. B. Moje & D. G. O'Brien (Eds.), *Constructions of literacy: Studies of teaching and learning in secondary classrooms and schools.* Mahwah, NJ: Erlbaum.

Moje, E., Brozo, W., & Haas, J. (1994). Portfolios in a high school classroom: Challenges to change. *Reading Research and Instruction, 33,* 275–292.

Moll, L. (1991). Literacy research in community and classrooms: A sociocultural approach. In C. Baker & A. Luke (Eds.), *Towards a critical sociology of reading pedagogy* (pp. 211–245). Philadelphia: Benjamins.

Momaday, S. (1996). *The Way to Rainy Mountain.* Albuquerque, NM: University of New Mexico Press.

Moore, D. W. (1996). Contexts for literacy in secondary schools. In D. J. Leu, C. K. Kinzer, & K. A. Hinchman (Eds.), *Literacies for the twenty-first century: Research and practice* (pp. 15–46). Chicago: National Reading Conference.

Moore, D. W., Alvermann, D. E., & Hinchman, K. A. (Eds.). (2000). *Struggling adolescent readers: A collection of teaching strategies.* Newark, DE: International Reading Association.

Moore, D. W., Bean, T. W., Birdyshaw, D., & Rycik, J. R. (1999). Adolescent literacy: A position statement. *Journal of Adolescent & Adult Literacy, 43,* 97–112.

Moore, D., & Moore, S. (1992). Possible sentences: An update. In E. Dishner, T. Bean, J. Readence, & D. Moore (Eds.), *Reading in content areas: Improving classroom instruction* (3rd ed., pp. 196–201). Dubuque, IA: Kendall/Hunt.

Mora, J. K., Wink, J., & Wink, D. (2001). Dueling models of dual language instruction: A critical review of the literature and program implementation guide. *Bilingual Research Journal, 25,* 435–460.

Morgan, W., & Beaumont, G. (2003). A dialogic approach to argumentation: Using a chat room to develop early adolescent students' argumentative writing. *Journal of Adolescent & Adult Literacy, 47,* 146–157.

Moulton, M. (1999). The multigenre paper: Increasing interest, motivation, and functionality in research. *Journal of Adolescent & Adult Literacy, 42,* 528–539.

Mountain, L. (2002). Flip-a-chip to build vocabulary. *Journal of Adolescent & Adult Literacy, 46,* 62–28.

Murray, D. (1984). *Writing to learn.* New York: Holt, Rinehart and Winston.

Nagy, W., & Herman, P. (1987). Breadth and depth of vocabulary knowledge: Implications for acquisition and instruction. In M. McKeown & M. Curtis (Eds.), *The nature of vocabulary acquisition* (pp. 19–35). Hillsdale, NJ: Erlbaum.

Nagy, W., & Scott, J. (2000). Vocabulary processes. In M. Kamil, P. Mosenthal, P. D. Pearson, & R. Barr (Eds.), *Handbook of Reading Research* (Vol. 3, pp. 269–284). Mahwah, NJ: Erlbaum.

Nagy, W., Herman, P., & Anderson, R. C. (1985). Learning words from context. *Reading Research Quarterly, 20,* 233–253.

Naipaul, V. S. (1984). *A house for Mr. Biswas.* New York: Vintage.

National Center for Education Statistics (2005). National trends in reading. Retrieved September 2, 2005 from http://nces.ed.gov/

nationsreportcard/ltt/results2004/nat-reading-scalescore.asp.

National Council of Teachers of Mathematics (2000). *Principles and standards for school mathematics.* Reston, VA: National Council of Teachers of Mathematics.

National Reading Panel (2000). *Report of the National Reading Panel: Teaching children to read.* (NIH Publication No. 00-4769). Washington, DC: National Institute of Child Health and Human Development.

National Reading Panel (NRP). (2000). *Teaching children to read: An evidence-based assessment of the scientific research literature on reading and its implications for reading instruction.* Reports of the subgroups (NIH Publication No. 00-4754). Washington, DC: National Institute of Child Health and Human Development.

National Research Council (1996). *National science education standards.* Washington DC: National Academy Press.

Neal, J., & Moore, K. (1991/1992). *The Very Hungry Caterpillar* meets *Beowulf* in secondary classrooms. *Journal of Reading, 35,* 290–296.

Neilsen, A. (1991). Examining the forces against change Fulfilling the promise of professional development. *Reflections on Canadian Literacy, 9*(2), 66–69.

Neilsen, J. (1990). *Hypertext and hypermedia.* Boston: Academic Press.

Neilsen, L. (1991). Of parachutes, mockingbirds, and bat-poets: A new paradigm for professional growth. *The Reading Teacher, 45,* 64–66.

Neilsen, L. (1998). Playing for real: Performative texts and adolescent identities. In D. Alvermann, K. Hinchman, D. Moore, S. Phelps, & D. Waff (Eds.), *Reconceptualizing the literacies in adolescents' lives* (pp. 3–26). Mahwah, NJ: Erlbaum.

Nelson, B. (1996). *Learning English: How school reform fosters language acquisition and development for limited English proficient elementary school students.* Santa Cruz, CA: National Center for Research on Cultural Diversity and Second Language Learning.

Neufeld, B., & Roper, D. (2003). *Coaching: A strategy for developing instructional capacity.* Washington, DC and Providence, RI: The Aspen Institute Program on Education and the Annenberg Institute for School Reform.

New London Group. (1997). A pedagogy of multiliteracies: Designing social futures. *Harvard Educational Review, 66,* 60–92.

Newmann, F. M. (1988). Can depth replace coverage in the high school curriculum? *Phi Delta Kappan, 69,* 345–348.

Nieto, S. (1994). Lessons from students on creating a chance to dream. *Harvard Educational Review, 64,* 392–426.

Nilsen, A. P., & Nilsen, D. L. F. (2000). Language play in Y2K: Morphology brought to you by Pokémon. *Voices from the Middle, 7*(4), 32–37.

Nippold, M., Duthie, J., & Larsen, J. (2005). Literacy as a leisure activity: Free-time preferences of older children and young adolescents. *Language, Speech, and Hearing Services in Schools, 36,* 93–102.

No Child Left Behind Act of 2001, Pub. L. No. 107-110, 115 Stat. 1452. Retrieved July 8, 2005 from http://www.ed.gov/policy/elsec/leg/esea02/index.html.

Nolan, T. (1991). Self-questioning and prediction: Combining metacognitive strategies. *Journal of Reading, 35,* 132–138.

Nolen, S. B., & Haladyna, T. M. (1989, March). *Psyching out the science teacher: Student motivation, perceived teacher goals and study strategies.* Paper presented at the annual meeting of the American Educational Research Association, San Francisco.

Northern Illinois University's Office of Public Affairs (2005, August 31). NIU literacy professor works to close reading achievement gap for African American adolescent males. Retrieved September 28, 2005 from http://www.niu.edu/PubAffairs/RELEASES/2005/aug/tatum.shtml.

Norton, D. (1990). Teaching multicultural literature in the reading curriculum. *The Reading Teacher, 44,* 28–40.

Nystrand, M., Gamoran, A., & Heck, M. J. (1992, April). *Using small groups for response to and thinking about literature.* Paper presented at the annual meeting of the American Educational Research Association, San Francisco.

O'Brien, D. (1998). Multiple literacies in a high-school program for "at-risk" adolescents. In

D. E. Alvermann, K. A. Hinchman, D. W. Moore, S. F. Phelps, & D. R. Waff (Eds.), *Reconceptualizing the literacies in adolescents' lives* (pp. 27–49). Mahwah, NJ: Erlbaum.

O'Brien, D. (2001, June). "At-risk" adolescents: Redefining competence through the multiliteracies of intermediality, visual arts, and representation. *Reading Online, 4.* Retrieved October 18, 2003, from http://readingonline.org/new literacies/lit_index.asp?HREF=/newliteracies/ obrien/index.html.

O'Brien, D. G., Stewart, R., & Moje, E. B. (1995). Why content literacy is difficult to infuse into the secondary school: Complexities of curriculum, pedagogy, and school culture. *Reading Research Quarterly, 30,* 442–463.

O'Dell, S. (1980). *Sarah Bishop.* Boston: Houghton Mifflin.

O'Neil, W. (1998). If Ebonics isn't a language, then tell me, what is? (pace James Baldwin, 1979). In T. Perry & L. Delpit (Eds.), *The real Ebonics debate: Power, language, and the education of African-American children* (pp. 38–47). Boston: Beacon.

Oakes, J. (1985). *Keeping track: How schools structure inequality.* New Haven, CT: Yale University Press.

Oakes, J. (1986). Keeping track, Part I: The policy and practice of curricular inequality. *Phi Delta Kappan, 68,* 12–17.

Obidah, J. E. (1998). Black-mystory: Literate currency in everyday schooling. In D. E. Alvermann, K. A. Hinchman, D. W. Moore, S. F. Phelps, & D. R. Waff (Eds.), *Reconceptualizing the literacies in adolescents' lives* (pp. 51–71). Mahwah, NJ: Erlbaum.

Offner, S. (1992). Teaching biology around themes: Teach proteins & DNA together. *The American Biology Teacher, 54,* 93–101.

Ogle, D. (1986). K-W-L: A teaching model that develops active reading of expository text. *The Reading Teacher, 39,* 563–570.

Ogle, D. & Blachowicz, C. (2002). Children searching and using informational text: A critical part of comprehension. In C. Block & M. Pressley (Eds.), *Comprehension instruction: Research-based best practice* (pp. 259–274). New York: Guilford.

Orner, M. (1992). Interrupting the calls for student voice in "liberatory" education: A feminist post-structuralist perspective. In C. Luke &

J. Gore (Eds.), *Feminisms and critical pedagogy* (pp. 74–89). New York: Routledge.

Otto, W. (1990). Getting smart. *Journal of Reading, 33,* 368–370.

Ovando, C. J. (2003). Bilingual education in the United States: Historical development and current issues. *Bilingual Research Journal, 27*(1).

Palincsar, A. S. (1986). The role of dialogue in providing scaffolded instruction. *Educational Psychologist, 21,* 73–98.

Palincsar, A. S., & Brown, A. L. (1984) Reciprocal teaching of comprehension-fostering and comprehension-monitoring activities. *Cognition and Instruction, 1,* 117–175.

Palmatier, R. A. (1973). A notetaking system for learning. *Journal of Reading, 17,* 36–39.

Palmer, R. G., & Stewart, R. A. (1997). Nonfiction trade books in content area instruction: Realities and potential. *Journal of Adolescent & Adult Literacy, 40,* 630–641.

Pang, V., Colvin, C., Tran, M., & Barba, R. (1992). Beyond chopsticks and dragons: Selecting Asian-American literature for children. *The Reading Teacher, 46,* 216–224.

Paris, S. G., Lipson, M. Y., & Wixson, K. K. (1983). Becoming a strategic reader. *Contemporary Educational Psychology, 8,* 293–316.

Paris, S., Wasik, B., & Turner, J. (1991). The development of strategic readers. In R. Barr, M. Kamil, P. Mosenthal, & P. D. Pearson (Eds.), *Handbook of reading research* (Vol. 2, pp. 609–640). New York: Longman.

Patterson, A., Mellor, B., & O'Neill, M. (1994). Beyond comprehension: Poststructuralist readings in the English classroom. In B. Corcoran, M. Hayhoe, & G. M. Pradl (Eds.), *Knowledge in the making* (pp. 61–72). Portsmouth, NH: Boynton/Cook.

Patterson, N. (1999, September). Making connections: Hypertext and research in a middle school classroom. *English Journal, 89,* 69–73.

Patterson, N., & Pipkin, G. (2001). Guiding readers to new understandings through electronic text. *Voices from the Middle, 8*(4), 64–66.

Paulu, N. (1995). *Helping your child with homework.* Washington, DC: U.S. Department of Education, Office of Educational Research and Improvement.

Pearson, P. D. (1998). Standards and assessment: Tools for crafting effective instruction? In J. Osborn and F. Lehr (Eds.), *Literacy for all: Issues in teaching and learning* (pp. 264–288). New York: Guilford.

Pearson, P. D., & Fielding, L. (1991). Comprehension instruction. In R. Barr, M. Kamil, P. Mosenthal, & P. D. Pearson (Eds.), *Handbook of reading research* (Vol. 2, pp. 815–860). New York: Longman.

Pearson, P. D., & Gallagher, M. C. (1983). The instruction of reading comprehension. *Contemporary Educational Psychology, 8,* 317–344.

Pearson, P. D., & Johnson, D. (1978). *Teaching reading comprehension.* New York: Holt, Rinehart & Winston.

Peltz, C., Powers, M., & Wycoff, B. (1994, March). Teaching world economics: An interdisciplinary approach for the middle-level classroom. *Middle School Journal, 25,* 23–25.

Peralta-Nash, C., & Dutch, J. A. (2000). Literature circles: Creating environment for choice. *Primary Voices K-6, 8*(4), 29–37.

Perry, T., & Delpit, L. (Eds.) (1998). *The real Ebonics debate: Power, language, and the education of African-American children.* Boston: Beacon.

Persky, H., Daane, M., & Jin, Y. (2003). *The nation's report card: Writing 2002.* Washington, DC: U.S. Department of Education, National Center for Education Statistics.

Phelps, S. (1984). A first step in content area reading instruction. *Reading World, 23,* 265–269.

Phelps, S. F., & Weaver, D. (1999). Public and personal voices in adolescents' classroom talk. *Journal of Literacy Research, 31,* 321–354.

Phelps, T. (1992). Research or three-search? *English Journal, 81*(2), 76–78.

Phillips, D. C. (Ed.). (2000). *Constructivism in education: Opinions and second opinions on controversial issues.* Chicago: University of Chicago Press.

Pierce, L. (1988). *Facilitating transition to the mainstream: Sheltered English vocabulary development* (Program Information Guide Series No. 6). Wheaton, MD: National Clearinghouse for Bilingual Education.

Pilgreen, J. (2000). *The SSR handbook: How to organize and manage a sustained silent reading program.* Portsmouth, NH: Boynton/Cook.

Poglinco, S. M., Bach, A. J., Hovde, K., Rosenblum, S., Saunders, M., & Supovitz, J. A. (2003, May). *The heart of the matter: The coaching model in America's choice schools.* A Consortium Paper for Policy Research in Education. University of Pennsylvania, Graduate School of Education, Philadelphia, PA.

Pressley, M. (1998). Comprehension strategies instruction. In J. Osborn & F. Lehr (Eds.), *Literacy for all: Issues in teaching and learning* (pp. 113–133). New York: Guilford.

Pressley, M. (2002). Comprehension strategy instr uction: A turn-of-the-century status report. In C. Block & M. Pressley (Eds.), *Comprehension instruction: Research-based best practice* (pp. 11–27). New York: Guilford.

Pressley, M., El-Dinary, P. B., & Brown, R. (1992). Skilled and not-so-skilled reading: Good information processing and not-so-good information processing. In M. Pressley, K. R. Harris, & J. T. Guthrie (Eds.), *Promoting academic competence and literacy in school* (pp. 91–127). San Diego: Academic Press.

Pressley, M., Hogan, K., Wharton-MacDonald, R., Mistretta, J., & Ettenberger, S. (1996). The challenges of instructional scaffolding: The challenges of instruction that supports student thinking. *Learning Disabilities Research & Practice, 11,* 138–146.

Pugh, S., & Garcia, J. (1990). Portraits in black: Establishing African American identity through nonfication books. *Journal of Reading, 34,* 20–25.

Purves, A. C. (1998). *The web of text and the web of God: An essay on the third information transformation.* New York: Guilford.

Quatroche, D. J., Bean, R. M., & Hamilton, R. L. (2001). The role of the reading specialist: A review of research. *The Reading Teacher, 55,* 282–294.

Rakow, S., & Gee, T. (1987, February). Test science, not reading. *The Science Teacher, 54,* 28–31.

Randall, S. N. (2000). Information charts: A strategy for organizing student research. In D. Moore, D. Alvermann, & K. Hinchman (Eds.), *Struggling adolescent readers: A collection of strategies* (pp. 198–205). Newark, DE: International Reading Association.

Raphael, T. (1982). Question-answering strategies for children. *The Reading Teacher, 36*, 186–191.

Raphael, T. (1984). Teaching learners about sources of information for answering comprehension questions. *Journal of Reading, 27*, 303–311.

Raphael, T. (1986). Teaching question-answer relationships, revisited. *The Reading Teacher, 39*, 516–522.

Raphael, T., & Gavelek, J. (1984). Question-related activities and their relationship to reading comprehension: Some instructional implications. In G. Duffy, L. Roehler, & J. Mason (Eds.), *Comprehension instruction: Perspectives and suggestions* (pp. 234–250). New York: Longman.

Raphael, T., & Pearson, P. D. (1982). *The effect of metacognitive awareness training on children's question answering behavior*, Technical report #238. Urbana, IL: Center for the Study of Reading.

Rasinski, T., Padak, N., McKeon, C., Wilfong, L., Friedauer, J., & Heim, P. (2005). Is reading fluency a key for successful high school reading? *Journal of Adolescent & Adult Literacy, 49*, 22–27.

Ratekin, J., Simpson, M., Alvermann, D., & Dishner, E. (1985). Why teachers resist content reading instruction. *Journal of Reading, 28*, 432–437.

Rawls, J., & Weeks, P. (1985). *Land of liberty*. New York: Holt, Rinehart and Winston.

Readence, J. E., Moore, D. W., & Rickelman, R. J. (2000). *Prereading activities for content area reading and learning* (3rd ed.). Newark, DE: International Reading Association.

Reif, L. (1990). Finding the value in evaluation: Self-assessment in a middle school classroom. *Educational Leadership, 47*, 24–29.

Reimer, K. M. (1992). Multiethnic literature: Holding fast to dreams. *Language Arts, 69*, 14–21.

Reinking, D., McKenna, M., Labbo, L., & Kieffer, R. (1998). *Handbook of literacy and technology*. Mahwah, NJ: Erlbaum.

Rekrut, M. (1997). Collaborative research. *Journal of Adolescent & Adult Literacy, 41*, 26–34.

Rekrut, M. (1999). Using the Internet in classroom instruction: A primer for teachers. *Journal of Adolescent & Adult Literacy, 42*, 546–557.

Rekrut, M. D. (1994). Peer and cross-age tutoring: The lessons of research. *Journal of Reading, 37*, 356–362.

Reppen, R. (1994/1995, Winter). A genre-based approach to content writing instruction. *TESOL Journal, 4*, 32–35.

Resnick, D. P., & Goodman, M. (1994). American culture and the gifted. In P. O. Ross (Ed.), *National excellence: A case for developing America's talent: An anthology of readings* (pp. 109–121). Washington, DC: U.S. Department of Education, Office of Educational Research and Improvement.

Reyes, M. L., & Molner, L. A. (1991). Instructional strategies for second-language learners in the content areas. *Journal of Reading, 35*, 96–103.

Reynolds, R., Taylor, M., Steffensen, M., Shirey, L., & Anderson, R. (1982). Cultural schemata and reading comprehension. *Reading Research Quarterly, 17*, 353–366.

Rhodes, L. K., & Shanklin, N. L. (1993). *Windows into literacy*. Portsmouth, NH: Heinemann.

Richardson, J. (2000). *Read it aloud! Using literature in the secondary content classroom*. Newark, DE: International Reading Association.

Richardson, J. S., & Morgan, R. F. (2000). *Reading to learn in the content areas* (4th ed.). Belmont, CA: Wadsworth/Thompson Learning.

Richgels, D., McGee, L., Lomax, R., & Sheard, C. (1987). Awareness of four text structures: Effects on recall of expository text. *Reading Research Quarterly, 22*, 177–196.

Ridgeway, V. G. (1997, December). *The use of e-mail to foster pedagogical dialogue within a content area reading discourse community*. Paper presented at the 47th Annual Meeting of the National Reading Conference, Scottsdale, AZ.

Rinaldi, A. (1993). *The fifth of March*. New York: Harcourt Brace.

Rinaldi, A. (1995). *A ride into morning*. New York: Harcourt Brace.

Robinson, F. P. (1961). *Effective study I* (Rev. ed.). New York: Harper & Row.

Rosenblatt, L. (1978). *The reader, the text, the poem: The transactional theory of the literary work*. Carbondale, IL: Southern Illinois University Press.

Rosenblatt, L. (1982). The literary transaction: Evocation and response. *Theory into Practice, 21*, 268–277.

Rosenblatt, L. (1985). Transaction versus interaction–A terminological rescue operation. *Research in the Teaching of English, 19*, 96–107.

Rosenshine, B., & Meister, C. (1992). The use of scaffolds for teaching higher-level cognitive strategies. *Educational Leadership, 49(7)*, 26–33.

Rosenshine, B., & Meister, C. (1994). Reciprocal teaching: A review of the research. *Review of Educational Research, 64*, 479–530.

Rosenshine, B., Meister, C., & Chapman, S. (1996). Teaching students to generate questions: A review of the intervention studies. *Review of Educational Research, 66*, 181–221.

Roskos, K., & Walker, B. J. (1994). *Interactive handbook for understanding reading diagnosis: A problem-solving approach* (pp. 5–7). New York: Merrill.

Rothenberg, S. S., & Watts, S. M. (2000). Students with learning difficulties meet Shakespeare: Using a scaffolded reading experience. In D. W. Moore, D. E. Alvermann, & K. A. Hinchman (Eds.), *Struggling adolescent readers: A collection of teaching strategies* (pp. 148–156). Newark, DE: International Reading Association.

Rozycki, E. G. (2005). Can we trust "best practices"? *Educational Horizons, 83*, 226–230.

Rubenstein-Avila, E. (2003). Facing reality: English language learners in middle school classes. *English Education, 35*, 122–136.

Ruddell, M. (1996). Engaging students' interest and willing participation in subject area learning. In D. Lapp, J. Flood, & N. Farnan (Eds.), *Content area reading and learning: Instructional strategies* (2nd ed., pp. 95–110). Boston: Allyn & Bacon.

Ruddell, M. R. (1997). *Teaching content reading and writing* (2nd ed.). Boston: Allyn & Bacon.

Ruddell, M., & Shearer, B. (2002). "Extraordinary . . . magnificent": Middle school at-risk students become avid word learners with Vocabulary Self-Collection Strategy. *Journal of Adolescent & Adult Literacy, 45*, 352–363.

Rudge, D., & Howe, E. (2004, November). Incorporating history into the science classroom. *The Science Teacher, 71*, 52–57.

Russell, M., & Plati, T. (2000). *Mode of administration effects on MCAS composition performance for grades four, eight, and ten.* Retrieved October 8, 2005 from www.bc.edu/research/nbetpp/statements/WE052200.pdf.

Samuels, B. (1989). Young adults' choices: Why do students "really like" particular books? *Journal of Reading, 32*, 714–719.

Sanacore, J. (1990). Creating the lifetime reading habit in social studies. *Journal of Reading, 33*, 414–419.

Sanacore, J. (2000). Promoting the lifetime reading habit in middle school students. *The Clearinghouse, 73*, 157–161.

Sanders, M. (1994). Technological problem-solving activities as a means of instruction: The TSM integration program. *School Science & Mathematics, 94*, 36–43.

Santa, C. M. (1988). *Content reading including study systems.* Dubuque, IA: Kendall/Hunt.

Santa, C., Havens, L., & Harrison, S. (1996). Teaching secondary science through reading, writing, studying, and problem-solving. In D. Lapp, J. Flood, & N. Farnan (Eds.), *Content area reading and learning: Instructional strategies* (2nd ed., pp. 165–180). Boston: Allyn & Bacon.

Sarroub, L., Pearson, P. D., Dykema, C., & Lloyd, R. (1997). When portfolios become part of the grading process: A case study in a junior high setting. In C. Kinzer, K. Hinchman, & D. Leu (Eds.), *Inquiries in literacy theory and practice* (pp. 101–113). Chicago: National Reading Conference.

Saunders, W. M., & Goldenberg, C. (1999). *The effects of instructional conversations and literature logs on the story comprehension and thematic understanding of English proficient and limited English proficient students.* Santa Cruz, CA: Center for Research on Education, Diversity and Excellence.

Scanlon, D., Deshler, D. D., & Schumaker, J. B. (1996). Can a strategy be taught and learned in secondary inclusive classrooms? *Learning Disabilities Research & Practice, 11*, 41–57.

Schallert, D., & Roser, N. (1996). The role of reading in content area instruction. In D. Lapp, J. Flood, & N. Farnan (Eds.), *Content area reading and learning* (2nd ed., pp. 27–38). Englewood Cliffs, NJ: Prentice Hall.

Schatz, E., & Baldwin, S. (1986). Context clues are unreliable predictors of word meanings. *Reading Research Quarterly, 21*, 439–453.

Schell, L. (1988). Dilemmas in assessing reading comprehension. *The Reading Teacher, 42*, 12–16.

Schimberg, A., & Grant, H. (1998, Fall). Whodun-it? A mystery thematic unit. *Science Activities, 35*, 29–35.

Schmidt, H. G. (1993). Foundations of problem-based learning: Some explanatory notes. *Medical Education 27*, 422–432.

Schoenbach, R., Braunger, J., Greenleaf, C., & Litman, C. (2003, October). Apprenticing adolescents to reading in subject-area classrooms. *Phi Delta Kappan, 85*, 133–138.

Schoenbach, R., Greenleaf, C., Cziko, C., & Hurwitz, L. (1999). *Reading for understanding: A guide to improving reading in middle and high school classrooms*. San Francisco: Jossey-Bass.

Schraer, W., & Stoltze, H. (1993). *Biology: The study of life* (5th ed.). Englewood Cliffs, NJ: Prentice Hall.

Schultz, K., & Fecho, B. (2000). Society's child: Social context and writing development. *Educational Psychologist, 35*, 51–62.

Schwarz, G. E. (2002). Graphic novels for multiple literacies. *Journal of Adolescent & Adult Literacy, 46*, 262–265.

Schwarz, G. (2004, October). Graphic novels: Multiple cultures and multiple literacies. *Thinking Classroom, 5*, 17–24.

Schwartz, R. (1988). Learning to learn vocabulary in content area textbooks. *Journal of Reading, 32*, 108–118.

Schwartz, R., & Raphael, T. (1985). Concept of definition: A key to improving students' vocabulary. *The Reading Teacher, 39*, 198–205.

Scott, J. C. (1990). *Domination and the arts of resistance*. New Haven, CT: Yale University Press.

Scott, T. (2005). Consensus through accountability? The benefits and drawbacks of building community with accountability. *Journal of Adolescent & Adult Literacy, 49*, 48–59.

Sefton-Green, J. (1999). Young people, creativity and new technologies: The challenge of digital arts. London: Routledge and the Arts Council of England.

Sewall, G. (1988). American history textbooks: Where do we go from here? *Phi Delta Kappan, 69*, 553–558.

Shaara, M. (1974). *The killer angels*. New York: Ballantine.

Shanahan, T. (1995). Avoiding some of the pitfalls of thematic units. *The Reading Teacher, 48*, 718–719.

Shealy, A. (2000, Spring/Summer). On becoming a teacher and writer. *Bread Loaf Rural Teacher Network Magazine*, 10–11.

Sheehan, A. D., & Sheehan, C. M. (2000). Lost in a sea of ink: How I survived the storm. *Journal of Adolescent & Adult Literacy, 44*, 20–32.

Shefelbine, J. (1990). Student factors related to variability in learning word meanings from context. *Journal of Reading Behavior, 22*, 71–97.

Simmons, J. (1990, March). Adapting portfolios for large-scale use. *Educational Leadership, 47*, 28.

Sinatra, G., Brown, K. & Reynolds, R. (2002). Implications of cognitive resource allocation for comprehension strategies instruction. In C. Block & M. Pressley (Eds.), *Comprehension instruction: Research-based best practice* (pp. 62–76). New York: Guilford.

Singer, H., & Donlan, D. (1982). Active comprehension: Problem-solving schema with question generation for comprehension of complex short stories. *Reading Research Quarterly, 17*, 166–186.

Singer, H., & Donlan, D. (1989). *Reading and learning from text*. Hillsdale, NJ: Erlbaum.

Skilton-Sylvester, E. (2002). Literate at home but not at school. In G. Hull & K. Schultz (Eds.), *School's out! Bridging out-of-school literacies with classroom practice* (pp. 61–90). New York: Teachers College Press.

Slavin, R. E. (1983). *Cooperative learning*. New York: Longman.

Slavin, R. E. (1984a). Students motivating students to excel: Cooperative incentives, cooperative tasks, and student achievement. *Elementary School Journal, 85*, 53–63.

Slavin, R. E. (1984b). Team assisted individuation: Cooperative learning and individualized instruction in the mainstreamed classroom. *Remedial and Special Education, 5*(6), 33–42.

Smith, C., & Bean, T. (1980). The guided writing procedure: Integrating content reading and writing improvement. *Reading World, 19*, 290–298.

Smith, F. (1971). *Understanding reading: A psycholinguistic analysis of reading and learning to read*. New York: Holt, Rinehart and Winston.

Smith, F. R., & Feathers, K. M. (1983a). Teacher and student perceptions of content area reading. *Journal of Reading, 26*, 348–354.

Smith, F. R., & Feathers, K. M. (1983b). The role of reading in content classrooms: Assumption vs. reality. *Journal of Reading, 27*, 262–267.

Smith, M., & Wilhelm, J. (2002). *Reading don't fix no Chevys: Literacy in the lives of young men.* Portsmouth, NH: Heinemann.

Smolen, L., Newman, C., Wathen, T., & Lee, D. (1995). Developing student self-assessment strategies. *TESOL Journal, 5,* 22–27.

Soetaert, R., & Bonamie, B. (1999). *New rules for the content game.* Retrieved September 26, 2003, from University of Ghent. http://memling.rug.ac.be/CLIL/content.html.

Spears-Bunton, L. (1990). Welcome to my house: African American and European American students' responses to Virginia Hamilton's *House of Dies Drear. Journal of Negro Education, 59,* 566–576.

Spears-Bunton, L. (1991, December). *Literature, literacy and resistance to cultural domination.* Paper presented at the meeting of the National Reading Conference, Palm Springs, CA.

Spears-Bunton, L. (1998). All the colors of the land: A literacy montage. In A. Willis (Ed.), *Teaching and using multicultural literature in grades 9–12: Moving beyond the canon* (pp. 17–36). Norwood, MA: Christopher Gordon.

Spiegelman, A. (1986) *Maus.* New York: Pantheon Books.

Spires, H. A., & Stone, P. D. (1989). The directed note-taking activity: A self-questioning approach. *Journal of Reading, 33,* 36–39.

Sprague, M., & Cotturone, J. (2003, March). Motivating students to read physics content. *The Science Teacher, 70,* 24–29.

Stahl, S. A. (1983). Differential word knowledge and reading comprehension: *Journal of Reading Behavior, 15*(4), 33–50.

Stahl, S. A., & Fairbanks, M. M. (1986). The effects of vocabulary instruction: A model-based meta-analysis. *Review of Educational Research, 56,* 72–110.

Stahl, S., & Clark, C. (1987). The effects of participatory expectations in classroom discussion on the learning of science vocabulary. *American Educational Research Journal, 24,* 541–556.

Stahl, S., & Kapinus, B. (1991). Possible sentences: Predicting word meanings to teach content area vocabulary. *The Reading Teacher, 45,* 36–43.

Standards for Middle and High School Literacy Coaches. (2006). Newark, DE: International Reading Association. Retrieved January 3, 2006 from http://www. reading.org/downloads/resources/597coaching_standards.pdf.

Standards for Reading Professionals-Revised 2003. Newark, DE: International Reading Association. Retrieved January 3, 2006, from http://www.reading.org/resources/issues/reports/professional_standards.html.

Stanovich, K. E. (1980). Toward an interactive-compensatory model of individual differences in the development of reading fluency. *Reading Research Quarterly, 16,* 32–71.

Stauffer, R. (1969). *Directing reading maturity as a cognitive process.* New York: Harper & Row.

Stauffer, R. (1976). *Teaching reading as a thinking process.* New York: Harper & Row.

Steffensen, M., Joag-Dev, C., & Anderson, R. (1979). A cross-cultural perspective on reading comprehension. *Reading Research Quarterly, 15,* 10–29.

Stein, N., & Glenn, C. (1979). An analysis of story comprehension in elementary school children. In R. O. Freedle (Ed.), *New directions in discourse processing.* Norwood, NJ: Ablex.

Steinbeck, J. (1989). *The pearl.* In R. Anderson, J. Brinnin, J. Leggett, & D. Leeming (Eds.), *Elements of literature* (pp. 674–712). Austin, TX: Holt, Rinehart & Winston.

Sternberg, R. J. (1987). Teaching critical thinking: Eight easy ways to fail before you begin. *Phi Delta Kappan, 68,* 456–459.

Sternberg, R. J., & Grigorenko, E. L. (2000). *Teaching for successful intelligence.* Arlington Heights, IL: Skylight.

Sternberg, R. J., Grigorenko, E. L., Jarvin, L., Clinkenbeard, P., Ferrari, M., & Torff, B. (2000, Spring). The effectiveness of triarchic teaching and assessment. *The National Center on the Gifted and Talented Newsletter,* pp. 3–8.

Stiggins, R., Frisbie, D., & Griswold, P. (1989). Inside high school grading practices: Building a research agenda. *Journal of Educational Measurement, 8,* 5–14.

Stodolsky, S. S. (1988). *The subject matters.* Chicago: University of Chicago Press.

Strategic Literacy Initiative (2004a). *Increasing student achievement through schoolwide reading apprenticeship, 2001-2004.* Retrieved September 22, 2005 from http://www.wested.org/cs/sli/print/docs/sli/widereading. htm.

Strategic Literacy Initiative (2004b). *Reading appren-ticeship classroom study: Linking professional development for teachers to outcomes for students in diverse subject-area classrooms, 2001–2004.* Retrieved September 22, 2005 from http://www.wested.org/cs/sli/print/docs/sli/classroom study.htm.

Strategic Literacy Initiative (2004c). *Studies of student reading growth in diverse professional development networks, 1999–2002.* Retrieved September 22, 2005 from http://www.wested.org/cs/sli/print/docs/sli/readinggrowth.htm.

Street, B. V. (1995). *Social literacies: Critical approaches to literacy in development, ethnography, and education.* New York: Longman.

Street, B. (2003). What's "new" in New Literacy Studies? Critical approaches to literacy in theory and practice. *Current Issues in Comparative Education, 5,* 1–14. Available on-line at http://www.tc.columbia.edu/cice/articles/bs152.pdf.

Strother, D. B. (1985). Adapting instruction to individual needs: An eclectic approach. *Phi Delta Kappan, 67,* 308–311.

Sturtevant, E. G. (1996). Lifetime influences on the literacy-related instructional beliefs of expe-rienced high school history teachers: Two com-parative case studies. *Journal of Literacy Research, 28,* 227–257.

Sturtevant, E. G. (2003, November). *The literacy coach: A key to improving teaching and learning in secondary schools.* Washington, DC: Alliance for Excellent Education.

Survey finds students, teachers show bias (2000, May). *The Council Chronicle,* p. 13.

Sutherland-Smith, W. (2002). Weaving the literacy Web: Changes in reading from page to screen. *The Reading Teacher, 55,* 662–669.

Swafford, J. (1988, December). *The use of study strategy instruction with secondary school stu-dents: Is there a research base?* Paper presented at the annual meeting of the National Reading Conference, Tucson, AZ.

Swanson, P., & de la Paz, S. (1998). Teaching effec-tive comprehension strategies to students with learning and reading disabilities. *Intervention in School and Clinic, 33,* 209–218.

Taba, H. (1967). *Teacher's handbook for elemen-tary social studies.* Reading, MA: Addison-Wesley.

Tatum, A. W. (2000). Breaking down barriers that disenfranchise African American adolescent readers in low-level tracks. *Journal of Adolescent & Adult Literacy, 44,* 52–64.

Tatum, A. W. (2005). *Teaching reading to black adoles-cent males: Closing the achievement gap.* Portland, ME: Stenhouse.

Taylor, B., & Beach, R. (1984). The effects of text structure instruction on middle-grade students' comprehension and production of expository text. *Reading Research Quarterly, 19,* 134–146.

Taylor, D., & Dorsey-Gaines, C. (1988). *Growing up literate: Learning from inner-city families.* Portsmouth, NH: Heinemann.

Taylor, M. (1976). *Roll of thunder, hear my cry.* New York: Dial.

Taylor, T. (1984). *The hostage.* New York: Bantam.

Taylor, W. (1953). Cloze procedure: A new tool for measuring readability. *Journalism Quarterly, 30,* 415–433.

Teemant, A., Pinnegar, S., Tharp, R., & Harris, C. (2001). The Mara Mills case: A video ethnogra-phy of biological science in a sheltered English class room. Center for Research on Educa-tion, Diversity & Excellence. Available on-line at http://www.crede.ucsc.edu/products/multi media/cdroms.html.

Temple, C. (2005). Critical thinking and critical literacy. *Thinking Classroom: A Journal of the International Reading Association, 6*(2), 15–20.

Temple, F. (1993). *Grab hands and run.* New York: Orchard.

Tharp, R., & Gallimore, R. (1988). *Rousing minds to life: Teaching, learning, and schooling in social context.* Cambridge, UK: Cambridge University Press.

Tharp, R., Dalton, S. S., & Yamauchi, L. (1994). Principles for culturally compatible Native American education. *Journal of Navajo Educa-tion, 11*(3), 33–39.

Thomas, H. K. (1999). The social construction of literacy in a high school biology class. In T. Shanahan & F. V. Rodriguez-Brown (Eds.), *48th Yearbook of the National Reading Conference.* Chicago: National Reading Conference.

Thomas, J. W., & Rohwer, W. D. (1986). Academic studying: The role of learning strategies. *Educational Psychologist, 21,* 19–41.

Thomas, W. (1986, February). Grading—Why are school policies necessary? What are the issues? *NASSP Bulletin, 70,* 22–26.

Thomas, W., & Collier, V. (2002). *A national study of school effectiveness for language minority students' long-term academic achievement.* Santa Cruz, CA and Washington, DC: Center for Research on Education, Diversity and Excellence.

Tierney, R., Clark, C., Fenner, L., Herter, R., Simpson, C., & Wiser, B. (1998). Portfolios: Assumptions, tensions and possibilities. *Reading Research Quarterly, 33,* 474–486.

Tierney, R., Readence, J., & Dishner, E. (2000). *Reading strategies and practices: A compendium* (5th ed.). Boston: Allyn & Bacon.

Tierney, R., Soter, A., O'Flahavan, J., & McGinley, W. (1989). The effects of reading and writing upon thinking critically. *Reading Research Quarterly, 24,* 134–173.

Trelease, J. (2001). *The new read-aloud handbook.* (5th ed.). New York: Penguin.

Trujillo, L. (2000, March 12). Latino or Hispanic? *The Arizona Republic,* pp. A1, A22.

Twain, M. (1961). *Life on the Mississippi.* New York: New American Library.

U.S. Department of Education (1998). *Pocket projections: Projections of education statistics to 2008* (NCES Report No. 98-017). Washington, DC: National Center for Education Statistics.

Valdez, P. (2001, November). Alternative assessment. *Science Teacher, 68,* 41–43.

Valencia, S., & Wixson, K. (2000). Policy-oriented research on literacy standards and assessment. In M. Kamil, P. Mosenthal, P. D. Pearson, & R. Barr (Eds.), *Handbook of reading research* (Vol. 3, pp. 909–935). Mahwah, NJ: Erlbaum.

Van Slyck, M., & Stern, M. (1999). A developmental approach to the use of conflict resolution interventions with adolescents. In L. R. Forcey & I. M. Harris (Eds.), *Peacebuilding for adolescents: Strategies for educators and community leaders* (pp. 177–193). New York: Lang.

Van Voorhis, F. L. (2003). Interactive homework in middle school: Effects on family involvement and science achievement. *Journal of Educational Research, 96,* 323–340.

Vaughn, T. H., & Vaughn, J. L. Jr. (1985). *Reading and learning in the content classroom: Diagnostic and instructional strategies.* Boston: Allyn & Bacon.

Vande Steeg, M. (1991). A new challenge for teachers. *The American Biology Teacher, 53,* 20–21.

Vogt, M., & Shearer, B. A. (2003). *Reading specialists in the real world: A sociocultural view.* Boston: Pearson Education.

Vygotsky, L. (1986). *Thought and language.* Cambridge, MA: MIT Press.

Vygotsky, L. S. (1978). *Mind in society: The development of higher psychological processes.* Cambridge, MA: Harvard University Press.

Wade, S. E., & Moje, E. B. (2000). The role of text in classroom learning. In M. L. Kamil, P. B. Mosenthal, P. D. Pearson, & R. Barr (Eds.), *Handbook of reading research* (Vol. 3, pp. 609–627). Mahwah, NJ: Erlbaum.

Wade, S. E., & Reynolds, R. E. (1989). Developing metacognitive awareness. *Journal of Reading, 33,* 6–14.

Walpole, S. (1998/1999). Changing texts, changing thinking: Comprehension demands of new science textbooks. *The Reading Teacher, 52,* 358–369.

Walpole, S., & McKenna, M. C. (2004). *The literacy coach's handbook: A guide to research-based practice.* New York: Guilford.

Walvoord, B., & Anderson, V. (1998). *Effective grading: A tool for learning and assessment.* San Francisco: Jossey-Bass.

Wandersee, J. H. (1987). Drawing concept circles: A new way to teach and test students. *Science Activities, 24*(4), 9–20.

Warger, C. L., & Rutherford, R. B., Jr. (1997). Teaching respect and responsibility in inclusive classrooms: An instructional approach. *Reclaiming Children and Youth, 6*(3), 171–175.

Watson, B., & Konicek, R. (1990). Teaching for conceptual change: Confronting children's experience. *Phi Delta Kappan, 71,* 680–685.

Weaver, C. (1988). *Reading process and practice: From sociopsycholinguistics to whole language.* Portsmouth, NH: Heinemann.

Weber, A. (2000). Playful writing for critical thinking: Four approaches to writing. *Journal of Adolescent & Adult Literacy, 43,* 562–568.

Webster's New World Dictionary of American English (Third College Edition). (1991). New York: Prentice Hall.

Weiner, B. (1986). *An attributional theory of motivation and emotion.* New York: Springer-Verlag.

Welner, K. G., & Oakes, J. (1996). (Li)ability grouping: The new susceptibility of school tracking systems to legal challenges. *Harvard Educational Review, 66,* 451–470.

Wenger, E. (1998). *Communities of practice: Learning, meaning, and identity.* Cambridge, UK: Cambridge University Press.

Wertsch, J. V. (1985). *Vygotsky and the social formation of mind.* Cambridge, MA: Harvard University Press.

Wertsch, J. V. (1991). *Voices of the mind.* Cambridge, MA: Harvard University Press.

Westera, J., & Moore, D. W. (1995). Reciprocal teaching of reading comprehension in a New Zealand high school. *Psychology in the Schools, 32,* 225–232.

White, R. M. (1995). How thematic teaching can transform history instruction. *The Clearinghouse, 68,* 160–162.

White, T., Graves, M., & Slater, W. (1990). Growth of reading vocabulary in diverse elementary schools: Decoding and word meaning. *Journal of Educational Psychology, 82,* 281–289.

Wigfield, A., Wilde, K., Baker, L., Fernandez-Fein, S., & Scher, D. (1996). *The nature of children's motivations for reading, and their relations to reading frequency and reading performance.* (Research Report No. 63). Athens: University of Georgia, National Reading Research Center.

Wiggins, G. (1993, Fall). Assessment to improve performance, not just monitor it: Assessment reform in the social sciences. *Social Science Record, 30,* 5–12.

Wiggins, G. (1998). *Educative assessment: Designing assessments to inform and improve student performance.* San Francisco: Jossey-Bass.

Willinsky, J. (1990). *The new literacy: Redefining reading and writing in the schools.* New York: Routledge.

Willis, A. (Ed.). (1998). *Teaching and using multicultural literature in grades 9–12: Moving beyond the canon.* Norwood, MA: Christopher Gordon.

Willis, A., & Palmer, M. (1998). Negotiating the classroom: Learning and teaching multicultural literature. In A. Willis (Ed.), *Teaching and using multicultural literature in grades 9–12: Moving beyond the canon* (pp. 215–250). Norwood, MA: Christopher Gordon.

Willis, S. (1993). Are letter grades obsolete? *ASCD Update, 35,* 1, 4, 8.

Wineburg, S. (1991). On the reading of historical texts: Notes on the breach between school and academy. *American Educational Research Journal, 28,* 495–519.

Winograd, P. N. (1984). Strategic difficulties in summarizing texts. *Reading Research Quarterly, 19,* 404–425.

Wolf, D., King, J. (Producers), & Van Sant, G. (Director). (2000). *Finding Forrester* [Motion picture]. United States: Columbia Pictures.

Wolf, K., & Siu-Runyan, Y. (1996). Portfolio purposes and possibilities. *Journal of Adolescent & Adult Literacy, 40,* 30–37.

Wolf, S., Edmiston, B., & Encisco, P. (1997). Drama worlds. In J. Flood, D. Lapp, & S. B. Heath (Eds.), *Handbook of research on teaching literacy through the communicative and visual arts* (pp. 492–505). New York: Macmillan.

Wolfe, R. R. (2000). Protein supplements and exercise. *The American Journal of Clinical Nutrition, 72,* 551–557.

Wong, B. (1997). Research on genre-specific strategies for enhancing writing in adolescents with learning disabilities. *Learning Disability Quarterly, 20,* 140–159.

Wong, B., Butler, D., Ficzere, S., & Kuperis, S. (1997). Teaching adolescents with learning disabilities and low achievers to plan, write, and revise compare-and-contrast essays. *Learning Disabilities Research & Practice, 12,* 2–15.

Wood, D., Bruner, J. S., & Ross, G. (1976). The role of tutoring in problem solving. *Journal of Child Psychology and Psychiatry, 17,* 89–100.

Wood, K. (1986). The effect of interspersing questions in text: Evidence for "slicing the task." *Reading Research & Instruction, 25,* 295–307.

Wood, K. (1988). Guiding students through informational text. *The Reading Teacher, 41,* 912–920.

Woods 100 helps to restore self-respect. (1978, December 30). *The Australian* (No. 4497).

Woodward, A., & Elliott, D. L. (1990). Textbook use and teacher professionalism. In D. L. Elliott & A. Woodward (Eds.), *Textbooks and schooling in the*

United States (Eighty-ninth Yearbook of the National Society for the Study of Education, Part I, pp. 179–193). Chicago: University of Chicago Press.

Worthy, J., Moorman, M., & Turner, M. (1999). What Johnny likes to read is hard to find in school. *Reading Research Quarterly, 34,* 12–27.

Wren, S. (2002). Ten myths of reading instruction. *SEDL Letter, 14*(3), 1–3. (A newsletter of the Southwest Educational Development Laboratory)

Wu, S., & Rubin, D. (2000). Evaluating the impact of collectivism and individualism on argumentative writing by Chinese and North American college students. *Research in the Teaching of English, 35,* 148–178.

Wysocki, K., & Jenkins, J. (1987). Deriving word meanings through morphological generalization. *Reading Research Quarterly, 22,* 66–81.

Yatvin, J. (2002). Babes in the woods: The wanderings of the National Reading Panel. In R. Allington, (Ed.), *Big Brother and the national reading curriculum: How ideology trumped evidence* (pp. 125–136). Portsmouth, NH: Heinemann.

Young, A. J., Arbreton, A. J., & Midgley, C. (1992, April). All *content areas may not be created equal: Motivational orientation and cognitive strategy use in four academic domains*. Paper presented at the annual meeting of the American Educational Research Association, San Francisco.

Young, J. P. (2000). Critical literacy: Young adolescent boys talk about masculinities within a homeschool context. *Reading Research Quarterly, 35,* 312–337.

Young, J. P., Mathews, S. R., Kietzmann, A. M., & Westerfield, T. (2000). Getting disenchanted adolescents to participate in school literacy activities: Portfolio conferences. In D. W. Moore, D. E. Alvermann, & K. A. Hinchman (Eds.), *Struggling adolescent readers: A collection of teaching strategies* (pp. 302–316). Newark, DE: International Reading Association.

Zeller, T. (2005, January 17). Measuring literacy in a world gone digital. *New York Times.* Retrieved January 18, 2005 from www.nytimes.com/ 2005/01/ 17/technology/17test.html.

Zimmerman, B. J. (1994). Dimensions of academic self-regulation: A conceptual framework for education. In D. H. Schunk & B. J. Zimmerman (Eds.), *Self-regulation of learning and performance* (pp. 3–21). Hillsdale, NJ: Erlbaum.

Zinsser, W. (1988). *Writing to Learn.* New York: Harper & Row.

Author Index

Subject Index

INTERFACES:

*les affaires et la technologie
à travers la vie de tous les jours*

BARBARA L. BLACKBOURN
GEORGIA INSTITUTE OF TECHNOLOGY

CATHERINE MARIN
GEORGIA INSTITUTE OF TECHNOLOGY

INTERFACES:

les affaires et la technologie
à travers la vie de tous les jours

John Wiley & Sons, Inc.
NEW YORK   CHICHESTER   WEINHEIM   BRISBANE   TORONTO   SINGAPORE

ACQUISITIONS MANAGER	**Lyn McLean**
FREELANCE DEVELOPMENTAL EDITOR	**Pat Ménard**
MARKETING MANAGER	**Leslie Hines**
PRODUCTION EDITOR	**Tony VenGraitis**
DESIGN SUPERVISOR	**Laura Boucher**
INTERIOR DESIGNER	**Sheree Goodman Design, Inc.**
COVER DESIGN	**Harry Nolan**
MANUFACTURING MANAGER	**Dorothy Sinclair**
PHOTO EDITOR	**Hilary Newman**
ILLUSTRATION COORDINATOR	**Anna Melhorn**
OUTSIDE PRODUCTION SUPERVISOR	**Carl Morse**

This book was set in Cheltenham by Ruttle Shaw & Wetherill, Inc. and printed and bound by Courier Stoughton at Westford. The cover was printed by Lehigh Press.

Library of Congress Cataloging in Publication Data:

Blackbourn, Barbara L.
    Interfaces : les affaires et la technologie à travers la vie de
tous les jours / Barbara L. Blackbourn, Catherine Marin.
       p.   cm.
    French and English.
    Includes index.
    ISBN 0-471-13893-2 (pbk. : alk. paper)
    1. French language—Business French. 2. French language—
Textbooks for foreign speakers—English. I. Marin, Catherine.
II. Title.
PC2120.C6B54 1997
448.2'421'02465—dc21

                                      97–1443
                                       CIP

Printed in the United States of America

10 9 8 7 6 5 4 3 2 1

$\mathcal{W}$elcome to **Interfaces!** Soon you will begin to *read* and *write* about, *listen* to French people speak about, and perhaps most importantly *talk* about many aspects of business and technology from an everyday life perspective. You'll begin from a personal standpoint, then consider a professional point of view.

     Interfaces targets an intermediate level of proficiency and was written to introduce you to the world of business and technology from an applied language vantage point. Each dossier begins with a daily living context. Using a dialogue as a point of departure, you methodically learn to speak, hear, read and write about business and technology first from a *personal,* then from a *professional* perspective. The importance, interrelationship, and impact of business and technology on everyday life is thus seen by focusing—both from within and without—on all three realms.

     Because each module is divided into three discrete yet interrelated dossiers, this program is readily adaptable to a semester or quarter system and fits both high school and college curricula. Each of ***Interfaces'*** six modules (for a total of 18 dossiers) is imbedded in a matrix of authentic French culture.

     Once again, welcome and enjoy!

BARBARA L. BLACKBOURN
CATHERINE MARIN

Overview of the Program

Interfaces is a fully integrated, applied language program that targets business and technology from an everyday life perspective—all at an intermediate level of proficiency in French.

Solid and traditional, yet innovative and stimulating, *Interfaces* is tight and cohesive. Complete with an entire *Audio Program* and *Guide d'étude* (Home Study Guide), *Interfaces* not only integrates all four language skills (reading, writing, listening and speaking) within an authentic matrix of French culture, but also enhances pronunciation and intonation as well as oral comprehension, grammar and structures through the use of systematic content-specific components designed and tested specifically for intermediate students.

Purpose

Interfaces provides a simple, straightforward and practical approach to the study of French. Its inviting and engaging dialogues give you easy access to various facets of the worlds of business and technology from a personal point of view.

In order to provide you with the vocabulary and structures necessary to markedly increase your proficiency in French, we offer highly supportive and encouraging clusters of activities, reinforced by audiocassettes. These activities give the linguistic tools you need to ask questions that will enhance your understanding of specific contexts.

To stimulate your learning we use multiple teaching styles and learning strategies. At the same time, we equip you with a certain knowledge of French culture and life as well as with the social skills necessary to interact appropriately while abroad.

To most efficiently prepare you for co-op positions and future employment, we went to French and Quebecer corporations and requested their input for the *Interfaces* program.

Strengths

The *Interfaces* program

- Integrates business, technology and everyday life
- Contains natural dialogues and current information

- Is practical and informative
- Is well-integrated both thematically and structurally
- Gives a "how to" approach to such varied and practical situations as

> Job hunting
>
> Opening a bank account
>
> Looking for the insurance best suited to one's needs
>
> Calming down and centering before a job interview or an important business meeting

- Approaches content areas from several different points of view or perspectives
- Teaches multiple communicative styles and strategies and appeals to *kinesthetic, visual* and *auditory* learners
- Highlights fundamental grammar and structures using the vocabulary inherent to the content areas in question
- Suggests small group activities and a constant interviewing and notetaking process to get at the heart of the subject matter in question and to elicit as much speech as possible with a high rate of retention
- Emphasises definition-giving, circumlocution and other vocabulary enhancing techniques
- Develops reading strategies through skimming, scanning, dictionary searches and cognate activities
- Builds a cultural matrix for you to explore (the French culture truly permeates the entire series)
- Reflects on and integrates team-building strategies and techniques
- Is permeated by many special touches, insights, words of wisdom, suggestions or advice, as well as cultural and lexical observations
- Systematically reviews pronunciation pitfalls using examples from the context in question
- Offers a lexicon of specialized items at the end of each dossier for those of you interested in preparing for the French C.C.I.P. certificate
- Is easily tailored to suit your needs thanks to the flexible nature of modules that are able to stand alone
- Provides a multitude of exercise and activity types, including role plays, skits, situations, and applications
- Juxtaposes the present and the past and asks you to constantly compare and contrast
- Incorporates summaries and charts for at-a-glance review
- Allows you to work at your own pace through the Home Study Guide (complete with an answer key)
- Uses systematic visual previews plus pre-activities, recycles lexical elements, grammar and structures and offers springboards for follow-up learning
- Provides native-speaker writing samples to study and teaches you the importance of French script
- Encourages you to want to learn more
- Is learner-friendly (with a generous use of annotation and glosses)

- Represents a cross section of French culture with characters of varying ages and backgrounds and addresses different registers of language
- Acquaints you with major French and Quebecer industries as well as examples of small businesses and mid-sized companies
- Aptly moves you from the self to the family to the community to the nation to the world
- Is complemented by a wealth of ancillaries (audiocassettes to accompany both the Textbook and the Home Study Guide, audio lab tapes and blackline masters)
- Has been tested, refined and enriched over the last 7 years by students' use, instructors' input and by native-speaker teams
- Is readily adaptable to semester or quarter systems and to both high-school and college curricula
- Is highly innovative and like *nothing* else on the market!

Developmental Process

To both highlight and capitalize on the strong points of Georgia Tech's existing programs, to better prepare our students for potential positions in an international market and optimize their learning, we needed materials that

- Targeted the intermediate level and encouraged stretching to the advanced level
- Were engaging, varied and appealing
- Fully integrated business, technology and everyday life.

To generate the original material for the intensive program in French, begun in 1991, we worked in small teams of 2–5 people. These informal, directed get-togethers were to give rise to a wealth of information in the form of proviso definitions, practical applications, vocabulary lists and the like. To generate applied language materials, we identified points of intersection among business, technology and everyday life. From these volumes, which we constantly modified, synthesized, refined and tested, we created a myriad of specific activities plus verb frames, role plays, skits, debates, etc., appropriate for the intermediate level. Outside reviewers were brought in to critique our program, and test sites were set up here and abroad. We began giving seminars and workshops on the teaching of business and technology almost immediately. In addition, with new teams of graduate-level native speakers every year as well as enthusiastic students, each successive session brought forth fresh ideas and helped refine and enhance the existing materials. Writing the **Interfaces** program was the next logical step.

In this final **Interfaces** text, the dialogues play a central role. As the focal point of each dossier, they were reshaped and refined during the developmental process and were to determine to a great extent the form the program as a whole was to take. These lively, tightly-knit dialogues (recorded on cassette by native speakers) integrate various registers of language. They closely link basic themes of business and technology and methodically incorporate geographical locations and methods of transportation. The personal flows naturally into the professional as each situation is encountered or elaborated upon.

Features of the **Interfaces** *Program*

The **Ouverture** in the form of an **Eventail de photos sur le même thème** (photo cluster) gives a quick visual preview of the theme for each module. Each dossier opens with a brief introduction and one or more **Pré-activités** that draw you into a mindset receptive to the subject matter in question by helping you recall words and expressions you have already used or seen.

Les mots pour le dire sections present the **Vocabulaire de base,** which provides the English equivalent of French words and expressions that you may not recognize immediately or might easily misspell. As a student of an intermediate proficiency level, you should master at least those terms printed in color. The **Cassette audio** complements the oral and written activities of this and subsequent sections.

Preceded by various activities (such as skimming, scanning, dictionary searches, and cognate recognition as well as pointed personal questions and other warm-up exercises), a glossed **Dialogue** uses the vocabulary words in a true-to-life context with authentic language. The dialogue is followed by exercises such as **Autrement dit** and **Avez-vous compris?** that integrate business, technology, and everyday life. Photos, illustrations, graphic art, and line drawings enhance understanding throughout the text.

The **Encadrés** interspersed throughout each module engage you through special touches and insights, words of wisdom, suggestions or advice and cultural or lexical observations. Some also serve as springboards for personal growth and creativity and draw forth the essence of the French that's a part of each of us. The **Réflexions sur le travail en équipe** section asks you to consider methods and processes to use when participating in a group and encourages you to build your own teamwork skills, brainstorm, and effect solutions. Certain boxes juxtapose the present and the past, others compare and contrast, and ask you to embrace the French culture, stretch in your creation of language, and express yourself in both a personal and a professional manner. Several box types are grouped under the heading **Quelques points de repère** and appear in each Dossier.

The **Lectures** come from recently published sources. Their **Activités et exercices** ask that you efficiently skim for the main idea of the reading, scan for specific information, and build upon your personal and professional vocabulary base.

The **Applications** and **La parole est à vous!** exercises provide small group activities, role plays, skit ideas, debate and roundtable discussion questions that ask you to put into action the material you have learned.

The **Lexique** component defines key words and specialized terms having to do with the content area in question and also uses them in context. These sections are of particular importance to those of you who plan to take the certification exam administered by the Chambre de Commerce et d'Industrie de Paris (C.C.I.P.). They constitute a big first step toward achieving that goal.

The **Expression écrite** sections provide native-speaker writing samples to study before fashioning the structures in question into your own paragraph. Facsimiles of the original hand-written versions of these paragraphs (provided by French people of various ages) may be found in the blackline masters of the *Instructor's Portfolio.*

The **Documents authentiques** found throughout the text (and complemented by other realia in the blackline masters of the **Instructor's Portfolio**) solicit discussion. You will be asked initially to formulate or answer questions, to compare and contrast, and eventually to narrate, describe and hypothesize.

At the end of each module, an **En guise de clôture** offers you an opportunity to pursue the subject matter of the preceding three dossiers even further. It contains three or more of the following: a literary text on the topic, a list of acronyms and abbreviations, familiar or slang expressions, money matters, and other helpful hints. **Récapitulons: Quelques aide-mémoire,** a summary-at-a-glance of the module's basic information in chart or table form, closes out each **En guise de clôture. Post-activités** and **Projets** (found in the *Instructor's Portfolio*) require that you creatively synthesize in writing what you have learned in the module. They also serve as "springboards" for subsequent dossiers or ask that you get to know yourself better and articulate that knowledge in such a way that you are better able to understand, communicate and interact with others.

Features of the Home Study Guide

Used in conjunction with your *Interfaces* textbook, the *Guide d'étude* (Home Study Guide) develops your oral comprehension skills, refines your pronunciation and offers you multiple grammar and structure exercises to complete at your own pace—all within the contexts of business, technology and everyday life.

The **Points grammaticaux** sections quickly, simply and methodically review major grammar concepts **(Verbes, Noms, Adjectifs** et **Adverbes)** and provide general activities to complete before class. Examples are chosen so that you will be exposed to the content area in question from several different points of view before studying more specific vocabulary with your instructor. After class, the boxes (called **Encadrés** and **Aperçus**) will help you fine-tune your grammar review by targeting specific verbs, nouns, adjectives and adverbs within the context being studied. The **Exercices de synthèse** will allow you to link and creatively use what you have learned in both your Textbook and Home Study Guide. The answers **(Corrigés)** for all the structures and boxes are given at the end of the *Guide d'étude* so that you may check your accuracy on a day-to-day basis and review any troublesome areas on your own.

Your **Cassette audio** is designed to help you 1) refine both your pronunciation and your intonation as you pattern your voice after that of native speakers for certain activities and specialized boxes; 2) learn to spell, count and read aloud in French as you mimic native speakers doing the same; 3) work on specific French phonemes or sounds in words from the context you are studying in the **Phonétique** sections; and 4) further prepare you for class as you develop your vocabulary and **Compréhension orale/aurale** by listening to native speakers talk about the lead-in photo clusters for each module from a visual, auditory and kinesthetic point of view. To enhance your ability to understand French-speaking people in a variety of situations, an **Echange** between native speakers finishes off each module's audio entry. Each of these verbal exchanges targets the content area in question one last time from a general point of view and is followed by a brief writing activity.

Artwork

Equipped with a detailed list of shots to photograph and videotape, Dr. Marin completed an extensive photo shoot exclusively for the *Interfaces* program. Interviewing strategic people in the process provided a wealth of information for the entire series.

In keeping with the simplicity and depth of the *Interfaces* approach, a teal color enhances pedagogical features. Simple icons have been designed to indicate at a glance both activity types and basic instructions. Color-banding, runners and boxes create readily recognizable sections and aid in the visual flow from dossier to dossier and module to module. The layout envisioned is simple and straightforward, yet multifaceted. It graphically blends the traditional and the hi-tech. Fundamentally, the external form of *Interfaces* has been designed to reflect its content.

Organization

The *Interfaces* textbook consists of six **modules** of three **dossiers** each plus a springboard section, **En guise de clôture,** which encourages you to stretch beyond the confines of, as well as to synthesize, the module's content.

Each **dossier** has four main sections **(Les mots pour le dire: Vocabulaire de base, Dialogue, Lectures,** and **Lexique),** which are complemented by an extensive array of exercise and activity types.

Each **Les mots pour le dire** section presents base-line vocabulary for the intermediate level (indicated in teal) plus specialized or incidental words you will encounter in the dossier.

Each **Dialogue** integrates business, technology and everyday life in a personable way. The natural flow and varied situations give easy and inviting access to the content of the dossier. The various characters, each with his/her own individual register, will nearly come to life for you!

The **Lectures,** a rich sampling from a variety of media including newspapers, magazines, brochures, prospectus, etc. allow you to delve more deeply into the general content area studied.

Going one step beyond the basic vocabulary section, the **Lexique** gives a simple definition of key terms in French plus a complete-sentence example to study. The **Lexique** component coupled with **Les mots pour le dire** with its *définitions provisoires* provide fertile ground for classroom games such as Password and Jeopardy.

Whereas the **Activités d'introduction** at the beginning of each dossier suggest a mindset and gently draw you into or guide you toward the content area, the **Remarques** and **Observations** address cultural and lexical concerns. The **Réflexions** ask students to consider teams and team make-up as well as teamwork skills and techniques.

Grouped under the heading **Quelques points de repère,** the **Le saviez-vous?** section offers advice, observations or choice tidbits of information. Visually stimulating with its white writing upon a dark gray slate background, **L'ardoise!** (the old-fashioned slate symbolizing traditional basics) juxtaposes the present and the past. **Les entreprises françaises!** section acquaints you with French industry in the sector being studied. **Une date importante!** and **Les chiffres parlent!** sections both signal dates, statistics and specific numbers useful in numeric review and serve as a point of departure or springboards for additional discussion.

The **Quelques points de repère** component lends itself particularly well to a note-taking assignment at home followed by *questions dirigées* in class.

The **Paroles de sagesse** are simple, one-to-three line proverbs, dictums or adages that you may simply contemplate, discuss with your study partner, or seek to apply to the content area or to your own life.

Expression écrite sections, written by native speakers who had not seen any of the material generated for *Interfaces,* offer another perspective on the subject matter and provide a natural example of how certain structures are used in French. After exploring the paragraph to find key elements, expressions or structures, students pattern their own composition after the model. The handwritten versions of these **Expression écrite** samples (rendered by a range of native speakers from ages 15 to 70+) add yet another dimension to the learning process as you are exposed to French penmanship, note the graphology of the French person writing the passage, or even seek to develop your own style of French script.

Finally each module offers you an opportunity to pursue the subject matter even further in its **En guise de clôture**. It contains a literary passage and three or more of the following: **Sigles et abréviations; Expressions familières; Conseils, suggestions; Pour réussir; La réussite: Sept ingrédients de base; Considération sur la diversité des individus; Un peu d'imagination; Une question d'argent; Une dernière question d'argent: L'indépendance financière. Quelques aide-mémoire,** summary charts of key concepts from each dossier, finish off the module.

*A*daptability

The dossiers of **Interfaces** are readily adaptable to both semester and quarter systems. Literally *any* section of **Interfaces** can stand alone, and yet its content is spiraled not only within the given dossier itself, but throughout the series. Thus, you are able to tailor **Interfaces** to your own specific desires or needs.

Although each of the six modules (accompanied by the corresponding Home Study Guide section) can be used alone as the subject matter for an entire course, we recommend that two modules (six dossiers) be studied each term for those on a quarter or trimester system and that three modules (nine dossiers) be completed for those on semesters.

By adding the blackline masters or more extensive use of the audiocassettes, a longer course would need very little, if any, outside material. The use of brand-new realia (from magazines, newspapers, T.V. broadcasts, satellite transmissions, etc.) is always a stimulating addition. Additional Francophone materials are a welcome plus!

*N*ote to the Students

- Study at least 20–30 minutes each day (4–6 days per week). A little each day is much more effective in language learning than "cramming" all the material into only one or two sessions.
- Push your pencil. Write out at least 3–4 examples per box or activity in complete sentences while thinking of their meaning and

pronunciation—even if it is just an example or fill-in-the-blank exercise.

- Buy a good French-French dictionary in addition to an inexpensive French-English one. Near the end of your study session each day, look up any important terms you don't recognize or that interest you. Take note of key words from the dictionary definition. Always indicate irregular stems for verbs, the gender of nouns, and any specific forms for adjectives and adverbs.

- Keep a notebook of these expressions. Review them along with your class notes at least once per week (or write notes in the margin of your Home Study Guide and skim them as you review each section).

- Develop a regular pattern of working with your study partner or in small groups at least twice per week.

- Tailor the use of your Home Study Guide to best suit your own goals. Note where you might need additional work and focus on those areas.

- Dare to stretch your language abilities and have fun while you are learning!

*S*upplements

Highly versatile, the **Guide d'étude** (or Home Study Guide) focuses upon the study and review of the four cornerstones of language (verbs, nouns, adjectives and adverbs). Basic phonetics (pronunciation, elision, liaison and intonation) and oral comprehension (both in **Photos et descriptions** and **Echange**) are systematically interwoven throughout the six modules. Its exercises, created from the raw material generated by small, directed teams of two or three educated native speakers—with an answer key for self-correction—provide a flexible review of grammar and phonetics within the contexts of business, technology and everyday life. When studying specific verb frames and flashes, you may choose to do the exercises quickly and only check for accuracy; you may opt to study all of the examples and attempt to get the gist of each sentence for yet another perspective on the content area; or you may do an in-depth analysis of each sentence, looking up words you might not know in the dictionary and noting parts of speech, gender, agreements and the like. The key element in the use of the **Guide d'étude** is the process of "pushing the pencil" and careful self-correction and evalution.

Since research shows that listening comprehension is the weakest skill exhibited by American students, the **Audio Program** consists of three 90-minute cassettes, 45 minutes per module. Each **Les mots pour le dire: Vocabulaire de base, Dialogue, L'ardoise!** section from **Interfaces** as well as the **Photos et descriptions, Phonétique** and **Echange** sections from the **Guide d'étude** are included. The variety of speakers, voices and accents as well as the extensiveness of the audio program will help alleviate this challenge.

The **Instructor's Portfolio** gives an overview of the program, comments on both theory and practice, includes blackline masters, supplemental exercises on **Transports et services,** an extra reading on a business trip aboad, and supplies a travel list and an additional project as well as lesson plans and the **Corrigés** for **Interfaces.**

The **Tapescript** supplies a transcript of all auditory components not found in **Interfaces** and the **Guide d'étude**. Thus for each module, the audio program includes: **Vocabulaire de base, Dialogues,** and **L'ardoise!** from *Interfaces* (three per module) plus **Photos et descriptions, Phonétique** and **Echange** from the *Guide d'étude.*

The **Corrigés** for *Interfaces* not only gives an array of response possibilities for the entire program but also gives your instructor the raw material necessary to bring you to an advanced proficiency level.

Welcome to *Interfaces.* May this enriching experience in learning be a fun, bold and even daring adventure for you!

BARBARA L. BLACKBOURN
CATHERINE MARIN

*M*any thanks to our Georgia Tech students and in particular to those who participated in the Georgia Tech Languages for Business and Technology Program. Their enthusiasm served as a constant inspiration to us as we created and refined our materials. Their faithful input truly helped shape this series.

We would like to express our gratitude to the staff at John Wiley & Sons—in particular, Carlos Davis, who believed in the concept of our program from the start, readily shared our vision, exhibited immediate enthusiasm and made *Interfaces* a reality.

Our Developmental Editor, Patricia Ménard, carefully read, critiqued and annotated the last three versions of our manuscript and provided us with constant encouragement, consistent praise and practical suggestions. We are grateful for her ability to keep us on task, for her flexibility in the on-going process and for the joy she clearly demonstrated in working on our project. Her excitement was always evident. Pat interfaced the entire series from start to finish. She was truly a treasure to us.

We thank Jennifer Williams for her ever-pleasant voice on the other end of the phone line, for her efficient responses to our many questions and requests, and for coordinating the final stages of preparation of the project for production, and we thank Carl Morse for his meticulous attention to detail and his painstaking care in copyediting our text and for seeing the book through the myriad stages of production.

We would also like to thank our generous colleague Frédéric CASTELLAN as well as many of the French graduate students who acted as animateurs during our intensive program for their contribution to this series. Of particular note were: Laurent BARBALAT, Julien BARES, Marie-Pierre BAUDOT, Johanne BEZY, Laurence BONTOUX, Etienne CAZAUDEBAT, Marie-Sylvie CENRAUD, Christelle FONTBONNE, Caroline GAUTIER, Fabien GROBON, Chantal JOURET, Pierre LAGRANGE, Daniel MICHIELS, Olivier MOUROUX, Christian PAJOT, Virginie QUILLIET, Denis ROYER and Katell SALLES. We thank each of them for the brainstorming discussions that generated the raw material for our intensive program and for their creativity, cooperative spirit, insight, teamwork, patience, hard work and enthusiasm in generating activities for the *Guide d'étude* (Home Study Guide).

Our heartfelt appreciation goes out to those in France who went out of their way to supply or share information, secure documentation and offer generous assistance in making the photo shoots possible. Their gracious giving of their time was invaluable to us and greatly contributed to the enrichment of our series. Our special thanks to M. ALIZON, Alexandre et Denise ARRIBAS, M. BLAINVEL, Françoise GODIVIER, Robert GAHINET, and the participants of the Agora workshop, Philippe

LE SPEGAGNE, Maryannick LE GOFF, M. et Madame LE GOFF, Paul et Marie-Armelle LE GOFF, Paul GUILLOU, Véronique TAILLIEZ, M. NOURY, Micheline et Clément JACQUINOT, M. GREHAIGNE, Mireille LE GARREC, Brigitte et Michel LEFEVRE, Anne-Marie SKYE, M. et Mme CASTELLAN, Inès SCHERB, Marcel LE TOUMELIN, Alain DUVAL, Allain BERNARD, Kricha ABDELLATIF, Jacques PETRUS, Joël PERON, Marie-Christine JEGO, Aline POLI, M. COTTEN, Mme LUCAS and Nicole NAOUR.

We'd also like to thank family and friends for making contacts, being interviewed, chauffeuring and lodging, offering generously of their time, energy, interest and enthusiasm—especially Francine et Eugène MARIN, Jean-Pierre MARIN, Anita et Jacky GUILLOTEAU, Jean-François MARIN, Vincent, Noémie et Corentin GUILLOTEAU, Nicole et Alain FOURRIER. Chantal LE GOFF-GUILLOU arranged a very fruitful visit in Brittany where she persuaded her family, friends and business connections to participate in our project. She dedicated an entire week just to facilitating our work abroad. She opened many doors and graciously accepted being photographed and interviewed herself as well. We are very grateful for her input, tireless energy, positive attitude and friendliness. Barbara also thanks Raymond Fisher for his constant willingness to brainstorm, his sense of direction, his ability to find solutions, his sensitive ear, caring support and encouragement as well as for the use of office materials and equipment. She lovingly acknowledges Beau and Nancy Blackbourn for their patience and understanding while their mom worked around the clock for months on end. And finally, she thanks Jonathan Bartleson for the motivation, insight, encouragement and enthusiasm he so willingly contributed on a daily basis throughout the writing of this program.

We wish also to express our gratitude to those French and French-speaking businessmen and women, government officials, specialists and colleagues from France, Quebec, Switzerland, the Ivory Coast, Martinique, Lebanon, the Atlanta metro area and the southeast who welcome the students from our intensive program into their companies or groups for tours and visits in French, readily share materials with us, encourage their students to participate in our program and even upon occasion offer co-op positions or internships to our graduates. Many thanks to Robert Banta, Corinne Barnes, le Consul de France Gérard BLANCHOT, Yves BERTHELOT, Jean-Michel BOCK, Marc BOUCHER, Steve Brichant, Pierre Brodeur, Jerry Brooks, Régent Cabana, Françoise Cloutier, Bertrand COMET-BARTHES, Jean-Lou CHAMEAU, Odille CORNET, Cyrille et Stéphanie DULAC, Michel DROUERE, Louise FORTIN, Sharon Gady, Vincent Garnier, Carlos GHOSN, Bob Hawkins, Monoela Jennings, Fred JENNY, David KEE, John Lyons, Jonathan Mann, John McIntyre, Pierre MERLOT, Marie MERLOT, Mathilde MERLOT, Marie-France MERLOT-BONARDI, Frédéric Jean MOREAU, Octavia NASSAR, H.B. Nicholson, Tony Papandrea, Daniel PARET, M. PIGNY, le Consul Adjoint Michel PINARD, Hans Püttgen, Virginia Rand-Hill, Heidi Rockwood, Elysée SAINT ELI, Marguerite SAMPAH, Jacques SEBAG, Marc SLAMA, Adam Steg, Fred Tarpley, Fabrice VERGEZ, Magda Walter, Rachel Ward, Claude WEGSCHEIDER, Les Amis des vieilles maisons françaises and l'Alliance Française.

Barbara dedicates this series to D.S.G.; Catherine, to her beloved cats, Diego, Freddie, Léone, Sarah, Rose and Sophie, whose voluptuous beauty and faithful affection helped to create a luxurious, peaceful and serene atmosphere at home so beneficial to the completion of such a long-term project, and to her husband, Frans de Waal. For more than a quarter of a century, he has generously provided her with unconditional love and support at all levels. From this passion, she derives an infinite source of

energy , joy, warmth, inspiration and satisfaction that makes work and
other facets of life so much fun.

B.L.B.
C.M.

---

*Index des
icônes utilisées*

 = *Guide d'etude (Home Study Guide)*

 = Activité en petits groupes

 = Activité de prise de notes

 = Elément du programme enregistré sur cassette

 = Lecture

 = Jeu de rôle

 = Travail écrit

 = Texte littéraire

---

xviii   INDEX DES ICONES UTILISEES

MODULE *I*

$\mathcal{B}$anque, Poste et télécommunications

1 Ouvrir un compte en banque

2 Banque et Minitel

3 Les télécommunications

Ouverture

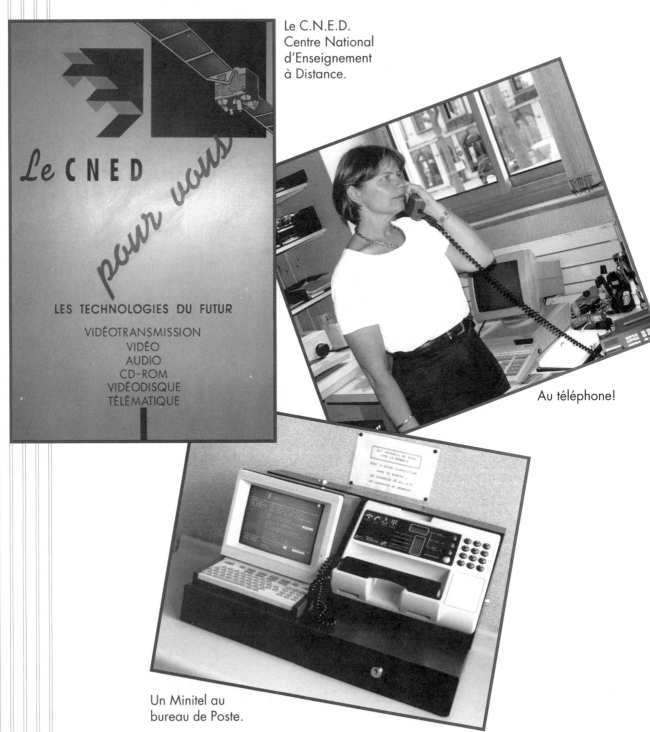

Le CNED
pour vous

LES TECHNOLOGIES DU FUTUR

VIDÉOTRANSMISSION
VIDÉO
AUDIO
CD-ROM
VIDÉODISQUE
TÉLÉMATIQUE

Le C.N.E.D.
Centre National
d'Enseignement
à Distance.

Au téléphone!

Un Minitel au
bureau de Poste.

L'enseigne de la banque:
Le Credit du Nord.

Retirer de
l'argent
à un guichet
automatique.

Des téléphones sans fil
dans un hypermarché.

*O*uvrir un compte en banque

Ce premier dossier du Module I va vous apprendre comment une personne résidant en France peut ouvrir un compte en banque et va également vous présenter quelques services offerts par les banques et la Poste en France.

*A*ctivité d'introduction

Le monde des finances

A. L'argent et les finances. Répondez aux questions suivantes par groupes de deux ou trois.

1. Quels mots associez-vous avec l'argent?
2. Quels mots associez-vous avec la banque?
3. Qu'avez-vous fait pour ouvrir votre premier compte *(account)* en banque?
   D'abord...
   Puis...
   Ensuite...
   Enfin...
4. Quels sont les avantages d'un compte en banque?
5. Comment choisit-on une banque?

Un distributeur de billets du Crédit du Nord au centre de Paris.

Les mots pour le dire

Jetez un coup d'œil *(glance)* sur la traduction des mots suivants mais concentrez-vous sur leur prononciation en français et sur les images qu'évoquent les noms, les adjectifs ou les actions décrites par les verbes ou les adverbes de la liste suivante.

Une plaque sur le mur extérieur d'un bureau de Poste indiquant ses heures d'ouverture.

Vocabulaire de base

VERBES

déposer de l'argent	*to deposit money*
faire la queue	*to stand in line*
ouvrir un compte	*to open an account*
prouver	*to prove*
toucher un chèque	*to cash a check*

NOMS

un carnet de chèques, un chéquier	*checkbook*
un CCP ou C.C.P. (Compte-Chèques Postal)	*checking account (at the post office)*
un compte à vue, un compte courant	*checking account*
un compte épargne	*savings account*
le domicile	*place of residence*
un dossier	*file*
un guichet	*teller's window*
une imprimante	*printer*
un ordinateur	*computer*
une pièce d'identité	*I.D.*
une quittance	*bill*
un relevé bancaire	*bank statement*
un renseignement	*(a piece of) information*

ADJECTIFS

bancaire	*banking*
postal(e)	*postal*
premier(ière)	*first*

ADVERBES ET EXPRESSIONS ADVERBIALES

d'abord	*first*
d'ailleurs	*besides, moreover*
demain	*tomorrow*
enfin	*finally*
ensuite	*then*
pas encore	*not yet*
puis	*then*

B. Orthographe et prononciation! Mettez-vous en groupes de quatre et épelez les termes suivants à haute voix.

1. un compte
2. un guichet
3. un relevé
4. un dossier

5. une pièce d'identité
6. une quittance
7. toucher un chèque
8. faire la queue

C. Définitions provisoires à terminer. Complétez les phrases suivantes.

1. Un carnet de chèques s'appelle aussi un _____.
   Comment est-ce que cela s'écrit?
   Ça s'écrit: *c.h.é.q.u.i.e.r.*
2. La machine qui permet de voir, sur papier, ce qu'on a écrit à l'ordinateur s'appelle une _____.
   Ça s'écrit: _____.
3. Lorsqu'on téléphone à quelqu'un pour obtenir des informations, on se renseigne ou on demande des _____.
   Ça s'écrit: _____.
4. Un passeport ou un permis de conduire sont des
   _____.
   Ça s'écrit: _____.
5. L'endroit où une personne habite est son _____.
   Ça s'écrit:_____.

D. Définitions provisoires à créer. En groupes de deux, écrivez une définition provisoire pour les mots suivants.

1. une banque
2. une quittance
3. un guichet
4. prouver
5. un compte épargne

Ouverture d'un compte en banque

HSG

➤ Do an initial run-through of the *Photos et descriptions* and *Phonétique* sections in your *HSG* to get an overview of the material.

E. Activité de pré-lecture. Répondez aux questions suivantes.

1. Quel âge faut-il avoir pour ouvrir son propre compte en banque aux Etats-Unis?
2. Quels sont les documents à fournir quand on va ouvrir un compte en banque et pourquoi?

F. A la recherche d'éléments précis. Dans le dialogue suivant, il y a plusieurs personnes qui se parlent.

1. Combien?
2. Qui?

3. Vincent, qui est-ce, par rapport à Noémie?

4. Et qui est Vincent par rapport aux employées de ce dialogue?

Ouverture d'un compte en banque

Noémie: N'oublie pas d'aller à la banque pour demander des renseignements. Je croyais que tu voulais ouvrir un compte en banque cette semaine, non?

Vincent: Ouais, j'ai le temps! D'ailleurs, je ne sais pas encore si c'est un CCP ou un compte en banque que je vais ouvrir. Je crois que je vais d'abord téléphoner au Crédit Agricole *(a famous French bank)* puisque c'est là que Papa et Maman ont leur compte. Je n'ai pas envie de faire la queue au guichet. Il y a toujours un monde fou.

Noémie: Tu exagères! D'ailleurs, ce n'est pas à un employé derrière un guichet à qui tu dois parler. Les agents qui s'occupent de *(take care of)* l'ouverture des comptes ont leur propre bureau et en général, on n'a pas besoin d'attendre. Tu entres dans la banque et c'est à droite, tu verras.

Vincent: Je téléphone tout de suite. Donne-moi le numéro de l'agence. Maman l'a écrit sur l'enveloppe de son relevé, là, sur son bureau, à côté de l'ordinateur, devant l'imprimante, près du dossier jaune. Là. Oui. Merci. Alors, le 02.41.86.82.34.

Une réceptionniste à l'accueil du Crédit Mutuel de Bretagne.

1ère employée du Crédit Agricole: Le Crédit Agricole, bonjour!

Vincent: Allô? Je voudrais avoir quelques renseignements, s'il vous plaît, au sujet de l'ouverture d'un compte...

1ère employée du Crédit Agricole: Un instant, Monsieur, s'il vous plaît... Ne quittez pas!

2e employée du Crédit Agricole: Allô, bonjour, Monsieur... vous désirez ouvrir un compte?

Vincent: Oui, et c'est la première fois... euh... quelles sont les démarches *(procedures, steps)* à suivre?

2e employée: Vous avez plus de dix-huit ans?

Vincent: Oui, j'ai eu dix-huit ans le 12 juillet.

2e employée: Bon, il faut vous présenter en personne et remplir un dossier. Vous voulez ouvrir un compte à vue ou un compte épargne?

Vincent: Un compte à vue, c'est la même chose qu'un compte courant?

2ᵉ employée:	Mais oui, Monsieur, effectivement.
Vincent:	Un compte à vue, je crois. Je voudrais avoir un carnet de chèques.
2ᵉ employée:	De toute façon, il faut que vous apportiez une pièce d'identité et un certificat de domiciliation.
Vincent:	Un certificat de quoi?
2ᵉ employée:	Un certificat de domiciliation, ou un justificatif de domicile, c'est-à-dire un papier qui prouve que vous habitez bien à l'adresse que vous donnez, comme une quittance de loyer, de gaz ou de téléphone, par exemple.
Vincent:	Bon, je suis étudiant et j'habite encore chez mes parents mais je cherche un appartement en ce moment.
2ᵉ employée:	Apportez un certificat de scolarité. Vous êtes étudiant à plein temps?
Vincent:	Oui.
2ᵉ employée:	Si vous n'avez pas de revenus, nous ne pourrons pas vous donner de chéquier. Ecoutez, passez à l'agence et je vous expliquerai à quelles cartes bancaires vous avez droit.
Vincent:	Je peux venir aujourd'hui même? J'aimerais que vous m'expliquiez également les différents comptes possibles et les avantages offerts (participe passé du verbe *offrir*—"offered") par le Crédit Agricole.
2ᵉ employée:	Mais certainement… Je vous rappelle que nos bureaux ferment à dix-sept heures trente.
Vincent:	Je passerai cet après-midi. Au revoir, Madame.
2ᵉ employée:	Au revoir, Monsieur. Merci et à tout à l'heure!
Noémie:	Est-ce que tu y vas en moto ou en bus?
Vincent:	En moto évidemment. Il n'y a pas de ligne directe. J'aurais au moins deux changements à faire.

➤ Listen to this dialogue on your audiocassette at least three times before your next class. Be ready to play any of the four roles as a warm-up activity.

➤ In France, besides being used in official contexts (such as train and school schedules, office hours, etc.), military time is frequently interchanged with standard time in everyday speech.

G. Associations! Complétez les phrases de la colonne 1 avec la partie correspondante dans la colonne 2.

1	*2*
Un instant, Monsieur, s'il vous plaît	quelques renseignements
Je voudrais avoir	merci
Je vous rappelle que nos bureaux	en personne
Il faut vous présenter	ne quittez pas
Au revoir, Monsieur	ferment à 17 h 30

H. A vous de compléter! Après avoir bien relu le dialogue, remplissez le blanc avec le mot qui convient.

1. Vincent _____ au Crédit Agricole.

2. Vincent veut demander des _____.

3. L'employée lui demande son _____.

4. Vincent ne peut pas ouvrir un _____ par téléphone.

5. Vincent doit aller à la banque pour _____ un dossier.

6. Ce n'est pas un compte épargne que Vincent veut ouvrir mais un

_____.

7. Si Vincent arrive à la banque après 17 h 30, les bureaux seront

_____.

8. Avant de raccrocher *(hanging up)*, l'employée dit

_____.

9. Vincent ira à la banque l'après-midi même et devra apporter une

_____ et un _____.

I. Vrai ou faux? Lisez les affirmations suivantes. Si elles ne sont pas correctes, changez-les de façon à ce qu'elles correspondent au texte.

1. Vincent veut ouvrir un compte en banque.

2. Noémie explique à Vincent où se trouve l'employé(e) qui s'occupe de l'ouverture *(opening)* des comptes.

3. Ça ne dérange pas Vincent de faire la queue à la banque.

4. La mère de Vincent sait qu'il va téléphoner à la banque.

5. Noémie téléphone à la banque pour avoir des informations.

6. L'employée explique à Vincent ce qu'il doit faire pour ouvrir un compte.

7. C'est la banque qui donne un certificat de domiciliation.

J. Autrement dit. Voici quelques définitions. Cochez (✓) la proposition qui vous semble la plus proche de la phrase ou de l'expression donnée.

1. Demander des renseignements, c'est
   a. essayer d'obtenir les idées de quelqu'un sur un sujet déterminé.
   b. aider quelqu'un à retrouver son chemin.
   c. interroger une personne pour obtenir des informations.

2. Quand on fait la queue, cela veut dire que
   a. plusieurs personnes attendent pour la même raison.
   b. on n'a pas beaucoup de patience.
   c. on essaie de passer avant son tour.

La façade d'une agence
de la Banque Populaire
et son logo.

3. Se présenter en personne veut dire

   a. qu'il faut être présenté par ses parents pour pouvoir ouvrir un compte.

   b. qu'il faut aller soi-même à la banque pour remplir les papiers.

   c. qu'il faut d'abord envoyer des papiers par la Poste, pour que la personne qui s'occupe de l'ouverture des comptes puisse préparer le dossier.

4. Une facture de téléphone, c'est

   a. un papier de la compagnie de téléphone qui indique combien on doit payer.

   b. un papier qui donne le nom des personnes à qui on a téléphoné.

   c. une sorte de brochure qui donne des renseignements généraux sur le téléphone.

5. «Je vous rappelle... » veut dire

   a. je me souviens bien de vous...

   b. je vous demande de vous souvenir que...

   c. je vous demande de me rappeler...

6. Remplir un dossier veut dire

   a. cacher un certain nombre de renseignements.

   b. poser des questions personnelles.

   c. répondre par écrit à des questions posées dans un formulaire.

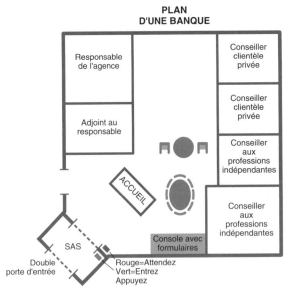

PLAN D'UNE BANQUE

➤ An "SAS" is an entrance to a building composed of two doors, approximately six feet apart, often linked to a security system.

REMARQUE
Plan d'une banque

Les banques sont souvent protégées *(protected)* par un système de sécurité. La porte d'entrée est alors fermée et il faut appuyer sur un bouton puis attendre qu'un petit signal vert s'allume pour pouvoir pousser la porte. Cela permet à la banque d'exercer un certain contrôle sur le nombre de clients qui se trouvent à l'intérieur et éventuellement de ne pas ouvrir la porte si un problème est pressenti *(foreseen)*.

La porte d'entrée d'une agence de la Société Générale.

 K. Applications. Après avoir étudié le plan de la banque qui précède, répondez aux questions suivantes par groupes de deux ou trois.

1. Pour entrer à la banque, que devez-vous faire? Notez au moins trois choses.
2. Vous voulez obtenir des informations. Expliquez en détail ce que vous devez faire.
3. Vous êtes un peu en avance et votre conseiller est occupé avec un autre client. Que faites-vous?
4. Expliquez et commentez le plan de l'agence. Que manque-t-il?
5. Si vous travailliez à cette agence, quel serait votre poste et pourquoi?

La porte d'entrée d'une autre agence de la Société Générale.

*O*bservations lexicales

Emprunter, prêter, payer

Faites bien attention à l'emploi des verbes *emprunter*, *prêter* et *payer!*

emprunter à quelqu'un = obtenir à titre de prêt ou pour un usage momentané.

> **EXEMPLE:** *Imaginez que j'ai besoin de 1.000 F. Voici le raisonnement que je fais:*
> *Je n'ai pas ces 1.000 F.*
> *La banque a ces 1.000 F.*
> *J'obtiens ces 1.000 F de la banque pour un certain temps.*
> *Je peux emprunter ces 1.000 F à la banque.*
> *J'emprunte 1.000 F à la banque.*
> *Je fais un emprunt.*

continued on page 12

continued from page 11

prêter = fournir une chose à condition qu'elle soit rendue un jour.

> **EXEMPLE:**   *La banque a 1.000 F.*
> *Elle me permet d'utiliser ces 1.000 F pendant un certain temps.*
> *La banque me prête 1.000 F.*
> *La banque me consent un prêt.*

payer = verser de l'argent en contrepartie de *(against)* quelque chose (objet, travail, etc.). *Payer,* c'est mettre quelqu'un en possession de ce qui lui est dû. Je dois 500 F à Céline: je la paie. Le client prend un livre dans le magasin puis il va à la caisse pour le payer. Rembourser, rémunérer. S'acquitter par un versement de ce qu'on doit.

> **EXEMPLE:**   *Je veux acheter un livre.*
> *Ce livre coûte 65 F.*
> *Je prends ce livre et donne en échange du livre un chèque de 65 F.*
> *Je paie 65 F pour pouvoir entrer en possession de ce livre.*

REMARQUE

Il y a souvent un complément d'objet direct lié au verbe *payer.*

- Son journal, Françoise le paie toujours comptant. ~ *cash en espèce*

- Francine paie le pain en espèces *(in cash),* mais elle préfère payer l'essence par chèque ou par carte bancaire.

La Caisse d'Epargne avec l'écureuil stylisé de son logo.

Autres verbes utiles liés à l'argent:

dépenser	Ne **dépense** pas trop d'argent pendant les fêtes de fin d'année!
changer	Avant de partir dans un pays étranger, je **change** de l'argent; des dollars en francs français, par exemple.
économiser	Il faut **économiser** pour avoir un peu d'argent en cas de problème et pour pouvoir faire face à de grosses dépenses dans l'avenir comme l'achat d'une voiture ou le départ en vacances.
mettre de côté	Tous les mois, Pierre et Martine **mettent** de l'argent **de côté** parce qu'ils veulent acheter une maison.
perdre	Nadine investit dans des SICAV *(appelés fonds mutuels au Québec)* pour limiter les risques de **perdre** son argent.
investir, placer	Où et comment est-ce que vous **investissez (placez)** votre argent?

L. A compléter! Remplissez les blancs des phrases suivantes avec un des verbes que vous venez d'étudier.

1. Chaque mois, j'essaie d' _____ environ *(approximately)* 1.000 F que je mets sur mon compte épargne logement. Je veux acheter un appartement dans deux ou trois ans.

2. Il me reste 150 marks. Il faut que je passe à la banque pour qu'elle me les _____.

[handwritten margin notes:]
② ① Faites une phrase originale avec chaque verbe

Pour vos placements en **SICAV**, votre bureau de Poste vous souhaite *la bienvenue !*

Quelques conseils pour bien choisir.

On ne choisit pas une SICAV uniquement en fonction de sa performance. Pour sélectionner celle qui vous convient, répondez simplement à ces quelques questions.

Combien voulez-vous investir ?
A La Poste, les parts de SICAV ont été déterminées pour être à la portée de tous (d'une centaine de francs à quelques milliers de francs).

Combien de temps voulez-vous placer votre argent ?
De quelques jours à plusieurs années, à La Poste, chaque SICAV est assortie d'une durée conseillée de placement. Une durée qui tient compte de l'objectif de gestion recherché : sécurité ou performance.

Quelle part de risque êtes-vous prêt à accepter ?
La Poste gère toutes ses SICAV dans une optique de sécurité et de régularité. Toutefois, les SICAV en actions, très dynamiques sur le moyen terme, peuvent connaître sur de courtes périodes de fortes fluctuations. C'est le devoir de La Poste de vous en informer et de vous conseiller des SICAV monétaires ou obligataires si vous recherchez en priorité la sécurité.

Grâce à ses compétences, La Poste vous offre autant de relais vers les performances des meilleurs placements. La gestion de vos SICAV est assurée par SOGEPOSTE, filiale de La Poste et de la Caisse des dépôts et consignations, reconnue pour sa compétence financière.

Alors, pour une bonne répartition de votre portefeuille, venez rencontrer le Conseiller Financier de votre bureau de Poste.

Dépliant de la Poste sur les SICAV.

① quelles sont des questions utiles à se poser pour choisir un placement

② chercher un avertissement bancaire.

---

3. Les Français _____ beaucoup d'argent dans les repas et la nourriture en général car c'est très important pour eux.

4. Le verbe *économiser* a deux synonymes. Je peux dire par exemple: Il faut _____ pour se préparer une bonne retraite. Je peux dire également *(also):* _____ une certaine somme tous les mois est une excellente habitude.

5. Cette femme était millionnaire mais elle _____ *(passé composé)* toute sa fortune lorsque son usine a fait faillite *(declared bankruptcy).* Je crois qu'elle va recommencer à zéro.

6. Il est difficile de savoir comment _____ son argent quand on n'est pas spécialiste, mais qui choisir pour se faire conseiller?

7. Lorsque nous avons acheté notre maison, mes parents nous _____ *(passé composé)* 50.000 F. Nous les leur _____ *(futur)* sur cinq ans.

8. Acheter son propre logement coûte très cher. En général, il faut passer par une institution financière pour _____ au moins les trois quarts du prix d'achat *(purchase price).* Nous _____ *(passé composé)* un compte épargne logement.

9. Combien _____ -tu _____ *(passé composé)* ta voiture? Pas plus de 75.000 F, j'espère!

Lecture 1

La carte Mozaïc

M. Activité de pré-lecture. Répondez aux questions suivantes.

1. A quoi sert selon vous une carte bancaire?

Pour pouvoir entrer dans la petite salle où se trouve le distributeur automatique de la Caisse d'Epargne, il faut insérer sa carte dans une fente puis tirer la porte.

① comment ce sytème est-il different d'ici.

② Démontrer les actions en disant ce que vous faites (role play)

Pour retirer de l'argent, il faut suivre les directives qui apparaissent sur l'écran.

Une personne vient de retirer 300 F de son compte au guichet automatique.

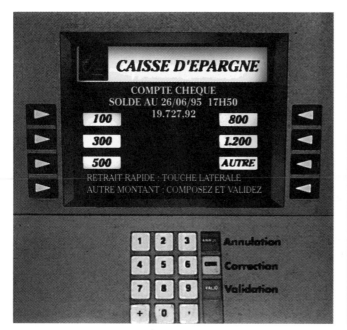
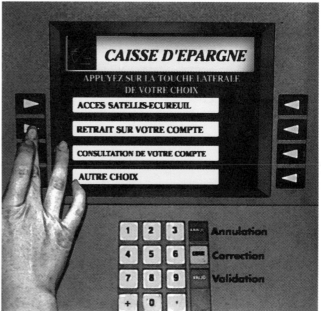

2. Est-ce que vous allez quelquefois retirer de l'argent à un distributeur automatique de billets? Si oui, pouvez-vous expliquer ce que vous faites exactement pour obtenir de l'argent?

D'abord...

Puis...

Ensuite...

Enfin...

3. Donnez quelques avantages et quelques inconvénients des distributeurs automatiques de billets. Donnez au moins trois exemples pour chacune des catégories.

N. Applications. Pour retirer de l'argent au guichet automatique, il faut suivre les directives qui apparaissent sur l'écran. Après avoir étudié les photos et dessins qui précèdent, mettez les étapes suivantes dans le bon ordre.

5 _____ Appuyez sur la touche latérale de votre choix (pour indiquer le montant de la somme voulue ou pour un autre montant), composez et validez.

1 _____ Entrez dans la petite salle où se trouve le D.A.B. en insérant votre carte dans la fente.

2 _____ Tirez la porte.

4 _____ Tapez votre code confidentiel.

8 _____ N'oubliez pas de prendre votre carte.

6 _____ Veuillez patienter, s.v.p.

3 _____ Insérez votre carte dans la fente du guichet automatique.

7 _____ Veuillez prendre vos billets.

O. Première lecture! Parcourez rapidement le texte suivant pour avoir une idée générale de leur contenu. <u>Soulignez les mots</u> que vous ne connaissez pas.

La carte Mozaïc — *une carte à puce "smart card"*

CARTE MOZAIC du Crédit Agricole pour les moins de dix-huit ans!

Mozaïc n'est pas une <u>carte</u> de <u>paiement</u>. En revanche *(in return, on the other hand)*, elle <u>permet</u> à son titulaire, au moyen d'un *(by using a)* <u>code</u> confidentiel, de retirer aux guichets automatiques des sommes qui ne peuvent <u>excéder</u> un montant *(une somme)* déterminé à l'avance: de 100 à 1 800 F par semaine, tous les montants, tous les rythmes sont possibles par tranches de 100 F. A vous de trouver le bon, celui qui s'accordera le mieux à votre budget tout en vous procurant autonomie et indépendance... en toute sécurité.

Crédit Agricole, janvier 1995.

> ➤ *Always* write down the gender (masculine or feminine) of a noun as you learn its meaning.

P. Mots à reconnaître. Faites une liste des dix mots du texte que vous pouvez comprendre parce qu'ils sont proches de l'anglais.

Q. Autrement dit. Voici quelques définitions. Cochez la réponse qui vous semble la plus proche du mot ou groupe de mots donné.

1. D'après ce passage, la carte Mozaïc est
   a. une carte de crédit.
   b. une carte de retrait *(withdrawal, debit)*.
   c. une carte de paiement.

2. Le titulaire *(holder, title bearer)* d'une carte est
   a. l'employé(e) de la banque qui a donné la carte.
   b. une personne qui a un titre.
   c. la personne à qui la carte appartient.

3. On se sert d'un code confidentiel pour
   a. avoir accès à son compte.
   b. téléphoner à la banque sans payer.
   c. emprunter de l'argent.

4. Un guichet automatique, c'est une machine qui
   a. permet de retirer de l'argent.
   b. compte la monnaie automatiquement.
   c. distribue des formulaires de banque.

R. Associations d'idées. Quels sont, d'après le texte et la liste suivante, les quatre mots ou groupes de mots qui sont associés à la carte Mozaïc?

danger   tarifs *(rates)* préférentiels

sécurité   tentation de trop dépenser

indépendance   jeunes de moins de dix-huit ans

guichet automatique

VIVEZ VOTRE BANQUE A L'HEURE DU MINITEL

Le bon sens en Direct

36 16 CATOUR

CA CRÉDIT AGRICOLE

VIVEZ DES MAINTENANT VOTRE BANQUE EN DIRECT

● VOS CODES CONFIDENTIELS : UN MOYEN EFFICACE

Pour éviter tout risque d'erreur ou de contrefaçon, votre accès confidentiel comporte un identifiant personnel de huit chiffres et un mot de passe de quatre caractères alphanumériques. Conservez-les précieusement : c'est la clé d'accès à toutes les informations qui vous sont personnelles. De plus vous aurez la possibilité de modifier votre mot de passe à tout moment : n'hésitez pas à utiliser cette faculté.
Dans un souci de sécurité, le service a été conçu de telle façon que toute utilisation anormale du mot de passe conduise à en inhiber l'accès.

● POUR EN SAVOIR PLUS

Si vous souhaitez de plus amples renseignements concernant l'utilisation de Touraine Télématique, faites le choix "Guide Vidéotex" dans le sommaire du service. Si vous avez des questions complémentaires, vous pouvez bien sûr consulter votre agence du Crédit Agricole.

● SI VOUS N'AVEZ PAS DE MINITEL...

Si vous n'avez pas encore de Minitel, renseignez-vous auprès de votre agence commerciale France Télécom. Vous y trouverez une gamme d'appareils dans laquelle vous pourrez choisir celui qui correspond le mieux à vos besoins. Et pour être sûr de ne pas vous tromper, vous pourrez même assister à une démonstration des différents modèles actuellement disponibles.

Dépliant de Crédit Agricole, 1995.

S. A vous la parole! Répondez aux questions suivantes en vous appuyant sur le texte de la page 16 et justifiez votre réponse.

1. Faut-il avoir 21 ans pour pouvoir obtenir une carte bancaire en France?

2. Faut-il être agriculteur *(farmer)* pour faire une demande de carte Mozaïc au Crédit Agricole?

3. Pourquoi faut-il un code confidentiel pour retirer de l'argent au guichet automatique?

Lecture 2

Quelques conseils pour votre sécurité

✓ **T.** **Activité de pré-lecture.** Répondez aux questions suivantes en essayant d'utiliser au moins une fois les verbes **être, permettre** et **pouvoir**.

1. Quelles sont les précautions à prendre pour ne pas avoir de problème avec une carte bancaire?
2. Que faut-il faire quand on perd sa carte?
3. Pourquoi faut-il apprendre son code confidentiel par cœur?
4. Y a-t-il d'autres numéros que vous connaissez par cœur? Pourquoi?

> ➤ When placing an international call from the United States, dial 011 first, then the country's code — e.g., 33 for France, 32 for Belgium, 31 for the Netherlands.

U. Les numéros de téléphone. Pour appeler le numéro de téléphone 03.87.54.14.02 à Metz des Etats-Unis, il faut faire le zéro onze, trente-trois, trois, quatre-vingt-sept, cinquante-quatre, quatorze, zéro deux: 011.33.3.87.54.14.02. Le numéro 33 est le numéro de la France, et le 03.87.54.14.02 est le numéro de l'abonné. Lisez à voix haute les numéros suivants.

1. 02.78.65.03.81
2. 01.42.98.67.13
3. 03.41.53.11.29

4. 03.54.86.99.10
5. 05.32.16.03.09
6. 02.55.33.11.22

> ➤ At home, practice saying aloud imaginary French telephone numbers with your study partner. Read each set of two digits as one number except for an initial zero — e.g., (33) 3.87.54.14.02 (a telephone number in Metz), you would read as *trente-trois. trois. quatre-vingt-sept. cinquante-quatre. quatorze. zéro deux.*

V. Première lecture. A la recherche d'un élément précis.

1. Dans le texte suivant, il y a un numéro de téléphone. Lequel?
2. Savez-vous à quoi correspond le 01 qui précède le numéro de téléphone?

HSG

> ➤ Review the forms of the imperative mood in your *Home Study Guide* before reading this segment.

Quelques conseils pour votre sécurité

Votre carte Mozaïc est un véritable passeport pour le retrait d'espèces en France et à l'étranger. Aussi conservez-la précieusement et respectez les règles de sécurité suivantes:

— Considérez votre carte comme de l'argent, ne la laissez pas chez vous, conservez-la toujours sur vous.

— Votre code confidentiel est votre signature personnelle, vous aurez à le composer pour chaque retrait, retenez-le par cœur.

— Assurez-vous que votre carte vous est bien restituée *(returned)* par le distributeur de billets après utilisation: ne l'oubliez pas!

Si malgré ces précautions il se produit une perte ou un vol, intervenez vite :

— Prévenez aussitôt le Centre National de Sécurité Eurocard (tél. 01.45.67.84.84)

ou votre agence ; si vous êtes à l'étranger, prévenez l'organisme Eurocard MasterCard le plus proche,

— faites une déclaration aux autorités de police ou aux autorités consulaires,

— confirmez par courrier à votre agence dans un délai de cinq jours la perte ou le vol de la carte.

En agissant ainsi, vous avez la certitude de :

— faire opposition,

— être protégé contre toute utilisation frauduleuse de la carte,

— obtenir une nouvelle carte très rapidement.

Brochure du Crédit Agricole: Petit Guide des multiples possibilités qu'offre la Carte Mozaïc, 1995.

W. A la recherche du mot juste! Trouvez dans le texte un mot de la même famille que les mots de la liste suivante.

> *MODELE:* *retirer* / ***un retrait***

1. régler
2. suivre
3. un oubli

4. perdre
5. voler

X. Mots de la même famille. Voici une liste de mots qui viennent du texte. Trouvez pour chacun d'entre eux au moins un mot de la même famille.

> *MODELE:* *passeport* / ***passer, un passant, un passage***

1. confidentiel
2. personnelle
3. composer

4. utilisation
5. consulaire
6. jour

Y. Autrement dit. Trouvez l'équivalent des expressions et mots suivants dans le texte.

1. gardez-la
2. la sûreté
3. un ensemble de lettres et de chiffres qui vous permet de vous identifier
4. soyez sûr que...
5. une machine qui donne de l'argent
6. l'action de prendre quelque chose qui appartient à quelqu'un d'autre
7. qui n'est pas loin de là
8. écrivez une lettre
9. empêcher que quelqu'un d'autre que vous ne se serve de votre carte
10. malhonnête *(dishonest)*
11. vite

Z. Avez-vous compris? Répondez aux questions suivantes en cochant la ou les réponses qui conviennent.

1. D'après ce texte, si vous perdez votre carte Mozaïc, vous devez:
   a. en acheter une autre.
   b. téléphoner au Centre National de Sécurité Eurocard pour prévenir et faire opposition.
   c. attendre cinq jours avant d'obtenir une nouvelle carte.

2. Quels sont parmi les mots suivants ceux qui sont associés à la carte Mozaïc?
   a. un chèque
   b. un code confidentiel
   c. un distributeur de billets
   d. une assurance
   e. une carte de paiement

3. Utiliser une carte bancaire n'est pas sans danger! Que peut-il se passer selon ce texte?

    a. On peut perdre sa carte.

    b. On peut oublier sa carte dans la machine.

    c. On peut oublier son code confidentiel.

    d. On peut oublier d'aller chercher sa carte avant de partir en voyage.

    e. On peut utiliser une carte qui n'est pas acceptée à l'étranger.

    f. On peut retirer plus d'argent que ce qu'on a sur son compte en banque.

    g. On peut être victime d'un vol.

 ✓ **AA. A vous la parole!** Répondez aux questions suivantes.

1. Demandez à vos voisin(e)s s'ils ou si elles ont déjà perdu une carte bancaire et si oui, ce qu'ils ou elles ont ressenti, pensé et fait?

2. Demandez à quelqu'un de votre groupe s'il ou si elle a été victime d'un vol. Si oui, demandez-lui d'expliquer la situation et les circonstances.

3. Demandez aux personnes de votre groupe ce qu'elles font pour ne pas perdre leur(s) carte(s) bancaire(s). Est-ce qu'elles prennent certaines précautions pour que leurs cartes ne soient pas volées? Si oui, lesquelles?

 BB. De la réflexion à l'écriture. Ce texte conseille la prudence. Relisez-le, puis écrivez un petit paragraphe d'une dizaine de lignes qui donne quelques exemples d'imprudences, c'est-à-dire de choses qu'il est préférable de ne pas faire avec sa carte bancaire.

> ➤ Begin with a one-sentence introduction, develop your ideas and finish with a one-sentence conclusion.

Quelques points de repère

Le saviez-vous?

- Presque tous les adultes résidant en France doivent avoir un compte courant bancaire ou postal car s'ils gagnent plus de 2.500 F par mois, leur salaire ne peut pas leur être payé en liquide. Ce salaire doit, légalement, être versé directement sur un compte.

Les entreprises françaises!

Il y a deux grands groupes de banques en France:

    1) Les banques qui font partie de l'Association professionnelle des banques comme la Société Générale, le Crédit Lyonnais, la Banque Nationale de Paris, Paribas, CCF et Indosuez.

    2) Les banques qui font partie du secteur mutualiste *(mutual benefit)* et coopératif comme le Crédit Agricole, le groupe des banques populaires et le Crédit Mutuel.

L'ardoise!

- Autrefois *(in the past)*, les gens faisaient du troc *(bartering, exchange)*, c'est-à-dire qu'ils échangeaient des marchandises contre d'autres marchandises. Maintenant, dans pratiquement tous les pays du monde, on vend ou on achète une marchandise; autrement dit on l'échange contre une monnaie. C'est la création de la monnaie qui a causé et facilité le développement extraordinaire du commerce.

- Autrefois, les petites gens se méfiaient des banques et préféraient garder leur argent chez eux et le cacher sous leur matelas ou dans un bas de laine. Les choses ont bien changé et rares sont les Français qui n'ont pas de compte courant et de compte épargne et qui n'ont pas fait appel à une banque pour faire un emprunt permettant l'achat d'un logement ou d'une voiture ou pour investir leur argent car avec l'inflation, garder son argent à la maison signifie, à long terme, perdre de l'argent.

➤ Until the fifties, pupils in France would use old-fashioned, hand-held slates to write upon when doing practice exercises in class. Each child had a little sponge to wipe the slate clean. For more permanent work or exams, small notebooks were used.

HSG

➤ Review the formation and use of the *imparfait* in your *Home Study Guide* before rereading this *"ardoise."*

Une date importante!

Les billets de banque en France existent depuis 1701 et les chèques depuis 1865.

Les chiffres parlent!

Le pouvoir d'achat des Français a triplé depuis 1949.

Réflexions sur le travail en équipe

Lorsqu'on travaille en équipe, la composition du groupe est extrêmement importante. Qui sont les personnes qui font partie de l'équipe? Comment sont-elles? Pourquoi sont-elles là? En quelle capacité? Quelle est leur fonction par rapport à la vôtre?

Lexique

[handwritten notes in margin:]
en liquide: comptant en espèce

un chèque en bois - bounced

① choisissez des mots. Etudiants écrivent une phrase originale

② Dessiner un chèque et indiquer le vocabulaire

un chèque en blanc: Remettre **un chèque en blanc** à quelqu'un, c'est signer un chèque sans en préciser le montant.

> Francine, je te laisse **un chèque en blanc** sur mon bureau. Quand la facture du téléphone arrivera, inscris le montant sur le chèque et envoie-le!

un chèque sans provision: On fait **un chèque sans provision** lorsqu'on remet un chèque à quelqu'un alors qu'il n'y a pas assez d'argent sur le compte pour que ce chèque soit réglé.

> Les commerçants préfèrent que les clients les payent en liquide car avec les paiements par chèque, il y a toujours le risque que **le chèque** soit **sans provision.**

un endossataire: C'est la personne qui endosse le chèque, c'est-à-dire la personne qui signe au dos du chèque pour pouvoir toucher ce chèque.

> Pour pouvoir déposer un chèque sur mon compte, je dois d'abord l'endosser. L'employé(e) de la banque doit vérifier que **l'endossataire** est bien la personne à qui le chèque est adressé.

l'intérêt *(m)*: **L'intérêt** est un certain pourcentage que l'on doit payer sur la somme d'argent empruntée. En France, les banques ne payent aucun **taux d'intérêt** à leurs clients sur la somme d'argent qu'ils laissent sur leur compte-chèques.

> Mon amie Denise a emprunté 10.000 F à sa banque pour acheter une voiture contre **un taux d'intérêt** de 13,75%.

le montant: Lorsque je fais un chèque de 2.000 F pour payer mon loyer, j'écris deux fois **le montant** de ce chèque: en chiffres et en lettres.

> Remplir un chèque veut dire inscrire **le montant** du chèque et le nom de la personne à qui ce chèque est adressé et y apposer sa signature, en général, en bas à droite.

le prélèvement automatique: On peut demander à sa banque de faire **un prélèvement automatique** pour payer certaines factures régulières comme le gaz, l'électricité, le loyer, une assurance vie, etc. Dans ce cas, c'est la banque qui règle la facture directement parce qu'elle a été autorisée à le faire.

> Grâce aux **prélèvements automatiques,** je suis sûre que mes factures sont payées à temps mais je dois faire attention à toujours garder suffisamment d'argent sur mon compte!

un reçu: Un reçu est un papier qui prouve que l'on a payé une certaine somme. Un bon de caisse, une quittance, un récépissé sont des exemples de **reçus.** Lorsque je suis en déplacement *(on a business trip),* mon entreprise me rembourse de tous mes frais à condition que je puisse présenter **les reçus** justifiant toutes mes dépenses. Si je ne le fais pas, je dois me contenter d'un forfait.

> Tu es allé acheter des timbres à la Poste hier? As-tu pensé à garder **le reçu?**

DES RELAIS DANS 32 PAYS

Pays	Montant par Postchèque	
Algérie	800	dinars algériens
Allemagne R.F.A.	400	deutsche Marks
Autriche	2 500	schillings
Belgique	7 000	francs belges
Chypre	100	livres chypriotes
Danemark	1 500	couronnes danoises
Espagne, Andorre, Baléares, Canaries	30 000	pesetas espagnoles
Finlande	1 000	marks finlandais
Grande-Bretagne, Guernesey, Ile de Man, Jersey	100	livres sterling
Grèce	25 000	drachmes
Hongrie	10 000	forints
Irlande	125	livres irlandaises
Islande	8 000	couronnes islandaises
Israël	350	shekels
Italie, Sardaigne, Sicile	300 000	lires
Japon	25 000	yens
Liechtenstein	300	francs suisses
Luxembourg	7 000	francs luxembourgeois
Malte	70	livres maltaises
Maroc	2 000	dirhams marocains
Norvège	1 300	couronnes norvégiennes
Nouvelle-Calédonie	22 000	francs CFP
Pays-Bas	300	florins néerlandais
Polynésie française	22 000	francs CFP
Portugal, Açores, Ile de Madère	30 000	escudos portugais
Saint-Marin	300 000	lires
Suède	1 400	couronnes suédoises
Suisse	300	francs suisses
Thaïlande	5 000	bahts
Tunisie	150	dinars tunisiens
Turquie	300 000	livres turques
Yougoslavie	700 000	dinars yougoslaves

Le tableau ci-dessus vous présente le réseau, ainsi que pour chaque pays la valeur de vos Postchèques en monnaie locale.

Dispositions valables en avril 1989 pouvant varier en fonction de la réglementation.

POSTCHÈQUES
POUR UN COMPTE-CHÈQUES INTERNATIONAL

RCS PARIS B 304 452 907 DGF / SF 90,5 - 04 / 89 - PPR 95310 St-Ouen-l'Aumône

EQUATEUR

LA POSTE
BOUGEZ AVEC LA POSTE

Un dépliant de la Poste.

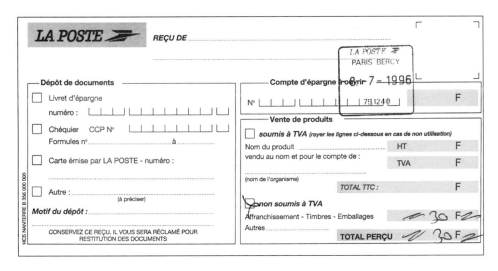

Un reçu de la Poste.

➤ Study the terms and definitions in the *Lexique* as well as those in the *Vocabulaire de base* on page 5. If you were to play *Mot de passe* (password) in class next time, would you be able to give simple definitions *in French* for all of the expressions?

le tiré, le tireur et **le bénéficiaire: Le tiré** est celui ou celle qui paie le chèque, **le tireur** celui ou celle qui émet le chèque (la banque) et **le bénéficiaire,** la personne ou l'entreprise qui encaisse le chèque, c'est-à-dire qui touche le montant spécifié sur le chèque.

Quand vous remplissez un chèque, n'oubliez pas de préciser le nom du **bénéficiaire;** autrement, n'importe qui pourrait toucher le chèque. En général, les noms du **tiré** et du **tireur** sont imprimés sur le chèque. **Le tiré** doit signer le chèque pour que **le bénéficiaire** puisse le toucher.

la banque encaisse la chèque après que le bene. l'a endossé

Paroles de sagesse

Ne cherchez pas à paraître plus que vous ne valez!

Expression écrite

D'abord, puis, ensuite, enfin

➤ Skim for the general idea of the paragraph.

Dans les activités intitulées *Expression écrite,* vous allez lire des paragraphes utilisant des mots faciles à employer qui vous aideront à vous exprimer *(express).*

Opérations effectuées à la banque

Personnellement, je ne vais à la banque que lorsque j'ai une opération particulière à y faire. Pour les opérations courantes, je me sers uniquement de ma Carte Bleue. Récemment, j'ai dû me rendre à mon agence afin d'effectuer un virement de mon compte épargne sur mon compte courant. En effet, j'avais besoin de disposer d'une certaine somme d'argent car je projetais d'acheter une voiture. D'abord, il m'a été nécessaire de calculer la somme d'argent maximum qu'il m'était possible de retirer de mon compte épargne logement afin d'y laisser le montant minimum exigé. Puis, je me suis rendue à mon agence afin d'effectuer toutes les opérations relatives à ce virement. Alors, l'employé du Crédit Agricole m'a rappelé le solde de mes deux comptes et a effectué le transfert par l'intermédiaire de son ordinateur. Puis, il m'a remis un reçu attestant de cette opération. Enfin, je lui ai demandé de me calculer le solde de mon compte une fois que je l'aurais débité du montant du prix de la voiture. L'ensemble de ces démarches ne m'a guère pris plus de quinze minutes. Si j'avais disposé d'un Minitel, j'aurais perdu encore moins de temps puisqu'il m'aurait été possible de les effectuer de mon domicile.

➤ Note the use of the past infinitive after the preposition *après*. This could be translated as *after having read,* but we tend to say *after reading* in spoken English.

CC. La parole est à vous! Après avoir lu le texte qui précède, écrivez vous-même un paragraphe au présent, au futur ou au passé sur le même sujet, c'est-à-dire sur ce que vous pouvez faire à la banque. Commencez par une phrase d'introduction, développez bien vos idées et finissez par une conclusion concise.

➤ After finishing your paragraph, read it aloud to your study partner. Ask him/her for input.

A la banque...

2ème jour : ① faites une revue du vocabulaire de chèque. Ecrivez un chèque au tableau.

② demander des définitions oraux, livre fermé

③ qu'est ce que faites au distributeur automatique?
(what are the steps...)

Dans le dossier suivant, vous allez en apprendre un peu plus sur les banques et commencer à étudier le Minitel.

Banque et Minitel

Dans le deuxième dossier du Module I, vous allez continuer à travailler sur le vocabulaire de base de la banque. Les banques sont informatisées et l'on peut effectuer un grand nombre d'opérations soi-même à un guichet automatique, en passant un simple coup de téléphone ou en se servant du Minitel. Ce dossier présente également différents usages du Minitel.

HSG

➤ For Dossier 2, reread *Points grammaticaux* and complete activities I and J in your *HSG*. In addition, review the irregular verbs *croire, ouvrir, vouloir* and *aller* and complete the corresponding exercises.

➤ Take detailed notes in French for reporting back and/or brainstorming.

➤ See photos of Minitels on pages 2, 17, 30, and 37.

➤ If you were now called on to write terms on the board during a brainstorming session, would you know how to ask for help in spelling words you might not recognize? If not, review Exercise C on page 6.

Activité d'introduction

Le Minitel

A. Introduction au Minitel. Répondez aux questions suivantes par groupes de deux ou trois.

1. Est-ce que vous savez ce qu'un Minitel est?
2. Après avoir regardé les photos de Minitels qui illustrent votre livre, nommez au moins trois points communs entre le Minitel et l'ordinateur. Tous les deux, ils ont...
3. Imaginez comment les différents membres d'une même famille peuvent utiliser le Minitel dans leurs activités quotidiennes *(daily)*. Donnez sept exemples.

Les mots pour le dire

Jetez un coup d'œil sur la traduction des mots suivants mais concentrez-vous sur leur prononciation en français et sur les images qu'évoquent les noms, les adjectifs, les adverbes ou les actions décrites par les verbes de la liste suivante.

Vocabulaire de base

V E R B E S

allumer (le Minitel)	*to turn on (the Minitel)*
déposer un chèque	*to deposit a check*
louer un appartement	*to rent an apartment*
perdre quelque chose	*to lose something*
retirer de l'argent	*to withdraw money*
taper	*to type*
tirer (le clavier)	*to pull out (the keyboard)*
toucher	*to cash; to touch*
vérifier le solde (de son compte)	*to verify; to check the balance (in/of one's account)*
verser de l'argent (sur son compte)	*to deposit, to make a direct deposit (into one's account)*
virer de l'argent, faire un virement	*to transfer money*

N O M S

une agence	*here: a rental office*
un chèque en blanc	*blank check*
le clavier	*keyboard*
un DAB (Distributeur Automatique de Billets) ou guichet automatique	*ATM machine*
une demande de carte bancaire	*application for a credit/banking card*
un dépôt	*deposit*
un identifiant	*personal secret code, PIN number*
un livret	*passbook*
le montant	*amount*
un mot de passe	*password*
un numéro d'accès	*access number*
un remboursement	*reimbursement*
le solde	*balance*
une somme	*sum*
un studio	*studio apartment*
un virement	*transfer*

A D J E C T I F S

autorisé(e)	*authorized*
crédité(e)	*credited*
pratique	*practical; convenient*
secret(ète)	*secret*
social(e)	*social*

A D V E R B E S   E T   E X P R E S S I O N S   A D V E R B I A L E S

déjà	*already*
en liquide, en espèces	*in cash*
hier	*yesterday*
non plus	*neither*
plutôt	*rather*
quand même	*all the same; anyway*

B. A vous! Mettez-vous en groupes de quatre et épelez les termes suivants à haute voix.

1. un numéro d'accès
2. le solde
3. un identifiant
4. le clavier

5. un remboursement
6. un virement
7. en espèces

Un distributeur automatique de billets.

C. Définitions provisoires à terminer. Complétez les phrases suivantes.

1. Lorsqu'on paie une certaine somme pour pouvoir habiter dans un appartement ou une maison, on paie un _____.
Comment est-ce que cela s'écrit?
Ça s'écrit: _____.

2. La partie de l'ordinateur sur laquelle on tape les lettres pour former des mots s'appelle le _____.
Ça s'écrit: _____.

3. Pour mettre le Minitel en marche, il faut l'_____.
Ça s'écrit: _____.

4. On va à un Distributeur Automatique de Billets pour _____ de l'argent.
Ça s'écrit: _____.

5. Lorsque quelque chose est utile et très facile à utiliser, on dit que c'est _____.
Ça s'écrit: _____.

D. Définitions provisoires à créer. Par groupes de deux, écrivez une définition provisoire pour les mots suivants.

1. un montant
2. un mot de passe
3. un studio

4. verser
5. taper

➤ Explain in simple French terms what each expression means. Have fun using circumlocution!

Dialogue

Vérifier le solde de son compte en banque par Minitel

E. Activité de pré-lecture. Répondez aux questions suivantes.

1. Vous ne savez pas combien il vous reste sur votre compte en banque. Que faites-vous? Cochez (✓) toutes les réponses qui vous paraissent correctes.

_____ Vous allez à la banque.

_____ Vous téléphonez à la banque.

_____ Vous ouvrez votre carnet de chèques et faites vos calculs.

_____ Vous consultez votre relevé de compte.

_____ Vous demandez à un ami.

_____ Vous attendez avant de faire votre prochain chèque.

2. Que faites-vous quand vous n'avez plus d'argent sur votre compte? Donnez cinq possibilités.

3. Comment faites-vous pour savoir si une certaine somme d'argent a bien été déposée sur votre compte? Donnez quatre possibilités.

F. Première lecture. Parcourez le texte du dialogue suivant (lisez rapidement et assez superficiellement), puis répondez aux questions suivantes.

1. Qui sont les deux personnes du dialogue, l'une par rapport à l'autre? Cochez la ou les réponses possibles.

_____ un frère et une sœur   _____ deux voisins

_____ un père et une mère   _____ deux collègues

_____ un oncle et une tante   _____ une patronne et un employé

_____ un fils et une mère   _____ une patronne et son secrétaire

2. Où se trouvent, selon vous, Vincent et Mme Amar? N'hésitez pas à deviner *(guess)*!

Vérifier le solde de son compte en banque par Minitel

Vincent: Maman, j'adore le studio que j'ai trouvé. Dommage que je ne le garde qu'un an. J'espère que je trouverai quelque chose d'aussi agréable à Dijon lorsque j'irai faire mon stage l'année prochaine. Tout le monde me dit que j'ai de la chance car Dijon est une ville intéressante et la Bourgogne une région magnifique. Au fait, est-ce que tu as déjà viré les 4.000 F sur mon compte de caisse d'épargne?

Mme Amar: Non, tu sais bien que j'attends le remboursement de la Sécurité Sociale.

Mme Amar et son fils se servent du Minitel.

Vincent allume le Minitel pour que sa mère vérifie le solde de son compte en banque.

Vincent: Ton compte n'a pas encore été crédité?

Mme Amar: Je ne crois pas. Je peux vérifier mon solde par Minitel, si tu veux.

Vincent: Oui, il faut absolument que je verse mon premier loyer pour le studio de la Place Viarme cette semaine; sinon l'agence va le louer à quelqu'un d'autre. J'ai promis de leur apporter un chèque demain! Est-ce que tu pourrais me laisser un chèque en blanc?

Mme Amar: Ecoute, Vincent, tu sais bien que ce n'est pas prudent. Tu pourrais perdre le chèque. Tu n'as pas ouvert de compte en banque hier?

Vincent: Si, et j'ai fait une demande de carte bancaire mais je ne l'ai pas obtenue tout de suite évidemment, et pas question d'avoir un chéquier parce que je ne suis pas salarié.

Mme Amar: Même si nous versons de l'argent sur ton compte tous les mois?

Vincent: Malheureusement, oui. Donne-moi un chèque en blanc, je te promets de faire très attention.

Mme Amar: Je préfère que tu téléphones à l'agence et que tu demandes exactement combien il faut que tu paies. Je peux te faire un chèque de ce montant-là au nom de l'agence. Bon, allume le Minitel et tire le clavier.

Vincent: Quel est le numéro d'accès du Crédit Agricole?

Mme Amar: Le 3616 et le code pour le Crédit Agricole, c'est CATOUR.

Vincent: Viens continuer, je ne connais pas ton identifiant... ton mot de passe non plus d'ailleurs...

Mme Amar: Voilà, j'arrive... Ah, tu as de la chance. Ça y est. Il y a eu un dépôt de 5.545 F. Voyons... oui, c'est bien de la Sécurité Sociale. Je vais faire un virement sur ton nouveau compte en banque tout de suite si tu veux.

Vincent: Oui, vire 800 F et donne-moi un chèque. On pourrait aussi aller au guichet automatique et retirer

Mme Amar: L'agence n'acceptera pas. Je crois d'ailleurs qu'on n'a même pas le droit de payer son loyer en espèces. Téléphone plutôt à l'agence! Bon, je vire 800 F et après on verra.

Vincent: Ce n'est quand-même pas pratique de ne pas avoir de chéquier!

Mme Amar: Tu sais, on utilise de moins en moins de chèques. Avec une carte bancaire et un code secret, tu pourras payer la majorité de tes achats. Tu as remarqué qu'il y a de plus en plus de magasins qui acceptent et même préfèrent la carte bancaire?

Vincent: Ouais. On voit le petit clavier spécial à la caisse. Il fait face au client. On tape son code secret, on attend, puis l'achat est autorisé par la banque.

Mme Amar: Ça va plus vite que d'écrire un chèque; et c'est plus sûr car si personne ne connaît ton code, même si tu perds ta carte, tu ne risques rien. Moi aussi, j'utilise ma carte de plus en plus souvent.

Vincent: Ce n'est pas la peine que je téléphone à l'agence; je peux aussi lire le contrat de location. Je vais le chercher. Il est sur mon bureau. Je l'ai rangé dans une chemise.

> ➤ With your study partner, take turns playing Vincent and Mme Amar. Be ready to play either of the roles for your next class, imitating as closely as possible the pronunciation and intonation patterns on your cassette.

> ➤ This is the present subjunctive of the verb *correspondre*; it's required because of the conjunction *pour que*.

G. Vrai ou faux? Si les propositions *(statements)* suivantes ne sont pas correctes, modifiez la phrase en question pour qu'elle corresponde à ce qui est dit dans le dialogue.

1. La mère de Vincent refuse de lui donner 4.000 F.
2. Vincent veut habiter dans son propre appartement.
3. La mère de Vincent se sert du Minitel pour avoir accès à son compte en banque.
4. Le numéro d'accès du Crédit Agricole est un code secret.
5. La mère de Vincent vérifie son relevé de compte pour savoir combien il lui reste à la banque.
6. Le versement de la Sécurité Sociale s'élève à 3.616 F.
7. La mère de Vincent ne veut pas que Vincent ouvre un compte en banque.

H. Choix multiple. Cochez la définition qui vous paraît correcte.

1. Virer de l'argent, c'est
   a. le transférer.
   b. le dépenser.
   c. l'économiser.

2. Vérifier le solde signifie

    a. demander combien d'argent liquide il nous reste.

    b. regarder combien d'argent on a sur son compte.

    c. regarder si on a encore assez de chèques.

3. Toucher un chèque, c'est

    a. vérifier s'il ne s'agit pas d'un faux chèque.

    b. recevoir la somme d'argent inscrite (écrite) sur le chèque.

    c. déposer la somme d'argent indiquée sur le chèque sur son compte en banque.

4. L'argent liquide, c'est

    a. des pièces et des billets.

    b. des pièces de monnaie en cours de fabrication *(being made, minted)*.

    c. de l'argent placé sur un compte en banque mais qui reste entièrement disponible *(available)*.

5. Mon compte est crédité quand

    a. ma carte de crédit est débitée directement de mon compte en banque.

    b. la banque a vérifié mon passé bancaire à la Banque de France.

    c. une certaine somme d'argent est arrivée sur mon compte et que je peux en disposer (l'utiliser, l'employer).

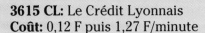

*O*bservations

Les codes et tarifs Minitel

Banques
Accès de chez vous à toutes opérations bancaires: Les banques facturent un abonnement *(bill for a subscription cost)* pour bénéficier de ce service en plus du prix de chaque connexion.

    3615 CL: Le Crédit Lyonnais
    Coût: 0,12 F puis 1,27 F/minute

    3614 BNP: La Banque Nationale de Paris
    Coût: 0,12 F puis 0,36 F/minute

    3614 SG: La Société Générale
    Coût: 0,12 F puis 0,36 F/minute

    3616 CBINFO: Si vous avez perdu votre Carte Bleue, composez ce code pour faire opposition.
    Coût: 0,12 F puis 1,27 F/minute

La Poste

    3614 LAPOSTE: Combien faut-il mettre de timbres pour une lettre pour les Etats-Unis ou un petit paquet pour la Côte-d'Ivoire? Quel est le code postal du village de votre grand-mère? Des informations pour les collectionneurs de timbres *(stamp*

collectors). Et bien sûr des infos sur les SICAV *(mutual funds)* et les plans d'épargne-logement.
Coût: 0,12 F puis 0,36 F/minute

3615 TELEFACT: Vous pouvez payer vos factures d'électricité (EDF) ou vos factures de téléphone (Télécom) par Minitel. Il faut d'abord remplir une fiche *(form)* autorisant le prélèvement direct de votre compte.
Coût: 0,12 F puis 0,99 F/minute

I. Avez-vous compris? Répondez aux questions suivantes.

1. Pourquoi est-ce que les gens consultent les services Minitel mentionnés dans la liste qui précède?

2. Comparez les prix des différents services Minitel.

3. Quel est le point commun entre toutes les connexions Minitel en ce qui concerne le prix?

4. Parmi les exemples proposés, quel est le service Minitel le plus cher? le moins cher?

5. En faisant des phrases complètes, comparez le prix des différents services Minitel suivants.

    a. du 3615 CL avec le 3614 BNP

    b. du 3614 BNP avec le 3614 SG

6. Quel genre d'information est-ce que vous pouvez obtenir à partir du 3614 LAPOSTE? Réfléchissez à tout ce qu'on peut faire à la Poste et trouvez au moins trois exemples qui ne sont pas mentionnés.

Lecture 1

TELESERVICE BNP: La banque à domicile

J. Activité de pré-lecture. Répondez aux questions suivantes en groupes de deux ou trois.

1. Est-il nécessaire d'aller à la banque pour avoir accès à son compte et effectuer certaines opérations?

2. En ce qui concerne votre compte en banque, mentionnez au moins trois choses que vous pouvez faire à distance et expliquez comment vous les faites.

3. Expliquez le préfixe «télé» dans les mots *le téléphone, la télévision, la télécopie.* Même sans avoir lu le texte qui suit, pouvez-vous deviner ce que veut dire «les téléservices de la banque»?

Ce guichet automatique se trouve à côté de la porte d'entrée d'un Crédit Mutuel de Bretagne.

TELESERVICE BNP: La banque à domicile

Le TELESERVICE BNP est un service de consultation, de gestion *(management)* et d'information à distance grâce auquel vous pouvez suivre vos comptes par Minitel et même par téléphone.

Nous l'avons créé et nous le développons en permanence pour vous offrir une gamme *(range)* de prestations *(services)* aujourd'hui sans équivalent sur le marché.

Savoir, décider, agir quand vous le voulez et où que vous vous trouviez.

Vous abonner au TELESERVICE BNP, c'est choisir de vous faciliter la vie et de gagner en efficacité *(efficiency)* dans la gestion de vos comptes.

Grâce à un accès permanent et confidentiel à votre banque, vous pouvez, en effet, à toute heure du jour et de la nuit:
— connaître le solde de vos comptes, vérifier que votre salaire a été viré, suivre vos factures Carte Bleue qui seront débitées ultérieurement…
— effectuer directement un virement d'un

compte à un autre, commander un chéquier ou faire opposition à votre Carte Bleue…
— vous informer sur l'ensemble des formules d'épargne, des solutions de crédit et des divers services que la BNP met à votre disposition *(disposal)* et, si vous le souhaitez, obtenir des conseils personnalisés (études de financement, gestion de patrimoine), recevoir une documentation et même ouvrir directement un compte par Minitel.

Un fonctionnement sûr et simple

Pour pouvoir utiliser le TELESERVICE BNP, il vous suffit de vous abonner *(to subscribe)*. Il vous en coûtera seulement 35 F par mois. Dès que votre souscription aura été enregistrée, un numéro d'abonné et un code confidentiel vous garantiront une totale sécurité d'utilisation.

Dépliant de la BNP: TELESERVICE BNP: la banque à domicile, 1995.

K. A la recherche du mot juste. Répondez aux questions suivantes.

1. Trouvez dans le texte le verbe de la même famille que les noms suivants.

- un abonnement
- la vérification
- un choix
- une disposition
- un virement
- l'ouverture

2. Trouvez dans le texte le nom de la même famille que les verbes de la liste suivante.

- gérer
- conseiller
- compter
- créditer
- se documenter

3. Trouvez dans le texte un synonyme pour chacun des mots suivants.

- un renseignement
- 24 heures sur 24
- une série de, un choix de
- versé
- simplifier
- faire

L. Vrai ou faux? Si les affirmations suivantes ne sont pas correctes, modifiez la phrase pour arriver à une affirmation qui corresponde au texte.

1. Le TELESERVICE BNP vous permet de faire le point sur vos comptes 24 h sur 24, 7 jours sur 7.

2. Le TELESERVICE BNP permet d'obtenir des informations sur vos comptes mais pas d'effectuer certaines opérations bancaires comme faire un virement, par exemple.

3. Vous pouvez gérer votre portefeuille-titres *(stock and bond portfolio)* par l'intermédiaire de TELESERVICE BNP.

4. N'importe qui peut avoir accès aux comptes bancaires des clients de la banque.

5. L'utilisation du TELESERVICE BNP est gratuite.

M. De la réflexion à l'écriture. Répondez par écrit à la question suivante.

Si les clients d'une banque font de plus en plus de transactions à la maison ou à un guichet automatique, qu'est-ce que cela va avoir comme conséquences pour cette banque? Pensez à différents changements possibles, tout spécialement en ce qui concerne le personnel de cette banque. Ecrivez au moins 10 lignes.

> ➤ Introduction, développement de vos idées et conclusion.

Lecture 2

Service: Banque en non-stop

N. Activité de pré-lecture. Répondez aux questions suivantes.

1. Quelles sont les heures d'ouverture de votre banque?

2. Est-ce que ces heures vous conviennent? Pourquoi?

3. Lisez le titre du petit extrait suivant. Avant même de lire le texte, essayez de deviner de quoi il va s'agir.

Service: Banque en non-stop

Enfin une banque pleine de bon sens *(common sense)* qui ne vous ferme pas la porte au nez en milieu de l'après-midi. Trois de ses bureaux à Paris sont ouverts en continu jusqu'à 19h (Champs-Elysées et rue de Rome) et même 20 h à la Défense. Autre avantage: un service téléphonique qui fonctionne 24 heures sur 24 (on peut l'appeler de n'importe quel pays *(country)* sans se soucier des décalages horaires *(time zone differences)*!), avec une personne physique au bout du fil qui peut faire en votre nom toute opération financière utile. Elle se nomme Citibank. Tous renseignements au:
    01.49.04.60.00.

Tiré de: *Madame Figaro:* samedi 15 janvier 1994, N° 15 366.

O. Autrement dit. Répondez aux questions suivantes en sélectionnant la ou les bonnes réponses. Attention, quelquefois il y a plus d'une réponse correcte!

1. Pourquoi le titre «banque en non-stop»?

a. Parce que les guichets de la banque sont toujours ouverts.

   b. Parce qu'on peut joindre *(contact)* la banque par téléphone à n'importe quel moment de la journée ou de la nuit.

   c. Parce que les employé(e)s de la banque font la journée continue *(do a full day's work with no break for lunch).*

2. Quels sont les avantages de cette banque par rapport aux autres banques?

   a. Elle a des employés qui parlent anglais.

   b. Elle offre un service téléphonique 24 heures sur 24.

   c. Elle a une entrée spéciale pour les handicapés physiques.

3. Que dit le texte du service téléphonique offert par Citibank?

   a. Il n'est pas pratique car il ne tient pas compte des décalages horaires.

   b. Il est pratique mais cher.

   c. Il est pratique car il est toujours accessible aux clients.

P. A vous la parole! Le texte contient quelques chiffres. Par groupes de deux, lisez ces chiffres à haute voix et expliquez à quoi ils correspondent.

Quelques points de repère

L'ardoise

Avant les ordinateurs, il y a eu un grand nombre de machines qui faisaient des calculs *(calculations)* elles-mêmes. Vers le milieu *(middle)* du XVIIe siècle en France, le mathématicien et philosophe Blaise Pascal avait inventé une machine à calculer qui permettait de faire des additions et des soustractions. Les premiers ordinateurs sont nés aux Etats-Unis et datent des années 50 *(from the 50's).* Autrefois, les ordinateurs étaient lourds, coûtaient très cher et occupaient toute une pièce dans une entreprise. Ils étaient fragiles et lents. Ce n'est que depuis les années 70 que les ordinateurs sont vraiment devenus de plus en plus petits, de plus en plus puissants et rapides tout en étant de moins en moins chers.

Le saviez-vous?

En France, lorsqu'une personne dépose un chèque sur son compte, elle ne peut pas avoir accès immédiatement à cet argent. Il faut qu'elle attende (subjonctif du verbe *attendre*) trois ou quatre jours au moins avant que son compte soit crédité et qu'elle puisse (subjonctif du verbe *pouvoir*) disposer de son argent.

Les entreprises françaises!

- Les principaux fabricants français de câbles à fibres optiques sont: FOI (Fibres Optiques Industrie) et CLTO (Compagnie Lyonnaise de Transmissions Optiques). Le groupe Pouyet-Quante (alliance franco-allemande) est le leader européen de la connexion dans les réseaux du câble. Depuis 1992, ce groupe s'est beaucoup développé à l'échelle internationale: la part du chiffre d'affaires générée à l'étranger a atteint 43% en 1994.

- *Zoom sur France Télécom:* C'est France Télécom qui commercialise le Minitel qui est une marque déposée. Un Minitel est un terminal avec lequel on peut avoir accès à un annuaire électronique et aux services de Télétel. Le Minitel s'adapte à une prise de téléphone et fonctionne à l'électricité, sur du 220 volts. France Télécom offre plusieurs modèles de Minitel du plus simple au plus sophistiqué.

Une date importante!

- Le mot «informatique» a été inventé en 1962, en France, par Philippe Dreyfuss.
- L'emploi du Minitel, expérimenté à la fin des années 70, s'est généralisé dès le début des années 80.

Les chiffres parlent!

- Un satellite est garanti 10 ans et un réseau câblé 25 ans.
- En 1993, il y avait 6.485.000 Minitels en service en France.

Magis
Le Minitel nouvelle génération.

France Telecom

La couverture d'un dépliant de France Télécom, 1995.

Réflexions sur le travail en équipe

Imaginez que vous faites partie d'une équipe. Pensez aux *systèmes* et aux *procédés* (méthodes pour parvenir à un certain résultat) qui vont être utilisés par ou dans le groupe (ou à ceux que vous pourriez employer dans certaines situations ou certains contextes) et faites-en l'évaluation.

Lexique

débiter: Débiter veut dire enlever une certaine somme d'argent d'un compte. **Le débit,** c'est le contraire du crédit et **débiter,** le contraire de créditer.

> J'ai envoyé un chèque de 1.400 F la semaine dernière à mon dentiste mais je ne sais pas si mon compte a été **débité.**

encaisser: Encaisser, c'est mettre dans sa caisse. Lorsque j'**encaisse** un chèque, je reçois la somme d'argent inscrite sur ce chèque. **Encaisser** est un synonyme de *toucher.*

> Je dois passer à la banque avant la fermeture car je voudrais **encaisser** un traveller chèque. Je n'ai pratiquement pas de liquide sur moi et je sors ce soir!

les frais *(m):* **Les frais** sont les dépenses qu'on a dans certaines situations. Lorsqu'un homme ou une femme d'affaires prend l'avion ou mange dans un restaurant avec un client pour conclure un contrat, toutes ces dépenses sont des **frais** professionnels et peuvent être remboursées par l'entreprise ou déduites *(deducted)* sur la déclaration d'impôts.

> Ma note de **frais** a doublé depuis que je n'habite plus à Paris!

l'informatique *(f):* **L'informatique** est le traitement automatique de l'information par ordinateur.

> **L'informatique** fait partie de notre vie quotidienne. Nous voyons des ordinateurs partout, dans les magasins, les banques, les écoles, et de plus en plus les ordinateurs ont leur place à la maison. **L'informatique** est également devenue une science que l'on peut étudier.

le porteur *(m):* **Le porteur** d'une carte bancaire est la personne qui possède cette carte.

> La grande majorité des **porteurs** de cartes bancaires se disent très satisfaits du service et utilisent leur carte au moins une fois par semaine pour retirer de l'argent dans un distributeur ou pour effectuer *(make)* un paiement.

rémunérer: Rémunérer est un synonyme de payer. Etre **rémunéré,** c'est recevoir un paiement pour un service.

> Les comptes courants en France ne sont pas **rémunérés.** Cela veut dire que même si vous avez une grosse somme d'argent sur votre compte pendant longtemps, vous ne gagnerez rien.

la télématique *(f):* **La télématique,** c'est tout ce qui touche les techniques et les services liés aux télécommunications et à l'informatique.

> La France a joué un rôle de pionnier en **télématique** grand public avec le Minitel.

le titulaire *(m):* **Le titulaire** d'un compte est la personne qui possède un compte en son nom. Le compte peut être un compte-joint ou en son nom personnel uniquement.

> Vincent est maintenant **titulaire** de son propre compte.

Le titulaire du compte compose son code secret.

 **aroles de sagesse**

Etre riche, qu'est-ce que c'est?

— avoir tout ce dont on a envie.
— être satisfait(e) de ce que l'on a et de ce que l'on est.

Réfléchissez aux domaines suivants:

- personnalité
- argent
- logement
- amis
- famille
- caractéristiques physiques et mentales
- poste, emploi
- loisirs
- talents
- *autres?*

***E**xpression écrite*

D'autres expressions adverbiales

Paragraphe sur l'achat d'un mandat *(money order)***.** Dans cette section, vous allez apprendre à articuler un récit à l'aide d'expressions adverbiales. Lisez le paragraphe qui suit et entourez (encerclez), les expressions adverbiales qui signalent une suite d'idées dans le récit.

Pour acheter un mandat

Si vous voulez envoyer un mandat, vous devez aller à la Poste demander une fiche au receveur puis la remplir. Après, lorsque la fiche est remplie, vous devez vous représenter au guichet. Le receveur enregistrera votre demande sur ordinateur. Ensuite, il faudra régler ce mandat. Le coût du mandat est de 20 francs plus la somme que vous voulez envoyer. La Poste n'accepte ni les chèques ni la Carte Bleue. Il faut donc payer en liquide. Si vous n'avez pas d'espèces, dans presque toutes les Postes, vous trouverez un distributeur automatique Carte Bleue. Vous retirerez de l'argent avant de régler le receveur qui enverra votre mandat et vous donnera un reçu.

Q. A vos plumes! Ecrivez un paragraphe semblable articulé de façon similaire sur un des sujets suivants:

Comment ouvrir un compte-chèques postal

Comment utiliser le Minitel pour virer de l'argent de son compte épargne à son compte courant

R. Une lettre à vos parents. Ecrivez une lettre à vos parents au présent ou au passé et employez au moins une dizaine de mots tirés des sections *Vocabulaire de base* ou *Lexique.* (environ quinze phrases)

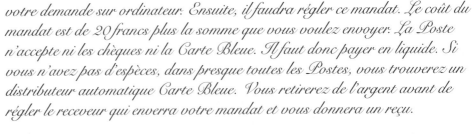

_____, _____
(ville)   (date)

Chers Maman et Papa,

(corps de la lettre)

Je vous embrasse tous les deux,

_____
(prénom)

Dans le dossier qui suit, vous allez étudier les domaines du téléphone et des télécommunications.

*L*es télécommunications

Le téléphone est une invention du XIXe siècle *(century)* mais il a beaucoup évolué du point de vue technique et propose aujourd'hui un grand nombre de services basés sur une technologie très sophistiquée à un vaste public. Rares sont les foyers *(homes)* qui n'ont pas le téléphone. Le téléphone joue un rôle important au niveau de la vie personnelle aussi bien que professionnelle. Ce dossier vous présente également différents appareils liés au téléphone comme le Minitel, le télécopieur, le répondeur.

HSG

➤ For Dossier 3, complete activities K–N of Module I in your *HSG* and study the irregular verb frames and flashes for *avoir* and *faire*.

*A*ctivité d'introduction

Le téléphone

A. Au sujet du téléphone. Répondez aux questions suivantes.

1. Combien d'appels téléphoniques passez-vous, en moyenne, par jour?
2. Pour quelles raisons est-ce que vous vous servez du téléphone?
3. Comment les différents membres d'une même famille peuvent-ils utiliser le téléphone dans leurs activités quotidiennes personnelles et professionnelles? Donnez au moins cinq exemples précis.
4. Quel genre de message est-ce que vous aimez et quel genre de message est-ce que vous détestez lorsque votre correspondant ne décroche pas le téléphone et que vous tombez sur son répondeur?

Téléphone public à carte.

Props
un téléphone
un fil

5. Est-ce que vous laissez facilement un message sur un répondeur lorsque vous ne réussissez pas à parler à la personne que vous appelez ou bien est-ce que vous trouvez difficile de parler à une machine? Expliquez.

6. Quel est le rôle et l'importance d'un téléphone dans une entreprise? Donnez au moins sept exemples.

Les mots pour le dire

Jetez un coup d'œil sur la traduction des mots suivants mais concentrez-vous sur leur prononciation en français et sur les images qu'évoquent les noms, les adjectifs ou les actions décrites par les verbes ou les adverbes de la liste suivante.

Vocabulaire de base	
V E R B E S	
brancher	*to plug in*
composer un numéro	*to dial a number*
décrocher	*to pick up (the phone)*
Ne quittez pas!	*Stay on the line!*
raccrocher	*to hang up (the phone)*
relier	*to hook, to link*
sonner	*to ring*
N O M S	
un appareil de téléphone	*telephone unit*
un appel	*call*
le cadran	*dial*
le combiné	*receiver*
un correspondant, un interlocuteur	*person with whom one is talking*
l'emploi *(m)*	*use*
un fichier	*file*
le fil	*cord*
une gamme	*line (of products)*
une ligne	*line*
un logiciel	*software (package)*
un mode d'emploi	*user manual*
la prise	*phone outlet, plug*
le réacheminement d'un appel, le transfert d'appel	*call forwarding*
un répondeur (automatique)	*answering machine*
une réunion par téléphone, une audioconférence	*conference call*
un signal d'appel, un bip sonore	*call waiting signal*
la sonnerie	*ring (of the telephone)*
la tarification, le tarif, le prix	*price*
une télécarte	*phonecard*
une télécopie, un fax	*fax*
un télécopieur	*fax machine*

Téléphone portatif dans un magasin.

ADJECTIFS	
amovible	*removable, detachable*
forfaitaire	*inclusive*
interrogeable à distance	*checkable by remote*
mensuel(le)	*monthly*
vieux (vieille)	*old*

> When the adjective *vieux* is used in front of a masculine singular noun beginning with a vowel or semi-vowel, the form *vieil* is used—i.e., *un vieil arbre, un vieil hôtel.*

ADVERBES ET EXPRESSIONS ADVERBIALES	
en biais	*gently sloping, oblique*
gratuitement	*at no cost*
en panne	*out of order*
sans fil	*cordless*
séparément	*separately*

> Be ready to give a simple definition in French of five of these highlighted terms. Use your French-French dictionary to prepare.

B. A vous! Mettez-vous par groupes de quatre et épelez les termes suivants à voix haute.

1. composer un numéro
2. la sonnerie
3. un interlocuteur
4. en biais
5. un remboursement
6. la tarification
7. une télécopie

C. Définitions provisoires à terminer. Complétez les phrases suivantes.

1. Lorsqu'on a une machine qui sert à enregistrer les messages téléphoniques qu'on reçoit, on a un _____. *répondeur*
   Comment ça s'écrit?
   Ça s'écrit: _____.

2. Lorsqu'on peut vérifier les messages qu'on a reçus sur son répondeur à la maison d'un autre appareil au bureau ou d'une cabine téléphonique, et qu'on peut même modifier le message que le correspondant entend lorsqu'il entre en communication avec le répondeur, on dit que ce répondeur est _____. *interrogeable à distance*
   Ça s'écrit: _____.

3. Pour que le téléphone marche, il faut le _____ de façon *brancher*
   à ce qu'il soit connecté aux réseaux électrique et téléphonique.
   Ça s'écrit: _____.

4. Le _____ est ce qui avertit *(warns)* une personne qui *signal d'appel / le bip sonore*
   est en communication téléphonique qu'une autre personne essaie de la joindre.
   Ça s'écrit: _____.

5. On appelle ce qui relie le téléphone à la prise, le _____. *fil*
   Ça s'écrit: _____.

D. Définitions provisoires à créer. En groupes de deux, écrivez une définition provisoire pour les noms suivants.

1. décrocher
2. une gamme
3. en panne
4. un télécopieur
5. un mode d'emploi

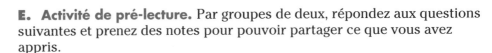

Dialogue

Changer de Minitel

E. Activité de pré-lecture. Par groupes de deux, répondez aux questions suivantes et prenez des notes pour pouvoir partager ce que vous avez appris.

1. Donnez quelques exemples de différences entre un vieil appareil de téléphone et un nouveau; entre un vieux téléviseur et un nouveau poste de télévision; entre un vieil ordinateur et un nouveau.

2. Que faites-vous quand vous voulez que vos parents changent un appareil qu'ils ont à la maison pour un appareil plus moderne, ou, si vous vivez avec quelqu'un, que dites-vous pour convaincre cette personne qu'il est temps de changer d'appareil?

3. Quand vous voulez appeler quelqu'un d'une cabine téléphonique, que faites-vous? Comment payez-vous votre appel? Décrivez les différentes étapes par lesquelles vous devez passer pour avoir votre correspondant au bout du fil.

Un téléphone dans son emballage sur le rayon d'un hypermarché.

② *quels sont les problèmes du vieux minitel?*

Changer de Minitel

Vincent: Qu'est-ce que tu fais?

Noémie: Tu vois bien! Je cherche des informations sur le Minitel.

Vincent: Ben oui! Mais des informations sur quoi?

Noémie: Sur les différentes écoles d'hôtellerie. J'ai promis à la voisine que je chercherais quelques adresses pour Emilie. J'ai trouvé des choses intéressantes mais qu'est-ce que le Minitel est lent! Les touches du clavier réagissent lentement et entre chaque commande, il faut attendre. Les informations n'apparaissent pas immédiatement sur l'écran. Ça m'énerve!

Vincent: C'est parce que c'est un vieux Minitel. C'est un des premiers Minitels! Tu sais que le gouvernement avait simplement prêté gratuitement ces Minitels pour lancer le concept et voir si ça pouvait marcher. A l'époque, c'était très moderne et on ne se plaignait pas de leur lenteur! Les choses ont bien changé!

Noémie: Il nous en faudrait un autre. C'est peut-être une bonne idée de cadeau de Noël!

Vincent: Ouais, mais cher! Justement, j'étais chez Céline cet après-midi. Ses parents viennent juste d'acheter un Sillage. C'est un téléphone, un répondeur et un Minitel en un. C'est France Télécom qui vient de sortir ça.

I 2

Noémie: Tu l'as essayé?

Vincent: Oui, quand je suis arrivé, Céline était en train de faire sa résa (réservation) au Minitel. Tu sais qu'elle va à Bruxelles pour une réunion de travail.

Noémie: Ah oui, c'est vrai. Elle prend le TGV évidemment?

Vincent: Ouais, ça lui fait moins de deux heures de train. C'est pas mal! Bref, ce que je voulais te dire, c'est que j'ai été impressionné par le nouveau Minitel. Il est beaucoup plus rapide que la vieille version et plus cool. Le style est ultra-moderne. L'appareil est bleu marine. Il n'y a qu'un seul clavier: les touches du téléphone et celles du Minitel étant les mêmes.

Noémie: Alors le clavier n'est pas amovible?

Vincent: Non, t'as pas besoin de tirer le clavier comme le nôtre. Il est fixe et l'écran aussi, derrière les touches. Il n'est pas perpendiculaire mais un peu en biais; ça permet une lecture facile.

Noémie: Moi, ce que je trouve encore mieux, c'est le Djinn Phone de France Télécom aussi. D'après ce que j'ai compris, c'est une sorte de logiciel que tu montes sur ton micro-ordinateur. Après ça, à partir de ton ordi, tu peux tout faire: tu peux téléphoner, envoyer des télécopies, consulter les services Minitel. Ça te donne tout: répondeur-enregistreur interrogeable à distance, fax personnel, Minitel, tu peux même transférer des fichiers à la vitesse de 14.400 bauds! Génial, quoi!

Vincent: Alors, pour que ton ordi te serve de répondeur et de télécopieur, faut qu'il reste allumé 24 heures sur 24?

Noémie: Sans doute, ouais mais je ne vois pas le problème.

Vincent: Et y a une version du logiciel qui marche avec Macintosh?

Noémie: J'ai pas l'impression.

Vincent: Alors, pas la peine de rêver!

Noémie: Dis donc, t'as encore des unités sur ta télécarte?

Vincent: Je viens d'en acheter une, pourquoi?

Noémie: Je sors avec des copains ce soir et j'ai promis à Céline de l'appeler vers 8 heures.

Vincent: Ecoute, je te la prête mais tu me la rends demain et tu restes pas des heures au téléphone; sinon tu me la rembourses ou tu m'en achètes une autre.

Noémie: D'accord, c'est sympa.

REMARQUES

Quelques mots et formes grammaticales empruntés au français parlé

Notez les exemples suivants tirés du Dialogue.

1. Il y a de nombreuses négations qui ne sont pas complètes.

   Tu restes pas des heures au téléphone. = Tu **ne** restes pas des heures au téléphone.

2. Certains pronoms personnels sujets ne sont pas écrits en entier.

   T'as pas besoin... = **Tu** n'as pas besoin...

continued on page 46

continued from page 45

3. Certains pronoms personnels sont complètement supprimés.

   Faut pas rêver. = **Il** ne faut pas rêver.

4. *Oui* est prononcé et écrit **ouais**.

5. Certains mots sont abrégés *(shortened)*.

   une résa = une réservation

   un ordi = un ordinateur

   sympa = sympathique

6. Certains mots font partie d'un vocabulaire familier à la mode parmi les jeunes. Attention, il vaut mieux ne pas les utiliser dans un contexte formel.

   Génial! = C'est vraiment très bien!

   C'est sympa. = C'est vraiment gentil de ta part.

   cool = très bien, à la mode

Faut-il utiliser ce genre de vocabulaire et de tournures grammaticales? Soyez extrêmement prudent car vous pouvez facilement choquer les personnes à qui vous parlez. Essayez de parler aussi correctement que possible, surtout dans une situation de travail ou lorsque vous vous adressez à des gens que vous ne connaissez pas bien.

F. A la recherche d'éléments précis. Cherchez dans le dialogue les renseignements demandés dans les questions suivantes.

1. Relevez sept mots qui se rapportent à l'informatique.
2. Trouvez dans le texte au moins trois mots ou expressions qui sont liés aux mots suivants.

   MODELE: *le Minitel de Noémie* / ***lent, vieux, énervant***

   a. le nouveau Minitel
   b. le Sillage
   c. Céline
   d. le Djinn Phone
   e. la télécarte de Vincent

G. A vous de compléter! Complétez les phrases suivantes avec un mot trouvé dans le dialogue.

vieux minitel
hôtelleries

1. Quand Vincent est arrivé, Noémie consultait le ________________.
2. Noémie voulait avoir des informations sur des écoles ________________.
3. Noémie est énervée parce que le Minitel est ________________.

viennent d'acheter

4. Les parents de Céline ________________ un Sillage.
5. C'est ____France Télécom____ qui vend le Djinn Phone.

transferer vite

6. Avec le Djinn Phone, on peut ________________ des fichiers.
7. Noémie demande à Vincent de lui prêter sa télécarte parce qu'elle veut ________________ Céline.

H. Autrement dit. Cochez la définition qui vous paraît correcte parmi celles que nous vous proposons ci-dessous.

1. Le clavier du Minitel, c'est
   a. la partie sur laquelle on peut lire le texte.
   b. la prise qui permet la connexion avec la ligne téléphonique.
   c. la partie de l'ordinateur où il y a les touches.

2. Les parents de Céline viennent juste d'acheter un Sillage. Cela veut dire
   a. qu'ils ont déjà acheté un Sillage.
   b. qu'ils vont bientôt acheter un Sillage.
   c. qu'ils sont juste en train d'acheter un Sillage.

3. Le Djinn Phone, c'est
   a. un appareil téléphonique qui a une sonnerie intéressante.
   b. un programme qui permet d'utiliser entre autres le Minitel à partir de l'ordinateur.
   c. un ordinateur qui est programmé pour téléphoner tout seul.

4. Une télécarte, c'est
   a. une carte de téléphone qui peut être utilisée dans les cabines publiques.
   b. une carte de téléphone qui permet de téléphoner à ses parents gratuitement.
   c. une carte qui permet de programmer la télévision.

5. Un logiciel, c'est
   a. une manière logique de penser qui permet de comprendre ce qu'un ordinateur fait.
   b. une personne qui répare les ordinateurs en panne.
   c. un programme qu'on utilise sur un ordinateur pour traiter des données.

L'écran et le clavier d'un Minitel.

l'ancien

I. Avez-vous compris? Après avoir bien relu le texte, répondez aux questions suivantes.

1. Pourquoi est-ce que Noémie pense que ce serait une bonne idée d'acheter un nouveau Minitel à ses parents pour Noël?
2. Pourquoi est-ce que Vincent préfère le Sillage au Minitel qu'il a à la maison?
3. D'après la description que le dialogue vous donne, qu'est-ce qui vous semble préférable, un Sillage ou un Djinn Phone? Pourquoi?
4. Quelle impression est-ce que les nouveaux produits de France Télécom vous donnent?

Un téléphone dans une cabine publique.

Observations culturelles

L'emploi du téléphone

En France, on n'utilise pas le téléphone de la même façon qu'aux Etats-Unis. La plupart des familles ont une seule ligne et deux appareils de téléphone. Il est rare d'avoir des prises de téléphone installées un peu partout dans la maison comme dans la cuisine ou la salle de bains. Le téléphone se trouve le plus souvent dans la salle de séjour et lorsqu'il y a un deuxième appareil, il est mis dans le bureau ou dans la chambre des parents. Les Français n'ont pas l'habitude de converser régulièrement au téléphone pendant plus d'une demi-heure avec leurs proches comme le font beaucoup d'Américains, les adolescents en particulier. En France, les appels sont beaucoup plus courts parce qu'il n'y a pas de forfait mensuel et qu'il faut payer chaque appel séparément. Les appels sont facturés par unité pour les communications locales et non globalement par appel, ce qui signifie que plus on reste longtemps au téléphone plus l'appel coûte cher. Les appels interurbains et internationaux sont facturés à la minute et ne sont pas bon marché.

Dans les entreprises, le téléphone joue un rôle primordial *(essential)* en France comme aux Etats-Unis pour les communications internes aussi bien qu'avec l'extérieur.

J. A la recherche d'éléments précis. Trouvez des mots de la même famille que les mots du texte suivants.

1. seule	**5.** mensuel
2. cuisine	**6.** séparément
3. proches	**7.** interurbains
4. appels	

K. Avez-vous compris? Répondez aux questions suivantes par groupes de deux ou trois.

1. En général, en France, dans quelles pièces de la maison est-ce qu'on ne trouve pas de téléphone? Donnez au moins quatre noms de pièces.

2. Pourquoi est-ce que les adolescents français téléphonent moins que les adolescents américains?

Lecture 1

Agoris 55, le fax personnel

L. Activité de pré-lecture. Répondez aux questions suivantes par groupes de trois ou quatre.

1. Avez-vous un télécopieur chez vous? Si oui, dans quels cas est-ce que vous (et les membres de votre famille) l'utilisez?

Le responsable de l'accueil dans un cabinet immobilier.

2. Dans quelles circonstances est-ce que cela peut être utile ou pratique d'avoir un fax à la maison?

3. Dans quel genre de bureau ou d'entreprise est-ce qu'il est indispensable d'avoir un télécopieur?

4. Qu'est-ce que vous attendez d'un fax? Quelles sont les caractéristiques que vous trouvez importantes?

Agoris 55
Le fax personnel

France Telecom

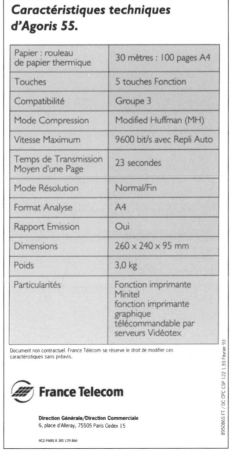

Caractéristiques techniques d'Agoris 55.

Papier : rouleau de papier thermique	30 mètres : 100 pages A4
Touches	5 touches Fonction
Compatibilité	Groupe 3
Mode Compression	Modified Huffman (MH)
Vitesse Maximum	9600 bit/s avec Repli Auto
Temps de Transmission Moyen d'une Page	23 secondes
Mode Résolution	Normal/Fin
Format Analyse	A4
Rapport Emission	Oui
Dimensions	260 x 240 x 95 mm
Poids	3,0 kg
Particularités	Fonction imprimante Minitel fonction imprimante graphique télécommandable par serveurs Vidéotex

Document non contractuel. France Télécom se réserve le droit de modifier ces caractéristiques sans préavis.

France Telecom

Direction Générale/Direction Commerciale
6, place d'Alleray, 75505 Paris Cedex 15

RCS PARIS B 380 129 866

895086S FT / DC CPC CSP 122 1.93 Février 93

Dépliant de France Télécom, 1993.

Agoris 55, le fax personnel

Un télécopieur très économique et simple d'emploi.

De coût extrêmement compétitif, Agoris 55 est un fax qui communique avec tous les télécopieurs d'aujourd'hui. Sa vitesse de transmission (9600 bits/s) lui permet d'envoyer une page A4 en 23 secondes en moyenne.

D'un encombrement minimal.

Agoris 55 est le plus petit télécopieur de la gamme (26 × 24 par 9,5 cm pour 3 kg). La place qu'il occupe est d'autant plus réduite *(reduced)* qu'il est conçu pour se poser sur votre Minitel. Il sait même profiter des capacités de numérotation de celui-ci. Mais si, par hasard, vous n'avez pas de Minitel, Agoris 55 fera naturellement équipe avec votre poste téléphonique.

Une imprimante Minitel à portée de la main.

Pour garder trace d'une interrogation de service Télétel (horaires *(schedules)* de trains, prix de produits, etc.) ou de l'Annuaire *(phone book)* Electronique, comptez sur Agoris 55. L'impression est on ne peut plus simple (appuyez sur le bouton «Impression»), rapide (10 secondes par écran), et de qualité (reproduction des niveaux de gris, inversion possible du noir et du blanc pour une meilleure lisibilité). Et afin de rendre l'opération encore plus efficace, quatre écrans peuvent être mémorisés pour impression ultérieure.

Un répondeur télématique à votre service.

Grâce à la fonction «répondeur télématique» d'Agoris 55, ce sont également les 6 millions de Minitels qui peuvent envoyer un message. Agoris 55 distingue automatiquement l'appel d'un Minitel de celui d'un télécopieur et enregistre ou imprime sans délai le message tapé par le correspondant.

Un photocopieur d'appoint.

Agoris 55, c'est aussi la possibilité de faire une photocopie ponctuelle sans avoir à sortir de chez vous ou de votre lieu de travail.

Le premier télécopieur domestique.

La petite taille d'Agoris et son faible prix en font le premier télécopieur qui trouve naturellement sa place à la maison. Pour télécopier votre réservation de vacances ou une demande d'informations, pour photocopier un papier administratif, ou pour imprimer un écran Télétel et garder trace de l'information retrouvée.

Le choix et la garantie France Télécom.

Agoris 55 est commercialisé dans toutes les agences France Télécom. En achetant votre télécopieur auprès de France Télécom, vous êtes assuré(e) de la compétence et de la pérennité de votre interlocuteur.

Autres modèles de la gamme Agoris commercialisés par France Télécom:
- Agoris 71, le fax professionnel,
- Agoris 75C, le fax répondeur professionnel.

Dépliant de France Télécom intitulé «Agoris 55: le fax personnel», 1993.

M. Vrai ou faux? Lisez seulement le titre en caractères gras de chaque section et répondez aux questions suivantes en indiquant la lettre V ou F selon le cas. Si une constatation est fausse, corrigez-la.

_____ **1.** Agoris 55 est un fax professionnel extrêmement sophistiqué.

_____ **2.** Agoris 55 peut également photocopier.

_____ **3.** Agoris 55 peut être combiné avec le Minitel.

_____ **4.** Agoris 55 est garanti par France Télécom.

N. A la recherche d'éléments précis. Les affirmations suivantes sont justes. Trouvez les phrases du texte qui correspondent.

✓ **1.** Agoris 55 peut transmettre *(transmit)* plus de deux pages par minute.

2. Agoris 55 n'est pas très grand.

3. Lorsqu'on veut imprimer plusieurs écrans, on peut le faire un peu plus tard car Agoris 55 a une mémoire.

4. Agoris 55 ne coûte pas cher.

5. On peut trouver Agoris 55 dans tous les points de vente *(outlets)* de France Télécom.

6. Il y a d'autres produits Agoris; Agoris 55 n'est pas le seul télécopieur de cette gamme.

✓ **O. Autrement dit.** Les extraits suivants sont tirés du texte. Regardez-les bien dans leur contexte et choisissez une des trois définitions proposées.

➤ Note key words or expressions that might be of use to you in *Mot de passe*.

1er paragraphe

1. simple d'emploi

a. L'utilisation d'Agoris 55 est simple comparée à des produits similaires.

b. Il n'est pas difficile de prendre la décision d'acheter Agoris 55.

c. Agoris 55 est facile à utiliser.

2. de coût extrêmement compétitif

a. Le prix auquel on peut l'acheter est intéressant comparé à des produits du même type.

b. Les vendeurs qui expliquent comment se servir de l'appareil Agoris 55 sont très compétents.

c. C'est pour faire face à la concurrence *(competition)* que France Télécom a lancé Agoris 55 sur le marché.

2e paragraphe

3. Agoris 55 fera naturellement équipe avec votre poste téléphonique.

a. Il faut absolument avoir un appareil de téléphone pour se servir d'Agoris 55.

b. Agoris 55 est fait de telle façon qu'il peut marcher avec votre appareil de téléphone.

c. Agoris 55 doit être branché sur le Minitel avant d'être connecté avec votre poste téléphonique.

6e paragraphe

4. Agoris 55 [...] trouve naturellement sa place à la maison.

a. Agoris 55 ne prend pas beaucoup de place quand on a une maison.

b. Agoris 55 est un fax professionnel qui peut être également utilisé à la maison.

c. Agoris 55 est un appareil qui a été conçu pour être utilisé à la maison.

7e paragraphe

5. Vous êtes assuré(e) [...] de la pérennité de votre interlocuteur.

    a. Contrairement à d'autres entreprises, France Télécom ne risque pas de disparaître.

    b. France Télécom assure ses clients que ses produits durent longtemps.

    c. France Télécom fait une remise *(rebate)* spéciale à ses clients du troisième âge *(senior citizens)*.

> ➤ Be prepared for a round-table discussion.

P. A vous la parole! Discutez des avantages et inconvénients d'Agoris 55, l'appareil présenté dans ce texte. Faites-en une liste pour pouvoir comparer vos idées avec celles du reste du groupe après avoir travaillé à deux ou trois.

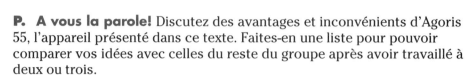

Lecture 2

Diatonis 5 de France Télécom

Q. Activité de pré-lecture. Répondez aux questions suivantes par groupes de deux ou trois.

1. Vous voulez monter une petite entreprise qui comprend six employé(e)s et trois bureaux plus un accueil *(reception area)*. De quel genre d'installation téléphonique pensez-vous avoir besoin? Faites une petite liste des appareils et services ou caractéristiques qui vous paraissent utiles.

2. Quand personne n'est au bureau, si vous ne voulez pas que le téléphone continue à sonner dans le vide lorsqu'il y a des appels, que faites-vous?

3. Que faut-il faire pour ne manquer aucun appel quand tous/toutes les employé(e)s sont en communication?

Les heures d'ouverture d'une agence France Télécom.

Diatonis 5 de France Télécom

Et comme par magie, vos téléphones se transforment en standard.

Un standard simple, moderne et évolutif.

DÉVELOPPER VOTRE COMMUNICATION INTERNE.

Etre efficace dans son activité, c'est d'abord bien faire passer l'information en interne. Diatonis 5 vous en donne les moyens:

- **L'appel intérieur à deux chiffres**
  Vous êtes, par exemple, le 41, votre assistante le 42, et le jour où un nouveau poste est installé, il suffit, très simplement, de lui affecter le 43.
- **L'offre d'entrée en tiers**
  Vous êtes déjà en communication et un appel urgent arrive sur l'autre ligne? La fonction «d'offre d'entrée en tiers» permettra à votre collaborateur d'intercepter l'appel et de vous le transférer sans aucun tracas *(hassle)*.
- **La conférence à trois**
  Si vous devez discuter d'un projet ou d'une affaire à plusieurs, la conférence à trois peut réunir sur la même ligne deux postes internes et un correspondant externe.
- **Le renvoi de poste**
  En cas d'absence, ou tout simplement pour ne pas être dérangé *(bothered)* pendant un temps donné, vous demandez que tous vos appels soient orientés vers un autre poste.

MÉNAGER UN ACCUEIL DE QUALITÉ

Avec Diatonis 5, éventuellement complété des options «Accueil» ou «Portier», vous vous dotez de moyens d'accueil proches de ceux d'une grande entreprise, tout en conservant la réactivité d'une structure de petite dimension.

- **L'avantage des sonneries différenciées**
  Grâce aux sonneries différenciées de Diatonis 5, vous savez, avant même de décrocher, si l'appel est intérieur ou extérieur. Si l'une de vos lignes est à usage privé, vous pouvez également en personnaliser la sonnerie.
- **La réception des appels par un seul poste ou par tous**
  Vous pouvez choisir le poste qui centralisera tous les appels extérieurs, ou bien au contraire permettre leur interception par n'importe quel poste de votre installation.
- **Vos correspondants vous joignent** *(get hold of you)* **plus facilement**
  Avec le signal d'appel intégré à Diatonis 5, vous pouvez répondre à un nouvel appel tout en étant déjà en ligne. Vos correspondants ont ainsi beaucoup plus de chances de vous trouver lorsqu'ils vous appellent.
- **Vous pouvez passer d'une pièce à l'autre**
  En cours de communication, vous pouvez passer dans une autre pièce, pour consulter un dossier, vérifier une facture, et reprendre votre correspondant sur un autre poste.
- **Le renvoi de nuit**
  En dehors de vos heures de travail (nuit, dimanche...), vous pouvez, si vous le décidez, demander le renvoi *(call forwarding)* de tous les appels professionnels sur une ligne privée.

Témoignage

«AVEC DIATONIS 5, AUCUN APPEL IMPORTANT NE M'ÉCHAPPE.»

«Prendre un appel, l'interrompre pour un message urgent, le transférer sur un autre poste et traiter le problème dans la minute, seul Diatonis 5 pouvait me permettre de réaliser cet exploit. Et maintenant, notre accueil téléphonique est, quoi qu'il arrive, extrêmement convivial!»

—MONSIEUR D. ENTREPRENEUR.

Dépliant de France Télécom intitulé «Diatonis 5», 1995.

R. A la recherche d'éléments précis du texte. Répondez aux questions suivantes.

1. Qui pourrait avoir le numéro 43?

2. Dans quel cas est-ce qu'un collaborateur doit intercepter un appel?

3. Donnez des exemples de situations dans lesquelles deux personnes de l'entreprise peuvent parler au téléphone avec une personne de l'extérieur?

4. Grâce à Diatonis 5, que peut-on faire lorsqu'on ne veut pas recevoir de coup de téléphone pendant un certain temps?

5. Comment sait-on si l'appel qui arrive vient de l'intérieur de l'entreprise ou de l'extérieur?

6. Grâce à quelle fonction les clients ont-ils plus de chances de trouver la personne à qui ils veulent parler quand ils appellent?

7. Pourquoi peut-il être utile de pouvoir passer d'une pièce à l'autre pendant une conversation téléphonique?

8. Grâce à quelle fonction de Diatonis 5 peut-on rediriger *(redirect, forward)* les appels arrivant au travail sur une ligne privée?

S. Autrement dit. Par groupes de deux ou trois, essayez d'expliquer les titres en caractères gras suivants.

1. **L'appel intérieur à deux chiffres**
2. **L'offre d'entrée en tiers**
3. **La conférence à trois**
4. **Le renvoi de poste**

T. En vos propres mots. Appuyez-vous sur le texte pour expliquer à deux ou trois ce que les fonctions «Accueil» et «Portier» peuvent être.

U. Vrai ou faux? Si les affirmations suivantes ne sont pas correctes, dites en quoi elles ne le sont pas en vous appuyant sur le texte.

1. Comme numéro intérieur, on ne peut choisir que 41, 42 ou 43. **Vrai?**

2. On peut discuter à trois mais aussi à quatre ou à cinq avec Diatonis 5. **Vrai?**

3. Les sonneries différenciées permettent aux clients de savoir si le correspondant qu'ils désirent est déjà en communication ou non. **Vrai?**

4. Le poste qui centralise tous les appels n'est pas fixe. C'est à l'entreprise de décider quel poste va recevoir les appels et cela peut être changé à tout moment. Diatonis 5 est un standard flexible. **Vrai?**

5. Lorsque vous quittez votre bureau au cours de votre conversation téléphonique, vous pouvez continuer cette conversation à un autre poste dans un autre bureau. Autrement dit, vous n'êtes pas obligé(e) de revenir à votre bureau pour terminer cette conversation. **Vrai?**

V. De la réflexion à l'écriture. Ecrivez le texte de quatre messages téléphoniques que vous laisserez sur votre répondeur. Deux de ces messages doivent être de nature personnelle et les deux autres professionnelle. Après les avoir écrits, travaillez bien leur prononciation pour être sûr(e) qu'ils soient bien compréhensibles une fois enregistrés *(recorded)*.

HSG

➤ Review the *Phonétique* section of Module I in your *HSG*.

Quelques points de repère

Le saviez-vous?

- Si vous ne voulez pas que votre numéro soit communiqué ou imprimé dans l'annuaire, vous pouvez le faire mettre sur une liste rouge. Pour bénéficier de ce service l'abonné devra payer 15 F par mois. Appartenir à la liste orange permet de ne pas recevoir de publicité. Ce dernier service est gratuit.
- On appelle souvent l'annuaire de téléphone "le bottin" du nom de Sébastien Bottin administrateur et statisticien français qui, en 1816, a publié une liste des commerçants de Paris.

Les entreprises françaises!

LES PTT

- Depuis 1991, la Poste et France Télécom ont obtenu le statut d'exploitants autonomes de droit public. Elles restent contrôlées par le Ministère de l'Industrie, des Postes et Télécommunications et du commerce extérieur ainsi que par le Parlement. Leur personnel continue à être fonctionnaire. La Poste a le monopole du transport des lettres et des papiers d'affaires ayant un poids qui ne dépasse pas 1.000 grammes. La Poste n'a pas le monopole du transport des colis, de la messagerie, des journaux et des imprimés. A ce jour France Télécom a le monopole du téléphone en France.
- La Poste en France offre de nombreux services. On peut aller à la Poste pour envoyer du courrier (il y a plusieurs formules d'acheminement plus ou moins rapides), des mandats *(money orders)*, des objets contre remboursement. A la Poste, on peut également acheter des timbres et des télécartes, consulter l'annuaire électronique par Minitel (service Télétel gratuit), téléphoner de cabines publiques, envoyer un fax, ouvrir un CCP (Compte-Chèques Postal) ou un compte épargne, faire un emprunt, investir de l'argent, etc.

Une date importante!

- Le téléphone est nationalisé en France depuis 1889.
- Les numéros verts (800 numbers) ont été créés en 1984.

Les chiffres parlent!

En 1993, il y avait dans la France entière, 170.000 publiphones dont 125.000 à cartes. Cela signifie que les téléphones publics qui fonctionnent encore avec des pièces de monnaie sont de plus en plus rares. L'emploi des cartes a fait tomber le vandalisme de façon spectaculaire parce qu'il n'y a plus rien à voler dans les téléphones publics.

L'ardoise

- Autrefois, les appareils téléphoniques des cabines publiques marchaient avec des jetons *(tokens)*, une sorte de pièce spéciale en métal. Pour pouvoir téléphoner dans un café, par exemple, il fallait d'abord acheter un jeton. Maintenant, on utilise des cartes qu'on achète dans un bureau de tabac ou à la Poste.

- Autrefois, les numéros de Paris commençaient par trois lettres. On disait par exemple: Odéon 24 32, mais on composait seulement les trois premières lettres "ODE" suivies des chiffres 24 32.

- Lorsque le téléphone n'était pas automatique, au début des années 50 et 60, en province, il était nécessaire de passer par la standardiste qui contrôlait un central téléphonique. Il fallait tourner plusieurs fois une manivelle pour appeler le bureau de Poste et dire par exemple: "Pour le 27 à Vernantes, je voudrais le 32 à Saumur, s'il vous plaît" et attendre que l'employé(e) de la Poste fasse la connexion.

- En 1940, en France, la moitié des abonnés seulement avait le téléphone automatique. Depuis 1939, le téléphone est automatique à Paris mais cela a pris presque 40 ans pour finir d'automatiser le reste du pays.

Une publicité pour France Télécom sur un minibus.

Réflexions sur le travail en équipe

Quand on fait partie d'une équipe, il est essentiel de bien réfléchir aux *objectifs* à accomplir ou au *but* à atteindre et de les formuler clairement.

Lexique

un abonné: Un **abonné** est une personne qui a une ligne de téléphone en son nom.

> L'annuaire téléphonique donne la liste des **abonnés** qui n'ont pas demandé à être sur la liste rouge.

l'annuaire *(m)*: **L'annuaire** est le gros livre ou le fichier électronique qui contient tous les numéros de téléphone et le nom des gens et des entreprises qui ont un abonnement.

> Il est très facile de consulter **l'annuaire** électronique de toute la France par Minitel; il suffit de taper le nom de la personne et la ville où elle habite, et le numéro apparaît sur l'écran. Ce service est gratuit.

effacer, effaçage: **Effacer** un message, c'est le faire disparaître. Après avoir écouté les messages qui ont été laissés sur mon répondeur, en général, je les **efface,** c'est-à-dire que je les détruis. On peut également **effacer** un tableau, par exemple; dans ce cas «effacer» veut dire enlever les mots écrits à la craie ou au feutre sur le tableau. **Effacer** le tableau veut dire le nettoyer.

> Avec mon nouveau répondeur qui est interrogeable à distance, je peux **effacer** mes messages à distance également, ce qui est pratique car quelquefois je pars pendant plusieurs semaines et lorsque j'ai beaucoup d'appels, mon répondeur pourrait être encombré. Je peux aussi à tout moment **effacer** le message que je laisse à mes correspondants et qui les accueille lorsqu'ils m'appellent et le remplacer par un autre message.

une facturation détaillée: En France, lorsqu'un abonné ne précise pas qu'il désire obtenir **une facturation détaillée,** la facture mensuelle qu'il reçoit ne lui donne que le montant total à payer. **La facturation détaillée** donne la liste de toutes les communications, leur durée ainsi que leur prix. Il faut payer un supplément pour bénéficier de ce service.

> Depuis que je reçois **une facturation détaillée,** j'ai remarqué que les enfants restent moins longtemps au téléphone car je peux savoir à qui ils téléphonent et combien de temps ils passent à bavarder avec leurs amis.

des frais *(m)* **de raccordement:** Lorsqu'on veut s'abonner au téléphone, qu'une ligne soit déjà installée ou non, il faut payer **des frais de raccordement,** somme forfaitaire qui s'élevait à 250 F en France en 1994. Raccorder signifie relier deux choses qui étaient séparées. Ici, il s'agit de relier le téléphone du nouvel abonné au réseau déjà existant. La France est un des pays européens les plus avantageux en ce qui concerne **les frais de raccordement.** Les Danois, par exemple, paient six fois plus que les Français pour le même service.

> Lorsqu'ils veulent avoir le téléphone, les retraités sont favorisés puisqu'ils sont dispensés de **frais de raccordement.** Ils n'auront donc à payer que leur abonnement et leurs communications.

les modalités de souscription: **Les modalités de souscription** sont les conditions, les caractéristiques concernant cette **souscription.**

> Pour connaître **les modalités de souscription,** adressez-vous directement à France Télécom.

un numéro azur: **Un numéro azur** (bleu) n'est pas gratuit mais il permet à la personne qui appelle l'abonné ayant **un numéro azur** de ne jamais payer plus que le prix d'un appel local même si l'abonné se trouve dans une autre région de France, par exemple. C'est l'abonné qui prend en charge la différence de prix.

> J'appelle souvent le service de publicité de cette entreprise pour laquelle je travaille en *free lance*. Comme l'entreprise a **un numéro azur,** je ne m'inquiète pas du prix de la communication!

un numéro vert: **Un numéro vert** est un numéro gratuit pour la personne qui l'appelle.

> Il y a en France plus de 15.000 entreprises qui offrent **un numéro vert** au public ou à l'intérieur même de la société pour les gens qui y travaillent.

un répertoire: **Un répertoire** est une sorte de liste de numéros de téléphone et de noms d'abonnés qui est mémorisée par le poste téléphonique. C'est un mini-annuaire qui est à la disposition de l'abonné et qui permet la composition automatique des numéros qui sont enregistrés dans **ce répertoire.**

> Mon nouveau poste téléphonique m'offre **un répertoire** de 40 numéros. J'y ai déjà enregistré les numéros de mes collègues et de tous les services et entreprises que j'appelle régulièrement. Cela me fait gagner beaucoup de temps.

un répondeur enregistreur numérique: Autrefois, **les répondeurs** contenaient une cassette et les messages étaient enregistrés sur cette cassette. Maintenant, **les répondeurs** numérisent la voix et il n'est plus nécessaire de passer par l'intermédiaire d'une cassette.

> Je suis contente d'avoir **un répondeur enregistreur numérique** car je n'ai plus de problèmes avec l'enregistrement de mes messages. Cela fait gagner du temps surtout quand on interroge le répondeur à distance. Autrefois, il fallait rembobiner la cassette et la bande pouvait se casser. Cela m'est arrivé plusieurs fois.

souscrire: **Souscrire** à un service, c'est prendre une sorte d'abonnement, c'est s'inscrire pour pouvoir bénéficier d'un certain service.

> Si vous êtes souvent absent de votre bureau, vous devriez **souscrire** à un service de Messagerie Vocale. Une Messagerie Vocale accueille vos correspondants et enregistre leurs messages 24 h/24.

une touche bis: Si votre téléphone a **une touche bis,** cela veut dire qu'il suffit d'appuyer sur cette touche pour que l'appareil refasse le numéro que vous venez juste de composer.

> J'ai essayé d'appeler les bureaux de la Sécurité Sociale aujourd'hui. Cela sonnait constamment occupé. Heureusement que j'ai **une touche bis** sur mon téléphone: cela m'a évité de recomposer le numéro à chaque fois que j'ai ré-essayé de les avoir au bout du fil.

$\mathcal{P}$aroles de sagesse

Ne vendez pas la peau de l'ours avant de l'avoir tué.

➤ Brainstorm with your study partner three situations where this sentence might be used.

HSG

➤ Complete the *Exercices de synthèse* and *Echange* sections of Module 1 in your *HSG*.

$\mathcal{E}$xpression écrite

L'infinitif, l'infinitif passé et le participe présent

Dans cette section vous allez étudier quelques constructions qui exigent l'infinitif, l'infinitif passé ou le participe présent. Pour l'infinitif la règle est la suivante:

Après toute préposition (sauf **après** et **en**), il faut employer l'infinitif.

Notez bien la formation de l'infinitif passé dans les exemples suivants.

Après avoir allumé son ordinateur, elle a ouvert un nouveau fichier.

Après être allée à la banque, elle est passée par le magasin d'ordinateurs.

Après s̲'être rendu compte qu'elle n'avait plus d'argent liquide sur elle, Chantal est partie en retirer au D.A.B. du Crédit Agricole.

L'accord du participe passé **rendu** ne se fait pas ici, à cause du mot «compte» qui est un complément d'objet direct qui suit le verbe.

Après m'être souvenu(e) de mon mot de passe, j'ai pu accéder au réseau Minitel.

Parcourez le texte qui suit pour en avoir une idée générale. Ensuite, lisez-le attentivement et faites bien attention aux infinitifs, aux infinitifs passés et au participe présent.

Un magasin de matériel informatique.

$\mathcal{L}'\mathcal{EDF}$

$\mathcal{L}'\mathcal{EDF}$ *(l'Electricité De France) est l'entreprise qui est en charge sur toute la France du réseau électrique. Pour des raisons commerciales, cette compagnie propose plusieurs moyens de paiements.* ***Après être mis*** *au courant, le client peut choisir* ***de payer*** *mensuellement sa consommation électrique ou* ***de payer*** *un fixe mensuel ajusté en fin d'année. Dans les deux cas, il faut payer sa facture avant le 23 de chaque mois* ***à moins d'avoir*** *une autorisation spéciale de retard de paiement.* ***Afin de faciliter*** *les démarches [steps] administratives, l'EDF propose* ***de payer*** *par débit automatique.* ***En choisissant*** *cette méthode, vous n'avez pas* ***à vous occuper*** *de votre paiement chaque mois.* ***Après avoir reçu*** *la facture chez vous, le montant est donc débité directement de votre compte bancaire.*

➤ Note the many infinitive constructions other than those which follow a preposition.

Pour y avoir droit, il vous faut envoyer un relevé d'identité bancaire ainsi qu'une autorisation de débit automatique à l'EDF.

W. Vérification. Cochez la bonne réponse.

   1. «Après» est suivi d'un
      a. infinitif
      b. infinitif passé
      c. participe présent

   2. «En» est suivi d'un
      a. infinitif
      b. infinitif passé
      c. participe présent

X. A vos plumes! En suivant le modèle de l'*Expression écrite* qui précède, écrivez un paragraphe (introduction, développement de vos idées et conclusion) en utilisant au moins trois infinitifs, deux infinitifs passés et un participe présent. Montrez comment les services de France Télécom peuvent vous être utiles quand vous ne connaissez pas le numéro de téléphone de quelqu'un et que vous devez contacter cette personne.

Avant de commencer un nouveau module, allons un peu plus loin avec la section «En guise de clôture».

En guise de clôture:
Allons un peu plus loin!

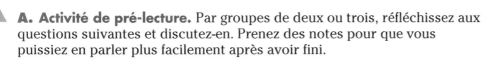

Texte littéraire

La Cigale et la fourmi

A. Activité de pré-lecture. Par groupes de deux ou trois, réfléchissez aux questions suivantes et discutez-en. Prenez des notes pour que vous puissiez en parler plus facilement après avoir fini.

1. Quand est-ce que vous allez voir votre voisin(e) pour lui demander de vous prêter quelque chose?
2. Faites une liste de sept choses que vous pourriez lui emprunter.
3. Quel genre de choses est-ce que vous n'aimeriez pas prêter à votre voisin(e) et pourquoi?
4. Qui serait mieux placé selon vous pour lui prêter ces choses?
5. Pensez au monde animal. Certains animaux sont associés à des stéréotypes, par exemple, le lion à la force, le chien à la fidélité. A quoi vous fait penser
   - un serpent?
   - une fourmi?
   - un chat?
   - un singe?

6. Y a-t-il des animaux qui sont plutôt associés à des images positives? Lesquels et pourquoi?

7. Quels animaux sont traditionnellement associés à des images négatives et pourquoi?

8. Quels sont les animaux qui doivent faire des provisions en vue de l'hiver?

9. Imaginez que vous avez besoin de nourriture et que vous n'avez pas d'argent. Que faites-vous?

10. En France, l'écureuil est le symbole de la caisse d'épargne. Pouvez-vous deviner pourquoi?

La Cigale et la fourmi

La Cigale, ayant chanté
Tout l'été,
Se trouva fort dépourvue
Quand la bise fut venue:
Pas un seul petit morceau
De mouche ou de vermisseau.
Elle alla crier famine
Chez la Fourmi sa voisine,
La priant de lui prêter
Quelque grain pour subsister
Jusqu'à la saison nouvelle.
«Je vous paierai, lui dit-elle,
Avant l'oût, foi d'animal,
Intérêt et principal.»
La Fourmi n'est pas prêteuse:
C'est là son moindre défaut.
«Que faisiez-vous au temps chaud?
Dit-elle à cette emprunteuse.
— Nuit et jour à tout venant
Je chantais, ne vous déplaise.
— Vous chantiez? J'en suis fort aise:
Eh bien dansez maintenant.»

—JEAN DE LA FONTAINE

B. Autrement dit. Faites correspondre les mots de la colonne A avec ceux du texte, placés dans la colonne B.

A	*B*
ne plus rien avoir	crier famine
rester en vie	se trouver fort dépourvu
mettre à la disposition de quelqu'un pour un certain temps	subsister
somme due à l'emprunteur en plus du capital	prêter
somme empruntée	le principal
en être très content	en être fort aise
aller dire qu'on a faim	l'intérêt

C. Avez-vous compris? Après avoir bien lu et relu le texte, répondez aux questions suivantes.

1. Quels sont les mots du texte qui ont un rapport avec la nourriture?
2. Quels sont les mots du texte qui ont quelque chose à voir avec l'argent ou l'échange de biens?
3. Quel est le problème de la Cigale?
4. Pourquoi la Cigale va-t-elle voir la Fourmi?
5. Pourquoi la Cigale s'adresse-t-elle à la Fourmi et non à quelqu'un d'autre?
6. Comment la Fourmi réagit-elle et pourquoi?
7. Comprenez-vous la réaction de la Fourmi? Qu'auriez-vous fait à sa place?
8. Quel est le caractère de la Fourmi?
9. Quel est le caractère de la Cigale?
10. Quel personnage trouvez-vous le plus sympathique, la Cigale ou la Fourmi? Pourquoi?
11. Vous identifiez-vous plutôt avec la Cigale ou avec la Fourmi?
12. Quelle est la morale de cette fable?
13. Que pensez-vous de cette morale? Peut-elle avoir des applications dans votre vie?
14. Qu'est-ce que les concepts de charité et de solidarité ajouteraient à cette fable?

➤ After having answered these questions in preparation for class, call your study partner and discuss two or three of them with him/her in French.

D. Un sketch *(skit).* La Cigale va à la banque pour emprunter de l'argent. Imaginez cette scène et jouez-la par groupes de deux, l'un(e) de vous étant la Cigale et l'autre la Fourmi. La Cigale doit expliquer pourquoi elle a besoin d'un prêt et la Fourmi pose des questions puis prend une décision et la justifie.

➤ Approximately fifteen exchanges per person.

 ## Sigles et abréviations

BNP	=	*Banque Nationale de Paris*
CB	=	*Carte Bleue (Carte VISA)*
CCP	=	*Compte-Chèques Postal*
DAB	=	*Distributeur Automatique de Billets*
M.	=	*Monsieur*
Mlle	=	*Mademoiselle*
Mlles	=	*Mesdemoiselles*
MM	=	*Messieurs*
Mme	=	*Madame*
Mmes	=	*Mesdames*
SME	=	*Système Monétaire Européen*

En matière d'actions

on pense trop souvent qu'on va

se retrouver fauché…

LA POSTE ➤

Dépliant de la Poste.

Actifs gérés par Sogéposte au 31.08.93 :

153,8 milliards de francs

soit une progression de 41,4 % sur un an

pour une gestion de 12 Sicav et

17 Fonds Communs de Placement.

Sogéposte, une équipe d'experts

au service de La Poste et de ses clients.

SOGEPOSTE

Filiale de La Poste
et de la Caisse des dépôts et consignations.

Les O.P.C.V.M. de La Poste sont gérés par Sogéposte et Ségur Gestion.

 ▊ **Expressions familières!**

avoir des ronds	=	*avoir de l'argent*
avoir du pognon plein les poches	=	*avoir beaucoup d'argent*
avoir un trou dans la main	=	*dépenser facilement son argent*
du fric, du pognon, de l'oseille	=	*de l'argent*
être fauché (comme les blés)	=	*ne pas avoir d'argent*
être radin	=	*être avare; ne pas être généreux financièrement; être près de son argent*
être sans un (sou)	=	*ne pas avoir d'argent*
faire son beurre	=	*gagner pas mal d'argent*
jeter l'argent par les fenêtres	=	*gaspiller son argent; ne pas être économe, raisonnable avec son argent*
la douloureuse	=	*l'addition*
La note était salée.	=	*C'était très cher.*
mettre du beurre dans les épinards	=	*cela mettra du beurre dans les épinards; cela facilitera la situation financière et aidera à apporter un petit supplément agréable*
ne pas arriver à joindre les deux bouts	=	*avoir des difficultés d'argent*
ne pas avoir le sou, être lessivé à sec	=	*ne pas avoir d'argent*
ne plus avoir un rond, un radis	=	*ne plus avoir d'argent*
banquer, casquer, raquer (J'ai été obligé(e) de raquer.)	=	*payer*
T'as pas cent balles?	=	*Tu n'as pas cent francs?*
un richard	=	*une personne riche*

Conseils, suggestions

Vous êtes directeur/directrice d'une banque et vous avez un rendez-vous très important dans un quart d'heure. Vous avez besoin de reprendre vos forces, votre énergie, de retrouver votre enthousiasme. Que faites-vous? Décrivez au moins trois choses que vous pouvez faire.

UNE AUTRE SUGGESTION:

LA RESPIRATION «ENERGISANTE»

Tout en comptant jusqu'à

5	Gonflez vos poumons en inhalant profondément par le nez.
20	Bloquez votre respiration et poussez les poumons contre votre diaphragme.
10	Expirez lentement et régulièrement par la bouche en éliminant tout l'air de vos poumons.

Répétez cet exercice une dizaine ou une quinzaine de fois.

AUTRES AVANTAGES DE LA RESPIRATION «ENERGISANTE»:
En plus de vous procurer immédiatement une bonne dose d'énergie supplémentaire, ce procédé facilite la circulation, augmente le niveau d'oxygène dans le sang, élargit la capacité des poumons et masse le cœur.

Dès que vous sentez un rhume venir, faites cet exercice trois ou quatre fois par jour et vous réussirez sans doute à l'éviter!

Récapitulons

Quelques aide-mémoire

1. A la banque, on peut

- ouvrir un compte-chèques ou un compte d'épargne.
- verser de l'argent sur son compte.
- toucher un chèque bancaire.
- acheter des chèques de voyage.
- échanger des devises; acheter des dollars américains avec des francs français, par exemple.
- changer de l'argent.
- faire de la monnaie.
- demander des renseignements sur les différents services de la banque.
- faire des transactions boursières.
- emprunter une certaine somme d'argent.
- commander un nouveau chéquier.
- retirer de l'argent à partir d'une carte de crédit.

- vérifier son solde.
- transférer de l'argent d'un compte sur un autre.
- faire une demande de carte bancaire (VISA, Carte Bleue, Eurocard, etc.).
- faire un retrait d'argent liquide.

2. A la Poste, on peut

Un bureau de Poste du 1er arrondissement, à Paris.

- ouvrir un compte-chèques ou un compte d'épargne.
- toucher un chèque postal.
- demander un mandat.
- acheter des timbres (de collection ou non).
- envoyer des lettres, paquets, colis, etc. par courrier normal ou en recommandé.
- passer un coup de fil.
- recevoir du courrier en poste restante.
- consulter l'annuaire téléphonique (par Minitel).
- verser de l'argent sur son compte.
- acheter une télécarte (carte téléphonique à puce).
- faire une demande de Carte Bleue.
- faire un retrait en espèces.
- acheter un aérogramme.
- acheter des boîtes ou emballages spéciaux.
- aller chercher son courrier à la boîte postale.

Une boîte aux lettres devant le Centre National d'Enseignement à Distance de Poitiers.

3. Avec un Minitel, on peut

- réserver une place dans un train.
- se renseigner sur les horaires de train.
- vérifier le solde de son compte en banque.
- passer une commande à partir d'un catalogue de vente par correspondance.
- trouver des informations sur des écoles et toutes sortes d'institutions.
- transférer de l'argent d'un compte à un autre.
- trouver le numéro de téléphone d'une personne résidant en France.
- lire le corrigé des épreuves du bac.
- savoir si une personne qui a passé le bac ou un autre examen est reçue ou non.
- avoir la liste des offres d'emploi *(job offers)* de l'ANPE (Agence Nationale Pour l'Emploi).
- laisser un message électronique à un abonné.
- payer une facture d'électricité, de téléphone ou de gaz.

- se renseigner sur le prix d'envoi de paquets par la Poste.
- obtenir des informations sur la Bourse.
- faire opposition si on a perdu sa Carte Bleue.

4. Avec un téléphone, on peut

- obtenir des renseignements en appelant des commerçants.
- savoir l'heure qu'il est en composant le numéro de l'horloge parlante.
- parler avec un(e) ami(e) de choses personnelles ou autres.
- prévenir sa collègue qu'on va arriver un peu en retard au travail.
- confirmer un rendez-vous d'affaires ou personnel.
- changer l'heure d'un rendez-vous.
- laisser un message sur le répondeur d'un correspondant qui est occupé ou absent.
- demander à la police ou à une ambulance de venir en cas d'urgence.
- appeler sa banque lorsqu'on a perdu sa carte bancaire.
- appeler un numéro vert pour obtenir gratuitement des informations.
- avoir une réunion avec plusieurs personnes à distance.
- composer automatiquement un appel urbain, interurbain ou international.
- avoir accès à la météo.
- connaître les résultats des grandes manifestations sportives du jour.
- donner des nouvelles à sa famille.

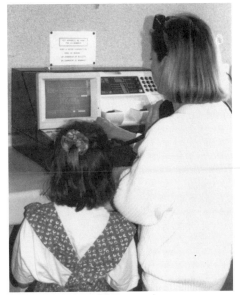

Une mère et sa fille consultent l'annuaire électronique sur Minitel à la Poste.

HSG

➤ Complete the *Exercices de synthèse* and the *Echange* sections of Module I in your *HSG*.

Préparez-vous à approfondir vos connaissances en informatique et à découvrir le réseau Internet dans le Module II!

Module *I I*

L'informatique
à la maison et au travail

Ouverture

La réceptionniste de l'hôtel France-Europe prépare la facture d'un client.

BIENVENUE SUR
NETSCAPE
VOTRE GUIDE POUR NAVIGUER SUR INTERNET

DECOUVERTE D'INTERNET | LA SOCIETE ET SES PRODUITS | BOUTIQUE NETSCAPE | AIDE | COMMUNAUTE | NOUVELLES ET REFERENCES

Un ordinateur dans un laboratoire.

La salle d'ordinateur d'une entreprise.

Postes à pourvoir en province et dans la région parisienne.

Quel article vous intéresse le plus?

*L'*ordinateur à la maison et au travail

Ce premier dossier du Module II vous présente d'abord une situation de la vie de tous les jours: deux jeunes filles qui travaillent à l'ordinateur, à la maison. Noémie aide Sarah qui est encore débutante.

Devenu indispensable dans le monde du travail en France, l'ordinateur a de plus en plus souvent sa place aussi à la maison. Parents et enfants apprennent à s'en servir! Ce dossier vous propose un vocabulaire de base en informatique et vous permet de le pratiquer.

*A*ctivité d'introduction

L'ordinateur

➤ Be ready to report your findings back to the class.

A. Votre avis sur l'ordinateur. Répondez aux questions suivantes par groupes de deux ou trois.

1. Est-ce que vous avez ou non un ordinateur chez vous? Expliquez pourquoi.
2. Donnez au moins quatre raisons pour lesquelles les gens ne se servent pas d'un ordinateur.
3. Comment est-ce que les différents membres d'une même famille peuvent utiliser un ordinateur? Donnez au moins sept exemples précis.
4. Si vous pouviez acheter exactement ce que vous vouliez, quel genre d'ordinateur aimeriez-vous avoir et pourquoi?
5. Quels sont le rôle et l'importance d'un ordinateur dans une entreprise? Donnez plusieurs exemples précis.

$\mathcal{L}$es mots pour le dire

Vocabulaire de base

VERBES

s'afficher sur l'écran	*to appear, pull up on the screen*
appuyer	*to press*
cliquer	*to click*
copier	*to copy*
créer un document	*to create a document*
déplacer	*to move*
dérouler	*to scroll*
imprimer	*to print*
maintenir (enfoncé)	*to maintain, keep (pushed in)*
modifier	*to modify*
numéroter	*to number*
ouvrir	*to open*
pointer	*to place the cursor*
reformater	*to reformat*
relâcher	*to release*
saisir un texte	*to type with a word processor*
sauver, sauvegarder	*to save*
sélectionner	*to select*
taper	*to type*
traîner	*to drag*

NOMS

un ascenseur	*elevator; scroll button*
une bande de déroulement	*pull-down*
une banque de données	*database*
un bouton	*button*
un clavier	*keyboard*
la corbeille	*trash*
le curseur	*cursor*
le disque dur	*hard disk*
la disquette, le disque souple	*floppy disk*
l'écran *(m)*	*screen*
un en-tête	*header*
la fente	*slot*
des jeux vidéo *(m)*	*video games*
la marge	*margin*
la mémoire	*memory*
le menu	*menu*
le moniteur	*monitor*
un ordinateur	*computer*
la police de caractère	*font*
une puce	*microchip*
la souris	*mouse*
les touches *(f)*	*keys*
un traitement de texte	*word processing package*
l'unité *(f)* centrale	*central unit*

continued on page 74

continued from page 73

ADJECTIFS

convivial(e)	*user-friendly*
minimal(e)	*minimal*
numérique, numérisé(e)	*digital, digitized*
portable, portatif(ve)	*portable*
puissant(e)	*powerful*
vif(ve)	*lively*

ADVERBES

automatiquement	*automatically*
également	*as well, equally*
lentement	*slowly*
rapidement	*rapidly, fast*

 Choose three terms from each category to look up in your French-French dictionary.

B. Epelez! Mettez-vous par groupes de quatre et prononcez les mots suivants à haute voix. Ensuite, énoncez une à une les lettres qui les composent.

1. un ordinateur
2. l'unité centrale
3. le disque dur
4. taper

5. une marge
6. sauvegarder
7. afficher sur l'écran

C. Définitions provisoires à terminer. Complétez les phrases suivantes avec le vocabulaire de base proposé ci-dessus.

1. Lorsqu'on a un programme qui sert à composer et formater un texte et qui d'une manière générale facilite l'écriture, on a un

   _____.

   Comment ça s'écrit? Cela s'écrit _____.

2. La partie du moniteur qui sert à visualiser le texte, c'est-à-dire sur laquelle le texte apparaît, s'appelle: _____

   Ça s'écrit _____.

Un ordinateur allumé.

3. Si vous n'aimez pas *Times,* vous pouvez changer de
_____ et choisir *Palatino,* par exemple. Faites
plusieurs essais et choisissez ce qui est le plus joli.

Ça s'écrit _____.

4. Grâce à mon ordinateur et par l'intermédiaire d'Internet, je peux
consulter des informations qui sont stockées ailleurs dans le monde
entier. Un autre mot pour l'ensemble de ces informations disponibles
est une _____.

Ça s'écrit _____.

5. Autrefois, les ordinateurs étaient énormes et très lourds, maintenant
on peut même avoir un petit ordinateur personnel qu'on peut
emmener avec soi. Avec ces ordinateurs _____ qui ne
pèsent pas plus d'un kilo, on peut travailler dans le train, dans
l'avion, à l'aéroport, à la bibliothèque, etc.

Ça s'écrit _____.

D. Définitions provisoires à créer. Par groupes de deux, écrivez une
définition provisoire pour les mots suivants.

1. la mémoire   **4.** puissant

2. la souris   **5.** numéroter

3. un en-tête

𝒟*ialogue*

Noémie et Sarah à l'ordinateur

E. Activité de pré-lecture. Par groupes de deux, répondez aux questions
suivantes.

➤ Be ready to share the information you find in the general
discussion.

1. Est-ce que cela vous arrive de demander l'aide d'un(e) camarade
lorsque vous ne savez pas faire quelque chose sur ordinateur? Si oui,
quel genre de choses? Donnez quelques exemples.

2. Si vous savez vous servir d'un ordinateur, qui vous a appris à le
faire? Comment avez-vous commencé à vous en servir?

3. Est-ce que vous avez des amis, des collègues ou des membres de
votre famille qui sont moins forts que vous dans le domaine des
ordinateurs et qui vous demandent de les aider? Si oui, donnez
quelques exemples.

4. Savez-vous, oui ou non, faire les choses suivantes sur ordinateur?
Cochez ce que vous savez faire.

_____ allumer l'ordinateur

_____ créer un document

_____ vous servir d'une souris

_____ taper un texte

_____ utiliser un tableur comme *Excel*

_____ ouvrir un fichier

_____ sauver/sauvegarder un texte

HSG

➤ Complete the *Photos et descriptions* and *Phonétique* sections of Module II in your *HSG.*

Noémie et Sarah à l'ordinateur

Noémie: Alors, elle avance cette disserte?

Sarah: Oui, mais je n'arrive pas à l'imprimer.

Noémie: Attends... avant d'imprimer, tu devrais reformater.

Sarah: Reformater?

Noémie: Oui, changer la présentation. Tu peux augmenter les marges, changer la police de caractères. Regarde, *Times,* c'est plus joli. Et puis, tu devrais ajouter un en-tête ou un pied de page pour numéroter les pages.

Sarah: Super! Apprends-moi... je veux le faire toute seule la prochaine fois!

Noémie: Tiens, donne-moi un disque souple pour faire un double de ta rédaction.

Sarah: Oh, c'est pas la peine.

Noémie: Si, si. Donne-moi un disque. Tu n'es pas prudente; il faut toujours garder un double de tous tes documents. C'est une habitude à prendre. Moi, une fois, au début, j'ai perdu un rapport que j'avais écrit parce que l'ordinateur ne pouvait plus lire ma disquette. Ça arrive! Le problème, c'est que je n'avais pas fait de double. Crois-moi, ça m'a servi de leçon!

Sarah: Alors comment je sauvegarde ce document sur disquette?

Noémie: D'abord, tu mets ta disquette dans la fente et elle apparaît sur l'écran, tu vois, en haut à droite, sous l'icône de ton disque dur. On dit qu'elle apparaît sur le bureau. Après, tu cliques une fois sur le nom de ta disquette pour lui donner un nom qui signifie quelque chose pour toi.

Sarah: Quoi par exemple?

Noémie: Je ne sais pas, moi. Ça dépend de comment tu t'organises. Si par exemple tu écris beaucoup de dissertations cette année, tu pourrais avoir une disquette «dissertations» et tu précises l'année. Ou bien tu mets le nom de ton prof. Un nom qui soit facile à reconnaître et qui t'aide à déterminer le contenu de ta disquette.

Sarah: Je pourrais choisir le nom de mon chat?

Noémie: Bien sûr, c'est possible mais pas très logique car si tu trouves cette disquette dans deux ou trois ans et qu'elle s'appelle «Diego», tu ne te souviendras plus de ce qui est dessus. Si tu mets «Dissertations 16e», tu sauras tout de suite! Mais fais comme tu veux, et de toute façon, ce n'est pas définitif.

Sarah: Bon, je vais écrire «Français seizième siècle».

Noémie: C'est un peu long! Tu as droit à plus de 20 caractères y compris les espaces et les signes mais essaie de trouver un titre assez court. C'est plus pratique!

Sarah: Bon, alors «Seizième». Et puis après?

> In spoken French the *est-ce que* is often omitted.

Noémie: Il faut que tu donnes un titre à ton document également et tu peux aussi créer un dossier général «Rédactions» dans lequel tu mettras celles que tu feras plus tard. Il faut que tu apprennes à être très organisée sinon, très rapidement tu seras débordée! Après, tu copies ton document sur ta disquette en le sélectionnant et en l'amenant sur ta disquette; tu vois, tu le prends et tu le traînes. Regarde, il est en train de se copier. Comme ça, il reste sur ton disque dur et il est maintenant également sur ta disquette. Tu peux double-cliquer sur la disquette, oui, et maintenant sur le document. Le voilà qui s'ouvre! Tu vois, il est bien là, mais c'est mieux de vérifier.

Sarah: Et maintenant comment est-ce que je fais sortir ma disquette?

Noémie: Elle sortira toute seule quand tu éteindras ton ordinateur, ou bien tu pointes sur la disquette avec ta souris et tu la fais descendre dans ta corbeille, ce qui la fait sortir également.

Sarah: Génial! Mais tu es sûre que ça n'efface rien de faire passer la disquette par la corbeille? Cela ne peut pas l'abîmer?

Noémie: Non, ne t'inquiète pas! Mais tu voulais l'imprimer ta disserte, non? Regarde, tu vas dans le menu et tu sélectionnes «imprimer». C'est simple!

Sarah: Quand c'est toi qui le fais, oui, c'est simple! Quand c'est moi, c'est différent car je panique! Je suis contente d'avoir terminé cette dissertation. Hier, il y a eu une coupure d'électricité à cause de la grève juste quand je commençais à travailler. Et ce matin, les journaux annonçaient quelques interruptions également!

Noémie: Oui, tu as eu de la chance!

F. A la recherche d'éléments précis. Trouvez au moins sept mots qui relèvent du domaine du traitement de texte et expliquez-les en vos propres mots ou bien utilisez-les dans une petite phrase qui aide à en comprendre le sens.

➤ You may choose to complete this exercise before class and practice saying two or three of the sentences aloud at home to make your French flow more freely during discussion.

G. Débutante à l'ordinateur. Qu'est-ce que Sarah sait faire et qu'est-ce qu'elle ne sait pas faire? Faites une petite liste correspondant à ces deux catégories.

✓ **H. Vrai ou non?** Corrigez les affirmations qui vous paraissent fausses de façon à ce qu'elles correspondent à ce qui est dit dans le texte.

➤ Even if a sentence is true, practice writing it out in long form using *Il est vrai que...*

1. Sarah en sait autant que Noémie dans le domaine des ordinateurs. Vrai?

2. Noémie pense qu'il est très important de sauvegarder un texte en double. Vrai?

3. Sarah est contente d'apprendre à mieux se servir de son ordinateur. Vrai?

4. Une disquette, ce n'est pas la même chose qu'un disque dur. Vrai?

5. On peut donner un nom aussi long qu'on le désire à la disquette. Vrai?

6. Lorsqu'on met une disquette dans la corbeille, on l'efface. Vrai?

7. Noémie n'avait pas oublié que Sarah voulait imprimer sa rédaction. Vrai?

I. Description. Trouvez au moins trois adjectifs qui se rapportent à Noémie et trois autres qui se rapportent à Sarah. Justifiez vos choix.

J. La parole est à vous! Discutez à deux ou trois quelle est la manière idéale d'apprendre à se servir d'un nouveau logiciel, d'un traitement de texte par exemple.

➤ Take notes in your reporter's notebook while discussing. Then write a one to three sentence synthesis for practice.

➤ Nationalisée depuis 1946, l'EDF (l'Electricité de France) est une entreprise qui fournit les résidents de France en électricité. L'EDF a le monopole de la distribution d'électricité mais pas de la production d'électricité. Si un particulier veut produire sa propre électricité, il en a le droit.

Lecture 1

EDF

K. Activité de pré-lecture. Répondez aux questions suivantes.

1. Que veut dire le mot «facturation»? Donnez plusieurs autres mots de la même famille.

2. Qui vous fournit en électricité et comment êtes-vous facturé(e)?

3. Si vous le désiriez, pourriez-vous être facturé(e) autrement?

EDF

EDF est en train de revoir tout son système informatique de facturation aux particuliers. Le but: facturer chaque mois, au lieu de tous les deux ou quatre mois, afin d'améliorer la trésorerie de l'entreprise.

Le Point: N° 1113 / 15–21 janvier 1994.

L'ÉNERGIE DE L'EXCELLENCE

L. Avez-vous compris? Parmi les réponses aux questions suivantes, cochez celles qui vous paraissent correctes. Attention, quelquefois il y a plusieurs réponses justes!

1. Les particuliers dont parle le texte sont
   a. tous les clients de l'EDF.
   b. certains clients de l'EDF seulement.
   c. les employés de l'EDF.
   d. les clients de l'EDF qui préfèrent étaler (*spread out*) leurs paiements.

2. Une facture, c'est un document qui
   a. donne le prix d'un service ou d'un produit à payer.
   b. indique la quantité et le prix des marchandises vendues.
   c. donne une autorisation d'achat.
   d. prouve qu'on a réglé un achat.
   e. promet le paiement d'une certaine somme.

3. Quel est le changement dont l'article parle?
   a. faire payer les clients plus souvent
   b. augmenter le prix de l'électricité
   c. envoyer une facture une fois par mois
   d. faire des retraits automatiques
   e. faire payer les clients par chèque et non en espèces

4. Qu'est-ce qui va permettre le changement annoncé?
   a. une révision du système informatique
   b. une modification dans la façon dont les factures sont faites
   c. le recrutement de personnel spécialisé en informatique
   d. le lancement (*launching*) d'une campagne publicitaire

5. Pourquoi est-ce que l'EDF a entrepris ce changement?
   a. pour gagner plus d'argent
   b. pour mieux régler ou contrôler ses rentrées d'argent
   c. pour aider ses clients à payer plusieurs petites sommes au lieu d'une grosse somme
   d. pour améliorer la situation financière de l'entreprise

M. A vous la parole! Discutez à deux ou trois les questions suivantes.

1. Comment et pourquoi est-ce que l'EDF a décidé de changer son système informatique?
2. En général, pour quelles raisons est-ce qu'une entreprise ou un particulier change d'ordinateur? Trouvez cinq arguments en faveur du changement et cinq autres contre.

➤ Discuss these arguments with your study partner. Be prepared for a mini-debate during your next class.

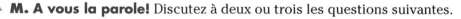

Lecture 2

Bill Gates

N. Activité de pré-lecture. Répondez aux questions suivantes par groupes de deux ou trois.

1. Que savez-vous des deux sociétés Apple et IBM? Pouvez-vous indiquer quelques différences entre IBM et Apple?
2. Le texte que vous allez lire est un extrait du livre «Big Blues chez IBM» de Paul Carroll publié par la maison Addison-Wesley. Le sous-titre du livre est «Le Déclin d'un empire américain». Expliquez le titre du livre en question.
3. Expliquez son sous-titre.

4. Que savez-vous sur Bill Gates?

5. Pensez à votre famille et aux gens que vous connaissez. A votre avis, est-ce que les jeunes apprennent plus facilement à se servir d'un ordinateur qu'une personne plus âgée? Expliquez.

Bill Gates

Note préliminaire: *Le livre* Big Blues Chez IBM *explique comment deux sociétés qui étaient ennemies ont pu collaborer et signer un accord en 1991. Un des résultats de cet accord a été la sortie de la ligne Power Mac. Le livre fait entrer ses lecteurs dans les coulisses* (behind the scenes) *des deux grandes sociétés IBM et Apple. Le livre présente également Bill Gates, le grand patron de Microsoft. La personnalité de Bill Gates a toujours fasciné les journalistes.*

Gates et Allen, pour étoffer *(to enrich, fill out)* leur co-entreprise nouvellement créée et baptisée Microsoft, entreprirent d'embaucher des jeunes programmeurs âgés d'une vingtaine d'années au plus pour préserver l'esprit bidouilleur *(nontraditionally creative)* de leur entreprise aux antipodes de la bureaucratie IBM. Alors que les gens d'IBM qu'il leur arrivait de rencontrer étaient généralement des cadres supérieurs d'âge moyen dont la première vision d'un ordinateur remontait au monstre terré dans sa pièce climatisée, les employés de Microsoft étaient si jeunes que la secrétaire, plus si jeune quant à elle, qui avait été embauchée alors que

Gates était en déplacement, essaya de l'empêcher d'entrer dans son bureau à son retour. Elle croyait qu'un freluquet *(whippersnapper)* de quinze–seize ans cherchait à s'installer de force dans le bureau du président de Microsoft.

Les gens d'IBM se prenaient totalement au sérieux tandis que Gates et sa bande traitaient leur travail comme s'il s'agissait d'un jeu.

Gates avait également le don de pouvoir se concentrer intensément sur un sujet, don que les adolescents sont capables d'exercer sur des choses comme des jeux vidéo mais qu'ils perdent lorsqu'ils entrent dans l'âge adulte et découvrent combien le monde est vaste. Le soir, lorsque les dirigeants d'IBM rentraient chez eux pour retrouver femme et enfants et se demander comment éliminer le chiendent *(crabgrass)* de leur pelouse, Gates entamait une nuit de travail. Il avait débranché son autoradio et mis sa télévision au grenier *(attic)* pour être le moins possible distrait de son travail.

«Les bonnes feuilles»: *SVM Mac,* No. 55, octobre 1994.

O. Synonymes. Voici quelques mots difficiles du texte. Relisez bien le passage duquel ils sont tirés et choisissez la définition ou le synonyme qui leur correspond le mieux.

1. *étoffer:* donner plus d'ampleur / réduire la taille / faire connaître

2. *embaucher:* augmenter le salaire / remplacer / engager

3. *l'esprit bidouilleur:* la mentalité conventionnelle / le sens de l'humour / le sens d'invention non traditionnel

4. *d'âge moyen:* ni jeune, ni vieux / dont la formation n'était pas extraordinaire / tous du même âge

5. *empêcher d'entrer:* faire en sorte qu'il n'entre pas / l'aider à entrer / le forcer à entrer

6. *le don:* l'incapacité / la flexibilité / le talent

7. *entamer:* éviter / commencer / finir

P. Autrement dit. Quels sont dans le texte les mots ou passages qui expliquent les idées suivantes?

1. Gates et Allen ont agrandi leur société.

2. Les employés de Microsoft étaient très créatifs.

3. La façon de travailler des employés de Microsoft et l'ambiance étaient complètement différentes de celles d'IBM.

4. Autrefois les ordinateurs étaient très grands et ils étaient installés dans une pièce séparée.

5. Bill Gates faisait très jeune.

6. Les employés d'IBM étaient plus intéressés par leur famille et leur propriété que par leur travail.

7. Bill Gates rentrait à la maison pour passer ses nuits à travailler sans être dérangé.

Q. L'un n'est pas l'autre! Le texte compare les employés de Microsoft avec ceux d'IBM. Quels sont parmi les mots et expressions suivants ceux qui s'appliquent à l'un ou à l'autre groupe? Indiquez la premiere lettre du nom de la compagnie en question devant chaque numéro.

_____ **1.** jeunesse

_____ **2.** vie régulière

_____ **3.** sens de l'humour

_____ **4.** jeu

_____ **5.** esprit bidouilleur

_____ **6.** soirées en famille

_____ **7.** temps libre passé à travailler dur

R. Vrai ou faux? Quels sont les mots ou les phrases qui, selon l'auteur du texte, caractérisaient Bill Gates à ses débuts? Ecrivez *V* ou *F* et corrigez les phrases qui ne sont pas justes. Bill Gates...

_____ **1.** faisait vieux pour son âge

_____ **2.** passait la soirée tranquillement avec sa femme et ses enfants

_____ **3.** voulait reprendre les méthodes d'IBM

_____ **4.** trouvait son inspiration en regardant la télé

_____ **5.** avait un pouvoir de concentration extraordinaire

_____ **6.** travaillait la nuit dans son grenier

_____ **7.** aimait employer des jeunes

S. A vous de jouer! Mettez-vous à deux. Un(e) de vous sera la secrétaire et l'autre Bill Gates. La secrétaire ne connaît pas Bill Gates. Elle ne peut pas croire qu'il est son patron et que le bureau dans lequel il veut entrer est bien le sien. Levez-vous et jouez cette scène!

HSG

Lecture 3

Faites votre compta sur petit écran

T. Activité de pré-lecture. Répondez aux questions suivantes par groupes de deux ou trois.

1. Pouvez-vous expliquer ce que c'est que la comptabilité? Donnez une définition provisoire en vous basant par exemple sur votre vie personnelle.
2. Pourquoi est-il important de bien tenir ses comptes?
3. En quoi l'emploi d'un ordinateur peut-il aider dans le domaine de la comptabilité?

Faites votre compta sur petit écran

- Des logiciels simples et bon marché permettent de se passer *(get by without)* d'un comptable *(accountant)* pour effectuer les opérations quotidiennes.
- Une solution adaptée aux besoins des entreprises de moins de dix personnes.

R ien de plus fastidieux que la saisie des écritures comptables: 20 577 francs à enregistrer à l'actif du compte «achats matières premières» *(raw materials)*, un loyer de 12 250 francs à ajouter aux charges d'exploitation, la consignation de 7 825,78 francs dans les recettes commerciales. Et c'est délicat. Une erreur est si vite arrivée! l'intervention d'un comptable professionnel est évidemment la meilleure solution. Mais les très petites entreprises n'en ont pas toujours les moyens.

Comment faire? On peut confier la corvée *(entrust the chore)* à un cabinet extérieur. Mais on peut aussi le faire en interne en utilisant un logiciel très simple d'usage.

«L'utilisation d'un tel logiciel ne dispense pas des services de l'expert-comptable. C'est toujours lui qui valide les comptes lors du bilan annuel. Mais les écritures sont saisies par ma secrétaire, témoigne Bertrand Savigny, gérant d'une petite société de services. Cela m'a permis de réduire sensiblement la facture du traitement comptable. Et je peux suivre au jour le jour les éléments clés de la situation économique et financière de l'entreprise, sans avoir à interroger sans cesse mon expert-comptable.»

Si les différents logiciels actuellement présents sur le marché sont tous vendus à des prix très voisins (environ 1000 francs), ils présentent toutefois des différences de conception et d'approche des problèmes concrets.

«Banc d'essai»: *L'Entreprise*, N° 118, juillet-août 1995. Article de Cécile Rémy.

U. A la recherche d'éléments précis. Relevez au moins six mots qui appartiennent au domaine de la comptabilité.

V. Avez-vous compris? Pouvez-vous deviner le sens de quelques-uns de ces mots? Essayez d'en rédiger une définition provisoire.

W. Autrement dit. Voici quelques mots ou groupes de mots tirés du texte et plusieurs explications possibles de ces mêmes mots. Cochez l'explication qui se rapproche le plus du sens du mot tel qu'il est employé dans le texte.

1. «Se passer d'un comptable» veut dire
   a. passer voir un comptable.
   b. ne plus avoir besoin de comptable.
   c. se contenter d'un seul comptable.

2. Un logiciel «bon marché» veut dire
   a. un logiciel qui vient de sortir sur le marché.
   b. un logiciel qui se vend bien.
   c. un logiciel qui ne coûte pas cher.

3. «Fastidieux» signifie
   a. ennuyeux et désagréable.
   b. inutile mais intéressant.
   c. rapide mais superficiel.

4. «Un cabinet» veut dire ici
   a. un bureau.
   b. un placard.
   c. une maison.

5. Si on peut se «dispenser des services de l'expert-comptable», cela signifie que ces services sont devenus
   a. inutiles.
   b. obligatoires.
   c. gratuits.

6. Selon ce texte, les prix des logiciels de comptabilité sont très «voisins». Cela veut dire que ces prix sont
   a. semblables.
   b. abordables.
   c. exagérés.

X. A vous de compléter! Les phrases suivantes sont incomplètes. Terminez-les après avoir bien relu l'article qui précède.

➤ Practice saying your completed sentences aloud so that when called on you can read them smoothly.

1. La profession de Bertrand Savigny est...

2. La secrétaire de Bertrand Savigny...

3. Depuis que Bertrand Savigny a adopté un logiciel de comptabilité, son comptable...

4. La facture du traitement comptable...

5. Sans consulter son expert-comptable, Bertrand Savigny...

6. Bertrand Savigny pourrait sans doute recommander un logiciel de comptabilité à une autre entreprise de services car...

Y. A vous de jouer! Jeu de rôle à faire par groupes de deux. Vous avez lu l'article sur les logiciels de comptabilité ci-dessus et vous expliquez à votre supérieur pourquoi il/elle devrait penser à adopter un de ces logiciels. Votre supérieur n'aime pas beaucoup les changements mais vous lui donnez une liste des avantages d'une telle solution et vous essayez de le/la convaincre.

Quelques points de repère

Le saviez-vous?

Evitez de vous abîmer la vue ou d'avoir des douleurs dans l'avant-bras quand vous travaillez de longues heures de suite sur ordinateur. Certains mouvements peuvent vous soulager. Ne restez pas les yeux fixés sur votre écran, levez les yeux régulièrement et concentrez-vous sur des objets placés à une distance différente pour que vos yeux puissent continuer à s'adapter et que la mise au point reste flexible. Quant à vos bras, dès que vous ne tapez plus, secouez-les légèrement pour les détendre *(relax)* et changez de position aussi souvent que possible. Massez-les *(massage them)* et faites des mouvements inverses à ceux que vous faites le plus souvent pour reposer vos muscles stressés. Votre corps est votre premier allié, ménagez-le et prenez-en soin.

Les entreprises françaises!

L'industrie informatique française exporte plus de 35% de sa production à l'étranger et certaines sociétés, comme Cap Gemini Sogeti, numéro un en Europe et occupant le 5e rang mondial, génèrent jusqu'à 70% de leurs revenus en vendant leurs produits à l'étranger! Bull est le leader français en ce qui concerne le matériel informatique. Parmi les dizaines de sociétés installées en France, citons parmi les plus connues et les plus performantes Sligos, Axime, GSI Industrie, Sema Group, Syseca. Matra Datavision et Dassault Systèmes sont davantage orientées vers l'industrie. De grands groupes industriels comme Schneider Electric, Merlin Gerin, Saint Gobain, Thomson et ITMI travaillent en collaboration avec de plus petites compagnies et laboratoires.

Une date importante!

En 1985, un grand pas en avant dans l'équipement informatique des écoles françaises a été fait lorsque Laurent Fabius, alors Premier Ministre du Président François Mitterrand a annoncé dans son plan «Informatique pour tous» qu'il allait équiper 160.000 établissements scolaires en ordinateurs.

Les chiffres parlent!

Chaque année en France et dans pratiquement tous les pays du monde, il y a des milliards *(billions)* de francs (plus de 35 milliards en 1993) de perte parce que les gens copient les programmes dont ils se servent au lieu de les acheter.

L'ardoise!

- On écrit de moins en moins à la main. Autrefois, le papier, le crayon ou le stylo étaient associés au processus de l'écriture. Le choix du papier, la couleur de l'encre, le type de plume utilisé étaient importants. L'écriture était liée à un certain nombre de plaisirs et de peurs. Certaines personnes par exemple éprouvaient l'angoisse *(anguish)* de la page blanche. L'emploi de plus en plus fréquent de l'ordinateur a changé le rapport personnel que l'on a avec l'écriture.

- Autrefois, les professeurs, chercheurs, ingénieurs, etc. donnaient leurs brouillons *(rough copies)*, projets de lettres, articles, rapports à taper à une personne chargée du secrétariat. Maintenant, grâce à la généralisation des ordinateurs personnels à la maison comme au travail, beaucoup de gens tapent eux-mêmes leurs documents ce qui a conduit à une redéfinition des responsabilités du service secrétariat.

Réflexions sur le travail en équipe

Pour qu'un groupe fonctionne bien, il faut qu'il y ait une bonne interaction entre tous les membres du groupe.

➤ What would such interaction look, sound and feel like to you?

Lexique

➤ Note words of particular use in *Mot de passe*.

une cartouche à encre: L'encre est le liquide noir ou de couleur qui permet de lire le document que l'on imprime sur papier. Ce liquide est contenu dans **une cartouche,** une sorte de petit réservoir.

Il faut que j'achète une nouvelle **cartouche à encre** car j'ai beaucoup imprimé ces derniers temps. La **cartouche** doit être presque vide.

un CD-ROM: Un **CD-ROM** est un disque qui permet de lire des données comme du son, des images ou des documents écrits, mais qui ne permet pas d'y en inscrire. Sur une disquette, par contre, on peut inscrire aussi bien que lire des données.

Sur mon vieux Macintosh, je n'avais pas de **CD-ROM**.

un fichier: Un **fichier** est le support informatique d'un document qu'on a créé. Ce sont des informations mises ensemble et traitées par ordinateur.

Tu devrais créer un nouveau **fichier** pour chaque domaine différent dans lequel tu travailles. Cela te facilitera la tâche en ce qui concerne l'organisation de tes données.

un logiciel: Un **logiciel** est un programme qui permet de réaliser certaines opérations sur ordinateur. Un traitement de texte comme *Word* est un logiciel. Certains **logiciels** permettent de faire les feuilles de paye à la fin du mois ou de remplir les déclarations d'impôts, ou d'effectuer certains calculs statistiques.

Je n'aime pas travailler avec *Word;* je trouve que *Nisus* est **un logiciel** beaucoup plus sophistiqué. Si tu veux, je t'apprendrai à t'en servir.

le matériel: Un ordinateur se compose d'éléments physiques qu'on appelle aussi **le matériel.** Le disque dur et la machine elle-même font partie du **matériel.** Bull est la compagnie française la plus importante dans le domaine du **matériel.**

Je ne crois pas que votre problème soit un problème de logiciel mais plutôt de **matériel.** La mémoire vive que vous avez à votre disposition est insuffisante. Vous avez un vieil ordinateur; il est temps d'acheter quelque chose de plus puissant!

un modem: Un **modem** est un appareil, un système électronique qui permet de transférer des données de l'ordinateur à une autre machine comme un autre ordinateur ou un fax, etc. ou bien d'avoir accès à des données qui sont stockées ailleurs, par l'intermédiaire d'une ligne téléphonique.

Le Powerbook de Macintosh est un portable qui comprend **un modem** incorporé. Où que vous soyez, il suffira que vous ayez accès à une ligne téléphonique pour pouvoir envoyer ou recevoir un fax, lire votre courrier électronique ou consulter des banques de données. C'est extrêmement pratique.

périphérique: Ce qui est **périphérique** est ce qui est situé à l'extérieur de l'ordinateur lui-même mais qui y est connecté comme une imprimante, un modem, un scanner, un disque dur supplémentaire portable, par exemple. **Un périphérique** opère sous la commande de l'ordinateur.

Les périphériques coûtent souvent plus cher que l'ordinateur lui-même.

la prévisualisation: Avant d'imprimer un document, on peut le **prévisualiser** de façon à mieux se rendre compte de la présentation de ce document sur la page.

Change tes marges pour que le document tienne sur une seule page. Si tu veux être sûre que ta lettre est bien proportionnée sur ta page et que tes marges ne sont pas trop étroites, tu peux la **prévisualiser.** Clique sur le petit rectangle, là, en haut à droite.

sauvegarder: Sauvegarder est un synonyme de sauver, ce qui signifie enregistrer des informations pour les conserver. On peut **sauvegarder** un fichier sur le disque dur ou sur une disquette.

Il faut toujours **sauvegarder** les documents au moins deux fois par mesure de sécurité. On peut les **sauvegarder** sur deux disquettes différentes pour diminuer le risque de perdre les données en question.

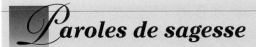

Paroles de sagesse

Paris ne s'est pas fait en un jour.

> ➤ Think of three applications of this principle. You may work with your study partner if you so choose.

Expression écrite

L'infinitif et l'infinitif passé

Dans cette section, repérez les infinitifs et les infinitifs passés <u>en les soulignant</u>. Notez aussi les prépositions qui les précèdent.

Un tableur

Pour mieux comprendre l'utilisation d'un tableur, on peut comparer son utilisation à celle d'une feuille de calcul en papier. Ainsi, sous sa forme papier, comme sous sa forme électronique, une feuille de calcul n'est pas une simple grille de lignes horizontales et verticales dans laquelle on peut entrer des données afin de faire toutes sortes d'opérations numériques.

Mais il y a une différence fondamentale entre le papier et l'écran. Sur le papier, après avoir fait la somme d'une colonne manuellement, on doit écrire le résultat avec un crayon. Si jamais l'un des nombres change, il faut sortir la calculatrice pour tout recommencer. Avec un tableur, il suffit de placer la formule représentant la somme de la colonne de nombres à la bonne position de la grille afin que l'ordinateur calcule le résultat et l'y affiche immédiatement. Si, plus tard, les nombres changent, le tableur recalcule la formule et affiche le nouveau résultat presque instantanément.

De plus, certaines cellules peuvent être liées entre elles afin de pouvoir utiliser le résultat du calcul de l'une comme élément de la formule de l'autre. Alors, après s'être occupé(e) de bien rentrer les données nécessaires, les formules mathématiques les plus complexes sont réduites à quelques commandes. Ainsi, à moins de pouvoir utiliser un tableur, certains calculs seraient quasiment infaisables à la main.

Z. A vos plumes! Créez maintenant votre propre paragraphe d'environ 150 mots sur les ordinateurs ou sur le traitement de texte que vous préférez en intégrant les prépositions suivies de verbes à l'infinitif ou l'infinitif passé comme dans le texte que vous venez de lire.

Dans le dossier suivant, vous allez étudier les problèmes d'ordinateur... et quelques solutions à ces problèmes!

Problèmes d'ordinateur

Que se passe-t-il quand un ordinateur ne marche plus ou quand un réseau est en panne *(broken down)*? Le deuxième dossier du Module II vous présente une autre dimension du monde informatisé et automatisé dans lequel nous vivons: les problèmes d'ordinateur. Les deux premières lectures donnent des exemples concrets de problèmes qui peuvent se poser et proposent des solutions. Le stress causé par de longues heures de travail à l'ordinateur forme le sujet du troisième texte.

Activité d'introduction

Les ordinateurs et vous!

A. La place des ordinateurs dans la vie quotidienne! Mettez-vous à deux ou trois et répondez aux questions suivantes.

1. Est-ce qu'il vous arrive d'aller à la banque ou dans une autre institution et de ne pas pouvoir faire certaines transactions parce que le système informatique est en panne? Que ressentez-vous et que faites-vous dans ces cas-là?

2. Dans notre vie de tous les jours, à la maison comme au travail, nous sommes très dépendants des ordinateurs, à la banque, à l'aéroport, à la bibliothèque, dans les magasins, etc. Est-ce que cette dépendance peut être gênante? dangereuse? Est-ce qu'elle vous inquiète? Discutez cette idée.

Les mots pour le dire

Vocabulaire de base

VERBES

activer	*to activate*
charger, recharger	*to charge, to recharge*
disposer de	*to have at one's disposal*
geler	*to freeze*
(se) mettre en marche	*to start, start working*
naviguer	*to surf*
régler	*to adjust*
relancer	*to restart*
relier, être relié	*to link, to be linked*

NOMS

une batterie, une pile	*battery*
une bogue, un bug	*bug*
le câble d'alimentation	*entry cable*
une case	*box*
le courant électrique	*electrical current*
le démarrage	*start-up*
le destinataire	*addressee*
la documentation	*documentation*
l'expéditeur *(m)*	*sender*
l'incompatibilité *(f)*	*incompatibility*
un informaticien	*computer specialist*
le menu Edition	*Edit menu*
le menu Fichier	*File menu*
le menu Pomme	*Apple menu*
le nettoyage	*cleaning*
le réseau	*net*
le service après-vente	*customer service*
la taille	*size*

ADJECTIFS

accessible	*accessible*
aisé(e)	*easy*
averti(e)	*advanced, warned*
cher(ère)	*expensive*
dispersé(e)	*scattered*
interconnecté(e)	*interconnected*
novice	*beginner*

ADVERBES ET EXPRESSIONS ADVERBIALES

entre	*between*
instantanément	*instantly*
en panne	*not working, down*
à plat	*low, empty*

B. Epelez! Mettez-vous par groupes de quatre et prononcez les mots suivants à haute voix puis énoncez une à une les lettres qui les composent.

1. la case
2. le réseau
3. en panne
4. le bouton de luminosité
5. activer
6. débrancher
7. schématiquement
8. à plat

C. Définitions provisoires à terminer. Complétez les phrases suivantes.

1. La grandeur ou la _____ d'un programme ou d'un fichier a beaucoup d'importance tout spécialement si vous n'avez pas beaucoup de mémoire vive.

   Comment ça s'écrit?

   Cela s'écrit _____.

2. Votre ordinateur est connecté ou _____ à la prise électrique par un câble qui l'alimente en électricité.

   Ça s'écrit _____.

3. Lorsque vous avez un gros problème d'ordinateur que vous ne pouvez pas régler vous-même, c'est l' _____ qui va s'occuper de le faire remplacer ou de le faire réparer.

   Ça s'écrit _____.

4. Quand l'ordinateur ne marche pas sur batterie, on a besoin de _____ pour le fournir en énergie.

   Ça s'écrit _____ .

5. Je touche aux boutons pour changer l'intensité de l'écran, pour obtenir une luminosité et un contraste différents mais je n'arrive pas à bien le _____.

   Ça s'écrit _____.

D. Définitions provisoires à créer. Par groupes de deux, donnez une définition provisoire pour les mots suivants.

1. la documentation
2. le démarrage
3. aisé(e)
4. accessible
5. naviguer

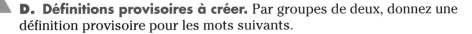

$\mathscr{D}$ialogue

Un problème d'ordinateur au bureau

E. Activité de pré-lecture. Mettez-vous à deux ou à trois et répondez aux questions suivantes.

1. Citez au moins quatre choses que vous faites quand vous avez un problème d'ordinateur. (Si vous n'avez pas d'ordinateur, imaginez ce que vous feriez.)
2. Expliquez quels problèmes vous avez déjà eus.

F. Lecture rapide. Parcourez le dialogue suivant et cochez toutes les bonnes réponses. Les interlocuteurs (les personnes qui se parlent)

1. sont des femmes et des hommes.

2. sont tous des hommes.

3. sont tous au même niveau hiérarchique dans la société en question.

4. travaillent tous à IBM.

5. travaillent peut-être dans un bureau de poste.

6. travaillent peut-être dans une banque.

7. sont des étudiants.

G. A la recherche de mots précis. Relevez au moins huit mots qui appartiennent au registre de l'informatique (qui ont quelque chose à voir avec les ordinateurs).

Un problème d'ordinateur au bureau

Michel: Tiens, c'est bizarre, mon ordinateur ne réagit pas normalement.

Bertrand: Comment ça?

Michel: Regardez, quand je tape quelque chose, c'est comme s'il n'enregistrait pas tout et puis je ne retrouve pas le fichier sur lequel j'ai travaillé hier. Ça y est. Je suis planté. J'ai dû faire une fausse manœuvre. Je n'arrive pas à sortir du programme.

Bertrand: Appelez Noémie Amar.

(Un peu plus tard...)

Michel: Est-ce que vous pensez que ça peut être un virus?

Noémie: Non, je n'ai pas l'impression, et puis il y a un programme sur votre machine qui contrôle toutes les disquettes que vous lisez et qui peut détecter et éliminer la plupart des virus. Cette souris ne réagit pas bien; elle a besoin d'un petit nettoyage... Voilà, ça va déjà mieux comme ça. Mais qu'est-ce qu'elle est lente! Vous savez que vous pouvez régler la vitesse de la souris? Vous voyez, j'ouvre le tableau de bord Souris. Le glissement de la souris va de «Lent» à «Rapide». Je clique sur le bouton qui correspond à «Rapide». Voilà. Tenez, je vais aussi changer la vitesse du double clic. Vous verrez, ce sera plus agréable.

Michel: Ah! Merci bien! Alors quel est le problème?

Noémie: Il y avait une prise qui n'était pas très bien enfoncée derrière. A part ça, je ne vois pas ce qui a pu poser un problème. Je vais faire redémarrer votre ordinateur. Ça ne fait pas de mal de le faire repartir en cas de problème. Au redémarrage, vous voyez, tout s'affiche normalement. Ça devrait aller. Alors, vous me dites que vous avez aussi perdu un fichier?

Michel: Oui, et ça m'ennuie parce que j'ai travaillé dessus pendant des heures hier.

Noémie: Et vous n'avez pas fait de copie?

Michel: Si, mais j'ai quand même bien travaillé une bonne demi-heure après cela.

Noémie: Est-ce que vous vous souvenez du nom de ce fichier? En principe vous devez avoir un programme sur cette machine qui sert à retrouver les fichiers qui ont disparu. Effectivement, c'est bien ce que je pensais, le voilà. Alors, je l'ouvre. Bon, regardez, vous le voyez votre document parmi cette liste?

Michel: Oui, «Compte 213 Denis», c'est bien celui-là. Mais vous en avez trouvé plusieurs versions?

Noémie: Oui, je vais saisir ces trois versions-là, leur donner un nom différent et vous pourrez les ouvrir toutes les trois pour voir celle qui est la plus complète.

Michel: Ouf! Vous m'avez sauvé la vie! Merci!

H. Avez-vous compris? Répondez aux questions suivantes.

> ➤ Feel free to work on these questions with your study partner before coming to class.

1. Pourquoi est-ce que Michel appelle Noémie?
2. D'après cette petite scène, qui est, selon vous, Noémie?
3. Quel est le diagnostic de Noémie?
4. Qu'est-ce que Noémie fait pour résoudre le problème de Michel?

I. Autrement dit. Lisez les définitions suivantes et cochez la réponse qui vous paraît correcte.

1. Faire une fausse manœuvre, c'est
   a. faire quelque chose qu'il ne fallait pas faire.
   b. ouvrir un fichier qui s'appelle «Fausse manœuvre».
   c. faire une erreur de calcul.

2. Redémarrer l'ordinateur, c'est
   a. ouvrir un programme.
   b. remettre l'ordinateur en marche.
   c. éteindre l'ordinateur.

3. Détecter un virus veut dire
   a. cacher la présence d'un virus.
   b. découvrir la présence d'un virus.
   c. bloquer l'action d'un virus.

4. Eliminer un virus signifie
   a. détruire ou faire disparaître un virus.
   b. créer un virus qui s'attaque aux autres virus.
   c. sélectionner un virus.

5. Une copie, c'est
   a. une reproduction sur papier.
   b. une imitation.
   c. un double.

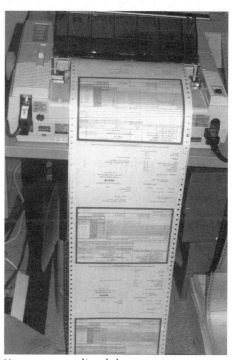

L'imprimante d'un laboratoire d'analyses médicales.

6. Ouvrir un fichier, c'est
   a. faire apparaître ce fichier sur l'écran.
   b. modifier ce fichier.
   c. créer un nouveau fichier.

HSG

➤ Should you need a quick review of the past tenses, see the *Points grammaticaux* of Module III in your *HSG*.

J. A vous de compléter! Le soir, à la maison, vous racontez ce qui s'est passé au bureau aujourd'hui. Terminez les phrases suivantes en vous aidant du dialogue.

1. Michel Marquet n'arrivait pas à sortir du programme parce que...
2. Il a appelé Noémie Amar...
3. Il a demandé à Noémie si...
4. Noémie a dit que...
5. Quand ils ont relancé l'ordinateur...
6. Michel avait perdu un fichier alors...
7. Noémie a retrouvé le fichier...
8. Michel était soulagé...

K. Autres scénarios possibles. Imaginez! Vous êtes Noémie Amar et votre voisin(e) joue le rôle de Michel!

1. L'ordinateur de Michel est infesté par un virus. Que dites-vous et que faites-vous?
2. Impossible de récupérer le fichier sur lequel Michel a travaillé la veille. Que dites-vous et que faites-vous?
3. Au redémarrage, l'écran reste noir. Que dites-vous et que faites-vous?

Observations grammaticales

Constructions avec «si»

Si vous avez dans la première partie de la phrase:	*alors vous avez dans la deuxième partie de la phrase:*
Si + verbe au présent →	verbe au futur, à l'impératif ou au présent

Si vous **venez** *(présent)* cet après-midi, vous **remplirez** *(futur)* le dossier.
Si tu **viens** *(présent)* cet après-midi, n'**oublie** pas *(impératif)* d'apporter ton ordinateur portable.
Si elle **travaille** *(présent)* pendant de longues heures à l'ordinateur, elle **aura** *(futur)* mal aux yeux.
Si nous ne **sauvegardons** pas *(présent)* notre fichier en double, nous **risquons** *(présent)* de le perdre!

➤ After reading these examples carefully, study the *futur* in the *Points grammaticaux* of Module II in your *HSG*.

Si vous avez dans la première partie de la phrase: *alors vous avez dans la deuxième partie de la phrase:*

Si + verbe à l'imparfait   →   verbe au conditionnel

Si j'**allais** *(imparfait)* cet après-midi à l'agence, je **pourrais** *(conditionnel)* remplir mon dossier.

Si vous **aviez** *(imparfait)* des problèmes d'ordinateur, vous **pourriez** *(conditionnel)* appeler Noémie Amar.

L. A compléter! Mettez les verbes indiqués au temps voulu.

1. Si les banques n'étaient pas automatisées

   a. les employé(e)s _____ *(faire)* un travail très différent.

   b. les distributeurs automatiques de billets _____ *(ne pas exister)*.

   c. on _____ *(ne pas pouvoir)* faire un virement d'un compte à un autre par Minitel.

   d. les employé(e)s _____ *(ne pas avoir)* d'ordinateurs pour faire leur courrier et _____ *(taper)* leurs lettres sur des machines à écrire traditionnelles.

2. Si, à cause d'un dérangement, les clients n'avaient plus accès à leur compte vingt-quatre heures sur vingt-quatre,

   a. ils _____ *(être)* obligés de faire leurs comptes eux-mêmes régulièrement.

   b. ils _____ *(aller)* en personne à la banque pour effectuer toutes leurs opérations bancaires.

   c. ils _____ *(se plaindre)* auprès de leur banque.

   d. ils _____ *(attendre)* avec impatience le rétablissement de ce service qui est si pratique quand il marche!

M. A vos plumes! Le système informatique de votre banque est en panne et vous voulez effectuer un certain nombre d'opérations bancaires. Que se passe-t-il? Complétez les phrases suivantes et faites attention à la concordance des temps.

1. Si je veux retirer une grosse somme d'argent de mon compte...

2. Si je veux déposer une certaine somme d'argent sur mon compte...

3. Si je fais une demande de carnet de chèques...

4. Si je veux virer 2.500 F de mon compte de dépôt à vue sur mon compte d'épargne...

5. Si je veux vérifier mon solde...

HSG

➤ Complete Exercises A–D of Module II in your *HSG.*

TELELION

Dialoguez avec votre banque

CREDIT LYONNAIS
LE POUVOIR DE DIRE OUI

VOS EFFETS DE COMMERCE

Dès leur arrivée au Crédit Lyonnais, soit 4 jours avant leur date de règlement, vous pouvez consulter vos effets sur TELELION PROFESSIONNELS.
Par minitel, vous décidez de les payer ou de les refuser, vous pouvez même changer d'avis jusqu'au jour du règlement.
Simplifiez-vous la gestion de vos effets avec le Bon à Payer télématique. Demandez-le à votre agence.

VOS REMISES CARTE BLEUE

Sur TELELION PROFESSIONNELS, vous consultez vos remises Carte Bleue, le détail des factures et les commissions perçues par le Crédit Lyonnais.

VOTRE CREDILION PROFESSIONNEL

Les professionnels peuvent aussi gérer leur crédit permanent professionnel par TELELION PROFESSIONNELS.

DES INFORMATIONS

TELELION, c'est aussi des réponses à vos questions, des informations pratiques, des informations financières, des conseils…

POUR EN SAVOIR PLUS SUR TELELION

Vous avez un minitel ?
Appelez nos pages de démonstration : composez 3614 CL.
Vous pouvez aussi demander une démonstration à votre agence : elle vous présentera en détail chacun des services.

POUR VOUS ABONNER

C'est possible directement sur votre minitel, à la suite des pages de démonstration : 3614 CL, ou en vous adressant à votre agence.
Si vous n'avez pas de minitel, votre agence commerciale France Télécom vous le fournira.

Dépliant du Crédit Lyonnais. (Suite, page 97).

*L*ecture 1

Comment réveiller un Mac qui dort?

N. Activité de pré-lecture. Répondez aux questions suivantes.

    1. Si l'écran de votre ordinateur reste noir, que faites-vous?

    2. Vous êtes en train de travailler sur votre ordinateur et tout d'un coup, votre écran devient noir. Que s'est-il passé selon vous?

TELELION
Le Crédit Lyonnais à domicile par minitel.

C'est facile :
les renseignements apparaissent sur l'écran de votre minitel par simple appel téléphonique en composant 3614 CL 310.

C'est pratique :
les informations sont disponibles directement, sans vous déplacer, 7 jours sur 7, jours et nuits.

C'est sûr :
votre code confidentiel garantit le secret des informations.

VOS COMPTES EN DIRECT

TELELION vous communique en permanence :
– le solde de vos comptes,
– les opérations des 30 derniers jours,
– les acquis de vos comptes d'épargne (intérêts, droits à prêts...)
– le détail de vos factures Carte Bleue qui seront débitées à la fin du mois en cours.

Ainsi, vous savez au jour le jour où en sont vos comptes et vos factures Carte Bleue.

La consultation de comptes par TELELION PROFESSIONNELS
comporte en plus :
– les dates de valeurs,
– la possibilité de rechercher une écriture par numéro ou par montant approximatif.

VOTRE PORTEFEUILLE-TITRES

TELELION vous indique la situation de votre portefeuille :
– son évaluation quotidienne globale et détaillée,
– le relevé de vos ordres de Bourse exécutés ou en cours,
– les revenus de votre portefeuille et leur fiscalité.

Pour mieux le gérer, TELELION met à votre disposition des informations financières.

VOS ORDRES DE BOURSE

En tout confort, par TELELION, vous passez des ordres de Bourse. Grâce à ce nouveau service, vos ordres donnés jusqu'à 21 h 30 arrivent directement en Bourse le lendemain.

Vos ordres au mieux sont exécutés à l'ouverture de la séance. Vous pouvez fixer un cours limite : votre ordre ne sera exécuté que si le cours est atteint. Il faut moins de 2 minutes pour passer un ordre. Vous pouvez aussi passer des ordres d'achat ou de vente de SICAV ou Fonds Communs de Placement du Crédit Lyonnais.

Comment réveiller un Mac qui dort?

L'écran noir:
Si vous n'entendez pas de bruit au démarrage, il est probable que vous avez débranché par mégarde le câble d'alimentation de votre ordinateur. Dans le cas d'un PowerBook, vos batteries doivent être à plat. Si votre machine reçoit sa dose de courant électrique, il s'agit d'un dysfonctionnement de l'unité centrale.

Direction service après-vente...
Si vous avez entendu du bruit au démarrage, ce qui indique que l'unité centrale s'est mise en marche normalement, jouez sur les boutons de luminosité et de contraste de l'écran, il est peut-être réglé au plus bas! Si vous possédez un Macintosh modulaire, vérifiez que le moniteur est bien connecté à la machine, qu'il est alimenté correctement et que vous l'avez allumé...

Extrait d'un article de Haïm Benamou, tiré de *SVM Mac*, octobre 1994. N° 55.

O. A la recherche d'éléments précis. L'auteur de l'article donne six raisons qui peuvent expliquer le fait qu'un écran reste noir. Relisez le texte et relevez trois de ces raisons.

P. Structures! Le texte «Comment réveiller un Mac qui dort» contient quatre constructions avec **si**. Isolez-les et dites à quel temps les verbes de la phrase sont.

Q. A vous de jouer! A deux, jouez une scène dans laquelle un(e) de vous a un écran qui reste noir et l'autre est le spécialiste qui pose des questions pour pouvoir régler le problème.

HSG

➤ Study the *Encadrés et aperçus* for the verbs *savoir, sortir* and *prendre* of Module II in your *HSG* and complete Exercises A–C.

Ecture 2

Ecran qui gèle

R. Activité de pré-lecture. Répondez aux questions suivantes.

➤ If you need a key term to explain this concept in French, consult your French-French dictionary.

1. Que veut dire le verbe «geler»? Qu'est-ce qui gèle normalement?

2. Pouvez-vous deviner ce que c'est qu'un écran qui gèle?

3. Savez-vous ce que vous pouvez faire lorsque l'écran de votre ordinateur gèle?

Ecran qui gèle

Ce type de problème, même pour un utilisateur averti, est le plus souvent difficile à résoudre car ses causes sont peu aisées à identifier. Toutefois, avec un peu de réflexion, on peut se tirer d'un mauvais pas.

Il peut s'agir d'un problème d'incompatibilité entre le programme et le fichier utilisé. Relisez la documentation, un certain nombre d'éditeurs consciencieux indiquent la liste des fichiers qui posent problème. Si vous venez d'ouvrir un document de grande taille, il est possible que votre logiciel ne dispose plus d'assez de mémoire vive.

Après avoir sélectionné *A propos de votre Macintosh* en passant dans le menu *Pomme*, regardez de combien de mémoire vive vous disposez. Ensuite, cliquez sur l'icône du programme que vous êtes en train d'utiliser puis demandez *Lire les informations* via le menu *Fichier*. Augmentez le chiffre qui se trouve dans la case *Mémoire souhaitée* en tenant compte de l'espace mémoire qui reste.

Autre possibilité, le programme a été mal écrit et comporte quelques bogues meurtriers. Là, vous ne pouvez rien y faire, sauf écrire une lettre vengeresse à qui de droit.

Extrait d'un article de Haïm Benabou, tiré de *SVM Mac*, N° 55, octobre 1994.

➤ Le mot «bogue» a été créé récemment. Officiellement, il est *au féminin:* **une bogue** ou **un bug.**

➤ You may choose to work on these sentences with your study partner.

S. A la recherche d'informations précises. Trouvez au moins cinq mots qui relèvent du domaine de l'informatique et employez-les dans une petite phrase.

T. Vrai ou faux? Relisez le texte et dites si les affirmations suivantes sont vraies ou fausses. Si elles ne sont pas vraies, changez les phrases de façon à ce qu'elles le deviennent.

_____ **1.** Un utilisateur averti est quelqu'un qui s'y connaît bien en ordinateurs.

_____ **2.** Lorsqu'un écran gèle, on ne peut rien faire.

_____ **3.** Un document de grande taille est un document qui utilise beaucoup de mémoire.

_____ **4.** *Fichier* et *Pomme* sont des menus qui existent dans tous les programmes.

_____ **5.** Une bogue ou un bug est une erreur qui peut poser des problèmes de fonctionnement dans un programme.

_____ **6.** Lorsqu'il y a une bogue, c'est à vous de corriger le programme.

U. Autrement dit. Les expressions et mots suivants sont tirés du texte. Pour chaque mot, nous vous proposons trois définitions. Choisissez la définition qui correspond le mieux à la signification du mot dans le texte.

1. *Résoudre un problème,* c'est
  a. trouver une solution à ce problème.
  b. comprendre ce problème.
  c. détecter un problème.

2. *Aisées à identifier* veut dire
  a. compliquées à expliquer.
  b. simples à utiliser.
  c. faciles à trouver.

3. *Se tirer d'un mauvais pas,* c'est
  a. sortir d'une situation grave, d'une situation où on ne veut pas se trouver.
  b. passer d'une situation grave à une situation encore plus grave.
  c. faire une erreur qui n'a pas de conséquences dramatiques.

4. *La documentation,* c'est
  a. un certain nombre d'informations.
  b. un papier prouvant que le matériel est sous garantie.
  c. un logiciel qui permet de résoudre un certain nombre de problèmes courants.

5. *Un bogue meurtrier* veut dire un(e) bogue
  a. qui se propage.
  b. qui résiste.
  c. qui a des conséquences dangereuses.

6. *A qui de droit* veut dire
  a. à la personne concernée.
  b. à un(e) avocat(e).
  c. à la personne qui pourra vous dire quels sont vos droits.

Lecture 3

Les stress calculés du travail sur écran

➤ Be ready to report your findings back to the class.

V. Activité de pré-lecture. A deux ou à trois, répondez aux questions suivantes.

1. Qu'est-ce que c'est que le stress?
2. Donnez plusieurs exemples précis de situations que vous trouvez stressantes.
3. Que ressentez-vous quand vous êtes stressé(e)?
4. Selon vous, est-ce que travailler à l'ordinateur peut être stressant? Justifiez et discutez votre réponse.

Les stress calculés du travail sur écran

Avec l'omniprésence de l'informatique, de la télématique et de la robotique dans le monde du travail, les postes sur écran sont légion aujourd'hui, mais cette modernisation ne se fait pas sans mal. Ces drôles de petites lucarnes sont accusées pêle-mêle de créer ou d'accentuer de nombreux troubles oculaires, de provoquer des maux de tête et de dos, d'induire enfin toutes sortes de difficultés psychologiques.

Pour confirmer ou infirmer ces dires, une enquête menée par la Direction régionale du travail et de l'emploi de Poitou-Charentes s'est penchée de 1986 à 1994 sur la santé des travailleurs sur écran. Une première analyse rendue publique en 1991 montrait que 60% des personnes travaillant sur écran ressentaient une gêne visuelle. Elle concluait que ce nouveau type de travail entraîne bel et bien une gêne visuelle fonctionnelle, proportionnelle à la durée d'utilisation de l'appareil. La seconde partie de l'enquête, portant cette fois sur les plaintes psychologiques et les maux de tête, vient d'être publiée. Anxiété, irritabilité pendant ou après le travail, troubles du sommeil, sont le lot de bien des salariés. Mais à la lumière de cette enquête, il semble exister des caractéristiques propres au travail sur «terminal»...

Chez ceux qui passent plus de 4 heures par jour sur ordinateur ou traitement de texte, les délais d'attente dus à l'indisponibilité de l'écran, l'effort de mémorisation des codes, la difficulté à comprendre certains messages, apparaissent comme des facteurs de gênes supplémentaires. De même que tout ce qui concerne l'environnement du poste de travail: nuisances visuelles, bruit, température inadaptée, position inconfortable. Globalement, les enquêteurs estiment que les salariés soumis à un rythme contraignant, passant au moins deux heures par jour en continu ou non devant l'écran dans de mauvaises conditions, seront anxieux, irritables, auront du mal à s'endormir.

France-Amérique, 31 décembre 1994–6 janvier 1995.

➤ Make note of key words and expressions for *Mot de passe.*

W. Le mot juste! Trouvez dans le texte l'équivalent des mots ou expressions suivants.

1. les emplois
2. se trouvent en grand nombre
3. le moniteur de l'ordinateur
   (trois mots dans le texte)

4. rendre plus fort

5. des problèmes d'ordre visuel

6. un trouble

7. les douleurs

8. avoir des troubles du sommeil

X. A vos plumes! Le texte mentionne l'environnement des travailleurs sur écran: *nuisances visuelles, bruit, température inadaptée, position inconfortable.* Expliquez chacune de ces catégories et donnez quelques exemples.

Y. Vrai ou faux? Mettez-vous à deux ou trois et lisez bien les affirmations suivantes. Pensez-vous que ces affirmations soient justes ou non et pourquoi? Ensuite essayez de voir si l'article défend la même opinion que vous et soulignez le passage dans lequel cette opinion est exprimée.

1. Ce sont surtout les secrétaires qui se plaignent de leur travail sur ordinateur.

2. Les employés qui travaillaient à l'ordinateur en 1986 avaient moins de problèmes qu'en 1994.

3. Les problèmes de ceux qui travaillent beaucoup à l'ordinateur sont principalement d'ordre psychologique.

4. Plus on utilise l'ordinateur plus on souffre de différents maux.

5. Plus de la moitié des gens qui travaillent sur ordinateur finissent par avoir des troubles des yeux.

6. Lorsque l'environnement du poste de travail n'est pas idéal, l'anxiété et l'irritabilité des travailleurs sur écran augmentent.

7. Certaines personnes qui travaillent sur ordinateur ont des difficultés à s'endormir.

Z. De la réflexion à l'écriture. Vous devez travailler au moins six heures par jour sur ordinateur. Décrivez ce qui serait pour vous l'environnement idéal, c'est-à-dire l'environnement qui éviterait autant que possible le stress lié à votre type de travail. Ecrivez un paragraphe d'environ 150 mots en commençant par une introduction et en finissant par une conclusion.

HSG

➤ For a review of the future *and* conditional stems, see the *Points grammaticaux* of Module II in your *HSG.*

*uelques points de repère*

Les chiffres parlent!

- En France, il n'y avait que 200.000 foyers «on-line» en 1995.

- En octobre 1995, 2.000 personnes sont venues à la soirée de lancement de *Windows 95* à Abidjan, la Côte-d'Ivoire.

- Le nombre de nouveaux serveurs web est estimé à plus de 6.000 par mois.

L'ardoise!

On avait reproché au téléphone d'avoir remplacé les lettres et d'avoir favorisé la communication orale immédiate au détriment de l'écriture. L'écriture a retrouvé une place de choix puisque la correspondance électronique se fait par écrit. Il faut taper ses messages pour pouvoir les envoyer. L'écriture a pourtant changé de visage. Les messages électroniques ont adopté un style moins formel, plus direct. Les longues formules de politesse ont pratiquement disparu. Les messages vont droit au but; c'est la rapidité qui prime.

Une date importante!

France Télécom perdra le monopole du téléphone en France en 1998. Cela devrait avoir une influence sur le prix des communications téléphoniques. Si les prix baissent, cela encouragera les Français à utiliser leur ordinateur à la maison et à se connecter avec le réseau Internet.

Le saviez-vous?

Le 6e Sommet de la francophonie a réuni les représentants de 47 pays ayant le français en partage, à Cotonou, la capitale du Bénin en décembre 1995. Les chefs d'Etat de ces 47 pays se sont engagés à promouvoir *(promote)* un espace francophone dans le domaine des nouvelles technologies et de la communication. Ils ont pris la résolution de se mobiliser pour occuper une place importante sur les autoroutes de l'information. Ils veulent favoriser la place d'une francophonie vivante dans le respect du pluralisme culturel sur les réseaux électroniques. Des serveurs francophones vont être créés et les logiciels de navigation vont être francisés pour faciliter la circulation de la langue française et des données en français sur les réseaux. Une action de sensibilisation à la nécessité du plurilinguisme sur les réseaux va être mise sur pied.

*R*éflexions sur le travail en équipe

Pour qu'un groupe fonctionne bien, il faut reconnaître que tous les membres de l'équipe ainsi que toutes les étapes d'un procédé sont interdépendants et puis agir en conséquence.

Le logo de France Télécom.

 # ℒexique

afficher: Afficher, c'est faire apparaître un graphique ou des caractères sur l'écran de l'ordinateur.

> **Affiche** l'icône de ton traitement de texte et clique dessus pour obtenir des informations sur ce progamme.

une application: Une application est une utilisation particulière de l'informatique dans un domaine particulier. **Une application** peut être un programme comme un traitement de texte.

> Est-ce que tu connais la version 3.0 du logiciel intégré *Works* de Microsoft? Dans une même **application,** ce logiciel inclut un traitement de texte, un tableur et une base de données. C'est très pratique si tu veux par exemple utiliser un graphique dans un document ou établir un mailing pour une lettre type.

le bouton de démarrage: Pour pouvoir allumer un ordinateur il faut appuyer sur un bouton qui se trouve souvent derrière ou bien sur une touche du clavier. Lorsqu'on a un problème, il est quelquefois utile de **redémarrer** en appuyant sur ce bouton.

> Si ton écran est gelé, **redémarre** ta machine en appuyant sur **le bouton de démarrage** et en recommençant à zéro.

brancher: Brancher un appareil, c'est faire la connexion électrique joignant des prises qui permettent de relier un système à un autre.

> Lorsqu'on allume un ordinateur et que l'écran reste noir, la première chose à faire, c'est de vérifier si l'ordinateur est bien **branché.** Lorsqu'il y a des orages, il est conseillé de débrancher son ordinateur.

cliquer: Lorsqu'on veut déplacer le curseur, on prend la souris et on la bouge. Lorsque le curseur est à l'endroit voulu, on **clique,** c'est-à-dire qu'on appuie rapidement une fois sur le bouton de la souris puis on le lache. Lorsqu'on veut ouvrir un document on **clique** deux fois de suite, rapidement: on **double-clique.**

> Tu devrais nettoyer la souris ou peut-être modifier la vitesse de fonctionnement. Je trouve qu'elle ne réagit pas assez rapidement quand je **clique.**

la corbeille: La corbeille fait partie du bureau. Elle est généralement affichée en bas et à droite de l'écran d'un Macintosh.

Pour éjecter une disquette, tu peux pointer l'icône de cette disquette, la tirer et la mettre dans **la corbeille.** Quand tu veux effacer un document ou te débarrasser d'un dossier, tu le tires dans **la corbeille** puis tu vides ta **corbeille.** L'option Vider **la corbeille** se trouve dans le menu Rangement.

démarrer: Lorsqu'on veut commencer à travailler sur un ordinateur, il faut d'abord l'allumer et le mettre en train de façon à ce que le système et tous les programmes soient prêts à fonctionner. On appelle ce processus **le démarrage.**

Démarre ton Mac et je vais te montrer comment activer ton télécopieur.

une disquette: Lorsqu'on utilise un ordinateur, on peut avoir accès à des données qui sont stockées sur un disque dur, un CD-ROM ou sur **une disquette.** Il y a plusieurs types de **disquettes.** Leur taille et leur capacité peuvent varier. On parle de **la disquette** originale lorsqu'on fait référence à **la disquette** qui contient le logiciel qu'on a acheté.

Est-ce que tu peux aller m'acheter une boîte de dix **disquettes?** C'est pour mon Power Mac. J'ai besoin de **disquettes** en double face.

une icône: L'icône est un petit symbole graphique, une sorte de petit dessin très simple qui permet de rapidement identifier et manipuler les fichiers aussi bien que les logiciels à l'intérieur d'un système. C'est la compagnie Apple qui a commencé à se servir d'**icônes** avec son micro-ordinateur Macintosh. Grâce au logiciel *Windows,* les ordinateurs PC ont maintenant un système similaire à leur disposition.

Tu vois, pour ouvrir ou activer mon traitement de texte, il suffit que je pointe **l'icône** avec la souris et que je clique. Voilà, c'est fait! C'est simple comme «bonjour»!

lancer: Lancer une application, c'est la faire démarrer, l'ouvrir et l'afficher sur l'écran pour qu'on puisse s'en servir.

Si tu veux **lancer** cette application, il va falloir que tu lui alloues (donnes) plus de mémoire.

un manuel: Un manuel est un livre qui donne un certain nombre d'informations sur une machine et explique comment s'en servir. Il y a plusieurs sortes de **manuels:** il y a des **manuels** d'auto-instruction, d'emploi, d'utilisateur, de formation et de référence.

Je ne me souviens plus comment activer mon fax. Passe-moi **le manuel** de mon Mac pour que je voie comment faire.

le menu Edition: L'édition est ce qui permet de modifier le texte.

J'ai plusieurs options d'**Edition** dans **le menu Edition:** je peux Annuler, Couper, Copier, Coller, Effacer, Tout sélectionner et Afficher le Presse-papiers. Je dois d'abord sélectionner une partie du texte pour pouvoir valider ces options.

pointer: Lorsqu'on prend la souris pour déplacer le curseur ou pour amener la flèche sur un dossier qu'on veut ouvrir, par exemple, on dit qu'**on pointe.**

Non, ne clique pas là où tu es, il faut d'abord que **tu pointes.**

tirer: Pour **tirer** un dossier du disque dur sur une disquette, par exemple, il faut prendre la souris, pointer sur ce dossier, enfoncer le bouton de la souris, puis tout en gardant le bouton de la souris enfoncé, on déplace le dossier grâce à la souris et on l'amène là où on veut le placer puis on relâche la pression du bouton.

Lorsque tu **tires** un dossier de ta disquette et que tu l'installes dans un autre dossier de ton disque dur, tu le copies automatiquement.

verrouiller: Verrouiller un fichier, c'est fermer un fichier pour qu'on ne puisse pas le modifier ou l'effacer par erreur.

Je ne peux pas vider ma corbeille. Il y a le message suivant qui s'est affiché sur mon écran: Impossible de vider la Corbeille, car tous les éléments qu'elle contient (hormis les dossiers) sont **verrouillés.** Pour supprimer un élément **verrouillé,** choisissez Vider la Corbeille tout en maintenant la touche Option enfoncée.

Paroles de sagesse

- Un homme averti en vaut deux.
- Deux précautions valent mieux qu'une.

➤ How might these adages apply to your life? Discuss them with your study partner.

Expression écrite

Premier aperçu de l'emploi de «connaître» et de «savoir»

Dans cette section, vous allez apprendre à utiliser des expressions courantes. Vous allez aussi essayer de faire la distinction entre les verbes «connaître» et «savoir». Lisez le texte suivant en faisant bien attention aux mots **en caractères gras** (in bold print).

➤ Just skim for the general idea of the paragraph.

Mon code secret

*Un code secret est associé à ma carte bancaire. **J'ai beau essayer** de m'en souvenir, il m'arrive de l'oublier. Je **connais** des personnes qui sont obligées de le noter dans un carnet pour s'en souvenir. Les cartes bancaires sont des cartes à puce: dans la carte, **il y a** une mémoire électronique qui **connaît** et reconnaît le numéro du code secret. Lorsque je paie par carte bancaire, il faut que je **sache** mon code car je dois le composer sur un clavier relié par réseau téléphonique au central bancaire. C'est ainsi que le vendeur vérifie que l'acheteur est solvable et que la carte lui appartient bien. **J'ai beau être très prudente,** samedi dernier, je me suis fait voler ma carte. Le voleur ne **savait** pas qu'il ne pourrait pas s'en servir puisqu'il ne* *connaissait pas le code. La carte a été avalée alors qu'il **était en train** d'essayer plusieurs codes à un D.A.B. Le voleur n'a donc pas réussi à l'utiliser parce que, après tout, cette carte **était à moi**, pas **à lui**. Heureusement pour moi et mon compte en banque!*

AA: Attention! Les expressions en caractères gras ne se traduisent pas littéralement en anglais. Etudiez les exemples qui suivent et donnez l'équivalent anglais des phrases qui ne sont pas encore traduites.

Cette disquette est **à moi, pas à lui.**	*This floppy is mine not his (belongs to me, not to him).*

N.B. Les pronoms disjoints sont: moi, toi, lui, elle, soi, nous, vous, eux, elles.

Ce compte épargne **est à elle, pas à vous!**	_____ _____
Le banquier était **en train d'**ouvrir le coffre quand l'alarme s'est déclenchée.	*The banker was (in the process of) opening the safe when the alarm went off.*
Nous étions **en train de** sauvegarder nos documents lorsqu'il y a eu une coupure de courant à cause de l'orage.	_____ _____ _____
Il y a plusieurs sortes de comptes en banque: par exemple, des comptes chèques ou courant, épargne ou épargne logement.	*There are several kinds of bank accounts: checking accounts, savings accounts (and a special saving account for the purchase of a home or lodging), for instance.*
Il y a des ordinateurs qui n'ont pas de souris.	_____ _____
J'ai beau utiliser ce nouveau traitement de texte depuis un an, je ne me sens toujours pas à l'aise.	*No matter how much I use this new word-processing software, I still am not comfortable (with it).*
Il a beau avoir relu trois fois le manuel, il ne sait toujours pas envoyer un fax directement de son ordinateur.	_____ _____ _____ _____

BB. La parole est à vous! Après avoir lu rapidement le texte ainsi que les traductions qui précèdent, écrivez un paragraphe au futur ou au passé sur une expérience peut-être un peu négative (au moins au début) à l'ordinateur.

Dans le dossier suivant, vous allez en apprendre un peu plus sur les ordinateurs et beaucoup plus sur Internet.

$\mathscr{L}$e réseau Internet

Le thème du sixième dossier est l'Internet, l'accès à l'Internet et différents emplois possibles de ce réseau dans le domaine personnel aussi bien que professionnel. Les ordinateurs peuvent non seulement être connectés entre eux à l'intérieur même d'un système mais peuvent également être reliés à d'autres ordinateurs faisant partie d'autres systèmes. Le réseau Internet permet de façon presqu'instantanée de transférer des informations et d'avoir accès à des données et des documents de toutes sortes: textes, chiffres, graphiques, photos, vidéos, etc. L'Internet n'est plus réservé à l'élite universitaire de quelques pays du monde. Il est devenu accessible à des millions de particuliers et occupe une place de plus en plus importante dans le monde des affaires.

$\mathscr{A}$ctivité d'introduction

L'Internet

A. Le réseau Internet. Mettez-vous à deux ou trois et répondez aux questions suivantes.

> ➤ Be ready to brainstorm your findings with the rest of the class.

1. Quels sont les avantages et les inconvénients de l'emploi du réseau Internet?

2. Est-ce que vous pouvez imaginer comment une entreprise pourrait se servir du réseau Internet?

Les mots pour le dire

Vocabulaire de base

VERBES

s'abonner	*to subscribe*
censurer	*to censure*
se connecter	*to connect*
diffuser	*to disseminate*
s'inscrire	*to register, sign up*
naviguer	*to navigate*
surcharger la mémoire	*to overload the memory*
visionner	*to view*
visiter un site	*to view/visit a home page*

NOMS

un abonné	*subscriber*
un abonnement	*subscription*
un appel interurbain	*long-distance call*
un appel urbain	*local call*
une connexion	*connection*
un guide de navigation	*navigation guide*
en ligne	*on line*
la messagerie électronique	*e-mail*
un modem	*modem*
un mot de passe	*password*
un outil de recherche	*research tool*
une recherche sur mots clés	*word search*
une rubrique	*heading; item*
la toile	*web*
un utilisateur	*user*
la vitesse	*speed*

ADJECTIFS

axé(e) sur	*built around, centered on*
bien conçu(e)	*well conceived*
bien fourni(e)	*well supplied*
bien structuré(e)	*well structured*
complet(ète)	*complete; full; no vacancy*
efficace	*efficient*
ennuyeux(se)	*boring*
étonnant(e)	*astonishing*
exceptionnel(le)	*exceptional*
expérimenté(e)	*experienced*
gigantesque	*gigantic*
gratuit(e)	*free*
indescriptible	*indescribable*
indispensable	*absolutely essential*
inégal(e)	*uneven*
limité(e)	*limited*

rapide	*fast*
surchargé(e)	*overloaded*
utile	*useful*

ADVERBES

approximativement	*approximately*
effectivement	*actually; effectively*
entièrement	*entirely*
facilement	*easily*
instantanément	*instantly*
rapidement	*rapidly*

➤ Note key words and expressions to practice for *Mot de passe.*

B. Définitions provisoires à terminer. Complétez les phrases suivantes avec le vocabulaire de base proposé ci-dessus.

1. Lorsqu'on entre dans un site sur Internet et qu'on prend connaissance des informations qui y sont proposées, on dit qu'on _____ ce site.

2. Lorsqu'on n'a pas le droit d'utiliser certains mots ou qu'on n'a pas le droit de montrer certaines images, on dit qu'on est _____.

3. C'est un mot qui fonctionne un peu comme une clé au sens qu'il me permet d'avoir accès à certaines informations ou d'entrer quelque part. C'est un mot _____.

4. Une personne qui a une ligne téléphonique en son nom est un _____.

5. Lorsqu'on paie une somme fixe tous les mois pour un certain service, on paie un _____.

6. Yahoo ou Netscape sont des _____. Ils permettent de naviguer sur le Web (la toile) et de trouver certains sites.

C. Définitions provisoires à créer. Par groupes de deux, écrivez une définition provisoire pour les mots suivants.

1. diffuser
2. une rubrique
3. se connecter
4. bien structuré
5. la messagerie électronique

Dialogue

Le responsable d'une agence discute avec l'un de ses employés

D. Activité de pré-lecture. A deux ou trois, répondez aux questions suivantes.

1. Vous rencontrez un(e) collègue dans les couloirs de votre entreprise.

Vous vous arrêtez pour bavarder quelques minutes. De quoi parlez-vous? Mentionnez au moins sept sujets possibles.

2. En sortant de votre bureau, vous rencontrez votre patron(ne). Est-ce que la conversation sera la même que celle que vous venez d'avoir avec votre collègue? Oui? Non? Pourquoi?

Le responsable d'une agence discute avec l'un de ses employés

En quittant la banque un vendredi après-midi, le responsable de la branche du Crédit Agricole d'une petite ville de province rencontre David Amar qui est un de ses employés. David Amar s'occupe des comptes commerciaux et il est passionné d'informatique.

Le responsable: Ah, Monsieur Amar, ça tombe bien. Je sais que depuis votre retour des Etats-Unis vous êtes abonné au magazine *Time*. Je voulais justement vous demander si vous aviez lu l'article sur Bill Gates dans le *Time* de cette semaine?

David Amar: Non, pas encore, pourquoi?

Le responsable: Eh bien, je dois vous avouer que depuis notre dernière petite conversation au sujet du réseau Internet, j'ai lu plusieurs articles sur les dernières technologies en informatique et sur tout ce qui touche aux autoroutes de l'information, etc. et hier, je feuilletais *Time*... Ma fille, celle qui est en Gestion à l'IUT (Institut Universitaire de Technologie) de Tours, le lit de temps en temps et me le rapporte lorsqu'il y a des articles qui pourraient m'intéresser...

David Amar: Il y a un article sur Bill Gates?

Le responsable: Oui, il paraît qu'avant la fin de l'année il sortira une nouvelle version de *Windows* qui permettra un accès extrêmement facile au réseau Internet. Il suffira d'appuyer sur un bouton et la connexion sera faite.

David Amar: Ah, ben, ça serait génial car c'est justement la difficulté d'accès d'Internet qui rebute les amateurs. Est-ce que Bill Gates veut contrôler l'Internet?

Le responsable: D'après l'article, oui... mais il y a évidemment une différence entre vouloir et pouvoir. S'il réussit, ce sera un coup de maître. En ce moment toutes les banques américaines et les compagnies de cartes de crédit s'intéressent énormément aux transactions financières sur Internet. C'est l'avenir! Lisez l'article et dites-moi ce que vous en pensez. En France, il n'y a pour l'instant que Le Crédit Mutuel de Bretagne qui s'y soit mis.

David Amar: En se connectant sur le service offert par le Crédit Mutuel, les clients peuvent accéder à l'ensemble du réseau Internet et naviguer sur la fameuse «toile d'araignée planétaire» et cela, sans souscrire ni

	donc payer aucun abonnement. C'est le Crédit Mutuel qui prend tout en charge. Il faut évidemment disposer d'un micro-ordinateur mais le coût d'accès est de 70 centimes la minute, ce qui est incroyablement bon marché!
Le responsable:	Effectivement! Le Crédit Mutuel est en train de profiter d'un nouveau créneau. C'est la banque de demain.
David Amar:	C'était déjà eux qui avaient lancé le premier service Minitel en 1982; toutes les autres ont rapidement suivi. Il faudra suivre leur effort de près. Je voulais justement vous dire que j'ai bien envie de m'abonner à Compuserve. Ils offrent un logiciel d'accès complet à Internet avec cinq heures de connexion gratuites par mois.
Le responsable:	Cinq heures? Ça paraît beaucoup comme ça, a priori, mais croyez-moi, ça va vite! Ma femme et moi étions chez un ami le week-end dernier, un fana (un amateur) du Web qui passe plus de dix heures par semaine à explorer la toile. Je préfère ne pas savoir à combien s'élèvent ses factures de téléphone! Il nous a fait une petite démonstration. Nous avons fait un tour du Louvre, puis nous sommes allés de site en site pendant une bonne heure. Je dois dire que nous étions fascinés.
David Amar:	Oui, c'est plus intéressant que la télévision! Est-ce que vous avez remarqué qu'il y a beaucoup de sites français qui sont bilingues? Certains sont même entièrement en anglais.
Le responsable:	Oui, cela nous a choqués. Ma femme parle couramment l'espagnol et l'allemand mais elle n'est pas très à l'aise en anglais. Alors cela l'a énervée. Bon, je me sauve.
David Amar:	Au revoir, Monsieur, et bon week-end!
Le responsable:	Oui, merci!

*O*bservation culturelle

Rapports entre patrons et employés

En France, les rapports entre patrons et employés restent généralement assez distants et sont plus formels qu'aux Etats-Unis. Même entre collègues, il n'est pas rare de s'appeler "Monsieur" et "Madame" et de se dire "vous" même si on travaille ensemble depuis des années.

E. Avez-vous compris? Répondez aux questions suivantes.

1. Qu'est-ce qui montre que cette conversation reste assez formelle? Citez plusieurs éléments.

continued on page 113

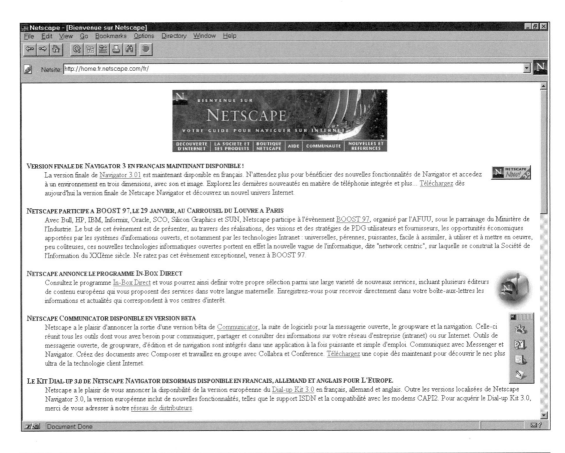

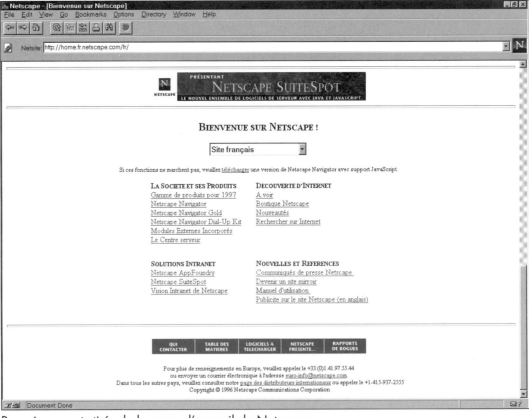

Renseignements tirés de la page d'accueil de Netscape.

continued from page 111

2. Il s'agit d'une conversation formelle; pourtant il y a quelques éléments personnels. Lesquels?

3. A votre avis, la facture de téléphone de l'ami du responsable est-elle élevée ou non? Expliquez.

4. Qu'est-ce qui a fasciné le responsable et sa femme?

5. Qu'est-ce qui a irrité la femme du responsable?

6. Comment est-ce que vous réagiriez si les sites des entreprises américaines installées aux Etats-Unis n'étaient pas en anglais mais entièrement dans une langue étrangère, en japonais ou en espagnol, par exemple?

F. Synonymes! Les termes de la colonne A sont tirés du dialogue. Faites correspondre chacun d'entre eux avec un mot ou groupe de mots de la colonne B.

> ➤ Note words or expressions that might be of use for *Mot de passe.*

A	*B*
feuilleter	simple
informatique	une entrée
génial	extraordinaire
rebuter	ce qui touche aux ordinateurs
un coup de maître	une action remarquable
un accès	lire rapidement
facile	décourager

G. A la recherche d'éléments précis! Après avoir lu attentivement le dialogue, complétez les phrases suivantes en cochant les réponses qui vous paraissent correctes. Attention, il peut y avoir plusieurs bonnes réponses correctes.

1. Cette conversation a lieu
   a. dans le bureau de Monsieur Amar.
   b. dans la rue.
   c. à la porte de la banque.
   d. dans le parking.
   e. chez le directeur.
   f. à un des guichets de la banque.

2. Ce dialogue est
   a. formel mais amical.
   b. froid mais poli.
   c. détendu et familier.
   d. tendu et sec.

3. David Amar
   a. a un abonnement au magazine *Time.*
   b. est allé aux Etats-Unis.
   c. a une sœur qui étudie la gestion.
   d. s'intéresse au réseau Internet.

continued on page 114

continued from page 113

    e. pense qu'un accès facile à l'Internet est improbable.

    f. va acheter la nouvelle version de *Windows.*

    g. va s'abonner à AOL *(America On Line).*

4. Le responsable de l'agence du Crédit Agricole

    a. s'intéresse à l'informatique.

    b. a des enfants.

    c. s'intéresse à ce qui se passe aux Etats-Unis.

    d. a un ordinateur à la maison.

    e. utilise le réseau Internet.

    f. comprend l'anglais.

    g. travaille pour une banque américaine.

    h. pense que le réseau Internet a un grand avenir dans le domaine des finances.

5. D'après ce dialogue, Bill Gates

    a. est abonné au magazine *Time.*

    b. s'intéresse au réseau Internet.

    c. va sortir une nouvelle version du logiciel *Windows.*

    d. veut introduire l'Internet sur le marché français.

    e. a déjà pris contrôle de l'Internet.

6. D'après le responsable,

    a. Bill Gates ne réussira sans doute pas ce qu'il est en train d'entreprendre.

    b. Bill Gates se fait des illusions sur l'avenir de l'Internet.

    c. Bill Gates veut rentabiliser le réseau Internet.

    d. Bill Gates veut acheter plusieurs banques.

7. Le responsable s'intéresse au réseau Internet

    a. parce que sa fille l'utilise à l'université.

    b. parce que ce réseau va jouer un rôle important dans le monde des finances.

    c. parce que sa banque est branchée sur ce réseau.

    d. parce qu'il a investi dans ce réseau.

8. Le Crédit Mutuel de Bretagne a

    a. ouvert un service bancaire en technologie Internet.

    b. multiplié ses services Minitel.

    c. suivi l'initiative des autres banques en proposant un service bancaire par l'intermédiaire d'Internet.

    d. annoncé son intention de proposer un service bancaire sur Internet.

HSG

➤ Study the verbs *dire* and *recevoir* in your *HSG* and complete Exercises D–F after studying the *Encadrés et aperçus* of Module II.

H. A vous de jouer! Mettez-vous à trois et imaginez que vous êtes le responsable de l'agence, sa femme et l'ami passionné de l'Internet. Cet ami vous donne une démonstration et vous explique ce qu'il fait. Qu'allez-vous explorer sur le Web et quelles remarques ferez-vous?

Lecture 1

Internet: Mode d'emploi

I. Activité de pré-lecture. Répondez aux questions suivantes.

  1. Que savez-vous d'Internet?

  2. Avez-vous un numéro de courrier électronique et utilisez-vous une messagerie ou malle électronique? Précisez.

  3. Expliquez le mot «réseau».

  4. Donnez plusieurs exemples de réseaux. Dans quels domaines en dehors de l'informatique est-ce qu'on peut parler de réseau?

➤ Practice saying your e-mail address aloud several times in French. Take note of the following symbols and their pronunciation:
- point /pwɛ̃/
- : deux points /døpwɛ̃/
- @ arrobas /aRobas/
- / barre oblique /baRoblik/ (or slash /slaʃ/)

Internet: Mode d'emploi

Que désigne et que signifie Internet?

Internet n'est en fait rien d'autre qu'un gigantesque réseau informatique ou, pour être plus précis, un réseau reliant entre eux tous les réseaux de la planète: réseaux d'universités, réseaux d'entreprises, réseaux de la NASA, du Pentagone et des bibliothèques nationales, ou réseaux de deux ordinateurs reliés entre eux par deux copains. C'est d'ailleurs *(moreover)* l'origine de son nom: inter-net, ce qui est entre les réseaux, ce qui les relie. A ce jour, on estime qu'Internet regroupe près de 20.000 réseaux. Plus de 30 millions d'utilisateurs répartis dans près de 50 pays naviguent ainsi sur le Net (dans le jargon Internet: "surfent sur le Net") et ont accès au contenu de millions d'ordinateurs qui communiquent entre eux.

A quoi cela sert-il?

On peut comparer Internet aux échangeurs des fameuses autoroutes de l'information. Le Net, c'est avant tout un gigantesque réseau de communication, d'échange, un espace de loisirs, d'information et de culture et, bien entendu, la plus fabuleuse base de données thématique au monde puisque le réseau vous permettra d'accéder à des milliers de bases interconnectées.

Communiquer avec l'e-mail

La principale utilisation d'Internet concerne le courrier électronique appelé e-mail (abréviation de "electronic mail"). La fonction e-mail vous permet d'écrire et de recevoir des messages sur votre ordinateur, quel que soit l'endroit où se trouvent l'expéditeur et le destinataire. Cela vous rappelle notre bon vieux Minitel? A ceci près que le Minitel est franco-français et ne concerne, schématiquement, que 6 millions d'utilisateurs dispersés sur près de 20.000 codes. Avec l'e-mail, vous avez accès aux boîtes aux lettres de 30 millions d'individus sur le même réseau. De Bill Gates, patron de Microsoft, au président Bill Clinton, en passant par tel chercheur du CNRS, l'écrivain Stephen King, votre ministre de la Culture, ou encore, plus simplement, votre copain qui vit à Sydney, tous sont instantanément accessibles et souvent pour bien moins cher que le prix d'une communication téléphonique.

Tiré de «Internet: Mode d'emploi,» article de Serge D. Grun. *CD Media* N°3, septembre 1994.

J. Premier paragraphe: A la recherche de mots précis! Répondez aux questions suivantes.

  1. Parcourez rapidement le texte qui précède et relevez au moins sept mots qui font référence aux Etats-Unis, soit des noms d'institutions américaines, soit des noms de personnes.

2. Dans le premier paragraphe, il y a trois chiffres. Lesquels? Expliquez à quoi ils correspondent.

3. Trouvez, dans le premier paragraphe, le synonyme des mots suivants.

➤ Note key words and expressions for *Mot de passe*.

a. immense

b. rattachant, joignant

c. du monde

d. de sociétés

e. deux amis

f. on calcule approximativement

g. rassemble

h. vocabulaire, langage particulier à un groupe

K. Deuxième paragraphe: Autrement dit. Lisez les deux définitions suivantes, puis, en vous basant sur le texte, cochez les réponses qui vous paraissent correctes. (Attention! Il y a plus d'une réponse correcte.)

1. Un échangeur d'autoroutes est

a. un ensemble de voies routières qui permet d'aller d'une autoroute à une autre.

b. une machine qui permet de réparer les routes.

c. une sorte de pont qui passe par-dessus l'autoroute.

d. une bretelle qui permet aux automobilistes qui se sont trompés d'autoroute d'aller dans la direction opposée.

e. un ouvrage qui permet d'aller d'une autoroute à une autre sans traverser ou couper les voies.

f. un raccordement entre différentes autoroutes.

2. Le Net permet

a. d'échanger des informations.

b. de recevoir et d'envoyer des messages.

c. de se détendre.

d. de contrôler ceux qui ont un ordinateur.

e. d'empêcher les pirates d'avoir accès à des informations secrètes.

g. d'avoir accès à des informations.

HSG

➤ Study *Les noms* of Module II in your *HSG*. Then, scan «Internet: Mode d'emploi» in order to answer the following questions.
1. Which two nouns ending in -*ier(s)* are masculine?
2. Which noun ending in -*age,* is in the text? M or F?
3. Which five words ending in -*eur(s)* within the text happen to be masculine?
4. Which two professions always used in the masculine form are cited in the excerpts?

Answers:
1. milliers, courrier.
2. message *(m)*.
3. ordinateurs, utilisateurs, échangeurs, expéditeur, chercheur.
4. écrivain, ministre.

L. Troisième paragraphe: Avez-vous compris? Répondez aux questions suivantes.

1. Citez deux points communs entre le Minitel et l'Internet.

2. Quelles sont les deux grandes différences entre le Minitel et l'Internet?

3. Quel est l'avantage de l'Internet selon la dernière phrase du texte?

M. D'autres mots pour le dire. Expliquez les mots suivants dans le contexte traditionnel de la Poste.

1. un expéditeur

2. un destinataire

3. un message

4. une boîte aux lettres

5. le courrier

Lecture 2

L'année de «l'e-cash»

N. Activité de pré-lecture. Répondez aux questions suivantes.

1. Regardez le titre de l'article suivant. Pouvez-vous en deviner le thème?

2. Expliquez le mot «cash» en français.

O. Après lecture rapide. Parcourez rapidement le texte qui suit et relevez les mots qui appartiennent au domaine de l'informatique ainsi que ceux qui ont affaire avec les finances en général. Faites-en deux listes séparées.

L'année de «l'e-cash»

Connaissez-vous «l'e-cash» (prononcez i-cache)? Ce mot qui va devenir à la mode, c'est la nouvelle dénomination de l'argent électronique et vous n'avez pas fini cette année, d'en entendre parler.

Avec la multiplication des réseaux informatiques auxquels vous pouvez accéder, de chez vous, grâce à un micro-ordinateur, les fournisseurs de services se sont avisés de l'existence de ce formidable créneau.

Que vient y faire l'argent? Au moins deux choses; d'abord permettre de payer des commandes passées via l'ordinateur dans les magasins électroniques de ces réseaux. Le plus grand problème actuel consiste d'ailleurs à sécuriser les transactions: un numéro de carte Visa qui s'y balade peut (trop) aisément y être piraté. Ensuite, accéder à des services financiers. La BNP et le CCF ont fait figure, en France, de pionniers et proposent de gérer des comptes et des placements via l'ordinateur.

Tiré du *Figaro économie*. Article de Jean-Michel Courévitch dans la rubrique «Points forts». Lundi 6 février 1995.

P. A la recherche d'éléments précis du texte. Relisez bien le texte ci-dessus pour trouver

1. deux noms de banques françaises.

2. le nom d'une carte de crédit.

3. la traduction de l'expression américaine «e-cash».

4. la prononciation du terme «e-cash».

Q. Avez-vous compris? Répondez aux questions suivantes.

1. Quel est le rapport entre l'informatique et l'argent dans ce texte?

2. Expliquez pourquoi il est difficile de sécuriser les numéros de carte Visa.

3. Qui pourrait vouloir pirater un numéro de carte de crédit et pourquoi?

R. Synonymes. Après avoir bien lu l'article qui précède, faites correspondre les termes de la colonne A qui sont tirés du texte avec les synonymes que nous vous proposons dans la colonne B.

➤ Note words and expressions to study for *Mot de passe*.

A	B
la dénomination	un espace libre
la multiplication	avoir accès à
accéder à	le nom
chez vous	à la maison
se sont avisés de	l'augmentation du nombre
un créneau	ont pris conscience de
actuel	se promener
sécuriser	être volé
se balader	qui existe au moment
être piraté	rendre sûr(e)

Lecture 3

Internet et l'entreprise

S. Activité de pré-lecture. A deux ou trois, répondez aux questions suivantes.

1. A votre avis, en quoi le réseau Internet peut-il ou non aider les entreprises?

2. Faites une liste du type d'entreprises qui pourraient bénéficier du réseau Internet et faites également une liste de quelques exemples d'entreprises pour lesquelles l'Internet ne représente pas un avantage clair.

> **Internet et l'entreprise**
> **Olivier Andrieu et Denis Lafont**
> **Editions Eyrolles**
>
> Enfin un ouvrage qui soulève les bonnes questions, celles que se posent les entreprises. "L'Internet peut-il procurer un avantage concurrentiel?", était déjà le thème d'un mémoire rédigé par Denis Lafont qui a enquêté auprès d'une série de sociétés connectées au Réseau. Aujourd'hui, il transforme l'essai en publiant "Internet et l'Entreprise" avec Olivier Andrieu. Les auteurs se complètent bien pour nous offrir une vision globale, marketing et pratique, de l'outil Internet. Quels sont ses points forts et ses dangers pour l'entreprise? Comment économiser sur sa facture télécom, augmenter sa productivité ou améliorer sa gestion des ressources humaines? Comment développer ses ventes, sa communication externe, la recherche et le développement? L'ouvrage va droit à l'essentiel. Il ne se contente pas de rappeler des généralités du style "l'Internet vous ouvre au marché mondial" ou "le courrier électronique vous permet d'économiser 30 à 40% sur votre facture télécom", mais apporte des réponses concrètes à des questions qui ne le sont pas moins. Les entreprises qui veulent se lancer dans le cyberspace trouveront ici tous les renseignements pratiques pour savoir comment procéder, à qui s'adresser et comment mettre en œuvre une stratégie Internet. L'ouvrage ne fait pas l'impasse sur les définitions de base ni sur la pédagogie du Net. Mais ce n'est pas son principal intérêt; ces informations ont déjà été souvent publiées ailleurs. Conçu comme un guide, sa consultation est aisée. Sur le fond, il est solide. Bien que l'évolution ultra rapide du réseau rende certaines informations partielles ou obsolètes, "Internet et l'Entreprise" n'est pas un livre de plus sur l'Internet.
>
> —JT
>
> @ *Internet Reporter*, article de J. Tournier, N° 5, déc. 95.

> ➤ Circle all of the adjectives in the passage. Which ones clearly let you know the gender of the nouns they modify?

Deux formulaires à remplir.
Tirés du magazine *Informatiques*.

T. Avez-vous compris? Donnez une définition provisoire ou un synonyme des mots suivants.

> ➤ Feel free to use your French-French dictionary to find key words for your definitions.

1. un ouvrage
2. soulever (une question)
3. rédigé
4. globale
5. aller droit à
6. l'essentiel
7. faire l'impasse sur
8. ailleurs
9. aisée

U. A vous de conclure! Lisez bien les questions suivantes et choisissez la réponse qui vous semble correcte parmi les trois qui vous sont proposées.

1. Cet article commence par le mot «enfin». Cela suggère que
   a. le journaliste est irrité.
   b. le journaliste est satisfait et soulagé.
   c. le journaliste est résigné.

2. Quel est le but de cet article?
   a. défendre l'emploi de l'Internet
   b. faciliter l'emploi de l'Internet
   c. présenter un livre sur l'Internet qui vise ou cible les entreprises

3. Que dit le journaliste sur les deux auteurs?

    a. Ils ne connaissent pas assez bien leur sujet.

    b. Ils sont des spécialistes de la pédagogie.

    c. Ils ont des qualités complémentaires.

4. Comment peut-on caractériser le livre en question?

    a. Il est utile et bien fait.

    b. Il n'est pas clair mais il est intéressant.

    c. Il est bien conçu mais difficile.

5. Quelle est la forme du livre?

    a. une série de questions et de réponses

    b. plusieurs chapitres organisés selon le type de l'entreprise

    c. un guide

6. Que dit l'auteur de l'article à propos «des généralités»?

    a. Ce livre présente des généralités mais c'est nécessaire car les entreprises ne savent encore rien sur le réseau Internet.

    b. Ce livre ne donne pas assez de réponses concrètes.

    c. Ce livre va au-delà des généralités et donne des informations précises.

7. Pourquoi est-ce que certaines informations sont incomplètes ou déjà dépassées?

    a. parce que les auteurs n'ont pas fait de recherches suffisantes

    b. parce que le fond du livre n'est pas assez solide

    c. parce que tout évolue extrêmement rapidement dans le domaine de l'Internet

8. *Internet et l'entreprise* n'est pas un livre de plus sur l'Internet. Qu'est-ce que l'auteur de l'article veut dire par là?

    a. Lisez ce livre. Vous ne serez pas déçu(e)!

    b. Si vous avez déjà lu des livres sur l'Internet et l'entreprise, alors vous n'aurez pas de mal à comprendre ce livre-là.

    c. C'est un livre qui ne se différencie pas beaucoup des autres livres écrits sur l'Internet ces derniers temps.

V. A vous de jouer! Mettez-vous à deux. Prenez les commentaires de ce journaliste et retournez-les de façon à dire exactement le contraire de ce qu'il dit. Une personne sera le journaliste négatif et l'autre un des auteurs du livre.

W. De la réflexion à l'écriture. Choisissez un des deux sujets suivants et écrivez un paragraphe d'une dizaine de lignes. N'oubliez pas de faire une petite phrase d'introduction et de conclusion.

    1. Premier sujet: Imaginez que vous devez expliquer ce que c'est que le réseau Internet à un ami francophone qui a entendu parler d'Internet mais ne sait pas vraiment ce que c'est.

    2. Deuxième sujet: Selon l'article 19 de la Déclaration universelle des Droits de l'homme: «Tout individu a droit à la liberté d'opinion et d'expression, ce qui implique le droit de ne pas être inquiété pour ses opinions et celui de chercher, de recevoir et de répandre *(disseminate)*, sans considération de frontières, les informations et les idées par quelque moyen que ce soit.» Expliquez en quoi l'Internet peut contribuer à la liberté d'expression. N'oubliez pas d'aborder également la question de la censure.

Quelques points de repère

Le saviez-vous?

En français, World Wide Web est quelquefois appelé «la toile», mais le plus souvent les Francophones disent «Le Web» ou même «W3» (prononcé *W3* ou *W cube*). Il y a encore beaucoup d'entreprises qui se demandent ce que l'Internet peut leur apporter mais un grand nombre d'entreprises sont convaincues que l'Internet va changer leur stratégie de mercatique *(marketing)* et leurs rapports avec leurs clients. Des dizaines d'entreprises françaises ouvrent un site sur le World Wide Web toutes les semaines. Un nouveau site peut être en cours de création lorsque vous essayez d'y accéder. Certains sites sont présentés en français, quelques-uns en anglais, et d'autres sont bilingues.

Il y a maintenant un serveur sur l'Internet qui a été conçu et réalisé exclusivement pour les étudiants. C'est le Cybermax. Les étudiants pourront consulter 300.000 ouvrages de la bibliothèque virtuelle, réaliser un certain nombre d'opérations pratiques comme réserver une place de spectacle ou consulter des annonces, offrant un emploi ou une formation ou bien discuter avec d'autres cybernautes.

Adresse: http://www.cybermax.fr

L'ardoise!

L'idée de la toile conceptuelle qui permet d'accéder à un grand nombre d'informations de façon non-linéaire est née en 1945. C'est Vannevar Bush, le conseiller scientifique du président américain Franklin Roosevelt qui, le premier, a exprimé la possibilité de créer des machines conceptuelles qui fonctionneraient comme le cerveau humain, c'est-à-dire par associations. Il a utilisé le terme de «web» pour décrire cette toile stockant des connaissances accessibles par une machine.

➤ La page d'accueil de Georgia Tech Lorraine à Metz, France. Version américaine.

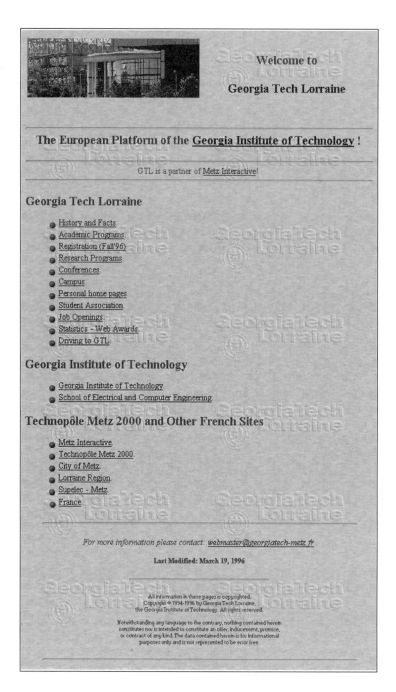

➤ Avoir sa page d'accueil en France toute en anglais n'est plus acceptable et L'Institut Georgia Tech a été obligé de créer une version bilingue.

Les chiffres parlent!

- Le marché français de la micro-informatique n'est pas aussi florissant que le marché allemand ou britannique. En 1994, les Français ont acheté 2,5 fois moins de micro-ordinateurs que les Allemands et 1,5 fois moins que les Britanniques. Le fait que les Français avaient déjà accès au Minitel depuis quelques années explique en partie ce retard.

- Le Web représentait 0,1% du trafic sur l'Internet en mars 1993 et 20% en avril 1995.

Une date importante!

La France a été connectée à l'Internet en 1994.

Un outil qui remplit 36 fonctions c'est quand même mieux que 36 outils n'ayant chacun qu'une fonction.

Djinn®

Et votre micro devient fax, Minitel®, transfert de fichiers.

Et pour répondre plus précisément à vos besoins, chaque modem de la gamme Djinn possède une fonction spécifique pour permettre en plus à votre micro :

- de devenir répondeur-enregistreur téléphonique pour environnement Macintosh
AppleDjinn Pro® 14400 :
1 790 F HT (2 158,74 F TTC)

- d'accéder au 3623 Télétel Vitesse Rapide®
Djinn Flash® 9600 :
990 F HT (1 193,94 F TTC)

- d'accéder au 3601 Kiosque Micro®
Djinn Flash® 14400 :
1 029 F HT (1 240,97 F TTC)

Pour plus d'informations et pour connaître les adresses des revendeurs tapez 3614 FRANCE TELECOM*.

France Telecom

Publicité de France Télécom.

Les entreprises françaises!

Voici l'adresse de quelques entreprises françaises présentes sur le Web.
Perrier: http://www.perrier.com/
Péchiney: http://www.pechiney.fr
Ilog: société francaise du secteur
informatique: http://www.ilog.fr

Pour trouver des sites en français, on peut
taper: http://www.inria.fr/
ou bien: http://wwwFranceNet.fr
ou encore: http://www.iway.fr

Quand le savoir-faire compte

Canada ▪ États-Unis ▪ Europe ▪ Asie-Pacifique

Réflexions sur le travail en équipe

Pour qu'un groupe fonctionne bien, il faut savoir qu'à n'importe quel moment pour améliorer ses résultats, il faut améliorer son système.

Lexique

une adresse: En courrier électronique, **une adresse** est un ensemble de chiffres, de lettres et de symboles qui permettent de contacter un utilisateur qui a un compte. *Exemple:*
catherine.marin@modlangs.gatech.edu

> En Europe, chaque **adresse** électronique finit par deux lettres qui identifient le pays dans lequel l'utilisateur a son compte. En France, ces deux lettres sont «fr».

browser ou **surfer: Browser** ou **surfer,** c'est aller de serveur en serveur sur le Web. Ce verbe vient du verbe anglais «to browse» qui signifie feuilleter ou parcourir (un texte). L'avantage de ce moyen de voyager dans l'espace informationnel est qu'il n'est pas linéaire.

> C'est Mathilde qui m'a appris à **surfer** sur le net. Je passe d'un site à l'autre. C'est facile, il suffit de cliquer sur ce qui est bleu pour avoir accès à l'information stockée.

un cyber-café: Un **cyber-café,** c'est un café où il y a un coin aménagé avec quelques ordinateurs à partir desquels, pour une certaine somme d'argent, on peut avoir accès au réseau Internet.

> Pour avoir la liste des **cyber-cafés** du monde entier on peut taper:
> http://www.flightpath.com/Brento/InternetCafes.HTLM
> Malheureusement, cette liste n'est pas complète!

➤ Read // as *deux barres obliques* /døbaRoblik/ (or deux slashes /døslaʃ/).

un emoticon: Un **emoticon** est un groupe de caractères qui permettent d'exprimer par écrit, de façon symbolique certaines réactions ou émotions et donc les communiquer ainsi par l'intermédiaire du réseau.
Par exemple:

(:-)	signifie un sourire
(:-(	signifie qu'on est triste
(:-D	signifie qu'on rit aux éclats
(:-/	signifie qu'on est déçu

— David, lis ce message que je viens de recevoir de Noémie. Est-ce que tu connais cet **emoticon?**
<:-o
— C'est le symbole qu'on emploie quand on est surpris, je crois.

un Internaute: Un **Internaute** est une personne qui se sert du réseau Internet et qui surfe sur le World Wide Web.

> Pour pouvoir surfer sur le réseau Internet, **les Internautes** consacrent moins de temps à la télévision.

un logiciel de navigation: **Un logiciel de navigation** est un logiciel qui permet d'entrer dans le réseau du World Wide Web, de trouver les différents sites qui existent et d'y accéder. On a besoin d'un tel programme pour pouvoir consulter les pages offertes sur le Web.

—Qu'est-ce que tu utilises comme **logiciel de navigation** sur le Web?
—En général, j'utilise Netscape.

un login: **Un login** est un identificatif qui permet à une machine de reconnaître qui veut se connecter.

Tiens, j'obtiens un message qui me dit que mon **login** n'est pas correct. Je recommence. J'ai peut-être tapé un espace de trop. Ah, voilà, ça marche.

un mot-clé: **Un mot-clé** est un mot important et représentatif qui peut servir d'outil de recherche.

J'ai fait une recherche sur ordinateur cet après-midi à partir d'une liste de **mots-clés** que j'avais constituée avec mon conseiller.

la netiquette: Le mot «netiquette» combine les deux mots «net» (qui signifie «réseau» en anglais) et «étiquette». **La netiquette,** c'est l'étiquette du réseau, c'est-à-dire un certain nombre de règles de savoir-vivre, un code de politesse, en usage sur tous les réseaux.

Ah, je vois que **la netiquette** n'est pas ton fort! Non, n'utilise pas de majuscules dans le texte de ton message car cela veut dire que tu cries et c'est impoli sur le réseau!

un parc d'ordinateurs: **Un parc d'ordinateurs** est l'ensemble des ordinateurs dont une entreprise ou un pays dispose.

J'ai lu récemment qu'au Québec, **le parc d'ordinateurs** serait de 1.7 million dont 400.000 dans les foyers et le parc de lecteurs de CD-ROM serait de 200.000. C'est un marché qui devrait intéresser les éditeurs français.

rebondir: Lorsqu'un message **rebondit,** c'est qu'il ne passe pas. L'envoi n'a pas réussi et le message revient à son point de départ. Cela arrive par exemple lorsqu'on a fait une faute dans l'orthographe d'une adresse électronique.

Je ne sais pas pourquoi le message que j'ai envoyé à Jean-Pierre **a rebondi** car je suis absolument sûre de l'adresse.

un site: **Un site,** c'est une sorte d'endroit virtuel sur le réseau d'Internet sur lequel on peut ouvrir une page et proposer un certain nombre d'informations aux usagers du réseau.

En ce moment, il y a des dizaines d'entreprises et de particuliers qui ouvrent **un site** sur Internet tous les jours.

le téléchargement: On parle de **téléchargement** quand on charge un logiciel à distance, à partir du réseau. On installe donc ce logiciel sur son micro-ordinateur en passant directement par le réseau et non à partir d'une disquette.

Les logiciels qui permettent de surfer sur l'Internet sont disponibles en **téléchargement** sur l'Internet.

➤ Think of three situations where this expression might be used. Then discuss them with your study partner.

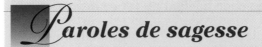

Paroles de sagesse

Il faut battre le fer quand il est chaud.

Expression écrite

Deuxième aperçu de l'emploi de «connaître» et de «savoir»

Dans cette section, vous allez réviser les expressions courantes étudiées à la page 105. Vous allez aussi reconnaître la distinction entre les verbes «connaître» et «savoir». Lisez le texte suivant en faisant bien attention aux mots que vous avez déjà étudiés aux pages 105–106 en caractères gras *(in bold print)*.

Mes parents et le courrier électronique

*Mes parents **savaient** bien que j'avais une adresse de courrier électronique mais ils ne comprenaient pas à quoi cela correspondait exactement. **J'avais beau** essayer de leur expliquer; ils ne voyaient pas l'avantage par rapport au fax, par exemple. **Il y avait** longtemps que je voulais leur faire une petite démonstration et lors de leur dernière visite je leur ai demandé s'ils **connaissaient** des gens qui se servaient de l'e-mail. Ils m'ont dit qu'ils ne **connaissaient** personne puis ma mère s'est souvenue que sa cousine Louise lui avait donné sa nouvelle carte de visite et qu'elle avait remarqué une adresse électronique dessus. Bref, je ne **savais** pas qu'on pouvait changer d'avis aussi rapidement. Ils sont arrivés sceptiques et sont repartis convaincus que le courrier électronique était une invention géniale.*

BANQUE NATIONALE

➤ Note that the *s* is pronounced on the second *tous* since it is a pronoun.

X. A vous de traduire! Après avoir étudié les distinctions entre les deux verbes «connaître» et «savoir», traduisez les phrases suivantes.

Connaître

Cette directrice de banque **connaît**-elle tous ses employés? Oui, elle les **connaît** tous.

Does this/that bank president know all her employees? Yes, she knows them all.

Connaissez-vous une banque qui accepte les chèques étrangers?

_____
_____

Je **connais** cette chanson.

I know (recognize) this/that song.

Elle **connaît** le nouveau PDG de cette entreprise mais ne l'ayant rencontré qu'une seule fois dans son bureau, elle n'est pas sûre de pouvoir le **reconnaître** ailleurs.

_____
_____
_____
_____
_____

Savoir

Sais-tu où se trouve la banque la
plus proche? Non je ne **sais** pas.

_____
_____

Nous ne **savons** pas pourquoi cet
ordinateur ne fonctionne pas.

_____
_____

Je **sais** comment transférer un
fichier du disque dur à une
disquette.

_____
_____
_____

L'employé de banque **sait** qu'il faut
vérifier l'identité du client avant de
lui donner accès à son compte.

_____
_____
_____

Savez-vous où se trouve la BNP?

_____

Je **sais** imprimer un document
maintenant. Il faut tout simplement
que je clique sur la bonne icône.

_____
_____
_____

Je **sais** cette chanson (= Je la
connais par cœur).

*I know this/that song (= I know it by
heart).*

Y. A vos plumes! Après avoir lu rapidement le passage qui précède ainsi
que les traductions, écrivez un paragraphe au futur ou au passé sur votre
première expérience sur Internet.

Avant de commencer le Module suivant, allons un peu plus loin avec
«En guise de clôture»!

MODULE *II*

En guise de clôture:
Allons un peu plus loin!

Texte littéraire

Et la lune battait son plein

A. Activité de pré-lecture. En groupes de deux, suivez les directives ci-dessous.

1. Cherchez les mots suivants dans un dictionnaire français-français et écrivez vous-même une phrase avec chacun d'entre eux.
   - l'argile
   - le sur mesure
   - un golem
   - un croquis

2. Expliquez les mots suivants, en français, à votre voisin(e).
   - un engouement
   - le doigté
   - un pseudonyme
   - un savant
   - une muse
   - quotidiennement
   - inverser
   - parapher
   - la matière grise
   - une pionnière

3. Répondez aux questions suivantes à deux ou trois.
   a. Quelle est l'importance du miroir dans le conte de fées «Blanche-Neige»?

b. Racontez le conte «Blanche-Neige» avec vos propres mots.

c. Pourquoi est-ce qu'un auteur choisit de signer son travail avec un pseudonyme? Essayez de trouver plusieurs raisons possibles.

d. Si vous deviez choisir un pseudonyme, lequel prendriez-vous et pourquoi?

B. Première lecture. Lisez le texte suivant. Au cours de cette première lecture, relevez au moins dix mots qui appartiennent au domaine de l'informatique.

Et la lune battait son plein

L'œil cathodique de son Mec+Ultra lui renvoya un reflet positif. Elle pouvait s'y fier. Nul n'était plus exigeant que ce miroir grisé qui reflétait, en caractères New York standard 12 points, le condensé bien carré de ses étonnements et de ses engouements. Elle pouvait juger, du premier regard, de l'efficacité des articles que d'un doigté léger elle confiait quotidiennement à son clavier. Et si l'effet n'était pas celui escompté, elle triturait ses textes jusqu'à ce que son vis-à-vis informatique affichât en toutes lettres à l'écran sa pleine satisfaction. La mémoire vive de son fidélisme ne la trahissait jamais. Mieux que le miroir magique de la reine de Blanche-Neige, ce très personnel computer était son golem. Statuette, non point d'argile, mais de silicium, qui portait, inscrit au front le mot *Vérité*.

Une dernière fois, elle fit défiler sur la surface lumineuse de son inséparable, son dernier reportage. L'aventure singulière d'un grand couturier parisien qui venait d'ouvrir la première boutique de sur mesure computorisé.

... Pas un seul vêtement dans son magasin, relut-elle. *Juste un cahier de croquis et une pile de coupons.*

D'une vive manipulation de la souris et des touches, elle effaça un mot, en rajouta un autre, déplaça une phrase, inversa un paragraphe.

Une fois le modèle et le tissu choisis, enchaîna-t-elle, *un appareil vous photographie sur toutes vos coutures, un microprocesseur mémorise votre morphologie, et un laser coupe l'étoffe à vos exactes mesures.* [...]

Plus que sa signature à taper, en bas et à droite de son texte. *Ada Azerty*

Son pseudo Azerty, elle l'avait trouvé en quelques secondes, en appuyant sur les cinq premières touches du clavier français de son nouveau Mec+Ultra. Si elle était restée en Californie, elle aurait continué à signer Qwerty, sur les caractères anglo-saxons de son ancien micro-ordinateur. Il était, bien entendu, hors de question qu'elle paraphât ses articles Grand-Jean, du nom rennais de son savant de père, qu'une chasse aux cerveaux avait transplanté, il y a quelques vingt-cinq ans, à Palo Alto, dans cette célèbre vallée entre San Francisco et San Jose, la plus fertile au monde en ces prisées matières grises dont on fait les puces, cortex et silicium. Exclu également qu'elle signât das Luzes, du nom carioca de sa sambiste de mère qui, pour elle et avec elle, embryon lové dans son ventre mulato, n'avait dansé qu'un seul carnaval.

Son nom de baptême Ada, en revanche, elle avait tenu à le garder. Pour cause. Elle portait le même prénom que la muse de l'informatique, Lady Ada Byron, comtesse de Lovelace, fille du poète Lord Byron et égérie du savant Charles Babbage, inventeur de la machine à calculer. Somptueux héritage. Le choix de son père n'était certes pas innocent. Il lui avait programmé une destinée à l'image de cette belle pionnière du XIXe siècle, première computer-woman et patronne des informaticiens. L'année de ses vingt ans, papa Grand-Jean lui avait offert, singulier cadeau d'anniversaire, le privilège de porter le même nom que le dernier-né des langages informatiques qu'il avait contribué à mettre au point. Ada en était fière. Dans son curriculum vitae, à la rubrique *Langues pratiquées,* elle inscrivait toujours, non sans une pointe de provocation:

Français, anglais, brésilien et... Ada.

Mariella Righini, *Et la lune battait son plein.* Editions Grasset & Fasquelle, 1985.

C. Choix multiple. Lisez bien les questions suivantes et cochez la réponse qui vous paraît correcte.

1. Qui est Ada Azerty?
   a. la muse d'un poète du XIXe siècle
   b. une spécialiste en informatique
   c. une jeune femme écrivain

2. Que veut dire «New York standard 12 points»?
   a. C'est un type de lettres utilisé par Ada Azerty.
   b. C'est le score d'un match de basket à New York.
   c. C'est le titre de l'article écrit par Ada Azerty.

3. Quel est le sujet de l'article dont il est question?
   a. la vie d'une jeune femme passionnée d'informatique
   b. le travail d'un savant français en Californie
   c. le travail d'un grand couturier qui se sert d'un ordinateur

4. Ada Azerty, c'est
   a. un pseudonyme.
   b. le vrai nom de l'écrivain en question.
   c. le nom de la mère de l'écrivain.

5. Un nom de baptême, c'est
   a. un pseudonyme.
   b. un nom de famille.
   c. un prénom.

6. Qui était le père d'Ada Azerty?
   a. un Américain spécialiste en informatique
   b. un Français qui travaillait aux Etats-Unis
   c. un poète anglais

7. Un Mec+Ultra, c'est
   a. un ordinateur.
   b. un logiciel.
   c. un informaticien.

D. Avez-vous compris? Répondez aux questions suivantes.

1. Qu'apprenez-vous sur la vie de la narratrice?
   Nom:
   Prénom:
   Pseudonyme:
   Nom de famille de la mère:
   Pays de résidence:
   Profession:
   Langues parlées:

2. Comment Ada a-t-elle choisi le nom Azerty?

3. Pourquoi Ada n'a-t-elle pas voulu garder le nom de famille de son père?

4. Quelle relation Ada a-t-elle avec son ordinateur?

Suggestions, conseils: Facteurs à considérer au travail

Considérez la valeur de chacun des éléments suivants dans le domaine du travail. Indiquez si une caractéristique (n')est...

0 (pas importante) ⎯⎯⎯⎯⎯⎯→ **10 (absolument essentielle)**

_____ 1. être traité(e) avec respect

_____ 2. être reconnu(e) pour la qualité de son travail

_____ 3. avoir un bon salaire

_____ 4. faire un travail intéressant

_____ 5. avoir la possibilité d'améliorer sa formation

_____ 6. bien aimer ses collègues

_____ 7. travailler pour des individus qui prennent l'opinion et les suggestions des autres en considération

_____ 8. avoir la liberté de travailler seul(e)

_____ 9. avoir la possibilité de travailler en équipe

_____ 10. avoir la possibilité d'influencer les autres

_____ 11. avoir un travail qui ait un impact sur la société

_____ 12. avoir la satisfaction de voir les résultats de son travail

_____ 13. travailler pour des supérieurs hiérarchiques efficaces

_____ 14. avoir une certaine sécurité d'emploi

_____ 15. avoir beaucoup d'avantages sociaux dont de longs congés annuels

_____ 16. avoir un emploi qui exige constamment de se surpasser

_____ 17. avoir le sentiment d'être bien informé(e) et fonctionner dans une équipe qui communique bien

_____ **18.** être mis(e) au courant des décisions cruciales au fonctionnement de l'équipe

_____ **19.** ?

_____ **20.** ?

E. A vos plumes! Après avoir réfléchi aux cinq facteurs de la liste précédente qui sont les plus importants pour vous, écrivez un petit paragraphe dans lequel vous élaborerez pourquoi ils le sont.

➤ With your study partner, practice these 18 examples in complete sentences using an impersonal expression plus *de*. **Modèle:** *Il est absolument essentiel (très important, indispensable, crucial, peu important (etc.) d'être traité(e) avec respect.* Then, think up at least two other factors to consider and rank them as well.

Récapitulons!

Quelques aide-mémoire

1. Avec un ordinateur, on peut entre autres
- créer un document.
- utiliser un logiciel, un traitement de texte, par exemple.
- programmer.
- sauvegarder un document ou un texte.
- faire des calculs.
- utiliser des banques de données.
- formater un document.
- créer un en-tête.
- faire des graphiques.
- avoir accès au réseau Internet par l'intermédiaire d'un modem.
- remplir sa feuille d'impôts.
- envoyer un message électronique.
- consulter son emploi du temps.
- regarder l'heure qu'il est.

Un ordinateur en marche au bureau.

2. Lorsqu'on a des problèmes d'ordinateur, on peut

- essayer de faire redémarrer la machine.
- vérifier si l'ordinateur est bien branché.
- regarder si toutes les parties du matériel sont bien connectées entre elles.
- consulter le manuel pour voir si un problème similaire y est décrit.
- envoyer le disque dur ou la partie qui pose problème en réparation.
- regarder si l'ordinateur est encore sous garantie.
- appeler le numéro vert de la maison mère ou du distributeur.
- téléphoner à un(e) ami(e) qui est plus fort(e) que vous en informatique.
- acheter un nouvel ordinateur.

3. Le réseau Internet permet

- d'envoyer des messages électroniques.
- de consulter des banques de données situées un peu partout dans le monde.
- de recevoir des informations.
- de communiquer rapidement et à bon marché avec tous ceux qui sont connectés au réseau où qu'ils soient.
- de faire un certain nombre d'opérations financières.
- d'être au courant de ce que les autres font.
- d'acheter certains produits.
- de browser le Web.
- de trouver l'adresse d'un ami qui travaille dans une université ou dans une grande entreprise.
- de faire de la publicité.
- d'envoyer un manuscrit à son éditeur.
- de se faire connaître.
- de vendre des produits.

Dans le Module III, vous allez vous pencher sur le monde du travail en vous concentrant d'abord sur les demandes et les offres d'emploi.

Module **III**

Demandes et offres d'emploi

7 Chercher un emploi

8 Recruter du personnel

9 L'entretien d'embauche

Ouverture

L'enseigne d'une Agence
Nationale Pour l'Emploi.

Quelques quotidiens
à un kiosque de la
gare de Nantes.

Le bureau d'une secrétaire d'une
agence de travail temporaire.

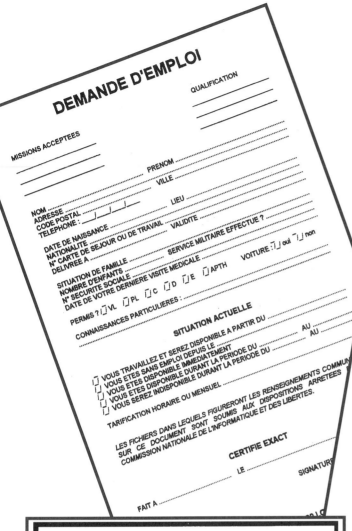

ETAT CIVIL

CURRICULUM VITAE.

Nom:
Prénom: GONZALES-MARTINEZ
Né le: Luis Carlos
à: 07/09/67
Adresse: Madrid, Espagne
Téléphone: 3, rue Chapon, 75003 Paris
Nationalité: 1 47 42 87 52
Célibataire   Espagnole
Libéré du service militaire

DIPLOMES.

Formation actuelle: préparation de l'examen d'entrée du C.F.P.A
(Institut d'études judiciaires Henri Motulsky-Paris X)

11/93   D.E.S.S Droit Européen des Affaires
         (Université Paris V-René Descartes)

09/92   MAITRISE Droit privé, mention Droit des Affaires
         (Université Paris X-Nanterre)

06/92   Diplôme d'Université D'ETUDES JURIDIQUES APPLIQUEES
         DE DEUXIEME CYCLE, mention DROIT ESPAGNOL
         (Université Paris X, en partenariat avec l'Université
         Carlos III de Madrid)

09/91   LICENCE Droit (Université Paris X)

06/90   D.E.U.G mention: Droit, spécialisation Espagnol
         (Université Paris X)

06/88   BACCALAUREAT Série B (économique)
         mention assez bien

LANGUE.

ESPAGNOL: Lu, écrit, parlé

EXPERIENCES PROFESSIONNELLES.

- Stagiaire à la S.C.P BORE-XAVIER, Avocats au Conseil d'Etat
  et à la Cour de Cassation. (06-07/93, dans le cadre des
  modalités d'obtention du D.E.S.S)
- Gardien-remplaçant en période estivale
  (Jean-marc Levet S.A, 1,rue Rembrandt, 75008)
  été de 1987 à 1993
- Agent de surveillance
  (S.E.V.I.P, 12,rue du Mont Thabor, 75001)
  du 18/11/89 au 26/03/90

Chercher un emploi

Le Module III est axé sur les demandes et offres d'emploi. Il s'ouvre sur le thème «chercher un emploi». A partir d'une conversation entre Cyril et Florine, une jeune fille qui est en train d'écrire son CV, vous allez commencer à réfléchir à ce qui constitue un bon CV. Dans ce premier dossier du Module III, vous trouverez également plusieurs CV et lettres de motivation authentiques. En France, les lettres de motivation et les lettres commerciales d'une manière générale diffèrent légèrement des lettres américaines, en particulier dans les formules de politesse qui servent de clôture. Vous travaillerez donc sur la rédaction *(editing, wording)* de telles lettres et sur la compréhension des petites annonces offrant des emplois. Le dernier texte illustrera le thème des débouchés pour ceux, jeunes et moins jeunes, qui cherchent un emploi mais n'ont pas de diplôme.

Activité d'introduction

Le thème de l'emploi

A. A la recherche d'un emploi. A deux ou trois, réfléchissez aux questions suivantes.

> 1. Vous cherchez un emploi. Que faites-vous? Cochez les réponses qui vous paraissent plausibles.
>   - Je regarde les petites annonces dans le journal.
>   - Je m'inscris dans un bureau de travail intérimaire.
>   - Je me présente au bureau du personnel des entreprises qui m'intéressent et leur laisse mon curriculum vitae.
>   - Je reste à la maison et j'attends que quelqu'un me téléphone.
>   - J'envoie des lettres de demande d'emploi.
> 2. Notez au moins trois autres choses que vous pouvez faire.
> 3. Faites la liste de quatre de vos points forts.
> 4. Faites la liste de quatre de vos points faibles.

➤ Donnez un synonyme d'«un bureau de travail intérimaire».

La secrétaire d'une agence de travail temporaire.

Les mots pour le dire

Vocabulaire de base

VERBES

décrocher (un entretien)	*to get, land an interview*
donner sa démission	*to resign*
embaucher	*to hire*
licencier	*to fire*
mettre à la porte	*to get rid of, fire*
pourvoir	*to provide, see to*
recruter	*to recruit*
rémunérer	*to remunerate*
renvoyer	*to dismiss, postpone*
signer	*to sign*
solliciter	*to solicit*

NOMS

l'approche *(f)* **directe**	*direct approach*
les attentes *(f)*	*expectations*
le but	*aim, goal*
un cadre	*middle-level or upper-level staff person, executive*
un candidat	*candidate*
une candidature	*application (for work)*
une candidature spontanée	*drop-in or stop-by application*
une carrière	*career*
un chasseur de têtes	*headhunter*
un contrat	*contract*
un curriculum vitae, un C.V. ou CV	*C.V., résumé*
un diplôme	*diploma*
un domaine de spécialisation	*major*

continued on page 140

continued from page 139

un dossier	*dossier, file*
un emploi	*job*
un entretien d'embauche	*job interview*
un finaliste	*finalist*
la gestion	*management*
une lettre de motivation	*cover letter*
un métier	*trade, business, calling, craft*
un poste	*position, job*
une profession	*profession*
une recommandation	*recommendation*
des références (f)	*references*
un rendez-vous	*appointment*
un salaire	*salary*

ADJECTIFS

agressif(ve)	*aggressive*
chronologique	*chronological*
ciblé(e)	*targeted*
clair(e)	*clear*
concis(e)	*concise*
courageux(se)	*courageous*
manuscrit(e)	*handwritten*
paresseux(se)	*lazy*
potentiel(le)	*potential*
précis(e)	*precise*
recherché(e)	*in great demand*
réciproque	*reciprocal*
spécifique	*specific*

ADVERBES

absolument	*absolutely*
attentivement	*carefully*
carrément	*squarely, bluntly, straight out*
franchement	*frankly*

➤ Note words or expressions that might be useful for *Mot de passe.*

B. Définitions provisoires à terminer. Complétez les phrases suivantes.

1. Quand une entreprise offre des emplois, qu'elle engage du personnel, on dit qu'elle _____.

2. Quand une entreprise ne peut pas garder un ou plusieurs employés, on dit qu'elle doit les renvoyer ou les _____.

3. En période de crise économique, il est difficile de trouver du travail. Un synonyme d'obtenir un emploi est _____ un emploi.

4. Lorsqu'on trouve un travail, l'entreprise propose un contrat écrit. Le candidat doit lire ce contrat puis le _____ s'il est d'accord avec les termes proposés.

5. Lorsqu'on cherche un emploi, on a une assez bonne idée du genre de travail qu'on aimerait faire et des conditions dans lesquelles on aimerait travailler, comme le salaire et les avantages sociaux liés au poste souhaité. L'employeur potentiel peut demander au candidat quelles sont ses _____, ce qui est une manière de demander ce qu'il désire.

6. Lorsqu'un chasseur de têtes contacte de lui-même une personne pour lui parler d'un poste qui pourrait l'intéresser sans que cette personne n'ait manifesté d'intérêt pour ce poste, on caractérise la méthode de ce chasseur de têtes d'_____.

C. Définitions provisoires à créer. Par groupes de deux, écrivez une définition provisoire des mots suivants.

1. embaucher
2. un candidat
3. un finaliste

4. un cadre
5. concis

HSG

➤ Do the *Photos et descriptions* section and complete Exercises A–C of Module III in your *HSG*.

Dialogue

Florine Guimaux rédige son curriculum vitae!

D. Activité de pré-lecture. Mettez-vous à deux ou à trois et répondez aux questions suivantes.

➤ Be ready to report your findings back to the class.

1. Vous faites votre CV pour la première fois. A qui vous adressez-vous pour savoir comment faire un CV et pourquoi?
2. Vous désirez faire une demande d'emploi. A qui montrez-vous votre CV et votre lettre de motivation avant de les envoyer? Pourquoi?

E. Première impression. Lisez rapidement le dialogue qui suit et devinez qui est Cyril par rapport à Florine. Pourquoi s'adresse-t-elle à lui? A-t-elle raison selon vous de lui demander conseil?

Florine Guimaux rédige son curriculum vitae!

Florine cherche un emploi. Elle vient de terminer son CV et le montre à Cyril. Voici leur conversation.

Florine: Cyril, tu as une minute? Est-ce que tu pourrais lire mon curriculum vitae et me dire ce que tu en penses?

Cyril: Ouais, vas-y. Donne-le-moi tout de suite. Tu n'as pas mis que tu as eu la mention «bien» au bac?

Florine: J'ai hésité et j'ai eu peur de paraître arrogante.

Cyril: Mais non, t'es folle. Au contraire, il faut mettre tout ce qui te distingue de la masse. N'oublie pas que ton CV est le premier contact entre l'entreprise et toi. Il faut donner envie à l'employeur potentiel de t'inviter pour un entretien d'embauche. C'est ça le but. Tu n'as pas mis non plus que tu as travaillé au Syndicat d'Initiative l'été dernier.

Florine: Non, parce qu'au fond, ce boulot-là n'avait rien à voir avec mon domaine de spécialisation.

Cyril: Peut-être, mais ça montre que tu n'as pas passé tous tes étés à ne rien faire. Ça montre que tu n'es pas paresseuse, que tu as de l'énergie.

Florine: Alors, tu crois que je devrais aussi ajouter que j'ai été monitrice à la Maison des Jeunes en 1994 et 1995, même si je n'étais pas rémunérée?

Cyril: Ben oui, pour la même raison. Et tu devrais préciser en quelques mots de quoi tu étais chargée. Ce sont tous ces détails spécifiques qui permettent de déterminer les compétences réelles et personnelles du candidat. Il faut aussi mettre que tu sais te servir d'un ordinateur. Et puis, entre parenthèses, tu fais la liste des traitements de texte et autres programmes que tu maîtrises.

Florine: Et qu'est-ce que tu penses de ma photo?

Cyril: T'en as pas une autre? C'est bien de sourire, mais là, tu ris... carrément. Ça ne fait quand même pas très sérieux. Mais pourquoi tu veux ajouter ta photo?

Florine: Certaines boîtes la demandent. Je la mettrai pas lorsque c'est pas exigé. Pour le reste, ça va?

Cyril: Une minute... y a une faute de frappe... là, regarde, tu as écrit «objetif» au lieu d'«objectif», et puis là, il y a une faute d'orthographe. Il y a deux «n» dans «professionnel», pas un!

Florine: Heureusement que tu l'as vue. Les profs nous ont assez répété qu'il suffit d'une faute d'orthographe pour qu'un dossier soit écarté.

Cyril: Il ne faut rien exagérer mais c'est vrai que ça fait mauvaise impression! En tête du CV, là, il est inutile de préciser chaque indication. Nom, prénom, adresse. Ça alourdit la présentation pour rien. Ecris:

GUIMAUX, Florine, Anne, Martine,
Née le 7 mai 1970
Célibataire
14 bis, rue du Général Buat, etc.

Ça suffit. Place-le au milieu de la page. Ça ressort mieux.

Florine: Et l'ordre de mes expériences professionnelles? Je les ai mises dans l'ordre chronologique évidemment.

Cyril: Oui, mais il est préférable de commencer avec les derniers parce que les employeurs sont plus intéressés par ce que tu viens de faire. C'est pas obligatoire mais je trouve que l'ordre chronologique inverse, c'est plus clair.

Florine: J'avais pensé opter pour une présentation plus originale dans le genre, «Vous êtes une société de... Vous cherchez à pourvoir un poste de... Mon profil peut vous intéresser...» et puis faire une liste de mes compétences et expériences professionnelles et ensuite préciser ma formation et finir par mon nom, mon adresse, etc. Qu'est-ce que t'en penses?

Cyril: Moi, personnellement, je préfère une présentation classique parce que tu prends un risque en voulant à tout prix être originale. Mais tu peux aussi avoir plusieurs CV, et selon le type de société à laquelle tu t'adresses, tu peux choisir telle ou telle version de ton CV. Pourquoi pas! Si tu penses qu'une entreprise cherche quelqu'un d'innovateur, vraiment dynamique, direct, cela peut te donner un avantage, justement, d'être différente.

Florine: J'aime bien l'idée de plusieurs versions. Je pourrais aussi en faire une sur papier blanc et l'autre sur un joli gris perlé. Merci, Cyril. Je retourne à mon ordi. Je vais retravailler cela tout de suite.

F. D'autres mots pour le dire. Trouvez dans le texte un synonyme des mots suivants.

1. prétentieuse
2. ce qui te met en valeur
3. un bureau de tourisme
4. ce travail
5. payée
6. quelles étaient tes responsabilités
7. soit éliminé
8. traditionnelle

G. La parole est à vous! Après avoir bien relu le dialogue, répondez aux questions suivantes.

1. Il y a au moins six mots, expressions et formes grammaticales qui appartiennent au domaine du français parlé. Faites-en une liste et écrivez à côté de chaque mot ou groupe de mots la forme correcte qui correspond.

ARRIBAS ORTIZ Dominique
4, rue des Hauts Pavés
49400 Saint Hilaire Saint Florent

2 41 50 46 12

Née le 30 août 1950
Deux enfants
Française

```
┌─────────────────────────────────────────┐
│  GRANDE HABITUDE DE L'ACCUEIL            │
│  SECRETARIAT ANGLAIS ESPAGNOL            │
└─────────────────────────────────────────┘
```

OBJECTIF :

          M'intégrer au sein d'un groupe dynamique
          et mettre à son service mes compétences
          commerciales et mon goût du contact.

FORMATION :

1967-68 :   BAC + 2

1972-74 :   Certificat The British Council

1992-93 :   Université Communale de Levallois-Perret
               Stage : "HOTESSE. DACTYLO. RECEPTION trilingue."
               Secrétariat. Word 5. Lotus 1,2,3.
               Anglais. Espagnol. Communication.
               Culture Générale. Accueil.
               Réception téléphonique.

EXPERIENCE PROFESSIONNELLE :

1968-72 :   Guide touristique.

1972-74 :   Standardiste bilingue.

1974-80 :   Secrétaire médicale.

1980-86 :   Période réservée à l'éducation de mes enfants.

1986-91 :   Suivre le mari en déplacement.

1993-94 :   Agent de bureau.

ACTIVITES ANNEXES :

          Lecture, musique, dance.

2. Montrez que Cyril connaît bien Florine. Donnez au moins trois exemples.

3. Pourquoi est-ce qu'un CV qui contient des fautes d'orthographe donne une mauvaise impression? Spécifiez au moins quatre raisons.

4. Est-ce que vous avez remarqué des différences entre le CV de Florine et les CV américains? Notez au moins trois différences.

5. Quelles sont les améliorations *(improvements)* proposées par Cyril? Faites une liste d'au moins sept éléments.

6. D'après ce dialogue, pourriez-vous faire un schéma rapide pour montrer comment Florine a choisi de présenter son CV?

7. Est-ce que le CV de Florine est écrit à la machine ou à la main? Justifiez votre réponse.

H. La lettre de motivation. Voici une liste des éléments qui composent une lettre d'affaires en français. Faites un schéma sur une feuille séparée d'une lettre écrite suivant un format français et indiquez où vous placeriez les éléments que vous venez d'étudier (vedette, signature, etc.) sur la page.

la suscription ou la vedette

la signature proprement dite

l'interpellation ou l'appel

la formule d'attaque

la ville + la date

le corps de la lettre

l'en-tête

les références

l'initiale du prénom et le nom de la personne qui signe

la formule de politesse

PJ (les pièces jointes)

l'objet de la lettre

la fonction de l'expéditeur de la lettre

ALVES Bernadette
Résidence Les Chênes Verts Bât. B -Appt. 8
76, Rue de Saumur
49000 LONGUE

Tel: 2 41 52 12 39

Longué, le 19 07.1996

Madame,

Après avoir poursuivi mes études et obtenu, à l'Université de la Sorbonne Nouvelle, une licence de langues Vivantes Etrangères, j'aimerais me lancer dans la vie active : c'est pourquoi, je sollicite auprès de vous un emploi.

Bien sûr, je reconnais n'avoir encore qu'une mince expérience, toutefois, j'espère avoir la chance de pouvoir exploiter mes connaissances, dans un domaine précis, afin de les développer, mais aussi, en acquérir de nouvelles...

En espérant vous rencontrer pour vous donner de plus amples informations, je vous prie de croire, Madame, à l'assurance de mes sentiments distingués.

Bernadette Alves

Alves

Véronique BOUCHER
12, rue Rousselle
92800 PUTEAUX
Tel. : 1 47 76 .20.33.
Fax : 1 46 86 98 41

En cours d'inscription au R.M.

Puteaux, le 26 avril 1996

Objet : Secrétariat à domicile

Madame, Monsieur,

Je me permets de vous adresser la présente afin de vous proposer mes services de secrétariat.

En effet, je travaille à mon domicile en tant que travailleur indépendant au prix de *17 francs hors taxe la page.*

Je vous remercie par avance de l'intérêt que vous voudrez bien porter à ce courrier et reste, bien entendu, à votre disposition pour tout renseignement complémentaire.

Je vous prie de croire, Madame, Monsieur, en l'assurance de mes sentiments distingués.

I. Autrement dit. Donnez une définition provisoire pour les mots suivants.

1. la vedette
2. la formule d'attaque
3. la signature
4. l'en-tête
5. le corps de la lettre

Observations culturelles

Les formules de politesse

Les formules de politesse sont très élaborées en français. Elles reflètent souvent la position de l'expéditeur par rapport au destinataire et peuvent suggérer une certaine hiérarchie. Une formule de politesse peut indiquer une relative soumission, du respect, une certaine sécheresse *(dryness; curtness)* ou au contraire un empressement et témoigner d'un désir de plaire. Elle peut se situer dans un contexte amical et personnel ou dans un contexte professionnel. Bien que les formules de politesse soient lues très rapidement et que le destinataire soit bien conscient de leur valeur figée et formelle, c'est-à-dire de la relativité de leur sincérité, elles sont importantes et doivent s'harmoniser avec l'ensemble du ton du reste de la lettre.

La signature

Tous les adolescents passent par une phase pendant laquelle trouver une signature personnelle, originale et inimitable est extrêmement important. Ils remplissent des pages entières de signatures avant de trouver la signature idéale qui correspond à leur personnalité. Ecrire son nom n'est pas la même chose que le signer, et une signature n'est pas nécessairement lisible; au contraire. On écrit rarement son prénom en entier mais on se sert de l'initiale de son premier prénom que l'on combine au nom de famille. On ajoute très souvent un trait qui souligne la signature. Voici quelques exemples de signatures françaises du même nom de famille qui est «Marin».

La date

En français, une lettre doit toujours commencer par une date, mais les dates sont présentées de façon légèrement différente des dates inscrites sur des lettres américaines.

EXEMPLE: Paris, le 12 mai 1997

J. Choisir une formule de politesse. Voici quelques formules de politesse avec lesquelles vous pourriez terminer une lettre. Comparez-les et dites quels sont leurs points communs et leurs différences. Expliquez dans quels cas vous choisiriez l'une plutôt que l'autre et pourquoi.

1. Je vous prie d'agréer, Monsieur le Directeur, l'expression de mes salutations empressées *(eager).*

2. Je vous prie d'agréer, Madame, l'expression de mes meilleures salutations.

3. Je vous prie de recevoir, Monsieur le Chef du personnel, l'expression de mes salutations les plus distinguées.

4. Je vous prie de croire, Madame la Directrice, à l'assurance de mes sentiments les plus dévoués.

5. Je vous prie d'accepter, Monsieur le Directeur, mes salutations les plus respectueuses.

6. Je vous prie d'accepter, ma chère Martine, mes salutations les plus amicales.

7. Je vous prie de bien vouloir agréer *(accept, receive kindly),* cher Monsieur, l'expression de mes sentiments les meilleurs.

8. Veuillez croire, Monsieur le Directeur, en l'expression de mes sentiments les plus respectueux.

9. Affectueusement vôtre.

10. Bien amicalement.

11. Veuillez accepter, Madame, mes salutations les meilleures.

12. Je vous prie de croire, Messieurs, en ma considération très distinguée.

13. Recevez, cher Monsieur, mes salutations les plus cordiales.

14. Bien à vous.

15. Veuillez croire, chère Madame, à mes sentiments dévoués.

16. Veuillez agréer, Monsieur le Préfet, l'expression de mon profond respect.

17. Recevez, Monsieur, nos salutations.

18. Je vous embrasse.

19. Grosses bises.

20. Amitiés.

K. A vous de classer! Pouvez-vous placer ces formules dans les catégories suivantes?

1. Formules indiquant le respect.

2. Formules indiquant la familiarité.

continued on page 148

➤ You may choose to talk through Exercise K with your study partner before coming to class.

HSG

➤ Study the *Phonétique* section of Module III in your *HSG* carefuly and complete Exercises D–I.

continued from page 147

3. Formules sèches indiquant une certaine irritation.

4. Formules suggérant une certaine égalité entre l'expéditeur et le destinataire.

L. Réflexions sur les formules de politesse. Comparez les formules de politesse courantes aux Etats-Unis ou dans votre pays d'origine et celles qui sont d'usage en France et dites ce que vous en pensez. Est-ce que vous préférez les formules françaises ou les formules américaines et pourquoi?

M. A la recherche de sa signature. Par groupes de deux ou trois, signez sur une feuille de papier en présence de vos voisins et commentez vos signatures. Depuis combien de temps avez-vous cette signature? Avez-vous travaillé sur sa forme définitive? Pourquoi?

N. Comment lire une date. Regardez la liste ci-dessous puis lisez les dates à voix haute en convertissant le chiffre indiquant le mois par le mois lui-même.

> *MODELE:* *Paris, le 17/04/1994*
> *se lit:* **Paris, le 17 avril 1994**

1. Saumur, le 14/12/93
2. Dijon, le 01/10/1981
3. Blois, le 18/11/1979
4. Lille, le 5/5/1995
5. Angers, le 6/9/1990
6. Aix-en-Provence, le 07/7/1972
7. Nice, le 02/6/1958

O. L'adresse. Remettez les éléments des adresses suivantes dans le bon ordre et lisez-les à voix haute.

> *MODELE:* *5 / Nantes / 44000 / place Viarme / Madame / Dubois*
> *se lit:* **Madame Dubois**
> **5, place Viarme**
> **44000 Nantes**

1. Alain / 41 / 49000 / Angers / Monsieur / rue du Maréchal Joffre / Gautron
2. boulevard de Strasbourg / Sébastien / 14 / Paris / 75010 / Leroi
3. Monsieur et Madame / avenue / Mauricet / 16 / Longué / 49160 / Victor Hugo
4. Monsieur / Jacques / "le Lion" / Rémin / 41310 / Authon

Lecture 1

Les petites annonces

P. Activité de pré-lecture. Répondez aux questions suivantes.

1. Dans quels cas est-ce que vous consultez les petites annonces?

2. Si vous cherchez un travail, quel genre de petites annonces allez-vous lire? Sur quels journaux ou magazines allez-vous vous concentrer et pourquoi?

3. Le message des petites annonces est quelquefois écrit en abrégé. Pourquoi? Faites une liste d'exemples d'abréviations courantes en anglais dans le domaine des petites annonces puis essayez de deviner quelles pourraient être les abréviations des mots français équivalents.

Les petites annonces

- **Valeo: l'équipement automobile**
Vous possédez un diplôme d'ingénieur mécanique, une expérience réussie de 2/4 ans dans la fonction Achats, (une expérience complémentaire Etudes sera appréciée).

- **Roche**
F. Hoffman-La Roche est un important groupe international chimique et pharmaceutique. Nous recherchons un ingénieur chimiste confirmé. Vous êtes Ingénieur Chimiste, avec de solides connaissances en synthèse organique et avez, nécessairement, cinq ans d'expérience en production...

- **Alcatel: radiotéléphone**
La Direction des Opérations et de la Maintenance, chargée de l'élaboration des offres et de l'exécution des contrats, recherche: 3 ingénieurs méthodologie d'installation débutants ou expérimentés...

- **Président Groupe International**
recherche: Chef de secrétariat particulier parfaitement bilingue anglais. A 35 ans environ, de niveau Sciences Po, vous justifiez d'une expérience professionnelle dans un poste similaire...

- **La ville de Montreuil-sous-Bois** (Seine-Saint-Denis) 100 000 habitants, recrute un collaborateur de cabinet du Député-Maire de niveau BAC + 4 minimum. Compétences particulières dans le domaine de la construction européenne, l'environnement et les finances publiques souhaitées. Qualités rédactionnelles et grande disponibilité nécessaires.

- **Eurocard Mastercard**
Société financière, spécialisée dans la gestion des moyens de paiement, recherche un cadre commercial. Agé de 28 ans environ, vous avez une formation type HEC, ESSEC, ESC, vous avez un excellent sens relationnel, parlez l'anglais. Une expérience de 2 à 3 ans dans une fonction similaire serait très appréciée mais n'est pas indispensable...

- **Le Nouvel Economiste** recherche stagiaires. *Mission:* vous développerez nos rubriques d'Annonces Classées dans une démarche à la fois marketing et commerciale. *Profil:* De formation Bac + 2 minimum, dynamique et doté d'un bon sens relationnel, vous désirez vous investir pleinement dans une expérience à la fois exigeante et passionnante.

Q. Avez-vous compris? Dans les extraits d'annonces offrant un emploi qui précèdent, colorez en une couleur les mots ou groupes de mots qui indiquent qu'ils s'adressent à des gens ayant déjà de l'expérience et colorez en une autre couleur les annonces qui ne rejettent pas les débutants.

R. A vous la parole! Quelle est l'annonce qui vous attire le plus et pourquoi?

S. A vos plumes! Cherchez dans un magazine ou un journal une annonce qui propose un poste qui vous attire et traduisez cette annonce en français.

T. Votre lettre de motivation. Réfléchissez à la lettre que vous pourriez écrire pour solliciter cet emploi.

1. Quelles sont les informations que vous désirez inclure et celles que vous ne donnerez pas. Faites-en une liste en style télégraphique.

2. La lettre accompagnant votre curriculum vitae sera-t-elle manuscrite ou tapée à la machine? Et votre CV? Pourquoi?

Roseline LE SERRE
Tel. 297.75.70.32

KERVIGNAC 23 JUIN 1995

Objet: Offre de service

Monsieur,

Depuis toujours et notamment depuis 10 ans je me passionne pour la cynophilie c'est la raison pour laquelle aujourd'hui je dirige une axe de recherche d'emploi dans le secteur animalier.

Votre clinique présente un intérêt majeur du fait de ma connaissance des chiens toutes races confondues. Ces fonctions dans un poste d'aide soignante vont permettre d'élargir mes compétences et de mettre à profit mon efficacité.

Méthodique et ambitieuse je désire exporter mon savoir faire en vue d'un développement au sein de votre cabinet (ou équipe).

Disponible pour vous rencontrer le plus rapidement possible. Espérant vous convaincre de l'intérêt de ma candidature au cours de l'entretien que vous voudriez bien m'accorder.

Je vous prie d'agréer, Monsieur, l'expression de mes sentiments distingués

3. Comment présenterez-vous votre lettre sur votre feuille de papier?
(Voir aussi lettres authentiques pages 145, 166 et 175.)

Lecture 2

Petites annonces abrégées

- 35 a./Parf. quadril. All./Angl./Esp./Bac+4 CI/Mobile Fce-étranger/Rech. poste de **consultant relations éco. int.**/A. Mauger/Tél: 54.45.87.58.70

- **Cadre export**/26a./2 a. exp. **Europe + Asie Sud Est** Bac + 5 Commerce/gestion inter./Rech. poste cial/mkg export ou acheteur import/Tél: (01) 39.57.76.25

- J.H. 40a./**Dipl.Cadre Com.Inter/ CESI/16 a. exp. com.** cherche poste com. exp. ds PME en dév./prod.High Tech./Angl./All./R. Ménier Tél: (01) 43.34.20.24

- **Allemand 42a./Responsable export**/ Tril. Fr./Angl./Flexible/Cherche nvelle activité export/Exp. **Extrême Orient**/Contacter MOCI PA réf. 89560

U. Avez-vous compris? Les abréviations utilisées dans le texte des petites annonces sont quelquefois très poussées et difficiles à déchiffrer *(decode)*. Les quatre annonces qui précèdent sont tirées du MOCI (Moniteur du Commerce International), un journal spécialisé en commerce. Lisez-les attentivement et essayez de décoder au moins 12 abréviations.

V. A vos plumes! Ecrivez une annonce telle qu'elle pourrait paraître dans un journal ou magazine francophone de votre choix. Utilisez au moins six abréviations.

Lecture 3

RCT: Radio Charpennes Tonkin (Lyon 93.3 FM)

W. Activité de pré-lecture. Par groupes de deux ou trois, réfléchissez aux questions suivantes.

> **1.** Quel rôle est-ce qu'une chaîne de radio locale peut jouer dans la recherche d'un emploi?
>
> **2.** Imaginez que vous avez envie de créer une émission de radio pour venir en aide aux chômeurs. Qu'est-ce que vous proposeriez comme rubriques?

RCT: Radio Charpennes Tonkin (Lyon 93.3 FM)

*C*ompétences, «le magazine des métiers et de l'emploi», invite les jeunes à partir à la découverte des activités professionnelles connues ou mal connues, à trouver un créneau porteur ou à choisir une formation adaptée. Christiane Réal, productrice et animatrice de l'émission, nous explique…

En quoi consiste «Compétences»?
Nous avons avant tout à cœur de ne pas jouer la carte du sinistrose, mais plutôt de faire passer un message d'espoir. Des professionnels viennent à l'antenne parler de leur métier avec passion. En connaître les multiples facettes permet de savoir où l'on met les pieds.

«Compétences» concerne-t-elle exclusivement les chômeurs?
Pas du tout! Elle est surtout dirigée vers les 16/26 ans. Les jeunes en cours de formation ont besoin d'information pour ne pas se tromper à l'heure où ils doivent prendre un certain nombre de décisions importantes. Ceux-ci prennent d'ailleurs

souvent la parole lors de l'émission pour poser des questions et apporter leurs réflexions.

Quels sont les métiers qui ont déjà été évoqués?
Depuis plus de deux ans, nous avons déjà eu l'occasion d'en aborder plus de deux cents. Les premiers qui me viennent à l'esprit sont ceux d'antiquaire, d'huissier, d'ingénieur et de nombreux métiers de l'artisanat.

Diffusez-vous d'autres rubriques sur l'emploi?
En dehors de cette émission, deux fois par jour, sont diffusées des offres d'emploi. Des offres de formations sont également proposées.

Combien de personnes l'émission concerne-t-elle?
RCT (Radio Charpennes Tonkin) émet dans un rayon de 80 km autour de Lyon et nous avons quelque 8 000 auditeurs.

Quels sont les horaires de l'émission?
«Compétences» est programmée tous les mercredis de 19h10 à 20h00.

Quels sont vos partenaires?
Nous collaborons entre autres avec la Jeune Chambre Economique, la Chambre des Métiers, la Direction Départementale du Travail et de l'Emploi, la Chambre d'Agriculture du Rhône (pour une série d'émissions sur les métiers «verts»), la Chambre de Commerce et d'Industrie de Lyon et bien sûr l'ANPE.

_____

Article tiré du magazine *Vive l'emploi!* N°5, janvier–février 1995.

X. A la recherche d'éléments précis. Répondez aux questions suivantes.

1. Trouvez dans cette interview quatre mots qui se rapportent au thème de la radio et expliquez-les.

2. Quel est le nom de l'émission de radio en question?

3. A quel groupe d'âge est-ce que cette émission s'adresse surtout?

4. Quel jour et à quelle heure est-ce que cette émission est diffusée?

5. Combien de personnes écoutent cette émission et où habitent-elles?

Y. Autrement dit. Cherchez dans le texte les phrases qui expriment la même idée que les expressions ou affirmations suivantes et soulignez-les.

1. Est-ce que votre émission s'adresse seulement aux gens qui n'ont pas de travail?

2. Les jeunes ne se contentent pas d'écouter notre émission; ils y participent activement.

3. Cette émission n'est pas la seule qui touche le thème de l'emploi. Tous les jours nous proposons une liste des emplois disponibles.

4. Nous travaillons avec divers organismes de la région.

Z. Vrai ou faux? Lisez les affirmations suivantes. Si elles ne correspondent pas à ce que vous avez compris du texte, reformulez-les.

1. «Compétences» ne parle que des métiers dans lesquels il y a des débouchés.

2. «Compétences» invite les jeunes à s'exprimer.

3. «Compétences» donne de nombreuses informations sur toutes sortes de métiers.

4. «Compétences» parle plus souvent de métiers artisanaux que de métiers qui exigent des diplômes de l'enseignement supérieur.

5. «Compétences» est une émission diffusée à l'échelle nationale.

LORIENT   **A.N.P.E.**

NOUVELLE PRESTATION DE RECHERCHE D'EMPLOI A COMPTER DE JUILLET 1995

LES ATELIERS INDIVIDUALISES DE RECHERCHE D'EMPLOI

Objectifs :
Les ateliers offrent un service individualisé permettant à chaque participant de :

➔ S'entraîner à aborder l'entreprise ;
➔ Acquérir et renforcer des techniques et des comportements adaptés de recherche d'emploi;
➔ Mettre en oeuvre des actes concrets de recherche d'emploi.

Publics :
Demandeurs d'emploi catégorie 1,2,3 et personnes bénéficiant d'un contrat emploi solidarité (CES), ayant un ou des objectifs d'emploi précis et clairement définis, disponibles pour se consacrer à une recherche active d'emploi et désirant approfondir ou renforcer un des éléments clés de sa recherche d'emploi.

Contenu :
* L'atelier individualisé de recherche d'emploi se déroule sur une ½ journée (3h30 environ) avec en moyenne 8 participants qui travaillent individuellement avec l'aide d'un animateur ANPE sur un des modules proposés et qui répond aux besoins des participants

☞ Rédiger un curriculum vitae,
☞ Utiliser les petites annonces,
☞ Rédiger une lettre de candidature spontanée,
☞ Téléphoner à une entreprise,
☞ Préparer un entretien d'embauche.

* Chaque participant ne peut s'inscrire à plus de deux modules de l'Atelier, sachant qu'un seul module de l'Atelier peut-être effectué par ½ journée.
Si des besoins existent dans tous les domaines de la recherche d'emploi, la STRE est plus appropriée.(2jours)

Si vous êtes intéressé par cette prestation individualisée et rapide, veuillez vous adresser à un conseiller.

6. «Compétences» est financée par la Chambre de Commerce et d'Industrie de Lyon.

Quelques points de repère

Le saviez-vous?

- La fête du travail est célébrée le 1er mai par un jour férié *(holiday)* national. C'est un jour de repos obligatoire *(required, mandatory)*. Traditionnellement, le muguet *(lily-of-the-valley)* est la fleur associée à cette fête et l'on peut acheter dans la rue, un peu partout, des petits bouquets de muguet ou un brin *(sprig)* de muguet que l'on met à sa boutonnière *(buttonhole)*.

- Depuis 1982, tout travailleur à plein temps, en France, a droit à 30 jours ouvrables (non compris week-end et jours fériés) payés par an.

L'ardoise!

Ce n'est que très progressivement que les conditions de travail ont été réglementées *(regulated)* pour protéger les travailleurs et leur permettre d'exercer leur métier et de vivre dans la dignité. Avant 1813, par exemple, il n'était pas illégal de faire travailler des enfants de moins de 10 ans dans des mines ou ailleurs. La longueur de la journée de travail s'est réduite petit à petit. Ainsi en 1841, une nouvelle loi a limité le nombre d'heures journalières de travail à 12 heures pour les enfants de 12 à 16 ans et en 1892 à 11 heures pour les femmes et les enfants de moins de 18 ans. Jusqu'au XXe siècle, les journées étaient longues et mal payées et les ouvriers ne bénéficiaient pas d'assurances sociales, de congés payés et d'autres avantages sociaux. Ils travaillaient dans des conditions d'hygiène qui laissaient souvent à désirer sans avoir les moyens de protester ou de changer leur situation.

Une date importante!

- Le SMIG, Salaire Minimum Interprofessionnel Garanti, a été instauré en 1950 et c'est en 1970 que le concept du SMIG a légèrement changé et que le SMIG est devenu le SMIC, Salaire Minimum Interprofessionnel de Croissance.
- L'Agence Nationale pour l'Amélioration des Conditions de Travail (l'ANACT) a été créée en 1973.

Les chiffres parlent!

Une femme enceinte *(pregnant)* a droit à 6 semaines de congés payés avant l'accouchement de son premier ou deuxième enfant et 10 semaines après la naissance de l'enfant. A partir du troisième enfant, elle a 8 semaines avant et 18 après.

Réflexions sur le travail en équipe

Considérez le modèle suivant. Ensuite, essayez de l'appliquer à n'importe quel(le) système, procédé ou méthode ainsi qu'à chacune des étapes qui en font partie.

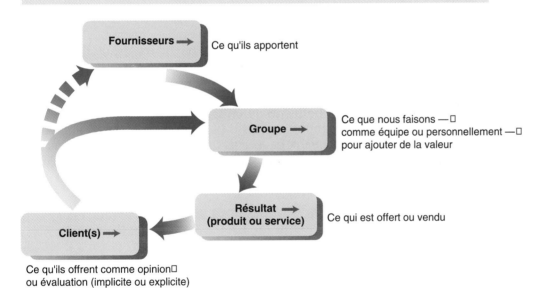

Fournisseurs → Ce qu'ils apportent

Groupe → Ce que nous faisons — comme équipe ou personnellement — pour ajouter de la valeur

Résultat (produit ou service) → Ce qui est offert ou vendu

Client(s) →

Ce qu'ils offrent comme opinion ou évaluation (implicite ou explicite)

Lexique

un concours: Un concours est une épreuve, c'est-à-dire une sorte d'examen qui permet à un certain nombre de candidats d'entrer en compétition pour un nombre de places qui est déterminé à l'avance indépendemment du niveau des candidats. Un concours est une méthode de sélection.

> Anna va se présenter **au concours** des bourses. Il y a 2.000 candidats pour 150 bourses disponibles. Je lui souhaite bonne chance!

les contraintes *(f)*: On parle de **contraintes** dans le domaine du travail pour décrire ce qui est gênant ou difficile ou bien ce qui peut poser des problèmes. Le travail de nuit peut représenter **une contrainte** car les horaires ne sont pas les mêmes que ceux de la plupart des gens. Pour d'autres, **des contraintes** peuvent être des voyages fréquents à l'étranger, ou encore des revenus irréguliers, ou un travail qui exige de longues périodes de solitude.

> Le métier de vendeur n'exige pas de diplôme mais il présente un certain nombre de **contraintes.** Il faut travailler debout pendant de longues heures d'affilée et le revenu est irrégulier lorsqu'il est constitué d'un fixe *(base salary)* et d'une prime *(commission, bonus)* qui dépend des ventes effectuées.

➤ Consultez votre carte de France pour voir où ces régions se trouvent.

un déplacement: On parle de **déplacements** quand on est obligé de voyager pour son travail. De nombreux représentants sillonnent leur secteur qui peut se composer de trois ou quatre régions avoisinantes comme le Poitou-Charentes, l'Aquitaine, le Limousin et le Midi-Pyrénées.

> Non, Madame Moreau ne peut pas prendre votre coup de fil. Elle est en **déplacement** jusqu'à lundi.

la disponibilité: Lorsqu'un emploi demande une grande **disponibilité**, cela veut dire que le candidat doit être assez libre et flexible et pouvoir travailler à des heures irrégulières ou le week-end ou bien qu'il doit pouvoir se déplacer. Une personne qui a des obligations familiales n'est souvent pas très **disponible.**

> C'est un travail vraiment intéressant mais qui exige **une disponibilité** totale car il faut pouvoir suivre la troupe de théâtre pendant les périodes de tournée ce qui signifie que six mois sur douze, on est en déplacement en France ou à l'étranger.

l'échelle *(f)*: On parle d'**échelle** lorsqu'on représente tous les niveaux de la société ou bien toutes les professions des plus intéressantes aux moins intéressantes ou bien des mieux payées aux moins bien payées. Lorsqu'on est **en haut de l'échelle,** cela veut dire qu'on fait partie de l'élite et qu'on est parmi les mieux payés de cette catégorie. Lorsqu'on est **en bas de l'échelle,** on est parmi les moins bien payés.

> Du point de vue salaire, il est vraiment **en bas de l'échelle** mais ce boulot lui permet d'acquérir un peu d'expérience et il adore travailler dans la forêt, en pleine nature, donc pour l'instant, il est content.

exercer: Exercer un métier veut dire pratiquer ou faire ce métier.

> Ce médecin **exerce** depuis peu mais il est vraiment excellent; tu devrais le consulter au sujet de ta migraine.

la formation: La formation est l'ensemble des études que l'on a fait et la préparation qu'on a eue à un certain travail. L'éducation d'une manière générale fait partie de **la formation** d'un individu.

> Il est médecin de **formation** mais il est devenu présentateur à la télévision dans un programme scientifique.

le niveau Bac + 4: Lorsqu'on parle de la formation d'une personne et des études qu'elle a faites on dit souvent «**Bac + un certain nombre d'années d'études**». Ainsi une personne qui a le **Bac + 3** a son baccalauréat, c'est-à-dire le diplôme national qui sanctionne la fin des études secondaires et 3 années d'études supérieures qui pourraient être une licence, par exemple. Une personne qui a son doctorat a au minimum le **Bac + 8**.

> Tu as vu cette annonce? On demande «**Bac + 2**» et quelques années d'expérience en laboratoire. Cela devrait t'intéresser. Regarde!

requérir: Ce métier **requiert** beaucoup de patience, c'est-à-dire demande, exige une grande dose de patience.

> Le métier de représentant **requiert** un certain nombre de qualités à savoir: une facilité d'élocution exceptionnelle, une grande mobilité et avant tout un sens du commerce bien développé.

un stagiaire: Un **stagiaire** est une personne qui fait **un stage,** c'est-à-dire un certain travail pendant une période déterminée dans le cadre de sa formation. Faire **un stage** permet de pratiquer ce qu'on a appris de façon théorique au cours des études. **Un stagiaire** peut être rémunéré ou non. Cela dépend de l'entreprise. Il est intéressant de faire **un stage** dans une ville, une région ou même un pays que l'on ne connaît pas car cela peut être très enrichissant.

> **Le stagiaire** espère que La Redoute (Vente par Correspondance) lui proposera un emploi à la fin du stage qu'il fait à Roubaix dans la région du Nord-Pas de Calais.

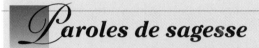

Paroles de sagesse

Il ne faut jamais dire: «Fontaine. je ne boirai pas de ton eau».

> ➤ Discuss the meaning of this adage with your study partner.

Expression écrite

Expressions adverbiales

Dans le récit qui suit, entourez les expressions adverbiales et faites bien attention à leur importance et au rôle qu'elles jouent dans le déroulement de l'histoire.

Le départ en vacances simplifié grâce au Minitel

Monsieur Orsay, cadre aux charbonnages de France, partait en vacances le 2 juillet. Comme il avait eu un emploi du temps particulièrement chargé, il n'avait pas eu assez de temps pour se rendre à l'agence de voyage. Il n'avait évidemment pas l'occasion d'aller à la banque en personne puisque les heures d'ouverture de la banque correspondaient à ses propres heures de travail. Heureusement, il possédait un Minitel à la maison.

Grâce au Minitel, il a pu rapidement préparer ses vacances. Il a tout d'abord transféré 20.000 francs de son compte épargne sur son compte courant pour couvrir entièrement les frais inhérents à son voyage en Provence.

Il a ensuite pu vérifier qu'il ne lui restait plus que 67.534 francs sur son compte après ce transfert. Cette somme-là était largement suffisante pour financer les études de ses enfants qui rentraient cette année-là à l'université.

Il devait aussi le soir même réserver des places de train pour toute sa famille. Grâce au système Socrate, il lui avait suffi de taper 3615 code SNCF pour entrer dans le réseau. Une fois connecté, il avait facilement pu choisir ses horaires, opter pour des billets de première classe dans une voiture non-fumeur, ainsi que sélectionner côté couloir pour sa femme et ses deux filles et une fenêtre pour lui-même et son fils. Il avait bien sûr pu bénéficier d'une réduction puisqu'ayant trois enfants, il possédait une carte Famille Nombreuse.

Ainsi, grâce à son Minitel, il avait pu organiser ses vacances sans perdre de temps inutilement.

AA. A vos plumes! Essayez maintenant d'écrire un paragraphe d'environ 150 mots sur un des deux sujets suivants.

- Le rôle de l'Internet ou des ordinateurs dans votre vie personnelle
- Comment vous comptez chercher et trouver un emploi qui soit vraiment fait pour vous

Essayez d'insérer logiquement au moins dix expressions adverbiales dans votre paragraphe.

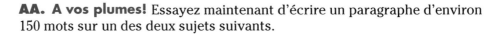

Dans le dossier suivant, vous allez voir comment les entreprises recrutent du personnel.

Recruter du personnel

Le point de départ du huitième dossier est le monde du secrétariat aussi bien en ce qui concerne les meubles, les objets, et d'une manière générale tout ce qui se trouve dans un bureau que le travail lié à un poste de secrétaire. Lorsqu'une entreprise offre des emplois, c'est souvent un(e) secrétaire qui s'occupe de placer des annonces ou de contacter une agence de travail temporaire ou même un chasseur de têtes. Lorsqu'une personne fait une demande d'emploi et est convoquée à un entretien d'embauche, c'est avec la/le secrétaire que le premier contact se fait. Cela est vrai également des clients d'un cabinet, d'un bureau ou d'une entreprise. Ce dossier présente également plusieurs facettes du processus de recrutement du personnel.

*A*ctivités d'introduction

Le processus de recrutement et le travail de secrétariat

A. Recruter du personnel. Imaginez que vous êtes le responsable d'une entreprise et que vous avez un poste à pourvoir. A deux ou trois, réfléchissez aux questions suivantes.

1. Quelles sont les étapes par lesquelles vous passerez? Nommez au moins sept étapes possibles.

2. En général, le recrutement du personnel est un travail qui se fait à plusieurs. Qui, selon vous, devrait faire partie du processus de recrutement et pourquoi? Faites une liste d'au moins six personnes.

Matériel de bureau.

Le bureau d'une secrétaire avec standard téléphonique.

B. Travail de secrétariat. Penchez-vous tout particulièrement sur le rôle d'un(e) secrétaire et répondez aux questions suivantes.

1. Quelles sont les responsabilités d'une entreprise qui embauche? Faites une liste de six responsabilités différentes.

2. D'une manière générale, quelles sont les activités journalières liées à un emploi de secrétariat? Faites une liste d'au moins six des activités d'un tel emploi.

3. Qu'y a-t-il sur le bureau d'un(e) secrétaire ou de toute personne qui fait un travail de type administratif? Faites une liste d'au moins huit de ces objets. A quoi ces objets servent-ils?

4. Qu'y a-t-il dans les tiroirs du bureau d'un(e) secrétaire et dans le vôtre? Pourquoi?

5. Comment peut-on personnaliser son bureau (la pièce ou le meuble) ou son lieu de travail en général?

6. Imaginez-vous dans un bureau. Quels bruits ou sons pouvez-vous associer avec les gens qui y travaillent et le matériel employé?

7. Et quelles émotions ou sensations peuvent être liées à un bureau et aux activités professionnelles qui s'y déroulent *(take place)*?

➤ N'oubliez pas de mentionner les objets personnels.

 Les mots pour le dire

Vocabulaire de base

V E R B E S	
accueillir	*to welcome*
annuler	*to cancel*
convaincre	*to convince*
convoquer	*to invite (a candidate)*
décacheter	*to open*
décrocher (le téléphone)	*to answer (pick up the receiver)*
déplacer un rendez-vous	*to change an appointment*
déranger	*to bother, disturb*

distribuer (le courrier)	*to distribute (the mail)*
écarter, être écarté(e)	*to put aside, be put aside*
être chargé(e) de	*to be responsible for*
être pris(e) au dépourvu	*to be caught unaware*
expédier	*to send*
figurer	*to be part of*
filtrer (les appels téléphoniques)	*to screen (calls)*
fixer un rendez-vous	*to make an appointment*
inciter à	*to incite to*
mettre en attente	*to put on hold*
mettre en communication avec	*to put through*
opter	*to opt*
peser	*to weigh*
prendre part à	*to take part in*
raccrocher (le téléphone)	*to hang up*
rejeter	*to reject*
susciter	*to instigate; to create*
trier (le courrier)	*to sort (the mail)*

N O M S

une agrafeuse	*stapler*
une boîte	*box; company* (fam.)
un boulot	*job* (fam.)
une carte de visite	*business card*
un classeur	*file; binder*
la colle	*paste, glue*
les compétences (f)	*specializations; proficiencies, skills*
la confiance	*confidence*
le courrier	*mail*
un déplacement	*business trip, (being out of town on business)*
la diffusion	*dissemination; broadcasting*
l'emploi du temps (m)	*schedule*
une enveloppe	*envelope*
l'expérience (f)	*experience*
une feuille de paie	*paycheck stub*
une feuille (de papier)	*sheet, piece (of paper)*
la force de conviction	*force of conviction*
le milieu professionnel	*professional environment*
un outil	*tool*
la paie	*paycheck*
du papier (à en-tête)	*paper; (letterhead) stationery*
des petites annonces	*want ads, classifieds*
les prétentions (f)	*expectations*
le profil	*profile*
un renseignement	*piece of information*
une tactique	*tactic*
un trombone	*paper clip*

A D J E C T I F S

annuel(le)	*annual*
célibataire	*single (unmarried)*

continued on page 162

continued from page 161

confirmé(e) (qui a fait ses preuves)	*confirmed (proven)*
dynamique	*dynamic*
exigé(e)	*required*
exigeant(e)	*demanding*
facultatif(ve)	*optional*
immuable	*unchanging*
indispensable	*absolutely necessary*
innovateur(trice)	*innovative*
mensuel(le)	*monthly*
onéreux(se)	*burdensome; expensive*
passionnant(e)	*exciting, thrilling*

ADVERBES ET EXPRESSIONS ADVERBIALES

actuellement	*now, at the present time*
aisément	*easily*
antérieurement	*beforehand*
exclusivement	*exclusively*
facilement	*easily*
immédiatement	*immediately*
inévitablement	*inevitably*
(in)suffisamment	*(in)sufficiently*
lors de	*at the time of*
au sein de	*in; within*
typiquement	*typically*

C. Définitions provisoires à terminer. Complétez les phrases suivantes.

1. Lorsqu'on décide de ne pas faire quelque chose, (par exemple de ne pas aller à tel ou tel rendez-vous d'affaires) il est préférable de téléphoner pour _____ ce rendez-vous ou bien pour le déplacer.

2. Ce verbe est un synonyme du verbe «envoyer». Je regarde sur l'enveloppe pour voir quel jour cette lettre a été _____.

3. Lorsque j'ai un choix, je peux _____ pour le plan A ou pour le plan B.

4. Quand on effectue très facilement un travail on peut dire qu'on le fait _____.

5. Lorsqu'on envoie un curriculum vitae, on peut joindre une photo. Ce n'est pas obligatoire, c'est _____.

6. _____ d'un entretien d'embauche, il est important de paraître à l'aise et sûr de soi mais pas trop arrogant.

D. A vous de créer des définitions provisoires! Par groupes de deux, écrivez une définition provisoire des mots suivants.

1. innovateur
2. dynamique
3. mettre en attente

4. potentiel
5. le profil

➤ Complete Exercises J–M of Module III in you *HSG*.

Observations pratiques

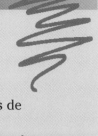

Pour mieux communiquer au téléphone!

Lorsque vous recevez un coup de téléphone professionnel:

- Décrochez rapidement. Evitez de laisser sonner plus de deux fois.
- Il n'est pas nécessaire de dire «Allô». Annoncez le nom de votre société immédiatement et dites qui vous êtes (prénom et nom de famille) ou quelle fonction vous occupez.
- Soyez poli(e), accueillant(e) *(welcoming):* la gentillesse *(kindness)* s'entend au téléphone et votre interlocuteur ou interlocutrice doit vous sentir disponible *(available).*
- Articulez et ne parlez pas trop rapidement.
- Sachez écouter ce que votre interlocuteur a à vous dire ou à vous demander.
- N'interrompez pas votre interlocuteur.
- Soyez concis(e) et ne donnez aucune information inutile.
- Prenez des notes et n'hésitez pas à demander à la personne qui appelle d'épeler son nom ou le nom de sa société.
- Répétez l'essentiel du message que vous avez noté, le nom et le numéro de téléphone de votre correspondant(e).
- Ne raccrochez votre combiné que lorsque votre correspondant(e) a raccroché.

Lorsque vous téléphonez dans le cadre de vos activités professionnelles:

- Avant d'appeler la personne que vous désirez joindre *(reach, contact),* prenez quelques notes dans l'ordre dans lequel vous voulez les aborder *(approach)* de façon à ne rien oublier.
- Gardez du papier et un stylo à proximité.
- Ayez votre emploi du temps et un calendrier sous la main.
- Téléphonez d'un endroit calme pour pouvoir vous concentrer et pour que le bruit ne gêne pas votre interlocuteur.
- Si votre appel concerne des documents, gardez-les près de vous pour pouvoir les consulter sans interrompre votre appel.
- Composez le numéro d'appel et dès que votre interlocuteur ou interlocutrice est au bout du fil et s'est identifié(e), dites qui vous êtes.
- Expliquez le plus simplement et brièvement possible la raison de votre appel.
- Soyez poli(e), patient(e) et flexible.
- Commencez toujours par ce qui est le plus important.
- Soyez bref(ève).
- Prenez des notes si nécessaire.

continued on page 164

continued from page 163

- Convenez de la suite à donner à votre appel.
- A la fin de la communication, reformulez de façon concise et claire ce que vous avez dit ou demandé ainsi que les termes de l'accord et ce qui a été décidé.
- Remerciez et prenez congé.
- Raccrochez.

E. A vous la parole! Répondez aux questions suivantes.

1. Quels autres conseils aimeriez-vous donner? Pouvez-vous ajouter quelques éléments aux deux listes qui précèdent?
2. En vous basant sur votre propre expérience, donnez quelques exemples de coups de téléphone qui manquent de professionnalisme.
3. Quelles sont les choses qui vous irritent lorsque vous téléphonez dans le contexte de vos activités professionnelles?

➤ Note key words in your reporter's notebook so you'll be free to circulate around the classroom to interview other students.

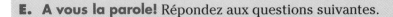

Dialogue

Un chef des ressources humaines et sa secrétaire

F. Activité de pré-lecture. Quand le chef du personnel demande à sa secrétaire de venir dans son bureau, quel genre de questions est-ce qu'il peut lui poser et quel type de tâches est-ce qu'il peut lui donner à faire?

Un chef des ressources humaines et sa secrétaire

Mme Lebrun: *(A l'intercom)* Madame Rémin, pouvez-vous passer dans mon bureau, s'il vous plaît?

Mme Rémin: Oui, Madame, tout de suite.

(Elle se dirige vers le bureau de Mme Lebrun et entre après avoir frappé légèrement à la porte.)

Mme Lebrun: Je viens de relire les dossiers de candidature. Il nous faut quatre hôtesses de caisse pour l'été. Convoquez les candidates des dix dossiers que j'ai mis à part. Ceux de la pile de droite, là. Gardez les douze dossiers de la pile de gauche et jetez les autres. Monsieur Durand et Madame Ligeon conduiront les entretiens. Voyez avec eux les heures qui leur conviendront le mieux en fin de semaine, au début de la semaine prochaine au plus tard. Dites-leur qu'il faut bien compter une vingtaine de minutes par candidate.

Mme Rémin: Très bien. Je téléphone aux dix candidates et leur envoie ensuite une convocation écrite?

Mme Lebrun: Oui, c'est cela. Téléphonez-leur dès cet après-midi.

Mme Rémin: Nous avons reçu aujourd'hui un dossier de candidature spontanée. Une jeune femme est passée elle-même le déposer. Je l'ai feuilleté. C'est une personne qui a déjà pas mal d'expérience comme hôtesse de caisse. Deux ans à Casino et sept ans chez Leclerc. Elle vient d'arriver à Perpignan, d'après ce que j'ai compris. Est-ce que cela vous intéresserait de parcourir ce dossier?

Mme Lebrun: Oui, tout à fait. La plupart des candidates n'ont pas d'expérience justement... Donnez-le-moi tout de suite. Je le lirai ce soir. Bon, rien d'autre pour l'instant, Madame Rémin. Ah si, pourriez-vous m'apporter un rouleau de Scotch, des trombones et des agrafes, s'il vous plaît? Cela fait plusieurs jours que je n'ai plus de Scotch et que j'oublie de vous en demander.

Mme Rémin: Bien sûr. Donnez-moi votre agrafeuse, si vous voulez; je vais vous la recharger tout de suite. Je suis en train de mettre à jour votre emploi du temps de la semaine prochaine. Il y a eu pas mal de changements dans vos rendez-vous.

Une secrétaire au travail.

Mme Lebrun: Bon, je verrai. Vous m'en donnerez une copie après la réunion de cet après-midi. Pendant la réunion, pas d'appels! Je ne veux être dérangée sous aucun prétexte. Il faut absolument que nous arrivions à une décision aujourd'hui en ce qui concerne toutes les dates de congés annuels. Ça ne va pas être facile d'expédier cela en deux heures!

Mme Rémin: Et si Monsieur Guimaux appelle? Il repart pour Marseille ce soir, si je me souviens bien.

Mme Lebrun: Ah oui, c'est vrai, Monsieur Guimaux! Je ne sais pas où j'ai la tête aujourd'hui! Vous faites bien de me le rappeler. Merci! Je lui avais demandé de m'appeler cet après-midi sans faute. Passez-le-moi dès qu'il appelle.

G. A la recherche d'éléments précis. Relevez au moins quatre mots ayant trait au thème du recrutement et cinq mots ayant un rapport avec le travail de secrétariat ou le matériel de bureau.

H. Vrai ou faux? A deux ou trois, lisez les affirmations suivantes à voix haute et dites si elles sont correctes ou non. Si elles ne le sont pas, modifiez la phrase de façon à ce que l'affirmation devienne correcte.

1. Mme Lebrun demande poliment à sa secrétaire de venir.

2. La secrétaire apporte les dossiers de candidature avec elle.

Jean-Pierre GILOU
6, rue Dupleix
56100 LORIENT

Tel : 297 52 22 46

Né le 2/09/1950 à Lorient

Marié - Epouse : Infirmière libérale
3 enfants (7 ans et jumelles de 4 ans)
Permis B + Véhicule

Attirance Professionnelle :
INSERTION SOCIALE ET PROFESSIONNELLE

FORMATION - CONNAISSANCES DE BASE

Secondaire Terminale A4
1ère année Lettre à la Faculté de Vincennes (auditeur libre)
Formation de 1 an à l'IGECO : Gestion des Entreprises commerciales
Formation à l'Aide psychologique par téléphone dans le cadre d'SOS Amitié

PARCOURS PROFESSIONNEL

1972
Service Militaire Armé dans les F.F.A.
Aide infirmier en service médecine

1973-1990
"Ardoisières de Plevin" Carrières d'ardoises
(Entreprise familiale de 45 personnes)
Fonction administrative et sociale, Gestion du personnel, Fonction de médiation sur le plan humain et financier, Suivi des paiements, Mise en place de la liquidation de l'entreprise pour cause familiale.

1990
Côté social et Associatif
- Parrainage d'une fratrie de cambodgiens (suivi pendant 10 ans)
- Garde d'enfants (confié avec accord tacite d'un éducateur - 5 mois)
- SOS Amitié
- SOS Enfants sans frontière
- Cadre personnel : Aide dans l'activité du conjoint
- Aide à 2 personnes âgées 2 fois/semaine

QUALITES

Capable d'écoute, de tolérance et de compréhension
Aime travailler dans une équipe
Communicatif et patient

CENTRES D'INTERET

Théâtre : Participant dans une petite troupe d'un club de loisir (2 pièces différentes par an)

DISPONIBILITE IMMEDIATE

Jean-Pierre GILOU
Tel : 297 52 22 46

Lorient le 23 Juin 95

Association Espoir
Morbihan
28 r. Mal Foch
56 100 Lorient

DEMANDE D'ENTRETIEN
A l'attention de Monsieur HUOME

Monsieur,

Depuis une vingtaine d'années je me suis investi d'une façon bénévole dans plusieurs associations à caractère social ou caritatif.

Tenant compte de cette expérience je voudrais m'orienter vers une formation ou un emploi d'aide médico-psychologique qui conviendrait à mes aspirations et à ma personnalité.

Votre organisme m'intéresse dans la mesure où je pense pouvoir y acquérir une bonne expérience et vous apporter ma disponibilité, mon fort désir d'optimiser mes chances sur un travail motivant.

Je souhaite avant tout vous rencontrer pour connaître votre avis de professionnel, je me permettrais donc de téléphoner à votre secrétariat pour me tenir à votre disposition.

Veuillez agréer, Monsieur, l'expression de mes meilleures salutations.

---

3. Mme Lebrun demande à sa secrétaire ce qu'elle pense de la sélection qu'elle a faite.

4. Mme Lebrun veut embaucher une nouvelle secrétaire.

5. Mme Lebrun respecte l'opinion de sa secrétaire.

6. Tous les dossiers seront conservés après les entretiens.

7. Mme Lebrun conduira elle-même les entretiens d'embauche.

8. M. Durand et Mme Ligeon pourront rencontrer les candidates quand ils le voudront.

9. Les candidates recevront d'abord une lettre qui leur dira qu'elles sont convoquées.

10. Ce sont les candidates qui devront téléphoner pour prendre rendez-vous.

11. Mme Lebrun n'aime pas être dérangée pendant les réunions importantes.

12. Mme Rémin a un peu peur de sa patronne.

I. D'autres mots pour le dire! Cherchez dans le texte l'équivalent des mots ou groupes de mots suivants.

1. les CV et les lettres de motivation

2. une caissière

3. j'ai séparé(s)

4. faites venir

5. remettre/donner/apporter

6. parcourir rapidemment

7. la majorité

8. je ne veux pas être interrompue dans mon travail

9. les vacances

10. terminer

11. je n'arrive pas à me concentrer

J. Avez-vous compris? Répondez aux questions suivantes.

1. Pourquoi est-ce que le chef des ressources humaines appelle sa secrétaire?

2. En quelles catégories est-ce que Mme Lebrun a classé les dossiers?

3. A votre avis, est-ce que la secrétaire a déjà une certaine expérience? Justifiez votre réponse.

HSG

➤ Complete Exercises N–P of Module III in your *HSG*.

K. La parole est à vous! A deux ou trois, réfléchissez aux questions suivantes et discutez-les.

➤ Be ready to report your findings back to the class.

1. Quelles sont les qualités essentielles d'une bonne secrétaire? Pourquoi?

2. Quels sont les défauts qui ne sont pas compatibles avec le métier de secrétaire? Pourquoi?

3. Aimeriez-vous être secrétaire? Pourquoi?

4. Traditionnellement, le métier de secrétaire est perçu comme typiquement et exclusivement féminin. Pouvez-vous expliquer pourquoi? Qu'en pensez-vous vous-même?

5. Qu'est-ce qui distingue les professions dites féminines de celles dites masculines? Faites une liste des professions appartenant à ces deux catégories et dites si vous êtes d'accord avec cette classification et pourquoi.

Lecture 1

Pas de temps à perdre pour recruter!

L. Activité de pré-lecture. A deux ou trois, discutez les questions suivantes.

1. Voulez-vous travailler dans une petite ou une grande entreprise? Pourquoi?

2. Réfléchissez à l'importance du recrutement pour une entreprise. Que se passe-t-il si l'entreprise recrute le candidat idéal? Que se passe-t-il si, au contraire, le candidat sélectionné ne répond pas aux attentes de l'entreprise? Nommez quelques conséquences dans les deux cas.

Pas de temps à perdre pour recruter!

*C*ontinent, intègre chaque année environ 200 jeunes diplômés, futurs chefs de rayon, responsables du personnel ou chefs comptables. «Pour identifier ces 200 jeunes motivés par notre métier, nous devons traiter des milliers de candidatures», explique Patrick Moreau, Directeur du Développement Social. Il est donc important de toucher tous ceux qui nous intéressent. L'annonce presse est un des moyens dont nous disposons.

En dix ans, le secteur du commerce a créé 140.000 emplois et il devrait en générer entre 180 et 200.000 d'ici l'an 2000. *Continent* ne fait pas exception à la règle puisque nous voulons recruter 200 jeunes diplômés en 1995. En 1996, nous ouvrirons deux très grands hypers à Chelles *(city in the Ile de France region)* et Marseille *(France's number one harbor located on the Mediterranean, southern France)* qui ont besoin chacun de 40 chefs de service confirmés pour constituer leur encadrement.

Monsieur Le Spégagne, manager à *Continent,* dans son bureau.

Le portrait robot du jeune diplômé pourrait être celui-ci: bac plus 2 minimum, ayant le goût du commerce, doublé d'un gestionnaire avisé et sachant animer une équipe. Dégagé des obligations militaires (pour les hommes), il a déjà une petite connaissance de la grande distribution. Pour trouver «l'oiseau rare», les responsables de recrutement participent à de nombreux forums et salons étudiants. Ils effectuent également nombre de présentations de *Continent* dans les écoles et les universités. Ces contacts directs suscitent beaucoup de candidatures spontanées. C'est un peu la partie immergée de l'iceberg, moins visible que les annonces de recrutement qui paraissent dans la presse, mais également très efficace.

Tiré de: Actualités *Continent*, N° 46, mai 1995.

M. Avez-vous compris? Répondez aux questions suivantes en cochant la ou les réponses qui vous paraissent correctes.

1. Le sujet du texte est
   a. le type de magasin que *Continent* veut devenir.
   b. le type d'annonce que *Continent* passe pour recruter du personnel.
   c. le recrutement de jeunes diplômés.
   d. le temps que les employés perdent au cours d'une semaine de travail.

2. Quel genre de diplômés est-ce que *Continent* cherche à recruter?
   a. des candidats qui ont déjà pas mal d'expérience
   b. des candidats qui ont le bac et qui ont fait quelques années d'études supérieures
   c. des candidats qui se sentent à l'aise dans une organisation de type militaire
   d. des candidats qui savent animer une équipe

3. Comment est-ce que *Continent* recrute?

   a. *Continent* fait passer des annonces dans la presse écrite.

   b. *Continent* va contacter les étudiants dans les écoles et universités.

   c. *Continent* s'adresse à l'ANPE.

   d. *Continent* distribue des offres d'emplois dans les boîtes aux lettres des futurs diplômés.

4. Que dit *Continent* des candidatures spontanées?

   a. Ce ne sont pas les candidatures les plus intéressantes.

   b. C'est la meilleure source de candidatures qui divergent de la norme.

   c. Elles sont le résultat des contacts directs de *Continent* avec le monde étudiant.

   d. Elles prouvent qu'il y a beaucoup de jeunes qui préfèrent s'adresser directement à l'entreprise.

N. A vous la parole! Après avoir bien relu le texte, répondez aux questions suivantes.

1. Quels types de postes est-ce que *Continent* pense offrir à ses 200 nouveaux employés en 1995 et 1996?

2. Pourquoi est-ce que *Continent* parle d'oiseau rare dans le contexte du recrutement de nouveaux employés? Qu'est-ce que c'est qu'un «oiseau rare» pour *Continent,* selon vous?

3. Pourquoi est-ce que l'auteur du texte parle de «la partie immergée de l'iceberg»?

4. Donnez d'autres contextes dans lesquels on peut aussi parler de la partie cachée de l'iceberg.

5. D'après vous, *Continent,* est-ce une grande ou une petite entreprise? Justifiez votre réponse.

Lecture 2

Bien recruter, c'est rentable!

O. Activité de pré-lecture. Répondez aux questions suivantes par groupes de deux ou trois.

1. Selon vous, comment est-ce que les entreprises font la sélection des candidats qui ont postulé *(applied)*?

2. Dans la langue française, il y a de nombreux mots et expressions anglais qui sont utilisés, surtout dans le domaine de la gestion et de la mercatique *(marketing).* Expliquez l'expression «turnover».

3. Quels sont les avantages et les défauts du grand taux de «turnover»?

Bien recruter, c'est rentable!

Une annonce passée dans *Le Figaro* en mars a provoqué 1.214 appels téléphoniques. Après présélection, nous avons envoyé 564 dossiers de candidature et finalement recruté une quinzaine de personnes!

Nous sommes très exigeants parce que nos métiers sont devenus complexes.

Les stagiaires reçoivent une formation longue et onéreuse et l'on ne veut pas se tromper.

En 1988 le taux de turnover des jeunes diplômés atteignait 38%, nous l'avons ramené aujourd'hui à 12%. Nous investissons sur eux au départ mais c'est payant à long terme.

Tiré de: Actualités *Continent* N° 46, mai 1995.

P. Avez-vous compris? Répondez aux questions suivantes.

1. Ce texte contient quelques chiffres. Faites-en une liste et dites à quoi ils correspondent.
2. Que dit le texte des stagiaires de *Continent?*
3. Que pense l'auteur du texte du «turnover» actuel de *Continent?*
4. Expliquez en quoi *Continent* peut dire que l'entreprise investit sur ses jeunes diplômés qui commencent à travailler en son sein?

Lecture 3

Comment figurer dans la short-list des chasseurs de têtes

Q. Activité de pré-lecture. A deux ou trois, réfléchissez aux questions suivantes et discutez-les.

1. Si vous étiez chef d'entreprise, dans quels cas est-ce que vous feriez appel à un chasseur de têtes et pourquoi ?
2. Si vous étiez vous-même chasseur de têtes, comment est-ce que vous vous y prendriez pour trouver les candidats qui correspondent au profil recherché par votre client?

Comment figurer dans la short-list des chasseurs de têtes

Tout commence par un message anodin: "Une certaine Isabelle cherche à vous joindre au téléphone. Elle veut vous parler d'un poste. Ne laissez pas passer la chance."

Huit mois! Bénédicte C. a dû patienter pendant tout ce temps avant de décrocher le poste pour lequel le directeur du cabinet Infraplan, Victor Ernoult, l'avait "approchée". Sa patience a payé, même

si, au départ, on lui avait parlé d'une fonction de directrice des ressources humaines de filiale, et qu'elle a finalement été embauchée pour s'occuper de la gestion des carrières au niveau de la holding.

LES DÉLAIS DE RECRUTEMENT DÉPASSENT SOUVENT SIX MOIS

Aujourd'hui, rares sont les personnes qui, contactées par un chasseur de têtes et intéressées par sa proposition, peuvent espérer une conclusion rapide de l'affaire. Avant 1991, les missions duraient, tout compris, entre deux et six mois. Lors de ces années fastes, on s'arrachait les candidats. Depuis, le volume annuel de recrutement a beaucoup diminué, et les entreprises peuvent prendre leur temps. Elles voient davantage de personnes et cherchent à "verrouiller" leur décision. Conséquence: les délais s'allongent, et, parfois, comme dans le cas de Bénédicte C., les définitions de poste évoluent en cours de route. [...]

Autre tendance de fond, qui s'est confirmée en dépit de la crise: l'approche directe n'est plus réservée au gotha des dirigeants qui émergent à plus de 800 000 francs de salaire annuel. Même pour des postes dits de "middle management", les entreprises recourent de plus en plus souvent à cette méthode car elle leur évite l'avalanche de candidatures que déclenche une petite annonce dans la presse. La tribu des chasseurs de têtes se compose néanmoins de deux groupes: ceux qui interviennent exclusivement sur le marché des top managers et ne pratiquent que l'approche directe, et ceux qui recrutent pour tous les niveaux d'encadrement et utilisent la petite annonce et/ou l'approche directe (l'"approche mixte"), en fonction de la difficulté de la mission ou du désir de leur client.

LE CADRE APPROCHÉ EST SOUVENT PRIS AU DÉPOURVU

Si la récession a douché les entreprises, elle a aussi rendu les cadres plus frileux. Il faut parfois toute la force de conviction d'un chasseur pour les inciter à quitter leur job. Pourtant, c'est souvent au moment où l'on s'y attend le moins que survient une proposition peut-être intéressante. Que faire pour ne pas rater l'occasion? L'improvisation a ses limites. Les étapes d'un recrutement par approche directe obéissent à un rituel quasi immuable. Mieux vaut donc le connaître pour donner le meilleur de vous-même.

Les quatre étapes vers le succès

1. Se faire repérer. Le fichier est l'outil de base des chasseurs de têtes. Il existe

plusieurs manières d'y figurer ou de se faire remarquer pour y entrer.
2. Etre bon au téléphone. Le tout premier contact avec le consultant se fait généralement par téléphone. La qualité de l'entretien est déterminante pour la suite des événements.
3. Préparer l'entretien avec le consultant. Au cours de cette phase très importante, le chasseur teste vos réelles motivations. Attention aux pièges!
4. Séduire le futur employeur et conclure le contrat. Il ne faut surtout pas vendre la peau de l'ours avant de l'avoir tué. La dernière étape peut réserver encore bien des surprises. Mieux vaut savoir les anticiper.

ÉCRIRE OU BIEN SE FAIRE REPÉRER

Le fichier est l'outil de base du chasseur de têtes. Pour y figurer, il existe de nombreuses méthodes.

Pour avoir une bonne chance de participer au sprint final, il faut - c'est une évidence - être dans la course dès le départ. Or ce départ, pour un chasseur de têtes, c'est le fichier. Il contient des milliers de dossiers de cadres ayant un profil susceptible de correspondre à une de leurs futures recherches. Avec la crise, les cabinets d'approche directe ont beaucoup réduit les dépenses liées à l'enrichissement systématique de leurs fichiers. Les cadres doivent donc être plus actifs que jamais s'ils veulent y figurer. L'effort en vaut la peine. Elisabeth Morin, associée du cabinet Sirca, estime en effet à une sur trois la proportion de missions où le candidat recruté est issu du fichier. [...]

UNE CANDIDATURE SUR DIX ABOUTIT DANS LE FICHIER

Celle de Telsearch, par exemple, intègre chaque année les informations contenues dans une quarantaine d'annuaires de grandes écoles. Les cadres diplômés d'un tel établissement ont donc tout intérêt à informer leur association d'anciens élèves de l'évolution de leur vie professionnelle. Pourtant, rien ne remplace la démarche consistant à écrire directement à un chasseur. Certains se contentent d'un CV avec une carte de visite, d'autres apprécient une lettre de motivation

continued on page 172

continued from page 171

manuscrite, surtout lorsqu'ils pratiquent la graphologie.[...]

LES CHASSEURS SURVEILLENT LES CERCLES PROFESSIONNELS

Avant d'adresser un mailing à tous les chasseurs de têtes de la place, la précaution élémentaire consiste à se renseigner sur leurs éventuels secteurs de spécialisation. Ces informations se trouvent dans la plaquette de présentation du cabinet. Elle contient souvent une autre information précieuse: la liste des principaux clients. Ce qui évite de s'adresser à ceux qui travaillent pour votre employeur. [...]

Au-delà de ces méthodes relativement classiques, il existe d'autres moyens de soigner son marketing personnel. Gérard Sakakini, associé de Leaders Trust International et président de l'Aprocerd, l'une des trois associations professionnelles, conseille de prendre part à des colloques, comme intervenant ou même comme simple auditeur. Les listes de participants que distribuent les organisateurs de la manifestation sont des sources d'informations appréciées des chasseurs.

Autre tactique conseillée pour qui souhaite se faire voir: être actif dans son propre milieu professionnel. [...] Plus largement, le réseau des relations de confiance peut également jouer un rôle efficace. "Il ne faut pas hésiter à faire savoir, de manière discrète, que l'on est prêt à bouger, suggère Jean-Pierre Gouirand, partner chez Heidrick & Struggles, le numéro 2 mondial de la profession; l'information finira tôt ou tard par nous atteindre."

Pour vous faire connaître

• ENTRETENEZ VOTRE RÉSEAU.

Gardez le contact avec vos ex-collègues. Une fois par an, vous pouvez, par exemple, inviter vos anciens patrons à déjeuner.

• VALORISEZ VOS SUCCÈS.

Si vous êtes à l'origine de bons résultats, faites en sorte que le mérite vous en revienne.

• ACTUALISEZ VOTRE CV.

Vous bénéficiez d'une promotion ou changez d'entreprise? Envoyez un mot au journal des anciens élèves de votre école ou à la rubrique "Carnet" des quotidiens.

• INTERVENEZ DANS LA PRESSE

Acceptez de répondre à des interviews ou écrivez des articles pour des revues. Sans exagérer, car vous pourriez lasser.

Article de Jean Botella. Tiré de *L'Essentiel du Management*, Nº 11, janvier 1996.

R. Vrai ou faux? Parmi les affirmations suivantes, relevez celles qui ne vous paraissent pas correctes et reformulez-les de façon à ce qu'elles correspondent à ce qui a été exprimé dans le texte qui précède.

1. Les chasseurs de têtes ne pratiquent que l'approche directe.
2. Les chasseurs de têtes n'hésitent pas à vous téléphoner pendant vos heures de travail.
3. Avant de rencontrer le futur employeur, il y a une séance *(session)* de préparation, une sorte de pré-entretien qui se déroule dans le bureau du chasseur de têtes.
4. Toutes les candidatures sont classées dans le grand fichier du chasseur de têtes.
5. Vous ne devez envoyer votre CV et votre carte de visite à un chasseur de têtes que si vous avez envie de changer d'emploi.
6. Les chasseurs de têtes apprécient les candidats qui sont actifs dans leur milieu professionnel.

7. Il faut rester discret et ne pas trop se faire remarquer. Quand on est vraiment fort, on n'a pas besoin de se faire de la publicité.

S. La parole est à vous! Répondez aux questions suivantes.

1. Pourquoi peut-on dire que la patience de Bénédicte C. a payé?

2. Pourquoi est-ce qu'en 1996, cela prenait beaucoup plus de temps pour conclure un recrutement qu'en 1991?

3. Expliquez: «Lors de ces années fastes, on s'arrachait les candidats».

4. Expliquez en quoi la définition du poste de Bénédicte C. a évolué en cours de route.

5. D'après les lignes «Autre tendance de fond... une petite annonce dans la presse», en quoi est-ce que le travail d'un chasseur de têtes a évolué ces dernières années?

6. Expliquez le concept de «l'approche directe».

HSG

➤ Study the verb frames and flashes for *écrire, venir* and *tenir* of Module III in your *HSG* and complete Exercises A–C.

T. A vos plumes! Ecrivez un petit paragraphe faisant le portrait robot d'un chasseur de têtes. Expliquez quels sont, selon vous, les qualités et traits de personnalité indispensables à un chasseur de têtes. Quel genre de formation a-t-il eue? Où habite-t-il? Quelles sont ses activités extraprofessionnelles? Quel type d'expérience a-t-il eue avant d'exercer ce métier?

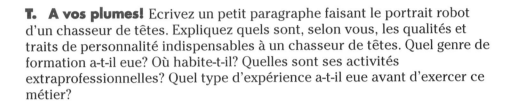

Quelques points de repère

Les chiffres parlent!

Le nombre des cabinets de recrutement s'est considérablement réduit ces dernières années à cause d'une conjucture économique peu favorable à l'embauche. Il y avait environ 1 200 cabinets de recrutement en France en 1996 alors qu'il y en avait 1 650 en 1992.

L'ardoise!

Autrefois, au cours d'un entretien d'embauche, les entreprises qui recrutaient pouvaient poser des questions comme "Etes-vous enceinte?" ou bien "Avez-vous l'intention d'avoir des enfants au cours des années à venir?" Maintenant, si des questions ayant trait à la vie personnelle du candidat ou de la candidate sont posées, il ou elle n'est pas obligé(e) d'y répondre.

- Si vous êtes nerveux(se) à l'idée de passer un entretien d'embauche, pensez que les personnes chargées de recruter le sont aussi car elles prennent un risque. Il est extrêmement important pour elles de prendre la bonne décision et de sélectionner le meilleur candidat.

- Lors d'un entretien d'embauche, un candidat est vulnérable car il a en général vraiment besoin de trouver un emploi et son avenir dépend de la décision des personnes qui conduisent l'entretien mais il est aussi en position de force car lui aussi, il a quelque chose à offrir: il a des compétences. Il a été convié *(invited)* à un entretien de sélection parmi de nombreux autres candidats, donc il est en bonne position.

- Un entretien d'embauche permet à une entreprise:
  1. de vérifier si le candidat ou la candidate correspond bien à l'idée que son dossier avait donné de lui (d'elle).
  2. de se faire une première impression de la personnalité de la personne pré-sélectionnée.
  3. d'obtenir des informations qui ne figuraient pas dans le dossier.
  4. de mesurer l'intérêt de cette personne dans l'emploi proposé.

- C'est à l'entreprise de montrer ses côtés positifs et de savoir convaincre et même séduire *(seduce)* le candidat.

Réflexions sur le travail en équipe

Pour obtenir les résultats les meilleurs, toute équipe devrait dans sa totalité choisir un système...
- qui met en valeur les compétences et la capacité de chacun de ses membres.
- qui subvient aux besoins des clients.
- qui maintient la qualité souhaitée.

Lexique

aborder: **Aborder** un sujet veut dire commencer à parler de ce sujet, prendre l'initiative de parler de ce sujet.

> Lors d'un entretien avec un chasseur de têtes, n'hésitez pas à **aborder** franchement le sujet des questions financières.

une convocation: Lorsqu'un candidat a retenu l'attention du service des ressources humaines, on lui envoie **une convocation** par lettre, c'est-à-dire qu'on lui envoie une lettre pour lui donner rendez-vous tel jour à telle heure pour un entretien.

> Allô, Nadine? Je viens juste de recevoir **une convocation** pour aller passer des tests chez Renault. Ce qui veut dire que je suis sur la «short-list»! Je suis enchantée!

date de disponibilité: Lorsque vous écrivez votre CV, il est recommandé de préciser votre **date de disponibilité**, c'est-à-dire la date à partir de laquelle vous pouvez commencer à travailler pour la nouvelle entreprise.

> Cette candidate n'a pas indiqué de **date de disponibilité**; je me demande quel préavis elle doit donner là où elle travaille actuellement.

donner suite à: Donner suite à une demande ou à une lettre de candidature veut dire entamer l'étape suivante qui peut être un examen, des tests ou un entretien. Lorsque la personne est déjà passée par ces étapes, **donner suite à** la candidature pourrait vouloir dire offrir un emploi.

> Nous sommes désolés de ne pouvoir **donner suite à** votre demande mais le poste qui vous intéressait est déjà pourvu.

un échelon: Un échelon est le barreau d'une échelle, c'est-à-dire une étape qui permet de monter. On parle d'**échelon** également lorsqu'on fait référence aux différentes étapes de la promotion à l'intérieur même d'une même fonction.

> Elle est extrêmement ambitieuse. D'**échelon** en **échelon** elle est arrivée assez rapidement à l'**échelon** supérieur, puis elle a décidé de changer d'emploi.

joindre: Lorsqu'on envoie une demande d'emploi, on **joint** à cette lettre un CV et quelquefois d'autres documents. **Joindre**, c'est donc «mettre avec».

> Françoise a fait une faute complètement stupide! Elle a oublié de **joindre** son CV à sa lettre. Alors, je suppose que sa demande ne va même pas être prise en considération.

une lettre d'embauche: Si une entreprise est intéressée par un candidat et qu'elle souhaite lui proposer un poste, elle lui envoie **une lettre d'embauche** et c'est alors au candidat lui-même d'accepter ou de refuser cette offre.

> Mme Huttin a laissé un message sur mon répondeur. Je vais recevoir **ma lettre d'embauche** en recommandé demain. Quel soulagement! Depuis le temps que je rêve d'habiter sur la Côte d'Azur, j'ai l'intention d'essayer de trouver un appartement entre Nice et Cannes. Je sais que cela ne va pas être bon marché.

une lettre de refus: Une lettre de refus est une lettre écrite par l'entreprise annonçant au candidat qui a postulé que sa candidature n'a pas été retenue.

> Il avait tellement peur de recevoir **une lettre de refus** qu'il ne pouvait pas rester à la maison à l'heure du passage du facteur.

opérationnel(le): Très souvent une petite annonce précise que l'entreprise offrant un certain poste demande que le nouvel employé soit **opérationnel** immédiatement, c'est-à-dire qu'il puisse exercer ses fonctions tout de suite.

Françoise Le Loup
Tel : 298.38.22.63   Guidel le : 30 Juin 95

Objet : Demande d'entretien
         pièce jointe annexe C.V.

Monsieur

Au cours de mes expériences passées, j'ai eu l'occasion de m'occuper d'enfants en difficultés et après une période de réflexion sur mon avenir professionnel, j'ai choisi de m'orienter en priorité vers le métier d'aide médico psychologique.

Votre établissement serait le lieu privilégié pour y vérifier mon orientation sur un contrat emploi solidarité ou une évaluation en milieu de travail du fait que j'envisage de suivre une formation au centre des aides médico psychologique de 5ᵀ AVÉ à Vannes.

Pourriez vous me recevoir rapidement afin de me donner une idée plus précise de ce métier, car je suis très motivée et je désire mettre toutes les chances de mon côté avant d'entreprendre une formation, je suis disponible et vous propose de me fixer un rendez-vous en vue d'évaluation de mes capacités (document explicatif ci joint)

En vous remerciant par avance d'encourager ma démarche et dans l'attente d'une rencontre, agréez monsieur mes respectueuses salutations.

> ➤ According to her cover letter, what has this candidate attached?

Isabelle HUBERT
132, Rue Racine
56700 HENNEBONT

Tel : 297.36.54.62

Mariée - 41 ans

> **18 ans Polyvalente Bureau**
> **Secrétariat Gestion Comptable**

FORMATION

1972	B.E.P. Sténo Dactylo Correspondancier
1993	"Utilisation de l'informatique dans tous les aspects de gestion dans les P.M.E. et P.M.I." au CERPPA - Lorient

Logiciels utilisés :
- Traitement de texte WORD 5.5
- Base de données, tableur intégré WORKS 2
- Gestion Commerciale : DIAPASON
- Gestion de la paie   : CRESUS
- Comptabilité   : ORDICOMPTA

EXPERIENCES PROFESSIONNELLES

1973-1991	Agent administratif à la Sté DAVUM Armatures - Caudan

- Facturation
- Salaires
- Accueil, Standard, Courrier administratif et devis
- Correspondant commercial
- Mise en place de l'informatique (Fichier)
- Saisie commandes et facturation sur micro-ordinateur MS DOS
(Réseau/Novell et Lotus)

1992	Opératrice de saisie à la S.B.C.D. - Lanester (2 mois)
1993	Stage pratique à la S.B.F.M. - Caudan

- Utilisation de l'informatique : EXCEL sous WINDOWS

DIVERS

Permis de conduire B + véhicule
Musculation, Randonnée pédestre
Lecture (policier, vécu, documents)
Musique (variétés, celtique, classique)
Mots croisés, jeux de société

Nous allons ouvrir une succursale qui devrait être **opérationnelle** début septembre dans la région du Nord-Pas de Calais, plus précisément dans la ville de Lille.

rédiger: Rédiger signifie *écrire, composer.*

C'est le service du personnel qui est chargé de **rédiger** les contrats.

retenir: Le verbe **retenir** a plusieurs significations. Employé dans un contexte de recrutement, **retenir** veut dire *garder, sélectionner.* Lorsqu'**on retient** une candidature, cela signifie qu'on est intéressé par ce candidat et qu'on veut lui proposer le poste en question ou tout du moins le faire venir pour un entretien.

Nous avons consulté tous les dossiers et c'est la candidature de Michèle Choutaux que **nous avons retenue** à l'unanimité.

vacant(e): Un poste est **vacant** lorsqu'il est libre, c'est-à-dire lorsqu'il existe mais que personne ne l'occupe. Une chaise peut-être **vacante** ou un appartement. En droit, des biens **vacants** sont des droits qui n'ont pas de propriétaires et on dit d'une succession qu'elle est **vacante** lorsqu'elle est ouverte et non réclamée.

Le poste ne restera pas longtemps **vacant.** Je sais que 150 candidats ont postulé et que le chef du personnel veut prendre une décision le plus vite possible.

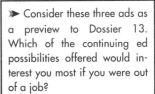

➤ Consider these three ads as a preview to Dossier 13. Which of the continuing ed possibilities offered would interest you most if you were out of a job?

➤ Study the definitions for the verb *accoucher* in your French-French dictionary. Then discuss the meaning of this adage with your study partner.

Paroles de sagesse

Petite négligence accouche d'un grand mal.

Expression écrite

Expressions interrogatives

Dans cette section, vous allez voir les expressions interrogatives les plus utilisées. Elles sont indiquées **en gras** dans le texte.

Dialogue: Réserver un vol
—*Agence de voyage Beau Soleil, bonjour.*
—*Bonjour, Madame. Est-ce que vous pourriez me donner des renseignements sur les vols Paris–Marseille, s'il vous plaît?*

—Oui, **quand** voulez-vous partir?

—Le 27 août.

—Et **quelle** serait votre date de retour?

—Le 2 septembre. **A quelle heure** est le premier vol?

—A 6 h 30.

—De l'aéroport d'Orly, **n'est-ce pas?**

—Oui, d'Orly Sud.

—**Quel** serait le billet?

—1.500 F T.T.C.

—Très bien, Réservez-moi une place sur ce vol.

—Les réservations sont payantes et coûtent 30% du prix du billet. **Comment** réglerez-vous le billet?

—Je paierai par Carte Bleue.

—**Quel** est votre nom, Madame, s'il vous plaît?

—Dutour. D.U.T.O.U.R.

—Dutour, oui. Et votre prénom?

—Christine.

—**Quelle** est votre adresse, s'il vous plaît?

—13, rue du Temple, dans le troisième.

—Et **quel** est votre numéro de téléphone?

—Le 01.48.25.72.55.

—Votre réservation est enregistrée et votre billet sera prêt à l'agence dès demain matin.

—**A quelle heure** est-ce que votre agence ouvre?

—Neuf heures quinze.

—Très bien, je passerai demain matin vers 9 h 30. Je vous remercie. Au revoir.

—Je vous en prie. A demain.

U. A vos plumes! En vous basant sur les expressions en gras du texte précédant et sur celles qui suivent, à vous maintenant de créer une conversation sur le recrutement du personnel. (15 échanges au minimum)

qu'est-ce que	que
qu'est-ce qui	où
qui est-ce que	pourquoi
qui est-ce qui	comment
qui	lequel, etc.

Dans le dossier suivant, vous allez examiner plusieurs facettes de l'entretien d'embauche.

*L'*entretien d'embauche

Le Dossier 9 se concentre sur l'entretien d'embauche. L'entretien d'embauche constitue une étape importante dans la recherche et l'obtention d'un emploi ainsi que dans le processus de recrutement. Après avoir envoyé un curriculum vitae et une lettre de motivation qui ont retenu l'attention du service des ressources humaines d'une entreprise, il faut se présenter en personne et savoir se montrer sous son meilleur jour *(in one's best light)* tout en essayant de se faire une idée de l'entreprise et de l'emploi en question pour pouvoir prendre une décision. De son côté, l'entreprise sonde le candidat et profite de l'entretien pour vérifier si le candidat répond bien à ses attentes à un niveau professionnel aussi bien que personnel. Que vous fassiez partie du groupe qui sélectionnera le candidat ou que vous soyez vous-même ce candidat, un entretien d'embauche se prépare. Les différentes lectures et activités de ce dossier illustrent le thème de l'entretien d'embauche et vous proposent des conseils *(advice)* qui vous permettront de mieux réussir votre entretien.

*A*ctivité d'introduction

L'entretien d'embauche

A. Préparation à l'entretien d'embauche. A deux ou trois, réfléchissez aux questions suivantes.

1. Imaginez que vous cherchez un emploi et que vous avez été convoqué(e) à un entretien d'embauche. Quels sont les sentiments qui vous animent et pourquoi?

2. Vous travaillez dans une entreprise et vous allez faire partie du groupe qui va sélectionner une personne qui travaillera en étroite collaboration avec vous, dans une petite équipe de trois. Vous vous préparez à l'entretien. Comment vous sentez-vous et pourquoi?

 *es mots pour le dire*

Vocabulaire de base

VERBES

avoir (perdre) confiance en soi	*to have (lose) confidence in oneself*
chercher un travail	*to search/look for a job*
décevoir	*to disappoint*
demander quelque chose	*to ask (for) something*
discuter	*to discuss*
douter	*to doubt*
employer	*to employ, give employment to; to use*
être sûr de soi	*to be sure of oneself*
évaluer	*to evaluate*
exagérer	*to exaggerate*
s'exprimer	*to express oneself*
s'informer	*to be/get informed*
payer, rémunérer	*to pay*
poser une question	*to ask a question*
prendre des initiatives	*to take the initiative*
se préparer à	*to prepare oneself, to get ready to*
se renseigner	*to get informed, to find out*
répondre à une question	*to answer a question*
travailler pour + substantif ou verbe	*to work for* + noun; *to work in order to* + verb
trouver du travail	*to find (some) work (to do)*
trouver un travail	*to find a job*

NOMS

des activités extraprofessionnelles	*extracurricular activities (outside of one's field)*
l'adjoint *(m)* **au responsable** *(m)*	*assistant commissioner*
un atout	*trump; asset, advantage*
un chef	*head, superior, leader*
un chef d'atelier	*foreman*
un chef de rayon, de service	*department head*
la/une communication	*call, conference/paper*
une confidence	*little secret*
un défaut	*character flaw, defect*
le dirigeant	*department or company head; director*
une fiche de paye, une feuille de paie	*payroll statement or stub*
l'honnêteté *(f)*	*honesty*
l'intégrité *(f)*	*integrity*
une interview (dans le domaine des média)	*interview (for/by the media)*
les loisirs *(m)*	*leisure time activities*
l'obtention *(f)*	*securing (of a job); obtaining*
un(e) patron(ne)	*boss*
un point faible	*weak point*
un point fort	*strong point*

un responsable	*department head; person in charge*
un service	*department*

ADJECTIFS

actif(ve)	*active*
arrogant(e)	*arrogant*
(un entretien) collectif(ve)	*(interview) in/as a group*
décontracté(e)	*relaxed*
déçu(e)	*disappointed*
dépendant(e)	*dependent*
direct(e)	*direct*
discret(ète)	*discreet*
essentiel(le)	*essential*
fermé(e)	*closed*
fort(e)	*strong*
franc(he)	*frank*
indépendant(e)	*independent*
indiscret(ète)	*indiscreet*
(un entretien) individuel	*one-on-one (interview)*
nerveux(se)	*nervous*
optimiste	*optimistic*
ouvert(e)	*open*
persévérant(e)	*persevering, resolute*
pertinent(e)	*pertinent*
pessimiste	*pessimistic*
rigoureux(se)	*rigorous, strict*
tendu(e)	*tense; tight*
timide	*timid*
travailleur(se)	*hard-working*

ADVERBES ET EXPRESSIONS ADVERBIALES

attentivement	*carefully*
certainement	*certainly*
inconsciemment	*unconsciously*
incontestablement	*unquestionably, indisputably*
nerveusement	*nervously*
probablement	*probably*
provisoirement	*tentatively*
sans doute	*probably*
sérieusement	*seriously*
sûrement	*surely*
ultérieurement	*subsequently*

B. Définitions provisoires à terminer. Complétez les phrases suivantes.

1. Lorsqu'on veut dire qu'il y a une grande chance qu'on fera quelque chose, on dit qu'on le fera _____.

2. Lorsqu'une personne n'est pas fermée mais qu'elle est, au contraire, prête à considérer des alternatives ou des idées et opinions différentes, on peut dire que cette personne est _____.

3. Une question _____ est une bonne question, une

question judicieuse, c'est-à-dire qui est importante et qui touche exactement le fond du problème.

4. Lorsqu'on a un entretien non pas en groupe mais face à face avec une personne à la fois, on dit qu'on a un entretien _____.

5. Un _____ est un point fort supplémentaire, un avantage, quelque chose qui distingue un candidat et joue en sa faveur.

6. Lorsqu'on veut avoir des informations sur quelque chose, on _____, c'est-à-dire qu'on pose des questions aux personnes compétentes et on essaie d'en savoir plus à ce sujet.

C. A vous de créer des définitions provisoires! Par groupes de deux, écrivez une définition provisoire pour les mots suivants.

1. des activités extraprofessionnelles
2. l'attitude
3. une confidence
4. décontracté(e)
5. provisoirement

➤ Feel free to look up key words or expressions in your French-French dictionary before coming to class.

➤ Il est très important d'arriver à un entretien bien préparé(e). Cela vous aidera à donner des réponses plus précises, plus claires et à poser des questions pertinentes et vous permettra de vous sentir plus à l'aise, plus détendu(e) au cours de *(in the course of)* l'entretien.

HSG

➤ Review the *Phonétique* section of Module III in your *HSG.*

Observations pratiques

L'entretien d'embauche

Un entretien d'embauche permet à la personne pré-sélectionnée

- de se faire une idée des conditions de travail.
- de compléter ses informations sur l'entreprise.
- d'obtenir de plus amples renseignements sur le poste libre.
- de se faire une première impression sur son futur patron et ses futurs collègues.

C'est au candidat de savoir se vendre et convaincre l'entreprise qu'il est le candidat qu'elle recherche. Il faut à la fois savoir se montrer motivé, sérieux, travailleur, honnête et agréable.

Le candidat ne sait pas quelles sont les qualités des autres personnes avec qui il se trouve en concurrence mais si l'entreprise ne l'avait pas jugé apte à tenir le poste, elle ne l'aurait pas invité. Les autres candidats ont certainement aussi des points faibles. Tout est encore possible. Le candidat a son avenir entre ses mains! L'entretien est donc un moment privilégié *(privileged)* dans la recherche d'un emploi. Il s'agit d'un côté comme de l'autre de tester ses interlocuteurs et de se montrer sous son meilleur jour!

Rien n'est joué à l'avance!

L'entretien d'embauche peut se faire de différentes façons. Le candidat peut avoir un entretien individuel avec une ou plusieurs personnes ou bien un entretien collectif au cours duquel il se trouve confronté à plusieurs interlocuteurs. Selon l'importance du poste à pourvoir, le candidat devra peut-être également passer une série de tests ou même une sorte d'examen. Un repas pris avec un ou plusieurs employés et responsables de l'entreprise peut faire partie du processus de sélection.

Différents styles d'entretien

- Un entretien peut consister en une série de questions extrêmement dirigées. C'est le recruteur qui a la situation en main et conduit la discussion.
- Un entretien peut se dérouler de façon plus décontractée et le candidat aura davantage d'occasions de s'exprimer.
- Un entretien ouvert sera basé sur des questions du type: «Parlez-moi de vous.» ou «Comment percevez-vous notre entreprise?»

Après l'entretien

Si l'entretien n'est pas suivi d'une offre d'emploi, il faut éviter de se laisser démonter *(be taken aback)* et douter de ses compétences. Un autre candidat correspondait sans doute mieux au profil du poste à pourvoir, mais cela ne veut pas dire qu'on ne vaut rien. Il faut persévérer et continuer à croire en soi!

D. A vous de jouer! A deux ou trois, imaginez que vous venez d'obtenir un entretien d'embauche. Signalez l'importance des éléments suivants en les numérotant de 1 à 10.

_____ les vêtements que je vais porter

_____ mes qualifications

_____ mes points faibles

_____ mes buts et mes objectifs de carrière

_____ mon comportement, mon attitude, ma façon d'être (mon sourire, ma façon de parler, mes gestes, les expressions de mon visage, etc.)

_____ le moyen de transport que je vais utiliser pour me rendre à l'entretien

_____ mes meilleurs traits de caractère

_____ mes points forts

_____ le salaire offert

_____ la ville ou la région où le poste en question est offert

E. Préparation à l'entretien d'embauche. Vous avez obtenu un entretien d'embauche dans l'entreprise de votre choix. Cet entretien aura lieu la semaine prochaine. Réfléchissez aux questions suivantes et répondez-y de façon personnelle.

1. Qu'est-ce que vous pensez faire la veille de l'entretien et tout particulièrement le soir?
2. A quelle heure comptez-vous vous lever?
3. Qu'est-ce que vous allez mettre comme vêtements?
4. Comment allez-vous vous rendre à l'entretien?
5. Avez-vous vraiment envie d'obtenir cet emploi? Comment allez-vous montrer votre enthousiasme?

continued on page 184

continued from page 183

6. Aimez-vous travailler en équipe ou préférez-vous diriger? Pourquoi? Comment?

7. Quels comportements ou attitudes pourraient prédisposer votre interlocuteur en faveur de votre candidature?

_____ Vous parlez beaucoup sans but précis.

_____ Vous écoutez attentivement ses questions et vous y répondez de façon logique et claire.

_____ Vous vous asseyez sans croiser les jambes et vous vous penchez un peu vers lui/elle.

_____ Vous mimez ses gestes et mouvements de façon subtile.

_____ Après avoir déterminé s'il/si elle est visuel(le), auditif(ve), ou kinésthésique, vous essayez de répondre à ses questions en utilisant son vocabulaire à lui ou à elle.

_____ Vous avez fait des jeux de rôle avec un(e) ami(e) avant d'aller à l'entretien.

_____ Vous vous êtes exercé(e) devant un miroir.

_____ Vous avez enregistré plusieurs essais ou tentatives sur cassette.

_____ Vous vous êtes habillé(e) d'une façon qui convient à l'emploi en question.

_____ Vous montrez une attitude ouverte et positive.

Dialogue

Entretien d'embauche

F. Activité de pré-lecture. A deux ou trois, travaillez sur les questions suivantes.

1. Laurence Martin est étudiante et elle cherche un emploi à temps partiel. Elle a remarqué une annonce indiquant que le supermarché Auchan embauchait. Elle a pris rendez-vous et se prépare pour aller à l'entretien. Quel genre de questions est-ce qu'on pourrait lui poser? Pensez au moins à trois questions possibles.

2. Pourquoi la personne conduisant l'entretien poserait-elle ces questions?

3. Et Laurence, quelles questions pourrait-elle poser?

Entretien d'embauche

Entretien entre M. Durand, Mme Ligeon, deux chefs de caisse du supermarché Auchan, et Laurence Martin.

M. Durand: Bonjour Mademoiselle, asseyez-vous, s'il vous plaît. Vous voulez bien vous présenter?

L. Martin: Bonjour, Monsieur. Je m'appelle Laurence Martin, je suis étudiante à l'Université de Perpignan et je suis actuellement en licence d'anglais. Comme j'ai beaucoup de temps libre, j'ai décidé d'essayer de trouver un emploi pendant quelques mois.

Mme Ligeon: Pourquoi avez-vous décidé de faire une licence d'anglais?

L. Martin: Eh bien, j'ai toujours aimé les langues étrangères. Je suis une personne très sociable et ouverte. Je suis attirée par ce qui est différent. J'aime voyager, rencontrer d'autres gens, apprendre à connaître et comprendre d'autres modes de vie, d'autres cultures.

M. Durand: Vous pourriez nous dire pourquoi vous avez choisi notre entreprise?

L. Martin: J'aimerais travailler dans votre entreprise car je pense qu'elle est leader sur le marché des supermarchés de la région de Perpignan. Cela m'intéresse aussi de travailler dans une grande entreprise et de voir comment elle fonctionne à l'intérieur.

M. Durand: Très bien. Maintenant pourriez-vous me parler de vos expériences antérieures?

L. Martin: Oui. Alors j'ai été serveuse dans un hôtel-restaurant en Angleterre il y a trois ans, pendant tout l'été. J'ai également été hôtesse à l'Office de Tourisme de Canet-plage il y a deux ans et réceptionniste au Camping «Mar Estang» à Argelès-plage l'été dernier.

M. Durand: Que pensez-vous de ces expériences d'emploi saisonnier?

L. Martin: Je pense que c'est une bonne chose car déjà cela permet aux jeunes de la région de trouver un travail deux mois par an, de commencer à participer à la vie active et puis bien sûr de gagner de l'argent. Je trouve que nous avons beaucoup de chance d'être dans une région touristique.

Mme Ligeon: Vous pourriez vous décrire, et nous dire par exemple quels sont vos qualités et vos défauts?

L. Martin: Je crois que je ne suis pas assez logique, que je ne suis pas toujours attentive à ce qui se passe autour de moi et je considère que ma spontanéité me pose aussi quelquefois des problèmes. Quant à mes qualités, je crois que je suis assez souriante et aimable lorsqu'il s'agit de travailler face à un public, je fais aussi tout mon possible pour que le travail que je fais soit bien réalisé. Je considère aussi que la ponctualité est très importante et je suis toujours à l'heure.

Mme Ligeon: D'accord. Quelles sont, selon vous, les qualités d'une hôtesse de caisse?

L. Martin: Je pense qu'une caissière doit être aimable et patiente avec ses clients. Elle doit aussi faire attention à sa

La caisse d'un hypermarché.

	propre caisse. Mais surtout je crois qu'elle doit être très souriante car c'est elle que le client regarde.
Mme Ligeon:	Je voudrais tout d'abord vous préciser que nous n'employons pas le terme «caissière» mais que nous utilisons le mot «hôtesse de caisse» car nous trouvons que c'est plus valorisant pour les employées. Et effectivement, nous considérons la qualité de l'accueil comme quelque chose d'essentiel. Nous demandons autant à nos hôtesses de bien savoir faire leur travail que de projeter une bonne image de la compagnie en étant souriantes et faisant tout leur possible pour que le client parte en gardant une bonne impression. Et que pensez-vous de la concurrence?
L. Martin:	Votre supermarché n'est pas le plus près de chez moi donc je vais souvent à Leclerc et à Casino. Je trouve qu'ils sont un peu plus lents et qu'ils font moins d'efforts de politesse. Néanmoins, je vous dirai franchement que c'est là que je vais faire mes courses car ils sont plus près et parce qu'il y a moins de monde.
M. Durand:	Vous devez aussi savoir que si vous travaillez chez nous, vous aurez des horaires qui changeront chaque semaine et vous devrez travailler deux dimanches en décembre. Est-ce que cela vous pose un problème?
L. Martin:	Pas du tout. Mes horaires sont flexibles et je n'ai aucune obligation à respecter dans la semaine.
M. Durand:	Bien, voilà. Je crois que nous avons fini. Avez-vous quelques questions à nous poser?
L. Martin:	Je voudrais juste savoir quand vous me donnerez une réponse?

M. Durand:	Nous ne pourrons pas vous donner de réponse avant la semaine prochaine.
L. Martin:	C'est parfait. Je vous remercie de m'avoir reçue. Au revoir, Madame, Monsieur.
M. Durand:	Au revoir, Mademoiselle.
Mme Ligeon:	Au revoir.

G. Vrai ou faux? Après avoir lu le dialogue, lisez les affirmations suivantes et décidez pour chacune d'entre elles si elles sont correctes ou non en mettant un "V" si elles le sont ou un "F" si elles ne le sont pas.

> ➤ Si une affirmation est fausse, corrigez-la.

_____ **1.** M. Durand demande l'âge de Laurence.

_____ **2.** M. Durand donne sa réponse immédiatement.

_____ **3.** M. Durand demande à Laurence de s'asseoir.

_____ **4.** Mme Ligeon pense que le fait que Laurence parle anglais peut être très utile pour une hôtesse de caisse.

_____ **5.** Mme Ligeon n'aime pas que Laurence appelle une hôtesse de caisse une «caissière».

_____ **6.** Mme Ligeon explique ce qu'elle pense des emplois saisonniers.

_____ **7.** M. Durand veut savoir quels sont les défauts et les qualités de Laurence.

_____ **8.** M. Durand demande à Laurence de lui donner le nom des concurrents d'Auchan.

_____ **9.** Laurence dit qu'elle fait toujours ses courses à Auchan.

_____ **10.** Laurence mentionne quelques-uns de ses défauts mais elle n'indique aucune qualité.

_____ **11.** Laurence a déjà été caissière chez Leclerc.

_____ **12.** Laurence explique que le service est excellent à Casino et que c'est pour cela qu'elle va y faire ses courses.

_____ **13.** Laurence a déjà eu quelques emplois saisonniers.

_____ **14.** Laurence demande quels seront ses horaires.

_____ **15.** Laurence dit qu'elle est très flexible du point de vue horaire.

_____ **16.** Laurence habite très près d'Auchan.

_____ **17.** Laurence devra attendre pour avoir la réponse d'Auchan en ce qui concerne l'emploi pour lequel elle postule.

H. A la recherche d'éléments précis. Etudiez le dialogue un petit plus en détail.

1. Laurence a déjà travaillé. Faites la liste de ses emplois précédents.

2. A la demande de Mme Ligeon, Laurence parle de ses défauts et de ses qualités. Faites la liste des défauts de Laurence.

3. Faites la liste des qualités de Laurence.

4. En vous basant sur ce dialogue et ce que vous pouvez percevoir/sentir de la personnalité de Laurence, pouvez-vous ajouter quelques défauts ou qualités sur vos deux listes précédentes?

5. Mme Ligeon demande à Laurence de lui dire quelles sont, selon elle, les qualités d'une hôtesse de caisse. Quelles qualités mentionne-t-elle?

6. Et selon vous, y a-t-il d'autres qualités qui sont importantes? Lesquelles et pourquoi?

7. Pourquoi Mme Ligeon n'aime-t-elle pas que Laurence emploie le terme «caissière»?

8. Connaissez-vous d'autres exemples d'emplois qui ont changé de nom pour des raisons similaires?

9. Laurence a-t-elle selon vous les qualités nécessaires pour être une bonne hôtesse de caisse? Justifiez votre réponse.

10. Mme Ligeon et M. Durand ne posent pas le même genre de questions. Que pouvez-vous dire de leurs différences dans la manière de conduire l'entretien?

I. La parole est à vous! Répondez aux questions suivantes.

1. Le directeur aurait pu poser d'autres questions à Laurence. Lesquelles?

2. Est-ce que Laurence aurait pu demander autre chose? A sa place, qu'auriez-vous demandé?

3. A quel supermarché allez-vous pour faire vos courses et pourquoi?

4. Comment sont les hôtesses de caisse de ce supermarché? Essayez de vous rappeler la dernière fois que vous êtes allé(e) faire des courses.

➤ Be ready to poll your class-mates. Have your reporter's notebook handy.

➤ Study the verb frames and flashes for *espérer, découvrir, connaître, être* and *pouvoir* of Module III in your *HSG* and complete Exercises D–H.

Les questions favorites

J. Activité de pré-lecture. A deux ou trois, réfléchissez à la question suivante et discutez-la. Si vous deviez faire partie d'un groupe responsable du recrutement du personnel, quelles questions aimeriez-vous poser aux candidat(e)s? Essayez de trouver quelques questions qui n'ont pas encore été posées jusqu'à maintenant dans ce dossier et expliquez pourquoi vous leur poseriez ces questions.

Les questions favorites

Les chasseurs de têtes ont tous une question préférée qu'ils posent à un moment ou à un autre de l'entretien. Piège ou pas, elle leur permet de mieux comprendre le candidat avant de l'évaluer.

Florian Mantione
Dirigeant de Florian Mantione Search.
Sa question: Quel est pour vous le

supérieur hiérarchique idéal?
- La réponse aide à savoir si le candidat est autonome, entreprenant, ou bien si son profil correspond plutôt à des fonctions d'exécutant.

Philippe Legrand
Dirigeant de Sud Expansion Partenaires.
Sa question: Dans l'absolu, quelle fonction souhaiteriez-vous occuper?

- Les candidats énoncent parfois des souhaits en totale contradiction avec le poste proposé. Il vaut mieux s'en apercevoir le plus vite possible.

Jean-François Petit-Archambault
Président du cabinet Orhus.
Sa question: Si vous disposiez de 5 millions de francs, qu'en feriez-vous?
- On distingue deux catégories: les entrepreneurs dans l'âme et ceux qui expliquent qu'ils placeraient cette somme avant de partir au soleil.

Jean-Michel Azzi
Directeur général de Maesina Self Marketing.
Sa question: Pouvez-vous me parler de vous pendant quelques minutes?
- Il faut pouvoir se résumer de manière concise. Cela traduit des qualités de synthèse, d'organisation et d'aptitude à la communication.

Geneviève Crouzet
Président d'Artémis Conseils.
Sa question: Quel est le fil directeur de votre parcours professionnel?

- Le candidat s'est-il laissé porter au cours de sa carrière? A-t-il pris des initiatives? A partir de ses réponses, on peut évaluer sa détermination.

Patrick Hayet
Dirigeant de Patrick Hayet-Conseil.
Sa question: Quelles sont vos activités extraprofessionnelles?
- La personnalité d'un rugbyman n'a rien à voir avec celle d'un golfeur. Cela donne une idée du contexte dans lequel le candidat est à l'aise.

Jean-Pierre Debette
Dirigeant du cabinet Momentum.
Sa question: Est-ce que vous estimez avoir de la chance dans la vie?
- La question est un peu brutale, mais elle complète bien l'impression générale donnée par l'entretien. Si la personne a la poisse *(rotten luck)*, c'est négatif.

Tiré d'un l'article de Jean Botella. «Comment figurer dans la short-list des chasseurs de têtes», *L'Essentiel du Management*, N° 11, janvier 1996.

K. D'autres mots pour le dire. Trouvez dans le texte les synonymes des mots suivants.

1. se former une opinion
2. le chef
3. indépendant
4. des désirs
5. un bureau
6. une sorte
7. investir
8. bref(ève)
9. un don naturel
10. la carrière
11. ne pas avoir de la chance

L. A la recherche du contraire. Trouvez dans le texte le contraire des mots ou groupes de mots suivants.

1. l'incapacité
2. dur(e), choquant(e)
3. la chance
4. positif

M. A vous la parole! Par petits groupes de deux ou trois personnes, discutez les questions suivantes.

1. Regardez bien le nom de la société dans laquelle les personnes interviewées travaillent. Que pensez-vous de ces noms?
2. Pourquoi, selon vous, y a-t-il certains noms qui sont partiellement en anglais?

3. Parmi les questions qui précèdent, quelle est celle que vous préférez et pourquoi?

4. Choisissez au moins trois questions parmi les questions favorites et posez-les à un membre de votre petit groupe.

Lecture 2

Interview de Paul Desmarais

N. Activité de pré-lecture. A deux ou trois réfléchissez aux questions suivantes et discutez-en.

1. Quelles sont selon vous les qualités les plus importantes chez un être humain? Pourquoi? Pensez à vos amis et à vos proches de façon générale, mais pensez aussi à vos collègues.

2. Quels sont au contraire les défauts que vous trouvez les plus désagréables? Pourquoi?

> ➤ Paul Desmarais a eu un cheminement exemplaire en matière d'expansion internationale des entreprises. A partir d'une petite compagnie d'autobus qu'il a sauvée de la faillite en 1951, il a bâti un empire qui se ramifie en Amérique du Nord, en Europe et en Asie.

Interview de Paul Desmarais

Vous avez appris depuis longtemps à travailler de très près avec les gens [...]. Quelles sont les qualités que vous admirez le plus chez un être humain?

Avant tout, chaque homme doit avoir le sens de l'humour, parce que sans humour, on ne peut pas passer à travers des échecs et de la misère! Et j'aime les bons travailleurs, les gens loyaux, qui ont de l'imagination et de l'énergie. J'aime avoir des gens qui se lèvent le matin et qui sont aussi énergiques toute la journée. L'honnêteté et l'intégrité sont essentielles. J'aime également les gens qui sont

indépendants d'esprit. Je n'aime pas avoir autour de moi des gens qui me disent ce que je veux entendre. J'aime les gens qui sont francs, qui sont capables de me dire qu'une chose n'est pas bonne, que je suis mal parti, que je fais fausse route, mais aussi bien entendu, que tout ira bien s'ils en sont convaincus.

Tiré d'une interview de Paul Desmarais, Président du Conseil et chef de la direction de Power Corporation. Interview par Claude Gravel. *FORCES* (revue trimestrielle québécoise), N° 109, novembre 1995, Montréal.

O. A la recherche d'éléments précis. Faites la liste de toutes les qualités énumérées par Paul Desmarais.

P. Autrement dit. Trouvez dans le texte les synonymes ou les contraires des mots suivants.

1. **Synonymes**
   - **a.** un être humain
   - **b.** les problèmes, les difficultés
   - **c.** fidèle
   - **d.** extrêmement important
   - **e.** je fais une erreur

2. **Contraires**
   - **a.** la réussite
   - **b.** le bonheur
   - **c.** amorphe
   - **d.** hypocrite

Q. La parole est à vous! Répondez aux questions suivantes.

    1. Etes-vous d'accord avec Monsieur Desmarais? Pourquoi?

    2. Quels sont les risques de la franchise dans la vie privée aussi bien que dans le monde du travail?

R. A vos plumes! Les qualités qu'on exige de ses employés sont-elles les mêmes que celles qu'on aimerait trouver chez un(e) ami(e)? Ecrivez un petit paragraphe de 150 mots environ sur les qualités que vous trouvez essentielles chez les gens qui vous entourent et expliquez pourquoi ces qualités sont si importantes pour vous.

HSG

➤ Study the noun and adjective frames of Module III in your *HSG* and complete Exercises I–N.

Q*uelques points de repère*

Une date importante!

Depuis 1972, la loi garantit officiellement une rémunération égale pour un travail égal, qu'on soit homme ou femme.

L'ardoise!

Autrefois, les recruteurs n'avaient pas recours à des tests de personnalité ou à la graphologie pour sélectionner les candidats. Il y avait également beaucoup moins de conventions sociales qui protégeaient les employés. Quand, pour une raison ou pour une autre, une entreprise voulait licencier *(fire)* un employé, elle le licenciait. De nos jours, les entreprises doivent se conformer à de nombreuses conventions sociales qui réglementent entre autres l'embauche et le licenciement et font valoir les droits des employés. Les entreprises ne peuvent pas renvoyer leurs employés sans raisons extrêmement sérieuses. Le recrutement devient alors une affaire délicate car l'entreprise prend un risque en embauchant une personne.

- Il y a des logiciels comme «Le Hiérarchiseur 500» qui aident à sélectionner et à recruter en comparant les candidats au profil du candidat idéal.
- En France, les femmes constituent 44% du total de la population active.
- Depuis 1990, il y a plus de 50% des médecins en France qui sont des femmes.

Réflexions sur le travail en équipe

Pour qu'un projet réussisse et atteigne une qualité optimum, il faut qu'il y ait un haut degré de compatibilité et de complémentarité entre les membres du groupe au niveau personnel, au niveau de l'équipe, entre les différents groupes et au niveau de l'organisme lui-même.

Lexique

l'aptitude *(f)*: **L'aptitude** est la capacité à faire quelque chose. On est **apte** à faire quelque chose quand on peut faire cette chose. Cette **aptitude** peut se référer à des capacités physiques, intellectuelles ou psychiques. **Une aptitude** peut également être une capacité acquise.

> Je ne crois pas que tu sois capable de devenir un bon conseiller car tu n'as aucune **aptitude** à la patience!

> L'entreprise va me faire passer des tests d'**aptitude** comme si mes diplômes n'étaient pas suffisants pour indiquer mon niveau!

autonome: Une personne est **autonome** lorsqu'elle peut effectuer certaines tâches par elle-même et qu'elle est capable de décider ce qu'il faut faire sans constamment demander l'aide d'un tiers ou d'un supérieur.

> Ce que j'aime dans ma profession, c'est qu'elle me permet d'être **autonome**. Tu sais que pour moi, la liberté et l'indépendance sont primordiales. Je voyage beaucoup, de Toulon à Rennes en passant par Lyon, Orléans et Le Mans. C'est quelquefois fatiguant mais je me sens libre comme l'air!

> Je comprends ton besoin d'**autonomie** mais moi, je n'aurais pas la discipline personnelle qu'un tel poste requiert.

se dérouler: «Se dérouler» est un synonyme de «se passer». On peut dire par exemple lorsqu'on a été témoin de quelque chose que la scène **s'est déroulée** sous nos yeux.

> L'entretien **s'est déroulé** sans surprise mais elle pense qu'elle a réussi à montrer son professionnalisme et à convaincre l'équipe de son efficacité.

un interlocuteur: Un **interlocuteur** est une personne avec qui l'on parle.

Pendant un entretien d'embauche, **les interlocuteurs** peuvent être le chef des ressources humaines et deux chefs de rayon par exemple, et bien sûr, le postulant lui-même, c'est-à-dire le candidat potentiel.

> Pendant l'entretien d'embauche, regarde bien tes **interlocuteurs** dans les yeux lorsqu'ils s'adressent à toi. Je sais que tu es très timide mais force-toi un peu parce que c'est essentiel. Il n'y a rien de pire que les regards fuyants. Ça donne très mauvaise impression.

se laisser démonter: Quand **on se laisse démonter,** on perd son assurance, sa confiance en soi. Certaines questions auxquelles on ne s'attendait pas du tout peuvent **démonter** pendant un entretien d'embauche.

> **Ne vous laissez pas démonter** par des questions indiscrètes. Vous n'êtes pas obligé(e) de répondre à des questions sur votre vie privée ou bien sur vos convictions politiques ou religieuses.

percevoir: Un candidat doit s'interroger sur la manière dont il va **être perçu** par les recruteurs, c'est-à-dire sur la façon dont il va être vu, jugé, évalué. Il doit se demander ce que les recruteurs vont penser de lui.

> C'est votre **perception** du poste qui nous intéresse. Dites-nous comment **vous percevez** le rôle du responsable de cette agence.

un(e) postulant(e): La personne qui postule, c'est-à-dire qui fait une demande d'emploi, est appelée **un postulant.**

> Nous avons eu plus de trois cents **postulants** pour ce poste. Nous avons été pris d'assaut par les candidatures et avons reçu une avalanche de coups de téléphone!

pourvoir un poste: Pourvoir un poste veut dire faire le nécessaire pour trouver une personne qui puisse remplir les fonctions correspondant à ce poste.

> L'année prochaine, M. Ligeon et Mme Rémin prendront leur retraite. Il y aura donc deux postes à **pourvoir** dans le service après-vente.

pourvu de: Quand on est **pourvu de** quelque chose, c'est qu'on est muni ou doté de ce quelque chose. On possède ce quelque chose.

> Il est **pourvu d'**un sens de l'humour extraordinaire.

> Il n'a pas besoin de s'inquiéter car il a la chance d'avoir un compte en banque bien **pourvu,** bien garni, bien rempli.

un recruteur: Un recruteur est une personne chargée de recruter pour elle-même ou pour une entreprise. Elle doit sélectionner de nouveaux employés.

> Il faut adresser ton CV et ta lettre de motivation au **recruteur** de ton choix.

HSG

➤ Complete the *Exercices de synthèse* and *Echange* sections of Module III in your *HSG*.

Paroles de sagesse

- Il n'est si petit métier qui ne nourrisse son maître.
- Un métier bien appris vaut mieux qu'un gros héritage.

Expression écrite

Formes négatives

Cette section vous donne un premier aperçu sur les investissements que vous allez étudier dans le Module VI. Le paragraphe suivant met l'accent sur les *formes négatives*. Lisez le texte et soulignez les expressions négatives qui s'y trouvent.

Mes investissements

Je n'étais pas satisfait(e) du rendement de mon compte épargne. J'avais l'impression de gaspiller mon argent. Alors, j'ai décidé d'étudier les différentes possibilités de placement ou d'investissement. Pourquoi ne pas me lancer à la Bourse [stock market] et devenir actionnaire et obligataire [stock/bond holder]? Mais comme il ne faut jamais prendre des décisions trop impulsives, avant d'acheter de tels titres (actions et obligations), il m'a fallu me renseigner sur de nombreuses sociétés afin de ne pas me tromper et pouvoir réaliser le maximum de profit avec le risque minimum. Il n'y a aucun investissement qui ne comporte quelques risques, mais une bonne connaissance du marché et des entreprises selectionnées, sans les éliminer complètement, peut cependant les minimiser.

En effet, pour obtenir des revenus de mes actions, il faut que l'entreprise dont je suis actionnaire ne perde pas d'argent mais au contraire réalise des bénéfices.

Après m'être informé(e) de mes droits et des choses à faire et à ne pas faire, je suis ainsi devenu(e) actionnaire d'une société, c'est-à-dire associé(e) de cette entreprise.

Je suis également devenu(e) créancier/créancière d'une entreprise en tant qu'obligataire. Pour les Français qui ne veulent pas investir à l'échelle nationale seulement, il existe aussi des SICAV (Sociétés d'Investissement à Capital Variable) qui sont des organismes de placement collectif en valeurs mobilières qui permettent d'avoir accès à certaines sociétés étrangères.

Cependant, à moins d'avoir une très bonne connaissance de la Bourse, il faut rester prudent avant de placer l'argent qu'on a épargné. Connaissez-vous le proverbe: «Il ne faut jamais placer tous ses œufs dans le même panier»? Cela veut dire qu'il est préférable d'avoir un portefeuille diversifié et de ne pas «tout miser sur le même cheval».

S. À vos plumes! À vous maintenant d'écrire un tel paragraphe (d'environ 150 mots) sur un des deux sujets suivants:

- vos choix en matière d'épargne en vue de votre retraite
- ce qu'il ne faut pas faire avant, pendant ou après un entretien d'embauche

**Avant de commencer le module suivant,
allons un peu plus loin avec «En guise de clôture»!**

MODULE **III**

En guise de clôture:
Allons un peu plus loin!

Texte littéraire

L'entretien d'embauche

A. **Activité de pré-lecture.** Répondez aux questions suivantes.

> **1.** Cherchez les mots suivants dans un dictionnaire français-français
> puis faites une petite phrase avec chacun d'entre eux dans le
> contexte du travail.
>
> - se raidir
> - une panoplie
> - hocher la tête
> - un plombier
>
> - une fiche de paie
> - faire la moue
> - mentir
> - se brouiller
>
> **2.** Que pensez-vous des demandeurs d'emploi qui mentent?
>
> **3.** Comment vous sentiriez-vous si vous ne réussissiez pas à trouver du
> travail?

L'entretien d'embauche

Il vint bientôt s'asseoir en face de moi; me jugea d'un coup d'œil. Je
me raidis, mais très vite je m'aperçus que de là où il était, en face de
moi, il ne pouvait pas voir mes chaussures. C'est toujours le point

faible de ma panoplie quand je vais chercher du boulot. Dans l'intérim, ils regardent. Il alluma une Gitane, m'indiqua le paquet du menton, je vis ses doigts jaunis, mais ses ongles étaient faits. Ses yeux étaient très rapprochés l'un de l'autre, Lambert a le genre de regard qui ne laisse rien passer de ce qu'il veut savoir. Il connaît les hommes, dans son métier, il faut apprendre à juger les gens tout de go, à s'en faire le portrait robot comme une photographie instantanée; il se trompe rarement, et il sait bien deviner jusqu'à quel point on est pauvre.

— Vous avez un c.v., des références?

— Non, je peux vous les apporter demain si vous voulez.

— Plus tard, nous verrons. Vous avez plus de quarante ans, n'est-ce pas ?

Je hochai la tête, ne parvenant pas à masquer ma surprise.

Lambert sourit, satisfait, et posa sa cigarette sur un cendrier bleu de suze Gentiane.

— A deux ans près, je devine à deux ans près, pas plus. Il n'est pas toujours facile de leur demander. Vous connaissez Manpower?

Je hochai de nouveau la tête, me demandant s'il était fou.

— Oui, mais qu'est-ce que...

Il reprit sa cigarette, la cala au coin de sa bouche et continua de parler comme s'il n'avait pas entendu ma question.

— Je suis un artisan, moi. Vous ne connaissez pas le bâtiment. Alors, je me demande si nous pourrons faire affaire. Il se passa la main sur le front, avec lassitude. Quand il me regarda de nouveau, bien en face, j'éprouvai de la gêne.

— J'ai déjà fait de l'intérim, monsieur, chez un plombier.

— Un plombier?

— Aux Lilas, je peux vous apporter mes fiches de paie.

Il fit la moue, j'avais envie de partir, car ce n'était pas lui qui m'aiderait à trouver un emploi. Mais Lambert était bavard, me racontant ce qui faisait la différence entre lui et Manpower. Depuis que je suis dans la mouise, je veux toujours parler avec des gens, mais lui, il me faisait mal à la tête, j'avais l'impression qu'il était un peu fou. Bientôt, je me levai, lui disant que j'étais disponible, et que s'il avait quelque chose à me proposer, qu'il me le dise car cela faisait près d'une heure que j'étais ici. Il roula des yeux ronds, passant sa main sous son menton luisant d'aftershave.

— Vous n'êtes pas envoyé par Manpower?

— Non monsieur, je cherche du travail, c'est tout.

Ma voix me parut digne et résignée.

— Merde, merde, gémit-il comme s'il était seul dans la pièce. Il se leva brusquement, posant ses deux mains à plat sur le bureau. Bon, j'ai cru que vous étiez le collaborateur qu'ils devaient m'envoyer, je me disais bien... Si vous voulez vous inscrire remplissez-moi ça. Je vous préviens, je n'ai pas grand-chose en ce moment.

Il me tendit la feuille sans me regarder, partit dans l'autre pièce.

— En capitales! cria-t-il.

Finalement je me rassis et je pris un stylo, je me mis à remplir la feuille photocopiée. Je les remplis toujours très lentement, car je suis obligé de mentir. Cela fait bien trois ans que je n'ai plus travaillé. Il y a longtemps, j'ai tenu un magasin de photo, mais j'ai fait faillite. Puis, en attendant de me refaire, j'ai travaillé dans des bureaux, comme expéditionnaire. Puis ça aussi s'est terminé, il y a trois ans.[...]

Je remplissais le formulaire lentement, tâchant de ne pas perdre pied.[...]

— Montrez-moi ça, vous finirez plus tard... Lômeur, Pierre, oui, oui, tiens tiens, vous habitez tout près, c'est pratique. Oui. Il fit claquer sa langue et me retendit la feuille, l'air sérieux. Continuez.

Je finis devant lui, sentant son regard sur moi. Je me levai pendant qu'il épluchait la feuille. Il me la retendit.

— Votre numéro de sécurité sociale, vous l'avez oublié. Très bien, monsieur Lômeur, apportez-moi vos références, excusez-moi encore pour cette histoire de Manpower, vous serez prioritaire si je trouve quelque chose dans vos cordes. Bon, il faut que je téléphone, j'attends une nouvelle secrétaire pour remplacer l'autre, à bientôt.

Il repassa derrière.

J'inscrivis mon numéro, je relus. Oui, je voulais bien travailler de nuit, oui, j'envisageais un déplacement si nécessaire, oui, j'acceptais des missions de moins d'une semaine, oui, oui, n'importe où, le salaire en rapport. Oui. Pourquoi devrais-je toujours dire oui? Je sortis, il parlait au téléphone, son regard planté dans mon dos. Je mis longtemps pour rentrer chez moi, crispé dans les rues. Je m'assis sur un banc, il faisait froid. Pourtant, malgré le froid, je n'étais jamais tombé malade depuis que je vivais sur la corde raide, en dehors de la société. J'avais sa carte dans ma poche, je la sortis, peut-être me donnais-je l'air occupé même s'il n'y avait personne à côté de moi à qui donner le change. Elle était un peu sale sur les bords, les caractères en italiques de son nom et de celui de sa société se brouillaient devant mes yeux. Ce jour-là, je connus la haine, comme jamais auparavant. Il me fallut faire un effort surhumain pour me lever du banc, reprendre ma route, ne pas rester là jusqu'à la fin. Quelle fin, je n'en verrai jamais la fin.

Extrait du roman, *Moi aussi un jour, j'irai loin* de Dominique Fabre. Paris, Nadeau, 1995.

B. A la recherche d'éléments précis. Répondez aux questions suivantes.

1. Qui allume une cigarette pendant l'entretien?
2. Est-ce que le narrateur a apporté son CV?
3. Quel âge a le narrateur?
4. Pourquoi le narrateur veut-il apporter ses fiches de paie?
5. Est-ce que le narrateur est affilié à Manpower?
6. Quel genre de formulaire est-ce que le narrateur remplit?
7. Pourquoi est-ce que le narrateur ment?
8. Quel genre de sentiment est-ce que le narrateur éprouve après son entretien?

C. Vrai ou faux? Si les affirmations suivantes ne sont pas correctes, changez-les de façon à ce qu'elles correspondent au texte.

1. Au début de l'entretien, Pierre Lômeur est un peu gêné car il pense que Lambert voit ses chaussures.
2. Pierre Lômeur prend une cigarette du paquet de Lambert après que celui-ci lui en offre une.
3. Lambert pense que Lômeur est envoyé par Manpower.
4. Il y a un malentendu entre les deux hommes car Lambert pense qu'il a été envoyé par Manpower pour un emploi de plombier.
5. Lambert est au téléphone quand Lômeur quitte le bureau.

6. Lômeur rentre chez lui directement car il fait froid.

D. Avez-vous compris? Répondez aux questions suivantes par écrit.

1. Qu'est-ce que Lômeur a fait comme métier et dans quoi est-ce qu'il a de l'expérience?

2. Faites une liste de la série de sentiments par lesquels Lômeur passe pendant et après l'entretien.

3. Montrez que Lômeur est prêt à accepter n'importe quel emploi.

4. Montrez que Lômeur a un bon sens de l'observation.

5. Quelle est l'atmosphère du texte?

Buts/Objectifs/Desseins

Si un but est la fin que l'on se propose d'atteindre ou l'intention que l'on a de faire quelque chose, pourriez-vous envisager la possibilité d'atteindre votre but, votre objectif ou votre dessein plus facilement si vous l'écriviez, le décriviez en détail et le visualisiez? Rendez vos buts, objectifs ou desseins aussi précis, aussi concrets que possible.

1. Le domaine personnel (votre bien-être et les enrichissements que vous apporte votre vie personnelle) est à la base de tout succès futur. Pendant cinq minutes, faites du remue-méninges *(brainstorming)* pour trouver au minimum quinze éléments qui sont liés pour vous au succès. Réfléchissez aux questions suivantes.

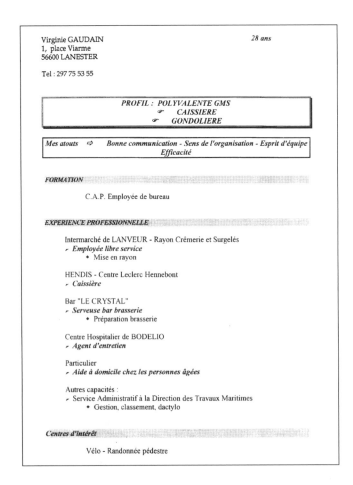

a. Qu'est-ce que vous aimeriez étudier ou apprendre juste pour votre propre plaisir?

b. Quelles abilités ou habiletés *(skills)* voudriez-vous perfectionner?

c. Comment aimeriez-vous être du point de vue personnel? Quelles caractéristiques comptez-vous cultiver?

d. Quelles sont les personnes qui vous inspirent? Qui aimeriez-vous connaître ou mieux connaître? A qui voudriez-vous ressembler du point de vue moral, intellectuel, physique, émotionnel, etc.?

2. Maintenant, pour chacun des buts, objectifs, desseins ou fins de la liste ci-dessus, indiquez *quand vous aurez atteint votre but* (par exemple, dans deux semaines, trois mois, un an, cinq ans, dix ans, en mai 2010, etc.).

3. Choisissez votre priorité numéro un pour cette année et écrivez un paragraphe où vous expliquez pourquoi vous comptez absolument réussir ce projet. Commencez par une phrase d'introduction, développez bien vos idées et finissez par une conclusion enthousiaste!

> ➤ Indicate what you would like to emulate next to the name of each of the fifteen individuals you choose.

Pour réussir

Pour que vous puissiez parvenir à une réussite réellement satisfaisante pour vous-même dans le domaine du travail, il faut

- que vous ayez une idée claire de ce que vous cherchez à accomplir, que vous ayez un but précis, bien défini.
- que vous choisissiez une profession qui vous permette de vous affirmer, de vous réaliser et qui reflète votre caractère et personnalité.
- que vous fassiez preuve d'intégrité, que vous agissiez en accord avec votre conscience, votre propre code d'honneur, en suivant une morale, en vous conformant à l'éthique sanctionnée par votre profession ainsi qu'en respectant le droit des autres.

A la fin de leur vie, les gens les plus satisfaits semblent être ceux qui ont fait preuve de générosité (temps, argent, compréhension, compassion), ceux qui ont eu une influence positive sur le monde, aussi bien dans le domaine personnel que professionnel. Lesquels de ces attributs possédez-vous déjà? Quels comportements, attitudes et caractéristiques avez-vous l'intention de développer?

Récapitulons!

Quelques aide-mémoire

1. Pendant un entretien d'embauche, on peut

- dire ce qu'on n'a pas écrit sur son CV.
- montrer qu'on est vraiment intéressé par l'emploi disponible.
- poser des questions sur les responsabilités liées à l'emploi en question.
- poser des questions sur les possibilités de promotion.
- parler de ses expériences passées et qui sont pertinentes.
- essayer de se montrer sous son jour le meilleur.

- se faire une idée de la personnalité de quelques-uns de ses futurs collègues et supérieurs.
- se faire une idée de l'ambiance et des conditions de travail dans l'entreprise en question.

2. Un CV est un document

- qui donne un certain nombre d'informations personnelles et professionnelles.
- qui présente les informations principales ayant trait à la formation d'une personne.
- qui donne une idée du parcours professionnel d'un(e) candidat(e).
- qui met en valeur les points forts d'un(e) candidat(e).
- qui accompagne une lettre de motivation.
- qu'on envoie à une entreprise pour essayer d'attirer et de retenir son attention.
- qu'on met à jour régulièrement.

3. Pour se préparer à un entretien d'embauche

- on se renseigne sur l'entreprise qui fait passer l'entretien.
- on s'exerce avec un(e) ami(e).
- on réfléchit à ce qu'on veut vraiment faire et à ce qu'on est réellement capable de faire.
- on s'interroge sur ce qu'on a à apporter à l'entreprise en question.
- on sélectionne ce qu'on va porter pendant l'entretien.
- on parle avec des gens qui ont passé un entretien dans la même entreprise ou dans une entreprise similaire.
- on essaie de savoir quel est le profil exact du candidat idéal recherché par cette entreprise et pourquoi.
- on réfléchit à comment on peut montrer qu'on est particulièrement intéressé dans l'emploi proposé.

4. Avant d'engager un nouvel employé, il faut

- comparer le dossier de tous les candidats.
- s'interroger sur les besoins exacts de l'entreprise.
- faire faire une étude graphologique des lettres de motivation et peut-être faire passer quelques tests psychologiques.
- inviter les meilleurs candidats à un entretien.
- se demander avec quelle personne on aimerait le mieux travailler à long terme.
- essayer de deviner quels sont les traits de la personnalité des candidats qui semblent attirants ou au contraire inquiétants.
- vérifier les références des candidats par téléphone.
- comparer la motivation, l'enthousiasme de tous les candidats.
- essayer de voir si ces personnes sont compatibles avec les autres membres de l'équipe.

Dans le Module IV, vous allez étudier les entreprises françaises.

Module **IV**

Les entreprises françaises

Ouverture

Une infirmière libérale passe à son cabinet pour lire son courrier et faire sa comptabilité.

Un mécanicien et ses outils.

La marchandise en vrac est stockée près du port de Lorient.

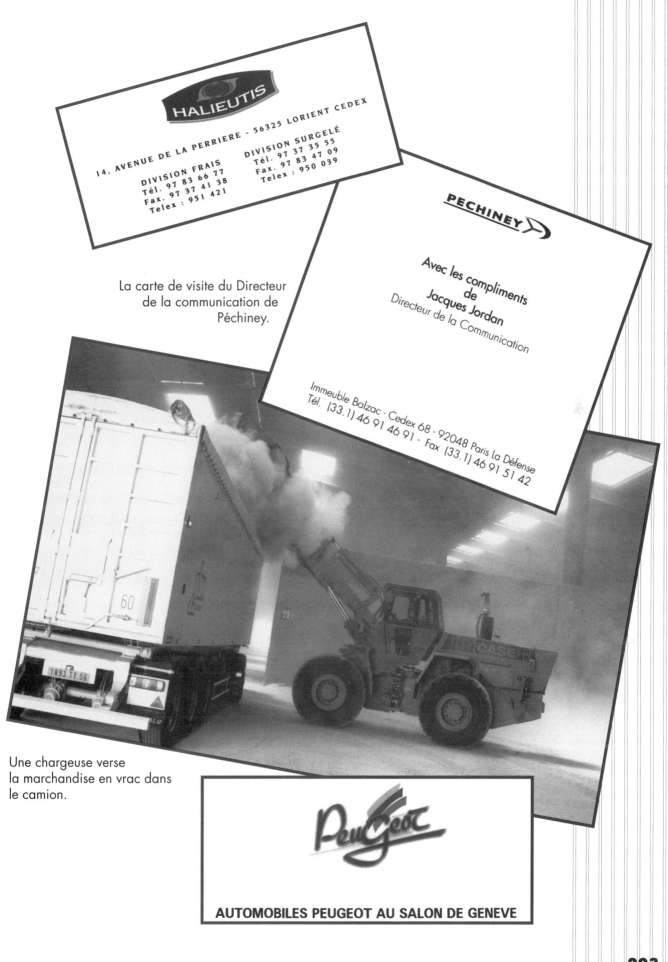

HALIEUTIS

14, AVENUE DE LA PERRIERE - 56325 LORIENT CEDEX

DIVISION FRAIS
Tél. 97 83 66 77
Fax. 97 37 41 38
Telex : 951 421

DIVISION SURGELÉ
Tél. 97 37 35 55
Fax. 97 83 47 09
Telex : 950 039

La carte de visite du Directeur
de la communication de
Péchiney.

PECHINEY

Avec les compliments
de
Jacques Jordan
Directeur de la Communication

Immeuble Balzac - Cedex 68 - 92048 Paris La Défense
Tél. (33.1) 46 91 46 91 - Fax (33.1) 46 91 51 42

Une chargeuse verse
la marchandise en vrac dans
le camion.

Peugeot

AUTOMOBILES PEUGEOT AU SALON DE GENEVE

*U*ne entreprise: Qu'est-ce que c'est?

➤ In Dossier 10, we will attempt to define what a company is.

En France, il y a entre 3 et 3,5 millions d'entreprises. Elles procurent *(offer)* un emploi à plus de 22 millions de personnes et c'est sur elles que la richesse du pays est basée. Le dixième dossier se concentre tout particulièrement sur ce que c'est qu'une entreprise et comment on crée une nouvelle entreprise. Les deux textes proposés comme lectures éclairent plusieurs éléments qui sont essentiels si l'on veut qu'une entreprise soit aussi performante *(productive)* que possible.

*A*ctivités d'introduction

Premier contact avec le monde des entreprises

➤ Note key words and expressions. Be ready to report your findings back to the class.

A. Définition. Qu'est-ce que c'est pour vous qu'une entreprise? Quelle définition en donneriez-vous? Prenez d'abord des exemples d'entreprises, puis, en vous basant sur ces exemples, essayez de formuler une définition plus générale.

B. Zoom sur la notion d'entreprise. Pour arriver à une définition plus complète de l'entreprise, interrogez-vous sur les questions suivantes.

Qu'est-ce que c'est qu'une entreprise pour...

1. un salarié?
2. l'enfant d'un(e) employé(e)?
3. l'Etat?
4. les actionnaires?
5. l'économie d'un pays?
6. la personne qui l'a fondée?
7. un syndicaliste du parti communiste?

C. La création d'une entreprise. A deux ou trois réfléchissez aux questions suivantes et répondez-y.

1. Qui crée une entreprise et pourquoi?

2. Que faut-il pour créer une entreprise? Répondez de façon détaillée et n'hésitez pas à donner beaucoup d'exemples.
- du point de vue matériel?
- du point de vue financier?
- du point de vue humain?
- du point de vue politique?

es mots pour le dire

Vocabulaire de base

VERBES

appliquer	*to apply*
croître	*to grow, increase*
se débrouiller	*to get by, manage, get out of difficulties*
se développer	*to get developed; to progress*
diversifier	*to diversify*
éclater	*to explode, burst*
évoluer	*to evolve*
exploiter (une idée, une personne)	*to cultivate, use; take advantage of*
fabriquer	*to make*
fonder	*to found, create*
marcher (bien, mal)	*to work (well, poorly)*
mettre au point	*to regulate, adjust; finalize, settle*
se monter	*to supply oneself with; to come to, amount to*
monter une entreprise	*to get a company up and running*
parvenir à	*to attain, reach; to succeed*
planifier	*to plan*
se réaliser	*to be realized, come true; to be fulfilled*
succomber	*to succumb, yield*
tenir à	*to cling to, be attached to; prize*
travailler à son compte	*to work for oneself*

NOMS

un ajustement	*adjustment*
un associé	*associate*
un chalenge, un challenge	*challenge*
le chiffre d'affaires	*turnover*
un commerçant	*merchant, shopkeeper*
une compagnie	*company*

continued on page 206

continued from page 205

un concessionnaire	*dealer(ship)*
le Conseil d'Administration	*board of directors*
le contrôle de qualité	*quality control*
un créneau	*niche*
la crise	*crisis*
un défi	*challenge*
la durée	*duration, length (of time)*
l'efficacité *(f)*	*efficiency*
une enseigne	*sign*
un entrepreneur	*entrepreneur*
l'expansion *(f)*	*expansion*
des fonds *(m)*	*funds*
un gérant	*manager*
la gestion	*management*
l'inefficacité *(f)*	*inefficiency*
la mondialisation	*world-wide application, globalization*
les moyens *(m)*	*means*
un patron, une patronne	*boss*
un P.D.G. ou P.-d.g. (Président-Directeur Général)	*CEO*
une P.M.E. ou PME (Petites et Moyennes Entreprises)	*small or medium-sized company*
la planification	*planning*
un régime	*system; regulations*
un responsable	*person in charge*
un secteur d'activité	*sector of activity*
un secteur de pointe	*hi-tech sector*
un service	*service; department*
une société	*company*
un souci	*worry, concern*

ADJECTIFS

commerçant(e)	*commercial*
compétitif(ve)	*competitive*
exploité(e)	*used, operated*
illimité(e)	*unlimited*
moyen(ne)	*average*
obsédé(e)	*obsessed*
paisible	*peaceful, calm, quiet*
passionnant(e)	*fascinating, enthralling*
prometteur(euse)	*promising*
propre	*one's own*
risqué(e)	*daring, off-color*
viable	*viable*

ADVERBES ET EXPRESSIONS ADVERBIALES

d'ailleurs	*moreover, besides*
ensuite	*then*
à fond	*totally, completely*
de moins en moins	*less and less*
de temps en temps	*from time to time*

D. Définitions provisoires à terminer. Complétez les phrases suivantes.

1. _____ une entreprise veut dire créer une nouvelle entreprise.

2. Lorsqu'une entreprise marche bien, qu'elle se développe et devient de plus en plus importante, on dit qu'elle _____. Ce verbe est le contraire de décliner, diminuer, baisser.

3. Quel est le _____ de cette entreprise, c'est-à-dire dans quel domaine est-ce qu'elle est spécialisée? Dans quelle branche est-ce qu'elle est active?

4. Si les choses ne vont pas exactement comme il faut, il peut être nécessaire de rectifier sa stratégie, de revoir ses plans ou de faire quelques _____, c'est-à-dire quelques changements de façon à s'adapter et à se conformer aux exigences du marché.

5. Cette nouvelle entreprise a bien démarré *(got off the ground)*. Ses débuts sont _____, c'est-à-dire pleins de potentiel. Ils annoncent une réussite à l'avenir.

6. On appelle _____ une personne dont la profession est de tenir un commerce, c'est-à-dire un magasin, une boutique, un restaurant ou un café. Ce mot est également un adjectif qui signifie qu'on a le sens des affaires, du commerce, qu'on sait vendre et plaire aux clients. Ma tante est extrêmement _____.

Un employé d'une maison d'Import-Export sur le port de Lorient.

E. Définitions provisoires à créer. Par groupes de deux, écrivez une définition provisoire pour les mots suivants.

1. évoluer
2. la mondialisation
3. une crise
4. un défi
5. un créneau

➤ Be ready to play *Mot de passe* in class. Would you be able to give simple definitions for most of the vocabulary words—in French, of course!

➤ You may use your French-French dictionary to note key words or expressions before coming to class.

HSG

➤ Study the *Photos et descriptions* section and complete Exercises A–C of Module IV in your *HSG*.

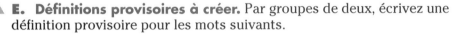

Dialogue

Deux amis discutent de leur avenir

F. Activité de pré-lecture. Mettez-vous à deux ou à trois et répondez aux questions suivantes.

1. Quelles qualités faut-il avoir pour fonder sa propre entreprise?
2. Dans quel domaine aimeriez-vous créer votre propre entreprise? Pourquoi?
3. Quels sont les avantages et les inconvénients de travailler à son compte? Faites une liste que vous discuterez.

Deux amis discutent de leur avenir

Charlotte: Je ne supporte plus mon patron. Tu sais, je pense de plus en plus souvent à m'installer à mon compte et créer ma propre petite entreprise. Je me vois très bien en Franche-Comté ou un peu plus au sud, dans la région Rhône-

Alpes, dans une grande ville comme Besançon ou Grenoble. Qu'est-ce que tu en penses?

Cyril: Tu es folle! Tu as gagné à la loterie nationale? Où est-ce que tu trouverais ton capital de départ? Il est hors de question que tes parents t'aident à ce que je sache!

Charlotte: Mes parents? Non, effectivement. D'ailleurs, même s'ils le pouvaient, je n'accepterais pas. Non, mais à mon avis, le capital de départ ne pose pas de problème. Je peux me lancer si je sélectionne un bon créneau. Après cela, ça ne devrait pas être trop difficile de trouver un partenaire ou bien de réussir à convaincre une banque de me consentir un prêt. Tiens, tu connais le magazine *L'Entreprise*? J'ai gardé le numéro de l'été dernier dans lequel on donne justement une liste de 111 créneaux pour réussir. Il y a plein d'entreprises offrant des services qui se montent et ça, ça n'exige pas de moyens exorbitants. Attends, je vais te montrer quelques exemples. Tiens, là, regarde. Ce mécanicien qui propose des vidanges ou révisions de voiture à domicile. Il a son camion équipé et pendant que tu travailles, lui, sur le parking de ton entreprise, il s'occupe de ta voiture! C'est l'idée exploitée par un certain Frédéric Degouy qui est maintenant PDG de «Dynacar» et possède cinq garages ambulants.

Cyril: C'est pas avec ses cinq garages ambulants comme tu dis qu'il va faire fortune!

Charlotte: Il a réalisé 6 millions de francs de chiffre d'affaires l'année dernière et pense créer sept filiales directes avant la fin de cette année puis un réseau de franchisés dans toute la France.

Cyril: Alors, là! Tu m'étonnes! Mais ça demande quand même un investissement de départ assez important. A combien lui revient un camion équipé?

Charlotte: 250.000 francs. Oui, c'est pas donné mais c'est relatif! Une minute, il y a d'autres choses qui demandent encore moins de fonds au départ. Que penses-tu de ça, écoute: Florence Boé, qui a fondé «Quat'Pat Services» à Neuilly-sur-Seine en janvier 1994. Elle s'occupe de chiens pendant l'absence de leur maître. Elle a déjà établi un réseau de 300 clients. Elle trouve des étudiants qui vont sortir ces chiens ou passer quelques heures avec eux ou bien elle trouve des familles d'accueil. Son chiffre d'affaires s'élève à 600.000 francs avec un investissement de départ de 100.000 francs. Ou bien «L'Age d'or Services» à Troyes. Il s'agit d'accompagner une personne âgée ou handicapée chez le médecin, chez le coiffeur ou bien aller avec elle faire des courses ou faire une promenade. Ça marche tellement bien d'après l'article que son créateur, Fabrice Provin, développe le concept en le vendant à des sortes de concessionnaires indépendants qui, moyennant une certaine somme, peuvent utiliser son enseigne.

Cyril: Et combien est-ce qu'il demande?

HACHETTE
Edition et Diffusion Francophones

JACQUES PÊCHEUR
RÉDACTEUR EN CHEF
LE FRANÇAIS DANS LE MONDE
DIAGONALES

58, rue Jean-Bleuzen, 92178 VANVES Cedex
Tél. (1) 46 62 10 50 · Télex HEDIF 631124 F · Fax (1) 40 95 11 33

➤ Une nouvelle forme juridique d'entreprise a été créée au début des années 90: L'E.U.R.L. (Entreprise Unilatérale à Responsabilité Limitée).

Charlotte: 67.602 francs de droit d'entrée, puis 14.825 francs par an.

Cyril: Et il a trouvé beaucoup de gens prêts à payer autant que cela pour exploiter son idée?

Charlotte: Oui, jusqu'à maintenant il y a 53 agences qui se sont ouvertes. Pas mal hein?! Toujours d'après l'article, il y aurait 7.000 personnes qui font appel à ces services. Ce numéro de *L'Entreprise* mentionne deux autres services qui marchent très bien et s'adressent partiellement aux gens qui sont vieux et ne peuvent plus se débrouiller tout seuls. A Paris et en banlieue, «Allô Linge» par exemple collecte le linge à domicile et le rapporte tout propre et repassé dans les 48 heures, ou bien «SOS Driver» à Orléans qui propose un chauffeur aux gens qui ont une voiture et qui pour une raison ou pour une autre ne veulent plus ou ne peuvent plus conduire. Il paraît que le marché français pour tout le troisième âge représenterait 1 milliard de francs!

Cyril: Oui, tu peux rêver en attendant de trouver ton créneau!

Charlotte: J'ai déjà trouvé! Créer les sites Internet pour les entreprises françaises qui veulent avoir leur place sur le Web! J'ai pas mal d'expérience dans ce domaine. Pourquoi ne pas m'installer à mon compte? Il y a une demande énorme en ce moment. Il faut que j'en profite!

Cyril: En ce moment oui, mais dans deux ou trois ans, qu'est-ce que tu feras?

Charlotte: Je verrai bien! Qui ne risque rien, n'a rien!

Cyril: Moi, je préfère rester salarié et avoir des revenus modestes, peut-être, mais réguliers. Je fais mes huit heures, ensuite je rentre chez moi bien tranquillement et il me reste encore du temps pour jouer au tennis, aller au cinéma, sortir avec mes amis. Je tiens à mes loisirs, moi! Les gens qui montent leur propre entreprise sont esclaves de leur travail. Ils travaillent comme des fous, 50 heures par semaine ou plus. Ils deviennent obsédés! Adieu les week-ends paisibles et sans soucis et les vacances au soleil!

Charlotte: Je ne suis pas d'accord! Quoi de plus passionnant que de fonder sa propre entreprise? C'est l'occasion idéale de se réaliser pleinement dans son travail. Si j'aime mon travail et que je m'y sens à l'aise, pourquoi compter les heures? Moi, je ne fais pas une distinction aussi radicale que toi entre travail et loisirs. Je veux faire quelque chose qui m'intéresse, et si ça m'intéresse, alors je me donne à fond.

Cyril: Eh bien, bonne chance et bon courage!

G. Avez-vous compris? Répondez aux questions suivantes.

1. Faites la liste des entreprises mentionnées dans le dialogue qui ont exploité un créneau nouveau ou original et qui ont bien démarré.

2. Il y a plusieurs chiffres cités dans ce texte. Ecrivez-les en toutes lettres *(write out in long form)* et dites à quoi ils correspondent.

3. Un dollar correspondant environ à cinq francs, commentez les prix qui figurent dans ce dialogue.

4. Expliquez en quoi on pourrait dire que Charlotte est optimiste, entreprenante et enthousiaste.

5. Peut-on qualifier Cyril de sceptique, ironique et prudent? Justifiez votre réponse.

H. La parole est à vous! Charlotte et Cyril ne sont pas du même avis. Complétez les phrases suivantes en vous appuyant sur ce qui a été dit dans le dialogue et finissez la phrase de façon différente selon la personne qui parle.

1. Charlotte: Emprunter le capital de départ...

2. Cyril: Emprunter le capital de départ...

3. Charlotte: Je vais te montrer quelques exemples de...

4. Charlotte: Frédéric Degouy...

5. Cyril: Je suis étonné que Frédéric Degouy...

6. Cyril: Tu rêves si tu crois que...

7. Cyril: Dans deux ou trois ans, tu...

8. Charlotte: Dans deux ou trois ans, je...

9. Cyril: Moi, je préfère être salarié car...

10. Charlotte: Moi, je préfère travailler pour moi-même car...

HSG

➤ Study the *Phonétique* section and complete Exercises D–I of Module IV in your *HSG.*

I. A chacun son opinion! Mettez-vous par petits groupes de deux ou trois personnes et discutez les questions suivantes.

1. Préférez-vous les idées de Charlotte ou celles de Cyril? Pourquoi?

2. Cyril fait une distinction nette *(clear)* entre ses loisirs et son travail. Et vous? Expliquez.

```
sarl  ATLANTIS
CONSEIL IMMOBILIER
4, rue Saint Jean
56108 LORIENT CEDEX
Tel. : 2 97 22 47 00
Fax : 2 97 22 48 12


                    Madame GUILLOU
                    CABINET INFIRMIER
                    Résidence PARVIS ST LOUIS
                    Place des halles St Louis
                    56100 LORIENT


                    Lorient, le 26 Juin 1995


Objet : Règlement Loyer


    Madame,

    Par la présente nous tenons à vous informer qu'à
    compter du 01 Juillet 1995, nous avons la gérance des
    locaux que vous occupez à l'adresse ci-dessus.

    En conséquence, à compter de cette date nous vous
    demandons de nous faire parvenir le règlement par
    chèque libellé à l'ordre de SOCIETE GENERALE 28000200.

    Vous souhaitant bonne réception de la présente,

    Nous vous prions d'agréer, Madame, l'expression de nos
    sentiments distingués.


                    Le Service Locations
```

Un magasin de chaussures.

Observation lexicale

Types d'entreprises françaises

- On peut classer les entreprises par leur taille. La plupart des entreprises en France sont des PME, c'est-à-dire des entreprises qui sont petites ou moyennes. De nombreuses PME sont familiales.

- On peut classer les entreprises par le secteur ou la branche dans lequel ou dans laquelle elles opèrent. Il y a trois secteurs différents.

  1. **le secteur primaire:** domaine des activités productrices de matières non transformées (l'agriculture, la pêche, la forêt, les mines);

  2. **le secteur secondaire:** domaine des activités productrices de matières transformées (l'industrie, le bâtiment);

  3. **le secteur tertiaire:** ce secteur comprend toutes les activités qui ne sont pas directement productrices de biens de consommation (le domaine du service: les commerces, l'administration, les professions libérales, le transport).

  Remarque: «La moitié des entreprises opère dans les services, le quart dans le commerce, un peu plus de 11% sont dans l'industrie et l'artisanat (qui toutefois regroupent 40% des salariés) et près de 14% dans le bâtiment et les travaux publics.»

  —Pol Guyomarc'h, *Dictionnaire de l'entreprise*

- On peut aussi classer les entreprises par la forme juridique sous laquelle elles opèrent. C'est l'origine des capitaux qui détermine la forme juridique de l'entreprise.

  1. **Il y a des entreprises individuelles.** Plus de 60% des entreprises françaises le sont. Un paysan qui travaille dans sa ferme et sur ses terres a une entreprise individuelle. Un petit commerçant comme un épicier, ou le propriétaire et gérant d'une maison de la presse, par exemple, a également une entreprise individuelle. Il en va de même pour un artisan (peintre en bâtiment, maçon, électricien, potier).

  2. **Il y a des entreprises sociétaires.** En France, environ 40% des entreprises sont sociétaires et elles emploient 90% des salariés. Les deux types de sociétés les plus courants sont les Sociétés Anonymes (S.A.) et les Sociétés à Responsabilité Limitée (S.A.R.L.).

  3. **Il y a des entreprises publiques.** Une entreprise est publique lorsque l'Etat est entièrement ou partiellement le propriétaire de cette entreprise comme c'est le cas pour la SNCF, la RATP, l'EDF et les P.T.T. Dans les années 80 et 90, la France a connu une vague de privatisation. Des entreprises qui avaient été nationalisées dans le passé sont redevenues des sociétés privées cotées en Bourse. En 1987, par exemple, Saint-Gobain, Paribas, TF1, Havas, la Société Générale, Matra etc. ont été privatisées.

> ➤ These are three possible ways to categorize French companies.

continued on page 212

continued from page 211

4. Il y a des entreprises coopératives. La raison d'être d'une coopérative n'est pas de s'enrichir mais de servir les intérêts de ses membres. La répartition du bénéfice se fait proportionnellement au travail qui a été effectué et non proportionnellement à l'investissement monétaire qui a été fait. Lorsqu'il y a un vote, chaque membre de la coopérative a une voix indépendamment de la part qu'il possède dans la coopérative.

J. La parole est à vous! Répondez aux questions suivantes par petits groupes de deux ou de trois.

1. Comment les entreprises sont-elles classées aux Etats-Unis ou dans votre pays d'origine? Comparez ce classement avec ceux qui précèdent.

2. Y a-t-il des entreprises publiques aux Etats-Unis? Lesquelles et pourquoi?

3. Discutez les avantages et les inconvénients des entreprises publiques.

4. Donnez des exemples de coopératives et discutez les avantages que les coopératives offrent.

5. Essayez de deviner quel est le secteur d'activités des sociétés françaises cotées en Bourse de la liste suivante.

Air France

Aérospatiale

L'Oréal

Danone

Bic

Canal+

Carrefour (hypermarchés)

Michelin

Le Club Méditerranée

Les Galeries Lafayette

Peugeot

Usinor-Sacilor (sidérurgie)

REMARQUE
L'organigramme

Un organigramme est un tableau schématique. Comme son nom l'indique, un organigramme représente l'organisation de l'entreprise. Il met en valeur les différents services et leurs rapports mutuels. Lorsqu'on lit un organigramme on peut donc avoir une idée de la fonction des différents services représentés et les liaisons hiérarchiques entre ces services.

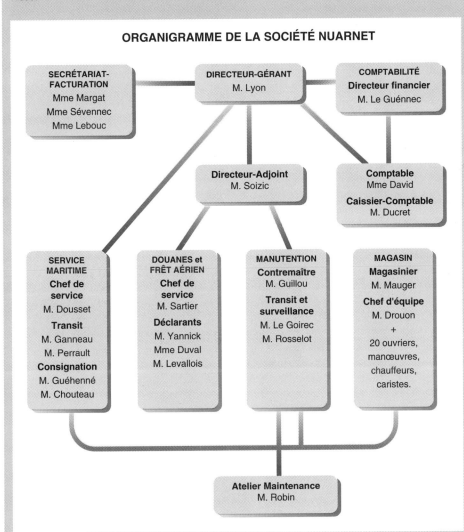

➤ Société d'import-export.

Lecture 1

Editorial sur la qualité totale

RIVE GAUCHE

Un grand magasin parisien.

K. Activité de pré-lecture. A deux ou trois, réfléchissez aux questions suivantes.

1. Expliquez l'importance d'une bonne communication dans la vie en général et au travail en particulier.

2. Essayez d'arriver à une définition de «la conscience professionnelle». Pour vous faciliter la tâche, vous pouvez partir d'un certain nombre d'exemples concrets.

3. Qu'est-ce que c'est pour vous qu'une entreprise qui marche bien?

Editorial sur la qualité totale

… [I]l y a deux choses que l'on n'apprend plus à l'école: la communication et la conscience professionnelle. Et quand on analyse les difficultés de certaines grosses maisons (le Crédit lyonnais en France, la banque Barings en Angleterre, chez nous je vous laisse le soin de trouver les exemples), on constate qu'il y a toujours une déficience dans les communications et une perte de la conscience professionnelle.

Quand, par contre, on analyse les causes de succès de certaines autres entreprises (les fabricants japonais d'automobiles et de produits électroniques, bien sûr) on découvre que la communication et l'application au travail sont régies par des règles quasi militaires. Tout le défi de la qualité totale est là.

Or, pour réussir à améliorer la qualité de vos produits et services, il faut exposer votre objectif, tenir des réunions de création ou de résolution de problèmes, motiver et sensibiliser les employés, expliquer à vos fournisseurs vos nouvelles exigences, exposer à vos clients les avantages de vos produits et services améliorés. Il vous faut combattre la force d'inertie et le refus du changement, convaincre de faire plus et mieux afin de répondre aux attentes du client.

Personne ne vous dit comment faire pour y parvenir. Et rares sont les cadres supérieurs qui admettent que la communication est un art régi par des règles qu'il faut connaître. Qu'il y a des techniques qu'il faut apprendre. Une institutrice d'enseignement supérieur m'avait chargé de tenir deux séminaires sur la communication dans la qualité totale: le premier n'a réuni qu'une poignée de participants; le second a dû être annulé.

Quant à la conscience professionnelle… ! Vous téléphonez à 9h05, la secrétaire est là, mais le patron… A 16h30, les bureaux à tapis sont souvent déjà vides. Traiter une affaire sérieuse entre le 15 décembre et le 10 janvier tient de l'exploit. Petits retards, oublis, approximations, erreurs d'inattention, débordements de travail dus au désordre, absences, etc. La qualité totale ne concerne pas que les simples employés, elle concerne d'abord les cadres. […]

La qualité totale, ce n'est pas une fantaisie. Elle concerne tout le monde et toutes les entreprises. […] La qualité, ce n'est pas une mode. C'est une question de survie.

Claude-Jean Devirieux (Editorial d'*Entreprendre*, le magazine des gens qui ont l'esprit d'entreprise, V. 8, N° 2, avril/mai 1995).

L. A la recherche d'éléments précis. Ce texte contient un grand nombre d'exemples de ce que les entreprises doivent faire et de ce qu'elles doivent éviter pour bien marcher. Faites une liste d'au moins six fautes commises par les entreprises.

M. Autrement dit. Les expressions suivantes sont tirées du texte qui précède. Expliquez-les dans le contexte qui vous est proposé.

1. des grosses maisons
2. une déficience dans les communications
3. des règles quasi militaires
4. la force d'inertie
5. le refus du changement
6. la communication est un art régi par des règles
7. les bureaux à tapis
8. des erreurs d'inattention
9. la qualité est une question de survie

N. Récapitulons! En trois ou quatre lignes, résumez l'essentiel de ce texte.

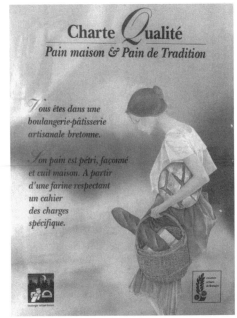

Vous êtes dans une boulangerie-pâtisserie artisanale bretonne.

Son pain est pétri, façonné et cuit maison. A partir d'une farine respectant un cahier des charges spécifique.

La charte qualité de la boulangerie-pâtisserie Le Goff, à Lorient.

> ➤ You may choose to work on Exercise M with your study partner before coming to class.

 *ecture 2*

Se lancer en affaires... et réussir!

O. Activité de pré-lecture. Répondez aux questions suivantes en groupes de deux ou trois.

1. Si vous deviez créer votre propre entreprise, comment est-ce que vous choisiriez les membres de votre équipe?
2. Qu'est-ce que c'est pour vous qu'une bonne équipe?
3. Quel est selon vous le rôle d'un chef d'équipe? Faites une liste d'au moins quatre de ses responsabilités.

Se lancer en affaires... et réussir!

Chercher à posséder son entreprise, c'est viser à la fois trois objectifs: un objectif personnel (mieux se réaliser), un objectif financier (faire des profits) et un objectif de gestion (assurer la survie, le succès et la pérennité de l'entreprise). Le futur entrepreneur pour réussir doit compter à la fois sur son dynamisme personnel et sur toutes les ressources mises à sa disposition, ainsi que sur l'assurance de collaborations utiles et d'encouragements désintéressés.

Bâtir une équipe gagnante

Se lancer en affaires, c'est d'abord structurer son projet, trouver son financement et constituer son équipe de travail, c'est-à-dire recruter et embaucher les personnes qui assumeront des fonctions

continued on page 216

continued from page 215

bien précises dans les opérations quotidiennes de l'entreprise.

RAISON D'ÊTRE ET IMPORTANCE D'UNE ÉQUIPE

Nous savons que, dans une petite entreprise, le dirigeant remplit généralement le rôle de chef d'équipe. Il veut une équipe de travail compétente et dynamique. Pour le faire, le dirigeant ou le chef d'équipe aura d'abord à définir clairement: Quels sont les besoins de l'entreprise pour sa bonne marche? Qui fera quoi? A partir de quand? Où? Quand? Comment? Avec quel effet?

Avant de recruter, le dirigeant d'entreprise aura à déterminer le nombre de personnes qu'exige chaque fonction, les tâches qui y sont reliées, la nature précise du travail, les conditions de travail, etc. Cette démarche permettra de bien identifier les qualités, les compétences, l'expérience à rechercher chez chaque futur membre de son équipe.

Dès le début de ses opérations, le dirigeant d'entreprise devra:

- établir ses besoins en employés à temps plein ou à temps partiel et leurs tâches;
- établir sa philosophie de gestion, les façons de communiquer ses messages, etc.;
- déterminer les conditions de travail qu'il peut offrir aux membres de son équipe et qui les motiveront;
- évaluer les avantages sociaux: vacances annuelles, jours fériés, congés de maladie, et s'il y a lieu, contribution à une caisse de retraite, assurance collective et assurance salaire.

Pour déterminer le salaire et autres conditions à offrir aux membres de son équipe, il devra préalablement tenir compte du chiffre d'affaires prévu ainsi que de la tâche à accomplir et des responsabilités inhérentes au poste. Il lui sera aussi utile de vérifier le salaire moyen offert par ses concurrents pour un travail équivalent.

STRUCTURATION DE L'ÉQUIPE

Travailler en équipe, c'est unir les efforts de deux ou plusieurs personnes en vue d'obtenir un meilleur résultat face à un travail ou à un mandat à accomplir. Cela implique que chacun respecte les différences de l'autre, au-delà des diplômes, de la personnalité et des habitudes.

Le dirigeant d'entreprise aura à:

- définir les tâches de chacun;
- déterminer les habiletés requises des candidats pour les accomplir (exigences académiques et formation requises, expérience nécessaire, langue(s) à utiliser);
- définir la nature des relations entre chacun.

LE RECRUTEMENT

L'embauche exigera cinq activités principales:

- faire le recrutement (offre d'emploi dans les média écrits, recours à une agence de placement ou autre maison spécialisée);
- après la réception des CV, inviter les meilleurs à répondre dans un premier temps par écrit à quelques questions pratiques: qu'est-ce que vous apporterez à l'entreprise de plus que ce qu'elle a déjà? Dans un plan d'action d'un an, quelles activités proposeriez-vous? Quels sont vos principaux défis d'avenir?
- tester les habiletés des candidats et s'assurer qu'ils répondent aux exigences du poste à combler;
- après l'entrevue, vérifier les références fournies;
- l'embauche, spécifier très clairement ce que vous attendez d'eux, et, si nécessaire, rédiger un contrat.

LES COMPÉTENCES ET QUALITÉS INDIVIDUELLES ATTENDUES DES CANDIDATS

Le dirigeant d'entreprise ou le chef d'équipe, tout en s'assurant de la compétence et de la motivation des membres de son équipe, devra vérifier s'ils possèdent:

- les connaissances et les compétences professionnelles requises pour exécuter et effectuer efficacement leur travail;
- un fort besoin de développement personnel et de réalisation de soi-même;

- une grande capacité d'établir des relations interpersonnelles positives;
- l'autonomie, la confiance en soi, l'esprit coopératif ainsi qu'un engagement total;
- le respect du rôle de chaque membre de l'équipe;
- une grande capacité d'adaptation;
- un jugement critique;
- la ponctualité et le respect des échéances;
- le souci de la tâche bien faite.

FONCTIONNEMENT DE L'ÉQUIPE

La première condition pour faire fonctionner une équipe gagnante, c'est que le chef d'équipe s'interroge sur ses objectifs, ses capacités et ses valeurs propres. Il déterminera aussi, préalablement, la nature des relations à établir avec les membres de sa future équipe.

RÔLE DU CHEF D'ÉQUIPE

- élabore des plans d'action et partage sa vision avec son équipe;
- distribue le travail et met en relation les personnes responsables du travail;
- s'assure de la diversité et de la complémentarité des membres de l'équipe;
- coordonne les efforts des membres et voit à l'intégration des activités en vue d'atteindre les objectifs fixés;
- recherche la participation de tous les membres de l'équipe (échanges et créativité);
- voit à la formation adéquate de chaque membre de l'équipe, les motive, les récompense et les félicite;
- contrôle et évalue le travail de chacun;
- facilite la libération de l'énergie créatrice de chacun et encourage le travail bien fait.

SES QUALITÉS ESSENTIELLES

- flair et détermination;
- esprit positif, réaliste et optimiste;
- confiance en lui et aux autres, capacité de déléguer;
- concentration sur les objectifs et les résultats;
- acceptation de prendre des risques calculés;
- capacité de distinguer l'essentiel du superflu;
- bon jugement.

RÈGLES DU TRAVAIL EN ÉQUIPE

Chaque membre de l'équipe doit se familiariser avec les règles du travail en équipe, partager avec ses collègues ses expériences et ses réalisations, et savoir mettre en commun ses sources d'information et ses contacts.

L'efficacité d'une équipe gagnante dépend de l'adhésion des membres à sept conditions fondamentales:

- Objectif commun;
- Rôle bien défini pour chacun et répartition équitable du travail;
- Complémentarité des compétences;
- Sentiment d'appartenance de chacun des membres à l'équipe;
- Participation active à l'information, à la discussion et à la prise de décision;
- Evaluation du travail accompli (auto-évaluation par chaque membre et par l'équipe).

Le respect de ces règles assure le fonctionnement d'une équipe compétente, durable et solidaire.

Edmond Bourque, Président et éditeur du magazine québécois *Entreprendre*, V. 8, No 2 avril/mai 1995.

CONTINENT
FRANCHISÉ INDÉPENDANT

M° le Spégagne.

KERYADO DISTRIBUTION K2 S A. · Rue du Colonel Muller
56100 LORIENT · Tél : 97 83 09 21   Fax : 97 83 49 46

➤ Qui est-ce?

➤ Consider brainstorming with your study partner before coming to class.

P. Avez-vous compris? Répondez aux questions suivantes.

1. Avant de composer une équipe à quoi faut-il réfléchir selon le début de ce texte?

2. Comment le salaire des employés est-il déterminé?

3. D'après ce texte, qu'est-ce qu'un chef attend des membres de son équipe?

4. Prenez point par point les éléments signalés dans ce texte comme faisant partie des responsabilités d'un chef d'équipe et expliquez-les avec vos propres mots.

5. Quelles sont d'après ce texte les qualités indispensables d'un chef d'équipe?

6. Expliquez en quoi avoir du flair et de la détermination est important. Donnez des exemples de situations dans lesquelles il faut effectivement avoir du flair et de la détermination.

7. Expliquez en quoi la capacité de déléguer est essentielle lorsqu'on travaille en équipe. Quelles qualités faut-il avoir pour pouvoir déléguer?

8. Commentez l'importance d'une répartition équitable du travail pour le bon fonctionnement d'une équipe. Que peut-il se passer si ce partage n'est pas juste?

9. Le texte souligne l'importance de la solidarité au sein d'une équipe. Donnez des exemples de solidarité et expliquez en quoi la solidarité solidifie une équipe.

Q. A vos plumes! Ecrivez un paragraphe bien structuré de 200 mots environ sur le sujet suivant: Préférez-vous travailler seul(e) ou en équipe? Expliquez pourquoi en donnant quelques exemples.

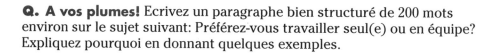

Quelques points de repère

Les chiffres parlent!

➤ Practice reading this segment aloud with your study partner until the numbers "roll easily off your tongue."

- En 1994, en France, parmi les voitures françaises, une Citroën Xanthia neuve coûtait 101.300 F, une Peugeot 106 3p kid: 56.700 F, une Peugeot 605 SV 24: 325.000 F, une Renault Twingo 1.2: 56.500 F, une Renault Saffrane Baccara biturbo: 426.000 F. Parmi les voitures étrangères, une BMW 850 CSI coûtait 722.500 F, une Golf GTI 115: 117.900 F, une Toyota Lexus LS 400: 432.000 F, une Honda Civic 1.3: 77.700 F. La voiture française la moins chère actuellement sur le marché est la Citroën AX "Spot": 41.000 F.

- *Production de véhicules en 1938*   Citroën: 68.109   Renault: 58.396   Peugeot: 47.213

  Production de véhicules en 1993   Renault: 1.264.628   Peugeot: 946.988   Citroën: 624.664

Les entreprises françaises!

L'Etat en France joue un rôle économique primordial. C'est l'Etat qui est le premier producteur, le client le plus important et également le premier employeur avec un chiffre total d'employés qui s'élève à 2 160 000 de personnes. L'Etat est aussi le numéro un des transports et le plus grand propriétaire foncier (terres) et immobilier (bâtiments) de France.

HSG

➤ Reread and practice the *Phonétique* section of Module IV in your *HSG.*

$\mathcal{R}$*éflexions sur le travail en équipe*

Pour faciliter une tâche, il faut toujours garder à l'esprit pourquoi tel ou tel travail va ou doit être fait, comment il va être accompli et quand il devra être terminé.

➤ Note key words and expressions used in the definitions. You may choose to just pass over words that you don't understand in the examples or look them up in your dictionary.

$\mathcal{L}$*exique*

l'actif *(m)*: **L'actif**, c'est l'ensemble des biens ou droits constituant le patrimoine d'une entreprise. **L'actif** est placé à la gauche du bilan.

> Cette année j'ai cédé **des actifs** pour renflouer mon entreprise.

un actionnaire: **Un actionnaire** est une personne qui possède des parts (ou actions) d'une entreprise. Il est propriétaire de cette entreprise en proportion du nombre d'actions qu'il possède.

> L'Etat est un **des actionnaires** de Renault.

un apport: **Un apport** est la somme de départ dont il faut disposer pour créer une SARL ou une Société Anonyme, par exemple.

> J'ai lu dans un magazine qu'il était possible de créer une SARL avec 5.000 F d'**apport** au lieu de 50.000 F. Le problème est qu'il faut envoyer un chèque de 495 francs pour recevoir le dossier qui explique soi-disant ce qu'il faut faire pour y avoir droit. Tu crois que c'est sérieux?

le bénéfice: **Le bénéfice,** c'est le gain ou profit réalisé par une entreprise. Une entreprise qui ne fait pas de **bénéfices** n'est pas viable.

> Renault n'a pas déclaré de **bénéfices** cette année.

le bilan: Chaque année, toute entreprise doit présenter **un bilan,** c'est-à-dire un tableau résumé de sa comptabilité.

> Cette année, **le bilan** de Peugeot est très positif.

le capital social: **Le capital social,** c'est le montant des richesses apportées à une société par les actionnaires. On trouve **le capital social** au passif du bilan des entreprises.

> **Le capital social** de Renault est de 50 milliards de francs.

le chiffre d'affaires: **Le chiffre d'affaires** est le total des ventes effectuées pendant la durée d'un exercice commercial.

> Renault réalise **un chiffre d'affaires** de plusieurs milliards de francs par an.

coté: Etre **coté** signifie avoir une valeur sur les marchés boursiers.

> A combien est **cotée** l'action de Renault actuellement?

des dividendes: **Les dividendes** correspondent à une rémunération. C'est ce qu'on gagne lorsqu'on possède des actions d'une société qui fait des bénéfices. **Les dividendes** peuvent être payés en liquide ou en actions.

> J'ai touché **des dividendes** sur les actions de Schneider que je possède.
> En 1989, Peugeot a déclaré **un dividende** de trois francs par action.

une entreprise de pointe: **Une entreprise de pointe** est une entreprise dont le domaine d'activité est hautement technologique. Elle consacre généralement des sommes importantes à la recherche et au développement.

> L'Aérospatiale est **une entreprise de pointe.** Elle est basée à Toulouse, dans l'Aquitaine, ainsi qu'aux Mureaux, près de Paris.

un exercice comptable: **Un exercice comptable,** c'est la période qui se termine par l'établissement des comptes d'exploitation et des bilans. Généralement, **un exercice comptable** dure une année.

> Cette année, **l'exercice comptable** de Renault fait apparaître une perte.

une fusion: Il y a **fusion** quand deux entreprises décident de se réunir pour ne former qu'une seule entité.

> Peugeot et Citroën **ont fusionné** en 1976.

un partenaire: **Un partenaire** est une sorte d'associé, c'est-à-dire une personne ou une entreprise avec qui l'on partage certaines activités et obligations.

> Renault n'avait trouvé un **partenaire** pour s'implanter sur le marché américain.
> Je cherche **un partenaire** pour jouer au tennis.

le passif: Le passif est l'ensemble des sources de financement d'une entreprise. Il est placé à droite du bilan.

Les dettes à long terme font partie **du passif**.

répartir: Répartir veut dire partager selon certaines règles ou consignes. Les dividendes d'une entreprise **sont répartis** entre les différents actionnaires.

Le PDG a décidé de **répartir** les parts du capital.

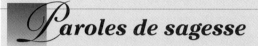

Paroles de sagesse

C'est en forgeant qu'on devient forgeron.

> ➤ After looking up the word *forgeron* in your dictionary, discuss what this adage means to each of you—in French, of course!

Expression écrite

Expressions adverbiales et conjonctions

Dans cette section, vous allez lire deux paragraphes. Le premier vous fait réviser certaines transactions effectuées à la banque. Dans le deuxième paragraphe, une jeune femme évoque le travail que son père faisait quand elle était petite. Encerclez toutes les expressions adverbiales ainsi que toutes les conjonctions et notez le temps du verbe associé à chacune d'entre elles.

À la banque

Hier, j'ai dû me rendre à la banque pour effectuer diverses opérations avant de partir en vacances. D'abord, j'ai demandé à l'employé de banque de me donner mon solde et les six dernières opérations réalisées sur mon compte. Lorsqu'il me les a donnés, j'ai vérifié que le montant de mon solde était bien le même que celui que j'avais calculé. Puis, j'ai demandé à l'employé de banque de virer 2.000 francs de mon compte épargne sur mon compte courant. Il m'a alors demandé de lui communiquer les numéros des deux comptes. Il a effectué cette opération sur son ordinateur et il m'a donné un petit relevé attestant de l'opération. Ensuite, je lui ai demandé de me commander des chèques de voyage en dollars pour une somme de 1.000 francs. Il a rempli une fiche que j'ai signée. Enfin, j'ai commandé un chéquier grâce au bordereau situé dans mon propre chéquier. Je l'ai rempli, signé et il l'a daté avec un tampon.

Mon père

Quand j'étais petite, mon père travaillait en tant que directeur du département d'alimentation du bétail à UNICOPA.

UNICOPA est une coopérative agricole de Bretagne et mon père était responsable de trois usines : Guigamp, Vannes et Guipava. Il était rentré dans l'entreprise alors que celle-ci n'en était qu'à ses débuts, et s'appelait encore La Morlaisienne. N'ayant aucune formation particulière, mon père a commencé comme «homme à tout faire» et a grandi peu à peu avec l'entreprise. Je me souviens qu'il était souvent absent de la maison mais quand il était là, il partait le matin à 8 heures, avec mes sœurs et moi. Il nous déposait à l'école puis allait directement au bureau. Généralement, quand il n'allait pas en tournée dans ses usines, ou quand il n'avait pas de déjeuner d'affaires, il rentrait à la maison à midi, ou plutôt, entre midi et une heure et demie. Cela dépendait de son boulot et on ne savait jamais ! Le soir, il revenait généralement vers 8 heures pour dîner. Et je me rappelle de longues conversations à propos de sa journée de travail, entre lui et ma mère… Souvent, le week-end, nous organisions une promenade familiale au siège social d'UNICOPA pour que Papa vérifie si tout allait bien. J'aimais ces promenades : les bureaux se trouvaient dans un ancien château, au milieu d'un joli parc, dont je m'imaginais être la propriétaire !

En fait, mon père passait beaucoup de temps à son travail, et c'était une fête lorsqu'il prenait quelques jours de congé pour voyager avec nous ou s'occuper du jardin.

R. A vos plumes! Essayez maintenant d'écrire un paragraphe d'environ 150 mots sur ce que vous avez appris au sujet des entreprises françaises. Commencez par une phrase d'introduction. Utilisez des expressions adverbiales et des conjonctions pour lier vos idées entre elles et les présenter de façon logique. Finissez par une phrase de conclusion.

La vitrine d'une petite boutique de vêtements au cœur de Paris.

Dans le dossier suivant, nous allons continuer à étudier le monde du travail.

Travailler dans une entreprise

Le Dossier 10 examinait l'entreprise du point de vue de ceux qui la créent ou qui la dirigent. Le Dossier 11 présente l'entreprise dans l'optique de ceux qui y travaillent. Que signifie travailler dans une entreprise? Que représente le travail dans la vie d'un être humain? Quels sont les devoirs, les responsabilités et les droits des salariés? Voici parmi d'autres quelques éléments qui sont abordés *(approached)* dans ce dossier.

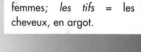

➤ *Mixte* = hommes et femmes; *les tifs* = les cheveux, en argot.

Activité d'introduction

Le monde des entreprises

A. Travailler. Mettez-vous par petits groupes de deux ou trois personnes et discutez les questions suivantes.

1. Que signifie pour vous travailler?
2. Quels sont les avantages et les inconvénients d'avoir à travailler?
3. Décrivez ce qu'est pour vous le travail ou l'emploi idéal.

Les mots pour le dire

Vocabulaire de base

VERBES

avancer	*to advance*
commander	*to lead, command*
échouer	*to fail*
encadrer	*to frame*
s'épanouir	*to bloom, blossom*
exécuter (des ordres)	*to carry out (orders)*
faire appel à	*to call for*
être fatigué	*to be tired*
être forcé de	*to be forced to*
s'inquiéter	*to get worried*
s'investir	*to invest oneself*
monter en grade	*to be promoted*
obéir	*to obey*
s'orienter	*to orient oneself; to move or turn toward*
s'ouvrir	*to open oneself*
pointer	*to check or punch in/out*
poursuivre	*to pursue, strive toward*
prendre en main	*to take care of*
promouvoir	*to promote*
suivre	*to follow*

NOMS

l'absentéisme *(m)*	*absenteeism*
l'administration *(f)*	*administration*
l'apprentissage *(m)*	*apprenticeship*
un atelier	*workshop*
un avocat, une avocate	*lawyer*
un cabinet	*office*
un comité d'entreprise	*company committee, board*
un comptable	*accountant*
la discrimination	*discrimination*
l'enrichissement *(m)*	*enrichment*
l'épanouissement *(m)*	*opening up, blooming*
un équilibre	*balance*
un fonctionnaire	*state employee, civil servant*
la formation continue	*continuing education*
un guichetier, une guichetière	*counter clerk*
le harcèlement sexuel	*sexual harassment*
un ingénieur	*engineer*
un jour de congé	*day off*
un ordre	*order*
la paie, la paye	*pay, wages*
le plaisir	*pleasure*
la rémunération	*salary, remuneration*

une subvention	*subsidy, grant*
une tâche	*task*
un traducteur, une traductrice	*translator*
un travailleur indépendant	*self-employed worker*
les trois huit *(m)*	*three eight-hour shifts*
une usine	*factory*
un vendeur, une vendeuse	*salesperson*

A D J E C T I F S

enthousiaste	*enthusiastic*
épanoui(e)	*fulfilled, happy*
équitable	*fair*
essentiel(le)	*essential*
fiable	*reliable*
intéressé(e)	*with a vested interest*
irréaliste	*unrealistic*
perspicace	*perceptive*
ponctuel(le)	*punctual*
respectueux(se)	*respectful*
stressant(e)	*stressful*
stressé(e)	*stressed out*
valorisant(e)	*actualizing, giving value to*

A D V E R B E S   E T   E X P R E S S I O N S   A D V E R B I A L E S

à l'heure	*on time*
en avance	*ahead of time, early*
en retard	*late*
trop tard	*too late*
trop tôt	*too early*

➤ Note key words or expressions to use for *Mot de passe*.

➤ Be ready for *Mot de passe!*

B. Définitions provisoires à terminer. Complétez les phrases suivantes.

1. Lorsqu'on est nommé à un emploi supérieur, on dit qu'on est promu ou bien qu'on _____ .

2. Dans de nombreuses usines, on exige des employés et des ouvriers qu'ils _____, c'est-à-dire qu'ils mettent une carte ou une feuille de papier dans une machine qui indique exactement à quelle heure ils sont arrivés et à quelle heure ils ont quitté leur lieu de travail.

3. Pour certaines professions libérales comme avocat, notaire, traducteur on ne parle pas de bureau pour se référer au lieu de travail mais de _____. On dit, par exemple: J'ai rendez-vous avec mon avocate à deux heures mais il faut que je lui téléphone parce que je ne me souviens plus si je dois me rendre directement au tribunal ou à son _____.

4. Un _____ est une personne qui travaille pour une administration publique.

AEROSPATIALE
ESPACE & DEFENSE

B.P. 2 - 78133 Les Mureaux cedex - France
Tel : (1) 34 92 12 34 - Telex : AISPA 695 988 F - Fax : (1) 34 92 12 54

Un employé de la Poste, un professeur d'université ou de lycée, un contrôleur de la RATP ou de la SNCF, en France, sont tous des _____.

5. Lorsqu'un(e) employé(e) est ennuyé(e) sur le lieu de son travail par des remarques ayant trait à son physique ou ses vêtements par un supérieur qui abuse de son pouvoir pour faire pression sur lui ou sur elle pour obtenir des faveurs d'ordre sexuel, on parle de _____.

6. Lorsqu'une décision n'est pas juste parce qu'elle avantage un employé au détriment d'un autre sans raison valable, on dit que cette décision n'est pas _____.

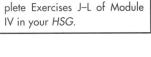

C. Définitions provisoires à créer. Par groupes de deux, écrivez une définition provisoire pour les mots suivants.

1. l'apprentissage *(m)*   **4.** une usine

2. un comptable   **5.** la paie

3. ponctuel(le)

➤ Study the nouns and complete Exercises J–L of Module IV in your *HSG*.

Dialogue

A la cafétéria, deux employés parlent de leur travail

D. Activité de pré-lecture. Mettez-vous à deux ou à trois et répondez aux questions suivantes.

1. De quoi est-ce que deux collègues peuvent se parler au travail?

2. Si vous deviez vous préparer à un entretien d'évaluation de votre travail avec votre supérieur direct, comment est-ce que vous vous sentiriez et pourquoi?

3. Quelle est l'importance d'un entretien d'évaluation pour l'employé et pour l'employeur?

A la cafétéria, deux employés parlent de leur travail

Luc Legrand: Alors, ça y est. Tu as fixé ton rendez-vous pour ton entretien d'évaluation?

Alex Rémin: Oui, mercredi prochain à 15 heures. Je suis un peu inquiet. C'est la première fois que je me fais évaluer.

Luc Legrand: Et ce ne sera pas la dernière! Franchement, il n'y a pas de quoi t'inquiéter, tu sais. Ils ne vont pas te manger! Tu as fait du bon boulot, tu es disponible, tu fonctionnes bien dans l'équipe, tu as su t'adapter et te montrer flexible. Je ne vois pas ce qu'on pourrait te reprocher!

Alex Rémin: N'empêche! Ce matin, ils m'ont remis un dossier qu'ils appellent «Bilan hiérarchique d'activité». Cela m'a impressionné! Ils m'ont même donné une cassette vidéo en complément au support écrit, soi-disant pour que j'aie une vision concrète de cet entretien mais au lieu de me rassurer, ça me rend encore plus nerveux.

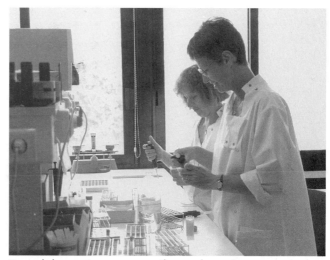

Deux laborantines au travail avec leurs éprouvettes.

Luc Legrand: Si tu veux, on peut la regarder ensemble cette cassette et je te dirai si ça correspond à la réalité. Remarque, moi aussi j'étais nerveux la première fois et de mon temps, il n'y avait pas encore de vidéo pour nous préparer!

Alex Rémin: Ce serait sympa. Oui, je veux bien. Est-ce qu'ils te disent vraiment comment ton travail est perçu et quels sont tes points forts?

Luc Legrand: Oui, mais ils passent plus de temps sur les points qu'on doit améliorer et sur la discussion des objectifs pour l'année à venir. En fait pendant l'entretien, ils suivent plus ou moins les points mentionnés. Montre-moi ça. Voilà: Tous les points qui sont répertoriés sous la catégorie «professionnalisme» y passent: efficacité, c'est-à-dire si tu es rapide, dynamique. Qualité du travail, c'est-à-dire si tu fais bien ton boulot, si tu termines ce que tu as commencé, si on peut compter sur toi, quoi. Organisation: ça c'est important. Ils veulent savoir si tu es autonome, si tu prends des initiatives, si tu maîtrises bien ce que tu fais. Adaptabilité et polyvalence, là, ils regardent si tu es capable de faire autre chose, si besoin est, et si tu es flexible. Hygiène, propreté: il ne s'agit pas de propreté personnelle mais celle des rayons, des caisses, des réserves. Tenue vestimentaire: ils sont très stricts là-dessus. Dans notre domaine, il faut toujours être tiré à quatre épingles, avoir les mains propres, enfin, bon, tu n'auras pas de problème de ce côté-là. Conscience professionnelle: ça, c'est crucial aussi. Ils veulent savoir si tu arrives à l'heure, si tu n'es pas trop souvent absent, si tu t'impliques dans ton boulot, si tu prends ton boulot vraiment au sérieux.

Alex Rémin: D'après la grille de correspondance qu'ils m'ont donnée, on peut être noté de A à E. Qu'est-ce que tu penses que je vais avoir?

Luc Legrand: Sans doute un «B».

Alex Rémin: B: «Salarié sans problème, ayant réalisé ses objectifs, polyvalent.» Qu'est-ce qu'il faut faire pour avoir un «A»?

Luc Legrand: La même chose, mais s'ils te donnent un «A», cela veut dire que tu es promotionnable dans l'année. Alors, à moins qu'ils n'aient vraiment l'intention de te faire passer à l'échelon supérieur, tu n'auras jamais que des «B». Mais un «B» te permet d'avoir droit à une bonne prime, c'est le principal. Tu ne vas pas être pénalisé au niveau de ton augmentation ou de ta prime avec un «B». Un «D» ou même, un «C», alors là, c'est une autre paire de manches!

Alex Rémin: Est-ce que tu as connu quelqu'un à qui on a donné un «C» ou un «D»?

Luc Legrand: Oui, tiens, Fabien, par exemple. Eh bien, l'année dernière, il ne s'entendait pas du tout avec son nouveau responsable. La situation était très tendue entre eux et Fabien n'était pas particulièrement poli, je dois dire. Il abat un boulot fou mais il n'est pas facile. Il faut savoir le prendre, Fabien! Cela a pété *(exploded)* plusieurs fois! Finalement, ce responsable a changé de rayon. Il faut dire que Fabien n'était pas le seul à avoir des problèmes mais on lui a quand même donné un «C», pas pour travail insuffisant mais pour comportement négatif.

Alex Rémin: Alors, qu'est-ce qu'il a fait?

Luc Legrand: Il était furieux. C'est vrai qu'il est très bosseur et sans lui, l'équipe aurait des problèmes! Il a protesté et a fait appel.

Alex Rémin: Sur le dossier, ça s'appelle «demander l'intervention de la strate hiérarchique supérieure»!

Luc Legrand: Ouais. Eh bien, la strate hiérarchique supérieure n'a pas voulu donner tort à la strate hiérarchique inférieure et il a dû garder son «C». Comme compromis, pour le calmer un peu, je crois qu'ils n'ont pas trop touché à sa prime. Comme prime, en tant qu'employé tu as droit à 3.500 F maximum mais ne t'attends pas à 3.500 F la première année. Je ne pense pas qu'ils te donnent plus de 1.500 F.

Alex Rémin: C'est déjà ça.

Luc Legrand: Les agents de maîtrise ont droit à plus d'un mois de salaire brut et la prime des cadres peut aller jusqu'à deux mois de salaire brut. Avec ça, ils peuvent bien partir en vacances, les cadres!

E. A la recherche d'éléments précis. En relisant le texte attentivement, faites une liste d'au moins dix mots qui se rapportent à l'entretien d'évaluation.

F. Avez-vous compris? Répondez aux questions suivantes.

1. Qui est Luc Legrand par rapport à Alex Rémin?
2. Avoir l'esprit d'équipe, qu'est-ce que c'est?
3. Pourquoi est-ce qu'Alex s'inquiète?
4. Comment est-ce que Luc rassure Alex?
5. Quelles sont les qualités de Luc?

G. Vrai ou faux? Lisez les affirmations suivantes et dites si elles sont correctes ou non. Modifiez celles qui sont incorrectes de façon à ce qu'elles correspondent à ce qui est dit dans le dialogue.

1. L'entretien d'évaluation a pour but d'établir le bilan hiérarchique d'activité des employés.
2. L'entretien de chaque employé est filmé en vidéo de façon à ce que l'employé puisse évaluer sa propre performance.
3. Alex Rémin a raison de s'inquiéter.
4. Lorsqu'un employé a fait de son mieux, a montré beaucoup d'enthousiasme pour son travail et a atteint ses objectifs de l'année, il aura automatiquement un «A».
5. Fabien est un collègue flexible mais un peu paresseux.
6. La prime dépend du travail qu'on a effectué et du genre de fonction qu'on occupe dans l'entreprise.

H. Zoom sur l'entretien d'évaluation et ses conclusions. Répondez aux questions suivantes, à deux ou trois.

> ➤ You may choose to brainstorm with your study partner before coming to class.

1. En vous aidant de ce qui a été dit dans le dialogue, pourriez-vous définir en une phrase à quoi correspondent les notes «A», «B», «C» et «D»?
2. Qui conduit *(leads)* cet entretien d'évaluation et quelles en sont les étapes *(stages)* importantes?
3. Qu'est-ce que le bilan hiérarchique d'activité détermine? Autrement dit, quelles en sont les conséquences?

Observations culturelles

Les congés payés

Légalement, tout employé en France a droit à des congés payés annuels à raison de 2 jours 1/2 ouvrables *(workdays)* par mois de travail accompli entre le 1er juin de l'année précédente et le 31 mai de l'année en cours, soit 30 jours ouvrables payés par an. C'est le minimum légal quelle que soit l'ancienneté de l'employé. Dans certains cas, l'employé peut bénéficier de quelques jours supplémentaires. Par exemple, les femmes de moins de 21 ans qui sont également mères de famille ont droit à 2 jours de plus par enfant et par an. Autre exemple: un employé faisant un travail particulièrement lourd ou travaillant depuis très longtemps dans la même entreprise peut obtenir de 1 à 6 jours supplémentaires *(extra)* par an. Une personne qui se marie ou une personne dont le conjoint, l'enfant ou un des parents meurt peut également obtenir un jour de congé rémunéré de son employeur.

   Une salariée enceinte (qui attend un enfant) a droit à un congé de maternité de six semaines avant la naissance et de dix semaines après la naissance du bébé quelle que soit son ancienneté. Elle percevra des indemnités journalières *(daily)* de la Sécurité Sociale qui s'élèvent à 84% de son salaire brut.

continued on page 230

continued from page 229

➤ Comparez et contrastez ces deux magasins de sport.

Un magasin de sport à Paris.

L'enseigne d'un magasin de sport.

Les Français ne travaillent pas pendant les jours de congés hebdomadaires *(weekly)* légaux, le samedi et le dimanche, ainsi que pendant les jours fériés, c'est-à-dire les jours réservés à la célébration d'une fête religieuse ou civile. Le contraire d'un jour ouvrable est un jour férié qui est un jour de repos, de congé officiel.

En France, il y a des jours fériés liés à des fêtes religieuses comme Pâques (dimanche et lundi), l'Ascension (40 jours après Pâques), la Pentecôte (dimanche et lundi), le 15 août (l'Assomption), le 1er novembre (la Toussaint), le 25 décembre (Noël). Les jours fériés d'origine civile sont le 1er janvier, le 1er mai qui est le jour de la fête du travail, le 8 mai célébrant la fin de la Seconde Guerre mondiale et le jour de la fête nationale, commémorant la prise de la Bastille, le 14 juillet.

Les «ponts»: Si par exemple le 1er mai est un jeudi, il est possible que l'entreprise donne le vendredi libre également pour permettre aux salariés d'avoir un long week-end. Donner ou prendre un congé supplémentaire pour permettre à plusieurs jours fériés de se suivre s'appelle «faire le pont».

I. La parole est à vous! Répondez aux questions suivantes, à deux ou trois.

1. Quelles sont les fêtes nationales et les jours fériés dans votre pays?

2. Comparez la situation en France et dans votre pays en ce qui concerne
   ▪ la durée de la semaine de travail.
   ▪ le salaire horaire minimum.
   ▪ les congés payés.
   ▪ les congés de maternité.

HSG

➤ Complete Exercises M–Q of Module IV in your *HSG*.

3. Regardez le calendrier de l'année prochaine: y a-t-il des possibilités de ponts? Lesquelles?

Lecture 1

Les entreprises parlent aux jeunes de 4^e

J. Activité de pré-lecture. En groupes de deux ou trois, discutez les questions suivantes.

➤ Be prepared to report your findings back to the class.

1. Quel(s) métier(s) trouviez-vous attirant(s) lorsque vous étiez plus jeune et pourquoi?

2. Quelles informations avez-vous obtenues sur les différentes carrières et différents métiers possibles? Est-ce que vous avez activement cherché des informations sur différents métiers possibles? Pourquoi?

3. Qu'est-ce que vous auriez aimé que les entreprises vous disent au sujet du monde du travail?

4. Pensez à votre métier actuel ou à votre futur métier. Quelles sont selon vous vos aptitudes et quelles sont vos aspirations?

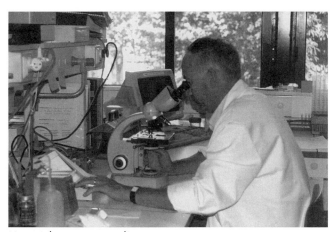

Un médecin se sert d'un microscope.

Une vendeuse d'un rayon poisson sert une cliente.

Les entreprises parlent aux jeunes de 4^e

Connaître des métiers intéressants pour t'orienter dans la vie scolaire et professionnelle

Si tu veux acheter une cassette, tu sais trouver les revues, regarder ou écouter la publicité, questionner les vendeurs.

Pour connaître les métiers, c'est la même chose, il faut beaucoup chercher, ta curiosité doit être sans limites.

- Interroge les personnes de ton entourage, leurs amis.

- N'hésite pas à demander à visiter les entreprises qui sont près de chez toi.
- Explore les expositions et les forums en demandant aux professionnels ce qu'ils pensent de leur métier.
- Recherche tous les documents possibles sur les métiers que tu veux connaître et sur les formations qui y préparent.

L'essentiel est de te lancer et d'avancer. Il faut aussi avoir toujours en tête trois ou quatre solutions pour éviter d'être déçu si la première n'est pas la bonne et pour cela disposer en

continued on page 232

continued from page 231

permanence d'un maximum d'informations et de conseils.

L'entreprise

Autour de toi, les adultes (parents, amis, voisins) parlent de leur travail à l'usine, au magasin, au bureau… La plupart de ces endroits sont des entreprises.

Il existe ainsi des milliers d'entreprises: des grandes, qui emploient beaucoup de monde, des moyennes et même de très petites dans lesquelles travaille parfois une seule personne, comme un plombier par exemple.

Chaque entreprise a un rôle utile: elle est au service de clients qui sont des particuliers ou d'autres entreprises.

Elle regroupe des personnes occupant chacune une place indispensable dans un but précis: concevoir, fabriquer des produits, objets ou services, les vendre, les entretenir.

Dans l'entreprise, quelle que soit sa taille ou son activité:

- tu gagneras ta vie tout en répondant aux besoins de ceux qui t'entourent;
- tu découvriras dans les ateliers ou dans les bureaux une occasion de faire de nouveaux amis avec qui tu développeras des activités productives et créatrices;
- tu poursuivras ta formation et assureras ainsi ton avenir.

Une entreprise ne se comprend que de l'intérieur. Une visite d'entreprise est très instructive si elle est bien préparée. Ce projet intéressant peut être réalisé avec certains de tes enseignants. A toi d'y participer pour découvrir: les machines, les métiers, l'organisation, l'ambiance.

Choisir un métier

Pour mieux apprécier un métier, demande-toi, après avoir interrogé ceux qui l'exercent déjà:

- Fait-il partie de ceux qui comportent un grand nombre d'emplois?
- Est-ce un métier qui est exercé dans de multiples branches?
- Est-ce un métier qui permet une bonne progression?
- Est-ce un métier qui permet l'accès à d'autres métiers?
- Est-ce un métier qui semble convenir à mes aptitudes et à mes aspirations?

Une formation adaptée

Une formation «adaptée» t'est indispensable: adaptée au métier que tu veux exercer, adaptée aux demandes des employeurs, adaptée à l'économie de demain. Quel que soit le choix que tu auras fait au départ, envisage dès ton entrée dans la vie professionnelle de progresser dans ta qualification par la formation continue qui peut également te permettre d'en changer le cas échéant. De nouveaux métiers apparaissent: sois curieux et pense à t'y préparer.

Les jeunes filles ne doivent pas s'arrêter à la recherche d'activités «traditionnellement féminines», sans pour autant les exclure.

Quelques conseils des employeurs

1. N'hésite pas à changer plusieurs fois de métier dans ta carrière. Chacun d'eux te fera progresser car chaque fois tu acquerras une formation complémentaire.
2. Envisage également de changer de lieu de travail, la mobilité géographique étant un atout considérable pour s'assurer un bon métier.
3. Ne désespère pas après un échec. Il y a de plus en plus de voies pour obtenir une qualification et exercer un autre métier. De plus, après l'entrée dans la vie professionnelle, la reprise d'études est possible.
4. N'oublie pas que la bonne connaissance d'une langue étrangère te sera très utile pour tous les métiers de demain en France ou à l'étranger.
5. Ne sois pas trop impatient, un bon métier s'acquiert dans la durée, par l'effort et l'expérience.

Notice réalisée par: JEUNESSE ET ENTREPRISES
Association reconnue d'utilité publique
4, rue Léo-Delibes — 75 116 PARIS
(Sous le patronage de l'Education Nationale et avec le concours de l'O.N.I.S.E.P. — Office National d'Information Sur les Enseignements et les Professions)

Des grues déchargent les bateaux dans le port de Lorient et mettent directement la marchandise en vrac sur des tapis ou dans des bennes allant dans les entrepôts.

K. Avez-vous compris? Répondez aux questions suivantes.

1. A quoi pouvez-vous voir que ce texte s'adresse à des enfants qui ont entre 13 et 15 ans? Donnez au moins trois éléments.

2. Pourquoi est-il important de ne pas se fixer sur un seul métier possible, selon le texte?

3. Comment choisit-on un métier d'après l'auteur du texte? Y a-t-il d'autres méthodes? Et vous-même, comment avez-vous choisi votre voie ou votre domaine de spécialisation?

4. Qu'est-ce que ce texte conseille aux filles tout particulièrement? Pourquoi?

5. Quel rôle est-ce que la curiosité peut jouer dans le choix d'une profession et plus tard dans l'exercice de cette profession?

6. Pourquoi est-il important d'interroger des gens qui exercent le métier qu'on pense choisir?

L. La parole est à vous! Discutez les questions suivantes par petits groupes de deux ou trois.

1. Quel est selon vous le meilleur conseil de ce texte? Pourquoi?

Le plan de la zone industrielle de Keryado, près de Lorient, en Bretagne.

➤ Listen to the *Photos et descriptions* segment on your audiocassette as you review the first section of Module IV in your *HSG*.

2. Qui peut jouer un rôle positif dans le choix d'une profession?

3. Pourriez-vous ajouter d'autres conseils? Lesquels?

4. Commentez les cinq conseils donnés par les employeurs.

Lecture 2

Le prix de l'équilibre

M. Activité de pré-lecture. A deux ou trois, réfléchissez aux questions suivantes.

1. Comment peut-on concilier sa vie professionnelle avec sa vie familiale et personnelle?

2. Pourquoi est-il souvent plus difficile pour une femme de faire carrière à un haut niveau?

Une infirmière libérale passe un coup de téléphone dans son bureau pour annoncer sa visite à un malade.

Le prix de l'équilibre

« Le nouveau conformisme prône l'équilibre personnel et loue l'engagement familial. Or, la réalité du travail rend la conciliation des vies professionnelle et personnelle de plus en plus difficile. Longues heures de travail, grande disponibilité, déplacements fréquents sont peu compatibles avec le développement personnel et les responsabilités familiales. Ceux et celles qui ont cru un temps à certains acquis déchanteront sans doute. La sociologue Mary Dean Lee, du département de gestion de l'Université McGill, a suivi 194 diplômés pendant cinq ans. Elle a observé que les hommes dont l'épouse demeure à la maison pour s'occuper des enfants gagnent plus que les autres diplômés, hommes ou femmes. Michel Tremblay, des HEC, était arrivé à une conclusion similaire lors d'une recherche dans les années 80 auprès de plus de 3.000 cadres. « La présence d'une personne qui assume les responsabilités familiales lève certains des obstacles à la progression de la carrière. Pour de nombreux cadres, leur femme constitue une ressource. » Nous ne sommes pas très loin de cette époque pionnière qu'a connue Monic Houde en début de carrière. « Peu de gens savait que j'avais un jeune fils, raconte-t-elle, je n'en parlais pas de peur de devoir en payer le prix. »

« Jacques Charuest est convaincu qu'encore aujourd'hui toute vérité n'est pas bonne à dire. « Dans certaines cultures organisationnelles, un cadre masculin marié prend un risque s'il invoque une responsabilité familiale. Il lance le message que son emploi et sa carrière ne sont pas sa première ou sa seule priorité. Certains s'en rappelleront au moment de décider qui sera promu et qui sera licencié. La situation est plus acceptable s'il est séparé ou divorcé ou si la responsabilité familiale invoquée concerne ses parents âgés. [...]

« Des centres d'intérêt à l'extérieur du bureau, des moments à soi, une bonne forme physique, tels seraient [...] les antidotes à l'intoxication par le travail. Ceux-ci sont toutefois inopérants s'ils ne sont pas associés à la passion et au plaisir. Louis Morin exprime ici ce que tous ressentent: « Il faut éprouver du plaisir à réaliser les objectifs professionnels et personnels que l'on se fixe et à relever les défis que chaque jour amène. Les gens malheureux sont des candidats au *burn out.* »

« Ils en rencontrent d'ailleurs beaucoup par les temps qui courent! Que font-ils quand ils les croisent? «Il m'arrive de suggérer à un collaborateur de rentrer chez lui et de jouer avec ses enfants,» répond Lorne Zakaib. «Il m'est arrivé d'obliger des cadres à prendre leurs vacances, raconte Marcel Boisvert. Je prends d'ailleurs les miennes religieusement. Je les incite souvent à s'inscrire à la formation en gestion du stress ou du temps que donne notre entreprise.» Guy Vaillant s'asseoit avec ceux qui abattent souvent des semaines de 65 heures. «Ce sont souvent des perfectionnistes qui ont besoin, par insécurité sans doute, de contrôler le moindre détail. Beaucoup de cadres pourraient réduire sensiblement leur semaine de travail s'ils éliminaient le temps non productif, déléguaient davantage, prenaient l'habitude de régler les questions au fur et à mesure, apprenaient à établir un ordre de priorités.»

«Leur message ne passe pas toujours. L'inquiétude rend sourd. «Dans un contexte d'insécurité et de restrictions, il est parfois difficile de convaincre, constate Lorne Zakaib. Quand je leur dis que ce qui compte, ce n'est pas le nombre d'heures, mais la contribution, et qu'une sortie en famille ou une partie de golf peut améliorer cette contribution, ils hésitent à me croire.» «Les gens ont tendance à résister au changement», rappelle pour sa part Marcel Boisvert.»

Jeanne Morazain : «Les gestionnaires: Mythes et réalités» pp. 48–50, paru dans *FORCES* No 108, 1995. Montréal.

COMPAGNIE MARCONI CANADA

600, boulevard Dr.-Frederik-Philips
Ville Saint-Laurent (Québec), Canada H4M 2S9
Téléphone: (514) 748-3148 Télécopieur: (514) 748-3100

CHANTAL GUILLOU-LE GOFF
INFIRMIÈRE LIBÉRALE
SOINS À DOMICILE

2 RUE DUPLEIX
56100 LORIENT

TÉL. 97 64 24 48

N. Autrement dit. Relisez bien le premier paragraphe du texte et expliquez les expressions suivantes d'après leur contexte. N'hésitez pas à vous servir d'un dictionnaire, français-français si possible, pour chercher la signification des verbes qui sont peut-être employés dans un sens que vous ne connaissez pas encore.

> ➤ Take notes to practice for *Mot de passe.*

1. prôner l'équilibre personnel
2. louer l'engagement familial
3. concilier vie professionnelle et vie personnelle
4. déchanter à propos des acquis sociaux
5. demeurer à la maison
6. lever des obstacles
7. leur femme constitue une ressource
8. en payer le prix

O. Avez-vous compris? Répondez aux questions suivantes.

1. Pourquoi, selon le texte, est-il difficile d'invoquer sa famille lorsqu'on ne peut pas faire certaines choses au travail?
2. Que faut-il faire, selon ce texte et selon vous, pour éviter le *burn out?*
3. Qu'est-ce qu'un atelier de gestion du stress ou de gestion du temps peut enseigner selon Marcel Boisvert?

> ➤ Essayez d'expliquer en français ce que c'est que le *burn out.*

P. La parole est à vous! Discutez les constatations et les questions suivantes à deux ou trois.

1. Jacques Charuest affirme que toute vérité n'est pas toujours bonne à dire. Expliquez ce qu'il veut dire puis donnez votre opinion à ce sujet.

2. Expliquez l'importance de la capacité de déléguer et d'établir des priorités en vous appuyant sur des exemples concrets et sur votre propre expérience.

3. Pourquoi, en général, résiste-t-on au changement?

Quelques points de repère

L'ardoise

Autrefois, les travailleurs n'avaient pas droit à des congés payés par leur employeur. En France, les congés payés ont été institués en 1936. C'est à partir de cette année-là que les employés et ouvriers ont commencé à aller en vacances à la campagne, à la mer ou à la montagne et que le tourisme a commencé à se développer.

Quelques dates importantes!

1813: Un décret interdit le travail des enfants de moins de 10 ans dans les mines.

1841: La journée de travail des enfants de 12 à 16 ans est limitée légalement à 12 heures par jour et à 8 heures par jour pour les enfants de 8 à 12 ans.

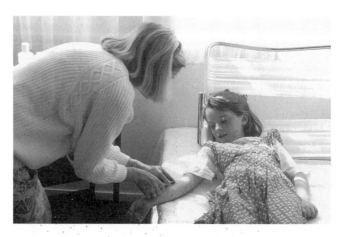

Une infirmière libérale fait une piqûre à une enfant.

1884: La liberté de créer des syndicats *(unions)* est garantie par une loi.

1893: Une loi fait respecter certaines normes d'hygiène et de sécurité de travail.

1909: Les femmes qui ont eu un bébé obtiennent légalement le droit de retrouver leur emploi après la naissance de leur enfant.

1919: La durée légale d'une journée de travail est limitée à 8 heures par jour.

1983: Tous les salariés peuvent prendre leur retraite à 60 ans, à taux plein *(full rate)*. Cependant il s'agit d'un droit et non d'une obligation!

L'enseigne d'une parfumerie et institut de beauté.

Le saviez-vous?

- De nombreux magasins et entreprises ferment leurs portes pendant un mois l'été, souvent en août. Dans ce cas, tous les employés doivent prendre leurs vacances en même temps. Les entreprises qui ne peuvent pas fermer s'organisent par roulement et l'employeur détermine quand chaque employé peut partir. Si le mari et la femme travaillent dans la même entreprise, ils ont droit à partir en vacances en même temps. L'ancienneté *(seniority),* la situation familiale, les enfants en âge scolaire sont parmi les facteurs importants qui détermine la priorité dans le choix de la période des congés payés.

- Depuis le 1er février 1982, en France, la semaine de travail est de 39 heures. Chaque employé peut être amené à faire un certain nombre d'heures supplémentaires mais il n'est pas autorisé à dépasser un total de 130 heures par an. Les heures supplémentaires sont rémunérées à un tarif spécial: les huit premières donnent droit à une majoration de 25% et les suivantes de 50%.

- L'Article 222-33 du Code pénal précise que «le fait de harceler autrui en usant d'ordres, de menaces ou de contraintes, dans le but d'obtenir des faveurs de nature sexuelle, par une personne abusant de l'autorité que lui confèrent ses fonctions, est puni d'un an d'emprisonnement et de 100 000 F d'amende.»

- L'AVFT est une Association contre les Violences faites contre les Femmes au Travail. Cette association a été fondée et a ouvert ses portes en 1985, à Paris.

Les chiffres parlent!

- Le SMIC (Salaire Minimum Interprofessionnel de Croissance) brut par mois: 6.249,62 francs (décembre 95).
- «La moitié des entreprises n'a pas de salarié, le seul actif étant le dirigeant et près de 93% des entreprises ont moins de 10 salariés. Environ 1% des entreprises ont plus de 500 salariés mais elles regroupent le tiers des salariés»

  — Pol Guyomarc'h, *Dictionnaire de l'entreprise*

Un panneau indiquant comment se rendre à l'hypermarché Rallye.

Réflexions sur le travail en équipe

Il doit y avoir un haut degré de constance et d'intégration entre le but de l'organisme, les groupes qui le constituent, la société et le pays dans lesquels il se trouve et le monde extérieur.

Lexique

l'ancienneté *(f)*: **L'ancienneté** se réfère au temps passé dans un emploi ou une fonction.

> L'avancement est décidé partiellement sur le critère de **l'ancienneté** et sur la productivité de l'individu en question.

être assujetti à: **Etre assujetti à** la loi signifie être soumis à la loi.

> Le patron ne peut pas licencier n'importe qui, n'importe comment. Il **est assujetti au** respect de certaines règles et s'il ne les suit pas, il peut se faire poursuivre en justice.

une augmentation: **Une augmentation** est une hausse, une majoration. **Une augmentation** est le contraire d'une baisse ou d'une diminution. Lorsqu'on obtient **une augmentation** de salaire par exemple, cela veut dire que l'on va gagner un peu plus.

> Les travailleurs ont fait grève pour obtenir **une augmentation** de salaire parce que cela fait trois ans que leur salaire n'a pas bougé.

bénévole: On est **bénévole** lorsqu'on fait quelque chose gratuitement, en général pour une bonne cause, sans y être obligé. La lutte contre la pauvreté passe souvent par **le bénévolat.**

> Les médecins qui travaillent pour l'organisation Médecins Sans Frontières par exemple, sont tous **bénévoles,** c'est-à-dire qu'ils offrent généreusement leur temps, leurs connaissances et leur expérience sans se faire payer en retour.

la durée légale du travail: **La durée légale de travail** est de 39 heures par semaine en France.

> **La durée légale de travail** a beau être de 39 heures, beaucoup de salariés n'osent pas protester lorsqu'on leur demande de travailler plus que cela et sans compensation car ils ont peur de perdre leur emploi.

une heure supplémentaire: Toutes les heures de travail qui sont effectuées au-delà de *(beyond)* 39 heures par semaine sont appelées **heures supplémentaires.**

> Mon frère adore faire **des heures supplémentaires** car son salaire est majoré de 25% de la 40e à la 47e heure et de 50% pour les heures suivantes, ce qui représente une différence appréciable.

des horaires individualisés: Lorsque les salariés sont autorisés à aménager leur temps de travail dans un cadre plus souple, on parle d'**horaires individualisés** ou variables ou flexibles ou bien encore à la carte.

Cette entreprise encourage ses employés à profiter d'**horaires individualisés** mais si elle accepte qu'un certain nombre d'heures soient mobiles, elle exige que les autres soient fixes.

un jour ouvrable: **Un jour ouvrable** est un jour normalement consacré au travail. Autrefois le verbe **ouvrer** voulait dire travailler.

J'ai droit à 2,5 **jours ouvrables** de congés payés par mois.

un litige: **Un litige,** c'est une dispute ou une contestation. En cas de **litige,** on peut essayer de négocier directement avec l'entreprise ou bien s'adresser au tribunal.

Il reste plusieurs **points de litige** entre le patronat et les syndicats qui représentent les grévistes *(strikers)*.

être muté: Lorsqu'une entreprise désire qu'un travailleur change de fonction et de lieu de travail, elle peut le **muter. Une mutation** est quelquefois le résultat d'une sanction mais elle peut au contraire signifier une promotion.

Elle travaillait à Paris, au CNED, et comme des centaines d'autres employés, elle **a été mutée** en province. Elle a refusé d'y aller car elle ne voulait pas déménager. Je crois surtout qu'elle pensait qu'elle allait s'ennuyer à Poitiers. Pourtant le Poitou-Charentes est une région formidable près du bord de la mer et plein de petites villes pittoresques comme Saintes, Cognac, La Rochelle, sans compter l'île d'Oléron et surtout l'Ile de Ré qui est mon île préférée. De plus le voyage Poitiers-Paris en TGV est très rapide et confortable. Franchement, je ne la comprends pas. Elle vivrait beaucoup mieux à Poitiers qu'à Paris!

un organisme à but non lucratif: **Un organisme** ou **une association à but non lucratif** n'a pas été créé(e) pour obtenir des gains, des bénéfices, c'est-à-dire pour gagner de l'argent.

Le week-end, elle travaille bénévolement pour **une association à but non lucratif** qui s'occupe de la réinsertion professionnelle de chômeurs de longue durée.

prendre sa retraite: Une personne qui a exercé une profession pendant un certain nombre d'années peut cesser *(stop)* ses activités professionnelles et toucher une pension qui lui permettra de subvenir à ses besoins. On dit qu'elle **prend sa retraite.** Cette personne est **un(e) retraité(e).**

Après 30 ans passés au service de son entreprise, mon père **a pris sa retraite** au mois de décembre de l'année dernière. Ma mère et lui ont acheté une grande propriété à l'ouest de Perpignan dans le Languedoc-Roussillon. Après Paris, c'est un véritable retour à la nature!

une sanction: Un travailleur qui a commis une faute grave peut **être sanctionné,** ce qui veut dire être puni. Le patron prend **des sanctions,** c'est-à-dire des mesures répressives, pour marquer sa désapprobation, son

Facture d'un salon de coiffure.

mécontentement. Lorsqu'**une sanction** disciplinaire a été prise injustement, elle peut être annulée. Dans ce cas, le travailleur **sanctionné** peut obtenir des dommages-intérêts, mais il peut également demander à être réintégré, c'est-à-dire retrouver ses fonctions précédentes.

> Ce vendeur a volé *(stole)* de la marchandise. Je me demande quelle va être **la sanction** prise par le patron mais je ne serais pas étonné s'il était renvoyé *(fired).*

volontaire: Etre **volontaire** veut dire qu'on s'offre **volontairement** pour faire quelque chose, c'est-à-dire de soi-même, librement, sans y être forcé. Lorsqu'on est **volontaire,** on n'est pas nécessairement bénévole, c'est-à-dire qu'**un volontaire,** contrairement au travailleur bénévole, peut être payé pour ses services.

> J'ai besoin de **trois volontaires** pour tester ce nouveau logiciel et rapporter au groupe les résultats du test.

➤ Complete Exercises R–X of Module IV in your *HSG*.

➤ After looking up the adjective *sot* in your dictionary, discuss this adage with your study partner.

*P*aroles de sagesse

Il n'y pas de sots métiers, il n'y a que de sottes gens.

*E*xpression écrite

Expressions adverbiales, expressions négatives, conjonctions

Dans cette section, vous allez réviser certaines opérations effectuées sur ordinateur. Dans le premier paragraphe, encerclez toutes les expressions adverbiales et négatives ainsi que toutes les conjonctions. Notez la forme du verbe associé avec chacune d'entre elles. Distinguez bien entre l'usage du passé composé et celui de l'imparfait. Dans le deuxième paragraphe, soulignez tous les infinitifs et infinitifs passés.

À l'ordinateur

J'étais à la maison il y a dix jours et j'étais en train de jouer à un jeu sur ordinateur quand je me suis rendu compte qu'il ne me restait qu'une journée pour taper mon rapport de stage. J'ai donc d'abord quitté le fichier «jeux». Puis, j'avais beau faire, je ne me rappelais plus où j'avais mis mes documents. Alors, j'ai cherché partout dans ma chambre et je les ai finalement trouvés dans le fond d'un de mes tiroirs. Ensuite, j'ai tapé mon rapport de stage sur mon ordinateur avec mon nouveau traitement de texte. Je connaissais bien les avantages de ce logiciel car j'avais déjà travaillé dessus avec une amie. Mais je ne savais plus comment insérer un tableau au milieu d'une page. Alors j'ai appelé mon amie qui m'a tout expliqué. Enfin, après avoir tapé mon rapport, je l'ai imprimé.

Un tableur

Pour se servir d'un tableur, il faut mettre un chiffre dans une case bien précise. Et à moins d'avoir un virus, l'ordinateur peut calculer toutes les opérations imaginables.

Après être allée voir mon comptable, j'ai décidé d'utiliser un tableur afin de tenir ma comptabilité personnelle. Après avoir suivi quelques cours d'informatique, où j'ai appris à m'en servir, j'ai acheté un logiciel avec un tableur très perfectionné. Avant de commencer à travailler avec le tableur, j'ai rassemblé tous mes papiers et mes documents pour rentrer les données dans l'ordinateur.

> ➤ *Excel* est un exemple de tableur.

Q. A vos plumes! Essayez maintenant d'écrire un paragraphe d'environ 150 mots sur ce que vous avez appris dans ce module au sujet du monde du travail. Commencez par une phrase d'introduction. Utilisez des expressions adverbiales et des conjonctions pour exprimer vos idées de façon logique. Finissez par une phrase de conclusion.

Dans le dossier suivant, nous allons nous concentrer sur quelques facettes du chômage et des conflits sociaux.

Le chômage et les conflits sociaux

Le troisième dossier du Module IV se concentre sur les phénomènes et problèmes liés au chômage. Quelle influence est-ce que le chômage a sur la santé des gens qui ont perdu leur travail ou qui n'en trouvent pas? En quoi est-ce que le taux important de chômage *(high unemployment rate)* actuel change la perception des Français, la façon dont ils envisagent leur avenir et celui de leurs enfants? Que peut-on faire pour sortir de l'impasse du chômage? Ce dossier aborde également mais brièvement le sujet des conflits sociaux et donne quelques exemples de conflits collectifs. Les textes proposés comme lecture éclairent quelques facettes des deux grands thèmes présentés dans ce dossier.

Un magasin de meubles dans la zone industrielle de Lorient.

*A*ctivité d'introduction

Le chômage

A. Faire face au chômage. Mettez-vous par groupes de deux ou trois personnes et réfléchissez aux questions suivantes.

1. Essayez de donner une définition du mot «chômage».
2. Qu'est-ce qu'une personne au chômage peut faire? Quelles sont ses options et quelles sont les difficultés qui se présentent à elle et auxquelles elle doit faire face?

$\mathcal{L}$es mots pour le dire

Vocabulaire de base

V E R B E S

affronter l'échec	*to confront defeat, deal with it*
s'arranger	*to work out*
avoir honte (de)	*to be ashamed (of)*
se battre	*to fight*
céder	*to give up, sell, dispose of*
conquérir, reconquérir	*to win, gain, conquer*
cotiser	*to pay one's contribution*
donner sa démission	*to resign*
faire face à	*to confront, to face*
s'inquiéter	*to worry*
être licencié	*to be fired*
mettre à la porte	*to fire*
mettre en cause	*to question, to call into question*
être privé(e) de	*to be deprived of*
se reconvertir	*to give up on old job and go into another field*
reculer	*to recoil*
se recycler	*to get retrained*
redouter	*to dread, fear*
(se) remettre en cause	*to question (oneself)*
renouveler (un contrat)	*to renew (a contract)*
repartir à zéro	*to start from scratch*
se replier sur soi	*to turn inward*
saisir (sa chance)	*to seize (the opportunity)*
supprimer	*to suppress*
surmonter	*to overcome*
tourner la page	*to turn the page*

N O M S

l'amertume *(f)*	*bitterness*
l'angoisse *(f)*	*anguish*
l'anxiété *(f)*	*anxiety*
l'appauvrissement *(m)*	*impoverishment; thinning; degeneration*
une chance	*chance, luck, occasion*
le chômage	*unemployment*
une chute	*fall*
la confiance en soi	*self-confidence*
la détresse	*distress*
la diminution	*reduction*
l'encouragement *(m)*	*encouragement*
une perte	*loss*
la récession	*recession*
la réinsertion professionnelle	*professional reintegration, return*

continued on page 244

continued from page 243

le rejet	*rejection*
un risque	*risk*
un SDF (Sans Domicile Fixe)	*homeless person*
un sens ou un sentiment de culpabilité	*feeling of guilt*
la sollicitude	*concern, solicitude*
la souffrance	*suffering*
un stage	*internship, co-op position*
la volonté	*desire, will*

ADJECTIFS

abattu(e)	*overcome*
ancien(ne)	*former, old*
anxieux(se)	*anxious*
décevant(e), déçu(e)	*disappointing, disappointed*
découragé(e)	*discouraged*
décourageant(e)	*discouraging*
démotivé(e)	*not motivated anymore*
déprimé(e)	*depressed*
encourageant(e)	*encouraging*
formé(e)	*formed*
humilié(e)	*humiliated*
précaire	*precarious*
prestigieux(se)	*prestigious*

ADVERBES ET EXPRESSIONS ADVERBIALES

encore	*still, yet, again*
grosso modo	*more or less, approximately*
jamais	*never*
notamment	*namely*
principalement	*principally, mainly*

➤ Please note key words and expressions used in these definitions to study for *Mot de passe.*

B. Définitions provisoires à terminer. Complétez les phrases suivantes.

1. _____ , c'est verser, donner, une somme régulière à un organisme en échange de certains avantages qui sont garantis.

2. Lorsqu'on s'attendait à trouver quelque chose de mieux et que le résultat ne correspond pas à ce qu'on espérait, on est _____ .

3. Lorsqu'on ne peut pas trouver de travail dans sa branche, il peut être nécessaire de se _____ , c'est-à-dire de changer de voie ou de domaine de spécialisation pour avoir une meilleure chance de trouver un emploi.

4. Lorsqu'on entre de nouveau dans la vie professionnelle après une absence temporaire on parle de _____ professionnelle. Il y a des ateliers individualisés de recherche d'emploi qu'on appelle aussi des ateliers de _____ professionnelle offerts par l'ANPE pour aider les demandeurs d'emplois à trouver du travail.

5. Une personne qui a perdu son emploi subit quelquefois un
_____ de la part de sa famille et de son entourage. Il y
a _____ quand les proches n'arrivent pas à accepter le
chômage de la personne en question et qu'ils l'excluent ou l'écartent
de leur vie.

6. Lorsqu'une personne a été licenciée et qu'elle a du mal *(difficulties)*
à trouver un nouvel emploi, elle peut passer par une période où elle
se sent mal. Elle est fatiguée sans raison, abattue, pessimiste et a des
idées noires. On dit qu'elle est _____.

C. Définitions provisoires à créer. Par groupes de deux, écrivez une
définition provisoire pour les mots suivants.

1. redouter

2. faire face à

3. la détresse

4. la souffrance

5. être démotivé(e)

HSG

➤ Study the verb frames and flashes for *créer, étudier, voir, boire* and *manger* within Module IV of your *HSG* and complete Exercises Y–Z.

Dialogue

Les conséquences du chômage

D. Activité de pré-lecture. Mettez-vous à deux ou à trois et répondez aux
questions suivantes.

1. Imaginez que vous avez perdu votre emploi. Quels seraient vos
sentiments?

2. Connaissez-vous des gens autour de vous qui sont au chômage?
Quelles sont les conséquences du chômage? Donnez au moins
quatre conséquences possibles liées au fait que l'on a perdu son
travail.

Les conséquences du chômage

M. Legrand: Tiens! Il y a un article intéressant dans *Valeurs mutualistes:* «Le chômage a-t-il une influence sur l'état de santé?» Ecoute ça: «Le chômage peut être pathogène par l'angoisse qu'il suscite et la misère qu'il est susceptible d'entraîner.»

Mme Legrand: Ah, bon... Tu devrais peut-être le donner à lire à Julien.

M. Legrand: Ça a l'air d'être un article sérieux basé sur une étude comparant un groupe de gens ayant une activité professionnelle avec un groupe de chômeurs.

Mme Legrand: Et alors?

M. Legrand: Et alors, les gens qui sont au chômage ont une moins bonne perception de leur santé et cela s'exprime par des malaises et une perte de confiance en soi.

Mme Legrand: Donc ils se plaignent davantage, mais est-ce que cela correspond à un état réel?

M. Legrand: Etat réel ou état ressenti, cela ne change rien à l'affaire. De plus, le groupe de chômeurs de cette étude avait tendance à prendre plus de médicaments et à consulter le médecin plus souvent. «Les symptômes évoqués par les chômeurs construisent un syndrôme cohérent marqué par la nervosité, l'anxiété, l'angoisse, l'insomnie, la perte de confiance en eux-mêmes et l'état dépressif, des vertiges, des évanouissements mais également de la constipation. Ce syndrôme qui est souvent identifié, dans le langage commun, comme un état de «déprime», est peu précis sur le plan médical.»

Mme Legrand: C'est un peu comme Julien.

M. Legrand: C'est vrai, tu as remarqué comme il se renferme? Il se replie sur lui-même, il ne sort plus, il devient taciturne. Si cette dépression continue, qu'est-ce qu'il va devenir?

Mme Legrand: Il est persuadé qu'il ne va pas pouvoir trouver de travail parce qu'il n'a pas d'expérience et qu'en Auvergne en ce moment, il n'y a aucune création d'emplois. Toutes les annonces d'emploi insistent sur l'expérience même pour les débutants! Tu crois qu'il va falloir qu'il déménage?

M. Legrand: Pour aller où? Je ne pense pas que cela ira mieux ailleurs! C'est effectivement décourageant. Comment peut-on avoir de l'expérience quand il faut déjà en avoir pour commencer? C'est un cercle vicieux.

Mme Legrand: C'est complètement absurde! Il faudrait qu'on l'aide à trouver un stage. Même s'il n'est pas rémunéré au moins, ça l'occupera et surtout, cela lui donnera peut-être une porte d'entrée sur quelque chose. Tu ne connais vraiment personne qui pourrait l'employer?

M. Legrand: Tu sais, un stage devient presqu'aussi difficile à trouver qu'un emploi. Je crois qu'il y a environ 800.000 étudiants chaque année en France qui sont obligés de faire un stage parce que cela fait partie de leur formation mais les entreprises ne proposent que 500.000 places. Toutes les demandes ne peuvent pas être satisfaites. Ce n'est pas possible.

Mme Legrand: Je ne comprends pas pourquoi les entreprises n'emploient pas plus de stagiaires car au fond, elles y gagnent!

M. Legrand: Oui et non, car il faut bien que ces stagiaires soient formés et cela prend du temps aussi. Cela représente un investissement de temps assez important de la part des entreprises et puis il y a la question de la rémunération.

Mme Legrand: La rémunération est quasi inexistante. Les stagiaires ne peuvent prétendre qu'à 30% du SMIC, même pas 2.000 francs par mois. C'est dérisoire! Et il y a beaucoup de stagiaires qui ne touchent aucune indemnité!

M. Legrand: Oui, mais quand il y a rémunération, je ne sais pas si les patrons sont exonérés des charges. Je crois que même s'ils ne paient que 30% du SMIC, ils doivent payer les charges sur l'intégralité de la somme.

Mme Legrand: Il faut quand même éviter que les entreprises ne voient les stagiaires que comme une main d'œuvre gratuite. Je trouve qu'il est normal que les stages soient indemnisés.

M. Legrand: De toute façon, à mon avis, il est préférable que les stages soient effectués dans le cadre d'une formation pour que les écoles contrôlent le contenu des stages. Cela évite les abus.

Mme Legrand: Si Julien avait déjà travaillé et qu'il avait perdu son emploi, il y a pas mal de choses organisées par l'ANPE qui visent la réinsertion professionnelle et aident les chômeurs à se repositionner par rapport au marché ou à s'entraîner à aborder l'entreprise. C'est vraiment dur pour les jeunes qui débutent car il n'y a pas grand-chose pour les aider.

M. Legrand: Cela ne fait que quatre mois qu'il cherche. J'ai entendu dire qu'il faut compter un an pour trouver un poste. Espérons qu'il ne va pas se décourager.

Mme Legrand: C'est facile à dire!

E. Avez-vous compris? Répondez aux questions suivantes.

1. D'après ce dialogue, qui est Julien par rapport à M. et Mme Legrand? Cochez les réponses qui peuvent être correctes.

_____ leur fils   _____ quelqu'un de leur famille, ou un proche

_____ un jeune collègue   _____ un jeune voisin

_____ un de leurs patients   _____ un jeune ami qui cherche un travail

_____ un jeune ami qui suit une thérapie   _____ leur petit-fils qui vient d'être licencié

2. Quel est le sujet de l'article dont parle M. Legrand? Cochez les réponses correctes.

_____ le chômage   _____ les conséquences du chômage sur la santé

_____ les raisons du chômage des jeunes   _____ les maladies qui sont liées au chômage

_____ les médicaments qu'il faut prendre quand on est au chômage   _____ la relation entre un adolescent qui est au chômage et sa famille

Une infirmière prend un médicament dans un placard de son cabinet.

3. Quels sont les symptômes de la dépression selon cet article? Cochez les réponses correctes.

_____ la nervosité   _____ l'agressivité

_____ le manque de sommeil _____ la fatigue

_____ la perte d'appétit   _____ la boulimie

_____ la peur   _____ le manque de confiance en soi

_____ les douleurs dans le _____ les maux de tête
      dos

_____ la paresse   _____ le manque d'intérêt dans ce
                                  qui se passe dans le monde

4. Qu'est-ce que Mme Legrand trouve absurde? Cochez les réponses correctes.

_____ le fait que les jeunes gens ayant des diplômes ne trouvent pas de travail

Un magasin situé dans une zone commerciale.

_____ le fait que pour commencer à travailler il faut déjà avoir de l'expérience

_____ le fait que les débutants n'ont pas d'expérience

_____ le fait qu'il n'y a aucun emploi pour ceux qui sont au chômage

_____ le fait que M. Legrand n'accepte pas d'aider Julien à trouver un travail

F. Description du moral de Julien. D'après M. Legrand, Julien est découragé, pessimiste, taciturne, fermé et déprimé. A deux ou trois, expliquez ces adjectifs, dites pourquoi Julien est ainsi, puis employez chacun de ces adjectifs dans une phrase qui montre clairement que vous les comprenez.

G. Autrement dit. Trouvez dans le texte des mots ou groupes de mots équivalents à ceux de la liste suivante.

➤ Note key words and expressions for *Mot de passe*.

1. être sûr de soi
2. avoir déjà travaillé
3. être sans emploi
4. débuter
5. pas payé

6. ce n'est pas logique
7. un travail
8. aller voir pour demander des conseils

HSG

➤ Study the verbs *de la maison d'être, souffrir, devoir* and *dormir* in Module IV of your *HSG* and complete Exercises AA–EE.

Lecture 1

Le chômage a-t-il une influence sur l'état de santé?

H. Activité de pré-lecture. Le texte suivant est un extrait de l'article discuté dans le dialogue de ce dossier. Il s'agit spécifiquement de la question de l'influence du chômage sur l'état de santé. Mettez-vous par petits groupes de deux ou trois et réfléchissez aux questions suivantes.

1. Est-ce que le fait de travailler peut avoir une influence, bonne ou mauvaise, sur la santé? Justifiez votre réponse.
2. Est-ce que la santé peut avoir une influence sur la façon dont on travaille? Comment?

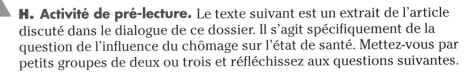

Le chomâge a-t-il une influence sur l'état de santé?

L'existence d'une relation entre le chômage et la santé est souvent affirmée sans que l'on en indique précisément le sens: est-on chômeur parce que malade, malade parce que chômeur, ou les deux à la fois?

Considérer le chômeur comme un futur malade, c'est inverser un lien qui faisait du malade ou de l'invalide un chômeur potentiel du fait de son incapacité à se faire embaucher et à exercer durablement une activité professionnelle, notamment en période de plein emploi.

La difficulté d'apprécier la nature des relations entre le chômage et l'état de santé des chômeurs tient à plusieurs

continued on page 250

continued from page 249

facteurs. Tout d'abord, les effets possibles du chômage sur la santé sont ambivalents. Le chômage peut être pathogène par l'angoisse qu'il suscite et la misère qu'il est susceptible d'entraîner, mais il agit également comme une mise à l'écart et donc à l'abri des risques professionnels et morbides liés à la fatigue et à l'usure au travail, qui peut se traduire par des effets bénéfiques sur l'état de santé.

On peut, en second lieu, se demander ce qui rend réellement le chômage pathogène: le licenciement, l'inactivité, la perte de statut social ou la diminution du pouvoir d'achat et les conséquences en termes d'appauvrissement? Au niveau d'une population, mesure-t-on alors l'effet du chômage ou l'effet plus général d'une pression due à la récession? Dans ce cas, des symptômes, des troubles ou des maladies peuvent résulter de deux événements a priori opposés: ils peuvent être liés au chômage ou au contraire à un surcroît d'activité professionnelle pour ceux que la peur du licenciement incite à réduire leur absentéisme ou à supporter des conditions d'activité détériorées.

Enfin, il est difficile d'imputer précisément telle pathologie ou tel symptôme particulier à la survenue du chômage, tant les manifestations évoquées peuvent prendre des formes diversifiées. [...]

Aujourd'hui, l'extension du chômage modifie la répartition de la population entre actifs et non actifs. Une part importante de la population voit dorénavant sa vie professionnelle, ou un moment de celle-ci, marquée par la succession et l'alternance d'emplois précaires ou à durée limitée et de chômage. Cette situation rend difficile toute caractérisation durable d'un individu comme chômeur ou actif pourvu d'un emploi en dehors du moment précis d'une enquête, et peut remettre en cause la fiabilité d'une approche comparative en l'absence de connaissance précise de l'ensemble de la vie professionnelle.

Tiré de la rubrique «Santé» de *Valeurs Mutualistes* MGEN (Mutuelle Générale de l'Education Nationale), N° 160, mai 1994.

I.   Autrement dit. Expliquez en français les mots du texte.

1. un invalide
2. pathogène
3. à l'abri *(m)*
4. une usure
5. un surcroît d'activité
6. modifier
7. l'alternance *(f)*

8. ambivalent
9. une mise à l'écart
10. morbide
11. des effets *(m)* bénéfiques
12. imputer
13. l'extension *(f)*
14. la fiabilité

J.   Antonymes. Trouvez dans le texte le contraire des mots suivants.

1. nier
2. ancien
3. le gain
4. l'expansion *(f)*
5. l'embauche *(f)*
6. un chômeur

7. en bonne santé
8. les causes *(f)*
9. l'enrichissement *(m)*
10. une diminution
11. sûr

K. Avez-vous compris? Après avoir relu et discuté le texte avec les membres de votre groupe, répondez aux questions suivantes.

1. Expliquez en quoi les effets du chômage sur le demandeur d'emploi peuvent être ambivalents.
2. Pourquoi, d'après ce texte, est-il difficile de faire une étude précise des caractéristiques du chômeur?

Lecture 2

Sortir du chômage. *Le couscous à la rescousse!*

L. Activité de pré-lecture. En groupes de deux ou trois personnes, discutez les questions suivantes.

1. Qu'est-ce qu'une femme divorcée, mère de trois enfants, qui se retrouve au chômage, peut faire?
2. Si vous avez une idée pour vous mettre à votre compte et que vous n'avez pas d'argent pour faire démarrer votre affaire, quelles sont vos alternatives? Essayez de faire preuve d'imagination!

Sortir du chômage. Le couscous à la rescousse!

Quand elle se retrouve au chômage, Fatima Hal, une jeune Marocaine, ne se prend pas la tête. Divorcée avec trois enfants à charge et deux jobs à mi-temps qui lui claquent dans les doigts, elle aurait pourtant de quoi... "Voyons, qu'est-ce que je sais faire? Mais le couscous, bien sûr!" Et elle décide de créer son restaurant. Sans un sou. "Pendant un an, je n'ai pas payé le loyer de mon appart..."

Son financement, Fatima ne le trouve pas auprès des banques — "Elles ne prêtent qu'aux riches" —, mais grâce à son imagination. "J'ai vendu à mes amis des bons pour de futurs repas." Ex-conseillère technique au ministère des Droits de la femme, ex-animatrice d'"îlots sensibles", elle connaît bien les milieux associatifs de femmes et d'immigrés. "J'ai cuisiné des dîners de 60 couverts dans les locaux de Femin'autres ou de Confluences." Fatima rode sa formule de l'achat de tickets pour des repas à venir. "L'idée a plu, parce qu'elle ne reposait sur rien. D'habitude, on mange et on paie après. Là, on mange après..." La jeune femme ajoute ironiquement: "Le fait d'être maghrébine m'a aidée. Georgina Dufoix, par exemple, m'a commandé un couscous pour 120 couverts, j'ai vendu beaucoup d'autres tickets au ministère."

Une année de labeur acharné, remplie par des milliers de couscous. "On parlait, dans la presse, d'un groupe de femmes maghrébines qui avaient créé leur restaurant. Bon, le groupe, c'était... moi toute seule."

Au bout d'un an, Fatima avait engrangé 100 000 F. Le Mansouria, ouvert en 1984, est devenu un restaurant où il vaut mieux réserver à l'avance. Du coup, les banques ont desserré le cordon: le Crédit Agricole d'Auxerre a permis à Fatima de s'agrandir et d'ouvrir un rayon traiteur. Les banques parisiennes restent réticentes. Savoureux, le couscous à la rescousse!

Tiré de l'article de Luc Bernard, *L'Événement du jeudi*, No 495 du 28 avril au 4 mai 1994.

M. Autrement dit. Dans ce texte, il y a plusieurs mots ou expressions qui sont familiers. D'après le contexte, devinez ce qu'ils veulent dire et précisez ce qu'il aurait fallu écrire en français plus formel.

1. se prendre la tête   **4.** sans un sou

2. un job   **5.** un appart

3. claquer   **6.** desserrer le cordon (de la bourse)

N. A la recherche d'éléments précis! Relisez attentivement le texte et trouvez les informations suivantes.

1. Combien d'enfants Fatima a-t-elle?

2. Quel est le pays d'origine de Fatima Hal?

3. Combien Fatima a-t-elle gagné entre 1984 et 1985?

4. Comment s'appelle le restaurant de Fatima Hal?

5. Quelle banque a donné un prêt à Fatima?

O. Choix multiple. Choisissez parmi les trois réponses proposées celle qui vous paraît correcte.

1. Fatima doit absolument travailler parce qu'elle

   a. est divorcée et qu'elle doit subvenir aux besoins de ses enfants.

   b. n'est pas une femme traditionnelle et qu'elle ne veut pas dépendre de son mari.

   c. a beaucoup de dettes.

2. Fatima décide de faire du couscous

   a. parce que quelqu'un lui suggère de se spécialiser en cuisine marocaine.

   b. parce qu'elle avait faim.

   c. parce que c'est une chose qu'elle sait vraiment bien faire.

3. Fatima ne s'adresse pas à une banque pour obtenir son capital de départ

   a. parce que sa famille avait assez d'argent pour la dépanner.

   b. parce que ses amis se sont cotisés pour lui venir en aide.

   c. parce qu'elle sait qu'aucune banque ne lui prêtera d'argent dans sa situation.

4. Comment est-ce que Fatima a financé son restaurant?

   a. Elle a demandé une aide financière au Ministère du Travail.

   b. Elle a vendu des repas à l'avance.

   c. Elle a travaillé dans un autre restaurant jusqu'à ce qu'elle ait gagné assez d'argent.

5. Comment est-ce que Fatima a réussi son affaire?

   a. en se faisant aider par ses enfants qu'elle n'avait pas besoin de payer

   b. en faisant appel au Crédit Agricole

   c. en faisant preuve d'imagination et en travaillant très dur

6. Comment sait-on que le restaurant de Fatima marche bien?

   a. Il faut faire une réservation à l'avance si on veut y manger.

   b. Il est souvent cité dans la presse.

   c. Fatima a maintenant de nombreux employés.

7. Que peut-on dire de Fatima?

   a. C'est une femme qui n'a pas su se débrouiller malgré l'aide dont elle a disposé.

   b. C'est une femme courageuse et déterminée.

   c. C'est une femme exceptionnelle qui sait faire travailler les autres.

P. La parole est à vous! Par petits groupes de deux ou trois personnes, discutez les questions suivantes.

1. En quoi est-ce que l'expérience de Fatima peut inspirer d'autres jeunes femmes qui traversent un moment difficile?

2. Montrez en quoi Fatima a su surmonter les handicaps liés au fait d'être un travailleur immigré en France et en quoi elle a même réussi à les tourner en son avantage.

Lecture 3

La première révolte contre la mondialisation

Q. Activité de pré-lecture. Par groupes de deux ou trois personnes, répondez aux questions suivantes.

1. Est-ce que vous savez ce qui s'est passé en mai 1968 en France? Si oui, essayez de l'expliquer à ceux qui ne le savent pas. Sinon faites les recherches nécessaires.

2. Discutez le concept de la «mondialisation» et de la «globalisation». En quoi est-ce que ces deux concepts ont changé l'économie et la vie de votre pays?

La première révolte contre la mondialisation

Décembre 1995 n'est pas mai 1968. Malgré sa force et sa diversité, le mouvement social qui agite la France depuis deux semaines n'a atteint, pour l'instant, ni l'ampleur, ni l'unité du soulèvement d'alors. Comme en 1968, les manifestations d'aujourd'hui révèlent une même crise, profonde, de la société française — «un malaise fin de siècle», selon l'expression du magazine américain *Newsweek*. Derrière des préoccupations disparates — crédits pour l'Université, retraite à cinquante ans pour les conducteurs de rames de métro, défense des services publics...— s'exprime une peur commune face au monde incertain qui émerge.

Pour la première fois dans un pays riche, on assiste aujourd'hui, en réalité, à une grève contre la «mondialisation», à une réaction massive et collective contre la «globalisation» financière et ses conséquences. Comme les autres grandes nations industrielles, la France se trouve plongée dans un véritable maelström, une révolution, celle pour simplifier, des deux «M»: le Marché, omniprésent, et les Multimédias. Cette double mutation

continued on page 254

continued from page 253

provoque un craquement des institutions et appelle la création de nouvelles régulations sociales et économiques. Elle inquiète une opinion mal préparée. Le mouvement actuel pourrait déboucher sur la contestation d'un autre «M»: Maastricht.

L'Europe est en effet souvent perçue en France comme le symbole de cette mondialisation redoutée. Cette crise est, en tout cas, d'ores et déjà, une sanction terrible pour les élites françaises.

Deux forces animent la révolution en cours dans l'économie mondiale: la généralisation des rapports marchands d'une part, le développement des technologies de l'information de l'autre. Il y a cinq ans encore, l'économie de marché n'englobait que 600 millions de personnes, soit, *grosso modo*, les populations des pays développés. Dans cinq ans, le marché couvrira plus de six milliards d'êtres humains. Cette extension du marché et son unification s'accompagnent d'une autre mutation profonde: l'émergence de la société de la communication et de l'information.

Cette double révolution n'en est qu'à ses tout débuts. Elle provoque pourtant déjà, dans les pays riches, et en Europe tout particulièrement, une profonde déstabilisation. Depuis la fin de la Seconde Guerre mondiale, les pays développés s'étaient dotés, tous et à des degrés divers, d'une organisation sociale et économique très particulière: un Etat-providence, un marché du travail structuré,

des services publics développés... Celle-ci est aujourd'hui radicalement remise en cause par les nouvelles concurrences et les nouveaux métiers.

D'ores et déjà, les pays européens — et leurs populations — commencent à en ressentir, douloureusement, les premiers effets. Ce sont l'explosion du chômage, la stagnation du pouvoir d'achat, la dégradation de l'environnement, le développement des inégalités et la crise financière de la protection sociale. C'est, pour reprendre l'expression de *Newsweek*, la fin de la «belle vie» qui menace. [...]

Cette grève contre la mondialisation menace de déboucher, maintenant et en France, sur une nouvelle remise en cause de Maastricht. La construction européenne y est en effet largement perçue comme le «cheval de Troie» de cette mondialisation.

Ce serait à cause de l'Europe que la France devrait réduire ses déficits publics et sociaux, libéraliser ses marchés et réformer ses services publics. Or il n'en est rien. La Suisse, la Malaisie et le Canada n'ont pas signé le traité de Maastricht. Aucun de ces pays ne revendique l'adhésion à l'Union européenne. Ils n'en sont pas moins contraints à des efforts similaires.

Tiré de l'article d'Erik Izraelewicz. *Le Monde*, Nº 15820 du jeudi 7 décembre 1995.

R. Avez-vous compris? Répondez aux questions suivantes.

1. En quoi est-ce que décembre 1995 diffère de mai 1968 selon le texte?
2. Pourquoi peut-on parler de «malaise de fin de siècle»?
3. D'après cet article, quels sont les groupes qui sont préoccupés par la situation et qui ont manifesté en décembre 1995?
4. Quels sont les trois «M» qui sont redoutés par les Français et pourquoi?
5. Quelle est la mutation profonde que la France est en train de vivre?

S. Autrement dit. Essayez de définir les concepts suivants en vos propres mots.

1. une réaction massive
2. un soulèvement
3. des préoccupations *(f)* disparates
4. une crise

5. un craquement des institutions

6. l'émergence *(f)*

7. une mutation

8. l'État-providence *(m)*

9. des services *(m)* publics développés

10. l'explosion *(f)* du chômage

11. la stagnation du pouvoir d'achat

12. la dégradation de l'environnement

13. le développement des inégalités

14. «la belle vie»

Quelques points de repère

Les chiffres parlent!

- En 1993, le salaire moyen des femmes était encore environ de 24% inférieur au salaire moyen des hommes.

- Les femmes représentent environ 36% des salariés mais 13% seulement des cadres supérieurs.

- 80% de la population active est salariée.

- 1% des Français possèdent 20% de la fortune totale des Français.

- En mai 1996, il y avait 11,8% de chômeurs en France.

L'ardoise!

Si le droit de grève est récent, les grèves, elles, sont un phénomène ancien. En 1539 par exemple, les typographes de Lyon avaient fait une grève qui avait duré quatre mois. Refuser de travailler a toujours été pour les ouvriers un moyen de pression efficace contre des conditions de travail et/ou un salaire inacceptables et dès le Moyen Age, ils se sont regroupés en associations pour se tenir informés et avoir davantage de pouvoir. Cependant faire une grève était très risqué dans la mesure où l'on pouvait perdre son emploi.

Une date importante!

- Depuis 1946, la Constitution française garantit le droit de grève, c'est-à-dire de la cessation totale du travail, dans le secteur privé et depuis 1950 dans le secteur public.

- L'ANPE (L'Agence Nationale Pour l'Emploi) a été créée le 13 juillet 1967 et placée sous l'autorité du Ministère du Travail. L'ANPE donne la liste des emplois disponibles, s'occupe de l'information, de l'orientation et du conseil des travailleurs. L'ANPE organise également des ateliers de formation pour aider les demandeurs d'emploi à trouver du travail. Elle propose aussi un appui *(support)* spécifique et personnalisé pour les personnes qui cherchent du travail et traversent une période difficile psychologiquement ou financièrement.

Le saviez-vous?

Un syndicat est une association qui a pour but de défendre les droits et les intérêts professionnels, matériels et moraux de ses membres.

La liberté syndicale est reconnue dans la Constitution française de 1946. Cette liberté est celle de créer un syndicat, c'est-à-dire de devenir membre d'un syndicat sans que cela ait de conséquences négatives pour l'employé syndiqué.

Certains syndicats représentent les employeurs. Citons par exemple:

- **le CNPF:** le Centre National du Patronat Français
- **la CGPME:** la Confédération Générale des PME (Petites et Moyennes Entreprises). C'est une association qui regroupe les entreprises de moins de 300 salariés.
- **la FNSEA:** la Fédération Nationale des Syndicats d'Exploitants Agricoles qui représente les exploitations agricoles.

Les autres syndicats représentent les employés. Voici les plus importants:

- **la CGT:** la Confédération Générale du Travail (1895)
- **la CFDT:** la Confédération Française et Démocratique du Travail (1964)
- **FO:** Force Ouvrière (1948)
- **la CFTC:** la Confédération Française des Travailleurs Chrétiens (1919)
- **la CGC:** la Confédération Générale des Cadres (1944)
- **la FEN:** la Fédération de l'Education Nationale

➤ Les syndicats sont en perte de vitesse. Le nombre d'adhérents continue à baisser et ils ont perdu beaucoup de leur pouvoir. Ils restent cependant le partenaire de choix de la direction pour discuter et négocier.

HSG

➤ Study the adjectives in Module IV of your *HSG* and complete Exercises A–C.

Réflexions sur le travail en équipe

La forme suit toujours la fonction. Il faut d'abord se demander quels sont le but et les objectifs de toute tâche à accomplir. La structure de l'équipe, le choix des responsables, la hiérarchie dans son ensemble (aussi bien au niveau de l'équipe que celui de l'entreprise) doivent servir le but et non vice-versa.

Lexique

les allocations *(f)* **de solidarité:** Les **allocations de solidarité** sont une somme versée par l'Etat à un travailleur au chômage qui ne reçoit plus d'indemnités de chômage parce qu'il ou elle est au chômage depuis trop longtemps ou à un jeune qui cherche un emploi mais qui n'a encore jamais travaillé.

Aussi longtemps que Pierre touchera l'allocation chômage, ça ira, mais après cela, s'il ne trouve toujours pas de travail, ça va être dur parce que **l'allocation de solidarité** est nettement plus basse que l'allocation chômage. Heureusement qu'il habite dans le Limousin où la vie est quand même moins chère que dans d'autres régions!

les charges (f) **sociales: Les charges sociales** sont les prélèvements obligatoires effectués sur les salaires. Les sommes prélevées sont versées dans différentes caisses d'organismes sociaux comme la Sécurité Sociale, les ASSEDIC, l'UNEDIC (l'Union Nationale pour l'Emploi Dans l'Industrie et le Commerce). Ce sont les employés et les employeurs qui ont à payer **les charges sociales.**

Un certain nombre de mesures ont été prises par le gouvernement pour alléger **les charges sociales** et encourager les employeurs à l'embauche.

un chômeur: Un chômeur est une personne qui est sans emploi, qui est disponible pour travailler et qui cherche un emploi.

Depuis qu'il est **chômeur,** Pierre va à l'ANPE tous les jours car il ne peut pas supporter d'être inactif et de rester à la maison.

la conjoncture économique: La conjoncture économique, c'est l'ensemble des conditions qui déterminent la situation économique.

Les Français espèrent que **la conjoncture économique** va s'améliorer cette année.

une cotisation: Une cotisation est une somme d'argent versée dans un certain but. Un travailleur verse **une cotisation** chômage. Un certain pourcentage de son salaire est prélevé tous les mois pour alimenter les ASSEDIC, c'est-à-dire les ASSociations pour l'Emploi dans l'Industrie et le Commerce. Ce sont les ASSEDIC qui, à leur tour, indemnisent les chômeurs.

Regarde sur ta fiche de paye à combien monte **ta cotisation** pour l'assurance chômage. Je me demande si tu payes plus que moi.

faire faillite: La faillite est la situation d'une entreprise qui ne peut pas payer ses dettes. Elle cesse ses paiements et doit être dissoute. Lorsqu'un commerçant **fait faillite,** par exemple, il est obligé de fermer son magasin.

En 1996, beaucoup d'entreprises boursières **ont fait faillite.**

l'indemnité de chômage: L'indemnité de chômage est la somme que les ASSEDIC versent mensuellement aux gens qui n'ont pas de travail et qui sont officiellement au chômage. Cette somme varie selon un certain nombre de facteurs comme le salaire touché par l'employé(e) lorsqu'il ou elle travaillait et la durée de la période de chômage.

Est-ce que vous savez comment **l'indemnité de chômage** est calculée et pendant combien de temps j'y aurai droit, s'il vous plaît?

liquider ses biens: Liquider ses biens veut dire vendre ce que l'on possède, matériel, stocks (quantité de marchandises en réserve), bâtiments, etc., de façon à pouvoir obtenir une certaine somme en liquide et pouvoir payer ses dettes, même si ce n'est qu'en partie.

Cette entreprise a fait faillite. Maintenant elle doit **liquider ses biens.**

la population active: La population active est l'ensemble des gens qui ont un emploi.

En France, en ce moment, les chômeurs constituent presque 12% de **la population active** alors qu'au Japon, ce chiffre reste au dessous de 3%.

le RMI: Le RMI a été créé par une loi du 1er décembre 1988. C'est le Revenu Minimum d'Insertion pour ceux qui n'ont plus de ressources. Une personne qui vit seule touche moins qu'un couple et lorsqu'il y a une ou plusieurs personnes à charge, une somme supplémentaire est alors perçue.

En 1993, en France, il y avait 725.000 personnes qui touchaient **le RMI.**

la Sécurité Sociale: La Sécurité Sociale est le principal organisme de protection sociale en France. **La Sécurité Sociale** comprend l'assurance maladie, les allocations familiales, l'assurance vieillesse, l'assurance accidents du travail. L'adhésion à **la Sécurité Sociale** est obligatoire.

—Est-ce que tu savais que **la Sécurité Sociale** perçoit environ 20% du PNB?
—Oui, et pourtant à cause du taux de chômage, elle est en pleine crise financière car il n'y a pas assez de gens qui cotisent.

la stagnation: Lorsque l'économie est en période de **stagnation,** cela veut dire qu'elle ne progresse pas, qu'elle est immobile.

Les profits de cette société sont **en stagnation** ce qui est mauvais signe.

➤ After checking the meaning of the noun *oisiveté*, brainstorm at least seven applications of this adage with your study partner.

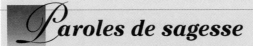

Paroles de sagesse

L'oisiveté est la mère de tous les vices.

Près du port de Lorient, une ensacheuse met la farine de poisson en sacs de 50 kg. Un ouvrier prend le sac qui arrive sur le tapis.

Expression écrite

Expressions adverbiales, expressions négatives, conjonctions

Dans cette section, vous allez lire deux petits paragraphes qui ont à faire avec l'argent et un troisième qui est au sujet du chômage. Indiquez le temps, le mode ou la forme de chacun des verbes utilisés.

➤ Note how the adverbial expressions and conjunctions used in these passages help you determine the correct form of each verb indicated.

➤ Note the negative exaggerations in *L'argent de poche*. In your opinion, what should the positive function of an allowance be? Think specifically about how children might be better taught money management through the concept of a budget and savings.

L'argent de poche

Mes parents ne m'avaient jamais donné d'argent de poche avant mes 10 ans et je ne pouvais rien m'acheter. Après mon anniversaire, ils ont commencé à me donner un peu d'argent chaque semaine mais je ne pouvais pas vraiment m'acheter beaucoup de choses. A partir de mes 15 ans, mes parents me donnaient 100 francs mais je ne pouvais ni m'acheter de vêtements ni aller au cinéma. Comme je n'avais pas encore 16 ans, je n'avais aucun moyen de gagner de l'argent. Lorsque j'ai eu 18 ans, je n'ai pas pu m'acheter de voiture car je n'avais pas assez d'économies. Je ne pouvais aller nulle part et je ne voyais personne.

Les investissements

Pour gagner un peu d'argent en Bourse [stock market], j'ai décidé d'acheter quelques actions et obligations [stocks and bonds]. Afin de connaître la procédure pour en acquérir, j'ai appelé mon banquier. Mais avant de lui téléphoner, j'ai écrit toute une série de questions que je voulais lui poser. Après avoir parlé à sa secrétaire, j'ai eu mon banquier en ligne et il m'a dit que je devais passer à sa banque pour en parler sérieusement. Donc, le lendemain, après être allée faire quelques courses, je suis passée à ma banque. Il m'a reçu dans son bureau et il m'a expliqué pourquoi à moins d'aimer les dangers financiers c'était moins risqué d'acheter des Sicav [mutual funds] et il a ajouté: «Il faut bien réfléchir avant de vous décider!» Le téléphone a ensuite sonné et il m'a dit, après s'être excusé, qu'il avait un autre rendez-vous.

Le chômage en France: Préoccupation des jeunes

A l'heure actuelle, les jeunes Français sont de plus en plus inquiets au sujet du chômage: si l'on se rapporte aux sondages, le chômage serait la principale préoccupation des jeunes à la sortie des écoles.

Il est vrai que le pays sort d'une crise économique assez grave, et la France connaît un taux de chômage particulièrement élevé, malgré les efforts du gouvernement pour favoriser l'emploi, et notamment l'emploi des jeunes. Il est assez malheureux de constater que le chômage peut toucher tout le monde. Il n'est pas rare de rencontrer des gens diplômés de Grandes Ecoles à qui il a fallu attendre plus d'un an avant de trouver du travail! D'ailleurs il a *été possible de remarquer, qu'à cause de cette situation, beaucoup de jeunes ont choisi de prolonger leurs études afin d'arriver plus tard sur le marché du travail, avec un meilleur «bagage intellectuel». Cependant, même dotés de hauts diplômes, certains jeunes se sont vus dans l'obligation d'accepter des emplois pour lesquels ils étaient surqualifiés, et sous-payés. D'autres ont dû se contenter d'aller pointer à l'ANPE, et de toucher les allocations-chômage.*

Heureusement, la situation tend à s'améliorer : l'embauche reprend petit à petit, et la peur de l'avenir s'atténue. Il faut espérer que les mesures prises par le gouvernement vont permettre aux entreprises d'embaucher de plus en plus de jeunes diplômés.

T. A vos plumes! Essayez maintenant d'écrire un paragraphe d'environ 150 mots sur ce que vous avez appris au sujet du chômage et du manque d'argent. Commencez par une phrase d'introduction. Utilisez des expressions adverbiales et des conjonctions pour exprimer vos idées de façon logique. Finissez par une phrase de conclusion.

En guise de clôture, allons un peu plus loin!

En guise de clôture:
Allons un peu plus loin!

Texte littéraire

Olivier au travail!

A. Activité de pré-lecture. Répondez aux questions suivantes à deux ou trois.

➤ Be ready to report back to the class.

1. Quand vous étiez petit(e), est-ce que vous admiriez certains adultes tout particulièrement dans le domaine de leur profession? Lesquels? Pourquoi?

2. Quelles professions vous paraissaient attirantes, fascinantes lorsque vous étiez jeune et pourquoi?

3. Quel était le premier emploi qui vous a donné l'impression de vraiment faire partie de la vie (professionnelle) adulte et pourquoi?

Olivier au travail!

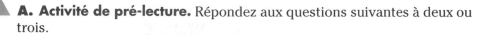

Dans la cour, il aidait à charger le papier sur des appareils Fenwick ou les diables qu'il faisait rouler à grand bruit dans les allées. Il portait de lourds fardeaux: rouleaux serrés de papier d'emballage, rames bien calées au creux de l'avant-bras et contre l'épaule. Il édifiait des tours gigantesques en entrecroisant et en alignant soigneusement les paquets.

➤ Un diable est un petit chariot à deux roues qui sert à transporter des caisses, des sacs, etc.

Il se rendait parfois dans le bureau vitré qui dominait les Entrepôts comme un mirador. De là, on voyait les buildings de papier, les manœuvres qui s'affairaient, les clients au comptoir de vente. Il frappait avant d'entrer, saluait la dactylo à chignon pointu et à bésicles qui tapait avec ardeur sur sa Corona... Les classeurs à rideaux souples en bois, les fichiers métalliques Kardex, les dossiers chargés de documents, les catalogues d'échantillons, les bottins, les registres lui paraissaient pleins de secrets précieux et respectables.

Il découvrit un autre aspect de sa tante Victoria. Celle qu'il voyait le matin en kimonos ornés de chrysanthèmes mauves, d'ibis noirs et de dragons jaunes apparaissait avec une simple blouse blanche et d'épaisses lunettes d'écaille tombaient sur son nez. Elle témoignait d'une activité intense, téléphonant, vérifiant des factures, établissant des prix de vente, des devis, ayant l'œil à tout. Au bureau, elle était toujours de bonne humeur, quiète, apaisée, débarrassée de tout vernis mondain. Olivier l'admirait et elle le sentait bien. Une sorte de complicité était née entre eux. Olivier ne disait plus «ma tante» et le mot «patronne» naissait à ses lèvres. Lui-même portait une salopette bleue, et, au repos, il croisait ses mains sur sa poitrine, sous le tissu, comme un débardeur costaud.

— Quand tu seras grand, disait la tante, tu pourras être chef de magasin!

Extrait de *Trois sucettes à la menthe*. — Robert Sabatier Paris: *France Loisirs,* 1979.

B. Vrai ou faux? Lisez les propositions suivantes et dites si elles sont vraies ou fausses et pourquoi.

1. Olivier est le neveu de la patronne.
2. La tante Victoria aime travailler au bureau.
3. Olivier a peur de sa tante.
4. Etre chef de magasin veut dire s'occuper de l'approvisionnement de l'entrepôt.
5. La tante est habillée de façon plus simple à la maison qu'au bureau.
6. La tante est flattée par l'admiration d'Olivier.
7. Olivier aide les employés des Entrepôts.
8. Olivier est fasciné par tout ce qu'il voit dans le bureau.
9. La tante est une femme très active qui s'occupe de tout.
10. La tante venait seulement au bureau pour voir si tout allait bien.
11. Olivier fait un travail de bureau.

C. Avez-vous compris? Répondez aux questions suivantes en cochant la bonne réponse.

1. Pourquoi est-ce qu'Olivier utilisait un diable?
   a. pour charger et transporter du papier
   b. pour taper une lettre à la machine
   c. pour classer des documents

2. Où est situé le bureau?
   a. au dessus de l'entrepôt de façon à pouvoir voir ce qui se passe

b. au sous-sol de l'entrepôt

c. dans la maison d'habitation de la tante Victoria

3. Dans ce texte, qu'est-ce que la dactylo fait?

    a. Elle parle au téléphone.

    b. Elle tape à la machine.

    c. Elle aide les clients.

4. Qu'est-ce que c'est qu'un devis?

    a. C'est une facture.

    b. C'est le prix qu'on propose pour faire un certain travail.

    c. C'est une sorte de chèque dont le paiement est garanti.

5. Pourquoi est-ce qu'Olivier avait envie d'appeler sa tante «patronne»?

    a. parce qu'elle était très autoritaire avec lui

    b. parce qu'elle est la femme du patron

    c. parce qu'il se rend compte que c'est elle qui dirige les Entrepôts

6. Qu'est-ce qu'Olivier porte?

    a. un costume chic pour travailler au bureau

    b. une tenue d'ouvrier

    c. un kimono

D. A vous la parole! A deux ou trois, discutez les questions suivantes.

1. Qui est le narrateur? De quel point de vue est-ce que cette histoire est racontée?

2. Quelle impression avez-vous des Entrepôts où travaillent Olivier et sa tante?

E. A vos plumes! Rédigez un petit paragraphe d'une centaine de mots sur la relation entre Olivier et sa tante. Commencez par une petite introduction et terminez par une conclusion.

Expressions familières: Le monde du travail et les relations humaines

la boîte	=	*l'entreprise, l'endroit où l'on travaille*
le boulot	=	*le travail*
boumer: Ça boume!	=	*Ça marche bien; le rendement du travail est bon*
la cafèt'	=	*la cafétéria*
ne pas coller	=	*ne pas aller, ne pas marcher*
(Ça ne colle pas!)		
un costard	=	*un costume*
être crevé, pompé, vidé	=	*être très fatigué*
un job	=	*un emploi*
un jus, un caoua	=	*un café (une tasse de café)*
un mec	=	*un homme*
une nana	=	*une femme*
piger	=	*comprendre*
un pote	=	*un ami, un copain*
prendre un pot	=	*boire quelque chose*

le resto	=	*le restaurant*
être bien sapé	=	*être bien habillé*
un toubib	=	*un médecin*

La Réussite: Sept ingrédients de base

A la maison aussi bien que dans le monde du travail, il y a sept éléments essentiels qui contribuent au succès d'un individu.

- **la responsabilité** (donnée d'abord, prise ou assumée ensuite)
- **le choix** (des choix simples d'abord, ceux qui sont plus difficiles ou moins évidents plus tard)
- **la liberté** (de créer, d'expérimenter, d'explorer, de faire des fautes, d'échouer sans être pénalisé[e])
- **l'écoute** (à condition que toutes les idées, celles qui ne sont pas bonnes y comprises, soient prises en considération — le concept d'un «sounding board» — pour que l'on puisse arriver plus facilement à ses propres solutions, par exemple; de façon à stimuler au maximum le processus de créativité; c'est le concept du remue-méninges)
- **l'encouragement** (le soutien moral systématique et non la critique négative)
- **l'entraide, la générosité** (aider les autres)

> ➤ Remue-méninges = une expression québécoise qui correspond à «brain-storming».

F. Application. Choisissez quelqu'un qui est important pour vous et répondez aux questions suivantes.

> ➤ Perhaps you'd like to brainstorm this application with your study partner or group.

1. Qui est-ce? Quelle relation avez-vous avec cette personne?
2. Faites une liste des responsabilités, choix et/ou libertés que vous pourriez lui donner.
3. Comment est-ce que vous pourriez lui montrer que vous l'écoutez, que vous l'encouragez dans le domaine de ses idées, de son travail et de son comportement?
4. Comment pourriez-vous lui communiquer votre enthousiasme?
5. Comment pourriez-vous l'aider à aider les autres?

Une fleuriste arrange un bouquet pour une cliente.

G. Jeu de rôle. Vous êtes diplômé(e) en informatique. Un(e) ami(e) qui cherche un emploi depuis plus d'un an a enfin obtenu un entretien d'embauche chez Bull. Comment allez-vous réussir à le/la motiver pour qu'il/elle réussisse son entretien? *(Minimum de sept échanges par personne).*

Quelques aide-mémoire

1. On travaille pour

- s'occuper.
- gagner sa vie.
- se développer au niveau personnel aussi bien que professionnel.
- réaliser ses rêves et son potentiel.
- avoir des contacts sociaux.
- être respecté.
- être utile.
- être actif.

2. Un organigramme

- indique qui est sous la direction de qui.
- précise qui est au même niveau de la hiérarchie que qui.
- indique qui est le/la responsable de quel département ou service.
- signale qui dirige quel département.
- montre la place de chaque service par rapport aux autres.
- précise le nom des chefs de service.
- renseigne sur l'importance de l'entreprise.
- donne une idée claire de la structure d'une entreprise.

3. Une entreprise peut être

- une petite boutique tenue par une personne seule ou un couple.
- une chaîne de magasins.
- un hôtel.
- une petite ou une grande exploitation agricole.
- une usine.
- un atelier artisanal.
- un cabinet de traduction.
- une agence de publicité.
- une compagnie de taxis.
- une clinique privée.
- une compagnie aérienne.

RENAULT

s.a.r.l. SOREPA
Garage des Deux Avenues
Agent
13, rue Mouton-Duvernet - 75014 Paris
Tél. 45 39 52 52 - Télécopie 45 39 16 65
R.C. Paris 313 742 033 - Siret 313 742 033 00019 - Code APE 501 Z

4. On peut aller à son travail

- en bus (autobus) ou en car (autocar). On attend le bus à l'arrêt de bus et l'autocar à certains arrêts mais aussi à la gare routière. Un bus est un moyen de transport en commun qui dessert les villes et reste à l'intérieur des villes en question. Le car va de ville en ville et s'arrête quelquefois entre ces deux grandes villes. Il peut desservir quelques villages sur sa route.
- en voiture, soit sa propre voiture soit celle d'un autre quand un(e) collègue passe vous chercher par exemple. Le port de la ceinture de sécurité est obligatoire pour les personnes assises sur les sièges à l'avant aussi bien qu'à l'arrière. Trouver une place de parking peut être difficile et coûteux.

La locomotive d'un Train à Grande Vitesse près d'une locomotive ancienne.

- à pied. C'est un excellent exercice pour ceux qui n'habitent pas trop loin de leur travail. Dans ce cas, avoir un parapluie est conseillé!
- en métro. Il y a une Carte Orange qui est très avantageuse et reste valable une semaine ou un mois. Le métro peut être bondé (extrêmement plein) aux heures de pointe. Attention aux pickpockets!
- à bicyclette, en vélo. C'est un moyen de transport très bon pour la santé mais un peu dangereux dans les grandes villes!
- en moto. Le port du casque est obligatoire.
- en taxi. C'est un moyen de transport qui peut revenir à cher si on couvre de grandes distances.
- en train. Il y a des trains de banlieue et des TGV pour les plus longues distances. Comme les gares sont au centre ville, c'est très pratique. N'oubliez pas que la population des centres villes est très dense. Beaucoup de gens vivent et travaillent au centre.
- en avion. Les hommes d'affaires peuvent faire Paris-Nice, aller et retour, dans la journée, ou bien se déplacer en avion pour arriver dans une ville et rester dans cette région pendant quelques jours. Les aéroports se trouvent en dehors des villes, donc cela perd du temps et il faut que la ville où ils vont soit très éloignée, plus de 4 heures de route, pour que cela soit intéressant du point de vue temps de prendre l'avion.

5. **Quand on fait un voyage d'affaires on peut avoir besoin des services**

- d'un bureau de réservation pour confirmer un vol ou changer une résa (réservation) déjà existante si on n'a pas de Minitel à portée de la main.
- d'un hôtel. Il est fortement conseillé de réserver une chambre à l'avance. Si vous avez besoin d'un plan de la ville, demandez-en un à l'hôtel. De nombreux magasins, en guise de publicité, en font imprimer et les mettent à la disposition des hôtels et des offices de tourisme.
- de restaurants ou de cafés. En France de nombreux accords sont entamés *(started)* pendant un dîner ou un déjeuner d'affaires. Les partenaires ne parleront pas nécessairement d'éléments précis d'un contrat éventuel mais ils seront de meilleure humeur et plus enclins

à atteindre un accord après un bon repas qui montre qu'on est pris au sérieux et qui fait preuve de politesse et de respect.

- d'un avocat. Il y a beaucoup moins d'avocats en France (en pourcentage) qu'aux Etats-Unis, mais il y a des notaires qui s'occupent de succession, d'héritage, de biens immobiliers, etc., et donc qui assument certaines des responsabilités d'un avocat américain.

- d'une compagnie d'assurance. On peut prendre une assurance-voyage ou vérifier et peut-être augmenter la couverture de certaines polices d'assurance auxquelles on souscrit déjà.

- d'un spécialiste, en informatique, en médecine ou dans n'importe quelle branche.

- d'un hôpital pour un contrôle, des vaccins ou autre. Si on tombe malade pendant le voyage, il sera peut-être conseillé de se rendre à la salle d'urgence.

- d'une banque ou d'une Poste.

- des transports en commun.

- d'un garage si on a des problèmes de voiture.

- d'un bureau de police si on a perdu ses papiers ou si on a été volé.

- d'un bureau de tabac, d'une maison de la presse ou d'un kiosque pour acheter un journal ou un magazine.

- d'un gendarme ou agent de police si on s'est trompé de route ou si on ne réussit pas à trouver une rue ou un bâtiment.

Dans le Module V, nous allons étudier différentes facettes du monde du travail.

Module V

Différentes facettes du monde du travail

Ouverture

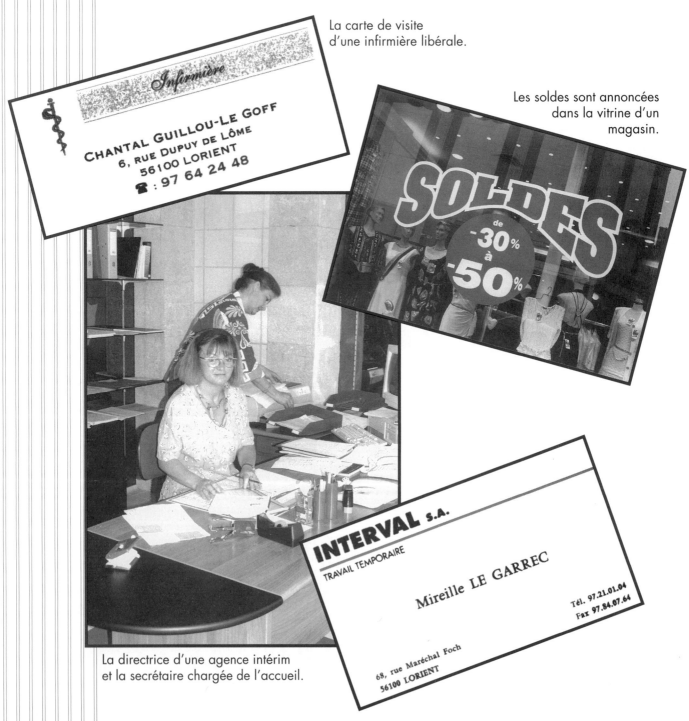

La carte de visite
d'une infirmière libérale.

Infirmière

CHANTAL GUILLOU-LE GOFF
6, RUE DUPUY DE LÔME
56100 LORIENT
☎ : 97 64 24 48

Les soldes sont annoncées
dans la vitrine d'un
magasin.

SOLDES
de -30% à -50%

La directrice d'une agence intérim
et la secrétaire chargée de l'accueil.

INTERVAL s.a.
TRAVAIL TEMPORAIRE

Mireille LE GARREC

Tél. 97.21.01.04
Fax 97.84.07.64

68, rue Maréchal Foch
56100 LORIENT

Une pub pour des téléphones portables.

Les bureaux du journal *Le Monde* à Paris.

*T*ravail temporaire et formation

C'est le travail temporaire qui fait l'objet du treizième dossier. Vous allez découvrir un type de travail qui a fleuri *(flourished)* en France au cours de ces quinze dernières années. De nombreuses agences intérim *(temporary work agencies)* ont ouvert leurs portes dans toutes les grandes villes françaises. Les gens qui veulent trouver un travail sont inscrits à l'ANPE, mais souvent, ils le sont également dans toutes les agences intérim de leur ville et il n'est pas rare que ces agences aient leurs bureaux dans le même quartier sinon dans la même rue. Ce dossier vous permettra de réfléchir à la notion de travail et de temps de travail et soulignera l'importance de la formation *(education)*. La formation représente le meilleur passeport pour l'emploi! Les diplômés de l'enseignement supérieur ont plus de deux fois plus de chances de trouver un emploi que ceux qui ont seulement achevé leur scolarité *(schooling)* obligatoire.

*A*ctivité d'introduction

Le monde du travail

A. Le travail temporaire et la formation. Mettez-vous par groupes de deux ou trois personnes et réfléchissez aux questions suivantes.

1. Dans quels cas une personne peut-elle être intéressée par un emploi temporaire?
2. Pourquoi une entreprise s'adresserait-elle à une agence intérim au lieu de recruter directement son personnel elle-même?
3. Qu'on ait déjà un emploi ou qu'on soit sur le marché du travail, pourquoi est-il important de continuer à se former?

Les mots pour le dire

Vocabulaire de base

VERBES

bâtir	*to build*
boucler les fins de mois	*to make ends meet*
consentir	*to consent, grant*
convenir	*to agree; to be appropriate*
coordonner	*to coordinate*
déroger (à la loi)	*to go against (the law)*
dispenser	*to exempt, excuse from*
être dé tenteur d'un contrat	*to be title holder of a contract*
mener à bien (un projet)	*to complete (a project)*
se mettre en relation avec	*to get in touch, make contact with*
se perfectionner	*to better oneself*
renouveler	*to renew*
rompre (un contrat)	*to break (a contract)*
suivre un cours	*to take a course*
titulariser	*to entitle*
en valoir la peine	*to be worthwhile*
se vanter de	*to brag about*

NOMS

un concours d'entrée	*competitive entrance exam*
la convention collective	*collective agreement concerning wage and work conditions*
des débouchés (m)	*job opportunities*
les démarches (f) (à suivre)	*steps (to take)*
l'engagement (m)	*agreement, promise*
sans engagement	*without obligation*
une formation en alternance	*alternate or rotational training*
la formation permanente	*continuing education*
des frictions (f)	*conflicts*
l'intérim (m)	*temporary work, job*
un(e) intérimaire	*temp*
un mi-temps (m)	*half-time job*
les obligations (f)	*obligations; bonds*
des perspectives (f)	*prospects*
un préavis	*notice, warning*
la répartition (des tâches ou des heures de travail)	*dividing up, distribution (of tasks and work hours)*
une reprise (de l'économie)	*recovery (of the economy); resumption*
le retournement	*return*
une rupture de contrat	*breaking of contract*
un smicard (une personne qui gagne le SMIC)	*minimum-wage earner*
la souplesse	*suppleness, pliability*
une subvention	*grant, subsidy*
un surcroît de travail	*additional work; excessive work*

> ➤ *L'intérim*—activité du personnel intérimaire; laps de temps pendant lequel une charge vacante est exercée par une autre personne.

continued on page 274

continued from page 273

ADJECTIFS

abordable	*affordable; approachable*
accessible	*accessible*
commode	*convenient*
conforme (à)	*true (to); matching*
gratuit(e)	*free*
hebdomadaire	*weekly*
imprévisible	*unforeseeable*
indispensable	*essential, absolutely necessary, vital*
modique (prix ou somme)	*modest (price or sum)*
sécurisant(e)	*giving a feeling of security*
vain(e)	*futile, fruitless, useless*
valorisant(e)	*self actualizing, giving a feeling of self worth*

ADVERBES ET EXPRESSIONS ADVERBIALES

à mi-temps	*half-time*
à plein temps, à temps complet	*full-time*
à temps partiel	*part-time*
auparavant	*before(hand); first; previously*
indéfiniment	*indefinitely*
suffisamment	*sufficiently*

➤ Note key words and expressions that might be useful for *Mot de passe.*

B. Définitions provisoires à terminer. Complétez les phrases suivantes.

1. Lorsqu'on possède un contrat de travail écrit en son nom, on dit qu'on est _____ d'un contrat.

2. Lorsqu'une entreprise est liée à l'un de ses employés par un contrat et qu'elle ne respecte pas les termes de ce contrat ou qu'elle décide sans avoir atteint un accord *(agreement)* avec son employé de renvoyer celui-ci, il y a _____ de contrat.

3. On est _____ quand on obtient un contrat définitif après avoir travaillé pendant une certaine période sans certitude de pouvoir continuer à exercer cette fonction.

4. Quand on choisit un domaine de spécialisation, on pense à ce que l'on aime faire mais on tient également compte des _____, c'est-à-dire des perspectives, des situations, des possibilités de travail que ce domaine peut offrir. S'il y a beaucoup de _____, on sera plus sûr de trouver un emploi.

5. Si une entreprise veut que vous essayiez un produit, elle peut vous envoyer un échantillon en précisant que c'est _____ de votre part. Cela veut dire que vous n'êtes pas obligé de garder ou d'acheter ce produit. Le fait d'accepter de voir ou d'essayer quelque chose ne vous oblige à rien.

6. On parle de _____ de travail lorsqu'il y a un surplus, c'est-à-dire une augmentation. Lorsqu'une entreprise reçoit beaucoup de commandes aux environs de Noël, on peut dire qu'il y a une situation de _____ de travail.

C. Définitions provisoires à créer. Par groupes de deux, donnez une définition provisoire pour les mots suivants.

1. un préavis
2. se perfectionner
3. une démarche

4. modique
5. des frictions (entre employé et patron)

Dialogue

Une directrice téléphone à sa secrétaire

D. Activité de pré-lecture. Mettez-vous par petits groupes de deux ou trois et répondez aux questions suivantes.

1. Pour quelles raisons est-ce que la directrice d'une agence intérim pourrait téléphoner à sa secrétaire de sa voiture? Donnez au moins quatre raisons possibles.
2. Quels sont les avantages et les inconvénients des téléphones portables ou portatifs?

Une directrice téléphone à sa secrétaire

Bien confortablement installée au volant de sa Peugeot 605, Mme Guimaux, qui dirige l'agence intérim Interval, arrive dans la zone industrielle de la banlieue d'Angers où elle a rendez-vous avec M. Bruneau, PDG d'une grosse entreprise de construction qui a besoin de plusieurs maçons. Profitant d'un feu rouge, elle prend son téléphone portatif et appelle sa secrétaire.

Mme Hubert: Agence Interval, bonjour.

Mme Guimaux: Mme Guimaux à l'appareil. Passez-moi Mme George, s'il vous plaît.

Mme Hubert: Un instant. Ne quittez pas. Elle est dans son bureau. Je vous la passe.

Mme George: Allô, Mme Guimaux?

Mme Guimaux: Oui, Mme George, pouvez-vous regarder mon emploi du temps de demain et me dire si c'est à 9h30 ou à 10h que je dois rencontrer Monsieur Robin?

Mme George: C'est à 9h30 et j'ai réussi à déplacer l'entrevue avec le directeur de la société Beuzeaut de vendredi 15h à mardi prochain à 10h30 comme vous me l'aviez demandé, mais il veut absolument vous parler aujourd'hui même avant 17 heures si possible. Je crois que c'est au sujet du chauffeur poids lourd que nous leur avons fourni la semaine dernière.

Mme Guimaux: Ah, bon, il y a un problème?

Mme George: Non, il n'a rien dit mais je n'avais pas l'impression qu'il s'agissait d'un problème.

LES TÉLÉPHONES DE VOITURE

VERSION MIXTE
(embarqué ou portable)

■ Légèreté
  Poids : 1,6 Kg

■ Faible encombrement
  dimensions : 200 X 115 X 75 mm

■ Autonomie perfomante en
  portable 4 jours en veille*

■ Fonction mains-libres
  intégrée au combiné

Evolution par accessoires

- Recharge batterie par chargeur
  secteur ou chargeur allume cigare en 2 H 30 mn
- Possibilité de fonction coupure autoradio ou alarme extérieure intégrée
  dans le kit d'installation
- Kit d'installation et kit "mains-libres" extérieur pour second véhicule.
- Batterie supplémentaire NiCd 1700 mA/h
- Autonomie standard avec batterie d'origine en portable
  ➞ veille : 30 h
  ➞ communicaton : 70 mn en 1,5 W
                    30 mn en 7 W

VERSION EMBARQUEE

Caractéristiques électriques

- Tension d'alimentation nominale 12V, négatif à la
  masse
- Puissances d'émission : 0,15W / 1,5 W / 7W
- Températures de fonctionnement : - 25°C à + 55°C

VERSION PORTABLE

* sous réserve de fonctionnalité disponible sur le réseau

Dépliant de France Télécom.

Mme Guimaux: Très bien, je vais l'appeler tout de suite. Ne me prenez pas plus de rendez-vous pour vendredi. Je dois quitter le bureau à 16 heures au plus tard. Et notre nouvelle annonce? Est-ce que vous avez contacté le *Courrier de l'Ouest* et *Ouest France?*

Mme George: Oui, elle passera dans le journal de samedi en deuxième page et toute la semaine prochaine.

Mme Guimaux: Si ce n'est pas trop tard, ajoutez que nous cherchons des plombiers, des électriciens et des couvreurs avec CAP et expérience. J'ai vu M. Deniau ce matin, il vient d'obtenir un gros chantier de rénovation des locaux du Laboratoire Bonnet. Vous savez, le laboratoire d'analyses médicales sur la place du Maréchal Joffre, la grande bâtisse à droite de la pharmacie.

Mme George: Oui, oui, je vois. C'est un beau bâtiment du XVIIIe siècle.

Mme Guimaux: Oui, je crois... une façade magnifique en tout cas. Le bâtiment est classé monument historique. Il nous faut d'excellents ouvriers. Je crois que ce chantier inclut également l'aménagement du grenier et que les travaux doivent être faits dans les délais les plus brefs… comme d'habitude! Cherchez dans nos fiches et voyez qui pourrait convenir. Il y a ce jeune homme qui est passé s'inscrire la semaine dernière. Est-ce que vous vous souvenez… un grand blond… Lemercier ou Lemeunier… Il était très qualifié, je me souviens. Bon, nous en discuterons à mon retour. Je vous laisse… A tout à l'heure. J'ai rendez-vous avec M. Bruneau dans quelques minutes.

Elle interrompt la conversation.

E. A la recherche d'éléments précis. Répondez aux questions suivantes.

1. Faites une liste des mots qui indiquent qu'il s'agit d'une conversation téléphonique.
2. Quelles sont les entreprises mentionnées dans ce dialogue qui ont déjà fait appel à l'agence Interval?
3. Faites la liste des professions qui sont recherchées en ce moment par l'agence Interval.

F. Avez-vous compris? Complétez les phrases suivantes par une ou plusieurs des alternatives proposées.

1. Mme Guimaux téléphone
   a. de la Poste.
   b. de sa voiture.
   c. de son téléphone portable.
   d. de son bureau.

2. Mme Guimaux téléphone
   a. à son bureau.
   b. à la secrétaire de M. Beuzeaut.
   c. à sa secrétaire.
   d. aux journaux régionaux.

3. Mme Guimaux demande à la secrétaire
   a. l'heure d'un de ses rendez-vous du lendemain matin.
   b. si elle est libre vendredi après-midi.
   c. de faire bien attention à ne pas prendre de rendez-vous en fin d'après-midi vendredi.
   d. si elle a reçu des coups de téléphone pendant son absence.

4. Mme George parle
   a. de son week-end.
   b. d'une annonce.
   c. de son patron.
   d. de deux rendez-vous.
   e. d'une secrétaire qui doit se faire remplacer.

5. D'après le texte, nous pouvons conclure qu'après son rendez-vous avec M. Bruneau, Mme Guimaux va

    a. rentrer immédiatement chez elle.

    b. repasser au bureau.

    c. aller au *Courrier de l'Ouest* pour vérifier le texte des annonces.

    d. retéléphoner à sa secrétaire pour lui dicter une lettre.

6. Mme George doit changer le texte de l'annonce qui va passer dans le journal

    a. en ajoutant quelques noms de professions dont l'agence va avoir besoin.

    b. en supprimant les noms de spécialistes dont l'agence n'a plus besoin.

    c. en expliquant quel type d'électricien et de maçon l'agence va avoir besoin spécifiquement.

    d. en précisant quand l'agence va avoir besoin de personnel supplémentaire.

HSG

➤ Study the *Photos et descriptions* and *Phonétique* sections of Module V in your *HSG* and complete Exercises A–E.

Lecture 1

La directrice d'une agence intérim parle de son travail

G. Activité de pré-lecture. En petits groupes de deux ou trois, répondez aux questions suivantes.

1. Qu'est-ce que c'est, selon vous, une agence intérim? Donnez-en une définition simple.

2. Avez-vous déjà travaillé pour ou dans une agence intérim? Pourquoi?

3. Quels sont les avantages et les inconvénients pour un employé de passer par une telle agence?

4. Vous êtes le directeur ou la directrice d'une agence de travail temporaire. Comment recrutez-vous votre personnel?

Une agence de travail temporaire en province.

La directrice d'une agence de travail temporaire au téléphone avec un entrepreneur en bâtiment qui cherche un électricien.

La directrice d'une agence intérim parle de son travail

Notre tâche consiste à mettre en relation les personnes qui cherchent un emploi avec les entreprises utilisatrices potentielles.

Ici, on travaille dans tous les secteurs, dans le bâtiment, l'industrie, les usines, le tertiaire. Il y a certaines agences qui sont très spécialisées dans certains domaines comme le tertiaire, l'industrie ou le bâtiment, mais ça, on le trouve dans les grandes métropoles style région parisienne ou les capitales régionales. Dans une ville comme la nôtre, on n'a pas tellement la possibilité de se spécialiser. On a automatiquement un secteur qui va marcher plus qu'un autre mais avec une balance puisque s'il y a un secteur qui marche comme l'industrie, on est tous dessus. Par contre, dès que l'industrie commence à tomber un petit peu, on retombe automatiquement sur ce qui marche. C'est pour cela qu'on essaie dans la mesure du possible d'équilibrer tous les secteurs.

Le seul secteur qui ne marche vraiment pas en ce moment, c'est le tertiaire, c'est-à-dire des secrétaires, des comptables, du personnel dit non-productif — et dans ces cas-là, le personnel est très rarement remplacé sauf en cas de maladie ou en cas de congé maternité. Le remplacement d'été qui autrefois marchait très fort est en ce moment en chute libre. Bon, notre agence ne fait pas que les remplacements, mais fait tout ce qui est surcroît de travail.

Le marché français actuel a subi quand même une crise violente. Il y a eu beaucoup plus de dépôts de bilan, de plans sociaux que de réelle embauche.

Donc aujourd'hui où il y a une très légère reprise, les entreprises commencent par reprendre du personnel par le biais du travail temporaire. Pourquoi? Parce que c'est une souplesse. Si ça repart, on prend du personnel. Si éventuellement ça s'arrête, quand les employés ont des contrats à durée limitée, on ne renouvelle pas leur contrat à la fin de la période en question. C'est donc plus facile. D'autre part, cela leur permet de ne rien gérer puisque le personnel mis en place n'est géré par l'entreprise qu'en ce qui concerne la productivité. La gestion pure, c'est-à-dire le salaire, les charges sociales, etc., c'est l'agence intérim qui s'en occupe puisque le personnel mis en disposition reste le personnel de l'agence elle-même. C'est l'agence qui paye son personnel et qui envoie une facture de prestation de service à l'entreprise. Donc cela passe dans ses frais généraux et non pas dans sa masse salariale.

D'autre part, cela coûte très cher à une entreprise de recruter du personnel. Quand une entreprise nous appelle, nos fiches sont là. C'est à nous de trouver la personne, de la mettre à la disposition de l'entreprise. Donc elle n'a pas la perte de temps et d'argent de faire passer une annonce, de lire les CV, de faire les entretiens. Une entreprise nous passe un coup de fil et nous dit: "Je veux deux maçons pour demain matin". C'est à nous de les trouver et de les envoyer.

Interview avec la Directrice de l'agence *Interval* de Lorient — juillet 1995

Un jeune homme vient de remplir des formulaires pour s'inscrire à l'agence de travail temporaire.

ETUDES EFFECTUEES ET DIPLOMES OBTENUS

ANNEE	NIVEAU ATTEINT	DIPLOME	ETABLISSEMENT

REFERENCES PROFESSIONNELLES

DATE	EMPLOYEUR	SOCIETE T.T.	FONCTION	DUREE

INTERVAL
68, rue Mal Foch - 56100 LORIENT
Tél. 97 21 01 04 - Fax 97 84 07 64

Nous vous remercions de joindre
une copie des documents suivants :

- PHOTO D'IDENTITE
- C.V.
- PIECE D'IDENTITE
- CARTE DE SEJOUR (pour les étrangers)
- CERTIFICATS DE TRAVAIL +
  DIPLOMES EVENTUELS
- PERMIS DE CONDUIRE (pour les chauffeur
  (ainsi qu'un extrait de casier judiciaire
  pour les chauffeurs PL)
- FICHE D'APTITUDE MEDECINE DU TRAV.

A très bientôt !

H. Avez-vous compris? Répondez aux questions suivantes.

1. Qu'est-ce que c'est, selon la directrice, qu'une agence intérim? Est-ce que sa définition diffère de la vôtre?

2. Pourquoi, selon la directrice, son agence n'est-elle pas spécialisée dans un seul secteur de l'économie?

3. Quel est, selon elle, le secteur qui marche le moins bien au moment où elle parle?

4. Est-ce que l'agence ne s'occupe que du personnel de remplacement?

5. Pourquoi les entreprises embauchent-elles du personnel par l'intermédiaire d'une agence intérim?

6. Qui rémunère les salariés qui sont employés par l'intermédiaire d'une agence intérim?

7. Que dit la directrice du processus de recrutement?

Lecture 2

La formation par alternance de la Chambre de Commerce et d'Industrie

I. Activité de pré-lecture. Par petits groupes de deux ou trois personnes, discutez les questions suivantes.

1. Quel est l'avantage de faire des stages en entreprise pendant la période des études? Prenez la perspective des apprenants mais n'oubliez pas non plus celle des entreprises.

2. Comment voyez-vous le stage idéal? Quel genre d'encadrement aimeriez-vous avoir de la part de l'entreprise?

3. Pensez-vous qu'un stage doit être rémunéré ou non et sur quelle base? Justifiez votre réponse.

La formation par alternance de la Chambre de Commerce et d'Industrie

Vous cherchez une formation par alternance sérieuse dans votre département? Pourquoi ne pas aller frapper à la porte de la Chambre de Commerce et d'Industrie de votre région?

Une formation par alternance est une formule où l'élève alterne les semaines de présence en entreprise et en institut de formation. Elle lui permet de mettre en application en entreprise les connaissances acquises pendant les cours.

Depuis 1974, la Chambre de Commerce et d'Industrie (CCI) de Versailles Val d'Oise-Yvelines forme les jeunes dans des secteurs porteurs d'emploi et répond ainsi plus précisément aux besoins des entreprises. Les taux de réussite aux diplômes d'état dans les écoles de la CCI sont exemplaires (82% en 1993) et on constate un taux de 90% d'insertion professionnelle à l'issue des formations. Le dispositif de la CCI

Versailles Val d'Oise-Yvelines comporte 13 instituts de formation par alternance et 7 écoles d'enseignement supérieur par alternance.

Aujourd'hui, ce système d'enseignement qui prépare à 120 métiers dans des domaines aussi divers que le secrétariat, la comptabilité, la vente, la parfumerie ou l'électronique peut accueillir jusqu'à 7 000 jeunes.

A qui la formation en alternance s'adresse-t-elle?

L'alternance s'adresse à des jeunes de 16 à 26 ans d'un niveau d'étude allant de la troisième jusqu'au Bac + 6. A partir du Bac + 2, l'élève est dirigé vers une école d'enseignement supérieur.

Déroulement des cours.

La durée des cours est de 39 heures par semaine et ils se déroulent sur 20 semaines de septembre à juin. L'inscription

continued on page 282

continued from page 281

se fait à partir du 15 mars. Les cours sont gratuits, mis à part une participation aux frais pédagogiques.

Quelles sont les entreprises formatrices?
Les entreprises d'accueil sont variées et fiables. Parmi les plus connues: Thomson, AXA, BNP, Mercedes Benz, BMW, Canon, Fougerolle, Spietrindel…

Quelles sont les conditions d'accueil en entreprise?
L'entreprise alloue au jeune une rémunération variant de 25% à 75% du SMIC. Elle doit impérativement confier à l'élève des missions qui sont en rapport direct avec le métier qu'il prépare.

Pour tout renseignement: Centre d'Information et d'Orientation Professionnelle:
    tél (01) 30 57 57 37
    ou (01) 30 75 36 00

Tiré de «Tout savoir sur la formation», article du magazine *Vive l'emploi!* Nº 5, jan–fév. 1995.

J. Autrement dit. Expliquez les expressions suivantes d'après leur signification dans le texte.

1. une formation par alternance
2. appliquer ses connaissances
3. des secteurs porteurs d'emploi
4. le taux de réussite aux examens est exemplaire
5. des domaines divers
6. le déroulement des cours
7. les entreprises d'accueil sont variées et fiables
8. l'entreprise alloue une rémunération au jeune

Le CNED (Centre National d'Enseignement à Distance) offre toutes sortes de cours à tous les niveaux dont certains transmis par satellite.

La porte d'entrée et la façade de la CCIM au sud de la Bretagne.

K. A la recherche d'éléments précis du texte.
Répondez aux questions suivantes.

1. Quel est le taux de réussite de la CCI aux examens nationaux?

2. Quel est le pourcentage de jeunes qui ont suivi une formation par alternance de la CCI et qui trouvent un emploi.

3. Combien d'écoles et d'instituts est-ce que la CCI de Versailles possède?

4. Combien y a-t-il de métiers parmi les formations possibles de la CCI?

5. Combien de jeunes est-ce que la CCI de Versailles peut former?

6. Combien coûte la formation par alternance offerte par la CCI?

7. Donnez au moins deux noms d'entreprises qui participent au programme de formation par alternance de la CCI.

8. Quelles conditions est-ce que la CCI pose aux entreprises avant de leur envoyer des jeunes en formation par alternance?

L. La parole est à vous! Par petits groupes de deux ou de trois personnes, dites ce que vous pensez de l'idée de la formation par alternance et pourquoi.

M. Jeu de rôle. Vous êtes un représentant de la CCI et votre partenaire est un représentant d'une entreprise qui ne participe pas au programme de formation par alternance. Vous essayez de le/la convaincre de l'importance d'un tel programme pour l'entreprise et pour les jeunes. Faites une liste de vos arguments et contre arguments.

CHAMBRE DE COMMERCE ET D'INDUSTRIE DE PARIS
DIRECTION DE L'ENSEIGNEMENT — EXAMENS POUR ÉTRANGERS
28 rue de l'Abbé-Grégoire - 75279 Paris Cedex 06 - Tél. (1) 49 54 28 00 (standard) - Accueil téléphonique (1) 49 54 28 65
Secrétariat des examens (1) 49 54 28 66 - Télex : 270 403 F DE CCIP - Télécopie (1) 49 54 28 90

CONGE INDIVIDUEL DE FORMATION
(C.I. F.)

"MODE D'EMPLOI"

⇨ Vous êtes salarié.

⇨ Vous êtes demandeur d'emploi après un Contrat à Durée Déterminée (CDD).

⇨ Nous vous proposons une REUNION D'INFORMATION COLLECTIVE pour vous informer sur :

① le CIF et le SALARIE
② le CIF et le DEMANDEUR D'EMPLOI
③ le CIF et L'EMPLOYEUR
④ le CIF et L'ORGANISME DE FORMATION
⑤ le CIF et le BILAN DE COMPETENCES

- Qu'est ce que le CIF ?
- Qui a droit au CIF ?
- Que finance le CIF ?
- Quelle est la durée du CIF ?
- Quelles sont les démarches à faire ?

CALENDRIER

● LORIENT (de 14 H à 16 H)

26 JUIN 1995

au :

FAF BRETAGNE
Immeuble Le Forum (4ème étage)
50 Rue Braille
56100 LORIENT

VOUS ETES INTERESSE ?   *INSCRIVEZ-VOUS*
EN NOUS CONTACTANT AU
99.29.72.30
FONGECIF BRETAGNE

La prochaine réunion est prévue le : 28/08/95

Exemple de formation offerte par l'A.N.P.E.

HSG

➤ Restudy the *Phonétique* section of Module V in your *HSG* and complete Exercises F–L.

Lecture 3

Un cours par correspondance: France Formation

N. Activité de pré-lecture. Discutez les questions suivantes par groupes de deux ou trois.

1. Dans quels cas est-ce que vous prendriez la décision de suivre un cours par correspondance?

2. Quels sont les avantages et les inconvénients d'un cours par correspondance?

3. Quelles qualités faut-il avoir pour pouvoir tirer parti au maximum d'un cours par correspondance?

Un cours par correspondance: France Formation

Vous voulez réussir? Choisissez dès maintenant une véritable qualification.

Pourquoi?

- Pour progresser dans votre métier actuel?
- Pour compléter votre formation initiale?
- Pour préparer un examen ou un concours national?
- Pour reprendre des études après une interruption de quelques années?

… en bref, pour améliorer votre cadre de vie en améliorant votre vie professionnelle…

Avec France Formation le contrat est clair

1. C'est vous qui décidez: après avoir choisi en toute connaissance de cause votre formation dans le Guide, vous commencez quand vous voulez. Vous pouvez vous inscrire à tout moment de l'année.
2. Vous jugez vous-même, grâce à un essai gratuit de 2 semaines du sérieux de notre méthode dès votre inscription.
3. Vous suivez votre propre rythme: en recevant vos cours par trimestre, vous avez une vision globale de votre formation et vous pouvez parfaitement vous organiser.
4. Nous vous accompagnons: vous pouvez contacter personnellement votre professeur principal pendant toute la durée de votre formation, et même après! Il est là pour vous guider et vous aider à progresser à votre rythme.
5. C'est simple pour vous: nous vous

proposons une formule de paiement unique, par mensualité.
Paramédical
Bâtiment, travaux publics
Comptabilité, gestion
Fonction publique
Secrétariat, bureautique
Informatique
Droit, banque, assurance
Enseignement général
Vente, commerce, distribution
Electronique
Tourisme
Langues

Pour bien choisir votre orientation, vous avez besoin du Guide des Formations! C'est un outil indispensable! Vous consulterez ainsi, tranquillement chez vous, ses 139 pages d'informations:

- une présentation complète de chaque formation (contenu, déroulement, durée, tests de niveau)
- les débouchés, les tarifs et les modalités d'inscription

Vous pouvez aussi recevoir le Guide en téléphonant à Lyon au 04 72 19 11 72, ou par Minitel: 3615 FRANCE FORMATION

FRANCE FORMATION — 69814 TASSIN CEDEX — est un établissement d'enseignement privé soumis au contrôle pédagogique de l'Etat.

Tiré d'une publicité placée dans le magazine *Vive l'emploi!* jan–fév. 1995.

O. A la recherche d'éléments précis du texte. Répondez aux questions suivantes.

1. Indiquez au moins deux raisons données dans le texte pour suivre un cours de France Formation.

Couverture du magazine *Eures*.

HATIER
INTERNATIONAL

Paris le 5 décembre 1994

Madame, Monsieur,

J'ai le plaisir de vous adresser, ci-joint, notre nouvelle méthode CADENCES.

CADENCES 1 s'adresse à de vrais débutants, adolescents/adultes, qui souhaitent acquérir rapidement les connaissances de base du français.

CADENCES 1 propose une centaine d'heures d'apprentissage correspondant à deux sessions d'un mois, à raison de 15 h. hebdomadaires ou à un cours extensif sur une année scolaire ou universitaire.

Directement issue des pratiques de la classe, CADENCES 1 conduit à une réelle compétence de communication en français par l'acquisition de savoirs linguistiques, communicatifs et culturels.

Notre objectif a été de proposer un ouvrage clair, pragmatique et accessible de tous points de vue.

CADENCES 1 se compose de :

- 1 livre de l'élève de 224 pages (comprenant les exercices)
- 1 guide pédagogique de 80 pages (avec un test d'évaluation pour chaque dossier)
- 2 cassettes audio

CADENCES 2 paraîtra en juillet 95.

Restant à votre disposition, nous vous prions de croire, Madame, Monsieur, à l'assurance de nos sentiments distingués.

Nicole LISSANDRE
PROMOTION

M. Lissandre

HATIER INTERNATIONAL - 31, rue de Fleurus 75006 Paris - Tél.: (1) 49 54 48 34 - Télex: 201 460 F - Fax: (1) 45 44 84 54

Banque : BFCE - 21, boulevard Haussmann 75009 Paris - Compte 30021/99999/04171194000/19
Les Éditions Hatier - SA au capital de 12 675 000 F - Siège social : 8, rue d'Assas 75006 Paris
RCS Paris B 352 585 624 - Siret 352 585 624 000 13

Promotion de la Maison d'édition HATIER pour une nouvelle méthode de français, langue étrangère.

2. France Formation insiste sur le fait que sa formule de cours est flexible. Donnez au moins deux exemples de cette flexibilité.

3. Quel genre de contacts est-ce que les étudiants ont avec leurs professeurs?

4. Dans quels domaines est-ce qu'il n'y a pas de formation offerte?

5. A quoi sert le Guide des Formations?

6. Que faut-il faire pour obtenir plus de renseignements sur les cours de France Formation?

P. Autrement dit. Expliquez avec vos propres mots les expressions et mots suivants.

1. votre formation initiale

2. reprendre des études

3. améliorer votre cadre de vie

4. en toute connaissance de cause

5. à tout moment de l'année

6. un essai gratuit

7. une formule de paiement par mensualité

8. un établissement d'enseignement privé

Agora se spécialise dans la formation.

Write key words and expressions in your reporter's notebook so you'll be ready to be interviewed.

Q. A vous maintenant! Comparez les deux types de formation proposés dans les deux textes qui précèdent, celui de la CCI et celui de France Formation en ce qui concerne les éléments suivants.

1. la flexibilité
2. le coût
3. l'efficacité
4. l'acquisition d'expérience
5. les résultats aux examens

Quelques points de repère

Une date importante!

Jusqu'en 1992, les entreprises n'avaient pas intérêt à avoir des employés à temps partiel car ces salariés leur coûtaient relativement plus cher que des employés à plein temps.

La loi du 31 décembre 1992, en réduisant le coût des charges patronales pour les employés à temps partiel tout en garantissant les droits de ces salariés, a encouragé les entreprises à offrir des emplois à temps partiel.

Ce n'est que depuis 1965 qu'un mari n'a pas le droit de refuser que sa femme exerce une profession à l'extérieur de la maison.

L'ardoise!

L'éducation est un droit qui n'a pas toujours été accessible à tous. De nombreuses études et écoles ont été pendant des siècles le privilège des hommes. Par exemple, c'est depuis 1924 seulement que les programmes scolaires de l'enseignement secondaire des filles et des garçons sont équivalents et que le Bac passé par les filles est reconnu comme ayant la même valeur que celui des garçons. Les femmes ont obtenu petit à petit le droit d'entrer dans toutes les grandes écoles. En 1918, par exemple, Centrale, une école d'ingénieurs, a ouvert ses portes aux femmes, et plus récemment, en 1972, la Marine marchande, ESSEC, HEC (écoles de commerce) ont fait de même.

Le saviez-vous?

Les Chambres de Commerce et d'Industrie (CCI) ont pour mission d'encourager l'activité économique dans le commerce, l'industrie et les services dans la ville et la région où elles sont implantées. Cette mission peut être divisée en trois axes principaux:

1. Représentation des commerçants et industriels auprès des pouvoirs publics. Rôle de conseil auprès des entreprises vis-à-vis des réglementations en vigueur et de leurs changements.

2. Assistance technique pour les PME en particulier. Conseil quant au fonctionnement individuel des entreprises, aide au développement des exportations ainsi qu'à l'expansion (nouvelles implantations) des entreprises.

3. Gestion de l'enseignement commercial: formation secondaire, supérieure et continue. La très grande majorité des écoles de commerce dépendent des CCI, les plus réputées sont toutes rattachées à une CCI (HEC, ESSEC, ESCP, ESCL, EDHEC et les Sup de Co de province). Gestion d'un certain nombre de services industriels et commerciaux: les CCI sont concessionnaires de l'Etat pour la construction et l'exploitation d'installations comme les ports maritimes et fluviaux, des aéroports, des zones industrielles ainsi que des centres de douanes.

Les domaines d'activités des CCI sont très larges en France. Ils sont le reflet de la relative décentralisation des pouvoirs au niveau du territoire, relative parce que les CCI sont soumises au contrôle administratif et financier de l'Etat.

Exemple de certificat remis par la C.C.I.P.

Les entreprises françaises!

LE TRAVAIL TEMPORAIRE

Les principaux groupes d'intérim implantés en France sont Ecco, Manpower, Bis, Adia et Sidergie.

LA FORMATION

Le CNED est le Centre National d'Enseignement à Distance. Le CNED fait partie de l'Education Nationale et est le numéro 1 de l'enseignement à distance. Il existe depuis plus de 50 ans et répond à une demande grandissante de formation à la carte. En 1980, il n'y avait que 200.000 inscrits. Aujourd'hui, le CNED forme près de 400.000 inscrits par an, dont 80% d'adultes, vivant en France et à l'étranger, répartis sur 150 pays du monde. La formation continue est un aspect important de son activité. Le CNED utilise les nouvelles techniques de la communication et propose des

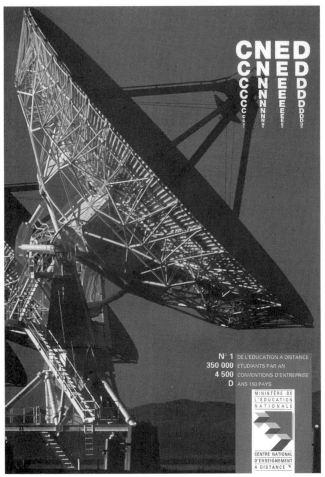

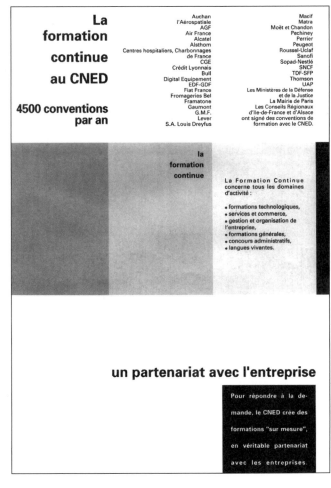

Diverses facettes du C.N.E.D.

➤ Review and practice the pronunciation of the French liaisons in the *Phonétique* section of your *HSG*.

formations avec un maximum d'interactivité en particulier grâce à des transmissions de vidéo par satellite, émissions interactives, diffusées à partir du centre situé près du Futuroscope de Poitiers et destinées à des sites équipés d'antennes paraboliques. Le CNED emploie 6.000 personnes dont 450 imprimeurs, 1.800 professeurs titulaires, 3.000 professeurs vacataires et 800 autres spécialistes de la chaîne de transmission du savoir. Le CNED propose 2.500 modules de formation différents. Le CNED crée des formations sur mesure et travaille en véritable partenariat avec les entreprises telles que le Crédit Agricole, Auchan, Digital Equipement, eaux minérales Vittel et Perrier, Elf France, Mairie de Paris, Conseil d'Etat, Ministère des Affaires Etrangères, Renault, Lyonnaise des Eaux, Peugeot, Dassault, Bull, UAP et Schlumberger.

*R*éflexions sur le travail en équipe

Le but de tout travail en équipe doit être précis, clair, simple et réalisable. De plus, ce but ne doit pas changer. C'est l'importance du but qui donne sens au travail à accomplir.

Lexique

aide *(f)* **au premier emploi des jeunes (APJ): L'APJ** est une mesure du gouvernement pour stimuler les entreprises à embaucher un jeune. Tout jeune de 16 à 26 ans, inscrit ou non à l'ANPE et non indemnisé par une assurance chômage, s'il est embauché à plein temps peut faire bénéficier son employeur d'une aide forfaitaire de 1.000 F par mois pendant 9 mois.

> Les moins de 26 ans en quête de leur premier emploi ont une meilleure chance de trouver quelque chose depuis que le gouvernement accorde **une aide du premier emploi des jeunes** aux entreprises qui les embauchent.

un contrat de retour à l'emploi (CRE): Un contrat de retour à l'emploi est accordé dans certaines conditions à des demandeurs d'emploi qui ont été inscrits à l'ANPE pendant un minimum de 12 mois au cours des 18 derniers mois, qui sont bénéficiaires de l'allocation de solidarité spécifique (ASS) ou du RMI, qui sont handicapés dans leur recherche d'un emploi ou qui ont plus de 50 ans ou aux femmes qui ont des enfants à charge. Ces personnes ont droit entre autres à une formation de 200 à 1.000 heures et leur employeur sera exonéré du paiement des cotisations patronales de la Sécurité Sociale pendant une période allant de 12 à 24 mois selon la situation.

> Josette devrait se renseigner car à mon avis, ayant 50 ans et encore trois enfants à charge, elle a droit à **un CRE,** ce qui l'aiderait peut-être à trouver un emploi.

la convention collective: La convention collective est un accord écrit qui a été conclu entre un ou plusieurs syndicats de salariés et les représentants des employeurs à l'issue d'une négociation. En général, **les conventions collectives** fixent le salaire minimal du secteur en question. Le numéro de **la convention collective** appliquée est inscrit sur le bulletin de salaire. Toutes les branches professionnelles n'ont pas nécessairement de **convention collective.**

> Le texte de la nouvelle **convention collective** a été affiché dans l'entreprise et puis remis au comité d'entreprise et aux représentants du personnel.

une dérogation: Une dérogation est une exception faite à une loi ou un principe.

> Je sais qu'il est interdit de renouveler *(renew)* ce genre de contrat mais nous pourrions peut-être obtenir **une dérogation.**

être en règle: On **est en règle** lorsqu'on a fait les choses comme il se doit, en suivant les règles existant dans ce domaine, en se conformant à l'usage.

> J'ai un permis de travail et un permis de séjour. Tous mes papiers **sont en règle.** Je peux donc officiellement chercher un travail dans ce pays.

à l'insu de: Lorsqu'on fait quelque chose sans le dire à quelqu'un, on le fait **à l'insu de** cette personne, c'est-à-dire sans qu'elle le sache.

> Si tu cherches un nouvel emploi, il est préférable que tu le fasses **à l'insu de** ton patron car celui-ci ne sera pas content et cela te compliquera la vie.

mener une mission à terme: **Mener une mission à terme** signifie finir cette mission, faire le travail qu'on s'était engagé à faire, jusqu'à la fin prévue dans le contrat.

Elle n'a pas **mené sa mission à terme** et n'a donc pas droit à l'indemnité de fin de mission (l'IFM) qui monte normalement à 10%.

une mission: On appelle «**mission**» une tâche qui est donnée à faire à quelqu'un, un certain travail à effectuer ou à réaliser en un temps donné.

Il est parti **en mission** à Paris pour trois jours.

le travail clandestin: Il y a différents types de **travail** qui sont considérés comme **clandestins**. Exemples: Un travail qui est effectué en dehors des horaires normaux, un travail qui dépasse la durée maximale légale, un travail fait pendant les congés payés, ou pendant les congés de maladie, ou pendant une période officielle de chômage.

Mais non, tu ne peux pas faire un travail qui soit officiellement rémunéré pendant tes vacances, ce serait **du travail clandestin!**

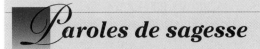

*P**aroles de sagesse*

Mieux vaut tenir que courir!

➤ Brainstorm with your study partner several situations where this adage might be used.

*E**xpression écrite*

Expressions négatives et conjonctions

Dans cette section, vous allez revoir certains usages du Minitel et aborder quelques concepts fiscaux *(tax-related)*. Encerclez toutes les expressions négatives ainsi que toutes les conjonctions des phrases suivantes.

Le Minitel

- *Je n'ai aucun problème pour réserver un billet de train car j'ai un Minitel.*
- *Depuis que j'ai un Minitel chez moi, je ne vais nulle part car je passe de nombreuses soirées à jouer avec.*
- *Grâce au Minitel, je ne regarde plus le Bottin (l'annuaire téléphonique).*
- *Le Minitel n'est pas encore bien connu aux Etats-Unis.*
- *Le Minitel ne pourra jamais se connecter à l'Internet.*
- *Certains Français n'aiment pas le Minitel car ils trouvent le prix des communications trop élevé et personnellement chaque fois que je reçois ma note de téléphone, je me promets de moins utiliser mon Minitel.*
- *Certaines entreprises françaises ne sont spécialisées que dans les services Minitel.*

Un Minitel.

Les Impôts

- *Si on gagne plus que 6.500 francs par mois, on doit payer des impôts [taxes].*
- *Le 15 février, j'enverrai ma déclaration 2042 à la perception [French IRS].*
- *Au Centre Des Impôts, on peut lire : «Payez vos impôts à temps, vous éviterez des pénalités».*
- *Si je travaillais à mon compte, je devrais payer toutes sortes de taxes.*
- *Si tu veux pouvoir payer tes impôts à temps, il faut que tu commences à économiser dès maintenant.*
- *Si nous étions comptables, nous consacrerions la majeure partie de notre temps à nous occuper de la déclaration d'impôts [tax returns] de nos clients.*
- *Pense à garder tes reçus si tu veux déduire tes frais de tes impôts.*

R. A vos plumes! En vous basant sur les phrases précédentes, essayez maintenant d'écrire un paragraphe d'environ 150 mots sur ce que vous avez appris au sujet du travail temporaire en France. Commencez par une phrase d'introduction. Utilisez des expressions adverbiales et des conjonctions pour exprimer vos idées de façon logique. Finissez par une phrase de conclusion.

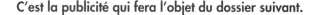

C'est la publicité qui fera l'objet du dossier suivant.

La publicité

Le quatorzième dossier se concentre sur quelques aspects de la publicité et de la mercatique. Depuis la Deuxième Guerre mondiale, la publicité a connu un essor *(expansion)* formidable. Elle est aujourd'hui omniprésente et prend de nombreuses formes: promotion dans les média, distribution d'objets publicitaires avec le logo de l'entreprise ou d'échantillons gratuits *(free samples)* par la Poste ou dans les magasins, etc.

Les média étant par définition un support de diffusion de l'information, c'est dans ce domaine que la publicité est la plus présente: impression d'encarts publicitaires ou d'annonces dans les journaux et les magazines, passage de spots publicitaires à la radio ou à la télévision, utilisation de panneaux d'affichage *(billboards)* publicitaire et de la publicité lumineuse dans les villes, envoi de catalogues, brochures, prospectus et réclames *(ads)* aux particuliers.

*A*ctivité d'introduction

La publicité et la mercatique

A. Premier contact avec la publicité et le marketing. Répondez aux questions suivantes.

1. Essayez d'arriver à une définition provisoire de la publicité et de la mercatique.
2. Où trouve-t-on des publicités? Dans quels média?
3. Quelles sont les publicités qui attirent le plus votre attention? Pourquoi?
4. Connaissez-vous des slogans publicitaires par cœur? Si oui, lesquels?
5. En vous basant sur des slogans dont vous vous souvenez, pouvez-vous faire une liste des caractéristiques d'un bon slogan?

6. Quelles réactions possibles pouvez-vous avoir devant une publicité qui vous plaît? Cochez les réponses qui vous paraissent vraisemblables.

Je souris.

Je suis irrité(e).

J'adore.

Je m'endors.

Je suis curieux(se) et je décide d'acheter le produit pour l'essayer.

Je la regarde attentivement.

Je la montre à un copain ou à une copine.

Je retiens le nom du produit.

Je jette la publicité dans la corbeille à papier.

7. Est-ce qu'il y a des publicités que vous détestez? à la radio? à la télévision? dans les journaux et magazines que vous lisez? Lesquelles?

8. Essayez d'analyser pourquoi vous ne les aimez pas.

9. Vous écoutez la radio. Quelle est votre réaction quand vous entendez un slogan publicitaire que vous détestez? Cochez les réponses possibles.

Je change de chaîne.

J'éteins la radio.

Je baisse le son.

J'augmente le son.

Je mets une cassette pour écouter quelque chose qui me plaît.

Je me concentre sur quelque chose d'autre.

J'essaie de penser à autre chose.

J'imite le speaker en le ridiculisant.

J'attends patiemment que le message passe.

J'écoute attentivement.

Les mots pour le dire

Vocabulaire de base

VERBES

changer d'avis	*to change one's mind*
conseiller	*to advise*
déconseiller	*to advise against*
déplaire à	*to displease*
détourner	*to turn away*
énerver	*to irritate, annoy (someone)*
s'évader	*to escape*
inciter à	*to incite to*
plaire à	*to please*
prévoir	*to foresee*
raisonner	*to reason*
rendre	*to render, make, give back*
rentabiliser	*to make profitable*
rêver	*to dream*
tromper	*to deceive*
zapper	*to channel surf*

continued on page 294

continued from page 293

N O M S

une affiche	*poster*
le besoin	*need*
une boîte aux lettres	*mailbox*
une bonne affaire	*good deal*
une chaîne	*channel*
la concurrence	*competition*
un consommateur	*consumer*
la consommation	*consumption*
un dépliant	*flyer*
l'embarras (m) du choix	*difficulty in choosing*
une émission	*program*
un encart publicitaire	*insert*
l'enjeu (m)	*stakes*
une étude (de motivation)	*study (of motivation)*
l'exclusivité (f)	*exclusivity*
un journal	*newspaper*
un lien	*link*
les média, les médias	*media*
la mercatique, le marketing	*marketing*
un message publicitaire	*advertisement*
un panneau d'affichage	*billboard*
la presse	*press*
la promotion, un article en promotion	*promotion, an item on special*
une réclame	*ad*
une revue, un magazine	*magazine*
un slogan	*slogan*
le son	*sound*
un spot	*commercial*
une stratégie	*strategy*
une tactique	*tactic*
une télécommande	*remote control*
un téléviseur, un poste de télévision, la télé	*TV set*
le zapping	*channel surfing*

A D J E C T I F S

attirant(e)	*attractive*
émotionnel(le)	*emotional*
humoristique	*humorous*
inacceptable	*unacceptable*
inconstant(e)	*fickle*
mensonger(ère)	*deceitful, misleading*
pratique	*practical*
rationnel(le)	*rational*
trompeur(se)	*deceitful, deceiving*

A D V E R B E S

constamment	*constantly*
inconsciemment	*unconsciously*
machinalement	*mechanically*
pratiquement	*practically*

➤ Note key words and expressions that might be useful for *Mot de passe.*

B. Définitions provisoires à terminer. Complétez les phrases suivantes.

1. Lorsqu'on passe d'une chaîne de télévision à l'autre, très rapidement, à l'aide de la télécommande, on dit qu'on _____.

2. Une _____ est un support papier qui présente souvent une photo et un texte. Une _____ sert à faire de la publicité, à annoncer quelque chose ou simplement à décorer.

3. Lorsqu'il y a beaucoup de choix et qu'on ne sait que choisir, on dit qu'on a _____ du choix.

4. La _____, c'est la raison véritable derrière quelque chose, ce qui explique cette chose ou ce comportement. Quand une entreprise veut vendre un produit, elle a besoin de savoir pourquoi les clients achètent telle ou telle chose. Alors elle fait faire une étude de _____ pour connaître les mécanismes cachés, les structures latentes de la conduite de ses clients.

5. Un _____ est en général une petite phrase qui est lancée lors d'une campagne publicitaire, qui attire l'attention et qu'on associe à un produit. «Du bo, du bon, Dubonnet!» est un _____ pour une boisson, un apéritif français. «On a toujours besoin de petits pois chez soi» en est un autre.

6. Lorsqu'une publicité ne dit pas la vérité, qu'elle trompe les consommateurs, on dit qu'elle est _____.

C. Définitions provisoires à créer. Ecrivez une définition provisoire pour les mots suivants.

1. plaire
2. rentabiliser
3. tromper
4. une stratégie
5. attirant

HSG

➤ Study the *Points grammaticaux* section of Module V in your *HSG* and complete Exercises M–R.

Dialogue

Vie de famille et publicité

D. Activité de pré-lecture. Répondez aux questions suivantes par groupes de deux ou trois.

1. Comment regardez-vous la télé? Est-ce que vous zappez beaucoup? Pourquoi?

2. Comment est-ce que vous réagissez lorsqu'un message publicitaire interrompt un programme télévisé?

3. Est-ce que vous vous laissez influencer par les publicités que vous voyez à la télé? Comment?

4. Quelles sont les meilleures heures et les meilleurs jours pour toucher un certain public qui regarde certaines émissions de télévision? Choisissez un produit et imaginez que vous êtes une

Page tirée de *L'officiel des spectacles*
du 14–20 septembre 1994, Paris.

entreprise. Vous devez choisir une heure et un programme pour faire
passer votre spot publicitaire. Expliquez quand et où vous allez le
placer et pourquoi.

Vie de famille et publicité

Emilie et Florine, deux amies de 21 ans, regardent la télé chez les parents de Florine.

Emilie: Ces pubs, ça m'énerve! Je n'arrive pas à m'habituer aux interruptions! Moi, je suis championne du zapping. Je préfère regarder ailleurs et passer d'une chaîne à l'autre plutôt que de supporter les messages publicitaires. Passe-moi la télécommande!

Florine: Ah, non! Moi, j'ai horreur du zapping. A la limite, je coupe le son. C'est pour cela d'ailleurs que j'peux jamais regarder la télé avec Papa ou Eric car ils n'arrêtent pas de zapper. C'est débile! Et puis y a des pubs qui sont marrantes! T'as vu celle de Peugeot dernièrement?

Emilie:	Non, j'crois pas... laquelle?
Florine:	La plus récente. Je l'ai vue avant-hier. Tu sais, quand on achète une Peugeot, on a une semaine après l'achat de la voiture pour la rendre, si on change d'avis ou si pour une raison ou pour une autre, on n'est pas content de la voiture. C'est nouveau!
Emilie:	Ah bon! C'est pas mal, ça!
Florine:	Oui, alors tu vois un jeune couple dans une voiture, une jeune femme et son mari ou son copain. C'est elle qui est au volant et visiblement c'est elle qui a choisi la voiture parce que pendant qu'elle conduit, lui, il n'arrête pas de critiquer la bagnole! Il essaie de l'influencer pour qu'elle aille rendre ou changer la voiture. Au bout d'un moment elle lui dit quelque chose comme: «Si ça continue comme ça, c'est toi que je vais changer, c'est pas la voiture!» C'est drôle, non?
Emilie:	Ouais... mais moi, j'ai pas la patience de regarder la pub. Ça y est, le film recommence. Remets le son!

Un peu plus tard...

Florine:	Tiens, hier après-midi, en sortant de la Fac, j'ai vu une publicité qui m'a hérissée.
Emilie:	Ah bon?
Florine:	Oui, j'allais à la Poste et en traversant la place de la mairie, j'ai vu deux copines qui regardaient une affiche et discutaient. Je me suis arrêtée pour leur dire bonjour. Elles m'ont demandé ce que je pensais de l'affiche en question. C'était une publicité pour la Caisse d'Epargne. Tu l'as peut-être déjà remarquée. L'affiche représente simplement un bébé assis dans une baignoire, avec comme slogan: «Il y a d'autres façons de payer moins d'impôts!»
Emilie:	Et alors?
Florine:	Et alors? Comment est-ce que tu peux dire ça! Comme si on avait un enfant pour pouvoir payer moins d'impôts! Avec ce qu'un enfant coûte et entraîne comme frais! Et puis, on ne peut pas comparer un enfant avec un compte épargne! C'est incroyable!
Emilie:	Oui, c'est effectivement une manière de raisonner un peu surprenante! Et qu'est-ce que tes copines en disaient?
Florine:	Alix était de mon avis. Elle était choquée et trouvait la publicité de fort mauvais goût mais Lucie riait de l'indignation d'Alix et disait qu'il fallait garder un sens de l'humour et ne pas prendre les choses trop au sérieux et que c'était juste pour attirer l'attention de manière amusante!

> ➤ Avoir des entants permet aux parents de payer moins d'impôts à l'Etat français.

Emilie:	Elle est où exactement cette affiche? Je passerai la voir demain avant de rentrer à la maison.
Florine:	Elle est sur le mur à droite de la Caisse d'Epargne justement. Je suis rarement choquée par une publicité mais celle-ci dépasse les bornes!

M. et Mme Guimaux, les parents de Florine, viennent de rentrer à la maison. Ils préparent le dîner avec Sarah et Eric, 16 et 14 ans.

Eric:	Alors, qu'est-ce qu'on mange ce soir?
M. Guimaux:	Ta mère et moi, on est rentrés tard, alors on a pris des plats cuisinés Findus. Alors, ça, et une salade et du fromage, bien sûr, ça ira pour ce soir. Je ne savais pas qu'Emilie restait dîner.
Emilie:	Oh, ne vous inquiétez pas pour moi!
Sarah:	«C'est bien connu, le Français ne mange pas assez de poisson.»
Eric:	«Je suis entièrement d'accord. Heureusement, il y a Findus!»
M. Guimaux:	Arrêtez donc de jouer aux perroquets et venez nous aider. Sarah, mets le couvert, et toi Eric, fais la vinaigrette pour la salade.
Sarah:	A propos de publicité, je viens de voir celle des glaces Gervais à la télé. Maman, est-ce que tu as pensé à prendre des cônes «Extrême» de Gervais? Je t'avais dit que j'en voulais. Miam... «Gervais, j'en veux!»
Mme Guimaux:	Non. Je ne peux quand même pas acheter tous les produits qui passent des réclames alléchantes à la télévision!
Eric:	Bien sûr que non, mais tu pourrais faire une petite exception pour Gervais. Tu sais bien que réclame ou pas réclame, c'est notre glace préférée!
Mme Guimaux:	Va en chercher tout de suite si tu veux, puisqu'Emilie est là et que nous n'avons pas de dessert pour ce soir. Nous pouvons faire une exception! Il est 7 heures et demie. Super U est encore ouvert. Mais cours, nous dînons dans dix minutes!
Eric:	Super! Donne-moi ton porte-monnaie. Je reviens tout de suite!

> ➤ Agreement on the past participle is being made as if *on* were *nous*.

Notez bien: Pour simplifier le travail sur le dialogue, nous l'avons divisé en trois parties distinctes. *Première partie:* Du début de la conversation entre Florine et Emilie jusqu'à la reprise du film «Remets le son». *Deuxième partie:* Suite de la conversation entre Florine et Emilie jusqu'à l'intervention d'Eric: «Alors, qu'est-ce qu'on mange ce soir?» *Troisième partie:* Conversation entre M. Guimaux, Mme Guimaux, Eric, Sarah et Emilie jusqu'à la fin.

Première partie du dialogue

E. Synonymes. Trouvez dans le texte un synonyme pour chacun des mots de la liste suivante.

1. irriter
2. être fort(e)
3. donner
4. détester
5. stupide

6. amusant(e)
7. opinion
8. conduire
9. sélectionner
10. la voiture

F. Autrement dit. Le début de ce texte contient un certain nombre d'éléments qui relèvent du français parlé. En voici une liste. Donnez la forme correcte ou le mot qui correspond à un registre un peu plus formel.

1. une bagnole
2. une pub
3. la télé
4. y a
5. c'est débile
6. t'as vu

7. j'crois pas
8. marrant
9. c'est pas
10. ouais
11. j'ai pas

G. Avez-vous compris? Répondez aux questions suivantes.

1. Florine et Emilie ont une attitude différente devant les messages publicitaires qui passent à la télé.

Que fait Emilie quand les messages commencent?

Que fait Florine?

Et vous? Pourquoi?

2. De quelle publicité en particulier est-ce que Florine et Emilie discutent?

3. Pourquoi est-ce que Florine raconte cette publicité?

4. Quel public est-ce que cette publicité vise *(target)* et pourquoi?

Deuxième partie du dialogue

H. Avez-vous compris? Répondez aux questions suivantes. Cochez les réponses correctes.

1. Comment pouvez-vous caractériser l'attitude de Florine envers la publicité. Elle est... ?

a. irritée
b. amusée
c. choquée

d. énervée
e. indignée
f. charmée

2. Comment pouvez-vous caractériser l'attitude d'Emilie?

a. un peu indifférente
b. comique

c. surprenante
d. très émotionnelle

3. Quelle relation Alix et Lucie ont-elles avec Florine?

　a. Elles sont des amies.

　b. Elles sont des collègues.

　c. Elles sont des cousines.

　d. Elles sont des voisines.

4. L'affiche qui est discutée est une publicité pour encourager les gens à faire certaines choses. Lesquelles?

　a. ouvrir un compte d'épargne

　b. faire fructifier leur argent

　c. avoir plus d'enfants

　d. utiliser des contraceptifs

　e. ouvrir un compte pour leur bébé

5. Comment Alix caractériserait-elle cette publicité?

　a. inacceptable

　b. choquante mais efficace (effective)

　c. amusante

　d. mal faite

　e. étonnante

> ➤ Que suggère cette publicité? Pouvez-vous reconnaître l'animal stylisé dont il s'agit?

6. Quelle est l'opinion de Florine?

　a. la même que celle de Lucie

　b. la même que celle d'Emilie

　c. la même que celle d'Alix

　d. la même que la vôtre

　e. la même que celle des gens de la Caisse d'Epargne qui ont eu l'idée de cette publicité

7. Qu'est-ce que cette publicité veut dire?

　a. A la Caisse d'Epargne, on peut investir son argent de façon à réduire ses impôts.

　b. A la Caisse d'Epargne, même les enfants peuvent ouvrir un compte.

　c. A la Caisse d'Epargne, il y a une crèche pour les enfants des employés.

Troisième partie du dialogue

I. Avez-vous compris? Répondez aux questions suivantes.

　1. De quelles publicités est-ce que cette famille parle?

　2. Qui aime les glaces Gervais?

　3. Quel est le slogan des glaces Gervais?

　4. Pourquoi est-ce que Mme Guimaux n'a pas acheté de cônes glacés Gervais?

　5. Pourquoi est-ce que M. et Mme Guimaux ont acheté des plats préparés Findus?

J. A compléter! Après avoir bien lu la troisième partie du dialogue, faites correspondre les éléments des deux colonnes A et B:

A	B
1. les Findus	est une marque de glace
2. Sarah	met le couvert
3. Eric	sont du poisson en plat préparé
4. Gervais	fait la vinaigrette
5. les parents	est un supermarché du quartier
6. Super U	ont fait les courses

K. Trouver le mot juste. Choisissez parmi la liste des adjectifs suivants ceux qui vous paraissent bien caractériser les membres de la famille et ce dont ils parlent. Rayez *(cross out)* ceux qui ne conviennent pas.

1. Sarah et Eric sont

gais, désagréables, moqueurs, gourmands, agressifs, indifférents, fiers, drôles, ouverts, gâtés, impolis, timides, actifs, tristes.

Et maintenant quels sont les adjectifs qui conviennent pour Sarah? Mettez ces adjectifs au féminin singulier. Sarah est...

2. M. et Mme Guimaux sont

très occupés, négligeants, autoritaires, gentils, préoccupés, dépensiers, distants, infantiles, attentifs, fermés, sérieux, affectueux, économes, violents.

Prenez les adjectifs que vous venez de sélectionner et mettez-les maintenant au féminin singulier. Mme Guimaux est...

3. La glace Gervais est

délicieuse, savoureuse, légère, calorique, sucrée, chère, crémeuse, rafraîchissante, acide, tentante, répugnante.

Prenez la liste des adjectifs proposés pour la glace Gervais. Si vous parliez des cônes Gervais, que diriez-vous? Faites les changements d'accord nécessaires. Les cônes Gervais sont...

4. Les produits Findus sont des plats

cuisinés, préparés, pratiques, végétariens, surgelés, frais, économiques, raffinés, salés, nouveaux, familiaux, chic, irrésistibles, indigestes, lourds, alléchants.

➤ Quels adjectifs associeriez-vous avec cette publicité?

➤ Note synonyms for *Mot de passe.*

5. Trouvez dans les listes d'adjectifs qui précèdent le contraire des adjectifs suivants:

frais	sérieux
dépensier	lourd
salé	économique
ouvert	désagréable
alléchant	distant

Observations lexicales

Pour décrire une réclame, une photo ou une scène

Si vous voulez décrire une réclame, une photo ou une scène, vous aurez besoin d'un vocabulaire précis pour pouvoir situer un élément ou un personnage par rapport à un autre. La liste qui suit vous fournit un bon point de départ.

au premier plan	au deuxième plan	au fond
à l'arrière plan	à droite	à gauche
en haut	en bas	au milieu
devant	derrière	un gros plan
un plan américain	un panorama	à côté de
près de		

L. Application. Répondez aux questions suivantes.

1. Faites rapidement un dessin qui correspond à la description suivante.

   Au premier plan, on voit une bouteille d'eau minérale en bas et à droite. Au fond, une montagne couverte de neige et au dessus du sommet, un ciel bleu vif. A gauche de l'image et au deuxième plan, une jeune femme skie. Derrière elle, on voit la neige qui brille au soleil et quelques arbres, au milieu de l'image mais à l'arrière plan, le public. Devant elle, au loin: la ligne d'arrivée.

2. A votre avis, il s'agit d'une publicité pour quel produit?

M. Allons un peu plus loin! Les questions suivantes touchent au domaine de la publicité et de la mercatique. Réfléchissez-y puis discutez-en par petits groupes.

1. Combien de temps est-ce qu'un produit dure sur le marché et pourquoi?

2. Pour quelles raisons achète-t-on un nouveau produit? une nouvelle voiture, par exemple? Cochez les réponses qui vous semblent possibles et n'hésitez pas à ajouter d'autres raisons si vous en trouvez. La voiture qu'on a déjà

   a. ne marche plus.

   b. est devenue dangereuse.

   c. consomme trop d'essence.

   d. a le moteur usé.

   e. est toute neuve.

   f. est encore en rôdage.

   g. paraît vieille.

   h. est trop grande.

   i. a la carrosserie abîmée.

   j. est le dernier modèle de la série.

3. Pourquoi achète-t-on une voiture de sport? Parmi les raisons suivantes cochez celles qui vous paraissent correctes.

   a. pour se faire plaisir

   b. parce que les vieilles voitures sont moins intéressantes

   c. pour avoir une voiture sûre

   d. parce qu'on en a envie

e. parce qu'on a besoin d'une voiture spacieuse

f. pour ne pas avoir de problèmes mécaniques

g. pour être remarqué

h. pour avoir une voiture plus rapide

i. pour donner l'impression qu'on est dynamique

j. pour faire jeune

k. pour impressionner les gens qu'on connaît

l. parce qu'on en a besoin

m. parce que ça coûte moins cher

n. parce qu'on est impressionné par la performance de cette voiture

o. pour avoir une voiture plus économique

p. parce que c'est agréable à conduire

q. pour avoir du succès

r. pour prouver à ses parents qu'on se débrouille bien financièrement

s. parce qu'une telle voiture réfléchit les qualités de son propriétaire

4. Distinguez les motivations conscientes et inconscientes de vos achats, autrement dit, vos mobiles rationnels de vos mobiles irrationnels. Prenez des exemples de mobiles rationnels parmi les deux listes qui précèdent.

5. Quels pourraient être vos mobiles inconscients? Inspirez-vous des deux listes qui précèdent mais n'hésitez pas à proposer d'autres explications.

6. Pourquoi achète-t-on une nouvelle paire de chaussures de tennis? Faites une liste similaire à celle qui vous est proposée pour justifier l'achat d'une voiture. On achète une nouvelle paire de tennis

parce que...   pour...

parce que...   pour...

7. Pourquoi achète-t-on une nouvelle savonnette?

parce que...   pour...

parce que...   pour...

8. Pourquoi achète t-on un nouvel ordinateur?

parce que...   pour...

parce que...   pour...

Acheter un nouvel ordinateur.

continued on page 304

GAP

Pour femme.

Ouvre le 31 août aux

Galeries Lafayette Montparnasse.

Venez chercher votre cadeau.

Dans la limite des stocks disponibles.

GALERIES
Lafayette

L'annonce de l'ouverture de GAP aux GALERIES LAFAYETTE.

continued from page 303

9. Pourquoi achète-t-on un nouveau jean?

parce que...   pour...

parce que...   pour...

10. Pourquoi faut-il faire une étude de marché avant de sortir un produit? Cochez les réponses correctes.

  a. pour savoir s'il y a un besoin

  b. pour savoir si on peut créer un besoin

  c. pour savoir qui achèterait un tel produit

  d. pour savoir combien le produit pourrait être vendu

  e. pour déterminer la concurrence

11. Choisissez un exemple de produit qui est sorti récemment sur le marché et répondez aux questions suivantes.

  a. Quel public ce produit vise-t-il?

  b. Quel âge?

  c. Quel sexe?

  d. Quelle classe sociale et économique?

  e. Quelle race?

12. Cherchez deux exemples de produits qui s'adressent pratiquement à tous les groupes de votre société et expliquez pourquoi il en est ainsi.

13. Faites une liste de produits qui visent spécialement un des groupes de votre société et expliquez en quoi ces produits ne conviennent pas à tout le monde.

  ▪ produits s'adressant aux jeunes enfants

Une réclame pour le magazine *Détours*.

- produits s'adressant aux adolescentes (jeunes filles)
- produits s'adressant exclusivement aux femmes
- produits s'adressant aux hommes
- produits s'adressant aux personnes âgées
- produits visant une race ou une culture spécifique
- produits s'adressant à un groupe de sportifs déterminés (joueurs de golf, de tennis, de football, etc.)
- produits visant les étudiants

N. A vous la parole! Que pensez-vous des affirmations suivantes? Discutez-en par petits groupes de deux ou trois personnes.

1. «Acheter, c'est s'identifier.»
2. «Acheter, c'est s'exprimer.»
3. «Choisir, c'est renoncer à autre chose.»
4. «On ne peut dépenser que lorsqu'on peut le justifier; sinon on se sent mal.»
5. «Acheter n'est pas toujours le résultat d'une décision rationnelle.»

HSG

➤ Study the *Encadré supplémentaire* on adjectives and complete Exercises S–Z of Module V in your *HSG*.

Lecture 1

Pour vendre, ils utilisent notre inconscient

O. Activité de pré-lecture. Par petits groupes de deux ou trois personnes, discutez les questions suivantes.

1. Pourquoi est-il important de bien connaître les motifs inconscients qui incitent les consommateurs à acheter?
2. Comment pourrait-on faire pour arriver à connaître les motifs inconscients des clients potentiels?

Pour vendre, ils utilisent notre inconscient

De plus en plus d'industriels font appel à l'hypnose pour connaître nos motivations d'achat.

Persuadée que nos motivations d'achats nous sont inconnues, une société d'études et de conseils, la Sorgem, utilise l'hypnose pour suivre le cheminement du désir qui nous incite à acheter. «L'hypnose permet de dépasser les barrières de chacun pour révéler les véritables motivations d'achat. Lors des entretiens sur tel ou tel produit, il ne s'agit pas de suggérer mais de prélever de l'information», explique Yves Krief, président de la Sorgem.

Vous êtes en voiture sur une autoroute déserte, le moteur ronronne, tout va bien. Votre esprit s'évade et vous transporte dans un autre lieu. Tout bruit environnant cesse de vous atteindre, et vous passez les vitesses machinalement. Cet état de douce

continued on page 306

continued from page 305

Publicité pour les produits surgelés d'HALIEUTIS.

rêverie, que chacun connaît, est déjà très proche de l'hypnose douce, car c'est notre inconscient qui est aux commandes.

Un plongeon dans nos désirs secrets

Comment se déroule une séance? Pendant trois heures, un psychothérapeute, accompagné d'un chargé d'études, plonge une personne volontaire et indemnisée (200 F) dans un état de relaxation extrême, grâce à sa voix et à l'évocation d'un souvenir agréable. Assis confortablement, les yeux fermés, le corps alangui, le débit lent mais étrangement précis, le sujet se remémore sa décision d'achat. Il remonte très loin dans sa mémoire.

Des indications précieuses

Ainsi, ce père de famille de 40 ans qui se souvient de son enfance, partant à la pêche avec son père dans une «automobile blanche… automatique… Florine… spacieuse. C'était comme si je roulais dans un lit». Des années plus tard, ce même homme achètera un véhicule ayant de fortes ressemblances avec celle que possédait son père afin de retrouver la sensation de confort et d'invincibilité.

Constructeurs automobiles, fabricants de cosmétiques, sociétés de transport, de plus en plus de sociétés ont recours à cette méthode pour mieux vendre leurs produits. Les réactions des hypnotisés sont très utiles et peuvent changer des stratégies de communication. […]

L'hypnose, pour les entreprises, est un instrument précieux, beaucoup plus efficace que les études de consommation classiques. Mais cela reste tabou. «En France, l'hypnose est associée à un phénomène de foire, les gens en ont peur. Mais les volontaires qui participent à nos séances sont très décontractés et quand ils se réveillent ils ont souvent envie de recommencer», certifie Yves Krief.

Extrait d'un article de Viviane Contri. Paru dans *Femme Actuelle,* N° 577, hebdomadaire du 16 au 22 octobre 1995.

P. Autrement dit. Les mots suivants sont tirés du texte. Expliquez-les avec vos propres mots.

1. inconnu
2. le cheminement
3. une barrière
4. prélever
5. s'évader
6. cesser
7. atteindre
8. un volontaire
9. se remémoriser
10. l'invincibilité
11. un tabou
12. décontracté

Q. Vrai ou faux? Lisez bien les affirmations suivantes et regardez si elles correspondent à ce qui est dit dans le texte. Modifiez les affirmations qui sont fausses de façon à ce qu'elles soient correctes.

1. Les psychologues utilisent l'hypnose pour pousser les gens à acheter certains produits.
2. Quand l'inconscient est aux commandes, on fait les choses machinalement.
3. Le jeune homme achète le même genre de voiture que son père parce que cette voiture est liée à des sentiments agréables et positifs.
4. Beaucoup de sociétés se basent sur les résultats d'études faites sous hypnose pour créer de nouveaux produits.

5. En France l'hypnose est depuis longtemps prise très au sérieux.

6. Les études faites sous hypnose sont plus intéressantes pour les entreprises que les études de consommation utilisant des méthodes plus traditionnelles.

7. L'hypnose n'est pas très agréable pour les volontaires qui se laissent tester et c'est pourquoi ils préfèrent ne pas recommencer l'expérience.

R. La parole est à vous! Discutez les questions suivantes.

1. Que pensez-vous de ces études faites sous hypnose?

2. Accepteriez-vous d'être interrogé sous hypnose si l'on vous demandait d'être volontaire? Pourquoi?

> ➤ Interview three classmates. Be ready to report your findings back to the class.

Lecture 2

Halte au zapping!

S. Activité de pré-lecture. Discutez les questions suivantes en petits groupes.

1. Pourquoi les gens choisissent-ils d'aller faire leurs achats dans un magasin plutôt que dans un autre?

2. Qu'est-ce qu'un magasin ou une chaîne de magasins peut faire pour attirer davantage de clients?

3. Que veut dire «faire du zapping»?

4. Que pourrait vouloir dire «faire du zapping» lorsqu'on parle de magasins dans lesquels les clients font leurs achats?

> ➤ Comparez et contrastez ces trois enseignes.

Le nom d'un magasin parisien.

La façade d'un salon de coiffure.

L'enseigne d'une boutique de vêtements.

Le rayon camembert
d'un hypermarché.

Halte au zapping!

Nos clients sont devenus versatiles, passant d'une enseigne à l'autre au gré des bonnes affaires. Or, notre fond de commerce, ce sont les clients fidèles qui font chez nous des achats réguliers et importants.

Pour grossir leur nombre, nous avons, depuis longtemps, mis l'accent sur les prix et le choix d'articles de qualité. Nous insistons désormais sur les services offerts et plus particulièrement, sur la practicité de nos magasins. C'est l'achat facile.

1.014, voilà le nombre d'hypermarchés recensés sur le territoire français. Autant dire que le consommateur n'a que l'embarras du choix pour faire ses courses. Sa boîte aux lettres est régulièrement alimentée par les dépliants publicitaires des différentes enseignes et c'est souvent dans son salon qu'il choisit d'aller dans tel ou tel hypermarché en fonction des promotions.

Ce phénomène s'accentue puisque la moyenne du nombre des magasins fréquentés par les clients est passée de 2,7 à 3,3 en trois ans.

Pas de doute, l'enjeu pour Continent consiste désormais à fidéliser ses clients.

La démarche n'est pas aisée car chaque enseigne met l'accent sur les prix et la qualité des produits.

Il faut impérativement créer un lien fort entre les consommateurs et nos magasins pour que Continent devienne leur enseigne préférée. Ce lien se matérialise aujourd'hui avec la carte Continent qui offre à nos clients les nombreux services et avantages du «Club Gagnant».

Tiré de *Actualités Continent*, N° 46, mai 1995.

Même les petits sachets d'emballage servent de support à la publicité.

T. A la recherche d'éléments précis. Répondez aux questions suivantes.

1. Il y a plusieurs chiffres dans ce texte. Lesquels? Quelle est leur importance?

2. Trouvez dans le texte le synonyme des mots ou groupes de mots suivants.

a. Arrêtez

b. changeants, inconstants

c. nous avons insisté sur

d. loyal, constant

e. d'un magasin différent à un autre

f. comptés

g. la France

h. faire ses achats

i. selon

j. augmente, s'accroît

k. facile

l. absolument

U. Vrai ou faux? Lisez les constatations suivantes puis indiquez si elles sont vraies ou fausses. Si elles sont fausses, corrigez-les. Si elles sont vraies, expliquez pourquoi.

1. Continent compte surtout sur ses clients fidèles.

2. Continent ne veut plus que ses clients aillent de magasin en magasin selon les promotions proposées.

3. Continent veut décourager l'achat facile.

4. Continent cherche plus à garder le même nombre de clients fidèles qu'à augmenter le nombre total de tous ses clients.

5. Il y a 1.014 hypermarchés «Continent» en France.

6. Les consommateurs n'ont pas encore assez de choix en France en ce qui concerne les hypermarchés où ils peuvent faire leurs achats.

7. Les Français ne reçoivent pas beaucoup de différents dépliants publicitaires dans leurs boîtes aux lettres.

8. Les dépliants publicitaires n'ont pas beaucoup d'influence sur les décisions prises par les clients.

9. Les Français fréquentent de plus en plus de magasins différents.

V. Mots clés. Voici une liste de mots tirés du texte. Encerclez les cinq mots essentiels à la compréhension du texte et expliquez votre choix.

a. Continent

b. boîte aux lettres

c. une bonne affaire

d. achats réguliers

e. l'enjeu

f. les produits

g. les consommateurs

h. fidéliser

i. l'accent

j. un dispositif

k. promotions

l. les prix

m. un lien

W. La parole est à vous! Par petits groupes de deux ou trois, répondez aux questions suivantes.

1. De quel point de vue ce texte est-il écrit?

2. Bien qu'il n'y ait pas de nom d'auteur, qui a pu écrire ce texte selon vous?

3. Quel est le message essentiel du texte? Rédigez-le en une seule phrase.

HSG

➤ Complete Exercises AA–DD of Module V in your *HSG* as well as the rest of the adjective flashes.

Quelques points de repère

Le saviez-vous?

- France Télécom se sert de l'espace fourni par les cartes de téléphone ou télécartes pour y placer un message publicitaire. Il y a donc une grande variété de cartes. Elles sont colorées et amusantes. Attention, ne jetez pas vos télécartes, collectionnez-les! En effet, les télécartes qui ont été émises à tirage restreint, c'est-à-dire à moins de 1.000 exemplaires prennent de la valeur! A la tête des télécartes recherchées: la «Longuet-Schlumberger». Cette carte, tirée à 80 exemplaires seulement lors de la visite du ministre dans une usine Schlumberger atteindrait 40.000 F au moins! Les collectionneurs

Les deux côtés d'une télécarte de France Télécom.

peuvent acheter un album spécial pour ranger et conserver leurs cartes.

- La publicité comparative a longtemps été interdite en France et en Europe. Elle est désormais autorisée à condition de ne pas être trompeuse, de ne pas engendrer la confusion dans l'esprit du public et de ne pas discréditer le concurrent.

L'ardoise!

L'usage intensif et envahissant de la publicité dans tous les média tel que nous le connaissons maintenant est un phénomène récent qui devient de plus en plus sophistiqué artistiquement et techniquement. Les clients potentiels blasés doivent être séduits, amusés, étonnés par des spots et une campagne qui coûtent des millions et qui peuvent à eux seuls assurer le succès ou l'échec d'une marchandise. Autrefois, la publicité se faisait surtout par une méthode aussi vieille que le monde, celle du bouche à oreille qui faisait ou défaisait la réputation d'une entreprise, d'un commerçant ou d'un produit en général.

Une date importante!

En novembre 1995, les ministres chargés de la consommation des Quinze se sont mis d'accord pour autoriser la publicité comparative mais dans des limites étroites pour éviter tout abus.

Les entreprises françaises!

- Les dix premiers groupes actifs dans le domaine de la publicité en France sont: EURO-RSCG France, Publicis Communication France, BDDP France, DDB-Needham France, Young & Rubicam France, Lintas, CLM/BBDO, Ogilvy & Mather, McCann Erickson France, Saatchi & Saatchi.
- Quelques exemples de slogans publicitaires français connus:

  «Il n'y a que Maille qui m'aille.» (pour la moutarde Maille)

  «SNCF, c'est possible.»

  «T'as le ticket chic, t'as le ticket choc!» (RATP: métro parisien)

  «Phillips, c'est déjà demain.»

  «Renault, des voitures à vivre.»

  «Bougez avec la Poste.»

  «Crédit Lyonnais, le pouvoir de dire Oui.»

  «Mammouth écrase les prix.» (hypermarché)

Le matériel ferroviaire

Les chiffres parlent!

De 1992 à 1994, les agences de publicité françaises sont devenues plus compétitives en réduisant leurs effectifs, bloquant les salaires, diminuant leurs frais tout en améliorant leur productivité. Malgré tous ces efforts, leur marge a chuté *(fell)* de 21% et leurs résultats d'exploitation ont baissé de moitié *(by half)*.

Réflexions sur le travail en équipe

Les systèmes, procédés et méthodes utilisés par une équipe doivent aider à planifier les tâches à accomplir, à communiquer et à prendre des décisions. Ils doivent également résoudre les problèmes qui se posent, faciliter les changements nécessaires et intégrer les améliorations voulues.

Pour perfectionner tout système, procédé ou méthode, il faut que tous les membres de l'équipe, à intervalles réguliers, évaluent leur travail, les résultats obtenus, ainsi que le fonctionnement de toute l'équipe. Pendant ces sessions de brainstorming («remue-méninges») chacun doit rester le plus ouvert possible aux commentaires ou critiques (constructives aussi bien que négatives) des autres. Après avoir opté pour tel ou tel changement, l'équipe devra essayer de repérer les points faibles pour pouvoir les corriger ou les éviter à l'avenir de façon à rendre le système, procédé ou méthode plus efficace.

Lexique

une brochure: **Une brochure** est un petit ouvrage broché ou relié qui donne des informations. Les entreprises peuvent sortir une brochure pour

(i)tineris

Messagerie Vocale
Guide Pratique

France Telecom Mobiles

La page de garde d'une brochure pour Itineris.

leur promotion. Une ville peut avoir une brochure touristique. Le contenu sera beaucoup plus développé que dans le cas du dépliant et du prospectus.

As-tu vu la nouvelle **brochure** du CNED? Elle est vraiment bien faite et donne envie de s'inscrire à un cours par correspondance!

une campagne: Une campagne publicitaire c'est une action qui, pendant une certaine durée déterminée à l'avance, vise à faire de la publicité pour une entreprise, un produit ou une personne.

Je me souviens bien de **la campagne** publicitaire de Guerlain qui essayait de vendre trois parfums différents de la gamme masculine «Héritage», «Vétiver» et «Habit Rouge». Cette **campagne** unique devait représenter Guerlain tout en respectant la particularité de chacun de ces trois parfums. Un véritable chalenge!

un dépliant: Un dépliant est une sorte de prospectus qui est plié plusieurs fois. **Un dépliant** donne des informations assez limitées.

Je me suis arrêtée au Syndicat d'initiative pour prendre quelques **dépliants** sur les villes de Chamonix, Aix-les-Bains et Annecy. Comme c'est la première fois que je suis en Haute-Savoie, je compte bien partir à la découverte de toute la région!

un mobile: Un mobile, c'est la cause, le motif d'une action. C'est ce qui pousse à agir.

Pierre aide souvent sa grand-tante bien qu'il ne l'aime pas. Je me demande quels peuvent être **ses mobiles**. Espère-t-il hériter? Je sais qu'elle est très riche.

une plaquette: Une plaquette est une sorte de brochure qui présente un produit, un service ou une entreprise.

Cette entreprise a sorti **une plaquette** en couleurs très impressionnante.

un prospectus: Un prospectus est destiné à promouvoir un établissement, une affaire ou un lieu touristique. Il s'agit souvent d'une simple feuille de papier qui ne contient donc pas beaucoup d'informations.

J'ai reçu **un prospectus** sur le nouveau restaurant du quartier. Nous devrions peut-être aller l'essayer.

la publicité: La publicité a pour but de promouvoir un produit ou une marque auprès des consommateurs, l'objectif étant pour l'entreprise de se faire connaître davantage et donc d'augmenter le volume de ses ventes.

Cette entreprise a fait énormément de **publicité** pour lancer sa nouvelle gamme de plats surgelés.

le publipostage: Le publipostage est de la publicité ou de la vente faite par voie postale, c'est-à-dire par l'intermédiaire de la Poste.

Ma boîte aux lettres est pleine de **publipostages** que je jette à la poubelle immédiatement.

Quels mots ciblant les affaires et la technologie reconnaissez-vous dans cette publicité pour le magazine *L'essentiel du management*?

Paroles de sagesse

Chassez le naturel, il revient au galop!

➤ Discuss with your study partner what this adage might mean.

Expression écrite

L'usage des noms

Dans cette section, vous allez revoir l'introduction de ce dossier du point de vue stylistique. Soulignez tous les noms et remarquez ceux qui ne sont pas précédés par un article.

La publicité en France

Depuis la Seconde Guerre mondiale, la publicité a connu un essor formidable. Elle est aujourd'hui omniprésente et prend de nombreuses formes: promotion dans les médias, distribution d'objets publicitaires avec le logo de l'entreprise, distribution d'échantillons gratuits par la Poste ou dans les magasins, etc.

Les médias étant par définition un support de diffusion de l'information, c'est dans ce domaine que la publicité est la plus présente: impression d'encarts publicitaires ou d'annonces dans les journaux et les

➤ Après quel type de ponctuation est-ce que les noms sont utilisés sans article?

magazines, passage de spots publicitaires à la radio ou à la télévision, utilisation de panneaux d'affichage publicitaire et de la publicité lumineuse dans les villes, envoi de catalogues, brochures, prospectus et réclames aux particuliers.

Avant d'écrire votre propre paragraphe, lisez celui qui suit en vous concentrant à nouveau sur les noms et leur emploi.

La publicité

De nos jours, la publicité prend de plus en plus d'importance dans notre vie de consommateurs. Elle est partout dans nos boîtes aux lettres, à l'abord des villes, à la radio, à la télévision... Elle fait maintenant partie du décor urbain et a littéralement envahi notre petit écran. Elle influence nos goûts, crée des besoins, répond à notre soif de nouveauté. Par exemple, à la télévision, le film du soir sera même interrompu par une page de publicité! Et les gens protestent de plus en plus à cause des longues interruptions réservées à la pub. Cependant, il existe des adeptes de la publicité: il y a même des émissions, comme «Culture Pub» sur TV6, entièrement dédiées à la publicité et à son histoire. Il est aussi amusant de remarquer qu'au delà de son indéniable aspect commercial, la pub est aussi devenue une nouvelle forme d'art, un moyen d'expression.

X. A vos plumes! Essayez maintenant d'écrire un paragraphe d'environ 150 mots sur ce que vous avez appris dans ce module au sujet du travail temporaire et de la formation. Commencez par une phrase d'introduction. Utilisez autant de noms que possible (sans article après les deux points [:]). Finissez par une phrase de conclusion.

Dans le dossier suivant, il s'agira de vente et d'achat et d'import-export.

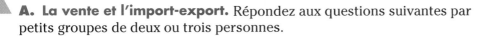

*A*chat et vente

Le Dossier 15 explore différents domaines qui se rapportent à l'achat et la vente en général. Il vous présente quelques aspects de l'import-export, de la douane, du monde des affaires à l'échelle internationale et vous fait connaître les produits français les plus exportés, les plus célèbres hors de France.

*A*ctivité d'introduction

Achat et vente

A. La vente et l'import-export. Répondez aux questions suivantes par petits groupes de deux ou trois personnes.

1. Définissez les termes «vendre», «exporter», «importer» avec vos propres mots.
2. Quels sont les éléments qui facilitent la vente? Pensez à la qualité des produits, la dimension humaine des contacts, l'infrastructure du pays, l'organisation de l'entreprise, etc.
3. Quels sont à votre avis les produits français les plus célèbres hors de *(outside of)* France et pourquoi? Faites une liste d'au moins six produits précis.

Un magasin situé dans une zone industrielle.

Les mots pour le dire

Vocabulaire de base

VERBES

annuler une commande	*to cancel an order*
commander	*to order*
dédouaner	*to clear customs*
différer	*to differ*
entamer des discussions, des négociations	*to start discussions, negociations*
expédier	*to send*
exploiter, opérer	*to operate*
faire parvenir	*to send something*
faire une réclamation	*to lodge a complaint*
fournir	*to furnish, supply*
freiner l'importation	*to slow down importing*
fusion et rachat d'entreprise	*M&A, mergers and acquisitions*
fusionner	*to merge*
liquider	*to wind up, settle, liquidate*
livrer	*to deliver*
passer une commande	*to place an order*
se plaindre	*to complain*
régler (une facture)	*to settle (a bill)*
rentrer dans ses frais	*to break even*
traiter avec (une entreprise)	*to deal with (a company)*
vendre à perte	*to sell at a loss*

NOMS

un acheteur	*buyer*
l'ALENA (l'Accord de Libre Echange Nord Américain)	*NAFTA*
la balance commerciale	*trade balance*
une balance déficitaire (excédentaire)	*adverse (favorable) balance*
le bénéfice net	*net profit, net earnings*
des biens de consommation	*consumer goods*
la CEE	*EEC, European Economic Community*
les chiffres bruts	*gross figures*
une clientèle haut de gamme	*top-of-the-line customers*
des denrées *(f)*	*goods*
la douane	*customs*
un douanier	*customs officer*
un droit de douane	*tariff*
un entrepôt	*warehouse*
l'expédition *(f)* **des marchandises**	*dispatch or shipment of merchandise*
les frais *(m)* **d'envoi**	*shipping costs*
une frontière	*border*
le gain	*payoff*
une gamme de produits	*line of products*

une gamme, une fourchette	*range*
une garantie réelle	*collateral*
le GATT (Accord général sur les tarifs douaniers et le commerce)	*GATT*
un grossiste	*wholesaler*
une holding	*holding company*
le libre-échange	*free trade*
la location	*leasing, rental*
une marge bénéficiaire	*profit margin*
la marge brute d'autofinancement	*cash flow*
la monnaie, des devises (f)	*currency*
le PIB, Produit Intérieur Brut	*GDP, Gross Domestic Product*
le PNB, Produit National Brut	*GNP, Gross National Product*
un point de vente	*outlet*
le protectionnisme	*protectionism*
un rabais, une réduction	*a reduction, discount*
un sous-traitant	*subcontractor*
la TVA	*VAT, Value-Added Tax*
la vente en gros	*wholesale sales*

ADJECTIFS

épuisé(e) (un article)	*out-of-stock (article)*
frontalier(ère) (un contrôle)	*border (control)*
garanti(e)	*secured*
non imposable	*tax free*

ADVERBES ET EXPRESSIONS ADVERBIALES

au détail	*retail*
en gros	*wholesale*

B. Définitions provisoires à terminer. Complétez les phrases suivantes.

1. Lorsqu'on commence à faire des négociations, qu'on ouvre la porte à des discussions, qu'on prend l'initiative de négocier, on dit qu'on _____ des négociations.

2. Lorsqu'on décide de cesser ses activités commerciales et qu'on commence le processus qui vise à régler tout ce qu'il faut régler pour en finir définitivement avec les affaires en question, on dit qu'on _____ ses affaires.

3. Un pays est entouré de _____, c'est-à-dire de lignes, de limites qui démarquent, qui séparent ce pays des pays voisins. A la _____, il peut y avoir contrôle des papiers d'identité et contrôle de douane pour les marchandises qui sortent du pays ou y entrent.

4. Le _____ est un ensemble de mesures qui sont prises pour empêcher ou rendre plus difficile l'entrée de produits étrangers. Un pays qui exerce le _____ cherche à éviter la concurrence pour protéger l'économie nationale.

5. Lorsqu'on ne fait ni bénéfice ni perte, on dit qu'on _____. Ce qu'on a gagné sert seulement à couvrir les frais qui ont été occasionnés.

6. Il y a deux sortes de vente. La vente au détail se fait dans les magasins. Le consommateur s'adresse alors aux commerçants qui ont un magasin offrant ces marchandises en petites quantités. Le consommateur peut acheter un stylo et un cahier dans une Maison de la Presse ou une papeterie par exemple. Il y a également la _____, c'est-à-dire la vente en grande quantité. Le propriétaire ou le gérant de la papeterie va acheter ses marchandises _____ chez un grossiste.

C. Définitions provisoires à créer. Par groupes de deux, donnez une définition provisoire pour les mots suivants.

1. vendre à perte   **4.** un rabais

2. la CEE   **5.** non imposable

3. des denrées

D. Autrement dit. Soulignez parmi les mots proposés le synonyme du verbe des propositions suivantes!

1. refuser une offre: décliner   regretter   renvoyer

2. régler une facture: recevoir   payer   inclure

3. annuler une commande: supprimer   confirmer   adresser

4. livrer la marchandise: enregistrer   vérifier   remettre à l'acheteur

5. faire parvenir un catalogue: envoyer   renvoyer   garder

6. fournir des marchandises: pourvoir   traiter   commander

7. différer une livraison: changer   retarder   avancer

8. expédier les marchandises: fabriquer   envoyer   assurer

HSG

➤ Study the verbs *pleuvoir/ falloir; (s)'appeler;* and *rire (paraître, plaire)* in Module V of your *HSG* and complete Exercises A–C.

Dialogue

Vendre ses produits aux Etats-Unis

E. Activité de pré-lecture. Mettez-vous par petits groupes de deux ou trois et répondez aux questions suivantes.

1. Définissez «un(e) intermédiaire», «faciliter les contacts» et «un fabricant» avec vos propres mots.

2. Pourquoi, selon vous, est-ce qu'un gouvernement cherche à exporter des produits de son pays à l'extérieur?

Vendre ses produits aux Etats-Unis

Une petite PME familiale française de robinetterie cherche à exporter sa nouvelle gamme de produits aux Etats-Unis. C'est l'idée de Paul Guimaux qui a passé un an aux Etats-Unis et qui croit à la possibilité d'un créneau dans leur secteur. Les deux frères discutent en attendant qu'une vendeuse s'occupe d'eux dans une quincaillerie.

François: Alors, est-ce que tu as appelé le Poste d'Expansion Economique d'Atlanta?

Paul: Oui, cet après-midi, à 4 heures. Avec les six heures de décalage horaire, cela faisait 10 heures du matin chez eux. J'ai parlé à la responsable du secteur habitat. Elle s'occupe de tout le sud-est des Etats-Unis. Elle s'apprêtait à venir en mission en France. Alors je l'ai invitée à venir voir ce que nous faisons. Elle m'a parlé d'un importateur de sanitaire du Mississippi qui venait de la contacter justement parce qu'il cherchait un certain type de robinet qu'il avait vu dans un magazine français. Elle l'a déjà mis en contact avec les fabricants français qu'elle connaît mais elle avait l'impression qu'il serait intéressé par ce que nous faisons. Je lui ai envoyé un catalogue par courrier immédiatement ainsi qu'une télécopie confirmant notre désir de la recevoir lors de son passage en France et lui demandant de nous faire parvenir davantage de renseignements.

Quelques melons au marché de Lorient.

François: Est-ce qu'ils font tout cela gratuitement?

Paul: J'ai l'impression qu'ils font pas mal de choses gratuitement mais quand ils aident un fabricant à trouver un importateur, ils sont obligés de facturer. Pour 1.500 F, un fabricant qui cherche un importateur d'un type particulier lui envoie une vingtaine de catalogues et elle, elle a toute une banque de données sur des sociétés américaines qui ont déjà manifesté un intérêt dans l'importation de ce genre de produits. Elle les appelle, leur envoie un catalogue, les rappelle pour voir s'ils sont décidés à rencontrer les fabricants. Si oui, l'étape suivante est l'organisation d'une mission de prospection. Elle peut même accompagner les fabricants au cours de cette mission, être présente pendant les réunions et discussions. Ce qui peut aider au niveau de l'anglais car ce n'est pas évident! Elle organise également des missions en France pour les importateurs qui souhaitent acheter un produit français. En gros, elle sert d'intermédiaire et de source d'information et facilite l'exportation des produits français aux Etats-Unis.

François: Après tout, elle travaille pour le gouvernement français!

Paul: Oui, le Poste d'Expansion Economique dépend du Consulat Général qui lui-même relève de l'Ambassade de France à Washington qui elle-même dépend du Ministère des Affaires Etrangères, de la DREE, c'est-à-dire de la Direction des Relations Economiques Extérieures.

François: Est-ce que tu sais si elle a déjà organisé quelque chose dans la robinetterie?

Paul: Oui, elle a préparé un stand au salon, «Kitchen and Bath Industry Show» qui est le plus important sur le territoire des Etats-Unis. C'est tout ce qui relève de l'aménagement des cuisines et des salles de bain. Aux Etats-Unis, tout ce qui touche à l'aménagement des cuisines et au sanitaire va toujours ensemble. Elle a aidé à trouver un décorateur sur place pour monter et aménager le stand. Ce décorateur a travaillé en collaboration avec une équipe française. Elle s'est occupée de trouver un bon emplacement et elle a recruté deux interprètes. Elle m'a expliqué que ça, c'était vraiment difficile. Elle a dû envoyer pas mal de documentation à ces interprètes pour qu'ils puissent arriver préparés, et elle leur a même donné des fiches qu'elle avait faites elle-même!

François: Et qui avait choisi les produits français exposés?

Paul: La Chambre de Commerce de l'Aisne et la DRIR.

➤ Délégation Régionale de l'Industrie et de la Recherche.

François: Est-ce qu'elle s'occupe aussi du suivi?

Paul: Oui. Elle dit que ce qui marche le mieux, ce sont les produits haut de gamme. Il y a, paraît-il, bon nombre d'Américains qui veulent des meubles ou accessoires européens, français en particulier et qui sont prêts à y mettre le prix.

François: Tu te rends compte, ça fait bien dix minutes qu'on attend et les deux vendeuses sont en train de discuter de je ne sais quel problème personnel. Elles nous ignorent royalement. J'ose à peine les déranger... c'est le monde à l'envers! Combien de temps est-ce qu'elles vont nous laisser poireauter comme ça?

Paul: Attends, je leur fais signe. Tu vois, c'est ça qui me manque le plus depuis mon retour des Etats-Unis. Tu ne peux pas savoir à quel point les commerçants sont aux petits soins envers les clients là-bas! Tu entres dans un magasin, tout de suite, un vendeur t'accoste et te demande s'il peut t'aider.

François: Oui, mais moi, je ne sais pas si j'aimerais ça... Je ne veux pas qu'on me saute dessus quand même!

Paul: Oui, je sais, moi je réagissais comme ça au début aussi. Dès qu'un vendeur ou une vendeuse s'approchait, j'essayais de l'éviter et je me sentais même agressé. Ça me mettait mal à l'aise. Puis j'ai appris à me relaxer et à dire quelque chose dans le genre «je veux simplement regarder, si j'ai besoin d'aide je vous ferai signe» et après ça, on me laissait effectivement tranquille. Mais tu peux vraiment demander n'importe quoi dans un magasin...

François: Par exemple?

Paul: Par exemple, si tu cherches quelque chose et qu'ils ne l'ont pas, ils vont te dire où tu peux le trouver, c'est-à-dire qu'ils t'envoient en fait à la concurrence! C'est quand même incroyable! Je me souviens une fois, comme je ne savais pas comment aller au magasin qui, selon la vendeuse, avait le genre de chaussures que je cherchais, elle a téléphoné au magasin en question pour demander comment je pouvais m'y rendre et m'a dessiné un plan! Va donc faire quelque chose comme ça en France!

François: Non évidemment... au bout de la troisième paire de chaussures que tu essaies, tu commences à te sentir coupable et tu n'oses pas envoyer la vendeuse en chercher d'autres, ça c'est sûr!

Paul: Autre chose qui m'avait énormément étonné aux Etats-Unis, c'est le fait que les vendeurs essaient de te faire profiter des meilleurs prix. Ils te disent des trucs dans le genre: «Si vous attendez la semaine prochaine, cet article sera en promotion et vous pourrez bénéficier d'une réduction de 30%.»

François: Non! C'est dingue, ça!

Paul: Si, je te jure! Ah! Voilà les vendeuses qui se décident enfin à s'apercevoir de notre présence!

Notez bien: Nous avons divisé le dialogue en deux parties. *Première partie:* Rôle du Poste d'Expansion Economique, du début jusqu'à la réplique de Paul qui se termine par «et qui sont prêts à y mettre le prix». *Deuxième partie:* L'attitude des vendeuses, de la réplique de François qui commence par «Tu te rends compte... » jusqu'à la fin du dialogue.

Première partie du dialogue

F. Autrement dit. Dans les deux premières répliques de Paul, trouvez l'équivalent des expressions ou mots suivants.

1. un domaine
2. désirent
3. un fax
4. envoyer
5. des informations
6. faire payer

7. recherche
8. entreprises
9. exprimé
10. source d'informations sur ordinateur
11. des baignoires *(f)*, lavabos *(m)*, cabines *(f)* de douche, bidets *(m),* etc.

G. Définitions de mots. Cochez la meilleure définition. Attention! Quelquefois les deux définitions peuvent être correctes.

1. exportation
   - On exporte un produit lorsqu'on s'en sert à l'extérieur.
   - On exporte un produit lorsqu'on l'envoie et qu'on le vend à l'étranger.

2. une mission de prospection
   - C'est un voyage qui permet de chercher des clients éventuels.
   - C'est un groupe de représentants qui est envoyé pour faire de la propagande.

3. l'aménagement des cuisines
   - C'est ce qui a à faire avec la disposition, l'arrangement des meubles et tout ce qu'on trouve dans une cuisine.
   - C'est l'organisation globale de l'espace et de l'équipement.

4. un stand
   - C'est un endroit réservé à un exposant dans une foire ou une exposition.
   - C'est une installation en général temporaire où l'on peut montrer un produit.

5. un emplacement
- C'est un endroit.
- C'est un espace où s'exercent certaines activités ou qui sert à un usage déterminé.

6. haut de gamme
- Ce mot réfère à la taille d'un produit qui est grand.
- Ce mot réfère à la bonne qualité et au prix élevé d'un produit.

7. un accessoire
- C'est un objet qui complémente le tout.
- C'est un objet qui est inutile.

H. Vrai ou faux? Lorsqu'une affirmation ne correspond pas à ce qui a été exprimé dans le dialogue, corrigez-la de façon à arriver à une affirmation correcte. Si elle est déjà vraie, ajoutez quelques détails supplémentaires.

1. Le Poste d'Expansion Economique est un institut privé.

2. Les fabricants français contactent le Poste quand ils veulent importer des produits américains.

3. Une mission de prospection est organisée pour que les fabricants puissent rencontrer les importateurs qui ont exprimé le désir de vendre les produits de ces fabricants.

4. Le Poste d'Expansion Economique sert de représentant officiel lors de la signature des contrats.

5. Le stand présentant les produits français dont le dialogue parle a été entièrement décoré et aménagé par des Français.

6. Tous les Français qui sont venus au salon parlaient couramment anglais.

7. Le rôle du Poste d'Expansion Economique s'arrête après la première mise en contact des parties intéressées.

8. Le Poste d'Expansion Economique fait tout pour que les fabricants français vendent leurs produits aux Etats-Unis.

9. Le Poste d'Expansion Economique fait quelquefois payer ses services.

10. Les interprètes doivent étudier avant de venir au salon car ils ou elles ne sont pas nécessairement spécialisés dans le domaine en question et ne connaissent donc pas le vocabulaire spécifique indispensable.

Deuxième partie du dialogue

I. Autrement dit. Trouvez dans le texte le synonyme des mots ou expressions suivants.

1. une personne qui a un magasin

2. parler

3. faire comme si on ne voit pas quelqu'un

4. presque pas

5. gêner, importuner, troubler

➤ Note synonyms that might be useful for *Mots de passe*.

6. donner beaucoup d'attention, bien s'occuper de quelqu'un

7. aborder, venir près de quelqu'un et lui parler

8. le commencement

9. changer de direction, fuir

10. se détendre

11. étonnant

12. se rappeler

13. une carte

14. bénéficier

15. les plus avantageux

16. en réclame

17. une remise

18. remarquer

J. Vrai ou faux? Après avoir relu la deuxième partie du dialogue, dites si vous êtes d'accord avec les affirmations suivantes.

1. Paul et François attendent parce que les vendeuses s'occupent d'autres clients.

2. Paul n'a pas aimé le service dans la plupart des magasins américains.

3. François a accompagné son frère Paul pendant son voyage aux Etats-Unis.

4. Paul trouve que la plupart des vendeurs en France sont gentils.

5. François croit qu'il n'aimerait pas qu'un vendeur vienne tout de suite lui proposer son aide.

6. François est très étonné d'entendre que les vendeurs américains font tout pour économiser de l'argent à leurs clients.

7. Paul dit qu'il plaisantait lorsqu'il prétendait que les vendeurs américains faisaient tout pour rendre service à leurs clients.

8. D'après Paul, les vendeurs français n'aiment pas qu'on les dérange.

9. D'après François, les vendeurs de chaussures n'aiment pas faire essayer un grand nombre de modèles différents.

K. La parole est à vous! Discutez les questions suivantes sur la qualité du service, en petits groupes de deux ou trois personnes.

1. Quelles qualités doit-on avoir pour devenir vendeur? Faites une liste d'au moins dix adjectifs qui peuvent caractériser un bon vendeur.

2. Quels sont les traits de personnalité et de caractère qui ne vous semblent pas souhaitables (*desirable*) chez un vendeur ou une vendeuse? Faites une liste d'une dizaine d'adjectifs et expliquez pourquoi vous les avez choisis.

3. Imaginez-vous dans un magasin. Pensez à

Madame Mahé vend son sel sur le marché de Lorient.

votre interaction avec le vendeur ou la vendeuse et complétez les phrases suivantes.

- J'aime...
- J'apprécie un vendeur qui...
- Je me sens à l'aise quand une vendeuse...
- Je suis favorablement impressionnné(e) quand un vendeur ou une vendeuse...
- Je pense qu'un vendeur doit...
- Je ne crois pas qu'une bonne vendeuse...
- Je déteste les vendeurs qui...
- Je préfère que la vendeuse ne...
- J'évite les vendeurs qui...

4. Que pensez-vous de l'expression «le client est roi»?

5. Donnez des exemples de situations où il est difficile pour un vendeur ou une vendeuse de garder son calme et de rester poli(e).

6. Quel genre de situation vous donnerait envie d'aller vous plaindre au supérieur du vendeur ou de la vendeuse en question?

HSG

➤ Study the verbs *se souvenir, acheter/vendre,* and *envoyer (essayer, payer)* in Module V of your *HSG* and complete Exercises D–F.

Lecture 1

Produits français qui ont conquis le monde

L. Activité de pré-lecture. Discutez les questions suivantes par petits groupes.

1. Réfléchissez aux domaines de l'industrie automobile et de l'aviation. Y a-t-il des noms de produits français appartenant à ces domaines qui vous viennent à l'esprit? Lesquels?

2. Quand on dit qu'un produit a conquis le monde, qu'est-ce que cela signifie?

3. Quels sont, selon vous, les produits américains qui ont conquis le monde?

4. Quels sont les produits français qui sont utilisés dans le monde entier?

GUILLEVIN INTERNATIONAL INC.

Produits français qui ont conquis le monde

Ils portent les couleurs de la France, parfois de façon inattendue. Du foulard de soie à la poêle à frire, des skis au yaourt [...]

Quels sont les produits français aussi bien connus de Hawaii à Hong-Kong que de Sydney à Djeddah? Le N° 5 de Chanel, bien sûr, ou encore la chemise Lacoste. Mais sait-on que le magazine *Elle* est édité dans vingt-trois langues et que les pneus Michelin sont disponibles dans 170 pays? Que la famille Haemmerlin, de Saverne, domine le marché mondial de la brouette, et les Selmer, de Paris, celui du saxophone?

Nous avons tenté d'identifier non pas les marques ou les raisons sociales, comme Yves Saint Laurent, Cardin ou Chanel dont la réputation est mondiale, mais les objets ou les services disponibles dans le plus grand nombre de pays. A l'exclusion des produits industriels, comme les contacteurs de Legrand, ou des biens intermédiaires, comme le ciment de Lafarge, peu repérables par les particuliers.

Le parfum Trésor de Lancôme, les carrés Hermès ou les bouteilles de Cointreau ne pèsent certes pas lourd dans le commerce extérieur de la France. Leurs chiffres d'affaires à l'exportation ne rivalisent pas avec ceux de nos gros constructeurs automobiles ou de nos bâtisseurs. Ce sont pourtant nos meilleurs

ambassadeurs. On remarquera qu'un sur trois peut figurer sur une table et qu'un sur cinq fait partie de l'univers magique du luxe. Comme pour confirmer les conclusions d'un récent rapport du Conseil économique et social: "Notre pays reste pour l'essentiel caractérisé par les produits et les activités de l'art de vivre à la française. L'économie rejoint ici la culture." Pourquoi pas?

Article tiré de Challenges économiques, *N° 83, juillet 1994.*

Que pensez-vous de cette devise?

M. Avez-vous compris? Après avoir lu le texte très attentivement, répondez aux questions suivantes.

1. Que dit le texte sur Saint Laurent, Cardin et Chanel?
2. Le texte parle-t-il des produits industriels ou des produits destinés à la consommation personnelle?
3. Qui exporte le plus? Lancôme, Hermès et Cointreau ou bien les constructeurs automobiles et les bâtisseurs?
4. Qu'est-ce que c'est selon vous qu'un produit de luxe? Donnez des exemples.
5. Que veut dire «ils sont nos meilleurs ambassadeurs»?
6. Que veut dire «l'art de vivre à la française»?
7. Expliquez «L'économie rejoint ici la culture.»

Lecture 2

Des créneaux inédits

N. Activité de pré-lecture. Discutez les questions suivantes par petits groupes de deux ou trois.

1. Qu'est-ce que c'est que la douane?
2. Pourquoi est-il important d'exporter des marchandises?
3. Quel genre de marchandises un pays est-il obligé d'importer?

Des créneaux inédits

«Le Québec compte de plus en plus d'entreprises qui relèvent avec succès les défis que pose l'internationalisation des marchés. Dero, fondée en 1964, est l'une d'entre elles. D'abord spécialisée dans

l'importation de pièces de lampes et d'éclairage, elle œuvre également depuis trois ans dans la fabrication de pièces de plastique par injection. Elle exporte ses «produits maison» tels que corbeille à

continued on page 326

continued from page 325

papier, seau à vin, pièces de ski, outils de jardinage, tous en plastique, depuis un an.

«Dero compte trois usines, 75 employés, un bureau à Casablanca, au Maroc, un bureau et un entrepôt à Puebla, au Mexique, ainsi qu'une représentante japonaise en poste à New York qui a pour mandat exclusif de développer le marché japonais. La société négocie actuellement avec la France et la Suisse. Elle n'hésite pas à sortir des sentiers battus pour étendre ses ramifications un peu partout dans le monde. «Pour une entreprise exportatrice comme la nôtre, le principal problème n'est pas de trouver de nouveaux produits, ni même de les fabriquer. C'est de les vendre en mettant sur pied un réseau de contacts et de distribution efficace», soutient Yves Robert, vice-président.

«Pour atteindre ses objectifs de ventes, Dero a appris à contourner les difficultés. «Les barrières à l'entrée de certains marchés compliquent parfois l'exportation de produits finis. Par exemple, au Maroc, où les droits de douane s'élèvent à 70%, il faut vendre nos produits à un prix beaucoup plus élevé qu'au Québec pour les rentabiliser», explique Yves Robert. C'est pourquoi, dans certains pays comme le Japon et le Maroc, Dero a entrepris de vendre ses moules à des partenaires locaux et de sous-traiter la production.»

Extrait de Carole Marcil, «Marchés actuels et marchés en émergence», paru dans FORCES, N° 109, 1995, p. 29, Montréal, Québec.

O. A la recherche d'éléments précis du texte. Répondez aux questions suivantes.

1. Depuis quand est-ce que la société Dero existe?

2. Quels sont les effectifs de Dero?

3. Dans quels autres pays est-ce que Dero a un bureau?

4. Quels sont les deux pays cités dans ce texte qui ont des droits de douane particulièrement élevés?

P. Phrases à compléter. Faites correspondre les parties de phrases de la colonne A avec celles de la colonne B.

A	B
1. Le Québec compte de plus en plus	est le vice-président de Dero.
2. Dero exporte	des corbeilles à papier et autres produits pour la maison.
3. La représentante japonaise	dans les pays qui ont de fortes barrières douanières.
4. Yves Robert	d'entreprises qui travaillent à l'extérieur du Canada.
5. Des partenaires sous-traitent la production	est installée à New York.

AIR CANADA POUR LE MONDE ENTIER

Q. La parole est à vous! Par petits groupes de deux ou trois, discutez les questions suivantes.

1. Donnez un autre titre au texte qui précède.
2. Discutez en quoi traiter avec des pays comme la France, le Maroc et la Suisse peut être attirant pour le Québec.
3. Quelles sont selon vous les difficultés auxquelles une entreprise doit faire face lorsqu'elle s'installe à l'étranger? Pensez tout particulièrement à l'environnement culturel.

R. Devinette! Choisissez cinq mots qui étaient nouveaux pour vous et essayez de les faire deviner aux membres de votre groupe en expliquant chaque mot sans le nommer.

Quelques points de repère

L'ardoise!

Autrefois, il y avait des barrières douanières entre tous les pays d'Europe. Chaque fois qu'un individu passait une frontière, il devait montrer une carte d'identité ou un passeport et ses bagages pouvaient être fouillés. Les entreprises devaient également passer par toutes sortes de formalités pour exporter ou importer des marchandises et elles devaient payer des droits de douane. L'Acte unique européen, signé en 1985, a permis l'établissement d'un grand marché intérieur permettant la libre circulation des personnes, des marchandises, des capitaux et des services entre les états membres de la C.E.E. (Communauté Economique Européenne).

Une date importante!

- Le Traité de Rome, signé le 25 mars 1957 a engagé la France, la République Fédérale Allemande, et le Benelux (Belgique, Pays-Bas, Luxembourg) dans une union douanière progressive qui a débouché sur le Marché Commun, la CEE et l'Union Européenne.
- Les accords de Maastricht ont débouché *(emerged)* en février 1992

sur un traité qui définit les étapes d'une union économique et monétaire (U.E.M.) entre les pays membres concernés. Les Danois ont refusé de ratifier ce traité.

- Le 30 septembre 1993, le Parlement européen votait en faveur de «l'exception culturelle» affirmant la volonté de l'Europe de défendre et de préserver son identité culturelle.

- Le 14 décembre 1993, les Etats-Unis et l'Europe ont atteint un accord global après avoir décidé d'exclure l'audiovisuel de la négociation du GATT. Les journaux américains ont attaqué ce qu'ils voyaient comme le protectionnisme français contre les biens culturels américains.

- Depuis 1993, le principe de la libre circulation des hommes, des marchandises, des services et des capitaux est appliqué entre les 15 pays membres de la CEE. C'est une conséquence de l'Acte unique qui avait été signé en 1985. Ce marché unique offre un espace d'échanges qui touche 348 millions de consommateurs. La construction de l'Europe a eu une grande influence sur l'économie française.

Le saviez-vous?

L'Union Européenne ou la CEE (Communauté Economique Européenne) regroupe les 15 pays suivants: la Belgique, la France, la RFA, l'Italie, le Luxembourg, les Pays-Bas depuis 1957; le Danemark, l'Irlande et le Royaume-Uni depuis 1973; la Grèce depuis 1981; l'Espagne et le Portugal depuis 1986; et l'Autriche, la Suède, la Finlande depuis 1994.

Les chiffres parlent!

- La France est la 5e puissance économique mondiale et la 4e puissance mondiale en ce qui concerne les exportations — après les Etats-Unis, l'Allemagne et le Japon.

- La France réalise 60% de ses échanges extérieurs en Europe. Les cinq principaux clients européens de la France sont: l'Allemagne, la Grande-Bretagne, l'Italie, le Benelux et l'Espagne.

- Sur les 16.000 sociétés à capitaux qui sont actives en dehors des frontières françaises, 34% se trouvent dans l'Union Européenne.

- 1.200 sociétés françaises sont implantées aux Etats-Unis.

- Les sociétés françaises atteignent un total de 16.000 filiales (*subsidiaries*) à l'étranger et elles emploient 2,5 millions de salariés.

- La production agricole française représente 23% de la production totale de la CEE.

- La France est le deuxième exportateur mondial dans le domaine de l'agro-alimentaire, derrière les Etats-Unis et devant les Pays-Bas. Des produits comme le vin, la bière, les produits laitiers font partie du secteur agro-alimentaire.

Les entreprises françaises!

HSG

➤ Complete the *Exercises de synthèse* and *Echange* sections of Module V in your *HSG*.

- La société Lafarge (matériaux de construction) réalise 64% de ses ventes hors de France.

- Essilor (optique) réalise 75% de ses ventes hors de France.

- Salomon (matériel de sport) réalise 91% de ses ventes hors de France.

Réflexions sur le travail en équipe

Une équipe devrait avoir le soutien des gestionnaires, la liberté de se concentrer sur son but et la capacité de gérer ses réunions, de planifier et faciliter ses discussions et de donner et recevoir des commentaires constructifs.

Lexique

accuser réception: Lorsqu'on **accuse réception,** on dit ou écrit qu'une chose envoyée a bien été reçue.

> Nous vous prions de bien vouloir **accuser réception** des marchandises dès leur livraison.

l'approvisionnement *(m)*: **Approvisionner,** c'est fournir en provisions, en marchandises. C'est faire en sorte qu'il y ait assez de nourriture, ou matériel selon le type d'**approvisionnement** dont on parle.

> Pendant la grève de la SNCF, **l'approvisionnement** était problématique car une grande partie des marchandises sont normalement acheminées par le train.

un arriéré: On a **un arriéré** lorsqu'on est en retard dans un paiement.

> Votre compte ayant **un arriéré** de plus de trois mois, nous nous voyons obligés de ne pas accepter de vous réapprovisionner aussi longtemps que nous n'aurons pas reçu votre paiement.

un bon de commande: Lorsqu'on veut commander des marchandises, on remplit **un bon de commande,** c'est-à-dire un imprimé ou un formulaire qui précise le type de marchandises souhaitées, leur quantité, leur prix et quelquefois, le mode de paiement.

> Remplissez ce **bon de commande** et n'oubliez pas de préciser vos nom et adresse ainsi que de joindre votre chèque.

l'emballage *(m)*: **Emballer** quelque chose veut dire l'envelopper d'une certaine manière, l'empaqueter, pour l'expédier par la Poste, par exemple. **Un emballage** peut être perdu ou consigné.

> Est-ce que vous pouvez m'expédier ce colis franco de port et d'**emballage?**

un escompte: Un escompte est une réduction du prix à payer si l'on règle une dette avant l'échéance.

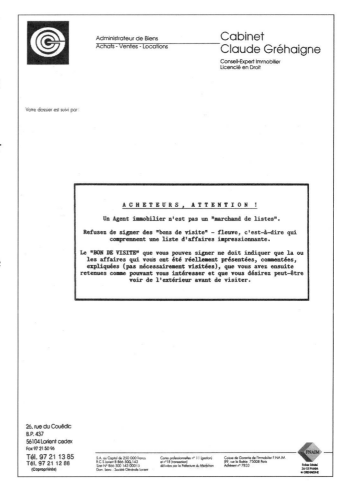

Un assortiment de
tartelettes, choux et
autres gâteaux.

Nous pourrons vous accorder **un escompte** de 5% si vous payez
avant le 1er décembre.

une facture: Une facture est un papier qui indique le prix et la quantité
des marchandises vendues ou qui précise le prix de services rendus qui
sont spécifiés sur le papier.

Sur **la facture,** vous avez écrit que vous m'avez envoyé trois caisses
de 12 bouteilles d'eau Evian mais je n'ai reçu que deux caisses.

les frais *(m)* **de port:** Lorsqu'on envoie des marchandises à un client, il y a
des frais de port, c'est-à-dire **des frais d'envoi.** En général, ce sont les
clients qui se chargent des coûts associés à l'envoi des marchandises.

Cela fera 1.895 francs plus 175 francs de **frais d'envoi** ou de **frais de
port.**

l'inventaire *(m):* **L'inventaire** est la liste précise des marchandises que
l'on possède en stock et qui sont, soit sur les étagères du magasin, soit
dans l'entrepôt.

Excusez-moi, notre magasin n'est pas ouvert au public aujourd'hui.
Nous faisons **l'inventaire annuel.**

un représentant: Un représentant est l'intermédiaire entre une maison qui
vend en gros et le commerçant qui fait de la vente au détail. **Le
représentant** vient présenter ses produits et espère qu'on lui passera une
commande. **Un représentant** a tout un secteur (géographique) dans lequel
il voyage beaucoup. Il va de magasin en magasin pour essayer de
convaincre les commerçants d'adopter les produits qu'il représente.

Le directeur régional organise un séminaire de deux jours pour
informer ses **représentants** sur les nouveaux produits et faire le
bilan de l'année.

le stock: Lorsqu'on a certaines marchandises **en stock,** cela veut dire
qu'on a ces marchandises en réserve, donc qu'on peut en disposer. Etre en
rupture de **stock** veut dire au contraire que, en général temporairement, on
n'a plus ces marchandises **en stock.**

Je ne peux pas **stocker** beaucoup de marchandises car je n'ai pas
d'entrepôt. Ce que j'ai **en stock,** c'est ce que vous voyez sur les
étagères et dans les boîtes sous les étagères.

➤ Essayez de préciser la différence entre un inventaire et
un assortiment.

la vente par correspondance: La vente par correspondance est faite à partir d'un catalogue et de bons de commande qui sont envoyés par courrier, par Minitel ou téléphone. Les marchandises sont ensuite expédiées au client par la Poste. *Les Trois Suisses* et *La Redoute* sont les deux entreprises les plus importantes de cette sorte en France.

La vente par correspondance s'est énormément développée ces dernières années. Les gens aiment faire leurs achats chez eux sans avoir à sortir. De plus, pour tous ceux qui habitent loin des grandes villes, cela augmente leur choix et leur permet d'acheter des choses qu'ils ne trouveraient pas dans leur petite ville ou petit village.

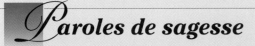

Paroles de sagesse

Que sert d'interdire ce qu'on ne peut pas empêcher?

> ➤ After looking up the verbs *interdire* and *empêcher* in your dictionary, discuss this adage with your study partner.

Expression écrite

Expressions adverbiales, expressions négatives, conjonctions

Dans cette section, vous allez lire un texte qui traite de l'exportation. Indiquez le temps, le mode ou la forme de chacun des verbes utilisés.

L'export

Lorsque l'on est à l'étranger, il apparaît clairement que les produits français qui s'exportent le mieux sont les produits de luxe.

Ceci se remarque surtout au niveau des cosmétiques et des parfums. Il est même amusant de voir à quel point l'image de la France est utilisée pour les produits de cette gamme: Les étiquettes sont écrites en français, les noms des parfums sont français, et même, parfois, la publicité se fait en français! On retrouve ce même phénomène au niveau de la mode, des habits, surtout pour la Haute Couture, et la maroquinerie.

Un autre domaine où l'image de la France se vend bien à l'étranger reste le domaine de la cuisine: Les bons petits plats traditionnels et la qualité de notre nourriture ne sont pas prêts de perdre leur renommée mondiale... Et même si MacDo a réussi à bien s'implanter en France, je ne connais pas encore de Français digne de ce nom qui ne sache apprécier un vrai bon repas, accompagné d'un bon vin du terroir!

Bref, il me semble qu'en fait ce que la France arrive le mieux à exporter, ce sont les choses que les Français apprécient: l'élégance, le chic, la bonne cuisine!

S. A vos plumes! Essayez maintenant d'écrire un paragraphe d'environ 150 mots sur ce que vous avez appris au sujet de l'import-export ou des achats et des ventes dans votre manuel ou votre guide d'étude. Commencez par une phrase d'introduction. Utilisez des expressions adverbiales et des conjonctions comme celles que vous avez vues dans le passage précédent pour exprimer vos idées de façon logique. Finissez par une phrase de conclusion.

Avant de commencer le module suivant, allons un peu plus loin avec «En guise de clôture.»

MODULE V

En guise de clôture:
Allons un peu plus loin!

Texte littéraire

Les sondages d'opinion

A. Activité de pré-lecture. A deux ou trois réfléchissez aux questions suivantes.

1. Imaginez que vous êtes une entreprise et que vous voulez savoir ce que vos clients pensent de vos produits. Que faites-vous?

2. Vous voulez découvrir ou tester de nouveaux marchés possibles. Comment vous y prenez-vous?

3. Aimeriez-vous faire des sondages d'opinion, c'est-à-dire interroger des gens dans la rue ou au téléphone et leur demander ce qu'ils pensent de tel ou tel produit? Pourquoi ou pourquoi pas?

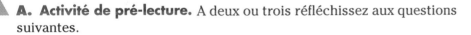

Les sondages d'opinion

Et pendant quatre ans, peut-être plus, ils explorèrent, interviewèrent, analysèrent. Pourquoi les aspirateurs-traîneaux se vendent-ils si mal? Que pense-t-on, dans les milieux de modeste extraction, de la chicorée? Aime-t-on la purée toute faite, et pourquoi? Parce qu'elle est légère? Parce qu'elle est onctueuse? Parce qu'elle est si facile à faire: un geste et hop? Trouve-t-on vraiment que les voitures d'enfants sont chères? N'est-on pas toujours prêt à faire un sacrifice pour le confort des petits? Comment votera la Française? Aime-t-on le fromage en tube? Est-on pour ou contre les transports en commun? A quoi fait-on d'abord attention en mangeant un yaourt: à la couleur? à la consistance? au goût? au parfum naturel? Lisez-vous beaucoup, un peu, pas du tout? Allez-vous au restaurant? Aimeriez-vous, Madame, donner en location votre chambre à un Noir? Que pense-t-on franchement de la retraite des vieux? Que pense la jeunesse? Que pensent les cadres? Que pense la femme de trente ans?

Que pensez-vous des vacances? Aimez-vous les plats surgelés? Combien pensez-vous que ça coûte un briquet comme ça? Quelles qualités demandez-vous à votre matelas? Pouvez-vous me décrire un homme qui aime les pâtes? Que pensez-vous de votre machine à laver? Est-ce que vous en êtes satisfaite? [...]

Il y eut la lessive, le linge qui sèche, le repassage. Le gaz, l'électricité, le téléphone. Les enfants. Les vêtements et les sous-vêtements. La moutarde. Les soupes en sachets, les soupes en boîtes. Les cheveux: comment les laver, comment les teindre, comment les faire tenir, comment les faire briller. Les étudiants, les ongles, les sirops pour la toux, les machines à écrire, les engrais, les tracteurs, les loisirs, les cadeaux, la papeterie, le blanc, la politique, les autoroutes, les boissons alcoolisées, les eaux minérales, les fromages et les conserves, les lampes et les rideaux, les assurances, le jardinage. [...]

Dans le monde qui était le leur, il était presque de règle de désirer toujours plus qu'on ne pouvait acquérir. Ce n'était pas eux qui l'avaient décrété; c'était une loi de la civilisation, une donnée de fait dont la publicité en général, les magazines, l'art des étalages, le spectacle de la rue, et même sous un certain aspect, l'ensemble des productions communément appelées culturelles, étaient les expressions les plus conformes.

—*Georges Pérec*

Tiré de *Les choses*. Editions J'au lu: Paris, 1973.

➤ Note synonyms for *Mot de passe.*

B. Synonymes. Trouvez dans le texte l'équivalent des mots ou groupes de mots suivants.

1. assez pauvres

2. crémeuse

3. des jeunes enfants

4. louer

5. le personnel appartenant à la catégorie supérieure des employés d'une entreprise

6. congelés

7. quelque chose pour allumer une cigarette

8. la partie du lit sur laquelle on se couche

9. les spaghetti ou macaroni

C. A la recherche d'éléments précis. Répondez aux questions suivantes.

1. Trouvez dans le texte des mots appartenant au vocabulaire de la nourriture ou l'alimentation.
2. Trouvez des mots qui ont à faire avec les appareils ménagers ou avec l'intérieur d'une maison.
3. Donnez quelques exemples de questions qui abordent des problèmes sociaux.

D. Avez-vous compris? Répondez aux questions suivantes.

1. Pourquoi est-ce que le texte présente une liste interminable de questions?
2. Quel effet cette juxtaposition de questions donne-t-elle?

E. Eliminez l'intrus! Pour chaque nom tiré de l'avant-dernier paragraphe du texte, nous vous proposons une liste d'adjectifs. Rayez l'adjectif qui ne peut pas qualifier le mot en question.

1. la lessive: blanche, parfumée, liquide, congelée
2. le linge: sale, satisfait, sec, neuf
3. le gaz: combustible, dangereux, invisible, modeste
4. les enfants: joyeux, énergiques, timides, publics
5. les vêtements: crus, sportifs, confortables, élégants
6. les sous-vêtements: sexy, intérieurs, chic, blancs
7. la moutarde: piquante, indifférente, jaune, onctueuse
8. la soupe: onctueuse, délicieuse, épicée, confortable
9. les cheveux: brillants, gras, teints, élevés
10. les étudiants: inutiles, intelligents, travailleurs, curieux
11. les ongles: cassés, vernis, rouges, libres
12. les sirops: sucrés, alcoolisés, doux, métalliques

F. A vous maintenant! Par petits groupes de trois, choisissez cinq autres noms dans la suite du texte et faites une liste semblable à celle qui précède.

G. A vous la parole! A deux ou trois, discutez les questions suivantes.

1. Vous-même, comme les personnages de ce texte, est-ce que vous désirez plus que ce que vous ne pouvez acheter? Donnez des exemples de ce que vous aimeriez acheter mais que vous ne pouvez pas vous permettre et expliquez pourquoi.
2. D'après ce texte, la publicité stimule ce désir. Expliquez pourquoi et comment.
3. Donnez un exemple de publicité qui vous donne envie d'acheter quelque chose.
4. En quoi est-ce que les magazines vous donnent envie d'acheter certaines choses?
5. Donnez plusieurs exemples de magazines qui peuvent vous faire rêver.
6. Est-ce que l'art des étalages peut effectivement influencer les acheteurs?

■ Sigles et abréviations

l'INSEE	=	*Institut National de Statistiques et d'Etudes Economiques.*
P et T	=	*Postes et Télécommunications*
PTT	=	*Postes Télégraphes et Téléphone*
RFi	=	*Radio France internationale*
RFo	=	*Radio France Outre-mer*
RMC	=	*Radio Monte Carlo*
RTL	=	*Radio Télévision Luxembourg*
SACEM	=	*Société d'Auteurs et Compositeurs de Musique*
T.V. ou télé	=	*Télévision*
TF1	=	*une chaîne de télévision française*
TMC	=	*Télévision Monte Carlo*

■ Considérations sur la diversité des individus

➤ Which of these characteristics would be most visible to you initially? Which would be most important in the choice of a life partner? In a friend, a colleague or team member?

la formation

l'expérience

le salaire

le statut juridique
- marié(e)
- célibataire
- divorcé(e)
- veuf/veuve

le statut militaire

la religion/la spiritualité

les choix politiques

la situation géographique

le statut des parents
- milieu social
- situation professionnelle
- situation familiale

le sexe

le groupe ethnique

les abilités physiques

les abilités mentales

les qualités

les défauts

l'âge

l'orientation sexuelle

l'orientation émotionnelle

la race

■ Projet: Les stratégies visuelles, auditives et kinesthésiques

Ce projet a pour but de faciliter une meilleure communication avec les autres, dans la vie quotidienne personnelle comme au travail.

Dans ce projet, vous allez apprendre à mieux communiquer avec les autres en identifiant, par l'usage qu'ils font de la langue et du *langage*, quelle partie de leur système neurologique domine au moment de l'interaction. De cette façon, vous pourrez entrer plus facilement dans leur système représentatif primaire.

Les descriptions suivantes sont extrêmement simplifiées mais vont vous aider à établir une première classification des trois types principaux (visuel, auditif et kinesthésique):

> ➤ *Langage:* les gestes, les attitudes, les expressions du visage, la distance que l'on maintient par rapport à son interlocuteur, plus l'échange verbal.

1. Les personnes à dominance ou dominante visuelle ont tendance à voir le monde en tableaux, en images. C'est parce qu'elles voient une succession rapide d'images ou d'aperçus que ces personnes parlent rapidement. Elles ne font pas nécessairement attention à ce qu'elles disent ou à la façon de le dire. En parlant, ces personnes créent souvent des métaphores visuelles; elles parlent de comment elles voient les choses. Elles reconnaissent les structures, les schémas, les images répétitives. Elles remarquent si une scène est claire ou obscure et enregistrent un grand nombre de détails tels que les couleurs, l'arrangement des meubles, la décoration, les vêtements portés et l'aspect physique des personnes présentes.

2. Les individus qui sont plutôt auditifs sélectionnent plus soigneusement leurs paroles. Leur voix résonne plus que celle des personnes visuelles. Ils parlent plus lentement, d'une façon plus mesurée, avec un rythme plus marqué. Ils attachent beaucoup d'importance au mot juste; et donc choisissent ce qu'ils disent avec beaucoup de soin. De plus, ils remarquent sons, musique, bruits, silence et ils utilisent des verbes comme *entendre* et *écouter*.

3. Les gens qui sont kinesthésiques ont tendance à fonctionner encore plus lentement. Ils réagissent foncièrement à leurs sentiments. Leur voix est très profonde et leurs paroles roulent lentement. Ils utilisent des mots comme *sentir, ressentir, toucher, frappé, surprenant* et *écrasant.* Etant sensibles, ils sont parfois la proie de leurs émotions auxquelles ils réagissent fortement sans nécessairement savoir bien les exprimer. Ils sont plus ouverts que les deux autres types au toucher. L'odorat et le goût sont également très développés chez eux. L'impact de l'ouïe ou de la vue peut les gêner, les submerger ou même les bouleverser. Par contre, certains sons ou images peuvent facilement les émouvoir.

> ➤ *Foncièrement:* profondément, intensément

Tout le monde possède des éléments de toutes ces catégories mais chacun privilégie le plus souvent à son insu un des systèmes représentatifs. Si nous réussissons à reconnaître et à employer le système préféré de l'individu avec qui nous avons affaire, nous pourrons mieux communiquer avec lui parce que notre message coïncidera avec le fonctionnement de son cerveau.

H. Elaboration du vocabulaire de base. En commençant par les paragraphes qui précèdent, trouvez les verbes, noms, adjectifs et adverbes typiques de chaque catégorie. Ensuite, complétez votre liste à l'aide de dictionnaires (anglais-français, français-français, ou un dictionnaire des synonymes) pour arriver à un total d'au moins quinze termes (cinq par catégorie).

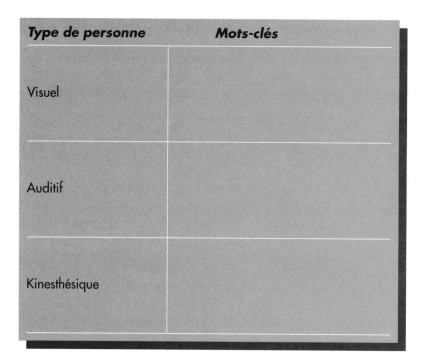

Type de personne	Mots-clés
Visuel	
Auditif	
Kinesthésique	

> You may choose to answer these questions as a self-evaluation before coming to class.

I. Interviews à faire en classe. Par groupes de deux, posez les questions suivantes à votre voisin(e) ou partenaire afin de déterminer s'il ou si elle est à dominance visuelle, auditive ou kinesthésique. Prenez de bonnes notes pour pouvoir partager les résultats de votre interview avec le reste de la classe.

1. Vous avez le travail de vos rêves. Qu'est-ce qui vous plaît *le plus* dans ce poste *(job)*?
    a. les personnes avec qui vous travaillez
    b. votre bureau
    c. les sons que vous entendez

2. Quelle ville associez-vous à votre enfance? Dites ce que vous aimiez *le mieux* dans cette ville.

3. Vous avez cinq semaines de congés payés par an. Vous êtes en vacances en ce moment. Que faites-vous? Qu'est-ce qui vous plaît *le plus* là où vous êtes?

4. En vous basant sur vos réponses, pensez-vous que vous êtes kinesthésique, visuel(e) ou auditif/auditive? Pourquoi?

HSG

> Review the *Phonétique* section on *liaisons* once per week until you feel comfortable with the material included there.

 *écapitulons!*

Quelques aide-mémoire

1. **Une entreprise s'adresse à une agence intérim**
    - lorsqu'une de ses employées va en congé de maternité.
    - lorsqu'elle a besoin d'un employé pour une durée limitée.

- lorsqu'elle ne veut pas avoir à passer par tout le processus de recrutement du personnel elle-même.
- lorsqu'un employé est en congé maladie de longue durée.
- lorsqu'elle n'est pas sûre que son besoin de personnel va durer.
- lorsqu'elle a besoin d'un spécialiste qu'elle ne sait pas où trouver elle-même.

2. Une bonne formation

- prépare à un métier.
- facilite l'apprentissage des connaissances nécessaires qui permettront d'exercer un métier.
- donne suffisamment de connaissances générales pour élargir l'horizon de la personne qui suit cette formation.
- augmente les chances d'une personne de trouver un travail.
- permet de se sentir à la hauteur des tâches à accomplir.
- exploite les talents naturels d'une personne et l'aide à réaliser son potentiel.
- permet de se sentir à l'aise.

3. Une bonne publicité

- attire et retient l'attention.
- doit donner envie d'acheter un produit.
- doit plaire.
- peut faire connaître un nouveau produit.
- peut lancer un produit.

Dans le Module VI, nous allons étudier entre autres comment gérer et investir notre argent, comment choisir une assurance et à quoi servent les impôts.

Gérer et investir son argent

Ouverture

Dépliant du
Crédit du
Nord.

Vivez tranquille...
Appuyez-vous sur
de solides garanties !

Dès aujourd'hui,
préservez votre avenir
et celui des vôtres.

ETOILE PROTECTION
ACCIDENT

Crédit du Nord
VOUS D'ABORD

A partir de
60 F/mois

BOURSE DE PARIS
SOCIETE DES BOURSES FRANÇAISES

La Bourse de Paris vue
de la place de la Bourse.

Publicité du Crédit du Nord
sous forme de petite carte.

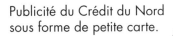

PRIV**A**TISATIONS
LLO
36.68.62.61
Les privatisations et la bourse en direct

Crédit
du
Nord

BOURSE

LIONVIE *

LIONVIE est un placement d'assurance-vie, à ce titre il bénéficie, en plus des qualités d'un placement rémunérateur, des avantages fiscaux propres aux contrats d'assurance-vie :

- réduction d'impôt,
- épargne exonérée d'impôt sur le revenu après 8 ans,
- transmission du patrimoine hors droits de succession (sous certaines conditions).

Ne pas confondre avec les assurances-décès qui, moyennant le paiement d'une cotisation, garantissent le versement d'un capital important en cas de décès.

VOUS POUVEZ BENEFICIER D'UNE RENTE A L'ISSUE DE VOTRE EPARGNE

Après 8 ans d'épargne, vous pouvez transformer votre capital en une rente. Elle vous sera alors versée régulièrement pendant toute votre vie, et vous permettra d'améliorer le niveau de votre retraite.

Notez que la rente perçue à l'issue d'un LIONVIE PEP est totalement exonérée d'impôts.

* Contrats collectifs d'assurance-vie souscrits par le Crédit Lyonnais auprès de sa filiale Les Assurances Fédérales-Vie

CREDIT LYONNAIS
LE POUVOIR DE DIRE OUI

Les Assurances Fédérales-Vie

Société Anonyme d'assurance au capital de 600 000 000 de F entièrement versé
Entreprise régie par le Code des Assurances
Siège Social : 27, avenue Claude Vellefaux - 75010 Paris
R.C.S PARIS B 612 023 275

F 93 960 07.92 YAP - Crédit Lyonnais S.A. au capital de 6 793 119 720 F - Lyon - RCS B 954 509 741 - PM 5731

LIONVIE

Valorisez votre épargne
en réduisant vos impôts

CREDIT LYONNAIS
LE POUVOIR DE DIRE OUI

Dépliant du
Crédit Lyonnais
qui suggère les
avantages fiscaux
de l'assurance LIONVIE.

LA POSTE   REÇU DE ....

RCS NANTERRE B 356 000 000

Dépôt de documents

☐ Livret d'épargne
numéro :

☐ Chéquier   CCP N°   à

Formules n° ....

☐ Carte émise par LA POSTE - numéro :
....

☐ Autre : ....   (à préciser)

Motif du dépôt : ....

CONSERVEZ CE REÇU. IL VOUS SERA RECLAME POUR
RESTITUTION DES DOCUMENTS

Compte d'épargne à ouvrir

N°

Vente de produits

☐ soumis à TVA *(rayer les lignes ci-dessous en cas de non utilisation)*   HT   F
Nom du produit ....   TVA   F
vendu au nom et pour le compte de :.   F

(nom de l'organisme)   TOTAL TTC:

☑ non soumis à TVA   106,80

Affranchissement- Timbres-Emballages
Autres............   TOTAL PERCU   106,80

PHILATELIE QUAI DES INDES
de LORIENT   28 11 1995

F

Un reçu
de la Poste.

*L*es impôts et les taxes

Les impôts *(taxes)* constituent une part essentielle des revenus de l'Etat. On peut les diviser en deux grandes catégories: les impôts directs qui sont fonction des revenus de toute personne morale (association ou entreprise) ou physique (individu) et sont calculés à partir d'une déclaration faite à l'administration fiscale, et les impôts indirects, ou encore taxes, qui frappent le consommateur *(consumer)* ou l'utilisateur. Ce premier dossier du Module VI aborde le domaine des impôts et des taxes principalement du point de vue des ménages *(households)* mais il inclut également quelques éléments qui ont trait *(have to do with)* aux

DIRECTION GÉNÉRALE DES IMPÔTS

impôts des entreprises comme la présentation d'un logiciel «liasse fiscale» *(tax bundle)* et une réaction de M. Jean Gandois, le président du CNPF, syndicat du patronat, qui appréhende *(dreads)* une augmentation de l'impôt sur les sociétés.

*A*ctivité d'introduction

Les impôts et les taxes

A. Réflexion sur les impôts et les taxes. Mettez-vous en groupes de deux ou trois personnes et réfléchissez aux questions suivantes.

1. A quoi servent les impôts?
2. Donnez des exemples de programmes ou projets qui sont financés par l'ensemble des taxes et des impôts d'un pays ou d'une région.
3. Comment devrait-on, selon vous, imposer entreprises et ménages? Sur quelle base ou selon quel barème et pourquoi?

Les mots pour le dire

Vocabulaire de base

VERBES

additionner	*to add*
être agacé (par)	*to be aggravated (by)*
alléger	*to lighten; to reduce*
alourdir	*to make heavy; to increase*
être assujetti(e) à l'impôt	*to be subject to taxation*
avoir droit à	*to be entitled to*
décéder, être décédé	*to die, to be deceased*
déclarer	*to declare*
déduire	*to deduct*
échapper à	*to escape from*
encaisser des revenus	*to collect revenues*
envisager	*to envisage, consider*
étaler sur (paiements)	*to spread (the payments) over*
imposer, être imposé(e)	*to tax, to be taxed*
inclure	*to include*
se munir de	*to take*
(se) plaindre	*to complain*
prélever	*to levy, impose*
remplir (un formulaire)	*to fill out (a form)*
solliciter (un délai de paiement)	*to ask for (a deferral)*
soustraire	*to subtract*

NOMS

un abattement	*tax allowance; dejection, despondency*
un allègement	*reduction*
une assiette fiscale	*(basis of) assessment*
un avantage fiscal	*tax advantage*
une baisse	*drop, lowering*
un barème	*calculation table, tax table grid; barometer*
le CDI (Centre Des Impôts), le fisc	*French equivalent of the IRS*
un comptable	*accountant*
un contribuable	*taxpayer*
une déclaration	*statement; tax return*
une déclaration annexe	*appended statement or return*
une dette	*debt*
un échéancier	*payment schedule*
une exonération	*exoneration; exemption*
des frais *(m)* de route	*travel expenses*
une hausse	*rise, increase*
l'imposition *(f)*	*taxation*
une imposition commune	*common tax*
un imprimé, un formulaire	*tax form*
une liasse fiscale (l'ensemble des formulaires de déclaration d'impôt)	*tax bundle*

continued on page 346

continued from page 345

la mairie	*city hall*
un ménage	*household*
la perception	*perception; tax collector's office*
le percepteur	*tax commissioner*
un prélèvement	*deduction; withdrawal*
les recettes *(f)* **fiscales**	*tax receipts*
le recouvrement des impôts	*tax collection or levying*
le régime de la communauté des biens	*joint ownership of property*
des revenus *(m)* **fonciers**	*land revenues*
un seuil	*threshold*
une surtaxe	*surtax*
une taxe	*tax; taxation; assessment*
une tranche d'imposition	*tax bracket*

ADJECTIFS

déductible, non-déductible	*deductible, non-deductible*
désavantageux(se)	*disadvantageous*
distribué(e), réparti(e)	*distributed*
fiscal(e) *(m pl,* **fiscaux)**	*fiscal, tax*
forfaitaire	*inclusive, contractual, outright*
imposable	*taxable*
imposé(e)	*taxed*
perçu(e)	*perceived*
plafonné(e)	*topped out; having reached its ceiling*
redevable	*liable, indebted for*
reportable	*deferrable, postponable*

ADVERBES ET EXPRESSIONS ADVERBIALES

à charge	*dependent*
effectivement	*indeed*
modérément	*moderately*

➤ Be ready to play *Password* during your next class.

B. Définitions provisoires à terminer. Complétez les phrases suivantes.

1. Lorsqu'on peut soustraire certains frais du montant de ses revenus, on dit que ces frais sont _____.

2. Une _____ est l'ensemble des formulaires que le contribuable remplit et envoie au Centre Des Impôts pour justifier le montant total des impôts qu'il doit payer.

3. Lorsqu'un contribuable ne peut pas payer la totalité de ses impôts en temps voulu, à la demande de celui-ci, le percepteur peut établir un _____, c'est-à-dire une sorte de calendrier qui autorise un délai dans les paiements, une répartition différente des paiements et qui précise les dates auxquelles les paiements partiels devront être effectués.

4. Le _____ est une sorte de tableau ou de grille indiquant certains chiffres auxquels on peut se référer lorsqu'on veut calculer quelque chose.

5. Lorsque les impôts sont augmentés, c'est-à-dire qu'ils deviennent plus élevés, on peut parler de _____. La _____ est le contraire de la baisse.

6. Le _____ est un Agent du Trésor, un fonctionnaire qui est chargé du recouvrement des impôts directs. Le _____ est donc une sorte de collecteur des impôts.

C. Définitions provisoires à créer. Par groupes de deux, donnez une définition provisoire pour les mots suivants.

1. solliciter un délai de paiement
2. forfaitaire
3. les impôts indirects
4. imposable
5. des impôts proportionnels aux revenus

HSG

➤ Study the *Photos et descriptions* and *Phonétique* sections of Module VI in your *HSG*.

ialogue

Discussion familiale au sujet du nouveau guide fiscal du Crédit Agricole

D. Activité de pré-lecture. Mettez-vous par petits groupes de deux ou trois et répondez aux questions suivantes.

1. Qui doit remplir une déclaration d'impôts et pourquoi?
2. Est-ce que vous remplissez votre déclaration d'impôts vous-même? Pourquoi?
3. Si vous ne voulez pas faire votre propre déclaration, que pouvez-vous faire?

Discussion familiale au sujet du nouveau guide fiscal du Crédit Agricole

M. Amar: Qu'est-ce que tu lis?

Mme Amar: Le nouveau guide fiscal du Crédit Agricole, tu sais, dans la série "Dossier Familial". C'est très bien fait mais je plains ceux qui doivent remplir leur déclaration d'impôts eux-mêmes. Il faut être systématique, extrêmement précis, avoir beaucoup de patience et vraiment savoir lire les petites lignes!

M. Amar: Oui, effectivement! Pas beaucoup de nouveautés pour la nouvelle année fiscale, je crois.

Mme Amar: Non, tu as raison. Il y a quelque chose d'intéressant là, regarde: "Si vous avez vendu vos SICAV monétaires ou obligataires de capitalisation le 31 décembre dernier et avez réinvesti dans les deux mois qui suivaient dans un achat immobilier, vous échappez à l'imposition sur les plus-values dans la limite de 600 000 F de cession pour une personne non mariée ou de 1 200 000 F pour un couple marié." Ah, oui, mais il faut être "soumis à une imposition commune." Dommage!

M. Amar: Oui, c'était une mesure pour tenter de relancer les investissements dans l'immobilier. Tu devrais passer ce guide à ta sœur. Ça pourrait l'aider.

Mme Amar: C'est une bonne idée! J'ai vu, par exemple, que lorsqu'on a divorcé dans l'année, on peut bénéficier des mêmes avantages fiscaux que lorsqu'on se marie. Pauvre Françoise, c'est un peu ironique quand même, tu ne trouves pas?

M. Amar: Peut-être, mais logique! Il faut remplir trois déclarations de revenus. Il faut en remplir une pour la période allant du premier janvier au jour du divorce ou de la séparation puis déclarer ensuite chacun séparément, sur un autre formulaire, ses revenus du jour du divorce au 31 décembre.

Mme Amar: Qu'est-ce que c'est compliqué!

M. Amar: Pas vraiment. En fait, ce qui se passe, c'est que le fisc considère les trois déclarations de revenus comme provenant de trois foyers fiscaux indépendants dont les revenus sont étalés sur un an. Donc ça peut faire une différence appréciable. De toute façon, tu sais, c'était toujours Françoise qui s'occupait des finances de la famille. Elle faisait même ses déclarations d'impôts elle-même. Elle s'est toujours super bien débrouillée dans ce domaine.

Mme Amar: C'est vrai. En fait Michel est plus à plaindre qu'elle!

E. A la recherche d'éléments précis du texte. Trouvez dans le dialogue le contraire des expressions ou mots suivants.

1. vague
2. Tant mieux!
3. ensemble
4. simple
5. négligeable
6. le mariage

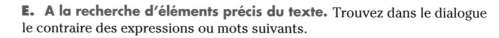

F. Autrement dit. Trouvez dans le dialogue un synonyme des expressions ou mots suivants.

1. considérer avec compassion
2. méthodique
3. des innovations
4. avec un maximum de
5. essayer
6. prêter
7. célibataire(s) ou divorcé(e)(s)
8. le Centre Des Impôts
9. répartis

➤ You might prepare this activity with your study partner.

G. Définitions provisoires à créer. Donnez une définition simple des mots et groupes de mots suivants.

1. un guide
2. un dossier
3. l'imposition
4. une imposition commune
5. un achat immobilier
6. relancer les investissements
7. des avantages fiscaux

H. Vrai ou faux? Lisez les affirmations suivantes. Si elles sont fausses, rectifiez-les de façon à ce qu'elles correspondent à ce qui a été exprimé dans le dialogue.

1. Mme Amar lit le guide fiscal parce qu'elle veut remplir elle-même sa feuille d'impôts.
2. Il y avait beaucoup de changements cette année dans ce qui était imposable ou non.
3. Mme Amar vient de divorcer.
4. M. et Mme Amar ne sont pas sous le régime de la communauté des biens.
5. Quand on vend ses SICAV monétaires, on ne paie pas d'impôts sur la plus-value.
6. M. et Mme Amar ont fait des investissements immobiliers pendant l'année fiscale dont il est question dans le dialogue.
7. Les gens qui ont divorcé dans l'année bénéficient d'un type d'imposition plus avantageux.
8. Françoise s'inquiète car c'était son mari qui remplissait toujours la déclaration d'impôts familiale.

I. Avez-vous compris? Répondez aux questions suivantes.

1. Relisez bien le passage que Mme Amar cite au sujet des SICAV monétaires. Pouvez-vous expliquer, avec vos propres mots, l'avantage fiscal dont il s'agit?
2. Pourquoi est-ce que les gens qui se marient ou divorcent dans l'année bénéficient d'avantages fiscaux? Comment est-ce que cela marche? Expliquez le principe dont il s'agit en vos propres mots.
3. Si vous suivez la logique de ce dialogue, pouvez-vous deviner qui est Michel?
4. Pourquoi Michel est-il plus à plaindre que Françoise d'après Mme Amar?

Observations fiscales

Si vous avez des difficultés de paiement ou si vous déménagez...

Si vous avez des difficultés de paiement, ne faites pas l'autruche! N'attendez pas. Prenez rendez-vous avec votre percepteur pour solliciter des délais de paiement ou un étalement du paiement des cotisations fiscales plus large et sans majoration. Si vous avez des difficultés réelles, le percepteur se montrera sans doute assez souple et vous pourrez proposer un échéancier raisonnable. Le but est de prouver que vous êtes prêt à payer votre dette.

Exemples de situations graves qui seront prises au sérieux par le fisc:

- Vous êtes au chômage.
- Vous êtes un agriculteur qui a été victime de calamités naturelles.

continued on page 350

continued from page 349

- Vous êtes un chef d'entreprise qui vient de créer son entreprise et vous venez de contracter de lourds emprunts.
- Votre conjoint est en longue maladie et vos revenus ont fortement baissé.
- Votre conjoint est décédé.
- Vous faites votre service militaire.

Si vous déménagez, vous changez de service fiscal puisque celui-ci dépend de l'adresse de votre domicile. Vous aurez un minimum de démarches à suivre. Vous devrez adresser une lettre recommandée avec avis de réception à votre Centre Des Impôts et à votre Trésorerie pour les prévenir de ce changement et leur faire part de votre nouvelle adresse. La première année, vous payerez la totalité de vos impôts à la trésorerie de votre ancien domicile. Ce ne sera que la troisième année (année de votre déménagement + 2) que vous payerez la totalité de ce que vous contribuez aux caisses de l'Etat à votre nouvelle perception.

J. Vrai ou faux? Après avoir bien lu les conseils qui précèdent, dites si les affirmations suivantes sont correctes ou non. Si elles ne sont pas correctes, modifiez les phrases pour qu'elles correspondent à ce qui est expliqué dans le texte.

1. Faire l'autruche veut dire ne pas vouloir faire face à la réalité.
2. Il faut prendre rendez-vous avec son percepteur pour qu'il puisse aider à trouver une solution aux difficultés de paiement.
3. Si vous êtes au chômage, le percepteur sera enclin à croire que vous avez de sérieuses difficultés financières.
4. Si votre femme ou votre mari est gravement malade, le percepteur comprendra que vous ne puissiez pas aller le voir en personne à la perception.
5. Si vous déménagez, vous devez toujours communiquer votre nouvelle adresse aux autorités fiscales.
6. Si vous changez de maison ou d'appartement mais que vous ne changez pas de Centre Des Impôts, la situation est simplifiée.
7. Dans le texte le mot «perception» est synonyme de «Centre Des Impôts».

K. Avez-vous compris? Dites quel est le thème général des deux conseils de la rubrique «Observations fiscales».

L. La parole est à vous! A deux ou trois, discutez les questions suivantes.

Est-ce que vous avez tendance à faire l'autruche lorsque vous êtes confronté(e) à des problèmes? Si oui, dans quel genre de situation et pourquoi? Si non, que faites-vous quand des problèmes surgissent à l'horizon et pourquoi?

HSG

➤ Complete the *Révisions générales* of the *Phonétique* section of Module VI in your *HSG*.

Lecture 1

Informations sur les impôts par Minitel

M. Activité de pré-lecture. Par petits groupes de deux ou trois, discutez les questions suivantes.

Dans le domaine des déclarations d'impôts, existe-t-il des livres qui peuvent procurer une certaine aide? Lesquels? Quel genre d'aide donnent-ils?

Informations sur les impôts par Minitel

Pour connaître le montant de vos impôts, pianotez sur le Minitel 3615 CA, mis en place par le Crédit Agricole, ou le 3615 IRSERVICE, mis en place par le ministère des Finances.

Munissez-vous de votre déclaration remplie avant de composer le numéro; vous aurez à vous y reporter pour répondre aux questions qui vous seront posées.

Tiré du *Guide Fiscal 95* du Crédit Agricole, Numéro spécial, février 1995.

N. Avez-vous compris? Répondez aux questions suivantes.

1. Combien y a-t-il de services Minitel qui peuvent aider les contribuables à calculer ce qu'ils devront verser à l'Etat?
2. Quelle est la banque qui offre un service Minitel dans le domaine des impôts?
3. Pourquoi faut-il avoir sa déclaration d'impôts sous les yeux lorsqu'on fait appel aux services Minitel en question?
4. Que veut dire «se reporter à sa déclaration»?

Comptables agréés du Québec

Partenaires en affaires

Lecture 2

CIEL: Une gamme performante de 16 logiciels au service de votre gestion

O. Activité de pré-lecture. Par petits groupes de deux ou trois, répondez aux questions suivantes.

1. Il existe un grand nombre de logiciels sur le marché qui répondent aux besoins spécifiques des entreprises en ce qui concerne leur comptabilité. En connaissez-vous? Si oui, lesquels?
2. Lorsque vous allez chez le médecin, chez le dentiste ou chez votre concessionnaire *(dealership)* pour faire réparer votre voiture, par exemple, l'employé(e) qui se trouve à la réception ou à la caisse se sert généralement d'un ordinateur. De quel genre de programmes est-ce qu'il/elle se sert? Qu'est-ce que ces logiciels doivent être capables de faire selon vous?

CIEL: Une gamme performante de 16 logiciels au service de votre gestion

CIEL liasse fiscale: 970F HT.

Un gain de temps bienvenu...

Logiciel permettant la saisie et l'édition de l'intégralité des liasses CERFA. Edition sur pré-imprimés ou papier vierge, sur imprimante matricielle ou laser. Les données peuvent être importées automatiquement, soit à partir de CIEL Comptabilité (V.5), soit à partir d'une balance en fichier ASCII. Modèles de saisie d'écritures extra-comptables.[…]

C'est une simple question de bon sens: un logiciel vendu en grand nombre n'a aucune raison d'être cher! Sur le principe de la diffusion de masse, CIEL commercialise depuis 1986, avec succès, des logiciels performants, à moins de 1 000F HT.

Des chiffres parlent d'eux-mêmes...

- Plus de 50 000 logiciels CIEL vendus à ce jour...
- Des logiciels choisis par des milliers de comptables de PME/PMI, d'artisans, commerçants, professions libérales et d'experts comptables. Des logiciels choisis par de grandes entreprises telles que IBM, Renault, Phildar...
- Les logiciels CIEL ont été sélectionnés par l'Education Nationale: l'assurance

pour elle, de former ses étudiants sur des logiciels largement utilisés par le monde professionnel.

L'innovation permanente pour devise

- Des logiciels à moins de 1 000F HT.
- Des versions complètes et non limitées, pas de prix d'appel sur des modules de base, que vous devrez forcément compléter plus tard… en payant à nouveau.
- Des logiciels qui privilégient la convivialité.
- De nouvelles versions régulières qui s'adaptent aux nouvelles exigences légales (la TVA intracommunautaire par exemple) et tiennent compte de l'avancement technologique en micro-informatique.
- De nouvelles versions *Windows* et *Macintosh*, pour tous ceux qui ont opté pour l'environnement graphique.

En bref…
Avec CIEL, vous choisissez l'expérience d'un leader et vous équipez votre gestion de logiciels au rapport qualité/prix unique. N'hésitez pas à comparer.

— Pierre-Yves MORLET, PDG CIEL.

P. Avez-vous compris? Répondez aux questions suivantes.

1. Relevez au moins sept termes appartenant au domaine de l'informatique.

2. Comment s'appelle le logiciel CIEL présenté dans ce texte?

3. Quel est le prix du logiciel en question?

4. A qui est-ce que ce logiciel s'adresse?

5. Est-on obligé d'adopter un logiciel CIEL pour le reste de sa comptabilité lorsqu'on choisit d'utiliser CIEL liasse fiscale?

6. Selon le PDG de CIEL, quels avantages y a-t-il à utiliser sa gamme de logiciels? Trouvez au moins trois avantages.

7. Pourquoi M. Morlet cite-t-il le nom des entreprises IBM, Renault et Phildar?

8. Pourquoi est-ce que l'Education Nationale se sert des logiciels CIEL, selon M. Morlet?

Q. Autrement dit. Répondez aux questions suivantes.

1. Expliquez le nom du logiciel en question.

2. Essayez d'expliquer avec vos propres mots ce que ce logiciel peut faire pour vous.

 HSG

➤ Listen to the *Phonétique* section again on your cassette for Module VI of your *HSG*.

Lecture 3

Tour de vis fiscal

R. Activité de pré-lecture. En petits groupes de deux ou trois personnes, répondez aux questions suivantes.

1. Quel genre de mesures est-ce qu'un gouvernement peut proposer pour réduire les dépenses de l'Etat?

2. Quel genre de mesures est-ce qu'un gouvernement peut proposer pour renflouer (remplir) les caisses de l'Etat?

Tour de vis fiscal

Alain Juppé hésite encore sur les hausses d'impôts
Le patronat accepte mal une augmentation de la taxe sur les bénéfices

Le gouvernement peine, décidément, à "boucler" son projet de loi de finances rectificative pour 1995. [...]

Ces hésitations s'expliquent par la situation dégradée des comptes de l'Etat. Le gouvernement sait qu'il ne peut se permettre d'afficher un déficit supérieur à 322 milliards de francs [...] mais le dérapage constaté en début d'année rend l'opération difficile. Pour rester dans l'épure, à défaut de pouvoir abaisser le déficit au-dessous de ce seuil, le gouvernement réfléchit donc encore à l'ampleur des nouveaux prélèvements fiscaux, ainsi qu'à leur répartition entre ménages et entreprises.

Une idée de dernière minute a été mise à l'étude. Elle consisterait à relever le taux supérieur de la TVA de 18,6% non pas à 20%, mais à 20,6%. Une autre idée chemine: celle de proroger jusqu'en 1999 cette hausse de la TVA, ainsi que la majoration de 10% de l'impôt de solidarité sur la fortune (ISF). [...]

La surtaxe envisagée pour l'impôt sur les sociétés sur le même modèle que celle décidée pour l'ISF, "passe" très mal dans les milieux patronaux. Déjà fortement agacés par la hausse du SMIC et par la modestie du plan d'allègement de charges sociales envisagé par le gouvernement, ceux-ci n'apprécient guère ce projet de hausse fiscale. Le président du CNPF, Jean Gandois, qui rencontre, mercredi, le chef de l'Etat, devrait lui délivrer le message suivant: les entreprises ont besoin de "signaux positifs", et sûrement pas qu'on alourdisse leurs charges fiscales.

Tiré de l'article «Alain Juppé hésite encore sur les hausses d'impôts» de L. Mauduit, paru dans *Le Monde* du 22 juin 1995.

S. Autrement dit! Relisez bien le texte qui précède et trouvez le synonyme des expressions ou mots suivants.

1. a des difficultés
2. terminer
3. affaibli
4. montrer publiquement

➤ Prenez des notes pour un match éventuel de *Mot de passe*.

5. plus grand que, plus élevé que

6. un manque, une dette

7. ce niveau

8. irrités

9. considérée

10. faire durer au-delà de la date fixée

T. A la recherche d'éléments précis! Trouvez dans le texte le contraire des expressions et mots suivants.

1. entamer, commencer

2. au lendemain de

3. améliorée

4. inférieur à

5. de longue date

6. cette baisse

7. la diminution

8. l'alourdissement *(m)*

9. négatifs

U. Vrai ou faux? Relisez bien l'extrait de l'article qui précède et vérifiez si les affirmations suivantes respectent le contenu exact du texte. Si cela n'est pas le cas, faites les modifications nécessaires pour qu'elles soient correctes.

1. Le gouvernement est absolument sûr des mesures qu'il veut prendre pour lutter contre les déficits.

2. C'est parce que le déficit est déjà si important que le gouvernement doit prendre des mesures.

3. S'il ne peut pas faire baisser le déficit, le gouvernement devrait se contenter de ne pas augmenter la dette.

4. Le gouvernement hésite entre deux taux de TVA.

5. L'impôt de solidarité sur la fortune va être augmenté.

6. Le gouvernement veut imposer les ménages plus que les entreprises.

7. Les milieux patronaux acceptent l'idée d'une augmentation des charges sociales à condition qu'elle soit temporaire.

8. Jean Gandois est le représentant de tous les syndicats.

9. CNPF est un syndicat et CNPF veut dire la Confédération Nationale du Patronat Français.

10. Jean Gandois va rencontrer le Président de la République pour lui offrir son soutien de principe.

V. Autrement dit. Expliquez les extraits suivants après avoir relu attentivement les passages dont ils sont tirés.

1. le gouvernement réfléchit à l'ampleur des nouveaux prélèvements

2. la surtaxe passe très mal dans les milieux patronaux

3. la modestie du plan d'allègement des charges sociales

4. alourdir leurs charges fiscales

W. Trouvez l'intrus. Un mot ne fait pas partie de chacune des trois séries suivantes. Lequel? Entourez-le!

1. gouvernement / hésitations / mesures d'urgence / signaux positifs / plan d'allègement

2. ménages / ISF / impôts plus lourds / rencontre avec le chef de l'Etat
3. entreprises / impôt de solidarité sur la fortune / CNPF / Jean Gandois / agacés

HSG

➤ Should you need extra practice on the agreement of adjectives, complete Exercises K–T in the *Activités supplémentaires* of Module VI in your *HSG*.

Quelques points de repère

Une date importante!

- Les Français doivent déposer leur déclaration de revenus à leur Centre Des Impôts (CDI) avant le 1er mars chaque année.
- La TVA (Taxe à la Valeur Ajoutée), remplaçant 11 taxes différentes, a été créée en 1954 pour les industries et a été généralisée à partir de 1968.

L'ardoise

La gabelle:

Le mot vient de l'italien *gabella* et de l'arabe *al-qabâla* qui veut dire «l'impôt».

La gabelle est un impôt du régime féodal qui a été créé par Philippe VI en 1340 et qui est lié au sel. Impôt indirect, la gabelle constituait la plus grosse ressource fiscale du royaume. Il y avait des pays de grande gabelle, des pays de petite gabelle, des pays de quart-bouillon, ce qui signifie donc que la gabelle n'était pas répartie de façon uniforme dans tout le pays. Il y avait même des pays complètement dispensés de la gabelle qu'on appelait les provinces franches. Les pays de grande gabelle payaient le plus: il y avait obligation d'acheter au moins 11 livres ¾ de sel par an.

Le saviez-vous?

- Toute personne qui est susceptible de payer des impôts est tenue de faire une déclaration de revenus.
- Si l'on n'a pas reçu de formulaire(s) à son domicile, il faut aller en chercher au Centre Des Impôts ou à la mairie.

- Vous ne payerez pas d'impôts si vous vivez seul et que votre salaire (ou pension) déclaré est inférieur à 57.695 F (chiffre de 1995). Ce montant monte en fonction du nombre de parts fiscales qui vous sont attribuées pour déterminer votre revenu imposable. Ainsi, pour une famille qui a plusieurs enfants ou autres personnes à charge, ce seuil peut atteindre 181.084 F (chiffre de 1995) pour 5 parts.
- Vous devez signer votre déclaration de revenus avant de l'envoyer. Si vous êtes marié(e) et que votre mari ou votre femme oublie de signer, votre déclaration sera quand même valable légalement car une seule signature suffit.
- Le fisc ne reconnaît pas l'union libre. Cela signifie que les personnes vivant ensemble sans être mariées sont considérées par le fisc comme des foyers fiscaux différents.
- Les frais de route peuvent être déduits *(deducted)* en fonction d'un barème forfaitaire qui a été établi par le fisc. Ce sont le nombre de kilomètres effectués et la puissance en chevaux *(horse power)* du véhicule qui déterminent le montant de la déduction.
- Certains revenus échappent à l'impôt. Par exemple: les allocations familiales, certains revenus mobiliers comme ceux d'un compte épargne logement, certains remboursements de frais, un certain nombre d'avantages en nature, une indemnité légale de licenciement.

Réflexions sur le travail en équipe

Chaque membre d'une équipe doit savoir exactement quel rôle il doit jouer, ce qu'il est tenu de faire et ce qu'on attend de lui pour pouvoir fonctionner de façon optimum au sein de l'équipe.

Lexique

un abattement: L'abattement est la fraction de la somme imposable qui est exemptée d'impôts. Obtenir **un abattement** revient donc à avoir une réduction de la somme imposable, donc une réduction d'impôts.

> Si votre enfant marié est rattaché à votre foyer fiscal, **l'abattement** auquel vous avez droit s'élève à 27.500 F.

l'assiette *(f):* On appelle **l'assiette** de l'impôt la matière imposable, c'est-à-dire les revenus, patrimoine, etc., qui servent de base au calcul de l'impôt.

> Les contrôles fiscaux sont chargés de rechercher les erreurs ou omissions dans le calcul de **l'assiette**.

un contribuable: Un contribuable est une personne qui paie des impôts. En 1988, en France, 52% des **contribuables** seulement étaient imposables.

> Les **contribuables** français sont mécontents car le gouvernement a annoncé une majoration de 2% de la TVA.

une déclaration d'impôts: La déclaration d'impôts est une synthèse des revenus annuels d'une personne, bénéfices et charges non-déductibles dans le cas d'une société. Pour une personne physique, ces revenus sont le salaire, les revenus immobiliers, dividendes et plus-values sur ventes de titres, rentes, etc. De ce revenu global sont déduits les exonérations auxquelles on a droit, ainsi que les dégrèvements (impôt dû seulement au dessus d'un certain seuil pour certaines sources de revenus). On obtient ainsi le revenu imposable.

Cette année, pour la première fois, je dois faire **une déclaration d'impôts,** ce qui m'inquiète un peu car tout le monde dit que c'est vraiment compliqué et ennuyeux.

un dégrèvement: Un dégrèvement d'impôt est une réduction d'impôt. Il y a un certain nombre de **dégrèvements** pour les contribuables qui sont âgés, handicapés, invalides, veufs ou veuves et qui ont des ressources modestes.

Après **les dégrèvements** auxquels il a droit, mon grand-père ne paie pratiquement pas d'impôts.

exonérer: Exonérer un contribuable, c'est le décharger de ses impôts. Un contribuable **exonéré** d'impôts n'a donc pas d'impôts à payer.

Est-ce que tu sais si un garçon qui fait son service militaire est **exonéré** d'impôts?

la fraude fiscale: On parle de **fraude fiscale** lorsque les contribuables, personnes physiques ou entreprises, ne déclarent pas la totalité de leurs revenus, et donc que ces contribuables paient moins d'impôts qu'ils ne le devraient.

En 1988, en France, le montant total de **la fraude fiscale** a été estimé à 106 milliards de francs.

les impôts directs: Les impôts directs sont ceux que les contribuables déterminent en remplissant leur déclaration d'impôts et paient d'eux-mêmes trois fois par an. Un impôt est un versement obligatoire que font les ménages et les entreprises. Ce versement alimente le budget de l'Etat.

En France, en 1993, la fiscalité **directe** a rapporté 280,2 milliards de francs et la fiscalité indirecte 283,7 milliards de francs.

les impôts indirects: Les impôts indirects sont ceux qui sont compris dans le prix de ce que les consommateurs achètent. Le prix de l'essence ou d'objets considérés comme étant superflus, comme le parfum incluent un fort pourcentage d'**impôts indirects.**

En France, la part **des impôts indirects** est très importante comparée à celle d'autres pays. Elle atteint entre 50 et 60% du total des impôts.

les impôts (m) **locaux: Les impôts locaux** sont les impôts qui sont perçus au profit de la commune, des départements, des groupements de collectivités locales, des Chambres de Commerce et d'Industrie.

Les impôts locaux sont plus élevés à Paris qu'en province.

un paradis fiscal: On appelle **paradis fiscal** un pays qui ne perçoit aucun impôt sur le revenu, comme Monaco, par exemple, ou qui ne perçoit qu'un impôt extrêmement faible comme les îles Vierges ou Hong-Kong.

Avec ses impôts de solidarité sur la fortune, sa forte imposition sur les revenus, la France est loin d'être **un paradis fiscal!**

une part: Pour savoir ce qu'un contribuable va devoir payer comme impôts sur ses revenus, il faut d'abord calculer le nombre de **parts** que cette personne ou ce foyer fiscal peut compter. Lorsqu'on est marié, qu'on a des enfants ou autres personnes à charge, on peut diviser son revenu imposable en un plus grand nombre de **parts**.

Lorsqu'on est célibataire et qu'on n'a personne à charge, on ne peut compter qu'**une** seule **part.**

le tiers provisionnel: Le **tiers provisionnel** est la partie *(fraction)* des impôts annuels sur le revenu qui est payée à l'avance.

Le mois prochain va être dur car nous devons payer notre **tiers provisionnel** et rembourser les 1.000 francs que nous avons empruntés à Maman!

➤ Après avoir cherché la définition de *à point*, discutez ce proverbe avec votre «partenaire» (un membre de votre groupe).

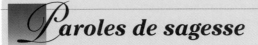

Rien ne sert de courir; il faut partir à point.

Expression écrite

«Si» et la forme conditionnelle

Dans cette section, vous allez apprendre à employer la conjonction «si» et la forme conditionnelle. En lisant les phrases suivantes, notez le temps du verbe de la proposition conditionnelle mais aussi celui de la proposition principale.

- **Si** on **gagne** plus que 6.500 francs par mois, on **doit** payer des impôts.
- **Si** tu **veux** être sûr(e) de toujours payer tes factures à temps, il **faut** demander un règlement par prélèvement.
- **Si** j'**étais** comptable, je **consacrerais** la majeure partie de mon travail à m'occuper de la déclaration d'impôt de mes clients.
- **Pense** à payer ta facture d'électricité **si** tu ne **veux** pas qu'on te coupe le courant.

Dans le texte suivant, repérez les formes conditionnelles et soulignez-les.

Pour payer ses impôts

Les impôts représentent une des sources de revenu les plus importantes pour l'Etat français. En effet, si les particuliers et les entreprises n'étaient pas taxés, l'Etat souffrirait d'un déficit budgétaire aigu.

Généralement, les particuliers remplissent leurs feuilles de déclaration d'impôt eux-mêmes. Si on ne reçoit pas chez soi le formulaire, il faut aller le chercher dans une mairie. Si un particulier a un revenu annuel inférieur à un certain seuil, il n'est alors pas imposé. Ensuite le montant dépend du revenu et est calculé par tranche. La tranche maximale d'imposition est supérieure à 50%. Si vous le désirez, il vous est possible de payer vos impôts en plusieurs paiements étalés sur l'année. Mais bien sûr, si vous préférez, vous pouvez payer en un seul versement. Dans ce cas, le bureau des impôts doit être en possession de votre paiement avant le 15 février de l'année.

Dans les entreprises, un comptable travaille à temps complet sur les transactions d'argent et s'occupe des procédures pour payer les impôts ainsi que les taxes.

Je n'aime pas payer mes impôts. Mais si je pouvais choisir, j'en payerais plus car cela signifierait que mes revenus seraient plus élevés!

X. A compléter. Finissez les phrases suivantes de façon originale.

1. Si j'avais un ordinateur, je...

2. Si j'arrive à l'heure à la banque, nous...

3. Si le Minitel n'existait pas, il...

4. Si l'employé de la Poste se dépêchait, je...

5. J'utiliserais mon ordinateur plus souvent si...

6. Si le Crédit Lyonnais est ouvert, elle...

7. Si les investissements en Bourse étaient moins risqués, vous...

Y. A vos plumes! Maintenant écrivez un paragraphe sur ce qu'il faut faire quand on a des impôts à payer ici aux Etats-Unis ou dans votre pays. Commencez par **Si j'avais des impôts à payer** + le conditionnel.

Dans le dossier suivant, nous allons étudier les assurances.

$\mathscr{L}$es assurances

Le Dossier 17, deuxième dossier du Module VI, présente quelques facettes du monde des assurances. Pour pallier *(attenuate)* les nombreux risques inhérents à la vie, sur la route, à la maison et au travail, les compagnies d'assurances conseillent la prudence et offrent tout un éventail *(range)* de protections diverses. Les assurances constituent également un moyen d'investissement, un placement *(investment)* qui joue un rôle important dans l'économie française.

$\mathscr{A}$ctivité d'introduction

Les assurances

A. Premiers pas dans le monde des assurances. Mettez-vous par groupes de deux ou trois personnes et réfléchissez aux questions suivantes.

1. Qu'est-ce que c'est qu'une assurance? Pouvez-vous, de façon très générale, expliquer le principe de l'assurance?

2. Quels sont les différents types d'assurances que vous connaissez? Faites une liste d'au moins sept types d'assurances et donnez une définition pour chacune d'entre elles.

3. Réfléchissez au coût *(cost)* des assurances pour les consommateurs *(consumers)*. Comment devrait-on, selon vous, calculer le montant des primes d'assurances?

Les mots pour le dire

VERBES

appliquer	*to apply*
assister	*to assist*
assurer, être assuré(e)	*to insure, to be insured*
avertir	*to warn*
avoir l'esprit tranquille	*to have peace of mind*
brûler	*to burn*
causer un préjudice	*to cause a loss*
cumuler	*to accrue, to pile up*
déclarer, être déclaré(e)	*to declare, to be declared*
dérober, être dérobé(e)	*to steal, to be stolen*
endommager	*to damage*
expertiser; faire expertiser	*to appraise, evaluate; to have evaluated*
inclure	*to include*
indemniser, être indemnisé(e)	*to compensate for; to be reimbursed for*
omettre	*to omit*
préconiser	*to recommend, advocate*
prendre effet	*to take effect, be operative*
prévoir	*to foresee*
protéger	*to protect*
rapatrier	*to repatriate*
rembourser, être remboursé(e)	*to reimburse, to be reimbursed*
se rendre au chevet de	*to be at the bedside of*
renouveler	*to renew*
résilier un contrat	*to terminate or cancel a contract*
souscrire	*to subscribe*
stipuler	*to stipulate*
voler, être volé(e)	*to steal, to be stolen; to be robbed*

NOMS

l'accord *(m)*	*agreement*
une aide matérielle	*material help*
une assurance multirisque	*multiple-risk insurance*
l'assuré(e)	*insured*
un bénéficiaire	*beneficiary*
un cambriolage	*theft*
la constatation	*statement*
un contrat de carte bancaire	*insurance automatically linked to the use of a bank or credit card*
un décès	*death*
les dégâts *(m)*, **les dommages** *(m)*	*damages*
une effraction	*breaking and entering*
les enjeux *(m)*	*stakes*
un faisceau de services	*an array of services*
des frais *(m)* **d'hébergement**	*lodging expenses*
les frais médicaux	*medical expenses*

continued on page 362

continued from page 361

une franchise	*deductible, exemption, immunity*
une garantie	*guarantee*
une hypothèse	*hypothesis*
l'imprudence *(f)*	*carelessness*
un incendie	*fire*
une lettre recommandée	*certified letter*
les lignes *(f)* **en petits caractères**	*lines in small print*
la perte	*loss*
un plafond	*maximum payment, ceiling*
une police d'assurance	*insurance policy*
une prestation	*benefit; performance*
la prime	*premium*
la protection	*protection, coverage*
le renouvellement	*renewal*
la responsabilité (civile)	*liability (personal)*
un sinistre	*disaster; accident*
la souscription	*subscription, contribution*
la validité, en cours de validité	*validity, valid*
un vol	*theft*

ADJECTIFS

accidentel(le)	*accidental, fortuitous*
blessé(e)	*wounded*
brûlé(e)	*burnt*
conseillé(e)	*advised*
couvert(e)	*covered*
décédé(e)	*deceased*
grave	*serious*
impayé(e)	*unpaid*
inclus(e)	*included*
majeur(e)	*major*
mineur(e)	*minor*
mort(e)	*dead*
onéreux(se)	*expensive*
prévu(e)	*foreseen*
tranquille	*peaceful*
tué(e)	*killed*

ADVERBES ET EXPRESSIONS ADVERBIALES

à l'avance	*in advance*
avec soin	*with care, carefully*
en cas de	*in case of*
en revanche	*on the other hand*
le cas échéant	*in the event, should the occasion arise*
sur place	*on site*
vivement	*sharply, brusquely; greatly, deeply*

➤ Prenez des notes afin de pouvoir mieux jouer à *Mot de passe.*

➤ Be prepared for *Mot de passe.*

B. Définitions provisoires à terminer. Complétez les phrases suivantes avec le vocabulaire qui précède.

1. Lorsqu'on est protégé par un contrat d'assurance, on dit qu'on est

_____.

2. Lorsqu'on décide de garder une assurance qu'on possède déjà mais qui va expirer, si l'on veut continuer à être couvert par le même contrat, on dit qu'on _____ son contrat.

3. Lorsqu'on assure le retour d'une personne dans son pays d'origine, on dit qu'on _____ cette personne. Lorsqu'une personne est blessée à l'étranger, elle peut avoir besoin d'être _____ par avion et d'être accompagnée par une infirmière, par exemple. Si la personne est décédée, son corps est _____ .

4. Ma maison a brûlé et tous mes meubles ont été détruits. Je vais acheter de nouveaux meubles pour remplacer ceux que j'ai perdus dans le sinistre, et l'assurance me _____ dans les limites prévues dans ma police d'assurance.

5. Lorsque je ne veux plus avoir de contrat avec une certaine compagnie d'assurances, j'ai l'option de ne pas renouveler ce contrat et donc de le _____ .

6. Lorsqu'un sinistre se produit, il y a de nombreuses choses qui sont détruites ou sérieusement abîmées. Un expert vient pour déterminer le montant des _____ qui ont été occasionnés _(entailed)_ par ce sinistre.

C. Définitions provisoires à créer. Par groupes de deux, donnez une définition provisoire pour les mots suivants.

HSG

➤ Study the _Points grammaticaux_ and complete Exercises J–K of Module VI in your _HSG_.

    1. un bénéficiaire   **4.** une franchise

    2. un cambriolage   **5.** un incendie

    3. une police d'assurance

Dialogue

Deux collègues discutent d'assurance-voiture

D. Activité de pré-lecture. Mettez-vous par petits groupes de deux ou trois et répondez aux questions suivantes.

    1. De quoi dépend le prix de votre assurance-voiture? Faites une liste de cinq éléments qui peuvent avoir une influence sur ce que vous payez.

    2. Comment avez-vous choisi votre assurance-voiture et pourquoi?

Deux collègues discutent d'assurance-voiture

Mme Vauclair: Est-ce que vous sauriez où je pourrais me renseigner sur les différences entre les assurances-voiture? Ma fille a décidé d'acheter une voiture le mois prochain et elle me demande de la conseiller en matière d'assurance.

Mme Amar: Je ne m'y connais pas beaucoup en assurances. Je sais que nous sommes assez contents de la nôtre

INFO SERVICE

NATIO ASSURANCES AUTOMOBILE

A la BNP, réduisez vos primes d'assurance automobile

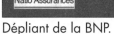
Natio Assurances

GROUPE
BNP

LA BNP, C'EST AUSSI D'AUTRES SERVICES ASSURANCES UAP...

Habitation

Santé

...A DES CONDITIONS INTÉRESSANTES

Renseignez-vous
auprès d'un conseiller
Assurances BNP.
Il vous établira gratuitement et
sans engagement
une étude personnalisée

GROUPE
UAP

GROUPE
BNP

LES AVANTAGES EXCLUSIFS RESERVES AUX CLIENTS DE LA BNP

▲ En tant que client de la BNP, vous profitez d'un **tarif étudié** et de solides garanties. Vous pouvez donc réduire sensiblement votre budget auto.

▲ Vous pouvez demander un **devis gratuit, sans aucun engagement** de votre part, à un conseiller Assurances BNP. Ainsi, vous pouvez comparer cette proposition avec votre assurance actuelle.

▲ Vous recevrez une **carte client**, Natio Assurances vous permettant d'être reconnu. En cas de sinistre, vous êtes sûr que votre dossier sera pris en main par l'UAP dans les meilleurs délais et vos indemnités réglées rapidement.

▲ Votre conseiller BNP habituel peut étudier avec vous une **solution crédit** vous aidant à passer le cap ou à acheter une nouvelle voiture.

NOTRE CONSEIL
Même si votre assurance actuelle n'arrive à échéance que dans quelques mois, informez-vous dès maintenant. Un conseiller Assurances BNP vous recevra et vous pourrez comparer tranquillement, chiffres à l'appui, le contrat qu'il vous proposera avec votre contrat actuel. Mieux encore, il vous aidera, le moment venu, à faire toutes les démarches nécessaires à votre changement d'assurance.

GROUPE
BNP

Dépliant de la BNP.

mais votre fille a moins de 25 ans; elle a donc un profil entièrement différent, même de celui de mon fils. Les assureurs estiment que les femmes sont de meilleures conductrices et les font bénéficier de conditions préférentielles. Cela peut aller presque du simple au double par rapport à un garçon du même âge. Justement, dans le dernier numéro de *50 millions de consommateurs*, il y a tout un dossier «Assurance auto».

Mme Vauclair: Ah bon, ça tombe bien! Faites-moi voir ça!

Mme Amar: Il est dans ma voiture. Je l'ai acheté pour Vincent qui rêve d'une voiture mais qui sait qu'il va automatiquement être très pénalisé à cause de son âge. Il a un copain qui a vingt ans et qui vient juste de passer son permis. Eh bien, il paie plus de 20.000 francs par an! Il est assuré aux Mutuelles du Mans, si je me souviens bien. Vincent veut potasser *(to study)* cela dans l'espoir de trouver des conditions plus intéressantes ailleurs. Une minute, je vais le chercher.

Mme Vauclair: Qu'est-ce que vous avez comme assurance, vous?

Mme Amar: Groupama. Regardez, là, au palmarès *(best of)* des «50», Groupama vient au quatrième rang après la

MAIF, FILIA MAIF et **MATMUT** et dans certaines catégories comme le contrat «tous risques», elle est même considérée comme très bonne juste derrière la MAIF.

Mme Vauclair: Comme nous n'avons pas la MAIF, ma fille qui n'est pas non plus dans le secteur public ne pourra pas l'avoir, malheureusement.

Mme Amar: Elle pourrait peut-être se renseigner auprès de la FILIA MAIF, car avec la MAIF, ce sont les deux seuls assureurs qui pratiquent une politique de solidarité entre générations et ne pénalisent donc pas les jeunes conducteurs qu'ils soient hommes ou femmes d'ailleurs.

Mme Vauclair: Je croyais que seuls les enfants d'assurés pouvaient bénéficier de ces conditions!

Mme Amar: Effectivement, vous avez raison. Pour elle, j'ai l'impression que ce sera UAP et Direct Assurance qui pourront lui proposer les tarifs les plus intéressants. Tiens, Direct Assurance propose un prix nettement inférieur aux autres compagnies pour les garçons de moins de 25 ans aussi. Il faut que je montre cela à Vincent!

ASSURANCE
AUTOMOBILE

" *Conduire en toute assurance,
je dis OUI.* "

Lion assurance
GROUPE CRÉDIT LYONNAIS

■ L'ASSISTANCE

En France et en Europe, en cas d'accident ou de maladie, vous bénéficiez du service "Assistance 24 h/24", dès le départ de votre domicile.

■ LA SIMPLICITÉ

Après accord, vous pouvez faire procéder à la remise en état immédiate de votre véhicule, sans expertise jusqu'à concurrence de 1500 FHT.

En option :

■ LA PROTECTION DU CONDUCTEUR

Cette garantie couvre le conducteur en cas d'accident dont il est responsable pour ses dommages corporels, frais médicaux et chirurgicaux. En cas de décès, un capital pouvant atteindre 2000000 F est versé. Une seule prime pour toute la famille, quel que soit le véhicule conduit (même prêté ou loué).

*Compagnie : La Lilloise d'Assurances

Lion Assurance - Société de Courtage d'Assurances - S.A. au Capital de 5 000 000 F - RCS Paris B 340856608 (87 BO 3910)

Vous appréciez
les services du Crédit Lyonnais,
découvrez son secteur Assurance.
Il protège au mieux votre famille
et vous-même, vos biens,
votre activité professionnelle et vos loisirs.
Vous aussi, vous avez tout à gagner à dire

"OUI, à l'Assurance d'un grand groupe".

Lion assurance
GROUPE CRÉDIT LYONNAIS

COUPON-RÉPONSE

Lion Assurance vous propose
une large gamme de
produits Assurances dommages :

❏ COMPLÉMENTAIRE FRAIS DE SANTÉ
❏ ASSURANCE FAMILIALE ACCIDENTS
❏ PRÉVOYANCE ACCIDENT-MALADIE
❏ LION HOSPITALISATION
❏ CONTRAT IMPATRIÉS-EXPATRIÉS
❏ PROTECTION JURIDIQUE
❏ MULTIRISQUE HABITATION
❏ TOUS RISQUES ŒUVRES D'ART ET OBJETS PRÉCIEUX
❏ MULTIRISQUE HABITATION "JEUNES 18-25 ANS"
❏ ASSURANCE AUTOMOBILE
❏ PROTECTION DU CONDUCTEUR
❏ ASSURANCE MOTO
❏ ASSISTANCE MOTO
❏ MULTIRISQUE PROFESSIONNELLE
❏ NAVIGATION DE PLAISANCE
❏ ASSURANCE SANTÉ CHIEN ET CHAT
❏ ASSURANCE MULTILOISIRS

Votre conseiller Lion Assurance est un professionnel de l'assurance. N'hésitez pas à l'interroger sur votre cas particulier. Il vous donnera tous renseignements et pourra au plus vite établir avec vous un devis personnalisé.

Lion assurance
GROUPE CRÉDIT LYONNAIS

Dépliant du Crédit Lyonnais

E. A la recherche d'éléments précis du dialogue. Lisez rapidemment le dialogue qui précède et relevez le nom des sept compagnies d'assurances françaises qui sont citées.

F. Autrement dit. Trouvez dans le texte les synonymes des mots ou groupes de mots suivants.

1. trouver des informations
2. dans le domaine de
3. les plus bas
4. pensent que
5. fait profiter
6. plus avantageuses
7. deux fois plus
8. puni
9. étudier sérieusement
10. les prix
11. elle tombe dans une catégorie différente

G. Antonymes. Trouvez dans le dialogue qui précède, le contraire des mots ou expressions suivants.

1. dernier
2. je suis spécialiste dans
3. similaire
4. plus mauvaises
5. une politique de discrimination
6. récompensé
7. le secteur privé
8. les mêmes conditions
9. vous avez tort
10. moins bien

H. Vrai ou faux? Lisez bien les affirmations suivantes. Si elles ne correspondent pas à ce qui est exprimé dans le texte, changez-les en conséquence.

1. Mme Vauclair cherche une nouvelle assurance pour elle-même.
2. Mme Amar a acheté *50 millions de consommateurs* pour Mme Vauclair.
3. Mme Amar et Mme Vauclair ont toutes les deux au moins un enfant qui a moins de 25 ans.
4. Les jeunes de moins de 25 ans sont toujours pénalisés en ce qui concerne le prix de leur assurance.
5. La fille de Mme Vauclair ne travaille pas dans le secteur public.
6. Le fils de Mme Amar va bientôt avoir sa propre voiture.
7. Certaines compagnies d'assurances n'assurent que les enfants dont les parents sont assurés chez elles.

HSG

➤ Study the verbs *mentir, (se) plaindre, (re)naître (mourir)* and *jeter (courir)* for a review of taxation and another point of view on insurance. Complete Exercises L–O of Module VI in the *HSG* with your study partner.

I. Avez-vous compris? Répondez aux questions suivantes, à deux ou trois.

1. Pourquoi est-ce que les jeunes hommes sont pénalisés par les compagnies d'assurances? Etes-vous d'accord avec cette mesure?
2. Comment les femmes de ce dialogue choisissent-elles leur compagnie d'assurances? Qu'en pensez-vous?
3. Pourquoi est-ce que cela vaut le coup de comparer les différentes compagnies d'assurances?

Lecture 1

Assurance-vie, une assurance épargne

J. Activité de pré-lecture. Répondez aux questions suivantes, à deux ou trois.

1. Expliquez le principe d'une assurance-vie.
2. Avez-vous une assurance-vie? Pourquoi?
3. Y a-t-il des cas où vous pensez qu'il est indispensable d'avoir une assurance-vie? Lesquels et pourquoi?

> ➤ Be prepared to interview a classmate and/or be interviewed. Take good notes so you'll be able to report your findings back to the class.

Assurance-vie, une assurance épargne

*A*vec près de 450 milliards de collecte l'an dernier, l'assurance-vie reste le placement favori des Français. Ils y consacrent plus de la moitié de leur épargne nouvelle. [...]

L'assurance-vie est un véritable placement financier. Son principe de base est que les versements effectués dans le cadre de ce type de contrat sont rémunérés selon le principe de la capitalisation. A la fin du contrat le souscripteur récupère le capital placé, augmenté des intérêts.

Aujourd'hui, la gamme des solutions assurance-vie est vaste et diversifiée. Il est ainsi possible de choisir entre un contrat classique en francs, ou bien d'opter pour des contrats libellés en supports financiers (Sicav, SCPI ou fonds communs de placement). Chaque catégorie de contrats correspond à des objectifs spécifiques et présente des avantages qui lui sont propres. A condition de le choisir judicieusement, un contrat d'assurance-vie permet de poursuivre des buts différents: vous pouvez chercher à répondre à des objectifs de constitution d'un capital, vous pouvez ménager des suppléments de revenus ou encore préparer la transmission de votre patrimoine. [...]

La constitution d'un capital

En tant que placement financier, l'assurance-vie permet de:

- **Constituer sans-risques un capital.** A condition, bien entendu, de privilégier les contrats libellés en francs, qui présentent l'avantage d'offrir un taux d'intérêt minimum garanti. Grâce à l'effet de cliquet, votre placement ne souffre pas des baisses des marchés financiers, les revalorisations sont définitivement acquises: si, après une bonne progression, les marchés financiers s'effondrent, votre capital restera au plus haut niveau atteint. Au terme, vous percevrez votre épargne majorée de la participation bénéficiaire, en franchise d'impôt si vous conservez le contrat au moins huit ans.

- **Gérer un portefeuille boursier.** Avec un contrat en unités de compte «valeurs mobilières» ou multisupports, votre argent sera investi dans des Sicav ou des fonds communs de placement. Cette formule présente un attrait majeur par rapport à la détention en direct de valeurs mobilières: l'absence de fiscalité au regard des plus-values boursières. Au terme, le portefeuille est converti en francs en fonction des cours des valeurs. Il est, à certaines conditions, possible de se faire remettre les titres détenus.

- **Réaliser indirectement un investissement immobilier.** Un contrat en unités de compte immobilier fait de vous un propriétaire immobilier sans le savoir, il vous décharge de la gestion et surtout en période de difficultés immobilières, vous évite tout problème de liquidité à la sortie puisque, au terme, vous n'avez pas de soucis de revente, l'assureur rembourse l'épargne acquise.

Tiré de la rubrique «Argent» parue dans *Dossier Familial* du Crédit Agricole, N° 244, mars 1995.

Assurance **VIE-ÉPARGNE**
Desjardins

NOUS VOUS OFFRONS
AUSSI
DE L'ASSURANCE VIE

Desjardins

Dépliant de la compagnie d'assurance Desjardins.

➤ Pour l'Exercice L, préparez des notes pour un débat ou une table ronde.

HSG

➤ For a review and self-test on adjectives and adverbs; complete Exercises J–K of Module VI in your *HSG*.

K. Autrement dit. L'idée principale du texte de la Lecture 1 est que les Français sont attirés par différentes formules d'assurance-vie parce qu'elles représentent un bon placement. Expliquez d'après le texte

1. en quoi on peut se constituer un capital sans-risques.
2. quel est l'avantage du portefeuille en bourse acquis par l'intermédiaire d'une assurance-vie.
3. en quoi investir en unités de compte immobilier peut être plus attirant que d'acheter soi-même des propriétés immobilières.

L. A vous la parole! A votre avis, est-ce qu'il y a de meilleurs investissements possibles que l'assurance-vie? Si nécessaire, faites des recherches et demandez l'avis de spécialistes pour vous faire une opinion et discutez de cette question lors de votre prochain cours.

Lecture 2

Interview de M. Lepetit, assureur maritime à la retraite

M. Activité de pré-lecture. Répondez aux questions suivantes.

   1. Cherchez les mots suivants dans un dictionnaire français-français puis faites une phrase avec chacun d'entre eux.

   a. une avarie   **f.** un secours

   b. en détresse   **g.** un sauvetage

   c. manœuvrer   **h.** un remorqueur

   d. l'abordage   **i.** périlleux

   e. l'échouement   **j.** un port

   2. Maintenant, expliquez de quoi, selon vous, l'assurance maritime peut s'occuper. Donnez quelques exemples.

> ➤ The flow of spoken French is depicted here. Don't pay much attention to the punctuation (or lack thereof).

Interview de M. Lepetit, assureur maritime à la retraite

L'assurance maritime, ce n'est pas du tout l'assurance «incendie particulier» ou «vol» ou «individuelle accident» du particulier, c'est classé dans l'assurance industrielle et bénéficie d'un droit très spécial. Je mentionnerai deux exemples: l'exemple de l'assistance, les droits de l'assistance et le droit de l'avarie commune.

Premier exemple, l'assistance. Alors, l'assistance, c'est un phénomène qui se produit fréquemment. Un bateau est en détresse et n'est plus en mesure de manœuvrer, soit par suite d'incendie, d'abordage, d'échouement ou de ce qu'on voudra et il fait appel à un secours extérieur. Le secours doit lui dire «moi, je viens mais tu signes un contrat» «no cure no pay». Si je ne réussis pas, tu ne me devras rien mais si je réussis, tu me devras une indemnité sérieuse».

On signe toujours un contrat «no cure no pay»: pas de sauvetage, pas de paiement. Dans ces contrats, la personne humaine n'est jamais en cause, ce sont des biens matériels dont il s'agit. On sauve les personnes sans indemnité, on les sauve comme assistance en mer, la personne n'a pas de valeur dans ce contrat là, c'est uniquement les biens.

Alors imaginons que le sauveteur soit un remorqueur qui vient tirer un bateau d'une situation périlleuse et qui l'amène au port sain et sauf, l'indemnité d'assistance sera fixée par des arbitres, nommés par les deux parties qui vont examiner la valeur des biens sauvés, la valeur des biens mis en jeu par le sauveteur pour parvenir au sauvetage, la durée du sauvetage, la durée de l'intervention et les risques de l'intervention. Et quand ils auront soupesé tout ça, ils fixeront une indemnité d'assistance qui est généralement très rémunératrice, pour encourager les sauveteurs et puis pour couvrir le cas où, intervenant, ils n'ont rien pu sauver. Donc, il y a des sociétés de sauvetage, notamment hollandaises, qui ont des remorqueurs un peu partout dans le monde. Elles ont tout le matériel qu'il faut, des bases à Singapour, partout et elles peuvent intervenir assez rapidement. Mais pas besoin d'être un sauveteur professionnel, n'importe quel autre navire qui passe par là peut assister, sauver. Ça, c'est l'assistance, c'est très particulier ce contrat «no cure no pay».

Deuxième exemple: l'avarie commune qui est une autre spécificité du droit maritime. L'idée en est très simple: prenez

continued on page 370

continued from page 369

un capitaine qui part avec son bateau en bois et ses voiles. Il part de la Martinique par exemple, et va en France avec une cargaison de sucre et de rhum. Il arrive quelque part dans l'Atlantique et il s'échoue sur un rocher qu'il n'avait pas vu. En fonction de l'heure de la marée, le temps, la direction des vents et d'autres considérations parce que c'est vivant la mer, il se dit «Il faut que je me tire de là très vite parce que si j'attends trop longtemps, je risque de perdre mon bateau. Il n'y a qu'une seule solution, je n'ai pas d'autres moyens, il faut que je jette à la mer la moitié de ma cargaison. Cela va alléger le navire, je pourrai me sauver avec le reste de ma cargaison.» Donc, il jette à la mer une partie de la cargaison, son bateau reflotte, il rentre, il arrive à Nantes sans autre problème. Il s'agit d'un sacrifice qui a été fait volontairement pour sauver le navire. Ça, c'est essentiel pour différencier l'avarie commune des autres cas. Alors comment régler économiquement, juridiquement ce problème? Est-ce que la cargaison qui a été jetée à la mer pour sauver le reste doit supporter seule les conséquences? Alors c'est là qu'intervient le procédé d'avarie commune. Le capitaine fait les déclarations nécessaires en arrivant au port et il dit par exemple: «j'ai jeté la moitié de ma cargaison à la mer».

Il y a des experts, des dispatchers, qui vont se pencher sur le problème et qui vont évaluer le bateau, évaluer la cargaison restante, évaluer ce qui a été jeté à la mer et puis qui vont faire une répartition. Imaginons, par exemple, que le bateau valait cent, que la cargaison valait cent et qu'on en a jeté à la mer cinquante. Il est donc arrivé à bon port cent cinquante de l'ensemble mais tout le monde va contribuer, c'est l'avarie commune, tout le monde va contribuer à pro-rata des biens sauvés, sur les biens sacrifiés. C'est-à-dire, sur deux cents, on en a perdu volontairement cinquante, c'est le quart, chacun paiera un quart de la valeur des biens sauvés et l'autre recevra la valeur de ses marchandises moins un quart, comme si elles avaient été sauvées. C'est très simple dans cet exemple-là, mais quand on imagine ce que pose comme problèmes, par exemple, un porte-container de 25.000 tonnes dans une situation similaire avec des montagnes de containers comprenant des marchandises diverses pour plusieurs destinataires différents! Cela peut devenir un problème très difficile à régler.

Interview avec Monsieur Lepetit, ancien assureur maritime. Mars 1995.

N. A la recherche d'éléments précis du texte. Trouvez au moins quatre mots qui se rapportent au monde maritime, autres que ceux que vous avez cherchés dans le dictionnaire avant la lecture du texte, et expliquez-les.

O. Avez-vous compris? Répondez aux questions suivantes, à deux ou trois.

1. Quels exemples de problèmes en mer est-ce que M. Lepetit signale?
2. Pourquoi faut-il encourager les sauveteurs à venir? Comment sont-ils encouragés?
3. Comment est-ce que l'indemnité d'assistance est fixée?
4. Dans quels cas les capitaines décident-ils de faire le sacrifice volontaire d'une portion ou de la totalité des marchandises qu'ils transportent?

P. Vrai ou faux? Si les affirmations suivantes ne vous semblent pas correctes, corrigez-les de façon à ce qu'elles le deviennent.

A propos de l'assurance maritime

1. L'assurance maritime est basée sur les mêmes lois que les autres assurances.

2. L'assurance maritime fonctionne comme les autres assurances sauf l'assurance incendie.

3. L'assurance maritime est une assurance de type industriel.

4. L'assurance maritime s'appuie sur un droit très spécial qui ne s'applique à aucune autre assurance.

A propos de «no cure no pay»

1. Si les marchandises sont sauvées, elles seront payées.

2. Si le bateau qui part au sauvetage a des frais, ils seront remboursés.

3. Si des membres de l'équipage tombent malades, l'assurance maritime couvre une visite chez le médecin et les médicaments nécessaires.

4. Si le bateau qui transporte les marchandises a un accident, les frais de transport de ces marchandises ne seront pas remboursés.

A propos de l'avarie commune

1. L'avarie commune veut dire que tout le monde met ses marchandises en commun.

2. Quelquefois, il est préférable de perdre une partie de la cargaison au lieu de risquer de tout perdre.

3. C'est le capitaine qui décide de la valeur de ce qu'il a perdu.

4. Le capitaine doit quelquefois prendre des décisions difficiles pour sauver son navire et/ou une partie de sa cargaison.

5. Dans l'exemple donné, il s'agit d'un capitaine qui avait eu un accident en pleine mer.

6. Le problème du capitaine est que son bateau était très abîmé.

7. Le problème du bateau était qu'il n'avait pas assez d'eau pour tenir à flots.

8. En jetant une partie de la cargaison, le capitaine veut alléger son bateau.

9. Le capitaine veut récupérer ce qu'il a jeté par dessus bord, une fois que le bateau sera en pleine mer.

HSG

➤ Review the *Phonétique* section of Module VI in your *HSG*.

Quelques points de repère

Les entreprises françaises!

- En 1946, 34 sociétés françaises d'assurances ont été nationalisées et divisées en 9 groupes. En 1968, il y a eu un nouveau regroupement de ces sociétés qui a abouti à 4 grands groupes.

- En 1994, le plus grand de ces groupes, UAP (Union des Assurances de Paris) a été privatisé. Les groupes qui ne sont pas complètement privatisés ont 25% de leur capital ouvert aux investisseurs.

- En 1995, les dix premières compagnies d'assurances en France étaient l'UAP, AXA, CNP, AGF, GAN, Predica, Groupama, Commercial Union France, les Mutuelles du Mans et Generali-France.

L'ardoise

Le concept d'assurance est très ancien. Il y a des groupes et des caisses de solidarité qui se sont formés de l'antiquité à la Renaissance dans plusieurs pays du monde pour aider, en cas de problème, les gens de certains métiers comportant de gros risques. En Europe, l'assurance-incendie, l'assurance-vie et l'assurance maritime sont parmi les plus anciennes. Ce n'est qu'au cours de la deuxième moitié du XIXᵉ siècle que les assurances se sont généralisées en France.

➤ Qui aurait besoin de la sorte d'assurance présentée ci-dessous dans le dépliant du Crédit Lyonnais?

PROTECTION JURIDIQUE

" A l'assurance d'être bien défendu, je dis OUI."

Lion assurance
GROUPE CRÉDIT LYONNAIS

---

l'assurance
d'être bien défendu !

EP

**EUROPÉENNE
DE PROTECTION JURIDIQUE**

95, rue Saint-Lazare 75009 Paris
Société Anonyme au capital de 10 000 000 de F - RCS Paris B 304 177 629
Entreprise régie par le code des assurances

Vous appréciez
les services du Crédit Lyonnais,
découvrez son secteur Assurance.
Il protège au mieux votre famille
et vous-même, vos biens,
votre activité professionnelle et vos loisirs.
Vous aussi, vous avez tout à gagner à dire
"OUI, à l'Assurance d'un grand groupe".

Lion Assurance : Société de Courtage d'Assurances - S.A. au Capital de 5 000 000 F - RCS Paris B 340 856 608 (87 BQ 39 101)

Réf. Dpl. 5 - 1992

SAPA

Lion assurance
GROUPE CRÉDIT LYONNAIS

COUPON-RÉPONSE

Lion Assurance vous propose
une large gamme de
produits Assurances dommages :

☐ COMPLÉMENTAIRE FRAIS DE SANTÉ
☐ ASSURANCE FAMILIALE ACCIDENTS
☐ PRÉVOYANCE ACCIDENT-MALADIE
☐ LION HOSPITALISATION
☐ CONTRAT IMPATRIÉS-EXPATRIÉS
☐ PROTECTION JURIDIQUE
☐ MULTIRISQUE HABITATION
☐ TOUS RISQUES ŒUVRES D'ART ET OBJETS PRÉCIEUX
☐ MULTIRISQUE HABITATION "JEUNES 18-25 ANS"
☐ ASSURANCE AUTOMOBILE
☐ PROTECTION DU CONDUCTEUR
☐ ASSURANCE MOTO
☐ ASSISTANCE MOTO
☐ MULTIRISQUE PROFESSIONNELLE
☐ NAVIGATION DE PLAISANCE
☐ ASSURANCE SANTÉ CHIEN ET CHAT
☐ ASSURANCE MULTILOISIRS

Votre conseiller Lion Assurance est un professionnel de l'assurance. N'hésitez pas à l'interroger sur votre cas particulier. Il vous donnera tous renseignements et pourra au plus vite établir avec vous un devis personnalisé.

Lion assurance
GROUPE CRÉDIT LYONNAIS

ETOILE PROTECTION
ACCIDENT

Une assurance "sur mesure" qui vous offre :

1 Une protection complète en cas d'accident : des indemnités hospitalisation, des prestations d'assistance assurées par EUROP ASSISTANCE, ainsi qu'une assurance décès et invalidité.

2 Un service téléphonique fonctionnant sans interruption 7 jours sur 7, 24 heures sur 24 : au bout du fil, une personne est toujours là pour vous aider.

3 Des garanties à effet immédiat : une indemnité d'hospitalisation et une assistance à domicile dès les premières 24 heures d'hospitalisation.

4 Un bénéficiaire librement choisi : il recevra le capital garanti, en cas de décès accidentel.

5 Une fiscalité avantageuse :
- un capital décès exonéré de droits de succession,
- un capital invalidité net d'impôts,
- des indemnités d'hospitalisation nettes d'impôts.

6 Des primes mensuelles minimes : vous choisissez vous-même le montant en fonction de la formule qui vous convient.

➤ Cherchez tous les termes qui ont à faire avec les impôts.

L'autre côté du dépliant du Crédit du Nord présenté à la page 342.

Une date importante!

L'assurance automobile est obligatoire en France depuis 1958.

Les chiffres parlent!

- En 1992, l'UAP employait 38.862 salariés, l'AXA, 27.400 et le Groupe Victoire, 16.968.
- Le chiffre d'affaires mondial de l'assurance française s'élevait à 819,7 milliards de francs en 1993.
- Le secteur de l'assurance dans sa totalité regroupe 600 entreprises qui emploient 1% de la population active française soit environ 211.000 personnes.

Réflexions sur le travail en équipe

Pour obtenir les meilleurs résultats possibles, il est important de travailler dans une atmosphère chaleureuse, de confiance, basée sur le respect réciproque.

Lexique

un agent: **Un agent** d'assurance représente les intérêts de la compagnie d'assurance et sert d'intermédiaire entre la compagnie et ses clients.

Autrefois, **les agents** avaient une indépendance beaucoup plus marquée car il n'y avait pas de fax et même si le téléphone existait déjà, il coûtait cher. **L'agent** prenait donc souvent des engagements sans les discuter d'abord avec ses supérieurs.

une avarie: **Une avarie**, c'est un sinistre. C'est le dossier, le réglement administratif. Aux bureaux d'une compagnie d'assurances, on parle toujours du service sinistre, c'est-à-dire de la gestion; mais **l'avarie** c'est le dommage lui-même. Le bateau qui s'échoue, il est **en avarie**. Ça devient un sinistre quand le cas arrive sur le bureau du dispatcher ou de l'assureur.

En cas d'**avarie**, consultez le commissaire **des avaries** qui représente l'assureur et peut envoyer un expert pour déterminer l'étendue des dommages et faire un rapport.

un commissaire-priseur: **Un commissaire-priseur** est une personne chargée d'estimer officiellement la valeur d'objets mobiliers.

Si vous ne connaissez pas la valeur d'une œuvre d'art ou d'un bijou, vous pouvez consulter **un commissaire-priseur**.

un courtier: **Un courtier** est une personne qui représente les intérêts du client, c'est-à-dire de l'assuré.

Les courtiers discutent avec les agents pour déterminer le taux de la prime ou le remboursement des dommages.

une exclusion: **Une exclusion,** c'est une cause de dommage que l'assureur n'entend pas garantir. Par exemple, ce qu'on appelle le vice propre est toujours exclu. C'est un vice inhérent à la nature de la marchandise.

Prenons l'exemple d'une cargaison de blé. Vous avez du blé que vous allez expédier de Lorient à Shanghaï. Il arrivent en mauvais état, pourri, moisi. On va nommer des experts pour obtenir une expertise. On va déterminer que ce blé n'était pas suffisamment sec pour faire le voyage de Lorient à Shanghaï; il était à un taux d'humidité trop important. Il faut préciser qu'on prend des échantillons quand on envoie des marchandises en vrac. Le blé n'était pas susceptible de faire le voyage et d'arriver en bon état. C'était donc du vice. Le dommage subi n'est pas la conséquence d'un risque de transport mais la conséquence d'un état de la marchandise avant son transport. Ce n'est pas un risque de transport, c'est un risque **exclu;** c'est **une exclusion.**

les facultés *(f)*: **Les facultés** sont les marchandises transportées par le navire ou l'avion.

Je viens de négocier un contrat pour assurer la cargaison de produits pharmaceutiques de Bordeaux à Madras. Le contrat signé est une police **facultés.**

l'indemnité *(f)*: **L'indemnité,** c'est la somme déterminée par un dispatcher qui représente le montant du dommage subi qui sera à la charge de l'assureur. **L'indemnité,** c'est donc la somme que l'assuré reçoit pour le dédommager. C'est le montant que l'assureur va verser après le sinistre.

Dans la presse, on lit souvent, par exemple: «Un Tel a mis le feu à sa maison pour toucher la prime d'assurance.» C'est faux, évidemment car il s'agit de **l'indemnité** et non de la prime!

la marchandise en vrac: La marchandise en vrac, c'est de la marchandise non-emballée, c'est du minerai de fer, c'est du charbon, c'est du blé, c'est tout ce qui se manipule sans emballage et qui est généralement chargé en grande quantité avec des moyens de chargement automatiques comme des tapis-roulant, des bennes, (ou des suceuses).

Les péniches transportent souvent de **la marchandise en vrac.**

la police d'assurance: La police, c'est le contrat **d'assurance** qui, pour une période déterminée, lie l'assureur et l'assuré et stipule les conditions de l'accord qui a été passé. **La police** précise le nom de l'assureur et celui de l'assuré, décrit les risques couverts ainsi que les exclusions éventuelles et indique le montant de la prime à payer.

Range **ta police d'assuranc**e dans un endroit sûr, dans un coffre à la banque, par exemple, parce que c'est un document extrêmement important qui prouve que tu es assuré.

la prime: La prime, c'est le montant que le client doit payer pour être assuré. Quand une personne a réglé **la prime** de son assurance, cette personne est assurée.

— A combien se monte **ta prime** d'assurance-incendie?
— Je ne sais pas. Attends, je vais regarder sur la police d'assurance qui est dans mon bureau.

un sinistre: Un sinistre, c'est un dommage. **Le sinistre,** c'est en quelque sorte l'événement qui ouvre droit à une indemnité. Par exemple, un incendie, c'est **un sinistre** et l'assuré touchera l'indemnité correspondant au dommage qu'il a subi, à condition bien sûr d'être suffisamment assuré. Au siège de la compagnie d'assurance, il y a une branche qui s'occupe uniquement **des sinistres,** c'est-à-dire des accidents ou de circonstances spéciales qui ont causé des dommages aux biens assurés.

Je ne me souviens pas des détails **du sinistre.** Je dois consulter le dossier avant de pouvoir répondre à votre question.

un souscripteur: Le souscripteur ou underwriter, qu'il soit salarié ou indépendant, c'est celui qui accepte le risque pour le compte d'un assureur ou pour le compte de Lloyds si c'est un underwriter de Lloyds.

Il y a de bons risques et de mauvais risques. Il est toujours difficile de trouver **un souscripteur** pour un mauvais risque, c'est-à-dire un risque qui a une grande chance d'avoir lieu et donc de causer des frais *(expenses)* à une assurance.

un tiers: Dans le domaine des assurances, lorsqu'on parle de **tiers** on veut dire une autre personne, un étranger. Il s'agirait alors de la victime d'un accident non causé par elle-même.

La responsabilité civile assure une personne pour les préjudices qu'elle peut causer à **un tiers.**

➤ Discutez ce proverbe avec votre «partenaire» (un membre de votre groupe).

*P*aroles de sagesse

Qui veut un cheval sans défaut doit aller à pied.

*E*xpression écrite

Formes négatives

Cette section va vous permettre d'améliorer votre connaissance des formes négatives. Dans le paragraphe suivant, observez les différentes expressions en caractères gras qui impliquent une négation. Regardez bien aussi comment elles sont utilisées.

Retour au Minitel

*De nos jours, le Minitel offre un service très apprécié. Il facilite de nombreuses opérations et, bien qu'il **ne** soit **pas** encore utilisé dans tous les foyers, il **n'**existe **aucune** administration que **ne** possède son Minitel. Il permet, par exemple, d'effectuer des réservations ou des achats de son domicile pour les personnes qui **ne** peuvent **ni** se déplacer, **ni** se libérer aux heures voulues. Il donne également accès aux corrigés et aux résultats des examens et des concours dès leur sortie, et permet ainsi de **ne pas** encombrer les standards téléphoniques et de **ne plus** être obligé(e) de se déplacer sur les lieux d'affichage des résultats. Il **n'**existe aujourd'hui presqu'**aucun** domaine qui **ne** possède son sevice Minitel. Il semble même que cet éventail de possibilités **ne** cesse **jamais** de s'élargir.*

Q. A vos plumes! A vous maintenant d'écrire un paragraphe d'environ 150 mots sur les assurances en utilisant les expressions négatives en gras dans le texte ainsi que celles qui suivent.

ne... nulle part	ne... que
ne... pas encore	ne... rien

> **Dans le dossier suivant, nous allons étudier la Bourse et plusieurs formes d'investissements.**

*L*a Bourse et les investissements

Le dix-huitième et dernier dossier vous invite à faire un premier pas *(step)* dans l'univers complexe de la Bourse. La Bourse est un marché financier qui permet une interaction entre les acheteurs et les vendeurs de valeurs mobilières *(securities)*. La Bourse constitue un rouage *(mechanism)* essentiel de l'économie et un lieu privilégié pour les investisseurs. Vous allez, entre autres, entendre une conversation téléphonique concernant l'achat et la vente d'actions cotées en Bourse et étudier le rôle de la Bourse. Les différentes lectures vous permettront d'explorer quelques facettes du monde des sociétés cotées en Bourse et leur rôle dans l'économie.

*A*ctivité d'introduction

La Bourse et les investissements

A. La Bourse. Mettez-vous par groupes de deux ou trois personnes et réfléchissez aux questions suivantes.

> **1.** Qu'est-ce que c'est que la Bourse? Pouvez-vous de façon très générale en expliquer le principe?
>
> **2.** Connaissez-vous le nom de quelques sociétés américaines cotées en Bourse? Lesquelles? Donnez au moins huit exemples.
>
> **3.** Connaissez-vous le nom de quelques sociétés françaises cotées en Bourse? Lesquelles? Donnez au moins six exemples.

Les mots pour le dire

Vocabulaire de base

VERBES

acheter, racheter	*to buy; to buy up, buy back*
baisser	*to lower*
céder	*to transfer one's property; to sell or dispose of*
coter, être coté	*to quote, to be quoted, to be listed*
se défaire de	*to get rid of*
déléguer	*to delegate*
se dévaloriser, se valoriser	*to drop in value; to appreciate*
échanger	*to exchange*
émettre	*to transmit, broadcast; to issue*
financer	*to finance*
fixer	*to fix*
fluctuer	*to fluctuate*
grimper	*to climb*
investir	*to invest*
monter	*to rise*
rapporter	*to earn; to bring back*
réaliser une bonne ou mauvaise affaire	*to make a good or bad deal*
recevoir	*to receive*
spéculer	*to speculate*
surveiller (les cours)	*to look after, watch, monitor (the market trends)*
tomber	*to fall*
varier	*to vary*
vendre, revendre	*to sell, resell*

NOMS

un acheteur	*buyer*
une action	*stock*
la Bourse	*stock market*
le capital	*capital*
une commission	*commission*
une cotation	*quotation, quoting (of a firm's shares on the stock exchange)*
le cours d'échange, de change	*exchange rate*
une créance	*claim, debt*
des demandeurs (m)	*plaintiffs, petitioners; person asking for; purchasers*
un dividende	*dividend*
un échange	*exchange*
une émission (d'obligations ou d'actions)	*issue, issuing (of bonds and stocks)*
une entreprise privatisée (publique)	*privatized (public) company*
une fluctuation	*fluctuation*

des frais (m) de courtage (m)	brokerage fee, costs
l'incertitude (f)	uncertainty
un indice boursier	stock market index
la liquidité	liquid assets; liquidity
le marché financier	financial market
le marché primaire (secondaire)	primary (secondary) market
la négociabilité	negotiability
une obligation	bond
une offre publique d'achat (une OPA)	public purchase offer
une offre publique d'échange (une OPE)	public exchange offer
des offreurs (m)	sellers
une part (de société)	share (in a company)
la performance	performance; how well a thing goes
un(e) propriétaire	owner
un titre	title
une transaction	transaction
la valeur boursière	security; stock or share
une valeur mobilière	transferable security
un vendeur	seller
le volume de transactions	transaction volume

ADJECTIFS

avantageux(se)	advantageous
boursier(ière)	having to do with the stock market
échangé(e)	exchanged
émis(e)	issued
fixé(e)	fixed
flottant(e)	floating
mobilier(ière)	transferable
négociable	negotiable
officiel(le)	official
réglementé(e)	regulated

ADVERBES ET EXPRESSIONS ADVERBIALES

antérieurement	beforehand
à court (long) terme	short (long) term
temporairement	temporarily

➤ Prenez des notes pour que vous puissiez mieux jouer à *Mot de passe.*

➤ Be ready for *Mot de passe.*

B. Définitions provisoires à terminer. Complétez les phrases suivantes.

1. Le _____ d'une action ou d'une obligation est déterminé par la confrontation de l'offre et de la demande pour ce titre sur le marché boursier.

2. Lorsque le capital d'une société est divisé en actions et que ces actions ont une valeur estimée, évaluée sur le marché boursier, on dit que ces actions sont _____ en Bourse.

3. Lorsque je veux vendre les actions dont je suis propriétaire, je peux les _____.

4. Lorsque j'achète des actions à un prix avantageux uniquement parce

que je m'attends à ce que leur valeur monte assez rapidement, je fais de la _____ parce que je compte sur une augmentation rapide de leur valeur pour les revendre ensuite.

5. Le cours des actions _____, c'est-à-dire qu'il change de jour en jour et même d'heure en heure, selon l'offre et la demande.

6. La _____, c'est le lieu où sont échangées des valeurs mobilières. C'est un marché financier.

C. Définitions provisoires à créer. Par groupes de deux, donnez une définition provisoire pour les mots suivants.

1. une entreprise publique

2. négociable

3. des frais de courtage

4. rentable

5. temporairement

HSG

➤ Study the verbs *(se)* ▪ *servir* and *suivre/valoir* and complete Exercises P–Q of Module VI in your *HSG*.

Observations

Introduction à la Bourse

▪ Il y a sept places boursières en France. Les six bourses régionales sont installées dans les villes de Bordeaux, Lille, Lyon, Marseille, Nancy et Nantes, la septième étant en plein centre de Paris dans le premier arrondissement. La Bourse de Paris, aussi appelée le Palais Brongniart du nom de son architecte, est de loin la plus importante.

▪ La Bourse contribue au financement des entreprises. Les émetteurs de titres (actions et obligations) peuvent être des sociétés publiques ou privées qui ont besoin de capitaux et font appel à la Bourse pour financer leurs investissements ou même leurs déficits. Pour l'émetteur, c'est une manière de subvenir à ses besoins financiers à meilleur marché que s'il s'adressait à une banque, par exemple.

▪ La Bourse est un lieu où les émetteurs et les investisseurs se rencontrent et où sont échangés des titres, à savoir principalement des actions, des obligations, des emprunts d'Etat, des bons du Trésor, des SICAV, ainsi que de nombreux autres instruments financiers plus spécifiques et complexes. C'est à la Bourse que sont déterminés les cours d'échange de ces produits. C'est aussi là que sont établis les cours de l'or, des métaux précieux et des devises étrangères. Les transactions sur titres sont effectuées par les Sociétés de Bourse uniquement, et la loi de l'offre et de la demande détermine le niveau des cours des titres.

▪ La Bourse assure donc la liquidité des valeurs mobilières. C'est là que les investisseurs peuvent vendre ou acheter des titres, tous les jours ouvrables de 10 heures à 17 heures sans interruption, grâce au système CAC (Cotation Assistée en Continu). Ce système a été mis en place en 1987.

Le marché des actions et obligations est divisé en deux parties: le marché primaire qui s'occupe de l'émission d'actions et d'obligations, c'est-à-dire de l'émission de nouveaux titres et le marché secondaire qui s'occupe uniquement de l'échange des valeurs mobilières, actions et obligations existantes, c'est-à-dire déjà émises. C'est sur le marché secondaire que les cours des valeurs mobilières varient. Il existe plusieurs autres marchés, les deux principaux sont le Marché à Terme et le Marché au Comptant. Pour le Marché à Terme, les transactions sur titres ne sont pas soldées *(sold)* immédiatement, mais le jour de la liquidation (dernier mercredi de chaque mois). C'est donc un marché ouvert à la spéculation: on peut revendre des titres que l'on n'a pas encore payés, ou bien vendre des titres que l'on ne possède pas encore. Au contraire, dans le cas du Marché au Comptant, toutes les transactions sont soldées immédiatement, et on ne peut pas faire de vente à découvert.

L'A.F.P. est située sur la Place de la Bourse à Paris.

Les Sociétés de Bourse exercent trois activités:

1. Elles négocient l'exécution des ordres d'achat et de vente de valeurs mobilières sur le marché. Elles ont donc une responsabilité de négociation.

2. Elles gèrent les flux de titres et de capitaux et font en sorte que les acheteurs obtiennent ce qu'ils veulent et que les vendeurs soient payés. C'est ce qu'on appelle la compensation.

3. Elles conservent les titres de leurs clients sous forme de comptes courants. Il s'agit de la conservation.

Malgré la forte volatilité des cours, la très grande variété des titres et des marchés qui caractérise la Bourse de Paris permet à chacun de satisfaire au mieux ses propres exigences: acheter des titres qui permettront peut-être un fort rendement mais dont le risque est élevé ou simplement diversifier son portefeuille en achetant des titres de nature différente, minimiser son risque financier en choisissant des SICAV, des bons du Trésor ou des parts d'emprunts d'Etat, etc.

Il faut malgré tout reconnaître que le London Stock Exchange garde sa suprématie par rapport aux autres Bourses européennes telles que la Bourse de Paris, grâce à une forte tradition de développement continu et d'avant-gardisme dans ce domaine.

D. A la recherche d'éléments précis. Après avoir lu très attentivement les informations qui précèdent, complétez les phrases suivantes.

continued on page 382

continued from page 381

1. Le premier rôle joué par les Sociétés de Bourse est celui de la
_____.

2. Le nom de l'architecte de la Bourse de Paris est
_____.

3. En France, il y a _____ places boursières.

4. Les sociétés publiques et privées qui ont _____ des titres sont cotées en Bourse.

5. Pour une entreprise, cela coûte moins cher de régler son financement en passant par l'intermédiaire de la _____ qu'en passant par une autre institution financière.

6. C'est la _____ qui détermine les fluctuations des cours des valeurs cotées en Bourse.

E. Avez-vous compris? Répondez aux questions suivantes.

1. Qui peut émettre des titres?

2. Qu'est-ce que c'est qu'un titre?

3. Quel est le rôle d'une Société de Bourse?

4. Où se trouvent les Bourses françaises?

5. Quelle est la Bourse européenne la plus importante?

6. Pourquoi est-ce que les entreprises font appel à la Bourse?

F. Trouvez l'intrus! Parmi les listes suivantes, rayez *(cross out)* le mot ou groupe de mots qui n'est pas à sa place.

1. *la Bourse:* des investisseurs, des émetteurs, le système CAC, l'intervention du Ministre des Finances, les Sociétés de Bourse

2. *un portefeuille diversifié:* des SICAV, des bons du Trésor, de grosses sommes en liquide, des actions, des obligations

3. *le marché secondaire:* des actions, des obligations, des valeurs mobilières, l'émission de nouveaux titres

4. *la grande liquidité de la Bourse:* la vente de titres, l'achat de titres, des délais très longs, des volumes importants échangés

5. *le Palais Brongniart:* Paris, Bordeaux, premier arrondissement, la Bourse, le cœur des marchés financiers français

G. Vrai ou faux? Les affirmations qui suivent, sont-elles correctes ou non?

1. Les cours de l'or sont déterminés au Palais Brongniart.

2. On peut faire des ventes à découvert sur tous les marchés de la Bourse de Paris.

3. La loi de l'offre et de la demande détermine le nombre d'investisseurs présents à la Bourse.

4. Il n'existe qu'une seule Bourse en France.

5. Pour investir son argent en France, il faut toujours passer par la Bourse.

6. La forte volatilité des cours fait référence au fait que les cours peuvent changer de valeur extrêmement rapidement.

HSG

➤ Study the *Encadré supplémentaire* on nouns and complete Exercises R–T of Module VI in your *HSG*.

Dialogue

Un intermédiaire d'une Société de Bourse au téléphone avec une cliente

H. Activité de pré-lecture. Mettez-vous par petits groupes de deux ou trois et répondez aux questions suivantes.

1. En vous basant sur votre simple bon sens, quels sont, selon vous, les avantages et les inconvénients d'investir son argent à la Bourse?

2. En quoi est-ce que la Bourse est un indicateur de la santé de l'économie d'un pays?

3. Si l'on ne veut pas passer par la Bourse, quelles sont les autres manières possibles de placer son argent?

Un intermédiaire d'une Société de Bourse au téléphone avec une cliente

Mme Amar: Allô? Pourrais-je parler à Monsieur Ploquin, s'il vous plaît?

La secrétaire: Oui Madame, c'est de la part de qui?

Mme Amar: Madame Amar.

La secrétaire: Oui, Monsieur Ploquin est sur une autre ligne. Pourriez-vous patienter quelques instants, — cela ne devrait pas être long — ou bien préférez-vous qu'il vous rappelle?

Mme Amar: Je préfère attendre.

La secrétaire: Bon. Alors ne quittez pas, Madame.

M. Ploquin: Allô? Madame Amar? Excusez-moi de vous avoir fait attendre. J'étais en communication. Alors voilà ce que j'ai fait pour vous aujourd'hui. Je vous ai acheté 750 Saint Gobain à 654.

Mme Amar: Elle était à 655,51 hier?

M. Ploquin: Oui, effectivement et elle ne va pas baisser beaucoup plus que cela. Je vous ai aussi pris 600 Accor à 619. En baisse par rapport à hier de 2,06 mais très stable puisque vous vouliez quelque chose de plus stable que vos EuroDisney que j'ai vendues à 8,70. Elles avaient encore baissé de 4,40 par rapport à hier.

Mme Amar: Ah, ça fait mal. C'était trop spéculatif.

M. Ploquin: Oui, pourtant je vous avais conseillé d'attendre encore.

Mme Amar: Non, non, je préfère vendre. Comment vont mes Legrand et mes Havas?

M. Ploquin: Très fort: 6700 et 430,50. Ce sont de grandes valeurs. Elles ne bougent pratiquement pas.

Mme Amar:	Bon, je vous rappellerai la semaine prochaine.
M. Ploquin:	Très bien. Au revoir, Madame Amar.
Mme Amar:	Au revoir, Monsieur.

I. A la recherche d'éléments précis. Répondez aux questions suivantes.

1. Le texte mentionne le nom de cinq actions différentes. Lesquelles?

2. Connaissez-vous au moins un de ces noms? Expliquez ce que vous en savez.

3. Complétez le tableau suivant avec les noms et les chiffres que l'on peut trouver dans le dialogue. Pour rendre compte de la stabilité de l'action en question, utilisez le signe + quand elle est en hausse, le signe 0 quand elle est stable et le signe - quand elle est en baisse.

Nom des actions	Cote de la veille	Cote du jour	Stabilité
Saint Gobain			
EuroDisney			
Accor			
Legrand			
Havas			

J. Avez-vous compris? Répondez aux questions suivantes en cochant la réponse correcte.

1. Que dit le texte de l'action Saint Gobain?
   a. Elle a baissé par rapport à la veille.
   b. Elle est en train de remonter.
   c. Elle est restée à la même valeur ces derniers temps.

2. Que dit Mme Amar des actions EuroDisney?
   a. Elles représentent un bon placement.
   b. Elles sont trop risquées.
   c. Elles ont été décevantes.

3. D'après M. Ploquin, les actions Legrand et Havas sont
   a. spéculatives.
   b. excellentes.
   c. en baisse.

Pour la bourse en direct...

Notez ici les quelques codes valeurs SICOVAM qui vous intéressent, par ex : ELF 12042.

Pour consulter votre sélection de valeurs notez votre mot de passe

➤ Notez bien la publicité pour la Bourse qui est sur l'envers de la carte Allô privatisations. L'autre côté de cette carte se trouve dans la section «Ouverture» à la page 343.

K. Vrai ou faux? Si les affirmations suivantes ne vous semblent pas correctes, modifiez-les de façon à ce qu'elles le soient et comparez vos affirmations ainsi corrigées avec celles du reste de votre groupe.

Monsieur Ploquin a

1. vendu les actions Legrand de Mme Amar.
2. conseillé à Mme Amar de ne pas vendre ses EuroDisney tout de suite.
3. acheté 619 actions Accor.
4. conseillé à Mme Amar d'acheter des actions moins spéculatives.
5. acheté ce jour-là 1.350 actions pour Mme Amar.

L. A compléter. Finissez les phrases suivantes d'après les informations que vous pouvez tirer du dialogue. Attention, répondez au passé!

1. Lorsque Madame Amar a appelé, Monsieur Ploquin n'a pas répondu au téléphone immédiatement parce qu'il _____.
2. Il annonce à sa cliente qu'il _____ 754 actions Saint Gobain.
3. On voit que Mme Amar connaît déjà cette action car elle sait que la veille, cette action _____.
4. M. Ploquin a vendu les actions EuroDisney car Mme Amar _____.
5. M. Ploquin précise que par rapport à la veille, les actions EuroDisney _____.
6. Mme Amar a demandé à son agent comment _____ ses actions Legrand et Havas.
7. M. Ploquin a annoncé que les actions Legrand et Havas _____.

HSG

➤ Review the usage of the three primary past tenses in French by completing Exercises L–O of Module VI in your *HSG*.

Lecture 1

L'investissement international au Québec

➤ Ensuite posez ces questions à une personne de votre groupe.

M. Activité de pré-lecture. Répondez aux questions suivantes.

1. Dans le monde des affaires, «l'heure est à la mondialisation». Expliquez ce que cela veut dire.
2. Voyez-vous autour de vous des signes ou des exemples du phénomène de mondialisation? Lesquels? Citez au moins quatre exemples.
3. On parle souvent du Canada et des Etats-Unis comme du «nouveau monde». Citez le nom de cinq pays appartenant au «vieux monde».

PERFORM

SAVOIR ET SAVOIR-FAIRE

420, RUE McGILL, BUREAU 100
MONTRÉAL (QUÉBEC) H2Y2G1
(514) 861-7000

L'investissement international au Québec

«Chaque matin, Margaret Coughtrie, gestionnaire de portefeuille à la Caisse de dépôt et placement du Québec, reçoit un très volumineux courrier en provenance d'Europe. Au bas mot, quinze centimètres d'analyses de firmes de courtage *(brokerage)*, de rapports annuels de compagnies, de communiqués de presse s'accumulent sur son bureau. A cette imposante correspondance s'ajoute un abonnement au *Financial Times* — le quotidien britannique imprimé sur du papier saumon — en plus des nombreux envois par télécopieur que lui font parvenir des courtiers, presque tous des Européens. Et puis, il y a les appels téléphoniques... A l'évidence, beaucoup de gens des «vieux pays» s'intéressent à Margaret Coughtrie.

«Cela s'explique. Cette jeune femme, originaire d'Ecosse, gère le portefeuille d'actions d'Europe continentale de la Caisse: rien de moins que 450 millions de dollars investis dans une quarantaine de compagnies de treize pays différents. Jour après jour, Margaret Coughtrie scrute, décortique *(peel)*, évalue, soupèse cette imposante masse d'informations afin de choisir les meilleurs titres boursiers d'Europe continentale. Son objectif: battre le marché, c'est-à-dire l'indice de référence Morgan Stanley International pour son secteur géographique,

l'équivalent du TSE 300 pour l'économie canadienne.

«Tout comme Margaret Coughtrie, une dizaine de gestionnaires et analystes de la Caisse vivent déjà à l'heure des marchés boursiers internationaux. Ils placent actuellement tout près de 10% de l'actif de l'institution, 4,4 milliards de dollars au total, sur les marchés boursiers américains, anglais, allemands, européens, japonais et sud-est asiatiques. Cinq autres gestionnaires placent environ 200 millions dans des fonds généraux et spécialisés, des banques d'affaires et des sociétés en commandite œuvrant à l'étranger. Si l'on ajoute les valeurs immobilières que la Caisse détient sur les marchés internationaux et les obligations de gouvernements étrangers de son portefeuille, c'est près de 5,6 milliards de dollars que l'institution place à l'extérieur du Canada, ou 12% du total de ses placements. Il y a dix ans, cette proportion n'atteignait que 2,3%.»

Extrait de Roger Poupart, «La Caisse de dépôt et placement du Québec: les nouvelles stratégies de développement international», paru dans *FORCES*, N° 107, 1994, p. 21, Montréal, Québec.

N. Avez-vous compris? Après avoir bien relu le texte, complétez les phrases suivantes en cochant les réponses qui vous paraissent correctes. Attention: quelquefois, il y a plus d'une réponse correcte.

1. Margaret Coughtrie

   a. écrit des articles financiers pour *Financial Times*.

   b. gère un portefeuille.

   c. préfère ne pas travailler avec les banques européennes.

   d. est la seule gestionnaire de la Caisse de dépôt et de placement du Québec.

2. Gérer un portefeuille signifie

   a. placer l'argent de clients qui ont fait des investissements.

   b. écrire les rapports annuels de compagnies pour lesquelles on travaille.

   c. acheter des titres boursiers.

3. Le *Financial Times* est

    a. un quotidien britannique d'informations générales.

    b. un journal qui est specialisé dans tout ce qui touche au monde des finances.

    c. un quotidien britannique qui offre un supplément spécial «Canada».

    d. un magazine économique.

4. D'après ce texte, Margaret Coughtrie obtient les informations dont elle a besoin par

    a. courrier.   **d.** la presse.

    b. téléphone.   **e.** ses contacts avec les courtiers.

    c. télécopie.

O. Synonymes. Margaret Coughtrie analyse soigneusement toutes les informations qu'elle reçoit. Quels sont, parmi les verbes de la liste suivante, les synonymes d'analyser qui sont employés dans le texte?

    1. étudier   **5.** décortiquer

    2. scruter   **6.** soupeser

    3. détenir   **7.** choisir

    4. s'accumuler   **8.** évaluer

P. A vos plumes! Faites une phrase avec les verbes suivants que vous utiliserez dans des contextes différents.

    1. scruter   **3.** évaluer

    2. décortiquer   **4.** soupeser

HSG

➤ Continue your review of the past by completing Exercises H–J of Module VI in your *HSG*.

Lecture 2

L'entreprise française la plus créatrice de richesses en 1994

Q. Activité de pré-lecture. A deux ou trois, discutez les questions suivantes.

    1. Que veut dire, pour une entreprise, conserver des racines familiales?

    2. Que signifie, pour une entreprise, avoir une stratégie internationale?

    3. Expliquez avec vos propres mots les mots suivants.

        a. stable

        b. diluer

        c. la croissance

    4. Dans quels contextes différents les trois mots qui précèdent peuvent-ils être utilisés? Donnez différents exemples.

L'entreprise française la plus créatrice de richesses en 1994

La MVA *(Market Value Added)*, c'est la valeur marchande d'une entreprise cotée. L'EVA *(Economic Value Added)*, c'est sa capacité à produire plus de capital qu'elle n'en utilise. [...]

Avec Carrefour, je mondialise!

L'entreprise française qui crée le plus de valeur est une société qui conserve ses racines familiales, qui pratique le même métier depuis trente-cinq ans, et qui conduit une stratégie internationale. Carrefour est classé N° 1 au Top 100 de la création de richesses, établi par le cabinet Stern, Stewart & Co. Selon la méthode MVA, 1 franc investi par les actionnaires de Carrefour générait 4 francs de valeur ajoutée. Du premier supermarché à Annecy, en 1960, au premier hypermarché à Sainte-Geneviève-des-Bois, en 1963; de la première ouverture en Espagne et au Brésil, dans les années 70, à l'achat d'Euromarché, en 1991, l'histoire de Carrefour suit une ligne droite: stabilité de l'actionnariat majoritaire et déplacement insensible du centre de gravité géographique. Le groupe bascule cette année dans le camp des entreprises mondialisées: 117 hypermarchés en France et 117 à l'étranger, mais dans quelques mois une demi-douzaine d'ouvertures hors de France (notamment en Argentine et au Brésil). A nos confrères de LSA, Daniel Bernard, le PDG du groupe, explique que "plus le groupe se mondialise, moins il court de risques. Passé un certain stade, les risques se diluent". L'essentiel, pour Carrefour, est de s'installer là où sont les gisements de croissance. Au premier semestre, ses ventes en France ont augmenté de 6,5% (ce qui n'est pas si mal au regard de la consommation nationale). Mais, dans le même temps, elles ont bondi de 23% dans les magasins brésiliens, et de 25% à Taïwan. Depuis son introduction, en 1970, à la Bourse de Paris, l'action Carrefour, hors dividende, a été multipliée par 118.

Tiré de *l'Expansion* N° 512 du 10 novembre 1995, Cahier N° 2.

➤ Dans quel arrondissement de Paris, la Bourse se trouve-t-elle?

BOURSE DE PARIS
SOCIETE DES BOURSES FRANÇAISES

DÉPARTEMENT COMMUNICATION
39, rue Cambon - 75001 PARIS
TÉL. : (1) 49 27 10 00 - TÉLÉCOPIE : (1) 49 27 14 33 - TÉLEX : 215 561 F
S.A. à Statut d'Institution Financière Spécialisée

R. A la recherche d'éléments précis du texte. Relisez le texte jusqu'à ce que vous puissiez répondre aux questions suivantes.

1. En quelle année et dans quelle ville est-ce que Carrefour est né?

2. Combien de magasins Carrefour y avait-il en France et à l'étranger en 1995?

3. Qu'est-ce qui montre que le groupe Carrefour était encore en plein développement en 1995?

4. Quand est-ce que Carrefour a été coté en Bourse pour la première fois?

5. Qui est Daniel Bernard?

6. Quelle est la différence entre le chiffre des ventes en France et à l'étranger?

S. Trouvez l'intrus! Voici quelques listes d'éléments qui caractérisent Carrefour. Dans chaque liste, il y a un élément qui ne correspond pas aux informations données sur Carrefour dans le texte qui précède. Rayez *(cross out)* cet élément et expliquez en quoi il ne convient pas dans le regroupement proposé.

1. Brésil, Argentine, Espagne, Taïwan, Mexique, France

2. Top 100, conservatrice, croissance, multipliée par 118, augmentation

3. 1950, 1960, 1963, 1970, 1991

4. un gisement de croissance, hypermarché, magasin, supermarché

T. La parole est à vous! A deux ou à trois, répondez à la question suivante. Si vous disposiez de capitaux assez importants, qu'en feriez-vous? Si vous décidiez de les investir, dans quoi les investisseriez-vous et pourquoi?

➤ Prenez de bonnes notes pour que vous puissiez partager vos réponses avec le reste du groupe.

Quelques points de repère

Le saviez-vous?

- Lorsqu'on veut expérimenter dans le domaine de l'achat d'actions, et qu'on veut s'initier à *(get acquainted with)* la Bourse, il est recommandé de faire partie d'un club d'investissement. Un club est un petit groupe de cinq personnes minimum qui élit un président, un secrétaire et un trésorier et qui investit le montant de la cotisation versée par les membres. Cette cotisation est une somme modique *(modest)* versée en général chaque mois. Les clubs bénéficient souvent de l'aide d'un conseiller de la Bourse ou d'une banque. Lorsque le club est composé d'un petit nombre de membres actifs et motivés, il constitue un bon moyen pour faire ses premiers pas en Bourse.

- Les spécialistes des finances en France lisent les grands quotidiens financiers internationaux comme le *Wall Street Journal,* mais ils lisent également la *Tribune Desfossés*, le *Figaro économie,* et des mensuels comme le *MOCI (Moniteur du Commerce International)* pour se tenir au courant de tout ce qui se passe tant au niveau économique que politique et social, pour pouvoir sentir le marché et être capable d'anticiper au maximum les fluctuations des valeurs boursières.

- Les actionnaires ont certains droits:

  1. *les droits pécuniaires:* Les actionnaires étant propriétaires d'une partie du capital d'une entreprise, ils ont également droit à une partie (proportionnelle) des bénéfices.

  2. *le droit de vote:* Les actionnaires ont droit de vote lors des assemblées générales en proportion de leur part de capital. Les actionnaires peuvent donc avoir leur mot à dire sur la gestion de l'entreprise en question.

  3. *le droit à l'information:* Les actionnaires peuvent prendre connaissance des diverses publications faites par les sociétés cotées spécifiant par exemple leur bilan annuel mais ils peuvent également avoir accès à d'autres informations telles que les procès-verbaux *(minutes)* des assemblées ou le rapport des commissaires aux comptes. Les actionnaires ont donc le droit de se renseigner sur la santé de l'entreprise dans laquelle ils ont investi.

L'ardoise

Avant l'informatisation de la Bourse, en 1991, les Agents de Change se rendaient à la Bourse tous les jours ouvrables et se rassemblaient autour d'un espace circulaire qui leur était réservé à l'intérieur de la Bourse. C'est là qu'ils suivaient le cours des actions et obligations et qu'ils procédaient à l'achat ou à la vente de valeurs mobilières en levant la main et en criant «J'ai» ou «Je prends». Depuis 1869, cet espace était appelé la corbeille à cause de sa forme. Un Agent de Change était un officier ministériel, c'est-à-dire qu'il était officiellement nommé par le ministre des Finances, ce qui lui donnait le droit de négocier des produits financiers, des obligations et des actions cotées en Bourse. Il servait d'intermédiaire entre les clients qui voulaient investir leur argent en Bourse et les sociétés cotées en Bourse qui, donc, faisaient appel au public pour se procurer les fonds nécessaires à leur développement.

Une date importante!

- La loi sur la réforme boursière du 22 janvier 1988 a instauré de grands changements dans les intermédiaires et les institutions liés à la Bourse. Une nouvelle structure a été mise en place. «Les Sociétés de Bourse» ont remplacé les anciens «Agents de Change». Ce ne sont plus des individus ayant un statut d'officier ministériel mais des sociétés commerciales de droit commun qui servent d'intermédiaire entre les investisseurs et la Bourse et qui négocient les valeurs mobilières. Les Sociétés de Bourse peuvent ouvrir leur capital aux banques, compagnies d'assurance, institutions financières, ainsi qu'aux sociétés industrielles et commerciales qu'elles soient de France ou de l'étranger.
- Depuis le 24 janvier 1991, la Bourse de Paris est entièrement informatisée et elle rassemble toutes les valeurs qui étaient cotées

➤ Trouvez tous les termes qui ont à faire avec les investissements.

FINANCES

Pour se retrouver chez soi.

La Poste :
une réponse appropriée
à chacun de vos besoins.

Rue de Tous les Jours :

**Tout ce qui concerne les dépenses
quotidiennes, la gestion de votre
budget...**

Allée des Propriétaires :

**Les meilleures solutions pour ache-
ter un appartement, une maison, ou
pour améliorer votre cadre de vie.**

Square du Sans Souci :

**Des formules d'épargne pour
mettre de l'argent de côté en cas
d'imprévu.**

Rond-Point des Projets :

**Des solutions sur mesure pour pré-
parer dès aujourd'hui les projets
que vous mènerez à bien demain.**

Allée des Revenus :

**Des placements performants qui
vous permettent de profiter de
revenus périodiques.**

Place des Valeurs :

**Des placements à fort rendement
pour une plus-value à long terme.**

7003272 DCF DEP PROPRIETAIRES 04/93. Montants et taux en vigueur au 31/03/93. RCS Nanterre B 356 000 000

RAPP COLLINS

LA POSTE

Dépliant de la Poste.

dans les six autres bourses françaises. Il n'est plus nécessaire que les intermédiaires des Sociétés de Bourse aillent à la Bourse en personne; ils ou elles peuvent faire toutes leurs transactions de leur bureau à partir de leurs terminaux.

Remarque: L'informatisation de la Bourse a conduit à reléguer les six places boursières régionales à un rôle extrêmement secondaire.

➤ Listen to the *Phonétique* section of Module VI in your *HSG* one more time.

Du point de vue de la MVA *(Market Value Added)*, les cinq meilleures performances entre 1989 et 1994, en France, ont été, dans l'ordre, NRJ (radio), Spir Communication (journaux gratuits), Guilbert (fournitures de bureau), Sodexho (restauration et services), TF1 (chaîne de télévision) et les cinq moins bonnes ont été Bouygues (bâtiments-travaux publics), DMC (textile), PSA Peugeot-Citroën (automobile), Vallourec (métallurgie), Thomson-CSF (électronique). (Information tirée de *L'Expansion* N° 512 du 10 novembre 1995, Cahier N° 2.)

Réflexions sur le travail en équipe

L'enthousiasme ou, d'une manière générale, une attitude positive contribue à l'harmonie du groupe et a un effet bénéfique aussi bien sur la créativité que sur la productivité de toute l'équipe.

Lexique

une action: **Une action** représente une fraction du capital social d'une société anonyme (S.A.). **Un actionnaire** est propriétaire d'une partie de ce capital. On peut acheter et vendre des **actions** à la Bourse.

> Est-ce que tu crois que je ferais un bon placement si j'achetais une centaine d'**actions** de l'Oréal?

le CAC 40: **Le CAC 40** est un indice de référence qui est composé de 40 valeurs qui ont été sélectionnées pour représenter l'ensemble du marché boursier français.

> Les investisseurs, les économistes et les hommes politiques surveillent l'indice **CAC 40** qui donne une bonne indication de la santé de l'économie du pays.

un cambiste: **Un cambiste** est une personne dont le métier consiste à s'occuper d'opérations de change. Pour travailler, **un cambiste** a besoin de plusieurs lignes téléphoniques et d'au moins un ordinateur et d'un ou plusieurs télécopieurs car toutes les transactions se font au moyen des technologies de pointe.

> Pierre est **cambiste;** il jongle avec les chiffres et est d'une rapidité extraordinaire. Il a l'œil sur tout et parle à plusieurs interlocuteurs à la fois et tout cela à une vitesse incroyable.

la cote: Le cours des valeurs de la Bourse publie **la cote** de chaque action, c'est-à-dire le prix auquel une action peut être achetée ou vendue. **La cote** varie selon l'offre et la demande.

> Regarde dans le journal **la cote** des actions Canal+, Peugeot et Carrefour pour voir si elles sont en hausse ou en baisse.

le courtage: **Le courtage** est la rémunération de la négociation faite au nom de quelqu'un d'autre. **Le courtage** est à la fois la profession des courtiers et la commission touchée pour effectuer ce travail. En général, **le courtage** ou les frais de **courtage** sont calculés sur un pourcentage de la somme investie pour un particulier ou une société.

Si je passais par une Société de Bourse, est-ce que tu sais à combien s'élèverait **le courtage?**

un investissement: Faire **un investissement,** c'est placer son argent pour le faire fructifier. C'est aussi utiliser une certaine somme d'argent pour le bénéfice futur de l'entreprise ou de l'individu. **Un investissement** peut comporter des risques lorsqu'il n'est pas garanti. On peut faire **un investissement** sûr ou risqué. En général, **un investissement** sûr rapporte moins d'argent qu'**un investissement** risqué réussi mais permet de ne pas perdre son argent. Acheter des actions à la Bourse fait partie **des investissements** risqués. Au contraire, placer son argent à la Poste sur un Plan Epargne Logement ne comporte pratiquement aucun risque. Ce placement donne droit à une rémunération de 6% nets d'impôt et à un prêt immobilier à 6,32%.

La société japonaise Fujitsu a investi 10% de son chiffre d'affaires en recherche et développement. Cela représente **un investissement** assez important.

une obligation: Une obligation est un titre négociable remis par une société anonyme ou une collectivité publique aux personnes qui leur ont prêté des capitaux contre une rémunération qui est définie par contrat. **Une obligation** peut être émise à un taux d'intérêt fixe ou variable. La durée d'un emprunt obligataire varie mais est rarement de moins de cinq ans.

Le portefeuille de cette entreprise comprend un ensemble de valeurs mobilières, actions et **obligations**, qui sont gérées par la B.N.P.

un placement: Placer de l'argent, c'est l'investir pour le faire fructifier. **Un placement** est une certaine somme d'argent investie.

Il y a des **placements** sûrs et des placements risqués. Mes parents préfèrent les **placements** qui sont garantis par le gouvernement parce qu'ils sont plus sûrs.

SICAV, FCP, OPCUM: Les **SICAV** (sociétés d'investissement à capital fixe) et les **FCP** (fonds communs de placement) font partie des **OPCVM** (organismes de placements collectifs de valeurs mobilières). Les **SICAV** et les **FCP** constituent deux types de portefeuille collectif de valeurs mobilières et de titres gérés par des spécialistes appartenant à une grande institution financière. Les fonds placés sont ceux d'épargnants qui veulent investir en Bourse sans avoir à intervenir en personne. Les **SICAV** fonctionnent comme des parts qu'on peut acheter et revendre comme un tout. Elles représentent une certaine sécurité de placement et leur valeur ne fluctue pas autant que celle des actions.

Une bonne partie de mon portefeuille est constitué de **SICAV** que j'ai acquises par l'intermédiaire de ma banque. Comme il y a près d'un millier de **SICAV** actuellement sur le marché, j'ai préféré demander l'avis d'un spécialiste pour m'aider à faire un choix.

la spéculation: On fait de **la spéculation** lorsqu'on veut réaliser un profit à relativement court terme, lorsqu'on veut gagner de l'argent en misant sur les changements de taux à la Bourse ou sur le changement de prix d'un terrain ou de tout bien immobilier ou non. En Bourse, par exemple, **la spéculation** part de l'espoir que l'action achetée est à la hausse. Lorsqu'on revend cette action qui a effectivement pris de la valeur, on réalise alors une plus-value intéressante.

> **Pierre:** Il a acheté un million de dollars dans l'espoir que le dollar va remonter.
>
> **Marie:** Mais c'est de **la spéculation**, ça. C'est dangereux!
>
> **Pierre:** Oui, mais s'il y a suffisamment de gens qui croient en la hausse du dollar, il va remonter!
>
> **Marie:** Cela n'empêche pas que c'est risqué.
>
> **Pierre:** Tu connais le proverbe: «Qui ne risque rien n'a rien!»
>
> **Marie:** C'est facile à dire quand il ne s'agit pas de son propre argent!

une transaction boursière: L'achat et la vente d'actions constituent **des transactions boursières**, c'est-à-dire des opérations financières effectuées dans le contexte de la Bourse. Une transaction est une sorte de contrat entre un acheteur et un vendeur.

> Les grands quotidiens indiquent le volume **des transactions boursières** de la veille pour donner une indication de la taille du marché financier.

les valeurs mobilières: Les valeurs mobilières sont des titres achetés et vendus à la Bourse des valeurs. Elles sont dites «mobilières» parce qu'elles peuvent changer de mains, c'est-à-dire changer de propriétaire. Elles peuvent être échangées sur un marché. Les deux principales **valeurs mobilières** sont les actions et les obligations.

> Il y a plusieurs critères qui permettent de juger **les valeurs mobilières** dont leur rentabilité et leur sécurité.

la valeur nominale: La valeur nominale d'une action est le prix de cette action lorsqu'elle a été émise. C'est donc son prix de départ.

> La société Blanchard a été constituée avec un capital de 150 000 F soit 1 500 actions d'**une valeur nominale** de 100 F.

HSG

➤ Complete the *Révisions générales* Exercises E–I of Module VI in your *HSG*.

➤ A discuter avec votre «partenaire» (un membre de votre groupe).

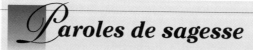
Paroles de sagesse

Il faut estimer ce qu'un individu fait et non ce qu'il peut faire.

Expression écrite

L'infinitif et l'infinitif passé

Comme dans la section à la page 59, le texte suivant emploie l'infinitif, l'infinitif passé aussi bien que le participe présent. Lisez-le, repérez les mots en question, et encerclez-les.

La Bourse et les investissements

Après avoir fait la richesse de nombreux initiés dans les années 1980, la Bourse était perçue comme l'endroit idéal pour faire fortune rapidement. En y plaçant son argent, on pouvait espérer des taux d'intérêt élevés. Les privatisations lancées par le gouvernement français afin de désengager l'état de l'économie, ont marqué le début de la popularisation du marché boursier. En effet à moins de faire partie d'un cercle restreint de connaisseurs, il faut avouer que la Bourse restait un monde mystérieux pour bon nombre de personnes. Après s'être révélées être un placement rentable et sans risque, les privatisations ont remporté un succès croissant dans l'opinion. L'état de grâce dont bénéficiait la Bourse a fini par prendre fin. Après être passés aux travers de plusieurs crises, les cours ont subi des baisses importantes. L'approche des petits porteurs vis-à-vis des marchés boursiers est devenue, par la force des choses, plus professionnelle. Ainsi, avant d'investir dans de nouveaux placements, nombre d'entre eux se constituent en club d'investissement.

U. A vos plumes! A vous maintenant d'écrire un paragraphe sur les investissements en utilisant toutes les expressions qui suivent.

- après avoir (+ infinitif passé)
- après être (+ infinitif passé)
- après s'être (+ infinitif passé)
- avant de
- afin de
- il faut
- à moins de
- pour
- en (+ participe présent)

Allons un peu plus loin avec «En guise de clôture»!

MODULE *VI*

En guise de clôture:
Allons un peu plus loin!

Texte littéraire

La dot de Nathalie

A. Activité de pré-lecture. Répondez aux questions suivantes.

1. Que veulent dire les mots suivants? Cherchez-les dans un dictionnaire français-français, puis employez-les dans une petite phrase.

   a. une dot
   b. la clarté
   c. un parti
   d. borné

   e. caser
   f. être ému
   g. confier
   h. un sou

   i. accourir
   j. rayonner
   k. congédier

2. Pourquoi les filles, autrefois, dans la plupart des sociétés, avaient-elles une dot?

➤ Prenez des notes pour *Mot de passe.*

La dot de Nathalie

[Nathalie] se laissait adorer par son père, sage encore, n'ayant eu aucun intérêt à ne pas l'être, d'un féroce et tranquille égoïsme, dans cette clarté si limpide de ses yeux.

   « Alors donc, monsieur, la voici en âge de se marier, et il y a justement un beau parti qui se présente, le fils du cartonnier, notre

➤ Faites attention a la prononciation du mot *dot*: /dɔt/.

397

voisin. Seulement, c'est un garçon qui veut s'établir, et il demande six mille francs. Ça n'est pas trop, il pourrait prétendre à une fille qui aurait davantage... Il faut vous dire que j'ai perdu ma femme, il y a quatre ans, et qu'elle nous a laissé des économies, ses petits bénéfices de cuisinière, n'est-ce pas?... J'ai quatre mille francs; mais ça ne fait pas six mille, et le jeune homme est pressé, Nathalie aussi...»

La jeune fille qui écoutait, souriante, avec son clair regard si froid et si décidé, eut une brusque affirmation du menton.

« Bien sûr... Je ne m'amuse pas, je veux en finir, d'une manière ou d'une autre. »

De nouveau, Saccard les interrompit. Il avait jugé l'homme, borné, mais très droit, très bon, rompu à la discipline militaire. Puis, il suffisait qu'il se présentât au nom de Mme Caroline.

« C'est parfait, mon ami... Je vais avoir un journal, je vous prends comme garçon de bureau... Laissez-moi votre adresse, et au revoir. »

Cependant, Dejoie ne s'en allait point. Il continua, avec embarras:

« Monsieur est bien obligeant, j'accepte la place avec reconnaissance, parce qu'il faudra que je travaille, quand j'aurai casé Nathalie... Mais j'étais venu pour autre chose. Oui, j'ai su, par Mme Caroline et par d'autres personnes encore, que monsieur va se trouver dans de grandes affaires et qu'il pourra faire gagner tout ce qu'il voudra à ses amis et connaissances... Alors si monsieur voulait bien s'intéresser à nous, si monsieur consentait à nous donner de ses actions... »

Saccard, une seconde fois, fut ému, plus ému qu'il ne venait de l'être, la première, lorsque la comtesse lui avait confié, elle aussi, la dot de sa fille. Cet homme simple, ce tout petit capitaliste aux économies grattées sou à sou, n'était-ce pas la foule croyante, confiante, la grande foule qui fait les clientèles nombreuses et solides, l'armée fanatisée qui arme une maison de crédit d'une force invincible? Si ce brave homme accourait ainsi, avant toute publicité, que serait-ce, lorsque les guichets seraient ouverts? Son attendrissement souriait à ce premier petit actionnaire, il voyait là le présage d'un gros succès.

« Entendu, mon ami, vous aurez des actions. »

La face de Dejoie rayonna, comme à l'annonce d'une grâce inespérée.

« Monsieur est trop bon... N'est-ce pas? en six mois, je puis bien, avec mes quatre mille, en gagner deux mille, de façon à compléter la somme... Et, puisque monsieur y consent, j'aime mieux régler ça tout de suite. J'ai apporté l'argent. »

« Il se fouilla, tira une enveloppe, qu'il tendit à Saccard, immobile, silencieux, saisi d'une admiration charmée, à ce dernier trait. Et le terrible corsaire, qui avait déjà écumé tant de fortunes, finit par éclater d'un bon rire, résolu honnêtement à l'enrichir aussi, cet homme de foi.

« Mais mon brave, ça ne se fait point ainsi... Gardez votre argent, je vous inscrirai, et vous paierez en temps et lieu. »

Cette fois, il les congédia, après que Dejoie l'eut fait remercier par Nathalie, dont un sourire de contentement éclairait les beaux yeux durs et candides.

— *EMILE ZOLA*

Tiré de *L'Argent* (1890). Paris: Editions Fasquelle, 1985.

B. A vous de compléter! En vous inspirant du texte, terminez les phrases suivantes.

1. Dejoie et sa fille viennent voir Saccard pour _____.
2. La femme de Dejoie était _____ de profession.
3. La femme de Dejoie est _____ quatre ans auparavant.
4. La femme de Dejoie avait économisé _____ francs.
5. Le fils du cartonnier veut _____.
6. Saccard offre à _____ de l'embaucher.
7. Saccard accepte de vendre des _____ à Dejoie.
8. Dejoie a apporté de _____ car il veut payer Saccard tout de suite.

C. Vrai ou faux? Lisez bien les affirmations suivantes. Si elles ne sont pas correctes, reformulez-les de façon à ce qu'elles le deviennent et comparez vos phrases ainsi transformées avec celles des membres de votre groupe.

1. Nathalie veut bien se marier avec le fils du cartonnier.
2. Le fils du cartonnier veut six mille francs de dot parce qu'il ne peut pas se marier avec une fille qui lui apporterait davantage.
3. Nathalie est gênée que son père parle de sa dot devant elle.
4. C'est Mme Caroline qui a envoyé Dejoie à Saccard.
5. Monsieur Dejoie est un capitaliste qui a une grande expérience boursière.
6. Monsieur Dejoie est sûr de pouvoir gagner au moins deux mille francs en six mois en plaçant ses quatre mille francs dans des actions de Saccard.
7. Saccard accepte de prendre l'argent de Dejoie immédiatement.

D. A vous la parole! Discutez les questions suivantes à deux ou à trois.

1. Pensez-vous que Dejoie soit prudent de confier ses quatre mille francs à Saccard?
2. Que se passera-t-il si Dejoie perd ses quatre mille francs parce que l'investissement n'était pas aussi sûr qu'il le croyait?
3. Pourquoi, selon vous, le fils du cartonnier insiste-t-il sur les six mille francs de dot?
4. Dejoie est-il un bon père?
5. Saccard a-t-il raison ou tort d'accepter l'argent de Dejoie? Pensez-vous qu'il a une obligation morale envers le père et sa fille?

E. Jeu de rôle! Mettez-vous à deux ou trois. Imaginez que vous êtes Dejoie ou sa fille et que vous demandez à Saccard de vous laisser investir dans son affaire. Contrairement à ce qui se passe dans le texte, celui-ci refuse. Insistez et expliquez bien votre situation et pourquoi il est très important que vous achetiez ses actions.

➤ Soyez prêt(e)(s) à faire un sketch *(skit)* et à le jouer en classe.

F. A vos plumes! Quels sont les rêves et les sentiments de Nathalie? Décrivez en un petit paragraphe d'une vingtaine de lignes la personnalité

HSG

de Nathalie telle que Saccard la voit et telle que vous la percevez après avoir lu cet extrait.

 Complete the *Exercises de synthèse* of Module VI in your HSG.

Une question d'argent

 Si un dollar permet d'acheter 5 F, 1.000 $ équivaut combien de francs?

Si vous investissiez 1.000 $ à un taux d'intérêt de dix pour cent, combien de temps est-ce que cela prendrait pour doubler cet argent?

Je mettrais _____ ans pour doubler mon investissement.
          (Devinez!)

En règle générale, si vous divisez 72 par le pourcentage d'intérêt auquel vous placez votre argent, vous obtiendrez le nombre d'années qu'il vous faudra pour doubler cette somme d'argent. Ainsi,

Après	*Vous aurez en dollars*	
7,2 ans	2.000	
14,4 ans	4.000	
21,6 ans	8.000	
28,8 ans	16.000	etc.

Casse-tête chinois:

Alors, qu'est-ce qui arriverait si vous aviez une carte de crédit et au lieu de payer la totalité du solde chaque mois, vous ne payiez que le minimum requis indiqué et que le taux d'intérêt exigé par la banque ou la société ayant émis votre carte de crédit s'élevait à 22%? (En laissant un solde mensuel de 500 $ sur votre compte, combien auriez-vous à repayer au bout d'un peu plus de trois ans?)

Une dernière question d'argent: L'indépendance financière

 Take these basic principles with you as you finish this course as our gift to you.

Si vous voulez devenir indépendant financièrement et vous sentir bien par rapport à votre situation financière:

1. Evitez de faire des dettes et emprunter de l'argent (sauf pour l'achat d'une maison).
2. Organisez votre budget en fonction de vos moyens et non de vos désirs ou des besoins que vous pensez avoir dès que vous touchez votre salaire.
3. Essayez de mettre immédiatement 10% de vos revenus de côté comme fonds d'urgence jusqu'à ce que vous ayez accumulé trois mois de revenus. Après cela, continuez à économiser ces 10% pour les investir.
4. Gardez 10% de vos revenus pour vos loisirs et passe-temps.

5. Soyez charitable. Donnez 10% de vos revenus à ceux qui en ont besoin, ainsi qu'à des organismes à but non-lucratif ou autres organisations bénévoles.

6. Commencez à investir le plus tôt possible et faites-le régulièrement (voir *Une question d'argent,* page 400).

7. Prenez votre situation financière en mains.
   - Achetez l'assurance-vie qui vous convient. (N'en choisissez pas une qui soit liée directement à un investissement, à un régime d'épargne ou à un abri fiscal ni à une assurance qui paie des dividendes).
   - Payez moins d'impôts en investissant dans un abri fiscal.
   - Evitez les intermédiaires. Gérez votre argent vous-même.

8. Commencez une tradition familiale dans le domaine de l'épargne et de l'investissement. Encouragez vos enfants à suivre les principes qui précèdent.

9. Cultivez une mentalité positive vis-à-vis de l'abondance. Sachez apprécier ce que vous avez et jouir de votre vie et de ce que vous possédez.

Récapitulons!

Quelques aide-mémoire

1. Une compagnie d'assurances
- vous propose un éventail d'assurances allant de l'assurance-automobile à l'assurance-vie en passant par l'assurance-accident.
- vous fait signer une police d'assurance qui devient un contrat entre elle et vous.
- vous explique les clauses de votre police.
- vous indique les exclusions, c'est-à-dire ce qui n'est pas couvert par votre police.
- vous demande de consentir à un prélèvement mensuel (annuel ou bi-annuel selon la police en question) de votre compte bancaire ou postal.
- envoie un expert pour déterminer la valeur des dommages subis lorsque vous avez été victime d'un sinistre.
- vous paie des indemnités si nécessaire.
- vous propose des moyens d'investir votre argent.
- vous protège contre certaines conséquences financières de certains accidents.

2. A propos des impôts
- Vous devez remplir une déclaration selon le type de revenus dont vous disposez.
- Si vous êtes Français ou si vous résidez en France, vous payez vos impôts en tiers provisionnels.
- La date limite pour faire parvenir votre déclaration au Centre Des Impôts est le 1er mars de chaque année.

- L'année fiscale est du 1ᵉʳ janvier au 31 décembre de l'année précédente.
- Vous êtes imposable en fonction de vos revenus.
- Vous pouvez bénéficier de délais de paiement si vous réussissez à convaincre votre percepteur qu'ils sont indispensables et raisonnables.
- Certaines personnes peuvent être exonérées d'impôts.
- Il y a des impôts directs et indirects.
- Ce sont les ménages et les entreprises qui se répartissent la totalité des impôts qui vont remplir les caisses de l'Etat.
- Les taxes sont des types d'impôts.

3. **Faire un investissement peut signifier**
   - placer son argent de façon à le faire fructifier.
   - acheter des actions ou des obligations.
   - acheter des Bons du Trésor.
   - acheter des biens mobiliers ou immobiliers.
   - faire une petite enquête au sujet d'une entreprise avant de miser sur elle.
   - prendre des risques.
   - perdre ses capitaux.
   - gagner de l'argent.
   - placer son capital dans une entreprise pour qu'elle puisse acheter du matériel ou acquérir des moyens de production.
   - choisir un Agent de Change qui pourra acheter des titres cotés en bourse en votre nom.
   - lire les grands quotidiens financiers.
   - se tenir au courant de la situation économique et sociale au niveau national et international.

HSG

➤ Complete the *Echange* section of Module VI in your *HSG*.

Nous vous souhaitons beaucoup de succès dans tout ce que vous entreprendrez à l'avenir... que ce soit dans le domaine des affaires, de la technologie ou de la vie de tous les jours!

APPENDICE I:

Cartes

La France et ses régions

LA MER DU NORD

L'ANGLETERRE

LES PAYS-BAS

L'ALLEMAGNE

LA MANCHE

Calais •

Lille •

LA BELGIQUE

LE LUXEMBOURG

NORD-PAS-DE-CALAIS

Le Havre •

HAUTE-NORMANDIE

• Rouen

PICARDIE

Reims •

Metz •

LORRAINE

Les Vosges

Strasbourg •

ALSACE

La Seine

Brest •

BASSE-NORMANDIE

Paris ⊛

ÎLE-DE-FRANCE

CHAMPAGNE-ARDENNE

BRETAGNE

Lorient •

PAYS-DE-LA-LOIRE

Orléans •

La Seine

Nantes •

• Angers

La Loire

• Tours

CENTRE

BOURGOGNE

Dijon •

FRANCHE-COMTÉ

Besançon •

Le Jura

LA SUISSE

L'OCÉAN ATLANTIQUE

Poitiers •

LA FRANCE

• La Rochelle

POITOU-CHARENTE

LIMOUSIN

Clermont-Ferrand •

Le Massif

Lyon •

RHÔNE-ALPES

L'ITALIE

Bordeaux •

La Garonne

AUVERGNE

Central

Grenoble •

Le Rhône

Les Alpes

AQUITAINE

MIDI-PYRÉNÉES

Toulouse •

LANGUEDOC-ROUSSILLON

PROVENCE-ALPES-CÔTE D'AZUR

Avignon •

Aix-en-Provence •

Nice •

Cannes •

MONACO

Marseille •

Les Pyrénées

ANDORRE

L'ESPAGNE

LA MER MÉDITERRANÉE

LA CORSE

Ajaccio •

0   100   200 Milles
0   100   200 Kilomètres

5°

Le Canada

LE YUKON

LES TERRITOIRES DU NORD-OUEST

LA COLOMBIE BRITANNIQUE

L'ALBERTA

LA SASKAT-CHÉWAN

LE MANITOBA

L'ONTARIO (*m*)

LA BAIE D'HUDSON

LA TERRE NEUVE

LE LABRADOR

LE QUÉBEC

LE NOUVEAU BRUNSWICK

ST PIERRE ET MIQUELON (FR)

L'ÎLE DU PRINCE EDOUARD

LA NOUVELLE ÉCOSSE

L'OCÉAN PACIFIQUE

L'OCÉAN ATLANTIQUE

Edmonton

Calgary

Vancouver

Seattle

Saskatoon

Regina

Winnipeg

Le Missouri

Minneapolis

Le Mississippi

Chicago

Le Lac Supérieur

Le Lac Michigan

Le Lac Huron

Le Lac Érié

Le Lac Ontario

Toronto

Ottawa

Montréal

Le Saint-Laurent

Québec

Halifax

Boston

New York

| 0 | 250 | 500 Milles |
| 0 | 250 | 500 Kilomètres |

70° 170° 160° 140° 120° 100° 80° 60° 10°

60°

50°

40°

70°

60°

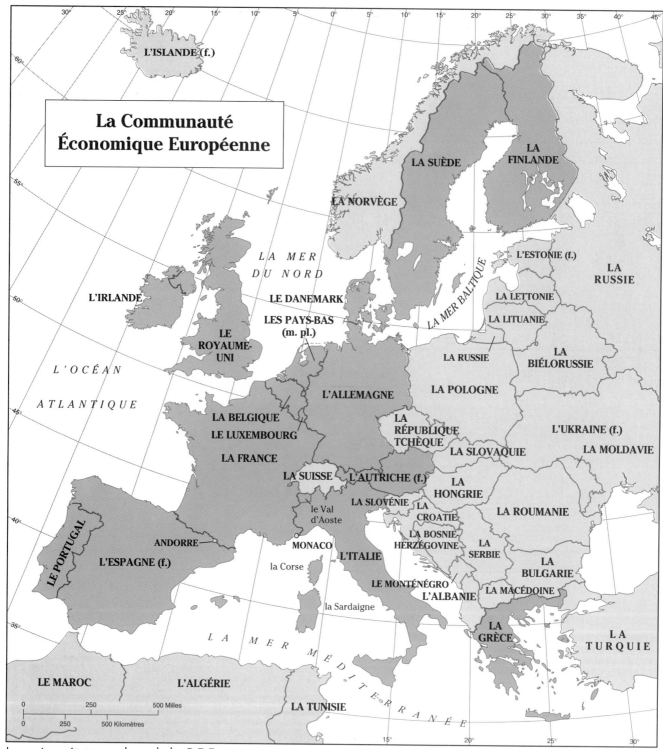

La Communauté
Économique Européenne

L'ISLANDE (f.)

LA MER
DU NORD

LA NORVÈGE

LA SUÈDE

LA FINLANDE

L'ESTONIE (f.)

LA RUSSIE

L'IRLANDE

LE DANEMARK

LES PAYS-BAS
(m. pl.)

LA MER BALTIQUE

LA LETTONIE

LA LITUANIE

LA RUSSIE

LA BIÉLORUSSIE

L'OCÉAN

ATLANTIQUE

LE
ROYAUME-
UNI

L'ALLEMAGNE

LA POLOGNE

LA BELGIQUE

LE LUXEMBOURG

LA FRANCE

LA RÉPUBLIQUE
TCHÈQUE

LA SLOVAQUIE

L'UKRAINE (f.)

LA MOLDAVIE

LA SUISSE

L'AUTRICHE (f.)

LA HONGRIE

LE PORTUGAL

ANDORRE

L'ESPAGNE (f.)

le Val
d'Aoste

MONACO

LA SLOVÉNIE

LA
CROATIE

LA BOSNIE-
HERZÉGOVINE

LA
SERBIE

LA ROUMANIE

L'ITALIE

la Corse

la Sardaigne

LE MONTÉNÉGRO

L'ALBANIE

LA MACÉDOINE

LA BULGARIE

LA GRÈCE

LA TURQUIE

LE MAROC

L'ALGÉRIE

LA MER MÉDITERRANÉE

LA TUNISIE

0   250   500 Milles

0   250   500 Kilomètres

Les quinze états membres de la C.E.E.

l'Allemagne *(f)*	la Finlande	le Luxembourg
la Belgique	la France	les Pays-Bas
l'Autriche *(f)*	la Grèce	le Portugal
le Danemark	l'Irlande *(f)*	le Royaume-Uni
l'Espagne *(f)*	l'Italie *(f)*	la Suède

APPENDICE *II:*

$\mathcal{V}$erbes

VERBES REGULIERS

Infinitif	Présent	Impératif	Passé composé	Imparfait
1. chercher	je **cherche**	**cherche**	j'ai **cherché**	je **cherchais**
(to look for)	tu **cherches**	**cherchons**	tu **as cherché**	tu **cherchais**
	il/elle/on **cherche**	**cherchez**	il/elle/on **a cherché**	il/elle/on **cherchait**
Participe présent:	nous **cherchons**		nous **avons cherché**	nous **cherchions**
cherchant	vous **cherchez**		vous **avez cherché**	vous **cherchiez**
	ils/elles **cherchent**		ils/elles **ont cherché**	ils/elles **cherchaient**

Infinitif	Présent	Impératif	Passé composé	Imparfait
2. investir	j'**investis**	**investis**	j'ai **investi**	j'**investissais**
(to invest)	tu **investis**	**investissons**	tu **as investi**	tu **investissais**
	il/elle/on **investit**	**investissez**	il/elle/on **a investi**	il/elle/on **investissait**
Participe présent:	nouns **investissons**		nous **avons investi**	nous **investissions**
investissant	vous **investissez**		vous **avez investi**	vous **investissiez**
	ils/elles **investissent**		ils/elles **ont investi**	ils/elles **investissaient**

Infinitif	Présent	Impératif	Passé composé	Imparfait
3. vendre	je **vends**	**vends**	j'ai **vendu**	je **vendais**
(to sell)	tu **vends**	**vendons**	tu **as vendu**	tu **vendais**
	il/elle/on **vend**	**vendez**	il/elle/on **a vendu**	il/elle/on **vendait**
Participe présent:	nous **vendons**		nous **avons vendu**	nous **vendions**
vendant	vous **vendez**		vous **avez vendu**	vous **vendiez**
	ils/elles **vendent**		ils/elles **ont vendu**	ils/elles **vendaient**

VERBES CHANGEANT DE RADICAL

In the list below, the letter at the right of each verb corresponds to the letter of the verb, or of a similarly conjugated verb, in the tables that follow.

acheter *(to buy)* A
amener *(to bring [someone])* A
annoncer *(to announce)* E
appeler *(to call)*, **s'appeler** *(to be called)* B
arranger *(to fix, arrange)* D
avancer *(to move forward)* E
célébrer *(to celebrate)* C
changer *(to change)* D
commencer *(to begin)* E
corriger *(to correct)* D
déménager *(to move one's residence)* D
déranger *(to disturb)* D

diriger *(to manage, run)* D
effacer *(to erase)* E
élever *(to raise)* A
emmener *(to take [someone] away)* A
employer *(to use, employ)* F
enlever *(to take off, remove)* A
ennuyer *(to bore, annoy)* F
envoyer *(to send)* (except in future and conditional) F
épeler *(to spell)* B
espérer *(to hope)* C
essayer *(to try)* F
essuyer *(to wipe)* F

Infinitif	Présent	Impératif	Passé composé	Imparfait
A. acheter	j'**achète**	**achète**	j'ai **acheté**	j'**achetais**
(to buy)	tu **achètes**	**achetons**	tu **as acheté**	tu **achetais**
	il/elle/on **achète**	**achetez**	il/elle/on **a acheté**	il/elle/on **achetait**
Participe présent:	nous **achetons**		nous **avons acheté**	nous **achetions**
achetant	vous **achetez**		vous **avez acheté**	vous **achetiez**
	ils/elles **achètent**		ils/elles **ont acheté**	ils/elles **achetaient**

Passé simple	Plus-que-parfait	Futur	Conditionnel	Subjonctif
je **cherchai**	j'avais **cherché**	je **chercherai**	je **chercherais**	que je **cherche**
tu **cherchas**	tu **avais cherché**	tu **chercheras**	tu **chercherais**	que tu **cherches**
il/elle/on **chercha**	il/elle/on **avait cherché**	il/elle/on **cherchera**	il/elle/on **chercherait**	qu'il/elle/on **cherche**
nous **cherchâmes**	nous **avions cherché**	nous **chercherons**	nous **chercherions**	que nous **cherchions**
vous **cherchâtes**	vous **aviez cherché**	vous **chercherez**	vous **chercheriez**	que vous **cherchiez**
ils/elles **cherchèrent**	ils/elles **avaient cherché**	ils/elles **chercheront**	ils/elles **chercheraient**	qu'ils/elles **cherchent**

Passé simple	Plus-que-parfait	Futur	Conditionnel	Subjonctif
j'**investis**	j'avais **investi**	j'**investirai**	j'**investirais**	que j'**investisse**
tu **investis**	tu **avais investi**	tu **investiras**	tu **investirais**	que tu **investisses**
il/elle/on **investit**	il/elle/on **avait investi**	il/elle/on **investira**	il/elle/on **investirait**	qu'il/elle/on **investisse**
nous **investîmes**	nous **avions investi**	nous **investirons**	nous **investirions**	que nous **investissions**
vous **investîtes**	vous **aviez investi**	vous **investirez**	vous **investiriez**	que vous **investissiez**
ils/elles **investirent**	ils/elles **avaient investi**	ils/elles **investiront**	ils/elles **investiraient**	qu'ils/elles **investissent**

Passé simple	Plus-que-parfait	Futur	Conditionnel	Subjonctif
je **vendis**	j'avais **vendu**	je **vendrai**	je **vendrais**	que je **vende**
tu **vendis**	tu **avais vendu**	tu **vendras**	tu **vendrais**	que tu **vendes**
il/elle/on **vendit**	il/elle/on **avait vendu**	il/elle/on **vendra**	il/elle/on **vendrait**	qu'il/elle/on **vende**
nous **vendîmes**	nous **avions vendu**	nous **vendrons**	nous **vendrions**	que nous **vendions**
vous **vendîtes**	vous **aviez vendu**	vous **vendrez**	vous **vendriez**	que vous **vendiez**
ils/elles **vendirent**	ils/elles **avaient vendu**	ils/elles **vendront**	ils/elles **vendraient**	qu'ils/elles **vendent**

inquiéter *(to worry)* C
jeter *(to throw)* A
lancer *(to throw, launch)* E
manger *(to eat)* D
menacer *(to threaten)* E
nager *(to swim)* D
négliger *(to neglect)* D
nettoyer *(to clean)* F
obliger *(to oblige)* D
partager *(to share)* D
payer *(to pay)* F
peser *(to weigh)* A
placer *(to put, set, place)* E

plonger *(to dive)* D
posséder *(to own)* C
préférer *(to prefer)* C
protéger *(to protect)* D
ranger *(to put in order, put away)* D
rappeler *(to recall, call back)* B
rejeter *(to reject)* B
remplacer *(to replace)* E
renoncer *(to give up, renounce)* E
répéter *(to repeat)* C
sécher *(to dry)* C
suggérer *(to suggest)* C
voyager *(to travel)* D

Passé simple	Plus-que-parfait	Futur	Conditionnel	Subjonctif
j'**achetai**	j'avais **acheté**	j'**achèterai**	j'**achèterais**	que j'**achète**
tu **achetas**	tu **avais acheté**	tu **achèteras**	tu **achèterais**	que tu **achètes**
il/elle/on **acheta**	il/elle/on **avait acheté**	il/elle/on **achètera**	il/elle/on **achèterait**	qu'il/elle/on **achète**
nous **achetâmes**	nous **avions acheté**	nous **achèterons**	nous **achèterions**	que nous **achetions**
vous **achetâtes**	vous **aviez acheté**	vous **achèterez**	vous **achèteriez**	que vous **achetiez**
ils/elles **achetèrent**	ils/elles **avaient acheté**	ils/elles **achèteront**	ils/elles **achèteraient**	qu'ils/elles **achètent**

VERBES CHANGEANT DE RADICAL *(suite)*

Infinitif	Présent	Impératif	Passé composé	Imparfait
B. appeler	j'**appelle**	**appelle**	j'**ai appelé**	j'**appelais**
(to call)	tu **appelles**	**appelons**	tu **as appelé**	tu **appelais**
	il/elle/on **appelle**	**appelez**	il/elle/on **a appelé**	il/elle/on **appelait**
Participe présent:	nous **appelons**		nous **avons appelé**	nous **appelions**
appelant	vous **appelez**		vous **avez appelé**	vous **appeliez**
	ils/elles **appellent**		ils/elles **ont appelé**	ils/elles **appelaient**

Infinitif	Présent	Impératif	Passé composé	Imparfait
C. préférer	je **préfère**	**préfère**	j'**ai préféré**	je **préférais**
(to prefer)	tu **préfères**	**préférons**	tu **as préféré**	tu **préférais**
	il/elle/on **préfère**	**préférez**	il/elle/on **a préféré**	il/elle/on **préférait**
Participe présent:	nous **préférons**		nous **avons préféré**	nous **préférions**
préférant	vous **préférez**		vous **avez préféré**	vous **préfériez**
	ils/elles **préfèrent**		ils/elles **ont préféré**	ils/elles **préféraient**

Infinitif	Présent	Impératif	Passé composé	Imparfait
D. manger	je **mange**	**mange**	j'**ai mangé**	je **mangeais**
(to eat)	tu **manges**	**mangeons**	tu **as mangé**	tu **mangeais**
	il/elle/on **mange**	**mangez**	il/elle/on **a mangé**	il/elle/on **mangeait**
Participe présent:	nous **mangeons**		nous **avons mangé**	nous **mangions**
mangeant	vous **mangez**		vous **avez mangé**	vous **mangiez**
	ils/elles **mangent**		ils/elles **ont mangé**	ils/elles **mangeaient**

Infinitif	Présent	Impératif	Passé composé	Imparfait
E. commencer	je **commence**	**commence**	j'**ai commencé**	je **commençais**
(to start, begin)	tu **commences**	**commençons**	tu **as commencé**	tu **commençais**
	il/elle/on **commence**	**commencez**	il/elle/on **a commencé**	il/elle/on **commençait**
Participe présent:	nous **commençons**		nous **avons commencé**	nous **commencions**
commençant	vous **commencez**		vous **avez commencé**	vous **commenciez**
	ils/elles **commencent**		ils/elles **ont commencé**	ils/elles **commençaient**

Infinitif	Présent	Impératif	Passé composé	Imparfait
F. payer	je **paie**	**paie**	j'**ai payé**	je **payais**
(to pay, pay for)	tu **paies**	**payons**	tu **as payé**	tu **payais**
	il/elle/on **paie**	**payez**	il/elle/on **a payé**	il/elle/on **payait**
Participe présent:	nous **payons**		nous **avons payé**	nous **payions**
payant	vous **payez**		vous **avez payé**	vous **payiez**
	ils/elles **paient**		ils/elles **ont payé**	ils/elles **payaient**

Passé simple	Plus-que-parfait	Futur	Conditionnel	Subjonctif
j'appelai	j'avais appelé	j'appellerai	j'appellerais	que j'appelle
tu appelas	tu avais appelé	tu appelleras	tu appellerais	que tu appelles
il/elle/on appela	il/elle/on avait appelé	il/elle/on appellera	il/elle/on appellerait	qu'il/elle/on appelle
nous appelâmes	nous avions appelé	nous appellerons	nous appellerions	que nous appelions
vous appelâtes	vous aviez appelé	vous appellerez	vous appelleriez	que vous appeliez
ils/elles appelèrent	ils/elles avaient appelé	ils/elles appelleront	ils/elles appelleraient	qu'ils/elles appellent

Passé simple	Plus-que-parfait	Futur	Conditionnel	Subjonctif
je préférai	j'avais préféré	je préférerai	je préférerais	que je préfère
tu préféras	tu avais préféré	tu préféreras	tu préférerais	que tu préfères
il/elle/on préféra	il/elle/on avait préféré	il/elle/on préférera	il/elle/on préférerait	qu'il/elle/on préfère
nous préférâmes	nous avions préféré	nous préférerons	nous préférerions	que nous préférions
vous préférâtes	vous aviez préféré	vous préférerez	vous préféreriez	que vous préfériez
ils/elles préférèrent	ils/elles avaient préféré	ils/elles préféreront	ils/elles préféreraient	qu'ils/elles préfèrent

Passé simple	Plus-que-parfait	Futur	Conditionnel	Subjonctif
je mangeai	j'avais mangé	je mangerai	je mangerais	que je mange
tu mangeas	tu avais mangé	tu mangeras	tu mangerais	que tu manges
il/elle/on mangea	il/elle/on avait mangé	il/elle/on mangera	il/elle/on mangerait	qu'il/elle/on mange
nous mangeâmes	nous avions mangé	nous mangerons	nous mangerions	que nous mangions
vous mangeâtes	vous aviez mangé	vous mangerez	vous mangeriez	que vous mangiez
ils/elles mangèrent	ils/elles avaient mangé	ils/elles mangeront	ils/elles mangeraient	qu'ils/elles mangent

Passé simple	Plus-que-parfait	Futur	Conditionnel	Subjonctif
je commençai	j'avais commencé	je commencerai	je commencerais	que je commence
tu commenças	tu avais commencé	tu commenceras	tu commencerais	que tu commences
il/elle/on commença	il/elle/on avait commencé	il/elle/on commencera	il/elle/on commencerait	qu'il/elle/on commence
nous commençâmes	nous avions commencé	nous commencerons	nous commencerions	que nous commencions
vous commençâtes	vous aviez commencé	vous commencerez	vous commenceriez	que vous commenciez
ils/elles commencèrent	ils/elles avaient commencé	ils/elles commenceront	ils/elles commenceraient	qu'ils/elles commencent

Passé simple	Plus-que-parfait	Futur	Conditionnel	Subjonctif
je payai	j'avais payé	je paierai	je paierais	que je paie
tu payas	tu avais payé	tu paieras	tu paierais	que tu paies
il/elle/on paya	il/elle/on avait payé	il/elle/on paiera	il/elle/on paierait	qu'il/elle/on paie
nous payâmes	nous avions payé	nous paierons	nous paierions	que nous payions
vous payâtes	vous aviez payé	vous paierez	vous paieriez	que vous payiez
ils/elles payèrent	ils/elles avaient payé	ils/elles paieront	ils/elles paieraient	qu'ils/elles paient

VERBES IRREGULIERS

In the list below, the number at the right of each verb corresponds to the number of the verb, or of a similarly conjugated verb, in the tables that follow. Verbs conjugated with **être** as an auxiliary verb in the compound tenses are printed in color. All other verbs are conjugated with **avoir**.

aller *(to go)* 1
avoir *(to have)* 2
boire *(to drink)* 3
connaître *(to know)* 4
courir *(to run)* 5
couvrir *(to cover)* 19
craindre *(to fear)* 6
croire *(to believe)* 7
découvrir *(to discover)* 19
devenir *(to become)* 30

devoir *(must, to have to; to owe)* 8
dire *(to say, tell)* 9
dormir *(to sleep)* 10
écrire *(to write)* 11
s'endormir *(to fall asleep)* 10
envoyer *(to send)* 12
être *(to be)* 13
faire *(to do, make)* 14
falloir *(to be necessary)* 15

mentir *(to lie)* 27
mettre *(to put, place)* 16
mourir *(to die)* 17
naître *(to be born)* 18
obtenir *(to obtain, get)* 30
offrir *(to offer)* 19
ouvrir *(to open)* 19
paraître *(to appear)* 4
partir *(to leave)* 27
permettre *(to permit)* 16

Infinitif	Présent	Impératif	Passé composé	Imparfait
1. aller	je **vais**	va	je **suis allé(e)**	j'**allais**
(to go)	tu **vas**	allons	tu **es allé(e)**	tu **allais**
	il/elle/on **va**	allez	il/elle/on **est allé(e)**	il/elle/on **allait**
Participe présent:	nous **allons**		nous **sommes allé(e)s**	nous **allions**
allant	vous **allez**		vous **êtes allé(e)(s)**	vous **alliez**
	ils/elles **vont**		ils/elles **sont allé(e)s**	ils/elles **allaient**

Infinitif	Présent	Impératif	Passé composé	Imparfait
2. avoir	j'**ai**	aie	j'**ai eu**	j'**avais**
(to have)	tu **as**	ayons	tu **as eu**	tu **avais**
	il/elle/on **a**	ayez	il/elle/on **a eu**	il/elle/on **avait**
Participe présent:	nous **avons**		nous **avons eu**	nous **avions**
ayant	vous **avez**		vous **avez eu**	vous **aviez**
	ils/elles **ont**		ils/elles **ont eu**	ils/elles **avaient**

Infinitif	Présent	Impératif	Passé composé	Imparfait
3. boire	je **bois**	bois	j'**ai bu**	je **buvais**
(to drink)	tu **bois**	buvons	tu **as bu**	tu **buvais**
	il/elle/on **boit**	buvez	il/elle/on **a bu**	il/elle/on **buvait**
Participe présent:	nous **buvons**		nous **avons bu**	nous **buvions**
buvant	vous **buvez**		vous **avez bu**	vous **buviez**
	ils/elles **boivent**		ils/elles **ont bu**	ils/elles **buvaient**

Infinitif	Présent	Impératif	Passé composé	Imparfait
4. connaître	je **connais**	connais	j'**ai connu**	je **connaissais**
(to know)	tu **connais**	connaissons	tu **as connu**	tu **connaissais**
	il/elle/on **connaît**	connaissez	il/elle/on **a connu**	il/elle/on **connaissait**
Participe présent:	nous **connaissons**		nous **avons connu**	nous **connaissions**
connaissant	vous **connaissez**		vous **avez connu**	vous **connaissiez**
	ils/elles **connaissent**		ils/elles **ont connu**	ils/elles **connaissaient**

plaindre *(to pity)* 6
se plaindre *(to complain)* 6
plaire *(to please)* 20
pleuvoir *(to rain)* 21
pouvoir *(to be able, can)* 22
prendre *(to take)* 23
promettre *(to promise)* 16
recevoir *(to receive, get)* 24
retenir *(to reserve)* 30

revenir *(to come back)* 30
rire *(to laugh)* 25
savoir *(to know)* 26
sentir *(to smell)* 27
se sentir *(to feel)* 27
servir *(to serve)* 27
se servir de *(to use)* 27
sortir *(to go out)* 27
souffrir *(to suffer)* 19

se souvenir de *(to remember)* 30
suivre *(to follow)* 28
tenir *(to hold)* 30
valoir *(to be worth; to deserve, merit)* 29
venir *(to come)* 30
voir *(to see)* 31
vouloir *(to wish, want)* 32

Passé simple	Plus-que-parfait	Futur	Conditionnel	Subjonctif
j'allai	j'étais allé(e)	j'irai	j'irais	que j'aille
tu allas	tu étais allé(e)	tu iras	tu irais	que tu ailles
il/elle/on alla	il/elle/on était allé(e)	il/elle/on ira	il/elle/on irait	qu'il/elle/on aille
nous allâmes	nous étions allé(e)s	nous irons	nous irions	que nous allions
vous allâtes	vous étiez allé(e)(s)	vous irez	vous iriez	que vous alliez
ils/elles allèrent	ils/elles étaient allé(e)s	ils/elles iront	ils/elles iraient	qu'ils/elles aillent

Passé simple	Plus-que-parfait	Futur	Conditionnel	Subjonctif
j'eus	j'avais eu	j'aurai	j'aurais	que j'aie
tu eus	tu avais eu	tu auras	tu aurais	que tu aies
il/elle/on eut	il/elle/on avait eu	il/elle/on aura	il/elle/on aurait	qu'il/elle/on ait
nous eûmes	nous avions eu	nous aurons	nous aurions	que nous ayons
vous eûtes	vous aviez eu	vous aurez	vous auriez	que vous ayez
ils/elles eurent	ils/elles avaient eu	ils/elles auront	ils/elles auraient	qu'ils/elles aient

Passé simple	Plus-que-parfait	Futur	Conditionnel	Subjonctif
je bus	j'avais bu	je boirai	je boirais	que je boive
tu bus	tu avais bu	tu boiras	tu boirais	que tu boives
il/elle/on but	il/elle/on avait bu	il/elle/on boira	il/elle/on boirait	qu'il/elle/on boive
nous bûmes	nous avions bu	nous boirons	nous boirions	que nous buvions
vous bûtes	vous aviez bu	vous boirez	vous boiriez	que vous buviez
ils/elles burent	ils/elles avaient bu	ils/elles boiront	ils/elles boiraient	qu'ils/elles boivent

Passé simple	Plus-que-parfait	Futur	Conditionnel	Subjonctif
je connus	j'avais connu	je connaîtrai	je connaîtrais	que je connaisse
tu connus	tu avais connu	tu connaîtras	tu connaîtrais	que tu connaisses
il/elle/on connut	il/elle/on avait connu	il/elle/on connaîtra	il/elle/on connaîtrait	qu'il/elle/on connaisse
nous connûmes	nous avions connu	nous connaîtrons	nous connaîtrions	que nous connaissions
vous connûtes	vous aviez connu	vous connaîtrez	vous connaîtriez	que vous connaissiez
ils/elles connurent	ils/elles avaient connu	ils/elles connaîtront	ils/elles connaîtraient	qu'ils/elles connaissent

Infinitif	Présent	Impératif	Passé composé	Imparfait
5. courir	je **cours**	**cours**	j'**ai couru**	je **courais**
(to run)	tu **cours**	**courons**	tu **as couru**	tu **courais**
	il/elle/on **court**	**courez**	il/elle/on **a couru**	il/elle/on **courait**
Participe présent:	nous **courons**		nous **avons couru**	nous **courions**
courant	vous **courez**		vous **avez couru**	vous **couriez**
	ils/elles **courent**		ils/elles **ont couru**	ils/elles **couraient**

Infinitif	Présent	Impératif	Passé composé	Imparfait
6. craindre	je **crains**	**crains**	j'**ai craint**	je **craignais**
(to fear)	tu **crains**	**craignons**	tu **as craint**	tu **craignais**
	il/elle/on **craint**	**craignez**	il/elle/on **a craint**	il/elle/on **craignait**
Participe présent:	nous **craignons**		nous **avons craint**	nous **craignions**
craignant	vous **craignez**		vous **avez craint**	vous **craigniez**
	ils/elles **craignent**		ils/elles **ont craint**	ils/elles **craignaient**

Infinitif	Présent	Impératif	Passé composé	Imparfait
7. croire	je **crois**	**crois**	j'**ai cru**	je **croyais**
(to believe)	tu **crois**	**croyons**	tu **as cru**	tu **croyais**
	il/elle/on **croit**	**croyez**	il/elle/on **a cru**	il/elle/on **croyait**
Participe présent:	nous **croyons**		nous **avons cru**	nous **croyions**
croyant	vous **croyez**		vous **avez cru**	vous **croyiez**
	ils/elles **croient**		ils/elles **ont cru**	ils/elles **croyaient**

Infinitif	Présent	Impératif	Passé composé	Imparfait
8. devoir	je **dois**	**dois**	j'**ai dû**	je **devais**
(to have to; must;	tu **dois**	**devons**	tu **as dû**	tu **devais**
to owe)	il/elle/on **doit**	**devez**	il/elle/on **a dû**	il/elle/on **devait**
Participe présent:	nous **devons**		nous **avons dû**	nous **devions**
devant	vous **devez**		vous **avez dû**	vous **deviez**
	ils/elles **doivent**		ils/elles **ont dû**	ils/elles **devaient**

Infinitif	Présent	Impératif	Passé composé	Imparfait
9. dire	je **dis**	**dis**	j'**ai dit**	je **disais**
(to say, tell)	tu **dis**	**disons**	tu **as dit**	tu **disais**
	il/elle/on **dit**	**dites**	il/elle/on **a dit**	il/elle/on **disait**
Participe présent:	nous **disons**		nous **avons dit**	nous **disions**
disant	vous **dites**		vous **avez dit**	vous **disiez**
	ils/elles **disent**		ils/elles **ont dit**	ils/elles **disaient**

Infinitif	Présent	Impératif	Passé composé	Imparfait
10. dormir	je **dors**	**dors**	j'**ai dormi**	je **dormais**
(to sleep)	tu **dors**	**dormons**	tu **as dormi**	tu **dormais**
	il/elle/on **dort**	**dormez**	il/elle/on **a dormi**	il/elle/on **dormait**
Participe présent:	nous **dormons**		nous **avons dormi**	nous **dormions**
dormant	vous **dormez**		vous **avez dormi**	vous **dormiez**
	ils/elles **dorment**		ils/elles **ont dormi**	ils/elles **dormaient**

Passé simple	Plus-que-parfait	Futur	Conditionnel	Subjonctif
je **courus**	j'**avais couru**	je **courrai**	je **courrais**	que je **coure**
tu **courus**	tu **avais couru**	tu **courras**	tu **courrais**	que tu **coures**
il/elle/on **courut**	il/elle/on **avait couru**	il/elle/on **courra**	il/elle/on **courrait**	qu'il/elle/on **coure**
nous **courûmes**	nous **avions couru**	nous **courrons**	nous **courrions**	que nous **courions**
vous **courûtes**	vous **aviez couru**	vous **courrez**	vous **courriez**	que vous **couriez**
ils/elles **coururent**	ils/elles **avaient couru**	ils/elles **courront**	ils/elles **courraient**	qu'ils/elles **courent**

Passé simple	Plus-que-parfait	Futur	Conditionnel	Subjonctif
je **craignis**	j'**avais craint**	je **craindrai**	je **craindrais**	que je **craigne**
tu **craignis**	tu **avais craint**	tu **craindras**	tu **craindrais**	que tu **craignes**
il/elle/on **craignit**	il/elle/on **avait craint**	il/elle/on **craindra**	il/elle/on **craindrait**	qu'il/elle/on **craigne**
nous **craignîmes**	nous **avions craint**	nous **craindrons**	nous **craindrions**	que nous **craignions**
vous **craignîtes**	vous **aviez craint**	vous **craindrez**	vous **craindriez**	que vous **craigniez**
ils/elles **craignirent**	ils/elles **avaient craint**	ils/elles **craindront**	ils/elles **craindraient**	qu'ils/elles **craignent**

Passé simple	Plus-que-parfait	Futur	Conditionnel	Subjonctif
je **crus**	j'**avais cru**	je **croirai**	je **croirais**	que je **croie**
tu **crus**	tu **avais cru**	tu **croiras**	tu **croirais**	que tu **croies**
il/elle/on **crut**	il/elle/on **avait cru**	il/elle/on **croira**	il/elle/on **croirait**	qu'il/elle/on **croie**
nous **crûmes**	nous **avions cru**	nous **croirons**	nous **croirions**	que nous **croyions**
vous **crûtes**	vous **aviez cru**	vous **croirez**	vous **croiriez**	que vous **croyiez**
ils/elles **crurent**	ils/elles **avaient cru**	ils/elles **croiront**	ils/elles **croiraient**	qu'ils/elles **croient**

Passé simple	Plus-que-parfait	Futur	Conditionnel	Subjonctif
je **dus**	j'**avais dû**	je **devrai**	je **devrais**	que je **doive**
tu **dus**	tu **avais dû**	tu **devras**	tu **devrais**	que tu **doives**
il/elle/on **dut**	il/elle/on **avait dû**	il/elle/on **devra**	il/elle/on **devrait**	qu'il/elle/on **doive**
nous **dûmes**	nous **avions dû**	nous **devrons**	nous **devrions**	que nous **devions**
vous **dûtes**	vous **aviez dû**	vous **devrez**	vous **devriez**	que vous **deviez**
ils/elles **durent**	ils/elles **avaient dû**	ils/elles **devront**	ils/elles **devraient**	qu'ils/elles **doivent**

Passé simple	Plus-que-parfait	Futur	Conditionnel	Subjonctif
je **dis**	j'**avais dit**	je **dirai**	je **dirais**	que je **dise**
tu **dis**	tu **avais dit**	tu **diras**	tu **dirais**	que tu **dises**
il/elle/on **dit**	il/elle/on **avait dit**	il/elle/on **dira**	il/elle/on **dirait**	qu'il/elle/on **dise**
nous **dîmes**	nous **avions dit**	nous **dirons**	nous **dirions**	que nous **disions**
vous **dîtes**	vous **aviez dit**	vous **direz**	vous **diriez**	que vous **disiez**
ils/elles **dirent**	ils/elles **avaient dit**	ils/elles **diront**	ils/elles **diraient**	qu'ils/elles **disent**

Passé simple	Plus-que-parfait	Futur	Conditionnel	Subjonctif
je **dormis**	j'**avais dormi**	je **dormirai**	je **dormirais**	que je **dorme**
tu **dormis**	tu **avais dormi**	tu **dormiras**	tu **dormirais**	que tu **dormes**
il/elle/on **dormit**	il/elle/on **avait dormi**	il/elle/on **dormira**	il/elle/on **dormirait**	qu'il/elle/on **dorme**
nous **dormîmes**	nous **avions dormi**	nous **dormirons**	nous **dormirions**	que nous **dormions**
vous **dormîtes**	vous **aviez dormi**	vous **dormirez**	vous **dormiriez**	que vous **dormiez**
ils/elles **dormirent**	ils/elles **avaient dormi**	ils/elles **dormiront**	ils/elles **dormiraient**	qu'ils/elles **dorment**

Infinitif	Présent	Impératif	Passé composé	Imparfait
11. écrire	j'**écris**	**écris**	j'**ai écrit**	j'**écrivais**
(to write)	tu **écris**	**écrivons**	tu **as écrit**	tu **écrivais**
	il/elle/on **écrit**	**écrivez**	il/elle/on **a écrit**	il/elle/on **écrivait**
Participe présent:	nous **écrivons**		nous **avons écrit**	nous **écrivions**
écrivant	vous **écrivez**		vous **avez écrit**	vous **écriviez**
	ils/elles **écrivent**		ils/elles **ont écrit**	ils/elles **écrivaient**

Infinitif	Présent	Impératif	Passé composé	Imparfait
12. envoyer	j'**envoie**	**envoie**	j'**ai envoyé**	j'**envoyais**
(to send)	tu **envoies**	**envoyons**	tu **as envoyé**	tu **envoyais**
	il/elle/on **envoie**	**envoyez**	il/elle/on **a envoyé**	il/elle/on **envoyait**
Participe présent:	nous **envoyons**		nous **avons envoyé**	nous **envoyions**
envoyant	vous **envoyez**		vous **avez envoyé**	vous **envoyiez**
	ils/elles **envoient**		ils/elles **ont envoyé**	ils/elles **envoyaient**

Infinitif	Présent	Impératif	Passé composé	Imparfait
13. être	je **suis**	**sois**	j'**ai été**	j'**étais**
(to be)	tu **es**	**soyons**	tu **as été**	tu **étais**
	il/elle/on **est**	**soyez**	il/elle/on **a été**	il/elle/on **était**
Participe présent:	nous **sommes**		nous **avons été**	nous **étions**
étant	vous **êtes**		vous **avez été**	vous **étiez**
	ils/elles **sont**		ils/elles **ont été**	ils/elles **étaient**

Infinitif	Présent	Impératif	Passé composé	Imparfait
14. faire	je **fais**	**fais**	j'**ai fait**	je **faisais**
(to do, make)	tu **fais**	**faisons**	tu **as fait**	tu **faisais**
	il/elle/on **fait**	**faites**	il/elle/on **a fait**	il/elle/on **faisait**
Participe présent:	nous **faisons**		nous **avons fait**	nous **faisions**
faisant	vous **faites**		vous **avez fait**	vous **faisiez**
	ils/elles **font**		ils/elles **ont fait**	ils/elles **faisaient**

Infinitif	Présent	Impératif	Passé composé	Imparfait
15. falloir	il **faut**	*(does not exist)*	il **a fallu**	il **fallait**
(to be necessary)				
Participe présent:				
(does not exist)				

Infinitif	Présent	Impératif	Passé composé	Imparfait
16. mettre	je **mets**	**mets**	j'**ai mis**	je **mettais**
(to put, place)	tu **mets**	**mettons**	tu **as mis**	tu **mettais**
	il/elle/on **met**	**mettez**	il/elle/on **a mis**	il/elle/on **mettait**
Participe présent:	nous **mettons**		nous **avons mis**	nous **mettions**
mettant	vous **mettez**		vous **avez mis**	vous **mettiez**
	ils/elles **mettent**		ils/elles **ont mis**	ils/elles **mettaient**

Passé simple	Plus-que-parfait	Futur	Conditionnel	Subjonctif
j'écrivis	j'avais écrit	j'écrirai	j'écrirais	que j'écrive
tu écrivis	tu avais écrit	tu écriras	tu écrirais	que tu écrives
il/elle/on écrivit	il/elle/on avait écrit	il/elle/on écrira	il/elle/on écrirait	qu'il/elle/on écrive
nous écrivîmes	nous avions écrit	nous écrirons	nous écririons	que nous écrivions
vous écrivîtes	vous aviez écrit	vous écrirez	vous écririez	que vous écriviez
ils/elles écrivirent	ils/elles avaient écrit	ils/elles écriront	ils/elles écriraient	qu'ils/elles écrivent

Passé simple	Plus-que-parfait	Futur	Conditionnel	Subjonctif
j'envoyai	j'avais envoyé	j'enverrai	j'enverrais	que j'envoie
tu envoyas	tu avais envoyé	tu enverras	tu enverrais	que tu envoies
il/elle/on envoya	il/elle/on avait envoyé	il/elle/on enverra	il/elle/on enverrait	qu'il/elle/on envoie
nous envoyâmes	nous avions envoyé	nous enverrons	nous enverrions	que nous envoyions
vous envoyâtes	vous aviez envoyé	vous enverrez	vous enverriez	que vous envoyiez
ils/elles envoyèrent	ils/elles avaient envoyé	ils/elles enverront	ils/elles enverraient	qu'ils/elles envoient

Passé simple	Plus-que-parfait	Futur	Conditionnel	Subjonctif
je fus	j'avais été	je serai	je serais	que je sois
tu fus	tu avais été	tu seras	tu serais	que tu sois
il/elle/on fut	il/elle/on avait été	il/elle/on sera	il/elle/on serait	qu'il/elle/on soit
nous fûmes	nous avions été	nous serons	nous serions	que nous soyons
vous fûtes	vous aviez été	vous serez	vous seriez	que vous soyez
ils/elles furent	ils/elles avaient été	ils/elles seront	ils/elles seraient	qu'ils/elles soient

Passé simple	Plus-que-parfait	Futur	Conditionnel	Subjonctif
je fis	j'avais fait	je ferai	je ferais	que je fasse
tu fis	tu avais fait	tu feras	tu ferais	que tu fasses
il/elle/on fit	il/elle/on avait fait	il/elle/on fera	il/elle/on ferait	qu'il/elle/on fasse
nous fîmes	nous avions fait	nous ferons	nous ferions	que nous fassions
vous fîtes	vous aviez fait	vous ferez	vous feriez	que vous fassiez
ils/elles firent	ils/elles avaient fait	ils/elles feront	ils/elles feraient	qu'ils/elles fassent

Passé simple	Plus-que-parfait	Futur	Conditionnel	Subjonctif
il fallut	il avait fallu	il faudra	il faudrait	qu'il faille

Passé simple	Plus-que-parfait	Futur	Conditionnel	Subjonctif
je mis	j'avais mis	je mettrai	je mettrais	que je mette
tu mis	tu avais mis	tu mettras	tu mettrais	que tu mettes
il/elle/on mit	il/elle/on avait mis	il/elle/on mettra	il/elle/on mettrait	qu'il/elle/on mette
nous mîmes	nous avions mis	nous mettrons	nous mettrions	que nous mettions
vous mîtes	vous aviez mis	vous mettrez	vous mettriez	que vous mettiez
ils/elles mirent	ils/elles avaient mis	ils/elles mettront	ils/elles mettraient	qu'ils/elles mettent

Infinitif	Présent	Impératif	Passé composé	Imparfait
17. mourir	je **meurs**	**meurs**	je **suis mort(e)**	je **mourais**
(to die)	tu **meurs**	**mourons**	tu **es mort(e)**	tu **mourais**
	il/elle/on **meurt**	**mourez**	il/elle/on **est mort(e)**	il/elle/on **mourait**
Participe présent:	nous **mourons**		nous **sommes mort(e)s**	nous **mourions**
mourant	vous **mourez**		vous **êtes mort(e)(s)**	vous **mouriez**
	ils/elles **meurent**		ils/elles **sont mort(e)s**	ils/elles **mouraient**

Infinitif	Présent	Impératif	Passé composé	Imparfait
18. naître	je **nais**	**nais**	je **suis né(e)**	je **naissais**
(to be born)	tu **nais**	**naissons**	tu **es né(e)**	tu **naissais**
	il/elle/on **naît**	**naissez**	il/elle/on **est né(e)**	il/elle/on **naissait**
Participe présent:	nous **naissons**		nous **sommes né(e)s**	nous **naissions**
naissant	vous **naissez**		vous **êtes né(e)(s)**	vous **naissiez**
	ils/elles **naissent**		ils/elles **sont né(e)s**	ils/elles **naissaient**

Infinitif	Présent	Impératif	Passé composé	Imparfait
19. ouvrir	j'**ouvre**	**ouvre**	j'**ai ouvert**	j'**ouvrais**
(to open)	tu **ouvres**	**ouvrons**	tu **as ouvert**	tu **ouvrais**
	il/elle/on **ouvre**	**ouvrez**	il/elle/on **a ouvert**	il/elle/on **ouvrait**
Participe présent:	nous **ouvrons**		nous **avons ouvert**	nous **ouvrions**
ouvrant	vous **ouvrez**		vous **avez ouvert**	vous **ouvriez**
	ils/elles **ouvrent**		ils/elles **ont ouvert**	ils/elles **ouvraient**

Infinitif	Présent	Impératif	Passé composé	Imparfait
20. plaire	je **plais**	**plais**	j'**ai plu**	je **plaisais**
(to please)	tu **plais**	**plaisons**	tu **as plu**	tu **plaisais**
	il/elle/on **plaît**	**plaisez**	il/elle/on **a plu**	il/elle/on **plaisait**
Participe présent:	nous **plaisons**		nous **avons plu**	nous **plaisions**
plaisant	vous **plaisez**		vous **avez plu**	vous **plaisiez**
	ils/elles **plaisent**		ils/elles **ont plu**	ils/elles **plaisaient**

Infinitif	Présent	Impératif	Passé composé	Imparfait
21. pleuvoir	il **pleut**	*(does not exist)*	il **a plu**	il **pleuvait**
(to rain)				
Participe présent:				
pleuvant				

Infinitif	Présent	Impératif	Passé composé	Imparfait
22. pouvoir	je **peux**	*(does not exist)*	j'**ai pu**	je **pouvais**
(to be able, can)	tu **peux**		tu **as pu**	tu **pouvais**
	il/elle/on **peut**		il/elle/on **a pu**	il/elle/on **pouvait**
Participe présent:	nous **pouvons**		nous **avons pu**	nous **pouvions**
pouvant	vous **pouvez**		vous **avez pu**	vous **pouviez**
	ils/elles **peuvent**		ils/elles **ont pu**	ils/elles **pouvaient**

Passé simple	Plus-que-parfait	Futur	Conditionnel	Subjonctif
je **mourus**	j'**étais mort(e)**	je **mourrai**	je **mourrais**	que je **meure**
tu **mourus**	tu **étais mort(e)**	tu **mourras**	tu **mourrais**	que tu **meures**
il/elle/on **mourut**	il/elle/on **était mort(e)**	il/elle/on **mourra**	il/elle/on **mourrait**	qu'il/elle/on **meure**
nous **mourûmes**	nous **étions mort(e)s**	nous **mourrons**	nous **mourrions**	que nous **mourions**
vous **mourûtes**	vous **étiez mort(e)(s)**	vous **mourrez**	vous **mourriez**	que vous **mouriez**
ils/elles **moururent**	ils/elles **étaient mort(e)s**	ils/elles **mourront**	ils/elles **mourraient**	qu'ils/elles **meurent**

Passé simple	Plus-que-parfait	Futur	Conditionnel	Subjonctif
je **naquis**	j'**étais né(e)**	je **naîtrai**	je **naîtrais**	que je **naisse**
tu **naquis**	tu **étais né(e)**	tu **naîtras**	tu **naîtrais**	que tu **naisses**
il/elle/on **naquit**	il/elle/on **était né(e)**	il/elle/on **naîtra**	il/elle/on **naîtrait**	qu'il/elle/on **naisse**
nous **naquîmes**	nous **étions né(e)s**	nous **naîtrons**	nous **naîtrions**	que nous **naissions**
vous **naquîtes**	vous **étiez né(e)(s)**	vous **naîtrez**	vous **naîtriez**	que vous **naissiez**
ils/elles **naquirent**	ils/elles **étaient né(e)s**	ils/elles **naîtront**	ils/elles **naîtraient**	qu'ils/elles **naissent**

Passé simple	Plus-que-parfait	Futur	Conditionnel	Subjonctif
j'**ouvris**	j'**avais ouvert**	j'**ouvrirai**	j'**ouvrirais**	que j'**ouvre**
tu **ouvris**	tu **avais ouvert**	tu **ouvriras**	tu **ouvrirais**	que tu **ouvres**
il/elle/on **ouvrit**	il/elle/on **avait ouvert**	il/elle/on **ouvrira**	il/elle/on **ouvrirait**	qu'il/elle/on **ouvre**
nous **ouvrîmes**	nous **avions ouvert**	nous **ouvrirons**	nous **ouvririons**	que nous **ouvrions**
vous **ouvrîtes**	vous **aviez ouvert**	vous **ouvrirez**	vous **ouvririez**	que vous **ouvriez**
ils/elles **ouvrirent**	ils/elles **avaient ouvert**	ils/elles **ouvriront**	ils/elles **ouvriraient**	qu'ils/elles **ouvrent**

Passé simple	Plus-que-parfait	Futur	Conditionnel	Subjonctif
je **plus**	j'**avais plu**	je **plairai**	je **plairais**	que je **plaise**
tu **plus**	tu **avais plu**	tu **plairas**	tu **plairais**	que tu **plaises**
il/elle/on **plut**	il/elle/on **avait plu**	il/elle/on **plaira**	il/elle/on **plairait**	qu'il/elle/on **plaise**
nous **plûmes**	nous **avions plu**	nous **plairons**	nous **plairions**	que nous **plaisions**
vous **plûtes**	vous **aviez plu**	vous **plairez**	vous **plairiez**	que vous **plaisiez**
ils/elles **plurent**	ils/elles **avaient plu**	ils/elles **plairont**	ils/elles **plairaient**	qu'ils/elles **plaisent**

Passé simple	Plus-que-parfait	Futur	Conditionnel	Subjonctif
il **plut**	il **avait plu**	il **pleuvra**	il **pleuvrait**	qu'il **pleuve**

Passé simple	Plus-que-parfait	Futur	Conditionnel	Subjonctif
je **pus**	j'**avais pu**	je **pourrai**	je **pourrais**	que je **puisse**
tu **pus**	tu **avais pu**	tu **pourras**	tu **pourrais**	que tu **puisses**
il/elle/on **put**	il/elle/on **avait pu**	il/elle/on **pourra**	il/elle/on **pourrait**	qu'il/elle/on **puisse**
nous **pûmes**	nous **avions pu**	nous **pourrons**	nous **pourrions**	que nous **puissions**
vous **pûtes**	vous **aviez pu**	vous **pourrez**	vous **pourriez**	que vous **puissiez**
ils/elles **purent**	ils/elles **avaient pu**	ils/elles **pourront**	ils/elles **pourraient**	qu'ils/elles **puissent**

Infinitif	Présent	Impératif	Passé composé	Imparfait
23. prendre	je **prends**	**prends**	j'**ai pris**	je **prenais**
(to take)	tu **prends**	**prenons**	tu **as pris**	tu **prenais**
	il/elle/on **prend**	**prenez**	il/elle/on **a pris**	il/elle/on **prenait**
Participe présent:	nous **prenons**		nous **avons pris**	nous **prenions**
prenant	vous **prenez**		vous **avez pris**	vous **preniez**
	ils/elles **prennent**		ils/elles **ont pris**	ils/elles **prenaient**

Infinitif	Présent	Impératif	Passé composé	Imparfait
24. recevoir	je **reçois**	**reçois**	j'**ai reçu**	je **recevais**
(to receive, get)	tu **reçois**	**recevons**	tu **as reçu**	tu **recevais**
	il/elle/on **reçoit**	**recevez**	il/elle/on **a reçu**	il/elle/on **recevait**
Participe présent:	nous **recevons**		nous **avons reçu**	nous **recevions**
recevant	vous **recevez**		vous **avez reçu**	vous **receviez**
	ils/elles **reçoivent**		ils/elles **ont reçu**	ils/elles **recevaient**

Infinitif	Présent	Impératif	Passé composé	Imparfait
25. rire	je **ris**	**ris**	j'**ai ri**	je **riais**
(to laugh)	tu **ris**	**rions**	tu **as ri**	tu **riais**
	il/elle/on **rit**	**riez**	il/elle/on **a ri**	il/elle/on **riait**
Participe présent:	nous **rions**		nous **avons ri**	nous **riions**
riant	vous **riez**		vous **avez ri**	vous **riiez**
	ils/elles **rient**		ils/elles **ont ri**	ils/elles **riaient**

Infinitif	Présent	Impératif	Passé composé	Imparfait
26. savoir	je **sais**	**sache**	j'**ai su**	je **savais**
(to know)	tu **sais**	**sachons**	tu **as su**	tu **savais**
	il/elle/on **sait**	**sachez**	il/elle/on **a su**	il/elle/on **savait**
Participe présent:	nous **savons**		nous **avons su**	nous **savions**
sachant	vous **savez**		vous **avez su**	vous **saviez**
	ils/elles **savent**		ils/elles **ont su**	ils/elles **savaient**

Infinitif	Présent	Impératif	Passé composé	Imparfait
27. sortir	je **sors**	**sors**	je **suis sorti(e)**	je **sortais**
(to go out)	tu **sors**	**sortons**	tu **es sorti(e)**	tu **sortais**
	il/elle/on **sort**	**sortez**	il/elle/on **est sorti(e)**	il/elle/on **sortait**
Participe présent:	nous **sortons**		nous **sommes sorti(e)s**	nous **sortions**
sortant	vous **sortez**		vous **êtes sorti(e)(s)**	vous **sortiez**
	ils/elles **sortent**		ils/elles **sont sorti(e)s**	ils/elles **sortaient**

Infinitif	Présent	Impératif	Passé composé	Imparfait
28. suivre	je **suis**	**suis**	j'**ai suivi**	je **suivais**
(to follow)	tu **suis**	**suivons**	tu **as suivi**	tu **suivais**
	il/elle/on **suit**	**suivez**	il/elle/on **a suivi**	il/elle/on **suivait**
Participe présent:	nous **suivons**		nous **avons suivi**	nous **suivions**
suivant	vous **suivez**		vous **avez suivi**	vous **suiviez**
	ils/elles **suivent**		ils/elles **ont suivi**	ils/elles **suivaient**

Passé simple	Plus-que-parfait	Futur	Conditionnel	Subjonctif
je **pris**	j'**avais pris**	je **prendrai**	je **prendrais**	que je **prenne**
tu **pris**	tu **avais pris**	tu **prendras**	tu **prendrais**	que tu **prennes**
il/elle/on **prit**	il/elle/on **avait pris**	il/elle/on **prendra**	il/elle/on **prendrait**	qu'il/elle/on **prenne**
nous **prîmes**	nous **avions pris**	nous **prendrons**	nous **prendrions**	que nous **prenions**
vous **prîtes**	vous **aviez pris**	vous **prendrez**	vous **prendriez**	que vous **preniez**
ils/elles **prirent**	ils/elles **avaient pris**	ils/elles **prendront**	ils/elles **prendraient**	qu'ils/elles **prennent**

Passé simple	Plus-que-parfait	Futur	Conditionnel	Subjonctif
je **reçus**	j'**avais reçu**	je **recevrai**	je **recevrais**	que je **reçoive**
tu **reçus**	tu **avais reçu**	tu **recevras**	tu **recevrais**	que tu **reçoives**
il/elle/on **reçut**	il/elle/on **avait reçu**	il/elle/on **recevra**	il/elle/on **recevrait**	qu'il/elle/on **reçoive**
nous **reçûmes**	nous **avions reçu**	nous **recevrons**	nous **recevrions**	que nous **recevions**
vous **reçûtes**	vous **aviez reçu**	vous **recevrez**	vous **recevriez**	que vous **receviez**
ils/elles **reçurent**	ils/elles **avaient reçu**	ils/elles **recevront**	ils/elles **recevraient**	qu'ils/elles **reçoivent**

Passé simple	Plus-que-parfait	Futur	Conditionnel	Subjonctif
je **ris**	j'**avais ri**	je **rirai**	je **rirais**	que je **rie**
tu **ris**	tu **avais ri**	tu **riras**	tu **rirais**	que tu **ries**
il/elle/on **rit**	il/elle/on **avait ri**	il/elle/on **rira**	il/elle/on **rirait**	qu'il/elle/on **rie**
nous **rîmes**	nous **avions ri**	nous **rirons**	nous **ririons**	que nous **riions**
vous **rîtes**	vous **aviez ri**	vous **rirez**	vous **ririez**	que vous **riiez**
ils/elles **rirent**	ils/elles **avaient ri**	ils/elles **riront**	ils/elles **riraient**	qu'ils/elles **rient**

Passé simple	Plus-que-parfait	Futur	Conditionnel	Subjonctif
je **sus**	j'**avais su**	je **saurai**	je **saurais**	que je **sache**
tu **sus**	tu **avais su**	tu **sauras**	tu **saurais**	que tu **saches**
il/elle/on **sut**	il/elle/on **avait su**	il/elle/on **saura**	il/elle/on **saurait**	qu'il/elle/on **sache**
nous **sûmes**	nous **avions su**	nous **saurons**	nous **saurions**	que nous **sachions**
vous **sûtes**	vous **aviez su**	vous **saurez**	vous **sauriez**	que vous **sachiez**
ils/elles **surent**	ils/elles **avaient su**	ils/elles **sauront**	ils/elles **sauraient**	qu'ils/elles **sachent**

Passé simple	Plus-que-parfait	Futur	Conditionnel	Subjonctif
je **sortis**	j'**étais sorti(e)**	je **sortirai**	je **sortirais**	que je **sorte**
tu **sortis**	tu **étais sorti(e)**	tu **sortiras**	tu **sortirais**	que tu **sortes**
il/elle/on **sortit**	il/elle/on **était sorti(e)**	il/elle/on **sortira**	il/elle/on **sortirait**	qu'il/elle/on **sorte**
nous **sortîmes**	nous **étions sorti(e)s**	nous **sortirons**	nous **sortirions**	que nous **sortions**
vous **sortîtes**	vous **étiez sorti(e)(s)**	vous **sortirez**	vous **sortiriez**	que vous **sortiez**
ils/elles **sortirent**	ils/elles **étaient sorti(e)s**	ils/elles **sortiront**	ils/elles **sortiraient**	qu'ils/elles **sortent**

Passé simple	Plus-que-parfait	Futur	Conditionnel	Subjonctif
je **suivis**	j'**avais suivi**	je **suivrai**	je **suivrais**	que je **suive**
tu **suivis**	tu **avais suivi**	tu **suivras**	tu **suivrais**	que tu **suives**
il/elle/on **suivit**	il/elle/on **avait suivi**	il/elle/on **suivra**	il/elle/on **suivrait**	qu'il/elle/on **suive**
nous **suivîmes**	nous **avions suivi**	nous **suivrons**	nous **suivrions**	que nous **suivions**
vous **suivîtes**	vous **aviez suivi**	vous **suivrez**	vous **suivriez**	que vous **suiviez**
ils/elles **suivirent**	ils/elles **avaient suivi**	ils/elles **suivront**	ils/elles **suivraient**	qu'ils/elles **suivent**

VERBES IRREGULIERS *(suite)*

Infinitif	Présent	Impératif	Passé composé	Imparfait
29. valoir	je **vaux**	*(does not exist)*	j'**ai valu**	je **valais**
(to be worth;	tu **vaux**		tu **as valu**	tu **valais**
to deserve, merit)	il/elle/on **vaut**		il/elle/on **a valu**	il/elle/on **valait**
Participe présent:	nous **valons**		nous **avons valu**	nous **valions**
valant	vous **valez**		vous **avez valu**	vous **valiez**
	ils/elles **valent**		ils/elles **ont valu**	ils/elles **valaient**

Infinitif	Présent	Impératif	Passé composé	Imparfait
30. venir	je **viens**	**viens**	je **suis venu(e)**	je **venais**
(to come)	tu **viens**	**venons**	tu **es venu(e)**	tu **venais**
	il/elle/on **vient**	**venez**	il/elle/on **est venu(e)**	il/elle/on **venait**
Participe présent:	nous **venons**		nous **sommes venu(e)s**	nous **venions**
venant	vous **venez**		vous **êtes venu(e)(s)**	vous **veniez**
	ils/elles **viennent**		ils/elles **sont venu(e)s**	ils/elles **venaient**

Infinitif	Présent	Impératif	Passé composé	Imparfait
31. voir	je **vois**	**vois**	j'**ai vu**	je **voyais**
(to see)	tu **vois**	**voyons**	tu **as vu**	tu **voyais**
	il/elle/on **voit**	**voyez**	il/elle/on **a vu**	il/elle/on **voyait**
Participe présent:	nous **voyons**		nous **avons vu**	nous **voyions**
voyant	vous **voyez**		vous **avez vu**	vous **voyiez**
	ils/elles **voient**		ils/elles **ont vu**	ils/elles **voyaient**

Infinitif	Présent	Impératif	Passé composé	Imparfait
32. vouloir	je **veux**	**veuille**	j'**ai voulu**	je **voulais**
(to wish, want)	tu **veux**	**veuillons**	tu **as voulu**	tu **voulais**
	il/elle/on **veut**	**veuillez**	il/elle/on **a voulu**	il/elle/on **voulait**
Participe présent:	nous **voulons**		nous **avons voulu**	nous **voulions**
voulant	vous **voulez**		vous **avez voulu**	vous **vouliez**
	ils/elles **veulent**		ils/elles **ont voulu**	ils/elles **voulaient**

Passé simple	Plus-que-parfait	Futur	Conditionnel	Subjonctif
je **valus**	j'**avais valu**	je **vaudrai**	je **vaudrais**	que je **vaille**
tu **valus**	tu **avais valu**	tu **vaudras**	tu **vaudrais**	que tu **vailles**
il/elle/on **valut**	il/elle/on **avait valu**	il/elle/on **vaudra**	il/elle/on **vaudrait**	qu'il/elle/on **vaille**
nous **valûmes**	nous **avions valu**	nous **vaudrons**	nous **vaudrions**	que nous **valions**
vous **valûtes**	vous **aviez valu**	vous **vaudrez**	vous **vaudriez**	que vous **valiez**
ils/elles **valurent**	ils/elles **avaient valu**	ils/elles **vaudront**	ils/elles **vaudraient**	qu'ils/elles **vaillent**

Passé simple	Plus-que-parfait	Futur	Conditionnel	Subjonctif
je **vins**	j'**étais venu(e)**	je **viendrai**	je **viendrais**	que je **vienne**
tu **vins**	tu **étais venu(e)**	tu **viendras**	tu **viendrais**	que tu **viennes**
il/elle/on **vint**	il/elle/on **était venu(e)**	il/elle/on **viendra**	il/elle/on **viendrait**	qu'il/elle/on **vienne**
nous **vînmes**	nous **étions venu(e)s**	nous **viendrons**	nous **viendrions**	que nous **venions**
vous **vîntes**	vous **étiez venu(e)(s)**	vous **viendrez**	vous **viendriez**	que vous **veniez**
ils/elles **vinrent**	ils/elles **étaient venu(e)s**	ils/elles **viendront**	ils/elles **viendraient**	qu'ils/elles **viennent**

Passé simple	Plus-que-parfait	Futur	Conditionnel	Subjonctif
je **vis**	j'**avais vu**	je **verrai**	je **verrais**	que je **voie**
tu **vis**	tu **avais vu**	tu **verras**	tu **verrais**	que tu **voies**
il/elle/on **vit**	il/elle/on **avait vu**	il/elle/on **verra**	il/elle/on **verrait**	qu'il/elle/on **voie**
nous **vîmes**	nous **avions vu**	nous **verrons**	nous **verrions**	que nous **voyions**
vous **vîtes**	vous **aviez vu**	vous **verrez**	vous **verriez**	que vous **voyiez**
ils/elles **virent**	ils/elles **avaient vu**	ils/elles **verront**	ils/elles **verraient**	qu'ils/elles **voient**

Passé simple	Plus-que-parfait	Futur	Conditionnel	Subjonctif
je **voulus**	j'**avais voulu**	je **voudrai**	je **voudrais**	que je **veuille**
tu **voulus**	tu **avais voulu**	tu **voudras**	tu **voudrais**	que tu **veuilles**
il/elle/on **voulut**	il/elle/on **avait voulu**	il/elle/on **voudra**	il/elle/on **voudrait**	qu'il/elle/on **veuille**
nous **voulûmes**	nous **avions voulu**	nous **voudrons**	nous **voudrions**	que nous **voulions**
vous **voulûtes**	vous **aviez voulu**	vous **voudrez**	vous **voudriez**	que vous **vouliez**
ils/elles **voulurent**	ils/elles **avaient voulu**	ils/elles **voudront**	ils/elles **voudraient**	qu'ils/elles **veuillent**

A

abattement *(m)* — tax allowance; dejection, despondency

abattu(e) — overcome

abonné(e) *(m, f)* — subscriber

(s')abonner — to subscribe

abordable — affordable, approachable

absentéisme *(m)* — absenteeism

absolument — absolutely

accessible — accessible

accidentel(le) — accidental, fortuitous

accord *(m)* — agreement

accueillir — to welcome

accuser réception (de) — to acknowledge receipt (of)

acheter — to buy

acheteur *(m)* — buyer

actif *(m)* — assets; member of workforce

actif(ve) *(adj.)* — active

action *(f)* — action; stock

actionnaire *(m, f)* — stockholder

activer — to activate

activités extraprofessionnelles *(f)* — extracurricular activities [outside of one's field]

actuellement — now, at the present time

additionner — to add

adjoint *(m)* **au responsable** *(m)* — assistant commissioner

administration *(f)* — administration

adresse *(f)* — address

affaire *(f)***, une bonne affaire** — deal, a good deal

affiche *(f)* — poster

(s')afficher sur l'écran *(m)* — to appear, pull up on the screen [of a computer]

affronter l'échec — to confront defeat, deal with it

agacé(e); être agacé(e) (par) — aggravated; to be aggravated (by)

agence *(f)* — rental office; office; agency

agent *(m)* — agent

agrafeuse *(f)* — stapler

ailleurs; d'ailleurs — elsewhere; moreover, besides

aisé(e) — easy, well-off

aisément — easily

ajustement *(m)* — adjustment

ALENA *(m)* **(l'Accord de Libre Echange Nord Américain)** — NAFTA

allègement *(m)* — reduction

alléger — to lighten; to reduce

allumer (le Minitel) — to turn on (the Minitel)

alourdir — to make heavy; to increase

amertume *(f)* — bitterness

amovible — removable, detachable

ancien(ne) — former, old

ancienneté *(f)* — seniority

angoisse *(f)* — anguish

annuaire *(m)* **téléphonique** — phone book

annuel(le) — annual

annuler — to cancel

antérieurement — beforehand

anxiété *(f)* — anxiety

anxieux(se) — anxious

appareil *(m)* **de téléphone** *(m)* — telephone unit

appauvrissement *(m)* — impoverishment; thinning; degeneration

appel *(m)* — call

appel *(m)* **interurbain** — long-distance call

appel *(m)* **urbain** — local call

application *(f)* — application

appliquer — to apply something to

apprentissage *(m)* — apprenticeship

approche *(f)* **directe** — direct approach

approvisionnement *(m)* — supplying or stocking up on provisions or supplies

approximativement — approximately

appuyer — to press

aptitude *(f)* — aptitude, ability, gift, talent

(s')arranger — to work out

arriéré *(m)* — unpaid balance

arrogant(e) — arrogant

ascenseur *(m)* — elevator; scroll button

assiette *(f)* — plate; subject matter of assessment

assiette *(f)* **fiscale** — basis of assessment

assister — to be present; to assist

associé(e) *(nom et adj.)* — associate

assujetti(e); être assujetti(e) à l'impôt *(m)* — to be subjected to; to be subject to taxation

assurance multirisque *(f)* — multiple-risk insurance

assuré(e) *(nom et adj.)* — insured

atelier *(m)* — workshop

atout *(m)* — trump; asset, advantage

attente *(f)* — expectation

attentivement — carefully

attirant(e) — attractive

audioconférence *(f)* — conference call

augmentation *(f)*	raise	**boulot** *(m)*	job *(fam.)*
auparavant	before(hand); first; previously	**bourse** *(f)*	scholarship; sack; change purse
automatiquement	automatically	**Bourse** *(f)*	stock market
autonome	autonomous	**boursier(ière)** *(nom et adj.)*	recipient of scholarship; having to do with the stock market
autorisé(e)	authorized		
avance *(f); à l'avance;* **en avance**	advance; in advance; ahead of time, early	**bouton** *(m)*	button
		bouton *(m)* **de démarrage** *(m)*	turn-on button
avancer	to advance		
avantage *(m)* **fiscal**	tax advantage	**brancher**	to plug in
avantageux(se)	advantageous	**brûlé(e)** *(nom et adj.)*	burned
avarie *(f)*	damage, mishap		
averti(e)	advanced, warned	**brûler**	to burn
avertir	to warn	**but** *(m)*	aim, goal
avocat(e) *(m, f)*	lawyer		
axé(e) sur	built around, centered on		

C

		cabinet *(m)*	office
B		**câble** *(m)* **d'alimentation** *(f)*	entry cable
baisse *(f)*	drop, lowering	**cadran** *(m)*	dial
baisser	to lower	**cadre** *(m)*	middle- or upper-level staff person in a leading position
balance *(f)* **commerciale**	trade balance		
balance *(f)* **excédentaire**	favorable balance	**cambiste** *(m, f)*	money changer or broker
		cambriolage *(m)*	theft, break-in
bancaire	banking	**campagne** *(f)*	countryside; campaign
bande *(f)* **de déroulement** *(m)*	pull-down	**candidat(e)** *(m, f)*	candidate
		candidature *(f)*	application (for work)
banque *(f)* **de données**	database	**candidature** *(f)* **spontanée**	drop-in or stop-by application
barème *(m)*	calculation table, tax table grid		
		capital(aux) *(nom et adj.)*	capital
bâtir	to build	**capital** *(m)* **social**	company assets
batterie *(f)*	battery	**carnet** *(m)* **de chèques** *(m)*	checkbook
battre	to beat	**carrément**	squarely, bluntly, straight out
(se) battre	to fight		
bénéfice *(m)*	benefit	**carrière** *(f)*	career
bénéfice *(m)* **net**	net profit, net earnings	**carte** *(f)* **de visite** *(f)*	business card
bénéficiaire *(m, f)*	beneficiary	**cartouche** *(f)* **à encre** *(f)*	ink cartridge
bénévole *(nom et adj.) (m, f)*	volunteer (somebody who gives his/her time and expertise for free)	**cas** *(m); en cas de*	case; in case of
		cas *(m)* **échéant**	in the event; should the occasion arise
besoin *(m)*	need		
biais *(m); en biais*	slant; on the bias; gently sloping, oblique	**case** *(f)*	box, pigeon-hole
		causer (un préjudice)	to cause (a loss)
biens *(m)* **de consommation** *(f)*	consumer goods	**CDI, Centre Des Impôts**	French equivalent of the IRS
		CD-ROM *(m)*	CD-ROM
bilan *(m)*	balance sheet, statement of account(s)	**céder**	to give up, sell, dispose of
		CEE	EEC, European Economic Community
blessé(e) *(nom et adj.)*	wounded		
bogue *(f),* **bug** *(m)*	bug	**célibataire** *(nom et adj.) (m, f)*	single (unmarried)
boîte *(f)*	box; company *(fam.)*		
boîte *(f)* **aux lettres** *(f)*	mailbox	**censurer**	to censure
bon *(m)* **de commande** *(f)*	order form	**certainement**	certainly
boucler les fins *(f)* **de mois** *(m)*	to make ends meet	**chaîne** *(f)*	chain, channel
		chal(l)enge *(m)*	challenge

chance *(f)*	chance, luck, occasion	**concis(e)**	concise
changer d'avis *(m)*	to change one's mind	**concours** *(m)*, **concours** *(m)* **d'entrée** *(f)*	competitive entrance exam
charge *(f); à charge*	burden; dependent	**(bien) conçu(e)**	(well) conceived
chargé(e) de	responsible for	**concurrence** *(f)*	competition
charger *(m)*	to charge, load	**confiance** *(f)* **(en soi)**	(self) confidence
chasseur *(m)* **de têtes** *(f)*	headhunter	**confidence** *(f)* **[faux ami]**	little secret [false friend]
chef *(m)*	head, superior, leader	**confirmé(e) [qui a fait ses preuves** *(f)***]**	confirmed [proven]
chef *(m)* **d'atelier** *(m)*	foreman		
chef *(m)* **de rayon** *(m)*, **de service** *(m)*	department head	**conforme (à)**	true to; matching
chèque *(m)* **en blanc**	blank check	**conjoncture** *(f)* **économique**	economic circumstances or climate
chèque *(m)* **sans provision**	rubber check; check with insufficient funds	**(se) connecter**	to connect
chéquier *(m)*	checkbook	**connexion** *(f)*	connection
cher(ère)	expensive, clear	**conquérir**	to win, gain, conquer
chercher un travail	to search, look for a job	**Conseil** *(m)* **d'Administration** *(f)*	board of directors
chiffre *(m)* **d'affaires**	turnover	**conseillé(e)**	advised
chiffres *(m)* **bruts**	gross figures	**conseiller** *(verbe et nom)*	to advise; adviser
chômage *(m)*	unemployment		
chômeur(euse) *(m, f)*	unemployed person who is actively searching for a job	**consentir**	to consent, grant
chronologique	chronological	**consommateur(trice)**	consumer
chute *(f)*	fall	**consommation** *(f)*	consumption
ciblé(e)	targeted	**constamment**	constantly
clair(e)	clear, light	**constatation** *(f)*	statement, notice
classeur *(m)*	file; binder	**contraintes** *(f)*	restraints
clavier *(m)*	keyboard	**contrat** *(m)*	contract
clavier *(m)* **numérique**	keypad	**contrat** *(m)* **de carte** *(f)* **bancaire**	insurance automatically linked to the use of a bank or credit card
clientèle *(f)* **haut de gamme** *(m)*	top-of-the-line customers		
cliquer	to click	**contribuable** *(m, f)*	taxpayer
colle *(f)*	paste, glue	**contrôle** *(m)* **de qualité** *(f)*	quality control
combiné *(m)*	receiver	**convaincre**	to convince
comité *(m)* **d'entreprise** *(f)*	company committee, board	**convenir**	to agree; to be appropriate
commander	to lead, command	**convention** *(f)* **collective**	collective agreement concerning wages and working conditions
commerçant(e) *(nom)*	merchant, shopkeeper		
commerçant(e) *(adj.)*	commercial	**convivial(e)**	user-friendly
commissaire-priseur *(m)*	commissioner	**convoquer**	to invite (a candidate)
commission *(f)*	commission	**coordonner**	to coordinate
commode	convenient	**copier**	to copy
communication *(f)*	call; presentation of a paper	**corbeille** *(f)*	basket, trash (on computer screen)
compagnie *(f)*	company	**correspondant(e)**	person with whom one is talking
compétence *(f)*	specialization; proficiency, skill		
		cotation *(f)*	quotation, quoting (of a firm's shares on the stock exchange)
compétitif(ve)	competitive		
complet(ète)	complete; full; no vacancy	**cote** *(f)*	quoted value
composer un numéro	to dial a number	**coter; être coté(e)**	to quote; be quoted, be listed
comptable *(m, f)*	accountant		
compte *(m)* **à vue,** **compte** *(m)* **courant**	checking account	**cotisation** *(f)*	contribution
compte *(m)* **épargne**	savings account	**cotiser**	to pay one's contribution
concessionnaire *(m, f)*	dealer(ship)	**courageux(se)**	courageous

courant *(m)* **électrique**	electrical current
courrier *(m)*	mail
cours *(m)* **d'échange** *(m)*, **de change** *(m)*	exchange rate
court terme *(m)*	short term
courtage *(m)*	brokerage
courtier *(m)*	broker
couvert(e)	covered
créance *(f)*	claim, debt
crédité(e)	credited
créer un document	to create a document
créneau *(m)*	niche
crise *(f)*	crisis
croître	to grow, increase
cumuler	to accumulate; to accrue
curriculum vitae *(m)*, **C.V. ou CV** *(m)*	CV, résumé
curseur *(m)*	cursor

D

d'abord	first
DAB *(m)*	ATM machine
débit *(m)*	debit
débouchés *(m)*	job opportunities
(se) débrouiller	to get by, manage, get out of difficulties
décacheter	to open [a sealed envelope]
décéder, être décédé(e)	to die, to be deceased
décès *(m)*	death
décevant(e)	disappointing
décevoir	to disappoint
déclaration *(f)*	statement; tax return
déclaration *(f)* **annexe**	appended statement or return
déclaration *(f)* **d'impôts** *(m)*	tax return
déclarer	to declare
déconseiller	to advise against
décontracté(e)	relaxed
découragé(e)	discouraged
décourageant(e)	discouraging
décrocher (le téléphone)	to pick up, answer (the phone)
décrocher (un entretien)	to get, land an (interview)
déçu(e)	disappointed
dédouaner	to clear customs
déductible, non-déductible	deductible, non-deductible
déduire	to deduct
(se) défaire	to get rid of
défaut *(m)*	character flaw, defect
défi *(m)*	challenge

dégâts *(m pl)*	damages
dégrèvement *(m)*	tax relief or deduction
déjà	already
déléguer	to delegate
demain	tomorrow
demander quelque chose	to ask (for) something
demandeurs (euses)	plaintiffs, petitioners; person asking for
démarches *(f)* **(à suivre)**	steps (to take)
démarrage *(m)*	start-up
démarrer	to start
démission *(f)*; **donner sa démission**	resignation; to resign
démotivé(e)	not motivated anymore
denrée(s) *(f)*	goods
directeur(trice)	department or company head
dépendant(e) *(nom et adj.)*	dependent
déplacement *(m)*	business trip (being out of town on business)
déplacer	to move
déplacer un rendez-vous	to change an appointment
déplaire à	to displease
dépliant *(m)*	flyer
déposer de l'argent *(m)*	to deposit money
déposer un chèque	to deposit a check
dépôt *(m)*	deposit
déprimé(e)	depressed
déranger	to bother, disturb
dérober; être dérobé(e)	to steal; to be stolen
dérogation *(f)*	exception
déroger (à la loi)	to go against (the law)
dérouler	to scroll
(se) dérouler	to come unwound or unrolled
désavantageux(se)	disadvantageous
destinataire *(m, f)*	addressee
détail *(m)*; **au détail**	detail; retail
détourner	to turn away
détresse *(f)*	distress
dette *(f)*	debt
(se) dévaloriser	to drop in value
(se) développer	to get developed; to progress
devises *(f)*	currency
différer	to differ
diffuser	to disseminate
diffusion *(f)*	dissemination; broadcasting
diminution *(f)*	reduction
diplôme *(m)*	diploma
direct(e)	direct
dirigeant(e)	director, leader

discret(ète)	discreet
discrimination *(f)*	discrimination
discuter	to discuss
dispenser	to exempt, excuse from
dispersé(e)	scattered
disponibilité *(f)*	availability
disposer de	to have at one's disposal
disque *(m)* **dur**	hard disk
disque *(m)* **souple**	floppy disk
disquette *(f)*	floppy, diskette
distribué(e)	distributed
distribuer	to distribute, pass out
diversifier	to diversify
dividende *(m)*	dividend
documentation *(f)*	documentation
domaine *(m)* **de spécialisation** *(f)*	major
domicile *(m)*	place of residence
dommages *(m pl)*	damages
dossier *(m)*	dossier, file
douane *(f)*	customs
douanier *(m)*	customs officer
douter	to doubt
droit *(m); avoir droit à*	right; to be entitled to
droit *(m)* **de douane** *(f)*	tariff
durée *(f)*	duration, length (of time)
dynamique	dynamic

E

écarter; être écarté(e)	to put aside; to set aside
échange *(m)*	exchange
échanger	to exchange
échapper à	to escape from
échéancier *(m)*	payment schedule (to reimburse a debt)
échelle *(f)*	ladder; level
échouer	to fail
éclater	to explode, burst
écran *(m)*	screen
effaçage *(m)*	deletion
effacer	to delete
effectivement	actually; effectively, indeed
efficace	efficient
efficacité *(f)*	efficiency
effraction *(f)*	breaking and entering
également	as well, equally
emballage *(m)*	wrapping
embarras *(m)* **du choix**	superfluity of choices
embaucher	to hire
émettre	to transmit, broadcast; to issue
émis(e)	issued

émission *(f)* **(d'obligations** *(f)* **ou d'actions** *(f)* **)**	issue, issuing (of bonds and stocks)
émission *(f)* **(de radio** *(f),* **de télévision** *(f)* **)**	program (radio, television)
émotionnel(le)	emotional
emploi *(m)*	use; job
emploi *(m)* **du temps** *(m)*	schedule
employer	to employ, give employment to, use
encadrer	to frame
encaisser (des revenus) *(m)*	to cash; to collect (revenues)
encart *(m)* **publicitaire**	advertising insert
encore; pas encore	still, again; not yet
encourageant(e)	encouraging
encouragement *(m)*	encouragement
endommager	to damage
endossataire *(m, f)*	endorsee
énerver	to irritate, annoy
enfin	finally
engagement *(m)*	obligation
enjeu *(m)*	stakes
ennuyeux(se)	boring
enrichissement *(m)*	enrichment
enseigne *(f)*	sign
ensuite	then
entamer des discussions *(f),* **des négociations** *(f)*	to start discussions, negotiations
en-tête *(m)*	header
enthousiaste	enthusiastic
entièrement	entirely
entre	between
entrepôt *(m)*	warehouse
entrepreneur *(m)*	entrepreneur
entreprise *(f)* **privatisée (publique)**	privatized (public) company
entretien *(m)* **collectif**	group interview
entretien *(m)* **d'embauche** *(f)*	job interview
entretien *(m)* **individuel**	one-on-one interview
enveloppe *(f)*	envelope
envisager	to envisage, consider
épanoui(e)	fulfilled, happy
(s')épanouir	to bloom, blossom
épuisé(e) (un article)	out of stock (articles)
équilibre *(m)*	balance
équitable	fair
escompte *(m)*	discount
esprit *(m); avoir l'esprit tranquille*	mind, spirit; to have peace of mind
espèces *(f); en espèces*	cash; in cash
essentiel(le)	essential

étaler (les paiements) (m) **sur**	to spread (the payments) over	**feuille** (f) **de paie** (f)	paycheck, payroll statement
étonnant(e)	astonishing	**feuille** (f) **(de papier)** (m)	sheet, piece (of paper)
étude (f) **(de motivation)** (f)	study (of motivation)	**fiable**	reliable
		fiche (f) **de paye** (f)	paycheck, payroll statement
(s')évader	to escape	**fichier** (m)	file
évaluer	to evaluate	**figurer**	to be part of
évoluer	to evolve	**fil** (m), **sans fil** (m)	cord, cordless
exagérer	to exaggerate	**filtrer (les appels** (m) **téléphoniques)**	to screen (calls)
exceptionnel(le)	exceptional		
exclusion (f)	exclusion; suspension	**finaliste** (m, f)	finalist
exclusivement	exclusively	**financer**	to finance
exclusivité (f)	exclusivity	**fisc** (m)	French equivalent of IRS
exécuter (des ordres) (m)	to carry out (orders)	**fiscal(e)** (m pl, **fiscaux**)	fiscal, tax
exercer (une profession)	to practice (a profession)	**fixé(e)**	fixed
		fixer	to fix
exercice (m) **comptable**	status at the end of an accounting period	**fixer un rendez-vous**	to make an appointment
		flottant(e)	floating
exigé(e)	required	**fluctuation** (f)	fluctuation
exigeant(e)	demanding	**fluctuer**	to fluctuate
exonération (f)	exoneration; exemption	**fonctionnaire** (m, f)	state employee, civil servant
exonérer	to exonerate	**fond** (m); **à fond**	bottom; totally, completely
expansion (f)	expansion	**fonder**	to found, create
expédier	to send	**fonds** (m pl)	funds
expéditeur(trice) (nom et adj.)	sender	**forcé(e); être forcé de**	forced; to be forced to
		force (f) **de conviction** (f)	force of conviction
expédition (f) **des marchandises** (f)	dispatch or shipment of merchandise	**forfaitaire**	fixed price; all-inclusive
		formation (f)	formation, education, training
expérience (f)	experience		
expérimenté(e)	experienced	**formation** (f) **continue**	continuing education
expertiser; faire expertiser	to appraise, evaluate; to have evaluated	**formation** (f) **en alternance**	alternate or rotational training
		formation (f) **permanente**	continuous training, continuing education
exploité(e)	used, operated		
exploiter	to cultivate; to use, take advantage of	**formé(e)**	formed, educated
		formulaire (m)	tax form
(s')exprimer	to express oneself	**fort(e)**	strong
		fourchette (f)	range; fork
F		**fourni(e) (bien)**	(well) supplied
		fournir	to furnish, supply
fabriquer	to make	**frais** (m pl)	expenses
facilement	easily	**frais** (m) **de courtage** (m)	brokerage fee, costs
facturation (f) **détaillée**	detailed billing		
facture (f)	bill	**frais** (m pl) **d'envoi** (m)	shipping costs
facultatif(ve)	optional	**frais** (m pl) **de route** (f)	travel expenses
faillite (f); **faire faillite**	bankruptcy; to go bankrupt	**frais** (m pl) **d'hébergement** (m)	lodging expenses
faire appel à	to call for		
faire face à	to confront, to face	**frais** (m pl) **médicaux**	medical expenses
faire parvenir	to send (something)	**franc(he)**	frank
faire une réclamation	to lodge a complaint	**franchement**	frankly
faisceau (m) **de services** (m)	an array of services	**franchise** (f)	franchise; deductible
		fraude (f) **fiscale**	tax evasion
fatigué(e)	tired	**freiner l'importation** (f)	to slow down importing
fax (m)	fax	**frictions** (f)	conflicts, friction
fente (f)	slot		
fermé(e)	closed		

frontalier(ière); contrôle *(m)* **frontalier**	border; border control	**illimité(e)**	unlimited
frontière *(f)*	border	**immédiatement**	immediately
fusion *(f)*	merger	**immuable**	unchanging
fusion *(f)* **et rachat** *(m)* **d'entreprise**	M & A, mergers and acquisitions	**impayé(e)**	unpaid
fusionner	to merge	**imposable, non imposable**	taxable, tax-free
		imposer; être imposé(e)	to tax; to be taxed

G

gain *(m)*	payoff	**imposition** *(f)*	taxation
gamme *(f)* **(de produits)** *(m)*	range, line (of products)	**imposition** *(f)* **commune**	common tax
garanti(e)	secured	**impôts** *(m)* **directs (indirects)**	direct (indirect) taxes
garantie *(f)*	guarantee	**impôts** *(m)* **locaux**	local taxes
garantie réelle	collateral	**imprévisible**	unforeseeable
GATT (Accord général sur les tarifs douaniers et le commerce)	GATT	**imprimante** *(f)*	printer
		imprimé *(m)*	tax form, printed matter
geler	to freeze	**imprimer**	to print
gérant(e)	manager	**imprudence** *(f)*	carelessness
gestion *(f)*	management	**inacceptable**	unacceptable
gigantesque	gigantic	**incendie** *(m)*	fire
gratuit(e)	free	**incertitude** *(f)*	uncertainty
gratuitement	at no cost	**inciter à**	to incite to
grave	serious	**inclure**	to include
grimper	to climb	**inclus(e)**	included
gros, en gros	big, wholesale	**incompatibilité** *(f)*	incompatibility
grossiste *(m, f)*	wholesaler	**inconsciemment**	unconsciously
grosso modo	more or less, approximately	**inconstant(e)**	fickle
guichet *(m)*	a teller's window	**incontestablement**	unquestionably, indisputably
guichetier(ière)	counter clerk	**indéfiniment**	indefinitely
guide *(m)* **de navigation** *(f)*	navigation guide	**indemniser; être indemnisé(e)**	to compensate for; to be reimbursed for
		indemnité *(f)*	compensation; allowance

H

		indemnité *(f)* **de chômage** *(m)*	unemployment compensation
harcèlement *(m)* **sexuel**	sexual harassment	**indépendant(e)**	independent
hausse *(f)*	rise, increase	**indescriptible**	indescribable
hebdomadaire *(m)* **(nom et adj.)**	weekly	**indice** *(m)* **boursier**	stock market index
heure *(f); heure supplémentaire; à l'heure**	hour; overtime; on time, per hour (wages)	**indiscret(ète)**	indiscreet
		indispensable	absolutely necessary, essential, vital
hier	yesterday	**inefficacité** *(f)*	inefficiency
holding *(f)*	holding company	**inégal(e)**	uneven, unequal
honnêteté *(f)*	honesty	**inévitablement**	inevitably
honte *(f); avoir honte**	shame; to be ashamed	**informaticien(ne)** *(m, f)*	computer specialist
huit; les trois huit *(m pl)*	eight; eight-hour shift(s)	**(s')informer**	to be/get informed
humilié(e)	humiliated	**ingénieur** *(m)*	engineer
humoristique	humoristic	**innovateur(trice)**	innovative
hypothèse *(f)*	hypothesis	**(s')inquiéter**	to worry
		(s')inscrire	to register

I

		instantanément	instantly
identifiant *(m)*	personal secret code (PIN number)	**insu** *(m); à l'insu de**	without the knowledge of, unbeknownst to

insuffisament	insufficiently
intégrité *(f)*	integrity
interconnecté(e)	interconnected
intéressé(e) *(nom et adj.)*	with a vested interest
intérêt *(m)*	interest
intérim *(m)*	temporary work
intérimaire *(nom et adj.)*	temp, temporary
interlocuteur(trice) *(m, f)*	person with whom one is talking
internaute *(m, f)*	Internet user
interrogeable à distance *(f)*	checkable by remote
interview *(f)*	interview (in the media world)
inventaire *(m)*	inventory
(s')investir	to invest oneself
investissement *(m)*	investment
irréaliste	unrealistic

J

jamais	never
jeu *(m)* **vidéo**	video game
jour *(m)* **de congé** *(m)*	day off
jour *(m)* **ouvrable**	workday
journal *(m)*	newspaper, journal

L

lancer	to launch
lentement	slowly
lettre *(f)* **de motivation** *(f)*	cover letter
lettre *(f)* **recommandée**	certified, registered letter
liasse *(f)* **fiscale**	tax bundle, tax return
libre-échange *(m)*	free trade
licencié(e) *(nom et adj.)*	holder of a Bachelor's Degree; fired
licencier	to fire
lien *(m)*	link, bond
ligne *(f); **en ligne**	line; on line
lignes *(f)* **en petits caractères**	lines of small print
limité(e)	limited
liquide *(m); **en liquide**	liquid; in cash
liquider	to wind up, liquidate
liquider ses biens *(m)*	to liquidate one's assets
liquidité *(f)*	liquid assets; liquidity
litige *(m)*	litigation
livrer	to deliver
livret *(m)*	passbook
location *(f)*	leasing, rental
logiciel *(m)*	software (package)

logiciel *(m)* **de navigation** *(f)*	navigational software
loisirs *(m pl)*	leisure-time activities
long terme	long term
lors de	at the time of
louer	to rent; to praise

M

machinalement	mechanically
magazine *(m)*	magazine
maintenir	to maintain, keep
mairie *(f)*	city hall
majeur(e)	major; of age
manuel *(m)*	manual, handbook
manuel(le)	manual [labor]
manuscrit(e)	hand-written
marchandise *(f)* **en vrac**	loose or bulk merchandise
marché *(m)* **financier**	financial market
marché *(m)* **primaire (secondaire)**	primary (secondary) market
marcher; marcher (bien, mal)	to walk; to work (well, poorly)
marge *(f)*	margin
marge *(f)* **bénéficiaire**	profit margin
marge *(f)* **brute d'autofinancement**	cash flow
matériel *(m)*	hardware, material
média(s) *(m pl)*	media
mémoire *(m, f)*	written report; memory
ménage *(m)*	household
mener à bien (un projet)	to complete (a project)
mensonger(ère)	deceitful, misleading
mensuel(le)	monthly
menu *(m)*	menu
menu *(m)* **Edition** *(f)*	Edit menu
menu *(m)* **Fichier** *(m)*	File menu
menu *(m)* **Pomme** *(f)*	Apple menu
mercatique *(f)*	marketing
message *(m)* **publicitaire**	advertisement
messagerie *(f)* **électronique**	e-mail
métier *(m)*	trade, business, calling, craft
mettre à la porte	to fire, to get rid of
mettre au point	to regulate, adjust; finalize, settle
mettre en attente *(f)*	to put on hold
mettre en cause *(f)*	to question, to call into question
mettre en communication *(f)* **avec**	to put through
(se) mettre en marche *(f)*	to start, to start working

(se) mettre en relation *(f)* **avec**	to get in touch, make contact with
milieu *(m)* **professionnel**	professional environment
mineur(e) *(nom et adj.)*	minor, underage
minimal(e)	minimal
(à) mi-temps *(m)*	half-time, part-time [job]
mobilier(ère)	transferable
mode *(m)* **d'emploi** *(m)*	user manual
modem *(m)*	modem
modérément	moderately
modifier	to modify
modique (prix ou somme)	modest (price or sum)
moins; de moins en moins	less; less and less
mondialisation *(f)*	world-wide application, globalization
moniteur *(m)*	monitor
monnaie *(f)*	change; currency
montant *(m)*	amount
monter	to rise; to climb
(se) monter	to come to, to amount to
monter en grade *(m)*	to be promoted
monter une entreprise	to get a company up and running
mort(e) *(nom et adj.)*	dead (person)
mot-clé *(m)*	key word
mot *(m)* **de passe**	password
moyen(ne)	average
moyens *(m pl)*	means
(se) munir de	to equip oneself with, to arm oneself with
muté(e)	transferred

N

naviguer	to navigate; to surf
ne... plus; non plus	not... anymore; neither
négociabilité *(f)*	negotiability
nerveusement	nervously
nerveux(se)	nervous
nettoyage *(m)*	cleaning
notamment	namely
novice *(m, f)*	beginner
numérique	digital
numérisé(e)	digitized
numéro *(m)* **azur**	toll-free number
numéro *(m)* **d'accès** *(m)*	access number
numéroter	to number

O

obéir	to obey
obligation *(f)*	bond; obligation

obsédé(e)	obsessed
obtention *(f)*	securing (of a job); obtaining
officiel(le) *(nom et adj)*	official
offre *(f)* **publique d'achat** *(m)* **(une OPA)**	public purchase offer
offre *(f)* **publique d'échange** *(m)* **(une OPE)**	public exchange offer
offreur *(m)*	purchaser
omettre	to omit
onéreux(se)	burdensome; expensive
opérer	to operate
opter	to opt
optimiste	optimistic
ordinateur *(m)*	computer
ordre *(m)*	order
organisme à but *(m)* **non lucratif**	non-profit organization
(s')orienter	to orient oneself; move or turn toward
outil *(m)*	tool
outil *(m)* **de recherche** *(f)*	research tool
ouvert(e)	open
(s')ouvrir	to open oneself
ouvrir un compte	to open an account

P

paie *(f)*	pay, wages
paisible	peaceful, calm, quiet
panne *(f)***; en panne**	breakdown; down
panneau *(m)* **d'affichage** *(m)*	billboard
papier *(m)***; papier à en-tête**	paper; letterhead stationery
paradis *(m)* **fiscal**	tax paradise [because no taxes are levied]
parc *(m)* **d'ordinateurs** *(m)*	computer or lab cluster
paresseux(se)	lazy
part *(f)* **(de société)**	share (in a company)
partenaire *(m, f)*	partner
parvenir à	to attain, reach, succeed in
passer une commande	to place an order
passif *(m)*	liabilities [financial]
passionnant(e)	exciting, thrilling, enthralling, fascinating
patron(ne)	boss
paye *(f)*	pay, wages
payer	to pay
P.D.G., PDG, P.-d.g. *(m)* **(Président Directeur Général)**	CEO
percepteur *(m)*	tax commissioner
perception *(f)*	perception; tax collector's office

percevoir	to perceive, detect; collect, be paid	**postal(e)**	postal
perçu(e)	perceived	**poste** *(m)*	position, job
perdre (quelque chose)	to lose (something)	**postulant(e)**	candidate
perdre sa confiance en soi	to lose confidence in oneself	**potentiel(le)**	potential
(se) perfectionner	to better oneself	**poursuivre**	to pursue, strive toward
performance *(f)*	performance; how well something does	**pourvoir**	to provide; to see to
persévérant(e)	persevering, resolute	**pourvu(e) de**	supplied, provided with
perspectives *(f)*	prospects	**pratique**	practical, convenient
perspicace	perceptive	**pratiquement**	practically
perte *(f)*	loss	**préavis** *(m)*	advance notice, warning
pertinent(e)	pertinent	**précaire**	precarious
peser	to weigh	**précis(e)**	precise
pessimiste	pessimistic	**préconiser**	to recommend, advocate
petites annonces *(f)*	want ads, classifieds	**prélèvement** *(m)*	deduction; withdrawal
PIB *(m)* **(Produit Intérieur Brut)**	GDP (Gross Domestic Product)	**prélèvement** *(m)* **automatique**	automatic withdrawal
pièce *(f)* **d'identité** *(f)*	ID	**prélever**	to levy, impose
place *(f)*; **sur place**	place, position; on site	**prendre effet** *(m)*	to take effect, be operative
placement *(m)*	investment	**prendre en main** *(f)*	to take care of, take charge of
plafond *(m)*	maximum payment, ceiling	**prendre l'initiative** *(f)*	to take the initiative
plafonné(e)	topped out; having reached its ceiling	**prendre part** *(f)* **à**	to take part in
(se) plaindre	to complain	**prendre sa retraite**	to retire
plaire à	to please	**préparer; se préparer à**	to prepare; to prepare oneself, to get ready to
plaisir *(m)*	pleasure	**presse** *(f)*	press
poste *(m)* **de télévision** *(f)*	television set	**prestation** *(f)*	benefit
planification *(f)*	planning	**prestigieux(se)**	prestigious
planifier	to plan	**prétentions** *(f pl)*	expectations
plaquette *(f)*	brochure, pamphlet	**prévisualisation** *(f)*	preview
plat(e)	flat, low, empty	**prévoir**	to foresee
plein temps, à temps complet	full-time	**prévu(e)**	foreseen
plutôt	rather	**prime** *(f)*	bonus; premium
P.M.E., PME *(f)* **(Petites et Moyennes Entreprises)**	small- or medium-sized company	**principalement**	principally, mainly
		pris(e) au dépourvu	caught unaware
PNB *(m)* **(Produit National Brut)**	GNP, Gross National Product	**prise** *(f)*	phone outlet, plug
		privé(e) de	deprived of
point *(m)* **de vente** *(f)*	outlet	**prix** *(m)*	price
point *(m)* **fort**	strong point	**probablement**	probably
pointer	to check, punch in/out; to place cursor, to point	**profession** *(f)*	profession
		profil *(m)*	profile
police *(f)* **d'assurance** *(f)*	insurance policy	**prometteur(se)**	promising
police *(f)* **de caractère** *(m)*	font	**promotion** *(f)*, **en promotion**	promotion, on special
ponctuel(le)	punctual	**promouvoir**	to promote
population *(f)* **active**	part of population that is working for wages	**propre**	clean; one's own
		propriétaire *(m, f)*	owner
portable	portable	**prospectus** *(m)*	flyer
portatif(ve)	portable	**protection** *(f)*	protection, coverage
porteur *(m)*	bearer, holder	**protectionnisme** *(m)*	protectionism
poser une question	to ask a question	**protéger**	to protect
		prouver	to prove
		provisoirement	tentatively
		publicité *(f)*	publicity

publipostage *(m)*	junk mail
puce *(f)*	flea; microchip
puis	then
puissant(e)	powerful

Q

quand même	all the same; anyway
queue *(f)*; **faire la queue**	tail, line; to stand in line
quittance *(f)*	a bill
quitter; Ne quittez pas!	to leave; Stay on the line!

R

rabais *(m)*	reduction, discount
raccrocher (le combiné)	to hang up (the phone)
racheter	to buy up, buy back
raisonner	to reason
repatriement *(m)*	repatriation
rapide	fast
rapidement	rapidly, fast
rapporter	to earn; to bring back
rationnel(le)	rational
réacheminement *(m)* **d'appel** *(m)*	call forwarding
(se) réaliser	to realize, be realized, come true; to be fulfilled
réaliser une bonne ou mauvaise affaire	to make a good or bad deal
rebondir	to bounce back
récession *(f)*	recession
recettes *(f)* **fiscales**	tax receipts
recevoir	to receive
recharger	to recharge
recherché(e)	in great demand
recherche *(f)* **sur mots** *(m)* **clés** *(f)*	word search
réciproque	reciprocal
réclame *(f)*	advertisement
recommandation *(f)*	recommendation
reconquérir	to regain, recover
(se) reconvertir	to give up an old job and go into another field
recouvrement *(m)* **des impôts** *(m)*	tax collection or levying
recruter	to recruit
recruteur *(m)*	recruiting officer or agent
reçu *(m)*	receipt
reculer	to retreat, to withdraw, to back out
(se) recycler	to get retrained
redevable	liable; indebted for
redouter	to dread, fear
réduction *(f)*	reduction, discount

référence(s) *(f)*	reference(s)
reformater	to reformat
régime *(m)*	diet; system; regulations
régime *(m)* **de la communauté des biens** *(m)*	joint ownership of property
règle *(f)*; **être en règle**	rule; to have a legal status, to operate within the law
réglementé(e)	regulated
régler; régler une facture	to adjust; to settle a bill; to pay
réinsertion professionnelle	professional reintegration, return to the workforce
rejet *(m)*	rejection
rejeter	to reject
relâcher	to release
relancer	to restart
relevé *(m)* **bancaire**	bank statement
relier	to hook, to link
remboursement *(m)*	reimbursement
rembourser; être remboursé(e)	to reimburse; to be reimbursed
(se) remettre en cause *(f)*	to question (oneself); to reconsider
remplir (un formulaire)	to fill out (a form)
rémunération *(f)*	salary, remuneration
rémunérer	to pay, to remunerate
rendez-vous *(m)*	appointment
rendre	to render; make; to return
(se) rendre au chevet de	to go to the bedside of
renouveler	to renew
renouvellement *(m)*	renewal
renseignement *(m)*	(a piece of) information
(se) renseigner	to get informed, to find out
rentabiliser	to make profitable
rentrer dans ses frais *(m)*	to break even
renvoyer	to dismiss, postpone, fire
répartir	to distribute
repartir à zéro	to start from scratch (again), to start over again
répartition *(f)*	dividing up, distribution of
répertoire *(m)*	repertoire; index; alphabetical list
(se) replier sur soi	to turn inward
répondeur *(m)* **(automatique)**	answering machine
répondre à une question	to answer a question
reportable	deferrable; postponable
représentant(e) *(nom et adj.)*	representative
reprise *(f)* **(de l'économie)** *(f)*	(economic) recovery
requérir	to require

réseau (m)	net
résilier un contrat	to terminate or cancel a contract
respectueux(se)	respectful
responsabilité (f) (civile)	(personal) liability
responsable (nom et adj)	department head; person in charge; responsible
retard (m); en retard	delay; late
retirer de l'argent (m)	to withdraw money
retournement (m)	return
réunion (f) par téléphone (m)	conference call
revanche (f); en revanche	revenge; on the other hand
revendre	to resell
revenus (m) fonciers	land revenues
rêver	to dream
revue (f)	magazine
rigoureux(se)	rigorous, strict
risque (m)	risk
risqué(e)	daring, risky, off-color
rompre (un contrat)	to break (a contract)
rubrique (f)	heading; item
rupture (f) de contrat (m)	breaking of contract

S

saisir (la chance)	to seize (the opportunity)
saisir un texte	to type with word processor and save in computer
salaire (m)	salary
sanction (f)	sanction
sans doute	probably, most likely
sauver	to save
sauvegarder	to save; to safeguard
SDF (Sans Domicile Fixe)	homeless person
secret(ète)	secret
secteur (m) d'activité (f)	sector of activity
secteur (m) de pointe (f)	hi-tech sector
sécurisant(e)	giving a feeling of security
Sécurité (f) Sociale	Social Security
sein (m); au sein de	breast; in, within, in the bosom of
sélectionner	to select
sens (m) de culpabilité (f)	guilt feeling
sentiment (m) de culpabilité (f)	guilt feeling
séparément	separately
sérieusement	seriously
service (m)	department; service
service (m) après-vente	customer service

seuil (m)	threshold
SICAV (f), FCP (m)	mutual funds
signal (m) d'appel (m), beep (m) sonore	call-waiting signal
signer	to sign
sinistre (m)	disaster, accident
slogan (m)	slogan
smicard(e) (une personne qui gagne le SMIC) (m, f)	minimum wage earner
social(e)	social
société (f)	society; company
soin (m); avec soin	care; with care, carefully
solde (m); en solde	balance; on sale
solliciter	to solicit
solliciter un délai	to ask for a deferral
sollicitude (f)	concern, solicitude
somme (f)	sum
son (m)	sound
sonner	to ring
sonnerie (f)	ring [of the telephone]
souci (m)	worry, concern
souplesse (f)	suppleness, pliability
souris (f)	mouse
souscripteur(trice) (m, f)	subscriber
souscription (f)	subscription, contribution
souscrire	to subscribe
soustraire	to subtract
sous-traitant (m)	subcontractor
spécifique	specific
spéculation (f)	speculation
spéculer	to speculate
spot (m)	commercial
stage (m)	internship
stagiaire (m, f)	intern; co-op
stagnation (f)	stagnation
stipuler	to stipulate
stock (m)	stock, supply
stratégie (f)	strategy
stressant(e)	stressful
stressé(e)	stressed out
structuré(e)	structured
studio (m)	studio (apartment)
subvention (f)	grant, subsidy
succomber	to succumb, yield
suffisamment	sufficiently
suivre	to follow
suivre un cours	to take a course
supprimer	to suppress
sûr (de soi)	sure (of oneself)
surchargé(e)	overloaded
surcharger (la mémoire)	to overload (the memory)

surcroît *(m)* **de travail** *(m)*	additional work; excessive work	**traducteur(trice)**	translator
sûrement	surely	**traîner**	to drag
surmonter	to overcome	**traitement** *(m)* **de texte** *(m)*	word processor
surtaxe *(f)*	surtax	**traiter avec**	to deal with
surveiller	to look after, watch closely	**tranche** *(f)* **d'imposition** *(f)*	tax bracket
susciter	to instigate, to create	**tranquille**	peaceful

T

		transaction *(f)*	transaction
tâche *(f)*	task	**transaction** *(f)* **boursière**	stock market transaction
tactique *(f)*	tactic	**transfert** *(m)* **d'appel** *(m)*	call forwarding
taille *(f)*	size	**travail** *(m)* **clandestin (au noir)**	clandestine or illicit work (under the table)
taper	to type	**travailler à son compte**	to work for oneself
tard	late	**travailler pour (+ substantif)**	to work for (+ *noun*)
tarif *(m)*	price list		
tarification *(f)*	pricing	**travailler pour (+ verbe)**	to work in order to (+ *verb*)
taxe *(f)*	tax, taxation, assessment		
télé(vision) *(f)*	television, TV set	**travailleur(se)**	hard-working
télécarte *(f)*	phone card	**travailleur(se)** *(m, f)* **indépendant(e)**	self-employed worker
téléchargement *(m)*	downloading over phone lines, via the Internet	**trier (le courrier)**	to sort (the mail)
télécommande *(f)*	remote control	**trois huit** *(m pl)*	eight-hour shift
télécopie *(f)*	fax	**trombone** *(m)*	paper clip
télécopieur *(m)*	fax machine	**tromper**	to deceive
télématique *(f)*	telematics [pertaining to the use of fiber optics and/or computers over telephone lines]	**trompeur(euse)**	deceitful, deceiving
		trouver du travail trouver un travail	to find [some] work [to do], to find a job
téléviseur *(m)*	TV set	**tué(e)** *(nom et adj.)*	killed
temporairement	temporarily	**TVA** *(f)*	VAT, Value-Added Tax
temps *(m)*; **de temps en temps**; **à temps partiel**; **plein temps, à temps complet**	time; from time to time; part-time; full-time	**typiquement**	typically

		U	
tendu(e)	tense; tight	**ultérieurement**	subsequently
tenir à	to cling to, prize; to be attached to; to value	**unité** *(f)* **centrale**	central unit
		usine *(f)*	factory
tiers *(m)*	third [party]	**utile**	useful
timide *(nom et adj.)*	timid	**utilisateur(trice)** *(m, f)*	user
tirer	to pull		
tirer le clavier	to pull out the keyboard	**V**	
titre *(m)*	title		
titulaire *(m, f)* **d'un compte**	title holder	**vain(e)**	futile, fruitless, useless
		valeur *(f)* **boursière**	security; stock or share
titulariser	to entitle; to tenure	**valeur** *(f)* **mobilière**	transferable security
toile *(f)*	web	**valeurs** *(f pl)* **mobilières**	stocks and bonds
tomber	to fall	**valeur** *(f)* **nominale**	nominal value
tôt	early	**validité** *(f)*, **en cours de validité**	validity, valid
touche *(f)*	key [on a keyboard]		
touche *(f)* **bis**	redial button	**valoir; en valoir la peine**	to be worth; to be worthwhile
toucher	to cash; to touch	**valorisant**	self-actualizing, giving a feeling of self-worth, giving value to
toucher un chèque	to cash a check		
tourner (la page)	to turn (the page)	**(se) valoriser**	to appreciate in value

(se) vanter (de)	to brag (about)	**visionner**	to view
varier	to vary	**visiter (un site)**	to view/visit (a home page)
vendeur(euse)	salesperson, seller	**vitesse** *(f)*	speed
vendre	to sell	**vivement**	sharply, brusquely; greatly, deeply
vendre à perte *(f)*	to sell at a loss		
vente *(f)* **en gros**	wholesale	**vol** *(m)*	theft; flight
vente *(f)* **par correspondance** *(f)*	mail-order sales	**voler; être volé(e)**	to steal; to be stolen
		volontaire *(nom et adj.)*	volunteer
vérifier le solde	to verify, to check the balance		
		volonté *(f)*	desire, will
verrouiller (un fichier)	to lock (a file)	**volume** *(m)* **de transactions** *(f)*	transaction volume
verser de l'argent *(m)*	to deposit money, to make a direct deposit		
viable	viable		
vieux (vieil, vieille)	old		
vif(ve)	lively	**z**	
virement *(m)*	transfer		
virer de l'argent, faire un virement	to transfer money	**zapper**	to channel surf
		zapping *(m)*	channel surfing

We are grateful to those who have generously granted us the use of copyrighted texts. The sources of these materials are cited on the page where the quoted matter appears.

We would like to thank also the many people who kindly supplied us with letters and documents of various types or graciously accepted being photographed and / or interviewed for our series.

All of the photographs in *Interfaces* were taken by coauthor Dr. Catherine Marin. Sources of realia are given on the pages where they appear.

Index de la majorité des noms propres, noms de grandes compagnies et groupes français ou travaillant en France citées dans *Interfaces*

INDEX